Fodor's 23rd Edition

W9-AGD-030

Southeast Asia

The complete guide, thoroughly up-to-date

Packed with details that will make your trip

The must-see sights, off and on the beaten path

What to see, what to skip

Mix-and-match vacation itineraries

City strolls, countryside adventures

Smart lodging and dining options

Essential local do's and taboos

Transportation tips, distances and directions

Key contacts, savvy travel tips

When to go, what to pack

Clear, accurate, easy-to-use maps

Books to read, videos to watch

Fodor's Travel Publications • New York, Toronto, London, Sydney, Auckland
www.fodors.com

Fodor's Southeast Asia

EDITORS: Karen Deaver, Mayanthi Fernando, Amy Karafin, Deborah Kaufman, Laura M. Kidder, Justine Rathbun, Bree Scott

Editorial Contributors: Maya Besa, Greg Bishop, Carissa Bluestone, Andrew Chilvers, Denise Dowling, Mick Elmore, Margaret Feldstein, Doreen Fernandez, Nigel Fisher, Bob Marriott, Michael Mathes, Mielikki Org, Elka Ray, Ilsa Sharp, Helayne Schiff, Holly S. Smith, Abby Tan, Mei-Yin Teo, Craig Thomas, Gisela Williams, Lara Wozniak

Editorial Production: Tom Holton

Maps: David Lindroth, *cartographer*; Rebecca Baer and Bob Blake, *map editors*

Design: Fabrizio La Rocca, *creative director*; Guido Caroti, *art director*; Jolie Novak, *senior picture editor*

Production/Manufacturing: Angela L. McLean

Cover Photograph: National Geographic Traveler/Paul Chesley/Photographers/Aspen

Copyright

Twenty-third Edition

ISBN 0–679–00611–7

ISSN 0160–8991

Special Sales

Fodor's Travel Publications are available at special discounts for bulk purchases for sales promotions or premiums. Special editions, including personalized covers, excerpts of existing guides, and corporate imprints, can be created in large quantities for special needs. For more information, contact your local bookseller or write to Special Markets, Fodor's Travel Publications, 280 Park Avenue, New York, NY 10017. Inquiries from Canada should be directed to your local Canadian bookseller or sent to Random House of Canada, Ltd., Marketing Department, 2775 Matheson Boulevard East, Mississauga, Ontario L4W 4P7. Inquiries from the United Kingdom should be sent to Fodor's Travel Publications, 20 Vauxhall Bridge Road, London SW1V 2SA, England.

PRINTED IN THE UNITED STATES OF AMERICA

10 9 8 7 6 5 4 3 2 1

Important Tip

Although all prices, opening times, and other details in this book are based on information supplied to us at press time, changes occur all the time in the travel world, and Fodor's cannot accept responsibility for facts that become outdated or for inadvertent errors or omissions. So **always confirm information when it matters,** especially if you're making a detour to visit a specific place.

CONTENTS

Contents

ON THE ROAD WITH FODOR'S

EVERY TRIP is a significant one. So here at Fodor's we've pulled out all stops in preparing *Fodor's Southeast Asia*. To guide you in putting together your experience, we've created multiday itineraries and neighborhood walks. And to direct you to the places that are truly worth your time and money, we've rallied the team of endearingly picky know-it-alls we're pleased to call our writers. Having seen all corners of the regions they cover for us, they're real experts. If you knew them, you'd poll them for tips yourself.

Greg Bishop, who updated Singapore Dining, Lodging, and Shopping, is a native of Nova Scotia, Canada. He has traveled extensively throughout Southeast Asia and has lived in Singapore for the past five years. Experiencing different cultures provides fascinating food for thought for his writing assignments. At press time he was relocating to Guadalajara, Mexico.

Thailand updater **Mick Elmore** arrived in Bangkok on Thanksgiving 1991, ending a four-month drive from Melbourne, Australia, with Peter Goldie in a beat-up old Chrysler. He's been stuck in traffic ever since. A journalist since 1984—first in Texas, then in Australia—he is now based in Bangkok, where he writes for wire services and magazines.

Doreen G. Fernandez is a professor of literature and communication at the Ateneo de Manila University. When she's not busy teaching, she writes books and newspaper columns on food. In her update of the Manila dining section for this guide, she was assisted by **Maya Besa,** a freelancer who writes about food on the Internet.

Nigel Fisher—who updated much of Thailand as well as Cambodia, Laos, and Burma—is editor of the monthly travel publication *Voyager International.* He has traveled extensively throughout Asia and the world, and uses Bangkok as his Eastern base.

Bob Marriott was born in Nottingham, England, but since 1966 has made his home in New Zealand. After teaching for many years, his passion for travel led him into a career as a freelance writer and photographer. His work has appeared in numerous publications in New Zealand, Great Britain, and Malaysia. In between articles and travel he is writing a novel set in Asia. Bob updated part of the Malaysia chapter for this edition.

Mielikki Org, who has written for *Fodor's China* and other publications, updated the Smart Travel Tips A to Z for this edition.

Several writers joined forces to bring you the best of Bali, Indonesia, and islands to the East. **Denise Dowling** first studied Indonesian language and culture during a semester abroad in Bali, and later returned as a journalist. She currently teaches journalism and is a freelance writer and editor for American, British, and Australian publications. She updated the islands of the Nusa Tengarra, including Lombok. **Margaret Feldstein,** who covered northern Bali, has traveled extensively in Southeast Asia and has been to Bali three times, beginning in 1995. **Holly S. Smith** is a freelance writer whose articles have appeared in various international magazines. She has also written several books including *Aceh: Art and Culture,* and *Java: Garden of the East,* and her current projects include a book on heroines in Aceh (a province in northern Sumatra) and a collection of short stories inspired by her backpacking adventures in Southeast Asia and South America. Holly covered southern and central Bali and updated Indonesia A to Z for this book. Western Bali updater **Gisela Williams** first went to island in 1992 as a student of the School for International Training and studied Bahasa Indonesian while living with a Balinese family near Ubud. She's now a freelance writer for several travel and fashion magazines.

Ilsa Sharp, who updated the Exploring, Nightlife and the Arts, Outdoor Activities and Sports, and A to Z sections of the Singapore chapter, is a British-born Chinese studies graduate and professional writer who was based in Singapore from 1968 to 98 and now commutes regularly to the region from her base in Perth, Australia. She is the author of several books on the history, culture, and wildlife of Singapore and the Asia-Pacific region.

Abby Tan, who updated the Philippines chapter, is a Manila-based journalist with an extensive career in newspapers, magazines, radio, and television. She has written about Southeast Asian travel, economics, finance, and politics. Among the books she has authored are the *Financial Times's Asia Pacific Communications Markets: Philippines,* the *ASEAN Media Directory,* and *Essential Philippines.* She has co-edited a world book publication *Women's Future, World's Future* and edited Web sites for several major international institutions.

Mei-Yin Teo is a Toronto-based travel writer whose articles have been published in *The Toronto Sun, The Toronto Star, Tandem,* and On Top of the World II Web site. She began a year-long trip around the world in February 2000 and traveled to Asia, Africa, Australia, the South Pacific, South America and Central America. Along the way, Mei-Yin updated part of the Malaysia chapter for this edition.

Lara Wozniak, who updated Java, Sumatra, and Sulawesi for the Indonesia chapter, Northern Borneo for the Malaysia chapter, and Thailand A to Z, is a U.S. lawyer and senior features writer for *Hong Kong iMail,* a daily English-language newspaper in Hong Kong. She also regularly contributes to American and British newspapers and magazines. She wrote the Nepal chapter for *Fodor's Nepal, Tibet, and Bhutan 1st Edition.*

Several writers combined their expertise on the Vietnam chapter. **Andrew Chilvers,** who contributed to the Ho Chi Minh City and Mekong Delta, has written for newspapers and magazines in England, New Zealand, Vietnam, Thailand, and Japan. **Michael Mathes,** a freelance writer based in Hanoi, loves to travel around the city by motorbike. He covered Hanoi and the northernmost reaches of Vietnam. **Elka Ray,** a freelance writer and editor, contributed to the Hanoi Dining, Lodging, Nightlife and the Arts, and Outdoor Activities and Sports sections. Past writing assignments include touring Vietnam's luxury beach resorts and interviewing some of the country's best-known pop divas. **Craig Thomas,** a recovering lawyer, is a freelance journalist based in Ho Chi Minh City. Craig worked on the Hue, Nha Trang, central coast, and central highland sections of the Vietnam chapter.

We'd also like to thank Amanresorts; Avis International; Sue from Biyu Nasak; Chia Boon Hee of BNE Travel Consultants, Singapore; Cathay Pacific; Lara Constantino; John Flood of TheDamai; Garuda Indonesia Airlines; Holiday Inn Senggigi; Hotel Tugu; Hyatt hotels; Mariflor Lopez-Vito; Malaysia Airlines; Malaysian Tourism Board of Kuala Lumpur and Sydney; Liam McMillan; Pak Astawa of Mimpi Resorts; Eddy Batubara of Nazareth Tours and Travel; Northwest Airlines; the Oberoi hotel; Emiliano Yu, Rolando Estabillo, Joy Pasiliao, and Gigi Ezequiel of Philippine Airlines; the Philippine Department of Tourism in New York, Iloilo, Cebu, and Baguio; the staff of Puri Lumbung; Richard from Rambutan Beach Cottages; Mr. R. Segar; Sheraton ITT; Singapore Airlines; Tania Goh and Tony Lim of the Singapore Tourism Board (STB) and Gerald Lee of the STB's office in Toronto; and the staff of Villa Ratu Ayu.

Don't Forget to Write

Keeping a travel guide fresh and up-to-date is a big job. So we love your feedback—positive and negative—and follow up on all suggestions. Contact the Southeast Asia editor at editors@fodors.com or c/o Fodor's, 280 Park Avenue, New York, NY 10017. And have a wonderful trip!

Karen Cure
Editorial Director

Southeast Asia

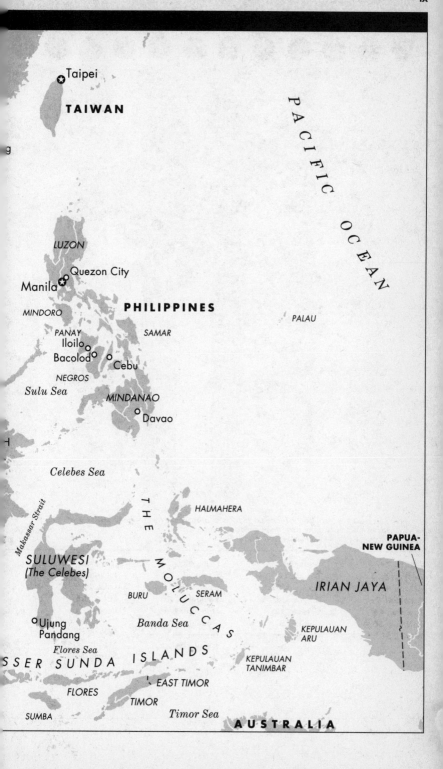

World Time Zones

Numbers below vertical bands relate each zone to Greenwich Mean Time (0 hrs.).
Local times frequently differ from these general indications,
as indicated by light-face numbers on map.

+11 +12 - -11   -10   -9   -8   -7   -6   -5   -4   -3   -2

Algiers, **29**
Anchorage, **3**
Athens, **41**
Auckland, **1**
Baghdad, **46**
Bangkok, **50**
Beijing, **54**

Berlin, **34**
Bogotá, **19**
Budapest, **37**
Buenos Aires, **24**
Caracas, **22**
Chicago, **9**
Copenhagen, **33**
Dallas, **10**

Delhi, **48**
Denver, **8**
Dublin, **26**
Edmonton, **7**
Hong Kong, **56**
Honolulu, **2**
Istanbul, **40**
Jakarta, **53**

Jerusalem, **42**
Johannesburg, **44**
Lima, **20**
Lisbon, **28**
London
(Greenwich), **27**
Los Angeles, **6**
Madrid, **38**
Manila, **57**

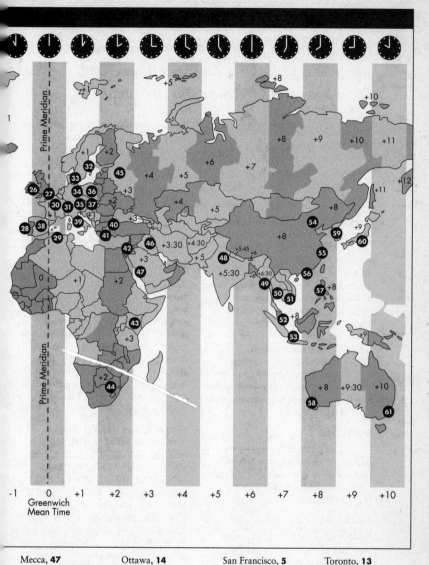

SMART TRAVEL TIPS A TO Z

*Basic Information on Traveling in Southeast Asia,
Savvy Tips to Make Your Trip a Breeze, and
Companies and Organizations to Contact*

AIR TRAVEL

Flights from the United States to Southeast Asia may be transpacific or transatlantic. Westbound, the major gateway cities are Los Angeles, San Francisco, Seattle, and Portland (Oregon). Eastbound, the major gateways are New York, Detroit, Chicago, and Dallas. Stopover points may include Bangkok, Hong Kong, Kuala Lumpur, Seoul, Singapore, Taipei, or Tokyo. Your best bet is to **use Bangkok, Hong Kong, Singapore, or Tokyo for your stopover,** as many airlines fly nonstop here from the West Coast and these cities have the greatest number of connecting flights. If time isn't an issue and you're leaving from the Midwest or the East Coast of the United States you can often **add a stopover in Europe or the Middle East to your transatlantic flight** for a small charge.

BOOKING

When you book, **look for nonstop flights** and **remember that "direct" flights stop at least once.** Try to avoid connecting flights, which require a change of plane.

CARRIERS

Northwest is the major U.S. airline that flies to Asia, with direct flights to Bangkok, Manila, and Singapore, among other cities. Continental, Delta, and United also fly to several Asian cities, including Singapore. From North America, China Airlines, Japan Airlines, Malaysia Airlines, Philippine Airlines, and Thai Airways International all fly to Asia from the West Coast. Connections from points east are usually made via U.S. air partners, but All Nippon Airways, Korean Air, and Singapore Airlines fly out of New York.

Northwest and United also serve Asia from Canada—as do Cathay Pacific, Japan Airlines, Korean Air, Malaysia Airlines, and Singapore Airlines—and Vietnam Airlines has an office in Montréal. The major carriers that fly to Asia from the United Kingdom include British Airways, Olympic Airways, Scandinavian Airways/SAS, and Thai Airways. Air New Zealand, Ansett, Malaysia Airlines, Qantas, and Thai Airways travel to Asia from most cities in Australia, New Zealand, and the South Pacific.

A number of smaller airlines connect the countries of Southeast Asia (☞ individual chapter A to Z sections), many of which have levels of comfort and service that equal or surpass those of Western carriers. Often, these airlines are less expensive, have more varied schedules, and will usually allow you to book last-minute and one-way tickets without penalty, since they generally don't offer advance booking discounts.

➤ MAJOR AIRLINES: **All Nippon Airways** (☎ 800/235–9262). **China Airlines** (☎ 800/227–5118). **Continental** (☎ 800/525–0280). **Delta** (☎ 800/221–1212). **EVA** (☎ 800/695–1188). **Japan Airlines** (☎ 800/525–3663). **Korean Air** (☎ 800/438–5000). **Malaysia Airlines** (☎ 800/552–9264). **Northwest Airlines** (☎ 800/225–2525). **Philippine Airlines** (☎ 800/435–9725). **Singapore Airlines** (☎ 800/742–3333). **Thai Airways International** (☎ 800/426–5204). **United** (☎ 800/241–6522).

➤ FROM AUSTRALIA AND NEW ZEALAND: **Air New Zealand** (☎ 0800/737000 or 0800/352266 in New Zealand; 132476 in Australia). **Ansett** (☎ 0800/267388 in New Zealand; 131767 or 1800/022146 in Australia). **Malaysia Airlines** (☎ 0800/777–747 in New Zealand). **Qantas** (☎ 008/808767 in New Zealand; 131313 in Australia). **Thai Airways** (300/651–960 in Australia).

➤ From Canada: **Cathay Pacific**
(☎ 800/233–2742). **Vietnam Airlines**
(☎ 514/281–1333).

➤ From the U.K.: **British Airways**
(☎ 0845/773–3377 or 0845/722–
2111). **Olympic Airways** (☎ 0187/
0606–0640). **Scandinavian
Airways/SAS** (☎ 0845/727–727).
Thai Airways (☎ 020/7499–9113).

CHECK-IN & BOARDING

Assuming that not everyone with a
ticket will show up, airlines routinely
overbook planes. When everyone
does, airlines ask for volunteers to
give up their seats. In return, these
volunteers usually get a certificate for
a free flight and are rebooked on the
next flight out. If there are not
enough volunteers, the airline must
choose who will be denied boarding.
The first to get bumped are passengers who checked in late and those
flying on discounted tickets, so **get to
the gate and check in as early as
possible,** especially during peak
periods.

Always **bring a government-issued
photo I.D. to the airport.** You may be
asked to show it before you are
allowed to check in.

CUTTING COSTS

The least expensive airfares to Southeast Asia must usually be purchased
in advance and are nonrefundable.
It's smart to **call a number of airlines,
and when you are quoted a good
price, book it on the spot**—the same
fare may not be available the next
day. Always **check different routings**
and look into using different airports.
Travel agents, especially low-fare
specialists (☞ Discounts & Deals,
below), are helpful.

A number of Web sites offer lower
fares when you **book tickets on the
Internet;** try cheaptickets.com, expe-
dia.com, priceline.com, or ticket-
planet.com. These sites will find
schedules, discounts, fares, and packages for you; you can even order and
pay for tickets and reserve seats and
meals on-line.

Consolidators are another good
source. They buy tickets for scheduled
international flights at reduced rates
from the airlines, then sell them at
prices that beat the best fare available
directly from the airlines, usually
without restrictions. Sometimes you
can even get your money back if you
need to return the ticket. Carefully
read the fine print detailing penalties
for changes and cancellations, and
**confirm your consolidator reservation
with the airline.**

When you **fly as a courier,** you trade
your checked-luggage space for a
ticket deeply subsidized by a courier
service. There are restrictions on
when you can book and how long
you can stay.

If you plan to visit multiple countries
in Southeast Asia, **check into "Circle
Pacific" or round-the-world (RTW)
fares.** These are flat-rate fares that are
subject to advance-purchase restrictions, usually of 7–14 days, and other
rules. Circle Pacific fares allow four
stopovers, although travel may not be
allowed to such countries as Vietnam,
Burma, Laos, and Cambodia. Additional stopovers can be purchased.
Around-the-world fares also have
routing restrictions and require one
transatlantic and one transpacific
crossing. These tickets are based on
either direction or mileage, and both
have their advantages: direction-based
fares can be less expensive, but
mileage-based fares allow backtrack-
ing and multiple visits to a single city.

➤ Consolidators: **Cheap Tickets**
(☎ 800/377–1000). **Discount Airline
Ticket Service** (☎ 800/576–1600).
Unitravel (☎ 800/325–2222). **Up &
Away Travel** (☎ 212/889–2345).
World Travel Network (☎ 800/409–
6753).

➤ Couriers: **Global Courier Travel**
(Box 3051, Nederland, CO 80466,
✍). **International Association of Air
Travel Couriers** (✉ 220 South Dixie
Hwy., Box 1349, Lake Worth, FL
33460, ☎ 561/582-8320). **Now
Voyager** (✉ 74 Varick St., Ste. 307,
New York, NY 10013, ☎ 212/431-
1616).

➤ Round-the-World Discounters:
Air Brokers International (☎ 800/
883–3273, ✍). **AirTreks** (☎ 800/350–
0612, ✍). **Avia Travel** (☎ 800/950–
2842, ✍). **Ticket Planet** (☎ 800/799–
8888, ✍).

SMART TRAVEL TIPS A TO Z

ENJOYING THE FLIGHT

For more legroom, **request an emergency-aisle seat.** Don't sit in the row in front of the emergency aisle or in front of a bulkhead, where seats may not recline. If you have dietary concerns, **ask for special meals when booking.** These can be vegetarian, low-cholesterol, or kosher, for example. On long flights, try to maintain a normal routine, to help fight jet lag. At night, **get some sleep.** By day, **eat light meals, drink water** (not alcohol), and **move around the cabin** to stretch your legs.

Some carriers have prohibited smoking throughout their systems; others allow smoking only on certain routes or even certain departures from that route. For flights within Asia, many airlines still have smoking sections, so **contact your carrier regarding its smoking policy.**

FLYING TIMES

See individual chapter A to Z sections for flying times to specific destinations.

HOW TO COMPLAIN

If your baggage goes astray or your flight goes awry, complain right away. Most carriers require that you **file a claim immediately.**

➤ AIRLINE COMPLAINTS: U.S. Department of Transportation Aviation Consumer Protection Division (✉ C-75, Room 4107, Washington, DC 20590, ☎ 202/366–2220, ✍). Federal Aviation Administration Consumer Hotline (☎ 800/322–7873).

RECONFIRMING

Most airlines require you to **reconfirm international flights 48 to 72 hours in advance.** Ask your airline or tour operator about its reconfirmation policy and keep this in mind as you travel.

AIRPORTS

The major Southeast Asian airports are in Bangkok, Denpasar, Jakarta, Kuala Lumpur, Manila, and Singapore. Other international hubs include Chiang Mai in northern Thailand; Hanoi and Ho Chi Minh City, Vietnam; Medan, Indonesia; Penang, Malaysia; Phnom Penh, Cambodia; Vientiane, Laos; and Yangon, Myanmar (☞ individual chapter A to Z sections for specific airport details).

AIRPORT TRANSFERS

Getting from the airport to downtown in Asia is rarely a problem, as a variety of transport is available at all hours. Bangkok, Kuala Lumpur, and Jakarta have nonstop airport shuttles that serve the train stations as well as the hotels. Shared hotel vans and taxis are the popular mode of transport in Hanoi, Denpasar, Phnom Penh, Bangkok, Medan, and Vientiane. It helps to **have a hotel brochure or an address in the local language for the driver.**

BIKE TRAVEL

Bikes are a refreshing means of transport, especially along the Mekong River in Thailand and Vietnam and in parts of Indonesia and Malaysia. In regions that are suitable for cycling, you can often rent bikes at guest houses, and most large cities have agencies that offer long-term rentals and bike maps.

BIKES IN FLIGHT

Most airlines accommodate bikes as luggage, provided they are dismantled and boxed. For bike boxes, often free at bike shops, you'll pay about $5 from airlines (at least $100 for bike bags). International travelers can sometimes substitute a bike for a piece of checked luggage at no charge; otherwise, the cost is about $100. Domestic and Canadian airlines charge $25–$50.

BOAT & FERRY TRAVEL

Boats and ferries are excellent means of transport throughout Southeast Asia; in fact, they sometimes constitute the most efficient and scenic way to get around in countries such as Indonesia and the Philippines. Unfortunately, traveling by boat over long distances can be inconvenient, as some boats cover routes only once a week. Eating facilities and toilets can also leave much to be desired. Boat and ferry arrangements can usually be made through your hotel or a travel agent. For more details, *see* individual chapter A to Z sections.

BUS TRAVEL

Most Asians don't own cars, so public transport is quite developed (and often crowded). Many countries offer luxury "super buses" that allow you to sightsee in comfort. For example, Indonesia, Thailand, Singapore, and Malaysia all have first-class buses with extra-wide, reclining seats, air-conditioning, video, scheduled box or buffet meals, and rest rooms. Most booking agents speak some English, and the fares are inexpensive compared to flying; if you have the time you might consider this option to see more of a country.

Tickets and schedules are available from terminals, hotels, and travel agents. You can usually buy a ticket on the spot, but for popular routes and longer distances, it's best to reserve in advance. Although hotels and travel agents usually accept traveler's checks and credit cards, **plan to pay in cash when you buy tickets at terminals.**

For local bus travel, the main problem is language; in many countries signs aren't in Roman letters. Even when numerals are the same and you know your route, city buses can be confusing, so **get written directions from your hotel clerk to show the driver.** For details on bus travel within or between specific cities or regions *see* individual chapter A to Z sections.

BUSINESS HOURS

Most businesses are open weekdays and Saturday from 9 to 5; they often close for one to two hours for lunch. *See* Opening and Closing Times *in* individual chapter A to Z sections.

CAMERAS & PHOTOGRAPHY

Cameras and film are widely available at reasonable prices throughout Southeast Asia, especially in Singapore. You can have your film developed at photo centers in major cities, but the quality may not be as good as at home.

Remember to ask permission or smile and make eye contact with people and children before photographing them. Note that photographing mosques is sometimes forbidden—if you're unsure of the proper etiquette, ask.

➤ PHOTO HELP: **Kodak Information Center** (☎ 800/242–2424). *Kodak Guide to Shooting Great Travel Pictures,* available in bookstores or from Fodor's Travel Publications (☎ 800/533–6478; $18.00 plus $5.50 shipping).

EQUIPMENT PRECAUTIONS

Always **keep your film and tape out of the sun.** Carry an extra supply of batteries, and **be prepared to turn on your camera or camcorder** to prove to security personnel that the device is real. Always **ask for hand inspection of film,** which becomes clouded after repeated exposure to airport X-ray machines, and **keep videotapes away from metal detectors.**

VIDEOS

Video cameras are a popular means of recording travels through Southeast Asia. Be sure to choose a reliable model, as camera repair shops are rare. Also bring spare tapes, as those sold in Southeast Asia may not be the same format as those used by your camera.

CAR RENTAL

Given the traffic situations within the city limits of major Southeast Asian destinations, it's probably best to **leave the driving to the cabbies and chauffeurs** who rule the roads here. **If you must rent a car, use common sense about when to do so.** In certain locations such as Bali (Indonesia), the east coast of Malaysia, or Phuket (Thailand), renting cars is common practice; in other locales traffic conditions and poor roads can make driving hazardous. Although hiring a car and driver (through your hotel or a travel agent) generally costs slightly more than simply renting a car, it's still relatively inexpensive.

Self-drive cars are available through large rental agencies, hotels, or travel agencies in major cities and tourist hubs. Although there are many inexpensive local agencies that waive the rules, if you want to be certain of the reliability of your vehicle it's best to **rent from a larger, well-known agency that can assist you if any**

problems occur. Western agencies usually offer either sedans or four-wheel-drive vehicles, all with standard transmission, cassette decks, and air-conditioning; vehicles from local agencies can range from mini-Jeeps to full-size vans, but they may not have air-conditioning or extra comforts. Although there are no car seat requirements in Asia, those with traveling with small children can **book infant and child seats in advance from Western agencies.**

➤ MAJOR AGENCIES: **Alamo** (☎ 800/522–9696; 020/8759–6200 in the U.K.). **Avis** (☎ 800/331–1084; 800/331–1084 in Canada; 02/9353–9000 in Australia; 09/525–1982 in New Zealand). **Budget** (☎ 800/527–0700; 0870/607–5000 in the U.K., through affiliate Europcar). **Dollar** (☎ 800/800–6000; 0124/622–0111 in the U.K., through affiliate Sixt Kenning; 02/9223–1444 in Australia). **Hertz** (☎ 800/654–3001; 800/263–0600 in Canada; 020/8897–2072 in the U.K.; 02/9669–2444 in Australia; 09/256–8690 in New Zealand). **National Car Rental** (☎ 800/227–7368; 020/8680–4800 in the U.K., where it is known as National Europe).

CUTTING COSTS

To get the best deal, **book through a travel agent who will shop around.** Payment must be made before you leave home. Thailand, Singapore, and Malaysia all have local agencies that may offer more reasonable prices. *See* Getting Around by Car *in* individual chapter A to Z sections.).

INSURANCE

Insurance isn't required in Asia but it's definitely recommended. When driving a rented car you are generally responsible for any damage to or loss of the vehicle as well as for any property damage or personal injury that you may cause. Before you rent, see what coverage your personal auto-insurance policy and credit cards already provide.

REQUIREMENTS & RESTRICTIONS

Most car rental companies require an International Driver's License. You can get one through the American or Canadian automobile associations, or, in the United Kingdom, through the Automobile Association or Royal Automobile Club. Most Western companies also have age requirements.

SURCHARGES

Before you pick up a car in one city and leave it in another, **ask about drop-off charges or one-way service fees,** which can be substantial. Note, too, that some rental agencies charge extra if you return the car before the time specified in your contract. To avoid a hefty refueling fee, **fill the tank just before you turn in the car,** but be aware that gas stations near the rental outlet may overcharge.

CAR TRAVEL

Travel by car can be efficient and convenient in Southeast Asian countries, but it's often better to let someone else do the driving. Use your judgment about when to travel by car. For example, you're better off using public transportation within Singapore, but for travel between Singapore and Malaysia, a car will be more convenient. In Thailand, exercise caution when driving along rural routes; highway robberies have occurred in the past.

AUTO CLUBS

➤ IN AUSTRALIA: **Australian Automobile Association** (☎ 02/6247–7311).

➤ IN CANADA: **Canadian Automobile Association** (CAA, ☎ 613/247–0117).

➤ IN NEW ZEALAND: **New Zealand Automobile Association** (☎ 09/377–4660).

➤ IN THE U.K.: **Automobile Association** (AA, ☎ 0990/500–600). **Royal Automobile Club** (RAC, ☎ 0990/722–722 for membership; 0345/121–345 for insurance).

➤ IN THE U.S.: **American Automobile Association** (☎ 800/564–6222).

EMERGENCY SERVICES

Larger, well-known agencies such as Hertz, Avis, and Budget will offer some assistance in emergency situations. Otherwise, passing locals will probably be glad to lend you a hand.

In Malaysia, you can also contact the Automobile Association of Malaysia. In Singapore, get in touch with the Automobile Association of Singapore.

➤ CONTACTS: **Automobile Association of Malaysia** (☎ 03/261–3713 or 03/261–2727). **Automobile Association of Singapore** (☎ 748–9911).

GASOLINE

Gas prices are about the same as what you usually pay at home. Gas stations can be found around major towns and cities and many are open 24 hours.

ROAD CONDITIONS

Road quality ranges from poor (in Vietnam and parts of the Philippines, crowded and bumpy, especially in rural areas) to excellent (smooth cement and asphalt, especially in the cities). For more details on road conditions, as well as information on road maps and rules of the road, *see* Getting Around By Car *in* individual chapter A to Z sections.

CHILDREN IN SOUTHEAST ASIA

Youngsters are not only welcomed in Southeast Asia, they're embraced with delight in most areas. Only the strictest business establishments and stiffest hotels and restaurants (ask before you book) frown upon children; otherwise, they're seen as a natural complement to life. You will be amazed at how many people will want to hold and play with your kids, and at how their presence will actually open conversations and cut through cultural boundaries. Because they'll be the center of attention, if your youngsters are very young or particularly shy, plan outings for off-peak hours. Many large hotels have playgrounds and special menus and activities for children; smaller places often have more personalized services. **Check to see what types of kid-friendly amenities a hotel offers.**

There are few formal sitting agencies in Asia. Large hotels and resorts have their own activity programs and baby-sitting services; smaller establishments will usually recruit a trusted family member or neighbor to provide any assistance you need. Some families hire a nanny from an au pair service before they depart.

If you are renting a car, don't forget to **arrange for a car seat** when you reserve.

FLYING

If your children are two or older, **ask about children's airfares.** As a general rule, infants under two not occupying a seat fly at greatly reduced fares or even for free. When booking, **confirm carry-on allowances** if you're traveling with infants. In general, for babies charged 10% of the adult fare you are allowed one carry-on bag and a collapsible stroller; if the flight is full, the stroller may have to be checked or you may be limited to less.

Experts agree that it's a good idea to use safety seats aloft for children weighing less than 40 pounds. Airlines set their own policies: U.S. carriers usually require that the child be ticketed, even if he or she is young enough to ride free, since the seats must be strapped into regular seats. Do **check your airline's policy about using safety seats during takeoff and landing.** And since safety seats are not allowed just everywhere in the plane, get your seat assignments early.

When reserving, **request children's meals or a freestanding bassinet** if you need them. But note that bulkhead seats, where you must sit to use the bassinet, may lack an overhead bin or storage space on the floor.

LODGING

Most hotels in Southeast Asia allow children under a certain age to stay in their parents' room at no extra charge, but others charge for them as extra adults; be sure to **find out the cutoff age for children's discounts.**

PRECAUTIONS

If you're traveling with a child in Southeast Asia, be sure to take a generous supply of Pepto-Bismol tablets, antibiotics such as Cipro, and rehydration salts for severe cases of diarrhea, motion-sickness tablets, Tylenol, and vitamins. Children, like adults, will need some time to adjust to the food, and you should be sure that everything is thoroughly cooked. Boiled water is fine for children to drink, and plenty of juices, milk, and mineral water will also be available. Make sure children wash their hands thoroughly before each meal.

SIGHTS & ATTRACTIONS

Places that are especially appealing to children are indicated by a rubber duckie icon in the margin.

COMPUTERS ON THE ROAD

In major cities, you'll find Internet access in hotels and cybercafés. (Indeed, those who remember the Love Bug crisis know that certain residents in the Philippines are particularly well-connected to the Internet.) In Indonesia, access is easiest in the tourist cities of Bali and Java; access from Vietnam is more difficult. Singapore is the best-connected Southeast Asian city. To keep in touch with friends, family, and contacts while abroad, **set up an e-mail account through providers such as Yahoo and Hotmail.** These accounts let you check mail from anywhere, and they're free of charge (although access can be slow during the busiest hours.)

With the exception of those in Vietnam and the Philippines, most hotels in Southeast Asia that serve foreigners have modem hook-up, either from your room or via a business center. Be sure to bring a surge protector. You should also carry several types of plug adaptors, since countries may use the U.S. flat, two-prong-type plug or the European flat, three-prong plug. Buy these before you leave, since they're hard to find in Southeast Asia.

CONSUMER PROTECTION

Whenever shopping or buying travel services in Southeast Asia, **pay with a major credit card** so you can cancel payment or get reimbursed if there's a problem. If you're doing business with a particular company for the first time, **contact your local Better Business Bureau and the attorney general's offices** in your own state and the company's home state, as well. Have any complaints been filed? Finally, if you're buying a package or tour, always **consider travel insurance** that includes default coverage (☞ Insurance, *below*).

➤ BBBs: **Council of Better Business Bureaus** (✉ 4200 Wilson Blvd., Suite 800, Arlington, VA 22203, ☎ 703/276–0100, FAX 703/525–8277 ✍).

CRUISE TRAVEL

If you're interested in visiting a variety of Southeast Asian cities, **consider a cruise to the region.** Southeast Asia is one of the hottest destinations in cruising, and you can sail in many different styles. Choices range from a traditional ocean liner to a clipper-type tall ship to a luxury yacht. Ports of call include Singapore, Bali, Komodo Island, Jakarta, and Ho Chi Minh City. To get the best deal, **book with a cruise-only travel agency.** (For more information, *see* Tours and Packages, *below*.)

➤ CRUISE LINES: **Crystal Cruises** (✉ 2121 Ave. of the Stars, Los Angeles, CA 90067, ☎ 800/446–6620). **Cunard Line Limited** (✉ 555 5th Ave., New York, NY 10017, ☎ 800/528–6273). **Orient Lines** (✉ 1510 S.E. 17th St., Suite 400, Fort Lauderdale, FL 33316, ☎ 305/527–6660 or 800/333–7300). **Princess Cruises** (✉ 10100 Santa Monica Blvd., Los Angeles, CA 90067, ☎ 310/553–1770). **Radisson Seven Seas Cruises** (✉ 600 Corporate Dr., Suite 410, Fort Lauderdale, FL 33334, ☎ 800/333–3333). **Renaissance Cruises** (✉ 1800 Eller Dr., Suite 300, Box 350307, Fort Lauderdale, FL 33335-0307, ☎ 800/525–2450). **Royal Caribbean Cruise Line** (✉ 1050 Caribbean Way, Miami, FL 33132, ☎ 305/539–6000). **Seabourn Cruise Line** (✉ 55 Francisco St., San Francisco, CA 94133, ☎ 415/391–7444 or 800/929–9595). **Silversea Cruises** (✉ 110 E. Broward Blvd., Fort Lauderdale, FL 33301, ☎ 305/522–4477 or 800/722–9955). **Star Clippers** (✉ 4101 Salzedo Ave., Coral Gables, FL 33146, ☎ 800/442–0551).

CUSTOMS & DUTIES

When shopping, **keep receipts** for all purchases. Upon reentering the country, **be ready to show customs officials what you've bought.** If you feel a duty is incorrect or object to the way your clearance was handled, note the inspector's badge number and ask to see a supervisor. If the problem isn't resolved, write to the appropriate authorities, beginning with the port director at your point of entry. *See* Customs *in* individual chapter A to Z sections for country-specific customs guidelines.

IN AUSTRALIA

Australian residents who are 18 or older may bring home $A400 worth of souvenirs and gifts (including jewelry), 250 cigarettes or 250 grams of tobacco, and 1,125 ml of alcohol (including wine, beer, and spirits). Residents under 18 may bring back $A200 worth of goods. Prohibited items include meat products. Seeds, plants, and fruits need to be declared upon arrival.

➤ INFORMATION: **Australian Customs Service** (Regional Director, ✉ Box 8, Sydney, NSW 2001, ☎ 02/9213–2000, FAX 02/9213–4000, ✎).

IN CANADA

Canadian residents who have been out of Canada for at least 7 days may bring home C$500 worth of goods duty-free. If you've been away less than 7 days but more than 48 hours, the duty-free allowance drops to C$200; if your trip lasts 24–48 hours, the allowance is C$50. You may not pool allowances with family members. Goods claimed under the C$500 exemption may follow you by mail; those claimed under the lesser exemptions must accompany you. Alcohol and tobacco products may be included in the 7-day and 48-hour exemptions but not in the 24-hour exemption. If you meet the age requirements of the province or territory through which you reenter Canada, you may bring in, duty-free, 1.14 liters (40 imperial ounces) of wine or liquor *or* 24 12-ounce cans or bottles of beer or ale. If you are 16 or older you may bring in, duty-free, 200 cigarettes and 50 cigars. Check ahead of time with Revenue Canada or the Department of Agriculture for policies regarding meat products, seeds, plants, and fruits.

You may send an unlimited number of gifts worth up to C$60 each duty-free to Canada. Label the package UNSOLICITED GIFT—VALUE UNDER $60. Alcohol and tobacco are excluded.

➤ INFORMATION: **Revenue Canada** (✉ 2265 St. Laurent Blvd. S, Ottawa, Ontario K1G 4K3, ☎ 613/993–0534; 800/461–9999 in Canada, FAX 613/991–4126, ✎).

IN NEW ZEALAND

Homeward-bound residents 17 or older may bring back $700 worth of souvenirs and gifts. Your duty-free allowance also includes 4.5 liters of wine or beer; one 1,125-ml bottle of spirits; and either 200 cigarettes, 250 grams of tobacco, 50 cigars, or a combination of the three up to 250 grams. Prohibited items include meat products, seeds, plants, and fruits.

➤ INFORMATION: **New Zealand Customs** (Custom House, ✉ 50 Anzac Ave., Box 29, Auckland, New Zealand, ☎ 09/359–6655, FAX 09/359–6732).

IN THE U.K.

From countries outside the EU, including those in Southeast Asia, you may bring home, duty-free, 200 cigarettes or 50 cigars; 1 liter of spirits or 2 liters of fortified or sparkling wine or liqueurs; 2 liters of still table wine; 60 ml of perfume; 250 ml of toilet water; plus £136 worth of other goods, including gifts and souvenirs. If returning from outside the EU, prohibited items include meat products, seeds, plants, and fruits.

➤ INFORMATION: **HM Customs and Excise** (✉ Dorset House, Stamford St., Bromley, Kent BR1 1XX, ☎ 020/7202–4227, ✎).

IN THE U.S.

U.S. residents who have been out of the country for at least 48 hours (and who have not used the $400 allowance or any part of it in the past 30 days) may bring home $400 worth of foreign goods duty-free. U.S. residents 21 and older may bring back 1 liter of alcohol duty-free. In addition, regardless of your age, you are allowed 200 cigarettes and 100 non-Cuban cigars. Antiques, which the U.S. Customs Service defines as objects more than 100 years old, enter duty-free, as do original works of art done entirely by hand, including paintings, drawings, and sculptures.

SMART TRAVEL TIPS A TO Z

You may also send packages home duty-free: up to $200 worth of goods for personal use, with a limit of one parcel per addressee per day (except alcohol or tobacco products or perfume worth more than $5); label the package PERSONAL USE and attach a list of its contents and their retail value. Do not label the package UNSOLICITED GIFT or your duty-free exemption will drop to $100. Mailed items do not affect your duty-free allowance on your return.

➤ INFORMATION: **U.S. Customs Service** (✉ 1300 Pennsylvania Ave. NW, Washington, DC 20229, www.customs.gov; inquiries ☎ 202/354–1000; complaints c/o ✉ 1300 Pennsylvania Ave. NW, Room 5.4D, Washington, DC 20229; registration of equipment c/o ✉ Resource Management, ☎ 202/354–1000).

DINING

Southeast Asia offers a fine and eclectic array of delicious cuisine, from the Spanish-influenced dishes of the Philippines to the delectable noodle and seafood options of Thailand and Malaysia, not to mention the myriad exotic fruits and vegetables available throughout the region. There tends to be something for everyone, whether it be spicy, vegetarian, grilled, or sweet. The restaurants we list are the cream of the crop in each price category.

MEALS & SPECIALTIES

Every country has its own dishes, but rice and noodles are staples throughout Southeast Asia. Vegetarian cuisine is also widely available. *See* the Dining sections of individual chapters for overviews of local specialties.

MEALTIMES

In most Southeast Asian countries, lunch is served between 11 and 2 and dinner from 5 to 10. Unless otherwise noted, the restaurants listed in this guide are open daily for lunch and dinner.

PAYING

Major restaurants usually accept credit cards. At small establishments in both cities and rural areas, expect to pay with cash.

RESERVATIONS & DRESS

Reservations are always a good idea: we mention them only when they're essential or not accepted. Book as far ahead as you can, and reconfirm as soon as you arrive. We mention dress only when men are required to wear a jacket or a jacket and tie.

DISABILITIES & ACCESSIBILITY

Those with disabilities who are planning a trip to Southeast Asia will find the amenities woefully nonexistent. However, the situation is quickly changing at many hotels and tourist sites as the need for access is universally recognized. Singapore, with its wide sidewalks and modern facilities throughout the main city area, is the best option for those who have disabilities, but the newer hotels in other countries are also incorporating wheelchair ramps, wide doors, and appropriate rooms into their plans. Although international airlines are also becoming well versed in making proper accommodations for those with disabilities, the smaller regional airlines may not be able to offer the same access or comfort; check before you book.

➤ LOCAL RESOURCES: **Association of the Physically Handicapped of Thailand** (✉ 73/7–8 Soi Theppresan (Soi 8), Thannon Tivanon, Talaat Kawan, Nonthaburi 11000, Thailand, ☎ 02/951–0569). **Disabled Peoples International** (✉ 78/2 Thanon Tivanon, Pak Kret, Nonthaburi 11120, Thailand, ☎ 02/583–3021).

LODGING

When discussing accessibility with an operator or reservations agent, **ask hard questions.** Are there any stairs, inside *or* out? Are there grab bars next to the toilet *and* in the shower/tub? How wide is the doorway to the room? To the bathroom? For the most extensive facilities meeting the latest legal specifications, **opt for newer accommodations.**

TRANSPORTATION

Unfortunately, most trains, buses, and cars in Southeast Asia are not equipped to accommodate wheelchairs. The best option is to hire a car and driver, especially if you have fold-up wheelchair.

➤ COMPLAINTS: **Disability Rights Section** (✉ U.S. Department of Justice, Civil Rights Division, Box 66738, Washington, DC 20035-6738, ☎ 202/514–0301 or 800/514–0301; TTY 202/514–0383 or 800/514–0383, FAX 202/307–1198, ✍) for general complaints. **Aviation Consumer Protection Division** (☞ Air Travel, *above*) for airline-related problems. **Civil Rights Office** (✉ U.S. Department of Transportation, Departmental Office of Civil Rights, S-30, 400 7th St. SW, Room 10215, Washington, DC 20590, ☎ 202/366–4648, FAX 202/366–9371) for problems with surface transportation.

TRAVEL AGENCIES

In the United States, the Americans with Disabilities Act requires that travel firms serve the needs of all travelers. Some agencies specialize in working with people with disabilities.

➤ TRAVELERS WITH MOBILITY PROBLEMS: **Access Adventures** (✉ 206 Chestnut Ridge Rd., Scottsville, NY 14624, ☎ 716/889–9096), run by a former physical-rehabilitation counselor. **Flying Wheels Travel** (✉ 143 W. Bridge St., Box 382, Owatonna, MN 55060, ☎ 507/451–5005 or 800/535–6790, FAX 507/451–1685, ✍).

DISCOUNTS & DEALS

Be a smart shopper and **compare all your options** before making decisions. A plane ticket bought with a promotional coupon from travel clubs, coupon books, and direct-mail offers may not be cheaper than the least expensive fare from a discount ticket agency. And always keep in mind that what you get is just as important as what you save.

DISCOUNT RESERVATIONS

To save money, **look into discount reservations services** with toll-free numbers, which use their buying power to get a better price on hotels, airline tickets, even car rentals. When booking a room, always **call the hotel's local toll-free number** (if one is available) rather than the central reservations number—you'll often get a better price. Always ask about special packages or corporate rates.

When shopping for the best deal on hotels and car rentals, **look for guaranteed exchange rates,** which protect you against a falling dollar. With your rate locked in, you won't pay more, even if the price goes up in the local currency.

➤ HOTEL ROOMS: **Steigenberger Reservation Service** (☎ 800/223–5652, ✍). **Travel Interlink** (☎ 800/888–5898, ✍). **VacationLand** (☎ 800/245–0050, ✍).

PACKAGE DEALS

Don't confuse packages and guided tours. When you buy a package, you travel on your own, just as though you had planned the trip yourself. Fly/drive packages, which combine airfare and car rental, are often a good deal.

ECOTOURISM

Tourism in consideration and in support of the environment is on the rise, and some tour groups offer special packages to Southeast Asia in light of this fact. Whether you're traveling with an ecotourist group or not, be as considerate to the environment when traveling as you would be in your own country. In Southeast Asia, this means holding on to litter until you come upon a trash receptacle (sporadically placed in some destinations), respecting nature and animals, trying not to waste water, and recycling when possible.

ELECTRICITY

To use your U.S.-purchased electric-powered equipment, **bring a converter and adapter.** The electrical current in the countries covered in this book is 220 volts, 50 cycles alternating current (AC), except in the Philippines, which, like the United States, runs on 110-volt, 60-cycle AC current.

If your appliances are dual-voltage, you'll need only an adapter. Don't use 110-volt outlets marked FOR SHAVERS ONLY for high-wattage appliances such as blow-dryers. Most laptops operate equally well on 110 and 220 volts and so require only an adapter. Surge protectors are highly recommended.

EMBASSIES AND CONSULATES

Embassies and consulates for New Zealand, Australia, Canada, the United Kingdom, and the United States are listed under Contacts and Resources in chapter A to Z sections.

EMERGENCIES

If you lose your passport, contact your embassy immediately. Embassy officials can also advise you on how to proceed in case of other emergencies. Your hotel may also be able to provide a translator if you need to report an emergency or crime to doctors or the police.

➤ EMERGENCY NUMBERS: **Indonesia** (☎ 118 for ambulance, 113 for fire, 110 for police). **Malaysia** (☎ 999). **The Philippines** (☎ 166 for police, 160 for ambulance or fire). **Singapore** (☎ 995 for fire or ambulance, 999 for police). **Thailand** (1699 for tourist police). **Vietnam** (☎ 15 for ambulance, 14 for fire, 13 for police).

ENGLISH-LANGUAGE MEDIA

English-language newspapers and magazines are available in Indonesia (*Jakarta Post, Indonesia Observer, Jakarta Now, What's On*); Singapore (*The Straits Times, 8 Days*); Thailand (*Bangkok Post, The Nation, Bangkok Metro*); and the Philippines (*Philippine Daily Inquirer, What's On in Manila, Expat, Panorama*). In Thailand, Singapore, Indonesia, Malaysia, and the Philippines (Manila only), English-language TV programs are sometimes available, such as CNN, the BBC World Service, and HBO. *Radio Thailand,* based in Bangkok, offers English-language news from 6 AM to 11 PM at 97 MHz FM.

ETIQUETTE & BEHAVIOR

In Southeast Asia, "saving face" is extremely important, and you'll find that being calm, respectful, and polite will greatly help overcome difficulties and misunderstandings. Raising your voice when things don't go as planned will only embarrass you and reduce your chances of being helped. Learning a few words of the local language to say "thank you," or simply a nod and a smile, is also helpful.

When visiting temples, don't wear shorts or tank tops; women should cover their knees and shoulders. Remove your shoes before entering the temple and and don't point the toes at any image of the buddha. Although beach attire is fine for beaches and crowded tourist spots, don't wear it on city streets or in offices.

In Thailand, you should never point your toes at people, and take care not to show the soles of your feet. Never use your left hand for anything (eating, shaking, gesturing, etc.) in Indonesia, Singapore, or Malaysia, as it's customarily the hand that's used for more hygienic purposes. Also, the head is considered a sacred part of the body and should never be touched.

GAY & LESBIAN TRAVEL

Many tourist areas—for example in Thailand, on Bali (Indonesia), and in the Philippines—offer a tolerant environment for gay and lesbian travelers. Other areas, however— such as the strict Muslim regions of Malaysia and most of Indonesia— aren't as tolerant. In more rural countries, such as Cambodia, Laos, and Vietnam, overt behavior isn't encouraged, either. Outside of major tourist spots, discretion is advised.

➤ GAY- & LESBIAN-FRIENDLY TRAVEL AGENCIES: **Different Roads Travel** (⊠ 8383 Wilshire Blvd., Suite 902, Beverly Hills, CA 90211, ☎ 323/651–5557 or 800/429–8747, FAX 323/651–3678). **Kennedy Travel** (⊠ 314 Jericho Turnpike, Floral Park, NY 11001, ☎ 516/352–4888 or 800/237–7433, FAX 516/354–8849, ✍). **Now Voyager** (⊠ 4406 18th St., San Francisco, CA 94114, ☎ 415/626–1169 or 800/255–6951, FAX 415/626–8626, ✍). **Skylink Travel and Tour** (⊠ 1006 Mendocino Ave., Santa Rosa, CA 95401, ☎ 707/546–9888 or 800/225–5759, FAX 707/546–9891, ✍), serving lesbian travelers.

HEALTH

Pay attention to what you eat and drink, wear sunscreen, and consume plenty of water or tea. You should also **bring your own prescriptions and medications,** as they may be unavailable or unreliable if bought in Southeast Asia. Many hotels can refer you to an English-speaking doctor. For serious health situations, it's best to be treated in your own country; otherwise consider flying to Singapore, which has the region's best medical facilities.

DIVERS' ALERT

Do not fly within 24 hours of scuba diving.

FOOD & DRINK

The major health risk is traveler's diarrhea, caused by eating contaminated fruit or vegetables or drinking contaminated water. Other diseases, such as cholera, hepatitis, and liver flukes, are more rare, but do occur. So **watch what you eat.** Stay away from ice, uncooked food, and unpasteurized milk and milk products, and **drink only bottled water** or water that has been boiled for at least 20 minutes, even when brushing your teeth. **Make sure food is cooked thoroughly** and that the restaurant is clean; avoid empty or unfrequented eateries. Food from street vendors is fine as long as the food is prepared in a hygienic manner, well-cooked, and hasn't been sitting around.

Mild cases of diarrhea may respond to Imodium (known generically as loperamide) or Pepto-Bismol (not as strong), both of which can be purchased over the counter. Drink plenty of purified water or tea—chamomile is a good folk remedy. In severe cases, rehydrate yourself with a salt-sugar solution (½ teaspoon salt and 4 tablespoons sugar per quart of water).

MEDICAL PLANS

No one plans to get sick while traveling, but it happens, so **consider signing up with a medical-assistance company.** Members get doctor referrals, emergency evacuation or repatriation, hot lines for medical consultation, cash for emergencies, and other assistance.

➤ MEDICAL-ASSISTANCE COMPANIES: **International SOS Assistance** (✉ 8 Neshaminy Interplex, Suite 207, Trevose, PA 19053, ☎ 215/245–4707 or 800/523–6586, FAX 215/244–9617, www.internationalsos.com; ✉ 12 Chemin Riantbosson, 1217 Meyrin 1, Geneva, Switzerland, ☎ 4122/785–6464, FAX 4122/785–6424; ✉ 331 N. Bridge Rd., 17–00, Odeon Towers, Singapore 188720, ☎ 65/338–7800, FAX 65/338–7611).

OVER-THE-COUNTER REMEDIES

You can buy Western medicines, such as aspirin. without a prescription in urban pharmacies and large hotels. Consult a physician—your hotel can refer you to one—for advice on local remedies.

PESTS & OTHER HAZARDS

According to the National Centers for Disease Control (CDC), there's a limited risk of malaria and dengue in certain areas of Southeast Asia. In most urban or easily accessible areas you need not worry. However, if you plan to visit remote regions or stay for more than six weeks, **check with the CDC's International Travelers hotline or Web site.** In areas where malaria and dengue, both of which are carried by mosquitoes, are prevalent, use mosquito nets, wear clothing that covers the body, apply repellent containing DEET, and use spray for flying insects in living and sleeping areas. Also **consider taking antimalarial pills,** but ask your doctor about the effectiveness and potential side effects of these drugs. There is no vaccine that combats dengue.

In the southern Philippines and parts of Indonesia, schistosomiasis can be present in freshwater and can enter through the skin; avoid bathing or splashing in freshwater lakes and rivers. Generally, animals shouldn't be approached because they may have rabies.

SHOTS & MEDICATIONS

Although the countries in Southeast Asia don't require or suggest vaccinations before traveling, the CDC may recommend one or more of the following precautions, depending on the country:

Tetanus-diphtheria and polio vaccinations should be up-to-date—if you haven't been immunized since childhood, **consider bolstering your tetanus vaccination.** You should also be immunized against (or immune to) measles, mumps, and rubella. If you plan to visit rural areas, where there's questionable sanitation, you'll need to **get a Havrix shot against hepatitis A.** If you're staying for longer than three weeks and traveling into rural areas, antimalarial pills and a typhoid vaccination are sometimes recommended. If staying for a month or more, you should be vaccinated against rabies and Japanese encephalitis; for six months or more, against hepatitis B. For news on current outbreaks of infectious diseases, ask your physician and check with the CDC.

➤ HEALTH WARNINGS: **National Centers for Disease Control** (CDC; National Center for Infectious Diseases, Division of Quarantine, Traveler's Health Section, ✉ 1600 Clifton Rd. NE, M/S E-03, Atlanta, GA 30333, ☎ 888/232-3228 or 800/311-3435, FAX 888/232-3299, ✆).

HOLIDAYS

See Opening and Closing Times *in* individual chapter A to Z sections for country-specific holidays.

INSURANCE

The most useful travel-insurance plan is a comprehensive policy that includes coverage for trip cancellation and interruption, default, trip delay, and medical expenses (with a waiver for pre-existing conditions).

Without insurance you will lose all or most of your money if you cancel your trip, regardless of the reason. Default insurance covers you if your tour operator, airline, or cruise line goes out of business. Trip-delay insurance covers expenses that arise because of bad weather or mechanical delays. Study the fine print when comparing policies.

If you're traveling internationally, a key component of travel insurance is coverage for medical bills incurred if you get sick on the road. Such expenses are not generally covered by Medicare or private policies. U.K. residents can buy a travel-insurance policy valid for most vacations taken during the year in which it's purchased (but check pre-existing-condition coverage). British and Australian citizens need extra medical coverage when traveling overseas.

Always **buy travel policies directly from the insurance company**; if you buy them from a cruise line, airline, or tour operator that goes out of business you probably will not be covered for the agency or operator's default, a major risk. Before making any purchase, **review your existing health and home-owner's policies** to find what they cover away from home.

➤ TRAVEL INSURERS: In the U.S.: **Access America** (✉ 6600 W. Broad St., Richmond, VA 23230, ☎ 804/285-3300 or 800/284-8300, FAX 804/673-1583, ✆), **Travel Guard International** (✉ 1145 Clark St., Stevens Point, WI 54481, ☎ 715/345-0505 or 800/826-1300, FAX 800/955-8785, ✆).

➤ INSURANCE INFORMATION: In Australia: **Insurance Council of Australia** (☎ 03/9614-1077, FAX 03/9614-7924). In the U.K.: **Association of British Insurers** (✉ 51-55 Gresham St., London EC2V 7HQ, ☎ 0207/600-3333, FAX 0207/696-8999, ✆).

LANGUAGE

See Contacts and Resources *in* individual chapter A to Z sections for country-specific information on languages.

LODGING

Accommodations in Southeast Asia range from shoebox-size rooms with community or "squat" toilets to five-star luxury hotels and villas. Every major city and important resort has at least one opulent hotel—and probably several—famous for service and amenities. The current trend in Southeast Asia, though, is to book a villa instead; these often have the same services and facilities as the major hotel chains but with the charm of a private home—and with equally convenient locations. If you can afford to splurge on accommodations, Southeast Asia is the place to do it, for the prices of even the very top hotels and villas are often still far lower than comparable digs elsewhere. Remember that you can bargain—even at upscale establishments.

For medium and large hotels in popular areas, **reserve your rooms at least two months prior to arrival.** This is especially true in December, during Chinese New Year, and at the end of Ramadan. International hotel chains have U.S. reservations offices, and you can reserve villas through a broker. If you do arrive in an Asian capital without a reservation, the information desk at the airport may be able to provide an immediate booking—often at a discount.

Most bottom-end accommodations are clustered in particular areas of cities or tourist hubs—and they're usually a little off the beaten path. Always **ask to see the room before committing to a stay in a budget hotel** and **comparison-shop for the best deal.** You can find budget dormitory and hotel accommodations at the YMCAs in Bangkok, Kuala Lumpur, Manila, and Singapore, or at hostels and homestays in Thailand, the Philippines, Indonesia, and Malaysia. They vary greatly in quality but are generally inexpensive and clean. You will also find some interesting, uniquely Asian lodging alternatives. In Sarawak, Malaysia, for example, you can stay in tribal longhouses and observe the native lifestyle, joining in meal preparation and evening entertainments. In northern Thailand, stays in village huts are part of many overnight treks to the hill tribes.

The lodgings we list are the cream of the crop in each price category. We always list the facilities that are available—but we don't specify whether they cost extra: when pricing accommodations, always ask what's included and what costs extra. Assume that hotels operate on the **European Plan** (EP, with no meals) unless we specify that they use either the **Continental Plan** (CP, with a Continental breakfast), **Breakfast Plan** (BP, with a full breakfast) or the **Modified American Plan** (MAP, with breakfast and dinner) or are **all-inclusive** (including all meals and most activities).

APARTMENT & VILLA RENTALS

If you want a home base that's roomy enough for a family and comes with cooking facilities, **consider a furnished rental.** These can save you money, especially if you're traveling with a group. Home-exchange directories sometimes list rentals as well as exchanges.

➤ VILLA AGENTS: **International Home Exchange** (✉ Box 915253, Longwood, FL 32791, ☎ 407/862–7211, 🖳). **P. T. Indovillas** (✉ Jl. Daksina #5, Batu Belig, Kerobokan, Bali, Indonesia, 62/361–733031, 🖳). **Vacation Rentals On-Line** (🖳).

HOSTELS

No matter what your age, you can **save on lodging costs by staying at hostels.** In some 5,000 locations in more than 70 countries around the world, Hostelling International (HI), the umbrella group for a number of national youth-hostel associations, offers single-sex, dorm-style beds and, at many hostels, rooms for couples and family accommodations. Membership in any HI national hostel association, open to travelers of all ages, allows you to stay in HI-affiliated hostels at member rates; one-year membership is about $25 for adults (C$26.75 in Canada, £9.30 in the U.K., $30 in Australia, and $30 in New Zealand); hostels run about $10–$25 per night. Members have priority if the hostel is full; they're also eligible for discounts around the world, even on rail and bus travel in some countries.

➤ ORGANIZATIONS: **Hostelling International—American Youth Hostels** (✉ 733 15th St. NW, Suite 840, Washington, DC 20005, ☎ 202/783–6161, 𝖥𝖠𝖷 202/783–6171, 🖳). **Hostelling International—Canada** (✉ 400–205 Catherine St., Ottawa, Ontario K2P 1C3, ☎ 613/237–7884, 𝖥𝖠𝖷 613/237–7868, 🖳). **Youth Hostel Association of England and Wales** (✉ Trevelyan House, 8 St. Stephen's Hill, St. Albans, Hertfordshire AL1 2DY, ☎ 01727/855215 or 01727/845047, 𝖥𝖠𝖷 01727/844126, 🖳). **Australian Youth Hostel Association** (✉ 10 Mallett St., Camperdown, NSW 2050, ☎ 02/9565–1699, 𝖥𝖠𝖷 02/9565–1325, 🖳). **Youth Hostels Association of New Zealand** (✉ Box 436, Christchurch, New Zealand, ☎ 03/379–9970, 𝖥𝖠𝖷 03/365–4476, 🖳).

HOTELS

All hotels listed in this book have private baths unless otherwise noted.

➤ TOLL-FREE NUMBERS: **Best Western** (☎ 800/528–1234, ✇). **Choice** (☎ 800/221–2222, ✇). **Four Seasons** (☎ 800/332–3442, ✇). **Holiday Inn** (☎ 800/465–4329, ✇). **Marriott** (☎ 800/228–9290, ✇). **Nikko Hotels International** (☎ 800/645–5687, ✇). **Radisson** (☎ 800/333–3333, ✇). **Renaissance Hotels & Resorts** (☎ 800/468–3571, ✇).

MAIL & SHIPPING

See Contacts and Resources *in* individual chapter A to Z sections.

MONEY MATTERS

Prices throughout this guide are given for adults. Substantially reduced fees are almost always available for children, students, and senior citizens. For more information on banks and exchange services, currency, costs, taxes, and tipping, *see* individual chapter A to Z sections.

CREDIT CARDS

Credit cards are widely accepted at hotels and restaurants, upscale shopping centers, and tourist shops throughout Southeast Asia. Throughout this guide, the following abbreviations are used: **AE**, American Express; **DC**, Diner's Club; **MC**, Master Card; and **V**, Visa. Note that the Discover card is usually only accepted in the United States.

CURRENCY EXCHANGE

For the most favorable rates, **change money through banks.** Although ATM transaction fees may be higher abroad than at home, ATM rates are excellent because they are based on wholesale rates offered only by major banks. You won't do as well at exchange booths in airports or rail and bus stations, in hotels, in restaurants, or in stores.

➤ EXCHANGE SERVICES: **International Currency Express** (☎ 888/278–6628 for orders, ✇). **Thomas Cook Currency Services** (☎ 800/287–7362 for telephone orders and retail locations, ✇).

TRAVELER'S CHECKS

Do you need traveler's checks? It depends on where you're headed. If you're going to rural areas and small towns, go with cash; traveler's checks are best used in cities. Lost or stolen checks can usually be replaced within 24 hours. To ensure a speedy refund, buy your own traveler's checks—don't let someone else pay for them: irregularities like this can cause delays. The person who bought the checks should make the call to request a refund.

PACKING

Pack lightly, because porters can be hard to find and baggage restrictions are tight on international flights—be sure to **check on your airline's policies before you pack.** And either **leave room in your suitcase or bring expandable totes for all your bargain purchases.**

If you'll be traveling through several different types of climate, your wardrobe will have to reflect this. Light cotton or other natural-fiber clothing is appropriate for any Southeast Asian destination; drip-dry is an especially good idea, because the tropical sun and high humidity encourage frequent changes of clothing. **Avoid exotic fabrics, because you may have difficulty getting them laundered.**

Southeast Asia is generally informal: a sweater, shawl, or lightweight linen jacket will be sufficient for dining and evening wear, except for top international restaurants, where men may be required to wear a jacket and tie. A sweater is also a good idea for cool evenings or overly air-conditioned establishments. An umbrella is helpful for shielding against both rain and sun.

The paths leading to temples can be rough, so take a pair of sturdy and comfortable walking shoes. Slip-ons are preferable to lace-ups, as shoes must be removed before you enter most shrines, temples, and homes.

It might be wise to **bring your favorite toilet articles** (in plastic containers, to avoid breakage and reduce the weight of luggage). Allow for the tropical sun by bringing along a hat and sunscreen. Mosquito repellent and coils are a good idea. Moist towelettes or baby wipes are great for cleaning off tropical grime and sweat, as well as for quick wash-ups before meals.

Small tissue packets are handy for spills and easier to tote than toilet paper, which is uncommon outside of resort areas. Women may want to bring their own feminine hygiene products, as there's a limited selection in most Southeast Asian stores.

In your carry-on luggage, **pack an extra pair of eyeglasses or contact lenses** and **enough of any medication you take** to last the entire trip. You may also ask your doctor to write a spare prescription using the drug's generic name, since brand names may vary from country to country. In luggage to be checked, **never pack prescription drugs or valuables.** To avoid customs delays, carry medications in their original packaging. And don't forget to carry with you the addresses of offices that handle refunds of lost traveler's checks. Keep money, traveler's checks, and your passport in a **money belt.**

CHECKING LUGGAGE

How many carry-on bags you can bring with you is up to the airline. Most allow two, but not always, so make sure that everything you carry aboard will fit under your seat or in the overhead bin, and get to the gate early. Note that if you have a seat at the back of the plane, you'll probably board first, while the overhead bins are still empty.

If you are flying internationally, note that baggage allowances may be determined not by piece but by weight—generally 88 pounds (40 kilograms) in first class, 66 pounds (30 kilograms) in business class, and 44 pounds (20 kilograms) in economy.

Airline liability for baggage is limited to $1,250 per person on flights within the United States. On international flights it amounts to $9.07 per pound or $20 per kilogram for checked baggage (roughly $640 per 70-pound bag) and $400 per passenger for unchecked baggage. You can buy additional coverage at check-in for about $10 per $1,000 of coverage, but it excludes a rather extensive list of items, shown on your airline ticket.

Before departure, **itemize your bags' contents** and their worth, and label the bags with your name, address, and phone number. (If you use your home address, cover it so potential thieves can't see it readily.) Inside each bag, **pack a copy of your itinerary.** At check-in, **make sure that each bag is correctly tagged** with the destination airport's three-letter code. If your bags arrive damaged or fail to arrive at all, file a written report with the airline before leaving the airport.

PASSPORTS & VISAS

When traveling internationally, **carry your passport** even if you don't need one (it's always the best form of I.D.) and **make two photocopies of the data page** (one for someone at home and another for you, carried separately from your passport). If you lose your passport, promptly call the nearest embassy or consulate and the local police. It's always good to **carry two spare passport photographs.**

ENTERING SOUTHEAST ASIA

To travel throughout most of Southeast Asia, you must have a passport that's valid for six months (having a passport that's valid for one year is advisable for longer stays). *See* individual chapter A to Z sections for specific passport and visa requirements.

PASSPORT OFFICES

The best time to apply for a passport or to renew is in fall and winter. Before any trip, check your passport's expiration date, and, if necessary, renew it as soon as possible.

➤ AUSTRALIAN CITIZENS: **Australian Passport Office** (☎ 131–232, ✆).

➤ CANADIAN CITIZENS: **Passport Office** (☎ 819/994–3500 or 800/567–6868, ✆).

➤ NEW ZEALAND CITIZENS: **New Zealand Passport Office** (☎ 04/494–0700, ✆).

➤ U.K. CITIZENS: **London Passport Office** (☎ 0990/210–410) for fees and documentation requirements and to request an emergency passport.

➤ U.S. CITIZENS: **National Passport Information Center** (☎ 900/225–5674; calls are 35¢ per minute for automated service, $1.05 per minute for operator service).

REST ROOMS

Hotels, restaurants, boats, bus and train stations, and airports that accommodate foreigners usually have Western toilets. Elsewhere the standard Southeast Asian model—squat toilets with or without a flush feature—will probably be the norm. As some cities' sanitation systems cannot handle toilet paper, a waste basket is sometimes provided for disposal. It's a good idea to **carry toilet paper and moist towelettes.**

SAFETY

CRIME

Southeast Asia is generally a safe region for travelers of all ages and walks of life. Still, let common sense be your guide. **Dress modestly and don't flash your money around.** Carry travelers checks, keep cash in a hidden money pouch, and use a credit card whenever possible. Pickpockets haunt crowded transport hubs, and scam artists love to draw in naive travelers, so **keep your valuables hidden or back in the hotel safe** and **check out what you buy before you lay down the money**—fake jewels, fake name-brand items (handbags, shoes, perfume), bait-and-switch gifts "prewrapped" for customs, and bogus shipping promises are the typical tricks of this region. Thankfully, most of this is limited to major tourist crossroads; in the more remote areas, where neighbors are on a first-name basis and doors remain unlocked at night, crime is rarely a problem.

POLITICAL STRIFE

There are several countries where the social and political climates have the potential for affecting your safety, including Cambodia, Indonesia, Malaysia, and Myanmar. Tourism to Cambodia is slowly on the rise, but you should proceed with caution by staying within the geographic boundaries set by guides—particularly in the Siem Reap and Angkor temple areas, where stray land mines and unexpected violence still pose a threat.

In the past few years, Indonesia has seen extreme strife in East Timor and has had its share of antigovernment demonstrations, particularly on the islands of Java and Sumatra. Although it was on the road to economic and political stability, at press time events in the Middle East spawned tension between Christians and Muslim fundamentalists in parts of the country. There were also bomb scares and threats to American institutions and citizens. Areas to avoid included Jakarta and Solo on Java; the city of Medan and all of Aceh province on Sumatra; the Moluccas; and East and West Timor. In addition, the state department advised travelers to avoid areas close to the southern Philippines (northern Sulawesi and northern Kalimantan), where terrorists were holding hostages. **Check with the state department for updates before departing.**

Antigovernment friction is more serious in Myanmar, where, depending on the latest political activity and the whims of the officials, you may be prohibited from venturing too far outside the capital. Finally, **don't travel with illegal drugs or with anyone carrying them.** People have been fined and imprisoned for accompanying drug-carrying travelers, even though they were completely unaware of their companion's luggage contents. The stakes in Southeast Asia for offenders are extremely high; some foreigners have even been executed for such violations.

SCAMS

Be wary of anyone offering you large discounts on tickets, tours, hotels, and items for sale (gemstones, antiques, etc.), especially in Thailand. Some self-proclaimed "travel agents" may not be travel agents at all, and overanxiousness may be a sign of inauthenticity. **Do not accept food or drink** from anyone you don't know very well, as assailants can slip in drugs that render you unconscious and then depart with your belongings.

WOMEN IN SOUTHEAST ASIA

Travel for women in Southeast Asia is generally safe. Nonetheless, take a few precautions, especially if you're traveling alone in Indonesia, Malaysia, and the southern Philippines. Dress conservatively, and don't respond to verbal comments and/or harassment. Take care when walking alone on beaches or desolate areas, and don't go out alone at night. Carry a sarong to cover your legs or shoulders when entering a temple and a large scarf to drape over your face if you're receiving unwanted attention. If you're lost or need assistance, try to consult local women when possible.

SENIOR-CITIZEN TRAVEL

There's no reason that active, well-traveled senior citizens shouldn't visit Southeast Asia, whether on an independent (but prebooked) vacation, an escorted tour, or an adventure trip. Before you leave home, however, determine what medical services your health insurance provider will cover; note that Medicare does not provide for payment of hospital and medical services outside the United States. If you need additional travel insurance, buy it (☞ Insurance, *above*).

To qualify for age-related discounts, **mention your senior-citizen status up front** when booking hotel reservations (not when checking out) and before you're seated in restaurants (not when paying the bill). When renting a car, ask about promotional car-rental discounts, which can be cheaper than senior-citizen rates.

➤ EDUCATIONAL PROGRAMS: **Elderhostel** (✉ 75 Federal St., 3rd floor, Boston, MA 02110, ☎ 877/426–8056, FAX 877/426–2166,⬳). **Folkways Institute** (✉ 14600 S.E. Aldridge Rd., Portland, OR 97236-6518, ☎ 503/658–6600 or 800/225–4666, FAX 503/658–8672).

STUDENTS IN SOUTHEAST ASIA

Students in Southeast Asia are sometimes entitled to discounts on entrance fees and transportation. Malaysia, for example, offers a student rail pass.

➤ I.D.s & SERVICES: **Council Travel** (CIEE; ✉ 205 E. 42nd St., 14th floor, New York, NY 10017, ☎ 212/822–2700 or 888/268–6245, FAX 212/822–2699,⬳) for mail orders only, in the U.S. **Travel Cuts** (✉ 187 College St., Toronto, Ontario M5T 1P7, ☎ 416/979–2406 or 800/667–2887 in Canada,⬳).

TAXES

See A to Z sections *in* individual chapters for country-specific tax information.

TELEPHONES

For details on making calls to, within, and from each country, *see* individual chapter A to Z sections.

LONG-DISTANCE SERVICES

AT&T, MCI, and Sprint access codes make calling long distance relatively convenient, but you may find the local access number blocked in many hotel rooms. First ask the hotel operator to connect you. If the hotel operator balks, ask for an international operator, or dial the international operator yourself. One way to improve your odds of getting connected to your long-distance carrier is to travel with more than one company's calling card (a hotel may block Sprint, for example, but not MCI). If all else fails, call from a pay phone. Many large hotels now rent mobile phones, too, which may be more convenient.

➤ ACCESS CODES: **AT&T Direct** (☎ 800/222–0300 for information on access codes). **MCI WorldPhone** (☎ 800/444–4141). **Sprint International Access** (☎ 800/877–4646).

TIME

Consult the World Time Zones chart at the front of this book to determine the time difference between your country and your destination. Thailand, Indonesia, and Vietnam are in the same time zone (Greenwich Mean Time + 7); the time will be one hour later (GMT + 8) in Singapore, Malaysia, and the Philippines.

TIPPING

For details on tipping *see* individual chapter A to Z sections.

TOURS & PACKAGES

Because everything is prearranged on a prepackaged tour or independent vacation, you'll spend less time planning—and often get it all at a good price.

BOOKING WITH AN AGENT

Travel agents are excellent resources. But it's a good idea to collect brochures from several agencies as some agents' suggestions may be influenced by relationships with tour and package firms that reward them for volume sales. If you have a special interest, **find an agent with expertise in that area**; ASTA (☞ Travel Agencies, *below*) has a database of specialists worldwide.

Make sure your travel agent knows the accommodations and other services of the place they're recommending. Ask about the hotel's location, room size, beds, and whether it has a pool, room service, or programs for children, if you care about these. Has your agent been there in person or sent others whom you can contact?

Do some homework on your own, too: local tourism boards can provide information about lesser-known and small-niche operators, some of which may sell only direct.

BUYER BEWARE

Each year consumers are stranded or lose their money when tour operators—even large ones with excellent reputations—go out of business. So **check out the operator.** Ask several travel agents about its reputation, and try to **book with a company that has a consumer-protection program.** (Look for information in the company's brochure.) In the United States, members of the National Tour Association and the United States Tour Operators Association are required to set aside funds to cover your payments and travel arrangements in the event that the company defaults. It's also a good idea to choose a company that participates in the American Society of Travel Agents' Tour Operator Program (TOP); ASTA will act as mediator in any disputes between you and your tour operator.

Remember that the more your package or tour includes the better you can predict the ultimate cost of your vacation. Make sure you know exactly what is covered, and **beware of hidden costs.** Are taxes, tips, and transfers included? Entertainment and excursions? These can add up.

➤ Tour-Operator Recommendations: **American Society of Travel Agents** (☞ Travel Agencies, *below*). **National Tour Association** (NTA; ✉ 546 E. Main St., Lexington, KY 40508, ☎ 606/226–4444 or 800/682–8886, ✎). **United States Tour Operators Association** (USTOA; ✉ 342 Madison Ave., Suite 1522, New York, NY 10173, ☎ 212/599–6599 or 800/468–7862, FAX 212/599–6744, ✎).

GROUP TOURS

Among companies that sell tours to Southeast Asia, the following are nationally known, have a proven reputation, and offer plenty of options. The classifications used below represent different price categories, and you'll probably encounter these terms when talking to a travel agent or tour operator. The key difference is usually in accommodations, which run from budget to better, and better-yet to best.

➤ Super-Deluxe: **Abercrombie & Kent** (✉ 1520 Kensington Rd., Oak Brook, IL 60521-2141, ☎ 630/954–2944 or 800/323–7308). **Absolute Asia** (✉ 180 Varick St., New York, NY 10014, ☎ 212/627–1950 or 800/736–8187). **TCS Travel Expeditions** (by private jet) (✉ 2025 1st Ave., Suite 450, Seattle, WA 98121, ☎ 800/727–7477 or 206/727–7300). **Travcoa** (✉ Box 2630, 2350 S.E. Bristol St., Newport Beach, CA 92660, ☎ 714/476–2800 or 800/992–2003).

➤ Deluxe: **Globus** (✉ 5301 S. Federal Circle, Littleton, CO 80123-2980, ☎ 303/797–2800 or 800/221–0090). **Maupintour** (✉ 1515 St. Andrews Dr., Lawrence, KS 66047, ☎ 785/843–1211 or 800/255–4266). **Tauck Tours** (✉ Box 5027, 276 Post Rd. W, Westport, CT 06881-5027, ☎ 203/226–6911 or 800/468–2825). **Uniworld** (✉ 17323 Ventura Blvd., Los Angeles, CA 91316, ☎ 818/382–7820 or 800/733–7820).

➤ First-Class: **Brendan Tours** (✉ 15137 Califa St., Van Nuys, CA 91411, ☎ 818/785–9696 or 800/421–8446). **DER Travel Services** (✉ 9501 W. Devon Ave., Rosemont, IL 60018, ☎ 800/937–1235, FAX 800/282–7474; 800/860–9944; for brochures). **General Tours** (✉ 53 Summer St., Keene, NH 03431,

☎ 603/357–5033 or 800/221–2216). **Orient Flexi-Pax Tours** (✉ 630 3rd Ave., New York, NY 10017, ☎ 212/692–9550 or 800/545–5540). **Pacific Bestour** (✉ 228 Rivervale Rd., River Vale, NJ 07675, ☎ 201/664–8778 or 800/688–3288). **Pacific Delight Tours** (✉ 132 Madison Ave., New York, NY 10016, ☎ 212/684–7707 or 800/221–7179).

➤ BUDGET: **Asialink** (✉ 1201 S. Las Vegas Blvd., Suite 109, Las Vegas, NV 89104, ☎ 702/382–5900). **Cosmos** (☞ Globus, *above*).

PACKAGES

Like group tours, independent vacation packages are available from major tour operators and airlines. The companies listed below offer vacation packages in a broad price range.

➤ AIR/HOTEL: **Absolute Asia** (☞ Group Tours, *above*). **DER Travel Services** (☞ Group Tours, *above*). **Orient Flexi-Pax Tours** (☞ Group Tours, *above*). **Pacific Bestour** (☞ Group Tours, *above*). **Pacific Delight Tours** (☞ Group Tours, *above*). **United Vacations** (☎ 800/328–6877).

➤ IN THE U.K.: **Bales Tours** (✉ Bales House, Junction Rd., Dorking, Surrey RH4 3HB, ☎ 01306/876881 or 01306/885991). **British Airways Holidays** (✉ Astral Towers, Betts Way, London Rd., Crawley, West Sussex RH10 2XA, ☎ 01293/723171). **Hayes and Jarvis** (✉ Hayes House, 152 King St., London W6 0QU, ☎ 020/8748–5050). **Kuoni Travel** (✉ Kuoni House, Dorking, Surrey RH5 4AZ, ☎ 01306/740500).

THEME TRIPS

➤ CUSTOMIZED PACKAGES: **East Quest** (✉ One Union Square West, Suite 606, New York, NY 10013, ☎ 800/638–34449). **Gecko Travel** (✉ 94 Old Manor Way, Portsmouth P06 2NL, United Kingdom, ☎ 023/9237–6799). **Global Spectrum** (✉ 1901 Pennsylvania Ave. NW, Ste. 204, Washington DC 20006, ☎ 202/293–2065 or 800/419–4446). **Pacific Experience** (✉ 63 Mill St., Newport, RI 02840, ☎ 401/849–6258 or 800/279–3639).

➤ ADVENTURE/TREKKING: **Asian Pacific Adventures** (✉ 826 S. Sierra Bonita Ave., Los Angeles, CA 90036, ☎ 323/935–3156 or 800/825–1680). **Geographical Expeditions** (✉ 2627 Lombard St., San Francisco, CA 94123, ☎ 415/922–0448 or 800/777–8183). **Himalayan Travel** (✉ 110 Prospect St., Stamford, CT 06901, ☎ 203/359–3711 or 800/225–2380). **Intrepid Small Group Adventures** (✉ 1311 63rd St., Suite 200, Emeryville, CA 94608, ☎ 510/654–1879 or 800/227–8747). **Mountain Travel-Sobek** (✉ 6420 Fairmount Ave., El Cerrito, CA 94530, ☎ 510/527–8100 or 800/227–2384). **Naturequest** (✉ 934 Acapulco St., Laguna Beach, CA 92651, ☎ 714/499–9561 or 800/369–3033). **Overseas Adventure Travel** (✉ 625 Mt. Auburn St., Cambridge, MA 02138, ☎ 800/955–1925). **Wilderness Travel** (✉ 1102 9th St., Berkeley, CA 94710, ☎ 510/558–2488 or 800/368–2794).

➤ ARCHAEOLOGY: **Archeological Tours** (✉ 271 Madison Ave., New York, NY 10016, ☎ 212/986–3054).

➤ BICYCLING: **Asian Pacific Adventures** ((☞ Adventure/Trekking, *above*). **Backroads** (✉ 801 Cedar St., Berkeley, CA 94710-1800, ☎ 510/527–1555 or 800/462–2848). **Global Spectrum** ((☞ Customized Packages, *above*).

➤ CRUISES: **Adventure Quest** (✉ 482 Congress St., Suite 101, Portland, ME 04101, ☎ 800/643–5630. **Emerald Cruises** (✉ 3450 Elliott Center Dr., Suite 101, Elliott City, MD 21043, ☎ 410/313–8883). **Orient Lines** (☎ 800/574–7829). **Uniworld** (☞ Group Tours, *above*).

➤ CULINARY: **Asialink** ((☞ Group Tours, *above*). **Geographical Expeditions** (☞ Adventure, *above*).

➤ ECOTOURISM: **Asia Transpacific Journeys** (☎ 800/642–2742). **Journeys International** (✉ 107 Aprill Dr., Suite 3, Ann Arbor, MI 48103, ☎ 734/665–4407 or 800/255–8735).

➤ LEARNING: **Earthwatch** (✉ Box 9104, 680 Mount Auburn St., Watertown, MA 02272, ☎ 617/926–8200 or 800/776–0188). **Myths and Mountains** (✉ 976 Tee Court, Incline Village, NV 89541-9004, ☎ 800/670–MYTH). **Smithsonian Study Tours and Seminars** (✉ 1100 Jefferson Dr. SW, Room 3045, MRC 702, Washington, DC 20560, ☎ 202/357–4700).

➤ NATURAL HISTORY: **Questers** (✉ 381 Park Ave. S, New York, NY 10016, ☎ 212/251–0444 or 800/468–8668). **Victor Emanuel Nature Tours** (✉ Box 33008, Austin, TX 78764, ☎ 512/328–5221 or 800/328–8368).

➤ SCUBA DIVING: **Asialink** (☞ Culinary, *above*). **Rothschild Dive Safaris** (✉ 900 West End Ave., #1B, New York, NY 10025-3525, ☎ 800/359–0747). **Tropical Adventures** (✉ 111 2nd Ave. N, Seattle, WA 98109, ☎ 206/441–3483 or 800/247–3483).

➤ YACHT CHARTERS: **Lynn Jachney Charters** (✉ Box 302, Marblehead, MA 01945, ☎ 617/639–0787 or 800/223–2050). **Ocean Voyages** (✉ 1709 Bridgeway, Sausalito, CA 94965, ☎ 415/332–4681 or 800/299–4444).

TRAIN TRAVEL

Trains are an option in most Southeast Asian countries; there's even luxury service between Bangkok and Singapore. Travel by train is reasonable, comfortable, and efficient in Thailand, Malaysia, and Singapore; in Indonesia and the Philippines, you're better off traveling by boat. Except for those in Singapore and Thailand, most trains don't have class designations. You can buy tickets, get schedule and fare information and, in Thailand and Malaysia, purchase discount passes through hotels, travel agents, and ticket counters at train stations. Expect to pay cash at counters; travel agents and hotels generally accept traveler's checks and credit cards. Plan to make reservations at least a day or two in advance. For more details, *see* the A to Z sections in each chapter.

On long trips bring edibles (fruit, instant noodles, drinks, etc.), as food and beverage selections may be limited. Go over your ticket very carefully with your travel agent or hotel clerk so that you understand the time of departure, the compartment and berth or seat number (if there is one), and date of your ticket. Most often, a train conductor will ask to see your ticket, so keep it in a convenient place.

TRANSPORTATION AROUND SOUTHEAST ASIA

Large Southeast Asian cities often have good local public transportation; you'll often have your pick of car, train, bus, boat, pedicab, motorcycle, or your own two feet to get around. *See* individual chapter A to Z sections for more information on the types of transportation that are available in each region.

TRAVEL AGENCIES

A good travel agent puts your needs first. Look for an agency that has been in business at least five years, emphasizes customer service, and has someone on staff who specializes in your destination. In addition, **make sure the agency belongs to a professional trade organization.** The American Society of Travel Agents (ASTA), with 27,000 agents in some 170 countries, is the largest and most influential in the field. Operating under the motto ìIntegrity in Travel,î it maintains and enforces a strict code of ethics and will step in to help mediate any agent-client disputes if necessary. ASTA also maintains a Web site that includes a directory of agents. (If a travel agency is also acting as your tour operator, *see* Buyer Beware *in* Tours & Packages, *above*.)

➤ LOCAL AGENT REFERRALS: **American Society of Travel Agents** (ASTA; ☎ 800/965–2782 24-hr hot line, FAX 703/684–8319, ✍). **Association of British Travel Agents** (✉ 68–71 Newman St., London W1P 4AH, ☎ 020/7637–2444, FAX 020/7637–0713, ✍). **Association of Canadian Travel Agents** (✉ 1729 Bank St., Suite 201, Ottawa, Ontario K1V 7Z5, ☎ 613/237–3657, FAX 613/521–0805). **Australian Federation of Travel Agents** (✉ Level 3, 309 Pitt St., Sydney 2000, ☎ 02/9264–3299, FAX 02/9264–1085, ✍). **Travel Agents' Association of New Zealand** (✉ Box 1888, Wellington 10033, ☎ 04/499–0104, FAX 04/499–0827).

VISITOR INFORMATION

For details on national and regional tourist offices *see* individual chapter A to Z sections.

➤ U.S. GOVERNMENT ADVISORIES: **U.S. Department of State** (✉ Overseas Citizens Services Office, Room 4811 N.S., 2201 C St. NW, Washington, DC 20520, ☎ 202/647–5225 for interactive hot line, 301/946–4400 for computer bulletin board, FAX 202/647–3000 for interactive hot line); enclose a self-addressed, stamped, business-size envelope.

WEB SITES

Do check out the World Wide Web when you're planning your trip. You'll find everything from current weather forecasts to virtual tours of famous cities. Fodor's Web site, www.fodors.com, is a great place to start your online travels. When you see a ✪ in this book, go to www.fodors.com/urls for an up-to-date link to that destination's site.

Many sites offer invaluable information about travel in Southeast Asia. Here are a few recommendations: for Thailand, wwww.amazingsiam.com, www.thailand-travelsearch.com, and www.tat.or.th; for Malaysia, www.tourism.gov.my; for Indonesia, www.indo.com; for Vietnam, www.govietnam.com and wwww.destinationvietnam.com; for Singapore, www.singapore-hotel.com/info.htm; for the Philippines, www.manilaguide.com and www.metromanila.com.

WHEN TO GO

You can depend on the coastal areas of Southeast Asia to be warm and the interior highlands to be cool most of the time, but from here on, the climate slightly differs from country to country. Thailand has three seasons: hot (March to June), rainy (June to October), and cool (November to February). Monsoon winds whip the rain into peninsular Malaysia from September to December but take another month or so to reach Sabah and Sarawak. November to January is Singapore's rainy season, although showers can still come regularly in June mornings and evenings. December to May is the dry season in the Philippines, with storms blowing in from June to November.

Indonesia, while generally divided into the November–April rainy season and the May–October hot season, is also divided between east and west: Sumatra, Kalimantan, and Java have markedly wet winter monsoons, while Bali and points east are far more arid and have much hotter dry seasons. The best time to visit northern Vietnam is from October to December, when the weather is cool and the least rainy. Chilly, wet weather starts in December and continues through March; sweltering heat is common from May to early October. The country's central highlands are cool year round and dry from December to March. In the south, the best weather is from December to April when it's dry; May to November generally brings the wet season. The rainy southwest monsoon sweeps through Cambodia and Laos, leaving them cool and dry from December to February and hot and parched by March and April. But remember, these are only generalizations. Winter mountain days can still be scorching, a brisk wind can bring a chill to the most dazzling dry-season beaches, and it can rain anywhere, at any time, so be prepared.

CLIMATE

For temperature charts, *see* individual chapter A to Z sections.

➤ FORECASTS: **Weather Channel Connection** (☎ 900/932–8437), 95¢ per minute from a Touch-Tone phone.

1 DESTINATION: SOUTHEAST ASIA

ASIA REVEALED

THE VAST, VARIED REGION of Southeast Asia encompasses every level of civilization. Bright, bustling Singapore—with its ultraluxury hotels, sophisticated restaurants, and world-class shopping—is tempered by the tribal villages of Borneo. Frenzied, feverish Bangkok meshes with the mountains of Malaysia, where cool highland retreats and frothing rivers provide escapes from the cities' chaos and heat. A large part of Southeast Asia's fascination lies in the quiet beauty found in its rice-paddy landscapes—the glimpse into a simpler time that the West has left behind. But no matter where you go, don't expect to escape modern life entirely. As tourism among these societies grows, it subtly or grossly changes them irrevocably.

WHAT'S WHERE

Indonesia

Indonesia is made up of five large and more than 17,000 small islands totaling more than 1,919,440 square km (741,052 square mi), with a population of 210 million. The capital city of Jakarta, on Java, is bursting at its seams with an influx of people swamping its Dutch-influenced past. Local markets are crammed with regional produce and crafts; museums display the heritage of former kingdoms; and the cuisine is a mixture of Indonesian, Chinese, and Dutch. Architecture—including some of the world's great Buddhist and Hindu monuments and the palaces of sultans in Yogyakarta and Solo—is one of the islands' stellar features.

Bali is only about 145 km (90 mi) long but has more than 3 million people and probably more than 10,000 temples. This is one of the very last completely traditional societies in which all facets of life—agriculture, economics, politics, technology, social customs, and the arts—are welded together by religion; in fact, this is the only Hindu stronghold in the Islamic archipelago. The beaches of Bali's south-

ern coast are highly developed to accommodate tourists, but it is in the interior that you can fully appreciate Bali's passionate and beautiful way of life.

To the east of Bali are the islands of the Nusa Tenggara, including: Lombok, a tropical haven for those who find Bali too commercialized; Sumbawa, an island of both mountains and plains; Komodo, home of the famous dragons; Flores, a dive paradise; Timor, site of an ongoing struggle for independence; and Sumba, an island of bold ikat patterns and the site of ancient battles.

North of the Nusa Tenggara is Sulawesi (formerly known as the Celebes). This orchid-shape landmass has unique flora and fauna; varied topography of rice fields, rain forests, mountains, and beaches; and ancient tribes that inhabit its Toraja highlands. To the north and west of Java, Sumatra shelters some of the world's largest tracts of virgin rain forest, while also offering tourists hill stations around Brastagi, and a cool resort at Lake Toba.

Malaysia and Brunei

Malaysia

The country's more than 329,748 square km (127,316 square mi) are divided into two parts: the peninsula and the states of Sabah and Sarawak on Borneo. Malaysia's population of 21.1 million is made up of about 49% Malays, 29% Chinese, 10% Indians, 1% other indigenous groups (mostly in Sabah and Sarawak) and others. Peninsular Malaysia, with 81% of the population, contains the chief cities, sights, and resorts. The scenery is spectacular, with jungles and rugged hills in the interior, plantations and superb beaches in some of the coastal areas.

The capital, Kuala Lumpur (population 2 million), is clean and comfortable, with striking Victorian-Moorish architecture. The city is a 50-minute flight from Penang (the other main tourist center) and is near the Genting and Cameron highlands. The island of Langkawi, between Penang and the Thai border, is a popular destination with deluxe hotels. Melaka, on the southwest coast, is the oldest city in Malaysia and has its share of historic charm. Off the southeast coast, Tioman Island is renowned for its scuba-diving facilities. Across the South China Sea on Borneo, Sarawak and Sabah are often considered frontier country. They have limited facilities (other than a few new luxury resorts) but offer virgin jungle, mountain scenery, and fascinating close-up glimpses of tribal life.

Brunei

Primarily a stopover between Sabah and Sarawak on Borneo, Brunei covers less than 5,760 square km (2,226 square mi). The tiny sultanate is rich in oil revenues but still has limited tourist facilities. Its population of 200,000 is found mostly in the sleepy tropical capital, Bandar Seri Begawan, and in *kampongs* (villages) on stilts at the waters' edge nearby.

The Philippines

The Philippines has a population of 72 million and an area of nearly 300,000 square km (115,831 square mi), including seven major and 7,100 minor islands. The economic, political, and cultural center is Manila (population 12 million). Tourism is concentrated in Cebu and the Metro Manila area, where there are modern hotels, restaurants, and shops. Elsewhere on the main island of Luzon, hill resorts, beaches, subtropical scenery, and friendly people are also draws. The nation contains about 55 ethnic groups, each with its distinctive language, customs, and traditions. The five major groups are the Ilocanos, Tagalogs, Visayans, Bicolanos, and Muslims.

Singapore

Singapore is something of an anomaly: an independent city-state with an efficient economy, a tightly run welfare system, and a remarkable multiracial social environment. Its population of 2.9 million contained in about 646 square km (249 square mi) has transformed its central shopping and business districts from what briefly was the mysterious and romantic "exotic Orient" to a bright, clean, modern tropical city—one that has the glamour of Hong Kong but without its brutal contrasts of wealth and squalor. Interwoven into the fabric of this tiny country are thriving pockets of Chinese, Indian, Malay, and Arabic culture.

Thailand

Thailand, with a population of 62 million and an area of almost 513,998 square km (198,455 square mi), has become one of the world's top tourist destinations. Most of the traffic flows through the capital city of Bangkok (population about 10 million), which is also a major gateway for Southeast Asia. The city has numerous hotels, restaurants, nightclubs, shops, and other tourist facilities.

Close to the capital lie important temples and ruins, mostly in smaller towns in the Bangkok basin—a hot, flat, wet, rice-growing plain that epitomizes subtropical Asia. The eastern and northeastern parts of the country are poor; those areas' riches lie in their fantastic ruins, their spicy food, and a traditional Thai lifestyle—as yet still untainted by tourism. In the north, Chiang Mai is now a city, but it retains some feel of its small-town past; on a cool mountain plateau, it has good hotels, a tranquil atmosphere, and numerous temples in the Lanna style (12th–13th centuries). A number of beach resorts have established themselves on the world map. Pattaya, south of Bangkok, was the first: it's Asia's largest—and possibly tackiest—resort. Phuket, an island in the Andaman Sea, is now the most popular seaside destination, though quieter Ko Samui in the Gulf of Thailand is preferred by many. Toward the Malaysian border are miles of sand beaches, fishing villages, and jungle regions.

Vietnam

Although it's rarely more than 150 km (90 mi) from the shores of the South China Sea at its western border, Vietnam snakes along the edge of the Indochinese peninsula for nearly 1,700 km (1,050 mi). The far northwest, bordered by China and Laos, is a remote mountainous region still inhabited by culturally unique hill tribes. Toward the coast lies Hanoi, the capital, surrounded by the fertile Red River Delta. The road north leads to the port of Haiphong on the Gulf of Tonkin, where the misty outcrops of Ha Long Bay were once the hideout of pirates but today are a renowned tourist attraction. South of Hanoi, Vietnam narrows; verdant fields hug hundreds of miles of largely unspoiled coastline, and low mountains and hills 50 km–200 km (30 mi–

125 mi) inland form the western border with Laos and Cambodia. The former imperial city of Hue, Danang, and the sight-rich town of Hoi An are found midway down the coast of this central region; the beach town of Nha Trang and the mountain resort of Dalat are toward the southern end, surrounded by a wider swath of low mountains known as the central highlands. South of the mountains, Vietnam flattens into a broad floodplain that is home to Ho Chi Minh City (formerly Saigon) and the lush Mekong Delta.

Other Destinations

Burma (Myanmar)
Isolated for so long and still under a repressive government, Burma is just now opening up to tourism. Only a few destinations have facilities for the Western traveler who requires comfort. Rangoon (Yangon) is a capital city reawakening; it's also home to one of the most glorious temples in the Buddhist world, Shwedagon Pagoda. Mandalay is the old capital of Myanmar kings. Pagan (Bagan), another ancient capital, still has thousands of pagodas remaining from the 11th century. Inle Lake is a tranquil haven of floating islands.

Cambodia
Cambodia is recovering from years of civil war and still requires some fortitude from its visitors. It is worth some inconvenience, however, to set eyes on Angkor, the long-lost, magnificent temple complex built in the 10th–13th centuries. To reach Angkor, you can fly direct from Bangkok or go by way of Phnom Penh, the country's capital, a city that's trying to overcome memories of the horrific "killing fields" of the late Pol Pot.

Laos
Laos sways to a slow rhythm of life, and the smiles of its people and charm of its small towns reward the visitor. You can see Vientiane, the capital city, in less than a day before proceeding north to Luang Prabang, with its enchanting palaces and temples. Southern Laos offers fascinating river journeys to thundering waterfalls and small villages settled along the banks of the Mekong Delta.

PLEASURES & PASTIMES

Beaches
Southeast Asia has some of the world's most exotic beaches, ranging from remote volcanic stretches in the Philippines to resort-strewn sites on Bali. The following is a brief rundown of the best beaches in each country.

Indonesia
Surfers head for the waves at Kuta Beach and the Bukit peninsula on Bali; divers stay along the east-coast reefs of Padangbai, Amed, and Tulamben, or at Western Bali Barat National Park. Bali's Jimbaran is more romantic, a quiet haven for sunset-lovers. Day-trippers from Jakarta head for Java's west coast, or north to Pulau Seribu. Lombok's Senggigi beach and Gili islands attract those who want to excape the tourist scene.

Malaysia
The peninsula's finest beaches are along its east coast and on islands just off the eastern shore. Several of these areas offer idyllic scenery and water-sports facilities. The beaches of Langkawi, Penang, and Pangkor, all islands off the west coast, are more developed, although hideaways with glorious private sands can be found on Langkawi and Pangkor Laut. In Sabah, there are fine sandy stretches and resorts along the west coast, not far from the capital, Kota Kinabalu.

Philippines
This tropical archipelago has an abundance of beaches, from pebble-strewn coastlines and black volcanic stretches to shady white expanses. Some of the most picturesque spots are on the smaller islands, particularly on Boracay, Iloilo, Palawan, and Cebu. Puerto Galera on Mindoro Island has several good beaches and is four hours from Manila by bus and ferry.

Thailand
With its long coastlines and warm waters, Thailand offers beach lovers lots of choices. Ko Samet, a popular Thai vacation spot, has many fine-sand beaches dotted with bungalows and cottages. On Phuket and nearby islands there are long, sandy beaches, cliff-

sheltered coves, waterfalls, mountains, and excellent scuba diving. Ko Samui, Ko Tao, and Ko Pha Ngan, in the gulf, have glistening white sand and crystal waters, and there are countless strands of sand along the western coast. Ko Chang, near Cambodia, is also becoming increasingly popular.

Vietnam

Vietnam's unspoiled beaches, clear waters, and coral reefs beckon travelers. The south-central coast, with Nha Trang as the resort hub, has some of Vietnam's most beautiful beaches, as does the much less crowded Dai Lanh, 83 km (51 mi) north of Nha Trang. Equally beautiful are the beaches of Danang and Hoi An. Vung Tau, the popular seaside resort, is not as beautiful but is convenient from Ho Chi Minh City.

Dining

Hotels usually have several restaurants, from coffee shops serving both Western and Oriental cuisine to posh places staffed by famous European chefs. At the other end of the scale are outdoor stalls and markets where you can eat happily for a song. Private villas usually provide a cooking staff—often professionally trained–who will shop for groceries, cook meals, and cater events.

Note: Though wine is available in Southeast Asia, it is relatively expensive. Furthermore, wine is not always the best accompaniment to local cuisines—whiskey or beer is often preferred. Mekong from Thailand is an excellent rice whiskey, and Thailand's Singha and Singapore's Tiger beers win international awards. Thailand also has a wide selection of locally brewed beers. If you're dining on European fare, consider Australian wines—they appear to survive the tropics better than do the French. If you want wine with Cantonese fare, check the wine list for Chinese wine (be sure that it's made from grapes and not rice)—Dynasty, for example, is a reasonable white Chablis-type wine.

Chinese

CANTONESE➤ Many Southeast Asian countries have significant ethnic Chinese populations, and Chinese restaurants are everywhere. The best-known regional Chinese cuisine is Cantonese, with its fresh, delicate flavors. Characteristic dishes are stir-fried beef in oyster sauce, steamed fish with slivers of ginger, and deep-fried duckling with mashed taro.

TEOCHEW➤ Though the cooking of the Teochew (or Chao Zhou), mainly fisherfolk from Swatow in the eastern part of Guangdong Province, has been greatly influenced by the Cantonese, it's quite distinctive. Teochew chefs cook with clarity and freshness, often steaming or braising, with an emphasis on fish and vegetables. Oyster sauce and sesame oil—staples of Cantonese cooking—don't feature much in Teochew cooking.

Characteristic Teochew dishes are *lo arp* and *lo goh* (braised duck and goose), served with a vinegary chili-and-garlic sauce; crispy liver or prawn rolls; stewed, preserved vegetables; black mushrooms with fish roe; and a unique porridge called *congee*, which is eaten with small dishes of salted vegetables, fried whitebait, black olives, and preserved-radish omelets.

SZECHUAN➤ The Szechuan style of cooking is distinguished by the use of bean paste, chilies, and garlic, as well as a wide, complex use of nuts and poultry. The result is dishes with pungent flavors of all sorts, harmoniously blended and spicy hot. Simmering and smoking are common forms of preparation, and noodles and steamed bread are preferred accompaniments. Characteristic dishes are hot-and-sour soup, sautéed chicken or prawns with dried chilies, tea-smoked duck, and spicy string beans.

PEKINGESE➤ This style of cooking originated in the Imperial courts. It makes liberal use of strong-flavored roots and vegetables, such as peppers, garlic, ginger, leeks, and coriander. Dishes are usually served with noodles or dumplings and baked, steamed, or fried bread. The most famous Pekingese dish is Peking duck: the skin is lacquered with aromatic honey and baked until it looks like dark mahogany and is crackly crisp.

HAINAN➤ The greatest contribution made by the many arrivals from China's Hainan island, off the north coast of Vietnam, is "chicken rice": whole chickens are poached with ginger and spring onions; then rice is boiled in the liquid to fluffy perfection and eaten with chopped-up pieces of chicken, which are dipped into a sour-and-hot chili sauce and dark soy sauce.

FUKIEN➤ This cuisine emphasizes soups and stews with rich, meaty stocks. Wine-sediment paste and dark soy sauce are used, and seafood is prominent. Dishes to order are braised pork belly served with buns, fried oysters, and turtle soup.

HUNANESE➤ The Hunanese cooking style is dominated by sugar and spices and tends to be more rustic. One of the most famous dishes is beggar's chicken: a whole bird is wrapped in lotus leaves and baked in a sealed covering of clay; when it's done, a mallet is used to break away the hardened clay.

HAKKA➤ This food is very provincial in character and uses ingredients not normally found in other Chinese cuisines. Red-wine lees are used to great effect in dishes of fried prawns or steamed chicken, producing delicious gravies.

Indian

SOUTHERN INDIAN➤ This cuisine is generally chili-hot, relies on strong spices like mustard seed, and uses coconut milk liberally. Meals are very cheap, and eating is informal: just survey the cooked food displayed, point to whatever you fancy, then take a seat at a table. A piece of banana leaf will be placed before you, plain rice will be spooned out, and the rest of your food will be arranged around the rice and covered generously with curry sauce. The really adventurous should sample fish-head curry, with its hot, rich, sour gravy.

NORTHERN INDIAN➤ Generally found in the more posh restaurants, northern Indian food is less hot and more subtly spiced than southern, and cow's milk is used as a base instead of coconut milk. Northern Indian cuisine also uses yogurt to tame the pungency of the spices and depends more on pureed tomatoes and nuts to thicken gravies. The signature northern Indian dish is tandoori chicken (marinated in yogurt and spices and cooked in a clay urn) and fresh mint chutney, eaten with *naan, chapati,* and *paratha* (Indian breads).

Malay and Indonesian

MALAY➤ This cuisine is hot and rich. Turmeric root, lemongrass, coriander, *blachan* (prawn paste), chilies, and shallots are the ingredients used most often; coconut milk is used to create fragrant, spicy gravies. A basic method of cooking is to gently fry the *rempah* (spices, herbs, roots, chilies, and shallots ground to a paste) in oil and then, when the rempah is fragrant, add meat and either a tamarind liquid, to

make a tart spicy-hot sauce, or coconut milk, to make a rich spicy-hot curry sauce. Dishes to look for are *gulai ikan* (a smooth, sweetish fish curry), *telor sambal* (eggs in hot sauce), *empalan* (beef boiled in coconut milk and then deep-fried), *tahu goreng* (fried bean curd in peanut sauce), and *ikan bilis* (fried, crispy anchovies). The best-known Malay dish is *satay*—slivers of marinated beef, chicken, or mutton threaded onto thin coconut sticks, barbecued, and served with a spicy peanut sauce.

INDONESIAN➤ Indonesian food is very close to Malay; both are based on rice and do not use pork (except for dishes prepared by the non-Muslim Indonesians). Menus on Bali, a Hindu island, often do not include beef; however, pork is a popular main dish here. *Nasi padang*—various dishes, such as curried meat and vegetables with rice, offering a range of tastes from sweet to salty to sour to spicy—originally comes from Indonesia. *Nasi goreng* (fried rice), *mie goreng* (fried noodles), and *ayam bakar* (grilled chicken) or *ikan bakar* (grilled fish) are ubiquitous. Chinese cuisine is also popular here.

Nonya (Nyonya or Peranakan)

When Hokkien immigrants settled on the Malay Peninsula, they acquired the taste for Malay spices and soon adapted Malay foods. Nonya (the cuisine was given this title, which is the Malay for word "woman" or "wife," because cooking was considered a feminine art) food is one manifestation of the marriage of the two cultures. Nonya cooking combines the finesse and blandness of Chinese cuisine with the spiciness of Malay cooking. Many Chinese ingredients are used—especially dried ingredients like Chinese mushrooms, anchovies, lily flowers, soybean sticks, and salted fish.

The Nonya cook uses preserved soybeans, garlic, and shallots to form the rempah needed to make *chap chay* (a mixed-vegetable stew with soy sauce). Other typical dishes are *husit goreng* (an omelet fried with shark's fin and crabmeat) and *otak otak* (a sort of fish quenelle with fried spices and coconut milk). Nonya cooking also features sourish-hot dishes like *garam asam,* a fish or prawn soup made with pounded turmeric, shallots, *galangal* (a hard ginger), lemongrass, shrimp paste, and preserved tamarind, a very sour fruit.

Philippine

Philippine cuisine starts with the same ingredients used in much of Southeast Asia—coconut and other native produce, meat, and fish. Added to these indigenous basics are layers of influences from several foreign cultures: Chinese (noodles, dumplings), Spanish–Mexican (rich stews, desserts), and American (fast foods). The result is a cuisine that reflects the country's history and society.

Thai

Although influenced by the cooking of China, India, Indonesia, and Malaysia, Thai cuisine is distinctly different in taste. It's characteristic flavors come from fresh mint, Thai basil, coriander, and citrus leaves; extensive use of lemongrass, lime, vinegar, and tamarind keeps a sour-hot taste prevalent. On first tasting a dish, you may find it stingingly hot (tiny chilies provide the fire), but the taste of fresh herbs will soon surface. Not all Thai food is hot; a meal is designed to have contrasting dishes—some spicy, others mild. The Thais don't use salt in their cooking. Instead, *nam pla* (fish sauce) is served on the side, which you add to suit your taste.

Popular Thai dishes include *mee krob,* crispy fried noodles with shrimp; *tom yam kung,* hot and spicy shrimp soup, and *tom kha gai,* small pieces of chicken in a coconut based soup (both are popular with foreigners); *gai hor bai toey,* fried chicken wrapped in pandanus leaves; and *pu cha,* steamed crab with fresh coriander root and a little coconut milk. Thai curries may contain coconut milk and are often served with dozens of garnishes and side dishes. Most meals are accompanied by rice and soup. For drinks try a local beer or whiskey or *o-liang,* the national drink—a very strong, black, iced coffee sweetened with palm-sugar syrup.

Shopping

Some people travel to Southeast Asia exclusively to shop. Finely tailored clothing and unique handicrafts can be found at rock-bottom prices here. Prices in department stores are generally fixed, but you can bargain in small shops and markets. The final price will depend on your bargaining skill and the shopkeeper's mood, but generally will range from 10% to 40% off the original price.

If you can, carry your purchases with you instead of trusting shopkeepers and postal services to ship them safely home. However, for larger items, such as ceramic vases or furniture, the upscale shops are generally reliable. Some credit card companies, such as American Express, guarantee that items purchased with their card will arrive home safely. With any purchase, make sure you get a receipt for the amount paid, both for potential returns and for customs. Also, check on customs and shipping fees to make sure your bargain doesn't turn into a costly white elephant.

The following is a quick rundown of some of the most popular buys in individual Southeast Asian countries.

INDONESIA➤ Batik, shadow puppets, and silver jewelry from Java and Bali; stone carvings and wooden masks, carvings, and furniture from Bali; gold and silver filigree from northern Sumatra.

MALAYSIA➤ Batik, pewterware, gold jewelry, silver, woven fabrics, and baskets.

PHILIPPINES➤ Traditional clothing, bamboo furniture, cigars, rum, rattan baskets, silver jewelry, and brassware.

SINGAPORE➤ Contemporary fashions, electronic equipment, antiques, and silk.

THAILAND➤ Silk, gems, jewelry, silverwork, ready-to-wear clothing, lacquerware, and pottery.

VIETNAM➤ Custom-made clothing, lacquerware, wood carvings, contemporary paintings, and pottery.

Sports

Bicycling is a popular diversion in Singapore, and mountain biking is fast catching on in parts of Malaysia and Thailand. There is fine **deep-sea fishing** around Pattaya (in the Gulf of Thailand) and Ranong and Phuket (in the Andaman Sea off Thailand's west coast). **Golf** aficionados will find quality courses in Thailand, Indonesia, Singapore, Malaysia, and the Philippines. If you plan to visit Thailand in March and April, look for **kite-fighting.** Many of Indonesia's wild rivers provide exciting **river rafting** opportunities. Southeast Asia's wealth of beaches and reef means that excellent spots for **scuba diving and snorkeling** abound. Particularly recommended are the waters near Phuket and several marine national parks in Thailand; the Indonesian reefs around Manado, Maluku, West Java, and Bali; a number of islands of the Philippines (Negros, Mindoro, Bohol, Cebu, and Palawan); the islands of Perhentian, Redang, Kapas, Tenggol off peninsular Malaysia; and Sipadan and Layang Layang off Sabah in Malaysian Borneo. **Surf's up** on Catanduanes island, off Southern Luzon in the Philippines and Bali's Bukit peninsula. **Tennis** facilities are available in Singapore and the Philippines, as well as at many resort hotels around the region. Thailand and the Philippines offer opportunities for **windsurfing.**

NEW & NOTEWORTHY

Indonesia

Hundreds have been killed since March 2000, when the Philippines military launched an offensive against the Moro Islamic Liberation Front (MILF) rebels. In July 2000 a bomb exploded at the attorney general's office, injuring no one; however, in August 2000 a bomb exploded outside the Jakarta residence of the Philippines ambassador to Indonesia, killing two people and wounding at least 18. Immediately after the bombings, Indonesian president Abdurrahman Wahid linked it to terrorists, although other commentators said a connection to political tensions in Indonesia shouldn't be ruled out, and the MILF denied any involvement. The following day, a bomb scare rattled the U.S. embassy in Jakarta. There have been other threats to American citizens and American institutions in Jakarta and Solo on Java, in Medan on Sumatra, and elsewhere. At press time the state department advised against travel to these cities as well to West Timor and the entire province of Aceh on Sumatra.

Some of the bloodiest violence has been the result of continued fighting between Muslims and Christians in the eastern Spice Islands. The islands are just below the southern region of the Philippines, where the Muslim separatists operate. The violence has rattled Jakarta's financial markets, sending share prices and the rupiah even lower. It has also caused the state department to advise Americans

against travel to the Moluccas, northern Sulawesi, and northern Kalimantan—Indonesian regions close to the southern Philippines.

Malaysia and Brunei

MALAYSIA➤ **New hotels** from such well-known management companies as Mandarin Oriental, Hyatt, Marriott, Pan Pacific, Regent, and Ritz-Carlton have all opened in the Golden Triangle. A number of lavish resorts have also opened on Langkawi. Strict adherence to Islam has curtailed licensing laws of Kelantan in the far northeast of the peninsula, although the east coast state of Terengganu is promoting its coastal and inland resorts. On Borneo, there has been a spate of hotel and resort construction in Sabah, most of it around Kota Kinabalu. In Sarawak, a number of new hotels have added additional rooms in both Kuching and Miri. Both Sabah and Sarawak are actively promoting tourism—especially **adventure and nature tourism.** Indeed, new lodges have made ecotourism on Sabah's east coast an attractive proposition.

The new Kuala Lumpur International Airport, with its gracefully contoured roof and polished marble floors, is a futuristic concept in passenger and cargo handling. It has a host of shopping and entertainment facilities, restaurants, cinemas, an art gallery, and two hotels. A fast rail connection to the city is nearing completion. Malaysia Airlines has bolstered its fleet with Boeing 777s, which are widely hailed as the world's most spacious and luxurious aircraft.

BRUNEI➤ Brunei recently entered the field of tourism, and it is actively cooperating with neighboring Sabah and Sarawak to encourage visitors to northern Borneo. Brunei's first **national park** established recently at Ulu Temburong offers a glimpse of virgin rain forest and its inhabitants. Bandar Seri Begawan's high-tech amusement park continues to charge no admission, making it a real draw for families.

Philippines

Although the terrorist group Abu Sayyaf began taking hostages in February of 2000, it was the April abduction of 21 people from the Malaysian island of Sipadan that brought the rebels, who comprise one of two main groups fighting for an independent Muslim state in the southern

Philippines, to the world's attention. Hostages were taken from Sipadan to the Philippine island of Jolo, where the Abu Sayyaf have kept—and released, for ransom—a steady stream of hostages (and "brides") since then. The islands that are dangerous are generally off the tourist track, but the U.S. State Department recently issued a warning to Americans traveling to the South, advising against travel to certain islands and to areas of Mindanao, where bombings and hijackings have occurred. Be sure to research the situation before you go. On a lighter note, a number of new **transportation projects** should make it easier to get around Manila and Luzon. Manila's Light Elevated Transit line is being expanded, and the Mass Rail Transit running along EDSA highway opened in February 2000. The expressway to the north, toward Central Luzon, has been improved and widened.

Singapore

Singapore is always adding **new and sparkling hotels** to its huge inventory of rooms—in excess of 30,000. Three of the newest, the Ritz-Carlton, the Inter-Continental, and the Four Seasons, are in the luxury category. The Raffles group opened the Merchant Court Hotel, which is designed for those who want convenience, comfort, and efficiency, but not the high tariff. The **convention center** at Suntec City has increased the number and size of conventions held in Singapore.

The **Singapore Art Museum**'s permanent collection encompasses some 3,000 works from throughout Southeast Asia. The entire collection is accessible through the museum's Electronic Gallery, called E-mage, where you can call up digital images of artwork on computer monitors. Other new museums include the **Asian Civilisations Museum** and the **Singapore Philatelic Museum**; both offer impressive exhibits in their respective areas.

Thailand

Although the troubled economy has slowed the rush to build **hotels,** 1998–99 still saw two new establishments open in Bangkok—Le Royal Meridien and the Peninsula. In late 1999 the Concorde in Bangkok opened, and the new Imperial, also in Bangkok, is scheduled to open in 2001. There may still be a shortage of hotel rooms in Phuket, since some tour operators moved many of their packages from Bali to Phuket when Indonesia was undergoing political troubles. Many travel agents have continued with these package deals despite Bali's return to prominence as a holiday haven. Demand for hotels is likely to be high in other resorts too, because more Thais are vacationing at home rather than abroad. Book your hotel well in advance, especially for peak periods.

Don't expect to find great bargains just because the Thai currency has dropped in value from 25 to 38 baht to the U.S. dollar. In response to the currency crisis the four- and five-star hotels in tourist centers changed their rates from baht to dollars. Moderately priced hotels still quote in baht but have adjusted their rates upward. Other costs in tourist areas are climbing, so although a vacation in Thailand should cost less than before the devaluation, not everything is cheaper in dollar terms. The real bargains are in **shopping.** Thai-made goods still have irresistible prices (and you can reclaim your VAT when you leave).

Bangkok Airways built an airport outside Sukhothai, which was once slightly off the beaten track. Now a daily flight arrives from Chiang Mai and Bangkok. The airline has also initiated direct flights between Bangkok and Siem Reap and between Singapore and Ko Samui. (Because Bangkok Airways is the only carrier with rights on Samui, flights there are already very expensive and are likely to become truly exorbitant.) There's also a **new airport** at Krabi with flights to and from Bangkok. Bangkok is going ahead with plans for a second airport at Nang-Ngu Kao, 32 km (20 mi) east of town, to relieve congestion at Don Muang, but its projected opening date of late 2004 may be delayed by a year or two. The elevated **skytrain,** which opened in late 1999, crosses the city from north to south and east to west; **new expressways** speed travel across town; and a subway is scheduled to open by 2003.

The elephant has a long history in Thailand (elephants were used to haul timber and move huge objects, including the teak pillars used in royal palaces and temples) and is revered for its strength, courage, and intelligence. In recent years, however, mechanization and restrictions on teak logging have made the domesticated elephant obsolete, and elephants and their mahouts have come to rely on the tourist industry as their only source of income. To make sure they are not mistreated, animal rights groups, including Friends of the Asian Elephant now monitor the treatment of elephants used in shows and treks. If you are going on an elephant-back trek and have concerns, check out how various companies treat their animals. Find out, for example, how many hours the elephants are worked each day and whether you will be riding in the afternoon.

Elephants shouldn't work more than five hours per day, and they should rest during the afternoon as they can become ill and thus temperamental if forced to work in the midday heat. A stick with a sharp hooked spike at the end is used by the mahout to control his elephant. If you see extensive over-use of these sticks, notify **Friends of the Asian Elephant** (✉ 350 Moo 8, Ram-Indra Rd., Soi 61, Tharaeng, Bangkhen, Bangkok 10230, ☎ FAX 02/ 945-7124, www.elephant.tnet.co.th), who will investigate the situation. Be as specific as you can in your complaint: note the trek company or elephant show, the address, the mahout's name, the elephant's name, and how frequently the mistreatment occurred.

New tourist destinations are opening up. Vacationing Thais have moved down the coast from Pattaya to Ban Phe, near Rayong, and hardier travelers go even farther, to the bungalow-dotted islands of the Ko Chang group, near the Cambodian border. Thailand's last tourist frontier is still its northeast (I-san), the country's poorest region, but new modern hotels, including a luxury guest house in Si Saket, are opening the region up to travelers who wish to visit Khmer temples and experience the essence of Thailand.

Vietnam

The government in Hanoi has loosened travel restrictions, beefed up travel facilities, and agreed to a number of joint ventures with foreign companies and investors. Unfortunately, the **new high-rise luxury hotels** that go up seemingly overnight tend to homogenize the cityscapes. Still, the Vietnamese are so keen on tourism that most lodging establishments—from mom-and-pop minihotels to five-star palaces— offer a wide range of **travel services.**

Tours, in particular, are widely available: everyone from the central government worker to the corner café owner runs excursions, so nearly every attraction in every corner of the country is accessible.

Although the country is undergoing a **major road-improvement program,** precarious road conditions and suicidal driving habits persist, making car travel nerve-racking. The government has put a lot of money into **reliable air service,** and state-run Vietnam Airlines has seen considerable improvements. Planes generally run efficiently and frequently. American carriers are negotiating with the Vietnamese government for regular air service from the United States to Vietnam.

Other Destinations

Burma (Myanmar)

Since changing its name from the State Law and Order Restoration Council (SLORC) to the State Peace and Development Council (SPDC) in 1997, the ruling party has opened the nation's doors to tourism and investment in an effort to prop up its dictatorship with foreign monies. Visas are now easier to obtain, and you can enter by land from Mae Sai in northern Thailand to Kengtung (this is periodically shut down, however, so inquire in advance at your embassy). Plus, you no longer need to purchase local currency at the official exchange rate (6 kyats to the dollar instead of 185 on the not-so-black market). The result has been a rapid increase in hotel construction, development of a rudimentary tourist infrastructure, and an opportunity to visit a country that has been off-limits for a long time.

Only your conscience can tell you whether, by supporting with your tourist dollar one of the most inhumane governments in the world, you are helping the civilian Burmese get an economic foothold and combat oppression.

Cambodia

Siem Reap, the base from which to visit the Khmer ruins of Angkor, is open to tourists; you can now fly in direct from Bangkok or even go by (torturous) road, and the hotels there have been refurbished to meet the needs of the international traveler. Phnom Penh has quieted down since most of the United Nations personnel have moved out and reduced the inflationary pressure. An express bus now runs between Phnom Penh and Ho Chi Minh City, Vietnam. Other parts of the country tend to be a little risky, with bandits and remnants of the Khmer Rouge roaming the forests.

Laos

Laos is opening up to foreign tourists in gentle steps, beginning with the Friendship Bridge crossing the Mae Khong river to Nong Khai. Visas are now obtainable there and at several other border crossings, as well as at the Vientiane airport (be sure you can show your outbound ticket and preferably a hotel reservation). New hotels are opening in Vientiane and the former capital, Luang Prabang. Outside these two cities, accommodation is pretty rudimentary and scheduled travel uncertain, but if you're an intrepid traveler you'll find your way around and you will be welcomed.

FODOR'S CHOICE

No two people will agree on what makes a perfect vacation, but it's fun and helpful to know what others think. We hope you'll have a chance to experience some of Fodor's Choices yourself in Southeast Asia. For detailed information about each entry, refer to the appropriate chapter.

Beaches

Indonesia

★ **Canggu, Bali.** This is the perfect afternoon stop on the way to view the sunset at Tanah Lot temple.

★ **Lombok Island.** Magnificent waves roll in on the deserted south-coast beaches.

Malaysia

★ **Langkawi.** With so many coves and beaches, you'll walk untrodden sands.

★ **Pangkor Laut.** A palm-grove beach on a private island with a charming hotel—what more could you want?

★ **Pantai Dalit, Sabah.** Golden sands stretch on either side of the Shangri-La Rasa Ria resort, from a limpid estuary to a jungled headland.

★ **The East Coast.** Magnificent beaches grace virtually the entire length of the peninsula.

Philippines

★ **Boracay Island, Panay.** One of the country's most beautiful beaches is here, with sands as fine as sugar.

★ **Mactan Island, Cebu.** Spend a few days lazing around at one of the resorts here.

★ **Santa Cruz Island, Zamboanga.** Rent a conoe to get to this island, which has a pink-coral beach and a lagoon.

Thailand

★ **Ao Nang Bay, Krabi.** Limestone pinnacles that rise curiously out of the blue sea will rivet your attention while you laze on the sands.

★ **Haad Tong Nai Pan Noi, Ko Pha Ngan.** Words can hardly describe such a perfect horseshoe bay.

★ **Nai Harn, Phuket.** As the sun sets dodging the tiny offshore islands, your tan will be golden.

★ **Pansea Beach, Phuket.** With a different beach for every day of your fortnight's Phuket island vacation, little Pansea Beach should be kept for the romantic interlude.

Vietnam

★ **Dai Lanh Beach, north of Nha Trang.** Sand dunes meet the sea at this semicircular beach, still virtually untouched by tourism.

★ **Doc Let, north of Nha Trang.** Doc Let is accessible only by hiring a private car, but beach-going doesn't get much better than these white sands and clear waters.

★ **Nha Trang.** Catch this beautiful resort beach before it becomes another Pattaya.

Dining

Indonesia

★ **Xin Hwa, Jakarta, Java.** Here spicy Szechuan dishes are served in refined surroundings. $$$$

★ **Sari Kuring, Jakarta, Java.** Very good Indonesian seafood is typified by the grilled prawns, which practically melt in your mouth. $$

★ **Ny Suharti, Yogyakarta, Java.** Forget charm and atmosphere and all the other items on the menu: you're here for the best fried chicken on the island, perhaps in all of Indonesia. $

Malaysia

⭐ **Mahsuri, Kuala Lumpur.** Treat yourself to a colonial curry tiffin, a sumptuous spread of delicately spiced dishes, available every Sunday at this historic mansion in KL's Lake Gardens. $$$$

⭐ **Lai Ching Yuen, in the Regent Hotel, Kuala Lumpur.** The city's best Cantonese fare is served in a room resembling two Chinese pavilions. $$$$

⭐ **Restoran Makanan Laut Selayang, Kuala Lumpur.** Delicious seafood is the specialty here, but if you're adventurous try the steamed river frogs and soups of squirrel, pigeon, or turtle. $$

⭐ **Restoran Paranakan, Malaka.** The tiger prawns in sweet santan curry at this restaurant serving up the best of Baba Nyonga fare are sheer heaven on a plate. $$

Philippines

⭐ **Lantaw Gardens, Cebu City.** The buffet here is served in an open-air, garden setting alongside a folk-dance show and scenic views of the city. $$$

⭐ **Bistro Remedios, Manila.** Pampanga regional cooking is served here in a 1950s-style Filipino home, complete with traditional furniture and paintings of Philippine landscapes. $$

⭐ **Alavar's, Zamboanga City.** This restaurant, a rambling house facing the sea, is famous for its wonderful seafood and its *buko* (coconut) juice. $$

⭐ **Ka Lui's, Puerto Prinsesa City.** Nothing is as fresh as the seafood here, served on a bamboo veranda. $$

Singapore

⭐ **Club Chinois.** Superior surroundings set the tone for "nouvelle Chinoise," the best of creative Cantonese and French cuisine. $$–$$$

⭐ **Dragon City.** Many Singaporeans claim that this is the best place to enjoy the emphatic cuisine of Szechuan. $$–$$$

⭐ **Banana Leaf Apolo.** Come for robust South Indian curries, including the famous Singaporean fish-head curry. $

Thailand

⭐ **Le Normandie, Bangkok.** For French food and an elegant evening out, this is the choice. $$$$

⭐ **Ban Klang Nam, Bangkok.** Superb seafood and other Thai delights are served here by the river with a view of ships at anchor. $$-$$$

⭐ **Huen Phen, Chiang Mai.** Eat well-prepared and authentic northern Thai fare in an old teak house full of handicrafts and antiques. $$

⭐ **Spice Market, Bangkok.** Newcomers to Thai food should come here to try one of the world's finest cuisines. $$

⭐ **Prachak, Bangkok.** The best roast duck in town is served for less than a dollar. $

⭐ **White Orchid, Phuket.** Try this tiny outdoor café for fresh fish and a welcome smile. $

Vietnam

⭐ **Camargue, Ho Chi Minh City.** Unique Eurasian cuisine is accented by an elegant open-air villa setting. $$$$

⭐ **Lemongrass, Ho Chi Minh City.** Masterful Vietnamese standards and tasteful Franco-Viet decor make this an expat standby. $$$

⭐ **Khazana, Hanoi.** Surprisingly delicious Indian cuisine made in a real tandoor oven is served in an opulent setting. $$

⭐ **Ngoc Suong, Nha Trang.** Try some of the world's freshest and finest seafood while dining in a delightful garden. $$

⭐ **Café des amis, Hoi An.** Five heavenly courses of seafood or vegetarian ambrosia are served nightly; come again the next night, as the unwritten menu changes daily. $

⭐ **Hue Restaurant, Hanoi.** Wonderful sugarcane-wrapped pork and other delicious standards are served at this casual sidewalk café. $

Lodging

Indonesia

⭐ **Amandari, near Ubud, Bali.** The peaceful gardens and luxurious cottages here are in a private village setting overlooking the lush Ayung River valley. $$$$

⭐ **Amanjiwo, Borobudur, Java.** The 35 suites all have views of Borobudur Temple from their private patios, 14 of which have swimming pools. $$$$

⭐ **Hotel Tugu, near Denpasar, Bali.** Art and artifacts abound here—in the public areas, the guest quarters, and the on-site museum. You can contemplate these works in your private cottage surrounded by quiet gardens. $$$$

★ **Mandarin Oriental, Jakarta, Java.** Expect refined, personal service in an atmosphere of understated elegance. $$$$

★ **The Oberoi, Medan Beach, Lombok.** The ultimate secluded retreat has private, thatch beach cottages within sight of Gili Air. $$$$

★ **Pool Villa Club, Senggigi Beach, Lombok.** Private hot tubs, private sundecks, and ivory marble bathrooms are just some of the luxuries offered in these two-story villas, which are just steps away from the white sands of Senggigi Beach. $$$$

★ **Kusuma Sahid Prince Hotel, Solo, Java.** A former prince's residence becomes your home away from home. $$$

★ **Hotel Majapahit, Surabaya, Java.** Built in 1910 and refurbished in 1996, this hotel with large grounds and personal service make you feel as if you're in a bygone era. $$$

Malaysia
★ **Datai, Langkawi.** Nature dictated the layout and structure of this luxury hideaway on the Andaman Sea. $$$$

★ **Palace of the Golden Horses, Kuala Lumpur.** Overlooking the lake at the Mines Resort, this Moorish-style building is palatial. The luxury of the lounges and opulence of the fittings make this probably the finest hotel in Asia. $$$$

★ **Regent Hotel, Kuala Lumpur.** Luxurious guest rooms and grand public spaces make this the smartest hotel in the city. $$$$

★ **Shangri-La's Tanjung Aru Resort, Kota Kinabalu.** Set in 25 acres of landscaped gardens with its own small beach, Sabah's finest resort offers what is arguably the friendliest service in Borneo. $$$$

Philippines
★ **Manila Peninsula, Manila.** The "Pen," with its understated grace, has well-kept rooms that are more like suites. $$$$

★ **Fort Ilokandia, Vigan, northern Luzon.** Reminiscent of Vigan's Old Quarter residences, the buildings of this hotel are nestled among sand dunes. $$$

★ **Insular Century Hotel, Davao City.** The airy rooms at this hotel—on 20 lush acres

of coconut groves, gardens, and beach—come with verandas. $$$

★ **Westin Philippine Plaza, Manila.** Luxurious and grand, the Plaza has an enormous lobby, a fabulous swimming pool, and rooms with views of Manila Bay. $$$

★ **Casa Amapola, Baguio City.** This quiet pension—once a family residence—retains a pleasing family-style informality. $–$$

Singapore
★ **Raffles Hotel.** Cliché though it may be, this world-famous hotel still oozes tradition and gentility in the midst of its modern, high-rise neighbors. $$$$

★ **The Ritz-Carlton, Millenia, Singapore.** Wallow in your bathtub and watch the ships lying at anchor in Singapore harbor. $$$$

★ **The Duxton.** In a city of skyscrapers, this boutique hotel in Chinatown is a wonderful alternative. $$$

★ **Regalis Court.** Housed in what was once a ballet academy, this Peranakan-style hotel is welcoming and economical. $

★ **RELC International Hotel.** For the best value in inexpensive lodgings, this is the spot. $

Thailand
★ **Chiva-Som, Hua Hin.** This spa resort, considered one of the world's best, has excellent service and elegant accommodation in a peaceful setting. $$$$

★ **Rayavadee Premier Resort, Ao Nang.** The only way to the duplex thatched cottages on this magical headland is by longtail boat. $$$$

★ **Oriental Hotel, Bangkok.** Nostalgia for the old days and views of the river bring people back here time and time again. $$$$

★ **The Regent, Bangkok.** For refined classical elegance and superb service, the Regent wins top honors. $$$$

★ **The Regent, Chiang Mai.** Surrounded by Lanna Thai architecture built around rice fields nestled in the hills, you'll take the luxury for granted. $$$$

★ **Santiburi, Ko Samui.** Steps away from your teak-floor bungalow are white sands shaded by swaying palms. $$$$

★ **Manee's Retreat, Si Saket.** Stay at this one-of-a-kind luxury guest house and experience the real Thailand. $$

★ **River View Lodge, Chiang Mai.** One of the few small, charming, and personable hotels in the north. *$$*

★ **Tara Mae Hong Son, Mae Hong Son.** This hotel blends into a valley and seems at one with nature. *$$*

★ **Panviman Resort, Ko Pha Ngan.** Staggered up the cliff side, the bungalows look over the bay. *$–$$*

★ **The Atlanta, Bangkok.** Music played at teatime and old movies shown after dinner are part of what makes this small hotel a throwback to better times. *¢*

Vietnam

★ **Delta Caravelle, Ho Chi Minh City.** The most popular hotel in the city has the best location and luxurious rooms with great city views. *$$$$*

★ **Hotel Continental, Ho Chi Minh City.** The setting for Graham Greene's *The Quiet American,* the Continental is the most elegant accommodation in town. *$$$$*

★ **Omni Saigon, Ho Chi Minh City.** This super-slick new pleasure dome offers every conceivable service. *$$$$*

★ **Hotel Sofitel/Metropole Hanoi, Hanoi.** Besides the beautifully renovated French-colonial architecture, there's impeccable food and service. *$$$$*

★ **Sofitel/Dalat Palace, Dalat.** Set on the cool slopes of rolling green hills, this perfectly restored Old World resort is an ideal retreat, especially for golfers. *$$$$*

★ **Hotel Majestic, Ho Chi Minh City.** New restorations have uncovered a slice of colonial Saigon in its heyday. *$$$$*

Other Destinations

★ **Strand Hotel, Rangoon, Burma.** Not only is this the best hotel in Rangoon (Yangon), it is also one of the best in Asia—all the conveniences of the late 20th century with impeccable Edwardian style. *$$$$*

Museums

Indonesia

★ **Puppet Museum, Jakarta, Java.** Watch a shadow-puppet play or view an extensive collection of traditional Indonesian puppets, as well as examples from Thailand, China, Malaysia, India, Cambodia, and elsewhere.

★ **Puri Lukisan Museum, Ubud, Bali.** Bali's "palace of paintings" incorporates an overview of the island's famed artisan immigrants and native talents in a setting of tropical gardens and Balinese folklore.

Malaysia

★ **Sarawak Museum, Kuching.** Over a century old, this museum offers a superb collection illuminating Borneo's diverse cultures and their lifestyles.

Philippines

★ **Metropolitan Museum of Art, Manila.** An impressive display of contemporary fine arts, pre-Columbian pottery, and exquisite pre-Hispanic gold jewelry distinguishes this museum.

★ **University of San Carlos Museum, Cebu City.** This extensive collection includes seashells, fauna, and anthropological relics, as well as traditional clothing and ornaments of various tribes.

Singapore

★ **Asian Civilisations Museum.** This cultural exhibition center has top-notch displays, many of which contain antiquities from mainland China.

★ **Images of Singapore/Surrender Chambers.** Wax figures and tableaux provide fascinating, three-dimensional recounting of Singapore's early days.

Thailand

★ **National Museum, Bangkok.** The history of Thai art and culture is all here.

The Natural World

Indonesia

★ **Danau Toba, Sumatra.** The largest lake in Southeast Asia and one of the highest in the world, Lake Toba sits nearly 3,000 ft above sea level, surrounded by green mountains that plunge into its 1,500-ft deep waters.

★ **Mt. Bromo, Java.** You can stand on the rim of this active volcano just before dawn and watch it spew steam from a bubbling cauldron.

★ **Keli Mutu, Flores.** Inside an extinct volcano cone, a trio of lakes mysteriously change colors.

Malaysia

★ **Batu Caves.** These dramatic and cathedral-like caves are the setting for an annual pilgrimage.

★ **Cameron Highlands.** Cool forested trails are a welcome relief from the steamy concrete towns of the lowlands.

★ **Firefly Resort.** Take an evening cruise and see thousands of fireflies twinkle like stars.

★ **Mt. Kinabalu from anywhere in Sabah.** Nature in its glory.

Philippines

★ **Banaue Rice Terraces, northern Luzon.** Like stairs to the sky, these spectacular rice paddies were terraced into the mountainsides more than 2,000 years ago.

★ **Chocolate Hills, Bohol.** More than 50 of these 120-ft-high limestone oddities dot a plain on this southern island.

★ **Mt. Mayon, southern Luzon.** What may be the world's most symmetrical (and still active) volcano towers 8,189 ft over the Bicol countryside.

★ **St. Paul Subterranean National Park, Palawan.** The world's longest known underground river courses beneath this rainforest park and through caverns full of stalactites and stalagmites.

Singapore

★ **Singapore Night Safari and Zoological Gardens.** The open plan of Singapore's zoo frees you from seeing nature's creations behind bars.

★ **Singapore Botanic Gardens.** Escape from brick and mortar to appreciate tropical flora.

Thailand

★ **Golden Triangle, northern Thailand.** Misty mountains lure hikers with great trekking and unique hill-tribe villages.

★ **Phang Nga Bay, off Phuket.** Go by boat to visit offshore caves and limestone rocks that rise mysteriously out of the sea.

Vietnam

★ **Hoa Lu, south of Hanoi.** A quiet ride in a bamboo boat on the winding river through this incomparable landscape is unforgettable.

★ **Halong Bay, off Halong City.** Jutting dramatically from the South China Sea, Halong Bay's limestone archipelago is a water-bound sculpture garden.

★ **Sapa, northern Vietnam.** Hill-tribe cultures thrive in the verdant highlands, undisturbed by the modern age.

Palaces and Unique Structures

Indonesia

★ **Kraton, Sultan's Palace of Yogyakarta, Java.** The original palace of Javanese sultans, built in 1756, is an extensive open complex of gardens and pavilions where there are performances of traditional Javanese dance and gamelan music daily.

★ **Pura Besakih, Bali.** The island's beautiful "Mother Temple" complex in the forested central mountains is the most visited cultural site on Bali.

Philippines

★ **Intramuros, Manila.** This ancient walled city, built by the Spaniards in the 16th century, is still formidable, with cannon emplacements atop the 30-ft-thick walls and a strategic location facing the bay.

★ **Malacañang Palace, Manila.** Notable colonial Spanish architecture and interior decor here demand a look, especially the three chandeliers in the reception hall; beautiful hardwoods used for the grand staircase; portraits and memorabilia of former presidents; and the exquisite music room.

Thailand

★ **Suan Pakkard Palace, Bangkok.** Five teak houses, including the gold-paneled Lacquer Pavillon, built in traditional Thai style stand on columns amid beautiful gardens and lotus ponds.

Sacred Places

Brunei

★ **Masjid Sultan Omar Ali Saifuddin, Bandar Seri Begawan.** This superb example of modern Islamic architecture was built in 1959 of imported white marble, gold mosaic, and stained glass.

Indonesia

★ **Borobudur Temple, Central Java.** It took perhaps 10,000 men 100 years to build this giant stupa, which illustrates the earthly and spiritual life of the Buddha with thousands of relief carvings and statues.

★ **Prambanan Temple Complex, Central Java.** These remarkable 9th-century temples celebrate the Hindu pantheon.

Philippines

★ **Quiapo Church, Manila.** This 16th-century church is home to the famed Black Nazarene, a dark-hardwood statue of Jesus of Nazareth said to perform miracles.

★ **San Agustin Church, Manila.** This old stone church has 14 side chapels, a trompel'oeil ceiling, and seats of hand-carved *molave*—a beautiful tropical hardwood—in the choir loft.

Singapore

★ **Sri Mariamman Temple.** The oldest Hindu temple in the city is also one of the most colorful and ornate.

★ **Sultan Mosque.** The focus of the Malay community is all golden domes and minarets.

Thailand

★ **Wat Benjamabophit, Bangkok.** Site of the famed Marble Temple, this wat's line of Buddha statues helps to harmonize the spirit.

★ **Wat Chaimongkol, Chiang Mai.** This is a small, serene temple by the Mae Ping River.

★ **Wat Phanan Choeng, Ayutthaya.** Memories and fate are embedded in this monument, built to commemorate the death of a king's beloved bride.

★ **Wat Phra Keo, Bangkok.** Ornate and dramatic, this is a spiritual magnet.

★ **Wat Traimitr, Bangkok.** Buddha's image shines with the love of gold here.

Vietnam

★ **Emperor Jade Pagoda, Ho Chi Minh City.** A Vietnamese "It's a Small World," this pagoda is lined with carnival-like sculptures and reliefs of gods and mythical figures.

★ **Marble Mountain, Quang Nam-Danang.** Remarkable cave temples house dozens of statues of the Buddha, some said to have magical powers.

Other Destinations

★ **Angkor Temple Complex, Cambodia.** This architectural marvel consists of more than 300 structures, including the monumental Angkor Wat, scattered across the jungle.

★ **Pagan Archeological Zone, Burma.** More than 2,000 ruined stupas, shrines, and monasteries remain from what was built during the Pagan Dynasty, about 1,000 years ago.

★ **Shwedagon Pagoda, Rangoon, Burma.** The 320-ft spire of this 2,500-year-old pagoda complex is covered with 70 tons of gold and encrusted with thousands of precious stones.

Shopping

Indonesia

★ **Antique wayang kulit on Bali or in Yogyakarta on Java.** These puppets conjure up the shadows of Hindu epics.

★ **Batiks and leather in Yogyakarta, Java.** Fabulous designs on batik and crafted bags in leather are real temptations.

★ **Silver filigree on Bali and in Yogyakarta on Java.** Delicate spiderweb creations in dainty, intricate shapes.

★ **Stone and wood carving on Bali.** Guardians sculpted in stone and masks in wood are essential to keep evil spirits at bay.

Malaysia

★ **Batik Malaysia Berhad, Kuala Lumpur.** The best quality and patterns of Malay fabric are found here.

★ **Kompleks Budaya Kraf, Kuala Lumpur and Langkawi.** All the regional crafts are here.

★ **Main Bazaar, Kuching.** The best of Borneo, with old (and new) antiques, basketware, mats and tribal artifacts.

★ **Selangor pewter, throughout Malaysia.** Malaysia is famous for its tin and has been producing pewter for centuries.

Myanmar

★ **Precious stones and lacquerware** are the specialties here.

Philippines

★ **Baguio Public Market, Baguio City.** Handicrafts, antiques, and fresh produce are available in abundance.

★ **Madrazo Fruit District, Davao City.** Most fruit vendors will let you sample the more exotic produce before you buy.

★ **Yakan Weaving Village, Zamboanga.** The handwoven cloth from this village is remarkable.

Singapore

⭐ **Arab Street.** Stores and shops spill out onto the sidewalk with an array of Malay and Indonesian wares.

Thailand

⭐ **Night Bazaar in Chiang Mai.** So much for so little, be it fake or authentic, is for sale here.

⭐ **Sapphires and rubies in Bangkok.** The center for gems is here.

⭐ **Thai silk in Chiang Mai, Bangkok, and I-san.** In all patterns, Thai silk is irresistible.

Vietnam

⭐ **Hoi An.** This perfectly preserved ancient port is almost entirely dedicated to seamstress boutiques and to souvenir shops that sell pottery and paintings by local artists.

⭐ **Linh Phuong Maison de Couture, Ho Chi Minh City.** This shop specializes in custom clothing made from Japanese and Vietnamese silks and cottons.

⭐ **Sapa Weekend Market.** Hill tribes from around the Sapa area convene at this colorful outdoor market to sell and exchange their chartreuse-embroidered, indigo-dyed clothing, as well as other handicrafts and food staples.

⭐ **Tien Dat, Hanoi.** The best tailor in town for casual custom clothing, Tien Dat has the finest silks and cottons.

GREAT ITINERARIES

The itineraries that follow suggest ways you can combine destinations for a trip that suits your interests, and give an idea of reasonable (minimum) amounts of time needed in various places. Don't try to see every one, but use this material for ideas on how to mix and match your destinations.

The Whirlwind Grand Tour

Southeast Asia is more diverse than Europe, yet there's a temptation on a first visit to cover the entire area on one European-style Grand Tour. Such a trip is physically and mentally taxing and cannot begin to do jus-

tice to the complexities of Asian cultures. Even with three weeks to see the capitals and a few highlights, it's best to skip a couple of places to spend more time in each.

Begin in exciting, exotic Bangkok, for a leisurely round of sightseeing interspersed with shopping. Go up to Chiang Mai in northern Thailand before flying into Burma to visit Mandalay, Pagan, and Yangon. From there, fly to Kuala Lumpur in Malaysia, before a stop in Singapore. Then it's on to Jakarta, Bali, and Manila.

Duration: 3 weeks

Transportation

Stopping in all the major regions of Southeast Asia requires the use of different airlines. Coming from the United States, you may want to use Thai Airways International or Continental, a U.S. airline that best covers the capital cities, as your major carrier. From Great Britain, British Airways serves many of Asia's capitals. From Australia, check out Qantas's fares and routes.

Itinerary

BANGKOK: FOUR NIGHTS➤ Arrive in Thailand's capital and catch some zzz's before taking in some of its 300 temples, old teak houses, markets, and restaurants. Go on a morning tour to Damnoen Saduak's floating market and a full-day tour to Ayutthaya, the ancient capital.

CHIANG MAI: TWO NIGHTS➤ Fly to Chiang Mai (or take the night train the evening before from Ayutthaya). Visit the major temples in and around town, including Doi Suthep. Spend a morning at the elephant training camp at Mae Sa and an afternoon browsing the craft showrooms and workshops along the Golden Mile.

MANDALAY AND PAGAN: THREE NIGHTS➤ Fly on Air Mandalay to upper Burma's unofficial capital for one night, before continuing to Pagan for two nights.

RANGOON (YANGON): ONE NIGHT➤ Fly to Rangoon for one night, and try to visit both the Shwedagon Pagoda and Bogyoke Aung San Market.

KUALA LUMPUR: TWO NIGHTS➤ Take the Malaysia Airways flight to the capital. Marvel at the Suria KLCC, one of Asia's finest shopping centers nestled beneath the world's tallest building, or explore the colonial heart of the city. Visit the Hindu shrine at the Batu caves, and take a trip to Malaka for a trishaw ride through the historic city streets.

SINGAPORE: ONE NIGHT➣ In Singapore, explore Chinatown, Little India, and the Arab district; take a stroll along the Padang, the heart of colonial Singapore; check out the shops on Orchard Road; and dine sumptuously on Singapore's multiethnic cuisines.

JAKARTA: ONE NIGHT➣ The Indonesian capital is a congested city of modern highrises and Dutch colonial buildings.

BALI: FOUR NIGHTS➣ Fly into Denpasar on Bali, but use one of the southern coastal beach hotels as your base for the first two nights. Move north to Ubud for the third and fourth nights; exploring the temples, crafts shops, and villages of this exotic island will take at least three days.

MANILA: THREE NIGHTS➣ Fly to the Philippine capital to explore the Spanish colonial sights, especially Intramuros, the walled city. The next day, visit Pagsanjan's waterfalls and rapids or the Villa Escudero and its museum and gardens.

The Indochina Tour

Take a circular tour of former French Indochina using Bangkok as a starting and ending point.

Duration: 3 weeks

Transportation
Continental, Northwest, and United have the best flights from the United States to Thailand. British Airways flies to Bangkok from London, Qantas from Australia. Use Bangkok Airways from Bangkok to Siem Reap, and either Air Cambodge or Vietnam Airlines for the hop to Phnom Penh.

Itinerary
THAILAND: THREE NIGHTS➣ Start in Bangkok with a leisurely round of sightseeing, shopping, and dining. Make a side trip to Ayutthaya, Damnoen Saduak's floating market, and the Bridge over the River Kwai in Kanchanaburi.

CAMBODIA: THREE NIGHTS➣ Fly directly to Siem Reap for two nights to visit the fantastic Khmer ruins at Angkor, then fly or take a boat down to Phnom Penh for a day.

VIETNAM: SIX NIGHTS➣ Fly to Ho Chi Minh City for a day, then fly to Danang and take a taxi to Hoi An for two nights. A tourist bus will take you, via Marble Mountain and Danang's Cham Museum, to Hue. Spend the night, and fly to Hanoi for the rest of your stay.

LAOS: THREE NIGHTS➣ From Hanoi take a plane to Luang Prabang, the former capital and still the country's artistic center. After two nights, fly to Vientiane for one night.

THAILAND: TWO OR MORE NIGHTS➣ Cross over the Mekong on the new Friendship Bridge to Nong Khai for the day. Take the night train to Bangkok to spend another day, and fly out that night or the following morning.

2 INDONESIA

In this land of contrasts and diversity, cultural attractions compete for your time with the pursuit of the pleasure principle. From the temples and beaches of Bali to the great architectural wonders around Yogyakarta, from fascinating animist rites on Sulawesi to the rush into the 21st century in Jakarta, Indonesia will enthrall you.

By Nigel Fisher
and Lois
Anderson

Updated by
Denise
Dowling,
Margaret
Feldstein, Holly
S. Smith,
Gisela
Williams, and
Lara Wozniak

THE SHEER SIZE OF INDONESIA is mind-boggling. This nation is the world's fourth most populous and covers more than 17,000 islands (more than one-third of them uninhabited) that stretch for more than 5,161 km (3,200 mi) from the Pacific to the Indian Ocean. From north to south, the islands form a 1,774-km-long (1,100-mi-long) bridge between Asia and Australia.

From Jakarta's tall steel-and-glass office buildings to Irian Jaya's thatched huts, Indonesia embraces an astonishing array of cultures. Today Indonesia's 210 million people—Asmat, Balinese, Batak, Dayak, and on down through the alphabet—speak more than 300 languages, though a national language, Bahasa Indonesia, is officially recognized as a means of binding the population together.

It's this size and diversity that make Indonesia so fascinating. You can relax in one of Bali's luxury resorts or take a river trip through the jungles of Borneo. If you do venture off the beaten path—really the way to fall in love with the country's charms—remember that patience is important. Since tourism has only recently become a priority for Indonesia, the infrastructure is often rudimentary. Only in areas slated for tourist development can you expect to find services that approach international standards. Elsewhere, expect only modest accommodations and casually scheduled transport.

Don't mistake this lack of development for a lack of history, however. The nation has seen a succession of conquerors and revolutions, even receiving its name from one of its earliest colonizers: *Indonesia* comes from two Greek words—*indos,* meaning Indian, and *nesos,* meaning islands—a testament to the Indian traders who roamed the islands in the 1st century AD. By the 7th century, powerful Buddhist and Hindu kingdoms had emerged, and by the 1300s the Majapahit Hindu empire had united much of what is now Indonesia. During the next two centuries, however, Arab traders began to set up communities and spread the teachings of Islam, the religion now followed by about 90% of the population, making Indonesia the world's largest Muslim country.

Contact with the West came in 1509, when Portuguese traders arrived. A century later they were displaced by the Dutch, and by the 18th century Dutch rule encompassed most of Indonesia, known to the West as the Dutch East Indies. Except for a brief interlude of British rule during the Napoleonic Wars of 1811–16, the Dutch remained in power until the outbreak of World War II. After the surrender of the occupying Japanese in 1945, a bloody fight for Indonesian independence ensued. In 1949 Indonesia won its sovereignty, and the name Dutch East Indies became one more piece of colonial history.

The man behind the independence movement was Sukarno (many Indonesians have only one formal name), who became president of the new republic and implemented a leftist nationalist policy. He forcibly prevented ethnic groups from forming their own republics and extended Indonesia's borders by annexing part of New Guinea, now the province of Irian Jaya. Despite imprisoning his opposition, he lost control of the movement, the economy suffered under an annual inflation rate of 650%, and Indonesia dissolved into chaos.

On the night of September 30, 1965, Communists (or so it was said) abducted and murdered six top generals and their aides and, it's alleged, were about to seize power. Major-General Suharto intervened, and blood flowed by the gallon. Anyone accused of being a Commu-

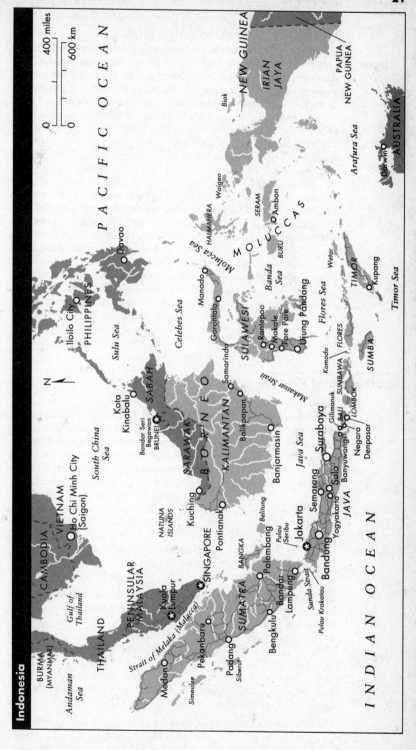

Indonesia

400 miles
600 km

P A C I F I C   O C E A N

NEW GUINEA

IRIAN JAYA

PAPUA NEW GUINEA

Biak

Waigeo

AUSTRALIA

Arafura Sea

Darwin

HALMAHERA

SERAM

Ambon

BURU

M O L U C C A S

Banda Sea

Wetar

TIMOR

Kupang

Timor Sea

Molucca Sea

Manado

Gorontalo

SULAWESI

Rantepao

Makale

Pare Pare

Ujung Pandang

Flores Sea

FLORES

SUMBAWA

Komodo

SUMBA

Celebes Sea

Sulu Sea

Iloilo City

PHILIPPINES

Davao

Makassar Strait

Samarinda

SABAH

Kota Kinabalu

Bandar Seri Begawan

BRUNEI

SARAWAK

B O R N E O

KALIMANTAN

Balikpapan

Banjarmasin

Java Sea

BALI

Gilimanuk

LOMBOK

Surabaya

Banyuwangi

Negara

Denpasar

South China Sea

VIETNAM

CAMBODIA

Ho Chi Minh City (Saigon)

THAILAND

BURMA (MYANMAR)

Andaman Sea

Gulf of Thailand

PENINSULAR MALAYSIA

Kuala Lumpur

SINGAPORE

NATUNA ISLANDS

Kuching

Pontianak

Belitung

BANGKA

Palembang

Pulau Seribu

Jakarta

Semarang

Solo

Yogyakarta

JAVA

Bandung

Bandar Lampung

Sunda Strait

Pulau Krakatau

Strait of Melaka (Malacca)

Medan

Pekanbaru

Siberut

Simeulue

SUMATRA

Bengkulu

Padang

I N D I A N   O C E A N

N

nist was slaughtered. Rampaging mobs massacred thousands—some estimates place the number of dead at 500,000.

Suharto became president in 1967 and ruled for seven consecutive terms until the growing economic and social turmoil that began with the 1997 Asian financial crisis—and the consequent devaluation of the rupiah by more than 75%—had the country riding waves of anxiety and expectation. Repressive policies toward the independence-minded people of Timor, the one island that remained more Portuguese than Dutch, didn't help either, particularly since Timor freedom fighters Bishop Carlos Ximenes Belo and José Ramos-Horta attracted the international spotlight when they shared the 1996 Nobel Peace Prize. In May 1998, after weeks of student demonstrations against Suharto's government, which culminated in riots that ricocheted throughout the islands, Suharto allowed Vice President B. J. Habibie to assume rule of the country. After more than 30 years of Suharto-controlled rule, peaceful parliamentary elections were held on June 7, 1999, followed by the election of President Abdurrahman Wahid on October 20. Stability for much of the country returned; however, at press time the political situation remained fluid as the new government faced continued civil strife in Aceh, Papua, and Maluku. In addition, threats to U.S. citizens and institutions were a concern in Jakarta and Solo on Java and Medan on Sumatra. (The state department was advising Americans to avoid travel to Indonesia, particularly to these cities and northern Sulawesi and northern Kalimantan.) East Timor voted for independence from Indonesia on August 30, 1999, and at press time was under the authority of the U.N.'s Transitional Administration.

Pleasures and Pastimes

Dance

Dance is everywhere on the islands: at celebrations, purification ceremonies, temple rituals, weddings, birthdays, processions to the sea. On Java, court dances are still performed at the sultan's palace in Yogyakarta and, in the summer, dance troupes of several hundred performers act out the Hindu legend of the *Ramayana* by full-moon light at the Prambanan Temple. For the Javanese, the slow, smooth movements are almost like a ballet in which each subtle turn of the head or lift of the finger has meaning. Sumatra's dance traits have the added elements of liveliness and simultaneous movements that include claps, snaps, kneeling dances, and chanting as music is played in the background for performances like the *saudati*. Other dances symbolize offerings of peace, such as northern Sumatra's *meusekat;* or, like the *tob daboh,* they can mimic battlelike action using dancers who are armed with real daggers.

On Bali, perhaps the island best known for its colorful and elegant performing arts, dancers move low to the ground, with bent knees, arched backs, and controlled steps, arms at right angles with elbows pointing up and fingers spread wide. The female dancers flutter their long-nailed fingers. They move slowly across the stage, then turn quickly but precisely with a staccato movement. Head movements are staccato, too, without facial expression except for darting and flashing eyes. They wear petaled or gold headdresses. The men have to act out battle and death scenes, and their movements are more varied.

Most dances are accompanied by the traditional gamelan orchestra of gongs, drums (mostly hand-beaten), a type of xylophone with bronze bars, violinlike instruments, and a flute. Balinese dancing is far more exuberant than Javanese, and the Balinese gamelan is sharper and louder, with more crescendo. Behind every dance is a legend with a moral theme.

BARONG

The Barong is a dance of Good versus Evil. The Good is Barong, a dragon with a huge, bushy, lionlike head and a long flower-bedecked beard. Bells ring as he snaps his head. The two dancers inside the costume use complicated motions to make Barong humorous and good natured, but ferocious when he meets Evil, in the form of the witch Rangda. Rangda's horrifying mask is white, with bulging eyes and tusks that extend from her mouth. Her long braided hair sweeps down to the floor amid menacing, red, mirrored streamers. She rushes threateningly back and forth across the stage. There are also beautiful female dancers with petaled headdresses, tasseled girdles, and gold-and-green sarongs, and male warriors whose prince is crowned with gold and flowers. Rangda forces the warriors to turn their *kris* (dagger) blades on themselves, but Barong's powers keep the blades from harming them. A bird dancer enters and is killed—the required sacrifice to the gods—and Rangda is banished.

LEGONG

The Legong is a glittering classical dance. The story involves a young princess kidnapped by an enemy of her father. Three young girls in tight gold brocade and frangipani headdresses perform several roles. Their movements are rapid and pulsating; they punctuate the music with quick, precise movements and flashing eyes. It's an exacting dance—girls start training for the roles at five and retire before they're 15.

KECAK

The dramatic Kecak, the Monkey Dance, depicts the monkey armies of Hanuman, who rescued Rama and his love, Sita, from the forests of Ceylon in the *Ramayana,* the great Hindu epic. No gamelan is used; all sound comes from the chorus, who, in unison, simulate both the gamelan and the chattering, moaning, bellowing, and shrieking of monkeys. This dance is often performed at night under torchlight. The dark figures, again in unison, make wild arm gestures and shake their fingers. (The Kecak isn't a classical dance but a product of the 20th century.)

Dining

Indonesian, Chinese, and Western cooking are available in every major town and resort. To meet the needs of an increasing number of Japanese tourists, you'll also find Japanese restaurants in Jakarta and on Bali.

Warungs are Indonesian street-food stalls, sometimes with benches and tables in the open, under canvas, or sheltered by a sheet of galvanized tin. The food here varies from drab to tasty, but it's always cheap: you can eat well for Rp 1,000. Warungs are often clustered together at a *pasar malam,* or night bazaar.

Rumah makan are just like warungs, only with fixed walls and roofs. Another step up is the *restoran,* a very broad category of small dining establishments. Most are Chinese-owned and serve both Indonesian and Chinese cuisine. Hotel dining rooms generally offer Chinese, Indonesian, and Western fare; the native specialties are usually toned down. If you enjoy spicy food, you'll be happier at more authentic eateries.

Nasi (rice) is the staple of the Indonesian diet. It's eaten with breakfast, lunch, and dinner, and as a snack, but it mainly serves as a backdrop to an exciting range of flavors. Indonesian food can be very hot, particularly in Sumatra. Your first sample might be *sambal,* a spicy relish made with chilies that's placed on every restaurant table. Indonesians cook with garlic, shallots, turmeric, cumin, ginger, fermented shrimp paste, soy sauce, lime or lemon juice, lemongrass, coconut, other nuts, and hot peppers. Peanut sauce is common; two dishes frequently encountered are *gado gado,* a cold vegetable salad dressed with spiced peanut sauce, and *saté* (or *satay*), slices of skewered, charcoal-broiled meat dipped in a flavored peanut sauce. *Mie* (noodles) are also used in a variety of popular fare, such as *mie goreng,* an entrée of stir-fried noodles with meat and vegetables.

You'll find dishes with such meats as *ayam* (chicken), *babi* (pork), *daging* (beef), and *kambing* (lamb), though, naturally, fresh fish and shellfish abound. *Ikan* (fish) is often baked in a banana leaf with spices, grilled with a spicy topping, or baked with coconut. *Udang* (shrimp) come cooked in coconut sauce, grilled with hot chilies, made into prawn-and-bean-sprout fritters, or, in Sulawesi, with butter or Chinese sweet-and-sour sauce. *Cumi-cumi* (squid) and *kepiting* (crab) are also featured.

For dessert, Indonesians eat fresh fruit: papaya, pineapple, rambutan, salak, and mangosteen. Because this is a mostly Muslim country, wine and alcohol—when available—are expensive additions to a meal; beer is your best bet. Hard liquor is generally only available in popular bars and Western restaurants in the major cities, although local whiskey brews, called *arak,* are found throughout the islands.

Most food comes cut into small pieces, and finger bowls are provided. Even in Jakarta, you'll see well-dressed Indonesians eating with their fingers. Visitors normally receive forks, although the combination of a spoon (held in the right hand to eat with) and a fork (held in the left hand to help push food into the spoon) is commonly used as well, just as in Thailand. In more remote areas, the right hand is the main eating implement. (The left hand, traditionally used in Asian lavatory hygiene, is considered unclean and is never used for dining, touching, or pointing.) Note that water in Indonesia isn't potable, so stick with the bottled variety. Ice used in restaurants and hotels is supposed to be the kind made under government supervision with the claim that it's safe; as you have no way to check whether the proper ice is used, you may want to forgo it.

Here are a few more food terms that appear frequently on Indonesian menus:

bakmi goreng—fried noodles with bits of beef, pork, or shrimp; tomatoes; carrots; bean sprouts; cabbage; soy sauce; and spices
dendeng ragi (or rendang)—thin squares of beef cooked with grated coconut and spices
gudeg—chicken with jackfruit
kelian ayam—Sumatran chicken curry
nasi campur—steamed rice with bits of chicken, shrimp, or vegetables with sambal; often topped with a fried egg and accompanied by *krupok,* delicious puffy prawn crisps
nasi goreng—fried rice with shallots, chilies, soy sauce, and ketchup; it may include pork (in Bali), shrimp, onions, cabbage, mushrooms, or carrots; it's often studded with tiny, fiery green peppers in Sumatra
nasi rames—a miniature rijsttafel
rijsttafel—literally, "rice table"; steamed rice with side dishes such as sayur lodeh, gudeg, or kelian ayam
sayur lodeh—a spicy vegetable stew
soto ayam—chicken soup, which varies from region to region but usually includes shrimp, bean sprouts, spices, chilies, and fried onions or potatoes; mie soto ayam is chicken noodle soup

Price categories throughout the chapter are based on the following ranges:

CATEGORY	COST*
$$$$	over $30
$$$	$20–$30
$$	$10–$20
$	under $10

Per person for a three-course dinner, excluding tax, service, and drinks.

Lodging

You'll find superb resorts—such as the Four Seasons on Bali and the Mandarin Oriental in Jakarta—that cost half what you might pay in the Caribbean. All such establishments generally include room service and air-conditioning as part of their long lists of amenities. (In general, large, high-end hotels have air-conditioning; smaller, budget establishments may not, so check ahead if it's important to you.) New hotels open all the time in Bali's popular areas; Ubud doesn't yet have any mammoth hotels, which has helped it maintain a small-town feel, but the number of small hotels (20–50 rooms) multiplies every year.

The government classifies hotels with star ratings, five stars being the most luxurious. Its criteria are somewhat random, however. (No hotel without a garage gets four stars, for example, despite the fact that many visitors don't need a garage.) Besides hotels, most Indonesian towns offer three types of rooming houses: *penginapan, losmen,* and *wisma.* Theoretically, the penginapan is cheapest, with thin partitions between rooms, and the wisma most expensive, with thicker walls. The term *losmen* is often used generically to mean any small rooming house. Facilities vary widely throughout the islands: some Bali losmen are comfortable and social, with shared living areas and rest rooms; others are quieter and more private, with separate sitting areas and individual baths. At the bottom range in the less touristed areas you'll usually get a clean room with a shower and an Asian toilet—either an in-ground porcelain "squatter" or a seatless Western "throne"—for less than Rp 44,800 a night. Losmen on Bali often include a light breakfast, and free tea, coffee, and snacks are part of the hospitality in many areas. Note that although there are a few luxury exceptions, as a rule the standards in accommodations on Lombok and islands farther east, as well as in some parts of Sumatra and Sulawesi, often fall below those in, say, Jakarta or Bali. Be prepared to rough it.

Price categories throughout the chapter are based on the following ranges:

CATEGORY	COST*
$$$$	over $150
$$$	$100–$150
$$	$75–$100
$	$40–$75
¢	under $40

For a standard double room in high season, excluding 10% service charge and 11% tax.

Scuba Diving and Snorkeling

Scuba diving is becoming popular, and licensed diving clubs have sprung up around the major resort areas. Bali (off Sanur and the north coast), Lombok's Gili Islands, Flores, and North Sulawesi have some of the world's best diving. The best times for diving in Indonesia are March–June and October–November.

Shopping

Arts and crafts in Indonesia are bargains by Western standards. If you have the time, custom-made items can be commissioned. Consider bringing pictures or samples of items that you'd like built or reproduced—anything from clothing and jewelry to furniture and board games.

From Java the best buys are batik cloth and garments, traditional jewelry, musical instruments, leather *wayang* puppets, and leather accessories. In Bali, look for batiks, stone and wood carvings, bamboo furniture, ceramics, silver work, traditional masks, and wayang puppets. Sumatra is best for handwoven cotton cloth; carved-wood panels and statues, often in traditional designs; and silver and gold jewelry. Sulawesi is known for its silver-filigree jewelry, handwoven silks and cottons, hand-carved wood panels, and bamboo goods. Be aware that machine-produced goods are sometimes sold as handcrafted.

Exploring Indonesia

Indonesia is an archipelago of more than 17,000 islands that stretches 5,200 km (3,224 mi) along the Equator from the Indian Ocean to the Pacific. It's the largest archipelago in the world, resting just above Australia and below peninsular Southeast Asia. Three of the planet's six largest islands are here, and some 210 million people who speak more than 500 languages are spread throughout 6,000 or so bits of land within this country. More than 90% of the population are followers of Islam, making Indonesia the world's largest Muslim nation.

Java is the archipelago's economic and political core, and it's also the most crowded island; 14 million people live in the capital area of Jakarta alone. Yet this is still a land of great natural power, with more than two dozen active volcanoes—including the infamous Krakatau—and 15 peaks that rise above 1,860 ft. The Great Britain–size isle is also a natural haven, with nearly two dozen national parks and reserves. Between these are clusters of five main cultural groups: the Islamic Sundanese and the reclusive Badui of West Java, the traditional Javanese of the central areas, the Tenggerese of the east, and the Madurese of Madura Island.

Bali is the country's most popular getaway for foreigners, just a pint-size nub of land 140 by 80 km (87 by 50 mi) in size. Its distinction is that it's the only Hindu island in an overwhelmingly Islamic country, yet the religions peacefully coexist. The dominant natural force in Bali is Gunung Agung, the "mother mountain," which the Balinese worship as the abode of the gods. Temples are built facing the volcano, and rituals are regularly performed in its honor.

Sumatra is the world's sixth-largest island, comprising more than 100 volcanoes that stretch 2,000 km (1,240 mi) north to south. More than 15 are currently active, including Gunung Leuser near Medan and Gunung Marapi near Jambi. This island also has some very large tracts of pristine rain forest, and much of its southern swamps have yet to be explored. The westernmost point in the archipelago is here, at Pulau Weh at the tip of the northern province of Aceh, also the region where Arabic traders originally landed in the 13th century before spreading the religion of Islam throughout the islands. Sumatra also encompasses Nias Island and the Mentawais in the Indian Ocean, where primitive cultures still exist, and the Riau Archipelago in the Melaka Strait, home to seafaring peoples. Near Medan is 1,797-square-km (1,114-square-mi) Lake Toba, the largest lake in Southeast Asia, where the Christian Batak culture thrives. The Bukittinggi area just to the west is the home of the matriarchal Minangkabau tribe.

To the southeast of Sumatra, the island of Borneo is the world's third largest, and the lower three-fourths, called Kalimantan, belongs to Indonesia. Its name means "river of diamonds," and it is, indeed, an island of powerful waterways—from the 720-km (446-mi) Mahakam to the 880-km (546-mi) Barito to the 1,140-km (707-mi) Kapuas, the archipelago's longest river. Naturally, then, life here is based on the rivers, where many of the approximately 300 Dayak cultures live in raised longhouses over the water. Kalimantan is also the site of several of the region's major natural havens, such as Tanjung Puting National Park and Tanjung Harapan orangutan reserve in the south.

Sulawesi is one of the world's most uniquely shaped islands; its four arms are bits of Australia, Antarctica, Borneo, and New Guinea that smashed together over the eons. As these islands slowly came together, they created a haven for some of the world's most unusual species, such as the anoa "dwarf buffalo," the babirusa "pig deer," and the black Celebes macaque. The island is also a shelter for unusual cultures, from the Bajau and Bugis sea gypsies in the south to the Christian Minihasans in the north. Perhaps the best-known and most intriguing culture here, though, is that of the Tanatoraja, where highland villages in the south-west peninsula are still the site of elaborate funeral celebrations, cliff-side graves, and life-size effigies of the dead.

Once known as the "Spice Islands," the miniarchipelago of Maluku lies just east of Sulawesi. A region that comprises 851 square km (527 square mi) of island volcanoes and coral atolls—more than 90% of it under water—Maluku has for centuries drawn international trade to the region and is one of the world's best dive areas. South of Maluku and just 500 km (310 mi) north of Australia, the "southeast islands" of Nusa Tenggara include Lombok, Sumbawa, Komodo, Flores, Sumba, and Timor, once known for their abundant sandalwood and wild horses. At the archipelago's far eastern edge is New Guinea, the second-largest island in the world, the western half of which is Indonesia's Irian Jaya. Even today, relatively few visitors make the journey to view the Stone Age Dani cultures of the interior Baliem Valley; even fewer have attempted the rugged slopes of 16,564-ft Puncak Jaya, the highest point in the archipelago, or explored the thick, mountainous rain forest and coastal swamps at the island's edges.

Great Itineraries

It could easily take an active traveler years to explore all of Indonesia, and even to see the limited number of destinations covered in this book would still require a whirlwind month or two. This guide discusses only those areas that have a range of amenities for all travelers and sights or attractions that are of particular interest. If you haven't been to Bali, then that island should be on your itinerary. It would be very easy to spend an entire vacation at one of Bali's resorts—**Kuta, Nusa Dua,** and **Sanur** are the best known—but assuming that you have the itch to see more, then Java's **Yogyakarta** and the famed temple of **Borobudur** should be your second destinations. Or consider visiting **Lombok** and the western islands of Nusa Tenggara as an extension of a holiday in Bali. North Sumatra, including the peaceful Lake Toba area and the rain forest of Gunung Leuser National Park, and south-central Sulawesi, including the beaches and waterfalls around Ujung Pandang and the mountainous Toraja highlands, are also recommended. **Jakarta,** while enmeshed in the typical trappings of big-city traffic, is actually worth a look for its cultural and historical sites, including a variety of museums, a cobblestone neighborhood known as Old Batavia, and a waterfront that has for centuries been a crux of Southeast Asian trade.

IF YOU HAVE 7 DAYS

Fly into Bali and spend the first two days exploring the temples and villages, using **Ubud** as your base; be sure to see at least one dance performance. Then take an hour's flight to **Yogyakarta** and spend two nights there, making sure to visit **Borobudur, Prambanan,** and the sultans' palaces in Yogyakarta and **Solo.** Return to Bali for a couple of days at a beach resort before flying out.

IF YOU HAVE 10 DAYS

Enter Indonesia by way of **Medan,** taking three days to visit **Brastagi** and **Lake Toba.** Depart from Sumatra and spend one night in **Jakarta.** On the fifth day, take the early morning flight into **Yogyakarta** and visit **Prambanan** in the afternoon. The next morning, drive out to **Borobudur** and then take the late afternoon flight to Bali. Split your final days between the beach and sightseeing around the island. Be sure to visit Ubud and other craft and cultural villages clustered southeast of the island's center.

IF YOU HAVE 14 DAYS

With two weeks in Indonesia, you could follow the 10-day itinerary and add a side trip from Bali to Sulawesi. Fly into **Ujung Pandang** for a night, taking the afternoon to explore the natural beauty of Bantimurung park, then proceed to **Rantepao** for a three-day exploration of Toraja. If time permits, head north and take a two-day dive trip on the coral reefs of Bunaken Marine Park near Manado.

When to Tour Indonesia

In June and July, popular areas (especially Torajaland) are crammed with visitors. Bali hotels also tend to be fully booked around Christmas and New Year's. Be sure to keep track of Muslim holidays, such as Ramadan, the fasting month when many establishments are closed during the day. During Idul Fitri, the Islamic New Year, and the weeks around Chinese New Year, vacationing Indonesians crowd the transport systems and hotels, so book early if you visit during these times. Be aware that many national museums are closed on Monday. Also, in observance of the Muslim holy day, museums and offices usually close by 11 AM on Friday. The best months for traveling are April–May and September–October, when you'll miss both the seasonal rains and the crowds. (*Also see* When to Go *in* Indonesia A to Z, *below.*)

Numbers in the text correspond to numbers in the margin and on the maps.

JAVA

Java could be a big country all by itself. It's the heart, soul, and financial center of Indonesia. And with more than 100 million people squeezed into an area about the size of Louisiana, it's the world's most populous island. Strangely enough, however, you can still find places of great solitude. This thin isle—about 1,100 km (684 mi) from east to west and between 100 km (62 mi) and 200 km (124 mi) wide—is full of volcanoes (many of them active), pounded by big surf from the Indian Ocean, and buffeted by the much calmer Java Sea. Divided into three provinces—West, Central, and East Java—and two special territories—Jakarta, the capital, and Yogyakarta, the cultural center—it's easy to see in bite-size sections. The road and rail systems are extensive (although in places they're pushed to their limits), the people are friendly, and English isn't as foreign a tongue as you might expect.

It seems that every bit of land—from the fertile valleys to the steep mountain slopes—is cultivated, taking advantage of the rich volcanic soil. But such landscaping is one of the few constants here. Java's long and varied history is evident at Borobudur, site of the world's largest Buddhist monument, or at Cirebon, a city on the north coast that dates back more than 500 years. There are ancient Hindu sites and remnants of old Javanese empires. Islam, which arrived in the 13th century and remains the most prominent religion, has its share of monuments, too. The Dutch made Java one of their colonies in the early 1800s, and their influence is still reflected in such cities as Bandung and Bogor in West Java. The capital, Jakarta—with its tall, modern buildings casting shadows on shacks and shanties—seems a tribute to a contemporary age in which the collision of new and old ideas has caused upheaval.

Indonesia, with Java leading the way, is entering an exciting yet worrying time. Exciting because of the promise of new freedoms and opportunities and worrying because of the uncertainty of economic crisis. As you travel, be prepared to see a huge gulf between rich and poor—particularly in Jakarta. Further, the floating rupiah and inflation are playing havoc with prices. With this come great bargains, but also considerable commercial instability. Companies—including travel agents, airlines, and other tourism-related businesses—open and close seemingly overnight. Some tolerance will be needed. Your patience and compassion, however, will be amply rewarded by the rich sights and experiences that Java, and the rest of Indonesia, offer.

Jakarta

Indonesia's capital is a place of extremes. Modern multistory buildings look down on shacks with corrugated-iron roofs. Wide boulevards intersect with unpaved streets. Elegant hotels and high-tech business centers stand just a few blocks from overcrowded kampongs. BMWs accelerate down the avenues while pedicabs plod along backstreets.

Although the government has tried to prepare for the 21st century, Jakarta has had trouble accommodating the thousands who have flocked to it each year from the countryside. Because of the number of migrant workers who arrive each day, it's difficult to accurately state the city's population, but 14 million is the general consensus. The crowds push the city's infrastructure to the limit. Traffic often grinds to a standstill, and a system of canals, built by the Dutch to prevent flooding in below-sea-level Jakarta, can't accommodate the heavy monsoon rains, so the city is sometimes under water for days. The heat and humidity take getting used to, though air-conditioning in the major hotels, restaurants, and shopping centers provides an escape. Early morning and late afternoon are the best times for sightseeing.

Exploring Jakarta

At Jakarta's center is the vast, parklike Merdeka Square, where Sukarno's 433-ft National Monument is topped with a gold-plated flame that symbolizes national independence. Wide boulevards border the square, and the Presidential Palace (the president doesn't live here), the army headquarters, City Hall, Gambir Railway Station, the National Museum, and other government buildings are here.

Immediately south of the square along Jalan M. H. Thamrin (*jalan* means "street") is the Menteng district, with many international hotels and embassies. Farther south (where Jalan Thamrin changes its name to Jalan Jentral Sudirman) is the downtown of New Jakarta, home to most banks, large corporations, and more international hotels. This area is also known as the Golden Triangle.

North and west of Merdeka Square, around the port of Sunda Kelapa at the mouth of the Ciliwung River, is the Kota area, known as Old Batavia. This is where the Portuguese first arrived in 1522. In 1619 the Dutch secured the city, renamed it Batavia, and established an administrative center for their expanding Indonesian empire.

Dutch rule came to an abrupt end when, in World War II, the Japanese occupied Batavia and changed its name back to Jayakarta. The Dutch returned after Japan's surrender, but by 1949 Indonesia had won independence and, abbreviating the city's old name, established Jakarta as the nation's capital.

Old Batavia

Old Batavia, known today as Kota, is down by the port, where the Dutch administration was centered. As Jakarta expanded after World War II, Old Batavia's stately colonial buildings fell into decay, its streets and sidewalks caved in, and its shophouses became warehouses and repair shops. Prior to the economic crisis, an appreciation for Jakarta's heritage was awakened, and a revitalization of Old Batavia began. Many of the old buildings were restored, and the area was rejuvenated. (Note that despite gentrification, it's best to visit Old Batavia by day; some of the streets are scary to walk along at night.)

A GOOD TOUR

To cover a lot of ground before the midday heat, a combination of walking and taking cabs is prudent for this tour. Start by taking a taxi to the **fish market** ①, which is best seen early in the day. If you walk through the back of the market, you can save on the entrance fee to **Sunda Kelapa Harbor,** where vessels dock with goods from Indonesia's outer islands. Head south and stop at the **Maritime Museum** ②, then veer left, over to Jalan Tongkol, which becomes Jalan Cengkeh. Turn right onto Jalan Kunir, and follow it a short distance to Jalan Pintu Besar Utara. Turn left and head down to the heart of Old Batavia, **Fatahillah Square** ③. On the west side of the square, which was the city's central plaza in the days of the Dutch, is the **Puppet Museum** ④ (often called the Wayang Museum); on the east side is the **Jakarta Fine Art Gallery** ⑤, in the former Palace of Justice. The old Town Hall, on the square's south side, is now the **Museum of Old Batavia** ⑥. Behind the Town Hall, on Jalan Pangeran Jayakarta and opposite the Kota Railway Station, is the **Portuguese Church** ⑦, the oldest in Jakarta. From the square, head south to explore **Glodok,** Old Batavia's Chinatown; wander around and marvel at all the activity in its narrow streets.

TIMING

To experience the fish market's frenzy, start your tour early, at around 7 AM. If you're visiting on a Sunday, there's an abbreviated wayang *kulit,* or shadow-puppet play, performed at 10 AM at the Puppet Museum. Since the heat builds as the day progresses, try to finish your walk soon after midday.

SIGHTS TO SEE

③ Fatahillah Square. At the heart of the old city is Fatahillah Square, cobbled with ballast stones from old Dutch trading ships. In its center is a fountain, a reproduction of one originally built here in 1728. Near the fountain, criminals were beheaded while their judges watched from the balconies of Town Hall (☞ Museum of Old Batavia, *below*). Just to the north is an old Portuguese cannon whose muzzle tapers into a clenched fist, a Javanese fertility symbol; childless women have been known to straddle the cannon to aid conception.

① Fish Market. The Pasar Ikan is as remarkable an introduction to the denizens of Indonesia's seas as a visit to an aquarium—and more chaotic and exciting. It's colorful, noisy, smelly, and slimy, and there are great photo opportunities. Be sure to come early, when it's in full swing. ⊠ *Sunda Kelapa Harbor.*

Glodok. Much of Chinatown has been demolished, but there are still sights and smells that evoke the days when Chinese were brought in

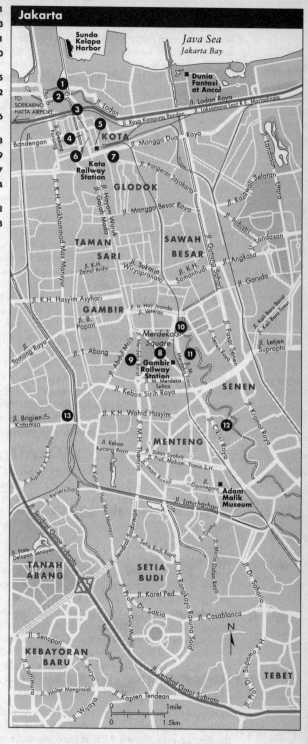

as laborers and worked to become merchants. Many now run successful businesses, and this has caused resentment from other ethnic groups. During the riots that rocked the capital in May 1998, ethnic Chinese were targeted by furious mobs who felt that the Chinese received unfair government protection. Though businesses were looted and burned throughout the city, Glodok was, obviously, hit hard. More than 1,000 people died in the rioting (mostly looters who were trapped in torched shopping malls), and many Chinese fled to neighboring countries. Some came back, but many of those who lost homes and/or loved ones vowed never to return. Today, there's little evidence of the riots, but for locals, the violence is a powerful part of the area's history. Wander around Glodok Plaza (a landmark shopping center and office building), and you can still find small streets crowded with Chinese restaurants and shops that sell herbal medicines. Glodok is also an entertainment district at night, but unless you know your way around, it's better left to the locals.

⑤ Jakarta Fine Art Gallery. The Belai Seni Rupa Jakarta is in the former Palace of Justice, built between 1866 and 1870, on the east side of Fatahillah Square. The gallery's permanent collection includes paintings by Indonesia's greatest artists; contemporary works, such as wood sculptures; and the Chinese ceramic collection of Adam Malik, a former Indonesian vice president. A museum in the southeast of the Menteng district, the **Adam Malik Museum** (✉ Jl. Diponegoro 29, ☎ 021/337400 or 021/337388), displays even more of his works. ✉ *Jl. Taman Fatahillah 2,* ☎ *021/676090.* 🎫 *Admission.* 🕐 *Tues.–Sun. 9–2.*

NEED A
BREAK?

Café Batavia (✉ Jl. Taman Fatahillah 2, ☎ 021/691–5531), on the north side of Fatahillah Square, is a friendly place in which to enjoy Indonesian hors d'oeuvres, an Indonesian or European entrée, or a bit of ice cream. Its collection of nostalgic bric-a-brac, including a sketch of Winston Churchill, makes it quite cheerful. Choose a table by the window and watch the goings-on in the square below.

---

② Maritime Museum. Two former Dutch East Indies warehouses have been restored to house the Museum Bahari. One warehouse has models of Indonesian sailing vessels; the other contains ancient maps and documents that tell the spice trade's history. Neither exhibit is thorough. ✉ *Jl. Pasar Ikan 1,* ☎ *021/669–0518.* 🎫 *Admission.* 🕐 *Tues.–Sun. 9–2.*

⑥ Museum of Old Batavia. On the south side of Fatahillah Square is the old Town Hall, built by the Dutch in 1707. It now houses the Museum Sejarah Jakart, commonly known as the Jakarta Museum. Batavia's history is chronicled with antique maps, portraits, models of ancient inscribed Hindu stones, antique Dutch furniture, weapons, and coins. Unfortunately, the exhibits have few explanations in English, and the museum is rather gloomy. Beneath the halls are the dungeons where criminals once awaited trial. Prince Diponegoro, an Indonesian patriot, was imprisoned here on his way to exile in Manado. All you see of the dungeons are the double-barred basement windows along Jalan Pintu Besar. ✉ *Jl. Taman Fatahillah 1,* ☎ *021/679101.* 🎫 *Admission.* 🕐 *Tues.–Thurs. 9–2:30, Fri. 9–noon, Sat. 9–1, Sun. 9–3.*

⑦ Portuguese Church. Opposite the Kota Railway Station, behind the Museum of Old Batavia, is the oldest church in Jakarta. It was built by the Portuguese—among the first Europeans to arrive in Indonesia—in the 17th century. Its exterior is plain, but inside you'll see carved pillars, copper chandeliers, solid ebony pews, and plaques that commemorate prominent Dutch administrators. ✉ *Jl. Pangeran Jayakarta.*

★ ♺ ❹ **Puppet Museum.** On the west side of Fatahillah Square, in a former Protestant church, is the Museum Wayang. Here you'll find an extensive collection of traditional Indonesian wayang kulit figures, the intricately cut leather shadow puppets used to perform stories from the Hindu epics the *Ramayana* and the *Mahabarata*. The museum also has wayang *golek* figures (wooden puppets used in performing Arabic folktales or stories of Prince Panji, a legendary Javanese prince associated with the conversion of Java to Islam), as well as puppets from Thailand, China, Malaysia, India, and Cambodia. An abbreviated wayang kulit is performed on Sunday at 10 AM. Also on display are puppets used in social education projects. ✉ *Jl. Pintu Besar Utara 27,* ☎ *021/679560.* 🔲 *Admission.* ☉ *Tues.–Thurs. and weekends 9–2, Fri. 9–1.*

Sunda Kelapa Harbor. At the back of the fish market is the wharf, where Makassar and Bugis *prahus* (sailing ships) are docked at oblique angles to the piers. They look like beached whales, but they still sail Indonesian waters as they have for centuries, trading between the islands. You can negotiate a small punt (about Rp 2,500–3,000) to take you on a 30-minute harbor tour. 🔲 *Admission.* ☉ *Daily 8–6.*

New Jakarta

In many developing countries, the capital becomes a symbol of national pride in shaking off the yoke of economic, and often colonial, servitude. In pre–economic crisis Jakarta, this attitude led to the construction of wide avenues, tall skyscrapers (many of which are bank offices), palatial government buildings, and extravagant monuments. Modern Jakarta has little aesthetic appeal, but it's an interesting example of how an evolving nation attempts to thrust itself into the modern age.

A GOOD TOUR

New Jakarta is almost impossible to cover on foot. The distances between sights are long, the streets aren't pedestrian-friendly, and the equatorial heat will melt you. Taxis are very cheap. Use them to get around.

Start your tour in vast Merdeka Square, at the towering **National Monument (MONAS)** ⑧, taking its interior elevator up to the top for a bird's-eye view of the city. Then head for the monument's basement to visit the Museum of National History. Next head west to the **National Museum** ⑨ and its outstanding collection of Indonesian antiquities and ethnic artwork. From the museum, you may want to ride around the square in a taxi. On the northwest corner is the Presidential Palace; on the northeast corner is the **Istiqlal Mosque** ⑩, Indonesia's largest (guided tours are available); and a bit farther down the east side is **Emmanuel Church** ⑪. Keep the taxi and continue south down Jalan Cikini Raya to the **Taman Ismael Marzuki** ⑫ (TIM), also known as the Jakarta Cultural Center, where you're bound to find a cultural performance in progress. (If you walk, it's about 15 minutes from the square's south side.) Directly west from TIM and about 10 minutes by taxi is the **Textile Museum** ⑬, with a collection of more than 300 kinds of Indonesian textiles and a workshop where batik-making is demonstrated.

TIMING

It shouldn't take much more than a half day to cover these sights. Do plan to spend at least a couple of hours in the National Museum. If possible, time your visit to coincide with one of the free tours given in English—Tuesday, Wednesday, and Thursday at 9:30 AM—and you'll appreciate the museum a thousand times more; on Sunday there's Javanese or Sundanese gamelan music from 9:30 to 10:30 AM.

SIGHTS TO SEE

⓫ **Emmanuel Church.** This classical Dutch Protestant church, off Merdeka square in the shadow of the **National Monument**, was built in 1835.

Today its modest simplicity seems wonderfully incongruous in contrast to the surrounding monuments' grandeur. ⊠ *Jl. Merdeka Timur 10.*

⑩ Istiqlal Mosque. On the northwest corner of Merdeka Square is Indonesia's largest mosque. If you haven't come to pray, you probably won't be encouraged to enter on your own. To appreciate the mosque's size and open layout, however, you can arrange to join a guided tour through your hotel or a travel agent. ⊠ *Jl. Veteren.*

❽ National Monument. Merdeka Square is dominated by the towering Monument Nasional (MONAS). Local wags have taken to calling the Russian-built tower commemorating Indonesia's independence "Sukarno's last erection." Some of this bitterness may stem from the fact that the World Bank supplied funds for 77 pounds of pure gold to coat the "flame of freedom" atop the column while many Indonesians starved. Regardless of how you feel about it, the monument serves as a useful landmark. Take its interior elevator up to just below the flame for a panoramic view of the city.

In the basement is the **Museum of National History,** with a gallery of 48 dioramas that illustrate Indonesia's history and struggle for independence. The Hall of Independence contains four national treasures: the flag raised during the independence ceremony in 1945; the original text of the declaration of independence; a gilded map of the Indonesian Republic; and the Indonesian coat of arms, which symbolizes the five principles of the Indonesian Republic (belief in one supreme god; a just and civilized humanity; unity of Indonesia; consensus arising from discussion and self-help; and social justice). ⊠ *Jl. Silang Monas, Merdeka Square,* ☎ *021/681512 museum.* ▨ *Admission (one price for both monument and museum).* ⊙ *Monument: Sat.–Thurs. 9– 4, Fri. 9–11. Museum: Tues.–Thurs. and Sat. 9–2:30, Fri. 9–11:30 AM.*

★ ❾ National Museum. On the west side of Merdeka Square stands the Museum Nasional, recognizable by the bronze elephant in front—a gift from the King of Siam (Thailand) in 1871. The museum has the most complete collection of Indonesian antiquities and ethnic artwork in the country. There are five sections: Hindu and Buddhist stone carvings from the 7th to 15th centuries; an exhibit of prehistoric skulls, weapons, and cooking utensils that date back 4,000 years; Indonesian ethnic crafts; a treasure room with gold trinkets, jeweled weapons, and Buddhist statues; and one of the largest collections of Chinese ceramics outside China. Free tours are given in English on Tuesday, Wednesday, and Thursday at 9:30 AM, and on Sunday you can hear gamelan music from 9:30 to 10:30 AM. To the right, as you face the museum, is the museum shop, which sells such items as shadow puppets and books on Indonesia. ⊠ *Jl. Merdeka Barat 12,* ☎ *021/381–2346.* ▨ *Admission.* ⊙ *Tues.– Thurs. and weekends 8:30–1, Fri. 8:30–11.*

⑫ Taman Ismael Marzuki. There's something happening at the Taman Ismael Marzuki (TIM) from morning to midnight. Most evenings, either the open-air theater or the enclosed auditorium stages some kind of performance, from Balinese dance to imported jazz, from gamelan concerts to poetry readings. Your hotel will have a copy of the monthly program. Two art galleries display paintings, sculpture, and ceramics. Also within the complex are an art school, art workshop, cinema, planetarium, and outdoor cafés. ⊠ *Jl. Cikini Raya 73,* ☎ *021/342605.* ▨ *Admission.* ⊙ *Daily 8–8. Planetarium shows: Tues.–Sun. at 7:30; Sun. at 10, 11, and 1.*

⑬ Textile Museum. With its rich collection of Indonesian fabrics and small workshop where batik-making is demonstrated, the Museum Tekstil will give you an idea of what to expect by way of design and quality in the textiles you'll come across as you travel about the country. ⊠ *Jl. K. Sasuit Tubun 4,* ☎ *021/365367.* ⊠ *Admission.* ☉ *Tues.–Thurs. and Sun. 9–2, Fri. 9–11, Sat. 9–1.*

Jakarta's Green Spaces

Jakarta has attempted to attract visitors and give local residents recreational opportunities. At the same time, the government has wanted to make Jakarta an example of the diversity that is Indonesia. Thus, many of the city's parks are celebrations of the nation's different ethnic and cultural groups.

A GOOD ROUTE

You may not want to visit both of these recreational attractions—choose the one that best satisfies your interests. North of Kota and stretching east along the bay is **Dunia Fantasi at Ancol;** billed as Southeast Asia's largest recreation area, it provides entertainment around the clock. About 12 km (7 mi) southeast of Merdeka Square and 30 minutes by taxi is the **Beautiful Indonesia in Miniature Park.** Its 250 acres hold 27 full-size traditional houses, as well as various museums.

TIMING

You may want to spend the afternoon at Dunia Fantasi at Ancol after touring Old Batavia, since it's north of Kota. However, avoid it on the weekends, when it's thronged with Jakarta families. You'll want to allow a good half day at Beautiful Indonesia in Miniature Park, perhaps arriving in time for lunch.

SIGHTS TO SEE

☾ **Beautiful Indonesia in Miniature Park.** The Batak house of North Sumatra, the Redong longhouse of the Kalimantan Dayaks, the cone-shape hut of Irian Jaya, and the Toraja house of South Sulawesi are just a few of the 27 full-size traditional houses—one from each Indonesian province—on display at the Taman Mini Indonesia Indah. There are even miniature Borobudur and Prambanan temples. Other attractions at the 250-acre park include a 30-minute movie, *Beautiful Indonesia,* shown daily from 11 to 5; the Museum Indonesia, with traditional costumes and handicrafts; a stamp museum; the Soldier's Museum, which honors the Indonesian struggle for independence; the Transportation Museum; and Museum Asmat, which highlights the art of the master carvers of the Asmat people of Irian Jaya. The park also has an orchid garden, an aviary, a touring train, cable cars, horse-drawn carts, paddleboats, and places for refreshment. English-speaking guides are available, if you call in advance. The park is about 12 km (7 mi) southeast of Merdeka Square and 30 minutes by taxi. ⊠ *12 km (7 mi) south of central Jakarta, off Jagorawi Toll Rd.,* ☎ *021/840–1702.* ⊠ *Admission.* ☉ *Museums, daily 9–3; outdoor attractions, daily 9–4.*

☾ **Dunia Fantasi at Ancol.** A village unto itself, this 24-hour park has hotels, nightclubs, shops, and amusement centers, including an oceanarium with dolphin and sea lion shows, a golf course, a race-car track, a four-pool complex with a wave pool, and water slides. Africa is represented by a comedy of mechanized monkeys, America by a Wild West town, Europe by a mock Tudor house, and Asia by buildings from Thailand, Japan, India, and Korea. Rides, shooting galleries, and food stalls surround these attractions, all set on 1,360 acres of land reclaimed from the bay in 1962. ⊠ *Taman Impian Jaya Ancol,* ☎ *021/682000, ext. 201.* ⊠ *Admission.* ☉ *Sat.–Thurs. 11–6, Fri. 1:20–10.*

Dining

All the major hotels have Western and Indonesian restaurants, and many of the latter also offer Chinese food. Outside the hotels, dining options

range from restaurants with a formal atmosphere and fine cuisine to
Western fast-food outlets, including the more upscale ones such as TGI
Friday's and Planet Hollywood, to inexpensive street stalls.

Chinese

$$$$ ✕ **Xin Hwa.** This elegant 100-seat restaurant in the Mandarin Orien-
★   tal hotel (☞ Lodging, *below*) prepares spicy Szechuan specialties, including sliced, braised chicken with hot-pepper oil and abalone soup
with fermented black beans. Try the excellent bird's nest soup and the
stir-fried lobster in a hot black-bean sauce. Dinner reservations are highly
recommended. ⊠ *Jl. M. H. Thamrin,* ☎ *021/391–6438. AE, DC,
MC, V. No lunch weekends.*

Contemporary

$$$ ✕ **Asiatique.** Marrying Asian spices with Western culinary concepts
isn't new in California, but it is in Jakarta. At this restaurant in the
Regent hotel (☞ Lodging, *below*), the chefs blend elements from dif-
ferent Asian cuisines to produce tempting combinations. You can order
most dishes as an appetizer or a main course; a broad selection of ap-
petizers is a good way to satisfy your curiosity. Especially tasty are the
lemongrass-spiked tandoori salmon and the fried chili and lobster
with peppers and lotus root. ⊠ *Jl. H. R. Rasuna Said,* ☎ *021/252–
3456. AE, DC, MC, V. No lunch.*

Eclectic

$$$ ✕ **Oasis.** Fine international cuisine, as well as a traditional rijsttafel,
ensure that the Oasis remains popular. A specialty is medallions of veal
Oscar—served in a cream sauce with mushrooms, crabmeat, and asparagus. The atmosphere lives up to the cuisine in this lovely old house
decorated with tribal art and textiles. A combo alternates with Batak
singers to provide music nightly. ⊠ *Jl. Raden Saleh 47,* ☎ *021/315–
0646. Reservations essential. AE, DC, V. Closed Sun.*

French

$$$ ✕ **Brasserie.** This cozy restaurant is in Kemang, a trendy neighborhood
south of the city where many expats live. The atmosphere in the din-
ing room and on the patio is casual, and the food—traditional French
dishes made with fresh, local ingredients—is good. The wine list has
an extensive selection of French varieties. ⊠ *Plaza Bisnis, Jl. Kemang
Raya 2,* ☎ *021/718–3422. AE, MC, V.*

$$$ ✕ **Le Bistro.** Candlelighted and intimate, with checked tablecloths and
copper pots, the ambience here puts you in the mood for the classic
Provençal menu—simple food from the south of France. Try the roast
chicken with rosemary and thyme. The circular piano bar at the back
of the dining room is the perfect spot for an after-dinner liqueur. ⊠ *Jl.
K. H. Wahid Hasyim 75,* ☎ *021/364272. AE, DC, V.*

Indian

$ ✕ **Omar Khayyam.** In addition to an Indian buffet lunch, this restau-
rant offers such specialties as curries and tandoori dishes. The decor
pays homage to the eponymous Persian poet: some of his poetry is inscribed on the walls. Try the chicken *tikka makhanwalla* (boneless tandoori chicken with tomato, butter, and cream sauce) or the marinated
fish that's wrapped in a banana leaf and deep-fried. ⊠ *Jl. Antara 5–
7,* ☎ *021/356719. Reservations not accepted. No credit cards.*

Indonesian

$$ ✕ **Handayani.** This neighborhood restaurant has friendly service and
some English-speaking staffers. Decor isn't its strong point—lines of
tables and chairs fill a bare room—but Handayani draws locals for its
food rather than its sparse interior. You may have to be a bit bold to
sample some of the dishes, such as chicken bowels steamed in banana

Dining ●

Lodging ○

Jakarta Dining and Lodging

leaves, beef intestine satay, and goldfish fried or grilled. If you're timid, try the lobster-size king prawns cooked in a mild chili sauce or the nasi goreng Handayani, a special version of the Indonesian staple. ✉ *Jl. Abdul Muis 35E,* ☎ *021/373614. DC, V.*

$$ ✕ **Natrabu.** Decor at this popular Padang (the spicy cuisine of the Minangkabau people in the Padang area of West Sumatra) restaurant is minimal: bare tabletops and side booths, red Sumatran banners hanging from the ceiling, and a model of a Minangkabau house set in a corner. Padang waiters wearing head scarves from the region deliver bowls of food from the moment you sit down. You can order, or you can select from the dishes they bring—you pay for the ones you try. ✉ *Jl. H. A. Salim (often called Jl. Sabang) 29A,* ☎ *021/335668. Reservations not accepted. MC, V.*

$$ ✕ **Pondok Laguna.** Here, the large dining room, divided by water
★   pools and falls, is always crowded with families and young couples. The noise level is fairly high and the service casual. Some of the staff speaks English; all are anxious to help foreign guests. Fish is the specialty—either fried or grilled and accompanied by different sauces that range from hot to mild. Everything is fresh and cooked to perfection. ✉ *Jl. Batu Tulis Raya 45,* ☎ *021/359994. Reservations not accepted. AE, DC, MC, V.*

$$ ✕ **Sari Kuring.** This restaurant, near Merdeka Square, serves very
★   good Indonesian seafood, especially the grilled prawns and the Thai fish à la Sari Kuring, marinated in spices then quickly fried. The restaurant is large but connected on many levels by stone steps, so there's some feeling of intimacy. If you can't get a table here, try next door at **Sari Nusantara,** where the fare is similar except for a slight Chinese influence in the cooking and fewer spices in the sauces. ✉ *Jl. Silang Monas Timur 88,* ☎ *021/352972. AE, V.*

Italian

$$ ✕ **Maxis Cucina Italiana.** Conveniently set in the Plaza Indonesia (☞ Shopping, *below*), it's a great place to relax after a hard day's shopping. Styled like a Mediterranean café with common redbrick walls, potted ferns, and plaster archways, it's a relaxing setting. The lasagna is filling, while the pasta with Gorgonzola cheese is a rare treat. ✉ *Level 1, No. 127 B, Jl. M. H. Thamrin,,* ☎ *021/327833. AE, V.*

Japanese

$$$$ ✕ **Sumire.** Tucked away in a corner of the Grand Hyatt (☞ Lodging, *below*), this seductive, dimly lighted restaurant has dark-wood antique furnishings, large rice-paper lanterns and walls, private tatami rooms, and a sushi bar. Sushi, sashimi, and Teppanyaki are all prepared by master chefs from Japan. Deep-fried beef tenderloins is a nice option for the non–fish eater; delicacies such as salmon roe, octopus, and eel are all excellent here. ✉ *Jl. M. H. Thamrin,* ☎ *021/390–1234, ext. 3430. Reservations essential. AE, DC, MC, V.*

$$$ ✕ **Nadaman.** This restaurant, in the Shangri-La hotel (☞ Lodging, *below*), offers a varied selection of traditional and newer Japanese dishes. The 56-seat main dining room is decorated with rice-paper lanterns and black-lacquer tables; there are also private rooms, some with tatami mats and one with tables and a sushi bar. ✉ *Jl. Jendral Sudirman Kav 1,* ☎ *021/570–7440. AE, DC, MC, V.*

Mexican

$$ ✕ **Green Pub.** The Green Pub's two branches are recommended not only for their Mexican food but for their live country-and-western music (6:30–9) and jazz (9:30–1). The decor is somewhere between that of a Western saloon and a Mexican ranch. The burritos and enchiladas are authentic, and the menu also includes such Tex-Mex dishes as bar-

becued spareribs. ⊠ *Jakarta Theater Building, Jl. M. H. Thamrin 9,*
☎ *021/359332;* ⊠ *Jl. H. R. Rasuna Said, Setia Budi Building 1,* ☎
021/517983. Reservations not accepted. AE, V.

Steak House

$$ ✕ **Gandy.** There are several Gandys in Jakarta, but this one is the most
interesting. Stepping into this popular place is like stepping back into
the 1960s: the staff wears uniforms that seem outdated by about 30
years but fit in well with the wooden decor and steak-house setting.
Some of the beef and imported lamb dishes—the specialties here—ar-
rive on a hot plate and keep cooking at your table. Things become lively
after 7 or 8 PM, when a jazz band with a singer performs. ⊠ *Jl. Hos.
Cokroaminoto 90,* ☎ *021/629–0539. AE, DC, MC, V.*

Thai

$$ ✕ **Tamnak Thai.** The friendly staff here serves good, standard Thai food
in the comfortable, 30-odd-table dining room or the separate VIP
room. The menu includes pictures—for the uninitiated—and the chef
will prepare dishes extra spicy or mild. Seafood dishes are standouts.
⊠ *Jl. Hos Cokroaminoto 78,* ☎ *021/315–0833. MC, V.*

Vietnamese

$$ ✕ **Paregu.** This place serves the best Vietnamese food in town. The
decor is simple, with Asian embellishments, and the service is top-notch.
Try the Vietnamese version of spring rolls; the fried rice with scram-
bled eggs, chicken, shrimp, and a blend of herbs and spices; or the herbed
seafood. ⊠ *Jl. Sudan Cholagogue 64,* ☎ *021/774892. No credit cards.*

Lodging

Jakarta has many world-class hotels with all the modern amenities and
countless budget establishments with few frills. Most accommoda-
tions are just south of Merdeka Square.

All the hotels will negotiate rates; in fact, most smile and blush at the
mere mention of presenting the published rate card: what's published
and what's real are two completely different things. You should be able
to knock at least 20% off the published rate.

All the hotels also are prepared for civil unrest. Hoteliers obviously don't
want to talk about it, but if you're concerned, ask what the plans are
in case of trouble. Be it guards, fences, or stockpiles of fresh food, the
Jakarta hotels are as secure as can be expected.

$$$$ 🏨 **Crowne Plaza Jakarta.** A majestic marble staircase graces the lobby
area, providing an expansive, calming ambience juxtaposed to the
bustling "Golden Triangle" commercial area of central Jakarta just out
the front door. Guest rooms have large working desks, extra-large beds,
and perfectly placed reading lamps, so you can take your work to bed
with you if you like. Fresh flowers, comfortable chairs, textured wall-
paper, and spacious bathrooms balance out the thoughtful business-
oriented design with homey touches. The upper-level lobbies have
rotating painting exhibitions, often of colorful local artists. The restau-
rants serve Spanish, Chinese, or Japanese food, and you can order con-
tinental foods in the cafés. ⊠ *Jl. Jend. Gatot Subroto Kav. 2–3, 12930,*
☎ *021/526–8833,* 🖷 *021/526–8832. 241 rooms, 18 suites. 3 restau-
rants, 2 bars, 2 cafés, pool, beauty salon, tennis court, health club, baby-
sitting, business services, meeting rooms. AE, DC, MC, V.* 🍷

$$$$ 🏨 **Grand Hyatt.** Glitter and shining-marble modernity characterize this
hotel with a four-story atrium lobby. Climb a palatial staircase (or take
the escalator) to the reception area; one more short flight up brings
you to the expansive Fountain Lounge, where you can watch the

stalled traffic on Jalan M. H. Thamrin. On the fifth floor is the pool garden and an extensive area of greenery. Rooms are spacious, and each has two bay windows; bathrooms have separate shower stalls and toilets. Furnishings are in the ubiquitous pastels, but pleasant nonetheless. Beneath the Hyatt is the Plaza Indonesia (☞ *also* Shopping, *below*), with restaurants, nightclubs, and more than 250 shops. In a city that sprawls, this proximity to a "social center" is an advantage. ⊠ *Jl. M. H. Thamrin (Box 4546), 10045, ☎ 021/390–1234 or 800/ 233–1234 in the U.S., ℻ 021/334321. 447 rooms, 20 suites. 6 restaurants, bar, pool, massage, 6 tennis courts, health club, jogging, squash, business services. AE, DC, MC, V.*

$$$$ 🏨 **Hotel Borobudur.** Billed as "your country club in Jakarta," this large, modern complex sits on 23 acres of landscaped gardens and has excellent facilities. Floor-to-ceiling windows at the back of the Pendopo Lounge look out onto the greenery, making it a delightful place for afternoon tea, cocktails, or snacks. Most of the compact guest rooms have a modern Javanese design; the Garden Wing has suites with kitchens. Request a room that overlooks the gardens and the pool or risk staying in one that faces the parking lot. ⊠ *Jl. Lapangan Banteng Selatan (Box 329), 10710, ☎ 021/380–5555 or 800/327–0200 in the U.S., ℻ 021/380–9595. 712 rooms, 140 suites. 5 restaurants, 2 bars, room service, pool, miniature golf, 8 tennis courts, badminton, health club, jogging, racquetball, squash, dance club, playground, business services, meeting rooms. AE, DC, MC, V.*

$$$$ 🏨 **Jakarta Hilton.** This massive complex, set on 32 acres and housing 1,104 rooms, comprises three buildings. Stay in the Main Tower or Garden Tower if you want Indonesian designs. A traditional Javanese wooden pavilion lobby gives way to a marble expanse at the reservation desks in both of these buildings. Rooms have sliding-door window shades that block out the intense Indonesian morning sun. For a more contemporary design, choose the Lagoon Tower with brighter, shinier hallways and traditional curtains. No matter which building you stay in, you're guaranteed large desks and three telephones in each room. The staff is friendly and helpful, and the diversity of restaurants, bars, and cafés means you don't have to leave the complex to tour the gastronomic globe. ⊠ *Jl. Gatot Subroto (Box 3315), 10002, ☎ 021/ 570–3600, ℻ 021/573–3089. 1,104 rooms, 115 suites. 6 restaurants, 2 bars, 2 cafés, 2 pools, beauty salon, massage, sauna, 12 tennis courts, jogging, squash, baby-sitting, business services, convention center, meeting room. AE, DC, MC, V.* 🐾

$$$$ 🏨 **Mandarin Oriental.** The elegant, circular lobby has three tall, beau-
★   tifully carved Batak roofs, each housing a Sumatran statue. Guest rooms are spacious and have top-quality furnishings: thick russet carpeting, floral bedspreads, off-white draperies on picture windows, and dark-wood furniture. Complimentary afternoon tea and hors d'oeuvres are delivered to your room. Most rooms are "executive," with butler service; for a nominal extra fee you can have complimentary breakfast and cocktails as well as use of the executive lounge and concierge services. The hotel's location is central, and with the Plaza Indonesia shopping complex and the Grand Hyatt across the square, there are shops, restaurants, and bars within a two-minute walk. On-site restaurants include the Xin Hwa (☞ Dining, *above*). ⊠ *Jl. M. H. Thamrin (Box 3392), 10310, ☎ 021/314–1307 or 800/526–6566 in the U.S., ℻ 021/314–8680. 438 rooms. 4 restaurants, bar, pool, sauna, health club, business services, meeting rooms. AE, DC, MC, V.* 🐾

$$$$ 🏨 **Le Meridien.** Centrally located, this hotel utilizes reoccurring dragon themes in its decor, from a dragon banister to dragon headboards, creating a nice mixture of traditional touches and architectures. The rooms are small compared to other comparably priced hotels, but

they have all the high-end amenities, including a separate shower and bath, nice views, glass-top desks and coffee tables, and rich reds and blues for the upholstery and bedspreads. ✉ *Jl. Jenderal Sudiman Kav. 18–20, 10220,* ☎ *021/251–3131,* FAX *021/571–1633. 225 rooms, 29 suites. 4 restaurants, 2 bars, massage, sauna, spa, exercise room, business services, conference center, meeting rooms. AE, DC, MC, V.* 🍴

$$$$ 🏨 **Regent.** The architects made the most of space and natural light at
★ this property, which sits on 6 acres in the Golden Triangle, the city's booming business district. In the lobby, 10 shades of granite and marble are set off by honey-color teak paneling and Indonesian art. Guest rooms are large—a minimum of 500 square ft—and double layers of masonry in between make them soundproof. Double-glazed, sliding glass doors lead out onto small balconies; framed Indonesian tapestries adorn the walls; and marble baths have deep tubs and separate shower stalls. Phones have two lines, modems, and voice mail. The Regent Club, on the 17th floor, has a commodious lounge where complimentary breakfast and evening cocktails are served against a backdrop of great city views. Service throughout the hotel is friendly. ✉ *Jl. H. R. Rasuna Said, 12920,* ☎ *021/252–3456 or 800/545–4000 in the U.S.,* FAX *021/252–4480. 378 rooms. 3 restaurants, bar, pool, sauna, 2 tennis courts, health club, business services, meeting rooms. AE, DC, MC, V.*

$$$$ 🏨 **Shangri-La.** At this opulent hotel, which regularly hosts dignitaries, chandeliers adorn the huge lobby and a string quartet plays classical music much of the day. Rooms have dark-wood furnishings, extra-large beds, and couches that you can sink into. The baths have tubs as well as separate shower stalls. A stay here includes free use of the well-equipped health club, which is like a resort in itself and has one of the city's best pools. The hotel's location in the Golden Triangle area makes it a convenient place for business travelers. ✉ *Jl. Jendral Sudirman Kav 1, 10220,* ☎ *021/570–7440 or 800/942–5050 in the U.S.,* FAX *021/570–3530. 628 rooms, 40 suites. 6 restaurants, 2 bars, deli, pool, beauty salon, massage, sauna, putting green, 3 tennis courts, health club, jogging, business services, meeting rooms. AE, DC, MC, V.* 🍴

$$$ 🏨 **Aston Grand Suites Hotel.** This all-suite hotel, formerly known as
★ Lippo Sudirman Grand Suites, combines the privacy of home with five-star hotel services. Expect a full-size refrigerator, rice cooker, and microwave in the kitchen, which also has maid's quarters off to the side. A white tile floor and mirrored wall decorate the living room, with a large-screen television in front of the three-seater couch. Bedrooms are also styled in whites and beiges, with thick carpets and complimentary terry-cloth robes and slippers. The two bathrooms (one with a shower, the other with a tub) have rich royal blue, forest green, or burgundy tiles, which stand out against the otherwise white, modern suite. The master bedroom has another television, and the second bedroom can be used as an office. For less than the cost of a double room at one of the more expensive hotels, you get all the amenities of an executive suite. There are 56 floors; whereas the higher ones have stunning views, they're more expensive. ✉ *Jl. Garnisun Dalam No. 8, Karet Samanggi, 12930,* ☎ *021/251–5151,* FAX *021/251–4090. 298 suites. 3 restaurants, 3 bars, kitchenettes, pool, wading pool, beauty salon, 2 saunas, 2 tennis courts, 2 squash courts, baby-sitting, nursery, 2 playgrounds, business services, meeting rooms. AE, DC, MC, V. www.aston-intl.com.*

$$$ 🏨 **Hotel Sahid Jaya Jakarta.** Expect friendly service and an impressive lobby with a traditional Javanese painted ceiling and intricately carved wooden panels in the lounge area. The staff, dressed in fanciful outfits, are exceedingly friendly, but the mystique diminishes some when you reach the room, which unfortunately has old carpets, worn Formica, and faux blond-wood furnishings. Still, the rooms are spacious, and the hotel is centrally situated near banks and businesses. ✉

86 *Jl. Jendral Sudirman, 10220,* ☎ *021/570–4444,* FAX *021/570–2208. 667 rooms, 61 suites. 7 restaurants, lounge, pub, pool, wading pool, tennis court, beauty salon, baby-sitting, laundry service, business services, convention center, meeting rooms. AE, DC, MC, V.* ☜

$$$ 🏨 **Hotel Wisata International.** Ranked as a three-star hotel by the government, the ungainly Wisata is off Jakarta's main thoroughfare. Corridors are long and narrow, guest rooms compact but clean. Each has a king-size bed; a TV and a safe take up most of the remaining space. Rooms on the executive floor are only marginally larger. Still, the price, the convenient coffee shop off the lobby, and the central location make the Wisata a reasonable choice. ✉ *Jl. M. H. Thamrin, 10230,* ☎ *021/230–0406,* FAX *021/324597. 165 rooms. Bar, coffee shop, meeting rooms. AE, DC, MC, V.*

$$ 🏨 **Jayakarta Tower.** This moderately priced hotel is within walking
★ distance of Old Batavia. The marble lobby is accented with hand-blown glass chandeliers and carved-wood panels. Each spacious room has a double or two twin beds with Javanese-pattern spreads, plus a table and two chairs and a vanity/desk. Executive rooms have minibars. For on-site meals, your choices are the Dragon (a Chinese restaurant) or a coffee shop that serves Western and Indonesian specialties; ask to see the Thai menu at both. The hotel is affiliated with KLM's Golden Tulip properties, so you can make reservations through the airline. ✉ *Jl. Hayam Wuruk 126 (Box 803), 11001,* ☎ *021/629–4408,* FAX *021/626–5000. 435 rooms. 2 restaurants, coffee shop, room service, pool, health club, meeting rooms. AE, DC, MC, V.*

$$ 🏨 **President Hotel.** Like many hotels in the Japanese Nikko Hotel group, the President has a spare, utilitarian atmosphere but is equipped with modern amenities. Guest rooms are simple and slightly worn, with blue-and-navy striped fabrics, plain wood furniture, and small bathrooms. But the complimentary slippers are a nice touch, and for the price, the service is first-class. The on-site Ginza Benkay restaurant serves Japanese food, the Kahyangan serves Japanese and Indonesian, and the Golden Pavilion serves Chinese. ✉ *Jl. M. H. Thamrin 59, 10350,* ☎ *021/230–1122,* FAX *021/314–3631. 354 rooms. 3 restaurants, bar, coffee shop, meeting rooms. AE, DC, MC, V.* ☜

$ 🏨 **Interhouse.** This hotel is in the Kebayoran expatriate neighborhood and shopping district. Rooms are comfortable, though not large, and have pleasant, homey furnishings and pastel color schemes. ✉ *Jl. Melawai Raya 18–20 (Box 128/KBYB), 10305,* ☎ *021/270–0408,* FAX *021/720–6988. 130 rooms. Restaurant. AE, V.*

$ 🏨 **Kebayoran Inn.** Just south of Jakarta's center is this quiet, residential-type lodging. The clean rooms are simply decorated, with an Indonesian batik or ikat here and there. ✉ *Jl. Senayan 87, 12180,* ☎ *021/716208,* FAX *021/560–3672. 61 rooms. Restaurant. AE, V.*

$ 🏨 **Marcopolo.** The staff at this basic, economical hotel is helpful, and
★ although the carpeted rooms are plain, they're clean and adequate. The restaurant serves good Chinese and European food. ✉ *Jl. T. Cik Ditiro 19, 10350,* ☎ *021/325409,* FAX *021/310–7138. 181 rooms. Restaurant, air-conditioning, pool, nightclub. AE, DC, V.*

Nightlife and the Arts

Nightlife

Owing to the political and economic crises, Jakarta's night scene is surely in for some volatile times; nightspots will, no doubt, quickly come and go. When you arrive, you'll have to check out what's happening. Hotel staffers are terrific resources, and concierges can make reservations for you if necessary. Another good resource is *Jakarta Week,* which lists upcoming events and is found at most hotels. The places detailed below seemed, at press time, the ones most likely to survive the test of both time and economics.

Bats. Expats flock to this bar in the Shangri-La (☞ Lodging, *above*) because it's the furthest thing from your run-of-the-mill hotel bar; it's more like a club in New York City. Okay, so there's a human-size Statue of Liberty above the bar, where the bartenders twirl and juggle the bottles like Tom Cruise in *Cocktail*, but the dance floor rocks on the weekends, and the multilevel layout with high ceilings means the smoke rises instead of getting into your eyes. ✉ *Jl. Jendral Sudirman Kav 1, 10220,* ☎ *21/570–8022, ext. 6400 or 6401.* ۞ *Daily 7 PM–2 AM.*

Fashion Café. The two-floor Fashion Café near the Shangri-La hotel has a high-energy, futuristic, techno design that makes for a terrific night out; wear black, and you'll fit right in. You can order such dishes as Naomi's Fish and Chips (named after fashion model Naomi Campbell) and Claudia's (as in Claudia Schiffer) New York Strip, or just stick to drinks at the bar. Sometimes there's a show. ✉ *Jl. Jendral Sudirman Kav 1,* ☎ *021/574–5111.* ۞ *Daily 11 AM–1 AM.*

Green Pub. After dinner at this pub-restaurant (☞ *also* Dining, *above*), consider hanging out with the expats and listening to music performed by local bands. ✉ *Jakarta Theater Building, Jl. M. H. Thamrin 9,* ☎ *021/359332.*

Hard Rock Cafe. You'll find the same American fare and rock-and-roll paraphernalia here as at its brethren in cities around the world. The live music starts at about 9 PM. The stage has a huge stained-glass-window backdrop that depicts Elvis Presley. ✉ *Sarinah Building, 2nd floor, Jl. M. H. Thamrin 11,* ☎ *021/390–3565.* ۞ *Daily 11 AM–1 AM.*

Harry's Captain's Bar. This comfortable spot in the Mandarin Oriental hotel (☞ Lodging, *above*) is good for a relaxed evening of jazz by a small international or local group. ✉ *Jl. M. H. Thamrin,* ☎ *021/ 321307.* ۞ *Nightly 8 PM–1 AM.*

Jaya Pub. This long-established piano bar is popular with older expats and Indonesians alike, in part because the owners are two former Indonesian movie stars, Rimi Melati and Frans Tumbuan. ✉ *Jl. M. H. Thamrin 12,* ☎ *021/327508.* ۞ *Daily noon–2 AM.*

O'Reiley's Pub and Bar. Built to resemble an Irish pub, this spot in the Grand Hyatt hotel (☞ Lodging, *above*) offers beer on tap. Stop by for a few drinks and some conversation early in the evening or a few pints and some live music later at night. ✉ *Jl. M. H. Thamrin,* ☎ *021/390– 1234.* ۞ *Daily 11 AM–1 AM.*

Planet Hollywood. You can't, it seems, have the Fashion and Hard Rock cafés without also having a Planet Hollywood. You can dine amid the movie memorabilia or just sip drinks and chat about your favorite films. There's live entertainment on Thursday, Friday, and Saturday after 10 PM. As it's in Jakarta's east section, it's best to take a taxi. ✉ *Jl. Gatot Subroto Kav 16,* ☎ *021/526–6727.* ۞ *Daily 1 PM–2 AM.*

Tanamur. Here's a place that just about every hotel staff member will suggest when asked for tips on nightspots. This Jakarta institution has good jazz and soft rock and is usually crowded. What goes on as couples huddle against the dimly lighted walls is better left unsaid; hostesses dance and drink with guests who don't have a date. ✉ *Jl. Tanah Abang Timur 14,* ☎ *021/353947.* ۞ *Nightly 9 PM–2 AM.*

The Arts

For information on Jakarta's art events, check the daily *Indonesian Observer* or the *Jakarta Post* newspapers.

DANCE AND THEATER

Beautiful Indonesia in Miniature Park. This park offers various regional dances on Sunday and holidays from 10 to 2 (☞ *also* Jakarta's Green

Spaces *in* Exploring Jakarta, *above*). ✉ *Off Jagorawi Toll Rd.,* ☎ *021/840–1702.*

Bharata Theater. Every night but Monday and Thursday, from 8:15 to midnight, this theater stages traditional wayang *orang* (dance-dramas) performances, depicting stories from the *Ramayana* or the *Mahabharata.* Sometimes the folk play *Ketoprak,* based on Javanese history, is also performed. ✉ *Jl. Kalilio,* ☎ *021/380–8283.*

Taman Ismail Marzuki. This arts center hosts plays, music and dance performances, art shows, and films. Monthly events schedules are distributed to hotels. ✉ *Jl. Cikini Raya 73,* ☎ *021/334720.*

PUPPET SHOWS

National Museum. Here there are biweekly performances using leather shadow puppets to depict stories from the *Ramayana* or the *Mahabharata,* or wood puppets to depict Islamic legends. ✉ *Jl. Merdeka Barat 12,* ☎ *021/381–1551.*

Puppet Museum. This museum frequently offers performances; call ahead for dates and times. ✉ *Jl. Pintu Besar Utara 27,* ☎ *021/692–9560.*

Outdoor Activities and Sports

Diving

Dive Indonesia (✉ Hotel Borobudur Inter-Continental, Jl. Lapangan Banteng Selatan, ☎ 021/380–4444, ext. 74222) specializes in underwater photography and arranges trips to Flores and Sulawesi. **Jakarta Dive School and Pro Shop** (✉ Indonesia Bazaar, Shop 32, Jakarta Hilton, Jl. Jendral Sudiman and Jl. Jendral Gatot Subroto, ☎ 021/570–3600, ext. 9008) offers open-water lessons and equipment rental.

Golf

At last count, greater Jakarta had 20 golf courses. The Indonesia Golf Course Association, together with the Indonesia Tourism Promotion Board, publishes *The Official Golf Map of Indonesia,* available free at travel agencies and tourist offices. There are two well-maintained, 18-hole courses open to the public, though both are extremely crowded on weekends. Greens fees are generally Rp 150,000 on weekdays and Rp 250,000 on weekends; caddy fees run Rp 25,000 (tips are appreciated). The **Padang Golf Jaya Ancol** (✉ Dunia Fantasi at Ancol, Taman Impian Jaya Ancol, ☎ 021/682000, ext. 221) has pleasant sea views. **Padang Golf Kemayoran** (✉ Jl. Asia-Afrika, Pintu 9, ☎ 021/654–1156) is popular with expats.

Running

The **Hash House Harriers/Harriettes,** a club known worldwide for mixing outrageous antics into its runs, has a chapter in Jakarta (✉ HHH Box 46/KBY, 12075, ☎ 021/799–4758). Men run Monday at 5 PM, women Wednesday at 5 PM, and there's socializing in between. Write or call for meeting places and routes.

Tennis and Squash

Many of Jakarta's hotels have tennis and/or squash courts where nonguests can play. Call first to reserve a court. The **Grand Hyatt** (✉ Jl. M. H. Thamrin, ☎ 021/390–1234), which has six courts; the 🎾 **Hotel Borobudur** (✉ Jl. Lapangan Banteng Selatan, ☎ 021/380–5555), which has eight courts; and the **Jakarta Hilton** (✉ Jl. Jendral Sudirman and Jl. Jendral Gatot Subroto, ☎ 021/570–3600), which has 12 courts, have both tennis and squash facilities.

Shopping

Indonesia is a shopper's paradise for locally produced items such as batik fabric, wood carvings, and clothing.

Department Stores

Pasaraya (⊠ Jl. Iskandarsyah 1½, in Block M, ☎ 021/736–0170). Jakarta's largest department store has Indonesia's latest in women's fashions and handicrafts.

Plaza Indonesia (⊠ Jl. M. H. Thamrin, ☎ 021/310–7272). Under the Grand Hyatt and across the square from the Mandarin Oriental, this is a central and convenient shopping center. Among its 250 stores are upscale boutiques ranging from DKNY to Versace, art and antiques galleries, bookshops, travel agents, restaurants, and the Japanese department store Sogo.

Plaza Senayan (⊠ Jl. Asia-Africa 8, ☎ 021/572–5555). One of the city's newest shopping complexes has upscale boutiques with designer-label fashions.

Sarinah Mataram (⊠ Jl. M. H. Thamrin 11, Menteng, ☎ 021/327425). This four-story department store not only sells a variety of goods from its convenient location but is also connected to the Hard Rock Cafe—a great place to rest your feet after all that shopping.

Markets

Jalan Surabaya Antiques Stalls (⊠ Pasar Barang Antik Jalan Surabaya, in Menteng residential area). The city's daily (9–6) "flea market" sells mundane goods at either end, but in the middle you might find delft-ware, Chinese porcelain, old coins, old and not-so-old bronzes, and more. You *must* bargain.

Pasar Melawai (⊠ Jl. Melawai, in Block M). This series of buildings and stalls offers everything from clothing to toys, cosmetics, and fresh foods. English is spoken; open daily 9–6.

Specialty Stores

ANTIQUES

For serious antiques shopping, try the stores along Jalan Paletehan I (Kebayoran Baru); Jalan Maja Pahit and Jalan Gajah Mada (Gambir/Kota); Jalan Kebon Sirih Timur and Jalan H. A. Salim (Mentang); and Jalan Ciputat Raya (Old Bogor Road). Unfortunately, due to the economic crisis many shops have gone out of business; although old favorites may be gone, new ones may spring up soon.

Madjapahit Art and Curio (⊠ Jl. Melawai III/4, ☎ 021/724–5878). This reputable store is near Block M.

HANDICRAFTS

Sarinah Mataram (⊠ Jl. M. H. Thamrin 11, Menteng, ☎ 021/327425). The department store's third floor is devoted entirely to handicrafts, which are also in abundance at its larger sister store, Pasaraya (☞ *above*).

TEXTILES

Batik Danar Hadi (⊠ Jl. Raden Saleh 1A, ☎ 021/323663). The batik selection here is quite large.

Batik Mira (⊠ Jl. Mar. Raya 22, ☎ 021/769–1138). This is the place for expensive but excellent-quality batik. Its tailors will do custom work, and you can ask to see the factory at the rear of the store.

Batik Semar (⊠ Jl. Tornang Raya 54, ☎ 021/567–3514). Here you'll find top-quality, unusual batik.

Bin House (⊠ Jl. Tewkbetung No. 10, ☎ 021/391–2079 or 021/315–2493). This shop carries Indonesian handwoven silks and cottons, including ikat, as well as antique textiles and objets d'art.

Plaza Indonesia (⊠ Jl. M. H. Thamrin, ☎ 021/310–7272). This is a good place for chic, fashionable batiks, especially on the first floor.

PT Ramacraft (⊠ Jl. Panarukan 25, ☎ 021/310–7785 or 021/314–3122). PT Ramacraft is the name of both the label and company run by Iwan Tirta, a famous batik fabric and clothing designer.

Jakarta A to Z

Arriving and Departing

BY AIRPLANE

Jakarta's airport, **Soekarno Hatta** (☎ 021/550–5307), is a modern show-piece, with glass-walled walkways and landscaped gardens. Although most of it isn't air-conditioned, it's breezy and clean. There's a small duty-free shopping area. Terminal One handles international flights, and Terminal Two serves all Garuda Indonesia Airways flights (both international and domestic) and all other domestic airlines. (For information on carriers and flights, ☞ Indonesia A to Z, *below*.) Between the two terminals, a **Visitor Information Center** (☎ 021/550–7088) is usually open Monday through Saturday 8 AM–10 PM, though sometimes it's closed seemingly because the staff feel like it. In both terminals there are **Indotel desks** (☎ 021/550–6451) where you can make hotel reservations, often at discounted rates.

From the Airport to Downtown: The airport is 35 km (20 mi) north-west of Jakarta. A toll expressway takes you three-quarters of the way to the city quickly, but the rest is slow going. To be safe, allow a good hour for the trip on weekdays.

Taxis *from* the airport add a Rp 2,300 surcharge and the Rp 7,000 road toll to the fare. The surcharge doesn't apply going *to* the airport. Blue Bird Taxi (☞ By Taxi, under Getting Around, *below*) offers a 25% toll-charge discount. The average fare to a downtown hotel is Rp 50,000.

Air-conditioned buses, with DAMRI in big letters on the side, operate every 20 minutes between the airport and six points in the city, including the Gambir Railway Station, Rawamangun Bus Terminal, Block M, and Pasar Minggu Bus Terminal. The cost is Rp 3,000.

BY BUS

Bus terminals are off Merdeka Square and Block M; buy tickets at the terminals or at travel agencies. **Pulo Gadang** (✉ Jl. Perintis Ke-merdekaan, ☎ 021/489–3742) serves Semarang, Yogyakarta, Solo, Surabaya, Malang, and Denpasar. Use **Cililitan** (✉ Jl. Raya Bogor, ☎ 021/809–3554) for Bogor, Sukabumi, Bandung, and Banjar. **Kalideres** (✉ Jl. Daan Mogot) is the depot for Merak, Labuhan, and major cities in Sumatra (which include a ferry ride as part of a bus journey).

BY TRAIN

Use the **Tanah Abang Railway Station** (✉ Jl. KH Wahid Hasyim, southwest of Merdeka Sq., ☎ 021/340048) for trains to Sumatra. (You get off the train for the ferry across the Sunda Straight to Suma-tra and then catch another train in Bandarlampang.) Trains for desti-nations other than Sumatra—to Bogor and Bandung or to the east Java cities of Semarang, Yogyakarta, Solo, Surabaya, Madiun, and Malang—start from one of two other stations: the **Kota Railway Station** (✉ Jl. Stasiun Kota, south of Fatahillah Sq., ☎ 021/678515 or 021/679194) or the **Gambir Railway Station** (✉ Jl. Merdeka Timur, east side of Merdeka Sq., ☎ 021/342777 or 021/348612). You can buy tickets from travel agencies (☞ Tour Operators and Travel Agents, *below*) or at the station at least an hour before departure.

Getting Around

BY BUS

Non-air-conditioned public buses charge a flat Rp 350; the (green) air-conditioned buses charge Rp 600. All are packed during rush hours, and pickpockets abound. The routes can be labyrinthine, but you can always give one a try and get off when the bus veers from your desired direction. For information, contact these companies: **Hiba Utama** (☎ 021/413626 or 021/410381), **P. P. D.** (☎ 021/881131 or 021/411357), or **Mayasari Bhakti** (☎ 021/809–0378 or 021/489–2785).

BY CAR

Though rental cars are available, they're not advised. Traffic is horrendous, and parking is very difficult. If you do decide to rent a car, be aware that traffic police supplement their income by stopping you, even for infractions that you never knew you made. The police will suggest Rp 70,000 to forget the matter; you're expected to negotiate, and Rp 30,000 should make you both happy. (Keep in mind that at press time, a low-ranking, unmarried civil servant's salary was about $20 U.S. a month, which explains the rampant bribery problem.)

You can rent cars from **Avis** (✉ Jl. Doponegoro 25, ☎ 021/331974). You can hire air-conditioned, chauffeur-driven cars for a two-hour minimum, at hourly rates of Rp 11,375 for a small Corona or Rp 21,000 for a Mercedes. Daily charters cost Rp 150,000 and Rp 250,000, respectively. Try Blue Bird Taxi (☞ *below*) or Avis (☞ *above*).

BY MOTOR BECAK

These dirty, little, orange put-puts are, believe it or not, very good for short, one-way trips. Flag them down on the street. Most rides are Rp 2,000 to 5,000; you *must* bargain for a price. Note that seating is tight for anyone bigger than average.

BY TAXI

Jakarta's air-conditioned, metered taxis charge Rp 2,000 for the first kilometer (½ mi) and Rp 800 for each subsequent 100 meters. You can flag taxis on the streets, and most hotels have cab stands. Be sure that the meter is on when you set off, and avoid taxis with broken meters or none at all, or you'll be seriously overcharged. For a radio-dispatched taxi, call **Blue Bird Taxi** (☎ 021/798–1001 or 021/794–1234).

Contacts and Resources

EMERGENCIES

Ambulance: ☎ 118. **City Health Service:** ☎ 119.

Doctors and Dentists. A group-practice clinic, **Bina Medica** (✉ Jl. Maluka 8–10, ☎ 021/344893) provides 24-hour service and English-speaking doctors. Dental services are provided at the **Metropolitan Medical Center** (✉ Jl. H. R. Rasvna Said Kav c-21, ☎ 021/520–3435 or 021/520–3441). English-speaking staff (including dentists) are available at the 24-hour clinic and pharmacy **SOS Medika Vayasan** (✉ Jl. Puri Sakti No. 10, ☎ 021/750–5973).

Pharmacies. Melawai Apotheek (✉ Jl. Melawai Raya 191, ☎ 021/716109) has a well-stocked supply of American medicines. **SOS Medika Vayasan** (☞ *above*) also has a pharmacy.

Police: ☎ 110. **Traffic accidents:** ☎ 118. **Fire:** ☎ 113.

ENGLISH-LANGUAGE BOOKSTORES

Major hotel shops carry English magazines, newspapers, paperbacks, and travel guides. For a wide book selection, try **PT Indira** (✉ Jl. Melawi V/16, Block M, ☎ 021/770584). The **Family Book Shop** (✉ Kemang Club Villas, Jl. Kelurahan Bangka, ☎ 021/799–5525) has several titles. The largest selection is at the **Times Bookshop** (✉ Jl. M. H. Thamrin 28–30, ☎ 021/570–6581), on Plaza Indonesia's lower floor.

TOUR OPERATORS AND TRAVEL AGENTS

Hotel tour desks will book the following tours or customize outings with a chauffeured car: "City Tour" (six hours) covers the National Monument, Pancasila Monument, Beautiful Indonesia in Miniature Park, and Museum Indonesia; "Indocultural Tour" (five hours) visits the Central Museum, Old Batavia, the Jakarta Museum, and a batik factory; "Beautiful Indonesia Tour" (three to four hours) takes you by air-conditioned bus through the Beautiful Indonesia in Miniature Park; and "Jakarta by Night" (five hours) includes dinner, a dance performance, and a visit to a nightclub. Tours beyond Jakarta include the following: a nine-hour trip to Pelabuhanratu, a former fishing village that's now a resort; an eight-hour tour to the safari park at Bogor and the Botanical Gardens, 48 km (30 mi) south of Jakarta at 600 ft above sea level, and to the Puncak Mountain Resort; and a two-day tour to visit Bandung and its volcano, with stops at Bogor and Puncak.

Gray Line (⊠ Jl. Hayam Wunuk 3–P, ☎ 021/639–0008) covers most of Jakarta and its surrounding attractions. If you show up at **Jakarta City Tourist Center** (⊠ Lapangan Binteng, Bantung Square, ☎ no phone), which opens at 8 AM, you can join any of the tours operating that day, usually at a discounted rate.

Travel agencies arrange transportation, conduct guided tours, and can often secure hotel reservations more cheaply than you could yourself. **Natourin** (⊠ 18 Buncit Raya, Jakarta 12790, ☎ 021/798–2300) has extensive facilities and contacts throughout Indonesia. **Jaksa Group** (⊠ Jalin Jaksa No. 29, Jakarta 10340 ☎ 021/3190–0607) will book flights, local tours, and inexpensive chauffeurs—which through this agency are less expensive than taxis. The agency also offers Internet and postal service. Although the following agents specialize in train travel, they can also help you with other travel needs: **Carnation Tours & Travel Service** (⊠ Jl. A. M. Sangaji 15 B, ☎ 021/350–9005 or 021/350–9006), **P. T. Bhayangkara** (⊠ Jl. Kebayoran Baru, ☎ 021/722–0252 or 021/720–7537), and **Iwata Nusantara** (⊠ Jl. Riau 19, ☎ 021/314–3810 or 021/314–8957).

Large government-owned travel agencies with branch offices at most Indonesian tourist destinations include the following: **Nitour** (⊠ Jl. Majapahit 2, ☎ 021/384–0956); **Satriavi Tours & Travel** (⊠ Jl. Prapatan 32, ☎ 021/231–0005); and **Pacto Ltd. Tours and Travel** (⊠ Jl. Taman Kamang 2, Block D 2–4, Kebayoran Baru, ☎ 021/719–6550), American Express's Indonesian representative.

VISITOR INFORMATION

The comprehensive *Falk City Map of Jakarta* is available at bookstores for Rp 9,200.

The **City Visitor Information Center** (⊠ Jakarta Theatre Building, Jl. M. H. Thamrin 9, ☎ 021/354094) has brochures, maps, and information on bus and train schedules to other Java destinations. The center is open Monday–Thursday 8–3, Friday 8–11:30 AM, and Saturday 8–2; that is, if the employees aren't all on break.

West Java

Java's western province has coastline, mountains, and fertile valleys that are intensively farmed. The province also has the impressive Ujung Kulon National Park, which is set on a peninsula in the island's southwestern corner. Just north of the park is Pulau Krakatau, an active island volcano. There are wild areas in the southeast corner, too, around the resort town of Pangandaran. Cosmopolitan Bandung, Indonesia's third-largest city, has a few reminders of the days when the Dutch flocked here to escape Jakarta's sweltering heat.

Most people in West Java are Sundanese and have their own language and cuisine (for a long time, the region was known as Sunda). The peo-

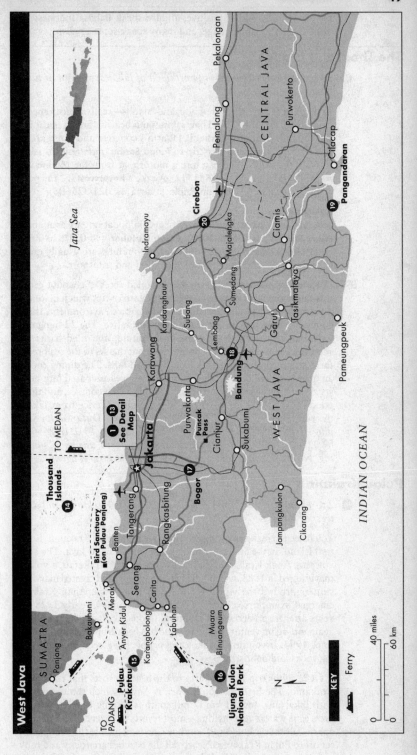

49

West Java

Java Sea

CENTRAL JAVA

INDIAN OCEAN

WEST JAVA

SUMATRA

TO MEDAN

TO PADANG

Thousand Islands

Bird Sanctuary
(on Pulau Panjang)

Pulau Krakatau

Ujung Kulon National Park

Jakarta

Bogor

Bandung

Cirebon

Pekalongan

Pemalang

Purwokerto

Cilacap

Pangandaran

Ciamis

Tasikmalaya

Garut

Pameungpeuk

Sumedang

Majalengka

Indramayu

Kandanghaur

Subang

Lembang

Karawang

Purwakarta

Puncak Pass

Cianjur

Sukabumi

Jampangkulon

Cikarang

Rangkasbitung

Tangerang

Banten

Serang

Merak

Bakauheni

Panjang

Anyer Kidul

Carita

Karangbolong

Labuhan

Muara Binuangeum

N

0   40 miles
0   60 km

KEY

Ferry

ple are friendly and inquisitive; all also speak Bahasa Indonesia, Indonesia's national language, and many speak some English.

The Thousand Islands

🔟 *16 km–32 km (10 mi–20 mi) northwest of Jakarta; an hour or two by boat.*

In the Java Sea are the little Thousand Islands—really a misnomer, because there are only 113. Their white-sand beaches are a retreat from the capital's heat and bustle. If Jakarta's concrete and noise are getting to you, consider a day trip to **Pulau Seribu** (*pulau* means island) to walk the sands. You can hire a motorboat from the **Marina Jaya Ancol** (✉ Jakarta, ☎ 021/681512) or take a **hovercraft** (✉ the port is at Jl. Donggala 26A, Tanjun Priok, Jakarta, ☎ 021/325608).

Lodging

Several islands have rustic getaways; accommodations are available on **Pulau Putri** (☎ 021/828–1093), **Pulau Matahari** (☎ 021/626–2622), and **Pulau Bidadari** (☎ 021/680048). Room rates are usually quoted as all-inclusive packages that include food and transport.

$$$ 🏨 **Kotok Island Resort.** Set on 42 unspoiled acres of coconut groves, this resort owns all but the island's very eastern tip, which belongs to a private Japanese club. In this back-to-nature environment, the accommodations are rustic, the plumbing primitive. The 22 bungalows have bamboo walls, basic bamboo furniture, and tiled baths with showers. Eight units are air-conditioned, but thanks to the sea breezes, the rest are comfortable with just overhead fans. The dining room— an open-air pavilion over the water—serves well-prepared Indonesian specialties. Licensed instructors give scuba-diving courses, and there's good snorkeling. The resort provides a launch service from Jakarta; the run takes 90 minutes. ✉ *Reservation office: Duta Merlin Shopping Arcade, 3rd floor, Jl. Gajah Mada 3–5, Jakarta,* ☎ *021/725–6302,* ⬛ *021/633–6120. 22 rooms. Restaurant, bar, beach, dive shop, snorkeling. No credit cards, unless you book through a travel agent.*

Pulau Krakatau

🔟 *2 to 4 hours by boat from Carita Beach, which is 150 km (95 mi) southwest of Jakarta.*

You'll need to make an overnight trip to see the famous Krakatau (Krakatoa) Island, in the Sunda Strait between Sumatra and Java. The active volcano, Anak Krakatau, is actually the child of Krakatau, a volcano that erupted in 1883, which killed 36,000 people and created marvelous sunsets around the world for the next two years. Anak Krakatau emerged from the sea between three other islands by early 1928—45 years after its predecessor's eruption. (Note: Access by boat is an on-again, off-again venture as the volcano has been erupting intermittently since 1993. If you do go, take care; people have been injured by flying rocks and debris.)

It's a 2½-hour trip from Jakarta to the beach resorts that run trips to Krakatau. The first one you'll reach is Anyer, which is most popular with Jakartans. Just 11 km (7 mi) south is Karang Bolong, which at press time wasn't very inviting—most resorts were fenced in and falling apart. Another 5 km (3 mi) south is Carita, which is the best place to set off to Pulau Krakatau. Nearly all the beaches are rocky and full of coral; as a result, the resorts have pools set within meters of the ocean. Due to the economic crisis and civil unrest in the late '90s, many of the former four-star hotels have fallen into disrepair. In hopes that stability will bring tourism revival, many new hotels are cropping up. Your best bet is to drive down the strip from Anyer to Carita and check out what's there. None of the hotels are up to Jakarta standards: the exteriors appear to be crumbling, but interiors are better maintained. On the weekdays, these resorts are ghost towns, so you can really bargain down your rates. On weekends and holidays, Jakartans flock to these resorts, and it's harder to get a deal on the price.

Dining and Lodging

$ ✕ **Villa Valentine.** The menu is written in Indonesian, but the staff will help you figure out what's what. Service is fast, and servings are huge: two to three main courses are more than enough for four people. The seafood is straight from the Java Sea, and the steak and french fries are a must-try. ✉ *Carita Beach, Labuan (diagonally across the street from the Sol Elite Marbella, below,* ☎ *0253/81064. No credit cards.*

$$ 🏨 **Clarion Suites Carita.** This all-suites hotel has huge rooms. If you're traveling with a family, the two-bedroom suites are perfect: both bedrooms are spacious and homey. The living room area is large and leads out to the balcony, overlooking the Java Sea. Each kitchenette has a refrigerator and a four-seat kitchen table. Bathrooms have showers only. ✉ *Jl. Raya Carita Km. 9, Carita Labuan, 42264,* ☎ *0253/81900 or 021/919–3575 in Jakarta,* ℻ *0253/81929 or 021/348–32846 in Jakarta. 65 suites. Restaurant, bar, kitchenettes, room service, pool, beach, boating, jet skiing, waterskiing. AE, DC, MC, V.*

$$ 🏨 **Hotel Mambruk Anyer.** The grounds here are huge; you could get lost but for the helpful groundskeepers to point the way. Rooms are basic with showers only, but they have refrigerators and full-length mirrors. The large wooden balcony has excellent ocean views. Be careful of the redbrick headboard: it hurts if you bump your head. ✉ *Jl. Raya Karang Bolong (Box 10), Anyer, 42166,* ☎ *0254/601602 or 021/791–90133 in Jakarta,* ℻ *0254/601723 or 021/791–90134 in Jakarta. 97 rooms. Restaurant, bar, lounge, refrigerators, pool, boating, jet skiing, waterskiing, billiards. AE, DC, MC, V.* ✍

$$ 🏨 **Resor Pantai Carita.** Vaulted ceilings and an open-air reception area are inviting and relaxing. Bedrooms pick up the theme with high ceilings and local touches like rattan headboards. The tile floors are soothing, and bathrooms have showers and baths. The exterior is in disrepair, but this detracts neither from the service nor the interior maintenance. ✉ *Jl. Raya Carita (Box 12), Labuan, 42264,* ☎ *0253/ 801127 or 021/3483–1122 in Jakarta,* ℻ *0253/801863 or 021/ 3483–0909 in Jakarta. 102 rooms, 48 bungalows. Restaurant, bar, lounge, room service, pool, wading pool, 2 tennis courts, snorkeling, boating, baby-sitting, laundry service, convention center, meeting room. AE, DC, MC, V.*

$$ 🏨 **Sol Elite Marbella.** From the common balcony you have excellent views of the banana trees in the jungle hills. Once you reach your room and look out your private balcony, you'll have stunning sea views. Rooms have large, dark-wood desks and two-poster beds. Tile floors and large balconies, refrigerators, and baths with showers are the other extras. The interior of the lounge, reception area, and even the elevators have fanciful tile work like a Spanish villa's. This is arguably the most upscale resort in the region; still, the exterior needs a paint job. ✉ *Jl. Raya Karang Bolong, Anyer, 42166,* ☎ *0254/602345 or 021/527–3636 in Jakarta,* ℻ *0254/602346 or 021/527–3536 in Jakarta. 580 rooms, 100 suites. 5 restaurants, bar, 2 pools, massage, 2 tennis courts, badminton, snorkeling, boating, jet skiing, baby-sitting, playground, convention center, meeting rooms. AE, DC, MC.* ✍

Ujung Kulon National Park

★ ⑯ *200 km (124 mi) southwest of Jakarta.*

Forty or so endangered Javan rhinos still hide in the jungles of Ujung Kulon National Park, a World Heritage Site with nearly 800 square km (309 square mi) of peninsular and island wilderness that few people venture to see. It's a great place to trek (the snorkeling is good, too), but getting here is tough; the easiest way is by boat. If you're adventurous and have the time (at least two or three days, though four or more is best) and the gear, you can arrange a guided tour in Jakarta or Carita or go on your own. Note that you'll need to buy supplies before setting out; there are no facilities in the park, although there are basic guest bungalows, a few small stores, and a World Wildlife Fund visitor center at the main entrance in Taman Jaya. Hotels in Jakarta can recommend tour operators (☞ *also* Tour Operators *in* West Java A to Z, *below*); a four-day, three-night trek usually costs Rp 2,240,000–Rp 3,136,000 per person, although you should negotiate for discounts. You can also hire a guide at the Taman Jaya park office.

Bogor

⑰ *60 km (37 mi) south of Jakarta.*

Sprawling, smoky Bogor hides several attractions. Drop in at Jalan Pancasan 17 to see a **gong foundry,** one of the few remaining on Java, where gamelan orchestra instruments are still made using traditional methods.

The white-porticoed **Presidential Palace**—first built in 1745 by Dutch governor general Gustav Willen Baron Van Imhoft and then rebuilt in 1856 after being destroyed by an earthquake—has fine painting and sculpture collections. The palace is on the west side of Bogor's main attraction, the **Kebun Raya Bogor** (Botanical Gardens), founded in 1817 by Indonesia's first English governor general, maintained by the Dutch, and adopted by Sukarno. The 275-acre garden has 15,000 species of plants, hundreds of trees, an herbarium, cactus gardens, and ponds with enormous water lilies. The park's monument is of Olivia Raffles, first wife of Sir Stanford Raffles, who died here at the Bogor Palace. Guides are available at Rp 6,000 an hour. ⌂ *Admission.* ◷ *Daily 8–5.*

Lodging

$$$ ⊞ **Novotel Bogor.** Bogor's best hotel looks like an alpine resort, albeit one that's surrounded by banana trees. The grounds are so lush that you can't help but think that the city's beautiful botanical garden provided inspiration. Rooms are spacious, and you can lounge by the pool or play golf or tennis. The hotel's only drawback is its location 4 km (2½ mi) from town. ⊠ *Golf Estat Gogor Raya, 16710,* ☎ *251/271555 or 800/221–4542 in the U.S.,* ℻ *251/271333. 179 rooms, 4 suites. Restaurant, pool, 18-hole golf course, 2 tennis courts, health club, jogging, business services. AE, DC, MC, V.*

En Route The road from Bogor to Bandung winds through tea plantations and rain forests, past waterfalls and lakes. This is the Puncak region, where on clear days you'll get views of the Gede, Pangrango, and Salak mountains. Just over Puncak Pass's summit is the Puncak Pass Hotel, a famous, scenic stop for travelers that serves excellent afternoon teas.

Bandung

 187 km (120 mi) southeast of Jakarta, 127 km (79 mi) southeast of Bogor.

On a 2,500-ft plateau and shadowed by majestic volcanoes, Bandung was transformed into a Dutch oasis at the turn of the 19th century. European architects put up Art Deco buildings, café society copied fashions from Paris and Amsterdam, and Bandung became Indonesia's cultural and intellectual heart. There was even speculation that the capital might be transferred here from Jakarta.

The city's status waned after World War II. With independence, the political focus shifted to the tightly centralized government in Jakarta, and the Sundanese reasserted their own complex language and customs. Today, Bandung is an appealing mix of European and Asian cultures. With overcrowding burdening Jakarta's infrastructure, Bandung has, in recent years, attracted high-tech businesses with its intellectual environment and its 13 universities, including the prestigious Institute Teknologi Bandung. Although brochures exaggerate the city's attractions, it does have a pleasant climate—warm days and cold nights—and it's small and pedestrian-friendly enough to cover on foot.

In the days when Bandung called itself the "Paris van Java," **Jalan Braga** was the "rue St. Honoré." In the last few years the city made a successful attempt to rejuvenate the area, and it's once again a nice place to walk. There aren't many remnants of Bandung's glory days, but the classic, Art Deco **Sheraton Hotel,** formerly the **Savoy Homann Hotel** (☞ *also* Lodging, *below*), has been restored. Near the Sheraton Hotel on Jalan Asia-Africa is the **Freedom Building** (Gedung Merdeka), where in 1955 Chou En-lai, Ho Chi Minh, Nehru, Nasser, and U Nu attended the famous Asia-Africa Conference of nonaligned nations.

Walking north back past the Sheraton, you'll reach the *alun-alun* (town square), the heart of Bandung. Just off the square is **Market Street,** which is worth a stroll at night, when book- and magazine-sellers take over one side and locally popular food stalls the other. If you continue north along Jalan Braga, you'll pass several cafés that offer great cakes and coffee. If you're looking for evening entertainment, karaoke bars have taken over some of the area's side streets.

At the **Geological Museum** (✉ Jl. Diponegoro), which is open Monday to Thursday 9–3, Friday 9–1, and is free, you'll find fossil replicas of Java Man (*Homo erectus,* a predecessor of Homo sapiens). North of the Geological Museum is the **Institut Teknologi Bandung,** designed by Maclaine Pont, a proponent of the Indo-European integrated style, exemplified here by the upturned, Minangkabau-style roofs; beyond the institute are the Dago Tea House and a waterfall with a splendid panorama of the city.

The hills that surround Bandung are known as Parahyangan (Abode of the Gods) and are sacred to the Sundanese. The first stop on a tour of this area is usually the pleasant hill town Lembang, just less than 10 km (6 mi) north of Bandung. The **Tangkuban Perahu Nature Reserve,** 10 km (6 mi) north of Lembang, contains Indonesia's only active volcano whose rim is accessible by car. From the preserve's entrance, the narrow road winds 4 km (2½ mi) to the crater's edge. The souvenir stands and hawkers are a nuisance, but the crater, boiling and seething with sulfurous steam, is dramatic. Several kilometers southeast of the crater are the **Crater Hot Springs,** with soothing public baths.

Dining and Lodging

$$$ ✕ **Braga Permai.** Sit at streetside patio tables and order from the large selection of Indonesian and Western dishes that make this restaurant popular. It's a good place for lunch, dinner, or a break from a walk along Jalan Braga (the cakes are great). At night a piano player adds to the ambience. ✉ *Jl. Braga 58,* ☎ *022/420–1831. AE, DC, MC, V.*

$$ ✕ **Sari Sunda.** This Sundanese restaurant first opened in the early 1990s and proved so successful that now there are three branches. This branch is in a wooden building with bamboo furniture and lots of plants—very relaxing. The Sundanese dishes are spicy but not spicy enough to stun your taste buds. You can't go wrong with the fried fish covered in sweet-spicy topping or the chicken steamed in bamboo. The fruit drinks are also highly recommended. ✉ *Jl. Lengkong Sesar 77,* ☎ *022/438125. AE, DC, MC, V.*

$ ✕ **Naripan Steak.** A 10-minute walk off Jalan Braga will bring you to this open-to-the-street, meat-lovers' grill. The dining room, with its basic tables and hard-back chairs, is sparse, but the food is tops. The satay beef and chicken are real treats. ✉ *Jl. Naripan 30,* ☎ *022/426–4453. No credit cards.*

$$ 🛏 **Sheraton Bandung.** Though this hotel is in a residential neighborhood 15 minutes by taxi from downtown, many travelers are drawn by its modern facilities, well-trained staff, and tranquillity. The best rooms overlook the circular courtyard and its pool. Dining is a relaxed affair, either on the terrace by the pool or inside with air-conditioning. The Sheraton-style architecture and ambience are more American than Indonesian. ✉ *Jl. Ir. H. Juanda 390 (Box 6530), 40065,* ☎ *022/250–0303 or 800/325–3535 in the U.S.,* 🖷 *022/250–0301. 111 rooms. Restaurant, pool, 2 tennis courts, business services. AE, DC, MC, V.*

$$ 🛏 **Sheraton Hotel.** It's neither the priciest nor the most up-to-date hotel
★ in town, but the Sheraton is loaded with character. Built in the 1880s, it acquired its Art Deco details in 1930. In the evening, guests gather at the bar in the central courtyard to listen to a band. Superior rooms are the size of small suites; most have sitting areas and look onto either the street (windows are double-glazed) or the courtyard. The English-speaking staff are very friendly. ✉ *Jl. Asia-Afrika 112, 40261,* ☎ *022/250–0303,* 🖷 *022/250–0301. 153 rooms. Restaurant, bar, coffee shop. AE, DC, MC, V.* 🌐

$ 🛏 **Lembang Grand Hotel.** Built in 1926 and used by the Dutch as a hill resort, the Grand offers simple accommodations just north of Bandung. ✉ *Jl. Raya Lembang 228, Lampang 40398,* ☎ *022/82393. 26 rooms. Pool, 2 tennis courts. MC, V.*

Outdoor Activities and Sports

In many villages near Bandung, Sunday morning is the time for the weekly *adu domba* (ram fights). Facing off two at a time, prize rams bang, crash, and lock horns until one contestant scampers off. It's as much a social event as a serious sport (though the wagerers take it seriously); don't miss it if you're around on a weekend.

Pangandaran

★ ⑲ *210 km (130 mi) southeast of Bandung, 370 km (230 mi) southeast of Jakarta.*

Pangandaran, a beach resort on a peninsula about halfway between Bandung and Yogyakarta, is popular with Bandung residents on weekends. If possible, visit during the week, when you share it only with the local fisherfolk. The Indian Ocean's surf pounds the black-sand beaches and can be dangerous. Still, there are sections protected by the bulb at the peninsula's end—great places to splash about in calmer waters.

Though the peninsula is small enough to see on foot, there are plenty of becaks if you get tired. You might take one to the national park's entrance, passing rows of booths along the way that sell mostly clothing. The staff at your hotel can recommend a guide who's familiar with the park's jungle terrain; they can also arrange longer trips to Green Canyon, a larger and more spectacular wilderness area a couple of hours away (☞ Tour Operators *in* West Java A to Z, *below*).

Dining and Lodging

$$ ✕ **Bunga Laut Restaurant.** Though this small, bungalow restaurant doesn't look like much, it has great Sundanese food—a bit spicy, but yummy. ⊠ *Jl. Bulak Laut 2,* ☏ *no phone. No credit cards.*

$ ✕ **Fish Market.** If you hanker for seafood, check out the open-air
★ restaurants here. Good choices include **Ditha,** in a bamboo building next to the road, and **Risma,** a concrete structure (its walls stop at waist level) next to the gravel parking area. At both you get to choose your fish and have it cooked however you want. ⊠ *Jl. Pantai Timur, about halfway up peninsula,* ☏ *no phone. No credit cards.*

$$$ ▣ **Pantai Indah Timur and Pantai Indah Barat.** The Indah Timur and its sister property, the Indah Barat, are the most upscale in the region. The grounds at both are very well kept, with many trees and brick footpaths. The wooden one- and two-story buildings fit in well with the environment. Rooms are spacious and comfortable though not luxurious. ⊠ *Jl. Kidang Pananjung 139,* ☏ *265/639004,* ℻ *265/379327. 21 rooms, 2 suites, 7 bungalows. 2 restaurants, pool, 2 tennis courts. AE, DC, MC, V.*

$$ ▣ **Adam's Home Stay.** The air-conditioned bungalows here are grouped near the pool, which is just a two-minute walk from the beach. There are also fan-cooled rooms in the old Dutch-era main house, which faces the ocean. The ocean view and sound of the waves from these rooms can't be beat, and the library-bookshop—which has English-language titles—is just down the stairs next to the restaurant. Stock up on reading material and have a cappuccino. ⊠ *Jl. Pamugaran Bulak Laut, 46396,* ☏ *265/639164,* ℻ *265/639164. 9 rooms, 3 bungalows. Restaurant, bar, pool, bicycles, library. MC (sometimes).*

Cirebon

⓴ *130 km (81 mi) northeast of Bandung, 250 km (155 mi) southeast of Jakarta.*

Cirebon is on a mangrove coast where, unfortunately, there are no beaches and few remaining mangroves. Over the centuries this port town has been influenced by many cultures; today it's something of a commercial crossroads and, as such, is a little wealthier than most Indonesian cities. The people here are friendly, and the distances between sights are manageable on foot. There are also plenty of fancy, painted becaks; you can catch a ride to almost anywhere in town for less than a dollar. City Hall, near the train station, is an Art Deco building right out of old Los Angeles or Miami. Cirebon also has a couple of cinemas that show slightly dated Hollywood movies, so if you missed something in the past year or two, this could be your chance to catch up.

Start your tour in the south of Cirebon at the **Kraton Kesepuhan,** a walled palace built in 1529 and set on 30 peaceful acres. The 13th generation of sultans still lives in a section that's closed to the public. You can get a look inside by visiting the museum. The ornate carriage (circa 1549) alone is worth the price of admission. Open Monday through Thursday and Saturday 8–4, Friday 7–11, 2–4, Sunday 8–5. Just north of Kraton Kesepuhan is **Mesjid Agung,** one of Java's oldest and most interesting mosques—note its tiered roof. From Kraton Kesepuhan it's a few minutes' walk north along Jalan Lemah Wungkuk to the **Kraton Kanoman,** a palace with tranquil grounds and a huge banyan tree in its courtyard. A few minutes up the road from Kraton Kanoman is the **Vihara Dewi Welasasih,** a colorful temple that's a testament to the Chinese influence in the city. On the coast near Vihara Dewi Welasasih there's an odd little **amusement park** with a few rides and a rickety old boardwalk over the water.

Dining and Lodging

$$ ✕ **Helena.** Seafood tops the menu at this big, air-conditioned dining hall; if you want it spicy, the chef will cook it Thai style. You'll also find a wide selection of Indonesian rice and chicken dishes. ⊠ *Jl. Ade Irma Suryani Nasution,* ☎ *231/201882. No credit cards.*

$$ ✕ **Jumbo Restaurant and Sea Food.** This restaurant in the heart of Cirebon has an extensive seafood menu as well as other chicken and meat dishes. The dark-wood dining room is quite comfortable. ⊠ *Jl. Siliwangi 191,* ☎ *231/203606. MC, V.*

$$$ 🏨 **Hotel Bentani.** Here you'll find all the amenities of a world-class hotel, but with more homegrown, personal service. Guest rooms are comfortable and spacious, and there are several on-site nightlife options, including karaoke. ⊠ *Jl. Siliwangi 69, 45121,* ☎ *231/203246,* ℻ *231/207527. 64 rooms, 20 suites. 2 restaurants, 2 bars, pool, sauna, health club, dance club. AE, MC, V.*

$$–$$$ 🏨 **Hotel Prima.** This hotel opened in 1991 across from the city hall. The rooms are comfortable, and the staff is friendly. ⊠ *Jl. Siliwangi 107, 45124,* ☎ *231/205411,* ℻ *231/205407. 88 rooms, 8 suites. Restaurant, bar, pool, 2 tennis courts. AE, MC, V.*

$$ 🏨 **Hotel Sidodadi.** Air-conditioning, clean rooms, and complimentary breakfast are all part of the package at this moderately priced establishment on Cirebon's hotel row. ⊠ *Jl. Siliwangi 72,* ☎ *231/202305,* ℻ *231/204821. 50 rooms. Restaurant. MC, V.*

West Java A to Z

Arriving and Departing

BY AIRPLANE

Jakarta is the hub for flights to points in West Java (☞ By Airplane under Arriving and Departing *in* Jakarta A to Z, *above*). There has been talk of making Bandung more of a gateway, but with the economic turmoil of the late 1990s, it may be a while till anything gets off the ground.

BY BOAT

Boat travel between Jakarta and Sumatra is an option, albeit a slow one. The KM *Lawit* and KM *Kerinci* make a 40-hour trip between Jakarta and Padang about every two weeks. There are also ferries every hour between Merak (110 km/68 mi west of Jakarta) and Bakauheni (on Sumatra's southern tip).

BY TRAIN

The trip to Bandung from Yogyakarta is eight hours, and there are three or more trains a day. The night train has *eksekutif* (first-class) compartments with reclining seats, air-conditioning, and blankets. The day train lacks these amenities but offers *biznis* (business class), with padded seats and windows that open.

Getting Around

BY AIRPLANE

There are flights to Bandung's Husein Sastranegara airport from Jakarta with **Merpati** (⊠ Jl. Asia Afrika 73, ☎ 022/441226) and **Garuda** (⊠ Jl. Asia Africa 181, ☎ 022/420–9467).

BY BOAT

Each Thousand Islands resort has its own boat transport; contact the resort directly to make arrangements. Boats for Pulau Krakatau leave Carita Beach at around 8 AM; the trip takes 2½ hours by speedboat (Rp 100,000), four hours on a slower boat (about Rp 40,000). It's best to visit with a reputable tour operator, and you can make arrangements for this in Jakarta or Carita. Don't venture out if the waters are rough, even though there are plenty of boatmen in Carita who will offer to take you despite high seas (avoid these people). Note also that sometimes you can't visit Pulau Krakatau due to volcanic activity.

Boats to Ujung Kulon National Park leave from Labuan, just south of Carita. You can take the *Wanawisata,* which costs about Rp 324,000 one way and takes about six hours. (You'll have to ask about its schedule, which is ever-changing). Alternatively, you can charter a boat (about Rp 400,000) that can carry as many as 20 people. Another option, and probably the best one, is to organize a three- or four-day tour with a travel agent in Carita (ask your hotel staff for recommendations).

BY BUS

The road from Jakarta to Bandung offers spectacular views, and many minibuses make the trip each day—though fretful passengers may spend more time watching the next curve than the scenery. The larger air-conditioned buses are a better bet. You can travel from Jakarta to Carita Beach by public bus in about three hours, but **P. J. Krakatau**'s (✉ Ujung Kulon Tours, Hotel Wisata International, Jakarta, ☎ 021/ 314–0252) minivans are a lot more comfortable.

BY CAR

You can rent a car and drive yourself, but it's not recommended unless you know the language and the country. It's best to hire a car with a driver to take you from major hubs to surrounding sights. Such arrangements don't cost much and leave you free to watch the scenery.

BY TRAIN

There are numerous trains between Jakarta's Gambir Station and Bogor each day (it's almost like a commuter service as many people live along the hour-long route). Four express trains make the four- to six-hour trip from Gambir to Cirebon daily. Trains between Surabaya and Jakarta also pass through Cirebon. The trip from Jakarta to Bandung—approximately three hours from Gambir Station, with nine departures daily—is quite scenic: the train travels through flat rice lands before climbing mountains along a curving track and over trestle bridges built by the Dutch. Rates are Rp 20,000 for eksekutif (executive class) with air-conditioning and reclining seats, Rp 7,000 for biznis (business class) with open windows and padded seats.

Contacts and Resources

EMERGENCIES

Hospital: Adventist Hospital (✉ Jl. Cihampelas 161, Bandung, ☎ 022/ 234386).

ENGLISH-LANGUAGE BOOKSTORES

In central Bandung there are several bookshops along Jalan Braga.

TOUR OPERATORS

The **Bandung City Tour** (☎ 022/520–4650) is a half-day bus trip to Bandung's major sites. Contact the **Indonesian Guide Association** (✉ Jl. Kidang Pananjung 21, Pangandaran, ☎ 265/639296) to arrange treks to wilderness areas around Pangandaran. Sudrajad Pujo Adi at **Kirana Wisata** (✉ Wisata International Hotel, Jl. M. H. Thamrin 48,

☎ 021/390–8008) has been taking visitors to Ujung Kulon National Park since 1990.

Bandung Tourist Information Office (✉ Alun-alun, Jl. Asia Afrika, ☎ 022/420–6644). **Bogor Tourist Information Office** (✉ Jl. Ir. H. Juanda 10, ☎ 251/338052)). **West Java Provincial Tourist Office** (✉ Jl. Soekarno-Hatta, Km 11, Bandung, ☎ 022/780–5739).

Central and East Java

Central Java—and the special province of Yogyajakarta within its borders—is Indonesia's cultural heart. The region nurtured some of the country's great Indian kingdoms in the 8th and 9th centuries, including the Buddhist Sailendras, who built the Borobudur temple, and the Hindu Sanjayans, who made Prambanan their religious center. Today visitors generally use Yogyakarta as a base for seeing these temples. However, if you prefer less commercialism and tourist hustling, the ancient city of Solo, 64 km (40 mi) to the east, is a good bet. From this quiet city you can easily drive out to Sukuh Temple and to Sangiran, the site where Java Man was discovered.

Five hours northeast of Yogyakarta is Surabaya, a good base from which to explore East Java, a province suited to adventurous travelers. It has three regions: the north coast, including Madura Island; the Brantas River basin; and the southern volcanoes. Mt. Bromo, an active volcano from whose rim you can peer down into nature's cauldron, is a highlight.

Yogyakarta

㉑–㉕ *618 km (371 mi) southeast of Jakarta, 431 km (251 mi) southeast of Bandung.*

Every Indonesian has a soft spot for Yogyakarta, or Yogya (pronounced *joeg-jakarta* or *joeg-ja*), a city of some 300,000 on a fertile plain in the shadow of three volcanoes. Dance and choreography schools, wayang troupes, and poetry workshops make it an artist's mecca. Every evening, classical drama and dance performances are staged in the city. Leading Indonesian painters and sculptors display their work in numerous galleries, and crafts shopping is a major activity. The batik here and in Solo (☞ *below*) is said to be superior even to that found on Bali.

Exploring Yogyakarta

Yogya sprawls. Unless you stay at the Garuda (☞ Lodging, *below*) or one of the less expensive city hotels, chances are you'll be a few miles from Jalan Malioboro, the main thoroughfare.

㉕ **Affandi Museum.** Out toward the airport, about 8 km (5 mi) southeast of Yogya, is the home and studio of Indonesia's best-known painter, Affandi (1907–90). A permanent collection of his works, along with paintings by young artists, is exhibited in an oval, domed extension to the traditional paddy-field house. ✉ *Jl. Laksda, Adisucipto 67,* ☎ *no phone.* 🎟 *Free.* ☉ *Daily 8–3.*

㉔ **Diponegoro Monument.** This is the reconstructed residence of Prince Diponegoro, who rebelled against the Dutch and led a bloody guerrilla battle in the Java War (1825–30). The house is now a museum that displays the prince's krises, lances, and other revered possessions. ✉ *Tegalrejo (4 km/2½ mi west of Yogyakarta),* ☎ *0274/563068.* 🎟 *Donation appreciated.* ☉ *Open by appointment only.*

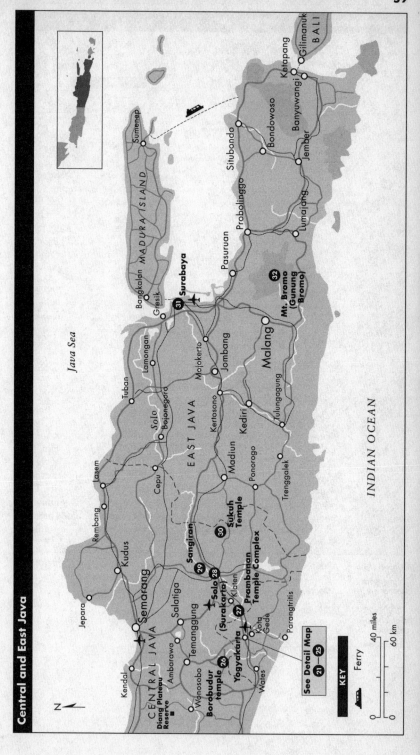

Central and East Java

KEY

⛴ Ferry

See Detail Map ㉑ — ㉕

0 — 40 miles
0 — 60 km

N

Java Sea

MADURA ISLAND

Sumenep

Bangkalan

Gresik

㉛ Surabaya ✈

Lamongan

Tuban

Rembang

Lasem

Kudus

Jepara

Semarang ★

Solo

Bojonegoro

Cepu

CENTRAL JAVA

Kendal

Ambarawa

Salatiga

Temanggung

Wonosobo

Dieng Plateau Reserve ■

Borobudur temple ㉖

Yogyakarta

Wates

Kota Gede

Parangtritis

㉗

㉘ Solo (Surakarta) ★

㉙

Sangiran

㉚

Sukuh Temple

Prambanan Temple Complex

Klaten

EAST JAVA

Kertosono

Madiun

Ponorogo

Trenggalek

Tulungagung

Kediri

Jombang

Mojokerto

Malang

Pasuruan

Probolinggo

Situbondo

㉜ Mt. Bromo (Gunung Bromo)

Lumajang

Jember

Bondowoso

Banyuwangi

Ketapang

Gilimanuk

B A L I

INDIAN OCEAN

60

Yogyakarta

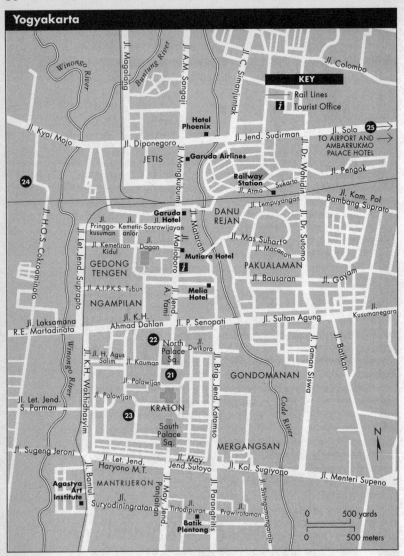

KEY
— Rail Lines
i Tourist Office

Jalan Malioboro. This is where the action is, day and night. It's the main shopping street, with not only established stores but also sidewalk vendors. They set up cardboard stands and sell handicrafts until about 9 PM, then convert to food stalls serving Yogya's specialties: nasi gudeg (rice with jackfruit in coconut milk) and ayam goreng (marinated fried chicken). Malioboro is a fascinating street; arrive by 8 PM, and you can catch both the shops and the food. Haggle over prices for items on the street or look for good deals at the indoor market, **Pasar Beringharjo,** at the top of the street; it's worth visiting just to see the stacked merchandise—everything from jeans to poultry.

★ ㉑ **Kraton.** At Malioboro's southern end stands the Kraton, or Sultan's Palace. The large, grassy square in front—a walled city within the city— is the **alun-alun,** where the townspeople formerly gathered to trade, gossip, and hear the latest palace news. The Yogya Kraton has special significance to Indonesians as the bastion against Dutch colonialism. During the War of Independence (1945–49), Yogya's Sultan Hamengku Buwono allowed the Indonesian freedom fighters—including guerrilla commander Suharto—to use the Kraton as a base. Built in 1756, it's a vast complex of pavilions and buildings, part of which—strictly off-limits to the public—is home to the present sultan. The complex is protected by 400 guards and maintained by 1,000 servants.

At the white, green-trimmed palace's center is the **Bengsal Kengono** (Golden Pavilion), an open hall with carved teak columns and a black-and-gold interior, where weddings, cremations, and coronations are held. The complex includes a gallery that displays a gamelan instrument collection. Try to time your visit to catch the Sunday classical dance rehearsal (10:30 and noon, except during Ramadan). In another pavilion is a sedan chair collection. The last one was used in 1877; a Rolls-Royce now transports the sultan. ☎ *No phone.* 🎟 *Admission.* ☉ *Sun.–Thurs. 8:30 AM–1 PM, Fri.–Sat. 8:30–11:30 AM.*

㉒ **Sono Budoyo Museum.** Of Yogya's several museums, the most interesting and well maintained is the Sono Budoyo Museum, on the square in front of the Kraton. Inside this traditional Javanese-style building is a crafts and batiks collection from Java and Bali. Its archaeological treasures include a small gold Buddha, and the display of wayang golek, the wood puppets used in Muslim theater, is charming. ☎ *0274/ 562775.* 🎟 *Admission.* ☉ *Tues.–Thurs. 8 AM–1:30 PM, Fri. and Sun. 8–11:30 AM, Sat. 8–noon.*

㉓ **Taman Sari.** Behind the Kraton is the recreational Water Palace, constructed by the same sultan who built the main palace. A large artificial lake, sunken bathing pools, underground passageways, and towers where gamelan orchestras serenaded the royal party were all part of this noble retreat. It was abandoned in the 18th century and fell into ruin; the restored sections give a sense of what the privileged enjoyed. Visit the ornate bathing pools used by the princesses, the underground mosque, and the tower from which the sultan watched his concubines lounge by the water. ☎ *No phone.* 🎟 *Admission.* ☉ *Sun.–Thurs. 8 AM–1 PM, Fri. 8–11 AM.*

Dining

For Western food, you can dine at the major hotels. Many also offer a performance of segments from the *Ramayana* for an extra fee. The Indonesian fare at local restaurants is inexpensive and good.

$$ ✕ **Pesta Perak.** Decorated with wrought-iron furniture and a sultan-
★ costumed maître d', Pesta Perak has excellent Javanese cuisine. Its rijsttafel includes satays, gudeg, and fish wrapped in banana leaves. An à la carte menu is also offered, but customers rarely choose this. A game-

lan trio plays traditional music. Use a *becak* to get there, and have it wait for you; the fare from Jalan Malioboro, including waiting time, is less than Rp 4,000. ✉ *Jl. Tentura Rakyat Mataran 8,* ☎ *0274/586255. MC, V.*

$$ ✕ **Pringsewu Garden Restaurant.** For alfresco dining at tables tucked between shrubs and trees, this restaurant is a delight. It offers some of the best fare in the region, served by a friendly, batik-attired staff. The cooking is from West Sumatra. Try the ayam goreng *mantega* (with a butter sauce) or the ikan *mas baket* (grilled and served in ginger sauce). ✉ *Jl. Magelang, Km 6,* ☎ *0274/564993. AE, DC, MC, V.*

$$ ✕ **Sintawang.** Though the tables are Formica, the restaurant is clean and offers a wide range of outstanding seafood, cooked either Javanese or Western style. Try the udang *bakar* (marinated and grilled), udang *pais* (spiced and grilled in a banana leaf), or ikan *asam manis* (in a sweet-and-sour sauce). ✉ *Jl. Magelang 9,* ☎ *0274/512901. Reservations not accepted. AE, DC.*

$ ✕ **Legian Garden Restaurant.** Choose a table next to the open windows at the terrace's edge and watch fellow tourists *jalan jalan* (amble around) on the street below. Since the food is pretty average (primarily Western, with a few Indonesian alternatives), you may just want to stop by for a beer. ✉ *Jl. Perwakilan 9 (off Jl. Malioboro), 1st floor,* ☎ *0274/564644. Reservations not accepted. No credit cards.*

$ ✕ **Ny Suharti.** It's worth the Rp 3,500 cab ride here from Malioboro ★ for the best fried chicken in Java. Forget charm and atmosphere and the other items on the menu: you're here for a bird—boiled, marinated in spices, then cooked up crisp. Order one for two people, with rice on the side, and enjoy it out on the veranda. If you pay by credit card, a 3% surcharge will be added to your bill. ✉ *Jl. Laksda Adisucipto, Km 7,* ☎ *0274/515522. Reservations not accepted. MC, V.*

$ ✕ **Via Via.** This little restaurant sets the standard for cheap, simple backpacker fare. The small Indonesian and Western menu is very good, as ★ are the fruit shakes. This is also a good place to pick up travel information. ✉ *Jl. Prawirotaman I, 24B,* ☎ *no phone. No credit cards.*

Lodging

There are accommodations to meet every pocketbook. The world-class Amanjiwo, which opened in 1997 near Borobudur temple, is one of the best hotels in Southeast Asia (with prices to match its reputation). In Yogya itself there are countless new medium-range hotels as well as two blocks of guest houses in the town's southern section. Just off Jalan Malioboro (across from the Garuda and 2 blocks from the railway station), there's a good selection of small budget hotels. With so many lodging options, prices are competitive. There are up to 50% discounts—just be sure to ask about them.

$$$$ 🏨 **Amanjiwo.** Superlatives don't do this hotel justice. Designed by ★ American Ed Tuttle, who also created Bali's Amankila and the Amanpuri in Phuket, Thailand, it has 35 suites, each in its own building; 14 have reasonably sized private pools, though there's also a 40-meter communal pool. Rooms are spacious with king-size beds; big, sliding-glass doors; outdoor sunken tubs; indoor showers; and two dressing areas with closets. The grounds are at the mountain base, and there are views of Borobudur temple from each suite. You can continue to pay homage to the temple while swimming laps in the pool, dining in the open-air restaurant, or relaxing in the bar. The hotel offers a sunrise tour of Borobudur (reservations are recommended). ✉ *About 6 km (4 mi) south of Borobudur temple and up a slight incline (Box 333), Magelang 56553,* ☎ *0293/88333,* 𝖥𝖠𝖷 *0293/88355. 35 suites. Restaurant, bar, café, pool, massage, bicycles, travel services. AE, DC, MC, V.* ✧

$$$$ ⛩ **Ambarrukmo Palace.** Built on a former royal country retreat's grounds, Ambarrukmo's guest rooms are large, decorated with light, Indonesian-pattern fabrics and mahogany furniture, and full of amenities. The best rooms have balconies that overlook the gardens. This hotel is very popular with American tour groups, and some rooms are a little worn; if yours isn't up to standard, don't be shy about asking for another. Every evening there's entertainment, usually dances from the *Ramayana.* ⌧ *Jl. Laksda Adisucipto, 55281,* ☎ *0274/588488,* FAX *0274/563283. 266 rooms. 2 restaurants, bar, minibars, pool, travel services. AE, DC, MC, V.*

$$$–$$$$ ⛩ **Melia.** Part of the Spanish-owned Sol Melia chain, this hotel is conveniently close to Jalan Malioboro. Some of its spacious, comfortable rooms have doors that connect them with other rooms—perfect options for families or other groups. The hotel is built around a big pool and garden area, where you can get a relaxing foot massage. ⌧ *Jl. Suryotomo 31, 55122,* ☎ *0274/589521,* FAX *0274/588070. 295 rooms. Restaurant, coffee shop, pool, massage, health club, shops, meeting rooms, travel services. AE, DC, MC, V.*

$$–$$$ ⛩ **Garuda.** The draws at this imposing old hotel are its central location and its moderate prices. Standard guest rooms are plainly furnished but do have all the latest conveniences, including a TV with a VCR and a minibar. Ask for one of the newer rooms as the older ones have a faint musty odor; note, however, that all rooms have suffered from the steady stream of tour groups (there are black scrape marks on walls and stains on carpets). The restaurants offer Indonesian and Western food. ⌧ *Jl. Malioboro 60, 55271,* ☎ *0274/ 566353,* FAX *0274/563074. 235 rooms. 2 restaurants, coffee shop, minibars, pool, tennis court, exercise room, business services, travel services. AE, DC, MC, V.*

$$ ⛩ **Radisson Yogya Plaza.** There is a pleasing freshness to this hotel, which calls itself a resort within a city. Guest rooms, most with king-size beds, are modern and functional; the best for light and peace are those overlooking the courtyard, where you'll find the pool and a café and terrace off to the side. In the evenings, a local band plays—sometimes a string quartet, sometimes a gamelan orchestra—and later there's a performance of the *Ramayana.* Off the large atrium lobby, which contains a comfortable sitting area, the dining room serves Western and Indonesian fare and excellent buffet breakfasts. The downside to this property is that it's more than a 30-minute walk from downtown Yogyakarta; a shuttle bus does run back and forth, but distance precludes a spontaneous walk. ⌧ *Jl. Gejayan, Complex Columbo, 55821,* ☎ *0274/584222,* FAX *0274/584200. 120 rooms. 2 restaurants, bar, pool, massage, 2 tennis courts, health club, business services, meeting rooms. AE, DC, MC, V.* ✧

$ ⛩ **Batik Palace Hotel.** For modest accommodations in Yogya's center, this hotel offers worn but clean rooms, each with twin beds, table, and chair. The lobby, decorated with batiks and crafts, is comfortable. ⌧ *Jl. Mangkubumi 46 (Box 115), 55153,* ☎ *0274/562229,* FAX *0274/ 562149. 38 rooms. Restaurant, pool. V.*

$ ⛩ **Data Guest House.** Along Jalan Prawirotaman to the south of the Kraton are a score of inexpensive guest houses. Data is one of the best, with clean rooms and reasonable prices, and its position down a narrow street makes it one of the quietest. The very basic double rooms (around Rp 134,400) have two narrow beds, cold-water showers, and fans—there are, however, no windows. Twice as much will get you a "garden view" (the guest house's fancy term for the courtyard), air-conditioning, and a hot-water shower. Since there are only eight of these deluxe rooms, reserve ahead. (Be sure you find Data Guest House—many other hotels in the neighborhood have "Data" in their names.)

✉ *Jl. Prawirotaman 26/1, 55153,* ☎ *0274/372064. 32 rooms. Breakfast room. AE, DC, MC, V.*

$　🏠 **Rose Guest House.** The rooms here are very modest, but they do have private baths and either air-conditioning or overhead fans. The rates include breakfast and airport transfers, an extremely good value. ✉ *Jl. Prawirotaman 22, 55153,* ☎ *0274/727991. 29 rooms. Restaurant, pool. No credit cards.*

Nightlife and the Arts

If you hanker for a beer and some local music, try the restaurants along Jalan Prawirotaman or Jalan Malioboro. Indeed, after dark Jalan Malioboro is transformed from a crowded market street into one long, open restaurant—the city's social hub. Magicians perform tricks, singers wander between tables strumming guitars, and conversations and coffee continue long into the night.

Most often there will be a gamelan orchestra playing in your hotel, but don't miss a performance in the sultan's palace. Portions of the *Ramayana* are performed at different venues throughout the city, but the most dramatic setting is at Prambanan (☞ *below*). Wayang kulit shows, usually based on stories from the *Ramayana,* are also performed.

DANCE, MUSIC, AND THEATER

The **Kraton,** the sultan's palace, hosts traditional gamelan music on Monday and Wednesday from 10:30 to noon. In addition, every Sunday from 10:30 AM to 12:30 PM, the **Kraton Classic Dance School** rehearses here. Actors perform stories from the *Ramayana* nightly at 7 in **Taman Hiburan Rakyat** (People's Park; ✉ Jl. Brig. Gen. Katamso). Shows last about two hours.

PUPPET SHOWS

Wayang kulit shows take place Sunday through Friday from 3 to 5 PM at the **Agastya Art Institute** (✉ Jl. Gedongkiwo MDIII/237, ☎ no phone).

Wayang kulit performances of the full *Ramayana* or *Mahabharata* are usually held every second Saturday of the month at **Sasono Hinggil,** just south of Yogya's Kraton, on the opposite side of the alun-alun. These plays begin at 9 PM and last until dawn. Shorter versions that last two to three hours are given at other times. Your hotel should have the schedule, or check at the information booth outside the theater.

At the **Ambar Budaya** (Yogyakarta Crafts Center; ✉ Jl. Laksda Adisucipto, opposite the Ambarrukmo Palace Hotel), hour-long wayang kulit performances take place every Monday, Wednesday, and Saturday at 9:30 PM.

Shopping

Shopping for batiks is a delight, and you should make time to watch batik being made at one of the many small factories. Yogyakarta is also a center for painters, and their works are displayed in scores of galleries. Leather goods here are usually well made and inexpensive. Yogyakarta may be a shopper's dream, but be selective—there's a lot of tacky merchandise alongside the treasures—and bargain gracefully. After you've offered your next-to-last price, walk away; you'll probably be called back. There are any number of scams to lure you into shops—for instance, the claim that a student art exposition is being held and the works are being sold without commercial profit. Don't believe it!

Jalan Malioboro is lined with shops; the handicraft stalls turn into food stalls around 9 PM. Most of the merchandise is junk, but it's worth picking through. This is a convenient area to buy T-shirts or shorts, but prices are on the high side.

You'll find good prices at the modern indoor market, **Pasar Bering-harjo,** at the top end of Jalan Malioboro, across from the Kraton. This fascinating market offers countless spices and foodstuffs, as well as pots and pans, clothes, and electronics.

HANDICRAFTS

In addition to batik, Yogya handicrafts include small hand-tooled leather goods, pottery (pieces decorated with brightly colored elephants, roosters, and animals from mythology are made in Kasongan, just south of Yogya), and wayang kulit and wayang golek. All the shops and stalls on Jalan Malioboro and around the Kraton sell puppets and other handicrafts. The **Yogyakarta Handicrafts Center** (⊠ Jl. Adisucipto, ☎ no phone), not far from the Ambarrukmo Palace Hotel, sells handicrafts by artisans with disabilities.

The patterned Indonesian textiles called batik—made by drawing on fabric with wax, then dyeing the unwaxed areas—can be found in all Yogyakarta stalls. Many batik-design prints are machine-made, however, so beware. Before you buy, try to visit a batik factory where you can watch the process and browse the showrooms.

One place to see batik being created is **Batik Plentong** (⊠ Jl. Tirtodipurun 28, ☎ 0274/562777), which has everything from yard goods to pot holders and batik clothing—all hand-stamped and hand-drawn. Visit **Iman Batik Workshop** (⊠ Jl. Dagen 76B, just off Jl. Malioboro, ☎ no phone), where Iman Nuryanto, the owner, holds changing local art exhibitions. Don't pay more than 50% of the asking price. The **Koperasi (Cooperative) Fine Arts School** (⊠ Jl. Kemetiran Kidul, ☎ no phone), south of the railway station, has batik designed by talented artisans—just be sure to bargain.

You'll find high-quality leather goods at **Kusuma** (⊠ Jl. Kauman 50, parallel to Malioboro, ☎ 0274/565453). There's room for modest bargaining, but no credit cards are accepted.

If you're interested in ceramics and pottery, head for **Kansongan,** 8 km (5 mi) southwest of Yogya. There are more than 30 pottery workshops in the little town, which is slowly being engulfed by Yogya but still far enough away to keep its identity. Pottery isn't the easiest merchandise to transport, but there are many pots and sculptures that are worth buying. Taxi drivers all know where Kansongan is, or you can take a bus heading toward Bantul, get out at the town entrance, and walk the last kilometer.

Many silversmiths have workshops and salesrooms in **Kota Gede,** 6 km (4 mi) southeast of Yogya. The largest in Kota Gede, **Tom's Silver** (⊠ Jl. Ngaksi Gondo 60, Kota Gede 3–1 A, ☎ 0274/525416) also offers the best workmanship. Also try **MD Silver** (⊠ Jl. Pesegah Kg. 8/44, Kota Gede, ☎ 0274/375063).

Borobudur Temple

★ ❷⑥ *42 km (26 mi) northwest of Yogyakarta.*

That Borobudur temple took perhaps 10,000 men 100 years to build becomes credible the moment you see its cosmic structure, in the shadow of the powerful volcanoes that the Javanese believe are God's abode. Try to go early in the morning—plan to end your two- to three-hour visit before noon, while the temperature is still relatively cool. Guided coach tours run from Yogya hotels, or you can hire a minibus and guide (usually more informed) through a Yogya travel agency. If you'd like to visit on your own, take the public bus that heads toward Samarung, then change at Muntilan for the Ramayana bus to Borobudur.

Borobudur was abandoned (the reasons are still debated) soon after completion in AD 850, and the forest moved in. The man who founded modern Singapore, Thomas Stamford Raffles (then Java's English lieutenant governor), and his military engineer, H. C. C. Cornelius, rediscovered the temple in 1814. A thousand years of neglect had left much of it in ruins, and the temple has undergone two mammoth restorations, first from 1907 to 1911, and then again from the 1960s to the 1980s with the help of UNESCO and $25 million.

The temple is a giant stupa (dome-shape structure): five lower levels contain 1,500 relief carvings that depict Siddhartha's earthly life in his passage to enlightenment. Start at the eastern staircase on the first level and walk clockwise around each gallery to follow the sequence of Lord Buddha's life.

Above the reliefs are 432 stone Buddhas. Even higher, above the square galleries, are three circular terraces with 72 latticed stupas that hide statues depicting Buddha's departure from the material world and existence on a higher plane. The top stupa symbolizes the highest level of enlightenment. Look out at the surrounding mountains from Borobudur's upper level and feel some of the inspiration that created this grand monument. If you go around each of the nine galleries, you'll have walked roughly 5 km (3 mi) closer to heaven. On weekends the complex is fairly crowded—another reason to come early. In 1990, a museum opened on the grounds, charging an additional admission that its contents don't justify. ☎ *No phone.* ✉ *Admission.* ⊙ *Daily 6:15–5.*

OFF THE
BEATEN PATH

CANDI PAWON AND MENDUT – About 1.5 km (1 mi) east of Borobudur, on the way back to the main road, is a small temple, **Candi Pawon,** built around the same time as Borobudur. It's thought that worshipers purified themselves here on their way to Borobudur. Another kilometer or so farther east is the small temple **Mendut,** also from the 9th century. The temple's exterior is superbly carved with some 30 large relief panels that depict scenes from Buddha's previous incarnations. Inside stands a magnificent 10-ft statue of Buddha, flanked by the bodhisattvas Avalokitesvara and Vajrapani.

Prambanan Temple Complex

★ ㉗ *16 km (10 mi) northeast of Yogyakarta, a 30-min drive via the Solo road.*

When the Sanjayan kingdom evicted the Buddhist Sailendras, the Sanjayans wanted to memorialize the return of a Hindu dynasty and, supposedly, undermine Borobudur. To this end they built Prambanan. When the 9th-century complex was rediscovered in 1880, it had fallen into ruin from centuries of neglect and enveloping vegetation. In 1937 reconstruction began, and the work continues to this day.

The temple was built with an outer stage for commoners, a middle stage for high-ranking nobility, and a main temple area for royalty. Of the original 244 temples, eight major and eight minor temples still stand, in the Prambanan plain's highest central courtyard.

The center temple, dedicated to Shiva, is the tallest (155 ft) and the best restored; Vishnu's is to the north; and Brahma's to the south. Originally the temples were painted—Shiva's red, Brahma's white, Vishnu's a dark gray—but only traces of the paint remain. To the temples' east are three smaller ones, which contained the gods' "vehicles": Shiva's bull, Vishnu's elephant, and Brahma's goose. Only the bull survives.

In part because the complex was dedicated to Shiva, and in part because Shiva's temple is the best restored, this is where you'll want to spend most of your time. Over the entrance is Kali's head, a protection against evil from land. On the balustrade, the *naga* (serpent) guards against evil from the sea. The base has medallions with lions (an imported figure) as well as half-bird, half-human figures flanked by trees of good hope. Above these, on the outer balustrade, are carvings of classical Indian dancers and celestial beings.

The balustrade's inner wall is carved with lively, sometimes frivolous, reliefs that tell the story of the *Ramayana*. From the east gate, walk around the temple clockwise to follow the story in sequence. The reliefs show free-flowing movement, much humor, and a love of nature. In contrast to Borobudur's reliefs, these carvings combine a celebration of earthly life's pleasures and pains with scenes from Hindu mythology. They're more fun to look at (monkeys stealing fruit and bird-women floating in air), but the drama they portray—the establishment of order in the cosmos—is just as serious.

In the main chamber, at the top of the east stairway, a four-armed statue of Shiva the creator and destroyer stands on a lotus base. In the south chamber, Shiva appears as divine teacher, with a big beard and big stomach. The statue in the western chamber is Ganesha, Shiva's elephant-headed son. And in the northern chamber, Shiva's consort, Durga, kills the demon buffalo. An **archaeological museum** was opened in 1990, but its exhibits won't add much to your appreciation of the temples' imposing architecture. However, you may want to stop at the information desk at the entrance to clarify any questions. Note that if you book through a tour operator, you can combine Prambanan with a visit to Borobudur or to Solo, 46 km (29 mi) northeast of Yogya. Minibuses go out to Prambanan from the Jalan Solo terminus in Yogya. If you hire a taxi, the round-trip will cost Rp 35,000. ☎ *No phone.* 🎟 *Admission.* ☉ *Daily 6–6 (last admission at 5:15).*

OFF THE
BEATEN PATH

CANDI SAMBISARI – The numerous other Buddhist and Hindu temples between Yogyakarta and Prambanan are in various states of ruin but merit at least a day of exploring. A great way to see them is to rent a bike and pack a lunch. Signs on the Yogya–Solo road point the way to the temples. Most are off the road, down small paths, and charge a small admission. Candi Sambisari, a small temple off the highway and 3 km (2 mi) back toward Yogya, is set in a sunken garden and is usually deserted—ideal for a quiet rest.

The Arts

Within walking distance of the temple is the **Prambanan theater complex,** where performances of the *Ramayana* are given in the evening, either at the Ramayana Theatre (open-air) or the Trimurti Theatre (indoor). The Ramayana ballet—an elaborate presentation with scores of dancers, a full-blown orchestra, and armies of people in monkey costumes—is performed at various times throughout the year. From January through March, shows are usually held on Thursday. April through June and October through December, there are at least three performances (Tuesday, Wednesday, and Thursday). July through September features up to five performances a week—always on Tuesday, Wednesday, and Thursday, and usually on Saturday and Sunday. Hotel tour desks can arrange tickets and transportation, or you can share a taxi from the Tourist Information Center in Yogyakarta (☞ Visitor Information *in* Central and East Java A to Z, *below*) at 6:30. Public buses pass the theater's entrance, but they can be unreliable, and drivers often overcharge foreigners. ⊠ *Jl. Raya Yogya-Solo, Km 16,* ☎ *0274/63918.* 🎟 *Admission.*

Solo

⓲ *60 km (37 mi) northeast of Yogyakarta, 40 km (25 mi) northeast of Prambanan.*

Solo (also known as Surakarta or Sala) is less Westernized than Yogya, with fewer tourists and much less hustling. The city has its own traditional batik designs and dance style. And although its people are devoutly Muslim, their daily life is less religious. During the unrest that led to Suharto's resignation, Solo was the scene of widespread looting, and many banks and businesses were torched. As was the case in Jakarta, the ethnic Chinese were singled out, partly because of an economic imbalance and partly because of cultural tensions that go way back. Conflict with the Chinese-Indonesians started in Solo in the 18th century when Chinese merchants supported a rebellion against Keraton Kartosuro. Then, in 1965, the "year of living dangerously," there were conflicts between political factions dominated by the Chinese and other groups. A riot on November 19, 1983, again targeted Chinese, and much of their property was damaged or destroyed.

On the town's west side is the **Kraton Mangkunegaran,** a palace complex of carved, gilded, teak pavilions. The outer center pavilion, or *pendopo,* serves as the audience hall and is typical of a Javanese royal building. The Italian marble floor laid in 1925, the guardian lions from Berlin, and the 50-ft roof supported by teak pillars make the pendopo very grand. Its ceiling is painted with a flame motif bordered by symbols from the Javanese zodiac, designed with the eight mystical colors (yellow to ward off sleep, green to subdue desire, purple to keep away bad thoughts, etc.). The effect is gaudy but dramatic.

The museum, in the ceremonial pavilion just behind the main pendopo, displays dance ornaments, masks, jewelry, chastity belts for men and women, and wayang kulit and wayang golek. At center stage is the enclosed bridal bed (originally a room reserved for offerings to the rice goddess). To the museum's left are the official reception rooms: a formal dining room, with a Javanese-style stained-glass window and an ivory tusk with carvings that depict the wedding of Arjuna, one of the heroes of the *Mahabharata;* a mirrored parlor area; and a "bathing" room for royal brides. ⊠ *Jl. Sugiyopranoto,* ☎ *no phone.* ☜ *Admission.* ⊙ *Mon.–Thurs. and Sat. 9–noon, Fri. 9–11 AM.*

Solo's second palace, **Kraton Kasuhunan** (sometimes called Kraton Solo), is being rebuilt because it suffered terrible damage (its elaborate ceremonial pavilion was gutted) during a 1985 fire. Luckily, the museum—one of Central Java's best—was unharmed by the blaze. It contains a priceless collection of silver and bronze Hindu figures and Chinese porcelain, but the real treats are three royal carriages given to the sultanate by the Dutch in the 18th century. The English-speaking guide will help you appreciate the collection. ⊠ *Jl. Coyudan,* ☎ *0271/ 44046.* ☜ *Admission.* ⊙ *Sat.–Thurs. 9–noon.*

Dining and Lodging

$$ ✕ **Kusuma Sari.** This spotless restaurant is excellent for Indonesian fare, be it ayam goreng or a snack such as *resoles ragout* (chicken wrapped in a soft pancake)—and you can dine until 11 PM nightly. The tile floors, glass-topped wood tables, and plate-glass windows don't offer a lot of atmosphere, but choose a table by the window and watch the flow of pedestrians and becaks on the town's main street. ⊠ *Jl. Slamet Riyadi 111,* ☎ *0271/37603. Reservations not accepted. No credit cards.*

$ ✕ **Ramayana.** For good, inexpensive local cuisine try this plain dining room, a two-minute walk from the Kusuma Sahid Prince Hotel

(☞ *below*). Dishes include such Indonesian staples as nasi goreng and satays. ⊠ *Jl. Imam Bonjol 49,* ☎ *0271/46643. No credit cards.*

$$$ ✕🏨 **Kusuma Sahid Prince Hotel.** Here three two-story buildings and ★ outlying bungalows are set back from the street on 5 acres of land-scaped gardens. The lobby veranda—the original *pendopo agung* (prince's courtyard)—is a wonderful place for tea or a cool drink. The quiet guest rooms are well maintained, and all the accoutrements—from the linens to the orchids—are fresh. Some rooms have a view of the enormous pool; those in the newer wing have up-to-date furnishings and climate control. The formal Kasuma Sahid restaurant is light and airy, with white linen and polished silver. The menu includes such Indonesian specialties as chicken with jackfruit and fish wrapped in banana leaves—with the restaurant's own special blend of spices. Western dishes with nouvelle French influences and Indonesian accents are featured as well. ⊠ *Jl. Sugiyopranoto 20, 57132,* ☎ *0271/46356,* ℻ *0271/44788. 103 rooms. Restaurant, bar, pool, shops, meeting rooms, travel services. AE, DC, MC, V.*

$ 🏨 **Wisata Indah.** Though the plastered walls are smudged and the bath-rooms are *mandi* style (a tub of water with a small bucket used to throw water over yourself; it doesn't sound like much, but it works quite well), the hot water is hot, the sheets are freshly laundered, and the staff is friendly and helpful. Outside each room are tables and chairs for breakfast (included in the price) and other meals that you can order from the bellboys. Negotiate the room rate before you sign in. ⊠ *Jl. Slamet Riyadi 173, 57132,* ☎ *0271/46770. 27 rooms. MC, V.*

The Arts

At Solo's **Kraton Mangkunegaran,** a gamelan orchestra performs each Saturday from 9 to 10:30 AM. Dance rehearsals are held on Wednesday from 10 to noon and on Monday and Friday afternoons.

Shopping

Solo's main shopping street is **Jalan Secoyudan.** In addition to a score of goldsmiths, you'll find antiques stores selling curios from the Dutch colonial days, as well as krises and other Javanese artifacts. Between Jalan Slamet Riyadi—which has many antiques shops—and Kraton Mangkunegaraan, and just off Diponegoro is **Pasar Triwindu,** Solo's daily flea market, where hundreds of stalls sell everything from junk to old coins to batik. Bargain like crazy.

Solo has its own batik style, often using indigo, brown, and cream as opposed to the brighter colors of Yogya's batiks. Prices are better in Solo, and there are some 300 batik factories. Aside from the shops along Jalan Secoyudan, visit **Pasar Klewer,** a huge batik market just outside the Kraton Solo, with a fine selection of goods on the second floor. An established shop that sells batik and has batik-making demonstrations is **Dinar Hadi Batik Shop,** on Jalan Dr. Rajiman ☎ (no phone).

Sangiran

㉙ *15 km (9 mi) north of Solo.*

In the late 19th century, Sangiran was the center for excavations in search of evidence to support Charles Darwin's theory of evolution. In 1891 Dutch physician Eugene Dubois discovered what he called "Java Man" (*Homo erectus*) in East Java not far from Sangiran, and the paper he published on his find rocked the scientific community. Afterward, older and more important Java Man finds were made, mostly around Sangiran. (Note that Sangiran isn't to be confused with Sanggarahan, a village just outside Yogya known for its pleasure houses.) The museum here contains good exhibits about these discoveries, including a

Java Man cranium replica (the originals are in museums around the world); models of these ancestors of the Homo sapiens who lived some 250,000 years ago; and fossils of other life forms, such as elephants. To get here you can take a bus to Kaliso, then walk 30 minutes to the site; or take a taxi (Rp 15,000 round-trip from Solo). ☎ *No phone.* ▨ *Admission.* ⊗ *Mon.–Sat. 9–4.*

Sukuh Temple

③⓪ *35 km (21 mi) east of Solo.*

Sukuh Temple stands mysteriously and exotically alone and contains elements of Hinduism, Buddhism, and animism. Looking like an abbreviated pyramid, the delightful temple is full of cult symbols and erotic-looking objects. The structure dates from the 15th century, but no one knows who built it or what traditions were practiced in it. The place has a mystical atmosphere, enhanced by the lush surrounding rice terraces. A hired car (Rp 20,000) is the most convenient way to get here; the journey takes a good hour along winding, hilly roads. You can also come by bus, but it requires three changes: at Tertomoyo catch the bus to Tawangmangu, then get off at Karangpandan for a minibus to Sukuh. ▨ *Admission.* ⊗ *Daily 9–4.*

Surabaya

③① *260 km (162 mi) northeast of Solo, 320 km (199 mi) northeast of Yogyakarta.*

Surabaya isn't on the traditional tourist route, but with a rapidly expanding business and industrial base—it's Indonesia's second-largest city and for centuries its most important eastern seaport—it's looking for visitors. Hope springs eternal in the human breast.

The city's rich history includes its capture by Kublai Khan in the 13th century and by the Japanese during World War II. On November 10, 1945, the Dutch and their allies virtually flattened the community while trying to reclaim it after the Japanese surrender. The Surabayans resisted and raised the Indonesian flag above the Hotel Majapahit. (November 10 is now celebrated throughout Indonesia as Revolutionary Heroes' Day, symbolizing the country's determination to throw off the colonial yoke.) Despite the history, the Hotel Majapahit and a 1950s Soviet submarine on display by the river are the only real sights.

Surabaya is the maritime jumping-off point for the little-visited island of Madura (famous for its bullfights) and for Sulawesi (☞ *below*); a transfer point for flights to Singapore, Hong Kong, and cities in Japan; and a good base from which to visit Mt. Bromo.

Dining and Lodging

$$$ ✕ **Indigo Restaurant and Bar.** Connected to the Hotel Majapahit (☞ *below*) and done in the same Art Deco style, this 130-seat restaurant—with its long, dark-wood bar and its booths—feels like a posh café. The good "Euro-Asian" food includes such dishes as pizza cooked in a wood-burning oven. The baked goods are delicious, and the coffee is strong. ⊠ *Jl. Tunjungan 65,* ☎ *031/545–4333. AE, DC, MC, V*

$$$ ✕ **Kuningan.** Fish is the specialty here, particularly shellfish. The traditional Chinese-style dining room is a comfortable place to peruse the extensive menu. ⊠ *Jl. Kalimantan 14,* ☎ *031/534–5103. MC, V.*

$$–$$$ ✕ **Cafe Venezia.** Set in a charming old villa that has a garden, this eatery is a great place to take a break. The intriguing mix of tasty food includes steaks and hamburgers as well as Japanese and Korean cuisine. ⊠ *Jl. Ambengan 16,* ☎ *031/534–3335. MC, V.*

$$$ **Hotel Majapahit.** Built in the town's center in 1910 by the Sarkies broth-
★ ers (of Singapore's Raffles fame), this is one of Indonesia's few heritage
hotels. Its expansive courts and green lawns became derelict after World
War II, but in 1994 the Mandarin Oriental Hotel Group took over; a $27
million restoration was completed in 1996. Although modern luxuries
were added, many of the original details were retained, including stained-
glass windows, terrazzo floors, and colonial-style balconies and veran-
das. Rooms on the ground floor are large, but those upstairs are slightly
quieter. The Presidential Suite, the largest of its kind in Indonesia, is more
than 8,600 square ft. Furnishings are Javanese, and some are antiques.
Batiks from Yogyakarta add color. There's a pool bar as well as three
restaurants: Sarkies for Oriental seafood, Indigo for Eurasian, and Shima
for Japanese. ⊠ *Jl. Tunjungan 65, 60011,* ☎ *031/545–4333,* 𝔽𝔸𝕏 *031/
545–4111. 135 rooms, 15 suites. 3 restaurants, bar, pool, tennis court,
health club, business services, meeting rooms. AE, DC, MC, V.*

$$$ **Hyatt Regency Surabaya.** This large, modern hotel has an 11-story
wing and the 27-story Regency Tower with Regency Club rooms,
meeting rooms, two business centers, and offices. An added convenience
is an airline ticketing office. Rooms are typical Hyatt—comfortable,
beige, fairly large, and furnished with wooden cabinets and king-size
beds. The main lobby is popular with locals who come to drink and
listen to live music. Expats gather in the tavern for drinks and light
meals. ⊠ *Jl. Jendral Basuki Rakhmat 106–128, 60275,* ☎ *031/531–
1234 or 800/233–1234 in the U.S.,* 𝔽𝔸𝕏 *031/531–2938. 500 rooms. 2
restaurants, coffee shop, lobby lounge, pool, exercise room, shops, business services, meeting rooms, travel services. AE, DC, MC, V.*

Mt. Bromo

★ ㉜ *Tosari, a village on the mountain, is 90 km (55 mi) southeast of
Surabaya.*

It's a thrill to approach the circular crater of this active volcano, one
of a triad of precipitous peaks, and then look down into what seems
like hell's depths—a bubbling cauldron of water, ash, and sulphur
that spews hot steam clouds. The sight's elemental eeriness is com-
pounded by having to get up very early in the morning, hike to the top
through the chilly air, and worship the sun as it rises.

Part of the pleasure of visiting Mt. Bromo (Gunung Bromo) is that you're
allowed much closer to the rim than at other volcanoes, but be sure-
footed: in 1994 one American peering down the 350 ft to the crater's
bottom fell in and never came out. Additionally, before you make any
Bromo-related travel plans, verify that the mountain is open: sometimes
the volcano is so active that the government prohibits visitors. However, the Tengger and Semaru peaks, which also surround the dusty
valley here, are popular trekking alternatives.

One way to visit Mt. Bromo is on an organized tour (☞ Guided Tours
in Central and Eastern Java A to Z, *below*) that gets you to the caldera's
rim just before dawn. You can either leave Surabaya in the afternoon
and stay overnight in a small bungalow hotel or leave in the morning's
wee hours and return by lunchtime. Either way, the predawn walk will
be chilly, so bring a sweater.

Central and Eastern Java A to Z

Arriving and Departing

BY AIRPLANE

Adisucipto Airport (☎ 274/566666) is 10 km (6 mi) east of Yogyakarta.
From Jakarta's Soekarno-Hatta Airport, **Garuda** (☎ 0274/56835 in

Yogyakarta, 031/532–1521 in Surabaya, or 021/231–1801 in Jakarta) offers several daily flights; flying time is about 45 minutes. Seats fill up quickly, so reservations are essential. There are also flights into Yogya from Denpasar (Bali) and Surabaya on **Merpati** (☎ 0274/514272 in Yogyakarta, 031/568–8111 in Surabaya, or 021/424–3608 in Jakarta). There are flights to Surabaya's **Juanda Airport,** about 20 km (12 mi) from downtown, on Garuda and Merpati from most Javanese cities, as well as from Bali and Lombok.

Between the Airport and Yogyakarta. A minibus runs until 6 PM from the airport to the terminal on Jalan Senopati for Rp 250; from here you can catch a three-wheel becak to your hotel. Taxis to or from downtown charge Rp 10,000. The major hotels send their own minibuses to the airport.

Between the Airport and Surabaya. A taxi to town is your best bet. Cabs cost about Rp 17,000 and work on a coupon system, so you need not bargain with the driver.

BY BUS
Night buses from Jakarta to Yogyakarta take about 14 hours and cost about Rp 12,250. Buses also run from Denpasar on Bali (12 hours), Bandung (7 hours), and Surabaya (8 hours). For information in Jakarta, contact **Antar Lintas Sumatra** (✉ Jl. Jati Baru 87A, ☎ 021/320970) or **P. T. ANS** (✉ Jl. Senen Raya 50, ☎ 021/340494).

BY CAR
Although the scenery may be beautiful, the long drive from Jakarta is slow going, and service areas are few and far between. It's advisable to hire a driver when traveling through Indonesia.

BY TRAIN
Trains from the Gambir Railway Station in Jakarta leave several times daily for Yogya's **Tugu Railway Station** (✉ Jl. Pasar Kembang, ☎ 274/589685). The trip takes 7–12 hours and costs Rp 6,700–Rp 21,500, depending on whether the train is an express or a local and on the ticket class. The most comfortable trip is via the *Senja Utama Express,* which has sleeping cars and leaves Gambir at 7:20 PM and arrives in Yogya at 4:50 AM. The fares are Rp 18,000 for B class, Rp 21,000 for A class, and Rp 44,000 for executive class. There are also day and night trains from Bandung (an eight-hour trip) and from Surabaya (seven hours) as well as service to Surabaya from Jakarta, Yogyakarta, and Solo. (Note: Trains to and from Jakarta and points east and west use Surabaya's Pasar Turi terminal on Jalan Gresik in the north of the city; the Gubeng Train Station, on Jalan Gubeng Sumatra in central Surabaya, is used by trains going to and from Solo, Yogya, and Bandung.)

Another line links Surabaya (from the Pasar Turi terminal) to Banyuwangi, on Java's eastern tip; from here ferries depart every 30 minutes for the 20-minute crossing to Bali. This is a slow train, though, and most non–air travelers to Bali prefer the night express buses. The train between Jakarta and Surabaya takes 14 hours overnight, but, oddly, sleepers aren't available. The executive class (Rp 21,000), however—with air-conditioning, reclining seats, and dinner service—is quite comfortable. Business and Economy classes cost less, but you'll feel worse for wear after an overnight trip. Another option is to break the trip in Cirebon, a charming coastal town four hours east of Jakarta on the fast train, and about 10 hours west of Surabaya.

Getting Around

BY BECAK

Becaks are the main form of public transportation in most Javanese towns and cities (except Surabaya and Jakarta, where they're banned since they're slow and cause traffic jams). Yogya alone has about 25,000 of them, most with paintings of mountains on their fenders. Solo has quite a few as well. In nice weather, they're a relaxing way to travel. The proper fare is about Rp 1,000 per km (½ mi); be sure to negotiate with your driver before starting out.

BY BICYCLE

In Yogya, you can rent bicycles for Rp 4,000 a day from the **Hotel Indonesia** (⊠ Sosromenduran IV, ☎ 0274/587659). The **Restaurant Malioboro** (⊠ Jl. Malioboro 67, ☎ no phone) also has rental bikes.

BY BUS

As a rule, you can simply go to the bus station in any Javanese city and catch a bus to most anywhere on the island. The shorter bus trips are tolerable; for longer hauls it's best to stick with trains. For day trips between cities, minibuses are favored. They leave for Solo throughout the day (7–5) from Yogyakarta's **Terminal Terban** (⊠ Jl. Diponegoro near Jl. P. Mangkubumi) or from Jalan Sudirman or Jalan Solo. From Solo's **Gilligan minibus station,** which is next to the main Tirtonadi Bus Terminal on Jalan Dr. Setiabudi in the northwest of town, take a *bemo,* or minivan (Rp 300), or a becak (Rp 750) the 3 km (2 mi) into town. To reach Mt. Bromo, you can take a bus from Surabaya's **Bungurasih Bus Station** to Probolinggo and change for a bemo up to Pasuruan; from there take a minibus up to Tosari. To get from Tosari to the crater's rim, another 7½ km (4½ mi), you can rent a four-wheel-drive vehicle or, if you're fit, make the two-hour uphill trudge.

BY TAXI

In Yogya you can catch taxis in front of the larger hotels; in general, they don't cruise the streets. Taxis are metered; the flag-fall charge is Rp 800 and covers the first kilometer. A shared taxi from Yogya to Solo costs Rp 2,500 per person.

BY TRAIN

The train from Yogya to Solo takes about one hour; from Solo to Surabaya takes about four. Executive class is air-conditioned and has comfortable reclining seats, business has padded seats but no air-conditioning, and third class can be chaotic.

Contacts and Resources

EMERGENCIES

Ambulance: ☎ 118. **Hospitals: Bethesda Hospital** (⊠ Yogyakarta, ☎ 0274/588876), **Dr. Sardjito Hospital** (⊠ Yogyakarta, ☎ 0274/587333), **RS Budi Mulia** (⊠ Surabaya, ☎ 031/534–1821), **RS Darmo** (⊠ Surabaya, ☎ 031/561–8824), and **RSUD Dr. Soetomo** (⊠ Surabaya, ☎ 031/550–1111). **Fire:** ☎ 113. **Police:** ☎ 110.

ENGLISH-LANGUAGE BOOKSTORES

There are several used-book stores along Jalan Prawirotaman in the south of Yogyakarta. In Surabaya the best bookshops are in the three main malls: **Surabaya Mall** (⊠ Jl. Kusuma Bangsa 116, ☎ 031/534–3002), **Surabaya Plaza** (⊠ Jl. Pemuda 31–37, ☎ 031/531–5088), and **Tunjungan Plaza** (⊠ Jl. Basuki Rachmat 8–12, ☎ 031/531–1507).

GUIDED TOURS

Hotels and travel agencies in Yogya can arrange the following tours, either in a private chauffeured car or as a group tour by bus:

Art and Handicrafts. A five-hour tour of the local crafts centers for leather puppets, wood carving, silver work, batik, and pottery.

Borobudur. An eight-hour tour of Yogyakarta; the countryside; and the Borobudur, Mendut, and Pawon temples.

Prambanan. A three-hour tour of the temple complex.

Yogya City. A three-hour tour that includes the sultan's palace, Sono Budoyo Museum, Kota Gede silver works, and batik and wayang workshops.

Yogya Dieng Plateau. A 10-hour tour of the Dieng Plateau, with its spectacular scenery, sulfur springs, and geysers, plus a visit to Borobudur.

In Surabaya, the largest tour agency is **Orient Express** (⊠ Jl. Jendral Basuki Rakhamat 78, ☎ 031/515253), which will meet you at the airport or anywhere else in Surabaya. Day tours (Rp 436,000 per person) depart Surabaya at 1 PM. Overnight tours (Rp 927,000 per person) depart at 3 PM for the Bromo Cottages in Tosari, where the accommodation is simple, modern, and clean. You rise at 3:30 AM and travel by jeep up Mt. Penanjakan (9,088 ft) for spectacular sunrise views. Afterward, the jeep takes you to the sea of sand—an area of sun-bleached volcanic ash—and then to the stairway to Bromo crater's rim; finally, it's back to the cottages for breakfast before returning to Surabaya.

You can also rent a chauffeured car and do the trip independently for about Rp 100,000, plus the fee for a jeep on the journey's last leg. Try **P. T. Zebra Nusantart** (⊠ Jl. Tegalsari 107, Surabaya, ☎ 031/511777); the firm also has a representative at the Surabaya Hyatt.

TRAVEL AGENCIES

Yogya's main companies include **Nitour** (⊠ Jl. K. H. A. Dahlan 71, ☎ 0274/375165) and **Satriavi Tours & Travel** (⊠ Hotel Ambarrukmo Palace, ☎ 0274/563559, ext. 7135). American Express cardholders can contact **Pacto Ltd. Tours and Travel** (⊠ Garuda Hotel, Jl. Malioboro 60, ☎ 0274/562906). The locally operated **Intan Pelangi** (⊠ Mutiara Hotel, Jl. Malioboro 18, ☎ 0274/562895) is also helpful.

In Surabaya: American Express cardholders can contact **Pacto Ltd. Tours and Travel** (⊠ Jl. Jendral Basuki Rachmad 106, ☎ 031/546–0628) and **Nitour Incorporation** (⊠ Jl. Urip Sumoharjo 63, ☎ 031/534–1247).

VISITOR INFORMATION

Yogyakarta's **Tourist Information Office** (⊠ Jl. Malioboro 16, ☎ 0274/566000) has maps, events schedules, and bus and train information. It's open Monday–Saturday 8–8. There's also a tourist booth at the railway station. The **Solo Tourist Information Office** (⊠ Jl. Slamet Riyadi 275, ☎ 0271/46501) is open Monday–Saturday 8–5.

In Surabaya you can try the **Surabaya Tourist Office** (⊠ Jl. Darmakali 35, ☎ 031/575448) or the **East Java Tourist Office** (⊠ Jl. Pemuda 118, ☎ 031/532–4499). Both are open weekdays 8:30 to 5.

BALI

The "magic" of Bali lies in that it's religiously distinct from the rest of Indonesia: unlike their Muslim neighbors, the Balinese are Hindus. Their faith also contains Buddhist elements and those of ancient, indigenous animist beliefs. Hindu culture came to Bali as early as the 9th century; by the 14th century, the island was part of East Java's Hindu Majapahit empire. When that empire fell to Muslim invaders, Majapahit aristo-crats, scholars, artists, and dancers fled to Bali, consolidating Hindu culture and religion here.

To the Balinese, every living thing contains a spirit; when they pick a flower as an offering to the gods, they first say a prayer to the flower. All over the island, from the capital city of Denpasar to the tiniest vil-lage, plaited baskets filled with flowers and herbs lie on the sidewalks, on the prows of fishing boats, and in markets. These offerings are made to placate evil spirits and honor helpful ones. Stone figures guard en-tries to temples, hotels, and homes. The black-and-white-checked cloths around the statues' waists symbolize the balance between good and evil. Maintaining that harmony is the life work of every Balinese.

The island's geography also contributes to Bali's religion and rituals: the focus of spiritual offerings is on Gunung Agung, the 9,866-ft "Mother Mountain," which is considered the island's holiest site. Agung is also known for its deadly eruption in 1963, but other active volcanoes rise 6,560–9,840 ft along Bali's mountainous interior. It's the ash fallout from these high summits, and the dependable rainfall from storms caught between them, that provide fertile valleys for the famed emerald rice terraces. At its edges, Bali is framed by thick man-grove swamps, sweeping white beaches, and lively coral reefs, offer-ing a variety of ecosystems for wildlife such as mouse deer, monkeys, dolphins, giant turtles, and more than 300 bird species, including the rare Bali starling.

Although the island is only 140 km (87 mi) long by 80 km (48 mi) wide, a week wouldn't be enough to fully appreciate Bali's beaches, temples, volcanoes, and towns. With Indonesia's most developed tourist infra-structure, Bali has several beach areas on its southern coast, where 90% of its visitors stay. Each has its own appeal, and all are within easy reach of one another.

Many travelers have discovered that the way to get a true taste of Bali is to stay in a villa. For the same cost (or less) you receive the same or even better amenities, more space per room, more privacy, and more personal service. As an added bonus, meals, laundry service, tours, and a car and driver are often included in the price. Hundreds of villa op-portunities are available throughout the island; the best are listed here. For villas that book guests through a broker, contact numbers and In-ternet addresses are provided. Note: All hotels and villas listed for Bali have air-conditioning, massage, laundry service, baby-sitting, travel ser-vices, and free parking unless otherwise noted.

Jimbaran

★ ❶ *1,100 km (682 mi) southeast of Jakarta, 3 km (2 mi) south of Ngu-rah Rai Airport, 20 km (12 mi) southwest of Denpasar.*

Once a sleepy fishing village, Jimbaran is now a playground for guests of several luxury resorts. On the western side of the Bukit Peninsula to the south of Kuta, the area's white-sand beaches, glowing sunsets, and sapphire waves create a captivating scene. An offshore reef makes the waters gentle enough for swimming.

OFF THE BEATEN PATH **PURA LUHUR ULU WATU –** About 15 km (9 mi) south of Jimbaran—at the end of the Bukit Peninsula—is this cliff-side temple overlooking the ocean. Originally constructed in the 11th century as one of Bali's six main territo-rial places of worship, Ulu Watu was rebuilt 500 years later and has been renovated several times since, giving the current structure a mix of old and new styles. The split-gate entrance imitates a curving set of

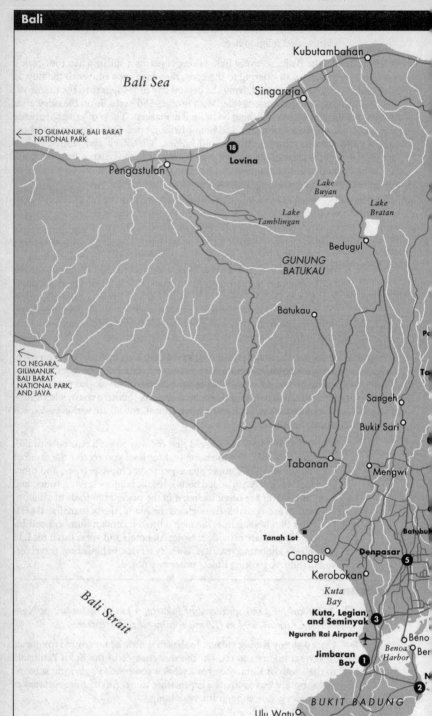

Bali Sea

Kubutambahan

Singaraja

← TO GILIMANUK, BALI BARAT
NATIONAL PARK

(18) **Lovina**

Pengastulan

*Lake
Buyan*

*Lake
Tamblingan*

*Lake
Bratan*

Bedugul

*GUNUNG
BATUKAU*

Batukau

← TO NEGARA,
GILIMANUK,
BALI BARAT
NATIONAL PARK,
AND JAVA

Sangeh

Bukit Sari

Tabanan

Mengwi

Tanah Lot

Canggu

Denpasar

Kerobokan

*Kuta
Bay*

**Kuta, Legian,
and Seminyak** (3)

Ngurah Rai Airport ✈

*Benoa
Harbor*

Beno

Ber

**Jimbaran
Bay** (1)

BUKIT BADUNG

Ulu Watu

Bali Strait

(5)

Batubul

Pc

Ta

N

(2)

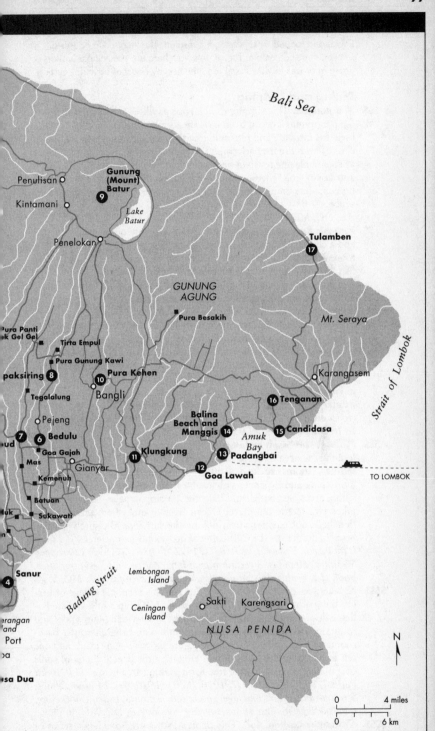

garuda wings and leads to the outer courtyard, where a second gate is framed by statues of Ganesha (the elephant-headed god and son of Shiva) and topped by a fearsome guardian. The inner court houses a smaller, three-tier temple. The sunsets from here are spectacular (visitors arrive in droves to view them), and the nearby beaches have fine surfing.

Dining and Lodging

$$–$$$ ✕ **Balangan.** This simple, thatch-roof pavilion looks over a sweep-
★ ing panorama of ocean from atop the forested Jimbaran hills. The ambience is intimate and refreshing, with just six alfresco tables and soft
classical music in the background. Watch kites whip over the trees below
as you nibble on French oysters, penne with grilled vegetable-basil pesto
and crispy goat-cheese croutons, linguini with chorizo sausages, or
homemade pumpkin ravioli. Try the roasted mango with caramel
sauce. ⊠ *Br. Cengiling 88,* ☎ *0361/410711. Reservations essential.
AE, DC, MC, V.*

$$ ✕ **Oasis Restaurant & Bakery.** Pastel hues, potted plants, a slick bar,
and a cheery bakery add to the class of this two-story restaurant. The
food is eclectic and beautifully presented: try the roll move (iced grilled
fish slices around sweet cucumber chunks), the chilli squid cilantro (spicy,
lightly fried squid curls), or the tangy, pan-seared tuna fillet with lemon
and capers, accompanied by au gratin potatoes. Desserts are light and
petite. ⊠ *Jl. Bypass,* ☎ *0361/702669. AE, DC, MC, V.*

$ ✕ **Restoran La Indonesia.** Along Jimbaran's main road, this thatched-
roof restaurant has authentic Balinese food. The interior is elegant and
the garden romantic, the mood heightened by soft gamelan music. Try
lawar (spicy mixed vegetable salad with shredded chicken), *tambusan
be pasih* (diced fish roasted in banana leaves), or *saur kare* (vegetables
in coconut-milk curry). If you can't decide, ask for the individual ri-
jsttafel sampler buffet. Note that Bali's famous dish, *bebek betutu*
(roast duck with vegetable stuffing), must be ordered a day in advance.
⊠ *Jl. Uluwatu 108,* ☎ *0361/701763. AE, DC, MC, V.*

$$$ ✕🏨 **Bali Cliff Resort and Hotel.** Positioned along rough-hewn cliffs over-
looking the ocean, this resort has one of the island's most spectacular
settings. Rooms are done up tastefully in pastels; suites and villas offer
more space and elegance, with marble floors, hand-carved furnishings,
sitting areas, spa baths, and balconies. A sloping, glass-enclosed tram
takes you to the multilevel Ocean Restaurant, where tables are in
thatched-roof pavilions overlooking the surf. For a leisurely Sunday
brunch, don't miss the Cliff coffee shop's exquisite buffet. ⊠ *Jl. Purah
Batu Pageh, Ungasan,* ☎ *0361/771992,* ℻ *0361/771993. 120 rooms,
50 suites, 10 villas. 3 restaurants, 3 bars, coffee shop, in-room safes,
pool, spa, health club, shops, theater, meeting rooms. AE, MC, V.* ✇

$$$$ 🏨 **Four Seasons Resort.** Set on 35 acres, this veritable village of luxury bungalows rises from the shore some 150 ft up a hill. Ornate Balinese doors lead into private courtyards, some with a plunge pool and
fountain. Bedrooms have peaked bamboo-and-thatch roofs; bathrooms have huge, deep tubs and separate showers—one inside and one
out in a small courtyard garden. Down by the beach, the pool spills
over a 20-ft waterfall into a free-form soaking area below. ⊠ *Jl. Bukit
Permai, 80361,* ☎ *0361/701010,* ℻ *0361/701020. 147 bungalows.
5 restaurants, pool, massage, spa, 2 tennis courts, beach, snorkeling,
windsurfing, boating, shops, meeting rooms. AE, DC, MC, V.* ✇

$$$$ 🏨 **The Ritz-Carlton, Bali.** This opulent, stunning hotel has a series of
pools that descend toward a breathtaking Indian Ocean view. Unpol-
ished marble surrounds the fountains and koi ponds, carved antique
wooden benches adorn the hallways, and a replica of Klungkung's
Kertagosa Palace mural graces the lobby ceiling. Most rooms in the
four-story main building have ocean views; all have a Western-style decor

with a Balinese flair. The thatched-roof villas have striking Balinese accents, *bale bungong* (cushioned lounging areas), and private plunge pools. ✉ *Jl. Karang Mas Sejahtera, 80364,* ☎ *0361/702222,* ℻ *0361/702555. 277 rooms, 16 suites, 36 villas. 6 restaurants, 6 bars, pool, spa, putting green, tennis court, beach, snorkeling, windsurfing, boating, children's programs (ages 4–12), meeting rooms. AE, DC, MC, V.* ✆

$$$–$$$$ 🏨 **Hotel Inter-Continental Bali.** Five stone garudas greet you from their posts in a large lotus pond at the entrance. Opulence readily mixes with tradition in the solid stone building, with hardwood floors, light-wood furniture, cream and rose cushions, and carefully hewn ornaments adorning the guest quarters. Cross the stone bridge over a wide, green lotus pond to reach twin dipping pools, where frigid showers spray from stone statues. Or, just have an afternoon swim at the beach—which has one of the island's best sunset views. ✉ *Jl. Uluwatu 45, 80361,* ☎ *0361/ 701888,* ℻ *0361/701777. 214 rooms. 2 restaurants, 2 bars, 3 pools, beach, snorkeling, windsurfing, boating, dance club, meeting rooms. AE, MC, V.* ✆

$$–$$$$ 🏨 **Villa Balquisse.** Walk through the ivy-covered, stone temple doorway and you're magically transported into a Mediterranean hideaway right in the midst of Jimbaran and just steps from the beach. There are actually two villa complexes here, each with its own set of thatched-roof bungalows awash in warm, tropical hues; a central sitting and dining pavilion decorated with unfinished antiques and colorful fabrics; and a beautiful, bluestone-tile pool. Villa 1 has a separate kitchen and three connected bedrooms to the side of its pool; Villa 2 has three double and two connecting bedrooms set back from the pool area. A full-service business office and toy-filled playroom face the large yard inside the entrance. The small restaurant—a single, long table beneath a poolside pavilion—serves exquisite, inexpensive gourmet fare. ✉ *Bookings: Indovillas,* ☎ *020/8353748,* ℻ *0361/733031. 7 rooms, 1 bungalow. Restaurant, minibars, 2 pools, business services. No credit cards. www.indovillas.com.*

$ 🏨 **Puri Bamboo Bungalows.** This small hotel offers comfortable accommodations and a convenient location. Each neat, two-story cottage has four rooms—two upstairs and two down—all with small, simply furnished bedrooms. Bathrooms have tubs and stone gardens; sinks are in the main room. Superior suites have porches, and deluxe suites include a sitting area. In the middle of the cottages, a pool with a swim-up bar is the center of activity, even though the beach is just steps away. ✉ *Jl. Pangeracikan, 80361,* ☎ *0361/701377,* ℻ *0361/701440. 20 rooms, 18 suites. Restaurant, bar, pool, beach. AE, MC, V.*

Nightlife

Right in town, the **Kakul Cafe** (✉ Jl. Bukit Permai 5c, ☎ 0361/702815) attracts a crowd on weekends. The **Monkey Forest Fun Pub and Disco** (☎ 0361/701888) at the Hotel Inter-Continental Bali is a popular hangout.

For the ultimate in chic, 1930s-style elegance, the sleek upstairs club at the **Oasis Restaurant & Bakery** (☞ *above*) is the place for drinks and a game of pool. On weekends, come to mingle with the beautiful people and listen to first-class live jazz and blues bands.

Shopping

Plan to spend a couple of hours at the excellent ceramic workshop and warehouse of **Jenggala Keramik Bali** (✉ Jl. Uluwatu II, Jimbaran, ☎ 0361/703310, ☉ daily 10–8), an enormous, modern, air-conditioned building with sleek displays of works by talented Balinese and Indonesian ceramic artists. But it's hardly a museum: although there are ceramic arts displays from the country's past (all for sale), there are also contemporary dishes, cups, general homewares, and other handy ceramic pieces in neat, Pier 1–style exhibits. Past the museum-quality displays is a workshop where you can throw and paint your own pottery, as well as a café that offers delicious baked goods, sandwiches, drinks, and desserts. Upstairs are more displays, as well as long desks and a library of books on ceramics, history, and home design. You can look down on the inner workings of a huge ceramic workshop and storehouse behind the public building and watch the wares being spun, fired, and painted before they line the shelves.

Nusa Dua

❷ *10 km (6 mi) southeast of Jimbaran Bay, 8 km (5 mi) southeast of Ngurah Rai Airport, 30 km (18 mi) southeast of Denpasar.*

Nusa Dua, a former burial ground, consists of two tiny islands linked to the mainland by a reinforced sand spit. Unlike Kuta and Sanur, this is a planned resort, with no indigenous community. Although you have to travel inland from here to see the real Bali, Nusa Dua's beaches are wide and peaceful, and its self-contained hotels are luxurious.

Dining and Lodging

$$$$ ✕🏨 **Amanusa.** The rough, winding road through the Bali Golf & Country Club and to Amanusa disguises the resort's opulence. Shining marble floors and thick columns welcome you into the stone main building, which towers above a reflection pond and a wide, sapphire-tile swimming pool. From here, the views of the forested peninsula stretch to the Indian Ocean, and most of the enormous villas—built into the land's gentle folds—partially share this vista. Each also has checkered-marble floors, rich teak furniture, a canopy bed, a garden, a sunken marble tub, and an outdoor shower. Individual *bale bungong* (sitting pavilions) are outside on the terraces; eight villas also have plunge pools. You can toast the sunset—seated beneath a canopy of bougainvillea beside the pool—while gamelan music is played. Afterward, the Terrace restaurant's candlelighted tables provide a romantic dinner setting above the peninsula's twinkling lights. Indonesian and Thai food are the highlights. Try the prawn salad with coconut, chili, lemon, and basil and the rich, red curry with chicken, peanuts, and coconut. Sumptuous desserts include chocolate-caramel-mousse cake and date pudding with butterscotch sauce. ✉ *Jl. Nusa Dua Selatan (Box 33), 80363,* ☎ *0361/772333,* 🆊 *0361/772335. 35 villas. 2 restaurants, pool, spa, golf privileges, 2 tennis courts, windsurfing, boating, mountain bikes, library, meeting rooms. AE, DC, MC, V.* ✍

$$$–$$$$ 🏨 **Bali Hilton International.** A spectacular floodlighted waterfall sets the scene before a semicircle of five-story buildings surrounding Balinese-theme courtyards and an enormous lagoon. Rooms have a mix of modern furnishings and Balinese decor; all have balconies with lagoon or sea views. A Japanese-speaking staff, Japanese newspapers, green tea, and slippers are available. The hotel's facilities are amenable to travelers with disabilities. ✉ *Jl. Raya Nusa Dua (Box 46), 80363,* ☎ *0361/771102 or 800/HILTONS in the U.S.,* 🆊 *0361/771616. 538 rooms. 7 restaurants, in-room safes, 3 pools, spa, 4 tennis courts, exercise room, squash, theater, meeting rooms. AE, DC, MC, V.*

$$$–$$$$ 🏨 **Grand Hyatt Bali.** Forty acres of gardens and cascading waterfalls are the setting for the Hyatt's four "ethnic village" compounds, each with its own small lagoon or swimming pool. Most rooms have king-size beds and small sitting enclaves with banquette seats. Bathrooms have separate shower stalls and wooden shutters that open to the bedrooms. Regency Club rooms feature balconies, marble bathrooms, private pools, and butler service. The hotel's Balinese character is heightened by the Pasar Senggol open-air night market of food stalls and an amphitheater where traditional dances are performed. ✉ *Jl. Raya Nusa Dua (Box 53),* ☎ *0361/771234 or 800/233–1234 in the U.S.,* ⨳ *0361/ 772038. 750 rooms. 5 restaurants, 4 bars, in-room safes, 6 pools, putting green, 3 tennis courts, health club, squash, shops, theater, children's programs, playground, meeting rooms. AE, DC, MC, V.* ♿

$$$–$$$$ 🏨 **Sheraton Laguna.** The garden setting here attracts an international crowd intent on relaxation and seclusion. The central courtyard has free-form swimming pools, lagoons, and waterfalls that are connected by stone steps and curving wooden bridges. Ground-level rooms have balconies or patios; upper suites have large balconies that drip with bougainvillea; and suites have large sitting areas and marble baths with oversize tubs. The luxurious spa has indoor and outdoor whirlpool baths, a long bathing pool with several waterfalls, and a massage and treatment villa with marble floors and a cushioned bale. ✉ *Jl. Raya Nusa Dua (Box 2077), 80363,* ☎ *0361/771327 or 800/325–3535 in the U.S.,* ⨳ *0361/771326. 211 rooms, 65 suites. 4 restaurants, in-room safes, pool, wading pool, spa, 2 tennis courts, exercise room, business services. AE, DC, MC, V.* ♿

Nightlife and the Arts

Some of the livelier resort locales include: **Club Taboh** (✉ Nusa Dua Beach Hotel, Jl. Raya Nusa Dua next to the Sheraton Nusa Indah, ☎ 0361/977120), which features karaoke and an all-night disco Tuesday through Sunday; the Grand Hyatt's **Lila Cita** (☎ 0361/771234), which has weekly fashion shows and live bands; and the Sheraton Laguna's **Quinn's** (☎ 0361/771–1237), which offers live entertainment nightly.

Along Jalan Pantai Mengiat, **Koki Bali** (☎ 0361/772406) has Balinese dancing at 8 PM every Tuesday and Thursday, the jazz bar at **Poco Loco** (☎ 0361/773923) rocks on weekends in peak season, and ✕ **Ulam** (☎ 0361/771590) is always crowded. Several dining establishments in the Nusa Dua Galeria shopping plaza have popular bars (all offer free transport to and from area resorts), including: **Arak Bali** (☎ 0361/774612), a classy restaurant specializing in seafood; **Harry's** (☎ 0361/772655), where Western-style fare caters to twentysomethings, and **Uno** (☎ 0361/773654), which attracts a Japanese crowd.

Balinese cultural performances are scheduled regularly at the **Galeria stage** (✉ Galeria Nusa Dua Shopping Centre, Jl. Raya Nusa Dua, ☎ 0361/771662). In summer live bands perform here Saturday night.

Outdoor Activities and Sports

The 18-hole, 6,839-yard, par-72 course of the **Bali Golf & Country Club** (☎ 0361/771791), on the Bukit Peninsula in Nusa Dua, has Rp 1,120,000 greens fees (including caddy) and Rp 241,920 club rental. Most of the hotels have mountain bikes and maps for the area's numerous cycling paths.

Shopping

Each Nusa Dua resort has at least one gift shop, but you'll find the best prices and selection outside the hotels. Along Jalan Pantai Mengiat, in the center of town, clothing shops and trinket stalls filled with carvings and textiles are tucked between small, open-air restaurants.

Kuta, Legian, and Seminyak

❸ *8 km (5 mi) northwest of Nusa Dua, 4 km (3 mi) northeast of Ngurah Rai Airport, 12 km (7 mi) southwest of Denpasar.*

Kuta beach—Bali's original tourist hangout—has fattened over the years into an extremely commercial, somewhat tawdry escape. Its once-splendid golden swatch of sand is now smothered by people and scattered with litter, and its main street, just 2 blocks from the beach, is crammed with boutiques, Western fast-food chains, bars, and carefree, drunken travelers. Still, the sunsets are stunning, the energy of the youthful vacationers (including many backpackers) gives the town a festive atmosphere, and there are enclaves of the real Bali down many a narrow, quiet street.

Just to the south of Kuta is Tuban, where enormous international hotels attract tourists. To the north, Legian is a bit more subdued than Kuta; it's for those who like to be close to the action but not right in it. Classy villas and boutique hotels targeting worldly, upscale travelers are springing up along the beaches and rice fields of Seminyak, a step north of Legian. More private rentals and luxury properties are beginning to fill in the coastline between Seminyak and Canggu, near the temple of Tanah Lot, making this part of the coast an exclusive hideaway for travelers who want to experience Bali in plush surroundings.

Dining and Lodging

$$$ ✕ **Fabio's.** This classic Italian restaurant is wide, open, and breezy, with soaring ceilings and lots of marble. The menu covers a detailed panorama of Italy, from pasta and pizza to risotto and an excellent selection of wines. Head for the windows in front of the large, clean kitchen to see your meal prepared. There's a romantic garden in back and a savvy bar up front, and live music Wednesday and Saturday. ✉ *Jl. Seminyak 66, Seminyak,* ☎ *0361/730562. AE, DC, MC, V.*

$$$ ✕ **La Lucciola.** Perfect margaritas and sunsets are why most people come to this chic beachside restaurant, but the cuisine and service are top-notch as well. Set in front of the sea along the golden sands of Berewa, the open, two-story building welcomes a casual, upscale crowd. By day, families come to play on the private beach (Rp 50,000 per person); by evening, a classier crowd settles in. The food is terrific: meaty chilli squid curls, succulent baked chicken, and crisp yet moist chocolate tarts. It's a wonderful place for that special night out. ✉ *Jl. Laksmana, Pantai Kayu Aya, Kerobokan,* ☎ *0361/730838. Reservations essential. AE, DC, MC, V.*

$$$ ✕ **Warisan.** Here, elite expatriates, artists, and their often famous guests relax around red cloth-covered tables, leisurely smoke cigarettes, and recount amusing tales of their international travels. The wine flows freely here—from probably the best list on Bali—with superb labels from France, Chile, Argentina, South Africa, and Australia. The fabulous cuisine is beautifully presented on colorful, oversize ceramic dishes: precisely arranged escargots burst with freshness, grilled rosemary chicken breast is meaty and succulent, and salmon asparagus penne combines a beautiful range of textures and tastes. Desserts are amazing, and it's worth coming here just for an afternoon treat and an espresso. ✉ *Jl. Kerobokan, Kerobokan,* ☎ *0361/731175. Reservations essential. AE, DC, MC, V. No lunch Sun.*

$$ ✕ **Bali Bakery Patisserie & Cafe.** This bright, clean café is split into two sections: a bakery decorated with baskets of rolls, bowls of long baguettes, and glass cases of exquisite cakes, and a café with little round tables and cozy booths. The extensive menu offers sandwiches and wraps, gourmet salads, and simple appetizers. Indonesian items and full dinners are also available—and make sure you try one of the beautiful pastries afterward. ✉ *Jl Raya Kuta 65, Tuban,* ☎ *0361/755149. AE, DC, MC, V.*

$$ ✕ **Verandah.** Set back from the main strip, this inconspicuous little
★   restaurant serves the best European fare on the island. The decor is dark, classy, tropical kitsch, with leopard-print bar chairs, ornately carved

wooden tables, and a raised seating area in back next to a mural of sunset and palm trees. Service is flawless, and each dish is an artwork of shapes, colors, and flavors. Selections are unusual, such as butterfly-sliced avocado and pear cocktail sauce sprinkled with blue cheese, or orange-marinated cold roast beef tenderloin served with goat's cheese, aubergine mousse, and balsamic vinegar—and those are just the appetizers. Main dishes are superb: thin-sliced Norwegian salmon drizzled with creamy avocado dressing; imported lamb chops with garbanzo Provençal sauce, served with a spinach and goat's cheese quiche; and delicate spinach and salmon terrine served with saffron sauce and garnished with caviar. Save room for the perfect desserts—you can even go back to the open kitchen and watch yours being created. For drinks and coffee, sit at the sleek bar up front; for romance, request a table in the garden. ⊠ *Jl. Seminyak 31B, Seminyak,* ☎ *0361/732685. Reservations essential. No credit cards. No lunch.*

$$ ✕ **Warung Kopi.** Marble-top tables facing the street in a pretty rear garden provide an oasis from the strip's noise. The menu is eclectic: Indonesian fish, vegetable, and rice dishes; Indian curries; Western beef and lamb. This is also a fine place to stop for just an appetizer or dessert; try the wicked chocolate brownies or the spiced orange carrot cake. Stop in Wednesday at 7 PM for the weekly Indian buffet. ⊠ *Jl. Legian Tengah 427, Legian,* ☎ *0361/753602. MC, V.*

$ ✕ **Made's Warung II.** This two-story, shop-encircled pavilion is an area hot spot, both for the food and the chance to see and be seen by the island's "in" clique. The menu is extensive, including European, Indonesian, Thai, and Indian dishes, and the popular bar's drink choices are just as vast. The Asian food, unfortunately, is bland; stick with Western fare and the terrific desserts. Prices are cheap and portions are large, though, and it's worth it just to hang out with the crowd. Note that there's parking in back. ⊠ *Jl. Seminyak, Seminyak,* ☎ *0361/732130. AE, DC, MC, V.*

$$$$ ✕🏠 **The Oberoi.** At Legian Beach's far western end, the Oberoi's 15 acres offer tranquillity, privacy, and friendly service. Thatched cottages have verandas, and the villas have balconies and garden courtyards; some luxury villas have private pools, and all have traditional Balinese inner courtyards. Hand-carved teak furnishings and locally made silk-screen prints and draperies are used throughout. Balinese dance is performed in the resort's amphitheater two or three evenings a week. Before the show, consider dining at the Kura Kura restaurant, where the Indonesian buffet and à la carte items have a Continental flair. The bebek betutu is a standout. ⊠ *Jl. Kayu Aya, Basangkasa, Legian Beach (Box 3351, Denpasar 80033),* ☎ *0361/730361 or 800/5–OBEROI in the U.S.,* ℻ *0361/730391. 60 cottages, 13 villas. Restaurant, bar, café, pool, spa, tennis court, health club, beach, windsurfing, theater, meeting rooms, car rental. AE, DC, MC, V.* ❧

$$$–$$$$ ✕🏠 **Le Meridien Nirwana Golf & Spa Resort.** Carved into Bali's southwestern coastline, this luxury resort fronts a new, spectacular golf course. Rooms feature plush modern furnishings and Balinese art; even standards have minibars, glass-wall showers, and wooden shutters that open the bathtub area to the rest of the room. The suites are apartment-size, with a desk and sitting area, separate bedroom, walk-in closet, and sumptuous marble bath. Villas have a private plunge pool, terrace, courtyard with sitting pavilion, and garden shower. The Tanah Lot temple sits just below the estate, and prime seaside panoramas are the highlight of dinner at the opulent Cendana Restaurant. An Indonesian rijsttafel is served on Sunday nights; reserve a terrace table next to the duck pond for sunset views. ⊠ *Jl. Kediri Tanah Lot (Box 198), Tanah Lot 82171,* ☎ *0361/815900,* ℻ *0361/815901. 245 rooms, 21 suites, 12 villas. 2 restaurants, bar, grill, lobby lounge, 3 pools, spa, 18-hole* golf course, 2 tennis courts, health club, beach, children's programs, business services, meeting rooms, car rental. AE, DC, MC, V. ✧

$$-$$$ ✕▥ **Umalas Stables.** This wonderful little hotel is one of Bali's best
★ hidden delights. A narrow, enclosed courtyard lined with gardens and fountains is flanked by a pretty, white, farmhouse-style line of stables housing competition-quality horses. Above, the elegant guest quarters are decorated in pale green floral fabrics and have windows that look over the surrounding rice fields. All have a TV, refrigerator, sitting area, and large, shower-only bathroom with marble accents. The hotel attracts many international riding professionals. There's a trotting circle next to the stables and a riding ring behind the estate. Once a month on Sunday the owners hold a "Children's Party," when kids of all ages are invited to spend the day with the horses and play in the freeform pool and on the playground. The poolside patio restaurant, open 8–5 daily, has a limited but good menu: pasta, curry, Indonesian dishes, and simple breakfast selections. ✉ *Bookings: Indovillas,* ☎ *0818/353748,* FAX *0361/733031. 4 rooms, 1 suite. Restaurant, refrigerators, pool, horseback riding, children's programs, playground. AE, DC, MC, V.* ✧

$$ ▥ **Poppies Cottages.** Here you can stay in a traditional thatched cottage for a fraction of what it would cost at a larger resort. Set amid fragrant gardens—highlighted by arching bridges, hidden pools, and flowing waterfalls—each cottage has one double bed or two single beds and a large, secluded balcony. Bathrooms have sunken tubs and are in screened, private gardens. A set of pools is nestled among rocks with landscaped sunbathing terraces and waterfalls, and the pavilion houses a small library and game area. The relaxed alfresco atmosphere and Indonesian and Western fare of Poppies Restaurant are enjoyable. Items range from Greek salads and *tom yam* (spicy Thai prawn soup) to grilled fish and succulent spareribs. ✉ *Poppies La., Kuta (Box 3378, Denpasar 80033),* ☎ *0361/751059,* FAX *0361/752364. 20 cottages. Restaurant, bar, 2 pools, library, car rental. AE, DC, MC, V.*

$ ✕▥ **Green Garden Bali.** Also known as the Puri Hijau (Green Palace), this small hotel is tucked back behind the Tuban shopping strip. Rooms are centered around a freeform pool with a waterfall tumbling from a high, rocky escarpment frothing with greenery. The decor is simple, with white-tile floors, floral spreads, and wood trim, and all rooms have desks, TVs, refrigerators, and bathtubs. The open-air restaurant serves large portions of Indonesian, Chinese, and Western fare. While you dine, try a free five-minute shoulder massage. ✉ *Jl. Kartika Plz. 9,* ☎ *0361/ 761023,* FAX *0361/754570. 25 rooms. Restaurant, bar, refrigerators, pool, beauty salon, spa, business services. AE, DC, MC, V.*

$$$-$$$$ ▥ **Gajah Putih.** This comfortable, two-story Italianate mansion is set at the sea's edge near Berawa beach. Spacious rooms are luxurious, but the feeling is casual and tranquil. The decor is tasteful and simple, with handwoven Indonesian ikat and batik fabrics in shades of maroon, brown, and navy that complement the graceful home. Five large, light-filled bedrooms surrounded by floor-to-ceiling windows have polished wood floors and solid, oversize antique furnishings, including hand-carved teak canopy beds and wardrobes. En suite marble bathrooms are grand, with double sinks, dipping pool–size sunken bathtubs, and teak walk-in closets. The ground-floor living area has light wicker furnishings, a large-screen entertainment center, and a pool table. The breezy upstairs terrace overlooks a grassy palm grove, the pool, and the tennis court; a spa, sauna, and fitness center were in the works at press time. The professional staff of 24 can serve every whim, from assisting with shopping to whipping up an elegant dinner party. ✉ *Bookings: Indovillas,* ☎ *0818/353748,* FAX *0361/733031. 5 rooms. Dining room, pool, tennis court, beach. AE, DC, MC, V. www.indovillas.com.*

$$$–$$$$ ⊞ **Villa Taman Wana.** Entering the secluded Taman Wana estate is like stepping into a luxurious garden sanctuary. Inside are three separate villa complexes: Villa Sumba has two separate bungalows connected to the main living area by skylit boardwalks; the larger bungalow has two bedrooms, each with separate baths, while the second, single bungalow faces a lap pool. Villa Tioman has two single bungalows, one facing gardens and the other fronting a freeform pool with a children's play area. Villa Lamu is a magnificent, three-bedroom home with sweeping forest views. The impressive freeform pool has a shallow beach end and a bridge arching over the center; a second, thin pool bubbles along the master bedroom deck. A second single bedroom has a separate entrance, and the loft bedroom (not air-conditioned) has a marvelous view. The upstairs sitting area, connected to the lower by a tree house–like suspension bridge, is comfortable and spacious. Two smaller, shower-only guest villas stand between the main house and the Villa Tioman complex. Living areas for all three villas feature modern kitchens, dining and bar areas, and sitting areas. The detailing in each villa is exquisite: shell-pink, tiled marble floors inlaid with teak; carved canopy beds; antique dressers and desks; and large garden bathrooms with huge terrazzo tubs. The well-trained, top-notch staff are discreet yet ready to tend to your needs at a moment's notice. Airport transfers, laundry, a personal cook, shopping services, and other amenities are included in the price. ⊠ *Bookings: Indovillas,* ☏ *0818/353748,* FAX *0361/733031. 7 bungalows, 1 house. Dining room, 4 pools, billiards, laundry service, airport shuttle. AE, DC, MC, V.* ✎

$$–$$$$ ⊞ **Puri Sienna.** Thoughtful touches make Puri Sienna a standout; look for decorative soaps, shampoos, and soft towels in the bathroom; umbrellas, flashlights, and mosquito spray cleverly set in the large, walk-in closets; and Balinese-crafted notebooks and pens at each bedside. The setting, between the main strip of shops and the beach, is not only convenient but stunningly beautiful. A lush, grassy lawn spreads out from the pool to the main house, which has an upstairs bedroom and office, open downstairs dining room, full kitchen, and comfortable living area. A single-bedroom villa stands off to the right, and the second villa behind it has two bedrooms with a comfortable little sitting area in between, as well as a shared deck that steps down into a lovely, bluestone-tiled swimming pool. All villas have luxury (shower-only) bathrooms and private kitchens. An additional three-story apartment complex was under construction at press time, which promises to be an excellent base for business travelers and families. ⊠ *Bookings: Indovillas,* ☏ *0818/353748,* FAX *0361/733031. 4 rooms. Dining room, in-room safes, kitchenettes, minibars, pool. AE, DC, MC, V.* ✎

$$–$$$$ ⊞ **Villa Sawah.** This clean, cozy country house has a welcoming, comfortable setting in the verdant hills of Kerobokan. A covered, wooden walkway forms a bridge between the main house and a one-story, three-bedroom annex, all surrounded by floor-to-ceiling windows framing the rice fields. The sunny, spacious main building features a comfortable living area, a long dining table, and a modern kitchen, as well as two small bedrooms and a full bath. Glass walls slide open to reveal the large terrace, which has a full view of a crescent-shape, sapphire-tile pool that runs along the outline of the rice terraces below it. In the annex, the master bedroom is nestled between a connecting children's room (with three antique beds and lots of toys) and a separate guest bedroom; all have large outdoor bathrooms with enormous terrazzo tubs and garden showers. A curving lotus pond follows the line of the rice fields to a children's *bale* next to the pool. ⊠ *Bookings: Indovillas,* ☏ *0818/353748,* FAX *0361/733031. 5 rooms. Dining room, pool. AE, DC, MC, V.* ✎

$$–$$$ 🏨 **Alam KulKul.** The sunny, breezy Alam KulKul is quiet and is just across the road from the beach. Cottages and suites are gathered into cozy gardens surrounded by high stone walls; standard rooms are in a large building at the property's back. The breathtaking Bali Villa, decorated with Balinese antiques, has a plunge pool and a garden bathroom with a sunken corner tub. Two Java Suites are decorated with island antiques and have garden tubs. Suites have contemporary furnishings and a garden sitting area—but those with a pool view aren't worth the higher price. ⊠ *Jl. Pantai (Box 3097), 80030,* ☎ *0361/752520,* FAX *0361/752519. 57 rooms, 23 villas. 2 restaurants, bar, minibars, 2 pools, beauty salon, spa, shops, children's programs, business services. AE, DC, MC, V.*☟

$–$$ 🏨 **Amarta Bungalows.** These new, classy "boutique bungalows," down a quiet lane between the beach and the shops, have the atmosphere and luxury of a small, private villa at a budget price. Centered around a kidney-shape pool of sapphire-blue tiles, this collection of two-story, thatch-roof bungalows has the graceful feel of a Balinese village. Gardens flow around the outer walls, and inside you'll find warm gold trim, hand-carved wooden furniture, and antique four-poster beds. Spacious garden bathrooms have stacked limestone rock walls, round bathtubs, and an outdoor shower. All villas have kitchenettes with microwaves and refrigerators, and breakfast and a daily fruit basket are included in the price. Note: Don't be afraid to ask for a rate discount. ⊠ *Jl. Abimanyu 2000X, 80361,* ☎ FAX *0361/734793. 8 villas. Kitchenettes, refrigerators, pool. AE, DC, MC, V.*

Nightlife and the Arts

The southwest coast can rock, be romantic, or provide rich cultural insights. In Seminyak, eclectic restaurant bars pipe in jazz or soft rock as sleekly dressed patrons sip martinis or wine, while those at the luxury hotel bars relax on wicker chairs at small, candlelighted tables facing the sea. For the gregarious, Kuta and Legian are 24-hour party towns: restaurants start the day with "hangover breakfasts" and liquid lunches; happy hour arrives midafternoon; bar-hopping buses lumber through the streets just after sundown; disco beats pound through the darkness long past midnight; and after-hours parties continue through dawn.

You'll find a list of nightlife hot spots in the *Bali Plus* booklet, distributed free at travel offices, hotels, and grocery stores, and in *Bali News,* another free publication. A new guide to Bali's entertainment scene is *the beat,* which is distributed free in restaurants throughout the island and covers restaurants, nightlife, movies, and music around the area. Many restaurants also schedule live music from week to week, so check their outdoor blackboards. A new magazine is *balio,* a large, eye-catching publication that offers the inside story on Bali's hot spots. The monthly English-Japanese *Bali Tribune* magazine details island happenings— look for its free postcards in area shops and restaurants. The glossy *Bali Echo, Hello Bali,* and even *Surf Time,* and the phone book–size *Bali Tourist Guide,* are good sources for after-hours ideas.

BARS

All Stars Surf Café (⊠ Jl. Kartika Plaza 8X, Tuban, ☎ 0361/754134) books live bands on weekends. If you like Caribbean music, head to the funky **Apache Reggae Bar** (⊠ Jl. Legian 146, ☎ 0361/761212). **Café Luna** (⊠ Jl. Seminyak, ☎ no phone) has live mixed music—and occasional go-go girls—on weekends, but the place always rocks. One of the area's best-known bars is the bustling **Goa 2001** (⊠ Jl. Seminyak, ☎ 0361/753922) at the seafood restaurant of the same name. The original **Made's Warung** (⊠ Jl. Pantai Kuta) was under renovation at press time, but the new place will be a hangout for mixing with the crowd on summer nights. The place for Irish drinkers is the wood- and shamrock-accented bar at **Paddy's** (✉ Jl. Kuta, ☎ 0361/752355). **The Soda Club** (✉ Jl. Double Six 7A, Legian, ☎ 0812/380–8846) has a free buffet on Friday 9–11 PM; the DJ-spun music rocks until 2.

The Arts

Although this area doesn't provide northern Ubud's genuine cultural performances, there are still numerous traditional dances and performances held here. The most accessible—and the most toned down—are at the larger hotels; many schedule special Balinese dance nights combined with an Indonesian buffet. Bali's short annual calendar creates year-round holidays and temple ceremonies, and foreigners are welcome to attend most celebrations.

CULTURAL PERFORMANCES

The **Jayakarta Hotel & Residence** (✉ Jl. Pura Bagus Taruna, ☎ 0361/751433) has a barbecue and a Balinese *Ramayana* cultural show on Wednesday, as well as an Indonesian rijsttafel night with a Legong dance on Friday; the respective costs are Rp 80,000 and Rp 75,000. The **Kuta Centre** (✉ Jl. Kartika Plaza, Tuban, ☎ 0361/756611) schedules free Balinese dance performances every Tuesday and Saturday 7–9 PM. The **Legian Beach Hotel** (✉ Jl. Melasti, Legian, ☎ 0361/751711) has occasional Legong dance performances, combined with a barbecue buffet, for Rp 143,360. The **Mentari Grill** (✉ Jl. Pantai 1, Kuta, ☎ 0361/751361) at the Natour Bali schedules the occasional "Nusantara Night," with Legong dances and an Indonesian buffet, for Rp 107,520.

Outdoor Activities and Sports

The spectacular new 18-hole, par-72 course at the **Le Meridien Nirwana Golf & Spa Resort** (✉ Jl. Kediri Tanah Lot (Box 198), Tanah Lot 82171, ☎ 0361/815900) has challenging greens set along the rugged west-coast cliffs.

Shopping

Along the main road you'll find hundreds of shops crammed with high-quality, inexpensive textiles, clothing, carvings, household goods, kites, chimes, and kitschy souvenirs—pretty much the same from store to store—in one open-air strip mall. Note that many of Seminyak's and Legian's newer clothing boutiques now have fixed prices marked—look for signs stating this, or ask the salesperson before you start bargaining. Credit cards are usually accepted at mall stores and newer boutiques in resort areas, but small shops generally only take cash. Note that in the listings, cities are only added when the shop address is off the main strip.

ANTIQUES AND SECONDHAND ITEMS

You can find antique wood items and architectural pieces at **Tata Kayu** (✉ Jl. Laksmana 38, Kerobokan, ☎ 0361/735072). One of the best selections of antiques in the area is at **Warisan** (✉ Jl. Kerobokan 68, ☎ 0361/733057).

HANDICRAFTS

Busana Indah (✉ Jl. Legian Kaja 502, ☎ 0361/751185) has a vast selection of cloth and batik. Next door at **Gunatama Textile** (✉ Jl. Legian Kaja 504, ☎ 0361/730996) are wonderful textiles, including a warehouse full of bolts of colorfully patterned Indonesian materials. Wonderful baskets and crocheted bags are woven on-site at **Isma'il Shop** (✉ Jl. Dhyana Pura 3, Seminyak, ☎ 0361/732737). **Mila Shop** (✉ Jl. Seminyak, ☎ 0361/733462) sells beautiful floral-pattern, hand-painted batik sheets, sheer fabrics, and sarongs.

OXXO (✉ Jl. Legian Kaja 501, ☎ 0361/730787) carries wayang puppets and other beautiful Indonesian treasures. Don't miss the excellent selection of wooden, hand-painted wayang golek puppets at **Rumah Wayang** (✉ Jl. Kartika Plaza 9X, Kuta, ☎ 0361/751650).

Handwoven baskets and crocheted items are the specialty of **You'N'Me** (✉ Jl. Pantai Kuta, ☎ 0361/758698).

JEWELRY

The showroom and workshop at **Mario Silver** (✉ Jl. Seminyak, ☎ 0361/730977) carries an extensive selection of jewelry and silver items; if you're staying in the area, pick-up service is available. **Ratu Silver** (✉ Jl. Legian 372, ☎ 0361/756632) sells a range of silver pieces.

WOMEN'S CLOTHING

Boko-Boko (✉ Jl. Seminyak, ☎ 0361/735386) offers a selection of women's dress and casual outfits. The wonderful, three-story **Dynasty** (✉ Jl. Legian, ☎ 0361/751844) sells beautiful, classy women's clothes and dresses. **Hana Hou** (✉ Jl. Seminyak 19, ☎ 0361/732768) has an eclectic dress selection. Beautiful satin party dresses and sequin bags are made at **Covex's Shop** (✉ Poppies La. I, Kuta, ☎ 0361/765678); items can be made to order in a few days. Try **Lucia** (✉ Jl. Pantai Kuta 24A, ☎ 0361/754462) for formal dresses and Chinese-style silks. **Studio Animale** (✉ Jl. Pantai Kuta, D1A 1–3, ☎ 0361/753830) has an extensive selection of women's casual wear and dress outfits. For delicate shell purses and other accessories, contact the excellent **joe-joe** (✉ Jl. Seminyak, ☎ 081/6581230).

Sanur

④ *12 km (7 mi) northeast of Kuta, 15 km (9 mi) northeast of Ngurah Rai Airport, 9 km (6 mi) southeast of Denpasar.*

Sanur was Bali's second beach resort, and today it's a good mix of Kuta and Nusa Dua: the former's energy without the frenzy, and the latter's class without the high prices. Hotels, restaurants, and shops are spread out, helping to keep the pace slow. The wide beach, which is framed by a shallow coral reef, is calm—perfect for snorkeling, boating, and windsurfing.

Dining and Lodging

$$$ ✕ **Jazz Bar & Grille.** This classy, two-story restaurant and club has intimate half-circle booths in front of a corner stage, where jazz bands create a soothing, sexy atmosphere nightly. Small round tables fill the space between the booths and the bar, and a curving staircase leads up to a more casual club with pool tables. The cuisine is international and homemade, with a full range of salads, sandwiches, and pastas from which to choose. Try the crispy coconut-batter prawns; the mini-calzones that ooze with mozzarella, olives, and ham; or the juicy grilled snapper marinated in lime juice. Or, just stop in for drinks and desserts. ✉ *Jl. Bypass, Sanur Raya 15–16,* ☎ *0361/285892. AE, DC, MC, V.*

$$–$$$ ✕ **Telaga Naga.** Set back off the main road in estate gardens, this beautiful restaurant surrounded by lotus ponds serves exquisite Cantonese and Szechuan cuisine. Dark-teak beams; small, close tables; and candlelight add romance to the bustling atmosphere as waiters rush between smartly dressed diners. The food is terrific and the portions are enormous—order the "small" size unless you're very hungry. Recommendations include sautéed chicken with dried red chili or the fried prawns with Szechuan sauce, both house specialties. ✉ *Jl. Danau Tamblingan,* ☎ *0361/288–1234. Reservations essential. No lunch. AE, DC, MC, V.*

$$ ✕ **Kafe Wayang.** Snuggled right up to the Jazz Bar & Grille (☞ *above*), this cozy little restaurant offers a quieter alternative. Close-set tables, Indonesian music, and the dual wayang kulit puppet emblem set an intimate scene. The menu is a fusion of Eastern and Western selections: toned-down rice and noodle dishes mixed with spiced-up salads, sandwiches, and grills. Note: You can call for free transport if you're staying in Sanur. ✉ *Jl. Bypass, Sanur Raya 12–14,* ☎ *0361/287591. AE, DC, MC, V.*

$$ ✕ **Spago.** Classy casual is the mood for this spacious art house set in a wide pavilion along Sanur's main road. This is one of the area's trendy hangouts, complete with a front bar, cozy sitting area, and a gallery of works by local artists. The cuisine is a mix of Western and Indonesian, with such tasty results as rosemary spring chicken on couscous, pumpkin gnocchi with garlic sauce and crispy bacon, and pepper-crushed tuna with papaya-mint salsa. Desserts—frozen cappuccino, lemon cheesecake—are petite. Wandering musicians strum jazz tunes most nights. ✉ *Jl. Tamblingan 79,* ☎ *0361/288335. AE, DC, MC, V.*

$$$–$$$$ ⊞ **Bali Hyatt.** For a hotel that's part of a large international chain, this has a surprisingly Balinese feel. Gardens cover the expansive grounds to the 6-km-long (4-mi-long) beach esplanade, where colorful *jukung* fishing boats depart each morning. Rooms are in four-story buildings, and though they're slightly worn, each has an island-style decor and a balcony. The most unusual feature is the green-tile pool with a waterfall replica of the entrance to the Goa Gajah (Elephant Cave). The hotel is within walking distance of local markets, shops, and restaurants. ✉ *Jl. Danau Tamblingan (Box 392, Denpasar 80001),* ☎ *0361/ 281234,* 𝔽𝔸𝕏 *0361/287693. 390 rooms. 5 restaurants, 4 bars, in-room safes, minibars, 2 pools, spa, 3-hole golf course, 2 tennis courts, jogging, beach, snorkeling, windsurfing, boating, children's programs, meeting rooms, car rental. AE, DC, MC, V.* ✍

$$$–$$$$ ⊞ **The Sanctuary.** Although its size is grand, this white, three-story mansion is actually a casual, fun place. The sunny living room, with wicker furniture and a polished-wood ceiling, has shelves filled with magazines, novels, games, and CDs. One bedroom is off the living room and another is next to the dining room; both have marble floors, en suite bathrooms with sunken tubs, and separate garden entrances. The second floor has another living room, a wraparound garden terrace, and a bedroom with a private deck and en suite bathroom. The third floor is a lookout and party pavilion, complete with a kitchen and bar, a pool table, and a telescope. A keyhole-shape pool is the highlight of the well-trimmed grounds, and a business office with 21st-century technology and meeting rooms is off to the right. Behind this is a separate guest villa with its own kitchen, dining pavilion, and plunge pool. Oriental rugs, Cambodian watercolors, and stone rubbings from Angkor Wat give the property a pan-Asian feel. A fitness center and tennis court were under construction at press time, and you can borrow the owner's golf clubs for a jaunt to one of three nearby courses. Laundry and a car and driver are included. ✉ *Bookings: Indovillas,* ☎ *0818/353748,* 𝔽𝔸𝕏 *0361/733031. 3 rooms, 1 villa. Dining room, 2 pools, kitchenettes, golf privileges, billiards, business services, meeting rooms, car rental. AE, DC, MC, V. www.indovillas.com.*

$–$$ ⊞ **Tamukami.** This little hotel combines the best of Bali's classic artistic styles with modern comforts. Buildings surround a beautiful yellow terrazzo deck and freeform pool with a waterfall tumbling down to a shallower children's section. Standard rooms, upstairs in the main building, have white walls, pretty batik floral curtains, dark-wood trim, blue ikat bedspreads, and are furnished with dark, carved antiques; the ground-floor superior rooms around the pool have the same decor but with inner sitting areas and porches, and studios add minibars and TVs.

Bungalows have dark, rich furnishings—in-room computers were on order at press time. A large conference room behind the lobby makes this an ideal base for small business groups. The colorful, cozy Alise Restaurant serves breakfast, mixed grills, and Western cuisine. ✉ *Jl. Tamblingan 64X,* ☎ *0361/282510,* ℻ *0361/282520. 12 rooms, 7 suites. Restaurant, bar, minibars, pool, business services, meeting rooms. AE, DC, MC, V.* ✥

Nightlife and the Arts

Bucu Warung (✉ Jl. Danau Toba 2, ☎ 0361/288462) schedules a mix of live Latin, rock, funk, and dance bands on weekends. **Jazz Bar & Grille** (☞ *above*) hosts live jazz and blues bands on weekends and often schedules live performances during the week—call for updates, and be sure to make reservations. Saturday is "Ladies Night," when ladies receive 50% off all food and drinks after 10 PM, and the "Sunday Jazz Jam" is also popular. **Kafe Wayang** (☞ *above*) also features mixed live music throughout the week, as well as a jam session on Friday nights; reserve a seat for these performances. **Mango Cafe** (✉ Jl. Danau Toba 15, ☎ 0361/288411) has live bands on Monday and Balinese children's Legong dances on Wednesday and Friday. **Spago** (☞ *above*), the classiest watering spot on the main drag, has wandering jazz musicians and live bands throughout the week.

Outdoor Activities and Sports

BOATING

You can hire the **Bali Hai** (☎ 0361/720331) for a luxurious excursion around the island as well as for dive and surf trips. For yacht charters, contact **Jet Boat Tours** (✉ Jl. Pantai Karang 5, ☎ 0361/28839).

SCUBA DIVING AND SURFING

Nusa Lembongan, the island opposite Sanur Beach and next to Nusa Penida, has surfing and diving opportunities. Both dive shops listed below rent boards and arrange transportation; you can also rent boards at the beaches, but they tend to be of lesser quality, and you'll be responsible for any damage done to them.

You can rent scuba equipment and get a ride out to the reef at Sanur from **Bali Marine Sport** (✉ Jl. Bypass Ngurah Rai, ☎ 0361/87872). **Ocean Dive Center** (✉ Jl. Bypass Ngurah Rai, ☎ 0361/88652) organizes reef dives.

Shopping

There are interesting shops along Jalan Bypass and Jalan Danau Tamblingan. Look for handwoven fabrics, jewelry, ceramics, baskets, and kites. The **Sanur Beach Market** is worth a browse for handcrafted souvenirs, but the **Sanur Art Market** is the best place for such shopping. **Bagus Drugstore,** on Jalan Duyung next to the Bali Hyatt, and **Alas Arum,** on Jalan Danau Tamblingan, sell groceries and have small bookshops (with English-language titles) and souvenir areas.

ANTIQUES AND SECONDHAND ITEMS

Miralin Collection (✉ Jl. Danau Tamblingan 136, ☎ 0361/286061) has an excellent selection of antique furniture, wood carvings, and wall hangings; contemporary pieces can be made to order. **Ayu Shop** (✉ Jl. Danau Tamblingan 138, ☎ no phone) has a similar selection.

CLOTHING

For women, **Animale** (✉ Jl. Danau Tamblingan 138, ☎ 0361/282646) has classy, contemporary dresses. Sanur also boasts the head office for **Mama & Leon** (✉ Jl. Danau Tamblingan 99A, ☎ 0361/288044), which carries beautiful pastel dresses and outfits for women and girls; you can also make your own beaded bracelets and choose special buttons at the front table. **Naga-Naga** (✉ Jl. Danau Tamblingan 56, ☎ 0361/286303) carries men's and women's clothing, all in a black-and-white theme. **Tigresse** (✉ Jl. Danau Tamblingan 71, ☎ 0361/270005) is a women's dress shop with pretty floral and cotton outfits.

GIFTS AND SOUVENIRS

Handwoven pillowcases, wall hangings, place mats, shawls, and older Balinese handicrafts can be found at **Bali Odina** (✉ Jl. Danau Tamblingan 60, ☎ 0361/286809). **Bé** (✉ Jl. Danau Tamblingan 80, ☎ 0361/284076) carries a variety of handmade gifts, such as paper products, notebooks, candleholders, and picture frames. **Gambir Art Market 2** (✉ Jl. Danau Tamblingan 50, ☎ 0361/288779) is a huge indoor shop that carries every type of souvenir: batik sarongs and clothing, woven baskets, wood carvings, metal items, and tourist kitsch—the walls are covered with Balinese paintings, and there's even a jewelry shop up front. If it's kites you want, try **Panca Sari Shop Kite Centre** (✉ Jl. Danau Tamblingan 10, ☎ 0361/286050), where you can buy any of Sanur's beautiful animal or boat kites or have one made in a day. **Pesamuan Studio** (✉ Jl. Pungutan 25, Sanur, ☎ 0361/281442) has an excellent selection of ceramics, art pieces, and gift items.

HANDICRAFTS

There's no better place in Sanur for textiles than **Nogo Bali Ikat Centre** (✉ Jl. Danau Tamblingan 98, ☎ 0361/288765), a large shop with hundreds of ready-made textiles and bolts of cloth; clothes and other items can be made to order as well. This is also a great place to learn about Balinese ikat weaving in general—look for the daily loom demonstration in front of the shop. **Sari Bumi** (✉ Jl. Danau Tamblingan 152, ☎ 0361/284101) in the Café Batujimbar has striking displays of pottery and other ceramics.

JEWELRY

Ispaknur Collection (✉ Jl. Danau Tamblingan 95, ☎ no phone) has lovely beaded jewelry, as well as many pretty seashells. A branch of the smart **Suarti** (✉ Jl. Danau Tamblingan 69, ☎ 0361/289092) silver jewelry shops highlights the beautiful handicrafts of Bali.

Denpasar

❺ *9 km (6 mi) northwest of Sanur, 16 km (10 mi) northeast of Ngurah Rai Airport.*

Most people don't stay overnight in this busy market town of about 400,000 people, but the island's capital is worth a day trip to visit its museums, markets, and monuments. You can book city tours through your resort, or you can see Denpasar on your own, by taxi or bemo.

Where Jalan Gajahmada intersects with Jalan Veteran is a large **statue of Brahma.** Its four faces look in the cardinal directions. To the left of the Brahma statue is the **Natour Bali Hotel** (✉ Jl. Veteran 3, ☎ 0361/225681), in a building dating from the Dutch colonial period.

Continue through this intersection past Puputan Square—a park on the right-hand side, with its Sukarno-inspired heroic statue of the common man—to reach **Pura Agung Jagatnatha,** Bali's state temple. (Go right at the end of the park onto Jalan Letkol, and the entrance is on your left.) The temple's center stupa is surrounded by a moat and rises eight levels; at the top is a statue of Shiva with flames coming from his shoulders. The stupa is supported by the cosmic turtle (on whose back the real world symbolically sits, according to Balinese legend) and protected by a huge carved face with a red cloth tongue. Nagas entwine the base; around the bottom are relief carvings.

Farther down Jalan Letkol is the **Bali Museum,** with Balinese art dating from prehistoric to present times. The buildings are excellent examples of Balinese temple and palace architecture. ✉ *Jl. Letkol,* ☎ *0361/222680.* 🎫 *Admission.* ⊙ *Tues.–Thurs. and weekends 8–5, Fri. 8–3:30.*

Another Denpasar attraction is **Taman Wedhi Budaya Arts Center,** where year-round dance performances are held (don't miss the island's annual summer arts festival, held here from mid-June to mid-July). Changing exhibits of modern paintings, batik designs, and wood carvings are also on display. ✉ *Jl. Nusa Indah,* ☎ *0361/222776.* 🎫 *Admission.* ⊙ *Daily 10–4.*

OFF THE BEATEN PATH
TANAH LOT – This famous temple stands on a small rocky islet 15 km (9 mi) west of Denpasar (it's accessible via a small causeway except at high tide, when it turns into an island). Though people flock here at sunset for the postcardlike setting, the Balinese deeply revere this pagoda-style temple. It has the added mystery of snakes that secret themselves in the rock holes and are said to guard the spirits residing at Tanah Lot. Cross the causeway to the temple, then return to the shore to watch it become silhouetted against the burning sky as the sun goes down.

Dining and Lodging

$$$$ ✕🏨 **Hotel Tugu Bali.** This memorable hotel is 11 km (8 mi) west of the
★ city in a bucolic landscape of rolling hills and rice paddies along the edge of the Bali Sea. Ornately carved teak doors and window frames and the ancient Chinese temple represent Balinese and Indonesian history. You enter the lower level of each two-story guest villa by a boardwalk over a lotus pond; access to the upper floors is via an outdoor spiral staircase. Each villa also has a back terrace with a plunge pool. Inside, you'll find marble floors, huge canopy beds, and exquisite antiques. You can also stay in (or just tour) the Puri Le Meyeur, a bungalow and monument to Belgian artist A. J. Le Meyeur De Merpres, and the Pavilion, which commemorates artist Walter Spies and is modeled after his home at the palace in Yogyakarta, Java. Other on-site amenities include an art gallery, the Puputan Museum, and a traditional medicine and spice stall. Even if you don't stay here, pop in for a glass of ginger tea at the small Tugu Restaurant. A dinner of such Thai dishes as stir-fried chicken with cashews, grilled red snapper, or crab soup is also an option. Just save room for dessert. ✉ *Jl. Batu Bolong, Canggu,* ☎ *0361/731701,* 🅵🅰🆇 *0361/731704. 25 villas. 2 restaurants, bar, pool, spa, library, business services, meeting rooms. AE, MC, V.* 🍴

Shopping

Along the Badung River (near the bridge off Jalan Gajahmada) is the large, two-story **Pasar Badung,** the liveliest market in town. Packed with spice vendors and farmers selling vegetables, meats, and flowers, it's busiest in the early morning, though commerce continues around the clock. The women who volunteer as guides get commissions from any vendor their charges patronize; of course, the price of anything purchased is raised accordingly. If you're in Denpasar in the evening, head for the **Kumbasari Night Market** in the riverside parking lot of the multilevel Kumbasari shopping center, a gathering place for locals. The **Kereneng Night Market,** a local favorite, at the bus terminal on Jalan Kambodja, is where you can taste such Balinese specialties as roast pig, sate, and coconut vegetable salads.

Crafts Villages

From Denpasar north, a strand of crafts villages is laced together by slim, twisting roads that slip between mountain folds and fertile rice fields. In just a day, you can cover the main sights; with a little more time, you can explore off-the-beaten-path shops that often double as the artisans' homes. In any case, these crafts villages are among the highlights of any trip to Bali, and the quality, variety, and affordability of the items sold in them will make a venture to these towns memorable.

Batubulan

Batubulan is 19 km (12 mi) northeast of Denpasar on the main road to Ubud and is famous for the stone-carvers whose workshops and displays line the road. You'll see small, open factories where boys chip at the soft sandstone and sculptures are for sale out front. Wares range from the classic guardian figures that stand before Balinese temples and houses to smaller statues. Most workshops make small carvings that are easier to transport home.

At 9:30 each morning, **dance-dramas** are performed at each of the village's three theaters, along the main road (the same show is done at all three). Travel agencies in Ubud and many hotels can make arrangements. Admission is around Rp 20,000.

Tohpati

Balinese batik tends to be more colorful than that of Java, and the designs are often floral rather than geometric. A good source of hand-drawn batiks is **Popiler** (☏ 0361/36498) in the village of Tohpati, on the northern outskirts of Batubulan. If you pay cash instead of using a credit card, you increase your bargaining power by around 20% for the yard goods, paintings, garments, and household items here. Behind the shop, you can watch girls outlining the designs with wax.

En Route   Take the road north to Singapadu, which peels off the main Batubulan road, and you'll reach the excellent **Taman Burung** (Bali Bird Park). Designed with Balinese thatched roofs, the aviaries of this first-class, 4-acre park house birds from around the world, including such rare species native to Indonesia as the Bali starling and birds of paradise from Irian Jaya. A 160-seat restaurant makes a good stop for a snack. ✉ *Jl. Serma Lok Ngurah Gambir, Singapadu,* ☏ *0361/299352.* ☐ *Admission.* ⊙ *Daily 9–6.*

Celuk

Celuk, 2 km (1 mi) northeast of Batubulan, is a village of silversmiths, and the town's main road is jammed with small shops. In workshops behind the stores, you can watch boys working the silver and setting semiprecious stones. As a rule, the jewelry you find here is 90%–92% silver, the tableware 60%–70%. Filigree pieces with detailed, imaginative designs—ships, flowers, butterflies—are among the best items to buy, but don't visit in the morning, when all the tour buses stop here; come in the afternoon when prices return to reasonable levels. If you have time, you can custom order pieces. Remember that with patience and a smile you might drive the cost of a $125 bracelet down to $80. (Bargaining is the rule, especially where prices are in dollars.)

At least 30 shops line the main road and surrounding streets, although a severe sidewalk shortage can make browsing on foot potentially life-threatening. The goods vary little from store to store—rings, earrings, pins, and hair clips are perennial favorites—but some establishments display more merchandise.

Sukawati

Four kilometers (2 miles) northeast of Celuk, Sukawati is known for its specialized crafts, including kites, mobiles, wind chimes, temple umbrellas, woven baskets, and shadow puppets. Stalls lining the road also sell baskets, hats, and furniture. **Pasar Seni,** the crafts market on the east side of the main road, sells works by some of the island's most talented artisans, but lines of tour buses stop here mid-morning, so arrive early. If you bargain determinedly, you may find some of the best prices in Bali. A kilometer (½ mi) west, the village of Puaya is one of the best places to shop for wayang kulit puppets and wayang topeng wooden masks.

Batuan

Batuan, 2 km (1 mi) north of Sukawati, is a weaving village and a painting center, where the famous black-and-white style of Balinese painting originated. Small galleries line the main road, and the backstreets have signs pointing to artists' homes. Impromptu visits are welcome in both.

You can't miss the giant elephants outside the **Antique Furniture Warehouse** (☎ 0361/298269), on the right side of the main road, which sells both antiques and reproductions. The hand-cut, painted shadow puppets sold on Bali are usually new, but you can buy antique ones at the **Jati Art Gallery** (⌂ along the main road, ☎ no phone), which also sells paintings, old masks and temple ornaments, handwoven ikat, batiks, wood carvings, and new puppets. **Mario Antique** (☎ 0361/298541) is a huge, open factory on the left side of the main road, where you can watch dozens of workers hone various pieces of furniture.

Find time to visit the 10th-century **Pura Puseh Pura Desa** (Temple of Brahma), where the seldom-seen *gambuh*—the oldest known form of dance drama on Bali—takes place at every full moon. Once performed only for royal celebrations or temple festivals, these dances are the ultimate in classical Balinese style and have influenced numerous other dramas, including the wayang *wong,* in which humans perform the roles of the wayang kulit shadow puppets, and the *legong,* a court dance performed by young girls. The gambuh dance dramas are accompanied by a gamelan orchestra that features the long, resonant flutes that are unique to the area. ⌂ *Jl. Raya, Batuan.* ☎ *Rp 15,000.* ☉ *Daily sunrise to sunset except during ceremonies. Dance performances at 8 PM.*

Kemenuh

On the main road in Kemenuh, 3 km (2 mi) northeast of Batuan, the house of **Ida B. Marka** (☎ no phone), a famous wood-carver, is open to the public, providing a rare look inside a Balinese home. The showroom is in front, but there's no pressure to buy. Behind are a courtyard and a cluster of buildings that serve as the family complex. The centerpiece is the building used for weddings and other rites of passage; this is where the oldest family member sleeps. Other structures include the family temple, a granary, and a cooperative workshop where other villagers help to carve and polish.

Mas

There are some 4,000 wood-carvers on Bali, and most of them live in Mas, 5 km (3 mi) northwest of Kemenuh. Unique crafts found here include framed wooden carvings of Balinese rural scenes, intricately detailed wooden Hindu goddess statues, wooden chessboards, and carvings of creatures and characters. The village is also known for its mask making, samples of which can be found in shops down the back lanes. The brightly painted masks, most of which represent characters in Balinese folklore, make great wall hangings.

Bedulu

❻ *5 km (3 mi) northeast of Mas, 26 km (16 mi) northeast of Denpasar.*

This was once the capital of the last Balinese kingdom to stand against Java's conquering forces in the 14th century. Today Bedulu's main claim to fame is the **Goa Gajah** (Elephant Cave), 2 km (1 mi) to the right of the intersection of Jalan Mas and Jalan Pengosekan (the entrance is on the right through a parking lot lined with souvenir vendors). Discovered in 1923 by a farmer, this cave temple is thought to have been built in the 11th century. In the courtyard, water spouts from the hands of six stone nymphs into two pools. It's believed that worshipers purified themselves here before passing through the mouth of the giant face of Boma carved on the entrance.

The cave is pitch dark—hope that your guide has a flashlight. To the left is a niche with a statue of Ganesha, the elephant-headed god and son of Shiva. In the center, to the right of a crumbled statue, are three *linga* (upright carved stones symbolizing male fertility), each with three smaller *yoni* (female forms).

The **Pura Saman Tiga** temple is on the left side of the road several yards beyond the Bedulu junction. Legend has it that this 11th-century temple was the site where a group of holy men once met to establish religious-tolerance laws. A little farther beyond the Bedulu junction is the **Bedulu Archaeological Museum** (☎ no phone), which houses numerous early Balinese artifacts, including pottery and sarcophagi. The museum is open Monday–Thursday 8–2 and Friday–Saturday 8–1.

Ubud

❼ *5 km (3 mi) northwest of Bedulu, 25 km (15 mi) northeast of Denpasar.*

Ubud gained fame as an art colony in the 1930s and has since grown into one of the island's main tourist and cultural centers, with galleries, crafts shops, and traditional Balinese dance troupes. Still, you can find quiet places in which to immerse yourself in Balinese culture, and the town offers many more opportunities to experience authentic Balinese life than do the coastal resort areas. It's also an excellent base from which to explore Bali's interior. Step out of town and walk the many trails that lead through the countryside to small temples and villages, and you'll find the "real Bali."

★ Ubud was placed on the world map when artists Walter Spies and Rudolf Bonnet introduced the Balinese to the three-dimensional form and convinced them that using real people, not courtly officials, in a free-flowing background was legitimate art. Exhibits at the **Puri Lukisan Museum,** set in gardens at the west end of the main street, show this art style's evolution from the 1930s to the present. Works are arranged chronologically, so you can see the transition from formal religious art to more natural, realistic depictions. ✉ *Jl. Raya (west of intersection with Monkey Forest Rd.),* ☎ *0361/975136.* ✆ *Admission.* ⊘ *Daily 8–4.*

For an overview of Balinese and Indonesian art styles, visit Ubud's finest painting collection at the **Neka Gallery,** at the east end of the main street. The works are organized by style in seven buildings, one of which has paintings by foreign artists, including Spies and Bonnet. Be sure to visit Building 6, devoted to works by Affandi, an Indonesian artist of international renown. Building 4 houses works by I Gusti Nyoman Lempadi, who is recognized as one of the first true Bali artists. ✉ *Jl. Raya,* ☎ *0361/975074.* ✆ *Admission.* ⊘ *Daily 9–4.*

★ The **Agung Rai Museum of Art (ARMA)** in Pengosekan, a small community just southeast of Ubud, is a cultural complex focused on a panorama of Balinese arts. The galleries exhibit prominent Indonesian and European artists' works, and a library and bookshop are also on-

Ubud and Vicinity

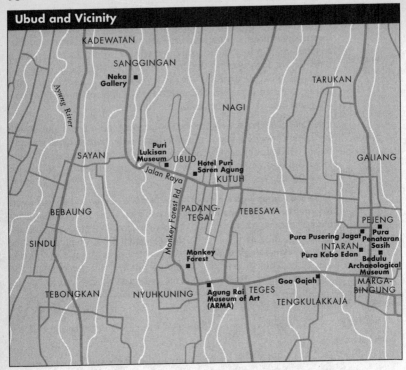

site. The museum offers dance, art, and music classes, and arts performances take place throughout the week. ⊠ *Jl. Pengosekan,* ☎ *0361/976659.* ⊠ *Admission.* ⊘ *Daily 9–6.*

In the center of Ubud is the beautiful **Hotel Puri Saren Agung,** which was once part of Ubud's royal palace. The structure was rebuilt after it was decimated by a 1917 earthquake; the current prince's living quarters are at the courtyard's end. Stop by for a look at the fine antiquities or to listen to the gamelan music that's played here nightly.

Across from Puri Saren is Monkey Forest Road, which has many souvenir and T-shirt shops and inexpensive restaurants. Farther along are small hotels and losmen, where you can find simple and very affordable accommodations. Keep walking and you'll reach the **Monkey Forest,** where a small donation gets you a close-up view of monkeys.

OFF THE BEATEN PATH — **TEGALALUNG** – The roads north out of Ubud pass through lovely countryside with patchwork rice fields in different stages of cultivation. Men ankle-deep in mud plant and weed while ducks paddle and dip for their lunch. Out in the fields stand shrines to Dewi Sri, the rice goddess, and raised wooden platforms where farmers rest or eat. In the village of Tegalalung, artisans carve intricate designs into wooden panels. You don't have to buy anything; just watch and marvel at the incredible craftsmanship.

Dining and Lodging

$$–$$$ ✕ **Ary's Warung.** This Ubud classic, set on the main road's busiest spot, combines a cozy front terrace with a larger adjacent bar and second-floor dining pavilion. Don't expect *warung* food though; the limited menu now includes only trendy, upscale fare with prices to match. Still, the restaurant itself has an international feel that turns romantic by evening candlelight. ⊠ *Jl. Raya,* ☎ *0361/975053. AE, MC, V.*

$$–$$$ ✕ **Indus.** Set along the high cliffs above the Ayung River, this two-story,
★ museum-size restaurant offers vast forest and rice-terrace panoramas
from every table. Stone steps between fountains lead to the marble-
floor first level, where another staircase climbs to a breezy upper-level
terrace. The cuisine is eclectic, filling, and healthy: Balinese paella
with fragrant yellow rice; char-grilled beef with mushroom gravy;
sweet-potato soup with fresh coconut milk; and Chinese greens with
tofu and mushrooms served on red rice. Desserts are far more sinful—
chunky banana chocolate cake, thick tiramisu, and light, creamy lime
tarts. If you don't want a full meal, just snuggle into one of the antique couches in the sitting area and order a pot of jasmine tea and a
treat from the bakery case. ✉ *Jl. Sanggingan,* ☎ *0361/977684. AE,
DC, MC, V.*

$$–$$$ ✕ **Terazo.** This local favorite is upbeat and upscale, with bright, mango-
color walls and works by leading local painters and sculptors. A back
terrace overlooks the first level, as well as the central, curving, green
terrazzo bar for which the restaurant was named. Italian cuisine is the
specialty, including a superb selection of pastas, but choices dabble into
Indonesian and international fare as well. Try the thick, smoky black-
bean soup; the tangy gazpacho; the spicy Thai beef stir fry; or the fresh-
grilled tuna. Fabulous desserts include a chilled lemon mousse and moist,
toasted walnut cake. ✉ *Jl. Suweta,* ☎ *no phone. AE, DC, MC, V.*

$$ ✕ **Bebek Bengil.** The "Dirty Duck" is a famous Ubud dining spot, an
elegant, pavilion-style restaurant settled into a rice-field backdrop.
This is the classiest place in town to try Balinese fare—the special, of
course, is bebek betutu—or, you can sample eclectic international
choices. Save room for a slice of strawberry cake, pungent Black Rus-
sian pie, or warm apple crisp. ✉ *Jl. Hanoman,* ☎ *0361/976645. AE,
DC, MC, V.*

$$ ✕ **Café Lotus.** In the center of Ubud, this large, busy restaurant has tables in a royal temple's courtyard gardens. Small waterfalls set the scene
against a magnificent lotus pond backdrop. Standard Western and Indonesian dishes—roast chicken, pasta, fried rice—are bland, but portions are sizeable. If you're just stopping in for a drink, sit on floor
cushions in the long, raised pavilion in back. ✉ *Jl. Raya,* ☎ *0361/
975660. AE, MC, V. Closed Mon.*

$$ ✕ **Jazz Café.** This cozy, classy café entertains an eclectic crowd with
live jazz and exquisite cuisine. Tasty selections include thick cream of
carrot soup, colorful pasta primavera, and spicy Thai curry. The
desserts are an added reason to linger: try the lemon crumble cake, or
the thick, chocolate fudge nut brownie. A raised area in back and two
garden pavilions offer more private, comfortable seating, with big, low
square tables and black ikat floor cushions. ✉ *Jl. Sukma 2, Tebesaya,*
☎ *0361/976594. AE, MC, V.*

$$ ✕ **Kokokan Club.** Tucked into folds of curving rice terraces in the Oos
River valley, the two-story, thatched-roof pavilion offers memorable
views and terrific Thai cuisine. Steamed spring rolls are fresh, coated
in thick, spicy peanut sauce; salads are crisp and zesty; and the thick
curries are flavorful. Even the standard *phad thai* (fried noodles) are
top-notch. Round tables, candlelight, and river breezes make this a popular dinner place, but the views are best in the late afternoon. ✉ *Jl.
Pengosekan,* ☎ *0361/96495. AE, MC, V.*

$$ ✕ **Murni's Warung.** This multilevel restaurant overlooking the forested
Ayung River valley is one of Ubud's original travelers' haunts. The rus-
tic, street-level dining room bustles with activity; reserve a table along
the river's edge for the best views. The Singapore-style bar below, with
comfortable wicker couches and Indonesian antiques, is the place to
sip tony cocktails to the river's sounds. The menu combines Indone-
sian and Western items, including pasta, curries, seafood, and sand-

wiches. Although the food is fair at best, portions are large. ⊠ *Jl. Raya,* ☎ *0361/975233. AE, MC, V.*

$–$$ ✕ **Bumbu Bali.** Along one of Ubud's busiest corners, this modest-look-
★   ing thatch-roof restaurant has made its mark by offering excellent Indian and Indonesian cuisine. As you enter, you'll hear romantic gamelan
music and the sound of trickling fountains. The open, candlelighted
dining room is a place to escape the rain; for more intimacy, sit in one
of the small garden pavilions around the green lotus pond. The menu
offers a variety of tasty and filling selections: try an Indian *thali* or one
of the Balinese meals, complete with a cone of fragrant yellow rice, served
on a traditional *wanci* ceremonial tray. If there's no room for dessert,
come back tomorrow for cardamom coffee cake, cool piña colada pineapple cake, or chocolate caramel pecan pie. ⊠ *Jl. Suweta,* ☎ *0361/
974217. AE, DC, MC, V.*

$ ✕ **Tutmak.** This cute travelers' favorite has expanded from a tiny cof-
fee shop into a full-blown deli-restaurant that gets everything right. Tables are staggered on wide steps up from street level to create a
comfortable, casual but chic bookstore atmosphere. Huge sandwiches
come with chips or beautiful organic salads. Vegetarian choices include
fabulous lasagnas, Middle Eastern plates, and Indian coconut fried rice
with almonds, peanuts, spinach, and spices. Save room for fantastic
desserts: mango or lime mousse, Scottish shortbread cake, and chocolate cake garnished with prunes and marinated with marsala. There
are also baked goodies in big jars: huge cinnamon muffins, thick
brownies, and admirable chocolate chip cookies—perfect accompaniments if you're just here for coffee. ⊠ *Jl. Dewi Sita,* ☎ *0361/975754.
No credit cards.*

$$$$ ✕⊞ **Amandari.** The traditional architecture and layout of this beau-
★   tiful gathering of luxury villas elegantly reflects local culture and customs. Walk along stone paths, past lotus ponds and tall, curving walls
to reach high, thatched-roof bungalows, most of which overlook the
forested Ayung River valley. The light-filled suites have marble floors,
heavy cream upholstery, dark-teak accents, and enormous bathrooms
with outdoor sunken tubs; six villas have private plunge pools, and a
sumptuous duplex with a spiral staircase is also available. The open-
air lobby leads back to a comfortable library, and the restaurant (one
of the island's most romantic dining spots) opposite stands above a dramatic pool with an infinity edge over the river. This resort is the ultimate in Balinese elegance, and it consistently tops the *Condé Nast
Traveler* magazine's annual international Gold List of small hotels. ⊠
Desa Kedewatan (Box 33), 80571, ☎ *0361/975333, 800/447–7462,
212/223–2848 in the U.S., or 0800/282684 in the U.K.,* 𝖥𝖠𝖷 *0361/975335.
30 suites. Restaurant, bar, pool, spa, tennis court, health club, hiking,
bicycles, library. AE, DC, MC, V.*

$$$$ ✕⊞ **Villa Pasti Indah.** At twilight, this small complex in the Payangan
hills looms like a dark castle nestled into a cleft between high rice-paddy
terraces. A brown river curves around the base of the property, which
is staggered up the sides of a steep hill. Stone steps lead up to the thatched-
roof, Japanese-style villas, which are surrounded by crushed limestone
walls and low bamboo fences for privacy. The interiors are magnani-
mous, with marble floors, stone walls, stepped-down sitting areas, VCRs
and DVD players, and two king-size beds each. Cavernous marble bathrooms have garden showers and Jacuzzi tubs. The lower villa has a
stone-inlaid plunge pool, a little yard, and a large, blossom-covered
tree house overlooking the busy road; the upper villa's plunge pool has
an infinity edge with a lush rice-paddy view. There's a kitchen on-site,
but the small restaurant offers basic—albeit expensive—Indonesian and
Western fare. Service at both the hotel and restaurant is Japanese-trained
and meticulously professional. Breakfast, laundry, and car hire are in-

cluded. ⊠ *Bookings: Indovillas,* ☎ *0818/353748,* FAX *0361/733031. 2 villas. Restaurant, in-room VCRs, refrigerators, 2 pools, shop, car rental. AE, DC, MC, V.*

$$$$ 🏨 **Four Seasons Resort at Sayan.** The journey to this 17-acre property begins with a walk along a wooden bridge above rice-terraced mountain slopes and the Ayung River. The path ends at a large elliptical lotus pond on the roof of the central three-story structure. A polished wood staircase descends to the reception area and a lounge and bar with a spectacular 180-degree vista. Two-story suites are in the main building; villas are set into the hillside all the way down to the riverbank. Rooms are accented with rich teak and stone and have custom-made furnishings and tapestries from Bali and Java. There's also a health club and, on a curving terrace, two sunken whirlpools that seem to hang out over the valley. ⊠ *Desa Sayan, 80571,* ☎ *0361/977577,* FAX *0361/ 977588. 18 suites, 28 villas. 2 restaurants, bar, pool, hot tubs, spa, health club, shops, library, meeting rooms. AE, DC, MC, V.*

$$–$$$$ 🏨 **Pita Maha.** A member of Ubud's royal family modeled the Pita Maha after a Balinese village and built it on the Oos River valley's edge. The villas' architecture is traditional, the interior touches tastefully luxurious: marble floors, ornate window panels, wicker furniture, woven mats. Tall, sliding glass panels open to private terraces; most villas also have plunge pools. Bathrooms have curving sunken tubs, decorative stone walls, and open gardens. The restaurant and large, infinity-edge pool look onto the river valley. Staying here also provides privileged access to local museums, temples, tours, and activities, compliments of the royal host. ⊠ *Jl. Sanggingan (Box 198),* ☎ *0361/974330,* FAX *0361/974329. 29 villas. Restaurant, 2 bars, in-room safes, pool, spa, shop, library. AE, MC, V.*

$$–$$$$ 🏨 **Villa Tugu.** Unusual combinations of light, angles, and color make this local artist's home intriguingly beautiful. A freeform, infinity-edge saltwater pool is the central focal point between the main three-bedroom home, the open dining pavilion, and the two-bedroom guest villa. Square stepping stones through lotus ponds lead between buildings, including a colorful modern kitchen painted in muted pastels. Awash in gold light, the main house follows suit and includes a large living area, three sizeable bedrooms, and a two-story artist studio. The villa has a Japanese-style bedroom and living area with sliding *shoji* screens, as well as a second bedroom with a canopy bed; both have marble bathrooms with huge sunken tubs. A bridge connects the second-floor office to a viewing tower that offers stunning rice paddy views. ⊠ *Bookings: Indovillas,* ☎ *0818/353748,* FAX *0361/733031. 5 rooms. Dining room, pool, car rental. AE, DC, MC, V.* ✍

$$–$$$ 🏨 **Kokokan Hotel.** Scattered in the hills above the sacred Tirta Tawar River, the stone-and-brick buildings of this charming hotel reflect their magic setting's aura. Rooms have marble floors, terraces, huge shower-only bathrooms, and ornate, hand-carved wooden doors and window panels. Balinese textiles and paintings accent the warm wood. Deluxe rooms have carved sandstone walls and sliding door panels that separate the large bedroom area from the bath. Room rates include a full breakfast; you can also dine in the poolside café or at the nearby Kokokan Club (☞ *above*). The on-site museum offers workshops that teach Balinese art forms such as gamelan playing, puppet and mask making, weaving, and dance. ⊠ *Jl. Pengosekan, 80571,* ☎ *0361/ 975742,* FAX *0361/975332. 15 rooms. Restaurant, café, pool, children's programs. AE, MC, V.*

$ 🏨 **Ananda Cottages.** This quiet hotel set amid Campuan's rice paddies is surrounded by beautiful gardens flowing with red and lavender hibiscus blossoms. Contemporary-style rooms are in the front building; these are large and light, all with a porch. Across the lush fields, brick, thatched-roof bungalows each have eight rooms, all with ornamental doors and windows, marble floors, antique furnishings, and ikat bedspreads. The top-floor superiors are cozy, romantically tucked under the eaves, all with air-conditioning, refrigerators, phones, and wonderful views. First-floor standards have porches and pretty garden bathrooms with tubs; some have air-conditioning, and you can request a refrigerator. ⊠ *Jl. Campuhan (Box 205, Denpasar 80364),* ☎ *0361/975376,* FAX *0361/975375. 57 rooms, 1 suite. Restaurant, bar, air-conditioning (some), refrigerators, pool. AE, DC, MC, V.*

¢ 🏠 **Honeymoon Guesthouse.** This romantic, wood-shuttered, colonial
★ Singapore-style mansion and adjacent guest quarters are indeed the perfect place for a honeymoon. Far down a back alley in Penestanan, the quiet grounds are also home to the famous cooking school (☞ *see* Classes *in* The Arts, *below*) touted by the town's well-known Café Luna and Indus restaurants. Fan-cooled standards are cozy and clean, all with bathtubs, and shelves of used books between the rooms. The best deals are for the deluxes, which feature carved teak beds and dressers, marble baths with sunken corner tubs, antique mirrors, and ornamental window frames; true romantics should take a room tucked under the thatched eaves. There are pretty touches everywhere: curving stone walkways, flowered teacups, and decorative door and window trim. The price includes a breakfast of fresh-baked croissants and other goodies from the Honeymoon Bakery across the alley. ⊠ *Jl. Bisma,* ☎ FAX *0361/973282. 12 rooms. Pool. AE, DC, MC, V.*

Nightlife and the Arts

Ubud no longer shuts down early—on weekends and in the tourist seasons, when the dance performances finish around 9 or 9:30, many cafés and restaurants are just starting to warm up. **Ary's Warung** (☞ *above*), in the heart of Ubud, is the upscale, jazzy, candlelighted gathering place for the town's beautiful people. Although the **Beggar's Bush** pub (⊠ Jl. Campuhan, ☎ 0361/975009), one of Ubud's original expatriate hangouts, was undergoing renovations at press time, the top-floor bar was still open, and it's always a good place to kick back with fellow travelers. The **Do Drop Inn** (⊠ Jl. Wanara Wana, ☎ 0361/975309), next to the football field, is a lively place to watch the games—and you can celebrate with the rowdy winners afterward.

The **Funky Monkey** café (⊠ Jl. Wanara Wana, ☎ 0812/3903729) has DJ theme parties Monday through Saturday from 9 PM to 1 AM; music might be anything from funk and worldfest to hip-hop, rhythm and blues, or acid jazz, depending on the night. Terrific live jazz by local musicians is the highlight at the classy new **Jazz Cafe** (☞ *above*). The **Kokokan Club** (⊠ Jl. Pengosekan, ☎ 0361/96495) in Pengosekan has live music on Saturday. **Nyoman's** (⊠ Jl. Ubud 33, ☎ 0361/977169) on the main strip attracts a crowd after everything else has shut down. **Sai Sai** (⊠ Jl. Wanara Wana, ☎ no phone) has weekly live rock music and the occasional gamelan; call or check the outdoor blackboard for a schedule. The new **Terazo** (☞ *see* Dining, *above*) is another of Ubud's classy haunts where the slender and stylish linger after dinner.

Ubud is the dance center of Bali, and you should see more than one of the varied performances during your visit—not a problem, as at least three troupes perform nightly. Dance shows at hotels are often commercially adapted and shortened; those held elsewhere around Ubud are more genuine.

Consult your hotel or the *Bali Tourist Guide* and the *Bali Guide to Events,* available free at most hotels and travel agencies, for current schedules. **Ubud Tourist Information** (☞ Visitor Information *in* Bali A to Z, *below*) has a weekly dance-performance schedule and sells tickets (Rp 5,000–Rp 7,000) that include transportation to shows not held in Ubud proper.

CLASSES

If you'd like to learn Balinese cooking, join in the classes held by the staff at the **Bumbu Restaurant** (✉ Jl. Suweta, ☎ 0361/974217), who will take you to the market and help you prepare a selection of lunch dishes; a recipe book and a "Bumbu Kitchen Team" apron are even included in the Rp 100,000 price. You can also sign up for classes, held at the **Honeymoon Guesthouse** (☞ *above*) and at **Indus** and **Café Luna** restaurants (☞ *above*). Three weekly courses are offered, each from 9 to 2 Monday, Tuesday, and Wednesday and costing Rp 100,000.

PERFORMANCES

Various classical Balinese dances and plays are held nightly at Ubud's **Puri Saren** (✉ Jl. Ubud, ☎ no phone) throughout the week. The regular dances here, all at 7:30 and Rp 20,000, are: Monday, Legong; Tuesday, *Ramayana* Ballet; Wednesday, Legong and Barong; Thursday, Gabor; Friday, Barong; Saturday, Legong; and Sunday, Legong of the *Mahabharata*. You can also watch the children of the Sadha Budaya Troupe practice their dance steps at the palace on Tuesdays 3–5:30 and Sundays 9:30–noon free of charge.

Kecak dances—including an exciting battle with blazing palm branches—are performed by candlelight during every full moon and new moon on the open temple stage at the **Agung Rai Museum of Art;** the performance begins at 7 PM and costs Rp 25,000 (✉ Jl. Hanoman, ☎ 0361/976659). For the same price, you can watch the Peliatan masters perform the Legong here each Sunday at 7:30 PM.

Outdoor Activities and Sports

GOLF

Forty-five minutes north of Ubud, the 18-hole, 6,432-yard **Bali Handera Country Club** (✉ Bedugul, ☎ 0361/788994) is in a volcanic crater and has beautifully landscaped gardens along its fairways. Greens fees are Rp 779,520 on weekends and Rp 645,120 during the week. Caddies cost Rp 62,720 a round.

RAFTING

It takes 2½ hours to drift and bump through gorges and rapids down the Ayung River, ending in the gentle valley near Ubud. Several companies organize rubber-raft trips for around Rp 492,800, including the reliable Australian outfit **Bali Adventure Rafting** (✉ Jl. Tunjung Mekar, Legian, ☎ 0361/751292). **Unda River Rafting** (✉ Jl. Kajeng 33, Ubud, ☎ 0361/975366) offers a new course along the Unda River—without all the steep step-climbing of the Ayung River tours—plus a free lunch buffet afterward. For more agencies that specialize in rafting tours, ☞ *also* Travel Agencies *in* Bali A to Z, *below.*

Shopping

Ubud's main street is lined with shops that sell art, textiles, clothing, and other handicrafts. The central market at the corner of Jalan Raya and Jalan Wanara Wana is open daily from dawn to dusk. The clusters of shops along Jalan Monkey Forest and the surrounding streets are also filled with bargains on jewelry, batik clothing and textiles, and handcrafted bags.

ANTIQUES AND SECONDHAND ITEMS

The fantastic **Rococo Antiques** (✉ Jl. Ubud, ☎ 0361/974805) displays beautiful furniture, textiles, and masks. **Dayu Collection** (✉ Jl. Hanoman, ☎ 0361/975428), next door to Rococo Antiques, has a smaller array of similar items. **Oman Gallery** (✉ Jl. Sanggingan, ☎ 0812/390–6610)

has an extensive display of antique crafts. **Panen Collection** (✉ Jl.
Dewa Sita, ☎ 0361/977734) carries beautiful antiques, textiles, and
batik. **Papadun** (✉ Jl. Sanggingan, ☎ 0361/975379) is a terrific place
to find antiques, especially old textiles and Sumatran wood carvings.
Tegun (✉ Jl. Hanoman 44, ☎ 0361/973361) features all sorts of col-
lectible Indonesian crafts and cloth. **Tips Handicraft Centre** (✉ Jl. Dewa
Sita, ☎ no phone) has beautiful antiques, wooden wayang golek puppets, masks, and baskets.

GIFTS AND SOUVENIRS

Ani's Collections (✉ Jl. Campuhan, ☎ 0361/975431), near the Campuhan bridge, displays a variety of Indonesian crafts. Stop into **Dhyma's
Dream** (✉ Jl. Hanoman, ☎ no phone) to buy wonderful household
items, handmade pillowcases, and small antiques. The **Eama Gallery**
(✉ Jl. Wanara Wana, ☎ 0361/973232) features hand-carved antiques
and beautiful small items.

For the big, colorful kites you see flying over the rice fields, go to the
Kites Centre (✉ Jl. Wanara Wana, ☎ 0361/298709), where you can
buy them or have one made to order. You can also try **Pusat Layang-
Layang** (✉ Jl. Pengosekan, ☎ 0361/298709). You'll find a wonderful
selection of wayang kulit and wayang golek puppets at **Wayan's Shop**
(✉ Jl. Ubud, ☎ 0361/977721).

HANDICRAFTS

Check out **Amnesia** (✉ Jl. Wanara Wana, ☎ 0812/393–3433), which
is indeed a gallery of unforgettable creations, including beautiful butterfly batiks, mobiles, painted boxes, and little glass candleholders. The
wonderful, museumlike shops **Kunang-Kunang** (✉ Jl. Campuhan, ☎
0361/975714 and ✉ Jl. Ubud, ☎ 0361/975716) are filled with all sorts
of Balinese and Indonesian crafts. **Le Chat** (✉ Jl. Wanara Wana, ☎ 0811/
388925) carries women's shirts and basic Balinese souvenirs. **Oleh-Oleh**
(✉ Jl. Ubud, ☎ 0361/973466) has a variety of Balinese and Indonesian crafts. **Panorama** (✉ Jl. Pengosekan, ☎ 0361/96336) sells basic
Bali kitsch. **Pondok Frog** (✉ Jl. Wanara Wana, ☎ 0361/975565) carries T-shirts and wood carvings and makes souvenirs to order.

JEWELRY

Look for the beautiful jewelry and stonework at **Aget** (✉ Jl. Wanara
Wana, ☎ 0812/393–1465); you can buy finished pieces or design your
own. **Alamkara** (✉ Jl. Dewi Sita, ☎ no phone) has a nice selection of
jewelry. **Alit's Silver** (✉ Jl. Wanara Wana, ☎ 0361/298101) can create gold and silver jewelry to order. **Budhi Ayu** (✉ Jl. Celuk, ☎ 0811/
385563) specializes in made-to-order gold and silver pieces. **Dewi Sri
Silver** (✉ Jl. Wanara Wana, ☎ 0361/975938) has classic silver pieces,
as well as Balinese souvenirs. At **Hari Ini Silver** (✉ Jl. Wanara Wana,
☎ 0361/974009), Balinese artists blend traditional designs with more
modern pieces and motifs. **Karang Silver** (✉ Jl. Pengosekan, ☎ 0361/
975445) has a shop full of pretty silver items. **Treasures** (✉ Jl. Ubud,
☎ 0361/976697) is one of the best places in Ubud to find beautiful
gold jewelry.

En Route Pejeng fell to the Javanese in the mid-1300s, but its temples still stand
as testament to a great kingdom. Take time to walk through the **Pura
Penataran Sasih,** Pejeng's former state temple, with its centuries-old
Moon of Pejeng bronze drum. The **Pura Pusering Jagat** is possibly the
crux of an ancient Balinese kingdom. At this temple, carvings and a
large urn depict tales of the *Mahabharata*. Don't miss the **Pura Kebo
Edan,** the "crazy buffalo" temple, with its famous 10-ft statue of its
namesake.

Tampaksiring

8 *19 km (12 mi) northeast of Ubud.*

This town is an excellent base for visiting three sacred Balinese sites. Since there are few accommodations or restaurants in the area, it's best to make Tampaksiring a day trip from Ubud.

Outside of town, follow signs to **Pura Gunung Kawi,** a monument to an 11th-century ruler and one of the oldest temples in Bali. From the access road, a stone stairway leads down to a lush valley. You pass beneath a stone arch to the canyon floor where there are two rows of memorial temples carved in niches in the face of two cliffs. According to legend, the giant Kebo Iwa carved these in one night with his fingernails.

Beyond the outskirts of Tampaksiring, the road forks. To the right is the famous temple at **Tirta Empul,** where people from all over Bali come to bathe in the holy spring. According to legend, the spring was created when the god Indra pierced a stone to produce magical waters that revived his army, whose soldiers had been poisoned by the demon king Mayadanava.

Gunung Batur

9 *11 km (7 mi) north of Tampaksiring, 62 km (37 mi) north of Ubud.*

West toward the villages of Penaka and Sebatu and north of Tampaksiring, the vanilla- and clove-bordered road climbs quickly. Roadside stalls sell fruits and vegetables rather than souvenirs and handicrafts. And then there's the majestic bulk of 5,632-ft Gunung Batur (Mt. Batur). Dark lava flows are visible within the volcano's vast crater—nearly 29 km (18 mi) in diameter and 600 ft deep—where a new volcano has arisen and cool Lake Batur has formed. Penelokan, a village at the old crater's edge, affords a great view of the lake and caldera.

An alternative route to Gunung Batur that captures Bali's enchanting rural scenes can be done in an afternoon, leaving around 3 PM to catch the day's best light. The narrow, two-lane Sayan–Kedewatan road along Ubud's eastern border passes a gathering of resorts through Payangan. Women carrying baskets of vegetables on their heads walk along the forest-lined route. As the lane heads north, you'll glimpse the Ayung River valley to the left; banana and palm trees crowd the right. The terrain then evens out into steeply stacked rice terraces that shine in the late afternoon light. About 12 km (8 mi) from the town of Kintamani, the forest occasionally opens to offer views of the river valley to the left and mountains to the right. The truly breathtaking scenes, however, begin 3 km (2 mi) outside Kintamani, when the triumvirate peaks of Gunung Agung, Gunung Batur, and Gunung Abang appear east to west. A thin pine forest surrounds the road as it climbs into the mountains and comes to the junction with the main northern road. Here, you can't help but stop to gape at the shadowy slopes surrounding Lake Batur far below.

The Gunung Batur region is known for its aggressive hawkers, so it's best to have a plan before arriving. Whether you plan to climb Gunung Batur or just admire its majesty from afar, the Lakeview Restaurant and Hotel in Penelokan is your best base. If you're just passing through, the Lakeview's large indoor dining area affords a panoramic view. If you have time to stay overnight, the hotel offers a great package for guests (Rp 313,600), which means you won't have to haggle over prices for a guide, and your transportation to and from the hotel will be provided for the early morning hike (it starts at 4 AM). The tour also includes a fantastic post-hike soak in a private hot-spring pool by the crater lake. You can arrange for a private guide of your own (☞ Tour Operators *in* Bali A to Z, *below*).

In the village of Penulisan, an old stairway leads to the ancient temple of **Pura Puncak Penilusan.** Until the TV tower was built next door, it was Bali's highest point. Most of the decaying sculptures are from the 11th century, but look closely and you will find older, pagan phallic symbols. The view, which stretches across Bali to the Java Sea, is breathtaking if it's a clear day. The temple feels even more romantic and mysterious, however, when shrouded in a foggy mist.

Dining and Lodging

¢–$ ✕⊞ **Lakeview Restaurant and Hotel.** Of the small, inexpensive hotels and restaurants in the Gunung Batur area, this is the best and most popular. The staff is friendly and helpful and the rooms are clean, but the accommodations are very basic. Superior quarters come with hot water and double or twin beds; deluxe rooms have double beds and include bathtubs. The indoor restaurant has decent Indonesian fare and memorable views. The hotel can arrange a guide for Gunung Batur (including a swim in the hot springs afterward) for Rp 313,600 per person. ✉ *Jl. Raya, Penelokan 80652,* ☎ *0366/51464 or 0366/31394. 20 rooms. Restaurant, bar, laundry service. AE, MC, V.*

Pura Kehen

❿ *35 km (21 mi) south of Gunung Batur. The drive south from Penelokan to Bangli is a quick run downhill. On the outskirts of Bangli is an S-curve; here take a left, and at the foot of the hill is Pura Kehen.*

Pura Kehen, a 12th-century temple dedicated to Shiva, is considered one of Bali's most beautiful: it rises up the mountainside and culminates in an 11-tier shrine. You step through an ornate entrance and into a courtyard with a giant holy banyan tree and a bell tower used to summon the villagers for ceremonies. The entrance to the inner courtyard is up steep steps. At the top center are the "closed gate" and a boma, which blocks evil spirits. Within the inner courtyard, the main shrine sits on a cosmic turtle, symbolizing the spiritual world, entwined by nagas, symbolizing the material.

OFF THE BEATEN PATH
PURA BESAKIH – Known as the Mother Temple of Bali, Pura Besakih is the most sacred of all. On Gunung Agung's slopes, the complex has 30 temples—one for every Balinese district—on seven terraces. It's thought to have been built before Hinduism reached Bali. The structure consists of three main parts, the north painted black for Vishnu, the center white for Shiva, and the south red for Brahma. You enter through a split gate.

Much of the temple area was destroyed in 1963 when Gunung Agung erupted, killing 1,800, but diligent restoration has repaired most of the damage. You aren't allowed into the inner courtyard, but there's enough to see to justify the steep 2-km (1-mi) walk from the parking lot past souvenir stands and vendors. Besakih is 40 km (25 mi) northeast of Bangli, 45 km (28 mi) north of Klungkung, and 60 km (35 mi) north of Denpasar. The temple can be reached from Bangli (if you're coming from Gunung Batur), Klungkung (the best route if you're coming from Ubud, Denpasar, or points south), or Candidasa—take the road inland to Amlapura, where the road splits; keep going to Rendang, then turn right to climb the 11 km (7 mi) to the temple.

Klungkung

⑪ *28 km (18 mi) southeast of Ubud, 46 km (29 mi) northeast of Denpasar.*

Klungkung is a former dynastic capital. In the center of town stands the **Kerta Gosa** (Hall of Justice), part of the 18th-century Royal Palace destroyed by the Dutch in the early 20th century and restored again by the remorseful Dutch two decades later. The raised platform in the hall supports three thrones—one with a lion carving for the king, one with a dragon for the minister, and one with a bull for the priest. The accused brought before this tribunal could look up at the painted ceiling and contemplate the horrors in store for convicted criminals: torches between the legs, pots of boiling oil, decapitation by saw, and dozens of other punishments to fit specific crimes. To the right of the Hall of Justice is the **Bale Kambang** (Floating Pavilion), a moat-encircled palace that was also decimated and rebuilt by the Dutch. Part of its painted ceiling's motif relates stories of the hero Sang Sutasoma, whose supernatural powers could turn arrows and spears into flowers. The **Museum Semarajaya,** across the courtyard from the Floating Pavilion, is also worth a look for its collection of island relics as well as black-and-white photos and newspaper clippings that depict palace life and relate historic events.

Goa Lawah

⑫ *10 km (6 mi) southeast of Klungkung.*

East of Klungkung, the road drops south to run along the coast and through the area of Kusamba, speckled with salt-panning huts' thatched roofs. Just beyond is Pura Goa Lawah, the bat cave temple, where thousands of bats hang from the ceiling over an ancient stone shrine. The cave is said to lead all the way to Gunung Agung.

Padangbai

⑬ *5 km (3 mi) northeast of Goa Lawah.*

Continuing east from Goa Lawah along the coast will bring you to Padangbai, a quiet village next to one of the island's main ports. Because most people simply pass through it en route to other sights, Padangbai has remained a charmingly offbeat center for water sports and romantic getaways. The only time the town seems at all frenzied is right after the four-hour ferry from Lombok arrives or when the occasional cruise ship docks—hawkers set up stands as passengers disembark. There's a tourist office at the docks, and there are plenty of boats for hire. There are also plenty of small losmen where you can while away the afternoons walking along the thin brown crescent of beach filled with colorfully painted fishing pontoons.

Balina Beach and Manggis

⑭ *5 km (3 mi) north of Padangbai.*

The curving stretch of Balina Beach, at Amuk Bay's other end, is just as serene as Padangbai—but with an upscale-resort feel. Several luxury hotels are set back into the forested slopes along the road between the village of Manggis, 11 km (7 mi) north of Padangbai, and Candidasa.

Dining and Lodging

$$$$ ✕🏨 **Amankila.** This hillside resort has Bandung Straits views. Luxurious thatched-roof pavilions are connected by raised cement walkways. Each guest villa has a terrace, a bedroom with a king-size canopy bed, and a bath with a sunken tub and separate shower; some villas have private pools. You'll feel like royalty basking in the sun beside the tri-level communal pool. The beach is a stiff, downhill climb, or you can ride to it in a chauffeured jeep. The large, warm library has an extensive collection of Indonesian travel and history books; in its cushioned sitting area, experts often present slide shows or give talks on topics related to local culture. At the Terrace restaurant, you choose from three menus—Indonesian, Nonya (Malay), and Western. The chef comes to your table to make recommendations, and the staff maintains this high level of service throughout your meal. Savory appetizers include the Thai-style crab and coconut salad and the *bosonboh,* a stir-fried salad with squid, tofu, bean sprouts, and vegetables. Succulent pork satay, juicy beef rendang, and curry *kapitan* (a wild-chicken curry flavored with lemongrass) are standout entrées. Each night a gamelan trio plays as the sun sets. ⊠ *Pantai Buitan (3 km/2 mi northeast of Padangbai turnoff), Manggis 80871,* ☎ *0366/21993, 800/447–7462, 212/223–2848 in the U.S., or 0800/282684 in the U.K.;* ℻ *0366/21995. 35 villas. 2 restaurants, bar, pool, massage, hiking, beach, snorkeling, windsurfing, library. AE, DC, MC, V.* ✍

$$$–$$$$ ╳⊡ **The Serai.** When sunlight washes the pale golden walls and marble floors, this resort's warmth is evident. Rooms are in two-story buildings with wood furnishings and cream-color upholstery. Superior rooms don't have tubs (only showers), but they do have outer sitting areas that face the pool and beach; in deluxe rooms the baths are fully equipped and the balconies have built-in sofas overlooking the pool and gardens. Outdoor activities and tours to local sights are available so you can experience the local flora, fauna, and culture. In the restaurant, the tables and chairs are arranged in a raised, sheltered pavilion surrounded by a lotus pond. Must-try Asian dishes include steamed duck breast, spicy prawn mango curry with yellow rice, and Thai green chicken curry. If you crave a Western dish, try the wild-rice mushroom risotto or the grilled peppered tuna. The on-site cooking school can teach you about Indonesian cuisine. ⊠ *Pantai Buitan (6 km/4 mi northeast of Padangbai turnoff), Manggis 80871,* ☎ *0363/41011,* ℻ *0363/41015. 58 rooms. Restaurant, bar, pool, beach, dive shop. AE, DC, MC, V.* ✍

$ ⊡ **Balina Beach Bungalows.** Popular with scuba and snorkel enthusiasts for its diving club, this hotel has one- and two-story thatched cottages near a sandy beach 3 km (2 mi) west of Candidasa. All rooms have private baths and ceiling fans. The best rooms, upstairs in the two-story bungalows, have sitting areas and terraces; the one-story garden-view rooms have open-air bathrooms and large corner tubs as well as large cushioned bales overlooking the rice fields. ⊠ *Pantai Buitan (8 km/5 mi northeast of Padangbai turnoff), Manggis 80870,* ☎ *0363/41002,* ℻ *0363/41001. 42 rooms. Restaurant, bar, pool, beach, dive shop. AE, DC, MC, V.*

Outdoor Activities and Sports

The **Balina Diving Association** (⊠ Balina Beach, ☎ 0361/80871) arranges dives out to Nusa Penida.

Candidasa

⑮ *3 km (2 mi) east of Balina Beach, 6 km (4 mi) east of Manggis, 14 km (9 mi) northeast of Padangbai.*

Candidasa, once a budget traveler's escape from the 24-hour partying of the southwestern beaches, now encompasses a throng of small hotels, restaurants, tourist shops, and travel agencies. Still, the area is more peaceful than Kuta or Legian and less expensive than Nusa Dua or Jimbaran. A lively coral reef 300 yards offshore calms the waves and makes the water ideal for snorkeling. If you prefer scuba diving, you can easily hire one of the many fishing boats that park close to the beach.

Dining and Lodging

$ ✕ **TJ's.** Don't let the dressed-down setting of chipped blue chairs, a mishmash of tables, and scuffed brick floors put you off—the food is terrific. There is Asian and Western fare, and a bar along the side wall serves up every drink you can imagine (it's a popular evening hangout). Among the best dishes are the Thai green chicken curry, the spicy Thai red prawn curry, and the nasi campur. ⊠ *Jl. Raya,* ☎ *no phone. AE, MC, V.*

$$ ▣ **The Watergarden.** This resort's name couldn't be more appropriate. Cool, thatched-roof cottages with high ceilings, marble floors, warm brick walls, and simple island furnishings are complemented by wide wooden terraces overlooking lily ponds. Each dwelling is nestled into gardens, with rushing waterfalls and koi ponds around every corner. From the beach across the road, the views of Gunung Agung are superb. ⊠ *Jl. Raya,* ☎ *0363/41540,* ℻ *0363/41164. 13 rooms. Restaurant, bar, pool, beach, snorkeling, library. V.*

$ ▣ **Fajar Candidasa Beach Bungalows.** Whistling songbirds and chuckling mynahs welcome you to this small hotel; indeed, dozens of birdcages decorate the reception area. Tall, redbrick, templelike bungalows and neat gardens line the walkway. All rooms have small terraces and oversize sunken tubs; only deluxe rooms have air-conditioning, however. The small swimming pool and terrace are right next to the ocean breakwater. The facilities are clean, and the grounds are quiet. ⊠ *Jl. Raya,* ☎ *0363/41539,* ℻ *0366/41538. 33 rooms. Restaurant, bar, pool, beach, boating. AE, MC, V.*

Tenganan

⑯ *8 km (5 mi) northwest of Candidasa.*

On the western side of Candidasa, the road turns inland to Tenganan, an ancient walled village of the Bali Aga—the people who lived on the island well before the conquerors of Java's Majapahit kingdom arrived. The village consists of two parallel streets lined on either side with identical walled compounds. Inside the compounds, houses face each other across a grassy central strip, where the public buildings stand (no cars are allowed). Tenganan people seldom marry outside the village, and they adhere to their traditions—it is, for example, one of the few places in Indonesia where double ikat is still woven and traditional Balinese script is transcribed onto palm leaves. Several unique and sacred types of music and dance are still performed here: the gamelan *selendeng,* the orchestra of the ancient Balinese; the gamelan *gambing,* composed of a pair of seven-key bronze xylophones and four wooden-key xylophones; and the *rejang* dance, which features ornate headdresses and costumes made of the fine *geringsing* cloth woven only in Tenganan.

Tulamben

⑰ *40 km (24 mi) northeast of Candidasa.*

The main road from Candidasa cuts west around the foothills of 3,854-ft Gunung Serayai and continues up and around the north coast. Although Tulamben isn't a large town, it's visited by many people who have one goal in mind: to dive the wreck of the *Liberty,* a World War II ship that sank just offshore. The reefs here add to the attraction, and the beaches are more serene than others nearby.

Dining and Lodging

$$–$$$$ ✕🏠 **Emerald Tulamben Resort.** Settled between Gunung Agung's slopes and the white-sand eastern beach, the Emerald Tulamben is the region's premier upscale hotel. Two-story cottages with brick walls and thatched roofs line the hillsides and are surrounded by blossoming bougainvillea gardens. Rooms have woven walls, canopy beds, bamboo furniture, and Balinese decor; all have air-conditioning, hot water, refrigerators, and private patios. Many have views of the three circular pools that step down toward the ocean. A cable car runs along the edge of the property, and an aquarium and glass-bottom boat are also on-site. The restaurant specializes in seafood but also offers Western and Indonesian fare. ✉ *Jl. Raya, Tulamben,* ☎ *0361/462673,* 𝔽𝔸𝕏 *0361/462407. 50 rooms. Restaurant, bar, coffee shop, pizzeria, pool, beach, dive shop, snorkeling, library, car rental. AE, DC, MC, V.*

$–$$ ✕🏠 **Mimpi Resort.** The accommodations are basic and pleasant at this dive resort set between the sea and Gunung Agung's foothills. Rooms have a traditional Balinese design with understated island decor; all have air-conditioning and private outdoor showers. The on-site restaurant has hearty Indonesian and Western fare. In addition to dive tours and snorkeling, the hotel also offers sea kayaking. ✉ *Desa Kubu, Karangasem,* ☎ *0363/21642,* 𝔽𝔸𝕏 *0363/21939. 40 rooms. Restaurant, bar, pool, spa, beach, dive shop, snorkeling. AE, MC, V.*

Lovina

★ ⑱ *70 km (42 mi) northwest of Tulamben.*

Calm seas, black-sand beaches, and lovely sunrises and sunsets are what you'll find at these peaceful northern settlements. The cluster of villages here—including Anturan, Bunut Panggang, Kalibukbuk, Temukus, and Tukad Mungga—is known as "Lovina," a pleasant name bestowed on this stretch of coastline in the 1950s by Prince Anak Agung Panji Tisna. It's far quieter than the popular tourist areas in the south and makes a great base from which to explore central Bali. Although a number of hotels and restaurants line the main Singaraja–Gilimanuk road that runs along the coast, the more luxurious places tend to be farther east. Travelers have long headed to Lovina for respite, but the larger and more upscale resorts have only surfaced in the last decade. The main tourist road in Kalibukbuk, Jalan Pantai Bina Rina, is where you'll find tourist conveniences like e-mail, a pharmacy, and the best dive operation, Spice Dive. (ATMs can be found along the Singaraja–Gilimanuk highway.) The food and entertainment establishments in Kalibukbuk tend to have a high turnover rate, so it pays to look for the popular places. Diving and snorkeling, dolphin-watching, trekking, and cultural explorations are the prime activities.

Dining and Lodging

$ ✕ **Biyu Nasak.** This unassuming restaurant, whose name means "ripe banana" in Balinese, is by far the best in the Kalibukbuk area and is an easy walk from Lovina Beach. It specializes in vegetarian dishes and seafood and serves up delicious versions of what might be considered travelers' comfort food: homemade garlic bread, tasty chocolate cake, grilled cheese sandwiches with tomato and avocado, and muesli and homemade yogurt for breakfast. The setting is cozy and calm, with a large selection of books, magazines, and children's toys available, plus a small gift shop. ✉ *Jl. Raya, Lovina Beach, Kaliasem,* ☎ 𝔽𝔸𝕏 *0362/ 41176. No credit cards.*

$ ✕ **Cafe Lumbung.** On the Kalibukbuk road leading to Lovina Beach, Cafe Lumbung is modeled after the Balinese rice barns (lumbungs) from which its name is derived. The high-ceilinged, airy room is set back from the street a bit, and the polite staff, who are well versed in English, serve up a menu of Indonesian and Western dishes. Chicken satay is served over its own mini-hibachi of coals, accompanied by a rich, chunky peanut sauce. ⊠ *Jl. Bina Ria, Kalibukbuk,* ☎ *0362/4119. AE, MC, V.*

$$$–$$$$ 🔲 **The Damai.** Opened in 1998, this tiny luxury hotel is Lovina's most elegant and romantic. About a 10-minute drive from downtown Lovina, it has a great view of the ocean (and the sunset). There are only eight bungalows, so the feeling is intimate and relaxed, with guests often gathering around the pool for after-dinner drinks. (The exceedingly friendly and helpful staff are likely to bring preheated blankets to the poolside gathering if the night air is cool.) Bungalows are decorated with lovely dark-wood furnishings and have an indoor toilet and sink with an outdoor shower. (Deluxe bungalows also have a Jacuzzi.) The Damai's prix-fixe dinner, which changes nightly, is fantastic—five courses of Asian-European dishes (like roast fillet of red grouper with bok choy and red beet saffron potato puree or chocolate fig cake with pineapple sorbet) are presented with four-star flourish. There's also a comprehensive wine list. Free transportation within Lovina is available to guests. ⊠ *Kayuputih, Lovina,* ☎ *0362/41008,* 𝖥𝖠𝖷 *0362/41009. 8 bungalows. Restaurant, bar, minibars, driving range, badminton, travel services. AE, DC, MC, V.* ✎

$$$–$$$$ 🔲 **Puri Bagus Lovina.** A comfortable midsize hotel, Puri Bagus Lovina is popular with tour groups. A large freeform swimming pool sits on the beach's edge and is surrounded by the café and restaurant. Rooms are spacious and have both indoor and outdoor showers. The hotel provides a weekly program of guided sightseeing tours in nearby areas, plus cultural activities at the hotel. There are occasional performances of traditional dance, accompanied by a large buffet of Indonesian, Western, and sometimes Japanese food. (If you're not staying at the hotel, it may be worth stopping by for dinner on one of these nights—call ahead to see if one is scheduled.) Part of a Balinese chain, Puri Bagus is not the place to come for an "authentic" Balinese experience—save for the thatched roofs, it could be in Florida. And while it offers some of Lovina's only upscale accommodations, the staff can at times seem downright unhelpful. ⊠ *Jl. Singaraja–Seririt,* ☎ *0362/21430,* 𝖥𝖠𝖷 *0362/ 22627. 40 villas. Restaurant, bar, café, refrigerators, room service, snorkeling. AE, DC, MC, V.* ✎

$$ 🔲 **Hotel Mas Lovina.** Also known as Las Brisas Cottages, these two-story thatched-roof cottages are painted pastel pink, making them look like oversized dollhouses. Bedrooms, which are upstairs, have long windows and pool and bay views. Downstairs, some accommodations have a living area, others have a kitchen—be sure to specify your preference when booking. Each cottage has a redbrick terrace, bamboo furniture, and a large shared backyard with fruit trees. A restaurant serving Indonesian, Western, Chinese, and Japanese food catches the breeze off the water. Children under 12 may stay with parents at no extra cost or can share their own room for half price. ⊠ *Jl. Raya Seririt,* ☎ *0362/41237,* 𝖥𝖠𝖷 *0362/41236. 20 rooms (10 cottages, 2 rooms each). Restaurant, bar, pool, beach, dive shop, travel services. MC, V.* ✎

¢–$$ 🔲 **Rambutan Beach Cottages.** An oasis set smack in the middle of Kalibukbuk's busiest area, Rambutan was opened by an Australian who now lives on the property with his Balinese wife and their young children. Because of this, it's a particularly welcoming place for young children, who will enjoy the seesaw, swing set, and slide. Rambutan's central location means you can explore Lovina's casual center on foot, not to mention walk along the area's best beach. Accommodations run the gamut from budget rooms with cold water only to standard rooms with hot water, plus deluxe rooms and new luxury villas with stone mosaic bathrooms. Rambutan's two large, attractive pools and 2½ hectares of lush grounds with winding paths make Rambutan the best value in Lovina. ✉ *Jl. Ketepang, Kalibukbuk,* ☎ *0362/41388,* FAX *0362/41057. 33 rooms. 2 restaurants, bar, 2 pools, badminton, Ping-Pong, playground. DC, MC, V (3% surcharge for credit cards).* 🕸

$ 🖼 **Aditya Beach Bungalows.** The ornate reception building, right on the main road in central Lovina, has an Indian flair but is actually an old Balinese structure. Guest quarters are down long paths through well-maintained gardens, and many have yards just steps from the sand. Rooms are large and open, with back entrances, raised front porches, tile floors, and very basic furnishings. Note: Check the toilet, tub, and refrigerator to make sure they're working, and keep food wrapped up, as ants can be a problem. The staff is very helpful and friendly, and a breakfast buffet is included in the price. ✉ *Jl. Raya Lovina (Box 134, Singaraja 81101),* ☎ *0362/41059,* FAX *0362/41342. 80 rooms. 2 restaurants, bar, café, refrigerator, pool, wading pool, spa, putting green, tennis court, travel services, car rental. AE, MC, V.* 🕸

Bali Barat National Park

Park entrance is 90 km (54 mi) southwest of Lovina, 140 km (87 mi) northwest of Denpasar.

With almost 200,000 acres of arid forests and mangrove swamps, Bali Barat (West Bali) National Park is a valuable natural treasure. Until recently, this has been one of the few areas left unsculpted by rice terraces, tourist complexes, and other human endeavors. Controversy was sparked a few years ago by the development of a hotel on park land. This has initiated some dissent among Indonesians who believe this allows them to use some of the land for farming. Unfortunately, the government has overlooked much of the park's regulation due to larger political problems throughout the country and lack of a secure leadership.

The park is home to several very rare species; foremost is the Bali starling, the island's mascot. Also known as Rothschild's mynah, this soft, white bird has a blue band around its eyes; the world's last 50 or so of these winged creatures are here, and an on-site breeding program is trying to save the species. Less rare but still of interest are several species of deer, including the mouse deer and the barking deer, several types of monkeys, leopards, and civets.

There are several unspoiled coral reefs off Menjangan Island, which is just north of the park's mainland. Local dive shops organize scuba and snorkeling trips. If you prefer to stay on land, there's a network of fairly flat trails around the park's edges. You can arrange guided treks at the park office in Cekik, 6 km (4 mi) west of the park entrance at Labuan Lalang (at the crossroads of the main Denpasar and Singaraja roads and on the left side just before Gilimanuk). Permits are required for travel within the park—dive shops usually take care of this, but for hiking trips, you'll need to stop at the park office yourself. Another option is a boat trip. You can hire craft at Labuan Lalang, along the Singaraja road. Nearby Pemuteran and Banyuwedang offer a small but upscale choice of resorts.

Bali A to Z

Arriving and Departing

BY AIRPLANE

About 13 km (8 mi) southwest of Denpasar, **Ngurah Rai International Airport** (☎ 0361/751011, ext. 1454) handles international and domestic flights. The Indonesian airlines work together to connect every region in the country; try: **Bouraq** (✉ Jl. Melati 51, Denpasar, ☎ 0361/ 223564), **Garuda** (✉ Jl. Melati 61, Denpasar, ☎ 0361/288011, ext. 1789), **Mandala** (✉ Jl. Diponegoro 98, Kerthawijaya Plz. D23, Denpasar, ☎ 0361/231659), and **Merpati** (✉ Jl. Melati 53, Denpasar, ☎ 0361/285071).

International carriers with offices in the south include: **Air New Zealand** (☎ 0361/289636), **KLM** (☎ 0361/756126), **Royal Brunei** (☎ 0361/ 757292), and **Singapore Airlines** (☎ 0361/261666).

Many airlines have offices in the Grand Bali Beach Hotel in Sanur, including **Air France** (☎ 0361/288511), **British Airways** (☎ 0361/288511), **Cathay Pacific** (☎ 0361/286001), **Continental** (☎ 0361/287774), **Japan Airlines** (☎ 0361/287576), **Malaysian Airlines** (☎ 0361/285071), **Quantas** (☎ 0361/288331), and **Thai Airways** (☎ 0361/288141).

Between the Airport and Hotels. With advance notice, most hotels can have a car or minivan waiting to meet you. Otherwise, order a taxi at the counter outside customs; the fixed fare varies depending on your hotel's location. You can also catch a bemo outside the airport, but make sure that you're going in the right direction and that if you enter an empty van you're not hiring it for yourself—unless that's your intention.

BY BOAT

Ferries make the 35-minute crossing every hour between Ketapang in eastern Java and Gilimanuk in western Bali for about Rp 1,000 for passengers and Rp 11,000 for vehicles. **Bounty Cruises** (✉ Benoa Harbour on Bali, ☎ 0361/733333) ferries passengers from the port of Benoa to Senggigi and the Gili islands on Lombok for $35 one-way and $70 round-trip, departing at 8 AM, arriving in Senggigi at 10:15, and arriving at Gili Meno at 10:45; the return journey starts at 1 PM, stops at Senggigi at 1:15, and arrives back at Benoa Harbour at 3:45. **Mabua Express** (✉ Benoa Harbour on Bali, ☎ 0361/772521 and ✉ Lembar Harbour on Lombok, ☎ 0364/37224) is the main passenger-only express service to Lombok; trips on the 40-m catamaran depart at 8 AM and 2:30 PM from Benoa and 5 PM from Lembar and take just two hours. This is the comfortable way to travel, with reclining seats, a bar, and facilities for people with disabilities. Travel in the Emerald or Lower-Deck classes costs $30 and includes a snack, juice, coffee, and transfers; Economy Class, which lacks the perks, costs $25.

BY BUS

Buses from Java to Denpasar use the ferry; an air-conditioned bus costs around Rp 17,000. Service is available from Jakarta (16 hours), Yogyakarta (16 hours), and Surabaya (8 hours). You can buy tickets in advance through any travel agent, or you can simply show up at the bus terminal a few hours before you'd like to depart.

Getting Around
BY BEMO

Bemos (minibuses) ply the main routes from Denpasar to Sanur and Kuta and from Kuta to Ubud. You can catch them at the main bemo terminals, where fares and schedules are posted, or simply flag one down along the road. Though crowded, bemos are inexpensive and give you a glimpse of everyday Balinese life.

BY CAR

Though one highway travels along the island's perimeter, most roads run north to south. One such thoroughfare heads from Denpasar to Sanur and Gianyar, traveling up through Ubud to Gunung Batur; another cuts off the southwestern highway to head north through Bedugul to Singaraja. On the Bukit Peninsula, the main highway splits just beyond the Ngurah Rai Airport; the east road goes to Nusa Dua, the west to Pura Uluwatu, and a smaller road links points in between.

Legally you must have an international driver's license to rent a car, though some agencies won't ask for it. If you plan to travel farther than Bali—to Lombok or Java, say—you need a permit from your rental agent; be sure to mention your itinerary before signing the contract. Daily self-drive rates run Rp 85,000–200,000, depending on the make; with a driver, expect to pay between 200,000 and 300,000 a day. Add Rp 100,000–Rp 400,000 per day for insurance depending on the model and year.

The highly recommended **Toyota Rent a Car** (✉ Jl. Bypass Nusa Dua, Jimbaran, ☎ 0361/703333, ✉ Jl. Raya Airport 99X, Tuban, ☎ 0361/763333, and ✉ Ngurah Rai International Airport, ☎ 0361/753744) has a top-notch fleet of sport-utility vehicles and compact cars. The company's rates are competitive, and it has on-the-spot mechanics and reliable, English-speaking drivers.

Although there are many small car-rental agencies, some are fly-by-night operations that rent out the family vehicle—without insurance or mechanic options—and then charge double or claim false dents and scratches when it's returned. If you must rent from a small company, check the vehicle before you sign anything—and document all prior damage with photographs and in writing.

Reliable operators include **Bagus Rent Car** (✉ Jl. Danau Tamblingan, at Jl. Duyung, Sanur, ☎ 0361/287794), **Bali Baru Wisata** (✉ Jl. P. Ayu 7, Denpasar, ☎ 0361/221096 and ✉ Jl. Legian 61, Legian, ☎ 0361/761155), **Calvin International Tours and Travel** (☞ Guided Tours, *below*), **Indo Trans Astri (ITA)** (✉ Jl. Kuta, Kuta, ☎ 0361/755518 and ✉ Ngurah Rai International Airport, Tuban, ☎ 0361/757850), **Nusa Dua Rent a Car** (✉ Jl. Pantai Mengiat 23, Nusa Dua, ☎ 0361/771905); **Pt. Dirgahayu Valuta Prima** (✉ Jl. Danau Tamblingan 66, Sanur, ☎ 0361/282657), **Sindhu Mertha** (✉ Jl. Danau Tamblingan 20, Sanur, ☎ 0361/288354), and **WBU Executive Travel** (✉ Jl. Danau Tamblingan 2, Sanur, ☎ 0361/282594).

BY TAXI

In the main tourist areas, you can flag a taxi down on the street or book one from any hotel or restaurant. Kuta, Sanur, Nusa Dua, and Denpasar have metered taxis. Make sure that the meter is used. The flag-fall is Rp 2,000, and it's about Rp 900 per km (½ mi), with a minimum Rp 6,000 charge if you call. You don't need to tip, but it's customary to round up to the next Rp 5,000 or so when you pay. A few reliable companies are: **Airport Taxi** (☎ 0361/751011, ext. 1611), **Bali Taxi** (☎ 0361/701111), **Pan Wirthi** (☎ 0361/723355), and **Praja Taxi** (☎ 0361/289090).

Contacts and Resources

BANKS AND CURRENCY EXCHANGE

You can find reliable banks—all with ATMs that usually accept international bank and credit cards—throughout Bali. Banks will change money as well, but moneychangers, which you'll find on every block in the tourist areas, often have higher rates.

Credit-card headquarters are: **American Express** (✉ Pan Indonesia Bank, Jl. Legian 80X, Legian, ☎ 0361/751058), **Diner's Club** (✉ Jl. Diponegoro 45, Denpasar, ☎ 0361/235559), and **Visa** (✉ Bank Duta, Jl. Hayam Wuruk 165, Denpasar, ☎ 0361/226578).

BUSINESS SERVICES

Large hotels have centers with basic phone, fax, photocopying, and computer services. **Bali Advisory Services** (✉ Jl. Danau Poso 108, Sanur, ☎ 0361/285336) can help with leases, contracts, and other business matters. You can get help with basic business services and gain Internet access at **C. V. Krakatoa** (✉ Jl. Seminyak 56, Seminyak, ☎ 0361/730824).

EMERGENCIES

Ambulance: ☎ 118. **Fire:** ☎ 113. **Police:** ☎ 110.

Hospitals and Dental Clinics: Clinic Bali Hyatt Sanur (✉ Jl. Danau Tamblingan, ☎ 0361/288271), **Kasih Ibu** (✉ Jl. Teuku Umar 120, Denpasar, ☎ 0361/223036), **Kuta Clinic** (✉ Jl. Raya Kuta, ☎ 0361/753268), **Nusa Dua Dental Clinic** (✉ Jl. Pratama 81A, ☎ 0361/771324), **Nusa Dua 24-Hour Clinic** (✉ Jl. Pratama 81A, ☎ 0361/771324), **Sangleh Public Hospital** (✉ Jl. Sangleh, Denpasar, ☎ 0361/227911), **Ubud Clinic** (✉ Jl. Ubud, Campuhan, ☎ 0361/974911).

Pharmacies: Bali Farma Apotik (✉ Jl. Melatig, Denpasar, ☎ 0361/22878), **Indonesia Farma Apotik** (✉ Jl. Diponegoro, Denpasar, ☎ 0361/27812). **Scuba-Diving Emergencies: Baruna** (✉ Jl. Raya Seririt, Lovina, ☎ 0362/41084) has a decompression chamber.

ENGLISH-LANGUAGE BOOKSTORES

Most large resorts sell some cultural and mass-market fiction books, and in major budget tourist areas, such as Kuta, used-book shops thrive on the main strip. **Ary's Book Shop** (☎ 0361/96351) in Ubud is one of the best for regional culture and history. Sanur's **Bagus Drugstore** (☎ 0361/287794) has a good selection of culture and nature books. The **Galeria Nusa Dua Shopping Centre** (✉ Jl. Raya Nusa Dua, in the center of town) supermarket has an entire section of regional travel and culture books, as well as paperback best-sellers and magazines.

TELEPHONES, THE INTERNET, MAIL

Satelindo (✉ Jl. Gatot Subroto Barat, Denpasar, ☎ 0361/412008, 24-hr information 021/54388888) sells Mentari cards that provide time for your mobile phone; the cards can easily be reloaded via phone or ATM.

There are many places to hook up to the Internet along the main west-coast strip from Seminyak to Kuta. **Bali@Cyber Café and Restaurant** (✉ Jl. Pura Bagus Taruna, Legian, ☎ 0361/761326, ✍) is a pleasant place in which to surf the net. You can make international calls, send faxes, pick up e-mail, and log on to the Internet at **C. V. Krakatoa** (✉ Jl. Seminyak 56, Seminyak, ☎ 0361/730284). **Goa 2001 Cybercafé** (✉ Jl. Seminyak, Seminyak, ☎ 0361/731178) has an air-conditioned office with a half dozen computer terminals. **Hello Internet Café** (✉ Jl. Diponegoro, Denpasar, ☎ 0361/246181) provides Internet and e-mail access. **Kapotajaya Wartel** (✉ Jl. Seminyak 16A, Seminyak, ☎ 0361/733202) has a range of international phone and Internet services. At **La Zale Internet Bar & Café** (✉ Jl. Kartika Plaza, Blok A3-2, Kuta, ☎ 0361/765202, and ✉ Jl. Legian 363, Legian, ☎ 0361/754422) you can surf in comfort. **Primantara Business Centre** (✉ Jl. Kartika Plz. 8, Kuta, ☎ 0361/752149) has Internet access and e-mail service and rents hand phones.

Some of the main post offices are: **Central Post Office** (✉ Jl. Puputan, Denpasar, ☎ 0361/223566) and **Kuta Post Office** (✉ Jl. Kuta, Gg. Selamat, ☎ 0361/754012).

International couriers include: **DHL** (✉ Jl. Hayam Wuruk, Denpasar, ☎ 0361/222526), **Federal Express** (✉ Jl. Bypass 100X, Jimbaran, ☎

0361/701727), **Tiki JNE** (✉ Jl. Bypass 65, Jimbaran, ☎ 0361/286294), and **TNT** (✉ Jl. Teuku Umar 88E, Denpasar, ☎ 0361/238043).

For shipping, try **Angkasa Jaya** (✉ Jl. Kuta 105A, Kuta, ☎ 0361/751390), **Bali Delta Express** (✉ Jl. Kartini 58, Denpasar, ☎ 0361/701727), **Pacific Express** (✉ Jl. Arjuna 21, Denpasar, ☎ 0361/235181), **Pt. Sumiando Graha Wisata** (✉ Jl. Padma Utara, Kuta, ☎ 0361/753425; ✉ Jl. Danau Tamblingan 22, Sanur, ☎ 0361/288570), and **United Parcel Service** (UPS; ✉ Jl. Imam Bonjol 336K, Denpasar, ☎ 0361/431870).

TOUR OPERATORS

Group bus or van tours range from full-day treks to temples, volcanoes, and caves to short in-town Denpasar trips or those that take you to Ubud's arts sights and nearby handicrafts villages. Some good all-purpose operators are **Aerowisata Tours & Travel** (✉ Jl. Bypass, Kuta, ☎ 0361/756769), **ANA Tourist Service** (✉ Poppies La. I 2, Kuta, ☎ 0361/755221), **Bali Nagasari Tours & Travel** (✉ Jl. Danau Tamblingan 102, Sanur, ☎ 0361/288096), **Calvin International Tours and Travel** (✉ Jl. Segara Batu Bolong 18, Kuta, ☎ 0361/751818), **Dewata Journey Service** (✉ Jl. Danau Tamblingan 16, Sanur, ☎ 0361/286631), **Kunang–Kunang** (✉ Jl. Pengosekan, Ubud, ☎ 0361/977388), **Lila Cita Gaya Tours** (✉ Jl. Danau Tamblingan 6, Sanur, ☎ 0361/288023), and **P. T. Putri Mandalika Tours & Travel** (✉ Jl. Hang Tuah Raya II, Sanur, ☎ 0361/287450).

Bali Avia (✉ Jl. Bypass 04X, Tuban, ☎ 0361/751257) helicopter tours run five circuits of Bali and the Bandung Straits islands; trips cost $550–$2,300 and charters run $1,150 per hour, with a maximum of four people.

Sea Trek (✉ Jl. Danau Tamblingan 64, Sanur, ☎ 0361/286992) offers charter trips to the islands east of Bali (all the way to Irian Jaya if you like) on the 16-passenger *Katharina,* a comfortable, teak-finished Buginese schooner with many modern amenities; charter trips are a specialty. Included are a top-notch, English-speaking crew of 12, professionally prepared meals, and day trips to remote villages and beaches.

The premier cruise from Bali to Lombok, Sumbawa, and Komodo is on the **Ombak Putih** (✉ Jl. Tirta Empul 14, Sanur, ☎ 0361/730191), a 36-m (120-ft), 24-passenger Buginese schooner that combines old-style sailing with modern-day comforts. Day trips to island beaches and villages; clean, comfortable rooms; extensive buffet meals; and top-notch service are all part of the package.

Cruises around Bali and/or to Nusa Lembongan are specialties of **P. T. Island Explorer** (✉ Jl. Sekar Waru 14D, Sanur, ☎ 0361/289856), **Quicksilver** (✉ Jl. Segara Kedul 3, Benoa Harbor, ☎ 0361/771997), **Sojourn** (✉ Benoa Harbour, ☎ 0361/287450), and **Waka Louka** (✉ Jl. Pratama, Tanjung Benoa, ☎ 0361/723629).

Agencies that specialize in dive trips are: **Bali Club Diver** (✉ Jl. Tamblingan 110, Sanur, ☎ 0361/287263), **Bali Diving Perdana** (✉ Jl. Danau Poso, Gang Tanjung, Sanur, ☎ 0361/286493), **Baruna** (✉ Jl. Raya Seririt, Lovina, ☎ 0362/41084), **Geko Dive** (✉ Jl. Silayukti, Padangbai, ☎ 0363/41516), **Nusa Dua Dive Center** (✉ Jl. Pratama 93A, Tanjung Benoa, ☎ 0361/774711), and **Sea Star Dive Center** (✉ Jl. Bypass Ngurah Rai 45, Sanur, ☎ 0361/286492).

For adventure tours—including white-water rafting, kayaking, trekking, and cycling—try: **Ayung River Rafting** (✉ Jl. Diponegoro 150B, Denpasar, ☎ 0361/283789), **Baleraf** (✉ Jl. Tamblingan 82, Sanur, ☎

0361/287256), **Bali Adventure Tours** (⊠ Jl. Bypass Ngurah Rai, Kuta,
☎ 0361/721480), **Bali International Rafting** (⊠ Jl. Tirta Ening 7, Bypass Ngurah Rai, Sanur, ☎ 0361/281408), and **Sobek** (⊠ Jl. Tirta Ening
9, Bypass Ngurah Rai, Sanur, ☎ 0361/287059).

TRAVEL AGENCIES
Nitour (⊠ Jl. Veteran 5, Denpasar, ☎ 0361/736096) is a reliable travel
agency and tour operator. **Pacto Ltd. Tours and Travel** (⊠ Bali Beach
Hotel, Jl. Tanjung Sari, Sanur, ☎ 0361/788449) provides tour and travel
services and also represents American Express. **Satriavi Tours & Travel**
(⊠ Jl. Cemara 27, Semawang, Sanur, ☎ 0361/287494) offers a comprehensive array of package tours and arranges custom trips. **Top Holiday Tour & Travel** (⊠ Jl. Legian Kaja 465, Legian, ☎ 0361/763087)
is an excellent one-stop shop for booking tours and transport tickets,
making reservations, mailing letters, changing money, and gathering
information on Bali.

VISITOR INFORMATION
Bali Tourist Information Center (⊠ Central Tourist Plaza, ground floor,
Jl. Benasati 7, Legian, ☎ 0361/754090). **Dipardi Bali** (⊠ Jl. Raya
Puputan Renon, Denpasar, ☎ 0361/238184). **Ubud Tourist Informa-
tion** (⊠ Jl. Raya, west of Monkey Forest Rd., ☎ 0361/973285).

NUSA TENGGARA

Dozens of islands that spill out eastward from Bali are part of the Nusa
Tenggara, the southeastern (*tenggara*) islands (*nusa*). They were formed
eons ago when shards of land broke from Sulawesi, 300 km (180 mi)
to the north, and from Australia, just 500 km (310 mi) south. Best known
are the stepping stones immediately east of Bali: Lombok, a serene haven
whose tourism industry is slowly growing; Sumbawa, a golden arc of
mountains and plains; Komodo, home of the dragons; Flores, a dive
paradise ringed by coral reefs; Timor, site of an ongoing struggle for
independence; and Sumba, island of bold ikat patterns and site of ancient battles. Between these islands are a smattering of islets: Rinca,
Roti, and the Solor and Alor archipelagos, to name a few.

Despite their relatively diminutive size, these arid islands are home to
many superlative natural sights. More than 40 volcanoes jut upward
from the sea in this province. The explosion of Sumbawa's Gunung
Tambora in 1814 was one of the largest in world history, and the 12,221-
ft summit of Lombok's Gunung Rinjani still rumbles threateningly from
time to time. Tiny Komodo is a mass of parched, dormant slopes
smothered in long, green-gold grasses. Flores has 14 active volcanoes
of its own. The islands' main wildlife includes birds—cockatoos, parrots, lories, and other Australian types—insects, and reptiles, such as
the famous Komodo dragon.

Most Nusa Tenggara inhabitants, like the people throughout much of
Indonesia, adhere to Islam. Still, there are subtle differences. The
Sasaks of Lombok resisted the influx of Hindu Balinese from the west
and have maintained unique brands of Islam. Farther east, the Sum-
bawanese have upheld the more traditional Muslim rites brought by
the Bugis and Makassarese of Sulawesi—although many people incorporate a healthy dose of animism into their practices. Animism is
also evident in the beliefs of the 1,000 or so villagers who live on Komodo. On Flores, 85% of the people are Catholic, thanks to missionaries who have been coming to this island since the 16th century.

The earliest outsiders were the intrepid 12th- and 13th-century traders
who discovered the islands' treasures of cinnamon, tortoiseshell, and

116

Nusa Tenggara

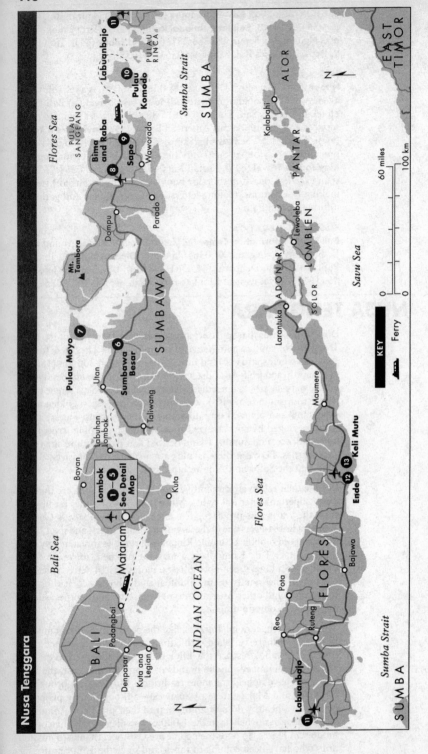

sandalwood during voyages around the Spice Islands of Maluku to the north. To this day, Nusa Tenggara remains well off the beaten path. Life has continued here in much the same way for five centuries. Even the modes of travel haven't changed much: aside from a few air routes (whose schedules are undependable), access is by daily ferries or weekly ships. Although there are long-distance buses that journey—on dusty mountain roads—between towns, in-town transport is primarily by horse-drawn cart or by bicycle. Development will no doubt work its way east from Bali, but these sunny islands are likely to remain untainted for a little while longer.

Lombok

The island of Lombok is just 45 km (27 mi) east of Bali, but it seems to exist several decades back in time. The beaches are superior to those of Bali, and the level of commercialism is substantially lower. Further, Lombok's drier climate is a distinct advantage during the rainy season (December–May).

Lombok, named for the island's well-known *lombok* (chili pepper), is home to two cultures: the Balinese Hindu and the Sasak Muslim. Most of the Balinese, who ruled the island until 1894, live on the island's western side around Ampenan, Mataram (the provincial capital), and Cakranegara (known for its handwoven textiles). Here you will find interesting Balinese temples, though none are as fully developed as in Bali. The Sasaks, who centuries ago came to Indonesia from northern India, live mainly in Lombok's central and eastern regions and comprise the majority of the island's 2.4 million population. Although they're included in the country's census of Islamic peoples, their religious practices are more animist and Hindu than Muslim. They're divided into two sects: the Wektu Telu (Three Prayers), whose rituals display more of a mix of doctrines, and the Wektu Lima (Five Prayers), who more stringently follow the guidelines of Islam.

Enjoy Lombok while you can, as the unspoiled atmosphere is changing fast: Senggigi Beach is now crowded with hotels, the beaches on the Gili coral atolls are already lined with low-priced bungalows, and more resorts at beaches to the south are planned, though property disputes had halted construction at press time.

Ampenan, Cakranegara, and Mataram

➊ *24 km (14 mi) north of Lembar (the port for Bali ferries), 1,200 km (744 mi) southeast of Jakarta.*

Most visitors are introduced to Lombok by way of Ampenan, Cakranegara, and Mataram—the string of towns that make up this island's most populated area. Each settlement has a separate function: western Ampenan is the port where travelers arrive by ship, ferry, and hydrofoil; Cakranegara, Lombok's former capital, is today a trading center; and Mataram is the island's administrative core and the site of the airport.

On the central town border between Mataram and Cakranegara is **Pura Meru,** the largest Balinese temple on Lombok. Constructed in 1720, Puru Meru is arranged around three courtyards full of small Meru shrines. The three most important—those to Shiva, Vishnu, and Brahma—are in the central courtyard.

Across from Pura Meru is **Taman Mayura,** once a Balinese royal palace, now a large artificial pool filled with lotus. In the pool's center is Bale Kembang, a floating pavilion that's similar to, but smaller and less ornate than, the one in Klungkung, Bali.

Lombok

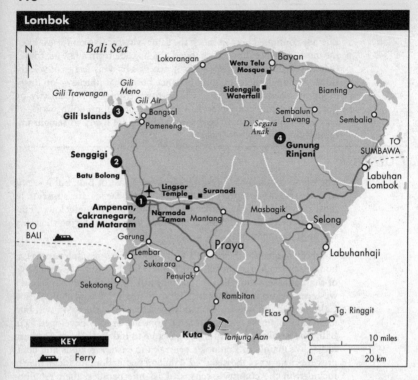

Bali Sea

KEY

🚗 Ferry

0 — 10 miles

0 — 20 km

The **Museum Negeri Nusa Tenggara Barat** (Museum of West Nusa Tenggara) has intriguing displays of island weaponry, decorative arts, and artifacts. ✉ *Jl. Panji Tilar No. 6,* ☎ *370/637503.* 🎫 *Rp 2,500.* ⏲ *Tues.–Sun. 8–2, Fri. until 11.*

OFF THE BEATEN PATH

NARMADA TAMAN – Lombok's most famous temple-palace complex is Narmada Taman (10 km [6 mi] east of Cakranegara), built in 1727. The architecture is an interesting mix of Hindu, Islamic, and Sasak, but the temple is notable for its man-made lagoon, which symbolizes the lake of the holy mountain, Gunung Rinjani, in north Lombok. The faithful explain that the replica's purpose was to permit an aging king to fulfill his religious obligations of throwing offerings into the mountaintop lake when he became too old to make the climb. However, more likely it was built so that the monarch could spy on the maidens washing in the pool. ✉ *Jl. Air Awet, Madan,* ☎ *0370/672490.* 🎫 *Rp 1,000.* ⏲ *Daily 7–7.*

Five kilometers (3 miles) north of Narmada is **Lingsar Temple,** built in 1714 by the first migrating Balinese and reconstructed in conjunction with Sasak Muslims as a symbol of their unity. Nearby is **Suranadi,** a cool hill town with a Hindu temple, especially venerated for its spring water and eels. Both promise good fortune.

Shopping

The best public market for handicrafts is in Cakranegara, on Jalan Hasanuddin. The Sweta market has moved east to Bertais, across the street from Mandalika bus terminal. Bertais is where you can shop for spices and beautifully made cane baskets that entrepreneurs buy and take back to Bali to sell at inflated prices. (Note that Bertais is also a hub for buses traveling to points east.)

Lombok Handicraft Center (✉ Jl. Hasannudin, Sayang) is also called Rungkang Jangkuk. If it's made in Lombok, one of the many stores at this complex is guaranteed to sell it. For a glimpse of the region's hand-woven textiles, head to **Slamat Riyadi** (⊠ Jl. Tanun, Cakranegara). For a glimpse of weavers at work, visit in the morning. Profits from **Lombok Pottery Centre** (⊠ Jl. Sriwijaya No. 111A, Mataram, ☎ 0370/640351; ⊠ Galleria Senggigi, Jl. Raya Senggigi, ☎ 0370/693370) are used to improved living conditions in pottery villages. For antiques and imitations, visit **Pak Sudirman** (☎ 0370/636315), who received a Presidential award for reviving Lombok's traditional crafts. There's a workshop in Ampenan and a Senggigi showroom with sporadic hours, so call for an appointment.

En Route   As you approach Senggigi from Mataram, you'll spot the **Batu Bolong** (Rock with a Hole) temple from alongside the road just a short way south. Perched above the ocean upon a huge outcrop that does, indeed, have a natural hole, the temple faces west toward Gunung Agung and the sunset. Beautiful maidens were supposedly tossed into the sea (as divine sacrifices) here in ancient days, reason enough why residents claim that sharks haunt these waters.

Senggigi

❷ *12 km (7 mi) northwest of Mataram.*

The narrow, curving strip of sand that comprises Senggigi was once a backpackers' escape from Bali's crowded beaches. Inexpensive accommodations are still available, but expensive resort hotels have begun to dominate the beach. Senggigi is still a pleasant place to relax, but it's no longer a quiet hideaway.

Dining and Lodging

$–$$ ✕ **Graha Restaurant.** Red-tile floors and red-check tablecloths add cheer to this thatched-roof restaurant. An outdoor terrace looks out over the sea, and soft jazz plays in the background. Specialties include grilled shrimp, *graha lumpia* (deep-fried spring rolls with sweet-and-sour sauce), and ikan *bumbu kuning* (fried and with a yellow sauce). Entrées come with garlic sauce and a choice of four kinds of sambal. ⊠ *Jl. Raya Senggigi,* ☎ *0370/693101. MC, V.*

$–$$ ✕ **Restaurant Naga.** The Chinese lanterns and eye-popping, vivid-yellow sign out front compel you to stop for a bite. Specialties include cashew chicken, Hong Kong duck, and Szechuan crab; specials might include Japanese seafood stew or baked spareribs. Free transport is available to and from area hotels. ⊠ *Jl. Raya Senggigi,* ☎ *0370/693207. MC, V.*

$ ✕ **Kafe Alberto.** For a quick meal of pizza, barbecued items, sushi, or homemade pasta, try this beachside, open-air restaurant, which offers traditional dancing lessons and Joget Gandrung and Putri Mandalika performances. ⊠ *Jl. Raya Senggigi,* ☎ *0370/693313 or 0370/693039. MC, V.*

$ ✕ **Lombok Coconut.** Over a meal of seafood, gourmet pizza, or pasta, you can chat about the dozens of stone carvings that decorate this restaurant's facade or about the birds that twitter in their cages. Eavesdropping on the often interesting conversations of other travelers is also an option. There's a money-back guarantee with every meal. ⊠ *Jl. Raya Senggigi,* ☎ *0370/693195. No credit cards.*

$$$$ ✕🏨 **Pool Villa Club.** The scent of coconut wood and teak greets guests
★   at these two-story villas on the Senggigi Beach Hotel grounds. Each has two ivory marble bathrooms and a sundeck and whirlpool facing a canal-shape swimming pool. An arched walk over the pool passes through frangipani and bougainvillea gardens, guarded by Hindi goddess fountains. Guests can drink at the swim-up bar with tree house–style swing chairs. Three restaurants, also open to nonguests, serve Italian, Asian, and French food. ⊠ *Jl. Raya Senggigi (Box 1001, Mataram*

83010), ☎ *0370/693210,* FAX *0370/693200. 16 villas. 3 restaurants, 2 bars, pool, spa, beach, snorkeling, windsurfing. AE, DC, MC, V.* 🍴

$$$–$$$$ 🏨 **Lombok Intan Laguna.** Beside the ocean it may be, but the Intan's focal point is its curving pool with arched stone bridge and round, thatched-roof bar. The two-story cottages have spacious rooms with tile floors, wood furniture, and indoor-outdoor bathrooms. Less expensive rooms are in a more modern, white, three-story building. At the open-air restaurant, the smell of flowers from the gardens is carried along on cooling sea breezes. A stay here puts you within walking distance of Senggigi's main shopping area. ✉ *Jl. Raya Senggigi (Box 1049, Mataram 83125),* ☎ *0370/693090,* FAX *0370/693185. 123 rooms. 2 restaurants, bar, pool, 2 tennis courts, exercise room, beach, shops. AE, DC, MC, V.* 🍴

$$$–$$$$ 🏨 **Senggigi Beach Hotel.** On a peninsula that juts into the Lombok Straits, this resort has thatched-roof cottages—each with several guest rooms—on 25 acres of grass, coconut trees, and white-sand beach. Modest rooms have twin beds, tables, chairs, and TVs; bathrooms have shower stalls rather than tubs. The open-sided dining room, overlooking the pool, serves mostly buffet-style breakfasts and dinners. ✉ *Jl. Raya Senggigi (Box 1001, Mataram 83101),* ☎ *0364/693210 or 0364/693219,* FAX *0364/693200. 148 rooms. Dining room, pool, spa, 2 tennis courts, badminton, beach, snorkeling, windsurfing, boating, travel services. AE, DC, MC, V.*

$$$–$$$$ 🏨 **Sheraton Senggigi Beach Resort.** The lobby, with its polished an-
★   tiques and bay views, immediately conveys the subtle elegance found throughout the resort. Landscaped grounds, thick with blossoms, embrace the three-story terraced buildings. Rooms have sumptuous wood and wicker furniture and Lombok craftwork; all look onto the gardens and the free-form pool, and many offer a glimpse of the beach. Two beachfront villas have private pools. The main restaurant offers indoor and outdoor dining, and the on-site stage is used for dance performances. ✉ *Jl. Raya Senggigi, Km. 8 (Box 1154, Mataram 83015),* ☎ *0370/693333 or 800/325–3535 in the U.S.,* FAX *0370/693140. 156 rooms. 3 restaurants, 3 bars, pool, spa, 2 tennis courts, health club, beach, snorkeling, windsurfing, boating, business services, travel services. AE, DC, MC, V.* 🍴

$$ 🏨 **Holiday Inn Resort Lombok.** This familiar Western establishment does a good job of mixing local traditions with foreign comforts. Stone walkways lead through gardens to connected chalets and larger, separate bungalows (each with several guest rooms); both types of accommodations have porches and large garden bathrooms. A layered pool surrounds a swim-up bar and Jacuzzi. Beside the pool is a dining terrace where local musicians stroll nightly. The adept travel staff can help arrange tours anywhere on the island. ✉ *Jl. Raya Mangsit (Box 1090, Mataran 83015),* ☎ *0370/693444,* FAX *0370/693092. 145 rooms, 14 bungalows. 2 restaurants, 3 bars, pool, massage, spa, health club, beach, snorkeling, windsurfing, boating, shops, laundry service, meeting rooms, travel services, car rental. AE, DC, MC, V.*

$–$$ 🏨 **Graha Beach.** Set on the beach, the Graha is one of the best of several inexpensive hotels and losmen in Senggigi. Clean, air-conditioned rooms have twin beds, tile floors, TVs, and private showers and toilets. There's a restaurant, small souvenir shop, and money exchange counter. Island tours can be arranged—prices are negotiable. ✉ *Senggigi Beach,* ☎ *0370/693101,* FAX *0370/693400. 39 rooms. Restaurant, beach, travel services, car rental. MC, DC, V.*

Nightlife and the Arts

Senggigi's main strip, Jalan Raya Senggigi, has a number of small bars and dance places that are busiest on Saturday nights. The **Indigo Bar**

(⌧ just north of Pacific Supermarket, ☏ 0370/693679) is a sleek lounge with plush blue couches and a teak bar. An acoustic band plays on weekends. The **Club Tropicana Bar and Restaurant** at Senggigi Square (☏ 0370/693463) has a dance floor with bands and DJs spinning salsa, pop, and rock. The **Sheraton Senggigi** (☞ *above*) (☏ 0370/693333) features various cultural performances weekly.

To explore local art, check out the shops at the **Pasar Seni** art market at the town's center, right on Jalan Raya Senggigi. Across from the post office, the **Pamour Art Gallery** (☏ 0370/693104) has exhibitions of Lombok and regional art, handicraft demonstrations, and an extensive collection of crafts and furnishings.

Outdoor Activities and Sports

For scuba and snorkeling trips to the Gilis, many travelers begin from Senggigi. On Jalan Raya Senggigi, try **Albatross** (☏ 0370/693399), which offers courses in English, Japanese, or European languages; **Blue Coral** (☏ 0370/693441), which claims to be the first PADI representative in Lombok; or the German-owned **Dream Divers** (☏ 0370/693738).

Gili Islands

❸ *5–8 km (3–5 mi) off the coast from Bangsal-Pameneng, which is 31 km (19 mi) northeast of Senggigi.*

A 30-minute drive north of Senggigi brings you to the Bangsal ferry dock, near Pameneng, where a small boat will zip you across to one of three coral atolls known collectively as the Gili Islands. All three islands have cottage bungalows that are popular with backpackers, most of which are simple bamboo huts (Rp 108,000–Rp 216,000) with a cold-water *mandi* (dip-bucket bath) and squat toilets; a few of the more upscale places have electricity. Most losmen rent snorkeling equipment, and dive trips can be arranged. Bring cash: credit cards are rarely accepted, and traveler's checks can be difficult to exchange.

Gili Air

Gili Air is closest to shore and requires only a quick 20-minute sea crossing in a motorized prahu. Here dazzling white sand meets crystal-clear water, and the coral reef is home to brightly colored tropical fish. The atmosphere is calm and uncluttered, the scenery simple and rural—a great place to clear your head.

DINING AND LODGING

$ ✕🏨 **Hotel Gili Air and Restaurant.** Gili Air's largest hotel has bungalows encircled by gardens. The modest, clean rooms have basic furnishings accented with island decor. Private bathrooms with flush toilets and running water are standard, and most rooms have beach and sea views; only 14 have air-conditioning and hot water, however. Continental breakfast is included in the price, and the on-site restaurant is open all day; pizzas are a specialty, and beachfront barbecues take place weekly. There's good snorkeling, and the friendly staff can help with tours around the islands. ⌧ *Desa Gili Indah, Pameneng,* ☏ 🇫🇦🇽 *0370/634435. 26 rooms. Restaurant, beach, snorkeling, travel services. MC, V.*

$$$$ 🏨 **The Oberoi, Lombok.** Hidden away on Lombok's northwest coast
★ and within sight of Gili Air, this resort offers the ultimate in upscale seclusion. Spacious terrace pavilions with lovely views are set on well-groomed grounds. High stone walls surround the private villas, each with a garden, fountain, and raised dining pavilion; some have plunge pools. Interiors have high, thatched-roof ceilings, marble floors, dark-teak furniture, oversized canopy beds; wicker seating areas; and garden or ocean views. Good-sized bathrooms have separate toilet and shower compartments, double marble sinks, large walk-through clos-

ets, and sunken tubs. Service is discreet and unobtrusive. The spa and fitness center offer deluxe traditional treatments. Two large pools face the ocean, and a boat is available to take you snorkeling at nearby reefs or to the Gilis. ⊠ *Pantai Medana, Tanjung (Box 1096, Mataram 83001),* ☎ *0370/638444,* ℻ *0370/632496. 20 villas, 30 terrace pavilions. 3 restaurants, 2 bars, in-room safes, pool, beauty salon, spa, health club, beach, snorkeling, windsurfing, library, laundry service, car rental. AE, DC, MC, V.* 🍃

OUTDOOR ACTIVITIES AND SPORTS

Blue Marlin (☎ 0370/634387) has an office in south Gili Air and can coordinate trips to the reefs. At Gili Air harbor, **Reefseekers Pro Dive** (☎ 0370/641008) is an excellent place to learn technique and ocean ecology (the owners also run a sea turtle nursery).

Gili Meno

For even more pristine waters, the next atoll, Gili Meno, has a greater abundance of sea life—red-lined triggerfish, starfish, five-line damsel, and the occasional shark—and, for scuba divers, there's unique blue coral 50 ft–80 ft below the surface. This is the quietest island, and it has earned its place as a divers' haven. Its accommodations and restaurants are basic, but that's part of its charm.

Gili Trawangan

Although it's the farthest island from Lombok, Gili Trawangan is the party island of the three Gilis, where most visitors come to get away from Bali crowds. The beaches are excellent here, and the diving is memorable. Despite the rapid rise in tourism, there are plenty of inexpensive accommodations and restaurants. **Hotel Villa Ombak** (☎ 0370/642753, ℻ 0370/642337) is the only resort on Gili Trawangan.

OUTDOOR ACTIVITIES AND SPORTS

Nearly on top of one another on Gili Trawangan's east side are **Albatross** (☎ 0370/630134), **Blue Coral** (☎ 0370/634497), and **Blue Marlin Dive Center** (☎ 0370/632424), which make regular dive excursions around the islands. A two-dive day trip is about Rp 537,600, and introductory through full-certification courses are available.

En Route Back on the mainland, on the way to Gunung Rinjani, consider a stop in **Bayan.** Its mosque stands on a stone platform and is said to be more than three centuries old—Lombok's oldest religious structure. This village is also rumored to be where the island's indigenous Wektu Telu (the less stringently Muslim of the island's two Sasak sects) religion was born. Among the highlights are the tall, spade-shape, traditional houses and rice barns. The settlements here are small, quiet clusters of life where men till the wide fields and women create beautiful original textiles. This is also a burgeoning tourist area where you're welcome to learn about and interact with the Sasak way of life.

Gunung Rinjani

❹ *77 km (50 mi) southeast of Bangsal, 82 km (51 mi) northeast of Mataram.*

Indonesia's third-highest mountain, after Puncak Jaya (16,564 ft) in Irian Jaya and Kerinci (12,600 ft) in Sumatra, 12,221-ft Gunung Rinjani is one of the most revered and feared summits in the country. Revered because, like Bali's Gunung Agung, it's considered a sacred summit, a place of the gods; feared because the mountain still occasionally shudders and spews fiery lava. Its beauty is stark and magnificent, a smoldering peak against blue sky and ocean, with the green crescent of Lake Segera Anak shimmering 6 km (4 mi) across outside the crater. The trek up the slope is breathtaking, both for the natural views and village scenes as well as the physical effort. (The hike to the rim and down to the lake can be dangerous and is best attempted by those who are in good shape and blessed with good balance.)

From Bayan, the trail around the rim has several approaches through the village settlements of Batu Koq and Senaru, 5 km (3 mi) and 8 km (5 mi) farther on. A 2-km (1-mi) side trip between them is to the Sendang Gila (Sindanggile) waterfall, where monkeys peer down from the trees alongside the path. Simple losmen abound here, as well as in the eastern villages of Sembulan Lawang and Sembulan Bumbung. Most trekkers plan on a three-day journey from Senaru or Batu Koq, taking time to explore nearby hot springs and falls one day and hiking up to the crater the next.

Take comfortable hiking boots, warm layers, a sleeping bag, a tent, a stove, cooking utensils, and a flashlight—most of which you can rent from losmen in Batu Koq and Senaru. Stock up on foodstuffs and water in Mataram, where there's more variety and where prices are lower. Several outfitters arrange organized treks (☞ Tour Operators *in* Nusa Tenggara A to Z, *below*).

Kuta and Environs

★ ❺ *143 km (89 mi) southwest of Bayan, 30 km (18 mi) southeast of Mataram.*

Once a tiny village on the shore of the Indian Ocean, **Kuta** is still quiet, but development plans by large hotels are on the horizon. The curving sandy beach, known as Putri Nyale Beach, is now cluttered with the activity of budget travelers who made this area famous, most of whom stay at one of the many losmen on the other side of the road.

Five kilometers (3 miles) southeast along the coast is the horseshoe-shape **Tanjung Aan,** one of the island's most beautiful beaches. Its fine, soft, white sands are usually deserted, except for windsurfers and a few vendors selling watermelons. All this may change—at press time the beach was slated for the development of several luxury hotels.

There are several small Sasak settlements just north of Kuta on the road to Mataram, including the village of **Rambitan.** Here, traditional Sasak houses and *lumbung* (a type of rice barn) are clustered together, and a few of the villagers sell batik sarongs at surprisingly low prices. Try to get a glimpse inside the houses, each of which has two main areas: the outer area where the men sleep and the inner one reserved for the women.

Farther north along the main road is **Penujak,** where lovely terracotta *gerabah* pottery is created; you'll also spot *gentong* (vessels), *jangkih* (traditional stoves), and wooden masks here. Cruise the main street to get a sense of design, selection, and quality. Although **Sukarara**'s fame as a traditional textile center has made it something of a tourist attraction (the costumed weavers at the looms in front of shops are just for show; the real weaving is done in the villages), it's definitely *the* place to see Lombok artisans' creative, colorful works.

Dining and Lodging

$$$ 🏨 **Novotel.** Kuta's only resort has a menu of activities that rivals Club Med. Aqua aerobics, pottery lessons, wood-carving demonstrations, and Sasak dance performances are just a sample of what guests can choose from, if they can be lured from the hotel's most enticing feature—Putri Nyale, a white-sand beach dwarfed by craggy limestone cliffs. Hotel architecture is equally dramatic, combining Sasak architecture with Sumbanese and African motifs. ✉ *Mandalika Resort,*

Pantai Putri Nyale (Box 5555, Mataram 83001), ☎ *0370/653333,* FAX *0370/653555. 85 rooms, 23 bungalows. 2 restaurants, bar, 2 pools, spa, health club, beach, snorkeling, boating, library, travel services, car rental. AE, DC, MC, V.* 🕾

$ ✕🏠 **Matahari Lombok Hotel and Restaurant.** This friendly establishment caters mainly to budget travelers, although its lovely setting and cleanliness make it seem more upscale. Three houses are available, one with 12 double rooms, one with 4, and one with 3—all with basic but pleasant local decor, but not all with private baths. Deluxe villas with garden bathrooms are poolside—the most unique is Lombok house, an A-frame with a loft bed. The restaurant offers Indonesian and Western dishes. The hotel is in the village but is within walking distance of the beach. ✉ *On Kuta's main thoroughfare,* ☎ *0370/655000 or 0370/654832,* FAX *0370/654909. 26 rooms. Restaurant, pool. MC, V.* 🕾

Sumbawa, Komodo, and Flores

Sumbawa

Sumbawa is an island of strict Islamic beliefs and stunning scenery, where boys race wild horses through golden plains, men practice bare-fisted *berempah* boxing in the high mountain villages, water buffalo are still used to pull plows through rice fields, and Gunung Tambora's lavender shadow towers over the bright central shoreline.

Sumbawa Besar

❻ *100 km (62 mi) east of Labuhan Lombok, 1,360 km (843 mi) southeast of Jakarta.*

Once the center of the Sumbawa sultanate that dominated the island's western half, Sumbawa Besar, or Big Sumbawa, is a rather small settlement. On the northwest coast, a two-hour drive from the ferry terminal at Poto Tano and less than an hour's flight from Mataram, it's usually just a pass-through point for those heading to the wildlife reserve at Pulau Moyo (☞ *below*). Still, this clean, quiet, welcoming town has a few noteworthy sights.

On Jalan Batu Pasak, the **Dalam Loka,** or old sultan's palace, is an assembly of raised wooden structures with tiered roofs built in 1885 and restored in the early 1980s. The original structure has 99 pillars to honor Allah's 99 names. You can stroll around the grounds for a look at Sumbawan architecture or ask for the manager, who can give you a tour of the rooms and explain the significance of the few vestiges of palace days—mostly drawings and decorations—on display inside.

Today, the sultans' descendants reside at the **Bale Kuning** on Jalan Wahidin, where many of the royal families' possessions are still kept; the tourist office (☞ Visitor Information *in* Nusa Tenggara A to Z, *below*) can arrange a visit with advance notification. A black-sand beach at **Kencana,** 11 km (7 mi) west of town, has decent reefs for snorkeling and views of northern Pulau Moyo.

DINING AND LODGING

A new mining project in southwest Sumbawa has encouraged more Western-style restaurants and accommodations in the Besar, such as **Hotel Cendrawasih** (✉ Jl. Cendrawasih No. 130A, ☎ 0371/24184). For Chinese food, try **Aneka Rasa Jaya,** on Jalan Hasanuddin, or have seafood at **Surabaya,** off Jalan Yos Sudarso.

$–$$ 🏠 **Tambora Hotel.** This midsize hotel, just five minutes from the airport, is your best option for an in-town stay. Rooms are simple and clean, and service is attentive. The hotel is a good base for day trips around the area, and it also has a minimart, an art shop, and a copy center on-site. Rates include breakfast. ⊠ *Jl. Kebayan,* ☏ *0371/21555. 49 rooms. Restaurant, travel services. AE, MC, V.*

$ ⌷ **Kencana Beach Cottages.** Just 15 minutes from the airport, this pleasant hotel is set in gardens surrounded by bamboo and palm trees. A gathering of colorful and very spacious traditional bamboo bungalows on stilts faces a black-sand beach where the clear water offers hints of the coral below. Wooden floors, white walls, high ceilings, and traditional woven art and paintings complete the elegantly simple decor. The location is quiet, but if you need more activity than just relaxing by the pool all day, there's plenty to keep you busy. The amicable staff at the on-site travel office can arrange trips to buffalo races, traditional villages, waterfalls, and Pulau Moyo. Before you set out, you can have a good breakfast, which is included in the room price. ⊠ *Jl. Raya Tano, Km 11, Badas,* ☏ *0371/22555,* FAX *0371/22439. 25 bungalows. Restaurant, bar, pool, massage, beach, dive shop, snorkeling, laundry service, travel services. No credit cards.*

Pulau Moyo

★ ➐ *20 km (12 mi) northeast of Sumbawa Besar.*

The focal point of the nature reserve on Moyo Island, just off Sumbawa's northeastern coast, is 402-ft Gunung Moyo. Although wildlife spotting is a draw, the main attraction is diving and snorkeling, and the island's remote location, extensive reefs, and upscale resort have made it the darling of expensive package tours. Some of the best reefs are around Tanjung Pasir and Aik Manis. For maps and permits, contact the **Dinas Perlindungan dan Pengawetan Alam (PHPA)**—otherwise known as the Forest Authority—office in Sumbawa Besar (☞ Visitor Information *in* Nusa Tenggara A to Z, *below*). For package tours, try the **Hotel Tambora** or the **Kencana Beach Cottages** (☞ *above*), the latter of which can charter a speedboat for two dozen people at a daily rate of about Rp 400,000. If you'd like to visit the island independently, you can take a half-hour ride in a local fishing vessel (around Rp 15,000 each way) from Aik Bari on the coast.

DINING AND LODGING

$$$$ ✕⌷ **Amanwana.** Its name, which means "peaceful forest," couldn't
★ be more appropriate. Nestled into a wooded setting facing a secluded beach, the large, luxurious tents mimic a mix of camping and island-bungalow features: simple yet spacious individual bale pavilions are surrounded by smooth terraces and protected by graceful, sloping canvas roofs held up by strong ropes and wooden poles. Despite their simple appearance, rooms are opulent and comfortable, with collectors' pieces of traditional art, polished wood floors, soft, sumptuous couches, king-size beds, writing desks, and large bathrooms. Although the pavilions are enclosed, only one wall is solid; the rest are panels that slide back to reveal huge glass windows, which afford a spectacular 270-degree view of the surrounding forest and bay. A library in the main building has an intriguing selection of books and works of art. The intimate, open-air bar-lounge has a thatched roof and overlooks the bay. ⊠ *Pulau Moyo,* ☏ *0371/22233 or 0361/771267 (for reservations),* FAX *0371/22288. 20 luxury tents. Restaurant, bar, dining room, lobby lounge, hiking, beach, snorkeling, windsurfing, boating, library, laundry service, travel services, airport shuttle. AE, DC, MC, V.* ✇

Bima and Raba

➑ *230 km (143 mi) east of Sumbawa Besar.*

Seven hours' drive from Sumbawa Besar, neighboring Bima and Raba are Sumbawa's main eastern settlements. Bima is the island's major port and the former sultanate that shared power over the island with the royal family of western Sumbawa; Raba is the main bus transit point 5 km (3 mi) east.

Things to see in these towns include the old **Sultan's Palace** in Bima on Jalan Sultan Ibrahim, which doubles as a museum of artifacts from the royal family and the region. Included in the collection are books, furniture, and weaponry. The palace is open 8–6 Monday through Saturday. There's a suggested donation of Rp 5,000; guides will be grateful for another Rp 1,000. For a contrast, explore the new **Royal Palace** on Jalan Sumbawa, where the sultans' descendents have a collection of formal attire, decorative jewelry, and royal valuables on display. Book an appointment to visit through the tourist office (☞ Visitor Information *in* Nusa Tenggara A to Z, *below*).

Sape

⑨ *50 km (31 mi) southeast of Bima and Raba.*

The muted clip-clop of horses' hooves on soft dirt roads echoes through the hills of Sape (*sah*-pay), Sumbawa's easternmost town. This sublime port—teeming with lively markets selling produce and colorful woven crafts—is the road traveler's stopping point en route to Komodo. Low, one-story homes line narrow streets traversed by horse-drawn carts (known here as Ben Hurs because they resemble the chariots used in the movie); occasionally, soulful Islamic music can be heard. The nearby rough, grassy mountains make for a good day's hike to supreme views over the town and the bay. Ferries to Komodo and Flores leave at 8 AM daily except Friday, and the morning crowd at the docks can be quite festive. For those stuck in town when the ferry breaks down—not an uncommon occurrence—things to do include visiting local weaving workshops, hiking in the hills, and practicing Indonesian with local tour guides who want to polish their English.

DINING AND LODGING

Most losmen will dish up a home-cooked meal for their guests. Fried rice, fried noodles, fried vegetables, or grilled fish with white rice are what you'll find across the board. There are a number of small losmen along the main road, each offering a half-dozen clean, quiet rooms with private Indonesian cold-water baths. Try **Losmen Friendship,** near the port, or **Losmen Mutiara,** a two-story, shared-bath hotel next to the docks.

Pulau Komodo

★ ⑩ *320 km (198 mi) east of Sumbawa Besar, 90 km (56 mi) east of Bima, 40 km (25 mi) east of Sape.*

On the approach to Komodo, a tiny island just 36 km (22 mi) long and 16 km (9 mi) across at its widest point, it's hard to imagine that it's home to the fearsome dragons described by late-19th-century explorers. Komodo's soft curves and parched golden grasses slide up over the topaz bay of lively coral reefs, glass-clear waters, and white-sand beach. But then you remember that this innocent-looking island is inhabited by 13-ft, 220-pound adult *ora*, as the dragons are known locally. Don't be frightened, though: although stories of European tourists and village children disappearing run rampant, a trip here is quite safe. The park office is right at the docks, and from it a mild 2-km (1-mi) walk along a sandy path brings you to the dragons' lairs. You'll see them sunning themselves in forest ravines or snuggling up in shallow caves inside cliff walls.

Local legends say that the dragons are descendents of a lost child who once took refuge in one of their burrows. Modern science reports that the dragons evolved from dinosaurs that lived in Asia some 130 million years ago. They're the largest lizards on earth, with a population of around 2,000, and they live only on Komodo, the nearby island of Rinca, and parts of Flores. Their soft, white eggs hatch in April or May, with a three-to-one ratio of males to females. The dragons have sharp hearing and a keen sense of smell (they can pick up the scent of carrion, their favorite treat, 7 mi away). They're fast, too, running at speeds of up to 18 mph and eating at a rate of six pounds of meat a minute. (At one time goats were slaughtered twice a week to attract the dragons, but these slaughters now take place much less frequently so that the dragons can be observed in the wild.) The dragons are also excellent swimmers—to the chagrin of those who are tempted to snorkel in the calm bay at the park's eastern edge. But the dragons aren't the only danger here: this is also an island of giant spiders, vipers, and scorpions. Thus, a guide must accompany everyone outside the main park compound, and you're encouraged to walk carefully and be aware of your surroundings at all times.

Travel to Komodo doesn't have to be the arduous journey of days past, thanks to luxury tour packages via speedboats from Bali, Lombok, and Flores. However, these are only short ventures; to stay longer and explore this fascinating island, you must prepare for a much simpler lifestyle. Komodo does have its amenities, namely an open-air restaurant that serves up simple fare, sells supplies, and rents a half-dozen raised wooden cabins. A 2-km (1-mi) low-tide beach walk from the park office, Kampung Komodo is a local settlement of a few dozen raised huts and colorful fishing boats. Here you can meet the islanders and hear their stories. English-speaking guides can be hired at the park office to translate.

Dining and Lodging

$ ╳☷ **Pulau Komodo Bungalows.** A half-dozen simple, raised wooden cabins grace the edge of a wide lawn and overlook grazing deer and scampering pigs. Each structure has four small bedrooms, a shared cold-water mandi, a common living area, and a wide balcony; the double rooms in front are the largest and coolest. The afternoon breeze eliminates the need for fans, as does the shortage of electricity, which only runs from 6 PM to 10 PM. A restaurant across the yard serves basic Indonesian fare, but you may want to bring your own food if you're staying more than one night. Note: Keep all luggage sealed and all food out of the rooms, as animals have been known to raid the cabins. This is the only place to stay on the island; otherwise, it's necessary to stay aboard a tour boat in the bay. ⊠ *Loh Liang, 100 yards northwest of PHPA office,* ☎ *no phone. 12 rooms. Restaurant, beach, snorkeling. No credit cards.*

Outdoor Activities and Sports

Komodo may be small, but there's plenty to do if you're the intrepid sort and have a few days. You can hire guides (Rp 25,000 for up to five people) to hike to the 1,731-ft Gunung Ara and other peaks. Overnight camping trips can also be arranged. You can spot still more wildlife on a side trip to Pulau Rinca, where dragon sighting is less commercialized than on Komodo. The snorkeling around this island's reefs is also spectacular. Divers can organize trips from Labuanbajo, Flores (☞ Outdoor Activities and Sports *in* Labuanbajo, *below*). Since there's no regular boat transport to Rinca, you must sign up for an organized tour or hire your own boat from Labuanbajo. At press time, **Reefseekers Pro Dive** (☞ Outdoor Activities and Sports *in* Gili Islands, *above*) planned to facilitate dive trips to the area from a neighboring island.

Flores

Originally named Cabo de Flores, or Cape of Flowers—owing to its blossoming coastlines—by 16th-century Portuguese traders, Flores is a rugged, arid island of smoldering volcanic peaks and teal bays ripe for exploring. Although they were once under the control of Sulawesi's Bugis and Makassarese peoples, the inhabitants of Flores are actually closer in culture to the early Melanesian civilizations that migrated west to the Indonesian archipelago. In addition, Flores's population is 85% Catholic, a significant statistic in an archipelago that's 90% Muslim. However, the island's draw is not really its culture, but rather its diving. The reefs here are some of Indonesia's best.

Labuanbajo

⑪ *100 km (62 mi) northeast of Sape on Sumbawa.*

A tiny settlement of one-story shops, homes, and losmen now does brisk business as a tourist jumping-off point for travelers heading by boat or plane west to Komodo, east to the gem-color lakes of Keli Mutu, or around the island on lengthy dive trips. Don't miss the Pasar Malam night market at the town's south end, where you can pick up a cheap bite to eat while finding inexpensive souvenirs. There are many simple, comfortable places to stay and numerous beaches and reefs to explore.

If you have an afternoon, check out **Batu Cormin,** a cave 4 km (2½ mi) outside of town. Several nearby islands have beaches that are worth visiting, including **Batugosok, Kanawa, Bididari, Sabolo Besar,** and **Sabolo Kecil;** the latter three also have excellent reefs for diving and snorkeling.

DINING AND LODGING

Most small losmen have their own small restaurants; peruse the diverse menus on a scenic stroll along the main road. There are more than a dozen small losmen along Jalan Yos Sudarso as well. Touts will try to strike bargains with you as you step off the ferry. Always insist on seeing accommodations first before making a deal, though; most places are simple and clean, but you never know if it's what you want until you see it. Walking along the main road is also a good way to check out the many travel booths and find out about the trips that they offer, as well as learn about additional accommodations and activities on the islands within an hour's boat ride of town.

$ ✕🏨 **Gardena Bungalows.** Just a few yards from the ferry dock, this hillside hotel offers traditional wooden bungalows with verandas above the bay in a garden setting. There's no air-conditioning, but fans are provided; all rooms also have beds with mosquito nets and private bathrooms with showers. This is a popular place, and the friendly staff can assist you with tours to Komodo and Rinca, snorkeling trips to Bididari and Sabolon islands, and bus and ferry tickets. A small restaurant serves Indonesian, Chinese, and Western fare; breakfast is included in the price. ⊠ *Jl. Yos Sudarso, 86554,* ☎ *0385/41258. 19 bungalows. Restaurant, laundry service, travel services. No credit cards.*

$ 🏨 **Puri Komodo Resort.** On a peninsula at Flores's northwest tip, this
★ back-to-nature retreat is a relaxing hideaway. The 50-acre resort sits on a long stretch of sugar-white sand at the edge of a huge coral reef, making it a prime spot for dive trips. The 13 basic, clean bungalows have breezy balconies and are equipped with American-style spring mattresses. Bathrooms are outside the rooms and include traditional bamboo showers with stone waterfalls; the toilet facilities are Western, however. The spacious two-story chalet has six rooms, each with a private indoor bathroom. The serene gardens are a lovely place to walk in the cool evenings before dining in the seaside restaurant. The resort

is 20 minutes by boat from Labuanbajo, but transfers and trips into town are free. Tours to Komodo, Rinca, and other area attractions can be arranged on-site. ✉ *Batu Gosok, 86554,* ☎ *0385/41319,* ℻ *0385/ 41030. 13 bungalows, 1 chalet. Restaurant, beach, snorkeling, travel services. No credit cards.* ✍

OUTDOOR ACTIVITIES AND SPORTS

Puri Komodo Resort (☞ Dining and Lodging, *above*) offers trips to Komodo and Rinca, as well as dive tours around Flores. **Kencana** and **Perama** organize boat trips to Komodo, Rinca, and other points around Flores. All of these are on Jalan Yos Sudarso, the town's 2-km (1-mi) main strip. Not all tours offer the same amenities, so it pays to check out what you'll get for your money; accommodations, food, equipment, supplies, entrance fees, and souvenirs may or may not be included.

Ende

⓬ *250 km (155 mi) southeast of Labuanbajo.*

At a mountain's base and on the sea's edge, Ende is a waiting point for many travelers catching ships to other parts of Nusa Tenggara and those heading east to Keli Mutu (☞ *below*). You can wander the lively **daily market** on Jalan Pasar at the waterfront for a taste of local culture. The **Ende Museum** on Jalan Perwira is actually a house where former President Sukarno was exiled by the Dutch in 1933 (☉ Mon.–Sat. 8–1). For those interested in architecture, the neighboring village of **Wolotopo** is a good place to see traditional woven textiles and the local style of raised wooden houses.

SHOPPING

To find quality ikat textiles from both Flores and Sumba, try the **market** on the corner of Jalan Pasar and Jalan Pabean. Eight kilometers (5 miles) east of Ende, the village of **Nggela** is the home of many traditional ikat weavers. The blankets sold here are good buys.

Keli Mutu

★ ⓭ *66 km (41 mi) northeast of Ende.*

A volcanic crater filled with a trio of gem-color lakes, Keli Mutu has attracted visitors for more than a century. The site's magic is that these three lakes change color—and no one knows why. (Scientists have theorized that the variations are caused by minerals in the soil or water.) In the 1960s, they were rust, navy, and cream; now they are teal, olive, and ebony. According to legend, souls of the dead inhabit the lakes and account for the variation in colors; sinners are condemned to the dark lake, old souls inhabit the cold turquoise waters, and young people rest in the green lakes. The view of the sunrise over the crater is one of the archipelago's most memorable.

The mountain is reached from Ende via the town of Moni, which is 14 km (9 mi) from the mountaintop. Trucks and minibuses make the journey up the 14-km (9-mi) road before dawn (before clouds shadow the view) and return between 7 and 8 AM, but many visitors prefer to ride up and then make the 2½-hour walk back down to Moni. There are also a number of hot springs and waterfalls just outside Moni. You can stay in a losmen in Moni or make this a day trip from Ende.

Nusa Tenggara A to Z

Arriving and Departing

By Airplane
Air Mark (☎ 361/759769 in Bali, 370/643564 in Lombok) and **Merpati** (☎ 0364/22226 in Bali, 370/636745 in Lombok) run shuttle ser-

vice, with flights every hour beginning at 8 AM, from Denpasar to Lombok's **Selaparang Airport** in Mataram. The last flight is around 5 PM. You can buy tickets at the airport an hour before departure. Note that flights tend to be late and are frequently canceled.

Elsewhere in the Nusa Tenggara, the main airports are at Sumbawa Besar, Bima, Labuanbajo, and Ende. Flights to Mataram on Lombok, Denpasar on Bali, Ujung Pandang on Sulawesi, and Jakarta on Java depart a few times weekly, but schedules are unpredictable and flights are often canceled. For details on air transport, contact **Merpati** (☎ 0374/42697 in Bima). The airport in Sumbawa Besar is just yards from the Hotel Tambora, but bemos make the journey from other points in town for around Rp 500. Bima's airport is 16 km (10 mi) from town, Rp 15,000 by taxi. The Labuanbajo airport is 3 km (2 mi) from town, a Rp 6,000 taxi ride. Ende's airport is just outside town at the junction of Jalan Ahmad Yani, Jalan Keli Mutu, Jalan El Tari, and Jalan Gatot Subroto; backpackers walk it, but you can also take a bemo for about Rp 500.

By Boat

Ferries make the four-hour crossing from Padangbai, east of Denpasar on Bali, to Lembar, south of Ampenan on Lombok, every two hours between 2 AM and 10 PM; the fare is about Rp 7,000. Since the ferry docks some distance from the tourist centers on both Bali and Lombok (it takes three bemos to travel from Lembar Harbor to Senggigi), a bus/ferry package—between Ubud, Kuta, or Sanur on Bali and Mataram or Senggigi on Lombok—is a good idea. Fares are reasonable (e.g., Rp 35,000 from Kuta to Senggigi), and most travel agents can make arrangements. Try **Dewi Sri Murni Tours** (☎ 0361/730272) in Kuta on Bali. On Lombok, contact **Perama Travel** (☞ Tour Operators, *below*).

The *Mabua Express* (☎ 0370/681195 in Lembar or 0361/721212 in Bali) luxury hydrofoil takes just 2½ hours to cross from Tanjung Benoa in southern Bali to Lembar. It leaves at 8 AM from Tanjung Benoa and at 5:30 PM from Lembar. The fare is Rp 179,200 in Emerald Class (lower deck) and Rp 224,000 in Diamond Class (upper deck); there is an extra charge to Kuta, Nusa Dua, or Sanur on Bali and to Bangsal, Mataram, or Senggigi on Lombok. The *Bounty* (☎ 0361/733333 in Bali, 0370/693567 in Lombok) is a 500-passenger catamaran that travels to Lombok, departing at 8 AM from Bali's Benoa Harbour. It returns to Bali at 1:30 PM from the harbor by Senggigi's art market. The price is Rp 313,600.

Ferries depart hourly between dawn and dusk (the last one is around 5 pm) from Labuhan Lombok for the 1½-hour journey to Poto Tano on Sumbawa's west coast; fares are around Rp 6,000 for air-conditioned (and smoke-filled) quarters and Rp 4,000 for deck class; vehicle transport costs Rp 8,000–Rp 20,000. Public ferries heading east from western Sumbawa no longer stop at Komodo. For the 10-hour journey to Labuanbajo, Flores, the cost is about Rp 15,000. In theory, the ferry departs at 8 AM every day but Friday, but check on the schedule and the ferry's condition before you show up at the docks (crossings have been canceled for weeks at a time due to boat repairs). Boats to Komodo may also be chartered at around Rp 100,000 for up to six people; most hotels or travel agencies can make arrangements.

The national fleet of **Pelni** (✉ Jl. Industri No. 1, Ampenan, ☎ 0370/637212) ships (large, cruise ship–type vessels) stop at Sumbawa Besar's satellite port of Badas, 7 km (4 mi) to the west, every two weeks. Pelni also pauses at Sumbawa Besar weekly, alternating journeys between

Lembar on Lombok and a route that encompasses Waingapu, Sumba, Ende, Flores, Kupang, and Timor. Costs range from about Rp 35,000 per segment for economy class (bunk beds in shared rooms of 100 or more, shared baths, and three simple meals a day) to about Rp 100,000 or more per segment for first class (a two-bed cabin and more elaborate meals).

From Labuanbajo, ferries depart every day but Friday at 8 AM for the 10-hour journey to Sape on Sumbawa (Rp 11,500). In Ende, the Pelabuhan Ipi dock is 3 km (2 mi) from town. The **Pelni office** (✉ Jl. Katerdral No. 2, ☎ 381/21043) has schedule details. A regular ferry also cruises south to the island of Sumba on Tuesday and east to Kupang on Timor on Saturday.

By Bus

Buses/ferries are an important form of transportation between islands in Nusa Tenggara. Sumbawa Besar has a new terminal, Karang Dima, which is 6 km (4 mi) northwest of town (in front of Tirtasari Hotel); vehicles leave for Lombok at 6, 8, and 9 AM and again at 3 PM and depart for Bima between 7 and 9 AM and at 8 PM, but check on the schedule first, since departure often depends on when the bus is full. Bima's terminal for points west is just outside the town center; buses to Lombok leave in the evening around 7:30 PM, and smaller buses to towns on Sumbawa run between 6 AM and 5 PM. Express buses to Lombok and Bali meet the ferries from Labuanbajo in Sape, Sumbawa's eastern port. Buses from Sape transfer in Bima for towns west. Those from Labuanbajo head east for Ende around 7 AM and then again around 4 PM when the ferry from Sape arrives.

Getting Around

By Bemo and Horse-Drawn Cart

Public transport on Lombok consists primarily of bemos and the *cidomo,* a horse-drawn cart that seats four or five and costs about Rp 1,000 per km (½ mi). Elsewhere in the Nusa Tenggara, bemos are the way to get around; most cost around Rp 500 for short distances, though the government-regulated prices were due to increase at press time; bargain with drivers for longer jaunts. Many areas still have horse-drawn carriages called *dokars,* also known as Ben Hurs in Sape.

By Bus and Taxi

The central bus terminal on Lombok is in Bertais, 2 km southeast of Sweta. Government-set fares are posted. Metered taxis are available from the airport and at hotels (though you can also hire them for a flat fee to take tours). In Lombok, they start at Rp 1,700 and then Rp 750 per km; prices are fixed from the airport (a taxi from the airport to Senggigi is Rp 15,000; to Kuta, Rp 62,000).

Unless you've hired your own vehicle to drive east through the other islands, buses are the only way to reach the small towns. Taxis are available in the larger settlements, but usually only for short-distance trips.

By Car

On Lombok, rental cars rent for Rp 150,000–Rp 250,000 a day (excluding a driver). Try **Toyota Lombok** ☎ (0370/626363); **Rinjani Rent Car** (☎ 0370/632259), on Jalan Bung Karno in Mataram across from the Hotel Granada; or **Metro Rent Car** (☎ 0370/632146), on Jl. Yos Sudarso in Ampenan, which rents small Suzuki jeeps for Rp 125,000–Rp 200,000, including insurance. In Senggigi, try **Arwidas** ☎ (0370/693843), which charges Rp 224,000–Rp 313,600 a day for a four-wheel-drive vehicle. You can also rent a car or hire a car and driver through major hotels.

Contacts and Resources

Emergencies
Scuba-Diving Emergencies: The closest decompression chamber is at Bali's Sanglah Hospital (⊠ Jl. Nias, Denpasar, ☎ 0361/227911).

LOMBOK
Ambulance: ☎ 118. **Fire:** ☎ 113. **Hospital: Klinik Senggigi Medical Services** (⊠ Jl. Raya Senggigi, near Pacific Supermarket, ☎ 0370/693210). **Police:** ☎ 110. Senggigi Tourist Police (☎ 370/693267 or 370/693110).

OTHER ISLANDS
Hospitals: Public Hospital of Sumbawa (⊠ Labuanbajo; head away from docks on main road and take first left after BRI Bank). **Public Hospital of Sumbawa** (⊠ Jl. Garuda, Sumbawa Besar, ☎ 0371/21087). **Police: Bima Police Station** (☎ 0374/21110). **Sumbawa Besar Police Station** (☎ 0371/21142).

English-Language Bookstores
Most major Lombok resorts have at least a few books, news magazines, and international papers available. Used bookstores come and go in the tourist areas of Senggigi and Kuta; ask at your hotel. The **Senggigi Supermarket and Department Store** (⊠ Jl. Raya Senggigi, ☎ 0370/693738) sells guidebooks, maps, and novels. In Kuta, **Kimen,** on Jalan Parawisata (next to Ocean Blue surf shop), has a variety of used books. Aside from this, however, you will find few bookshops selling English-language material on the island. Lombok guidebooks are available at some resorts, but the selection is often better in Bali.

If you're desperate for reading material on the other islands, local hotels usually have a few books to trade, or you can trade with fellow travelers. Unfortunately, outside of the more touristed areas, the bookstore concept hasn't caught on in Indonesia.

Tour Operators

LOMBOK
Bidy Tour and Travel (⊠ Jl. Ragigenep 17, Ampenan, ☎ 0370/632127 or 0370/634095) offers treks, island cruises, dive packages, visits to villages, and fishing trips. The agency can also help with general travel arrangements. **Perama** (⊠ Jl. Pejanggik No. 66, Mataram, ☎ 0370/635936; ⊠ Jl. Raya Senggigi, Senggigi, ☎ 0370/693007) coordinates treks to Gunung Rinjani, day tours of Lombok, and land/sea adventure tours to Komodo. **Pt. Lombok Independent Tours** (⊠ Jl. Gunung Kerinci 4, Mataram, ☎ 0370/632497) arranges farmhouse stays, monkey walks, and rain-forest treks. **Satriavi Tours & Travel** (⊠ Senggigi Beach Hotel, ☎ 0370/693080 or 0370/693210) organizes a variety of island tours, including treks to Gunung Rinjani. **Spice Island Cruises** (☎ 0361/286283) travels from Bali to Lombok, Sumbawa, and Komodo.

FLORES
Grand Komodo Tours and Travel (⊠ Jl. Sukarno Hatta 45, Bima, ☎ 0374/42018; ⊠ Jl. P. W. Papu, Labuanbajo, ☎ 0385/4127) organizes dive trips throughout Nusa Tenggara on live-aboard boats. **Puri Komodo Resort** (⊠ Batu Bosok, Labuanbajo, ☎ 0385/41319 or 0385/41310) coordinates a variety of tours and treks.

Travel Agencies
The following Lombok companies can make travel arrangements: **Lombok Indah Tour and Travel** (⊠ Booth at Pacific Supermarket, Senggigi, ☎ 0370/693838). **Nazareth Tours and Travel** (⊠ Jl. Koperasi 62, Ampenan, ☎ 0370/631695). **Perama** (⊠ Jl. Yos Sudarso, Labuanbajo).

Visitor Information

The **Regional Office of Tourism** (⊠ Jl. Langko No.70, Ampenan, ☎ 0370/631730, 631829, FAX 0370/637838) is open Monday–Thursday 7–2, Fridays 7–11, and Saturday 7–12:30.

The **Labuanbajo Tourist Office** (⊠ Dinas Pariwisata, ☎ 0385/41170) keeps odd hours, though scheduled hours are weekdays 7–2 and Saturdays until noon; if you want information, it's best to stop by as soon as you get off the ferry from Sape.

The **Bima Tourist Office** (⊠ Jl. Soekarno Hatta, ☎ 0374/44331) is open 7–3 Monday through Friday and Saturday until noon. The **PHPA Office Information Booth** (⊠ Jl. Yos Sudarso, Bima, ☎ no phone) provides general information on Komodo and Rinca. It's open Monday–Thursday 8–4 and Friday–Saturday 8–11. The **Sumbawa Besar Tourist Office** (⊠ Jl. Bungur No. 1, ☎ 0371/23714) opens Monday–Thursday 8–4 and Friday–Saturday 8–11. For information on the national parks, try the **PHPA Office** (⊠ Jl. Garuda 12, Sumbawa Besar, ☎ 0371/21358), which is open 8–2 weekdays.

SULAWESI

To the north and east of Bali and Java is the island of Sulawesi, formerly called the Celebes. Four long peninsulas radiate from a central mountainous area, giving the island an orchid shape. Its topography is dramatic—from rice fields, rain forests, and mountains to bays where sugar-white sand crescents gently slip into sapphire water and dazzling coral reefs. Sulawesi is actually a puzzle of land masses that were pieced together over millions of years, its arms once connected to Borneo, New Guinea, and even Antarctica. The island also inherited plenty of natural power from the "ring of fire" into which it was born, for Sulawesi has 11 active volcanoes. The crushing tectonic forces that pushed the island's arms into place resulted in a mountain chain that stretches 1,300 km (806 mi) from north to south. Still, no point on the island is more than 100 km (62 mi) from the sea.

With its pieces sliding together from all over Earth, Sulawesi is the home of many unique species; in fact, two-thirds of its mammals and one-third of its birds are found nowhere else in the world. Included in its rare cast of wildlife are the *babirusa* (deer pig) and two types of *anoa* (pygmy buffalo). Several national parks, including Morowali, Lore Lindu, Tangkoko Batuangus Dua Saudara, and Pulau Manado Bunaken Tua, are prime trekking and wildlife-watching spots—if you're the adventurous sort. At present, Sulawesi is virtually unspoiled, its tourist infrastructure confined mostly to the southwestern port of Ujung Pandang, central Tanatoraja, and northeastern Manado.

The earliest human inhabitants were seafaring tribes who sailed through the straits from other parts of Asia and from Australia. The first major settlement was southern Soppeng, which was soon overshadowed by Mankasara—now Ujung Pandang—and northern Manado, both busy trading hubs on the way to and from Malaku's Spice Islands. Mankasara in particular rose to prominence in the 16th century as the aggressive Bajau "sea gypsies" and Bugis tribes took over the waters. In fact, the Bugis were so feared by Asian and Western traders venturing into the region that they became the basis for the modern-day term "Boogey (Bugi) Man." However, it took just a century or so for the Dutch to dominate trade in the region and later take over much of the island, changing the capital's name to Makassar in the process. As Islam spread through the lower peninsula in the early 1600s, the Dutch began working their way north and inland to a region the Bugis called Tanatoraja, the fabled "Land of the Kings"—a secluded, mountainous area where head-hunting, witchcraft, human sacrifice, and elaborate funeral rites were practiced. It was well into the 1900s before missionaries arrived bringing Christianity, and well into the 1940s before the Dutch relinquished power, allowing the island to become part of the Republic of Indonesia.

Today, more than 12 million people live on Sulawesi; around four-fifths follow Islam, and the rest—mostly in Tanatoraja and northern Manado—are Christian. The people's physical attributes and their traditions have Arabic, Austronesian, Chinese, and Indian roots; indeed, the island's culture is its primary attraction. There are the southern Bugis, who once sent bands of pirates to prowl the waters and raid ships and whose glorious 200-ton, dual-masted *pinisis* can still be seen in the water at Ujung Pandang and at the Maru Masa shipyards, 7 km (4 mi) from Bira at the peninsula's opposite end. The Bajau, too, are expert sailors who still spend nearly all their time on the water; their village homes are clustered together over the south coast's bays. Perhaps the most famous culture here, though, is that of Tanatoraja, where traditional clan houses—the carved and painted *tongkonan*—are built on stilts and topped by massive, curving roofs. To the north, the Minihasans around Manado follow Christian beliefs (20% of them are Catholic, 80% are Protestant) introduced by 15th-century Spanish and Portuguese missionaries.

Travel on Sulawesi is challenging at best. Most of the numerous flights between the southwest peninsula and Tanatoraja and northeastern Manado were, at press time, suspended owing to the political and economic crises. With the Ujung Pandang–Manado highway recently completed, buses are a viable alternative until the airlines reestablish service; however, the central terrain is mountainous, vehicles are rarely in good condition, and trips are often arduous. Sea travel is the third, and perhaps most pleasant, option if you have the time—ships only call weekly or biweekly at various island ports. Renting a car and driving yourself isn't advised, and, unfortunately, if you're planning to venture far from Ujung Pandang, long-distance drivers aren't always available. On this island, perhaps more than any other, you must keep your traveler's sense of humor, making every effort to consider the journey as much a part of the fun as the destination.

Ujung Pandang

❶ *1,630 km (1,011 mi) northeast of Jakarta, 770 km (477 mi) northeast of Denpasar, 322 km (200 mi) north of Labuanbajo.*

Most visitors fly into Ujung Pandang and use it as their base for travel throughout Sulawesi. The city has several old forts and palaces that can easily be seen on short trips along the coast just outside of town. Ujung Pandang's port is busy and colorful, with everything from small, slim prahu outriggers to sleek pinisi to huge modern Pelni (a state-owned company) ships. Natural wonders are also plentiful, including vast, empty beaches, waterfalls, and gardens less than a two-hour drive away.

Benteng Ujung Pandang, better known as Ft. Rotterdam, is by the harbor in the center of the Old City. Once a fortified trading post for the Sulawesi Gowan dynasty, the fort was captured and rebuilt by the Portuguese in 1545, then captured by the Dutch in 1608 and reinforced again. Several municipal offices are housed in the complex, including

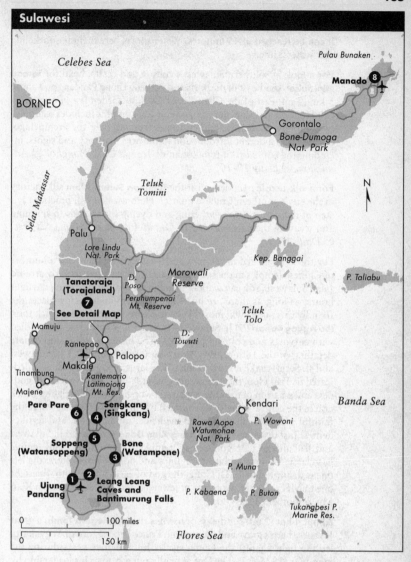

the Conservatory of Dance and Music. You can occasionally see un-official dance performances (the children practice on the stage in the fort's center) as well as the official ones frequently held on Saturday night at 8; the staff at your hotel should have a schedule. The fort also includes the **Galigo Museum,** the state's museum, which is divided into ethnology and history sections. The ethnographic museum is the more interesting, with a large collection of artifacts from different areas of Sulawesi. *Free to fort; admission for museums.* *Fort: Daily 8–6. Museums: Tues.–Sun. 8–12:30.*

The lovely blossoms at the **Clara Bundt Orchid Garden,** just south of the fort off Jalan Hasanuddin, include those from varieties from all over the world. Some of the plants here grow to more than 13 ft high. There's also an extensive seashell collection that includes several giant clams. *Jl. Mochtar Lufti 15,* *0411/22572.* *Free.* *Daily 10–4.*

Across the harbor from Ujung Pandang is **Samalona Island,** which has been developed into a recreational center, mostly appealing to locals. It can be reached in 45 minutes. Water sports here include snorkeling and waterskiing.

For a look at southern Sulawesi's culture and crafts, head for **Taman Mini Sulsel,** southeast of the ports and Benteng Ujung Pandang and about 5 km (3 mi) east of the Clara Bundt Orchid Garden (☞ *above*). This combination amusement park and cultural complex includes examples of architecture, textiles, and costumes from all over the archipelago, but it makes a decent introduction to the area's history and sights, including the curved-roof tongkonan of Toraja. ⊠ *Jl. Dangko.* ⊠ *Admission.* ⊙ *Daily 10–10.*

For a silk-textile overview, visit the **Tenunan Sutera Alam** silk factory in the city's southern Chinese quarter. Here women still practice each step of their craft, from gathering and dyeing the strands to spinning and weaving the garments. ⊠ *Jl. Ontah 408,* ☎ *no phone.* ⊠ *Free.* ⊙ *Daily 10–3.*

For those interested in religion and architecture, there are a number of Chinese temples in the southern part of the city, particularly around Jalan Sulawesi. You can wander through them anytime during daylight hours, as long as there are no religious ceremonies taking place; the friendly caretakers will most likely be pleased to provide a quick tour. **Ibu Agung Bahari** (⊠ Jl. Sulawesi 41), is a 350-year-old structure filled with carvings and colorful paintings. The brilliant colors and ornate detailing of the 18th-century **Tian Hou Gong Temple** (⊠ Jl. Sulawesi and Jl. Serui) make it hard to miss. The large wooden building is dedicated to Tian Hou, the "Heavenly Queen," who is both a fertility goddess and a patron of the sailors who still worship here. Her figure, which graces the central altar, is surrounded by three lower levels, where the faithful also worship venerated medicine, motherhood, and fertility deities. Just down the street is **Long Xian Gong Temple** (⊠ Jl. Sulawesi and Jl. Bali), or "Dragon Ghost" temple, built in 1868. This temple has classic Chinese architectural lines and houses three altars: the left one is dedicated to Tu Di Gong, the god of earth and wealth; the right one to Mi Lo Fo, the protector of jewelers; and the central one to Xian Mu, a mother of the gods.

About 4 km (2 mi) southeast of town is the **Diponegoro Tomb,** a great Javanese hero's grave and monument. Prince Diponegoro of Yogyakarta led the fight against the Dutch successfully for five years during the Java War (1825–30). The Dutch finally put a stop to his leadership by summoning him to their headquarters on the pretense of negotiating peace and then taking him prisoner. His sentence was exile to Sulawesi and imprisonment at Ft. Rotterdam, where he spent his final 26 years. ⊠ *Jl. Diponegoro.* ⊠ *Free.* ⊙ *Daily sunrise–sunset.*

Four centuries ago, the kingdom of Gowa—which merged with the kingdom of Tallo to form the island's first true center of power—was the site of the Makassar rulers' palace and a key port. The ruins of "Old Gowa" begin 7 km (4 mi) south of Ujung Pandang at **Sombaopu,** the fort that protected the sultanate with massive brick walls (10 ft thick and 23 ft high) and a clever locale overlooking the sea. The Dutch—in cahoots with Makassar rival Bugis troops—decimated the fort in 1669, and the elements pounded the ruins for the next three centuries. Indonesian archaeologists restored them in the late 1980s. Besides strolling around the fort area, you can also visit the historical museum, which displays artifacts and ammunition uncovered in the excavation, as well as four "living cultural villages" that represent four of the region's ethnic groups' crafts and rituals. ⊠ *Off Jl. Tallo along the Ujung Pandang–Sunguminasa Hwy.,* ☎ *no phone.* ⌷ *Admission.* ☉ *Daily 8–5.*

The **Tomb of Sultan Hasanuddin** and other kings of Gowa are in a cemetery between the fort and the Sungguminasa Palace (☞ *below*). Besides the grave of Hasanuddin, the most famous of the Gowan kings and a national hero for his ferocious battle against the Dutch, you'll also find the **Pelantikan stone**, or *tomanurunga*, the coronation stone of the kingdom of Gowa. Kingdom legends tell of the goddess Tomanurunga, who started the line of Gowan kings when she married a mortal named Karaeng Bayo at this site. Afterward the stone became the place where the sultans were crowned. Fifteen minutes' walk from the tomb is the 1603 **Mesjid Katangka,** Ujung Pandang's oldest mosque (now rebuilt) and the site of more graves.

The traditional, raised, wooden palace of **Sungguminasa** (4 km/2½ mi south of Sombaopu) was built in 1936. The **Ballalompoa Museum** here is a must-see, full of ornate royal jewelry and ceremonial costumes. ⊠ *Jl. Cenderawasih, off Jl. Tallo and the Ujung Pandang–Sungguminasa Hwy.,* ☎ *no phone.* ⌷ *Admission.* ☉ *Mon.–Thurs. 8–1, Fri. 8–10:30, Sat. 8–12.*

North of the city are several noteworthy sights. The remains of **Tallo,** Gowa's 16th-century satellite kingdom and ally, are 3 km (2 mi) north of Ujung Pandang in the rice paddies off Jalan Tallo Umar. Just 4 km (2½ mi) north of town is **Paotare,** the harbor where the Bugis bring their pinisi to unload cargo, mend sails, and prepare for the next voyage. Watching these elegant wooden schooners set off along the warm, bright water is a timeless sight. Sunsets from here are singular, but the pier has missing planks and gaping holes, so watch your step. **The ports of Sukarno and Hatta** along Jalan Martadina southwest of Paotare are a good place to watch large modern ships and two-masted prahu glide in from all parts of Indonesia.

Dining and Lodging

$$ ✕ **Shogun.** On the waterfront road, Sulawesi's original Japanese restaurant is clean and busy. Menu items include such traditional fare as sushi and sashimi. Try anything served with the fresh local seafood. Sake is a nice complement to an evening meal. ⊠ *Jl. Penghibur 2,* ☎ *0411/324102. AE, MC, V.*

$$ ✕ **Surya Supercrab.** This restaurant serves some of the best seafood in Ujung Pandang—count on crowds and a wait for a table. The large, bright room has no notable decor or atmosphere, but the crab-and-asparagus soup is delicious, as are the gigantic prawns. ⊠ *Jl. Nusakambangan 16,* ☎ *0411/317066. No credit cards.*

$$–$$$ ✕⌷ **Radisson Ujung Pandang.** What this hotel lacks in charm it makes up for in efficiency and a grand waterfront location. Rooms are boxlike but comfortable and well equipped, with such amenities as hair dryers and in-room safes. The coffee shop looks out onto the water and offers a combined Western and Asian menu—tiger prawns with a hint of lemongrass and barbecued duck in a light curry sauce. There's also a Chinese restaurant that serves both Szechuan and Cantonese fare. *Jl. Somba Opu 235, 90111,* ☎ *0411/333111,* FAX *0411/333222. 90 rooms. Restaurant, coffee shop, in-room safes, health club, meeting rooms. AE, DC, MC, V.*

$$–$$$ ⌷ **Hotel Sedona.** This comfortable, deluxe, 10-story hotel has a scenic location on the southern Losari Beach. The spacious lobby has polished marble floors and floor-to-ceiling windows that offer sweeping sea views. Rooms and suites are awash in pastels and decorated with contemporary furnishings tailored for modern travelers, including

queen-size beds, desks, minibars, and sizable baths; six rooms have terraces. A large ballroom and meeting rooms with many facilities make this hotel popular with business travelers. ⊠ *Jl. Somba Opu 297, 90111,* ☎ *0411/870555,* FAX *0411/870222. 218 rooms, 12 suites. 3 restaurants, 2 bars, minibars, pool, health club, beach, shops, laundry service, business services, meeting rooms. AE, MC, V.* ✍

$$–$$$ ☷ **Makassar Golden Hotel.** Right on Losari Beach, this hotel has Toraja-style roofs on its main building. Most of the comfortable rooms and cottages face the sea and have wall-to-wall carpeting, with beige decor and woven, Toraja-design bedcovers. All rooms have private baths, minibars, and TVs. ⊠ *Jl. Pasar Ikan 50, 90111,* ☎ *0411/314408,* FAX *0411/320951. 50 rooms, 10 cottages. Restaurant, coffee shop, minibars, pool, beach, dance club, laundry service, meeting rooms. AE, DC, MC, V.*

$ ☷ **Hotel Ramayana.** Between the airport and Ujung Pandang, Hotel Ramayana is clean but purely utilitarian. It's conveniently located across from the Liman Express office, which runs buses to Tanatoraja. ⊠ *Jl. G. Bawakaraeng 121, 90111,* ☎ *0411/442478,* FAX *0411/442479. 35 rooms. Restaurant, travel services. No credit cards.*

Nightlife and the Arts

Sunset viewing and snack munching are the prime activities on the patios of the expat hangouts **Kios Semarang** and **Eva Ria** along Jalan Penghibur. Local bands often play at the **Makassar Golden Hotel** (⊠ Jl. Pasar Ikan 50–52, ☎ 0411/314408). Dancers can try the disco at the **Marannu City Hotel** (Jl. Sultan Hasanuddin 3–5, ☎ 0411/315087).

Shopping

Ujung Pandang's position at the crossroads of trade routes between east and west Indonesia, as well as those north and south between Asia and the South Pacific, makes it one of the most diverse shopping spots in the country. Start east of the waterfront and south of Benteng Ujung Pandang at **Jalan Somba Opu,** which is lined with crafts shops filled with shells, spices, carvings, silks, gold, fine Gowan brasswork, and musical instruments. **Asia Art and Curio** (⊠ Jl. Somba Opu, ☎ no phone) has a variety of antiques. **Asia Baru** (⊠ Jl. Somba Opu, ☎ no phone) is a good place for porcelain. **Kanegbo Art Shop** (⊠ Corner of Jl. Somba Opu and Jl. Pattimura, ☎ no phone) sells silk textiles, baskets, and pieces of fine, regionally made jewelry. The **Maryam Art Shop** (⊠ Jl. Pattimura 6, 2nd floor, ☎ no phone) has old pieces of artwork and furnishings.

Leang Leang Caves and Bantimurung Falls

❷ *38 km (24 mi) northeast of Ujung Pandang.*

The extensive underground chambers of the **Leang Leang Caves** (also known as the Maros Caves) make up an archaeological park that protects some of the archipelago's most valuable prehistoric artwork. In the midst of breezy, forested hills, the park's rugged limestone cliffs hide Mesolithic paintings of wildlife and human images from 5,000 to 10,000 years ago. Visit Leang Pettae and Leang Peta Kere to see eerie sets of human handprints, or Ulu Leang and Leang Burung I and II to see fossils. More than 60 caves have been found in the region, including Salukan Kalang, which at 11 km (7 mi) is the island's longest.

Three kilometers (2 miles) northeast of Leang Leang is a serene forest haven with cool streams, quiet caves, and the thundering **Bantimurung Falls,** made famous by 1800s naturalist Alfred Russel Wallace, who came here to collect butterflies. Although the park is overrun with locals on weekends and holidays and it now takes patience to find the spectacular giant bird wings so common in Wallace's day, the area is nevertheless a good place to observe Sulawesi's natural beauty.

Bone

❸ *79 km (49 mi) northeast of Bantimurung, 110 km (68 mi) northeast of Ujung Pandang.*

In the 17th century, this town (formally known as Watampone) was a regional core of power and a semiautonomous state ruled by the rebel king Aru Palakka. The Dutch eventually conquered the city—three times—and remnants of their presence include colonial houses along some of the streets. The Dutch weren't the only outsiders to live in Bone, though; the seafaring Bugis also maintained a presence, and an 1881 Bugis house, the **Bola Soba,** is behind the Hotel Watampone on Jalan Sudirman. The former palace is now the **Museum Lapawawoi,** with an extensive collection of photos, royal-succession charts, and an array of court artifacts. The museum is open daily 8–5; there is an admission fee. Bone is also a base for visiting one of the peninsula's largest cave systems, the **Mampu Caves,** 40 km (25 mi) south of town.

Dining and Lodging

$ ✕ **Pondok Selera.** This small, friendly place is consistently recommended as the best restaurant in town. The back garden is a pleasant spot to enjoy savory Indonesian and Chinese dishes. Any of the seafood entrées with hot rice and mixed vegetables will satisfy. ⊠ *Jl. Biru 28,* ☎ *no phone. No credit cards.*

$ 🏨 **Wisma Bola Ridie.** Owned by a descendant of the last prince of Bone, this hotel is in a charming 1930s Dutch building. Its name means "The Yellow House," and its yellow exterior is a symbol of South Sulawesi nobility. Large, comfortable rooms, tile floors, and congenial hospitality all add to the delightful setting, five minutes' walk from the main town. Breakfast and tea are included in the price. ⊠ *Jl. Merdeka 6,* ☎ *0419/21412. 6 rooms. No credit cards.*

$ 🏨 **Wisma Watampone.** This modern-style building with touches of Sulawesi decor offers more Western comforts than expected outside of Ujung Pandang, including air-conditioning and private baths in all rooms. Quarters are simple, spacious, and clean, and the English-speaking staff members are happy to assist with travel plans. ⊠ *Jl. Biru 14,* ☎ *0419/21362,* 🖷 *0419/22367. 20 rooms. Restaurant, coffee shop, pool, laundry service. AE, MC, V.*

En Route Forty kilometers (25 miles) northwest of Bone (via Uloe) are the **Mampu Caves,** a network of underground limestone passages that are part of Sulawesi's largest cave system. You can hire guides in the village next to the site, who will point out an imaginative variety of characters found in the unusual stalactite and stalagmite shapes. Local lore has it that these images are a lazy local princess's former court, turned to stone when she dropped her spool, promised to marry whoever picked it up, then broke her vow when it was returned by a dog.

Sengkang

❹ *65 km (40 mi) northwest of Bone, 175 km (109 mi) northeast of Ujung Pandang.*

Sengkang (Singkang) is an unexpectedly pleasant lakeside resort town in the southwestern peninsula's center. A large, shallow lake—Danau Tempe—gives the town a relaxed, mountain-hideaway feel, and the scenic gardens, lush hills, and "floating" houses (Bugis houses raised on stilts) have made it quite a draw. There are also numerous weaving co-operatives in the area where you can observe the creation of silk textiles from the worm to the loom to the market shelves. Check out **Toko Sumber Sutera** (✉ Jl. Magga Amirulla 140, ☎ no phone) for an idea of selection and price.

Soppeng

❺ *25 km (15 mi) southwest of Sengkang, 75 km (46 mi) northwest of Bone.*

Soppeng, or Watansoppeng, is another silk-production hub. Along the northern road from here to Pangkajene are mulberry-tree groves where silkworms are cultivated; many of the worms that hatch here are sent to Sengkang. Among the town's other attractions are its gardens, some of the most prized in the region, and the hundreds of fruit bats that live in the trees near the central mosque. Soppeng's true richness, however, lies in its cultural treasures, such as the **Taman Purbakala Kompleks Makam Kuno** (Sultans' Graves), a gathering of unique stone structures just outside town on the road to Ompo.

Pare Pare

❻ *70 km (43 mi) northwest of Soppeng, 180 km (112 mi) north of Ujung Pandang.*

From Ujung Pandang, the four-hour drive north to Pare Pare—halfway between Ujung Pandang and Rantepao in the Tanatoraja region—takes you through rice fields and past the Makassar Strait. Bugis houses, which are built on stilts and have crossed roof beams, line the road. At some you'll see fish hanging from the rafters, curing in the sun. With 90,000 people, Pare Pare is Sulawesi's second-largest town. The Bugis *bago* ships—smaller and more agile than the 100-ton pinisi cargo ships—and other craft sail from its port. At the **Museum Bangenge,** 2 km (1 mi) south of town at Cappa Galung, you'll find a collection of traditional weapons, costumes, and ornaments overseen by curator Haji Hamzah, a descendent of the last ruler of the region's Bacu Kiki kingdom. ✉ *Desa Cappa Galung,* ☎ *no phone.* 🎫 *Admission.* ◷ *Daily 10–4.*

Dining

$ ✕ **Bukit Indah.** Perched on a hill, this smart, pristinely clean restaurant has a bay view and catches a nice breeze. The crab-and-corn soup is delicious; if you feel daring, try the fried frogs' legs. To reach Bukit Indah, take a right turn up the hill from the main street just before entering downtown Pare Pare. (Note that six clean, simple rooms are available if you wish to stay the night.) ✉ *Jl. Sudirman 65,* ☎ *0421/21886. No credit cards.*

$ ✕ **Sempurna.** On Pare Pare's main street is a clean, Formica-furnished, air-conditioned restaurant that serves tasty Indonesian and Chinese fare. Seafood dishes dominate the menu; try the sweet-and-sour shrimp. ✉ *202 Jl. Bau Massepe,* ☎ *0421/21573. No credit cards.*

En Route   The route from Pare Pare north to Tanatoraja wasn't paved until 1980; before then, the rutted, stony track took hours to cover. Even today, travel on this narrow, two-lane road can be arduous, if not terrifying, as it winds along steep, jagged cliffs before it twists and turns inland, climbing into limestone hills forested with pines and palms. Shimmering in the distance are the steely blue mountains that barred intruders for centuries. Farther north are the smooth tucks and folds of soft, green mountain slopes. The sky is enormously wide and, in the dry season, the air is clear and warm, allowing a glimpse of what regional legends maintain is the realm of gods.

NEED A
BREAK?
About 54 km (32 mi) before Makale is a roadside restaurant, **Puntak Lakawan,** with a terrace that affords spectacular views of Tanatoraja. Stop for the vistas, the strong coffee, and the "tourist only" Western toilet facilities—not for the food.

Tanatoraja (Torajaland)

★ ❼ *Makale is 328 km (205 mi) northeast of Ujung Pandang, 110 km (68 mi) northeast of Pare Pare; Rantepao is 17 km (11 mi) northeast of Makale.*

The so-called Land of the Kings, which dominates south-central Sulawesi, was put in the international limelight in the early 1900s, when word of its animist cultures and their traditions first reached the West. Then, as now, people were captivated by tales of Tanatoraja's graceful tongkonans, whose curving roofs point east and west to the heavens out of respect for ancestors; of its life-size *tau tau* (wooden effigies) that mark graves in limestone cliffs; of its wedding ceremonies and their elaborate gold and silk brocade costumes; of its exciting *sisemba* kickboxing contests and buffalo fights; and of its funerals involving hundreds of people and dozens of animal sacrifices.

The more popular sights are between Makale, the administrative center, and Rantepao, the commercial and tourist hub to the north. From Rantepao a network of roads peels off into the countryside to Toraja villages. To see the highlights, you'll need at least three full days; plan on a week to visit the more remote villages. If you drive to the area, add a day each way for the trip to and from Ujung Pandang. Although the dry season runs from April to October, many of the celebrations take place in July and August when the crops are harvested. This is when most people visit the area—particularly the towns around Rantepao. To avoid crowds, schedule a trip around these months or venture into the northwestern or eastern regions, which are the least infiltrated by Western visitors.

A good way to experience Tanatoraja is by hiking from one village to the next through hills and rice paddies along small, rugged paths. (Be sure to wear strong, ankle-supporting shoes and a hat—for sun protection—and bring binoculars so that you can clearly see the tau tau.) A trip that combines bus travel and short hikes is another option, though the going will be slow. You can also hire a minivan or a jeep. Regardless of how you travel, a good, professionally trained guide is essential. Such a guide will not only serve as your translator, but also your ambassador and teacher—explaining the culture's beliefs and ceremonies, relating local legends, and introducing you to the lesser-known settlements.

Of all the rituals, the funeral ceremony is probably the most important to the peoples of the Tanatoraja, and you should attend one if you get the chance. Funerals here are celebrations of life after death rather than a lament for the departed soul. They can take months to arrange, with relatives arriving from all over the archipelago, and can last for days. Palm wine is drunk, feasts are shared, and animals are slaughtered. Wealth is measured in buffalo (it's believed that the dead arrive in the hereafter riding a large white buffalo): the more buffalo sacrificed at the funeral, the more honor to the dead, the family, and the clan. Even those who have converted to Christianity continue the funeral ritual to demonstrate their prestige, keep tradition, and make sure the dead have plenty of influence with the gods.

Another large ritual takes place when a clan erects a new tongkonan. At these housewarming ceremonies the whole clan—often hundreds of people—is present. Buffalo, chickens, and pigs are sacrificed, both as dishes for the huge feast and as a show of prestige. All tongkonan face north—toward the land of the gods, according to one legend. Another legend contends that they face the direction from which the first settlers sailed (they are then purported to have used their upturned boats as shelters, hence the buffalo-horn shape of the roofs today). Houses are raised and have high gables with geometric designs and, perhaps, a few buffalo skulls; they also usually face a row of large rice barns.

Makale

Set amid the mountains and around a man-made lake, Makale is the entrance to Tanatoraja. Although it gleams with whitewashed Dutch churches and has an interesting market, this cool highland town attracts few visitors. Indeed, if you're in the area during peak season, you might consider making this your hub rather than crowded Rantepao. Although Makale isn't within walking distance of the main sights, you can easily hire a vehicle and a guide here. The **town market,** held every six days off Jalan Pasar Baru, is a riot of color and activity. Several trails on the outskirts of town lead to small villages—perfect for day hikes and picnics. A path from Jalan Ihwan Rambe runs west toward **Tondon,** where there are several secluded tau tau.

Rantepao and Environs

Rantepao is a small, easygoing town of dirt roads, cool mountain breezes, and a quietly booming tourist business year-round. Its big event occurs every sixth day, when the "weekly" market at the town crossroads attracts shoppers from miles around. Even on off days, the market shops sell wood carvings, cloth, and other Toraja-crafted goods. Rantepao's inexpensive restaurants and hotels are clean, comfortable, and friendly, and its semi-backwoods location and Christian-animist character give it an honest, genteel aura.

Some of the best-known Tanatoraja villages and sights are a short walk or drive from Rantepao. (Note: When you visit a village, plan to give a small donation of at least Rp 1,500, as tourism helps with these communities' upkeep. Also bring gifts of cigarettes or food to show your respect.) In **Karasik,** a traditional village on the town's southern outskirts, a group of elegant tongkonan surround several megaliths. Four kilometers (2 miles) south of Rantepao is **Kete Kesu,** a wood-carving village with hanging graves beneath the cliffsides; you'll also spot coffins and piles of bones along the thin forest paths. Ten minutes' walk from Kete Kesu is **Sulukeng,** where megaliths mark several graves.

In **Londa,** 8 km (5 mi) south of Rantepao, long, twisted passageways run deep into the cliffs and are lined with skulls and bones. Coffins are tucked into some of the cave shelves as well, many with more than one body inside (it's customary to bury family members together). You don't need a guide for the caves, but you will need a bright flashlight; if you don't have one, there are plenty of guides—many of whom speak English and are excellent storytellers—with gas lamps for hire near the snack stands outside. Within walking distance of the Londa caves is **Pabalsenam,** a tree of hanging graves for babies who died before teething. Five kilometers (3 miles) south of Londa is **Lemo,** one of the best places for viewing tau tau in the cliff faces; try to arrive here early in the morning, because the figures face east and are bathed in shadows by midday.

At **Marante,** 5 km (3 mi) northeast of Rantepao, you'll find burial caves in a limestone cliff as well as the remnants of poles used to support

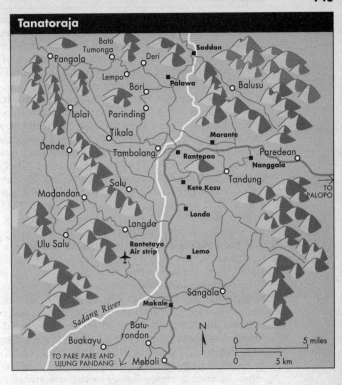

Tanatoraja

hanging coffins, some old carved coffins, and a funeral bier shaped like a traditional house—a ship to carry the deceased to the next life. At one end of the village is a modern home with a prow projecting from the roof and a wooden buffalo head attached to its front post—a fabulous anachronism.

Ten kilometers (6 miles) east of Rantepao is quiet **Nanggala.** Here the tongkonan are built on poles with soaring prow-shape roofs and are lined up facing north; *lumbung* (granaries, smaller than the houses but similar in shape) stand opposite. The tongkonan is cared for by the clan leader. A noble clan may decorate all the walls with carved and painted designs symbolizing the buffalo, the sun, and important crops. A middle-ranking clan is permitted to decorate only the front gable. When you see a wooden buffalo head or buffalo horns affixed to the front pole of the house, you're looking at a noble clan's house.

In the very old village of **Palawa,** 7 km (4 mi) north of Rantepao, hundreds of sacrificed buffalo horns hang on the houses. Eight of the traditional homes contain shops that sell Toraja carvings, textiles, old coins, and, well, junk. In **Saddan** (3 km/2 mi northeast of Pulawa), Toraja women weave and sell their colorful textiles, which have mainly primary colors in geometric patterns.

DINING AND LODGING

$ ✕ **Pondok Torsina.** A few miles south of Rantepao, this small hotel and
★ restaurant serves good Indonesian food on a veranda overlooking the rice paddies. Try the asparagus soup, shrimp in spicy butter sauce, or grilled fish. If possible, make arrangements a day in advance to have the *piong*, a traditional Toraja meal cooked in bamboo. The Toraja owner is very helpful in filling in any information gaps left by your guide. ✉ *Tikunna Malenong,* ☎ *0423/21293. No credit cards.*

$ ✕ **Restaurant Rachmat.** Right across from the traffic circle in the center of town, this Chinese-operated restaurant has design elements based on a traditional Toraja house. The menu includes standard Indonesian, Toraja, and Chinese dishes and caters to tour groups, so it can be busy and noisy. Local specialties include fried buffalo steak and black rice. ⊠ *Jl. Abdul Sari 8. No credit cards.*

$$$ ✕⊡ **Marante Highland Resort.** At this hotel just outside Marante, request a room in one of the traditional structures with roofs that look like upside-down boats. These are decorated with Indonesian fabrics and have terraces that overlook the landscaped grounds, and all rooms have long bathtubs. The pool has an adjoining terrace café, the coffee shop serves Western food and a few Indonesian dishes, and the barbecue restaurant offers an array of Southeast Asian dishes. The hotel staff can arrange excursions to the surrounding villages and cliffside graves. ⊠ *Jl. Jurusan Palapo (Box 52, Rantepao 91831),* ☎ *0423/216169,* FAX *0423/21122. 111 rooms. 3 restaurants, pool, shops, meeting room, travel services. AE, DC, MC, V.*

$$ ✕⊡ **Hotel Misiliana.** The lovely setting for this massive collection of traditional bungalows is a hilly, landscaped area 4 km (2 mi) northeast of town. The courtyard garden has a row of tongkonan with rice barns opposite; guest rooms surround the courtyard and are in two- or four-unit bungalows designed to complement the houses. The rooms themselves are spotless and have twin beds with colorful native spreads as well as modern tile baths. Set-menu breakfasts and dinners are included in the room price. A cultural show takes place some evenings. ⊠ *Jl. Pongtiku 27 (Box 01), 91831,* ☎ *0423/21212,* FAX *0423/21512. 96 rooms. 2 restaurants, bar, coffee shop, pool, tennis court, laundry service, business services, meeting rooms, travel services, car rental. AE, DC, MC, V.*

$$ ✕⊡ **Toraja Prince Hotel.** This large complex in the hills 4 km (2 mi) northeast of town is as upscale as you'll get in the region. The buildings have flourishes of traditional architecture. Rooms are spacious, comfortable, and clean; bright Torajan textiles complement the dark woods. The Japanese restaurant is a refreshing alternative to the abundance of Indonesian fare in town; a second restaurant serves Torajan, Chinese, and Western dishes. The friendly, professional management team operates a very thorough travel service. ⊠ *Jl. Pakubalasalu, 91831,* ☎ *0423/21430,* FAX *0423/21304. 95 rooms. 2 restaurants, bar, pool, shop, laundry service, travel services. AE, MC, V.*

$ ✕⊡ **Pia and Poppies Hotel and Restaurant.** Mr. Paul worked for years
★ as a chef at different Bali resorts before returning to Rantepao and opening this inn. His wonderful property is sleepy and serene, with panoramic valley views from the terrace, and skylighted, rock-inlaid showers. Mr. Paul and his family also preside over one of the most sophisticated Torajan dining rooms around; save room for the pumpkin soup. ⊠ *Jl. Pongtiku 27A (a few blocks south of Rantepao on the road to Makale), 91831,* ☎ *0423/21121,* FAX *0423/25059. 10 rooms. Restaurant, bar. No credit cards.*

$$ ⊡ **Toraja Cottages.** Just 3 km (2 mi) east of Rantepao, and set among gardens, this hotel consists of rows of attached cottages around the main building. The small, clean rooms have twin beds. Westernized Indonesian food is served in a veranda restaurant with rattan furniture. People like to gather in the small bar off the lobby. ⊠ *Kampung Bolu (reservations: Jl. Somba Opu 281, Ujung Pandang 91831),* ☎ *0423/21089 or 0411/84146 in Ujung Pandang,* FAX *0423/21304 or 0411/873083 in Ujung Pandang. 58 rooms. 2 restaurants, bar, pool, shops, travel services. AE, DC, V.*

Manado

8 *2,500 km (1,550 mi) northeast of Jakarta, 1,900 km (1,178 mi) north-east of Ujung Pandang, 1,600 km (992 mi) northeast of Rantepao.*

As the hub for ships sailing between the Philippines, Borneo, and the Spice Islands and as the capital of a collection of northern states united in the province of Minihasa, Manado is a cosmopolitan city. Yet despite its international flavor and port town status, it's a surprisingly clean, open, congenial place.

★ For most people, *the* reason to come here is scuba diving. Bunaken Manado Tua National Marine Reserve's waters and reefs offer some of the world's most spectacular dive sites. Live coral gardens and diverse marine life make for fascinating and colorful exploration. Most trips begin from Manado or Malayang village, where powerboats zip to **Pulau Bunaken,** the main island of this archipelago (10 km/6 mi offshore), in just over an hour. Dive operations know this territory well and offer a variety of trips to the reefs around Pulau Bunaken. Area dive sites include the **Manado Wreck,** the 196-ft skeleton of a Dutch ship that sunk during World War II; the reefs off **Pulau Manado Tua,** a dormant volcano now covered with forest; and the coral gardens around **Pulau Siladen, Pulau Montehage,** and **Pulau Nain.**

When you come up for air, Manado has an abundance of markets, little shops, museums, and memorials. The **Sam Ratulangi Monument,** on Jalan Sam Ratulangi, honors the "father" of the Minihasan people, who was east Indonesia's first governor. The **Ibu Walanda Maramis Monument** memorializes a pioneer of the Indonesian women's movement. The **Toar Lumimuut Monument** on Jalan Sudarso commemorates the legendary goddess Lumimuut and her son—who, as the stories go, mistakenly married each other. **The Provincial Museum of Northern Sulawesi** on Jalan Supratman provides a good overview of the region's culture. There is an admission fee to the museum, which is open Monday–Thursday 8–5, Friday 8–11, and Saturday 8–2.

Lodging

$$–$$$ ▣ **Novotel Manado.** Right on the waterfront esplanade near the Matahari Department store, this large hotel is one of the town's most luxurious. Standard rooms are comfortable and have touches of local decor amid the mainly Western furnishings. Suites have spacious sitting areas; for a fine bay view, request one of the two suites that have balconies. A sixth-floor pool also commands a stunning bay view; the bar here is an early-evening hot spot. Blue Banter Marina, Tour, and Diving Center, in front of the hotel, offers dive tours to area reefs as well as dive classes and provincial tours. ⊠ *Jl. Piere Tendean, 95111,* ☎ *0431/ 855555,* 𝔽𝔸𝕏 *0431/851194. 190 rooms, 14 suites. Restaurant, 2 bars, coffee shop, pool, health club, dive shop, laundry service, business services, meeting rooms, travel services. AE, DC, MC, V.*

$$ ▣ **Hotel New Queen.** Just 10 minutes from the airport, this establishment offers clean, convenient accommodations at reasonable prices. Rooms are basic in decor but have refrigerators. The price includes airport transfers, breakfast, dinner, or laundry service. ⊠ *Jl. Wakeke 12–14, 95111,* ☎ *0431/855551,* 𝔽𝔸𝕏 *0431/853049. 35 rooms. Restaurant, bar, coffee shop, refrigerator, laundry service, meeting room. AE, DC, MC, V.*

$$ ▣ **Nusantara Diving Center (NDC).** Manado's best-known dive orga-
★ nization also runs a hotel and restaurant right on Molas Beach, 5 km (3 mi) north of town. You can check in, make your scuba plans, and be out on the Bunaken reefs the next day. Rooms are basic and small, and not all of them have air-conditioning. But the place is friendly, and most guests don't mind the limited indoor space as they're here for the

diving. The on-site dive shop has all the equipment necessary for dive and snorkel tours and classes, and the travel desk can organize trips to the countryside, including visits to area volcanoes. All-inclusive dive, boat, and hotel packages are available. ✉ *Molas Beach, 95001,* ☎ *0431/863988,* 𝖥𝖠𝖷 *0431/860638. 43 rooms. Restaurant, 2 bars, beach, dive shop, dance club, travel services. AE, MC, V.* ✇

Outdoor Activities and Sports

Package rates for the three top dive operators in the area run Rp 648,000–Rp 972,000, including equipment, boat, and meals. **Barracuda** (✉ Jl. Sam Ratulangi 61, Manado, ☎ 0431/62033) has a fleet of dive boats as well as several chalets on Molas Beach so that you can put together hotel and dive packages. **Murex** (✉ Jl. Sudirman 28, Manado, ☎ 0431/66280) also has a dive resort and a number of boats that run to the Sangihe and Talaud islands north of Manado, among other places. The **NDC** (☞ Lodging, *above*), considered one of the friendliest and most professional outfits in the region, offers all-inclusive hotel, dive tour or class, and boat packages.

Sulawesi A to Z

Arriving and Departing

BY AIRPLANE

Garuda (☎ 0411/322705) flies to Ujung Pandang's **Hasanuddin Airport** (☎ 0423/62411) from Jakarta and Surabaya on Java and from Denpasar on Bali, among other places.

Merpati (☎ 0411/24114 in Ujung Pandang; 0423/21485 in Rantepao) once flew each morning between Ujung Pandang and the **Rantetayo Airport** (☎ 0423/62423) near Rantepao; this is the only air route to Tanatoraja, and at press time flights were suspended. However, due to the popularity of this region, service was expected to resume; contact your travel agent or Merpati for updates. In any case, even when flights are scheduled, the runway can become unserviceable in the rainy season, causing frequent cancellations.

All flights to Manado's **Sam Ratulangi Airport** (☎ 0431/51060) from the south are via Ujung Pandang on **Garuda** (☎ 0431/51544). **Merpati** (☎ 0431/64027) may also have flights to different points on the island. **Bouraq** (☎ 0431/62757) serves the city from Gorontalo on the northeast peninsula, Palu in the central area, and the northeast island of Ternate. Internationally, you can enter Manado nonstop from Davao in the Philippines or from Singapore (☞ *also* Arriving and Departing *in* Indonesia A to Z, *below*).

Between the Airport and Downtown. The Hasanuddin Airport is 22 km (14 mi) east of Ujung Pandang; a taxi to town costs about Rp 25,000. You can buy a coupon inside the terminal, next to the baggage claim. You can also hire a minivan—perfect for groups or those with lots of dive gear—outside the arrivals area for around Rp 10,000. Rantetayo Airport is 24 km (15 mi) southwest of Rantepao. You can catch a bus into town or book one for a ride to the airport from your hotel for about Rp 5,000. From Sam Ratulangi Airport, 13 km (8 mi) east of Manado, metered taxis run roughly Rp 13,000.

BY BOAT

Pelni (✉ Jl. Angkasa 18, Jakarta, ☎ 021/421–1921) ships from Surabaya (☎ 031/21041) pass through **Ujung Pandang** (☎ 0411/331393) every seven days and moor at Pelabuhan Hatta Harbor, a short becak ride from the town's center. Because Ujung Pandang is the gateway to eastern Indonesia, many other shipping companies take passengers from here aboard freighters to Maluku and other eastern islands and to Kalimantan, on Borneo. **Manado**'s port is Bitung, 30 km (19 mi) from town, where **Pelni** (⊠ Jl. Sam Ratulangi 7, Manado, ☎ 0423/62844) ships pass through en route to Ambon, Jayapura, Ujung Pandang, and other points along the Sulawesi coast.

Getting Around

Because the country between Ujung Pandang and Rantepao is breath-taking both from the ground and from above, the ideal way to visit Tanatoraja is to make the outbound journey by road and return by air.

BY BECAK

For short journeys, bicycle rickshaws are popular. Bargain hard—an in-town trip should cost about Rp 1,000, even if the driver begins by asking Rp 10,000.

BY BEMO

In Ujung Pandang, bemo minivans run along Jalan Jendral Sudirman/Rat-ulangi, Jalan Hasanuddin/Cenderawasih, and Jalan Bulusaraung/Mesjid Raya to Leang Leang (sometimes detouring to the airport). Public minibuses to towns outside Ujung Pandang leave from Jalan Sarappo whenever they're full.

BY BUS

The best bus service north from Ujung Pandang to Tanatoraja and points in between is **Liman Express** (☎ 0411/315851). Buses run from Man-ado to Gorontalo and all the way south to the Ujung Pandang; how-ever, as the "highways" are often unpaved, in a state of disrepair, or washed out altogether, for road trips in the Minihasa province it's far more convenient to hire a car and driver from one of the many travel agencies; for longer distances it's more convenient to fly.

The bus to Tanatoraja from Ujung Pandang takes 9 to 12 hours, de-pending on weather and road conditions, plus an hour lunch break. There are morning and evening departures in both directions. At Rp 15,000–Rp 35,000, it's an economical way to go. Since the country-side is not to be missed, make sure to make at least one daylight trip.

BY CAR

You can hire a car and driver through most hotels and travel agencies in Ujung Pandang, Rantepao, Makale, and Manado. For in-town and short regional excursions from Ujung Pandang, taxis are widely used; ask at your hotel for recommendations and count on Rp 350,000–Rp 600,000 per day. In Tanatoraja, travelers often hire minibuses to shut-tle them between sights, with prices around Rp 54,000 an hour or Rp 432,000 a day. Taxis may be hired for around Rp 32,500 an hour in Manado.

BY TAXI

You can hail cabs on the street in Ujung Pandang or pick one up out-side a hotel. Taxis are metered; the fare is roughly Rp 1,000 per km (½ mi). Two large companies are: **Amal Taxi** (☎ 0411/313131) and **Omega** (☎ 0411/22679). Taxis are available in Tanatoraja and Man-ado, but bemos and *mikrolets* (a Manado-style bemo) are more pop-ular. In Manado, you can also try **Dian Taksi** (☎ 0421/862421).

Contacts and Resources

EMERGENCIES

Police: ☎ 110 or 7777. **Ambulance:** ☎ 118. Hospitals: **Elm Hospital** (⊠ Jl. A Yani, Rantepao); **Pancaran Kasih** (⊠ Jl. Sam Ratulangi, Man-ado); **Rumah Sakit Umum** (⊠ Jl. Yos. Sudarso, Manado); **Rumah Sakit Umum** (⊠ Jl. Gunung Bawakaraeng, next to Hasanuddin University, Ujung Pandang); **Stella Maris Hospital** (Jl. Panghibur, Ujung Pandang).

Pharmacy: **Kimia Firma** (✉ Jl. A Yani, Ujung Pandang). **Scuba Diving Emergencies:** The only public decompression chamber is operated by **Baruna Watersports** (✉ Jl. Bypass Ngurah Rai 300B, Kuta, ☎ 0361/753820) on Bali.

All of Ujung Pandang's and Manado's major hotels have shops or kiosks with English-language newspapers, magazines, and the occasional guidebook or novel.

In Ujung Pandang, **Toraja Highland Tours and Travel** (✉ Jl. Rambutan 3, ☎ 0411/852495) offers a full range of southern-province tours and specializes in trips to Toraja. **Intravi** (✉ Jl. Urip Sumoharjo 225, ☎ 0411/319747) is also a reputable agency. Besides arranging tours, **Pacto Ltd. Tours and Travel** (✉ Jl. Jendral Sudirman 56, ☎ 0411/873208) represents American Express. **Ramayana Tours** (✉ Jl. Bulukunyi 9A, ☎ 0411/871791) has particularly good Tanatoraja tours because many of its guides come from there. It also offers excursions to the southeast peninsula, famous for boat-building and a reclusive Muslim village, and arranges customized trips such as jeep treks across the island or canoe visits to the weavers of Galumpang in central Sulawesi. In Manado, try **Helista Tour and Travel** (✉ Jl. Bethesda 75, ☎ 0423/628880), which also offers dive tours, or **Manado Land and Sea** (✉ Jl. Diponegoro 5, ☎ 0431/64476).

Ceria Nugraha (✉ Jl. Usmar Jafar 9, 90111, ☎ 0411/311846) and **Limbunan** (Jl. Gunung Bawakaraeng 40–42 [Box 97], 90111, ☎ 0411/323333) are reliable agencies in Ujung Pandang. In Tanatoraja, try **Ramayana Satrya** (✉ Jl. Pong Tiku, Rantepeo, ☎ 0423/21615). In Manado, **Pandu Express** (✉ Jl. Sam Ratulangi 91, ☎ 0431/851188) and **Pola Pelita Express** (Jl. Sam Ratulangi 113, ☎ 0431/852231) offer a range of travel services.

In Ujung Pandang, the **South Sulawesi Tourist Office** (✉ Jl. A. P. Pettani, ☎ 0411/443225) is open Monday–Thursday and Saturday 7–2, Friday 7–11. The **North Sulawesi Provincial Tourism Office** (✉ Jl. 17 Augustus, ☎ 0431/64911) can help with maps and dive details; it's open Monday–Thursday 7–2, Friday 7–11, and Saturday 7–12:30. The **Manado Tourist Office** (✉ Jl. 17 Augustus, ☎ 0431/64299) has general information on the area and is open Monday–Thursday 7–2, Friday 7–11, and Saturday 7–12:30. If you're headed to one of the region's national parks, contact the **National Parks Office** (✉ Jl. Babe Palar 67, ☎ 0431/62688). It's open Monday–Thursday 9–4, Friday 9–11, and Saturday 9–12:30. The **Tourist Information and Booking Center** (✉ Bunaken Souvenir Shop, Jl. Sam Ratulangi 178, Manado) also has maps and regional information available. Its hours are Monday–Thursday 9–4, Friday 9–11, and Saturday 9–4.

SUMATRA

Although Sumatra's amenities have improved in recent years, this is still an island for the adventurous and the tolerant—not for those who need exact schedules, fixed prices, and luxury. The world's fifth-largest island (about the size of Japan or Spain), and Indonesia's northernmost one, lies off the Malaysian peninsula's west coast. Its rubber and palm-oil plantations and oil and gas fields make it a gold mine for the country. Medan, North Sumatra province's capital, is an important commercial center. West Sumatra province's capital, Padang, is a large port. But not all of Sumatra's resources have been exploited, not all of its lands developed: it has rain forests that teem with wildlife as well as beautiful lakes, mountains, and beaches.

Before Jakarta exploded into the violence that led to the end of President Suharto's 32-year-rule, riots in Medan (in May 1999) caused large business areas of the city to close. Medan is a commercial center and has one of Indonesia's largest ethnic-Chinese populations, which is often targeted by disenfranchised Indonesian workers who believe the Chinese receive unfair government assistance. The city is also home to several universities whose student bodies often agitate for more political freedom. And then there is Aceh—the province on Sumatra's northern tip—whose zealous Muslim inhabitants have always wanted more independence from Jakarta. (The Dutch never fully controlled this region, and the Indonesian government only did so with strong-arm tactics; you should still check with your embassy before visiting Aceh.) All the turmoil aside, the Sumatrans are an intriguing and diverse people—from the former headhunter Bataks in the north to the matrilineal Miningkabau tribes in the west. Many islanders are also freewheeling entrepreneurs who understand the value of tourism; some speak a little English, and most are friendly and quick to offer help and information.

To do Sumatra right, you'll need at least a week. It's best to enter at Medan in the north and travel overland to Padang on the west coast (or vice versa). Taxis and a comprehensive bus system link small towns, and domestic airlines connect provincial capitals.

North Sumatra

Outside of Medan, the bustling provincial capital, much of North Sumatra remains wilderness. Among its highlights are the 100-km-long (62-mi-long) Danau Toba and its island, Samosir, which are in a volcano's caldera; Gunung Leuser National Park's rain forests; and the Bukit Lawang Orangutan Rehabilitation Center. Although many sights are along the Trans-Sumatran Highway, which runs the length of Sumatra from north to south, others take more effort to reach. Luckily, the people are friendly and helpful, making much of the island a joy to see—regardless of infrastructure problems.

Medan

❶ *1,350 km (840 mi) northwest of Jakarta, 625 km (390 mi) northwest of Singapore, 575 km (360 mi) northeast of Padang.*

Medan, North Sumatra's capital and Indonesia's fourth-largest city, developed into a bustling plantation town in the early 20th century and is now only second (after Jakarta) in terms of business importance. More than 2 million people jostle about in a city designed for 500,000. Cars, taxis, bemos, motor scooters, bicycles, and pedestrians compete for positions on streets that are in various states of repair.

The two major in-town sights are the large, multidome **Mesjid Raya Mosque** (near the intersection of Jl. Mesjid Raya and Jl. Sisinga Mangaraja in the southeast of town), built in 1906 and one of Indonesia's largest, and the Sultan's Palace, the **Istana Sultan Deli** (✉ Jl. Katamso, just west of the mosque), built in 1880. Special permission from the tourist office (☞ Visitor Information *in* North Sumatra A to Z, *below*) is required to visit inside the palace.

The **Orangutan Rehabilitation Station** in Gunung Leuser National Park is just a 2½-hour drive from town. You can hire a taxi and a guide for

North and West Sumatra

Banda Aceh

Andaman Sea

Takengon

ACEH

Langsa

Blangkejeren

Pulau Simeulue

NORTH SUMATRA

Medan ❶

Brastagi ❷
Lingga ▪

Tebingtinggi

Pematangsiantar

Ambarita
Tuk Tuk ❸
Tomok

Prapat ▪
Binanga

Tanjungbalai

**Danau Toba and
Pulau Samosir** ❹

Sibolga

Rantauprapat

Langgapayung

Pulau Nias

Padangsidempuan

Mentawai Strait

WEST SUMATRA

MALAYSIA

Kuala Lumpur ☆

Strait of Melaka (Malacca)

Pulau Rupat

RIAU

Bonjol ❺

**Danau
Maninjau** ❼ ❻ **Bukittinggi**

Padangpanjang ❽ **Batusangkar**

Padang ❾

Pulau Siberut

Rengat

Mentawei Islands

Sungaipenuh

Muarabungo

JAMBI

Jambi

Pulau Pagai

Bangko

INDIAN OCEAN

Bengkulu

SOUTH SUMATRA

Palembang

N

0   100 miles

0   150 km

Kotabumi

about Rp 810,000. It's best to leave Medan by about 11 AM to reach the park by 2 PM. You will then have a 30-minute walk in tropical heat up to the ranger's hut. A further 15-minute hike up the mountain takes you to the feeding platform where rangers, at 3:30 PM, spend 35 minutes feeding and inspecting the orangutans, preparing them for life in the wild. You need to be relatively fit to make the 45-minute hike, which involves rugged terrain and crossing a creek by raft, but the experience is worth it.

Dining and Lodging

Western fast food has arrived in Medan. There's a McDonald's near the Mesjid Raya Mosque, a Pizza Hut in Deli Plaza, and, it seems, Kentucky Fried Chicken is everywhere else. For more upscale Western fare, try the restaurants in the larger hotels. On the Asian side, many eateries—including the food stalls in the park across from the mosque—serve good Padang cuisine. Padang food originated, of course, in Padang on Sumatra's west coast, but it is known throughout the archipelago. Dishes are similar to curries, and most are quite spicy.

$$–$$$ ✕ **Miramar.** Near several antiques shops in central Medan, this restaurant serves Chinese and Padang dishes (seafood is a specialty) in an air-conditioned dining room with big, padded chairs around large tables. The menu has pictures, and the service is good. ⊠ *Jl. Pemua 11,* ☎ *061/325491. AE, MC, V.*

$$ ✕ **RM Famili.** A short walk down Jalan Sisingamangaraja from the Mesjid Raya Mosque, this is a great place to sample Padang food. There are many selections in a glass display case as you walk into the large, open-air dining room. Smiling waiters will bring small plates of food to your table and serve you rice. You eat what you want and pay accordingly. It's best to get a seat close to the waterfall fountain to drown out the traffic noise outside. ⊠ *Jl. Sisingamangaraja 33,* ☎ *061/718787. No credit cards.*

$–$$ ✕ **Tip Top.** Opened in 1935, Tip Top is a Medan institution. It offers Indonesian, Chinese, and Padang food (all of it good) and some Western food (not as good). The front dining room opens onto a very busy street, but there are quieter, air-conditioned dining rooms in the back. The cake and coffee are tops. ⊠ *Jl. Jendral A. Jani 92,* ☎ *061/24442. No credit cards.*

$$$ 🏨 **Hotel Danau Toba.** The city's first major hotel (circa 1972) is more like an urban resort with its lagoonlike pool (complete with landscaped islands), its many restaurants, and its karaoke bar and disco. Despite their age, public areas and guest rooms are well maintained. ⊠ *Jl. Imam Bonjol 17, 20235,* ☎ *061/557000,* ℻ *061/530053. 268 rooms, 4 suites. 4 restaurants, 4 bars, pool, massage, health club, dance club, meeting rooms. AE, DC, MC, V.*

$$$ 🏨 **Novotel Soechi.** This central Medan establishment has a cybercafé with eight terminals, which makes it a good choice for those who can't bear to be disconnected from cyberspace. Rooms are of a good size, and some adjoin—perfect for families or other groups. There's a 24-hour restaurant on-site and a good selection of dining and shopping options in the adjoining Hong Kong Plaza. ⊠ *Jl. Cirebon 76-A, 20235,* ☎ *061/561234,* ℻ *061/572222. 232 rooms, 15 suites. Restaurant, 4 bars, café, pool, tennis court, health club, business services, meeting rooms. AE, DC, MC, V.*

$$ 🏨 **Natour Dharma Deli Medan.** Although this hotel, part of Indonesia's Natour chain, is right in central Medan, it has a lovely pool with bar service and shaded areas—the perfect escape from urban buzz and equatorial sun. Though rooms are on the boxy side, each is comfortably furnished with two queen-size beds, two chairs, a coffee table, a desk, and satellite TV. The coffee shop serves Indonesian, Chinese, and

Western food. ⊠ *Jl. Balai Kota 67, 20111,* ☎ *061/455–7011,* FAX *061/ 327153. 180 rooms. Bar, coffee shop, pool, massage, exercise room. AE, DC, MC, V.*

$$ 🏨 **Tiara Medan Hotel.** The clean, smart Tiara is one of Medan's best hotels. Guest rooms are spacious and well maintained, and the staff is friendly and quick to help. The lobby restaurant offers standard Chinese, European, and Indonesian fare for lunch, and the more formal Amberita Restaurant serves dinner. ⊠ *Jl. Cut Mutiah, 20152,* ☎ *061/ 519414,* FAX *061/51076. 316 rooms, 16 suites. 2 restaurants, bar, coffee shop, pool, beauty salon, 2 tennis courts, health club, squash, business services, meeting rooms, travel services. AE, DC, V.*

$ 🏨 **Hotel Sri Deli.** This wooden, brightly painted, four-story hotel is near the mosque. Rooms are clean, and each has its own bath (with hot water)—a real plus in a budget hotel; some rooms have air-conditioning as well. Some of the friendly staff speak a little English, and many tour guides hang out downstairs. ⊠ *Jl. S. M. Raja 30, 20214,* ☎ *061/ 713571. 53 rooms. Café. No credit cards.*

¢ 🏨 **Garuda Plaza Hotel.** Enter the shining marble lobby or the restaurant fit for a wedding banquet, and you'll be surprised that this is a budget hotel. Rooms are cozy and boast minibars, 24-hour room service, and cable television—extras that are unexpected given the cost. The pool is perfect for swimming laps. ⊠ *Jl. Sisingamangaraja No. 18, 20213,* ☎ *061/736–1234 or 061/736–4411. 151 rooms. 1 restaurant, 1 bar, coffee shop, in-room fax, pool, barbershop, beauty salon, laundry service, meeting rooms, airport shuttle. AE, DC, MC, V.*

¢ 🏨 **Guest House Prim Indah.** This basic hotel offers a bargain deal: an air-conditioned double room costs only Rp 179,200, including breakfast and transfers from Medan's airport. While the rooms are spacious, there's no television and no baths (only showers, which run hot and cold water). The restaurant serves Western and Indonesian food, the staff is friendly, and the hotel is only 20 minutes from the airport. ⊠ *Jl. Duta Wisata 58, 20356,* ☎ *061/786–3325 or 061/786–3324,* FAX *061/786–3324. 4 rooms. Restaurant, pool, tennis court. D, MC, V.* ✍

Shopping

For a variety of contemporary goods, try **Deli Plaza** (⊠ Jl. Guru Patimus) in the north of town. In central Medan, the many shops in the **Hong Kong Plaza** (⊠ Jl. Cirebon) are your best bets.

Jalan Jendral A. Yani has several good curio and antiques shops selling wares from all over Indonesia (note that only hard currency is accepted, and haggling is de rigueur): **Toko Bali** (⊠ Jl. Jendral A. Yani 68, ☎ 061/512556), **Dagang Sepalat** (⊠ Jl. Jendral A. Yani 61, ☎ no phone), **Rufino** (⊠ Jl. Jendral A. Yani 56, ☎ 061/567165), and **Selatan** (⊠ Jl. Jendral A. Yani 44, ☎ 061/518149). If the heat and the bargaining tire you, take a break at the nearby Tip Top or Miramar restaurants (☞ Dining and Lodging, *above*).

Brastagi

❷ *68 km (41 mi) southwest of Medan.*

Brastagi (or Berastagi), two hours from sweltering Medan on one of two routes to Danau Toba, is a refreshing hill station 4,600 ft above sea level and set between two volcanoes. It retains an Old World air from the days when Dutch planters came here to escape the heat.

Several groups of the Karo Bataks have their villages in the highlands, and one worth visiting is **Lingga,** 15 km (9 mi) southwest of Brastagi and just a little off the road to Danau Toba. Here you can see 250- to 300-year-old multifamily tribal houses still in use today. Karo Bataks, as well as the Toba Bataks, are descendants of proto-Malay tribes who originally inhabited the border areas of what is now Myanmar (Burma) and Thailand. They chose this mountainous region for its isolation, and their patrilineal society remains virtually intact—despite the increasing numbers of sightseers.

Dining and Lodging

$$–$$$
★
✕⌂ **Bukit Kubu Hotel.** This wonderful, old, colonial-style hotel is the area's best. Ask for a double suite with a mountain view (the price is only Rp 54,000 more than a standard room). Lunch is served on a terrace; dinner, inside, is in the formal dining room. Starched linen and billowing lace curtains are reminiscent of the 1930s, when Dutch planters came here to relax. Today, the hotel is popular with wealthy folk from Medan who come for weekends. ⊠ *Jl. Sempurna 2, 22151 (booking office: Jl. Jendral Sudirman 36, Medan 20100),* ☎ *0628/91524 or 061/ 519636 in Medan. 40 rooms. Restaurant, laundry service. AE, V.*

$
⌂ **Hotel International Sibayak.** Swim in one of the country's largest heated swimming pools at this sprawling hotel, which provides modern facilities (like a convention center for groups of 600) amid dense jungle and views of Mts. Sibayak and Sinabung. Rooms are spacious with basic hotel decor. At the hotel's Indonesian restaurant, check out the spicy grouper (*ikan kerapu asam cekala*) cooked in red and green chili peppers, red onions, garlic, and coconut. ⊠ *Jl. Merdeka, 22151,* ☎ *0628/91301,* ℻ *0628/91307. 130 rooms. 2 restaurants, bar, pool, tennis court, billiards, convention center. AE, MC, V.*

Prapat

❸ *120 km (75 mi) southeast of Brastagi, 176 km (110 mi) south of Medan.*

From Brastagi it's an easy two-hour bus or taxi ride south to Prapat, the resort town near Danau Toba where ferries leave for Pulau Samosir. The last 30 minutes of the journey are the most dramatic. The road winds through vegetation to a pass, where the lake suddenly appears below. (Note that if you're coming directly from Medan—a four-hour drive—you can take the Trans-Sumatran Highway. The views aren't quite as fantastic and you'll miss charming Brastagi, but the route is fast.) If you arrive in Prapat late and miss the last boat (about 4:30 PM) there are a few good places to eat and to rest.

Dining and Lodging

$$–$$$
✕ **Singgalang.** The first version of this family restaurant opened 40 years ago. This new edition, an air-conditioned dining room just off the highway, carries on the tradition of offering good Chinese and international fare. (There are also a couple of fan-cooled guest rooms if you're stuck for a place to stay.) ⊠ *Trans-Sumatran Hwy. 52,* ☎ *0664/ 41260. AE, DC, MC, V.*

$
✕ **Trogadero.** For good Indonesian cuisine—satays, nasi goreng, and the like—try this one-room restaurant near the water. It's easy to relax in the easygoing atmosphere. ⊠ *Jl. Haranggaol 110,* ☎ *0664/41148. No credit cards.*

$$$–$$$$
⌂ **Niagara.** One of Prapat's best hotels is on a hill behind town with spectacular lake views and a big pool. Guest rooms are spacious and comfortable, and the huge dining room has an international menu. There's a free shuttle bus into town. ⊠ *Jl. Pembangunan 1, 21174,* ☎ *0664/41028,* ℻ *0664/41233. 178 rooms, 4 suites. Bar, dining room, pool, 4 tennis courts, bicycles, dance club. DC, MC, V.*

$$
⌂ **Natour Hotel Prapat.** The best quarters here are in the bungalows on landscaped slopes that face the lake. Rooms, though worn, are comfortably large and well furnished and have patios. Like all Natour ho-

tels, this one is not spectacular, but it's a bargain. ⊠ *Jl. Marihat 1, 21174,* ☎ *0664/41012,* 𝔽𝔸𝕏 *0664/41019. 85 rooms. Bar, dining room, beach. AE, V.*

$ 🏨 **Risis Hotel.** This clean, whitewashed hotel on the street that leads to the market square is a good bet if you're on a tight budget. Some rooms have private baths; all have bare walls and floors and minimal furniture. Although there's no on-site restaurant, Trogadero (☞ *above*) is nearby. ⊠ *Jl. Haranggaol 39, 21174,* ☎ *0664/41392. 20 rooms. No credit cards.*

Danau Toba and Pulau Samosir

★ ❹ *Samosir Island is 45 minutes by boat from Prapat.*

Danau Toba, Southeast Asia's largest lake and one of the world's highest, sits 2,950 ft above sea level, surrounded by steep slopes that plunge headlong into the water to depths of 1,475 ft. Prapat may be the major resort town *on* the lake, but most visitors prefer to stay *in* the lake—on Samosir, a hilly 777-square-km (300-square-mi) island that's home to the Toba Bataks. The island remains agriculturally based. Even the people who run guest houses in touristed Tuk Tuk (☞ *below*) continue to plant rice fields.

In **Tomok,** you'll find the tombs of King Sidabutar, who ruled in the 1800s; his son; his grandson; and several warriors of rank. Nearby are several Batak houses with curving roofs and intricately carved beams and panels. To reach these attractions, walk ½ km (¼ mi) up from the ferry dock past stalls selling souvenirs, artifacts, and batik cloth. Keep in mind that the actual purchase price is 30%–40% of the initial asking price.

Tuk Tuk, on a peninsula that juts into the lake, has been greatly developed as a tourist hub during the last 10 years (indeed, some areas are virtual guest-house ghettos, with one lodging after another). Still, quiet retreats remain, and a stay in one can be pleasant. There are few vehicles; many visitors get around by bicycle, just as the easygoing locals do. (Note that the locals are fond of chess and are usually eager to play.) To reach Tuk Tuk, it's best to take the passenger ferry (a 45-minute ride), which stops at several hotels on the peninsula. **Ambarita** is a village where, in the past, miscreants had their heads lopped off. You can still see the courtyard where the king held council. Ancient, weathered stone chairs and tables form a ring in front of the chief's traditional house. The village is a nice two-hour bicycle outing from Tuk Tuk.

At Samosir's northern tip is **Simanindo,** site of a fine old traditional house, once the home of a Batak king. The village has been declared an open-air museum, and the one house not to miss is the Long House (Rumak Bolon), with its fine carvings and the sculpted depiction of the god Gajah Dompak. His job was to frighten off evil spirits, and by the look of him, he must have been good at it.

In nice weather, consider making the pleasant ride (by motorcycle) to the small **Danau Sidihoni** toward the center of Pulau Samosir island. On the way, contemplate the fact that you'll be visiting what has to be the world's only lake on an island in a lake on an island.

Passenger boats cost Rp 1,500 one-way to Tuk Tuk, slightly more for Ambarita and Simanindo. They leave from Prapat's lakeshore market. A little way down the coast there's a car ferry to Tomok. The passenger boats are more frequent and enjoyable. For a more extensive look at the island, you can charter a powerboat for a three-hour trip to Tomok, Tuk Tuk, Ambarita, and Simanindo, which will cost about Rp 40,000.

For travel around Samosir, minibus taxis make irregular trips, and there are motorbikes for rent (about Rp 20,000 a day).

Dining and Lodging

Accommodations here are pleasant, albeit a bit rustic. All hotels have restaurants, but you should try eating at a few places since the best lodging doesn't necessarily have the best food.

$–$$ ✕ **Bagus Bay.** For a good selection of Indonesian food, very edible pizza and sandwiches, and terrific fruit shakes, check out this big, open-air eatery. You'll also find an extensive used bookshop with some English-language titles. Once a week (the days vary), there's an evening performance of traditional dance and music put on by local Bataks. ✉ *Jl. Slamet Riyadi, Tuk Tuk,* ☎ FAX *0625/41481. No credit cards.*

$–$$ ✕🏠 **Toba Vegetarian Restaurant.** Toba has seven guest rooms, four of them in a Batak house that was moved here and refurbished. It has hot water and a balcony facing the lake. Room 7, on the second floor, is the best room. The food here is good, especially the freshly baked cakes and the dark German bread. ✉ *Jl. Slamet Riyadi 111, Tuk Tuk 22395,* ☎ *0271/37603. 7 rooms. Restaurant. No credit cards.*

$$$ 🏠 **Toledo.** This is one of the bigger resorts, but fits well into the environment. Though the hotel caters to tour groups, you can stay here without feeling overwhelmed. Ask for a room with a patio facing the lake; make your second choice a room next to the pool. Activities here include boat rides on the lake and outings to island sights. ✉ *On both sides of the road along the Tuk Tuk peninsula's northeast side, Tuk Tuk 22395,* ☎ *0271/46356,* FAX *0271/44788. 140 rooms. Restaurant, bar, pool, massage, beach, boating, shops, meeting rooms, travel services. AE, DC, MC, V.*

$$ 🏠 **Carolina Cottage.** Tuk Tuk's first accommodation remains its best.
★ Rooms—in Batak houses at the lake's edge—all have spectacular views and baths; most also have hot running water. The service is friendly and helpful. For convenience and a great view, request a room by the beach and the swimming area. Continental breakfasts, snacks, and dinners are served. ✉ *On a small lane off Jl. Slamet Riyadi, Tuk Tuk 22395,* ☎ *0625/41520,* FAX *0625/41521. 50 rooms. Restaurant, bar, beach. No credit cards.*

En Route On the Trans-Sumatran Highway from Prapat to Bukittinggi is Binanga (sometimes known as Lumban Binanga), and 15 km (9 mi) southwest of Prapat are five traditional houses. Park at the side of the highway (you'll see a sign) and walk down the hill past some new houses and terraced paddy fields to these 100- to 200-year-old Batak houses. Few tourists come here, so Binanga isn't as busy as Samosir's villages.

Mentawei Islands

You can surf at the beaches of the remote and isolated Mentawei Islands, which are off Sumatra's west coast. Take an overnight trip on a teak vessel to the islands (☎ 0751/34978 or 021/828–1239 in Jakarta), which are about 70 nautical miles west of the mainland. The trip takes 7 to 10 hours. You leave at 9 PM but arrive at the first of the five or six surfing sites at about 6 AM. Surfing here is along magnificent barrels, reputedly some of the world's best.

North Sumatra A to Z

Arriving and Departing

BY AIRPLANE

You can fly to Medan on several airlines. **Garuda Indonesian Airways** (☎ 061/514877) and **Silk Air** (☎ 061/537744) have daily hour-long flights from Singapore to Medan's **Polonia Airport** (☎ 061/538444), right on the town's south edge. **Malaysia Airlines** (☎ 061/519333) flies from Penang, Malaysia. There are also flights to Jakarta on Java and Padang in West Sumatra. **Merpati** (☎ 061/321888) also serves Medan. The only way into Medan from the airport is by taxi. A fixed rate of Rp 8,000 applies.

BY BOAT
The least expensive and more adventurous way to reach Medan is on one of the daily five-hour "fast boats" from Penang, Malaysia. The Melaka Straights often get rough. Contact **Kuala Perlis-Langkawi Ferry Service** (☎ 04/262–5630) in Penang or **Perdana Express** (☎ 061/545803) in Medan.

Getting Around
BY AIR
If you only have enough time for a few of Sumatra's highlights, the best strategy is to use Medan as a sightseeing hub and then fly to Padang to see its area sights—or vice versa. For details on airports and carriers in Medan, *see* By Airplane *in* Arriving and Departing, *above.*

BY BUS
Buses range from the air-conditioned express variety to crowded local vehicles. Long-distance bus travel—such as the 14- to 16-hour journey from Medan's Amplas bus station to Padang—can be an adventure. (Motion sickness is a concern, as is all the smoke from the clove Kretek cigarettes popular with so many passengers.) Short day trips by bus are quite tolerable, however. Bus stations are never far from town centers, and you'll generally find a bus leaving for nearby destinations within 30 minutes of your arrival at the station. A travel agent can arrange the bus trip, too. In Medan, contact **Trophy Tours** (☞ Tour Operators and Travel Agents, *below*).

BY CAR
Although many sights are along the Trans-Sumatran Highway—a well-sealed two-lane (for the most part) highway—renting a car and driving yourself is a risky business on Sumatra. It's best to hire a car and driver—leaving the work to someone who knows the terrain and the language. A travel agent (☞ Tour Operators and Travel Agents, *below*) and the staff at major hotels can make arrangements.

BY TAXI
In Medan, you'll find car and motorcycle taxis at hotels, the bus station, the airport, and the dock. Some taxis have meters; with others, you must negotiate the fare before you get in. The original asking price will usually be about 20% to 40% higher—if you look gullible, it will be higher still—than what you should pay. For a shared taxi, try **Indah Taxi** (✉ Brig-jen Katamso 60, ☎ 061/510036).

Contacts and Resources
EMERGENCIES
Ambulance: ☎ 118. **Fire:** ☎ 113. **Hospital:** Dr. M. Jamil (✉ Jl. Perintis Kemerdekaan, ☎ 061/22355 for English speakers). **Police:** ☎ 110.

ENGLISH-LANGUAGE BOOKSTORES
Try the bookshop in the **Tiara Medan Hotel** (✉ Jl. Cut Mutia, Medan, ☎ 061/574000). The **Toko Buku Bookshop** (✉ Jl. Ahmad Yani 48, Medan, ☎ no phone) is another good bet.

TOUR OPERATORS AND TRAVEL AGENTS
Trophy Tours (✉ Jl. Brig-jen Katamso 33, Medan, ☎ 061/555666) can help with tours and trips on Sumatra as well as with other travel arrangements. **P. T. Tri Jaya Tour & Travel** (✉ Villa Prim Indah, Jl. Duta

Wisata 58, Medan, ☎ 061/786–3325, FAX 061/786–3324, ✍) offers tailor-made tours on Sumatra and other Indonesian islands.

VISITOR INFORMATION
The **tourist office** at Polonia Airport—between the domestic and international terminals—has lists of accommodations in the region. The staff will happily make reservations and arrange ground transportation.

Some information can be obtained from **North Sumatra Regional Office of Tourism** (✉ Jl. Ahmad Yani 107, Medan, ☎ 061/538101). More helpful is the **Provincial Tourist Service** (✉ Jl. Jendral A. Yani 107, Medan 20151, ☎ 061/511101).

West Sumatra

Much of mountainous West Sumatra remains covered in virgin jungle with volcanoes, rivers, elephants, endangered tigers, and rhinos—a nature-lover's delight. It has three regions: the volcanic highlands, a coastal plain, and islands covered in jungle. The long plain is heavily inhabited, the highlands and islands less so. Nearly 90% of the population are members of the matrilineal Minangkabau tribe (here women inherit the family property). Extended families live in *rumah gadang* (big houses) with roofs that have a series of curving spikes—similar to buffalo horns—that point skyward.

Bonjol

❺ *600 km (372 mi) south of Medan, 220 km (136 mi) north of Padang.*

There's really not much here—just a funky concrete globe of the world, a park, some coffee stalls, and a souvenir shop—but it *is* right on the equator and hence merits a little respect. You can get a certificate that you visited at the souvenir shop, which might make Bonjol worth a stop if you're driving south from Medan to Padang on the Trans-Sumatran Highway. If you're a geography junkie, you can also make Bonjol a day trip from Bukittinggi (☞ *below*).

Bukittinggi

❻ *120 km (75 mi) southeast of Bonjol, 550 km (341 mi) southeast of Prapat, 94 km (58 mi) north of Padang.*

Nestled in the highlands north of Padang, picturesque Bukittinggi is the area's cultural and tourist hub. At 3,051 ft above sea level on the Agam Plateau, it offers cool relief from the heat. The Dutch called it Ft. de Kock; although some foundations and a few rusty cannon are all that remain of the actual fort, the hilly site offers good views.

The **Jam Gadang** clock tower is the landmark of Bukittinggi's center. The nearby town market is a lively place to shop for local items or sample local food. The **Rumah Gadang Museum,** a refurbished, 19th-century Minangkabau home that's also near the clock tower, offers free dance performances on Sunday and public holidays.

At the town's south end are the extensive **Japanese Tunnels,** dug with forced labor during World War II as a defense against the Allies. They're worth the small admission charge, and it's easy enough to tour them by yourself because there are lights along the main tunnel. If you want a more extensive look, you can hire a guide—preferably one who knows the history and carries a flashlight. Nearby the Japanese Tunnels is **Sianok Canyon,** which winds south of the city. A one-hour walk through the canyon from Bukittinggi brings you to the village of

Kota Gadang, whose inhabitants are known for their silver work—particularly silver filigree. Even if you're not in the market, the walk here makes a nice half-day outing.

Pandai Sikat (12 km [8 mi] south of Bukittinggi) is known for its furniture and woodworking factories, but it's also a weaving center with several hundred looms turning out cloth. The furniture is beautiful to some, a bit overdone for others, and too big for most travelers to transport home. However, there are some smaller wood carvings for sale here, too.

Dining and Lodging

$ ✕ **Lapan Nasi Sederhana.** It doesn't look like much—just a room that is open to the street and food displayed in a glass case—but the Padang dishes are spicy and good. Point to what you want, and it will be brought to your table with a bowl of rice. This place is popular and can be packed. ✉ *Jl. Minangkabau 61,* ☎ *no phone. No credit cards.*

$ ✕ **Simpang Raya.** Like its Padang cousin, this branch serves a good selection of such Indonesian staples as nasi goreng and satays in a simple dining room. Expect crowds at lunchtime. ✉ *Jl. Sudiman 8,* ☎ *0751/22163. No credit cards.*

$$$ ◫ **Melia Comfort Pusako.** The Melia's location 4 km (2 mi) from the town's center gives it the feel of a resort. Rooms here are spacious and have mountain views. You can bike into town or ask the hotel staff to arrange for transportation. They can also coordinate golf outings at a local course. ✉ *Jl. Soekarno-Hatta 7, 26129,* ☎ *0752/32111,* FAX *0752/32667. 184 rooms, 7 suites. 2 restaurants, bar, pool, massage, 2 tennis courts, health club, bicycles, business services. AE, DC, MC, V.*

$$$ ◫ **Novotel.** In a building that looks like a cross between a medieval fort and a Middle Eastern palace, this hotel is a commanding presence above the town's center. It also has many of the amenities you would expect of an international chain establishment, including a pleasant pool and gardens. You can walk or bike around town from here, and the on-site Shaan Holidays office will arrange guided tours of the area or trips to the local golf course. ✉ *Jl. Laras Datuk Bandaro, 26113,* ☎ *0752/35000,* FAX *0752/23800. 93 rooms, 6 junior suites, 1 suite. Restaurant, bar, pool, bicycles, travel services. AE, DC, MC, V.*

$-$$ ◫ **Benteng Hotel.** This budget hotel—a simple concrete structure—offers rich views from its location right next to what remains of Ft. de Kock on the highest hill in town. The basic rooms have TVs, well-kept old furniture, hot water in private baths, and air-conditioning—though you hardly need it with the cool highland breezes. The staff is friendly. ✉ *Jl. Benteng 1, 26113,* ☎ *0752/21115,* FAX *0752/22596. 15 rooms. Restaurant, bar. MC, V.*

Danau Maninjau

❼ *40 km (25 mi) west of Bukittinggi.*

Smaller than Danau Toba and, perhaps, not as spectacular, this lake is still quite beautiful. The steep crater walls are mostly forested, though there are terraced rice fields in places. The drive here from Bukittinggi is something of a thrill; the final descent from the crater's rim to the lake involves 44 hairpin turns. You can calm your nerves with a swim in the lake's deep blue waters.

Batusangkar

❽ *50 km (31 mi) southwest of Bukittinggi.*

According to legend, Batusangkar is the cradle of Minangkabau culture, and it has many unique traditional houses as well as a countryside full of terraced rice fields. It's best to visit with a driver and guide from Bukittinggi or Padang. Be sure to stop in Balimbang village, which has many traditional Minangkabau houses, including one reputed to be 350 years old.

Padang

9 *575 km (360 mi) southeast of Medan, 900 km (560 mi) northwest of Jakarta, and 490 km (304 mi) southwest of Singapore.*

West Sumatra's capital is also the largest port in the west of the island. Sitting on a coastal plain, it's hot and has the laid-back atmosphere and attitude that often accompanies such a climate. Many of the city's structures have Minangkabau roofs with their hornlike spikes. The clip-clop of horse-drawn carts is a more common sound than the ear-splitting whine of motorcycle taxis so often heard in Medan. The city's old quarter, next to the river, is worth a stroll. The century-old shops look a bit worn (somehow, this adds to their appeal), and the boats in the river are colorfully painted. But the highlight here is the food. Don't miss the chance to sample spicy Padang food *in Padang.*

In a traditional Minangkabau house on the corner of Jalan Diponegoro and Jalan H. O. S. Cokroaminoto, the **Adiyawarman Museum,** open daily 9 to 5, has a collection of regional antiques.

Although Padang is on the coast, most of its beaches aren't that great. The exception is **Bungus Bay,** 20 km (12 mi) south of town. The sand is soft and white, and the surf is calm. Further, this crescent-shape bay is surrounded by rice fields and hills. Several islands just off the coast from Padang also have beautiful beaches.

Dining and Lodging

$$–$$$ ✕ **Sari.** One of Padang's fancier restaurants is near a quaint little mosque with loudspeakers that blast the call to prayer early in the evening. Seated in the air-conditioned dining room or on the patio, you can order local and imported steaks or Indonesian and Padang dishes. ⊠ *Jl. Thamrin 71B,* ☎ *0751/31838. MC, V.*

$$ ✕ **Simpang Enam.** This restaurant tops the competition. Although the
★ menu has a selection of Chinese dishes, anything made with the fish, fresh from the waters nearby, will be delicious (the pepper crab is a good choice). You order in the simple air-conditioned dining room and then watch through a window as the chefs cook your meal. ⊠ *Jl. H. O. S. Cokroaminoto 44,* ☎ *0751/25044. AE, V.*

$–$$ ✕ **Simpang Raya.** In an old house off a busy road, Simpang Raya has a good selection of Indonesian staples, including a noteworthy chicken satay. There are tables in an air-conditioned room, in a fan-cooled room, and on a patio. ⊠ *Jl. Aziz Chan 24,* ☎ *0751/24894. No credit cards.*

$$$ ▦ **Hotel Bumi Minang.** This upscale hotel offers international service (it's big enough to hold regional conferences) but still provides traditional hospitality. Expect tastefully decorated rooms with blond woods, wicker, and off-white cushions. Service is friendly and helpful. ⊠ *Jl. Bundo Kandung 20–28, 25118,* ☎ *0751/37555,* ℻ *0751/37567. 164 rooms. 6 restaurants, bar, lounge, pool, sauna, 2 tennis courts, exercise room, business services, convention center, meeting rooms. AE, D, MC, V.* ✆

$$$ ▦ **Sol Inn Pusako, Sikuai Island Resort.** A 20-minute boat ride from Padang, this resort has 99-acre Sikuai Island all to itself. Each of its 54 timber cottages has a balcony view of the beach. Though the decor is nothing fancy, rooms are spacious and comfortable with air-conditioning, hot water, and TVs. The restaurant serves Indonesian, Japanese, Chinese, and Western cuisine. You can work off all that food by participating in one of the resort's many water-sports activities. ⊠ *Jl. Muara 38,*

Padang 25118, ☎ *0751/35311 or 800/336–3542 in the U.S.,* FAX *0751/ 22895. 54 cottages. Restaurant, 3 bars, 2 pools, jogging, beach, dive shop, snorkeling, boating, jet skiing, fishing. AE, DC, MC, V.*

$$–$$$ 🏨 **Batang Arau Hotel.** In Padang's old quarter and next to the river, this
★ former bank—yes, bank—was converted into a hotel in 1995. Though each room is unique, all are outfitted with solid wooden furniture, iron beds, and are decorated in local Minangkabau style. Two rooms have balconies. Breakfast is included in the rate. ✉ *Jl. Batang Arau 33, 25118,* ☎ *0751/27400,* FAX *0751/31404. 6 rooms. Bar, billiards. AE, V.*

$$ 🏨 **Paradiso Village, Cudadak Island.** For a very basic island escape— one where your days are filled only with sunbathing and reading—try Paradiso Village, a 90-minute boat ride or a 90-minute drive and a 10-minute boat ride from Padang. The resort offers two-story bungalows with mosquito nets and fans, although sea breezes usually keep things cool enough. The reasonable room rates include all your meals—very reasonable, indeed. ✉ *Rimbun Sumatra Tours, Jl. Batang Arau 33, Padang 25118,* ☎ *0751/31403,* FAX *0751/31404. 10 bungalows. Restaurant, beach. AE, MC, V.*

$–$$ 🏨 **Wisma Mayang Sari.** This small establishment in an old Dutch-era house still feels like someone's home. Rooms are basic, though each has air-conditioning or a fan, a private bath with hot water, and a refrigerator. Breakfast is included in the price. ✉ *Jl. Jendral Sudiman 19, 25118,* ☎ *0751/22647. 15 rooms. Refrigerators. V.*

West Sumatra A to Z

Arriving and Departing

BY AIRPLANE

Daily flights from Jakarta and four flights a week from Medan to Padang's **Tabing Airport**, north of town, is served by **Garuda** (☎ 0751/30737), **Merpati** (☎ 0751/38103), and **Silk Air** (☎ 0751/38120), a Singapore airline.

BY BOAT

If you're a patient traveler with a lot of time, boat travel is another option. Check with **Pelni** (☎ 0751/33624) about its service. The line travels weekly to many of the nearby islands and also has service to Jakarta and coastal cities on mainland Sumatra.

BY BUS

If you're a glutton for punishment, take the overnight bus on the Trans-Sumatran Highway from Jakarta to Padang. The Padang bus station is on Jalan Pemuda near the intersection with Jalan M. Yamin.

Getting Around

BY AIRPLANE

There are regular flights between Padang and Medan. For more information, *see* Arriving and Departing *in* North Sumatra A to Z, *above.*

BY BUS

There are 14- to 16-hour bus trips between Padang and Medan—not the most comfortable way to go. For hops between nearby towns, however, bus travel is fine, though some local buses don't have air-conditioning and can be crowded. You can buy your ticket at the bus station—usually near the town center—right before you depart, or you can have a travel agent make arrangements for you in advance. In Padang contact **Lintas Andalas Terminal** (✉ Jl. Pemuda, ☎ 0751/23216).

BY CAR

Despite the relatively good condition of the Trans-Sumatran Highway, driving a rental car yourself can be dangerous unless you already know the country and speak the language. It's best to make arrangements to hire a car and driver through a travel agent (☞ Tour Operators and Travel Agencies, *below*) or the staff of a major hotel.

You can pick up cabs or becaks at hotels, bus stations, airports, and docks. If your cab isn't metered, be sure to negotiate the price before you get into the car; don't hesitate to bargain hard. In both Padang and Bukittinggi, horse-drawn carts are another public transport option. You can also share a cab with four or five strangers and split the cost. For a shared taxi in Padang, contact **Safa Marwa** (✉ Jl. Pemua 33, ☎ 0751/25244). **Patax** (✉ Jl. Pintu Kebun, ☎ 0752/21163) is a good company in Bukittinggi.

Contacts and Resources

EMERGENCIES

Ambulance: ☎ 118. **Fire:** ☎ 113. Hospitals: **RSUP Dr. M. Djamil** (✉ Jl. Perintis Kemerdekaan, Padang, ☎ 0751/26585) or **General Hospital** (✉ Jl. A. Rivai, Bukittinggi, ☎ 0752/21013). Pharmacy: **Yani** (✉ Jl. A Yani 42, Padang, ☎ 751/27948). **Police:** ☎ 110.

ENGLISH-LANGUAGE BOOKSTORES

In Padang try **Gramedia** (✉ Jl. Damar 63, ☎ 0751/37003), a few blocks north of the museum and bus station. It has a few English-language pulp-fiction titles. In Bukittinggi, on Jalan Ahmad Yani, there are several used bookshops with some English-language novels.

TOUR OPERATORS AND TRAVEL AGENCIES

In Padang, **Pacto** (✉ Jl. Tan Malaka, ☎ 0751/33335) can help you with a variety of travel arrangements. **Rimbun Sumatra Tours** (✉ Jl. Batang Arau 33, ☎ 0751/31403) is, as its name suggests, good for tours.

In Bukittinggi try: **Pt. Maju Indosari** (✉ Jl. Muka Jam Gadang 17, ☎ 0752/21671) or **Shaan Holidays** (✉ Jl. Pemuda 9, ☎ 0752/32530).

VISITOR INFORMATION

In Padang, contact the **Indonesian Tourist Promotion Office** (✉ Jl. Khatib Sulaeman 22, ☎ 0751/55231). In Bukittinggi, contact the **Bukittinggi Tourism Information Office** (✉ Jl. Syech Bantam 1, ☎ 0752/22403).

INDONESIA A TO Z

Arriving and Departing

By Airplane

AIRPORTS

International flights to Jakarta's **Soekarno Hatta** Airport (☎ 021/550–5307) land at Terminal One, with the exception of Garuda Indonesia Airways flights, which are processed through Terminal Two. Medan's **Polonia Airport** (☎ 061/538444) and **Bali's Ngurah Rai International Airport** (☎ 0361/751026) are also major international gateways.

Many travelers use one airline into an Asian capital such as Bangkok, Seoul, Singapore, Taipei, or Tokyo, then transfer to one of the numerous Asian airlines that fly to Indonesia. Others take advantage of international routes that utilize less common entry points such as Davao, the Philippines, to Manado, Sulawesi; Darwin, Australia, to Kupang, Timor; and Kuching, Malaysia, to Pontianak, Kalimantan.

CARRIERS

Garuda Indonesian Airways (☎ 021/231–1801 in Jakarta, 0361/227825 in Denpasar, and 061/514877 in Medan), the national carrier, once offered a direct flight from Los Angeles to Jakarta or Bali; at press time, however, this service was suspended.

Continental Airlines (☎ 800/525–0280 in the U.S. and Canada, 0800/776424 in the U.K., 0361/287774 in Bali, and 021/344417 in Jakarta), connects more than a dozen points in Southeast Asia and Micronesia. It also has the shortest flight to Bali from the American west coast, via Honolulu and Guam.

Northwest Airlines (☎ 800/225–2525) flies to 19 major transit points in Asia, from which you can connect with a flight to Indonesia.

Other airlines with service from North America include: **Cathay Pacific** (☎ 021/380–6664 in Jakarta and 0361/286001 in Denpasar), **Japan Airlines** (☎ 021/570–3883 in Jakarta and 0361/287576 in Denpasar), **Malaysia Airlines** (☎ 021/522–9682 in Jakarta, 0361/285071 in Denpasar, and 061/519333 in Medan), **Singapore Airlines** (☎ 021/520–6881 in Jakarta, 0361/287940 in Denpasar, and 061/537744 in Medan), and **Thai Airways International** (☎ 021/314–0607 in Jakarta, 0361/288141 in Denpasar, and 061/510541 in Medan).

From London, **Garuda** (☞ *above*) flies to Jakarta and Bali. **Cathay Pacific** (☞ *above*) also flies to Bali.

Qantas (☎ 021/230–0277 in Jakarta and 0361/288331 in Denpasar) has nonstop flights from Sydney. **Air New Zealand** (☎ 021/573–8195 in Jakarta and 0361/756170 in Denpasar) and **Ansett Australia** (☎ 021/315–4462 in Jakarta and 0361/289636 in Denpasar) offer nonstop service from both Australia and New Zealand.

FLYING TIMES

Transpacific flying times to Bali are approximately 19 hours from Los Angeles, 23 hours from Chicago, 25 hours from New York, and 22 hours from Vancouver. Flying the eastbound route, the flight time from New York is 23 hours to Jakarta and 25 hours to Bali. Allowing for stops, it's 26 hours from Toronto and Montréal to Jakarta and 28 to Bali. From London it's 16 and 18 hours to Jakarta and Bali, respectively. From Sydney and Melbourne, it's 7 and 4 hours to Bali and 9 and 6 hours to Jakarta. From Auckland, it takes 9 hours to reach Bali and 11 hours to Jakarta. (For details on flying times within Indonesia, *see* By Airplane *in* Getting Around, *below*.)

By Boat

High-speed ferries depart from Penang, Malaysia, every day but Sunday to Belawan (the port of Medan), Sumatra, five hours later. Return trips depart around noon from Belawan every day except Monday. Contact **Perdana Express** (☎ 061/545803 in Medan) or **Kuala Perlis-Langkawi Ferry Service** (☎ 04/262–5630 in Penang).

Another popular ferry route is that from Singapore to the Riau Archipelago's Batam—there are departures every hour during the day—where you can pick up a domestic flight to anywhere in Indonesia. Another ferry route from Singapore is to Tanjung Pinang, also in the Riau Archipelago and just a 90-minute ferry ride, and from there you can take a Merpati flight to other Indonesian destinations.

Getting Around

By Airplane

Reservations are strongly advised on popular routes—between Jakarta and Yogyakarta, for example. Expect delays, especially during the monsoon rains, which can make air travel impossible. Besides the major air hubs in Medan, Jakarta, and Bali (☞ Arriving and Departing, *above*), official air entry points include: Ambon, Maluku; Balik-papan, Kalimantan; Bandung, Java; Batam, Riau; Biak, Irian Jaya; Man-ado, Sulawesi; Mataram, Lombok; Padang, Sumatra; Pekanbaru, Sumatra; Pontianak, Kalimantan; and Surabaya, Java.

CARRIERS

Garuda Indonesian Airways (☞ Arriving and Departing, *above*), **Merpati** (☎ 021/424–3608 in Jakarta), and **Sempati** (☎ 021/835–1612 in Jakarta) cover all 27 provinces. **Bouraq** (☎ 021/628–8827 in Jakarta) flies into small towns with limited landing facilities, such as destinations in Kalimantan on Indonesian Borneo. Note: Always check with the airlines the day before your flight, because flights are often canceled, and schedules change owing to the country's finan-cial crisis.

FLYING TIMES

Flying within Indonesia requires patience and flexibility, as schedules run on the infamous *jam karet,* or "rubber time," and long hauls may incorporate unscheduled stops. From Jakarta it's 40 minutes to Ban-dung, 1¼ hours to Yogyakarta, and 1½ hours to Surabaya on Java; 1½ hours to Denpasar on Bali; 2 hours to Ujung Pandang on Sulawesi; 2¼ hours to Medan on Sumatra; and 2¼ hours to Mataram on Lombok. From Denpasar, it's 40 minutes to Mataram and almost 1½ hours to Ujung Pandang.

PASSES

Garuda Indonesia offers a **Visit Indonesia Pass** for $300 good for three flights within Indonesia, and additional flight coupons for $100 each. It's best to buy the pass before your arrival (allow at least a week for processing), but if you don't have time to purchase one before your trip, you can buy one in Indonesia if you show a local airline office a copy of your international tickets. One hitch to the deal, though, is that you must fly in and out of the country on Garuda Indonesia; other-wise, a $60 surcharge is added.

By Bajaj

Although scooting through traffic in these three-wheel orange con-traptions can be faster, more exciting, and less expensive than taxis, keep in mind that they are also hot (no air-conditioning) and loud (no glass in the windows). A few blocks will cost Rp 500–Rp 1,000; 1 km (½ mi) will run Rp 2,000–Rp 5,000, depending on your negotiating skills. Drivers are notorious for overcharging, so bargain hard—and finalize the price *before* you get in.

By Becak

These three-wheeled pedicabs are useful for short distances. Jakarta has only 2,000 pedicabs remaining, with 318 in the central portion of the city, but elsewhere in Indonesia they're plentiful. A few blocks will cost Rp 200–Rp 500; 1 km (½ mi) can run Rp 1,000–Rp 3,000. Becak drivers are tough bargainers, but if one doesn't meet your price, an-other may. Just be sure to determine the fare beforehand.

By Bemo

A bemo is a converted minivan, good for short trips. Most bemos fol-low regular routes and will stop anywhere along the way to pick up or discharge passengers. You pay when you get out. Try to learn the fare (they vary according to distance) from another passenger; other-wise you'll be overcharged. An empty bemo will often try to pick up Western travelers, but beware: unless you clarify that it's on its regu-lar route, you will be chartering it as a taxi.

By Boat

Ferries run between many of the islands. Hotel travel desks and travel agencies have schedules; you buy your tickets at the terminals. For longer trips, **Pelni** (✉ Jl. Angkasa 18, Jakarta, ☎ 021/421–1921; Jl. Martadinata 38, Ujung Pandang, ☎ 0411/331393), the state-owned shipping company, serves all the major ports with ships accommodating 1,000 to 2,000 passengers in four classes. First-class cabins are air-conditioned and have private bathrooms—but don't expect comfort or opulence; this is not a luxury cruise. Schedules and tickets are available from Pelni's head office or at travel agencies. Official entry and exit points by sea are: Ambon, Maluku; Batam, Riau; Belawan, Sumatra; Benoa, Bali; Dumai, Riau; Jakarta and Surabaya, Java; Padangbai, Bali; Semarang, Java; and Tanjung Pinang, Riau.

By Bus

Buses are an important form of surface transportation in Indonesia, though they offer varying degrees of comfort. Long-distance expresses have air-conditioning, reclining seats, rest rooms, meals, videos—even karaoke. Local buses, however, can be crowded and hot. It's an inexpensive means of transport—the 14-hour trip between Jakarta and Yogyakarta, for instance, costs Rp 17,500 on an air-conditioned express. Tickets and schedules are available from terminals, travel desks, or travel agencies. Tourist offices also provide schedules. The only international land crossing from Indonesia is between Kuching, Malaysia, and Pontianak, Kalimantan.

For Java and Sumatra, contact **Antar Lintas Sumatra** (✉ Jl. Jati Baru 87A, Jakarta, ☎ 021/320970). For Java, Bali, and Sumatra, try **P. T. ANS** (✉ Jl. Senen Raya 50, Jakarta, ☎ 021/340494), **Java Indah Express** (✉ Jl. Diponegoro 14, Denpasar, ☎ 361/227329), or **Lorena** (✉ Jl. Hasannudin 3, Denpasar, ☎ 361/234941). To book a seat on one of the smaller vehicles that run east through Nusa Tenggara, try the numerous Denpasar transport agencies on Jalan Diponegoro and Jalan Hasannudin; otherwise, you can ask the drivers at any ferry terminal if seats are available. **Liman Express** (✉ Jl. Timor, Ujung Pandang, ☎ 0411/442478) makes daily runs to Tanatoraja on Sulawesi.

By Car

Given the traffic situations within the city limits of major Indonesian destinations, it's probably best to leave the driving to the cabbies and chauffeurs who rule the roads here. If you must rent a car, use common sense about when to do so. On Bali, renting cars is common practice and relatively safe, but in other locales traffic conditions and poor roads can make driving hazardous. Although hiring a car and driver (through your hotel or a travel agent) generally costs 25%–50% more than simply renting a car (about Rp 324,000–Rp 540,000), it's still relatively inexpensive.

EMERGENCY ASSISTANCE

Prompt assistance is part of the service at major international car-rental agencies as well as at the more popular local companies. Otherwise, you're pretty much on your own. However, if you break down or run into trouble, Indonesians are in general very helpful and will be able to direct you to the nearest auto service facility—if not actually stay with you and help you fix your vehicle.

GASOLINE

Gas prices are actually much lower than in the States, the equivalent of around $1–$1.25 for a U.S. gallon. Stations are few and far between, so don't set out with less than a quarter tank, and check your fuel gauge frequently to make sure that it works. Pertamina is the major gas station operator, but there are numerous small vendors alongside the roads; be sure, however, that you know how to ask for the right type of fuel.

PARKING

Except at the larger resort hotels, where guests usually park free in designated lots or garages, parking in Indonesia is for the most part "take what you find"; curbside is your only option.

RENTALS

Self-drive cars are available through large rental agencies, hotels, or travel agencies in major cities and tourist hubs, including Jakarta, Yogyakarta, and Bali. Most Indonesian car-rental companies require your license from home *and* an International Driver's License. You can get one through the American or Canadian automobile associations, or, in the United Kingdom, through the Automobile Association or Royal Automobile Club. Most Western companies also have age requirements. For example, Avis requires that you be at least 25 years old, Hertz 21 years old, and National 18 years old.

Always discuss your itinerary with the agent before signing the contract. Some rental contracts may limit the areas to which you can drive. For example, you need a special permit—really just a letter from the rental agency—to cross from Bali to Lombok.

Western agencies usually offer either sedans or four-wheel-drive vehicles, all with standard transmission, cassette decks, and air-conditioning; vehicles from local agencies can range from mini-jeeps to full-size vans, but they may not have air-conditioning or extra comforts. The rental charge for a four-wheel-drive vehicle from an international firm starts at about $45 a day. For details on agencies, *see* the A to Z sections *in* specific regions.

ROAD CONDITIONS

Indonesia's main roads are paved and in good condition, but side and back roads can be poor. Tourist areas are often very congested, with small trucks, bemos, scooters, bicycles, and pedestrians adding to car traffic. Off the main highways, expect village animals—cows, goats, dogs, chickens—to appear in the road without warning.

RULES OF THE ROAD

The most important rule to remember here is that there are no rules: drivers routinely ignore red lights and policemen, yet stop mid-road for a chat with a passing vehicle or to buy cigarettes from a wandering vendor. Keep your eyes open and your reflexes sharp at all times. Driving is on the left, and passing is on the right. Road signs reading HATI HATI mean "warning" and exclamation points mean "Caution!" for a variety of reasons: sharp curves, steep embankments, construction, or bad roads in general. Hint: Tap your horn as a warning before passing on two-lane roads and as you round blind curves on less-used thoroughfares.

There are no formal seat belt laws, but make sure yours works and that you wear it. Although they aren't required in Indonesia, it's wise to use car seats if you're traveling with young children. To get such a seat, you'll need to rent your car in advance through a Western agency and request it when booking.

By Horse Cart

Horse-drawn carts are disappearing fast, but they remain popular in Yogyakarta, Denpasar, Lombok, Sumbawa, and other tourist areas. The typical fare for distances up to a km (½ mi) is Rp 200–Rp 500.

By Taxi

Registered taxis and hired cars may be hailed on city streets—look for the yellow number plates. Except in Jakarta, Surabaya, parts of Bali, and at most airports, you negotiate the fare with the driver before setting out. Most hotels have taxi stands.

By Train

Java is the only island with reliable train service. The line runs from Jakarta through Yogyakarta to Surabaya and Banyuwangi, and it's a worthwhile mode of transport if you have time. Executive and business classes include air-conditioning, comfortable swivel seats, TV, and meals. Economy offers fan-cooled cars and open windows that let you view the lush countryside as it slides by. Early morning departures are best for avoiding the midday heat. Night trains are also a viable alternative though sleeper cars are rarely offered. Schedules and tickets are available through hotel travel desks, travel agencies, or at the train stations; be sure to get tickets well in advance. Between Jakarta and Yogyakarta, it's around Rp 55,000 in executive class, Rp 23,000 in business, and Rp 14,000 in economy; to Surabaya, it's around Rp 57,000 in executive, Rp 38,000 in business, and Rp 10,000 in economy. For more information, contact the **Regional Operational Office** (KADAOPS; ⊠ Jl. Taman Stasiun 1, Jakarta Kota, Jakarta, ☎ 021/6929083).

Contacts and Resources

Customs and Duties

ON ARRIVAL

Two liters of liquor and 200 cigarettes may be brought into Indonesia duty-free. Restrictions apply on the import of radios and television sets. Of course, no drugs, weapons, or pornography are allowed; neither are cassette players nor printed matter in Indonesian or Chinese. Note: Carry all prescription medicines in their original containers and keep a copy of the doctor's slip with you.

ON DEPARTURE

You may not export more than 50,000 rupiah per person. Other forbidden exports include valuable antiques (generally more than 100 years old and worth $100 or more), artifacts, cultural treasures, and products made from endangered plants and animals, such as furs, feathers, and the tortoiseshell items sold in Bali.

Electricity

The electrical current in Indonesia is 220 volts, 50 cycles alternating. If you're coming from North America, you'll need an adapter and a converter unless you have dual-voltage appliances, in which case you'll need only an adapter. Electricity may flicker out at anytime, even in Jakarta and Bali. Carry a small flashlight with extra batteries and keep computers charged at all times.

Embassies and Consulates

AUSTRALIAN

Consulate: (⊠ Jl. Prof. Mochtar Yamin Kav 51, Renon, Denpasar, ☎ 0361/235092). **Embassy:** (⊠ Jl. H. R. Rasuna Said Kav. C15–16, Jakarta, ☎ 021/522–7111).

CANADIAN

Embassy: (⊠ Jl. Jendral Sudirman Kav 29, 5th floor, Wisma Metropolitan 1, Jakarta, ☎ 021/510709).

NEW ZEALAND

Embassy: (⊠ Jl. Diponegoro 41, Jakarta, ☎ 021/330680).

UNITED KINGDOM
Consulate: Medan (✉ Jl. Ahmad Yani 2, ☎ 061/518699). **Embassy: Jakarta** (✉ Jl. M. H. Thamrin 75, ☎ 021/330904).

UNITED STATES
Consulates: Denpasar (✉ Jl. Hayam Wuruk 188, ☎ 0361/233605); **Medan** (✉ Jl. Imam Bonjol 13, ☎ 061/322200); **Sanur** (✉ Jl. Segara Ayu 5, ☎ 0361/288478); and **Surabaya** (✉ Jl. Raya Dr. Sutomo 33, ☎ 031/568–2287). **Embassy: Jakarta** (✉ Jl. Medan Merdeka Selatan 5, ☎ 021/3442211).

Health and Safety

Drink only bottled water, and avoid ice in any beverage (although ice at luxury hotels, such as those on Bali, is often made from distilled water and may be safe). It's best to steer clear of raw, unpeeled fruits and vegetables, raw seafood, and undercooked meat. Although malaria is rare in the tourist areas, it has not been eradicated from the outer regions, so it's best to take precautions. Inoculations for hepatitis and tetanus should also be up-to-date. If you're a hiker or diver, be aware that these islands are home to a number of dangerous and poisonous creatures—know what to watch out for before you head into the wild.

Owing to the downward spiral of the Indonesian economy and general political dissatisfaction, large public demonstrations and riots have occurred in Jakarta, Bandung, Medan, and Ujung Pandang. Tourists should be safe in any case, but be wary of the social climate before you travel, pay attention to travelers' advisories, and steer clear of areas embroiled in political upheaval, especially during elections.

Crime against travelers mainly occurs in large cities and tourist areas, where small-time thieves prey on unseasoned visitors, so a little caution in how you act can go a long way. Dress modestly and don't flash your money around. Carry traveler's checks and keep large amounts of cash in a hidden money pouch or locked in hotel safes. Pickpockets haunt crowded transport hubs, and scam artists love to draw in naive travelers. Check out what you buy before you lay down the money—fake jewels, fake name-brand items (handbags, shoes, perfume), bait-and-switch gifts "prewrapped" for customs, and bogus shipping promises are the typical tricks of this region.

Although it's common practice for Indonesian men and women to walk hand-in-hand with friends of the same sex, gay and lesbian travelers should practice discretion, even in Bali, since homosexuality is not readily accepted in this overwhelmingly Muslim country. For advice and information on gay and lesbian activities, contact the organization **Gaya Nusantara** (✉ Jl. Mulyosari Timur 46, Surabaya, ☎ 031/593–4924).

Language, Culture, and Etiquette

Although some 300 languages are spoken in Indonesia, Bahasa Indonesia has been the national language since independence. English is widely spoken in tourist areas.

Indonesians are extremely polite. Begin encounters with locals by saying "*Selemat pagi*" ("Good morning"), "*Selamat siang*" ("Good day"), "*Selamat sore*" ("Good afternoon"), or "*Selamat malam*" ("Good evening"), depending on the time of day. Two phrases you'll use often are "*Terima kasih*" ("Thank you") and "*Ma'af*" ("Excuse me" or "I'm sorry"). Shaking hands has become a common practice, and Indonesians are very tactile, so expect to be touched often in conversation. Smiling is the national pastime, so do it frequently and you'll have a much easier time traversing language barriers. Some etiquette no-nos are pointing with your index finger (gesture with your whole hand instead), crossing your arms, and placing your hands on your hips (signs of anger). Most important, avoid touching food or people with your left hand, which is considered unclean.

The more formal or sacred an occasion, the more formally dressed you should be. When visiting mosques, women should wear something on the head and shouldn't enter during menstruation. Men should wear long trousers and have at least their upper arms covered. Don't walk in front of those who are praying. At Balinese temples, you must wear a sash to enter; these are usually rented on-site for a few rupiah. Shorts (and other above-the-knee clothing) are considered improper temple attire, so avoid them or borrow a sarong when visiting any holy place.

Mail

POSTAL RATES

Two kinds of airmail are available: *pos udara* (regular) and *kilat* (express). Kilat rates to the United States or the United Kingdom are Rp 1,200 and Rp 1,300 respectively for postcards and Rp 1,600 and Rp 1,700 for 1 gram (.035 oz.) letters. Postcards are Rp 600 to all other foreign countries. Pos udara letters of less than 21 grams (.735 oz.) are Rp 1,600 to North America and Europe and Rp 1,200 to Australia and New Zealand.

RECEIVING MAIL

For letters or packages to reach you in any major town in the islands, have them sent to the main post office—usually open Monday through Thursday 8–4, Friday 8 AM–11 AM, and Saturday 8 AM–12:30 PM. You can have mail sent to you "poste restante" care of local post offices. Just be sure that letters addressed to you have your surname (underlined and in capital letters), followed by your first name, to avoid filing confusion. A small fee may be charged to pick up a letter. Most hotels will also accept mail and hold it. Do not have anyone send cash.

WRITING TO INDONESIA

Indonesian addresses are straightforward. All you need for a proper address are the name, street address (Jl. or Jln. stand for "Jalan," or road), number (though many addresses in small towns won't have this), town, island, and postal code. Finally, be sure to follow all this information with "Republik Indonesia."

Money and Expenses

COSTS

Prices in Indonesia depend on what you're buying. The basic cost of living is low and domestic labor is cheap, but you'll pay a premium for anything imported. Thus, camera film is expensive, food is not. Regionally, costs rise in direct relation to tourism and business development. Prices in Bali and Jakarta are relatively high, particularly at deluxe hotels and restaurants. Sumatra and Sulawesi, by contrast, are bargains.

Major cities have shopping complexes and department stores where prices are fixed, but at small shops and street stalls, bargaining is expected and part of the shopping experience. Bargaining is, in fact, having a dialogue with the vendor, and a certain respect is established between you and the seller. It's also an art, so try to develop your own technique. Start by offering half the asking price, even a third in the tourist areas. You'll finish somewhere in between. Shops with higher-quality merchandise are likely to take credit cards, but payment in cash puts you in a better bargaining position. The keys to good negotiation in Asia are a positive attitude and flexibility.

Sample Prices: Cup of coffee, 25¢–$2; small bottle of beer, $1–$4; small bottled water, 25¢–$2; can of soda, 50¢–$3; bottle of house wine, $7–

$15; sandwich, $2–$7; 2-km (1-mi) taxi ride, 75¢–$3 (depending on traffic); city bus ride, 10¢–$2; museum: 25¢–$3.

Indonesia's unit of currency is the rupiah. Bills come in denominations of 100, 500, 1,000, 5,000, 10,000, 20,000, 50,000, and 100,000 Rp, coins in 25, 50, 100, 500, and 1,000 Rp. The exchange rate at press time was Rp 7,595 to the U.S. dollar, Rp 5,144 to the Canadian dollar, Rp 12,060 to the U.K. pound sterling, Rp 4,535 to the Australian dollar, and Rp 3,780 to the New Zealand dollar. Check current rates at www.xe.net. Note that money changers will not exchange the old US$100 bills (with the smaller head) at a decent rate, if at all, due to problems with widespread counterfeiting. Bring new bills only.

SERVICE CHARGES, TAXES, AND TIPPING
High-end hotels charge 21% tax, of which only 10% is the regular government tax also seen on the bill at moderate hotels; the rest comprises various service charges. Departing passengers on international flights pay an airport departure tax of Rp 50,000. Domestic airport taxes are from Rp 5,500 to Rp 11,000, depending on the point of departure.

The more expensive tourist restaurants include a service charge; if not, tip 10%. Above the hotel service charge, plan to tip bellboys $1 per bag; you may also want to tip room-service personnel if you request a special service. Porters at the airport should receive about 50¢ per bag. Taxi drivers aren't tipped except in Jakarta and Surabaya, where 50¢, or small change, is the minimum. For a driver of a hired car, $2.50 for half a day would be the minimum tip. Private guides expect a gratuity, perhaps $3–$5 per day.

Opening and Closing Times
Banks are open from around 9 AM to 3 PM or 4 PM, but they may close during the lunch hour. Bank branches in hotels may stay open later. **Government offices** are open Monday–Thursday from approximately 8 to 3 and Friday 8–11:30 AM. Some are also open on Saturday 8–2. **Offices** have varied hours, usually around 9–5 weekdays and a half day on Saturday. Most **museums** are open Tuesday–Thursday and weekends 9–2 (although some larger museums stay open until 4 or 5), Friday 9–noon. **Shops** are generally open Monday–Saturday 9–5. Offices and stores in Muslim areas are open only until 11 AM on Friday.

NATIONAL HOLIDAYS
Start of Ramadan, the Islamic month of fasting (Nov. 17, 2001; Nov. 6, 2002); New Year's Day; Idul Fitri, the end of Ramadan (Dec. 16, 2001; Dec. 6, 2002); Isra Miraj Nabi Mohammed, Mohammed's Ascension (Feb./Mar.); Good Friday (Apr. 13, 2001; March 29, 2002); Easter (April 15, 2001; March 31, 2002); Ascension Day (May 24, 2001; May 9, 2002); Waicak, Birth of Buddha (May/June); Haji, commemorating Mecca pilgrimages (July); Independence Day (Aug. 17); Birth of Mohammed (Oct.); Christmas Day.

Outdoor Activities and Sports
Swimming pools, health clubs, tennis, badminton, and sometimes squash and racquetball are available at the major hotels. There are golf courses near the larger cities and in resort areas. Special adventure tours can be arranged through tour operators. Traditional sports include bull races in Madura, Java; bullfights (bull against bull) at Kota Baru, near Bukittinggi, Sumatra; and cockfighting (though it is illegal) in Java, Bali, and Sulawesi.

For scuba-diving information, contact the Indonesian diving organization, **Possi** (⊠ Jl. Prapatan 38, Jakarta, ☎ 021/348685), or try

Pulau Seribu Paradise (☎ 021/380–8426) in Jakarta, **Baruna Water Sports** (☎ 361/753820) at Kuta Beach in Bali, or **Nusantara Diving Center** (☎ 437/3988) in Manado. A helpful guide for divers interested in Indonesian reefs is *Underwater Indonesia* (by Kal Muller, Periplus Editions, Singapore, 1995).

Passports and Visas

The Indonesian government stipulates that passports must be valid for at least six months from arrival date, and all travelers must have proof of onward or return passage. Unlike other countries in the region, these regulations are strictly enforced in Indonesia. For stays up to 60 days, visas are not required for citizens of Australia, Canada, New Zealand, the United Kingdom, and the United States as long as you enter the country through one of the major gateways. These include the airports at Ambon, Bali, Balikpapan, Bandung, Batam, Biak, Jakarta, Kupang, Manado, Mataram, Medan, Padang, Pekanbaru, Pontianak, and Surabaya, as well as the seaports of Ambon, Balikpapan, Batam, Belawan, Benoa, Jakarta, Kupang, Manado, Padangbai (Bali), Pontianak, Semarang, Surabaya, and Tanjung Pinang. The only international land crossing allowed is between Kuching, Malaysia, and Pontianak, Kalimantan. Other ports of entry may require a visa.

Telephones

CALLS TO INDONESIA

To call Indonesia from overseas, dial the country code, 62, and then the area code, omitting the first 0.

LOCAL CALLS

Prior to the economic crisis, efforts were being made to upgrade and standardize Jakarta's phone system, but there has been little progress since (hence, some phone numbers in Jakarta have five or six digits and others have seven). Further, upgrades have not even been started in some parts of Indonesia—phone numbers vary in length and service varies in quality. Phone numbers change frequently, too. If you have difficulty reaching a contact, consider asking a local—perhaps your guide—to help you contact an Indonesian-speaking operator. You're even better off using hotel phones despite the small surcharges; that way you don't need to amass quantities of coins, and an operator can help with translation and information. Your best chance of finding a phone is in hotel lobbies, at the Telekom agency, or the privately run *Wartel* offices. Some travel agencies have phones you can use for local calls, and the staff will let you send and receive faxes for a small fee.

For local calls, three minutes costs Rp 100. Older public phones take Rp 100 coins, but the newer ones accept only phone cards, available at newsstands and kiosks in most towns. For long distance, dial the area code before the number. For operator and directory assistance, dial 108 for local calls, 106 for the provinces.

INTERNATIONAL CALLS

Major Indonesian cities are now hooked into the International Direct Dialing (IDD) system via satellite. Dial 001 plus the respective country code. For towns without the IDD hookup, go through the operator (in tourist destinations many speak English). If you want to avoid using hotel phones, the most economical way to place an IDD call is from the nearest Kantor Telephone & Telegraph office. For international directory assistance, dial 102.

You can make collect calls to Australia, Europe, and North America; for other countries, you need a telephone credit card. Reduced rates on international phone calls are in effect 9 PM–6 AM daily. For most Western countries, Indonesia also has special "home country" phones in its Telekom offices and many hotels. With these you can contact an operator in your home country just by pushing a button. Like a collect call, the bill is charged to the person you're calling, or you can use one of the calling cards that are sold everywhere.

AT&T, MCI, and Sprint long-distance services make calling home relatively convenient, but you may find the local access number blocked in many hotel rooms. First ask the hotel operator to connect you. If the hotel operator balks, ask for an international operator, or dial the international operator yourself. One way to improve your odds of getting connected to your long-distance carrier is to travel with more than one company's calling card (a hotel may block Sprint, for example, but not MCI). If all else fails, call your phone company collect in the United States or call from a pay phone in the hotel lobby. Here are some long-distance access codes in Indonesia: **AT&T** (☎ 001–801–10), **MCI** (☎ 001–801–11), and **Sprint** (☎ 001–801–15).

Visitor Information

OUTSIDE INDONESIA

Australia has an **Indonesian Embassy** (✉ 8 Darwin Ave., Yarralumla ACT 2600, ☎ 06/2733222) and an **Indonesian Tourist Office** (✉ Level 10, S. Elizabeth St., Sydney NSA 2000, ☎ 02/923–33630). In Canada, contact the **Embassy of Indonesia** (✉ 287 MacLaren St., Ottawa, Ontario K2P 0L9, ☎ 613/236–7403). New Zealand also has an **Indonesian Embassy** (✉ 70 Glen Rd., Kelburn, Wellington, ☎ 04/475–8697). In the United Kingdom, contact the **Indonesian Tourist Office** (✉ 3 Hanover St., London W1R 9HH, ☎ 0171/493–0030). In the United States, contact the **Indonesian Embassy** (✉ 2020 Massachusetts Ave. NW, Washington, D.C. 20036, ☎ 202/775–5200). You can also check out the country's tourism Web site (✎).

WITHIN INDONESIA

The Directorate General of Tourism in Indonesia (✉ 81 Karmat Raya, Jakarta, ☎ 021/310–3117). For details on specific tourist offices throughout the country, *see* the A to Z section *in* each region.

When to Go

Indonesia's low-lying regions are uniformly hot and humid year-round. Temperatures can reach 90°F (32°C) soon after midday, and they drop no lower than 70°F (21°C) at night. The weather at higher altitudes is up to 20°F (11°C) cooler.

The best months to visit Indonesia are April–May and September–October, when crowds are lighter and you're not so likely to get drenched: the west monsoon, from November through March, brings heavy rains. It can drizzle for several days in a row or pour half the day, with only occasional dry spells. Since most of Indonesia's attractions are under the open sky—temples and other architecture, beaches, and outdoor festivals—the monsoon can very literally dampen your enjoyment. Like many locals, you may want to keep an umbrella on hand at all times for protection from both rain and sun.

In the peak tourist months, June–August, popular areas (especially Tanatoraja) are crammed with visitors. Bali hotels also tend to be fully booked around Christmas and New Year's; transport and accommodations in the rest of the country are full around Muslim holidays. Unless you plan to stay only on Bali, consider carefully before visiting during Ramadan, the Islamic month of fasting, when many restaurants, offices, and tourist attractions are closed until sundown.

CLIMATE

The following are average temperatures in Jakarta:

Jan.	84F	29C	**May**	88F	31C	**Sept.**	88F	31C
	74	23		74	23		74	23
Feb.	84F	29C	**June**	88F	31C	**Oct.**	88F	31C
	74	23		74	23		74	23
Mar.	85F	30C	**July**	88F	31C	**Nov.**	85F	30C
	74	23		74	23		74	23
Apr.	86F	30C	**Aug.**	88F	31C	**Dec.**	85F	30C
	74	23		74	23		74	23

FESTIVALS AND SEASONAL EVENTS

Festival dates depend on the type of calendar prevalent in the region where they take place. Most of Indonesia uses the Islamic calendar; the Balinese use a lunar calendar. The **Indonesia Calendar of Events,** with listings for the entire archipelago, is available at Garuda airline offices, or contact tourist information offices.

Dec.–Jan.: **Idul Fitri,** two days marking the end of Ramadan (a month of fasting during daylight), is the most important Muslim holiday. Festivals take place in all the villages and towns of Muslim Indonesia. **Kesodo** ceremonies are held by the Hindu Tenggerese at the crater of Mt. Bromo on Java.

Mar.: **Nyepi,** the Balinese New Year, falls on the vernal equinox, usually around March 21. New Year's Eve is spent exorcising evil spirits, which are first attracted with offerings of chicken blood, flowers, and aromatic leaves, then driven away with noise as masked youths bang gongs and tin pans. The island falls silent: no fires or lamps may be lighted, and traffic is prohibited.

May: **Waicak Day,** a public holiday throughout Indonesia, celebrates the Buddha's birth, death, and enlightenment. The **Ramayana Ballet Festival** is held at the Prambanan temple near Yogyakarta during the full-moon week each month, beginning in May and continuing through October. A cast of 500 performs a four-episode dance-drama of the *Ramayana* epic.

July: **Galungan,** Bali's most important festival, celebrates the creation of the world, marks a visit by ancestral spirits, and honors the victory of good over evil. Celebrants make offerings in family shrines and decorate their villages. On the 10th and last day they bid farewell to the visiting spirits with gifts of *kuningan,* a saffron-yellow rice.

Aug.: **Independence Day** is celebrated on the 17th throughout Indonesia with flag-raising ceremonies, sports events, and cultural performances.

Oct.: The town of Pamekasan on Java holds **bull-racing finals** in mid–October. A jockey stands on skids slung between two yoked bulls. The animals are decorated, and there's mass dancing before they run. The winner is the bull whose feet cross the finish line first. **Sekaten** commemorates the birth of Mohammed. In Yogyakarta the sultan's antique gamelan—a unique Indonesian musical instrument—is played only on this day. The concert is performed in the gamelan pavilion of the kraton, the sultan's palace complex. Then the celebrants form a parade, carrying enormous amounts of food from the kraton to the mosque, where they distribute it to the people.

3 MALAYSIA AND BRUNEI

Malaysia offers a rich olfactory experience. In city streets the acrid aroma of diesel fumes blends with that of chilies frying in vendor stalls, sweet incense from Indian shops, pungent curry powders from spice merchants, and hints of frangipani and other flowers abloom. The steaming jungle has a damp, fermenting scent. In neighboring Brunei, the smell of money permeates. This tiny country is one of the richest in the world, and with Malaysia it shares not only a tropical climate and jungle terrain but also a mix of Malay and Muslim traditions.

By Nigel Fisher

Updated by
Bob Marriott,
Mei-Yin Teo,
and Lara
Wozniak

THE EARLIEST INHABITANTS of the Malay Peninsula were Neolithic Negrito peoples whose descendants—the Orang Asli—still live simply in jungle uplands. Several waves of progressively more Mongoloid groups brought Iron and Bronze Age cultures to the peninsula and spread out over the entire archipelago. Later, with the emergence of the Java-based Majapahit, the Malay Peninsula came under the influence of a Hindu-Javanese empire that exerted little political control but strong cultural influence. This was once seen in the *wayang kulit* (shadow puppet plays)—a form of storytelling performed in villages in Kelantan until banned by the extremist Islamic state government in 1992—as well as in traditional ceremonies and customs (such as batik-making and folktales) that are still practiced today.

In the 15th century, Islam entered Malaya (as the peninsula was once called) from northern Sumatra and became the official religion of the powerful state of Melaka (Malacca) during the reign of Sultan Iskandar Shah. Islam solidified the system of sultanates, in which one person and his family provided both political and religious leadership. (Today Malaysia still has nine sultans; every five years one is elected to serve a term as constitutional monarch. The head of government in this parliamentary democracy is the prime minister.)

For the next 200 years the peninsula was a hornets' nest of warring sultanates, marauding pirates, and European adventurers who, while searching for spices and gold, introduced guns and cannons. The Portuguese conquered Melaka, and were followed by the Dutch, who established a stronghold in Java and outposts in Sumatra and Melaka. An 1824 treaty gave the British Dutch-held Melaka, which became part of the British Straits Settlements along with Singapore and Pinang (Penang). With the British dominating Malaya and the Dutch in Sumatra, the two regions—which shared similar histories, cultures, and religious customs—began to split and follow the lead of the Europeans.

In the mid-19th century, war and famine forced millions of Chinese to flee their homelands and seek employment in Malaya's rapidly expanding tin industry. Soon after their arrival, the rubber industry began to flourish. Rubber requires intensive labor, and still more workers were brought in from India. Other groups came from India to trade, open shops, or lend money. While in India the British trained many civil servants and professionals who also came to Malaya. This Indian community maintained strong ties with home. (To this day Indians sometimes request brides or grooms from an ancestral village—many marriages are still arranged—and often retire in their native land.)

These patterns of life in Malaya continued until World War II. Malays continued their traditions in *kampungs* (communal villages), where time flowed slowly. Sultans prospered under British protection, combining the pleasures of East and West. The Chinese became the peninsula's economic backbone, and the Indians performed various middleman roles. The British maintained a benevolent rule. Each community flourished separately, with little cultural exchange.

The war had little impact on life in Malaya until the Japanese attack on Pearl Harbor and subsequent invasion of Malaya. Japanese forces landed in the northeastern state of Terengganu and moved rapidly down through the jungle, taking Singapore in March 1942. Life on the Malay Peninsula changed overnight. The British had farthest to fall. Many women and children were evacuated to Australia, but the men remained. Former planters, bankers, executives, and soldiers were thrust from a life of ease into hardship or jail. Many perished during the construc-

Malaysia

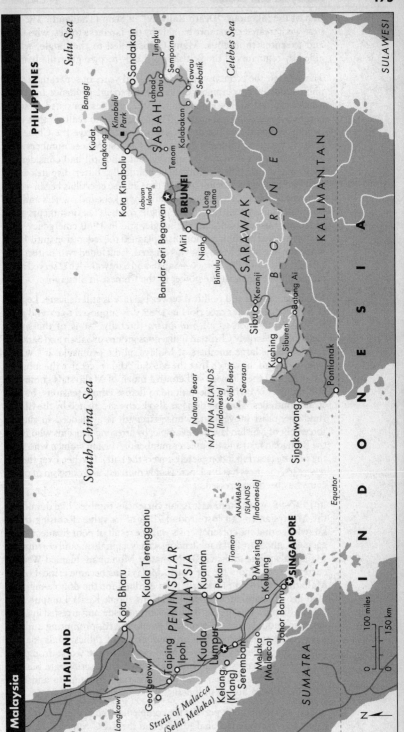

THAILAND

Langkawi
Georgetown
Taiping *PENINSULAR*
Ipoh *MALAYSIA*
Kuala
Lumpur
Kelang (Klang)
Seremban
Melaka (Malacca)
Strait of Malacca (Selat Melaka)
Johor Bahru
SINGAPORE
Kota Bharu
Kuala Terengganu
Kuantan
Pekan
Mersing
Keluang
Tioman

South China Sea

SUMATRA

INDONESIA

Equator

0   100 miles
0   150 km

N

NATUNA ISLANDS (Indonesia)
Natuna Besar
Subi Besar
Serasan

ANAMBAS ISLANDS (Indonesia)

Singkawang
Pontianak
Kuching
Siburen
Batang Ai
Keraniji
Sibu
Bintulu
Niah
Miri
Bandar Seri Begawan
BRUNEI
Long Lama
Labuan Island
Kota Kinabalu
Langkong
Kudat
Bangji
Sandakan
Tungku
Semporna
Tawau
Sebatik
Lahad Datu
Kalabakan
Tenom
■ Kinabalu Park
SABAH
SARAWAK
B O R N E O
KALIMANTAN

Sulu Sea
PHILIPPINES
Celebes Sea
SULAWESI

tion of the infamous "Death Railway" in Siam (Thailand). The Chinese were treated even more harshly by the Japanese forces, who jailed and executed thousands. Many Chinese fled to the jungle, where, aided by remnants of the British army, they formed guerrilla bands.

The war left the economy floundering, and years of separatism made unification and development difficult. Prior to independence and under a federation of Malaysian states in 1957, politics consisted of struggles between two racial groups. The Malays, who realized that independence would remove British protection and leave the Chinese in control, became politically active. The Chinese, whose numbers were greatly diminished by the occupation but who still had considerable economic clout, failed to organize politically. Bitter disputes raged among the local leadership. In 1948 the Chinese guerrillas began a campaign of terrorism, harassing plantation workers and owners and ambushing Malays and British on jungle roads. (The insurgents were gradually pushed back into the jungle, and in 1960 emergency policies were lifted.) Ethnic factionalism plagued the federation until 1963, when the nation of Malaysia was created. It included two British protectorates in northern Borneo—Sabah and Sarawak—that served as an ethnic balance against the power of the Chinese in Singapore.

Malaysia's racial and political power balance is still delicate. Legislation introduced after race riots in 1969 was supposed to extend positive discrimination to all *bumiputra* (literally "sons of the soil"), including the largely Christian indigenous groups of Sabah and Sarawak as well as the large numbers of Malays on the peninsula. It's widely acknowledged, however, that the Muslim Malays receive the most assistance, and the Chinese still control much of Malaysia's commerce and industry. Much has been done to defuse ethnic tensions, but the strain continues. The situation has also been exacerbated by the Islamic fundamentalist movement, whose strength is evidenced in the enforcement of Muslim law (for example, by arresting Muslims who break the Ramadan fast) and the greater number of Muslim women who wear the *tudung* (scarf that completely covers the hair). Further, over the last few years, the press has been increasingly muzzled, and criticism of politicians has been suppressed.

In 1997–98, when Southeast Asian currencies tumbled like dominoes, the Malaysian ringgit lost around 70% of its value. Refusing to acknowledge that the currency crisis was the result of poor financial management, uncontrolled bank lending, crony capitalism, and corruption, Malaysia's prime minister, Dr. Mahathir Mohamad, blamed Western currency speculators for the crash. Malaysians became critical of Dr. Mahathir, who had previously been credited for the double-digit annual growth rate. Street demonstrations shook Kuala Lumpur after Anwar Ibrahim was fired as deputy prime minister and arrested in 1998. Periodic antigovernment protests have followed, prompting authorities to issue an indefinite ban on outdoor public rallies. Malaysia was further challenged by the severe haze created by the worst drought of the century—thanks to El Niño—and by the indiscriminate burning of the rain forest to clear land for plantations in Sumatra and Kalimantan, in neighboring Indonesia.

But the situation didn't prevent the completion and opening of the new Kuala Lumpur International Airport and the KlCC complex. In 1998, Malaysia also hosted the Commonwealth Games, which involved building a world-class stadium complex and accommodations for thousands of athletes. Early in the new millennium, the economy has substantially improved. Massive road, bridging, and building projects are underway, and few fail to be impressed by how the country is developing.

Pleasures and Pastimes

Malaysia offers some of the world's best coral reefs; long stretches of white sand (both developed and deserted); the highest mountain between the Himalayas and New Guinea; hill resorts that provide recreation and escape from the tropical sun; spectacular limestone outcroppings and impressive caves in Sarawak's Gunung Mulu National Park; vast areas of primary jungle; and networks of rivers perfect for white-water rafting. Though there are increasingly more amenities and facilities throughout the country, the major destinations remain Melaka, Kuala Lumpur, Pinang, and Langkawi on the west coast; Kuantan and Tioman Island on the east coast; the Cameron and Genting highlands in the center; Kota Kinabalu in Sabah; and Kuching in Sarawak.

Beaches

Despite its countless beautiful beaches, resorts are a relatively new concept in Malaysia. Still you'll find some terrific establishments on Langkawi Island (a pet project of the prime minister), even though its beaches are only so-so. Although Pinang was the first region to promote beaches, its Batu Ferringhi Beach pales in comparison with those on the Pangkor Islands (off the west coast) and along the eastern coast from Terengganu to Johor. The lovely islands of Perhentian and Redang embody the idea of tropical paradise, complete with scuba diving and other resort facilities. Farther south, around Cherating, you'll find miles of tranquil sandy stretches and traditional Malay fishing villages. Several islands off Mersing, notably Tioman, offer resorts that range from super-luxurious to the simple feet-in-the-sand variety.

On Borneo, Sarawak's rivers tend to carry silt to the ocean, making for muddy waters. Damai Beach, just outside Kuching, has a resort complex, but Sarawak's best beach is in the somewhat remote Similajau National Park. In Sabah, there are countless beaches along the west coast, with resorts in Tanjung Aru and Tuaran, near Kota Kinabalu, which also offers five lovely islands in a marine national park just minutes from downtown.

Dining

Ordering a meal from street vendors (paying each for the individual dish he or she makes) and sharing a table with locals is a great way to immerse yourself in Malaysian cuisine and culture. Just look at what others are eating, and if it appeals to you, point and order. You're likely to find a mix of food—Chinese, Malay, and Indian—in one cluster of stalls. One Chinese favorite is the *popiah,* a soft spring roll filled with vegetables. The *meehon* and *kweh teow* (fried noodles) are also tasty and cheap. Perhaps the best-known Malay dish is *satay*—slivers of marinated beef, chicken, or mutton threaded onto thin sticks, barbecued, and served with a spicy peanut sauce. Be cautious with the local *nasi kandar*—the chilies rule the spicy prawns and fish-head curry. Malaysia's breakfast dish, *nasi lemak* (a bundle of rice with salt fish, curry chicken, peanuts, cucumber, and boiled egg), is worth a taste.

Because fruit is so plentiful and delicious, Malaysians consume lots of it, either fresh from the ubiquitous roadside vendors or fresh-squeezed—try star fruit, watermelon, and orange juice. Mangoes, papayas, rambutans, mangosteens, and finger-size bananas are widely available. The "king" of fruits is the durian, but be prepared: the smell isn't sweet, even though the taste is (it's sort of like vanilla pudding). Hotels have strict policies forbidding durians in guest rooms, so you'll have to select a fruit, have the seller cut it open, and then eat the yellow flesh on the spot.

Authentic Malay food isn't as widely available in sit-down restaurants as Chinese or even American fast-food fare. Thai and Japanese restaurants are plentiful, and the food of the Nonyas or Straits-born Chinese (a fusion of Malay and Chinese cuisines) is perennially popular. In Kuala Lumpur, you'll find establishments that serve a variety of Indian cuisines—southern, northern, and Muslim. Eating rice and curry from a banana leaf with your hand (right hand only, please), as is done in the southern Indian restaurants, is an experience you'll no doubt savor. The following terms are likely to appear on the menus in Malaysia:

asam—sour; a reference to the sourness provided by the tamarind fruit used in some dishes

dim sum—Chinese snacks, eaten at breakfast or lunch, made with meat, prawns, or fish, and usually steamed or deep fried

garoupa—a local fish with tender flesh and a sweet flavor

green curry—a Thai curry made with green chilies, lots of fresh herbs, small green *brinjals* (eggplants), and chicken or red meat

ice kacang—shaved ice heaped over red beans, jelly, sweet corn, and strips of green mung-pea flour, sweetened with syrup and drenched with coconut milk or evaporated milk

kacang—(pronounced *ka-chang*); signals the presence of beans or nuts

kaya—a jam made from steaming a mixture of eggs, sugar, and coconut cream

kerabu—a hot-and-sour Nonya salad of chicken, jellyfish, unripe mango, squid, beef, or almost anything else, dressed with onions, lemongrass, lime juice, and small chilies

rendang—meat simmered for hours in spices, chilies, and coconut milk until nearly dry

roti—bread

sambal—a thick, hot condiment of chilies, local roots, and herbs; if it has plenty of shrimp paste, it's known as *sambal belacan*

tandoori—meat or seafood roasted in a clay oven, northern Indian style

tom yam—a very sour, hot, and lemony Thai soup usually made with seafood

Price categories are based on the ranges below.

CATEGORY	COST*
$$$$	over $30
$$$	$20–$30
$$	$8–$20
$	under $8

Per person, based on three dishes shared between two people, excluding tax, service, and drinks

Golf

Golf is part of the British legacy in Malaysia, and you'll find around 200 courses—many of them excellent—throughout the country. Kuala Lumpur's Mines Resort and Golf Club, which hosted the 1999 world championships, is the finest, along with the Royal Selangor and the Saujana Golf and Country Club, also in Kuala Lumpur, the Bukit Jambul Golf and Country Club in Pinang, the Datai Bay Golf Club in Langkawi, the Borneo Golf and Country Club in Sabah, and the Damai Beach Golf Course near Kuching.

Hiking

The Malaysian Tourism Promotion Board, or MTPB (☞ Visitor Information *in* Malaysia and Brunei A to Z, *below*), has a useful brochure that describes the country's 19 national parks and their trails and lodging options. (In some places, particularly Sarawak, the accommodations are surprisingly upscale.) Hiking opportunities range from full-scale backpacking through dense jungle to short treks combined with road and river transport. The best climb in Southeast Asia is Sabah's Mt. Kinabalu. Paths around the park headquarters there offer rewarding but less arduous walking. Trekking in Sarawak's Gunung Mulu National Park ranges from a grueling hike to the razor-sharp Pinnacles to three to four days following the Headhunter's Trail. The trekking in the remote Kelabit Highlands, also in Sarawak, is excellent. On peninsular Malaysia you can arrange jungle hikes in Taman Negara, a national park north of Kuala Lumpur. For leisurely hikes in cooler temperatures, try the hills of the Cameron Highlands.

Jungle Treks and River Trips

Rain forest threaded by rivers and rapids still covers much of Borneo. Intrepid travelers can trek through the jungle interior on foot or by Jeep, ride a longboat upriver (transportation in the interior is often by river, where boats take the place of buses), and stay overnight in a tribal longhouse. The tourist industry is only now being developed in these regions, so you won't trip over other visitors. And though you'll find signs of modernity in even the most remote longhouses, native lifestyles and hospitality are largely unaltered. Insects hum, invisible creatures croak and grunt, water gurgles and sighs. Equally mysterious are the groaning and screeching of trees that, burdened by age and debris, finally crash through the jungle growth. Sabah's scenic white-water rivers also guarantee exciting outdoor adventures.

Lodging

You'll find many new luxury hotels—shining marble-and-glass towers that provide smiling service and every comfort—particularly in Kuala Lumpur. Hotels in smaller provincial capitals aren't quite as grand, though they certainly provide quality and comfort. In bare-bones establishments the furnishings may be worn and the plaster walls may have cracks, but the bed linen will be fresh and the bathrooms clean. Resorts run the gamut from modern, self-contained complexes with many amenities to cramped, down-at-the-heel Chinese hotels where the shared bath is down the hall.

Hotels with distinctive Malaysian charm and character include the Desa Utara Pedu Lake Resort in Kedah, which is based on a kampung concept and stretches across 300 acres of rain forest; the Palace of the Golden Horses which dominates the Mines Resort in Kuala Lumpur; and the Hyatt Regency in Kuantan, where the views over the South China Sea are hypnotic. More exotic options include a Dayak longhouse in Sarawak, or a beach bungalow (with primitive plumbing) on a small island off the peninsula's east coast.

Bathrooms in the city generally have Western-style commodes; Asian-style squat facilities are common in rural areas. Better hotels have in-house movies available on color TVs. The government censors the media, including the channels offered by Astro and Mega satellite broadcasting, although all major hotels offer CNN. All hotels are air-conditioned unless otherwise stated, and room service is available in all the $$$ and $$$$ hotels.

A homestay program is currently being developed in the region. Lodge with a family, perhaps in a kampung, and experience local culture, customs, and food in an intimate setting. Accommodation can be basic, but will be clean and cheap. For more information, contact the MTPB (☞ Visitor Information *in* Malaysia and Brunei A to Z, *below*).

Price categories are based on the ranges below.

CATEGORY	COST*
$$$$	over $115
$$$	$90–$115
$$	$60–$90
$	under $60

For a standard double room in high season, excluding service charge and tax.

Scuba Diving

Sipadan Island, off Sabah's east coast in the Celebes Sea, is one of the best dive spots in the world. Here you can explore a spectacular 2,000-ft wall of vertical coral and swim with sea turtles. Islands off Semporna, and the atoll of Layang Layang off Sabah's west coast also offer spectacular diving. Sarawak has the Luconia Shoals, which are accessible via Miri or Brunei. Off the peninsula, you should head for Tioman Island; the small islands around Mersing; or the islands of Perhentian, Redang, Kapas, and Tenggol—all off Terengganu on the east coast.

Shopping

Malaysia's hand-printed batiks, with layers of rich colors and elaborate traditional designs, have become high fashion worldwide. You can buy shirts and simple skirts and dresses or lengths of fabric. Look for *songket*, traditional hand-woven brocade. Pewter is another specialty, since it's made from one of the country's abundant raw materials, tin. The best-known manufacturer is Selangor Pewter, which markets its goods through its own showrooms as well as in department stores, gift shops, and handicraft centers.

Handicrafts, especially those from Sarawak, are well made and appealing. Typical items are rattan baskets, handwoven straw goods, and handmade silver jewelry from Kelantan. The Iban people create weavings called *pua kumbu*, which have primitive patterns and a faded look like that of an antique carpet. Tribal sculptures also have an allure. Perhaps the most unusual handcrafted material is *kain songket*, an extraordinary tapestrylike fabric with real gold threads woven into patterns.

Exploring Malaysia and Brunei

Malaysia is composed of two parts: Peninsular Malaysia (known as Malaya before the formation of Malaysia in 1963) and the two Borneo states of Sabah and Sarawak. (Borneo, the world's third-largest island, also includes the sultanate of Brunei and the Indonesian province of Kalimantan.) Peninsular Malaysia has 11 states. Those covered in this guide are Kedah, Perak, Pinang, Negeri Sembilan, Melaka, Johor, Pahang, Terengganu, Selangor, and the federal territory of Kuala Lumpur.

Although Sabah and Sarawak have a much larger area than the peninsula, the land is largely covered by rain forest or plantations; 80% of the people live on the peninsula. Malaysia's population of some 21.1 million is about 49% Malay; 29% Chinese; 21% Indian and various minorities; and 1% non-Malay indigenous groups including the Kadazan, Iban, and other tribes of Borneo. Although Malaysia is officially a Muslim country, freedom of worship is permitted. The Chinese are mostly Buddhist or Christian, the Indians Hindu or Muslim. Sabah and Sarawak are primarily Christian, as a result of 20th-century missionaries who converted most of the non-Muslim natives.

This mix of cultures is one of Malaysia's main fascinations. It's especially noticeable in the cities, where, interspersed with businessmen in Western garb and teenagers in T-shirts and jeans, you'll see Malay women in floral-print sarongs, conservative Muslim women with traditional head coverings, Chinese in the pajama-type outfits called *samfoo,* and Indian men in *dhotis* (saronglike garments). It manifests itself in a lively and varied food scene, with a proliferation of vendors who sell everything from exotic fruits and juices to Hokkien noodles and Malay satay. And it proclaims itself joyously in the street festivals and religious ceremonies that different cultures celebrate throughout the year.

On the west coast of the peninsula is Kuala Lumpur, Malaysia's capital and the gateway through which most people enter the country. It's a sprawling, clamorous, modern city that nevertheless retains many reminders of the past. The beach resort island of Pinang is a wonderful place to tool about in a trishaw or pedicab through streets lined with lively shops and graceful colonial architecture. North of Pinang is the duty-free island of Langkawi, whose idyllic setting has attracted the attention of resort developers. For a sense of Malaysia's colonial history, a visit to Melaka, with ruins and restored buildings from successive European colonizers, is a must.

The peninsula's east coast is less developed, allowing a glimpse of a quieter Malaysia. Terengannu's islands of Perhentian, Redang, Kapas, and Tenggol, as well as a couple of coastal spots, offer superb beaches and a range of resorts. Farther south, around Kuantan and Cherating you'll find outstanding beaches and first-rate resorts; Mersing, south of Kuantan, is the jumping-off point for several islands, including Tioman, where the film *South Pacific* was shot. The scenery of this island is as idyllic today as it was then; several resort hotels offer a perfect base for a water-sports or jungle-hiking vacation. Much of the rest of the peninsula is covered with rubber estates, oil palm plantations, and cool hill stations. Sabah and Sarawak deliver all the adventure that the word *Borneo* promises, including trips through dense jungle on foot or by longboat to visit the descendants of headhunters at their long-houses—a rare opportunity to learn about a culture so very different from what you've left at home.

Great Itineraries

If you seek only sun, sea, and relaxation, Pangkor Laut, Pinang, Langkawi, Kuantan, the east coast, or around Kota Kinabalu in Sabah are ideal. Alternatively, the diversity of Malaysia is such that a trip could be specifically geared to special-interest travel, such as river trips in Borneo or hiking through the national parks. The itineraries below are as diverse as possible within limited time frames.

IF YOU HAVE 3 DAYS

With this time limit, you'll probably want to focus on seeing **Kuala Lumpur,** though you really should try to get out into the country; **Melaka,** with its colonial past, is only a two-hour drive away. You could also limit Kuala Lumpur to only one day and spend two in **Pinang** or at the beach on the island of **Pangkor Laut.**

IF YOU HAVE 7 DAYS

Start your visit with two full days in **Kuala Lumpur** before going north to the **Cameron Highlands** to stay at The Smokehouse Hotel for a night. Then continue north up to **Pinang** to spend a couple of nights in **Georgetown,** renting a car one day to tour the island. Then take a plane to **Langkawi** for two days of sun and a beach vacation.

IF YOU HAVE 10 DAYS

Although 10 days won't permit you to cover all of Malaysia's highlights, it does offer some flexibility. Give yourself a full day in **Kuala Lumpur** and then pick up a car to drive to the **Cameron Highlands** for a night. The next day, continue on to Pinang and spend the night in **Georgetown.** On the following day, drive over the mountains to the east coast and

Kuantan. You'll want to rest up and spend a couple of nights there or slightly up the coast at **Cherating.** On the sixth day drive down to **Johor Bahru** to drop off the car and pick up a flight to **Kota Kinabalu** in Sabah. Give yourself at least a couple of days here. From Kota Kinabalu you may want to fly into **Bandar Seri Begawan** in Brunei for the night before continuing on to **Kuching** in Sarawak. Spend a minimum of two nights in Sarawak, making sure that you have a chance to go into the interior for a river trip and a visit to a Dayak village. From Kuching, you can take a direct flight back to peninsular Malaysia or Singapore.

When to Tour Malaysia and Brunei

The wet season runs from late October through February on peninsular Malaysia's east coast (where flooding is common), in Sarawak, and on Sabah's east coast. Sabah's west coast is more likely to receive heavy rain from May through July. Islam is the state religion of Malaysia, but freedom of worship is practiced. Islamic law is more strictly enforced in the northern states (in government-owned establishments, alcohol is not served). However, in Kuala Lumpur and other cities, tolerance is greater—reflected in part by the nightlife. During the month of Ramadan, Muslims aren't allowed to eat or drink from sunup to sundown; Muslim restaurants are therefore usually closed during the day. Incidentally, the stress of fasting during Ramadan makes believers a little grumpy and not their normal hospitable selves. (☞ *also* When to Go *in* Malaysia and Brunei A to Z, *below.*)

Numbers in the text correspond to numbers in the margin and on the maps.

KUALA LUMPUR

Malay, Chinese, Muslim, and European influences, plus a blend of modern sophistication and Old World charm make Malaysia's capital, Kuala Lumpur, a city of delightful contrasts. Narrow streets packed with colonial shops and houses open onto broad tree-lined avenues that sit in the shadows of enormous skyscrapers. Gardens bursting with tropical flowers and graced with cool fountains provide peaceful havens in the midst of bustling commercial centers. Kuala Lumpur or as it is commonly called, KL, was founded by miners who discovered tin at the confluence of two muddy rivers. With its population of around 2 million today, the city shows few signs of its humble beginnings.

New buildings push skyward alongside massive hotel complexes that provide excellent service and accommodation. Huge air-conditioned shopping centers sell brand-name goods and designer labels, and the city has dining options to suit every taste, from plush restaurants to wayside stalls. KL as a whole is a safe place, the people are pleasant and polite, and visitors are rarely hassled to buy goods in shops or markets.

The new International Airport stands at the crossroads of the world's major air routes, making KL an important destination in Southeast Asia. Yet in spite of all its changes, the city has not lost its character and remains a simulating gateway to a surprising and beautiful country.

Exploring Kuala Lumpur

394 km (246 mi) northwest of Singapore, 481 km (300 mi) south of Alor Setar (near the Thai border).

In the last 20 years, KL has mushroomed outward and upward in a most confusing manner. Most visitors spend their time in a section known as the Golden Triangle, which has the city's best hotels and shopping areas, as well as a number of sights. Here you'll find symbols of Malaysia's boom time, with the towering Petronas Twin Towers and the KL Tower as the most recent additions. The city's colonial center is marked by the Sultan Abdul Samad Building, which faces the open green (Merdeka Square) and the quaint Tudor-style Royal Selangor Club. Nearby Chinatown is still a busy center for trading and commerce.

Downtown Kuala Lumpur

A GOOD TOUR

Take a cab to Chinatown and start at **Sri Mahamariamman** ①, the city's major Hindu Temple on Jalan Tun H.S. Lee. Coming out of the temple turn right and follow to Jalan Sultan. Turn left, then take the first right into Jalan Panggong and another left when you reach Jalan Bolai Polis. On your left is **The Old China Café**, and the Sikh Temple of Gorwarara Sahip is immediately opposite. Just beyond, turn right into Jalan Petaling, where about 50 yards on your left is **Chan See Shu Yuen** ②, the most atmospheric temple in Chinatown. Retracing your steps up Jalan Petaling, you could detour left down Jalan Hang Lekir for **See Yeoh Temple** ③, then at the top of Jalan Petaling spend a little time bargaining at the street stalls that line each side. They stock umbrellas, cheap clothing, wallets, music cassettes, watches, and fashion jewelry. (At night the street is closed to auto traffic and becomes a full-scale market.) At the junction of Jalan Chen Lock, turn left to the **Central Market** ④, across the road and about 100 yards on your right. This is a renovated Art Deco building with food stalls and a lively market. Look for bargains in silk and pottery, then exit through the back entrance. Turn left onto Jalan Benteng, then follow around to the right before turning left over the Klang River bridge. The bridge leads right to the giant flagpole in **Merdeka Square** ⑤, where you might want to sit awhile and admire the lovely flower gardens.

From Merdeka Square you can take a cab to see the classic architecture of the **Railway Station** ⑥, the contemporary **Masjid Negara** ⑦, and the exhibits at the **Muzium Negara** ⑧. If you have a little more time, consider a stroll through the greenery of **Taman Tasik Perdana** ⑨.

To continue the walking tour from Merdeka Square, head north, passing the magnificent **Sultan Abdul Samad Building** ⑩, which is on your right. Just beyond this, on the right, you can detour down Jalan Tun Perak to **Masjid Jamek Bandaraya** ⑪, and walk about 500 yards to the **Menara Maybank** ⑫, which houses the Numismatic Museum. Otherwise pass under the LRT track and continue north on **Jalan Tuanku Abdul Rahman,** where you can take one of the very short (50 yards), larongs on your right to **Masjid India** ⑬, a modern Indian mosque. This area is known as Little India and on Saturday nights hosts a large open-air market. Staying on Jalan Tuanku Abdul Rahman you pass a few turn-of-the-century shophouses, bookstores, and small open-fronted restaurants. Note the numerous colorful carpet shops, (the locals call this part Carpet Street), and look on the left for the **Coliseum Theatre** ⑭, one of the capital's first movie houses, and the **Coliseum Cafe** next door. If you're hungry, stop in for a sizzling steak, probably the best in town, and a British pint. The busy Kamdar Department Store is directly across the road. Continue north to the **Selangor Pewter Showroom** ⑮, almost at the junction of Jalan Tuanku Abdul Rahman and Jalan Dang Wangi. The Odeon Theatre is on the right-hand corner and on the left the **Kompleks Pertama** ⑯, which faces the **Sogo,** both massive shopping complexes.

From the junction of Jalan Tuanku Abdul Rahman and Jalan Dang Wangi, you can continue by cab or on foot, depending on your energy level. If you choose to keep walking, turn right along Jalan Dang Wangi past the Campbell Department store until you reach Jalan Ampang. Turn left, then right onto Jalan Sultan Ismail. Cross carefully to the left-hand side where you will pass the Concorde Hotel before turn-

Kuala Lumpur

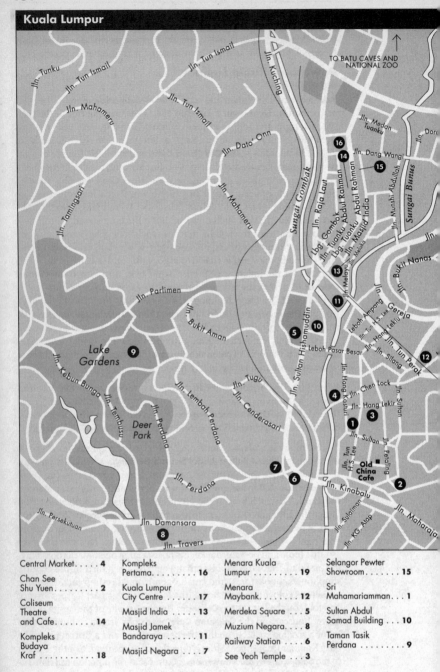

TO BATU CAVES AND
NATIONAL ZOO

Central Market **4**	Kompleks Pertama **16**	Menara Kuala Lumpur **19**	Selangor Pewter Showroom **15**
Chan See Shu Yuen **2**	Kuala Lumpur City Centre **17**	Menara Maybank **12**	Sri Mahamariamman . . . **1**
Coliseum Theatre and Cafe **14**	Masjid India . . . **13**	Merdeka Square . . . **5**	Sultan Abdul Samad Building . . . **10**
Kompleks Budaya Kraf **18**	Masjid Jamek Bandaraya **11**	Muzium Negara . . . **8**	Taman Tasik Perdana **9**
	Masjid Negara **7**	Railway Station . . . **6**	
		See Yeoh Temple . . . **3**	

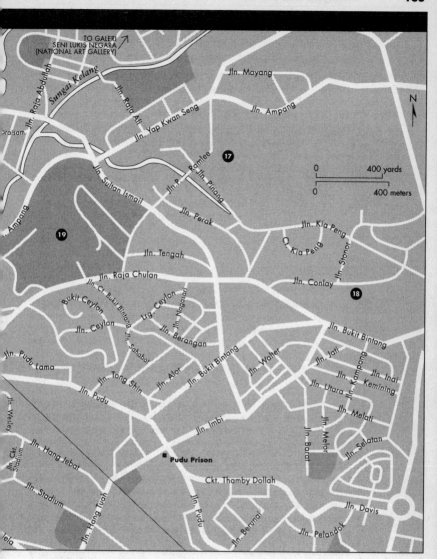

TO GALERI
SENI LUKIS NEGARA
(NATIONAL ART GALLERY)

Jln. Mayang

Jln. Ampang

Jln. Raja Abdullah

Sungai Kelang

Jln. Raja Alī

Jln. Yap Kwan Seng

raisam

Jln. P. Ramlee

Jln. Pinang

17

N

0   400 yards

0   400 meters

Jln. Sultan Ismail

Jln. P.

Jln. Perak

Jln. Kia Peng

Ampang

19

Jln. Tengah

Ct. Kia Peng

Jln. Stonor

Jln. Raja Chulan

Jln. Conlay

18

Bukit Ceylon

Jln. Ct. Bukit Bintang

Lrg. Ceylon

Jln. Nagasari

Jln. Bukit Bintang

Jln. Ceylon

Jln. Sahabat

Jln. Berangan

Jln. Jati

Jln. Inai

Jln. Kampong

Jln. Pudu Lama

Jln. Tong Shin

Jln. Alor

Jln. Bukit Bintang

Jln. Walter

Jln. Kemining

Jln. Utara

Jln. Wesley

Jln. Pudu

Jln. Melati

Jln. Imbi

Jln. Melor

Jln. Selatan

Ckt. Stadium

Jln. Hang Jebat

Jln. Barat

Pudu Prison

Jln. Stadium

Ckt. Thamby Dollah

Jln. Hang Tuah

Jln. Davis

Jln. Pudu

lela

Jln. Berunai

Jln. Petandok

ing left onto Jalan P. Ramlee. This takes you to the **Kuala Lumpur City Centre** ⑰, and the gleaming spires of the Petronas Twin Towers. After a browse through the stunning Suria KLCC shopping complex you can take a rest amid the flower gardens with their sparkling fountains.

Alternatively, from the Kompleks Pertama on Jalan Tuanku Abdul Rahman take a cab to the **Kompleks Budaya Kraf** ⑱, where a wide range of handicrafts from all over Malaysia is on display. From here you can walk up Jalan Stonor and turn left onto Jalan Kia Peng, which leads via Jalan Pinang to **Kuala Lumpur City Centre.** An elevator ride to the top of the **Menara Kuala Lumpur** ⑲ (KL Tower) provides a spectacular view of the city.

TIMING

The walking part of this tour can take four to six hours depending on the time spent shopping and browsing. Be careful crossing roads as scooters appear out of nowhere, weave in and out of traffic, and are not averse to using the footpath. Drink and eat regularly and carry a bottle of water; the local water is perfectly fine to drink. KL is probably the safest city in southeast Asia, so don't hesitate to talk to locals as they are usually friendly and helpful.

SIGHTS TO SEE

❹ **Central Market.** This lively bazaar, housed in an Art Deco building in the heart of KL, was once the city's produce market. Today it's the commercial, cultural, and recreational hub of downtown daily from 10 to 10. You can wander through its many shops and stalls that sell herbs (for cooking or for medicine), kites, batik clothing, jewelry, antiques, rattan baskets, and wood and bamboo crafts. In addition, food vendors offer Malaysian dishes at reasonable prices.

❷ **Chan See Shu Yuen.** Built in 1906, this temple has an impressive roof decorated with figures depicting Chinese mythology. Just off the southern end of Jalan Sultan, the temple is somewhat isolated from the rest of Chinatown.

⓮ **Coliseum Theatre and Cafe.** The landmark Coliseum, one of KL's first movie houses, shows Malaysian and Indonesian films with Chinese subtitles, so it's not really the place to stop for a movie unless you're a linguist. Consider, however, taking a break at the **Coliseum Cafe** (☞ *also* Dining, *below*), a favorite local watering hole that may well serve the best steak in town. ✉ *98–100 Jln. Tuanku Abdul Rahman,* ☎ *03/292–6270.*

Galeri Seni Lukis Negara. The new art gallery opened in November 1999. It spans almost 6 acres, and is flanked by the National Theatre and the National Library. Amenities include a creative center, a sculpture garden, and a photography and graphics studio. There is also a bookshop and café. ✉ *Jln. Temerloh, off Jln. Tun Razak,* ☎ *03/402–54990.* ✪ *Daily 10–6.* ✆ *Free.*

Jalan Tuanku Abdul Rahman. Locals still often refer to this street by its old name, Batu Road, as it was once the main road to the Batu Caves. Regardless of what you call it, the street is home to a number of colorful sari shops, bookstores, stationery shops, Indian Muslim restaurants, and stores of an indeterminate nature. By day you can shop and stop for some people-watching and a bowl of steaming noodle soup at one of the open-air coffee shops with marble-top tables and bentwood chairs.

Across the road from the Coliseum Theatre lots of little shops and vendors press on in the shadow of the bustling Kamdar department store. This area is sometimes called Carpet Street due to the number of shops selling brilliant floor coverings, many in silk, from Belgium, China, India, and the Middle East. Sit in comfort on a pile of rugs and haggle an hour away. Farther along the Peiping Lace Shop sells Chinese linens, lace, jewelry, and ceramics. Neighboring China Arts, a branch of Peiping Lace, is full of decorative coromandel screens, carved writing desks, teak and camphor chests, and antique vases.

★ ⓲ **Kompleks Budaya Kraf.** The two-story Handicraft Complex, once called the Karyaneka Handicraft Centre, is the ideal place to learn about Malaysia's handicrafts and do some serious souvenir shopping. At the entrance there are several shops; at the back is a museum with exhibits on batik, wood carving, ceramics, silver, pewter, and brass. ⊠ *53 Jln. Conlay.* ☎ *Free.* ☉ *Daily 10–10.*

⓰ **Kompleks Pertama.** Pertama (which means "first") is typical of most KL shopping centers: it has clothing, shoe, appliance, and record shops. It also has such recreational facilities as a video-game room, a pool hall, and a nightclub. ⊠ *Jln. Dang Wangi and Jln. Tuanku Abdul Rahman.*

⓱ **Kuala Lumpur City Centre.** The massive KLCC development is dominated by the **Petronas Twin Towers Complex.** Completed in 1996 and currently the world's tallest building, the Twin Towers are linked by a skybridge at the 41st and 42nd floors. It is a city within a city as more than 50,000 people work here on a daily basis. The buildings include the **Suria KLCC,** a shopping and entertainment center that has two department stores, 300 specialty shops, restaurants, food courts, and a cinema complex. A park and gardens rich with tropical flowers and fountains surround the area, and the Mandarin Oriental Hotel stands alongside.

⓭ **Masjid India.** Outside the modern Indian Muslim mosque, in the center of Little India, street vendors sell local *ubat* (medicine) or *jamu* (cosmetics) with all the theatricality of carnival barkers and snake-oil salesmen. They lure potential customers with elaborate stories and "magic" acts in which audience members participate.

⓫ **Masjid Jamek Bandaraya.** At the confluence of the Klang and Gombak rivers is the city's oldest (and most charming) mosque, its two minarets only slightly taller than the coconut palms on the grounds. It was designed by a British architect and was completed in 1909. A vendor beside the main gate sells tape recordings of those hypnotic prayer chants.

❼ **Masjid Negara.** The contemporary architecture of the National Mosque features a towering 240-ft minaret spire, a purple roof, and geometric-pattern grillwork. Though not the largest mosque in Asia, it can accommodate 10,000 worshipers. The entrance is on Jalan Lembah Perdana. Signs remind you to dress modestly, to remove your shoes when entering, and to be aware that certain areas are off-limits, especially during prayer times. The mosque complex also houses a library and a mausoleum. ⊠ *Jln. Sultan Hishamuddin.* ☉ *Sat.–Thurs. 9–6, Fri. 2:45–6.*

⓳ **Menara Kuala Lumpur.** For a dramatic overview of KL and the surrounding area, take an elevator ride up the 1,380-ft Kuala Lumpur Tower. In addition to an observation platform you'll find food outlets, a revolving restaurant, and gift and souvenir shops. On a clear day, you can see the Straits of Melaka from here. ⊠ *Jln. Puncak (off Jln. P. Ramlee).* ☎ *RM8.* ☉ *Daily 10–10.*

⓬ **Menara Maybank.** On the imposing hill at the corner of Jalan Tun Perak and Jalan Raja Chulan stands the Maybank Building, designed to resemble the handle of a kris (dagger with a wavy blade), the national emblem. At the top of the escalators, you can walk around the soaring (five-story) bank lobby during business hours. The **Numismatic Museum,** which exhibits Malaysian bills and coins from the past, can supply information on the nation's major commodities and adjoins a gallery of contemporary art. ☎ *03/230–8833.* ☎ *Free.* ☉ *Mon.–Sat. 10–6.*

⑤ Merdeka Square. Once known as the Padang, this open green square has been the site of everything from rugby and cricket matches to Merdeka (Independence) Day celebrations. With its colorful flower gardens, this is a lovely place for a quiet stroll in the evening, or just to sit and watch the world go by. At the back of the square is the black-and-white, pseudo-Tudor **Royal Selangor Club,** once called the "Spotted Dog," and for years the haunt of British colonials.

⑧ Muzium Negara. The distinctive architecture of the National Museum makes it easily identifiable; the building is modeled after an old-style Malay village house, enlarged to institutional size. Burial totem poles from Sarawak line the path to it. On its facade, two large mosaic murals depict important moments in history and elements of Malay culture.

The **Cultural Gallery,** to the left as you enter, emphasizes Malay folk traditions and Chinese culture in Malaysia. A model Nonya (Peranakan or Straits-born Chinese) home exhibits classical Chinese furniture and such exquisite antiques as carved canopy beds and a table-and-chair set with mother-of-pearl inlay. The **Historical Gallery** has models of homes from different regions, traditional costumes, a collection of ceramic pottery, gold and silver items, and other artifacts. Displays trace the stages of British colonization from the late-18th century to the British withdrawal in the mid-20th century. Photos and text outline the Japanese occupation during World War II and Malaysia's move toward independence. The **Natural History Exhibit** upstairs is devoted to indigenous wildlife, with stuffed flying lemurs, birds, insects, and poisonous snakes.

Behind the museum, the **Transportation Shed** has displays of every form of transport used in the country, from a Melaka bullock cart—with its distinctive upturned roof—to the pedal trishaws that are still used in Pinang. Don't miss the Malay-style house, called **Istana Satu** (First Palace). Built on stilts, the simple little wooden structure is open and airy—perfectly suited to the tropics—and has decorative wood carvings. ✉ *Jln. Damansara,* ☎ *03/238–0255.* 💳 *RM1.* ☼ *Sat.–Thurs. 9–6, Fri. 9–12:15 and 2:45–6.*

⑥ Railway Station. The imposing Moorish structures that make up the city's main railway station and the administrative offices of **Kereta-api Tanah Melayu (KTM),** the national rail system, have become a common postcard shot of KL. Built in the early 20th century and renovated since, the station was designed by a British architect to reflect the Ottoman and Mogul glory of the 13th and 14th centuries. The KTM building itself blends Gothic and Greek designs and has wide, distinctive verandas.

③ See Yeoh. Chinatown's oldest temple was founded by Yap Ah Loy, the first head of KL's Chinese community, in 1885. It's somewhat disappointing inside, however, especially compared with the Chan See Yeun temple nearby.

⑮ Selangor Pewter Showroom. Tin was a major Malaysian export, so it was only natural that the country would develop a pewter industry. The most famous name is Selangor, and this showroom has a full range of the sorts of wares made in Malaysia for more than 100 years. Most designs are simple and of superior quality. A few items, such as a photo frame encrusted with Garfield the Cat, are pure kitsch. In its Heritage Collection, Selangor has replicas of *caping,* fig leaf–shape "modesty discs" that nude children once wore to cover their genitals; now teenagers wear them on chains as pendants. In the back of the shop you can see a pewter-making demonstration. ✉ *223 Jln. Tuanku Abdul Rahman.*

① Sri Mahamariamman. A temple was built on this site by the Tamil community from southeast India back in 1873. The exuberantly colored figures that adorn the five-tier *gopuram* (gateway) were created only in 1960 and refurbished in mid-1998. During the annual Thaipusam festival, the chariot from this temple is taken through the streets on its way to Batu Caves.

NEED A
BREAK?

The **Old China Cafe** (☞ *also* Dining, *below*), a charming antiques-filled café-restaurant, is a great place to stop for a snack after visiting Sri Mahamariamman. Try the *pie-tee* (crunchy savories) or *bubur cha–cha*, an intriguing dessert of sweetened coconut milk with diced yam and sweet potato. Even if you're not hungry, it's worth popping in to have a drink and soak up the atmosphere. ⊠ *11 Jln. Balai Polis,* ☎ *03/232–5915.* ⊘ *Daily 11–11.*

---

⑩ **Sultan Abdul Samad Building.** This massive structure—erected in 1897 and bedecked with Moorish arches, copper domes, and a clock tower—is considered the center of the Old City. (Preservationists fought to have it restored in the early 1980s.) Originally occupied by the state secretariat (Dewan Bandaraya), it now houses the judicial department and high courts, along with a handicrafts museum and salesroom called **Infokraf Malaysia.** ⊠ *Jln. Sultan Hishamuddin,* ☎ *03/293–4929 (Infokraf).* ◻ *Free.* ⊘ *Sat.–Thurs. 9–6.*

⑨ **Taman Tasik Perdana.** Behind the National Museum are the scenic Lake Gardens, more than 200 acres where you can enjoy a leisurely stroll and join city dwellers relaxing, picnicking, and boating on the lake. Inside you'll find a **bird sanctuary,** a **butterfly park,** and a **deer park**—transport around the gardens is available at nominal cost. Also in the park are the **National Monument,** a bronze sculpture dedicated to the nation's war dead, and an **orchid garden** with more than 800 species (the gardens are open daily from 10 to 6).

Around Kuala Lumpur

In the past couple of decades, KL has grown so much that sights once considered part of the countryside are now thought of as part of the suburbs. Two outlying sights worth seeing are the Batu Caves and the Zoo Negara (National Zoo); you can readily reach both by cab or bus. To get a glimpse of KL's outskirts as well as several in-town attractions, consider taking the tourist board's "Country Tour" (☞ Tour Operators *in* Kuala Lumpur A to Z, *below*).

SIGHTS TO SEE

★ **Batu Caves.** About 11 km (7 mi) north of KL, these vast, beautiful limestone caverns were discovered in 1878 by American naturalist William Hornaday, who was searching for new species of moth larvae. To reach the caves you must climb a flight of 272 steps; a wide path with an iron railing leads you through the recesses, and colored lights illuminate stalagmites and other formations. The caves are the site of the spectacular but gory Thaipusam festival (held around February). The main cave houses a Hindu temple dedicated to Lord Subramaniam; behind the immense Dark Cave (it's 1,200 ft long and 400 ft at its highest point) is a third cave—the Art Gallery—with elaborate sculptures of figures from Hindu mythology. The caves are open daily 7 AM–9 PM. To get to them, take a taxi (about RM30–RM40 round-trip) or Bus 68 or 70 from Lebuh Ampang in Chinatown.

OFF THE
BEATEN PATH

FIREFLY PARK RESORT – A new attraction in Kuala Selangor approximately 80 km (50 mi) west of KL near the coast. Take an after-dark boat trip on the Selangor River to view thousands of fireflies twinkling like tiny fairy lights in the Berembang trees. It's romantic, relaxing, and unforgettable. Air-conditioned chalets are available at RM120 per unit Mon.–Fri. and RM150 for Sat.–Sun.; the rate includes breakfast. ⊠ *Jalan Haji Omar, Kampung Bukit Belimbing, 45000 Kuala Selangor,* ☎ *03/889–*

1208, FAX *03/889–1234.* ✆ *Firefly viewing RM10.* ⊙ *Daily 7:45 PM–10:30 PM. www.firefly-selangor-msia.com.*

Zoo Negara. The National Zoo is 14 km (9 mi) north of KL center, and you can reach it by taxi (about RM20 round-trip) or by Bus 17 or 174 from Lebuh Ampang in Chinatown. The zoo sprawls over a large area of gardens; a shuttle bus (RM1) takes you around and stops at major attractions. Be sure to check out the indigenous species, which include tigers, bearded pigs, rhinoceros, civet cats, and orangutans. Vividly colored coral-reef fish do much to dispel the gloom of the aquarium that's at the back of the zoo. ⊠ *Jln. Ulu Klang,* ☎ *03/406–9887.* ✆ *RM6.* ⊙ *Daily 9–6.*

Dining

Eating establishments in KL are as varied and diverse as the city itself, and new restaurants are popping up all over, from the suburbs to the city center. Indian, Chinese, Japanese, Thai, and Nonya cuisine are all available, along with the Malay food. There are plenty of Western choices, too, especially along the Bintang Walk which stretches from the J. W. Marriott hotel to the Lot 10 shopping center. Here, pavement cafés with familiar names like Starbucks Coffee, Piccolo Paradise, Caesars Bistro, and Häagen-Dazs, are packed until the early hours of the morning.

There are many restaurants in the Golden Triangle, in the area around Jalan Bukit Bintang and Jalan Sultan Ismail, and in Chinatown and central KL. Still, don't hesitate to try places that are farther afield, perhaps in the trendy suburb of Bangsar (about 3 km/2 mi south of the city center and about RM3–RM4 by taxi) or to the north of KL. Eating out almost everywhere is informal. Jackets and ties are seldom worn except at the swankiest hotels. Expensive restaurants add a 10% service charge—in which case you don't need to tip. In addition, some expensive restaurants are classified as "tourist class" and charge 5% sales tax. Lunch is normally served from 11:30 AM to 2:30 PM, dinner from 6:30 to 11 (last orders for food are taken between 9:30 PM and 10 PM). Seafood restaurants are usually open from 5 PM to 3 AM.

Golden Triangle
CHINESE

$$$$ ✕ **Lai Ching Yuen.** The extensive menu at this widely acclaimed Can-
★ tonese restaurant in the Regent Hotel (☞ Lodging, *below*) features shark's fin, bird's nest, abalone, pigeon, chicken, duck, and barbecue specialties. The dining room is designed as two Chinese pavilions; illuminated glass etchings, modern Chinese art, silver panels, a Burmese teak ceiling, and silver-and-jade table settings create an elegant ambience. Traditional music on Malay instruments accompanies dinner. ⊠ *160 Jln. Bukit Bintang,* ☎ *03/241–8000. Reservations essential. Jacket and tie. AE, DC, MC, V.*

$$ ✕ **Teochew Restaurant.** Soothingly decorated in cream and brown, this spacious eatery has well-spaced tables and screened-off private dining rooms. It's popular on weekends and holidays, when 100 varieties of dim sum are served for breakfast and lunch. Typical Teochew Chinese dishes include noodles made entirely of fish; sea cucumber stuffed with scallops, crab, mushrooms, and water chestnuts; and sizzling prawns. Try also the *oh wee,* a sweet yam dessert with ginkgo nuts that's served with tiny cups of bitter Teochew tea. ⊠ *270–272 Jln. Changkat Thamby Dollah, off Jln. Pudu,* ☎ *03/241–5851. Reservations essential. AE, DC, MC, V.*

CONTEMPORARY

$$$$ ✕ **Regent Grill.** This gourmet restaurant in the Regent Hotel (☞ Lodging, *below*) aims to impress. Wood paneling, leather upholstery, and stark earth-tone walls make the white German Schoenwald china and Schoff Zweisel crystal stand out. The menu varies, but frequent items are panfried goose liver and honey-braised endive, or dill-marinated salmon rolls in Turkish dough. As might be expected from the name, charcoal-grilled prawns, salmon, and beef are always featured. A set menu offers appetizers and desserts from a buffet and your choice of a red or white meat, fish, or pasta main course. The wine list is comprehensive—there are some 300 selections, and many are surprisingly affordable. ⊠ *160 Jln. Bukit Bintang,* ☎ *03/241–8000. Reservations essential. Jacket and tie. AE, DC, MC, V. No lunch.*

$$$–$$$$ ✕ **FIC's.** The food at this restaurant in the Kuala Lumpur Hilton (☞ Lodging, *below*) is excellent, and the decor is striking. A spiral staircase winds down into two spacious dining areas that are separated by a man-made stream. Huge windows look out onto an enclosed garden, and granite slabs on the floor and walls are inset with metal letters that spell out recipes or wine descriptions. The European cuisine, which often features Mediterranean or Asian accents, avoids heavy sauces and uses plenty of fresh herbs. You can order from the à la carte menu or the set lunch (RM49) and dinner (RM72) menus. Dishes vary from month to month, but one constant is lamb shank braised in wine and served with potato puree, shiitake mushrooms, deep-fried onions, and fresh herbs. The crème brûlée is to die for. ⊠ *Jln. Sultan Ismail,* ☎ *03/242–2122. Reservations essential. AE, DC, MC, V.*

ECLECTIC

$$$ ✕ **Citrus Rouge.** Situated beside its sister restaurant, Scalini (☞ *below*), Citrus wears several hats at once. You'll find a counter where you can enjoy modern European cooking; a glass-enclosed restaurant; and a large, partially open section with a dining area, a long bar, and a dance floor (there's music and a DJ). The cuisine is a mixture of French and Italian. Try the langoustine à la Campanola, with mushroom, spinach, beef bacon, and thyme sauce. The service is very friendly. ⊠ *19 Jln. Sultan Ismail,* ☎ *03/242–5188. AE, MC, V.*

$ ✕ **West 57th Street Cafe.** A tiny gift shop opens onto a small, intimate dining area at this hip haunt of local entertainers and the "in crowd." The pale green drapes may not be to everyone's taste, but the food is delicious. A typical menu is New Yorkers' Pasta with prawns, salmon, chicken, meat balls, and cheese. The open-faced chicken pie and the chicken and seafood mayo are memorable. ⊠ *Lower ground floor, Bukit Bintang Plaza,* ☎ *03/248–5563. AE, MC, V.*

FRENCH

$$$$ ✕ **Lafite Restaurant.** The Shangri-La Hotel's (☞ Lodging, *below*) Lafite Restaurant—named for France's finest vineyard—serves classic French and innovative cuisine in a romantically lit setting with fine crystal, oil paintings, and pastel wallpaper and upholstery. An impressive wine cellar is the dining room's centerpiece. In addition to the à la carte menu, which is modified periodically, you can partake of a buffet lunch (weekdays only) or dinner. The buffet selections are extensive: at least six main courses and a daily roast are offered, as are many salads and desserts. ⊠ *11 Jln. Sultan Ismail,* ☎ *03/234–3900. Reservations essential. Jacket and tie. AE, DC, MC, V.*

INDIAN

$$$ ✕ **Bharaths.** This classy restaurant serves tempting fare like samosa, crab cutlet, chicken sixty-five, mutton masala, fish curry, ginger tea, and mango lassi. South Indian food doesn't come any better. ⊠ *Lot 415, Level 4, Suria KLCC,* ☎ *03/263–2631. AE, MC, V.*

Kuala Lumpur Dining and Lodging

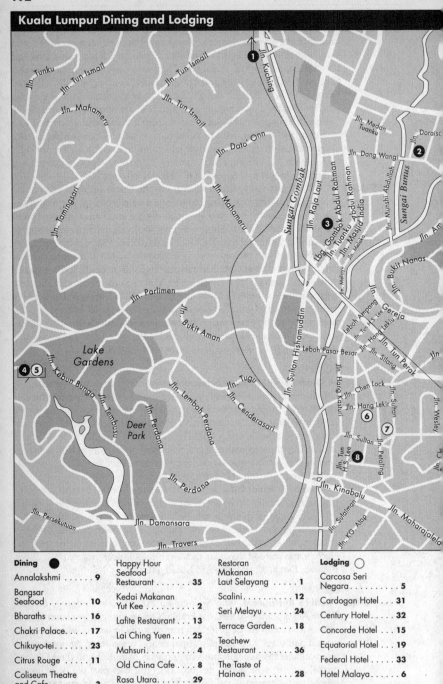

Dining ●

Annalakshmi **9**

Bangsar
Seafood **10**

Bharaths **16**

Chakri Palace **17**

Chikuyo-tei **23**

Citrus Rouge **11**

Coliseum Theatre
and Cafe **3**

FIC's **21**

Happy Hour
Seafood
Restaurant **35**

Kedai Makanan
Yut Kee **2**

Lafite Restaurant . . . **13**

Lai Ching Yuen **25**

Mahsuri **4**

Old China Cafe **8**

Rasa Utara **29**

Regent Grill **26**

Restoran
Makanan
Laut Selayang **1**

Scalini **12**

Seri Melayu **24**

Terrace Garden **18**

Teochew
Restaurant **36**

The Taste of
Hainan **28**

West 57th
Street Cafe **30**

Lodging ○

Carcosa Seri
Negara **5**

Cardogan Hotel . . . **31**

Century Hotel **32**

Concorde Hotel . . . **15**

Equatorial Hotel . . . **19**

Federal Hotel **33**

Hotel Malaya **6**

Kuala Lumpur
Hilton **22**

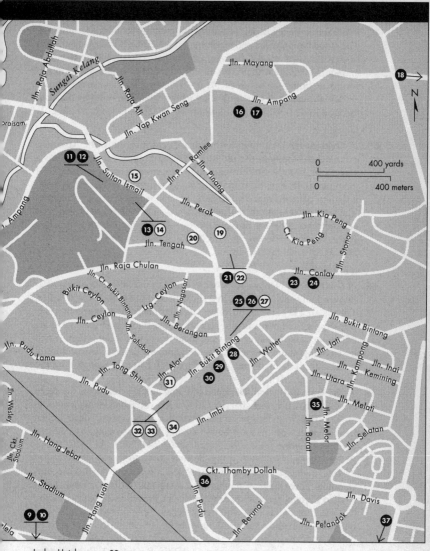

ITALIAN

$$$–$$$$ ✕ **Scalini.** The ever-popular Scalini has three dining areas—four if you count the garden, which is sometimes opened to accommodate patrons. The mood is minimalist and modern; the menu mainly Italian. You'll find pizza (baked in a wood-fired oven), beef carpaccio, clam and mussel soup, and squid-ink pasta with prawns as well as broad beans and shiitake mushrooms or honey-glazed duck breast. The wine list has varieties from around the world; if you don't want a bottle, you can order by the glass (around RM16). ⊠ *19 Jln. Sultan Ismail,* ☎ *03/245–3211. AE, MC, V.*

JAPANESE

$$$ ✕ **Chikuyo-tei.** Despite its rather dismal entrance (into the basement of an office complex) the oldest Japanese restaurant in the city has a warmly lit, woody interior with tatami rooms and other sectioned-off dining areas. It serves excellent *unagi kabayaki* (grilled eel) and *nigirisushi,* a variety of sushi made with tuna, herring, salmon eggs, and squid. The *teppanyaki*—meat, seafood, and vegetables sliced, seasoned, and cooked on a hot plate in front of you—is popular. ⊠ *See Hoy Chan Plaza, Jln. Raja Chulan,* ☎ *03/230–0729. Reservations essential. AE, DC, MC, V. No lunch Sun.*

MALAYSIAN

$$ ✕ **Seri Melayu.** Here you can opt to eat Malay style—seated on a *tikar* (woven mat)—while taking in a show of Malaysian music and dance. There's an à la carte menu as well as a buffet with an excellent selection of spicy and mild curries, vegetable dishes, and *kuih* (cake). Dishes not to be missed include the rich, meaty rendang; *ulam* (vitamin-rich herbs that you dip into a spicy sauce); and, for dessert, *pengat* durian, made with that oh-so-controversial fruit. ⊠ *1 Jln. Conlay,* ☎ *03/245–1833. AE, D, MC, V.*

$$ ✕ **The Taste of Hainan.** Designed by Zang Toi, this place has the decor of an opium den in Shanghai circa 1930. Here you'll find Hainanese cooking at its best, from freshwater prawns with a garlic and chili dip to grilled fresh salmon with mustard butter, cream, and crispy ginger. ⊠ *Lot 10 Shopping Centre, Jln. Sultan Ismail,* ☎ *03/244–7701. AE, MC, V.*

$ ✕ **Rasa Utara.** The decor here may be somewhat impersonal, but the Malay dishes—including many Kedah specialties from the north—are outstanding. There are reasonably priced set menus (written in English and Malay) for two, four, or six or more diners, as well as à la carte choices. The meal for two comes with rice, chicken curry, mixed vegetables, an omelette, fruit, and a soft drink for only RM15 per person. The *roti jala* (pancakes with chicken or beef curry) are lovely. Consider refreshing yourself with a glass of coconut water. ⊠ *B5003, Basement 1, Bukit Bintang Plaza, Jln. Bukit Bintang,* ☎ *03/241–9246. AE, DC, MC, V.*

SEAFOOD

$$ ✕ **Happy Hour Seafood Restaurant.** This restaurant has a friendly, corner–coffee shop atmosphere. Steamed, baked, or fried crabs filled with rich red roe are specialties. Other good choices are the prawns steamed with wine and ginger or the deep-fried garoupa. ⊠ *53 Jln. Barat (off Jln. Imbi),* ☎ *03/248–5107. AE, DC, V. No lunch.*

Chinatown and Central Kuala Lumpur

CHINESE

$ ✕ **Kedai Makanan Yut Kee.** This 65-year-old, family-run Hainanese
★ restaurant is one of the few that hasn't been torn down in the name of progress. Big and airy but rather noisy from the city traffic, the casual dining area is filled with marble-top tables and regular customers who insist on their favorite seats. Recommended is *roti babi*, a sandwich with pork filling dipped in egg and deep-fried (douse it liberally with Worcestershire sauce). The black coffee is the best around, and

the Swiss roll filled with kaya makes a fine dessert. As befits the coffee-shop feel, meals are served starting at 7 AM; service stops at 6 PM. ⊠ *35 Jln. Dang Wangi,* ☎ *03/298–8108. Reservations not accepted. No credit cards. Closed Mon.*

CONTINENTAL

$$ ✕ **Coliseum Theatre and Cafe.** The aroma of sizzling steak—the house specialty—fills the air in this café. It was established before World War II, and a nostalgic, slightly seedy colonial ambience prevails: the waiters' starched white jackets are a bit frayed, and the walls are cracked and brown with age. Steaks are served with brussels sprouts, steak fries, and salad. Another favorite here is crab baked with cheese. ⊠ *98–100 Jln. Tuanku Abdul Rahman,* ☎ *03/292–6270. Reservations not accepted. No credit cards.*

NONYA

$$ ✕ **Old China Cafe.** This charming café-restaurant, tucked away at the bottom end of Chinatown, is an absolute treasure. Set in a Chinese guildhall that was built at the turn of the century, it has large mirrors, calligraphy, photographs, and other memorabilia from that period. All the tables, chairs, porcelain pieces, and other fixtures are antiques. The Pinang-born chef offers a delectable range of Nonya dishes, including curry *kapitan* (chicken in spiced coconut milk) and *udang asam pedas* (prawns in sour hot gravy). ⊠ *11 Jln. Balai Polis,* ☎ *03/232–5915. AE, MC, V.*

Farther Afield

CHINESE

$$ ✕ **Restoran Makanan Laut Selayang.** Food, not decor, is this restau-
★ rant's raison d'être. You can eat outside, under a zinc roof, or in a simple air-conditioned room that seats 30 at three large, round tables. Adventurous diners can try steamed river frogs and soups of squirrel, pigeon, or turtle. Also good are the deep-fried soft-shell crabs and the prawns fried with butter, milk, and chilies. The house specialty is *fatt thieu cheong* ("monk jumps over a wall"), a soup of shark's fin, sea cucumber, dried scallops, mushrooms, and herbs, which must be ordered in advance. ⊠ *Lot 11, 7½ mi, Selayang,* ☎ *361–389010. AE, V.*

CONTINENTAL

$$$ ✕ **Terrace Garden.** Soothing shades of green and gray, white walls, black-framed windows, and pale green trellis dividers blend well in this restaurant converted from a house. Dolly Lim runs the place sweetly and efficiently, the service is very friendly, and there's live music every night but Sunday. The chef recommends either the char-broiled spareribs or the sea bass with martini sauce and black pepper. ⊠ *308 Jln. Ampang,* ☎ *03/457–2378. Reservations essential. AE, DC, MC, V.*

ECLECTIC

$$$$ ✕ **Mahsuri.** In the dining room of the Carcosa Seri Negara hotel (☞
★ Lodging, *below*)—which is made up of a pair of colonial mansions—a new Swiss chef offers excellent continental and Malaysian cuisine. The afternoon tea here is famous (partake of it, and you won't want dinner); the curry tiffin is a must if you happen to be in KL on a Sunday. You can enjoy this sumptuous spread of Anglo-Indian and Malay dishes on a wide veranda or in an air-conditioned restaurant. To work off the excess weight you may have gained after your thoroughly British Pimms cocktail and a meal, you can indulge in a game of croquet on the lawn. ⊠ *Taman Tasik Perdana,* ☎ *03/282–1888. Reservations essential. AE, DC, MC, V.*

INDIAN

$$ ✕ **Annalakshmi.** This Bangsar restaurant, decorated with Indian artifacts and antiques, is an elegant place to go for Indian vegetarian food.

It's staffed by volunteers of the Temple of Fine Arts (a group devoted to the propagation of Indian arts and culture), and the food is so beautifully spiced that it's a real treat even for confirmed carnivores. Although there's an à la carte menu, you'll be able to sample a much wider range of dishes at the buffet full of savories, spiced vegetable dishes, curries, side dishes, breads, and desserts. ⊠ *46 Jln. Maarof,* ☎ *03/282–3799. AE, D, MC, V.*

SEAFOOD

$$$ ✕ **Bangsar Seafood.** In the trendy suburb of Bangsar, which has some of KL's hottest restaurants and pubs, this restaurant offers 30 tables in the open air and another 30 inside. Feast on market-fresh seafood (some of it still swimming in tanks) cooked just about any way you want. ⊠ *Jln. Telawi Empat,* ☎ *03/282–2555. AE, MC, V.*

THAI

$$ ✕ **Chakri Palace.** This restaurant displays Thai paintings, vases, and carvings and has a varied menu including fish, vegetable, curried meat, and salad dishes. Some favorites are *pla kao sam rod* (deep-fried garoupa with Thai chili herbs), *gung phad nor-mai parang* (asparagus with prawn), and a delicious mango and sticky rice dessert, *khow neow ma-moung.* ⊠ *Lot 417b, Level 4, Suria KLCC,* ☎ *03/382–7788. AE, MC, V.*

Lodging

Many hotels are north of the train station, with some of the best near the intersection of Jalan Sultan Ismail and Jalan Bukit Bintang, the heart of the commercial district and one corner of the Golden Triangle. The range is broad. Establishments at the top level can compete with the world's best in terms of luxury and service; at the lower level, you can find nearly unbeatable prices. There are particularly good deals in hotels on Jalan Tuanku Abdul Rahman and in Little India.

$$$$ 🏨 **Carcosa Seri Negara.** These two colonial mansions in the Lake Gardens, just 10 minutes from downtown, once housed the governor of the Straits Settlement. There are seven suites in Carcosa, the main house, and six more an eight-minute walk away in Seri Negara, the guest house. Carcosa has recently been completely renovated with new decor and furnishings. Seri Negara was damaged by a serious fire in 2000, but renovations are in the works and should be complete by April or May 2001. A stay here isn't ideal for families or scene-makers; come if you want luxurious Victorian accommodation—including your own butler—with all the modern conveniences. The Mahsuri dining room (☞ *also* Dining, *above*) is one of KL's best. If you don't stay or dine here, at least stop by for the lavish afternoon tea or the Sunday curry tiffin. ⊠ *Taman Tasik Perdana, 50480,* ☎ *03/282–1888, 212/223–2848 or 800/447–7462 in the U.S.,* FAX *03/282–7888. 13 suites. Restaurant, pool, 2 tennis courts, massage, sauna, exercise room, business services, meeting rooms. AE, DC, MC, V.*

$$$$ 🏨 **Kuala Lumpur Hilton.** KL's first high-rise luxury hotel still maintains its world-class standards for service and quality. The mood of crisp elegance is set in the lobby, with fresh flowers and glowing chandeliers. The pastel-decorated rooms have bay windows, sitting areas, and desks. Rooms with the best views look down onto the hotel's pool, the KLCC, and the Petronas Twin Towers. FIC's (☞ *also* Dining, *above*) restaurant serves outstanding contemporary Western fare. ⊠ *Jln. Sultan Ismail, 50250,* ☎ *03/248–2322 or 800/HILTONS in the U.S.,* FAX *03/244–2157. 581 rooms. 4 restaurants, bar, coffee shop, pool, 2 tennis courts, health club, squash, business services, meeting rooms. AE, DC, MC, V.* 🐾

$$$$ 🏨 **Palace of the Golden Horses.** This hotel's sheer opulence is breath-
★ taking. The lobby's domed ceiling is handpainted with gold-embossed
horses, which reflect on the marbled floor, and the equine theme continues throughout the interior. The building is a magnificent example
of modern Malaysian-Moorish architecture, perched majestically at the
head of a lake. This superb hotel is world class both as a luxury resort
and a conference center. There's also an outstanding variety of dining
and entertainment, and the views over the lake are stunning. Only 20
minutes' drive south from the city center, and 30 minutes from KLIA.
✉ *Jln. Kuda Emas, The Mines Resort City, Seri Kembangan, Selangor
Darul Ehsan, 43300,* ☎ *603/943–2333,* FAX *603/943–2666. 401 rooms,
80 suites. 5 restaurants, 2 lounges, pool, health club, spa, windsurfing, boating, jet skiing, waterskiing, business services, meeting rooms.
AE, MC, V, www.signature.com.my.*

$$$$ 🏨 **Regent Hotel.** This hotel, across from the Star Hill Shopping Cen-
★ tre, opened in 1990 and has maintained its crisp newness. Spacious guest
rooms have plenty of light, a decor of natural woods and pastel fabrics, and opulent marble bathrooms with huge tubs and separate glass-
enclosed showers. The large atrium lobby is tiered, with each level
separated by flower boxes. The fifth-floor pool overlooks the city and
a crowded public pool across the avenue. The Regent Grill and the Lai
Ching Yuen (☞ Dining, *above*) restaurants vie for top culinary honors with the Hilton's and Shangri-La's European and Chinese restaurants. ✉ *160 Jln. Bukit Bintang, 55100,* ☎ *03/241–8000 or 800/
545–4000 in the U.S.,* FAX *03/242–1441. 468 rooms. 3 restaurants, coffee shop, tea shop, pool, sauna, health club, squash, business services,
meeting rooms. AE, DC, MC, V.*

$$$$ 🏨 **Shangri-La Hotel.** Since opening in 1985, this central hotel has attracted a glamorous set that parades through its spacious, opulent lobby.
Businesspeople favor it for its business services, meeting rooms, and
proximity to the city's financial institutions. All guest rooms are large
and furnished with dark-wood furniture to give them a traditional feel.
The higher floors are quieter, and guests paying a premium to stay on
the Horizon Floor receive more personalized service. In addition to the
gourmet Japanese, French, and Chinese dining rooms, there's a poolside café for daytime relaxation and a pub for congenial evening socializing. The Gourmet Corner offers delicatessen treats that are ideal
for lunch or afternoon tea. ✉ *11 Jln. Sultan Ismail, 50250,* ☎ *03/232–
2388 or 800/942–5050 in the U.S.,* FAX *03/230–1514. 722 rooms. 4
restaurants, pub, pool, 2 tennis courts, health club, dance club, business services, meeting rooms. AE, DC, MC, V.* 🐾

$$$ 🏨 **Century Hotel.** The old-fashioned values of consideration and civility
are well in evidence and the friendliness of the staff is genuine at this com-
fortable hotel in the heart of the city. The restaurant serves excellent food,
the bar is a quiet haven, and the pool is terraced and landscaped. All this
plus the city's main shopping complexes are right at the doorstep. ✉ *17–
21, Jln. Bukit Bintang, 55100,* ☎ *603/243–9898,* FAX *603/2162–8644.
381 rooms, 37 suites. 2 restaurants, bar, café, in-room safes, refrigera-
tors, pool, exercise room, business services. AE, DC, MC, V.*

$$$ 🏨 **Equatorial Hotel.** This 16-story hotel near the Hilton doesn't have
a warm or appealing layout, but it serves well the businessperson on
a budget. Deluxe rooms are spacious and equipped with such amenities as hair dryers and phones in the bathrooms. Rooms in the rear are
quieter. The basement café serves a "hawker" buffet of authentic local
dishes, and the reasonably priced lunches at the Kampachi Japanese
restaurant have become deservedly well-known. ✉ *Jln. Sultan Ismail,
50250,* ☎ *03/2161–7777 or 800/44–UTELL in the U.S.;* FAX *03/221–
1161. 300 rooms. 4 restaurants, bar, pool, business services, meeting
rooms. AE, DC, MC, V.* 🐾

$$$ ⊞ **Federal Hotel.** In the heart of the shopping district, this old-style hotel is distinguished by a revolving restaurant on its roof and an 18-lane bowling alley downstairs. The front of the hotel, with its street-level coffee shop, is decidedly urban, but the landscaped pool area has a tropical atmosphere. The guest rooms have large windows and the usual amenities. ⊠ *35 Jln. Bukit Bintang, 55100,* ☎ *03/2161–7777 or 800/ 44–UTELL in the U.S.,* FAX *03/221–1161. 450 rooms. 4 restaurants, coffee shop, pool, meeting rooms. AE, DC, MC, V.*

$$$ ⊞ **Park Avenue Hotel.** Formerly the Prince, this high-rise is near the major shopping district. An 18th-floor restaurant serves Western fare. ⊠ *Jln. Imbi, 55100,* ☎ *03/242–8333,* FAX *03/242–6623. 300 rooms. 2 restaurants, coffee shop, pool, dance club, business services. AE, MC, V.*

$$–$$$ ⊞ **Concorde Hotel.** This large, centrally located property has bright, fresh rooms, and the price is right. Pay more for the concierge floor if you want more personalized service, including complimentary breakfast. The large lobby is often filled with tour groups. ⊠ *2 Jln. Sultan Ismail, 50250,* ☎ *03/244–2200,* FAX *03/244–1628. 600 rooms. 3 restaurants, coffee shop, pool, health club, 3 concierge floors. AE, DC, MC, V.*

$$ ⊞ **Cardogan Hotel.** This is mainly a business hotel with few frills, but the clean, smart rooms—most of which have king-size beds—have air-conditioning, TVs, and minibars. The staff is cheerful, and the coffee shop is good for a quick meal. Best of all is the Golden Triangle location, close to many restaurants and hawker stands. ⊠ *64 Jln. Bukit Bintang, 55100,* ☎ *03/244–4856,* FAX *03/244–4865. 61 rooms. Coffee shop, minibars, exercise room, business services. MC, V.*

$$ ⊞ **Hotel Malaya.** Right in the heart of Chinatown, this 10-story hotel has a bright modern lobby with marble floors and a cheerful restaurant that serves local and Western cuisine. All rooms are spotless and have minibars, international-direct-dial (IDD) telephones, TVs, and tea-and coffee-making facilities. Standard rooms are small and lack windows; it's better to choose a superior or deluxe room. ⊠ *Jln. Hang Lekir, 50000,* ☎ *03/232–7722,* FAX *03/230–0980. 238 rooms. Restaurant, bar, minibars, meeting rooms, free parking. AE, DC, MC, V*

$–$$ ⊞ **Swiss Inn.** This hotel fills two buildings that are between Jalan Sultan and Jalan Petaling, in the heart of Chinatown. The main entrance is on Jalan Sultan, but the terrace restaurant—a great place to watch the world go by—is right on Jalan Petaling. The pleasantly furnished rooms have a faintly Old World feeling, with dark-wood dressing tables and wardrobes. To be sure that your quarters will have a window, request a superior or deluxe room. ⊠ *62 Jln. Sultan, 50000,* ☎ *03/232–3333,* FAX *03/201–6699. 110 rooms. Restaurant, bar, café. AE, DC, MC, V.*

$ ⊞ **Lodge Hotel.** Across from the Hilton in the Golden Triangle, the Lodge offers basic air-conditioned accommodations. Everything is a little shabby—carpets have stains, and bathrooms need some plaster repair—but the rooms are clean, and the service is friendly. The pool is tiny, but the coffee shop stays open, albeit sleepily, 24 hours a day. ⊠ *Jln. Sultan Ismail, 50250,* ☎ *03/242–0122,* FAX *03/241–6819. 46 rooms. 2 restaurants, bar, coffee shop, pool. AE, DC, V.*

Nightlife and the Arts

The free weekly *Day & Night* magazine has a good restaurant guide, the latest on the entertainment scene and plenty of useful maps. It's available at some hotels and MTPB offices (☞ Contacts and Resources *in* Kuala Lumpur A to Z, *below*). The "Time Out" pages in Thursday's *Sun* include an excellent calendar of all that's going on in town as well as restaurant reviews. The "Metro Diary" column of the daily *Star* also lists such happenings.

Most government-sponsored events are of the folk- rather than the fine-arts variety. Free, traditional cultural programs are regularly presented on Friday evening from 8 to 9 on Level 2 of the **Putra World Trade Center** (✉ Jln. Tun Ismail). The **Central Market**'s outdoor stage (☎ 03/274–6542) is the site of free performances Saturday and Sunday at 7:45 (with the occasional weeknight show as well). Offerings include fashion shows and jazz concerts. The Central Market puts a schedule of events in its monthly leaflet, which is distributed at hotels and MTPB offices.

Dance Clubs

Pubs close at around 11 PM, which is about when the action at the discos cranks up (it continues until 1 AM or 3:30 AM on Saturday and public holidays). Sometimes you'll find live bands as well as DJs, and many establishments have restaurants. Be prepared for cover charges at some places and a drink minimum at others.

At **Barbarran Bar & Dance Club** (✉ Ground floor, Wisma Equity, Jln. Ampang, ☎ 03/266–4677) DJs play a fusion of funk retro and dance music. Happy hour Monday to Saturday 5–10 PM, Sunday all night long. The **Beach Club Cafe** (✉ 97 Jln. P. J. Ramlee, ☎ 216/19919) serves Asian food inside and runs a casual restaurant outside. The club holds dancing and disco raves Sunday–Thursday until 3 AM, and Friday–Saturday until 3:30 AM. **Conlay Club** (✉ 6 Jln. Conlay, opposite Ceri Malayu restaurant, ☎ 603/244–3198) is one of the more permanent hot spots with a bistro and bar, a small dance floor, karaoke, and pool tables. It gets lively on weekends. **Emporium Grand Cafe** (☎ 03/248–1000) has funky decor and a trendy crowd plus Mediterranean dining. The dance floor is open from 10, with R&B, hip-hop, and fusion jazz.

Hotel Lounges

At the lounges and clubs of the major hotels, the atmosphere is international and the tabs are pricey. Most have entertainment every night but Sunday. A live combo often plays at the **Blue Moon Lounge** (✉ Equatorial Hotel, Jln. Sultan Ismail, ☎ 03/261–7777). You'll find a piano bar and a singer in the **Lobby Lounge** (✉ Pan Pacific Hotel, Jln. Putra, ☎ 03/442–5555). The **TMF** (✉ Kuala Lumpur Hilton, Jln. Sultan Ismail, ☎ 03/249–3317) has happy hour from 5 to 9 PM; Monday is "boyz night out," and ladies' night is Thursday with free standard drinks from 7 to 11 PM.

Pubs and Bars

Once upon a time, pubs were modeled after their British counterparts. Nowadays you'll find American-style bars with country-western, blues, jazz, or pop bands; Irish pubs; karaoke bars; wine bars, and other cosmopolitan places. Bangsar, just south of the city center, is the hottest area for pubs and bars, which come and go with amazing speed. It's best to take a cab here and cruise between Jalan Telawi and Jalan Maarof to see where it's all happening.

Coliseum Bar (✉ 98 Jln. Tuanku Abdul Rahman), in the famous old Coliseum Hotel, is totally unpretentious; it's easy to chat with locals over a beer here. The **Hard Rock Cafe** (✉ Wisma Concorde, 2 Jln. Sultan Ismail, ☎ 03/244–4062) is adjacent to the Concorde Hotel; by 10 PM a line forms outside. For a quiet drink try the **Long Bar** at the Century Hotel (✉ 17–21, Bukit Bintang, ☎ 603/243–9898). Lively **Modesto's** (✉ The Embassy, Jln. Ampang, ☎ 03/248–9924)—which is jam-packed on weekends—has darts, pool, and other amusements. The **Pub** (✉ Shangri-La Hotel, 11 Jln. Sultan Ismail, ☎ 03/232–2388) has a cozy wood-paneled ambience in which to relax, have a pint and a snack, and play backgammon. At **Riverbank** (☎ 03/274–6651), a small spot in a corner of Central Market, you can sit on the terrace above the river while a DJ inside plays music. **Succo Sound Bar** (☎ 03/

382–1988 is a very trendy bar in the KLCC with a fantastic view of the fountain and the park.

Outdoor Activities and Sports

Beaches

The nearest beach to KL is at Port Dickson, about 1½ hours away. Intercity buses from Pudu Raya station take you to the Port Dickson terminal; from there local buses will drop you off anywhere you want along the coast road. Alternatively, you can charter a taxi for around RM150 round-trip. The beach stretches for 16 km (10 mi) from Port Dickson (a good place to begin a walk is the fifth milestone from town) to Cape Rachado, with its 16th-century Portuguese lighthouse. On the coast road, stalls sell the fruits of the season. Be aware that the sea isn't suitable for swimming; the water is shallow and often polluted. The Mines City Resort, built around what was once the world's largest and deepest tin mine, is a 20-minute drive south of the city. This 150 acre man-made lake has facilities for swimming, sailing, wind-surfing, and water- and jet-skiing.

Golf

Hotels can make arrangements for you to use local courses, including the **Royal Selangor Golf Club** (☎ 03/984–8433), whose two 18-hole championship courses have an outstanding reputation. Greens fees are RM250, which covers caddy fee plus 5%. The **Saujana Golf and Country Club** (☎ 03/746–1466) has two 18-hole courses. It's a 30 minute drive from the airport and 25 minutes from KL city center. Fees on weekdays are RM 170; on public holidays and weekends you'll spend RM 290. Caddy fees are an additional RM 21.

Horse Racing

Malaysians have a passion for horse racing, and a regional circuit includes race days in KL, Pinang, Ipoh, and Singapore. Races are held on weekends year-round. Off-course betting is permitted at all the courses, regardless of where the actual race is being run; punters get to watch the action on huge TV screens. For information call the relevant **Turf Club** (☎ 03/958–3888 in Sungei Besi near KL; 04/229–1412 in Pinang; 05/242–1522 in Ipoh).

Shopping

Malaysia's shopping scene has been transformed in the last five years. There's a wider range of better-quality goods than ever before, prices have dropped considerably, and watches and electronics are now cheaper in KL than in Singapore. Prescription eyeglasses (ready in a day or two) and high-fashion items are also surprisingly inexpensive, and you can pick up locally made jeans and shirts for much less than in North America and Europe. If you can't find a particular product or service, call **Infoline** (☎ 03/230–0300), a telemarketing company whose staff members will try to steer you in the right direction.

Centers and Markets

CENTERS

The upscale **Star Hill,** (✉ opposite the Regent Hotel on the corner of Jln. Bukit Bintang and Jln. Gading), may be the most beautiful complex in the Golden Triangle. It has a branch of a well-known Singapore department store as well as high-fashion outlets and food centers with inexpensive local and international fare. Billed as "Malaysia's premier shopping center," **Suria KLCC** (☎ 603/382–2828) is part of the new development on the grounds of what was once the Selangor Turf Club. The center is in a six-story, crescent-shape complex in front of the Petronas Twin Towers. Pass beneath the striking skylight of its main entrance and on to any of the 300 shops and two department stores. There are restaurants and also a cineplex.

Lot 10, Bukit Bintang Plaza, and **Sungei Wang Plaza** are three popular shopping centers on Jalan Bukit Bintang and Jalan Sultan Ismail—you may not even realize when you pass from one to the other since they share much of the same space. The Sungei Wang has 500 retail outlets including Parkson Grand (the largest chain store in Malaysia). You'll also find major department stores like Isetan (Lot 10) and Metrojaya (Bukit Bintang), as well as bookstores, boutiques, pharmacies, camera and electrical outlets, food courts, and a cybercafé. **Low Yat Plaza** (⊠ behind Bukit Bintang) is the latest addition to the shopping scene and while not as large as the other three, still has a wide range of outlets.

Those interested in computer hardware and software should head for **Imbi Plaza** (⊠ Jln. Imbi). **The Mall** (⊠ Jln. Putra) has a department store and numerous specialty shops, including an excellent bookstore. **The Weld** (⊠ Jln. Raja Chulan) is decidedly upscale, with a marble interior and such shops as Crabtree & Evelyn, Benetton, Bruno Magli, and Etienne Aigner. For arts and crafts try **Yow Chuan Plaza** (⊠ Jln. Tun Razak).

MARKETS

At KL's street markets, stalls sell everyday goods, from leather handbags to pocketknives to pop music cassettes. Bargaining is the rule, and only cash is accepted. The large market on Chinatown's **Jalan Petaling** starts late each morning and runs well into the night. On Saturday nights there's a market in the Larong Tuanku Abdul Rahman. This runs parallel to Jalan Tuanku Abdul Rahman and exits on Jalan Dang Wangi.

Specialty Items

ANTIQUES

China Arts (⊠ 235 Jln. Tuanku Abdul Rahman, ☎ 03/292–9250), next to the Peiping Lace Co., has Chinese arts and crafts. **Eastern Stamps, Coins and Antiques** (⊠ Sungei Wang Plaza,, ☎ 03/248–7217) is conveniently located and has some interesting pieces. For Nonya antiques, try **Le Connoisseur** (☎ 03/241–9206) in Yow Chuan Plaza. The shop is normally open only in the afternoon, but call Mrs. Cheng to visit at other times. For Chinese arts and crafts, look in at **Peiping Lace Co.** (⊠ 223 Jln. Tuanku Abdul Rahman, ☎ 03/298–3184).

ART

Art Folio (⊠ 2nd floor, City Square, 182 Jln. Tun Razak) offers expensive oil paintings, watercolors, and ceramics. There's a selection of Chinese brush paintings and ceramics at **Art House** (⊠ 2nd floor, Wisma Cosway, Jln. Raja Chulan). Watercolors and portraits finished or in progress can be found at the **Central Market** (⊠ Jln. Cheng Lock, ☎ 03/2274–9966). **Collectors' Focus** (⊠ 3rd floor, Lot T, City Square, 182 Jln. Tun Razak) has art at affordable prices. Top-quality artwork from Malaysia and other Southeast Asian countries is on sale at **Valentine Willie Fine Art** (⊠ 1st floor, 17 Jln. Telawi 3, Bangsar Baru, ☎ 03/284–2348).

HANDICRAFTS

Batik Malaysia Berhad (⊠ Jln. Tun Perak, ☎ 03/291–8606) has a wide selection of batik fabrics, shirts, dresses, and handicrafts. The stalls of the **Central Market** (☞ *above*) offer handicrafts as well as many other souvenirs, including portraits, painted tiles, jewelry, and antiques. For the widest range of Malaysian handicrafts—including rattan baskets, straw handbags, wood carvings, Kelantan silver jewelry, and batik fashions—try the new **Kompleks Budaya Kraf.** (⊠ Jln. Conlay, ☎ 03/262–7533).

At the **Selangor Pewter Factory** (⊠ 4 Jln. Usahawan 6, ☏ 03/422–3000), a few miles north of the city in the suburb of Setapak, you can see how pewter is made (from refined tin, antimony, and copper) and then formed into pitchers, candelabra, and the like. You can buy duty-free souvenirs here, too. The factory is open Monday–Saturday 8:30–4:45 and Sunday 9–4. The best selection of modern pewter designs is available at the **Selangor Pewter Showroom** (⊠ 231 Jln. Tuanku Abdul Rahman, ☏ 03/298–6244).

JEWELRY

Jewelry by Selberan, with showrooms in **KL Plaza** (☏ 03/241–7106) and **Yow Chuan Plaza** (☏ 03/243–6386) does fine work with precious gems.

Kuala Lumpur A to Z

Arriving and Departing

BY AIRPLANE

Kuala Lumpur International Airport (KLIA; ☏ 03/8777–8888). The new airport in Sepang, around 60 km (37 miles) south of KL, opened in mid-1998 and now handles all domestic and international service.

From the Airport to Downtown. A normal limousine to the city costs RM70; a more luxurious limo, RM90. Regular taxis aren't available. KL City Bus offers service to downtown (the trip takes about 1½ hours) aboard air-conditioned coaches; the fare is about RM25. The nearly completed Express Rail Link (ERL) will provide public transport between the city and airport in just 30 minutes—and your bags will be checked in before boarding the ERL.

BY BUS

Regional buses bring you to the main **Puduraya Terminal** (⊠ Jln. Pudu, across from the Maybank Building), where you can get a taxi or local bus to your city destination. KL–Singapore express buses cost RM22; KL–Butterworth, RM17. For Kota Bharu and other destinations on the east coast, buses and shared taxis use the **Putra Bus Station** (⊠ Jln. Tun Ismail, across from Putra World Trade Center).

BY CAR

Roads into and out of KL are clearly marked, but traffic jams are legendary. It's best to avoid the morning and late-afternoon rush hours if possible. Tropical downpours also cause delay. It's strongly recommended that you hire a taxi or chauffeur-driven car to get around the city and its immediate environs rather than driving yourself; if you want to rent a car to travel farther afield, pick it up just as you are leaving the city. Luxury hotels in KL generally have parking lots, and guests are usually given a 50% discount on regular rates.

BY TRAIN

All trains from Butterworth and Singapore deposit passengers at the **railway station** (☏ 03/227–47434) on Jalan Sultan Hishamuddin, a short distance from the city center. (There are always cabs at the taxi stand here.) The second-class train fare (in an air-conditioned car) to KL from either Singapore or Butterworth is approximately RM34; first class is about RM68.

Getting Around

Conditions in KL aren't ideal for walking as distances between sights seem a long way in the heat and humidity and crossing streets requires a reckless disregard for danger (best to wait until a few locals form a group and cross with them). Taxis are very reasonably priced, so the best plan is a combination of foot and cab travel. Arm yourself with a map, choose the sights you wish to see, and dress in comfortable walking shoes and loose, light clothing (cotton fabrics are cooler than synthetics). When it's a long way to your next destination or you're tired, just take a cab. The Light Rail Transit has two lines, the Putra and the Star, with stations at KLCC, Pasar Seni (for Central Market and Chinatown), Masjid Jamek (for Merdeka Square area) and Bandaraya, ideal for the Sogo and Pertama shopping centers.

BY BUS

Buses cover most of the metropolitan area, and stops are usually marked. Note, however, that bus route maps simply don't exist, so before you get on a bus, ask the driver whether his route serves your destination. Just tell the conductor where you want to go, and have small change ready, because ticket sellers don't like to break large bills. The fares are 90 sen from one destination to another throughout. The two major bus terminals are Pudu Raya on Jalan Pudu and the Klang terminal on Jalan Sultan Mohamed.

BY CAR

Major car-rental agencies in KL are: **Avis** (✉ 40 Jln. Sultan Ismail, ☎ 03/241–7144), **Budget** (✉ 32 Jln. Imbi, ☎ 03/242–4693), **Hertz** (✉ 19 Jln. Pinang, ☎ 03/925–2211), and **SMAS** (✉ 21 Jln. Mahara Jalela, ☎ 03/248–1199). In view of the distance to the KL International Airport, it might be sensible to check with the rental agency about whether or not you can drop off the car there just before your departure.

BY TAXI

Taxis—which are metered and air-conditioned—are plentiful, except during rainstorms or rush hour. You can catch them at stands, hail them on the street, or request them by phone (pickup costs extra). Most taxi drivers speak passable English, but make sure they understand where you want to go and know how to get there before you set off. Also make sure that the driver turns on the meter—cabbies are notorious for not using their meters and charging visitors more than twice the correct fare. The flag fare is RM2 for the first 2 km (1 mi), and 20 sen for each additional 200 meters. A 50% surcharge applies between midnight and 6 AM, and extra passengers (more than two) pay an additional 20 sen each per ride. Luggage, if placed in the trunk, is an additional RM1. You can also hire a cab by the hour for around RM40 for the first hour and RM30 per hour afterward.

There's an RM1 surcharge for booking a cab by phone. Radio-dispatch taxi companies include: **Comfort Radio Taxi** (☎ 03/733–0507), **Destination Transport** (☎ 03/626–2525), **Koteksi** (☎ 03/781–5352), **Mesra Radio Taxi Service** (☎ 03/443–0659), and **Teletaxi** (☎ 03/221–1011).

BY TRAIN

Two LRT lines are now in operation. In the city the Star Line travels north to south connecting Pudu, Hang Tuah, Plaza Rakyat, Masjid Jamek, Bandaraya, and Sultan Ismail, and goes on to the Putra World Centre. The Putra LRT connects with the main railway at KL station, then connects with the Star Line at Masjid Jamek, going on to Dang Wangi, Kampong Baru, KLCC, and City Square. They operate 6 AM to 12 midnight. For information and a route map, stop by any of the stations, clearly visible as the rail runs on raised ramps above the road, or contact the **LRT Customer Service Hotline,** (☎ 019/217–5558 for Putra or ☎ 03/494–2550 for Star).

Contacts and Resources

EMERGENCIES

Ambulance, Police, and Fire: ☎ 999. **Doctors and Dentists:** The telephone directory lists several government clinics (look under the heading "Kementerian Kesihatan") that treat walk-in patients for a cash fee; these are open during normal business hours. Alternatively, ask your hotel to make a recommendation. There's a pharmacy in every major shopping center, though it will be open only during business hours.

ENGLISH-LANGUAGE BOOKSTORES
Because English is widely used in Malaysia, reading material is easy to find, especially on Jalan Tuanku Abdul Rahman; **Minerva Book Store** at Number 114 is recommended. You'll also find bookshops in major shopping centers, including **Berita Book Centre** (⊠ 002–003, 1st floor, Bukit Bintang Plaza), **MPH** (⊠ 002, ground floor, Bukit Bintang Plaza), and **Times Books** (⊠ D3, 3rd floor, Star Hill Plaza).

TOUR OPERATORS
The **MTPB** (☞ Visitor Information, *below*) maintains a list of all licensed tour operators; you can also get brochures in most hotel lobbies and information from local travel agents. **Globalria Resorts &Tours** (⊠ 66, Damai Kompleks, Jln. Lumut, ☎ 03/444–5291/2, FAX 03/444–5631) organizes package tours, drivers, and guides for a variety of destinations throughout the country. The **Malaysian Tourist Information Center** (MATIC; ☞ Visitor Information, *below*) offers a daily, three-hour "Country Tour" that leaves from the MATIC office at 9:30 AM and takes in Kompleks Budaya Kraf; Ambassadors' Row; the remains of a rubber plantation; pewter and batik factories; a butterfly and insect farm; the oldest Malay house in the KL area; and the Batu Caves. The cost is RM25. **Mayflower Acme Tours** (⊠ 18 Jln. Segambut Pusat, ☎ 03/625–87011; Ming Court Hotel lobby, ☎ 03/261–1120) is one of the biggest operators. **Reliance** (⊠ 3rd floor, Sungei Wang Plaza, Jln. Sultan Ismail, ☎ 03/248–0055) is a major tour operator.

TRAVEL AGENCIES
American Express (⊠ MAS Bldg., 5th floor, Jln. Sultan Ismail, ☎ 03/216–10000). **Thomas Cook** (⊠ Wisma Bouftead, Jln. Raja Chulan, ☎ 03/241–7022). *See also* Tour Operators, *above*.

VISITOR INFORMATION
The staff at the **KL Visitors Center** (⊠ 3 Jln. Hishamuddin, ☎ 03/230–1369) supplies city maps, directions, and assistance in finding hotels weekdays 8–4:15 and Saturday 8–12:45 PM. The **MATIC** (⊠ 109 Jln. Ampang, ☎ 03/216–43929) is in a restored colonial mansion that's open daily from 9 to 6. You can pick up information on KL and the rest of Malaysia, and the staff is very helpful. In addition you can make arrangements to visit the National Park (Taman Negara) at a private agency here. City and country tours depart from MATIC at 9:30 AM (☞ Tour Operators, *above*), and there are cultural shows given on the first floor every Tuesday, Thursday, Saturday, and Sunday at 3:30 PM; admission is RM2. There are also information counters at the airport and the railway station. The **MTPB** (⊠ 26th floor, Menara Dato Onn, Putra World Trade Center, Jln. Tun Ismail, ☎ 03/293–5188) has information on all of Malaysia. It's open Monday to Thursday 8–12:45 and 2–4:15, Friday 8–noon and 2:30–4:15, and Saturday 8–12:45 PM.

NORTHWEST COAST AND CENTRAL HIGHLANDS

North of KL and inland you'll find cool, lovely highlands. Off the coast of Perak state are the delightful resort islands of Pulau Pangkor and Pangkor Laut. Farther north, the state of Kedah is known mainly for the resort island of Langkawi. The recently completed North–South Highway makes travel along the west coast rapid and easy.

205

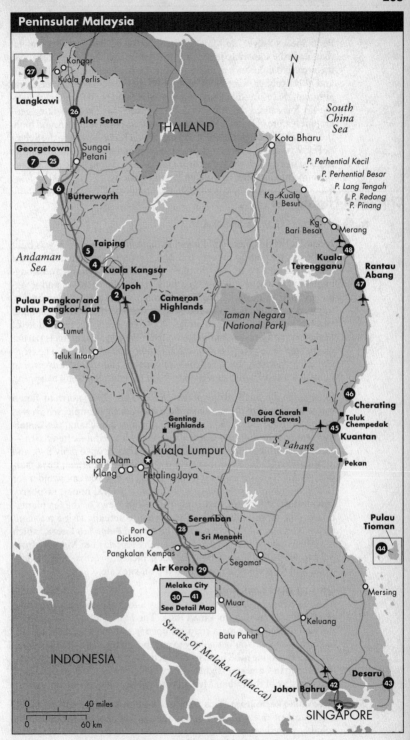

Peninsular Malaysia

Perak

Perak means "silver" in Malay, although it's a far less glamorous metal that made the state rich. It once had the richest tin field in the world, and this attracted thousands of migrant Chinese to the region during the 1880s and '90s. Rubber plantations took over when the tin boom ended, and although there are still plenty of tin deposits, the low price for this commodity has caused the mines to cease operation. The most striking geographic feature of Perak is the strange limestone peaks found around Ipoh, the capital. Although the royal town of Kuala Kangsar, where the Sultan of Perak resides, has romantic royal palaces and mosques, most visitors to the state head for the Pangkor islands or inland (and just over the border into Pahang state) to the Cameron Highlands.

Cameron Highlands

★ ❶   *190 km (118 mi) north of KL.*

A colonial atmosphere still lingers at this hill station, which was built for British plantation owners and civil servants. The genteel, civilized tone is epitomized by The Smokehouse Hotel (☞ Dining and Lodging, *below*), where you can sip a pink gin by the fireplace and imagine yourself in dear old England. Though you'll see tea plantations, terraced vegetable gardens, and jungle, much of the landscape makes you feel as if you're hallucinating—it's Great Britain in the middle of Malaysia (and only 322 km/200 mi from the equator). This is particularly true once you pass through the town of Tanah Rata. The tropical air gives way to a Scottish crispness; Tudor and Edwardian bungalows and English row houses (built for laborers) begin to appear.

En route to the small village of Brinchang, 3 km (2 mi) north of Tanah Rata, you'll pass the large, lavish **Sam Poh** Chinese temple, which was built in 1965. Another 4 km (2½ mi) north of Brinchang, the **Butterfly Farm** and the **Butterfly Garden** have many beautiful—often flashy—local species fluttering among the flowers. They're open daily 8–6, and admission is RM3. Even more interesting is the **Robertson Rose Garden,** 4 km (2½ mi) northwest of Brinchang, where you can wander for free (daily from 10 to 4) among the roses, buy local honey, raspberry jam, and dried flowers, and enjoy marvelous views of the tea plantations in the surrounding hills. If you want to actually visit a tea plantation, you can take a free tour of the **Sungai Palas Tea Estate,** which is just beyond the rose garden and is open every day but Monday from 8:30 to 4:30. You'll learn how the tea is picked, processed, and packaged, and then enjoy a cup of it in the on-site café.

Dining and Lodging

Most Cameron Highlands eateries are very informal places that don't take reservations; many are in Tanah Rata. The Malay food stalls opposite the post office on the main road are open in the evening and sell good, inexpensive food. You're unlikely to pay more than RM5–RM8 per person for a satisfying meal here. In Tapah, the small town you pass through heading up to Cameron Highlands, try the local *roti canai* (pancake and curry) at any of the Indian Muslim coffee shops along the main street.

$–$$ ✕ **Jasmine Restaurant.** This restaurant is best known for its rijsttafel, a set meal of rice with lots of curries and condiments. Another reasonably priced set meal consists of four Chinese dishes. ✉ *45 Main Rd., Tanah Rata,* ☎ *05/491–1703. No credit cards.*

$–$$ ✕ **Restoran Orient.** For a warming "steamboat," where pieces of meat, seafood, and vegetable are dipped into boiling stock in a sort of fondue set in the center of the table, try this popular spot. There's also a standard Chinese menu. Like all the restaurants on the Main Road, this one is fairly basic but comfortable. ⊠ *38 Main Rd., Tanah Rata,* ☎ *05/491–1633. No credit cards.*

$$$$ ✕▥ **The Smokehouse Hotel.** To really breathe the true spirit of this hill
★ station, consider a stay at this a-little-down-at-heel but ever-so-charming hotel. Stuffed with delightful British clutter, the suites have superb mountain views and plenty of odd corners in which to sit and think. You can dine in style on typically English dishes, such as a roast beef dinner (around RM90). Just as in colonial India, British "rules of deportment" are followed here: you order from the bar and wait until the maître d' invites you to your table; later you can return to the bar and linger over brandy or port. Late-afternoon tea—with scones, strawberry jam, and cream—in the gardens is another delightful option. ⊠ *Golf Course Rd., Tanah Rata 39100,* ☎ *05/491–1215,* FAX *05/491–1214. 13 suites. Restaurant, bar. AE, MC, V.*

Outdoor Activities and Sports

Time at the Cameron Highlands is best spent breathing in the glorious mountain air and walking. Although the highly touted jungle walks are exciting, the trails aren't well marked, and trail maps are merely suggestive. It's best to hire a guide so that you can relax and admire the scenery rather than worrying about whether the search party will find you. **C. S. Travel & Tours Sdn. Bhd** (⊠ *47 Jln. Besar*) can recommend a guide. You can also inquire about one at **The Smokehouse Hotel** (☞ *above*). The official trails vary in length and difficulty. You can walk the relatively easy Trail 4 in about an hour, passing a waterfall and a lookout tower with views over Brinchang.

Ipoh

❷ *121 km (75 mi) north of Brinchang in the Cameron Highlands, 205 km (127 mi) northwest of KL.*

The third-largest town on peninsular Malaysia has a number of magnificent colonial buildings around its *Padang,* or open green. The railway station, city hall, and Hongkong Bank are particularly noteworthy. The main attractions, however, are the Chinese temples built inside caves just outside Ipoh. Also of interest is an abandoned mansion on a rubber estate.

The remains of **Kellie's Castle**—a mansion with Moorish arches, apricot-color bricks, and a four-story tower—stand in the Kinta Kelas Rubber estate 12 km (7½ mi) south of Ipoh. Named after the Scottish rubber planter who built it, the grandiose mansion was never completed because Kellie died while on a trip to Portugal. You can see a painted statue of Kellie himself, wearing a *solar topee* (pith helmut) and a planter's jacket, on the facade of the nearby Tokong Sri Maha Mariamman Temple, which he reputedly built after a number of Tamil laborers working on his mansion died of a mysterious illness. 🔲 *3RM.* ⊙ *Daily 8–7.*

Some 6 km (4 mi) south of Ipoh is the oldest and largest cave temple, **Sam Po Tong,** founded in the 1890s by a Buddhist monk. Landscaped gardens lead to a huge chamber, which is filled with 40 statues of the Buddha and has a pool of tortoises that are considered sacred. 🔲 *Free.* ⊙ *Daily 8–4:30.*

The **Perak Tong** cave temple, 6 km (4 mi) north of town, has a 49-ft statue of the Buddha and impressive wall paintings of various Chinese deities. The temple, built in 1926, can be very atmospheric when worshipers ring the huge, century-old bell during their devotions. At the back, if you climb 385 steps up from the cave (mounting hours are 9–4), you'll be rewarded with a view of the surrounding countryside. 🔲 *Free.* ⊙ *Daily 8–5.*

Dining and Lodging

Ipoh is renowned for its Cantonese cuisine, particularly the noodles. There are a number of simple coffee shops along Jalan Bandar Timah (Kedai Kopi Kong Meng, at Number 65, is famous for its *kway teow,* meltingly soft fresh rice-flour noodles with chicken and seasonings).

$　　✕ **FMS.** You can enjoy a simple Western meal at what is probably Malaysia's oldest restaurant. Named after the Federated Malay States, of which Perak was a member in 1906 when the restaurant opened, it was redecorated in an indeterminate style in the 1950s. However, the beer is cold and the fish-and-chips are fine. Or try the restaurant upstairs, also called FMS, which serves local food. The decor is deliberately nostalgic with old photographs, radios, and a collection of antique Coca-Cola memorabilia. ✉ *2/2A Jln. Sultan Idris Shah (opposite the Padang),* ☎ *05/253–7678. No credit cards.*

$$$　　✕🏨 **Casuarina Parkroyal Hotel.** Although slightly outside of Ipoh, this is one of the most amenity-rich hotels in the area. There's a swimming pool and nice views from the rooms facing it. A tourism information office on the first floor can answer any questions. If you hanker for expensive Western cuisine, the upscale restaurant serves up a good steak. ✉ *18 Jln. Gopeng, 30250,* ☎ *05/255–5555,* ℻ *05/255–8177. 200 rooms. Restaurant, bar, pool, health club, shops, car rental. AE, DC, MC, V.* ⊛

$　　🏨 **Majestic Station Hotel.** If you're a nostalgia freak who wants to know what it was like to stay in a hotel during the colonial era, consider a room at the Majestic Station. On the top level of the magnificent Moorish Ipoh railway station, which is all colonnades and cupolas, the hotel was recently renovated with an eye toward retaining a charming, old-fashioned ambience. Request one of the rooms that opens onto the veranda, where ceiling fans whir lazily above. Although these rooms aren't luxurious, they do have wood parquet flooring; dark-wooden furniture; refrigerators (in some); TVs; IDD phones; air-conditioning; and spotless, thoroughly modern bathrooms. ✉ *Ipoh Station, 3rd floor, 30000,* ☎ *05/255–5605,* ℻ *05/255–3393. 86 rooms. Restaurant, café, meeting rooms. AE, MC, V.*

Pulau Pangkor and Pulau Pangkor Laut

❸　*84 km (52 mi) southwest of Ipoh, 175 km (109 mi) northwest of KL.*

Just off the coast and part of Perak state, Pulau Pangkor is an island known for its fishing and its western shore beaches. Aside from the major stretches of sand at Teluk Nipah, Teluk Belanga, and Pasir Bogok, there are quieter coves at Tortoise Bay and Teluk Chempedak. The jumping-off point for the island is the small coastal town of Lumut, a one-hour taxi ride from Ipoh (it costs about RM50–60 one way for an air-conditioned cab). An express ferry runs to and fro about every 30 minutes. What really makes a journey here worthwhile is a stay in the exclusive resort on Pulau Pangkor Laut—a private islet just south of Pulau Pangkor. If you like to travel in style all the way, you can arrange limo service from KL or Pinang through the resort; the cost is about RM450.

Dining and Lodging

$$$$　✕🏨 **Pangkor Laut Resort.** As you approach Pulau Pangkor Laut, you
★　　will see what looks like a traditional Malay fishing village but what is really a collection of smart resort villas. Set on stilts that are connected by walkways 15 ft above the ocean, the water villas have private balconies and peaked roofs that keep the air circulating (helped, of course, by air-conditioning). The two villas that contain suites have private decks, huge bathrooms with baths that are suspended over the water, and raised platforms with glass-paned trapdoors that reflect light from the sea below. Those who prefer terra firma should opt for a villa on the palm-stud-

ded beach or in the forested hills. These villas also have oversize baths (those for beach villas are outside) as well as cream-color cotton spreads and polished wood floors. The resort has everything you need for the perfect beach vacation, including a spa village (which will open in late 2001), many land and water activities, and a variety of restaurants. The Fisherman's Cove offers a dinner menu of seafood specialities. When it comes to dining in style, the romantic Samudra, poised on stilts over the bay, is the place to be. ⊠ *Pulau Pangkor Laut, 32200,* ☎ *05/699–1100,* FAX *05/699–1200. 126 villas. 5 restaurants, 3 bars, 2 lounges, 3 pools, massage, spa, 3 tennis courts, health club, hiking, squash, dive shop, snorkeling, windsurfing, boating, library. AE, DC, MC, V.* 🐚

Kuala Kangsar

❹ *50 km (31 mi) northwest of Ipoh, 255 km (158 mi) northwest of KL.*

The royal capital of Perak state for the past 250 years is set on a bend of the Perak River. The charm of Kuala Kangsar is such that one Victorian writer admitted liking it "better than any place that I have been at in Asia." This very Malay town's most famous landmark is the exuberant **Ubudiah Mosque,** an Arabian Nights' fantasy completed in 1917 and built of black-and-white Italian marble topped by gilded domes. (Ask permission before entering the mosque, and avoid visiting it during Friday's midday prayers.) ⊠ *Jln. Istana.*

The Sultan of Perak lives in the modern, white-marble Istana Iskandariah, which is closed to the public. However, you can visit another royal residence, the **Istana Kenangan,** which now houses the **Royal Museum.** A fine example of traditional Malay woodworking skills, this building was constructed entirely without nails. Notice the carved friezes and split bamboo wall panels. The museum has an interesting collection of old photographs of sultans and various British gentlemen. ⊠ *Jln. Istana,* ☎ *no phone.* 🎟 *Free.* ☉ *Daily 9:30–5, closed Friday 12:15–2:45.*

Taiping

❺ *32 km (20 mi) north of Kuala Kangsar; 291 km (180 mi) northwest of KL.*

Taiping's main claim to fame is that it's the wettest town on the peninsula. Despite the fact that the town's Chinese name means "everlasting peace," Taiping (then known as Larut) was the scene of fierce fighting between rival Chinese tin miners in the 1870s. This predominantly Chinese town has a scenic garden, Taman Tasik (Lake Gardens), built around a couple of disused tin-mining pools. Taiping's biggest attraction is Malaysia's smallest and oldest hill station—**Bukit Larut** (☎ 05/807–7241 for superintendent/reservations), formerly known as Maxwell Hill. The 3,395-ft ascent to the resort was once made by sedan chair; today, you can travel by government Land Rover (which leaves every hour from 8–5) or walk for two to three hours along the 13-km (8-mi) road. You'll find the same wooden bungalows, lawns, flower beds, pine trees, and misty morning views that enchanted and soothed the colonials. You can stay either in one of three well-equipped bungalows—requesting that the caretaker arrange meals for you—or in the three-bedroom Rest House, which serves Malaysian dishes. There's not much to do apart from relaxing, strolling, or playing tennis. But inactivity is part of Bukit Larut's charm.

Pinang

Tucked between the states of Perak and Kedah, Pinang (Penang) state is most famous for its eponymous island—a major vacation destination and home to the state capital of Georgetown. Known as the Pearl of the Orient for its natural beauty, Pulau Pinang respects tradition but is neither stodgy nor sleepy. The island offers gracious colonial architecture, vibrant Chinese communities, Indian temples and mosques, beach resorts, and some of Malaysia's most exciting food.

Thanks to its safe anchorage and strategic position in the Straits of Melaka, the island caught the eye of an English trader in the late 1700s. He persuaded the Sultan of Kedah to grant him the island in exchange for British protection, and Pinang quickly grew into a thriving and cosmopolitan entrepôt. Today the island's population is primarily Hokkien Chinese, though a sizable Indian community thrives, particularly in Georgetown, and many Malays reside in the countryside.

Butterworth

❻ *78 km (48½ mi) northwest of Taiping, 164 km (102 mi) northwest of Ipoh.*

Butterworth is Pinang state's major industrial area. Its only truly noteworthy characteristic is that it's the main jumping-off point for Pulau Pinang. If you're driving, you'll probably cross the 14-km-long (8-mi-long) bridge that joins the southeast corner of island with the mainland, not far from Penang International Airport. There's also a 24-hour car-and-passenger ferry service (☞ Arriving and Departing By Boat *and* By Car *in* Northwest Coast and Central Highlands A to Z, *below*).

Georgetown

❼–㉕ *7 km (4½ mi) west off the shore of Butterworth, 370 km (230 mi) northwest of KL.*

Georgetown is a great place to tour on foot, by bicycle, or by trishaw; of course, you'll have to stop frequently to browse in the city's many intriguing shops and to sample its world-famous cuisine. In recent years, many streets have been renamed, but locals prefer to use the older—often simpler—colonial names (understandably, you're more likely to hear "Pitt Street" than "Jalan Masjid Kapitan Keling").

The best place to begin a tour is near the Swettenham Pier, where there are offices of the Penang Tourist Association and the MTPB (☞ *also* Visitor Information *in* Northwest Coast and Central Highlands A to
❼ Z, *below*). Opposite the tourism offices is a **Victorian clock tower,** donated to the city by a Pinang millionaire to commemorate Queen Victoria's diamond jubilee. The tower is 60 ft tall, one foot for every year of her reign up to 1897.

Head from the Victorian clock tower up Jalan Tun Syed Barakbah past
❽ **Ft. Cornwallis,** the harborside site where city founder Captain Sir Francis Light of the British East India Company first landed on the island in 1786. On the outside, the 1810 compound's moss-encrusted ramparts and cannons give the impression of a mighty fortress, but it never saw any real action. On the inside are an open-air amphitheater, shade trees, and public toilets. 🎫 *RM1.* ☉ *Daily 8:30–7.*

❾ The **Esplanade**—an open, grassy field next to Ft. Cornwallis—is a pleasant site for a stroll, especially in the evening, when the sea breezes roll in and the hawkers set up their stands. The Esplanade is often used for festivals and recreational sports. A monument surrounded by palms honors soldiers who died in World War I.

Pinang's hub used to be Lebuh Pantai (Beach Street), near the ferry terminal in the heart of the banking district. But the city center has gravitated toward the huge new KOMTAR (☞ *below*) shopping and office complex. Even the city government has moved to this complex, and

211

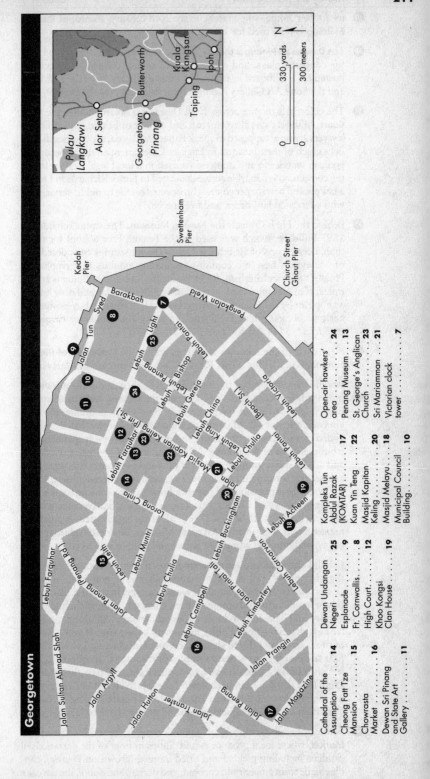

Georgetown

Cathedral of the
Assumption **14**
Cheong Fatt Tze
Mansion **15**
Chowrasta
Market **16**
Dewan Sri Pinang
and State Art
Gallery **11**

Dewan Undangan
Negeri **25**
Esplanade **9**
Ft. Cornwallis **8**
High Court **12**
Khoo Kongsi
Clan House **19**

Kompleks Tun
Abdul Razak
(KOMTAR) **17**
Kuan Yin Teng **22**
Masjid Kapitan
Keling **20**
Masjid Melayu **18**
Municipal Council
Building **10**

Open-air hawkers'
area **24**
Penang Museum . . . **13**
St. George's Anglican
Church **23**
Sri Mariamman **21**
Victorian clock
tower **7**

⑩ its former home—the stately, early 20th-century **Municipal Council Building** is now used for special exhibitions.

⑪ The **Dewan Sri Pinang** is the city's major auditorium, seating some 1,300 for concerts, plays, and other events. Coming cultural activities are posted on a billboard in front. The **Pinang Library** is on the first floor and the **State Art Gallery** is on the third floor. ▨ *Free.* ☉ *Daily 9–5.*

⑫ The colonial structure across from Dewan Sri Pinang houses the **High Court.** Malaysia's legal system is based on that of Britain, and although lawyers are now supposed to speak Bahasa Malaysia, the courts still conduct much of their business in English. Cases are open to the public, so you can wander in and immerse yourself in a local legal drama. Inside the compound is a marble statue dedicated to James Richardson Logan, a lawyer and newspaper editor who devoted his life to public service and who advocated law, order, and free speech.

⑬ Behind the High Court is the **Penang Museum.** The statue outside the 1897 building, which was used as the Penang Free School for more than a century, is of Sir Francis Light. The museum is considered one of Malaysia's best and contains fascinating exhibits that emphasize Pinang's multiculturalism. Right beside the museum building is an old railcar that was once used on the Pinang Hill funicular and now houses a shop run by the Pinang Heritage Trust. Here you can buy postcards, heritage books, prints, coins and old porcelain. ⊠ *Lebuh Farquhar,* ☎ *04/261–3144.* ▨ *RM1.* ☉ *Sat.–Thurs. 9–5.*

⑭ Next door to the museum and art gallery is the **Cathedral of the Assumption,** one of the oldest Roman Catholic churches in Malaysia.

⑮ Beyond the cathedral, at the top of Lebuh Leith, is one of the most stunning traditional houses in all Malaysia, the **Cheong Fatt Tze Mansion.** Built in the early part of this century by a Chinese immigrant who amassed a fortune in Malaya and Indonesia, the house has exquisite, gilded carved screens, cast-iron columns, intricate mosaic panels made from pieces of broken pottery, Art Nouveau stained-glass windows, and ornate spiral staircases. Its 38 rooms and five courtyards were used as a setting for the film *Indochine.* Rescued from dereliction in 1990, the bright-blue mansion and five shophouses (once housing for the staff and lesser wives of Cheong Fatt Tze, and now a bar-restaurant complex [⊠ 20 Leith St., ☎ 04/227–0076]) are being restored. A one-hour mansion tour is given at 11 AM every Monday, Wednesday, Friday, Saturday, and Sunday; admission is free and tours cost RM10.

Lebuh Leith runs into **Jalan Penang,** the city's main shopping strip. In the labyrinth of stalls along it and in its alleyways, you'll find such basics as underwear, belts, handbags, and luggage. In the first block a series of handicrafts and antiques shops carry gift items including Asian jewelry and Thai and Indonesian wood carvings. All along the road, trishaw drivers—mostly older men—will solicit you. If you take one of them up on an offer to sightsee, consider heading up Lebuh Muntri past some of the city's best examples of traditional architecture, turn left onto Lorong Cinta (Love Lane), turn right, and pass the museum. From here you can head back down Jalan Masjid Kapitan Keling, passing the famous temple of Kuan Yin and Masjid Kapitan Keling (☞ *below*) Turn right onto Lebuh Buckingham and proceed back to Jalan Penang.

⑯ South of Lebuh Campbell, off Jalan Penang, is the indoor **Chowrasta Market,** where local produce is sold. Shops in front of the entrance sell produce including pickled and dried nutmeg (grown on Pinang); candies made from ginger root, coconut, and durian; and *dodol,* durian cake that's sold in little triangular pieces or foot-long rolls. In the morning, the market spills out onto three of the surrounding streets, where you'll find everything from freshly netted prawns to wooden Chinese clogs to barbecued wafers of sweet pork and bowls of noodles.

⑰ At the bottom of Jalan Penang is the **Kompleks Tun Abdul Razak (KOMTAR),** named to honor Malaysia's second prime minister. The complex is totally out of scale with the neighboring buildings and can be confusing owing to its size and many entrances. Still, you can conduct business (all the government offices are here), shop, eat, and even sleep here. The **Shangri-La Penang** hotel (☞ Lodging, *below*) is connected to the complex via a small department store on level two; there are a number of fast-food outlets that serve hamburgers, fried chicken, and pizza in the center of the mall; the third-floor **Tourism Information Centre** has helpful staffers who sell maps and brochures and give advice; and **Chin's Art Gallery,** next to the Malaysia Airline System (MAS) office on the ground level will engrave your initials in a stone *chop* (seal) for RM60–RM150, depending on the size and quality of the stone. Among the tower's busiest tenants are hip young tailors with trendy haircuts and smart outfits who scurry about fitting customers with garments cut from the bolts of fabric they stack in every corner of their tiny shops.

⑱ At the junction of Lebuh Acheen and Jalan Masjid Kapitan Keling is Pinang's oldest mosque. The **Masjid Melayu,** also known as the Acheen Street Mosque, was restored and repainted in 1998. The walk along quiet back lanes to reach it is as interesting as the mosque itself, which has Chinese architectural touches in its design.

⑲ On the north side of Lebuh Acheen, look for a small sign posted above an entrance to an alley announcing the **Khoo Kongsi Clan House,** a complex of structures that may be the most elaborately decorated in Malaysia. Be aware that it's closed for renovation until sometime in 2001. The **Leong San Tong** (Dragon Hall) temple is a showcase of Chinese architecture and art, constructed by 19th-century master craftsmen. Virtually no surface is unadorned. Notice the relief sculptures depicting Chinese legends and the heavily gilt dragons. Visitors are welcome daily 9–5. The open theater across the square is used for opera performances.

Not only is Jalan Masjid Kapitan Keling often referred to by its colonial name, Pitt Street, but it's also called the Street of Harmony because temples, mosques, and churches from four major religions are
⑳ situated along and just off it. The **Masjid Kapitan Keling,** the oldest mosque in Pinang, is at the Lebuh Buckingham intersection. Built in the early 1800s, the mosque continues to serve the Indian Muslim community. (You need permission to enter.) Also along this section of Pitt Street is a row of small jewelry shops run by Indians who deal in gold and semiprecious stones. Many are also licensed money changers. These street bankers can handle almost any type of foreign currency and work much longer hours than regular banks. Some are also numismatists who sell to collectors.

Past the gates of the Teochew Association House, on the corner of Pitt
㉑ and Lebuh Chulia, is the temple in the heart of the Indian district, **Sri Mariamman,** on Lebuh Queen. The entrance is topped by a gopuram covered with statues of Hindu deities. Inside, the ceiling features the symbols for the planets and signs of the zodiac. The most prized possession of the faithful is a statue of Lord Subramaniam, which is covered with gold, silver, diamonds, and emeralds. The statue is paraded about during the Thaipusam festival. You can enter the temple, with permission.

㉒ The **Kuan Yin Teng** temple is dedicated to the goddess of mercy and is the busiest in the city—perhaps because it's associated with fertility. Built in 1800, it serves the Cantonese and Hokkien communities. A

㉓ block east of Kuan Yin Teng, on Lebuh Farquhar, is the stately **St. George's Anglican Church,** with its gracious flowering trees and gazebo. Built in 1818 by convicts, this symbol of the British role in Pinang's early history is now attended mostly by Indians.

㉔ On the corner of Lebuh Light and Lebuh King, at an **open-air hawkers' area,** old Chinese men often bring their caged pet birds when they come for a cup of coffee and a breath of morning air. In this area, you may also see elderly men writing letters on old portable typewriters. These public scribes serve clients who need help dealing with the bureaucracy or illiterates who simply want to write a friend.

Traveling east on Lebuh Light, before you reach the Victorian clock tower
㉕ you'll see the **Dewan Undangan Negeri,** a majestic colonial building with massive columns. This is the state assembly, and the luxury cars parked out front belong to its illustrious members. You're now across from Ft. Cornwallis again—near the ferry if you're hopping back to the mainland and a waterfront cab ride away from the beach hotels.

Dining

In Pinang, food is still prepared in old, time-consuming ways, giving it an authenticity not always found in other Malaysian cities. For elegant dining with attentive service, the major hotels are your best bet, but with hundreds of hawker centers all over the island, it would be a shame not to sample some of Malaysia's best stall food. You can find excellent Chinese food (including a renowned oyster omelette) every night at the stalls around the junction of Macalister Road and Lorong Bahru, near the junction of Macalister Road and Jalan Penang. Even nicer is the long line of stalls along Gurney Drive, about 10 minutes by taxi out of Georgetown on the road north to Batu Ferringhi. There are other hawker centers at Lebuh Chulia, Lebuh Kimberley, and the Esplanade.

Local stall-food specialties include: *char* kway teow (flat rice noodles fried smooth and soft with bean sprouts, prawns, and eggs), Hokkien *mee* (noodles, pork, and bean sprouts in a spicy shrimp soup topped with fried onions), the famous Pinang *rojak* (savory fruit and vegetable salad with a pungent dressing), and Pinang *laksa* (rice-flour noodles in a sour, fishy gravy topped with herbs, shredded cucumber, and pineapple). For dessert consider trying *cendol* (green mung-bean noodles and red beans in fresh coconut milk and rice) or the Nonya *bubur cha cha* (sweet potatoes, yams, and red beans in coconut milk sweetened with palm sugar).

CHINESE

$ ✕ **E. T. Steamboat.** At this restaurant named after the do-it-yourself Chinese stew, waiters bring vegetables, seafood, tofu, and a fondue pot full of rich broth to your table; you custom-cook your own dinner. For variety, try *lowbak* (pork rolls) or the spicy tom yam soup. ✉ *4 Jln. Rangoon,* ☏ *04/226–6025. No credit cards.*

CONTINENTAL

$$$ ✕ **Brasserie.** Modern French music sets the mood at this restaurant in
★ the Shangri-La Penang hotel (☞ Lodging, *below*). You select a main course from the menu—which has a wide range of Western options— and then help yourself from the buffet for soups, salads, and dessert. Menus change weekly and include roast prime rib, sushi, and fresh oysters. There's a buffet every evening and a brunch on Sunday. ✉ *Jln. Magazine,* ☏ *04/262–2622. Reservations essential. AE, DC, MC, V.*

$$ ✕ **Eden.** A downtown restaurant with funky decor, Eden makes fresh
★ oxtail soup every day and is famed for its shredded lamb in black pepper sauce. The lunch menu caters to Westerners, with sandwiches, salads, and ice-cream sundaes. ✉ *15 Jln. Hutton,* ☏ *04/263–9262. AE, DC, MC, V.*

INDIAN

$ ✕ **Hameediyah.** This simple downtown restaurant excels with its nasi kandar rice—served with spicy mutton, fish, and chicken curries—or *murtabak,* an Indian-style pizza filled with spicy mutton and onions. ⊠ *164 Lebuh Campbell,* ☎ *04/261–1095. No credit cards. Closed Fri.*

MALAYASIAN

$$ ✕ **The Istana Malay Theater Restaurant.** This authentic Malaysian restaurant is home to the Pinang Cultural Center. Here you can enjoy traditional Malay cuisine including satay, chicken curry, and sautéed okra with prawn paste while watching an excellent performance of Malaysian music and dance. ⊠ *No. 288, Jln. Teluk Bahang,* ☎ *04/ 885–1175. AE, DC, MC, V.*

NONYA

$$ ✕ **Dragon King.** People come here for the food—a blend of Malay and Chinese cuisines—not the atmosphere or modest decor. Try the spicy curried chicken and the kerabu mango salad. Come early; the place closes at 9 PM. ⊠ *99 Lebuh Bishop,* ☎ *04/261–8035. MC, V.*

$$ ✕ **Hot Wok.** Considered one of Pinang's best Nonya restaurants, this place is on the ground floor of a block of modern shophouses next to Island Plaza (RM10 by taxi from Georgetown or around RM15 from Batu Ferringhi). The atmosphere is relaxed and friendly and the furniture mostly ornate antique Peranakan pieces, with plenty of British colonial clutter (cigarette posters, portraits of Queen Elizabeth) in one of the two dining rooms. The menu includes all the Pinang Nonya classics. Try the *inche kabin,* spiced deep-fried chicken with a dip based on English Worcestershire sauce, and the pork *cincalok,* intriguingly flavored with preserved tiny shrimps. The mango kerabu is uncompromisingly spicy but excellent; request that the chef tone down the chili a little if you can't take it hot. ⊠ *125 Desa Tanjung, Jln. Tanjung Tokong,* ☎ *04/899–0858. AE, DC, MC, V.*

Lodging

$$$$ 🏨 **Equatorial Hotel.** Although not in Georgetown proper and far from the beaches, this hotel is close to the airport, has an 18-hole golf course and is geared toward business travelers. Note the unique 10-story atrium garden with bubble elevators. One restaurant, The View, offers a range of Provençal cuisine; the view, by the way, is of the island's coastline. Here you can see the spectacular Pinang bridge and watch ships moving through the straits. ⊠ *1 Jln. Bukit Jambul, Bayan Lepas 11900,* ☎ *04/643–8000 or 800/44–UTELL in the U.S.,* ⛛ *04/644–8000. 668 rooms. 4 restaurants, bar, coffee shop, pool, 2 tennis courts, 18-hole golf course, health club, squash, business services, meeting rooms. AE, DC, MC, V.* ✍

$$$$ 🏨 **Shangri-La Penang.** The glitziest hotel in Georgetown is linked with the KOMTAR shopping and office complex downtown. Its comfortably decorated rooms offer great views of the city. The Shang Palace, a Cantonese restaurant, serves dim sum daily and the Brasserie (☞ Dining, *above*) prepares Continental cuisine. Guests are a mix of tourists and business travelers seeking modernity and efficiency. ⊠ *Jln. Magazine, 10300,* ☎ *04/262–2622, 800/942–5050 in the U.S., or 081/747– 8485 in the U.K.,* ⛛ *04/262–6526. 426 rooms, 16 suites. 3 restaurants, coffee shop, lobby lounge, pool, health club, dance club, business services, meeting rooms. AE, DC, MC, V.*

$–$$ 🏨 **City Bayview.** You'll get a lot for your money at this well-equipped, modern high-rise, including a convenient downtown location, great views, and a pool. It began life as the Merlin, the first of Pinang's modern hotels, and underwent extensive renovation in 1998. There's a Japanese restaurant, a newly spruced-up revolving restaurant on the 14th floor, and a Chinese restaurant which serves Cantonese and Szechuan dishes. ⊠ *25A Lebuh Farquhar, 10200,* ☎ *04/263–3161,* ⛛ *04/263–*

4124. 350 rooms. 3 restaurants, bar, coffee shop, lounge, pool, dance club, meeting rooms. AE, DC, MC, V.

$ 🖼 **Malaysia.** All the rooms in this hotel, conveniently located on upper Jalan Penang, have baths, TVs, and refrigerators. ⊠ *7 Jln. Penang, 10000,* ☎ *04/263–3311,* FAX *04/263–1621. 126 rooms. Coffee shop, pub, refrigerators. AE, DC, MC, V.*

Nightlife and the Arts

BARS

Downtown Georgetown still has seedy bars, with dim lights and ladies of indeterminate age and profession—but it's not hard to find more tasteful options. The entertainment hub on Jalan Gottlieb is where it's all happening. At the bright-blue **20 Leith Street** (☎ 04/261–6301)— a row of five converted houses that were once part of the Cheong Fatt Tze mansion—there's a small beer garden, a northern Indian restaurant, and a Japanese restaurant with a bar, pool tables, a dartboard, and music videos. If you want a look at a tacky bar that was popular with the Australian armed forces when they were based in Butterworth, try the **Hong Kong Bar** (⊠ 371 Lebuh Chulia, ☎ 04/261–9796). Pool enthusiasts should check out **Screwball 8 Penang** (⊠ No. 7C–7E, ground floor, Asas Centre, Jln. Gottlieb, ☎ 04/227–6317).

DANCE CLUB

Royce Bistro (⊠ 11–G–1/11–G–2 New Bob Centre, Jln. Gottlieb, ☎ 04/228–0388) is popular with the young, hip crowd because it has the longest happy hour in Pinang—from 2:30 to 9:30 daily.

LOUNGES

For a drink and a panoramic city view, head for the revolving restaurant atop the **City Bayview** hotel (⊠ Farquhar St., ☎ 04/263–3161). In the **Shangri-La Penang**'s (⊠ Jln. Magazine, ☎ 04/262–2622) lobby lounge, a string quartet—playing everything from classical pieces to waltzes to pop—alternates evenings with a Latin combo.

Outdoor Activities and Sports

GOLF

Pinang has two 18-hole golf courses that are open to the public—Batu Gantung and Bukit Jambul. For information, fees, and tee times, call the golf section of the **Penang Turf Club** (☎ 04/226–6701) or the **Bukit Jambul Country Club** (☎ 04/644–2255).

HIKING

For hiking, your best bet is the tropical **Rima Rekreasi** (Recreational Forest), 1½ km (1 mi) past the village of Teluk Bahang. The forest also has a museum, a playground, and picnic tables. A nature book called *Trails of Penang Island* is available at tourist information centers for RM15 (☞ Visitor Information *in* Northwest Coast and Central Highlands A to Z, *below*).

RUNNING

In Air Itam (Ayer Itam), about 9 km (6 mi) southwest of Georgetown, runners or walkers can explore the track around the reservoir that provides Pinang with drinking water. The path cuts through a tropical forest and across a dam. Take a bus to Air Itam and walk the rest of the way up, which is a workout in itself. It's best as an early morning outing.

Shopping

Jalan Penang is the main shopping street, with Lebuh Campbell and Jalan Burmah as offshoots. For a wide selection of goods—including some that are duty-free—sold in air-conditioned surroundings, a trip to the KOMTAR complex is a must. Most shops are open 11–8. The newest shopping areas are Bukit Jambul and Jambul Sunshine Square, on the way to the airport.

The **Chowrasta Market** (☞ Exploring, *above*) on Jalan Penang is primarily a fresh produce market with additional shops and stalls outside. Upstairs, clothing and miscellaneous goods are available. On Sunday morning, a **flea market** with a mixture of junk and antiques is held on Jalan Pintal Tali.

ANTIQUES

The **Eccentric Gift Shop** (⊠ Jln. Burmah, ☎ 04/227–4181), in the Midlands Park Centre, has antiques and bric-a-brac as well as handicrafts from Vietnam, Indonesia, and other Asian countries. You'll find several curio and junk shops along Jalan Pintal Tali, but try **Lorong Kulit Market,** which is open every morning, for particularly interesting finds. **Saw Joo Ann** (⊠ 39 Lebuh Kimberley, ☎ 04/261–9851) is the place to go for high-quality Malaysian artifacts. (If it's not open during normal business hours, ask at the coffee shop next door and someone will let you in to browse.)

HANDICRAFTS

On Upper Jalan Penang, shops sell crafts from Malaysia, Thailand, Indonesia, China, and India. The best selection of batik prints is at **Craft Batik** (⊠ 32 Jln. Kelawei, ☎ 04/229–3770) where you can see how batik is made. **Penang Butterfly Farm** (⊠ 803 Mk. 2, Jln. Taluk Bahang, ☎ 04/885–1253) sells objects from all over Southeast Asia.

Batu Ferringhi

14 km (8 mi) northwest of Georgetown.

Most of Pulau Pinang's northern coast is broken up into small rocky coves—except, that is, for the shore at Batu Ferringhi. In the 1960s, this beach—its fine, golden sands shaded by casuarina and coconut trees—made Pinang one of the best-known vacation islands in Southeast Asia. Since then the north coast has been greatly developed, and today a strip of resorts starts from about 12 km (7 mi) northwest of Georgetown and extends all the way to Teluk Bahang.

Though not Miami Beach, Batu Ferringhi does have a similar ambience—a strip of fancy hotels that primarily provide blocks of rooms to package tours. (You'd never want to pay the published room rate here unless you don't mind your fellow guests paying half that amount.) Batu Ferringhi may be a popular choice for a week's stay, but it has fewer charms for day-trippers (public facilities, such as showers and changing rooms, are nonexistent). Don't go to a great effort to drive out unless you're really desperate for a day at the beach.

Dining and Lodging

$$$ ✕ **Eden Seafood Village.** This huge, open-air, beachfront restaurant is a supermarket of seafood and caters to tourists with a nightly cultural show. Its Chinese-style specialties include crab cooked in a spicy, chili-tomato sauce, steamed prawns in ginger sauce, lobster, and fried squid. ⊠ *Batu Ferringhi,* ☎ *04/881–1852. Reservations essential. AE, DC, MC, V.*

$$ ✕ **End of the World Restaurant.** By the jetty in Teluk Bahang, 5 km (3 mi) beyond Batu Ferringhi, this simple, open-air place specializes in seafood. It's so highly regarded that people drive out all the way from Georgetown just for dinner. Everything is good, though the black-pepper crab is especially recommended. ⊠ *144–A Jln. Hassan Abbas, Teluk Bahang,* ☎ *04/885–1189. No credit cards. No lunch.* ☽ *Daily 5–11:30.*

$$$$ ✕🏨 **Penang Mutiara Beach Resort.** The luxury starts in the white-mar-
★ ble lobby, with its fountains and floor-to-ceiling windows. It continues in the rooms, all of which have ocean views, rattan furniture, batik
wall prints, and Malay-pattern rugs; ceiling fans, shutters, and balconies
that drip with bougainvillea add to the overall tropical elegance. Dining options include tasty Japanese fare at Tsuru-No-Ya, and the outstanding La Farfalla, whose chic, retro-style decor and impeccable
service are matched by sublime northern Italian cuisine. (The chef has
a way of combining ingredients in inventive ways, as evidenced by the
beef capaccio with blade olive pâté or the red tagliolini with sole and
asparagus in saffron sauce.) ✉ *Jln. Teluk Bahang, Teluk Bahang
11050,* ☎ *04/885–2828 or 800/44–UTELL in the U.S.,* 📠 *04/885–
2829. 438 rooms. 4 restaurants, 2 bars, 2 pools, 4 tennis courts, health
club, windsurfing, parasailing, waterskiing. AE, DC, MC, V.* 🍴

$$$$ ✕🏨 **Shangri-La's Rasa Sayang Resort.** There's enough activity—pro-
grammed and otherwise—here to keep you busy day and night. If you
need a break, have a seat by the large pool (the one between the main
building and the beach) and wait for it to be transformed—as it is each
evening—into a colorfully floodlighted fountain. The resort has a Japanese restaurant (which pleases the many Japanese who stay here) as
well as a Chinese restaurant and one that serves European fare. ✉ *Batu
Ferringhi Beach, 11100,* ☎ *04/881–1811, 800/942–5050 in the U.S.,
or 081/747–8485 in the U.K.,* 📠 *04/881–1984. 514 rooms. 3 restaurants, bar, coffee shop, lounge, 2 pools, putting green, 4 tennis courts,
health club, squash, volleyball, snorkeling, windsurfing, boating, meeting rooms. AE, DC, MC, V.* 🍴

$$$ ✕🏨 **Casuarina Beach Hotel.** Spacious rooms, a low-key pace, and at-
tentive service make this established resort a favorite. Named for the
willowy trees that mingle with the palms along the beach, the hotel
has a pleasant pool area and offers champagne brunches and country-
and-western music nights. Il Ritrovo, an Italian bistro that's decorated
with travel posters and candles in wine bottles, is a standout among
the hotel's three restaurants. Its excellent three-course meal is good value:
you can start with a perfect *antipasti tutti mare* (seafood antipasto),
followed by an impressive range of pasta, veal, lamb, and chicken dishes
and classic Italian *dolci* (sweets). A local band plays diners' requests.
✉ *Batu Ferringhi Beach, 11100,* ☎ *04/881–1711,* 📠 *04/881–2155.
180 rooms. 3 restaurants, bar, pool, tennis court, snorkeling, windsurfing,
boating. AE, DC, MC, V.* 🍴

$$$ 🏨 **Holiday Inn Penang.** This two-building hotel has a 23-story garden
wing, a seven-story oceanfront beach wing, and a large pool. It's popu-
lar with Australians and Britons, and it offers such activities as bike rides
and jungle walks, snooker and Ping-Pong tournaments, and tennis and
windsurfing lessons. Rooms face either the hill or the sea. Nonguests can
use the hotel's facilities during the day for a fee (subject to availability).
✉ *72 Batu Ferringhi Beach, 11100,* ☎ *04/881–1601 or 800/HOLIDAY
in the U.S.,* 📠 *04/881–1389. 364 rooms. 2 restaurants, 2 bars, pool, 2
tennis courts, health club, hiking, Ping-Pong, windsurfing, children's programs. AE, DC, MC, V.* 🍴

$$$ ✕🏨 **Shangri-La Golden Sands Resort.** The beachfront Golden Sands has
lush landscaping around two pools and an open-air lounge and café with
a spectacular indoor-outdoor garden effect. Rooms will be upgraded by
September 2000. Organized activities like jungle walks and golf com-
petitions are common, and special poolside events, such as theme din-
ners or barbecues, are held most nights. The hotel's most popular
restaurant, Peppino, serves a wide variety of antipasti, pizzas, and pasta.
✉ *Batu Ferringhi Beach, 11100,* ☎ *04/881–1911, 800/942–5050 in the
U.S., or 081/747–8485 in the U.K.,* 📠 *04/881–1880. 395 rooms. 2 restau-
rants, bar, coffee shop, 2 pools, wading pool. AE, DC, MC, V.* 🍴

$$ ⊡ **Lone Pine.** Built in 1948, this was the first hotel on Batu Ferringhi Beach. Today, it's completely refurbished and most guest rooms open out to a terrace, balcony, or private courtyard. The air-conditioned rooms are furnished in dark wood and have all the amenities of a large hotel. ⊠ *97 Batu Ferringhi Beach, 11100,* ☎ *04/881–1511,* ℻ *04/881–1281. 50 rooms. Restaurant, bar, refrigerators, pool. AE, DC, MC, V.* ✫

Nightlife and the Arts

CULTURAL EVENTS

Eden Seafood Village (☎ 04/881–1852) in Batu Ferringhi holds a cultural show for diners every evening. The show features Malay dancers, Indians laden with bells, and noisy Chinese lion dancers.

The **Pinang Cultural Center** (⊠ Jln. Teluk Bahang, Teluk Bahang, ☎ 04/885–1175), re-creates a kampung with a *balai* (community center), an Orang Ulu longhouse, and an antique Malay House. A 1½-hour tour (conducted every day from 6–7:30), introduces you to all aspects of Malaysian culture. A dinner and show from 7:30–10:30 includes a performance of traditional dance and music. ⊠ *Show RM48; dinner and show RM110; tour, dinner, and show RM135.*

LOUNGE

The Penang Mutiara Beach Resort's serene **Palmetto Lounge** (⊠ Teluk Bahang, ☎ 04/881–2828) has a resident pianist and a live band.

Kedah

The state of Kedah, the nation's "rice bowl," surrounds Pinang state to the east and the north, and it includes the vacation islands of Langkawi. Kedah may well be one of Malaysia's most historic states. Here you'll find 7th-century Hindu/Buddhist ruins and a sultanate that dates from pre-Islamic times. The Thais ruled the state from 1821 until 1846, and though it still shares a border with Thailand, this border was greatly reduced when the state of Perlis was created out of Kedah's northwest corner in 1842.

Alor Setar

➂ *93 km (57½ mi) north of Butterworth, 462 km (287 mi) northwest of KL.*

Alor Setar (pronounced, and sometimes spelled, without the "e"), the capital of Kedah, has a number of attractive mosques and royal residences, most of which are in the center of town. A good place to begin is on Jalan Raja at the **Balai Besar,** the Thai-influenced Great Audience Hall, once used for royal receptions. The current open-sided structure with columns and wood carvings was built in 1904 to replace an 18th-century building. Nearby, the three-tier, octagonal **Balai Nobat** was built to house the sacred musical instruments of the royal orchestra. Unfortunately, you can only go inside if you make prior arrangements in the government office across from it.

The **Muzium Diraja** (Royal Museum) was built in 1763. Used as a royal residence until 1983, it houses a collection of memorabilia and photographs of previous sultans. Some of the rooms remain as they were when the last sultan lived here. ⊠ *Jln. Raja,* ☎ *04/732–7937.* ⊠ *Free.* ☉ *Sat.–Thurs. 10–6, Fri. 10–12 and 2:30–6.*

On the corner of Jalan Pekan Melayu and Jalan Kampung Perak sits the **Masjid Zahir,** an imposing Moorish-style mosque built in 1927 with the usual onion domes and minarets. On Jalan Tengku Ibrahim you'll find the building that houses the **Bali Seni Negeri** (State Art Gallery). The gallery's collections aren't really worth your time, but you should make a point of pausing to look at the lovely colonial architecture (1912) of the former courthouse.

If you're interested in seeing some stone artifacts recovered during the archaeological excavations at Lembah Bujang (literally "Bachelor Valley"), as well as antique Chinese ceramics, head for the **Muzium Negeri** (National Museum) about 2 km (1 mi) north of Alor Setar. ✉ *Jln. Lebuhraya Darulaman,* ☎ *04/733–1162.* ☜ *Free.* ☺ *Sat.–Thurs. 10–6, Fri. 10–12 and 2:30–6.*

Before you leave town, soak up some local atmosphere at the "Wednesday Centre" or **Pekan Rabu,** a market somewhat confusingly opened every day of the week from early morning until early evening. A large modern building on Jalan Tuanku Ibrahim, right in the middle of town, houses a range of stalls where you can find everything from handicrafts to local Malay delicacies.

Langkawi

★ ㉗ *30 km (19 mi) off the coast from Kuala Perlis, which is 171 km (106 mi) northwest of KL.*

Langkawi is an archipelago of 104 islands (there are only 99 at high tide) north of Pinang and just south of Thailand. A couple of decades ago, it was a Robinson Crusoe hideaway; today it's one of Malaysia's hottest destinations, and the government hopes to see it become even more popular. (Prime Minister Mahathir is from Kedah state, and he has thrown his not inconsiderable weight behind its development.) Virtually all the development—including the building of an international airport—has taken place on the major island, Pulau Langkawi, after which the whole group is named. To further encourage tourism, the whole region is a duty-free zone. (Though beer, wine, and spirits are much cheaper here than elsewhere in the country, you may have a hard time finding alcohol outside your hotel owing to the region's devout Muslim population. Indeed, most activity is focused around the hotels and resorts.)

The main town of Kuah—which is 4 km (2½ mi) from the ferry terminal in the southeast of Pulau Langkawi—has a few hotels and shopping blocks. Most resorts are along the island's southwest coast, particularly around Pantai Cenang, Pantai Tengah, and Teluk Burau; a few more sit along the northwestern and northeastern coasts. In the northwestern corner, there are also pristine rain forests. Though Langkawi is still largely rural—and many of its residents live simple, traditional lifestyles—it has a good system of well-maintained and well-signposted roads, making driving around easy. Try to get out and explore the beaches not only on the main island but also on the other 100 islands. There are boats for hire as well as organized trips (☞ Tour Operators *and* Visitor Information *in* Northwest Coast and Central Highlands A to Z, *below*). Take a boat, pick an island, snorkel, dive, and laze away the day on your own beach.

Pulau Langkawi has a number of theme parks, most of them of limited appeal to non-Malaysian visitors. You could, however, spend half a day or so exploring these parks and learning about the archipelago's legends (Langkawi is often billed as the "Isles of Legends"). Some of these tales are rendered in stone at **Lagenda Park,** between the ferry terminal and a large square dominated by a vast, ugly statue of an eagle. Visit late in the afternoon or risk sweltering in the heat (there's no shade anywhere, and no refreshment stands). ☜ *RM5.* ☺ *Daily 9–9.*

★ In the north of Pulau Langkawi, far from the resorts, is the huge **Kompleks Budaya Kraf Langkawi.** Here handicrafts from all over Malaysia are a sold in a lavish mosquelike series of white-stone galleries. The complex has a sister operation in KL (☞ Exploring *in* Kuala Lumpur, *above*). ⊠ *Teluk Yu,* ☎ *04/959–1913.* ☉ *Daily 9–6.*

Head north to the **Galleri Perdana,** which houses more than 10,000 state gifts presented to the Malaysian prime minister. Some are amazingly tacky and others are quite impressive. Don't miss the collection of automobiles. ⊠ *Kilim,* ☎ *04/959–1498.* ☑ *RM3.* ☉ *Tues.–Thurs. and weekends 10–5, Fri. 10–12:15 and 3–5.*

You certainly won't be the only one around if you take a trip to the popular **Pulau Payar Marine Park,** about 45 minutes south of Pulau Langkawi by catamaran, for a look at a coral reef. The excursion offered by Sriwani Tours & Travel (☞ Tour Operators *in* Northwest Coast and Central Highlands A to Z, *below*) is recommended. The trip includes hotel transfers, a high-speed catamaran ride to the park, lunch, and a stop at a glass-bottom reef-viewing platform from which you can snorkel.

Dining and Lodging

Although the best places to eat in Langkawi are generally inside the resorts, there are a few independent restaurants that merit a visit. Around Kuah you'll find some simple, locally owned stalls that offer good food. (Note, however, that alcohol isn't served, and English is rarely spoken.) Your lodging choices range from luxurious, expensive resorts to local hotels with ultracheap, fan-cooled rooms.

$$ ✕ **Bon Ton Coconut Village.** Housed in an open-sided, Balinese-style pavilion, Bon Ton is just south of the airport and north of Pantai Cenang. The very good East–West cuisine, delightful ambience for both lunch and dinner, and rich cakes (they're legendary) have made this restaurant popular with Pulau Langkawi's "in crowd." You'll also find a gift shop at the entrance to the restaurant pavilion, as well as the Warung Kopi, an informal stall hawking inexpensive local food—it's run by the same team that operates the main establishment. ⊠ *Mukim Kedawang, Pantai Cenang,* ☎ *04/955–3643. AE, MC, V.*

$$ ✕ **Charlie's Place.** This restaurant, which is part of the Langkawi Yacht Club, just east of Kuah, has sea breezes and sea views to complement your meal. Downstairs you'll find authentic Asian cuisine and the upstairs Captain's Deck offers good Western and Continental food. Try the grilled lamb chops. ⊠ *Jln. Dato Syed Omar, Kuah,* ☎ *04/966–4078. AE, DC, MC, V.*

$$$ ✕🔲 **Rebak Marina Resort.** A private island 15 minutes off the coast of Langkawi is home to this exclusive resort, which offers a 128-berth marina. The Balinese-style lobby is open-air, spacious guest rooms have wooden floors and canopy beds, and the sea-facing rooms provide a wonderful view of a palm-fringed beach. The Marina Cafe is an all-day dining restaurant facing the marina. Though the menu is quite limited, the food, which includes Malaysian and Mediterranean cuisine, is good. Hang out at the lobby bar and strike up a conversation with one of the sailors checking e-mail. ⊠ *Pulau Rebak Besar, Kuah 07007,* ☎ *04/996–5566,* FAX *04/966–9973. 106 rooms. 2 restaurants, bar, lounge, pool, 2 tennis courts, health club, hiking, squash, windsurfing, marina, fishing, meeting room. AE, DC, MV, V. www.glemarie.com.*

$$$$ 🔲 **Datai.** Tucked away on Pulau Langkawi's northwestern tip (a 40-
★ minute drive from most attractions), this hideaway resort faces the turquoise Andaman Sea and is backed by a rain forest. The large, open-air main building—which serves as a reception area and lounge—overlooks a small valley that carves its way steeply down to the beach, a 10-minute walk away. Open-air corridors link the lobby to the guest quarters, many of which also look down into the valley. The large rooms are decorated in silk and red *merbau,* a warm Malaysian hardwood that shines from the floors to the walls. Each room has a bedroom with

a king-size bed; a living room with a bar and two daybeds; and a grand bathroom with two vanities, a shower, a bath, and luggage space. Villas and suites are almost twice as big and have decks with sun lounges and elevated verandas. Though the food here isn't innovative, it's high quality (note that only hotel guests are permitted to eat in the restaurants). Fine Thai cuisine is available every evening in the gorgeous open-sided Pavilion restaurant. If you need pampering, visit the Mandara Spa, a series of luxurious villas specializing in creative interpretations of Asian treatments. ⊠ *Jln. Teluk Datai, 07000,* ☎ *604/959–2500, 603/263–5112 in KL, 800/447–7462 in the U.S, or 0800/181535 in the U.K.,* 𝔽𝔸𝕏 *604/959–2600 or 603/245–3540 in KL. 54 rooms, 40 villas, 14 suites. 3 restaurants, bar, minibars, 2 pools, 18-hole golf course, 2 tennis courts, health club, hiking, beach, windsurfing, boating, mountain bikes, shop, library, meeting rooms. AE, DC, MC, V.* 🏊

$$$$ 🏨 **Pelangi Beach Resort.** Management intended to re-create the atmosphere of a kampung here, but with such facilities as a pool with a swim-up bar, the atmosphere is really that of a large (25 beachfront acres) resort—albeit one where the service, amenities, and architecture are tops. In the center of the large lobby is a relaxing lounge where you can take tea or sip cocktails. Guest rooms are small, and the extensive use of (compressed) wood and heavy carpeting makes them seem even smaller; fortunately, they come with balconies as well as air-conditioning and fans. About a third face the sea, another third a man-made lake, and the remainder the back lot (as usual, room rates reflect these views). The beach isn't spectacular, but at low tide you can wade across to a nearby island for privacy. ⊠ *Pantai Cenang 07000,* ☎ *04/952–8888 or 03/261–0393 in KL,* 𝔽𝔸𝕏 *04/952–8899. 331 rooms, 55 suites. 3 restaurants, pool, sauna, 3 tennis courts, exercise room, squash, travel services. AE, DC, MC, V.* 🏊

$$$ 🏨 **Berjaya Langkawi Beach & Spa Resort.** Set below the forest-covered hills in the far northwest of Pulau Langkawai, the Berjaya reflects its Malay heritage in the architecture. All rooms have a balcony or terrace that overlooks the bay. Perhaps the main attraction here is the outstanding spa (open to guests and nonguests alike) with its wide range of health and beauty treatments—everything from Oriental reflexology to flotation-tank treatments to aromatherapy facials. ⊠ *Burau Bay 07000,* ☎ *04/959–1888,* 𝔽𝔸𝕏 *04/959–1886. 400 rooms. 3 restaurants, bar, 3 pools, massage, sauna, spa, steam room, 2 tennis courts, exercise room, beach, dance club. AE, DC, MC, V.* 🏊

Northwest Coast and Central Highlands A to Z

Arriving and Departing

By Airplane

Penang International Airport (☎ 04/643–0811) in Bayan Lepas (about 18 km/11 mi south of Georgetown) is served by Malaysia Airline System (MAS), Singapore Airlines, Cathay Pacific, and Thai Airways International. Pinang is about a 40-minute flight from KL. Airport taxis use a coupon system with fixed fares. A one-way ride into the city costs RM19; to Batu Ferringhi it's RM35. A public bus (Yellow No. 83) just outside the airport entrance will take you to the KOMTAR terminal in the city center for RM1.25. Buses run hourly 7 AM–10 PM from the airport and 6 AM–9 PM to the airport.

Langkawi International Airport (☎ 04/955–1311) is at Padang Matsirat, in the southwest of Pulau Langkawi and about 20 km (12 mi) from Kuah. There are several daily MAS flights from Pinang, and KL as well as flights from Singapore (SilkAir as well as MAS), Japan, and Taiwan. MAS flights are often fully booked, so make reservations far in advance and reconfirm them. Unless your resort can arrange for pickup, you'll need to take a taxi from the airport. Cabs are plentiful and fares are fixed; pick up a coupon at the taxi counter. You should-n't have to pay more than RM10–RM40 to any destination.

Ipoh's **Sultan Azlan Shah Airport** (☎ 05/312–2459) is served by daily flights from KL. It's 5 km (3 mi) west of the city, and taxis charge RM10 for the trip.

By Boat

Ferries to Pinang from Butterworth operate 24 hours a day, running about every 20 minutes 6 AM–midnight, every 40 minutes from 11:20 PM to 2 AM, hourly from 2 to 4 AM and every 40 minutes from 4:40 to 6 AM. The fare is RM7 per vehicle *and* 60 sen per person. Daily express ferries ply between Pinang and Sumatra, Indonesia, departing from Georgetown at 8:30 AM and arriving at Medan's port of Belawan five hours later (no visa required for American and British citizens). The return trip departs from Belawan at 10 AM. The one-way fare is RM96, two-way is RM160. The terminal office is next to the tourist information office on Jalan Tun Syed Sheh Barakbah, near Ft. Cornwallis.

An air-conditioned express ferry departs from Pinang to Langkawi at 8 AM, 9:15 AM, and 2:30 PM daily and makes the return journey at 5:30 PM. The hour-long trip costs RM35 one way, RM60 return. You can also reach Langkawi aboard a ferry from Kuala Kedah (near Alor Setar). Ferries depart every half hour between 7:30 AM and 7 PM daily; the trip takes a little over an hour and costs RM15 one way. There's also ferry service from Kuala Perlis, near the Thai border; the trip takes 45 minutes and costs RM12 one way. Ferries to Langkawi from Thailand depart three times daily from Satun, on the Thai border; the journey takes 1½ hours and costs RM19 one way.

By Bus

On the mainland, the **main bus station** (☎ 04/634–4928) serving Pinang is on the Butterworth side near the ferry terminal. On the island, you can book tickets from the KOMTAR building on the ground level as the buses leave from here. The fare from KL to Pinang is around RM20.

By Car

To reach Pulau Pinang, you can either drive across the Penang Bridge from Butterworth (RM7 toll) or take your car across on the ferry (☞ By Boat, *above*). No bridge connects the mainland to Langkawi. However, with 24-hour advance notice, a vehicular ferry service is available from Kuala Kedah to Langkawi for RM80.

By Train

The train station serving Pinang is next to the bus and ferry terminals in Butterworth. You can buy a ticket at the **Butterworth Station** (☎ 04/323–7962) or at a booking station at the Pinang **ferry terminal** (✉ Pengkalan Weld, Georgetown, ☎ 04/261–0290). It's not a long walk from Butterworth station to the ferry, but you'll have to carry your own luggage. On the Pinang side, taxis will be waiting.

The Ekspres Langkawi rail service runs from KL to Alor Setar, where you can take a bus or taxi to Kuala Kedah for the ferry service across to Langkawi.

Getting Around

By Bus

Three bus companies operate on Pulau Pinang. Blue buses, which run to the north of the island (including Batu Ferringhi), and through George-town toward Ayer Itam, leave from the station near the Pengkalan Weld ferry terminal. Yellow buses run to the central and southern parts of the island. Transit Link buses run north, south, and central. All buses pass through the station at KOMTAR. You buy tickets from conductors on the bus and pay according to the distance you travel. For information on routes and schedules, call 04/262–9357 for Yellow buses; 04/226–6367 for Transit Link buses; and 04/226–8652 for Blue buses.

There's no bus service in Langkawi. You must take a taxi or hire a car or motorbike.

By Car
Avis (☎ 04/643–9633 and 04/811–1522), **Hertz** (☎ 04/263–5914 and 04/643–0208), and **National** (☎ 04/643–4205) have counters at Pinang airport and in Georgetown. In Langkawi, rental cars are available at the airport through **Angkaland Tours & Travel** (☎ 04/955–5797) and **Bayou Tours & Travel** (☎ 04/955–7007).

Instead of renting a vehicle and driving to the Cameron Highlands yourself, consider hiring a chauffeured, air-conditioned car. From the KL International Airport the five- to six-hour drive will cost about RM350 (the six-hour drive south from Pinang costs about the same). A few words of caution if your destination is The Smokehouse Hotel: despite assurances that drivers will go all the way up the mountain to the hotel, they may try to leave you at the taxi station in Tanah Rata. Your best recourse is to refuse to pay the fare until the driver has arranged for a second taxi to go the rest of the way up the hill.

By Taxi
You can pick up what's known as an "outstation taxi" from cab stands next to the bus stations in all major Malaysian towns. On Pulau Pinang, you'll find stands near many hotels. The minimum charge is RM5, more for air-conditioned cars. Though taxis have meters, the drivers prefer not to use them. Establish the price before you get in. Two companies are **Syarikat Georgetown Taxi** (☎ 04/261–3853) and **CT Radio Taxi Service** (☎ 04/229–9467). There are always taxis available at Langkawi airport and ferry terminal, as well as in Kuah. Your resort will phone a cab if you wish to hire one.

By Trishaw
Pulau Pinang's Georgetown is one of the few places in Malaysia where trishaws—large tricycles with a carriage for passengers and freight—are not only available, but also provide a safe, pleasant, and inexpensive way to sightsee. (Not only tourists but some residents—mainly elderly Chinese women and children heading for school—rely on them.) Don't be alarmed if your trishaw heads the wrong way up a one-way street; Pinang motorists are used to making allowances for these vehicles. Negotiate the route and fare before you get in. A short trip is likely to cost only RM5. If you want to hire a trishaw for longer, the usual hourly rate for one passenger is from RM20–RM25. The driver will, of course, ask for more, but negotiate.

Contacts and Resources

Emergencies
Pulau Pinang. Ambulance and police: ☎ 999; the **Penang Adventist Hospital** (☎ 04/226–1133) also sends ambulances. **Fire:** ☎ 994. Hospitals and clinics: **Hospital Besar** (✉ Jln. Residency, Georgetown, ☎ 04/229–3333) or the **Loh Guan Lye Specialists Centre** (✉ 19 Jln. Logan, Georgetown, ☎ 04/228–8501). All hospitals and clinics are able to dispense medication.

Pulau Langkawi. Ambulance and police: ☎ 999. **Fire:** ☎ 994. Hospitals and clinics: **Daerah Langkawi** (✉ Jln. Bukit Tekuh, ☎ 04/966–3333).

Perdana Polyclinics (✉ Lot 110, Pusat Daganan Kelana Mas, Kuah, ☎ 04/966–8526). All hospitals and clinics can provide medication.

English-Language Bookstores

Once you're outside the major tourist areas, English is a rare commodity. It's best to stock up on reading material at major resorts or in shops in KL, Pinang, or Langkawi. On Pulau Pinang, the **Times Bookstore** is on the first floor of the Penang Plaza shopping complex (✉ 126 Jln. Burmah, Georgetown), and in the Lifestyles Department on the fourth floor of the KOMTAR building. Other Georgetown bookstores include: **United Happy Stores** (✉ 519 Lebuh Chulia, ☎ 04/261–1293) and **Popular Bookstore** (✉ KOMTAR Building, ☎ 04/263–0682).

On Langkawi, major resorts have their own souvenir and gift shops that sell books and magazines. You can also try **Book Village** (✉ Rumah Rok Rafeah, Lubuk Semilang, ☎ 04/955–5568).

Tour Operators

Several companies offer general tours of Pulau Pinang. The most popular is a 73-km (45-mi), 3½-hour drive around the island. From Batu Ferringhi it goes through Malay kampungs and spice orchards; stops at the Snake Temple; cruises past the Universiti Sains Malaysia campus and through Georgetown; and then returns via the beach road. The principal tour companies also offer such excursions as "Pinang Hill and Temples," "City and Heritage," and "Pinang by Night," in addition to trips to the world's largest butterfly farm (at Teluk Bahang) and the Botanical Gardens. Operators can also arrange a waterfront and Pinang Bridge trip, and a Monkey Beach excursion.

Pinang's major companies include: **Mayflower Acme Tours** (✉ Georgetown, ☎ 04/262–8198; Tan Chong Building, 23 Pengkalan Weld, Georgetown, ☎ 04/262–8196) and **Tour East** (✉ Golden Sands Hotel, Batu Ferringhi, ☎ 04/881–1662; Penang Plaza, 4th floor, Georgetown, ☎ 04/261–9563). The **Penang Tourist Guides Association** (☞ Visitor Information, *below*) offers tours of Georgetown for RM32.

At least 10 tour companies in Langkawi can arrange coach tours to such main-island sights as Mahsuri's Tomb, as well as to nearby islands. Try **Mayflower Acme Tours** (✉ Sun Village, ☎ 04/955–1330) or **Reliance Sightseeing** (✉ Langkawi Mall, ☎ 04/966–5033). For cruises by high-speed catamaran down to Pulau Payar Marine Park, contact **Sriwani Tours & Travel** (✉ Jetty Point Complex, near Kuah, ☎ 04/966–7318).

Travel Agencies

On Pulau Pinang try: **American Express** (✉ Pan Chang Building, 274 Lebuh Victoria, Georgetown, ☎ 04/262–3724). On the ground floor of Georgetown's KOMTAR complex on Jalan Penang you'll find a branch of **MAS** (☎ 04/262–0011), as well as **Ace Tours and Travel** (☎ 04/262–1169), which often sells airline tickets for less than MAS.

Langkawi also has an office of the **MAS** (✉ Fair Shopping Mall, Jalan Persiaran Putra, but for cheaper air tickets, visit the travel agencies on Jalan Chulia.

Visitor Information

In Georgetown, **Tourism Malaysia** (☎ 04/643–0501 airport; 04/262–0066 KOMTAR) has a counter at the airport and an office opposite the clock tower near Ft. Cornwallis; hours are weekdays 8:30–4:30 and Saturday 8:30–1. The **Penang Tourist Guides Association (PTGA)** (☎ 04/261–4461) and the **Penang Tourist Centre Berhad (PTCB)** (☎ 04/261–6633) distribute information from centers on Level 3 of the KOMTAR building and downtown near Ft. Cornwallis at the intersection of Lebuh Pantai and Lebuh Light. The PTGA is open daily from 10 to 6 and the PTCB is open weekdays 8–4:30 (closed from 1 to 2) and Saturday 8–1.

In Langkawi, there's a tourism information counter at the airport where you can pick up free brochures. For more detailed information, try the **Langkawi Tourist Information Centre** (⊠ Jln. Persiaran Putra, Kuah, ☎ 04/966–7789). It's open Sat.–Wed. 9–5 and Thurs. 9–1.

THE SOUTHERN PENINSULA AND THE EAST COAST

Although the peninsula's southern tip and eastern coast are becoming more developed, they're still very much places for visitors with a sense of adventure. Along coastal roads—from Desaru all the way up to the Thai border—towns and resorts are few; beaches, though tempting, have few facilities; and public transportation is sporadic.

Increased tourism has brought some development to the coastal towns of Pahang state. In Terengganu state, changes have been wrought both by tourism and the discovery of petroleum a couple of decades ago. Still, along the state's coast you're as likely to find a hotel consisting of simple thatch chalets as you are a luxury resort with all the trimmings. The tourist infrastructure of the offshore islands, the best known of which is Pulau Tioman, has been developed, and many now have scuba facilities. Outside these areas, however, the east coast still putters along with an economy based largely on fishing and agriculture. But that's really what makes it a delight.

Negri Sembilan

Between KL and Melaka is an area called Negri Sembilan (Nine States). Although it's not a major tourist destination it does offer you the chance to see a different side of Malaysia. Negri Sembilan is unique in that its Malay peoples are originally from the matriarchal Minangkabau tribe of western Sumatra, and their traditional law, or *adat*, differs from that of other Malays.

Seremban

28 *64 km (40 mi) southwest of KL, 320 km (200 mi) northwest of Singapore.*

Negri Sembilan's capital is a busy city with attractive botanical gardens and a cultural center where there are several examples of early Minangkabau architecture. In both Negeri Sembilan and West Sumatra, roofs have a buffalo-horn shape, commemorating the victory of a Sumatran buffalo over a buffalo representing the invading Javanese. (The tribal name of "minangkabau" means "victory of the buffalo.")

The main reason for leaving the North–South Highway, which bypasses Seremban, is to visit the **Taman Seni Budaya Negeri.** Just 3 km (2 mi) outside Seremban itself and close to the highway, this center showcases local culture. Exhibits in the main museum aren't remarkable, but on the grounds are three superb original wooden houses that were reconstructed here almost 50 years ago. The most elaborate of these, the **Istana Ampang Tinggi**, is a fine example of the wood-carver's art. ⊠ Jln. Labu. 🎫 *Free.* 🕐 *Tues., Wed., and weekends 10–6, Thurs. 8:15–1, Fri. 10–12:15 and 2:45–6.*

OFF THE
BEATEN PATH**SRI MENANTI** — Thirty kilometers (18 miles) east of Seremban is what was once the royal capital, Sri Menanti. Here you can visit an ancient royal burial ground; the "new" *istana* (palace), which was built in the 1930s; and the old istana—constructed in 1902 in the Minangkabau style (built entirely without nails) and used by the sultan until 1931. The drive to Sri Menanti takes you through hilly country, where bougainvillea and hibiscus abound. 🖾 *Free.* ⊙ *Tues., Wed., and weekends 10–6, Thurs. 8:15–1, Fri. 10–12:15 and 2:45–6.*

Melaka

The state of Melaka (Malacca), once an important Muslim sultanate, has been reduced to a tiny wedge of land along the strait named after it, with Negri Sembilan to the north and Johor to the south and east. However, the state's eponymous capital—Malaysia's oldest city—is full of interesting sights. On its northern outskirts, the region of Air Keroh (Ayer Keroh) has been developed as a recreational area with a number of attractions.

Air Keroh

㉙ *70 km (42 mi) southeast of Seremban, 134 km (85 mi) southeast of KL.*

You could spend a pleasant half day in Air Keroh, either on your way south from KL to Melaka City or as a side trip from Melaka City (a taxi from town should cost around RM7). Start at the **Hutan Rekreasi** (Recreational Forest), where you can stroll along paths through undisturbed vegetation and learn about the various plants from the helpful labels. A canopy walk is being built along the edge of the forest which will provide splendid viewing. If you want to spend the night, chalets with all facilities can be hired for around RM50. There is also a campground where you can sleep cheap (50 sen per night). 🖾 🕿 *06/232–8401.* 🖾 *Free.* ⊙ *Daily 7–6.*

If you haven't yet seen a Malaysian zoo, you could have a look at the small **Melaka Zoo** near the Recreational Forest. It has around 50 species of wildlife from Southeast Asia and Africa. 🕿 *06/232–4053.* 🖾 *RM3.* ⊙ *Weekdays 10–6, weekends 9:30–6:30.*

The **Taman Rama Rama** resolves any question you may have had about whether or not Malaysia is a lepidopterist's paradise. At this attractive butterfly farm, some 200 local species fly freely. 🕿 *06/232–0033.* 🖾 *RM4.* ⊙ *Daily 8:30–5:30.*

If you have time for only one attraction, head straight for **Taman Mini Malaysia,** attractive gardens where traditional houses typical of all 13 Malaysian states are showcased. The grounds also contain the **Mini ASEAN Village,** where you can view structures from Malaysia's neighbors in the Association of Southeast Asian Nations (ASEAN). 🕿 *06/231–6089.* 🖾 *RM3.* ⊙ *Weekdays 10–6, weekends 9:30–6:30.*

Melaka City

㉚–㊶ *10 km (6 mi) south of Air Keroh, 155 km (97 mi) southeast of KL.*

Remarkably well-preserved old buildings, ancient ruins, tombs and temples, give Melaka a unique charm. Founded by a Sumatran prince in the year 1400, Melaka was captured by the Portuguese in 1511, then by the Dutch in 1641. In the years following, the city thrived; it was once considered the most important port in Southeast Asia.

The British took over of Melaka in 1824, and apart from the Japanese occupation during World War II, held control until Malaysian independence in 1957. Every culture that ruled Melaka made its mark, leaving a fascinating patchwork of tradition, history, and religion. Buddhism, Hinduism, Christianity, and the Islamic faith peacefully coexist, and in the old part of town you might come across a mosque squeezed between a Hindu and a Buddhist temple. To embrace the essence of this picturesque city take a trishaw ride through its historic streets.

The center of historic Melaka is Dutch Square (you can't miss the windmill), in front of the Stadhuys and Christ Church. This is backed by St. Paul's Hill and its various historic sights. There are several museums within walking distance of both the square and the hill. Across the river from the Stadhuys is the old Chinatown, with its temples, antiques shops, and fine examples of 19th-century Melaka architecture.

③⓪ Start at one of the city's oldest Portuguese ruins, dating from 1521, **St. Paul's Church,** atop St. Paul's Hill. Note the huge headstones with inscriptions in Dutch, Latin and Portuguese. The statue at the summit commemorates St. Francis Xavier, who was buried here before being moved to his permanent resting spot in Goa, India, where he began his missionary career.

③① Come down the hill and explore the **Porta de Santiago,** an entrance gate that is all that remains of A Famosa, a Portuguese fortress. This gate has become the symbol of the state of Melaka.

③② Near the Porta de Santiago is the **Muzium Budaya,** whose exhibits on Muslim culture and royalty are housed in a re-creation of a traditional wooden palace known as the Sultanate Palace. ⊠ *Jln. Kota,* ☎ *06/282–7464.* ▨ *RM2.* ⊗ *Mon., Wed., Thurs., and Sat.–Sun. 9–6, Fri. 9–12:15 and 2:45–6. Closed Tues.*

Firmly aground on the riverbank—on your left as you head toward Dutch Square—is a re-creation of a Portuguese ship that sank off the coast of
③③ Melaka. It houses the **Maritime Museum,** which offers a glimpse of the sailing vessels and trade at the height of the Melaka sultanate in the 14th century. ⊠ *Off Jln. Merdeka,* ☎ *no phone.* ▨ *RM2.* ⊗ *Mon., Wed., Thurs., and Sat.–Sun. 9–6, Fri. 9–12:15 and 2:45–6. Closed Tues.*

③④ The **Stadthuys** complex in Dutch Square is good and solid, in true Dutch style. Note the thick masonry walls, the heavy hardwood doors, and the windows with wrought-iron hinges. The complex was erected between 1641 and 1660 and used until recently for government offices. It has now been restored and converted into a museum with artifacts from both the Dutch and Portuguese eras. Across from the Stadthuys
③⑤ is another fine example of Dutch architecture. **Christ Church** was built in 1753 of salmon-pink bricks brought from Zeeland (Netherlands) and faced in red laterite. Look for tombstones in the floor that display Armenian script. Follow Jalan Gereja (on the right of Christ Church)
③⑥ for about 100 yards to the **St. Francis Xavier's Church,** built in 1849 by Reverend Farve.

Head back to the Dutch Square windmill and you'll be right by a small bridge leading to Melaka's west bank. Cross the Melaka River to the
③⑦ **Chinese quarter,** its narrow streets lined with traditional shophouses, ancient temples, and clan houses (note the interesting carved doors). From the bridge, continue straight until you reach **Jalan Hang Jebat (Jonkers Street),** a wonderful place to hunt for and bargain over antiques. Continue along to Jalan Hang Kasturi, turn right and follow
③⑧ to **Hang Jabat's Mausoleum,** commemorating one of the 15th-century champions of justice in Melaka who was killed in a duel.

Walk back to Jalan Tukang Emas, turn right and head for Jalan Tokong,
③⑨ or Temple Street. On your left is the **Cheng Hoon Teng Temple,** one

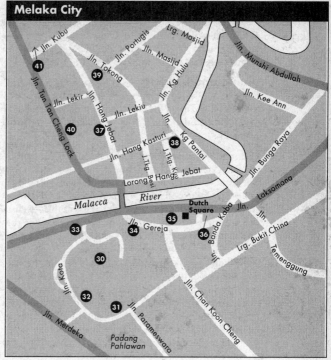

of the country's oldest Chinese temples. You'll recognize it by its ceremonial masts, which tower over the surrounding houses, and by the porcelain and glass animals and flowers that decorate its eaves. Built in the Nanking style, the temple embraces three doctrines: Buddhist, Taoist, and Confucian. You can tell the monks apart by their robes; the Taoists, for example, expose their right shoulder. On your way out, you can buy sandalwood (the scent that permeates the temple) as well as papier-mâché houses and cars and symbolic money ("hell money"), used to burn as offerings during funerals. From the temple, retrace your steps, turning right onto Jalan Hang Lekiu and right again onto Jalan Hang Jebat, where you'll find good pork satay at No. 83, and several coffee shops that sell wonderful noodles.

From Jalan Hang Jebat take a left onto Jalan Kubu, then another left onto Jalan Tun Tan Cheng Lock. This street was once called Millionaires' Row because of its glorious mansions, built by wealthy Babas (Peranakan men) in the 19th century. The **Baba and Nyonya Heritage Museum** is set in a superb town house that's furnished with many items that belonged to the original owners. The museum offers a good deal of insight into the lifestyle and architecture of the Peranakans (Straits Chinese), whose culture and cuisine assimilated many Malay elements. *48-50 Jln. Tun Tan Cheng Lock,* ☎ *06/283–1273.* ⊠ *RM7.* ⊙ *Daily 10–12:30 and 2–4:30.*

From the Baba and Nyonya museum, take a taxi to **Bukit China** (Chinese Hill), about 10 minutes northeast of the city center, for a glimpse of more Chinese history. Six centuries ago, a Ming emperor's envoy set up the first trade arrangements in this ancient Malay capital; a daughter of the emperor was sent to Melaka as wife to Sultan Mansor Shah. She and her 500 ladies-in-waiting set up housekeeping on Bukit China. The early Chinese traders and notables who lived and died in Melaka were buried on this hill, and their 17,000 graves remain, making this the largest Chinese cemetery outside China. Stop off at the **Sultan's Well,** at the foot of Bukit China. Tossing a coin into the well—a custom that dates from the founding of Melaka by Raja Iskandar Shah in the 14th century—is said to ensure your return to the city.

Dining and Lodging

For a delicious, inexpensive dinner, head for the row of stalls known as Glutton's Corner. It used to be on the seafront, but reclamation has pushed it far inland, where it now takes up almost one side of Jalan Merdeka.

$$ ✕ **Bunga Raya Restaurant.** Also known as Madam Fatso's (after its not-so-slender proprietor), Bunga Raya is perfect for a seafood feast. The place is basic—bright neon lights over a semi-open-air cluster of tables—but the food is good. There are huge Sri Lankan crabs (live for steaming or for transformation into chili crab) as well as good steamed fish and prawns. Ask Madam or her daughter for recommendations on what's best the night you visit. ⊠ *40, Jln. Merdeka,* ☎ *06/283–6456. MC.* ⊙ *Daily 12:30 PM–1:30 AM.*

$–$$ ✕ **Jonkers.** Melaka's prettiest place to eat also has some of the most delicious food, but unfortunately it's open only from 11 AM to 5 PM. In the historic heart of the town, it's housed in a lovingly resorted Peranakan town house. You pass through a tastefully stocked gift shop before entering an open internal courtyard with a well surrounded by colorful tiles. The light, tasty offerings include several imaginative East–West dishes, a Nonya set lunch, and excellent cakes. ⊠ *17 Jln. Hang Jebat,* ☎ *06/283–5578. AE, MC, V.*

$–$$ ✕ **Restoran Paranakan.** For a superb, reasonably-priced meal you
★ need look no further. The chicken randang and deep-fried cuttlefish are simply delicious, as are the tiger prawns in sweet santan curry. ⊠ *107, Jln. Tun Tan Cheng Lock,* ☎ *06/284-500. AE, MC.*

$$$ ✕⊞ **Century Mahkota Hotel.** The newest luxury hotel in town sits on reclaimed land behind the Mahkota Parade shopping complex. The hotel is glossy and spacious and has a good number of recreational facilities. Rooms are tastefully furnished and well equipped. You can enjoy freshly made pizza at the Pizza Terrace, international fare at the Cafe Mahkota, or a variety of Asian cuisines at the aptly named Spices restaurant. Though the hotel is a short walk from several sights, there's free shuttle service to the center of town. ⊠ *Jln. Merdeka, 75000,* ☎ *06/ 281–2828,* FAX *06/281–2323. 295 rooms. 3 restaurants, 2 bars, piano bar, 2 pools, beauty salon, golf privileges, 2 tennis courts, squash, business services, meeting rooms. AE, DC, MC, V.* ✆

$$$ ⊞ **Renaissance Melaka Hotel.** Operations at this 24-story hotel run
★ smoothly, making it a good choice whether you're visiting on business or for pleasure. Guest rooms are bright (be sure to ask for one that overlooks the gardens), decorated in pastel colors, and equipped with IDD phones, color TVs and VCRs, and refrigerators; rooms on the Renaissance Floor have private concierge services. In the evening there's usually live entertainment in the Utan Fun Pub on level 2. Special package rates may be 60% lower than the listed room rates; ask about discounts when making reservations. ⊠ *Jln. Bendahara, 75100,* ☎ *06/ 284–8888,* FAX *06/284–9269. 295 rooms. 2 restaurants, bar, no-smoking floors, refrigerators, pool, exercise room, squash, business services, meeting rooms, travel services. AE, DC, MC, V.* ✆

$$ ⊞ **City Bayview.** This modern 14-story high-rise stands in contrast to the older buildings of Melaka. The look of the hotel is strictly functional (read: no personality), but the rooms, with motel-like furniture and IDD phones, are clean and satisfactory. ⊠ *Jln. Bendahara, 75100,* ☎ *06/239–7888,* FAX *06/236–7699. 181 rooms. 2 restaurants, coffee*

shop, pool, exercise room, dance club, laundry service, business ser-vices, meeting rooms. AE, DC, MC, V.

Nightlife

Melaka's sights are brought to life nightly in a **sound-and-light show,** in which the city's history is told to the accompaniment of Malay music, sound effects, and illuminated monuments. The first show is at 8:30 PM; the second, narrated in English, is at 9:30 PM. They're held in the stadium between Jalan Merdeka and Jalan Parameswara. Check with the Tourist Office as performance times can vary.

Johor

The state of Johor, which covers the southern tip of the peninsula, has huge oil palm and pineapple plantations, old rubber estates, canning factories, and a considerable amount of industry. The state was founded by the Sultan of Melaka in 1511, when he was ousted by the Portuguese, and it has been ruled with an iron hand by subsequent sultans ever since. The capital, Johor Bahru, is at the very tip of the peninsula and is con-nected to Singapore by a causeway—built in the '20s, bombed by the British, and rebuilt by the Japanese during World War II—and, farther east by a bridge that opened in 1998. Eastern Johor state is less de-veloped, and its attractive beaches and lovely islands are attracting more and more visitors, especially from Singapore.

Johor Bahru

42 *368 km (229 mi) southeast of KL, 206 km (128 mi) southeast of Melaka, 1 km (½ mi) north of Singapore.*

At the southern tip of peninsular Malaysia and connected to Singapore, the royal and administrative capital of Johor state, Johor Bahru (JB), suf-fers from a lack of town planning that stands in sharp contrast to Sin-gapore's orderliness. There's no center and streets follow no grid or other logical plan but rather run into one another higgledy-piggledy. The pace used to be noticeably different, too, but JB's days as a laid-back escape from the planned sterility of its neighbor are over. Because labor costs are lower than in Singapore, the last few years have seen rapid commercial and industrial development. The pace is picking up, taxis are smarter, and there are new first-class hotels; congestion and pollution are also on the rise. JB is a good jumping-off point for exploring the peninsula's east and west coasts, but there's not a lot here to compete with Malaysia's other attractions.

The town's major sight is the **Istana Besar** (⊠ Jln. Tun Dato Ismail), the old palace of the sultans of Johor. This neoclassical, rather institutional-looking building, erected in 1866, has been converted into a museum; it holds hunting trophies as well as ceremonial regalia and ancient weapons. You can see the displays daily 9–5 for RM18. The new sul-tan's palace, the **Istana Bukit Serene** (⊠ Jln. Straits View), was built in 1933 and is noted for its gardens, which are popular with joggers.

Masjid Sultan Abu Bakar (⊠ Jln. Gerstak Merah, off Jln. Tun Dato Is-mail), built in 1890 in European Victorian style, is one of Malaysia's most beautiful mosques, with sparkling white towers and domes sur-rounding the main prayer hall. It can accommodate more than 2,000 worshipers. At the cemetery on Jalan Muhamadiah, the **Sultan Abu Bakar Mausoleum** has been the final resting place for the Johor royal family since it left Singapore. You can't enter the mausoleum, but a number of impressive Muslim tombs surround it.

Dining and Lodging

Although there are smart restaurants at Johor's top hotels, the local favorite dining option is outdoors at one of the Tepian Tebrau food stalls along the seafront on Jalan Skudai. Seafood steamboat is the specialty, but Malay curries and Chinese dishes are also offered.

$$–$$$ ✕ **Straits Garden Seafood.** This popular spot is a short distance (RM5 by taxi) from the center of town. The Filipino band that plays here can be a little exuberant, but you can always ask for a quieter seat near the fishponds. The tiger prawns, either grilled or fried, are expensive but are a must. ✉ *Jln. Skudai,* ☎ *07/237–5788. AE, DC, MC, V. No lunch.*

$$$$ ✕⌂ **Hyatt Regency Johor Bahru.** The grand, modern Hyatt is built on a slight rise facing the Straits of Johor. The mammoth building forms an arc around landscaped gardens through which a two-tier pool meanders. Guest rooms are large (more than 350 square ft) with all the latest technological gadgetry in bedside controls. You can increase the feeling of space by opening the wooden shutter between the bedroom and the spacious bathroom. Four restaurants offer you the choice of Western, Japanese, Szechuan, and Italian cuisine. ✉ *Jln. Sungai Chat (Box 222), 80720,* ☎ *07/222–1234,* FAX *07/223–2718. 400 rooms. 4 restaurants, bar, pool, 2 tennis courts, health club, business services, meeting rooms. AE, DC, MC, V.* ⌨

$$$ ⌂ **Puteri Pan Pacific.** This hotel opened in 1991 adjacent to the Kotaraya Complex—the city's newest and most prestigious office and shopping mall. The design makes use of round, timber-clad columns and colorful batiks in an open-court lobby. Guest rooms, decorated in pastels, are fully equipped with modern amenities. ✉ *Jln. Salim (Box 293), 80000,* ☎ *07/223–3333,* FAX *07/233–6622. 500 rooms. 5 restaurants, in-room safes, pool, business services. AE, DC, MC, V.*

Desaru

43 *94 km (58 mi) east of JB, 436 km (270 mi) southeast of KL.*

Since the west coast of Johor and nearby Singapore have few decent beach resort areas, Desaru was developed to fill the bill. The beach here is, indeed, beautiful (just beware of the dangerous currents), and there's also a seaside golf course. This is an area that has not yet attracted a lot of capital, but the potential is there and further development is planned.

Dining and Lodging

$$$–$$$$ ✕⌂ **Desaru Golden Beach Resort.** At this full-service luxury resort set in seaside gardens, all the rooms have color TVs, VCRs, minibars, and balconies with views of the South China Sea. A wide variety of facilities—including the nation's longest swimming pool—is available, and pickup in Singapore can be arranged. As there's nowhere to eat in Desaru outside the hotels, you can try one of the three establishments here (the Chinese seafood restaurant is noteworthy), or you can walk along the beach to the restaurants at the Desaru Perdana Beach Resort (☞ below). ✉ *Tanjung Penawar (Box 50), Kota Tinggi 81907,* ☎ *07/822–1101,* FAX *07/822–1480. 100 rooms, 4 suites, 116 villas. 3 restaurants, bar, minibars, pool, 4 tennis courts, golf privileges, miniature golf, hiking, beach, dive shop, bicycles, dance club, recreation room, playground, meeting rooms. AE, MC, V.*

$$–$$$ ✕⌂ **Desaru Perdana Beach Resort.** The newest hotel along Desaru's beach, this luxurious resort consists of a series of five-story buildings grouped around a huge pool. Rooms are equipped with all the modern amenities. One on-site restaurant serves international and Malaysian food, another Chinese fare; the third is Desaru's only Japanese restaurant. ✉ *Tanjung Penawar (Box 29), Kota Tinggi 81900,* ☎ *07/822–2222,* FAX *07/822–2223. 188 rooms, 22 suites. 3 restaurants, coffee shop,* *pool, hot tub, sauna, 2 tennis courts, golf privileges, hiking, volleyball, beach, baby-sitting, meeting rooms. AE, MC, V.*

Outdoor Activities and Sports

GOLF

The **Desaru Resort Golf Club** (⊠ Kota Tinggi, ☎ 07/822–2333) is open to guests at all Desaru hotels. It has an undulating 18-hole course designed by Robert Trent Jones, Jr. and made more difficult by strong sea breezes. Greens fees are RM150 on weekends, RM 90 weekdays; caddies cost RM 20.

Pahang

Until relatively recently, Pahang—the largest and arguably the most beautiful state on the peninsula—was isolated from the rest of the country by jungle-covered mountains. Access was by sea and then by plane until the construction of the road (now a highway for most of the distance) across from KL and a coastal road linking it with JB. Most of a huge national park, the Taman Negara, falls within Pahang's boundaries, and there are also miles of glorious beaches and many quaint Malay fishing villages. The lush island of Tioman is part of Pahang (though it's reached via the low-key market town of Mersing in neighboring Johor state), and there are beaches north of Kuantan, the state capital, up through Cherating.

Pulau Tioman

④④ *Two hours by ferry from Mersing, which is 146 km (91 km) north of Desaru, 161 km (100 mi) northeast of JB, and 353 km (218 mi) southeast of KL.*

The largest of the islands off the shore of Mersing (in Johor state) was used as the setting for Bali Hai in the movie *South Pacific*. The mountainous, tropical Pulau Tioman hasn't changed much since then, but virtually every beach now has tourist accommodations. You can sunbathe in sandy coves, swim in clear waters, try the 18-hole international golf course, or walk through jungle-clad hills (the highest is Gunung Kajang at 3,400 ft). In addition, there are plenty of water-sports options (brightly colored fish and coral make for especially enjoyable snorkeling), and you can hire boats and rent bicycles to get around.

Express ferries to Tioman stop at several of its bays; they generally depart in the morning and are dependent on the tide. The trip takes about two hours and costs around RM25–RM30 one-way. Timetables are posted inside the R&R Plaza near the Mersing jetty. Though there are many tour operators around the jetty, **Zaid Mohammed Lazim** (⊠ 17 Jln. Abu Bakar, R&R Plaza, ☎ 07/799–4280) can not only book your ferry ride but also make reservations at the island lodging of your choice. (Note that you can also fly from KL or Singapore to Tioman; for details, ☞ Arriving and Departing *in* The Southern Peninsula and the East Coast A to Z, *below*).

Tioman, although peaceful and quiet by most standards, does get a little busy. For a really quiet haven, check out the other nearby islands. Three of them have resorts with simple bungalow accommodations, including: **Sea Gypsy Village Resort, Pulau Sibu** (☎ 07/222–8642), **Rawa Safarai's Island Resort, Pulau Rawa** (☎ 07/799–1204), and **Radin Resort & Safaris, Pulau Besar** (☎ 07/799–4152).

For boats to other islands, inquire at the tour operator offices on the Mersing jetty or stop by the Mersing Tourist Information Centre (☞ Visitor Information *in* The Southern Peninsula and the East Coast A to Z, *below*) about 400 yards from the wharf. The helpful staffers can provide maps and information and recommend reliable hotels in Mersing and on the islands.

Dining and Lodging

If the room rates at the Berjaya Tioman Beach Resort (☞ *below*) seem too steep, you can drop by to use its facilities but stay at one of the inexpensive chalets around Kampung Tekek and Kampung Air Batang. The best places to eat are inside the various resorts; the only independent restaurant worth mentioning is Liza in the main bay of Tekek just north of the Berjaya resort. Here you'll pay around RM20 for a meal of Western food (slightly more if you order seafood).

$$$$ ✕🏨 **Berjaya Tioman Beach Resort.** A complete renovation in 1993 transformed this property into a full-service hotel and resort complex. Rooms are decorated in soft colors and equipped with TVs and minibars. If the attractive 18-hole golf course and the large pool aren't enough to keep you occupied, the activities desk can arrange pony rides, diving and snorkeling excursions, and boat trips around the island. ⊠ *Box 4, Mersing, Johor 86807,* ☎ *609/419–1000,* ℻ *609/419–1718. 400 rooms. 4 restaurants, 4 bars, coffee shop, pool, 18-hole golf course, 2 tennis courts, dive shop, windsurfing, boating, jet skiing, meeting rooms. AE, MC, V.*

En Route   Although there are numerous traditional kampungs and colorful fishing villages along the east coast between Mersing and Kuantan, the only main town is **Pekan** (107 km/66 mi north of Mersing). It's the home of the sultan, and you can see his modern palace—with its manicured lawns and, of course, its polo field—but only from outside the gates. Don't bypass this town, as the signposts suggest; drive through the center instead. Built on the western shore of a river, it's a delightfully old-fashioned community with two-story shophouses along its main street.

Kuantan

🖑 *177 km (110 mi) northwest of Mersing, 259 km (156 mi) northeast of KL.*

The east coast's major beach and resort area is just north of the state capital, Kuantan (to get here from the capital, take Jalan Teluk Sisek just past the Hotel Suraya). At the sandy, crescent-shape bay of Teluk Chempedak you'll find several hotels, four or five restaurants and bars, discos, and a small but attractive beach. Sunbathers come for the company of other vacationers rather than for solitude. If you prefer privacy, continue a few miles north, where smaller hotels dot a long stretch of virtually untrodden sand.

OFF THE BEATEN PATH   **GUA CHARAH** – Some 25 km (15 mi) into the jungled hills west of Kuantan are the Gua Charah (Pancing Caves). Traveling from Kuantan, you first pass rubber and oil-palm plantations before arriving at the bottom of a small hill. Now comes the hard part: to reach the caves, you must climb 220 steps. Buddhists still live here, and there are many altars. Don't miss the cave with the reclining, 30-ft-long Buddha, carved by a Thai monk who devoted his life to the task.

Dining and Lodging

$$$ ✕🏨 **Hyatt Regency Kuantan.** Here, breezes from the South China Sea
★   blow through lush, cultivated gardens and ripple across two swimming pools just steps from the golden beach. Rooms are in three courts that are also near the shore. It's worth paying the premium rate for a room that faces the sea (rather than one that faces the hills at

the back) so that you can sleep with your balcony doors open to the sounds of the surf. Guest rooms are carpeted and have either king-size or twin beds as well as bathrooms with separate shower stalls. A six-story business wing at the rear of the main hotel has conference rooms and 52 business suites. The Kampung Café is set on stilts facing the sea and is made all the more romantic by candlelight that's reflected off sparkling crystal and silver. The food is a mix of Malay and European; the seafood dishes are the best. ⊠ *Teluk Chempedak, Pahang Darul Makmur 25730,* ☎ *09/566–1234,* ℻ *09/567–7577. 275 rooms, 52 suites. 3 restaurants, café, 2 pools, sauna, golf privileges, 3 tennis courts, exercise room, squash, beach, dance club, business services, meeting rooms. AE, MC, V.* ⊗

$–$$ 🏠 **De Rhu Beach Resort.** Set on endless sands along the South China Sea, this modern resort hotel has a wide-open lobby and a clientele of both business-seminar participants in shirts and ties and bathing suit–clad sun worshipers. At night, both types of guests relax in the bars or the disco. Guest rooms have utilitarian furnishings, king-size or twin beds, and adequate bathrooms. A light-filled coffee shop serves Malay and European fare, and there's a Japanese restaurant. ⊠ *152 Sungai Karang, Beserah 26100,* ☎ *603/4142–6661,* ℻ *603/4142–3331. 162 rooms. 2 restaurants, 2 bars, coffee shop, 2 pools, 2 tennis courts, health club, squash, beach, dance club, meeting rooms. AE, DC, MC, V.* ⊗

$ 🏠 **Tanjung Gelang Motel.** This small, Chinese-owned establishment has simple chalets that face the beach and are packed rather tightly together. The motel's main advantage is its price (RM80–RM100 a night); there are no frills, just the basics and a small restaurant that serves Chinese and European food. Still, the De Rhu Beach Resort and all its facilities are right next door. ⊠ *Jln. Kemaman (Km 15), Pahang Darul Makmur 26100,* ☎ *09/544–7254,* ℻ *09/544–7388. 48 rooms. Restaurant. AE, MC, V.*

Cherating

46 *30 km (18 mi) northeast of Kuantan, 289 km (175 mi) northeast of KL.*

Half an hour's drive north of Kuantan is the peaceful village of Cherating, a rustic haven for beachcombing along miles of white, clean beaches that are fanned by gentle breezes rustling through the coconut trees. Club Med was one of the first to stake its claim on a fine stretch of sand here, responding to the spirit of the place with its Malay-style bungalows built on stilts. Since then, numerous resorts have sprung up along the main highway, but they always seem to have more than enough empty rooms to offer good discounts.

Opportunities for turtle-watching—one of the east coast's most popular attractions—begin at Cherating and continue north. The best viewing place is said to be Chendor Beach, an hour north of Kuantan or 20 minutes up from Cherating. Most nights between May and September (the peak month is August), enormous leatherback turtles slowly make their way ashore to lay around 100 eggs each. Signs at the hotels will tell when and where to go, and the crowds do gather to watch as the 1,000-pound turtles laboriously dig their "nests" before settling down to their real work.

OFF THE BEATEN PATH **TASIK CHINI –** Drive inland from Cherating for an hour, then hop on a boat for a 40-minute ride to this tranquil and beautiful lake. You'll see wild orchids, monkeys, squirrels, lizards, and birds and visit an Orang Asli village. Contact any local tour agent to arrange a trip.

Dining and Lodging

$$$$ ✕🏨 **Club Med Cherating.** This Malaysian-style Club Med village is on its own bay, surrounded by 200 acres of parkland. Accommodation is in twin-bedded bungalows with air-conditioning and showers. As with all Club Meds, use of all sports facilities and participation in such activities as arts-and-crafts workshops are included in the price, as are buffet-style meals. The resort was refurbished in 1994 and is quieter and more low-key than the Club Meds found in the Caribbean. ✉ *Jln. Kuantan–Kemaman (Km 29), 26080,* ☎ *09/581–9131 or 03/261–4599 in KL,* ℻ *09/581–9524. 600 rooms. 2 restaurants, pool, 6 tennis courts, aerobics, archery, exercise room, squash, beach, windsurfing, children's programs. AE, MC, V. All-inclusive.* 🏊

$$$$ ✕🏨 **Impiana Resort Cherating.** This low-rise sprawl of modern luxury on 32 acres at the edge of Cherating's beach offers you more independence than Club Med. The vast lobby, flooded by natural light and cooled by sea breezes, is the focal point. Beyond is the two-tier pool, and beyond that the sea. You can have Malay, Chinese, or Western food from the three restaurants or try a little of everything at the evening buffet. Standard rooms are in the main building; there are also two-bedroom suites. Most guest quarters face the sea, and all have four-poster wooden beds, ceiling fans, and air-conditioning. For recreation, there's a fully equipped water-sports center. ✉ *Km 32, Jln. Kuantan–Kemaman, Cherating, Pahang 26080,* ☎ *09/581–9000,* ℻ *09/581–9090. 108 rooms, 7 suites. 3 restaurants, bar, beach, jet skiing, meeting rooms. AE, DC, MC, V.* 🏊

$$ ✕🏨 **Cherating Holiday Villa Beach Resort.** From the central building that houses the reception and dining area, buildings fan out toward the beach, enclosing a pool and gardens. The structures vary, with each taking some architectural aspect, usually a roof style, from a different region of Malaysia. Rooms are equally diverse: from modern, Western-style accommodations to chalets designed in the Malay style with bare, wooden floors and a minimum of furniture. Most are wood-paneled, with sliding glass doors facing the pool (rooms on the second floor offer more privacy). The restaurant serves dinners that are a mix of Italian-inspired fare and Malay cooking; a beach barbecue is held twice a week. ✉ *Lot 1303, Mukim Sungei Karang, 26080,* ☎ *09/581–9500 or 03/2162–2922 in KL,* ℻ *09/581–9178 or 03/2162–2937 in KL. 94 rooms. 2 restaurants, coffee shop, 2 pools, 3 tennis courts, badminton, exercise room, squash. AE, MC, V.* 🏊

$ 🏨 **Cherating Beach Mini-Hotel.** If your reason for staying in Cherating is beachcombing, then this budget hotel is perfect. The chalets are very small and sparsely furnished, but the beach is at the front door. The staff is wonderfully low-key and friendly, and the restaurant does its best to cook up European food (though it's better at Malaysian dishes). ✉ *Batu 28 Kampung, Jln. Kemaman, 26080,* ☎ *09/581–9335,* ℻ *09/581–9352. 20 chalets. Restaurant. No credit cards.*

Taman Negara

176 km (109 mi) from Kuantan to Jerantut, 250 km (155 mi) northeast of KL.

Malaysia's oldest protected area, Taman Negara (National Park), sprawls across the borders of Pahang, Terengganu, and Kelantan states, roughly in the center of the Malay peninsula. Covering 4,343 square km (1,677 square mi), the park is where a large percentage of the peninsula's plant and animal life is protected. Access is by road or rail to Kuala Tembeling or Jerantut, and then a three-hour boat ride to the headquarters area at Kuala Tahan. Within the park, you can trek, explore the rain forest by canoe, stay overnight to watch for mammals, or go fishing.

The best accommodation in the park is the privately run **Taman Negara Resort** (☎ 09/266–3500, FAX 09/266–1500) where the luxurious two-story, two-bedroom bungalows have their own kitchens and balconies and go for almost RM600 per night; less expensive are the twin-bed chalets with attached bathrooms for RM201. You can make reservations through the resort itself or through MATIC in KL (☞ Visitor Information *in* Kuala Lumpur A to Z, *above*).

Terengganu

The sultanate of Terengganu, like that of Kelantan to the north, paid annual tribute to Siam (Thailand) until it came under British control in 1909. Separated from the western part of the peninsula by jungle-covered mountains, Terengganu state remained a peaceful backwater with an overwhelming Malay population largely engaged in fishing and small-scale agriculture until the discovery of petroleum a couple of decades ago.

The recent establishment of several luxurious coastal and inland resorts, an increase in the number of accommodations and scuba facilities on the offshore islands, and the gradual development of Lake Kenyir as an ecotourism destination all make a visit to Terengganu less of a challenge than it used to be. Its endless beautiful beaches where giant sea turtles come ashore to lay their eggs, its exquisite coral-girt islands, its traditional villages and handicrafts, and its jungled interior are more accessible than ever before.

Rantau Abang

㊼ *150 km (93 mi) northwest of Kuantan, 399 km (211 mi) northeast of KL.*

Not so much a village as a scattering of guest houses along the coastal road, the protected, 10-km (6-mi) stretch of beach of Rantau Abang is one of the places where the giant leatherback turtle comes ashore to lay its eggs (between May and September each year). These magnificent and endangered turtles lumber ashore after dark to dig a hole and deposit around 100 eggs in the sand. They then cover the hole and head back to sea, leaving the eggs to hatch around 50 to 60 days later. These eggs are transferred to protected hatcheries, and when the baby turtles emerge, they're transferred to the beach to begin their watery existence. Amazingly, the hatchlings will return to exactly the same spot some 20 years later to breed and repeat the cycle.

The **Turtle Information Centre** has a video and other displays relating to the turtles. Admission to the center is free, and it's open May–August, Saturday–Thursday 9–1, 2–6, and 8–1, and Friday 9–12 and 3–11; from September to April, the hours are daily 8–12:45 and 2–4.

Lodging

$$$$ 🏨 **Tanjong Jara Resort.** The finest place to stay in the area, this award-
★ winning resort serves up beautiful views of the beach, the South China Sea, and landscaped tropical gardens. The rooms are large and intricately designed using native timbers. This is an experience that is unmistakably Malay with a touch of sheer luxury. ✉ *Batu 8, Off Jln. Dungun Terengganu, 23000,* ☎ *609/845–1100,* FAX *609/845–1200. 100 rooms. 2 restaurants, snack bar, 2 pools, massage, 2 tennis courts, priviliges, windsurfing, boating, dive shop, fishing, business services. AE, V, DC, MC www.tanjongjararesort.com.*

$$ 🏨 **Awana Kijal Beach & Golf Resort.** Roughly 60 km (37 mi) south of Rantau Abang, this huge beachfront resort has plenty of activities—from golf to arts-and-crafts workshops. (If you're seeking peace and quiet, try elsewhere—especially during school holidays.) The lobby soars up to an impressive height, but despite allusions to classical Malay architecture, the decor and furnishings throughout are of questionable taste. Most rooms face the sea, although they don't have balconies. ⊠ *Jln. Kemaman-Dungun (Km 28), 24100,* ☎ *09/864–1188 or 03/200–6288 in KL,* ℻ *09/864–1688. 268 rooms. 5 restaurants, 2 bars, pool, wading pool, 18-hole golf course, tennis court, health club, Ping-Pong, beach, snorkeling, fishing, playground, business services, meeting rooms. AE, DC, MC, V.* 🐾

Kuala Terengganu

48 *209 km (130 mi) north of Kuantan, 162 km (101 mi) north of Cherating, 455 km (282 mi) northeast of KL.*

Kuala Terengganu, the state capital, is basically a big village trying to get used to being a town. Giant mango trees shade old, wooden houses with terra-cotta roofs. Next to such houses sit modern office blocks constructed with the wealth provided by the petrochemical industry.

The true heart of the town is the **Central Market,** where a fascinating array of fresh and dried produce is sold on the ground floor. This is where you'll find *keropok lekur,* a local specialty made of pureed fish and sago flour that's boiled or deep fried. (Keropok is also dried into wafers that can later be fried to a crisp; buy a packet to take home.) Upstairs in the market there's a collection of tiny shops where you can bargain for batik, kitchen implements, and local handicrafts; there are also food stalls that serve tasty, inexpensive Malay cuisine.

Near the market is a jetty where boats leave for **Pulau Duyung,** a large island in the Terengganu estuary famous for its traditional boat building. Recent completion of a bridge makes it easier than ever to get there. Opposite the jetty, on Jalan Sultan Zainal Abidin, you'll find a complex of traditional buildings, including the **Terengganu Tourist Information Centre** (☞ Visitor Information *in* The Southern Peninsula and the East Coast A to Z, *below*), beside some souvenir shops. You can pick up a range of brochures and get helpful advice here.

One of the few old sights in town is **Bukit Puteri** (Princess Hill), where the remains of a fort and several cannons can be seen atop the small hill. You pay RM1 to climb the stone steps at the side of the tourism office; unfortunately, it closes daily at 5:45 PM, too early to see the sunset. Around the corner from Bukit Puteri, on Jalan Masjid Abidin, is the attractive **Istana Maziah,** the sultan's old palace, now used only for ceremonial functions (the new, architecturally uninteresting palace is on the main road south). Completed in 1903, Istana Maziah and its grounds are closed to the public, but you get a good view of it from the road.

The small **Chinatown** of this overwhelmingly Malay community (it's one of the very few in the country where Malays predominate) is basically one street, Jalan Bandar. Walk along this road, which runs to one side of the Central Market, and notice the beautiful old houses and shops, particularly Number 151. This attractive building with faded decorative tiles is the home of Teratai, a shop with a good range of arts and crafts. Down the street, the small Chinese temple of Ho Ang Kong, dedicated to a fishing god, is picturesque and serene.

If you have time for only one sight in Kuala Terengganu, then it must be the **Terengganu State Museum,** 5 km (3 mi) southwest of the town center. A taxi trip (RM7) or bus ride (50 sen) takes you through the still-charming district of Kampung Losong to the museum complex. Set in landscaped gardens on the Terengganu River, the main part of the museum is housed in four large blocks that cleverly echo the traditional style of a Terengganu house. You might want to bypass several of the 10 galleries, but don't miss the Bangunan Utama (Main Building), where there are displays of textiles, traditional clothing, handicrafts, and royal regalia.

Located nearer the river is a **fisheries museum** (where you can see some lovely old carved and painted canoes); a **maritime museum** (check out the two huge wooden boats permanently beached on the lawn); and a group of magnificent old wooden houses reconstructed in the gardens. The finest of these is the **Istana Tengku Long,** built in 1888 and constructed entirely without nails. The curving roof gables have gilded wooden screens, carved with verses from the Koran. The istana and other houses are often closed, but if you ask, the security guard will open them so you can look around inside. ⊠ *Bukit Losong,* ☎ *09/ 622–1444.* ⊠ *RM5.* ☉ *Sat.–Thurs. 10–6, Fri. 10–12 and 3–6.*

Dining and Lodging
There are surprisingly few restaurants in Kuala Terengganu, apart from a few Indian Muslim places downtown. Your best bet is to eat in one of the two major hotels.

$$$ ✕☵ **Primula Parkroyal Hotel.** This premier hotel is right on the beach less than a mile from the town center. The spacious, carpeted rooms have all the modern conveniences, and most have small verandas. The pool area and gardens are very attractive, and recreational activities are organized daily. The hotel also counts a medical clinic among its amenities. The Rhusila Coffee House offers buffets for breakfast, lunch, and dinner, as well as an interesting à la carte menu with local and Western dishes. Try a steamboat or a pizza at the casual poolside Pelangi restaurant. ⊠ *Jln. Persingahan (Box 43), 20904,* ☎ *09/622– 2100,* ℻ *09/623–3360. 249 rooms. 2 restaurants, bar (no alcohol served), pool, beach, bicycles, shops, children's programs, business services, meeting rooms. AE, DC, MC, V.*

$$ ✕☵ **Yen Tin Midtown Hotel.** As its name implies, this hotel offers comfortable, well-equipped rooms right in the center of town. The Midtown Cafe on the second level is famous for its roti jala and its ulam. Likewise, if you hanker for a steak or fish-and-chips you won't find better in the area, but they do not serve alcohol. ⊠ *Jln. Tok Lam, 20100,* ☎ *09/623–5288,* ℻ *09/623–4399. 144 rooms. Restaurant, business services, meeting rooms. AE, DC, MC, V.*

$$$$ ☵ **Aryani.** If you want a tiny patch of paradise where the most strenuous activity is taking in a dip in the pool to the sounds of a live gamelan orchestra, head 45 km (28 mi) north of Kuala Terengganu to the Aryani, outside the village of Merang (not to be confused with Marang, south of Kuala Terengganu). Owned and designed by a member of the Terengganu royal family, this resort is a blissful combination of pavilions, gardens, lotus ponds, discreetly situated villas, and white-sand beach. It's all reminiscent of a small resort on Bali, and indeed, you'll find Indonesian as well as local handicrafts used in the decor. The hotel's spa is in a restored, century-old Malay house; a traditional Malay body massage here is a must. If you crave activity, you can rent a bike or ask the staff to arrange a diving or snorkeling expedition to nearby Pulau Redang or a trip to Lake Kenyir, the Sekayu Falls, or the museum in Kuala Terengganu. ⊠ *Jln. Rhu Tapai-Merang, 21010,* ☎ *09/ 653–2111 or 03/269–6410 in KL,* ℻ *09/653–1007. 40 rooms. 3 restaurants, pool, spa, beach, library. AE, DC, MC, V.*

Outdoor Activities and Sports
Situated on the edge of the largest man-made lake in Southeast Asia, **Tasik Kenyir Golf Resort** (☎ 609/666–8888, ℻ 609/666–8889, ⚐) is a slice of heaven about 80 km (50 mi) inland from Kuala Terengganu.

The golf course is on an island and patrons are ferried over by boat. When you've had enough golf, take advantage of the surrounding lake area and fish, boat, swim, or trek through the rain forest. Accommodation at the resort is in Malay style chalets set among the trees—it's 100 to 110 RM per person per night, golf included.

Pulau Besar, Pulau Kecil, and Pulau Redang

Pulau Redang is 50 km (31 mi) off the coast from Merang; Pulau Besar and Pulau Kecil are 21 km (13 mi) off the coast from Kuala Besut.

Scattering the waters of the South China Sea—from Terengganu's border with Kelantan state down almost to Pahang—islands with white-sand beaches, limpid waters, and coral reefs beckon. Owing to the strong winds, rain, and rough seas during the year-end northeast monsoon, the season for visiting these islands is from March to October. Facilities for snorkeling and scuba diving are available at all the major hotels.

Accessible from the village of Merang, which is 40 km (25 mi) north of Kuala Terengganu, **Pulau Redang** is about two hours by boat from the coast. Redang (which is composed of Redang, Pulau Pinang, and seven islets) is part of a marine park, but this hasn't protected its once-tranquil villages, forest, and bays. Trees were felled and hilltops were bulldozed to create a nine-hole golf course, and villagers have been relocated to make room for new resorts. Although Redang still offers excellent scuba diving and snorkeling, it's no longer an untouched tropical paradise.

The **Perhentian Islands** are a 1½-hour boat ride from Kuala Besut, 123 km (76 mi) north of Kuala Terengganu. Part of a marine park, Perhentian is composed of two islands, Besar (Big) and Kecil (Little), each with a scattering of simple villages and range of accommodations.

Lodging

$$$$ 🏨 **Berjaya Redang Beach Resort.** Situated at Pulau Redang's northernmost bay, this resort has an exquisite beach of powdery-white sands lapped by turquoise waters. Unfortunately, the chalets are crowded too closely together for privacy. Still, the rooms are air-conditioned and have all the facilities you'd expect of a top hotel, including TVs with VCRs. The hotel also operates its own ferry service to and from Merang. ✉ *Teluk Dalam Kecil (Box 126, Main Post Office), 20928,* ☎ *09/697–3988 or 03/242–9611 in KL,* FAX *09/697–3899 or 03/245–5408 in KL. 152 rooms. 2 restaurants, 3 bars, pool, tennis court, hiking, volleyball, beach, dive shop, snorkeling, meeting rooms. AE, DC, MC, V.*

$$ 🏨 **Perhentian Island Resort.** This Pulau Besar resort offers the least cramped and most tasteful accommodations of any hotel on Terengganu's islands. On a private beach backed by jungle you'll find comfortable chalets, each with four, twin bed–equipped rooms. The hotel has its own ferry service to the mainland. ✉ *Teluk Pauh,* ☎ *010/903–0100 or 03/244–8530 in KL,* FAX *03/243–4984 in KL. (Mailing address: Menara Promet, 22nd floor, Jln. Sultan Ismail, Kuala Lumpur 50250). 106 rooms. Restaurant, pool, tennis court, volleyball, beach, dive shop, snorkeling, windsurfing. AE, DC, MC, V.*

The Southern Peninsula and the East Coast A to Z

Arriving and Departing

By Airplane

Senai Airport (☎ 07/599–4500) is 25 km (16 mi) north of JB (there are air-conditioned buses into the city). MAS offers direct flights to JB from KL, Pinang, Kota Kinabalu (Sabah), and Kuching (Sarawak). MAS flies into **Sultan Ahmad Shah Airport** (☎ 09/538–2023), 15 km (9 mi) west of Kuantan from KL and Kuala Terengganu; SilkAir flies in from Singapore. **Sultan Mahmud Airport** (☎ 09/666–4201) is 13 km (8 mi) northwest of Kuala Terengganu and has direct flight service from KL and Kuantan. **Kerteh Airport** (☎ 09/666–3062) serves the town of Kerteh and surrounding petrochemical industrial estates and is 12 km (7 mi) from the Awana Kijal Resort south of Rantau Abang. **Pulau Tioman** (☎ 09/419–1395) has a small airport at Kampung Tekek; MAS has service from KL and Kuantan; SilkAir flies from Singapore.

By Boat

The ferry between Dumai (on Sumatra in Indonesia) and Melaka takes four hours, costs RM80, one way, and RM150 round-trip. It departs (usually) everyday at 10 AM. Citizens of Canada, the United States, and the United Kingdom don't need a visa to enter Indonesia. Boats to Tioman and other islands off Mersing run from the Mersing jetty; you can find the latest timetables and make reservations at Mersing's R&R Plaza or at ticket offices belonging to the individual resorts—all are near the jetty. An express ferry from Pulau Tioman to Singapore is operated by **Tioman Island Resort Ferries** (☎ 65/271–4866 in Singapore).

By Bus

Johor Bahru, as the southern end of the line for peninsular Malaysia, has comprehensive, efficient, and inexpensive bus service. Departures are frequent from the main terminal, which is 3 km (2 mi) north of town, and both air-conditioned and non-air-conditioned buses are available. Bus 170 makes the run across the causeway between Johor Bahru and Singapore.

Melaka is served by frequent express buses from KL's Puduraya Terminal (☞ Arriving and Departing by Bus *in* Kuala Lumpur A to Z, *above*); the trip costs RM7. There are also frequent direct buses—so many that you don't need to book in advance—to Singapore. Express buses also link Kuantan with KL, JB, and Kuala Terengganu. Kuala Terengganu has express service to Ipoh, KL, JB, Kuantan, and Kota Bharu; these operate out of the Central Bus Station at Jalan Syed Hussain.

By Car

The North–South Expressway between KL and JB bypasses Seremban and Melaka, though exits for these towns are clearly indicated. An expressway from KL toward Kuantan goes as far as Karak, where it's replaced by a regular two-lane roadway. The coastal road north from Kuantan to Kuala Terengganu is well marked, mainly straight and easy to follow.

By Taxi

Either privately chartered or shared taxis between major destinations are a good proposition (a private charter fare is four times as much as a shared fare). You can pick up what's known as an "outstation taxi" from cab stands next to the bus stations in all major Malaysian towns. A chartered taxi from KL to Melaka costs approximately RM80– RM90. A round-trip will cost slightly less than twice the one-way fare, but a KL taxi driver is unlikely to know his way around Melaka. Cabs to Kuantan from KL cost around RM140, from JB, RM120. From Kuantan to Kuala Terengganu by shared taxi will cost RM20.

By Train

As train service to the south and the east coast is far less frequent, much slower, and more expensive than buses or long-distance taxis (especially since the completion of the North–South Highway), it's not worth using except for perhaps KL–JB trips. Melaka doesn't have a train station, but you can get off in Tampin, 38 km (24 mi) north of the city and take a taxi into town (about RM3). For information, call **Malayan Railways,** (☎ 06/282–3091) also known as KTM, or the **Tampin train station** (☎ 06/441–1034).

Getting Around

By Trishaw

In Melaka, the best way to get around the historical area is on foot or by trishaw, which will cost you a minimum of RM5 and around RM20 per hour. You can also take a trishaw in Kuala Terengganu. In all other towns, a local taxi will be both inexpensive (RM5 for about 3 km/2 mi) and efficient.

By Car

You can rent cars at the following places throughout the region: **Kuantan: Orix Car Rental** (⊠ Kuantan airport, ☎ 09/538–8394) and **Mayflower Car Rental** (⊠ Kuantan airport, ☎ 09/538–3490).

Melaka: Hawk (⊠ 126 Jln. Bendahara, ☎ 06/283–7878).

Johor Bahru: Budget (⊠ Senai Airport, ☎ 07/598–1625) and **Hertz** (⊠ Johor Information Centre, ☎ 07/222–3591).

Kuala Terengganu: Kapas Rent A Car (⊠ Kuala Terengganu Airport, ☎ 018/896–6676; 101/983–3103 [mobile-phone numbers]); Primula Parkroyal Hotel, ☎ 09/622–2100), **Orix Car Rental** (⊠ Kuantan Airport, ☎ 09/538–3894), and **Kijal Travel & Tours** (⊠ Awana Kijal Beach & Golf Resort, Km 28 Jln. Kemamam-Dungun, ☎ 09/864–1188).

Contacts and Resources

Emergencies

Ambulance and Police: ☎ 999. **Fire:** ☎ 994. Hospitals and Clinics: **Johor Public Hospital** (☎ 07/223–1666); **Kuantan Public Hospital** (☎ 09/513–3333); or **Melaka Public Hospital** (☎ 06/556–2333). **Scuba-Diving Accidents:** The only decompression chamber on the peninsula is at the Malaysian Navy Base in Lumut, on the coast near Ipoh. Dive masters should be able to fill you in on emergency procedures.

English-Language Bookstores

Books and magazines in English are very limited outside hotel sundry shops in this region. In Melaka, the long-established **Lim Brothers** (⊠ Jln. Laksamana, ☎ 06/282–3866) has some pleasant surprises. You'll find the best selection at **MPH** (⊠ Mahkota Parade shopping complex, ☎ 06/283–2960), also in Melaka. JB also has a branch of **MPH** (⊠ Plangi Leisure Mall, Jln. Serampang, ☎ 07/335–2672).

Tour Operators and Travel Agencies

Most of the tour operators cited below can help you make general travel arrangements including airline reservations and hotel bookings. Several companies organize day trips to Melaka from KL in an air-conditioned limousine (RM250–RM300) or by bus (about RM70). These may be arranged through most hotels. The best-known tour guide in Melaka is **Robert Tan Sin Nyen** (⊠ 256-D Jln. Parameswara, ☎ 06/284–4857). You can take a 45- or 90-minute **river tour** (☎ 06/283–6538) of the city from the dock on Jalan Quayside.

In Kuantan, tour operators include **East Coast Holidays** (⊠ No. 13, Telok Cempedak, 25050, ☎ 09/566–5228 or 09/567–3228, FAX 09/567–5223), **E.C.P.** (☎ 09/581–9535), and **Jelai Holiday** (☎ 09/513–9862). **Kijal Travel & Tours** (⊠ Awana Kijal Beach & Golf Resort, Km 28, Jln. Kemamam-Dungun, ☎ 09/864–1064) offers fishing and snorkeling trips, handicraft and shopping tours, treks to Sekayu Falls, and nighttime turtle-watching forays to the Rantau Abang area. **Kapas Travel & Tours** (✉ Primula Parkroyal Hotel, ☎ 09/622–2100) offers a range of city tours in Kuala Terengganu; day trips to Sekayu Falls, Lake Kenyir, and Pulau Kapas; and turtle-watching, fishing, scuba diving, and boating excursions.

Visitor Information
MTPB (✉ Tun Abdul Razak Complex, ground floor, Jln. Wong Ah Fook, JB, ☎ 07/222–3591). **Melaka Tourist Information Center** (✉ Jln. Kota, ☎ 06/283–6538). **Mersing Tourist Information Centre** (✉ 1 Jln. Abu Bakar, ☎ 07/799–5212). **Pahang Tourist Information Centre** (✉ Jln. Mahkota, Kuantan, ☎ 09/517–1623). **Terengganu Tourist Information Centre** (✉ Jln. Sultan Zainal Abidin, Kuala Terengganu, ☎ 09/622–1553).

NORTHERN BORNEO

Until the period of colonial expansion in the 18th and 19th centuries, the Sultan of Brunei held sway over all of northern Borneo. However, with the granting of Sarawak to James Brooke (the first "white rajah"), and the sale of the northern tip of Borneo (Sabah) to the British North Borneo Company, the lines on the map were redrawn. Today, Brunei consists of two tiny pieces of land surrounded by Sarawak, with Sabah adjoining Sarawak's northern border. The eastern and southern borders of Sarawak adjoin Kalimantan, the Indonesian portion of the island of Borneo. Although both Sarawak and Sabah became part of Malaysia, Brunei has remained an independent sultanate.

Sarawak

Sarawak's modern history began in 1841 after an English adventurer, James Brooke, was formally ceded land around the Sarawak River in exchange for settling a rebellion against the local rajah, an uncle of the Sultan of Brunei. Raja Brooke instituted a benevolent family regency that lasted until the Japanese occupation during World War II. Sarawak then became a British colony as the Brookes could not afford to restore it following the war. In 1963, the Federation of Malaysia was formed by the incorporation of Malaya with Sarawak and Sabah (Singapore was initially part of Malaysia, but left after two years). Sarawak, like neighboring Sabah, was permitted to retain a number of special rights, including control over immigration.

The native peoples of Sarawak are ethnically different from those of the peninsula, and the Chinese who have settled here are better integrated, often through intermarriage with non-Muslim natives. Although proud to be Malaysians, the peoples of Sarawak have a very strong sense of their unique history and identity. Despite the fact that modern trappings such as generators and satellite TV have reached far into the interior, many tribespeople still live in communal wooden longhouses, with as many as 60 or even 100 families—entire villages, really—under one roof.

Sarawak is Malaysia's largest state, with some 1.9 million people inhabiting its 124,450 square km (48,342 square mi). Almost 500,000 live around the capital city of Kuching, a pleasant, fairly modern town that still retains many of its Victorian buildings and Chinese shophouses. Some 30% of Sarawak's population is Iban, 27% is Chinese, and 20% is Malay; the rest is a mixture of indigenous ethnic groups. As in Sabah, Christians outnumber Muslims.

Sarawak's principal attractions are its magnificent national parks—particularly Gunung Mulu with its spectacular caves, and the archaeo-

Northern Borneo

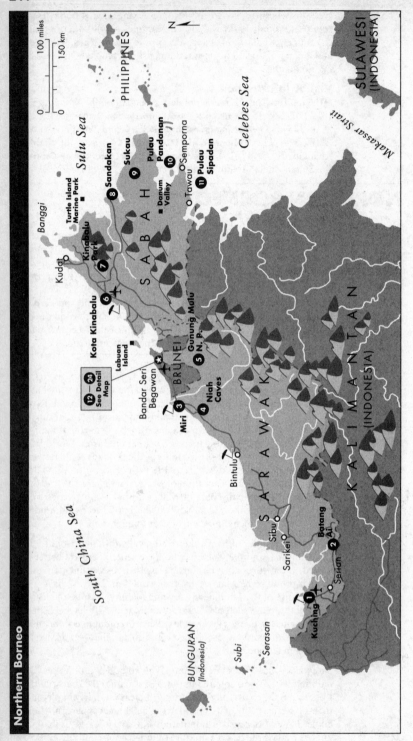

logically important Niah Caves National Park—as well as the native longhouses. Some tour operators have built comfortable lodges adjacent to upriver longhouses, so you can stay overnight and learn about the lifestyle and culture of the local people without sacrificing too many creature comforts.

Kuching

● *920 km (575 mi) southeast of KL, 832 km (520 mi) southwest of Kota Kinabalu.*

Kuching is one of the most charming cities in the region, and a walk around the Old Town near the river will give you some feeling for its history. You'll note the gentle, unhurried pace as you stroll along the landscaped waterfront, which runs along the Sarawak River and has benches, food stalls, gardens, and a small stage where performances are often held. The lookout tower at the upriver end of the waterfront affords a fine view of downtown Kuching and the surrounding countryside.

One of the finest Brooke-era buildings is the white courthouse, completed in 1874. Topped by ironwood shingles, the building has shady verandas and Romanesque columns; the clock tower was added in 1883. Behind the courthouse on Jalan Tun Haji Openg stands the pavilion, a pleasant architectural mishmash that's being transformed into a costume and textile museum. Opposite, the post office is an attractive building with Corinthian columns.

At the downriver end of the waterfront, next to the Kuching Hilton, is the town's oldest building. At the 1843 **Tua Pek Kong** Chinese temple, you can watch worshipers lighting incense and making paper offerings. This temple is on a site considered highly auspicious by the Chinese, where the Mata Kuching River, after which the city was named, once flowed into the Sarawak River (the Mata Kuching has long since disappeared into a drainage tunnel).

★ A stroll through the waterfront's **main bazaar** takes you past curio and antiques shops where you can find everything from a beaded Dayak baby carrier to a strand of old beads. Wonderful for basketwork, wood carvings, and souvenirs, the bazaar also has fascinating old coffee shops, stores that sell such items as processed birds' nests and Sarawak pepper, and old-style provision shops.

The small streets off the bazaar lead to **Jalan Carpenter,** the heart of Kuching's Chinatown. Here you'll find a couple of interesting temples, some restaurants and food stalls, and a number of goldsmiths and other artisans.

Across the river is **Ft. Margherita,** built in 1879 by Rajah Charles Brooke (James Brooke's nephew). Take a quaint *tambang* (river taxi) across and explore the fort, which now houses a rather funky police museum displaying cannons and other weapons as well as memorabilia from the Communist insurgency that threatened Sarawak in the '60s and '70s. A little upriver from Ft. Margherita sits the **Astana,** built in 1870 as Charles Brooke's palace. Consisting of three bungalows, complete with military ramparts and a tower, the Astana is now the official residence of Sarawak's head of state and isn't open to the public.

★ The highlight of Kuching is the comprehensive and beautifully curated **Sarawak Museum.** In the original building, opened in 1891, there are exhibits of local insects and butterflies, sea creatures, birds, and other wildlife, as well as displays on body tattoos, burial items, face masks, and carvings. In the newer building across the road, you'll find temporary exhibitions downstairs, as well as an excellent selection of books inside the souvenir shop. Upstairs are reproductions of the dwellings of Sarawak's different ethnic groups (including several longhouses) that are full of artifacts. There's also a model of the Niah Caves and a good collection of ceramics and beads. ⊠ *Jln. Tun Haji Openg,* ☎ *082/244232.* 🎫 *Free.* ⊙ *Daily 9–6.*

The award-winning **Sarawak Cultural Village** at Damai Beach (☞ Outdoor Activities and Sports, *below*), contains the life-size dwellings of seven major Sarawak ethnic groups, all set in a lovely garden at the foot of Mt. Santubong. People from the different communities live and work in the various longhouses, farmhouses, or kampung dwellings, and they give demonstrations of such things as woodcarving, cooking local cakes, weaving, or using a blowpipe. Entrance to the village includes admittance to a cultural show with lively dances. A restaurant serves local dishes, and there's a good souvenir shop where you can buy CDs of tribal music. ⊠ *Santubong,* ☎ *082/422411.* 🎫 *RM45.* ⊙ *Daily 9–5; cultural shows daily at 11:30 and 4:30.*

Bako National Park is close enough to Kuching (a mere 37 km/23 mi northeast by road, followed by a 20-minute boat ride) for a day trip; all tour operators offer such packages. If you have the time, however, it's worth staying overnight; accommodations range from hostels to comfortable chalets, and there's a basic restaurant and a small store. Despite being the smallest national park in Sarawak, Bako has many natural sights: mangrove swamps, rain forests, proboscis monkeys, carnivorous pitcher plants, wonderfully sculpted rock formations known as the Sea Stacks, and a beautiful beach. Before going, book your lodgings and obtain an entry permit at the visitor center next to the Sarawak Museum in Kuching. ☞ Visitor Information *in* Northern Borneo A to Z, *below*). 🎫 *RM3.* ⊙ *Weekdays 8–4, Sat. 8–12:45.*

Dining and Lodging

$$ ✕ **Beijing Riverbank.** The food here—light refreshments and drinks downstairs, a more elaborate Cantonese and Western menu upstairs— is acceptable. What really draws people to this modest building shaped like a Bidayuh tribal head house is its location overlooking the river. ⊠ *Kuching Waterfront,* ☎ *082/234126. MC, V.*

$$ ✕ **Lok Thian.** This large restaurant is renowned for its gourmet Chinese food, including Cantonese barbecue. The ground floor has a Thai restaurant; Chinese and Japanese food are served upstairs. ⊠ *319 Jln. Padungan,* ☎ *082/331310. AE, DC, V.*

$$ ✕ **Tsui Hua Lau.** Better for a Chinese banquet than a dinner for two, this brightly lighted, two-story restaurant has an extensive menu with Cantonese, Szechuan, and Shanghainese fare. The unusual entrées include braised turtle, sea cucumber, and bird's nest soup. The barbecued duck and Szechuan-style shredded beef meet high standards. ⊠ *22 Ban Hock Rd.,* ☎ *082/414560. AE, DC, V.*

$ ✕ **Topspot Food Court.** Don't miss the chance to eat as the locals do in the somewhat unlikely setting of the landscaped roof of a parking garage. Clean and brightly lighted during the evening, the food court has stalls that serve a wide range of cuisines, including several with excellent fresh seafood. Choose your own fish or prawns and specify how you want them cooked. There are also Chinese clay-pot specials (food slow-cooked in an earthenware pot) and Malay satay. ⊠ *Top floor of parking garage on Jln. Bukit Mata Kuching,* ☎ *no phone. No credit cards.*

$$–$$$ ✕🏨 **Holiday Inn Kuching.** The first international hotel in Kuching enjoys an unrivaled location right on the river. The rooms are compact, with standard amenities. The view of the road is rather dreary, so request a room with a river view. The Executive Floor has rooms with

locally inspired furnishings and a shared lounge with a splendid view of the river. The gaudily decorated Meisan Szechuan restaurant serves spicy Szechuan fare; you'll also find a variety of dim sum at its popular Sunday brunch (reservations essential). Note that if you'd like to trade an in-town lifestyle for one at the seashore, you can make arrangements to split your stay between this property and one of the two Holiday Inns on Damai Beach (☞ *below*). ⊠ *Jln. Tuanku Abdul Rahman (Box 2362), 93100,* ☎ *082/423111, 800/HOLIDAY in the U.S., or 0171/722–7755 in the U.K.,* ℻ *082/426169. 305 rooms. 2 restaurants, bar, pool, sauna, tennis court, exercise room, dance club, playground, business services. AE, DC, MC, V.*

$$$$ ★ 🏨 **Kuching Hilton.** This 15-story luxury hotel on the Sarawak River, just across from Ft. Margherita, has become a landmark for quality service and fine dining. Its spacious rooms have light-wood furniture, including a desk. The Penthouse Floor and the two Executive Floors have such extra amenities as separate check-in, personal butlers, and private lounges. The serene, ground-floor Waterfront Cafe is a great place to watch the river traffic. Its menu has Malay, Chinese, and Indian favorites plus Western specialties. It's also the best place in town if you're longing for a fresh salad, good bread, and delicious noodle dishes. ⊠ *Jln. Tuanku Abdul Rahman (Box 2396), 93748,* ☎ *082/ 248200 or 800/HILTONS in the U.S.,* ℻ *082/428984. 322 rooms. 4 restaurants, bar, pool, exercise room, business services, meeting rooms. AE, DC, MC, V.* ✆

$$$ 🏨 **Holiday Inn Resort Damai Beach.** This is one of two Holiday Inn resorts set virtually side by side on a stretch of beach about 24 km (15 mi) from Kuching. (A shuttle bus serves the two resorts from the Holiday Inn Kuching.) The beach itself is only so-so, but the setting—backed by lush rain forest and cradled by Mt. Santubong—is glorious. The large, well-furnished rooms have an outdoorsy feeling, owing to their glass patio doors. For a little more seclusion, opt to stay in one of the 80 deluxe rooms or 20 suites; they're housed in buildings with various indigenous architectural styles on the breezy slopes overlooking the main hotel. The word *damai* means "harmony and peace," but to find it here you must walk away from the hotel's many activities. ⊠ *Damai Beach (Box 2870), 93756,* ☎ *082/846999, 800/HOLIDAY in the U.S., or 020/7722–7755 in the U.K.,* ℻ *082/428911. 282 rooms, 20 suites. 3 restaurants, snack bar, pool, sauna, golf privileges, miniature golf, 2 tennis courts, exercise room, hiking, squash, snorkeling, windsurfing, boating, bicycles, dance club, recreation room, business services, meeting rooms. AE, DC, MC, V.*

$$$ 🏨 **Holiday Inn Resort Damai Lagoon.** Newer than the adjacent Holiday Inn Resort Damai Beach (☞ *above*), this resort has an enormous lagoon-shape swimming pool. Some of its pleasant rooms are in an austere multistory block; others are in attractive Malay-style chalets near the pool and the beach. As with its sister hotel, Damai Lagoon offers many recreational options, including water sports and jungle treks. ⊠ *Damai Beach (Box 3159), 93756,* ☎ *082/846900, 800/HOLIDAY in the U.S., or 020/7722–7755 in the U.K.;* ℻ *082/846901. 256 rooms. Restaurant, 2 bars, 2 snack bars, pool, hot tub, massage, sauna, golf privileges, 2 tennis courts, health club, hiking, squash, snorkeling, windsurfing, boating, bicycles, business services, meeting rooms. AE, DC, MC, V.*

$ 🏨 **Borneo Hotel.** This well-located, well-established hotel is a good deal. Its rooms are modestly furnished, but they're clean and have air-conditioning, TVs, phones, and private baths. The staff is friendly, and the small restaurant serves good local curries. ⊠ *30C-F Jln. Tabuan,* ☎ *082/244122,* ℻ *082/254848. 65 rooms. Restaurant, deli, piano bar. AE, DC, MC, V.*

Nightlife and the Arts

Evening entertainment in Kuching tends to run along the lines of karaoke lounges and bars. The Holiday Inn Kuching has a popular world-music lounge known as **Tribes** (⊠ Jln. Tuanku Abdul Rahman, ☎ 082/423111); it's open Monday–Saturday 4 PM–1 AM. The town's favorite disco is **Peppers** (⊠ Jln. Tuanku Abdul Rahman, ☎ 082/248200) in the Kuching Hilton. For traditional dance performances, you can't beat the cultural show at **Sarawak Cultural Village** (☎ 082/846411) in Santubong.

Outdoor Activities and Sports

BEACHES

Damai Beach is about 24 km (15 mi) northwest of Kuching (35 minutes by taxi), at the foot of Mt. Santubong. The two Holiday Inn resorts here (☞ Lodging, *above*) allow nonguests to use their facilities for windsurfing, catamaran sailing, kayaking, and waterskiing. To be honest, the sea here doesn't really invite swimming (it's rough in monsoon season and shallow and murky at other times), but the forested hills backing the beach make it a very pleasant spot to relax.

GOLF

The **Sarawak Golf Club** (☎ 082/440966) at Petra Jaya, about 15 minutes from downtown Kuching, is open to guests of major hotels. Greens fees are RM105–RM157, caddies RM8–RM12. The **Damai Beach Golf Course** (⊠ Jln. Santubong, ☎ 082/846088), designed by Arnold Palmer, is close to the Damai resorts and is open to nonmembers. Greens fees are RM150–RM180, caddy fees are RM15–RM25, and you can rent carts for about RM30.

Shopping

The handicrafts in Sarawak are among the most fascinating in all of Malaysia. Especially distinctive are the handwoven Iban textiles or *pua kumbu,* whose intricate designs have ceremonial significance. Baskets, hats, and mats are made from a variety of materials including rattan, palm leaves, and reeds; their designs vary according to the ethnic group. Wood carvings often bear the motif of the hornbill, the national emblem. Pottery designs show a Chinese influence, as do brass and silver objects. Many tribal artifacts from Indonesian Kalimantan are also sold in Kuching.

The best place to browse for antiques, curios, handicrafts, and other souvenirs is the **main bazaar,** which runs parallel to the waterfront. There are close to 20 shops whose irresistible bric-a-brac literally spills out onto the pavement. Try the **Atelier Gallery** (No. 104); **Nelson's Gallery** (No. 84), which is run by the most knowledgeable antiques dealer in town; and **Arts of Asia** (No. 68). Although prices are amazingly low to start out, bargaining is expected (just be sure to ask whether the item you're haggling over is a genuine antique or a skillful copy). Goods can be shipped anywhere, and major credit cards are accepted in most shops.

A **Sunday market** in the parking lot of Bank Bumiputra on Jalan Satok sells everything from fruit to heirlooms. The market actually starts on Saturday afternoon and is a good place to catch the local atmosphere.

Batang Ai

❷ *Approximately 100 km (62 mi) southeast of Kuching.*

Few people visit Sarawak without making a trip to a tribal longhouse. Some are as close as a 1½-hour drive from Kuching; others involve a longer drive followed by a boat trip. You can visit for a day or stay for a week. Either way, your hosts welcome you with a mixture of hospitality and polite indifference.

The Skrang River was the first area to be used by tour operators as a destination for longhouse excursions. However, with the construction of the huge Batang Ai hydroelectric dam and the opening of the four-star Hilton Batang Ai Longhouse Resort (☞ Lodging, *below*), there are more accommodation options now than before. Many operators use the resort (to reach it you must make a half-hour boat ride across the lake) as the hub for day trips to or overnight stays at longhouses along the rivers that feed the Batang Ai Reservoir (☞ Tour Operators and Travel Agencies *in* Northern Borneo A to Z, *below*.). Popular longhouse destinations are the Engkari River and the Batang Ai (*batang* means "river" in Iban). At the huge Batang Ai National Park (where you have a good chance of spotting wild orangutans) your only lodging option is camping.

The route to Batang Ai takes you by car or bus through pepper plantations, run mostly by Chinese families, where you can pause and look at one of Sarawak's major exports being grown and dried. Most tours also stop at the interesting market in the little town of Serian and later make a break for a local meal. The entire trip from Kuching to the Batang Ai Lake takes around 4½ hours. Note that most visitors stay in separate accommodations near the longhouse, rather than actually sleeping in the longhouse itself. These purpose-built lodges are simple but adequate, with mosquito netting, flush toilets, and running water. The attraction is seeing, close at hand, a lifestyle that has changed little in centuries. Tour operators can advise you on dress and comportment.

Lodging

$$$$ 🏨 **Hilton Batang Ai Longhouse Resort.** This resort, which opened in 1994, is an alternative to the spartan accommodations available on longhouse tours. Designed on the lines of a traditional Iban timber longhouse, it stands on a small island in Batang Ai Lake, surrounded by hills and with a patch of rain forest behind. Rooms are comfortably furnished with native woods and have air-conditioning and ceiling fans. Another longhouse contains a large dining room with a terrace that overlooks the lake. Treks and longboat excursions to Iban communities are the main options for daily activities. Hilton International will make travel arrangements through a local tour operator. ✉ *Reservations: Kuching Hilton, Jln. Tuanku Abdul Rahman (Box 2396), Kuching 93748*, ☎ *082/248200 or 800/HILTONS*, 🗚 *082/428984. 100 rooms. Restaurant, meeting rooms. AE, DC, MC, V.* 🍽

Miri

❸ *544 km (340 mi) northeast of Kuching.*

This once sleepy fishing village is now the administrative capital of northeastern Sarawak, thanks primarily to Shell, which began exploiting its offshore oil in 1910. Several flights daily link this economic center with Kuching, Bandar Seri Begawan in Brunei, and Kota Kinabalu in Sabah. You'll find comfortable hotels; karaoke clubs and bars; and the exotic Tamu Muhibbah native market, which sells all sorts of weird produce—from edible stems harvested in the jungles to sago worms, a local delicacy eaten either blanched or barbecued.

Most visitors use Miri as a jumping-off point for the famous Gunung Mulu National Park (several flights daily) and the archaeologically important Niah Caves, a bus or taxi ride away. It's also possible to travel by bus from here to Kuala Belait, and then cross the border into Brunei. Miri was once a popular hub for trips up the Baram River to the longhouses of the Kayan and Kenyah tribes. However, increased logging activities in the region have made such trips less attractive. Enthusiastic scuba divers can visit the Luconia Shoals, northwest of Miri, on a live-aboard dive boat that operates between April and October.

Lodging

$$$ ⊞ **Holiday Inn Miri.** On the beach at the mouth of the Miri River, this international hotel is slightly closer to town than its neighbor, the Rihga Royal (☞ *below*). Popular with both leisure and business travelers, it has a swimming pool and a gym as well as the usual room amenities. The Western food served in the coffee shop is often surprisingly good, and there's also a popular Chinese restaurant. ⊠ *Jln. Temenggong Oyang Lawai, 98998,* ☎ *085/418888,* FAX *085/419999. 168 rooms. Restaurant, bar, coffee shop, pub, pool, health club, beach, dance club, business services, meeting rooms. AE, DC, MC, V.*

$$$ ⊞ **Rihga Royal Hotel.** On the edge of the beach and a five-minute taxi ride from the town center, this modern hotel sits on 20 acres of landscaped grounds. Three buildings surround a courtyard that fans out to the grounds, the pool, and the guest chalets. Rooms throughout are smart, efficient, and functional; each has air-conditioning that's individually controlled and coffee- and tea-making facilities. A cascading waterfall is the centerpiece of the atrium lobby, off which is a pub for a convivial chat and a game of darts. ⊠ *Jln. Temenggong Oyang Lawai, 98998,* ☎ *085/421121,* FAX *085/421099, 170 rooms. 3 restaurants, pub, pool, health club, dance club, business services, meeting rooms. AE, DC, MC, V.* 🍸

Niah Caves

❹ *109 km (68 mi) south of Miri.*

The Niah Caves in Niah National Park are the most important archaeological site on Borneo, yielding evidence of human habitation some 25,000 to 30,000 years ago. Artifacts uncovered include stone, bone, and iron tools; wall paintings; Chinese ceramics; and 1,000-year-old wooden coffins. Unfortunately, most of these items have been removed to Kuching's Sarawak Museum for safekeeping, and the Painted Cave, where the wall paintings and coffins remain, is closed to the public for reasons of preservation.

However, the caves are still worth visiting, especially when birds' nests are gathered twice a year. Edible nests formed from the hardened saliva of a couple of varieties of swiftlet are scraped off the walls and roofs of the cave in a death-defying operation by collectors, who scale flimsy poles and ropes to climb as much as 100 ft above the cave floor. The collectors are convinced that the risks are justified by the high price paid by the Chinese, who believe that the nests have medicinal properties and generally make them into a soup. Year-round, the local Ibans gather dung from the cave floors for fertilizer.

The park is about a 1½-hour bus or taxi ride (RM80) from Miri. If you're adventurous you can walk 45 minutes along a well-maintained boardwalk through the rain forest to explore the caves with or without a guide. The park offers a range of accommodations, including comfortable chalets, and there's a canteen that serves drinks and basic meals. You can make lodging reservations at the Miri visitor center (☞ Visitor Information *in* Northern Borneo A to Z, *below*).

Gunung Mulu National Park

❺ *35-minute flight or eight-hour trip by both bus and boat from Miri.*

The most dramatic feature of Sarawak's vast Gunung Mulu National Park is the world's largest limestone cave system, set amid virgin rain forest. Although the complex ecosystem of the forest is impressive, it's the "show caves" (those open to the public) that are unforgettable. Strategic lighting and boardwalks make it possible to explore four caves: Deer Cave, which could hold London's St Paul's Cathedral five times over; Lang's Cave, with its beautiful stalactites and stalagmites; Clearwater Cave, which has a river running through it and is the longest cave in Southeast Asia; and Wind Cave, with lovely flowstones and other interesting formations. Those with a sense of adventure can arrange with a tour operator to travel underground from one cave passage to another. Hikers can visit the sharp limestone Pinnacles or trek out from the park along the Headhunters' Trail, finishing the trip by boat downriver to Limbang.

The park offers a variety of accommodations near its headquarters at Mulu, and there are private hotels just outside the park's boundaries. The hostels that are run by various tour operators are very basic, but fortunately, a surprising degree of comfort in the midst of the jungle is offered by the attractive Royal Mulu Resort. Access from here to the park headquarters is by longboat.

The best way to reach Mulu is by the Twin Otter planes run by MAS (generally there are four flights per day from Miri). The trip takes 35 minutes and offers a panoramic view of the rain forest, especially over Brunei, where logging has not encroached. An alternative way to reach Mulu is by bus from Miri to Kuala Baram, then by a series of express boats and longboats up the Baram River; this takes at least eight hours and because of deforestation and erosion along the river, it's a depressing rather than scenic ride.

Lodging

$$$ 📷 **Royal Mulu Resort.** This charming resort consists of a series of timber chalets and larger buildings with rooms, all linked by boardwalks and set high on stilts at a river junction. The attractively furnished guest quarters have parquet floors, private baths, air-conditioning, and satellite TVs. The resort also has a pool, a walk-in aviary, and a library with interesting reference books. *Reservations through Rihga Royal Hotel:* ✉ *Jln. Temenggong Oyang Lawai, Miri 98998,* ☎ *085/790100,* 🖷 *085/425057. 88 rooms. Restaurant, bar, pool, library, meeting room. AE, DC, MC, V.* 🐎

Sabah

Sabah—known as the "Land Below the Wind" because it lies below the typhoon belt—occupies the northern tip of Borneo. It shares its southwestern border with Sarawak and the rest of its southern border with the Indonesian province of Kalimantan. Its primary resource is timber, from which fortunes have been made. Although vast tracts of forest have been replaced by oil palm plantations, a sizable portion of land is protected in national parks or conservation areas. These majestic forests and freshwater swamps contain abundant wildlife—and relatively few people. Although the state's area is some 75,500 square km (29,388 square mi), it only has about 2 million people, of which the Kadazans are the largest ethnic group. Along the west coast, the Bajaus grow rice and raise ponies; on the east coast a group related to the Bajau, but who speak a different language, are mostly fishermen. The Chinese, who run much of Sabah's commerce, live mostly in the towns and make up about 10% of the population.

Borneo's forbidding interior made it far less attractive to early traders and explorers than neighboring areas, so Sabah remained unexploited by the British until the late 19th century. In 1963, it joined Sarawak,

Malaya, and Singapore (which later seceded) in forming the Federation of Malaysia. Most Sabahans are Christians, although the official religion of Malaysia is Islam. Sabah's native arts, crafts, and social customs are still retained, and Bahasa Malaysia, the national language, is still a second tongue for most Sabahans.

The capital, Kota Kinabalu, is a relatively new town, rebuilt after it was destroyed by Allied bombing during World War II. It contains few sights but is an important transportation hub. Most travelers to Sabah visit Mt. Kinabalu, the legendary mountain in the less-developed interior. At 13,450 ft, this is the highest peak in Southeast Asia outside the Himalayas, and it's part of a huge national park. You can hike from the park headquarters to the summit and back in two days. For beachcombers, the seas around Sabah offer a kaleidoscope of marine life. You can scuba dive in some of the world's top dive spots or simply snorkel or putter about the reefs in a glass-bottom boat.

Kota Kinabalu

❻ *1,584 km (990 mi) east of KL.*

The capital, called Jesselton when Sabah was known as British North Borneo, was razed during World War II. It was renamed in 1967, four years after Sabah became part of the Federation of Malaysia. Little of historic interest remains—the oldest part of the city is vintage 1950s. The multistory shophouses sell hardware and other practical goods; the upper floors are dwellings. The central market on the waterfront sells produce and handicrafts. Next to the central market is a smaller collection of stalls that sell produce from the Philippines.

Kota Kinabalu's main draw is the **Sabah Museum,** on a hilltop off Jalan Penampang about 3 km (2 mi) south of the city center. The building resembles a traditional longhouse, and its exhibits are a good introduction to local history, archaeology, botany, and ethnography. Perhaps the most interesting feature is the group of full-sized traditional houses in the garden setting of **Kampung Warisan** (Heritage Village), on the slopes behind the museum parking lot. Within the museum you'll find many antique *tajau* (Chinese ceramic jars)—heirlooms with a practical purpose that are common throughout Asia. ✉ *Jln. Kebajikan,* ☎ *088/253199.* 🎟 *Free.* ☻ *Museum Sat.–Thurs. 10–6; Heritage Village Sat.–Thurs. 9–1 and 2–5.*

Three seas wash the shores of Sabah, and they're all accessible from Kota Kinabalu. Just offshore are five small, delightful islands that make up the **Tunku Adbul Rahman Marine Park** (☎ 088/211652 for the Sabah Parks Office in Kota Kinabalu). You can make a day trip to picnic and snorkel among the reefs at **Pulau Gaya** and walk the 20 km (12 mi) of trails through the mangrove swamps and tropical forests. **Pulau Sapi** is popular with sun worshipers and snorkelers (note that it can get very crowded). **Pulau Mamutik** is a quiet little island where a well-known dive operator has a base. **Pulau Manukan** is the most developed island, with chalets for rent, a restaurant, a small swimming pool, and a campground. **Pulau Sulug,** the island farthest offshore, is the least visited. However, a dive operator has plans to erect a number of chalets here.

OFF THE   **KAMPUNG BAVANGGAZO –** This small, peaceful kampung is in the Kudat
BEATEN PATH district, about three hours north of Kota Kinabalu. The people who live
             here are members of the Rungus tribe, a subgroup of the Kadazan tribe
             and the most traditional of Sabah's people. Here you'll learn about the
             Rungus farmers' lifestyle, sample local food and rice wine, see a cultural

show, and stay in a longhouse (beds have mosquito netting, and proper toilet and shower facilities are available). You'll also see handicrafts being made and can buy the finished products at remarkably low prices. Either make arrangements with a tour operator (☞ Tour Operators and Travel Agencies *in* Northern Borneo A to Z, *below*) or rent a car and drive. The whole operation is run as a cooperative by the villagers; contact the Sabah Tourism Promotion Corporation (☞ Visitor Information *in* Northern Borneo A to Z, *below*) for information and reservations if you opt to visit independently.

Dining and Lodging

$$–$$$ ✕ **Port View Seafood Restaurant.** This place has grown from a simple, open-sided eatery to a brightly tiled and gaily decorated (even if pink is not to everyone's taste) restaurant that's very popular with Asian tour groups. The seafood is spanking fresh (even live, if you want); the steamed prawns and butter prawns are superb. ⊠ *Jln. Haji Saman (opposite Marine Police base),* ☎ *088/221753. AE, MC, V. No lunch.*

$$ ✕ **Nam Xing.** Locals who patronize this Chinese restaurant order the dim sum for breakfast or lunch, but there are also tasty seafood dishes—chili crab, squid, and prawns. The noise and gusto of the clientele provide a lively distraction from the bland decor. ⊠ *32 Jln. Haji Saman,* ☎ *088/212900. No credit cards.*

$ ✕ **Wishbone Cafe.** Located in the Jesselton, an attractive boutique hotel, this perennially popular restaurant is informal but comfortable and always busy at lunchtime. Local food (the Hainanese-style chicken rice is recommended) and simple Western fare are available. The service is very good. ⊠ *69 Jln. Gaya,* ☎ *088/223333. AE, DC, V.*

$$$$ ✕▥ **Hyatt Kinabalu.** Rooms are spacious and comfortable; many have views of the port and nearby islands. Those on the Regency Club floors have extra amenities. The hotel also has the best Japanese restaurant in town, the Nagisa, and a very popular pub, Shenanigan's. You can get good pizzas and cakes—perfect for picnics—in the delicatessen. ⊠ *Jln. Datuk Salleh Sulong, 88994,* ☎ *088/221234, 800/223–1234 in the U.S.,* 𝖥𝖠𝖷 *088/225972. 288 rooms, 14 suites. 3 restaurants, 2 bars, pool, business services. AE, DC, MC, V.* ☟

$$$$ ✕▥ **Shangri-La's Tanjung Aru Resort.** This luxury establishment is
★ near the airport and 10 minutes from downtown (there's a shuttle into town and to Shangri-La's Rasa Ria Resort about an hour away). No longer a quiet getaway, it has become a major resort that bustles with activity when it's full. Wicker furniture gives the rooms an airy feel; each room also has a balcony that overlooks the hotel's 25 landscaped acres and the sea beyond. There's a marina that arranges windsurfing, scuba diving, waterskiing, and sailing excursions as well as trips to the nearby marine park islands. You can play tennis and pitch-and-putt golf or go biking; the small beach is a great place to relax, build sand castles, or play volleyball. Tour operators in the hotel's shopping arcade offer white-water rafting excursions and trips to Sepilok, Sukau, and Danum Valley. Of the four restaurants, Peppino is noteworthy for its Mediterranean food with Italian accents. ⊠ *Jln. Aru (Locked Bag 174), 88999,* ☎ *088/225800 or 800/942–5050 in the U.S.,* 𝖥𝖠𝖷 *088/ 244871. 500 rooms. 4 restaurants, bar, 2 pools, 4 tennis courts, exercise room, volleyball, beach, dock, dive shop, snorkeling, windsurfing, waterskiing, boating, bicycles, shops, dance club, business services, travel services. AE, DC, MC, V.* ☟

$$$$ ▥ **Shangri-La's Rasa Ria Resort.** Set on 400 acres of tropical vegetation
★ along a long sandy beach, this resort is about an hour's drive from Kota Kinabalu International Airport. The split-level rooms are a touch on the small side, but with all there is to do here, you probably won't be spending much time inside. In addition to tennis and the usual water sports,

you'll find horseback riding, crab catching, and golf at the nearby 18-hole Dalit Bay Golf and Country Club among the list of activities. At the adjacent nature reserve, the stars are a pair of orangutans. The only drawback to this resort is the lack of a nearby village or town with alternative places to eat. ⊠ *Pantai Dalit (Box 600), Tuaran 89208, ☎ 088/792888 or 800/942–5050 in the U.S., FAX 088/792777. 330 rooms. 4 restaurants, bar, grocery, pub, pool, outdoor hot tub, golf privileges, 2 tennis courts, health club, hiking, horseback riding, beach, dive shop, snorkeling, windsurfing, boating, jet skiing, bicycles, video games, children's programs, business services. AE, DC, MC, V.*

$$$ 🏨 **Promenade Hotel.** Promenade is near the waterfront overlooking
★ Pulau Gaya and a five-minute drive from the city center. It caters more to Malaysian businessmen than to leisure travelers. Rooms are small though adequately furnished; only the lobby has fancy decor. The pub, Le Rendezvous, is a popular place at night. ⊠ *4 Lorong Api Api 3, Api Api Centre, 88000, ☎ 088/265555, FAX 088/246559. 451 rooms. 2 restaurants, pub, pool, exercise room, dance club, business services. AE, DC, MC, V.*

$ 🏨 **Casuarina Hotel.** Two minutes' walk from Tanjung Aru Beach and less than 10 minutes from the airport, this attractive boutique hotel is nicely furnished. The staff is very friendly, and there's a free shuttle service to downtown. ⊠ *Lorong Ikan Lais, off Jln. Mat Salleh, 88100, ☎ 088/243899, FAX 088/223000. 44 rooms. Restaurant, bar. AE, MC, V.*

Nightlife and the Arts

CULTURAL SHOWS

The best place to see a cultural show with a variety of Sabahan dances is at the **Malam Kampung** (Village Night; ☎ 088/225800 for reservations) in the Pulau Bayu restaurant of Shangri-La's Tanjung Aru Resort (☞ Dining and Lodging, *above*). Held every Sunday at 8, the evening includes a buffet of Malaysian food or selections from the à la carte menu. Cultural shows are given at the **Monsopiad Cultural Village** (☎ 088/761336) in a rural setting about 20 minutes from town. Although the House of Skulls—a minimuseum devoted to the trophies of the famous, long-dead headhunter, Monsopiad—is open daily, the cultural performance and buffet dinner are normally given only for groups. Check with any Kota Kinabalu tour operator (☞ Tour Operators and Travel Agencies *in* Northern Borneo A to Z, *below*) about trips to see the show.

DANCE CLUBS

Try the Promenade Hotel's **Le Rendezvous** (⊠ 4 Lorong Api Api 3, Api Api Centre, ☎ 088/265555). You can kick back and smoke a cigar (on sale here), drink wine and beer, and, when you get drunk enough, join the locals who visit for the karaoke. The Hyatt hotel's **Shenanigan's** (⊠ Jln. Datuk Salleh Sulong, lower level, ☎ 088/221234) is the most popular place in town, with lively music and a friendly atmosphere. For a relaxing evening where you can sip a drink, play pool or board games, and enjoy light meals and the occasional live show, try the spacious, two-level **Something Al's** (⊠ Jln. Aru, ☎ 088/266480) at Shangri-La's Tanjung Aru Resort.

Outdoor Activities and Sports

BEACHES

The closest beaches to Kota Kinabalu are on the islands of the **Tunku Adbul Rahman Marine Park** (☎ 088/211652 for the Sabah Parks Office in Kota Kinabalu), a 15-minute speedboat ride from the small jetties in front of the Hyatt hotel downtown. Except for Pulau Sapi, which tends to get crowded, peace and privacy prevail. Pretty coral formations and marine life attract snorkelers and divers (☞ Diving, *below*. Tour operators (☞ Tour Operators and Travel Agencies *in* Northern

Borneo A to Z, *below*) will arrange trips complete with a picnic lunch or barbecue.

DIVING

Kota Kinabalu is a great place to arrange trips to some of the world's best dive spots. Sipadan, an oceanic island off Sabah's southeast coast, is renowned for its 2,000-ft wall dive, turtles, and pelagic fish. North of Sipadan, islands such as Mabul and Pandanan offer pristine corals and rich marine life. Far off Sabah's west coast is the atoll of Layang Layang, where a dive resort gives enthusiasts a chance to discover the underwater world and see the thousands of migratory birds that nest here.

Borneo Divers (✉ 4th floor, Wisma Sabah, Locked Bag 194, Kota Kinabalu 88999, ☎ 088/222226), a 5-star PADI facility, arranges diver training and excursions to most of Sabah's dive sites. They were the first company to offer dive trips to Sipadan, where their chalets occupy a prime location. **Tanjung Aru Dive Centre** (✉ The Marina, Shangri-La's Tanjung Aru Resort, WDT 14, Kota Kinabalu 89459, ☎ 088/256676) offers diver training and dives around Kota Kinabalu, and runs a small, exclusive dive resort on Pandanan island, off Sabah's east coast.

GOLF

There are three private golf courses within Kota Kinabalu and several others within a two-hour drive of the city; note that it's best to make arrangements to play in advance through your hotel. The 18-hole course of the **Sabah Golf and Country Club** (✉ Jln. Kolom, ☎ 088/247533) at Bukit Padang is quite popular. Greens fees are RM70–RM150. Also popular is the 27-hole course of **Sutera Harbour Golf and Country Club** (✉ Sutera Harbour Blvd., ☎ 088/252266), where greens fees are RM200–RM250; golf carts are compulsory and cost RM25. The 9-hole course of the **Kinabalu Golf Club** (☎ 088/234904) is near the beach at Tanjung Aru. Greens fees are RM105 and caddies cost RM27 (note that visitors aren't permitted to play on weekends). Other fine courses are those at Karambunai and Pantai Dalit, north of Kota Kinabalu, and the Borneo Golf and Country Club, south of town at Bongawan. The Mt. Kinabalu Golf Course, at around 6,000 ft on the slopes of Mt. Kinabalu, offers some spectacular vistas and a cooler climate at its 18-hole course.

Shopping

To see how the locals shop, visit the Sunday morning **street fair** on Jalan Gaya. Stalls sell everything from fresh fruit to orchids, clothing to bric-a-brac, and basketwork to puppies. For a wide assortment of goods, try the **Centrepoint** complex on the Coastal Highway, where stores sell clothing, shoes, photographic equipment, and souvenirs; you'll also find money changers and several restaurants, including those that serve Western fast food. The **Wisma 2020** complex has a large department store and a wide range of shops; there are food stalls on the fourth floor.

Sabah handicrafts are less elaborate than those of Sarawak, but they do have character. In Kota Kinabalu, **Borneo Craft** (✉ Ground floor, Wisma Merdeka, ☎ 088/237936) has a small but interesting collection of local handicrafts, as well as a good range of books on Borneo. **Rafflesia Gift Centre** (✉ Wisma Merdeka, ☎ 088/239287) has a wide range of handicrafts and souvenirs. They also have a branch, **Classic Batik & Craft**, on the ground floor of Centrepoint complex. The gift shop inside the **Sabah Tourism Promotion Corporation** (✉ 51 Jln. Gaya, ☎ 088/218620) is worth checking out for trinkets, batiks, carvings and other reasonably-priced handicrafts. If you're driving to Mt. Kinabalu, stop at the handicraft stalls at **Nabalu Market,** where the locally made basketwork is interesting and cheap, and the vendors are as colorful as the products they sell.

Kinabalu Park

❼ *90 km (55 mi) east of Kota Kinabalu.*

Kinabalu Park, about 1½ hours from Kota Kinabalu, is regarded as having the richest assemblage of plants in the world within its 754 square km (467 square mi). Nature lovers can walk miles of well-marked trails through jungle dense with wild orchids, carnivorous pitcher plants, bamboo, mosses and vines, and unusual geologic formations. The wildlife is shy, but you're likely to see a variety of birds (some endemic), squirrels, and tree shrews. To reach the Kinabalu Park Headquarters on your own, take one of the frequent minibuses that depart from the Padang in Kota Kinabalu for Ranau (the one-way fare is RM8); they pass the park's entrance. The cost to enter the park is RM2. Many Kota Kinabalu tour operators (☞ Tour Operators and Travel Agencies *in* Northern Borneo A to Z, *below*) also offer organized trips. For general information, contact the **Sabah Parks Office** (☎ 088/211652) in Kota Kinabalu.

★ For some, the main event is scaling **Mt. Kinabalu,** at 13,450 ft the highest mountain in Southeast Asia outside the Himalayas; it's also a place of spiritual significance (souls of the departed are believed to reside here) for the Kadazan people. Hikers can trek from the park headquarters to the peak and back in two days. The view from the summit on a clear morning is worth every step, so most people catch their second wind at 11,000 ft in the rest house at Panar Laban (☞ *also* Lodging, *below*) before leaving at 2 AM to reach the summit by dawn.

Poring Hot Springs, on the southeastern side of Kinabalu Park about 40 km (25 mi) from the park headquarters, is popular for day trips. If you have the time, however, stay overnight in the chalets. The hot sulphur springs are piped into attractive open-air baths; there's a pool of mountain-temperature water for a refreshing plunge afterward. You can also make the steep 3,000-ft climb to Poring's canopy walkway, which is strung high above the ground and offers a bird's-eye view of the rain forest. If you like your entertainment to be less strenuous, visit the Butterfly Farm to see many live, native—often amazing—species. Good, inexpensive food is available in the restaurant overlooking a pool.

On the east side of Mt. Kinabalu, **Mesilau Plateau** is reached via the vegetable-growing district of Kundasang about 30 minutes from the park headquarters. Just beyond the scenic 18-hole Mt. Kinabalu Golf Course, you'll find a series of beautiful wooden hostels and chalets, together with a restaurant and an information center. There are also plans to create a trail from here up to Panar Laban.

Lodging

Although there's a range of accommodations in Kundasang, about 5 km (3 mi) from the park, it's infinitely better to stay in the park's superb forested environment. Accommodations at Panar Laban, the park headquarters, Poring Hot Springs, and Mesilau Plateau were privatized in mid-1998; everything else is still managed by Sabah Parks. Beds in the heated rest house at Panar Laban cost RM25 per person and bunk beds in the nearby mountain hostel cost RM5. At the park headquarters, you'll find the Nepenthes Villas (two bedrooms with twin beds plus a sitting room and a kitchen) for RM250 a night and the Twin Bed Cabins offer (you guessed it) twin beds with attached bathrooms for RM50. Two hostels offer dormitory-style accommodations for RM10 per person. Make advance reservations for any of the park lodgings through **Kinabalu Gold Resorts** (⊠ 3rd floor, Block C, Kompleks Karamunsing, Kota Kinabalu, ☎ 088/243629, ℻ 088/242861, ✍).

$ ⚅ **Hotel Perkasa.** The Perkasa sits on a hilltop about 6 km (4 mi) from the park headquarters. It overlooks the vegetable farms of Kundasang, and it faces Mt. Kinabalu, to which excursions can be arranged. Rooms offer a mountain view as well as heaters—a rarity in the tropics—to warm the brisk mountain air, but that's the extent of the luxury. The hotel is a 2½-hour drive from the airport in Kota Kinabalu. ✉ *WDT 11, Ranau 89300,* ☎ *088/889511,* 𝔽𝔸𝕏 *088/889101. 74 rooms. Restaurant, bar, golf privileges, tennis court, exercise room, business services, travel services. AE, DC, MC, V.*

Sandakan

❽ *386 km (241 mi) east of Kota Kinabalu.*

The coastal town of Sandakan was the capital of British North Borneo until it was completely destroyed by the Allies toward the end of the Japanese occupation during World War II. The capital was transferred to Jesselton (now Kota Kinabalu), but Sandakan came back to life in the 1970s as the center for the logging industry. That natural resource has been largely exhausted and the land is now replanted with oil palm plantations. No longer a boomtown, Sandakan is nonetheless worth visiting as it's within a couple of hours of some of Borneo's most accessible wildlife sights.

No visit to Sabah is complete without a trip to the **Sepilok Orang-Utan Rehabilitation Center,** set in a rain-forest reserve just 25 km (15 mi) from Sandakan. Here, illegally captured animals are prepared for a return to the wild. You can watch the twice-daily feeding of the semi-wild orangutans, who come in from the forest for a meal of bananas and milk until they're ready to go it alone. During the various fruiting seasons, when plenty of food is available in the wild, the number of animals visiting the feeding platform is likely to be greatly reduced, so ask your tour agent or a local before booking. From Sandakan's Labuk Road station, buses depart for the center at 9:20, 11:30, 1:30, and 3 each day. To arrive in time for the first feeding, take a minibus for "Batu 14," or take a taxi and ask the driver to wait for you (around RM25). ☎ *089/ 531180.* ⚅ *RM10.* ⊙ *Daily 8–6; feeding times 10 AM and 2:30 PM.*

Three islands, Selingan, Bakungan, and Gulisan (almost one hour by speedboat north of Sandakan), and their surrounding waters make up the **Turtle Islands Marine Park**(☎ 088/243629). Throughout the year, green and hawksbill turtles come to their shores to dig nests and lay their eggs in the warm sands. The eggs are then gathered by rangers and transferred to hatcheries in an effort to conserve these endangered marine animals. To visit the islands, tour operators in Kota Kinabalu or Sandakan (☞ Tour Operators and Travel Agencies *in* Northern Borneo A to Z, *below*) can arrange for a boat and an overnight stay at one of the three chalets on Selingan.

Sukau

❾ *134 km (83 mi) southeast of Sandakan.*

The Kinabatangan, Sabah's largest river, flows through a vast tract of freshwater swamp that's home to a rich variety of wildlife, including the orangutan; the big-nosed, pot-bellied proboscis monkey found only in Borneo; and a host of glorious birds. The village of Sukau, on the mid-reaches of the Kinabatangan and about two hours by road from Sandakan, is a focal point for wildlife-viewing trips along the river and its tributaries. Five tour operators maintain simple but comfortable tourist lodges along the Kinabatangan and take visitors by boat at dusk and at dawn to look for proboscis monkeys. Make arrangements in Kota

Kinabalu with Wildlife Expeditions or Borneo Eco Tours (☞ Tour Operators and Travel Agencies *in* Northern Borneo A to Z, *below*).

<table>
<tr><td>OFF THE
BEATEN PATH</td><td>DANUM VALLEY – Anyone with a serious interest in discovering the complex beauty of the virgin rain forest should make a trip to the Danum Valley Conservation Area. To get here you must fly (40 minutes) from Kota Kinabalu to Lahad Datu on Sabah's east coast and then drive 85 km (53 mi). Apart from the field center, where scientists carrying out studies of the forest are based, there's accommodation at the Borneo Rainforest Lodge (☎ 088/244100), where fan-cooled wooden chalets on stilts are clustered near the Danum River. From here you can follow trails through the forest, watch for birds and other wildlife from the stunning canopy walkway, and go on night drives. Nature interpretation is provided by knowledgeable guides; you'll also gain a greater understanding of conservation by visiting some of the projects where experiments in reforestation are being conducted.</td></tr>
</table>

Pulau Pandanan

➓ *Reaching Pandanan involves a 45-minute to an hour flight from Kota Kinabalu to Tawau, followed by a 1½-hour minibus ride to Semporna, and then a 45-minute speedboat ride.*

Many beautiful coral-fringed islands are found to the east and northeast of Semporna; as yet, only one of these has been developed as a dive resort. Pasir, a private resort on the minute island of Pandanan, offers simple but comfortable accommodation and excellent macro diving. To make arrangements for a dive excursion here, contact the Tanjung Aru Dive Centre (☞ Scuba Diving *in* Outdoor Activities and Sports *under* Kota Kinabalu, *above*).

Pulau Sipadan

➕ *45-minute flight from Kota Kinabalu to Tawau, followed by a 1½-hour minibus ride to Semporna, and then a 1-hour boat ride from Semporna.*

Until a decade ago, the tiny oceanic island of Sipadan, around 30 km (18 mi) south of Semporna, was visited only by nesting sea turtles. Jacques Cousteau's proclamation that the island was "an untouched piece of art" combined with the establishment (in 1989) of a small dive resort changed all that. Scuba divers began arriving in ever-increasing numbers to explore the pristine waters and coral reefs.

The island rises 2,000 ft directly from the floor of the Celebes Sea, offering a dive wall that goes on forever. Unchecked development has resulted in a total of five resorts now on the island, with even more divers coming in daily from a Japanese-owned resort on nearby Mabul Island. Federal legislation was introduced in early 1998 to restrict the number of divers to 80 per day, but at press time, this wasn't being enforced. Sipadan still offers a remarkable diving experience, even if it is being challenged by the presence of too many people. For trips and accommodations, contact Borneo Divers (☞ Scuba Diving *in* Outdoor Activities and Sports *under* Kota Kinabalu, *above*).

Brunei

Surrounded by both the Malaysian state of Sarawak and the South China Sea, Brunei is a tiny nation unlike any other in Southeast Asia. Since 1929, when oil was discovered off its shores, the sultanate of Brunei Darussalam—no larger than the state of Delaware and with a population of only 280,000—has become one of the richest countries in the world. Although

Brunei shares with its Malaysian neighbor a tropical climate and a jungle terrain, its people enjoy an unmatched standard of living.

In the 16th century, Brunei was nominally in control of an empire that stretched as far north as Manila. The nobility, however, was cruel and unpopular, and its power was gradually eroded by internal politics and revolts. In 1841, the first white rajah of Sarawak, James Brooke, obtained a grant for the land around the Sarawak River from the Sultan of Brunei. For the next 60 years, Brooke and his successor extended Sarawak's borders farther and farther, so that by the beginning of the 20th century, Brunei was a tiny, insignificant state. It became a British protectorate in 1888. Britain helped quell a rebellion against the sultanate in 1962; political stability followed, and Brunei was granted full independence in 1984.

Brunei's 29th sultan, Hassanal Bolkiah, has ruled since 1967, when his father abdicated. Like his predecessors, he takes his role as a guardian of Islamic values seriously and has banned the sale of alcohol in Brunei. His fabulous personal fortune (he's estimated by *The Guinness Book of Records* to be the world's wealthiest man) also makes him a major player in global politics: his US$10 million contribution to the Nicaraguan rebels linked his name with the Iran-Contra arms scandal. Bragging about his extravagance—his passion for polo ponies, Italian sports cars, the Boeing jet he gave his daughter for her 18th birthday—is a national pastime. His 50th birthday celebrations included hiring Michael Jackson to perform; Whitney Houston did the singing honors at the wedding of his daughter. He's also famous for his beneficence. His government uses oil revenues to finance free public education, health care, and cultural programs. He has even donated an amusement park to the citizens of Brunei, making it the only one in the world where admission and rides are free. Brunei's business and real-estate investments abroad have ensured that the sultanate's prosperity will continue long after its oil and gas are exhausted.

You can get a quick overview of Brunei with a full day in Bandar Seri Begawan, its capital. The city is situated on a wide river, and many of its citizens dwell at the Kampung Ayer (Water Village) in houses built on stilts. If you're looking for adventure and undisturbed wilderness, consider a trip inland. More than 80% of Brunei is forest, mostly primary rain forest dominated by giant dipterocarp trees and populated by eagles, bears, wildcats, bats, and monkeys of all kinds—not to mention ants, snakes, and other of the less attractive jungle dwellers. You can take a day trip to Ulu Temburong National Park, although it's really better to plan an overnight stay.

Bandar Seri Begawan

12–**24** *900 km (560 mi) northeast of Kuching, 300 km (186 mi) southwest of Kota Kinabalu.*

Unlike most Asian cities, where imposing modern office buildings and hotels dominate the skyline, Bandar Seri Begawan (BSB) has a traditional look. Its buildings are appealing—and the space around them is well landscaped—but few are more than six stories tall. This low profile makes the downtown mosque's stately minarets and huge golden dome—the first thing you see as you drive in—all the more impressive. Combining walking trips with short taxi or bus rides, you can easily visit all the main attractions in a day; indeed, many sights are near the mosque in the central district, with the sultan's palace and several fine museums a short distance away.

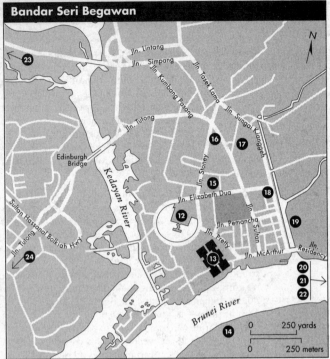

Start near the Brunei River at one of the city's most famous landmarks,

★ **12** the beautiful **Masjid Sultan Omar Ali Saifuddin.** This superb example of modern Islamic architecture was built in 1959 of imported white marble, gold mosaic, and stained glass—all made possible by petrodollars. The exterior is constructed of granite from Hong Kong, the interior is covered with marble from Italy, the chandeliers come from England, and the prayer rugs were brought from Iran. Be sure to take the elevator up the 145-ft minaret for a terrific view of the city. The mosque's beauty is further enhanced by being partly surrounded by a lagoon, where a religious stone boat called the *Mahaligal* floats year-round, as elegant and ornate as the mosque itself. ⊠ *Jln. Elizabeth II and Jln. Stoney.* ⊗ *Public viewing: Sat.–Wed. 8–noon, 1:30–3:30, and 4:30–5:30, Fri. 4:30–5:30.*

From the mosque, walk down Jalan Pretty toward the river, passing

13 the attractive shopping and commercial **Yayasan Hassanal Bolkiah complex.** The architecture is inspired by traditional Malay houses, and the buildings are set around a large courtyard. This is BSB's most upscale shopping area, and it's a good spot to grab a coffee and croissant (perhaps at the Delifrance Cafe) or to discover local food at the sparkling clean stalls in the air-conditioned, third-floor food court.

In front of the Yayasan you'll see wide steps (beside the Port View Seafood restaurant; ☞ *also* Dining and Lodging, *below*) leading to the river. This is one of the main departure points for the small boats that zip at alarm-

14 ing speed across the river to stilt houses of **Kampung Ayer.** Almost one-third of the city's population lives in these solidly built wooden homes (actually, there are 28 separate kampungs linked by concrete-and-wood bridges and by systems for water, electricity, and sewage). Schools, clinics, and small mosques stand among the houses, all of which all bristle with TV antennae. Each kampung used to have its own specialty trade such as boatbuilding, weaving, or making brassware. Today, however, most of the residents commute by water taxi or private boat to work on terra firma, generally in some branch of government service. You can hire a boat (expect to pay around B$20 for half an hour), explore the waterways, and follow some of the boardwalks that link the homes. You may even be invited in for a drink by the friendly inhabitants.

Ask your boatman to return you to the city side of the river, and then retrace your steps to the mosque. Across from it on Jalan Queen Elizabeth Dua, note the scenes of village life depicted in the mosaic mural on the facade of the **public library.**

⑮

Continue down Jalan Queen Elizabeth Dua and turn left onto Jalan Sultan. Follow it (you'll pass the Brunei History Centre, which really doesn't merit a visit) until you reach the **Royal Regalia Building,** which opened in 1992 to celebrate the sultan's silver jubilee. The semicircular building, with its lavish marble floors and carpets, is basically a museum devoted to the life and times of the current sultan. There are a great many photos (women will enjoy studying the costumes and shoes of notable ladies), a wonderfully ornate crown, the coronation carriage, and even a golden hand and forearm that the sultan used to support his chin during the coronation ceremony. ⌧ *Free.* ⏰ *Sat.–Thurs. 8:30–5, Fri. 9–1:30 and 2:30–5.*

⑯

The **Royal Ceremonial Hall,** across Jalan Sultan from the Royal Regalia Building, isn't officially open to the public. Still, you can get a glimpse of the impressive interior with its pillars leading up to the royal throne at the end.

⑰

Continue south along Jalan Sultan and turn left back onto Jalan Queen Elizabeth Dua; at Jalan Sungei Kianggeh turn right. This road runs along the river and passes the town's main **Chinese temple,** where Chinese opera is performed on an outdoor stage during important festivals. On the opposite side of the river, accessible via a footbridge, is the **Tamu Kianggeh,** a native market where interesting produce is sold (most of the activity takes place fairly early in the day).

⑱

⑲

At the bottom of Jalan Sungei Kianggeh, turn left and cross the bridge onto Jalan Residency. About 1 km (½ mi) along this road and on your right is the **Brunei Arts and Handicrafts Centre.** The eight-story building, shaped like the scabbard of a kris, contains workshops for silversmithing, brassmaking, weaving, and basketmaking. The silver goods—including such oddities as miniature cannons and boats—are exquisite. Crafts are for sale in the showroom, but prices are steep. ☎ 02/240676. ⌧ *Free.* ⏰ *Mon.–Thurs. 8–12:15 and 1:30–4:30, weekends 8:30–2.*

⑳

In front of the center, you should be able to pick up a Central Line bus (B$1) to take you the 4 km (2½ mi) to the **Brunei Museum.** The obligatory gallery on oil and gas donated by Shell Petroleum is of limited interest. It's best to head right upstairs to the Islamic Art Gallery, where there are some outstanding ceramics, jewelry, prayer rugs, Korans, and other items from around the Islamic world. ☎ 02/244545. ⌧ *Free.* ⏰ *Tues.–Thurs. and weekends 9:30–5, Fri. 9:30–11:30 and 2:30–5.*

㉑

At the back of the Brunei Museum steps lead down to the **Malay Technology Museum.** Exhibits here focus on the Malays' traditional crafts, such as boatmaking, fishing, house-building, metalworking, and goldsmithing. In Gallery Three, there are interesting displays—including models of houses—relating to the Kedayan, Murut, Dusun, and Iban people. ☎ 02/242862. ⌧ *Free.* ⏰ *Sat.–Mon. and Wed.–Thurs. 9–5, Fri. 9–11:30 and 2:30–5.*

㉒

From the Malay Technology Museum you can take a bus to the Jalan Cator bus station in the center of BSB. From here take a taxi or a Circle Line bus to the **Masjid Jame 'Asr Hassanil Bolkiah,** the largest mosque

㉓

in Brunei. No expense was spared in the construction and furnishing of this superb mosque to mark the 25th anniversary of the sultan's accession to the throne. Generally referred to by the locals as the Kiarong Mosque (after a nearby village), it's set in immaculate gardens and is a symphony of golden domes, minarets, and blue tiles. ☎ 02/440676. ⌖ Free. ⊙ Sat.–Wed. 12–1:30 and 4:30–5:30.

② If you have time, take a bus or taxi back to town and on to the **Istana Nurul Iman** (Sultan's Palace), about 3 km (2 mi) west of the city along Jalan Tutong. It's officially closed to the public except for a three-day open house during the annual Hari Raya Puasa festival, when you can greet the sultan or his two official wives (gender segregation is the rule of the day; only women are permitted to meet the wives, and only men can meet the sultan). Built in the shape of a Borneo longhouse at a cost of US$500 million, it's the largest (1,788 rooms including a throne room that seats 2,000) and one of the most opulent homes in the world. The sultan, his first wife, and their children actually live here; in addition, the sultan's oldest son has his own palace, as does the sultan's second wife. If you can't visit the interior, drive by just to glimpse the massive arched roofs, gold domes, and expanses of imported marble. Near the palace wall is a sculpture garden, a permanent ASEAN exhibit that features modern works from neighboring countries, all based on the theme "Harmony in Diversity."

OFF THE BEATEN PATH

JERUDONG PARK – Combining Moorish architecture with all the latest high-tech rides (maintained by a crew of Western technicians), this state-of-the-art amusement park is a cross between an Arabian Night's fantasy and Disneyland. It has been unkindly said that the park was created to give people something to do at night after alcohol sales were banned in 1991. Be that as it may, entrance to the park and all the attractions within it are absolutely free. In addition to some adrenaline-pumping rides (especially the "Pusing Lagi"), there's a spectacular musical fountain with a laser light show. Just opposite the entrance is a collection of food stalls, where you can enjoy a meal before entering. The only hitch to Jerudong Park, which is near the sultan's private polo grounds about 20 km (12 mi) out of town, is getting here and back. There's no public bus service, and it's almost impossible to pick up a taxi when you wish to return. The best way is to arrange round-trip transportation (about B$60 per person) with your hotel. ☎ No phone. ⌖ Free. ⊙ Sun.–Wed. and Fri. 5–midnight, Thurs. and Sat. 5 PM–2 AM.

ULU TEMBURONG NATIONAL PARK – Brunei's only national park is on the small wedge of land separated from the rest of Brunei by the Limbang district of Sarawak, Malaysia. Getting here is half the fun. You take a 45-minute speedboat ride through the mangrove swamps from BSB to the small town of Batang. From here you take a vehicle along Temburong's only road to Batang Duri, where you transfer to a longboat for a delightful ride through beautiful rain forest—where Iban boatmen skillfully negotiate the rapids—to the park headquarters. From here on, travel is on foot, and you need to be fit—the steep hillsides mean you're always either climbing or descending. A highlight of the park is its canopy walk, a somewhat intimidating structure of aluminum towers and walkways strung high above the forest floor. Provided you've got a good head for heights and the fitness for the demanding trek along the trail to the start of the walkway, you get a fantastic view from the top—not just of acre after acre of forested hills, but also of the plant and animal life. You may spot gibbons (especially if you go early in the morning), hornbills, and orchids. Sunshine Borneo Tours and Travel (☞ Tour Operators and Travel Agencies *in* Northern Borneo A to Z, *below*) offers day trips to Ulu Temburong—complete with a barbecue lunch—and can also arrange for longer stays.

Dining and Lodging

Although it has a few noteworthy restaurants, BSB isn't a great place for eating out. Hotel coffee shops are popular with locals as well as visitors, and you'll find low-cost hawker food at the open-air stalls near Edinburgh Bridge and along the river on Jalan Kiangggeh, near Jalan Pemancha. There are also food stalls—albeit slightly more expensive ones—on the third level of the Yayasan Hassanal Bolkiah complex. Note that many restaurants close at 10:30 PM. Compared with its neighbors, Brunei is an expensive place, accommodations are limited, and advance reservations are advised. Apart from Jerudong Park House and the Sheraton, most hotels are plain, but clean and comfortable. All listed below have a private bath, air-conditioning, and a TV in each room. For price categories, *see* the charts *in* Pleasures and Pastimes, at the start of this chapter.

$$$ ✕ **Port View Seafood.** Right on the riverbank opposite the Yayasan Hassanal Bolkiah complex, this attractive new restaurant has plate-glass windows that overlook the water and Kampung Ayer on one side. Although the emphasis is on seafood, *halal* Chinese dishes (prepared without pork) are also available. ✉ *Jln. MacArthur,* ☎ 02/231465. *AE, DC, MC, V. No lunch.*

$$ ✕ **Fratini.** This relatively new restaurant on the ground floor of the Yayasan Hassanal Bolkiah complex is a welcome addition to BSB's dining scene. The food is Italian—with lots of pasta dishes and pizza options—though you'll find other cuisines as well. ✉ *G24, Block C, Yayasan Hassanal Bolkiah Complex,* ☎ 02/232892. *AE, DC, MC, V.*

$$ ✕ **Rasa Sayang.** On the fifth floor of a central business district office/shopping complex, the Rasa Sayang has excellent dim sum at lunchtime. The Malaysian waitresses are happy to help you make your selections, which include everything from steamed buns to barbecue ribs. For something more substantial, the fish dishes (particularly pomfret with onions and a soy-based sauce) are better than the beef. ✉ *Top floor, Bangunan Guru 2 Melayu,* ☎ 02/223600. *AE, DC, V.*

$$$$ ✕▥ **Sheraton Utama.** The smartest, most professionally managed hotel in BSB is in the central business district. Rooms are on the dark side owing to their small windows (the best view you'll get is one of the pool), but light fabrics and furnishings add some cheer. Superior rooms, with two queen-size beds or a king, are worth the extra B$20, and two- and three-room suites are also available. Bathrooms are functional rather than luxurious, though they're equipped with toiletries and bathrobes. The formal dining room, Deal's, offers the only respectable European fare beyond the coffee-shop variety. In a small, personable room with Regency-style decor, the German chef serves Dover sole, U.S. prime beef, and New Zealand lamb, as well as local seafood. Recipes are simple but professionally executed. The more casual Café Melati serves a buffet breakfast, lunch, and dinner from 7 AM to 10:30 PM. On most evenings, there are barbecue or fondue dinners poolside. The bar is a friendly meeting place. ✉ *Jln. Tasek (Box 2203), 1922,* ☎ *02/244272, 800/325–3535 in the U.S., or 0800/353535 in the U.K.,* ☏ *02/221579, www.sheraton.com. 156 rooms and suites. 2 restaurants, bar, pool, exercise room, business services. AE, DC, MC, V.*

$$ ▥ **Brunei Hotel.** In the heart of the central business district, this hotel has neat, clean, minimally furnished but pleasant rooms with oak trim. The Coffee Garden restaurant serves local and Western food (seafood is the best thing to order); there's usually a theme buffet in the evening. The VIP Room serves classic Cantonese fare. ✉ *95 Jln. Pemancha (Box 50), 1900,* ☎ *02/242372,* ☏ *02/226196. 75 rooms. 2 restaurants. AE, DC, V.*

$$ ▥ **Terrace Hotel.** This hotel offers clean rooms at modest prices. You'll also find a pool surrounded by well landscaped grounds. ✉ *Jln. Tasek Lama (Box 49), 1900,* ☎ *02/243553,* ☏ *02/227302. 80 rooms. Bar, coffee shop, dining room, pool, beauty salon. AE, DC, MC, V.*

Shopping

The **open market** alongside the Kianggeh River is a fun place to browse for inexpensive goods. The best place to shop for a wide assortment of items is the attractive **Yayasan Sultan Hassanal Bolkiah** complex, generally referred to simply as the Yayasan. There's a large basement supermarket opposite a good drugstore and bookstore (where you can pick up secondhand books). On the ground floor of the same block are the **Delifrance Cafe**; the Italian restaurant **Fratini** (☞ *also* Dining and Lodging, *above*); and a branch of the **Body Shop.** On the upper level, you'll find a reasonable bookstore—the **Times Bookshop**—as well as trendy boutiques; the third level has an air-conditioned food court. The department store in the other block is rather disappointing.

The showroom at the **Brunei Arts and Handicrafts Centre** (☞ *above*) has the best selection of local work, but its prices—especially for finely worked silver—are high. Popular items include kris (ornamental daggers) and *kain songket,* a cloth containing gold or silver thread.

Gold jewelry (24 karat) is popular among Brunei's citizens, so goldsmiths offer a wide selection. Check out **Chin Chin Goldsmith** (✉ 33 Jln. Sultan, ☎ 02/222893). At **Million Goldsmith and Jewelry** (✉ Teck Guan Plaza, Jln. Sultan, ☎ 02/429546), you'll find necklaces, brooches, and bracelets in interesting designs.

Northern Borneo A to Z

Arriving and Departing

By Airplane

SARAWAK

Malaysia Airlines is the primary carrier to Sarawak, although Royal Brunei also flies into **Kuching International Airport** (☎ 082/454242); this spacious airport is about 11 km (7 mi) south of town, and the unmetered taxis charge RM15 for the trip. Singapore Airlines has two flights a week from Singapore to Kuching, and Dragonair operates flights linking Hong Kong and Kuching. Royal Brunei also operates daily flights from BSB to Kuching and Miri.

SABAH

Malaysia Airlines is the primary carrier to Sabah; in addition, Royal Brunei, Singapore Airlines, TransAir, and Dragonair fly into **Kota Kinabalu International Airport** (☎ 088/238555). A taxi ride from the airport to the city center costs RM12; purchase the taxi voucher from the counter marked TEKSI.

BRUNEI

Brunei International Airport (☎ 02/331747) near BSB, is sleek, modern, and efficient. The national carrier, Royal Brunei Airlines, has routes throughout Southeast Asia, as well as to Europe and Australia. Malaysia Airlines flies to Brunei from Kuching in Sarawak and Kota Kinabalu in Sabah. Singapore Airlines, and Thai Airways International also serve Brunei. The quickest way to get downtown from the airport is by taxi, although air-conditioned minibuses (B$2) leave from the covered bus depot about 100 yards from outside the arrival hall. Taxis are unmetered, but the fare is currently fixed at B$22.

By Boat

You can get to Brunei from Limbang in northern Sarawak via a riverboat that takes half an hour and costs about B$7; there's also service to Brunei from Lawas, Sarawak. Express boats run between Muara, which is about 30 minutes and B$2 by air-conditioned minibus from BSB, and the Malaysian island of Labuan (there are express boats to the island from Kota Kinabalu in Sabah); the trip takes about one hour, and the fare is B$20. It's much cheaper to do the trip in reverse, as the fare from Labuan to Muara is RM20.

Getting Around

By Airplane

Sarawak has an excellent system of internal air links, with frequent MAS flights between Kuching, Sibu, Bintulu, Miri, Limbang, and Lawas. Smaller destinations such as Mulu, Mukah, Kapit, and Bario can be reached via the subsidized MAS Rural Air Service. Sabah has flights connecting Kota Kinabalu with Tawau, Lahad Datu, and Sandakan on the east coast, while the Rural Air Service operates from Kota Kinabalu to Kudat, and links Kudat with Sandakan. There are no internal flights in Brunei.

By Boat

SARAWAK

In a land where rivers are often still the major highways, boats are an essential means of transport. Fast, air-conditioned express boats link Kuching with Sibu, where you can get other express boats up the Rajang River to Kapit and on up the Baleh River. There are also express boats along another river system, the Baram, operating from Kuala Baram north of Miri up to Marudi and Long Lama. Canoes equipped with outboard engines, known locally as longboats, ply the smaller rivers.

BRUNEI

Water taxis—small, open boats—to the Kampung Ayer are available from several places, including near the market off Jalan Sungai Kianggeh and the steps near the Yayasan shopping complex. Bargain with drivers for fares; a complete tour should cost between B$20 and B$25. Trips to the Temburong District of Brunei involve travel by speedboat through a network of mangrove forest.

By Bus

SARAWAK

Long-distance buses—from Lundu, on the northwest coast, to Kuching and from Kuching right up through Sri Aman, Sibu, Bintulu, and Miri—advertise their timetables in the daily English-language newspapers. In Kuching, the main terminal is the Jalan Penrissen Bus Station, south of town. A handy map showing the various local bus stations in Kuching and their routes is available at the Visitors' Information Centre near the Sarawak Museum (☞ Visitor Information, *below*).

SABAH

Private buses, both minibuses and large air-conditioned coaches, serve the towns and the countryside, and link Kota Kinabalu with Kudat in the north as well as Sandakan, Lahad Datu, and Tawau on the east coast. It's also possible to travel by bus south to Lawas in Sarawak. Kota Kinabalu's main terminal for long-distance buses is near the Padang; this is also the departure point for minibuses to Ranau, which pass in front of Kinabalu Park. Local buses leave for Tanjung Aru from opposite the post office; minibuses leave from an empty lot in front of Centrepoint shopping complex.

BRUNEI

A paved road links Kuala Belait, 112 km (70 mi) southwest of BSB, with the Malaysian town of Miri in Sarawak. It's slow going and involves a river crossing by ferry and two immigration-control stops. And if you want to go on to BSB, you have to take another bus. The best way to do the trip from Miri right to BSB is aboard one of the air-conditioned, private minibuses owned by **Mr. Nee Tien Poh** (☎ 02/222945 in BSB;

085/433898 in Miri). The extra comfort and speed is well worth the cost (B$60).

By Car

SARAWAK AND SABAH

Four-wheel-drive vehicles are recommended for driving in the interiors of both states. Car-rental prices are high—starting at RM140–RM160 a day. In Kuching, try: **Mayflower Car Rental** (⊠ Kuching airport, ☎ 082/236889) or **Pronto Car Rental** (⊠ Kuching airport, ☎ 082/410110). In Kota Kinabalu, try: **E&C** (☎ 088/239996) or **Kinabalu Rent A Car** (☎ 088/232602), which has desks at the airport and at major hotels.

BRUNEI

Two rental agencies have counters at the airport: **Avis** (☎ 02/426345) and **National Car Rental** (☎ 02/424921). Rates are B$100–B$150 per day.

By Taxi

SARAWAK AND SABAH

Cabs are more expensive here than on the peninsula, and they're unmetered. Always agree on the price with your driver before setting out. To ensure that things go smoothly, ask at your hotel about nearby taxi stands, the usual fares to various destinations within cities, and how to arrange trips to rural areas. Hiring a car with driver for three hours in Kuching or Kota Kinabalu costs about RM80; it should be slightly cheaper outside the state capitals.

In Kuching, drivers gather in front of the Holiday Inn and opposite the Crowne Plaza. Shared taxis and minibuses congregate near the bus terminals, and river taxis leave from marked departure points (*pangkalan*) along the waterfront. In Kota Kinabalu you can always find a cab near the Hyatt downtown. Summoning cabs by telephone isn't very reliable, but you can try a **taxi company** (☎ 088/51863 or 088/25669) in Kota Kinabalu.

BRUNEI

You can hire a private taxi for sightseeing, but drivers often speak little English. Hotels will arrange such service for around B$50 an hour, often with a minimum of three hours.

By Train

SABAH

Sabah State Railways (☎ 088/254611) runs the only rail service on Borneo from Kota Kinabalu south to Tenom. The 49-km (31-mi) stretch between Beaufort and Tenom passes through the spectacular Crocker Range and Padas Gorge. The locomotive from Beaufort to Tenom (RM2.25) is very slow and uncomfortable; however, a quaint small railcar takes 1½–2 hours and costs RM8.85.

Contacts and Resources

Emergencies

SARAWAK AND SABAH

Major private hospitals maintain high standards and doctors speak English. Your hotel will be able to arrange for a doctor or dentist should the need arise. Pharmacies are well stocked and the pharmacists speak English (if not the counter staff). Scuba divers should note that the only decompression chamber in the region is in Labuan, off Brunei Bay.

Hospitals: Normah Medical Centre (⊠ Jln. Tun Datuk Patinggi, Kuching, ☎ 082/440055); **Sabah Medical Centre** (⊠ Kingfisher Park, Kota Kinabalu, ☎ 088/424333). **Police:** ☎ 082/241222 in Kuching; 088/242111 in Kota Kinabalu.

Brunei's medical services are of a high standard and are staffed by English-speaking doctors and nurses. **Ambulance:** ☎ 995. **Fire:** ☎ 995. Hospital: **Jerudong Park Medical Centre** (✉ Jerudong Park, ☎ 02/671433).

English-Language Bookstores

SARAWAK AND SABAH
In Sarawak, Kuching is the best place to find English-language books and magazines. Recommended shops include: **The Curio Shoppe** (✉ Kuching Hilton, Jln. Tuanku Abdul Rahman, ☎ 082/248118), **The Curio Shoppe** (✉ Sarawak Museum, Jln. Tun Haji Openg, ☎ 082/253977), and **Mohamed Yahiah Sons** (✉ Holiday Inn Kuching, Jln. Tuanku Abdul Rahman, ☎ 082/254282).

In Sabah, Kota Kinabalu shops include: **Borneo Craft** (✉ Ground floor, Wisma Merdeka, ☎ 088/237936), or **Iwase** (✉ Ground floor, Wisma Merdeka, ☎ 088/233757).

BRUNEI
In BSB, try: **Far Eastern Books** (✉ G4 Guan Teck Plaza, Jln. Sultan, ☎ 02/242539) or **Times Bookshop** (✉ 1st floor, Yayasan Sultan Haji Hassanal Bolkiah Complex, ☎ 02/220964).

Tour Operators and Travel Agencies
Note that many of the companies cited below can help you make general travel arrangements—airline reservations, hotel bookings, and so on—as well as organize tours.

SARAWAK
It takes about three hours to see Kuching's historic sites, including a drive past the central market and a Malay village and a stop at the Sarawak Museum. You can take guided nature walks within the orangutan sanctuary at Semenggoh; visit a crocodile farm; or take a trip to the Bako National Park or the Kubah National Park, where the Matang Wildlife Centre is. Tour organizers also arrange backpacking and spelunking excursions into mountain regions and ancient caves.

In Kuching you'll find the itineraries and prices comparable at: **Asian Overland Services** (✉ 286A, 1st floor, Westwood Park, Jln. Tabuan, ☎ 082/251162), **Ibanika** (✉ Lot 435, Lorong 9, Jln. Ang Cheng Ho, ☎ 082/424022), and **Singai Travel Services** (✉ 2nd floor, Lot 168, Chan Chin Ann Rd., ☎ 082/412778). **Borneo Adventure** (✉ 55 Main Bazaar, ☎ 082/245175) has won awards for its longhouse tours and also offers a wide range of other tours in Sarawak, Sabah, and Brunei. In Miri, **Tropical Adventure** (✉ Ground floor, Mega Hotel, Jln. Merbau, ☎ 085/419337) specializes in adventure tours to Gunung Mulu National Park and the Bario Highlands; they also offer dive trips on live-aboard boats to Luconia Shoals from April to October.

SABAH
A Kota Kinabalu city tour covers the highlights in just two hours. Country tours often stop at Mengkabong, a stilted village of Bajau fisherfolk 30 km (18 mi) out of Kota Kinabalu. On the way you'll pass rice fields; rural kampungs; and the town of Tamparuli, famed for a nearby suspension bridge. Other excursions include the Sunday market at Kota Belud, a day trip to Tenom, and the Sepilok Orang-Utan Rehabilitation Center. Two- and three-day trips are offered to the wildlife haven of Sukau in the Kinabatangan region, to the Turtle Islands off Sandakan, and to Danum Valley. Tour operators also offer whitewater rafting as well as hiking safaris into the interior (including visits to native villages); some specialize in dive trips.

Tour operators in Kota Kinabalu include: **Borneo Adventure** (✉ 10th floor, Gaya Centre, Jln. Tun Razak, ☏ 088/238731); **Borneo Divers** (✉ 4th floor, Wisma Sabah, Jln. Tun Razak, ☏ 088/222226), which offers diving courses and excursions to Sipadan and the reefs of Tunku Abdul Rahman National Park and has packages with Malaysia Airlines; and **Borneo Eco Tours** (✉ 12A, 2nd floor, Lorong Bernam 3, off Jln. Kolam, ☏ 088/234009).

Several operators are based at Shangri-La's Tanjung Aru Resort (near the airport and 10 minutes from downtown), including: **Borneo Expeditions** (☏ 088/222948); **Tanjung Aru Tours & Travel** (☏ 088/256676), which offers resort diving and scuba training and has a private dive resort on Pandanan Island north of Sipadan; and **Wildlife Expeditions** (☏ 088/246000), which specializes in trips to Sepilok, Sukau, the Turtle Islands, and the Danum Valley.

BRUNEI

Two tour companies specializing in tours of Brunei are based in BSB. The best-known operator is **Sunshine Borneo Tours and Travel** (✉ Block A, No. 4, 1st floor, Abdul Razak Complex, Km 3½, Jln. Gadong, ☏ 02/446812). It organizes tours of the capital, river trips, and tours to Iban longhouses both in Brunei and across the border in Sarawak, and day trips to Ulu Temburong National Park. **Freme Travel Service** (✉ Unit 4038 Wisma Jaya, Jln. Pemancha, ☏ 02/335025) offers similar tours in both Brunei and neighboring Sabah and Sarawak.

Visitor Information

SARAWAK

Sarawak has an efficient network of tourist information offices, and staffers are unfailingly friendly and helpful; these centers also handle accommodation bookings and issue visit permits for the various national parks in the vicinity. They include: **Visitors Information Centre** (✉ 31 Jln. Masjid [next to Sarawak Museum], Kuching, ☏ 082/410944); **Visitors Information Centre** (✉ 32 ground floor, Jln. Cross, Sibu, ☏ 084/340980); and **Visitors Information Centre** (✉ 452 Jln. Melayu [opposite Tamu Muhibbah], Miri, ☏ 085/434181).

In Kuching, the **MTPB** (✉ Rugayah Building, Jln. Song Thian Cheok, ☏ 082/246775) has information on all of Malaysia but not a great deal on Sarawak itself. The **Sarawak Tourist Association** maintains a small information center on the Kuching waterfront (☏ 082/240620) and at the Kuching airport (☏ 082/456266).

SABAH

The **Sabah Tourism Promotion Corporation** (✉ 51 Jln. Gaya, ☏ 088/219400) has an office that's conveniently located in downtown Kota Kinabalu. In Kota Kinabalu you'll also find an office of the **MTPB** (✉ Wing On Life Building, Jln. Segunting, ☏ 088/211732).

BRUNEI

Brunei only recently began to actively encourage tourism and cannot match the tourism information services of its neighbors. There's a tourist information booth at the airport, where you can pick up the brochure *Explore Brunei*, but there is no tourism office in downtown BSB.

MALAYSIA AND BRUNEI A TO Z

Arriving and Departing

By Airplane

AIRPORTS

The brand-new **Kuala Lumpur International Airport** opened in June 1998 and is the major gateway to Malaysia. This large, modern facility, 51 km (32 mi) from downtown, has updated check-in, baggage-handling, and security procedures; two hotels; and bus links into the capital. Given the congestion in and around KL, getting to the airport can take as long as two hours; the direct rail link, nearing completion, should cut this time down to approximately 30 minutes. The old airport at Subang is now used mainly for charters and internal flights.

Brunei International Airport (☎ 02/331747) near BSB, is a modern gateway.

CARRIERS

Malaysia Airlines (☎ 03/746–3000 in KL), the national carrier, offers six weekly flights from Los Angeles to KL with a stop in Tokyo or Taipei, and three weekly flights from New York to KL with a stop in Dubai. MAS also has frequent flights to KL from six cities in Australia and daily from Auckland, New Zealand. Among the many airlines that serve Kuala Lumpur are **British Airways** (☎ 03/232–5797), **Air Canada** (☎ 03/248–8596), **Singapore Airlines** (☎ 03/292–3122), and **Thai Airways International** (☎ 03/201–2900). During the day, both MAS and Singapore Airlines fly hourly between KL and Singapore; you can cut the fare in half by buying a standby air-shuttle ticket at the airport.

Brunei is served by its national carrier, **Royal Brunei Airlines** (☎ 02/242222 in BSB), which has direct daily flights to London, and three flights a week to Frankfurt. The airline also has services to Perth, Darwin, and Brisbane in Australia and to Bangkok. Daily flights connect Brunei with both Singapore and KL. Singapore Airlines also serves Brunei.

FLYING TIMES

The flying time to KL is 19 hours from Los Angeles, 17 hours from Vancouver, 15 hours from New York (eastward), 12½ hours from London, 8 hours from Sydney, and 10½ hours from Auckland. The flying time to Brunei is 16½ hours from London, 8 hours from Brisbane, 2½ hours from Bangkok, and 2 hours from KL and Singapore.

Getting Around

By Airplane

Malaysia Airlines flies to 35 towns and cities in the country (for air hub information, ☞ Arriving and Departing by Airplane *in* individual region's A to Z sections). Domestic flights are relatively inexpensive and often fully booked, especially during school holidays and festivals. Still, there's no need to reconfirm reservations. There are no internal flights within Brunei.

AIR PASSES

Malaysia Airlines offers a **Discover Malaysia** pass that enables international visitors to travel on domestic routes for about half the normal fare. You may make flight reservations and purchase tickets overseas or in Malaysia. There's a catch, though: you must show that your entry into Malaysia will be or is on Malaysia Airlines.

By Boat

There's no passenger service between peninsular Malaysia and Sabah and Sarawak, nor from Singapore to Brunei. In Malaysian port cities there's regular **ferry service** to the nearby islands. To get to Pangkor, catch the ferry in Lumut; for Langkawi, ferries leave from Kuala Perlis, Kuala Kedah, and Pinang. Ferries to Pulau Redang leave from Merang, and those to the Perhentian islands leave from Kuala Besut. Launches serve Tioman Island from Mersing and the islands of the Tunku Abdul Rahman Marine Park from Kota Kinabalu. Frequent passenger launches run from BSB to Limbang, and express boats to Labuan depart from Brunei's port of Muara.

By Bus

Bus service is extensive and cheap, but generally only coaches traveling between major cities are air-conditioned. Local buses are often crowded, noisy, and slow, but it's a great way to people-watch and sightsee at the same time. Brunei has an excellent public bus service in BSB, using small, air-conditioned coaches. For information on schedules, contact the nearest tourism information service or ask at your hotel. Buses generally run between 6 AM and 6 PM.

By Car

EMERGENCY ASSISTANCE

The **Automobile Association of Malaysia** (✉ 191, Jln. Tun Razak, KL, ☎ 03/2162–5777 or 03/2612–2727) can offer advice in case of a roadside emergency. There's no such service in Brunei; in case of mechanical problems, contact your car-rental agency.

GASOLINE

Stations charge about RM1.08 per liter (RM4.86 per gallon) and generally offer full service; in KL however, government policy has forced many gas stations to operate self-service pumps. In the cities, most stations operate 24 hours; elsewhere, they're closed at night. Fuel costs B53 cents per liter (B$2.38 per gallon) in Brunei, and service stations generally close at night.

PARKING

Except for KL, Georgetown, and JB, on-street parking is generally adequate in Malaysia. In some towns, meters are installed (and closely monitored), though you're just as likely to have a parking attendant issue you a receipt. Major cities also have multistory parking garages. In Brunei, parking is generally on the street, though BSB has a parking garage.

RENTAL AGENCIES

In Malaysia, you usually don't need an International Driver's License to rent a car; a valid permit from home is adequate. Cars are available for hire only in major towns. Rates run from as little as RM70 a day in Langkawi to around RM170 in Kota Kinabalu, with unlimited mileage. Inquire about special three-day and weekend rates. These can offer significant rate reductions. One-way rentals are possible for additional drop-off fees. In Brunei, both self-drive and chauffeured cars are available in BSB. Major car-rental offices in Malaysia include Avis, Budget, Hertz, Mayflower, and Thrifty; in Brunei, you'll find Avis and National Car Rental systems. For details on these and smaller, local agencies, *see* Getting Around By Car *in* the individual region's A to Z sections.

ROAD CONDITIONS

The North–South Expressway is a first-class highway that runs along the western side of the peninsula from the Thai border past Butterworth (near Pinang), Ipoh, KL, and Melaka, down to JB, where it's linked by a causeway and a new bridge to Singapore. The East–West Highway runs from Butterworth across to Kota Bharu. Other roads, especially near industrial centers, have heavy traffic day and night. Slow-moving trucks, motorcycles, and bicycles make driving somewhat treacherous. Back roads are narrow but paved, and the pace is relaxed—you'll weave around dogs sleeping in the road. Mountain roads are often single-lane, and you must allow oncoming cars to pass. Brunei has one major road that links BSB with Kuala Belait in the southwest; note that you can't drive to the Temburong area of Brunei unless you drive through Limbang in Sarawak.

RULES OF THE ROAD

In both Malaysia and Brunei, seat belts are compulsory for drivers and front-seat passengers, and stiff fines are imposed on those caught without them. Driving is on the left side of the road. The police use radar traps frequently, and fines are heavy—about RM300 for driving 20 kph over the limit. Don't be tempted to bribe your way out of a fine; however, given the traditional courtesy of Malaysians and Bruneians, a smile from a helpless tourist sometimes saves the day. Some common traffic signs in both countries, include: AWAS (caution), JALAN SEHALA (one way), KURANGKAN LAJU (slow down), and IKUT KIRI (keep left). Directions are *utara* (north), *selatan* (south), *timur* (east), and *barat* (west).

By Taxi

Both Malaysian and Bruneian taxi operators near bus terminals call out destinations for long-distance, shared-cost rides; drivers leave when they get four passengers. Single travelers who want to charter a taxi pay four times the flat rate and leave whenever they want. The quality of service depends on the condition of the vehicle and bravado of the driver.

City taxis are plentiful and relatively cheap. Taxis on peninsular Malaysia are metered. However, taxi drivers in KL will sometimes attempt not to use the meter and, instead, charge you a fixed price. Console yourself with the thought that the locals, too, are subjected to such treatment, especially during rush hour or when it's raining hard. Taxis in Sabah and Sarawak are not metered—set the fare with the driver in advance. Between midnight and 6 AM, rides cost 50% more than what's on the meter. In Brunei, taxis are metered in the capital; a 50% surcharge is added 9 PM–6 AM.

By Train

Malayan Railways (☎ 03/273–9118, ✍) known as KTM, offers relatively comfortable service on the peninsula. On long trips movies are shown, but the passing scenery is always more interesting. In some sections the route goes through jungle and you may see wild monkeys. Sleepers are available on overnight service for a supplemental charge. Dining-car food is simple, cheap, and tasty. For information on the rail line in Sabah, *see* Getting Around By Train *in* Northern Borneo A to Z, *above*.

A luxury (and superexpensive) train service, the **Eastern & Oriental Express,** (☎ 800/524–2420 in the U.S.) which is modeled after the *Orient Express,* makes the 41-hour trip between Singapore and Bangkok with stops in Malaysia at KL and Butterworth.

RAIL PASSES

Foreign visitors can buy the KTM Railpass, which permits unlimited travel for 10 days (US$55) or 30 days (US$120), at main railway stations in Malaysia and in Singapore. Prices are reduced for children between 4 and 12 years old and for youths under the age of 30 and who hold the ISIC, YIEE Card, or Youth Hostel Card.

Contacts and Resources

Customs and Duties

MALAYSIA

Such items as cameras, watches, pens, lighters, cosmetics, perfume, portable radio cassette players, cigarettes (up to 200), and liquor (1 liter) may be brought into Malaysia duty-free. If you're bringing in dutiable goods, such as video equipment, you may have to pay a deposit (up to 50% of the item's value) for temporary importation, which is refundable when you leave. If you have to pay a tax or deposit, be sure to get an official receipt. The importation of illegal drugs into Malaysia carries the death penalty. There are restrictions on the export of antiquities. If in doubt about any purchase, check with the director of the Muzium Negara in KL. Currency controls implemented in 1998 require a special permit to bring in more than 1,000 ringgits in the form of cash or other negotiable instruments. There's no limit on the amount of foreign currency that can be brought in.

BRUNEI

You're allowed to import 200 cigarettes or 250 grams of tobacco and 60 milliliters of perfume or 250 milliliters of toilet water. The import of alcohol is restricted to two bottles (about 2 quarts) of liquor and 12 cans of beer for non-Muslims over 17 years of age. A declaration must be completed on arrival. The importation of illegal drugs into Brunei also carries the death penalty.

Electricity

The electrical current in both Malaysia and Brunei is 220 volts, 50 cycles alternating current (AC). You should bring an adapter and converter, or, if your appliances are dual voltage, just an adapter. Wall outlets take a variety of plug styles, including plugs with two round oversize prongs and plugs with three prongs. It's a good idea to bring a surge protector for your laptop.

Embassies and Consulates

MALAYSIA

Australia (⊠ 6 Jln. Yap Kwan Seng, Kuala Lumpur, ☎ 03/242–3122). **Canada** (⊠ Plaza MBF, 5th floor, Jln. Ampang, Kuala Lumpur, ☎ 03/2161–2000). **New Zealand** (⊠ Menara IMC, Jln. Sultan Ismail, Kuala Lumpur, ☎ 03/238–2533). **United Kingdom** (⊠ 185 Jln. Ampang, Kuala Lumpur, ☎ 03/248–2122). **United States** (⊠ 9 Jln. Langat, Kuala Lumpur, ☎ 03/2168–5000).

BRUNEI

Australia (⊠ 4th floor, Teck Guan Plaza, Jln. Sultan, BSB, ☎ 02/229435). **United Kingdom** (⊠ Hongkong Bank Chambers, Jln. Pemancha, BSB, ☎ 02/226001). **United States** (⊠ 3rd floor, Teck Guan Plaza, Jln. Sultan, BSB, ☎ 02/229670).

Health and Safety

FOOD AND DRINK

As a rule, food handlers in both Malaysia and Brunei are inspected by health-enforcement officers, but the best advice is to patronize popular places: consumers everywhere tend to boycott stalls with a reputation for poor hygiene. Avoid eating precooked food from outdoor food stalls, where lack of refrigeration increases the risk of contamination; places where food is cooked for you only when ordered are recommended. Bottled water is widely available and preferred by many locals; ice is, by law, made from boiled water.

OTHER PRECAUTIONS

As elsewhere in Southeast Asia, you should find out whether there are stinging jellyfish in the water before you wade in. Some trees in the rain forest can cause allergies; if you are trekking with a guide, you'll be warned of any possible dangers. Gay and lesbian travelers should be aware that both Malaysia and Brunei officially frown upon such relationships; to avoid embarrassment, discretion is recommended.

Language, Culture, and Etiquette

MALAYSIA

The official language is Bahasa Malayu, though local variations can differ greatly from the official version. English is widely spoken in government, business, and tourism establishments, and it's the interracial lingua franca. The Chinese generally speak several dialects, including Cantonese, Teochew, Hakka, and Hokkien; the Indians are primarily Tamil speakers. In Sabah and Sarawak, as many as 50 tribal languages are spoken, though all schoolchildren throughout the country are educated in the national language.

Being neatly dressed is respected by Malaysians. As this is officially a Muslim country, conservative dress is recommended. Revealing clothes, shorts, and short skirts should be worn only at resorts. To enter mosques, women must wear something, a scarf for example, over their heads (in some mosques, women are requested to wear a coverall that's handed to them at the door by mosque officials). Everyone must remove their shoes before entering a mosque or any private home. Avoid using the left hand to give or receive anything, as this is considered offensive to Muslims.

BRUNEI

The official language is Malay, but English and the Hokkien Chinese dialect are widely spoken. Bruneians are even more conservative in dress than most Malaysians, so it's prudent to dress modestly. As in Malaysia, remove your shoes before entering a mosque or a private home, and avoid using the left hand to give or receive anything.

Mail

Addresses in Malaysia and Brunei do not always include street numbers; often the name of a large office building, a shopping complex, or a hotel is sufficient. Note that in addresses for a shop in a large complex, you might see a digit with a decimal in it, such as 3.26. The "3" indicates the floor or level within the complex, and the "26" indicates the shop number on that floor or level.

POSTAL RATES

In Malaysia, stamps and postal information are generally available at hotel front desks. Postcards cost 55 sen to the Americas, 50 sen to Europe, Australia, and New Zealand; airmail letters cost RM1.10 (½ oz) to the Americas, 90 sen to Europe, and 55 sen to Australia and New Zealand. Aerograms are the best value of all, at 50 sen—regardless of where they're being sent.

Brunei charges B30 cents for postcards, B45 cents for aerograms, and B90 cents for airmail letters to any overseas destination. Obtain stamps from your hotel or the post office.

RECEIVING MAIL

American Express (✉ Bangunan MAS, 5th floor, Jln. Sultan Ismail, Kuala Lumpur, ☎ 03/213–0000; 4th floor, Shell Building, Jln. Sultan, BSB, ☎ 02/228225) will hold mail for 30 days at no charge, as long as you can produce identification and either an American Express card or American Express traveler's checks. In addition, you can have mail sent to you labeled "poste restante" care of the main post office in various cities or towns; check both your first name and surname as the locals sometimes file mail by the first name that appears on the envelope.

Although postal codes are officially in use in both countries, mail will still be delivered without them. Address envelopes in the normal fashion and you can expect them to reach their destination. The efficiency of the Malaysian mail system is such that many Malaysians prefer to use courier service for urgent mail, and register all important mail (another RM1).

Money Matters

COSTS

The Malaysian ringgit, like other Asian currencies, lost dramatically against the U.S. dollar and other currencies in mid-1998. This means that for many visitors, the country offers real value. As might be expected, prices in the cities are higher than elsewhere, though mostly rural Sabah is the most expensive state in the country. Prices in most shops and larger stores are fixed, but you can discreetly ask for a discount. In street markets, flea markets, and antiques stores, bargaining is expected. Taxes on alcohol mean that a glass of beer or bottle of wine is surprisingly expensive in Malaysia. Brunei is a rich country, and the Brunei dollar is strong. Things here cost almost twice as much as they do in Malaysia.

Sample Costs in Malaysia: Cup of coffee/tea in a hotel, RM5.50; cup of tea in open-air *kedai,* RM1; small bottle of water RM1.10; bottle of beer, RM8.50; bowl of noodles at a stall, RM3.50; 2-km (1-mi) taxi ride, RM2; city bus ride, 90 sen.

Sample Costs in Brunei: Breakfast of toast, eggs, and coffee, B$10–B$15; coffee in a hotel B$5; bowl of noodles B$3–B$4; taxi ride, B$4 for first mile, B60 cents per mile thereafter; city bus ride B$1.

CURRENCY

Malaysian ringgit are issued in denominations of RM1, RM5, RM10, RM20, RM50, RM100, RM500, and RM1,000. The ringgit is divided into 100 sen, and there are coins worth 1, 5, 10, 20, and 50 sen and RM1. The exchange rate at press time was RM3.80 to the U.S. dollar, RM2.61 to the Canadian dollar, RM6.00 to the pound sterling, RM2.28 to the Australian dollar, and RM1.89 to the New Zealand dollar.

Brunei dollars are issued in notes of B$1, B$5, B$10, B$50, B$100, B$500, and B$1,000. Coins come in denominations of 1, 5, 10, 20, and 50 cents. The Brunei dollar is at par with the Singapore dollar, which also circulates in Brunei. At press time the exchange rate was B$1.70 to the U.S. dollar, B$2.70 to the pound sterling, B$1.17 to the Canadian dollar, B$1.03 to the Australian dollar, and B$0.85 to the New Zealand dollar.

SERVICE CHARGES, TAXES, AND TIPPING

In Malaysia, a 5% tax is added to bills of hotel and restaurants classified as tourist class, along with a 10% service charge in a system that the locals call "plus plus." (You'll see the "++" symbols where this applies.) In nontourist-class restaurants and local coffee shops, tipping isn't expected. All departing passengers pay an airport tax of RM40 to international destinations, RM10 to Singapore and Brunei, and RM5 for domestic destinations. Tip porters RM1 per bag. It would be insulting to tip less than 50 sen. Malaysians usually tip taxi drivers with their coin change. Otherwise, when you want to acknowledge fine service, 10% is generous, though not expected.

In Brunei, there's a service charge of 10% in hotels and also in air-conditioned restaurants. Hotel porters should be given B$1 per bag. The driver of a hired car appreciates B$10 for a morning's work, but there's no need to tip taxi drivers. Departing passengers pay an airport tax of B$12 on international flights, B$5 to Singapore or Malaysia.

Opening and Closing Times

In Malaysia: Restaurants normally serve lunch from 11:30 AM to 2:30 PM and dinner from 6:30 PM to 11 PM, with last orders at 9:30 or 10 PM. **Shops** are generally open 9:30 AM–7 PM; department stores and supermarkets, 10–10. Many places are closed Sunday, except in the states of Johor, Kedah, Perlis, Kelantan, and Terengganu, where Friday is the day of rest. **Banks** are open weekdays 9:30–3 and Saturday 9:30–11:30. **Post offices** are open from Monday to Thursday 8–5 and Friday 8–12.30. **Government offices** open Monday–Thursday 8–12:45 and 2–4:15, Friday 8–12:45 and 2:45–4:15, and Saturday 8–12:45.

In Brunei: Government offices are open from 7:45 to 12:15 and 1:30–4.30, except on Friday and Sunday, when they are closed. Most **shopping centers** open daily from 10–10. Restaurants generally close early, between 9 and 10.

NATIONAL HOLIDAYS

Note that the dates of some religious holidays change from year to year.

In Malaysia: Chinese New Year (Jan./Feb.), Labor Day (May 1), Hari Raya Aidilfitri (Jan.), King's Birthday (June 4), Hari Raya Aidel-Adha (Mar.), National Day (Aug. 31), Prophet Muhammad's Birthday (Aug.), Deepavali (Nov.), Christmas (Dec. 25).

In Brunei: Hari Raya Aidilfitri (Jan.), National Day (Feb. 23), Anniversary of the Royal Brunei Army (May 31), Sultan's Birthday (July 15), Prophet Muhammad's Birthday (Aug.).

Passports and Visas

IN MALAYSIA

Citizens of Australia, Canada, New Zealand, the United States, and the United Kingdom do not need visas for stays of less than 90 days. All visitors must be in possession of a passport that's valid for three months from the date of arrival on peninsular Malaysia, and for six months on the date of arrival in Sabah or Sarawak.

IN BRUNEI

All visitors must be in possession of a valid passport. For stays of up to 14 days, citizens of Canada and New Zealand don't need visas. United Kingdom citizens can stay for up to 30 days and American citizens up to 90 days without a visa. Australians must obtain visas in advance (note that you can't get them in Sabah or Sarawak). To apply for visas, Australians should contact any Royal Brunei Airlines office or the **Brunei High Commission** (✉ 16 Bulwarra Close, O'Malley, Canberra ACT 2606, Australia, ☎ 02/6290–1801).

Student and Youth Travel

The **Youth Hostels Association** (✉ 9 Jln. Vethavanam, off Jln. Ipoh, Kuala Lumpur, ☎ 03/971–7373) operates hostels throughout Malaysia. However, these are generally out of the way and no cheaper than other budget accommodations. (The same is true of YMCA and YWCA lodgings.) Many national parks, especially in Sarawak and Sabah, offer either camping sites or inexpensive hostels.

Telephones

CALLS TO MALAYSIA AND BRUNEI

To call Malaysia from overseas, dial the country code, 60, and then the area code, omitting the first 0. The area code for KL is 3; for Pinang and Langkawi, 4; for Melaka, 6; for Tioman and JB, 7; for Cherating and Kuala Terengganu, 9; for Kuching, 82; and for Kota Kinabalu, 88. To call Brunei from overseas, dial the country code, 673, and then the area code, omitting the first 0. The area code for BSB is 2.

LOCAL CALLS

Malaysia: Public pay phones take 10 sen, 20 sen, 50 sen, and RM1 coins (time unlimited on local calls). Remember to press the release button, which allows your coins to drop down, when the person you call picks up the receiver. Phone cards are becoming popular for use at public pay phones. There are three types of cards Kadfon, Unicard, and Cityfon, which can only be used in phone booths where instructions for use are displayed. The cards come in denominations from RM5 to RM50 and can be purchased at airports, Shell and Petronas gas stations, and most 7-Eleven and Hop-In stores. A limited number of pay phones accept major international credit cards. For assisted local calls, dial 102. Dial 103 for directory information.

Brunei: Pay phones use phone cards in values of B$10, B$20, B$50, and B$100, on sale at Telecom offices and post offices.

LONG-DISTANCE AND INTERNATIONAL CALLS

In Malaysia: You can make direct-dial calls overseas from many hotel-room phones. If you want to avoid the hotel charges, local phone books give pages of information in English on international calling, rates, and locations of phone offices. Pay phones where international calls can be made have an orange IDD sign over them, and can generally be found outside post offices. For assisted international calls, dial 108.

When calling the States, you can dial the following **access numbers** to reach a U.S. long-distance operator: **AT&T** (☎ 1800–800011); **MCI** (☎ 1800–800012); **Sprint** (☎ 1800–800016). To use AT&T's **UKDirect** to Britain, dial 1800–800044.

In Brunei: You can make direct-dial international calls from the major hotels or from the Central Telegraph Office on Jalan Sultan. To call the operator for assistance on overseas calls, dial 01; for directory information, 113.

Visitor Information

MALAYSIA

For information and brochures, contact the **Malaysia Tourism Promotion Board** (MTPB; ✉ 595 Madison Ave., Suite 1800, New York, NY 10022, ☎ 212/754–1113, www.tourism.gov.my; 57 Trafalgar Sq., London WC2N 5DU, ☎ 020/7930–7932).

BRUNEI

Brunei does not have any tourism information offices either at home or abroad. Before coming, inquire at the local office of Brunei's national airline, Royal Brunei Airlines. They may be able to give you a copy of their in-flight magazine, *Muhibbah*.

When to Go

Malaysia's equatorial climate is fairly uniform throughout the year: temperatures range from the low 90s during the day to low 70s at night. The mountains may be 10° cooler than the lowlands. Relative humidity is usually about 90%. Rain is common all year, but showers don't last long and shouldn't slow you down much. A rainy season brought on by monsoons lasts from November through February on the east coast of the peninsula, from October through April in Sarawak, and from October through February in Sabah. The heavy rains can cause delays. During school holidays, locals tend to fill hotels, so book in advance if you plan to visit in early April, early August, or from mid-November to early January.

Brunei lies between 4° and 6° north of the equator, and temperatures don't vary much from one season to the next: it's hot and humid year-round, and the equatorial sun is fierce. (The annual mean temperature is 80°F.) Though sudden, brief rainstorms are prevalent throughout the year (particularly November–May), the wettest months are December and January. Even during the monsoon season, be prepared for blasts of heat between downpours. There's no peak tourist season.

CLIMATE

The following are average temperatures in KL:

Jan.	89F	32C	May	91F	33C	Sept.	89F	32C
	72	22		74	23		74	23
Feb.	91F	33C	June	91F	33C	Oct.	89F	32C
	72	22		74	23		74	23
Mar.	91F	33C	July	89F	32C	Nov.	89F	32C
	74	23		72	22		74	23
Apr.	91F	33C	Aug.	89F	32C	Dec.	89F	32C
	74	23		74	23		72	22

FESTIVALS AND SEASONAL EVENTS IN MALAYSIA

Malaysia's multiracial society celebrates numerous festivals, since each ethnic community retains its own customs and traditions. The dates of some holidays are fixed, but most change according to the various religious calendars.

Jan.–Feb.: During **Chinese New Year,** Chinese families visit Buddhist temples, exchange gifts, and hold open house for relatives and friends. The Hindu festival **Thaipusam** turns out big crowds for a street parade in Pinang and a religious spectacle at the Batu Caves near KL. Indian devotees of the god Subramaniam pierce their bodies, cheeks, and tongues with steel hooks and rods. **Hari Raya Puasa or Aidilfitri** marks the end of Ramadan, the fasting month. It's a time of feasting and rejoicing and often includes a visit to the cemetery followed by mosque services. Tourists are welcome at the prime minister's residence in Kuala Lumpur during open-house hours. (Because the Islamic calendar follows the lunar cycle, each Gregorian year Ramadan begins roughly 10 days earlier.)

May–June: The **Kadazan Harvest Festival** is celebrated May 30 and 31 in Kota Kinabalu, Sabah, with feasting, buffalo races, games, and colorful dances in native costumes. The Sabah Fest, which runs in the capital for two weeks from mid-May, features cultural performances, sales of handicrafts, and special food in major shopping complexes and hotels. **Gawai Dayak,** a weeklong harvest festival, is celebrated in Sarawak with dances, games, and feasting in the longhouses. The official celebration is held in Kuching on June 1. The **Dragon Boat Festival** features boat races off Gurney Drive in Pinang early in the month. On June 5 every state marks the **King's Birthday** (Yang Di-Pertuan Agong) with parades. In KL's Merdeka Stadium, a trooping of the colors is held.

Aug.–Sept.: Merdeka Day, on August 31, is Malaysia's Independence Day. Arches are erected across city thoroughfares, buildings are illuminated, parades are arranged, and in KL there's a variety show in Lake Gardens. On **All Souls' Day,** or the Feast of the Hungry Ghosts, Chinese honor their ancestors by burning paper objects (for the ancestors' use in the afterlife) on the street. Chinese opera is performed in various locations in Pinang and other cities.

Oct.–Nov.: During **Deepavali,** the Hindu festival of lights that celebrates the triumph of good over evil, houses and shops are brightly decorated.

Dec.: During the **Chingay Procession** in late December, Malaysian Chinese parade through the streets of Pinang and JB doing stunts with enormous clan flags on bamboo poles, accompanied by cymbals, drums, and gongs. It's a noisy, colorful, folksy pageant. **Christmas** is widely celebrated, with decorations, food promotions, music, and appearances of Father Krismas.

FESTIVALS AND SEASONAL EVENTS IN BRUNEI

Brunei's Muslim festivals are generally low-key affairs involving visits to the mosque and to relatives. **Royal Brunei Armed Forces Day** on May 31 consists of military parades and displays at the Taman Haji Sir Omar Ali Saifuddien in BSB. On the **Sultan's Birthday,** celebrated July 15, parades and festivities take place throughout the country, with fireworks and night markets in the evening.

4 PHILIPPINES

A feast of islands awaits you in the Philippines. Luzon has historic Metro Manila, with its vibrant nightlife, the breathtaking Cordillera and Sierra Madre mountain ranges to the north, and Spanish-era architecture and churches. The Visaya Islands have some of the country's best sandy stretches and music lovers, and Mindanao has towering Mt. Apo and rare flora and fauna. All three regions enjoy translucent seas, tropical beaches, and highlands to trek.

By Luis H.
Francia

Updated by
Maya Besa,
Doreen
Fernandez,
and Abby Tan

T HIS ARCHIPELAGO OF 7,107 ISLANDS, extending between Taiwan to the north and Borneo to the south, seems like a misplaced Latin American country. Indeed, Filipinos are often referred to as the "Latins of the East." Although the dominant racial stock is Malay—akin to the indigenous populations of Indonesia, Borneo, and Malaysia—most people's names are Hispanic and their faith Roman Catholic (the Philippines is the only predominantly Catholic nation in Asia). To add to this cultural mix, the government is headed by a democratically elected president and English is widely spoken here, making the Philippines the fourth-largest English-speaking nation in the world, after the United States, the United Kingdom, and India. These features reflect four centuries of Spanish and American colonization. As celebrated Philippine writer Carmen Guerrero Nakpil put it, the Philippines "spent more than 300 years in a convent and 50 in Hollywood."

The cultural potpourri began around the 10th century, when the native Malays intermarried with Arab, Indian, and Chinese traders. By the 14th century, Islam had established itself in southern Mindanao with the conversion of tribal royalty. Muslim tenets started to spread north to the Visayas and Luzon, but in 1521, Ferdinand Magellan—a Portuguese navigator in the service of the Spanish throne, heading the first expedition to circumnavigate the world—landed on the island of Homonhon, off the coast of Samar, and claimed the country for Spain. Magellan moved on to Cebu (which was then known as Zubu and which was, as now, an important trading port) and was killed shortly thereafter by Lapu-Lapu, a native chieftain. Spanish rule was uneasy, periodically interrupted by regional revolts that culminated in the 1896 nationwide revolution, the first of its kind in Asia. Nationalist aspirations were aborted, however, when the United States, after defeating Spain in the Spanish-American War, took over in 1898—but not without the ensuing bitter, five-year Philippine-American War, a conflict characterized by guerrilla tactics on the part of the poorly armed Philippine soldiers.

American rule, interrupted by Japanese occupation during World War II, came to an end on July 4, 1946, when Manuel Roxas took over as the first postcolonial president. Except during the dictatorial rule of Ferdinand Marcos from 1972 until 1986 (when he was ousted by the bloodless four-day People Power revolution), the government has since been a democratically elected one. The new constitution adopted in 1987 under President Corazon Aquino limits presidential tenure to one term of six years. Elections in 1992 to determine her successor resulted in former general Fidel V. Ramos's winning the presidency. The current president is Joseph Estrada, Ramos's vice president and a former screen actor, elected in 1998.

After more than two decades of unrest, a nationwide Communist insurgency—with its roots in agrarian and social injustice—has been on the decline, with ongoing peace talks between rebel leaders and the government. A Muslim secessionist movement in southern Mindanao has come to terms with Manila, though radical splinter groups engage the Philippine military from time to time. The military, after several coup attempts in the late '80s, has adjusted to civilian leadership.

Because of its colonial history and its people's innate warmth, the Philippines today is a country open to visitors and tolerant of cultural idiosyncrasies. Filipinos are a gregarious, fun-loving people whose hospitality is legendary. ("No" is a word frowned upon; a Filipino will find countless ways to decline a request without sounding negative, smoothing over a potentially disruptive moment. Westerners should be aware that insistent straightforwardness can be counterproductive.) Filipinos love to joke and tease and have a good sense of the absurd. These qualities come in handy in a society full of paradoxes and contradictions, where medieval Catholic values coexist with tropical hedonism; a freedom-loving people still contends with such feudal practices as private armies; and poverty persists amid sunshine and rich natural resources.

Pleasures and Pastimes

The Philippines may not have world-class museums or a monumental ruin at every turn, but the nation's three island groupings—Luzon (the largest), the Visayas, and Mindanao—have twice the coastline of the continental United States and offer diverse attractions. The indigenous tribes—from the Ifugao in northern Luzon to the T'boli in Mindanao—offer glimpses of ancient traditions. The outstanding beauty of the land, the many picturesque towns and villages, the abundance of uncrowded islands and beaches, the excellent dining, and the hospitality and gaiety of the people offer rewards all their own.

Beaches

The Philippines has an abundance of beaches, from pebble-strewn coastlines and black volcanic stretches to brilliant white expanses of sand. The advantage of being on a tropical archipelago (remember, more than 7,000 islands!) is that you're never far from the sea. Some of the loveliest beaches—Boracay, Panay, Bohol, and Cebu—are in the Visayas region. Palawan is possibly the least developed island and the wildest in terms of flora and fauna.

Churches

The heart of the typical Philippine town is its Catholic church—along with the adjacent plaza and the town hall—where communal rites are observed and in front of which you can witness the languorous rhythms of daily life. Churches from the Spanish colonial era are evident in most of the country, except of course in the Muslim south and in the higher reaches of northern Luzon. These churches have been dubbed "earthquake baroque" for the massive walls and buttresses built (not always successfully) to withstand earthquakes; their ornate facades combine classical Western influences with folk art motifs. Some of the more distinctive churches are in the Ilocos region (along the coast of northern Luzon), in the metropolitan Manila area, and in the Visayas, particularly on such islands as Cebu, Bohol, Leyte, and Panay.

Dining

Including as it does both patently Asian and Western dishes, Philippine food may puzzle you. History is responsible: on a matrix of native (Austronesian or Malay) dishes akin to those in the rest of Southeast Asia, Chinese traders input their culinary culture, Spanish colonizers added touches of Spain and Mexico (through which the islands were governed), Indian and Arab interaction influenced the food of Mindanao, and U.S. colonization brought in American cooking.

The indigenous cuisine consists of seafood or meat broiled or stewed in vinegar (for preserving without refrigeration) or sour-stewed in broth with tamarind or tomato (which are cooling in hot weather), or in other liquids such as coconut water (*pinais*) or coconut milk (*laing*). Coconut is prominent—as a vegetable (the bud, the heart of palm), as a drink (called *tuba* when its taken from the sap, *lambanog* when it's distilled), as coco milk or cream in which to cook fruits and vegetables (*ginataan*), and as flesh grated into desserts and sweets.

The Philippines

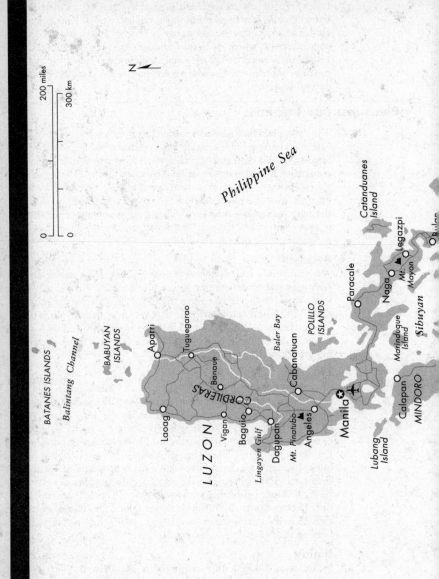

Rice is a staple: when steamed to go with meals, it's a shaper of other tastes; when ground into flour, it's transformed into myriad cakes for snacks and feasts. One such cake is *bibingka,* baked on and beneath hot coals and topped with freshly grated coconut, salted duck's eggs, and slices of *carabao* (water buffalo) milk cheese; another is leaf-wrapped *suman,* sticky rice cooked with coconut milk and eaten with ripe mangoes.

The Chinese connection is apparent in such foods as vegetable- or pork-filled *lumpia* (spring rolls), and especially in *pansit* noodles (rice, mung bean, wheat; fresh or dried; fat or thin) sautéed with vegetables, pork, or seafood—the ingredients differ from region to region and from cook to cook.

Spanish dishes have become fiesta food: *lechon,* spit-roasted suckling pig; chicken *relleno* stuffed with pork, sausage, and spices; paella rich with crabs, prawns, sausages, ham, and clams; *pochero,* a beef stew given local character with a vegetable relish; *callos,* tripe with chickpeas and pimientos; *caldereta,* goat or beef stew with olive oil, bell peppers, and olives.

The American regime, which began in 1898, brought in convenience (sandwiches and salads), quick cooking (fried chicken, hamburgers), and a new food culture. The East–West range is therefore wide, but it has been made more Philippine through time by local ingredients, dipping sauces (such as *patis,* a fish sauce, or *bagoong,* a salted shrimp or fish paste), cooking styles, and general fine-tuning.

In a nation with some 90 ethno-linguistic groups, there are, of course, regional variations. The Bicol people (from southeast Luzon) like chili-hot food; so do the Maranaws, who live around Lake Lanao in Mindanao. Dare to try the Bicol *pinangat* (shrimp or pork wrapped in taro leaves, cooked with coco cream, ginger, and chilies) or the Maranaw catfish (cooked with turmeric, coco milk, and chilies). The Ilocano north favors *pinakbet,* a vegetable stew made with bagoong, and often with the bittersweetness of *ampalaya* (bitter melon). It is now the pan-Philippine vegetable dish—everyone cooks it with regional variations (steamed or sautéed, for example, with shrimp or with pork). Leyte and Samar (eastern Visayan provinces) folk have many dishes cooked in coconut milk (such as prawns or chicken with ginger). Tagalog dishes lean toward a controlled sourness, as in beef, pork, or chicken *sinigang.* The food of the Pampanga province (60 km/37 mi north of Manila) is one of the richest regional cuisines; it includes a plethora of sweets and such exotica as *betute* (stuffed frogs).

You can sample many of these regional cooking styles—and most international cuisines—in Metro Manila restaurants, as well as in food malls, street stalls, and market *turo-turo* (point-point) counters that offer an array of cooked foods. But venturing into the provinces is the best way to get a real taste of the Philippines. Price categories throughout the chapter are based on the following ranges:

CATEGORY	COST*
$$$$	over $24
$$$	$17–$24
$$	$10–$17
$	under $10

per person for a three-course dinner, excluding tax, service, and drinks.

Lodging

Major urban areas, such as Manila, Cebu, Baguio, and Davao, have lodgings for every type of traveler, from the hedonist with deep pockets to the backpacker who must count pennies. Large towns usually feature a couple of reasonably priced, comfortable hotels and lower-scale inns and pensions. In the more rustic areas, accommodations tend, not surprisingly, toward the basic. Popular beach areas have resorts made up of anything from pricey air-conditioned cabanas to inexpensive cottages. Small cities and towns offer mostly family-run hotels, sometimes short on amenities but generally well maintained and clean and with a courteous and helpful staff. For the more expensive hotels and beach resorts, it's best to make reservations during the peak season (November to February). Price categories throughout the chapter are based on the following ranges:

CATEGORY	COST*
$$$$	over $220
$$$	$100–$220
$$	$60–$100
$	under $60

for a standard double room in high season, excluding 10% service charge and 13.7% tax.

Mountain Climbing

Mt. Pulog in the Cordilleras, Mt. Mayon in southern Luzon, Mt. Kanlaon on Negros Island, Mt. Hibok-Hibok on Camiguin Island, and Mt. Apo in Mindanao all have trails and local guides for hire.

Shopping

The Philippines can yield great bargains if you know what to look for and where. There are handicraft stores all over the country, usually near the public market in small- to medium-size cities and towns and in shopping centers in such large urban areas as Manila, Cebu, and Baguio. In Manila, the country's commercial capital, you'll find regional goods, though prices are higher than elsewhere. Focus on handicrafts special to the region you're visiting. Look for handwoven rattan baskets, blankets, and backpacks from northern Luzon; handwoven cloth from northern Luzon, Iloilo City, and southern Mindanao; items crafted of shell from Cebu City and Zamboanga City; handwoven *pandan* (a type of screw pine) mats with geometric designs from Zamboanga City and Davao City; brassware from southern Mindanao; bamboo furniture from central Luzon; gold and silver jewelry from Baguio City and Bulacan province; and cigars from the Ilocos region. Bargaining is acceptable in public markets, flea markets, and small, owner-run stores. Department stores and big shopping areas have fixed prices.

Water Sports

The tropical waters are ideal for a variety of water sports, from scuba diving to waterskiing. Many resorts in different regions offer equipment and facilities. The country has some of the best dive sites in the world, with more than 40 known spots, most around Palawan, the Visayas, and Batangas Province (on Luzon). Many more wait to be discovered. Most resorts rent out snorkeling equipment; the tonier ones have scuba gear as well. Surfers have discovered the Philippines, though there are still only a handful of surf centers. Most are on the island of Siargao, northeast of Mindanao, on the Pacific coast.

Exploring the Philippines

Great Itineraries

To truly appreciate what the country has to offer, you need at least two weeks, given the variety of attractions and their diverse locations. If you have less time, however, here are some suggested itineraries.

IF YOU HAVE 3 DAYS

With such little time, your best bet is to concentrate on **Metro Manila,** with an all-day trip to Pagsanjan Falls, a two-hour drive from the city, and a stop at Tagaytay Ridge to view Taal Volcano (a volcano within a lake within a volcano). In the city, two days should be sufficient to visit such sights as Intramuros, Malacañang, the Coconut Palace, Rizal Park, and such colorful neighborhoods as Binondo, Quiapo, and the tourist districts of Ermita and Malate.

IF YOU HAVE 7 DAYS

Spend two days exploring **Metro Manila,** then either join a tour or proceed on your own to the Cordilleras in northern Luzon. Plan on an overnight stay in **Banaue** to visit the magnificent rice terraces, built more than two millennia ago. Nearby is **Sagada,** a picturesque town with unique limestone formations and burial caves. From Sagada, proceed to **Baguio** and spend two days there.

IF YOU HAVE 10 DAYS

Spend two days in **Metro Manila,** then head north to the rice terraces in **Banaue** and to **Baguio.** On the sixth day, fly back to Manila and take a connecting flight to **Cebu.** Two days in the Queen City of the South should suffice to see its sights and to spend a lazy day at a beach on nearby Mactan Island. The last two days could be spent either in **Zamboanga City,** on the western coast of Mindanao, or **Davao City,** on the eastern coast. Both have local culture and beach resorts. Zamboanga is an older city, the southernmost bastion of Spanish rule in the archipelago; Davao City is a boomtown, near the country's tallest peak, Mt. Apo, and the site of huge agribusiness and trading concerns.

When to Tour the Philippines

The ideal time to visit is from mid-October to February (the peak tourist season being from late November to February), right after the monsoon rains and before the start of the scorchingly hot period from March to May. Besides having perfect beach weather, the hot months coincide with the Lenten season, when reenactments of Christ's Passion take place in towns and cities, and flagellants, whipping themselves into a bloodied frenzy, stagger through the streets, particularly in Central Luzon. There are fiestas every month, but during May every town in the country seems to have some kind of celebration. If you happen to be in the Philippines in the rainy season, from June to mid-October, be sure to pack a raincoat and waterproof shoes. (☞ When to Go *in* Philippines A to Z, *below.*)

Numbers in the text correspond to numbers in the margin and on the maps.

METRO MANILA

The urban sprawl that is metropolitan Manila (it's made up of the cities of Manila, Makati, Pasay, Quezon, Caloocan, and Pasig, plus 12 towns) is a fascinating, even surreal, combination of modernity and tradition. In Manila's streets you'll see horse-drawn *calesas* (carriages) alongside sleek Mercedes-Benzes, Japanese sedans, passenger buses, and the ubiquitous passenger jeepneys—once converted World War II Jeeps but now manufactured locally.

Built by the Spanish conquistadors in 1571 as Intramuros, a fortified settlement on the ashes of a Malay town, Manila spread outward over the centuries, so that the oldest districts are those closest to Intramuros. Yet very few buildings attest to the city's antiquity, since it suffered extensive damage during World War II; more than any city except for

ONE LAST TRAVEL TIP:

Pack an easy way to reach the world.

MCI WORLDCOM WORLDPHONE.

123 456 7891 2345
J.D. SMITH

Wherever you travel, the MCI WorldCom Card℠ is the easiest way to stay in touch. You can use it to call to and from more than 125 countries worldwide. And you can earn bonus miles every time you use your card. So go ahead, travel the world. MCI WorldCom℠ makes it even more rewarding. For additional access codes, visit **www.wcom.com/worldphone**.

EASY TO CALL WORLDWIDE

1. Just dial the WorldPhone® access number of the country you're calling from.

2. Dial or give the operator your MCI WorldCom Card number.

3. Dial or give the number you're calling.

China (A)	108-12
Hong Kong	800-96-1121
Indonesia ◆	001-801-11
Japan ◆	00539-121▶
Korea	00729-14
Malaysia ◆	1-800-80-0012
Philippines ◆	105-14
Singapore (A)	8000-112-112
Taiwan ◆	0080-13-4567
Thailand (A) ★	001-999-1-2001
Vietnam (A) ÷ ●	1201-1022

(A) Calls back to U.S. only. ◆ Public phones may require deposit of coin or phone card for dial tone.
▶ Regulation does not permit intra-Japan calls. ★ Not available from public pay phones. ÷ Limited availability.
● Local service fee in U.S. currency required to complete call.

EARN FREQUENT FLIER MILES

AmericanAirlines® A'Advantage®

CHINA AIRLINES

▲Delta Air Lines SkyMiles®

TWA®

///UNITED Mileage Plus®

US AIRWAYS DIVIDEND MILES

Bureau de change

Cambio

外国為替

In this city, you can find money on almost any street.

NO-FEE FOREIGN EXCHANGE

The Chase Manhattan Bank has over 80 convenient
locations near New York City destinations such as:

> Times Square
> Rockefeller Center
> Empire State Building
> 2 World Trade Center
> United Nations Plaza

Exchange any of 75 foreign currencies

 CHASE

THE RIGHT RELATIONSHIP IS EVERYTHING.®

Warsaw, Hiroshima, and Nagasaki. Among Manila's older districts are the centrally located, bay-front Ermita and Malate, which make up the Tourist Belt (so-called because of its many hotels, clubs, restaurants, boutiques, and coffee shops). At the upper end of the scale is Makati City, the country's financial center, with its wide, well-kept boulevards; high-rise apartment and office buildings; ultramodern shopping centers, and well-guarded walled enclaves of the fabulously rich.

Because Metro Manila is a conglomeration of cities and towns, it lacks a defined center, and you certainly won't find an easy-to-navigate grid layout. Adding to the confusion is a lack of consistent urban planning. Like many cities in developing nations, Metro Manila has its share of congestion, pollution, haphazard planning, and poverty. The large slum of Tondo is currently being converted into a housing area, but it was once dominated by a huge pile of garbage known as Smoky Mountain for the endless burning of trash fires. The poor still live in cardboard shanties and scavenge for a living. But the 10 million inhabitants of the "noble and ever loyal city"—as Manila was described by its Spanish overlords—have a joie de vivre that transcends their struggles. Manilans bear their burdens with humor and a casual grace, and the fortuitous blend of Latin and Southeast Asian temperaments makes for an easygoing atmosphere, where play is as important as work. The nightlife here may well be Southeast Asia's liveliest—comparable to that in Bangkok—with myriad restaurants, discos, coffeehouses, nightclubs, topless bars, music lounges, and beer gardens. Certainly the bands—rock, Latin, or jazz—have a reputation for being the finest in Southeast Asia. Enjoy the city's mix of the terrible and marvelous.

Exploring Metro Manila

Metropolitan Manila has a roughly crescent shape, with Manila Bay and the scenic Roxas Boulevard that runs along it forming the western boundary. The Epifanio de los Santos Highway (EDSA) forms the eastern border. The Pasig River divides the city into northern and southern sections, with the oldest districts, including the ancient walled city of Intramuros, near where the river empties into Manila Bay.

Intramuros

Manila's ancient walled city, built by the Spaniards in the 16th century, is a compact 7.5 square km (3 square mi). Within this small area, churches, schools, convents, offices, and residences were constructed—the latter reserved for the Spanish and Spanish mestizos only. In its heyday, Intramuros—with its seven drawbridges and its encircling moat—must have presented a magnificent sight to visiting galleons. The moat, filled in by the Americans to prevent the spread of disease, is now used as a golf course, but the 30-ft-thick walls are still formidable, with cannon emplacements and a strategic location facing the bay.

A GOOD WALK

Ft. Santiago ① is where the Spanish established their first settlement and where you should begin your explorations. Across from the fort is **Manila Cathedral** ②. Walking along General Luna Street, which borders the cathedral, you'll come to **San Agustin Church** ③. Across the street is the Barrio San Luis Complex, which includes **Casa Manila** ④. General Luna Street ends near one of Intramuros's fortified gates, Puerta Real, which has a display of antique church silver. Bearing left onto Muralla Road, note the famed (if largely reconstructed) walls—gray, stately, and seemingly invincible. You'll pass lookout towers and other fortifications. Muralla Road winds around in a semicircle, bringing you to Puerta Isabel. This gate houses a fascinating display of baroque floats bearing statues of saints.

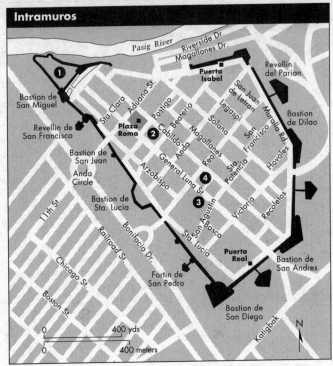

TIMING

It's best to explore the Walled City early in the morning to beat the heat. Exploring Intramuros on foot should take about half a day, or rent a *caretela* (a horse-drawn cart that can carry several people) on the grounds for about P300.

SIGHTS TO SEE

4 Casa Manila. The main attraction of the **Barrio San Luis Complex** is not the shops but this splendid re-creation of a 19th-century Spanish patrician's three-story domicile. It's complete with a carriage entrance, an inner courtyard, and a grand stairway. Upstairs is a display of period furniture and accessories. ⊠ *General Luna St.,* ☎ *2/527–4084.* ☞ *Admission.* ☉ *Daily 9–6.*

1 Ft. Santiago. This stone fort overlooking the mouth of the Pasig River is on the site where the original Malay Muslim settlement stood. Previously used by the Spanish, Americans, and Japanese, it's now a pleasant park with an open-air theater where plays in Pilipino (the national tongue) are staged among the ruins. The fort has a grim history: Philippine revolutionaries (including the national hero José Rizal) were imprisoned here by the Spanish; they often drowned in the dungeons, which were below the high-tide level. ☞ *Admission.* ☉ *Daily 8 AM–9 PM.*

2 Manila Cathedral. Dedicated to the Immaculate Conception of the Virgin Mary, this Romanesque edifice (a reconstruction of the original 1600 structure) has three arched doorways that form an imposing facade. The middle door is made of bronze, with eight panels that portray the cathedral's history. Inside, the clerestory's stained-glass windows depict the history of Christianity in the Philippines. Underneath the main altar is a crypt where the remains of the former archbishops are entombed. Fronting the church is **Plaza Roma,** where bullfights were once staged. Its centerpiece is a monument to three Philippine priests executed in 1872 for their nationalism. ✉ *Gen. Luna and Postigo Sts.,* ☎ *2/527–5836.* ⊙ *Mon.–Sat. 6–5, Sun. 6–6.*

★ ❸ **San Agustin Church.** The second-oldest stone church in the country has 14 side chapels and a trompe-l'oeil ceiling. Up in the choir loft, note the hand-carved 17th-century seats of *molave,* a beautiful tropical hardwood. Adjacent to the church is a small **museum** run by the Augustinian order, featuring antique vestments, colonial furniture, and religious paintings and icons. ✉ *Gen. Luna and Real Sts.,* ☎ *2/527–4060 or 2/527–4052.* ⊡ *Admission to museum.* ⊙ *Church daily 7–7:30 AM and 5–6 PM; museum daily 9–noon and 1–5.*

North of the Pasig River

This is a poor and crowded part of the city, but it also has an old, historic feel. The streets are narrow, with a mix of small businesses and residential buildings. Manilans say a foreigner should come here to get a true feel for down-home Philippine neighborhoods.

SIGHTS TO SEE

Binondo. Forbidden by the Spanish from living in Intramuros, Chinese merchants and their families settled north of the Pasig River, and a sizable community—now known as Binondo—grew here in the 18th century. Bounded by the river, Claro M. Recto Avenue, Del Pan Street, and Avenida Rizal, Manila's Chinatown is a jumble of small streets packed with jewelry shops, sporting-goods and clothing stores, apothecaries, kung fu schools, movie houses that show Hong Kong flicks, magazine stalls, seedy hotels, brothels, and restaurants that usually offer Fukien cuisine (which emphasizes minimally seasoned, fresh seafood). Stroll about, especially on Ongpin, the main street, or stop a *calesa* and have the driver take you around.

❺ **Binondo Church.** This 16th-century church still has its original stone walls. Note the replica of St. Peter's dome at the main altar and the Madonna encased in glass. The first Philippine saint, Lorenzo Ruiz, started here as an altar boy. ✉ *Paredes St. at Plaza Calderon de la Barca,* ☎ *2/242–4041.* ⊙ *Daily 6 AM–7 PM.*

★ ❽ **Malacañang Palace.** Once the seat of the colonial Spanish and American governor-generals, this palace is the official residence of Philippine presidents and is sometimes referred to as the Philippine White House. During her term, Corazon Aquino preferred to live in the guest house, a symbolic gesture meant to disassociate her from the dictatorial Ferdinand Marcos. Now open to the public, Malacañang's colonial Spanish architecture and interior decor are worth a look, especially the three chandeliers in the reception hall, the beautiful hardwoods used for the grand staircase, the portraits of former presidents, and the exquisite music room. The Marcoses' personal effects are gone (those shoes and that bulletproof bra!), and the rooms converted to the Malacañang Heritage Museum, featuring memorabilia of past presidents. ✉ *J. P. Laurel St.,* ☎ *2/734–7421 or 2/733–3721.* ⊡ *Admission.* ⊙ *Mon.–Fri. 9–3.*

★ ❼ **Quiapo Church.** East of Binondo, not far from the foot of Quezon Bridge and facing Plaza Miranda—where orators of varying skills and persuasions harangue passersby—is this 16th-century church, later enlarged. Its crowded environs are as close to an authentic Philippine neighborhood as you can get in Manila. On side streets vendors sell amulets and herbal cures for a wide variety of ailments. The church is home to the famed **Black Nazarene,** a dark hardwood statue of Jesus of Nazareth made by a Mexican craftsman and brought via galleon from Mexico in the 18th century. Many believe that praying to the statue can produce miracles. It isn't unusual to see supplicants crawling on their knees from the entrance to the altar. As part of the Quiapo Fiesta, each January 9

290

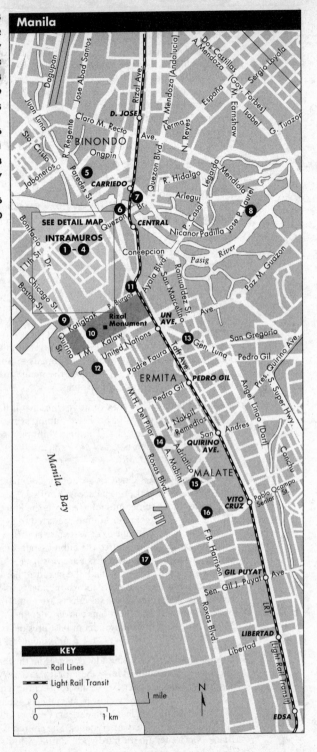

Manila

KEY

— Rail Lines

▪▪▪ Light Rail Transit

0   1 mile

0   1 km

N

the Nazarene is paraded through the district's narrow streets by bare-chested male devotees who compete for the honor of pulling the float that carries the statue. ⊠ *Plaza Miranda and Quezon Blvd.,* ☎ 2/733-4945. ◷ *Daily 6 AM–8 PM.*

❻ Quinta Public Market. Inexpensive handicrafts, from handwoven mats to rattan baskets and straw brooms, are the specialty of this market near Quiapo Church. You'll find more handicrafts in the small arcade right beneath the nearby bridge. You can also get a snack or light meal of native dishes. Be mindful of your wallet or bag, and be especially wary of people offering to buy your dollars. ⊠ *Below Quezon Bridge.* ◷ *Daily 5 AM–8 PM.*

South of the Pasig River: The Tourist Belt and Around Manila Bay

The Ermita and Malate districts that form the so-called Tourist Belt are bordered by Roxas Boulevard to the west, Taft Avenue to the east, Intramuros to the north, and Pablo Ocampo Senior Street to the south. On Roxas are nightclubs, the Cultural Center of the Philippines complex, hotels, restaurants, apartment buildings, Rizal Park, and Intramuros. On Taft Avenue are the Light Rail Transit line, universities, shops, stores, and several hospitals. In between are bars and cocktail lounges, the infamous go-go joints (especially on M. H. del Pilar and A. Mabini streets), massage parlors, coffeehouses, more restaurants and hotels, office buildings, boutiques, and shopping malls.

SIGHTS TO SEE

☝ ⑫ Children's Museum. Known as *Museo Pambata*, this interactive collection of computers, educational toys, environmental displays, and crafts is designed for children under 12. Kids learn while they play. ⊠ *Roxas Blvd., Ermita,* ☎ 2/523-1797. 🎟 *Admission.* ◷ *Tues.–Sun. 9–5.*

★ ⑰ Coconut Palace. South of Malate on Roxas Boulevard is this $10 million project of former first lady Imelda Marcos, so named because more than 70% of the construction materials were derived from the coconut tree. The grandiose structure, within the Cultural Center complex, faces Manila Bay and was constructed for Pope John Paul's visit in 1981 (he refused to stay here). Each of the seven (the Marcoses' lucky number) palatial suites is named and styled after a different region of the country. The Pangasinan Room, for example, features *pina* (pineapple fiber) bedcovers and a fabulous mother-of-pearl table set. Several of Imelda's jet-set friends stayed here at one time or another, among them Van Cliburn and Brooke Shields. ⊠ *Roxas Blvd. in Cultural Center complex,* ☎ 2/832–0223 or 2/831–1756. 🎟 *Admission.* ◷ *By appointment only Tues.–Sun.; 5-person minimum.*

⑭ Malate Church. Photographers love to shoot the picturesque, well-kept facade of this gray-stone church, an intriguing mixture of Romanesque and Baroque styles. Its interior, however, is unremarkable. Between the church and Roxas Boulevard is Rajah Sulayman Park, the centerpiece of which is a statue of Rajah Sulayman, a pre-Spanish (16th-century) ruler of Manila. ⊠ *Remedios and M. H. del Pilar Sts.* ◷ *Mon.–Sat. 5:30–noon and 3–7, Sun. 5:30 AM–8 PM.*

NEED A
BREAK?

Around Malate Church are innumerable places for lunch or a snack. You can walk eastward (away from the bay) on Remedios Street and choose from several cafés around Remedios Circle. Besides the cafés listed in Nightlife and the Arts (☞ *below*), try the 24-hour **Aristocrat Restaurant** (⊠ Roxas Blvd. at San Andres St., ☎ 2/524–7671), a favorite with everyone from gangsters to businesspeople; prices are reasonable, and the food is decent.

⑨ Manila Hotel. On the edge of Rizal Park and a short stroll from the Rizal Monument is the doyen of Philippine hotels, built in 1912 (☞ *also* Lodging, *below*). This is where General Douglas MacArthur lived during much of his time in the Philippines; Ernest Hemingway also stayed here once. The spacious lobby is gracious in an Old World way; note the ceiling and woodwork, made entirely of precious Philippine hardwoods, the floors of Philippine marble, and the *capiz* (translucent-shell) and brass chandeliers. ⊠ *Rizal Park at Bonifacio Dr.,* ☎ 2/527–0011.

NEED A   Manila Hotel has an airy, pleasant poolside coffee shop, **Café Ylang-**
BREAK?   **Ylang** (☎ 2/527–0011). The menu offers solid local and Continental fare; in the afternoon you'll find a mouthwatering dessert buffet that's ever so hard to resist.

⑮ Manila Zoo. This small zoo in the Tourist Belt has the usual assortment of wild animals, including such local species as the *tamaraw* (a peculiar water buffalo), the rare mouse deer (the smallest deer in the world), and the Palawan pheasant. ⊠ *Quirino Ave. at Adriatico St.,* ☎ 2/525–8157. ◨ *Admission.* ⊙ *Daily 7–6.*

★ **⑯ Metropolitan Museum of Art.** This impressively designed museum has exhibits of classical and contemporary fine arts. Each year there are four major exhibitions by renowned Filipino and foreign artists. In the basement galleries you'll find displays of pre-Columbian pottery and an exquisite collection of pre-Hispanic gold jewelry from the Central Bank collection. ⊠ *Roxas Blvd., Central Bank complex, across from Cultural Center,* ☎ 2/523–7855 or 2/521–1517. ◨ *Admission.* ⊙ *Mon.–Sat. 10–6.*

⑪ National Museum. Once the site of Congress, this building now houses displays that range from archaeological treasures to paintings, including an impressive array of the 19th-century artist Juan Luna's works. Three nearby government buildings have been incorporated into the museum, alleviating the crowded displays. Two permanent exhibitions have been installed: "The Story of the Filipino People" and "The Treasures of San Diego," which features a sunken 17th-century galleon's treasures. ⊠ *Rizal Park at Padre Burgos St.,* ☎ 2/527–1209 or 2/527–0278. ◨ *Admission.* ⊙ *Tues.–Sun. 9–5.* ◈

⑬ Paco Park. On the south side of the Pasig River, this petite but beautiful circular park of moss-covered stone—with a picturesque chapel in the middle that's a favorite site for weddings—was a cemetery until it was declared a national park in 1966. Its two concentric walls served as burial niches for the Spanish elite and, for a while, the national hero José Rizal. No burials have been performed here since 1912. Free concerts are offered on Friday at 6 PM. ⊠ *San Marcelino and General Luna Sts.,* ☎ 2/525–7853. ◨ *Admission.* ⊙ *Daily 8–5.*

⑩ Rizal Park. Stretching from Taft Avenue toward the bay is a 128-acre oasis where Manilans can jog, do tai chi, stroll through the **Chinese Garden**, a pleasant arboretum, or just lie on the grass. The park is named after José Rizal, a national hero who was, among other things, a doctor, linguist, botanist, novelist, poet, educator, and fencer. Executed in 1896 by the Spanish because of his reformist views, he was originally buried at Paco Park but now lies under the **Rizal Monument**, designed by Swiss artist Richard Kissling and erected in 1912. Nearby, towering above the statue, is a stately 50-ft obelisk marking the spot where three local 19th-century priests were garroted by the Spanish for their nationalist views. The 24-hour guards, like honor guards everywhere, try to be as impassive as possible. Rizal's poem *Mi Ultimo Adios* (My Last Farewell), composed just before his death, is inscribed on a bronze slab set into a nearby octagonal wall; in addition to the original Spanish, it appears in English and several other languages. ☎ 2/526–2394 *(park administration).* ☒ *Admission to Chinese Garden.* ⊙ *Park daily dawn–dusk; Chinese Gardens daily 8–6.*

OFF THE
BEATEN PATH

A RIDE ON THE LRT – The Light Rail Transit (LRT) is an excellent way to travel beyond the usual tourist sights. For only a few pesos, you can ride from one end of the 15-stop line and back (a 1¼-hour trip), taking in the heart of Manila. Baclaran, the southernmost terminal, is not far from Baclaran Church, which is packed on Wednesday with devotees for special services to the Virgin Mary. Moving north, you'll pass through congested neighborhoods and can often peer into offices, apartments, and backyards. It's worth getting off at the R. Papa station, taking a pedicab, and visiting the remarkable Chinese Cemetery (there's a small entrance fee). The mausoleums are virtual mansions with architectural styles that range from Chinese classical to Baroque, a reminder that wealth makes a difference even in death. At the last stop, Monumento, walk a short distance to the monument marking the spot where Philippine revolutionaries began their struggle against Spain.

Dining

Reservations are a good idea on holidays and weekends. Most places close only on Christmas, New Year's Day, All Souls' Day, Maundy Thursday, and Good Friday. Hours are normally noon to 2:30 for lunch and 7 to 11 for dinner; some restaurants are also open for breakfast (7–10) and *merienda* (afternoon snack, 4–6). Few require formal dress; jackets or the long-sleeve *barong tagalog* for men suffice at even the most upscale establishments, and most others draw the line only at athletic shorts and tank tops. Restaurants build a 10% VAT into their charges. Ask whether or not a service charge is included; if it isn't, a 10%–15% tip is expected.

Chinese

$$ ✕ **The Good Earth.** Each of this restaurant's three locations will intrigue: ★ the Magallanes tea room is within an art gallery; a curio-antiques shop leads to the Greenhills restaurant; and the Malate place is within a disco-restaurant-bar complex. In all three, the cuisine of Henry Cheung is Chinese with a difference: not for banquets, but for thoughtful, pleasurable dining. Take, for example, the *dacquitos* filled with minced duck, or the eggplant-and-shrimp cylinders on a sauce whimsically named Lily on a Pond. There are noodles in clear broth, and steamed fish with ham, but also prawns garnished with crab fat and *wasabi*-spiked sauce, a perfect *char siu* (roast pork), and chili-spiced shrimp with walnuts. ☒ *101 Building, Magallanes Commercial Center, Makati City,* ☎ *2/853–0293 or 2/853–0294. AE, DC, MC, V. Closed Sun.;* ☒ *Silhouette Tower, 5 Eisenhower St. at Annapolis St., Greenhills, San Juan,* ☎ *2/723–8982 or 2/744–5754. AE, DC, MC, V. Closed Mon.;* ☒ *Republic of Malate, 1769 A. Mabini St., Malate,* ☎ *2/303–3533 or 2/303–3534. AE, DC, MC, V. No lunch Mon.*

$ ✕ **North Park Noodle House.** All kinds of homemade noodles are served dry or in savory broth, with Nanking or anise-seed beef, prawn dumplings, wontons, Szechuan pork in bean sauce, and the like at all three locations of this beloved noodle house. *Congee* (rice porridge) comes regular (with pork or chicken balls, fresh grouper fillet, century egg, or beef) or superior (whisked fine, with crystal prawn, shiitake mushrooms, sea abalone). It's soothing comfort food, and a range of accompaniments—pot stickers, vegetables in oyster sauce, garlic squid, sausages and roast meats—make for varied Chinese meals. The service at all locations is brisk, the opening hours are long, delivery is possible, and the food, though casual, is of high quality. ⊠ *1200 Makati Ave., Makati City,* ☏ *2/895–3471, 2/896–3482, or 2/896–3490;* ⊠ *206 Wilson St., Greenhills, San Juan,* ☏ *2/725–9439, 2/725–8653 or 2/725–7348;* ⊠ *689 Banawe Ave., Quezon City,* ☏ *2/412–9505, 2/412–9459, or 2/413–7063. No credit cards.*

Contemporary

$$$–$$$$ ✕ **Le Soufflé.** This restaurant's long-running reputation for excellence is now exhibited in both **Le Soufflé** at the Fort and **Le Soufflé Bistro** in the Ortigas area, with the same creative team of chef-owners in command. Guests' requests are gladly entertained, and special menus are designed by arrangement. Creations range from spiced wild-rice risotto to an ethereal onion soup crowned with a cheese soufflé, from baked duck and shiitake mushrooms in phyllo pastry to milkfish bellies with toasted garlic chips. Pastry chef Jessie Sincioco's dessert repertoire shines with many-flavored dessert soufflés, a sublime whiskey-laced bread pudding, and iced *halo-halo* parfait; literally "mix-mix," the latter is a new take on a traditional Philippine snack—mixed, sweetened fruits and beans topped with crushed ice. ⊠ *The Fort Global City, Fort Bonifacio, Taguig,* ☏ *2/887–5107 or 2/887–5108;* ⊠ *2F Wynsum Corporate Plaza, Ruby Rd., Ortigas Center, Pasig City,* ☏ *2/634–8971, 2/636–1614. AE, DC, MC, V.*

$$$ ✕ **Aqua.** Tucked away in a corner of a Makati business complex is this
★ new restaurant specializing in modern European food. Inside, green glass and *capiz*-shell adornments create a simple and elegant environment. Specialties include a salad of organic greens and Asian slaw; seared duck *foie gras* with pumpkin risotto and honey balsamic reduction; and Blue Mountain quail ravioli with savoy cabbage and smoked bacon. A divine *calamansi* (Philippine lime) soufflé drizzled with raspberry syrup, torched meringue on Champagne strawberry-mint soup, or Valrhona chocolate cake with white-chocolate sherbet are spectacular finishing touches. ⊠ *Tower 1, The Enterprise Center, 6766 Ayala Ave., Makati City,* ☏ *2/886–5767 or 2/886–5768,* ℻ *2/886–5769. AE, DC, MC, V. Closed Sun..*

$$$ ✕ **Grassi's.** Old Grassi's favorites still claim diners' loyalty: soft-shell crab tempura on mango-pimiento dressed greens, arugula salad with pan-fried scallops and green papaya, king salmon with ginger and fried fennel leaves. Young chef Toby Wettach has also expanded the menu. Try creamy risotto with pan-fried duck liver and sun-dried tomatoes; steamed "sandwich" of shiitake mushrooms between sea bass and salmon fillets wrapped in leeks, on arugula mashed potatoes; and especially, succulent roasted quail in a coffee-herb crust atop pumpkin polenta. The white-chocolate mousse or sherbet terrine of lime, mango, and kiwi are worth the trip. A more casual spin-off, **Grassi's Café** has opened across town in a spanking development rising from the ashes of an old power plant. ⊠ *5F Benpres Building, Meralco Ave. and Exchange Rd., Pasig City,* ☏ *2/632–1203 or 2/632–1204. AE, DC, MC, V. Closed Sun. Grassi's Café:* ⊠ *Rockwell Center, Amapola and Estrella Sts., Makati City,* ☏ *2/729–6740, 2/729–6741. AE, DC, MC, V.* ☺ *Open daily, till 1 AM on weekends.*

$$$ ✕ **Sala.** Chef-owner Colin Mackay and his crew redesign the menu in
★ this small, fashionably elegant spot regularly, changing a dish a day so that the menu emerges completely new every six weeks. Executive lunches are a marvelous bargain, but the *à la carte* menu may have such treasures as duck breast with red-pepper chutney, sesame-crusted seared tuna with Asian coleslaw, grilled lamb loin accompanied by a Gorgonzola tart and roasted pear, or an herb crêpe filled with spinach, ricotta, and roasted tomato. And the savory rosemary bread deserves

special mention. Precious desserts might be walnut baklava with ginger ice cream, or apricot polenta with orange torte and lemon ice cream. Service is very fine and friendly. ⊠ *610 J. Nakpil St., Malate,* ☎ *2/524–6770. AE, DC, MC, V. No lunch Sun..*

$$$ ✗ **Soleil.** Sleek minimalist interiors complement imaginative cuisine by young Colombian chef David Pardo. His approach is contemporary French, which he blends with compatible traditions. Patrons are loyal to their favorites: *mozzarella di bufala* salad with grapes and anchovies; Lucban *longaniza* (local sausage) risotto with Spanish paprika; or seared Chilean sea bass with shiitake mushrooms in Madeira. He continues to invent such dishes as lobster ravioli with citrus-tarragon cream, and coconut-crusted prawns, scallops, mussels, and squid in an herbal broth. Intriguing desserts are prune Armagnac tart with cinnamon ice cream, chocolate soufflé with crème fraîche, and tarragon ice cream. The dishes are quiet, understated pleasures. ⊠ *2289 Pasong Tamo Extension, Makati City,* ☎ *2/867–4450 or 2/867–4451,* FAX *2/ 867–4452. AE, DC, MC, V. Closed Sun..*

Cuban

$$ ✗ **Café Havana.** *Arroz a la Cubana,* a dish from the Phil-Hispanic repertoire, appears here, along with *Cubano* favorites like spare ribs *habanera* with guava sauce, the rich *encendido* ("set on fire") stew, black beans, fried plantains and more. Weekends especially, *mojitos* (Hemingway's favorite rum drink, they say) and sultry salsa rhythms spill out onto the street, and dancing on tabletops is not uncommon. The upstairs Hemingway cigar lounge carries Cuban, Dominican, and Manila stogies. ⊠ *1903 Adriatico and Remedios Sts., Malate,* ☎ *2/521–8097 or 2/524–5526. AE, DC, MC, V.*

Eclectic

$$$–$$$$ ✗ **Tivoli Grill.** This bright dining room at the Mandarin Oriental (☞
★ Lodging, *below*) sets French and other cuisines in casual elegance. Roasted duck breast on Parmesan polenta, and hazelnut-crusted *lapu-lapu* on sun-dried tomato-and-scallop risotto are listed alongside salmon *paksiw* (cooked in garlic and vinegar) with eggplant, bitter melon, and chilis over steamed rice. Caramelized mango and mascarpone cream in puff pastry coexists with passion-fruit and raspberry parfait on star anise–scented fruits. The wine list is generous, the service refined, and the chamber music soothing. ⊠ *Mandarin Oriental Hotel, Makati Ave., Makati City,* ☎ *2/750–8888. AE, DC, MC, V.* ☉ *Breakfast and lunch Mon.–Fri., dinner daily.*

$$ ✗ **Uva.** First on the table at this casual restaurant, named for the Italian word for grape, are crisp-fried root chips (potato, taro, purple yam) to dip in garlicky hummus. Among the starters is *lumpia* Napoleon, the chef-owner's award-winning recipe of heart of palm, leek threads, sweet soy, and candied garlic in pastry layers. Chilean sea bass here comes with baby bok choy and asparagus and is dressed with *sake* and a sprinkling of *togarashi* (small Japanese chili). Yellowfin tuna bears a Japanese touch too, with *ponzu* (sauce of rice vinegar, soy sauce, mirin, and bonito flakes) and pickled ginger. End with fruit sorbet with lemongrass water and burnt-orange snaps. ⊠ *Tomas Morato at Timog Ave., Quezon City,* ☎ *2/929–1570 or 2/929–1572. AE, DC, MC, V. No lunch Sat. and Sun..*

French

$$$$ ✗ **Prince Albert Rotisserie.** Three decades of excellent French cuisine comprise the record of this elegant dining room at the Hotel Inter-Continental Manila (☞ Lodging, *below*). Resident chef Cyrille Soenen's à la carte menu has duck liver marinated in Medoc wine served with mango chutney, and grilled sea scallops with mesclun greens, sun-dried toma-

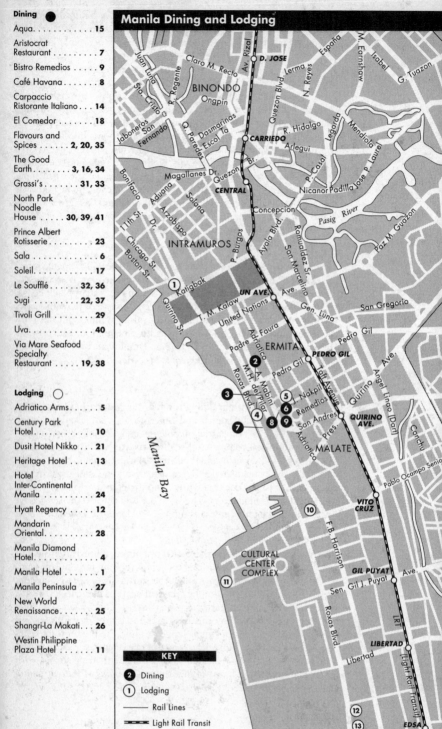

Manila Dining and Lodging

KEY

❷ Dining

① Lodging

—— Rail Lines

▭▭▭ Light Rail Transit

Ramon Magsaysay Blvd.
Altura Ext.
41
Santai
V. Santa Mesa Mapa
Old Valenzuela
Finaglobanan
Blumentrit
40
F. Manalo
P. Guevarra
P. Sanchez
Blumentrit
Wilson
39
Mabini
San Juan R.
Gen. Kalentong
Gen. Blumentrit
Mencias
Shaw Blvd.
33 - 38
Laura
Old Panaderos
New Panaderos
Boni Avenue
Dr. Jose Fabella Rd.
Pedro Gil
M. Roxas
E. Pascua
Pasig River
Boni Avenue
Cong. Augusto Francisco
Florentino Torres
Estrada
Zobel Roxas Avenue
J.P. Rizal
Imelda Avenue
Vito Cruz St.
Kamagong
Pasong Tamo
Senior St.
South Super Highway
Estrella
31
30
Yakal
Malugay
Sen. Gil J. Puyat Ave.
14
H.V. de la Costa Sr.
Tordesillas
29
28
Ayala Ave.
Paseo de Roxas
MAKATI Ave.
15
27
26
20
25
18
19
24
Pasay Road
23
E. de los Santos Hwy. (EDSA)
21
22
N
Cementina
32
16
17
0   1 mile
0   1 km

toes, Parmesan shavings, and truffle oil—for starters. Exquisite entrées include tender fillet of roast lamb coated in herb mousse, sea bass fillet with truffle sauce, and suckling pig scented with tandoori spices. Desserts like mango-pineapple brochette on a vanilla skewer served with tea sorbet fascinate. ☒ *1 Ayala Ave., Makati City,* ☏ *2/815–9711. AE, DC, MC, V. No lunch Sat. Closed Sun.*

Italian

$$ ✕ **Carpaccio Ristorante Italiano.** This friendly neighborhood restaurant has cool, low-lit interiors, casual tables around a glowing central bar, friendly and brisk service, and simple, satisfying food. You can start with beef, lamb, salmon, or tuna carpaccio, naturally; or a salad of grilled eggplant and buffalo mozzarella on tender greens with balsamic vinaigrette. Pastas and pizzas here are mostly *classico* (tomato and basil, pesto). Entrées might be cod or salmon fillet, saltimbocca, Black Angus rib eye, or osso buco with thick risotto. Daily set menus and blackboard specials (gnocchi, crêpes, chicken cacciatore) freshen up the choices. Cap a meal with lemon-scented *panna cotta* (custard), tiramisu, or homemade gelato. ☒ *7431 Yakal St., San Antonio Village, Makati City,* ☏ *2/843–7286. AE, DC, MC, V. Closed Sun.*

Japanese

$$–$$$ ✕ **Sugi.** The Japanese and Philippine chefs here work with a wide-ranging menu: sushi, tempura, *teppanyaki* (cooked on a grill built into the table) steak, sukiyaki, grilled *gindara* (silver cod), *shabu-shabu* (thinly sliced, blanched beef with a dipping sauce), and *soba* (buckwheat) and *udon* (wheat) noodles served hot or cold. Specials, refreshed regularly, may be enoki mushrooms bundled with crisp bacon, *kana koura age* (creamed crab with mushrooms), or emperor's soup (slivers of squid, prawn, mushrooms, and radish sprouts served in a tiny pot with a spout). The decor is simple Japanese, and the service warm and enthusiastic. ☒ ☒ *Greenbelt Mall, Ayala Centre, Makati City,* ☏ *2/816–3885 or 2/816–3886;* ☒ *Greenhills Commercial Center, Ortigas and Connecticut Aves., San Juan,* ☏ *2/725–0208 or 2/723–9496. AE, DC, MC, V.*

Philippine

$$ ✕ **Bistro Remedios.** Housed in a 1950s-style Filipino home, this first-
★ ever Philippine bistro is open for breakfast, lunch, and dinner and has a menu favoring Pampanga cuisine—*betute,* pork-and-spice stuffed frogs; *gule Magalang* of squash flowers and tendrils with broiled catfish—but also accommodating other regional fare—Tagalog *sinigang* of lake fish (in a soured broth); Visayan *binacol* (chicken soup with young coconut); Bicolano *laing* (taro leaves cooked with coconut milk and chilis); and *pospas paro* (porridge of rice, shrimps, chili leaves, and ginger), said to possess medicinal potency. Finish off the culinary tour with *durian* (the fruit famous for its caramel taste but controversial for its smell) ice cream, *manyaman* (sweet potato, wild rice, fresh fruits), or Maria Clara's secret: mango, rice cake, coconut cream. Imaginative yet authentic, Bistro Remedios distills hometown flavors and charm. ☒ *1911 Adriatico St., Malate,* ☏ *2/523–9153 or 2/521–8097. AE, DC, MC, V.*

$ ✕ **Aristocrat Restaurant.** Since opening in 1936, the Aristocrat has been run by four generations of the Reyes family, and features the native dishes with which their grandmother started. There are many branches, but the one on Roxas Boulevard, by the bay, is the signature outlet. Open 24 hours, it offers basic fare at moderate prices: barbecued chicken or pork with Javanese rice, a sweet-spicy Indonesian sauce, and papaya pickles; *pansit luglog* (noodles with a shrimp-and-duck-egg sauce); honey chicken; *lumpia Shanghai* (tiny pork-filled crisp rolls); *adobo* (meat or vegetables cooked in vinegar and spices) and *kare-kare* (oxtail, tripe and vegetables in a sauce thickened with ground roasted rice and peanuts). Or have a farmer's breakfast of garlic rice, dried beef or sausages or marinated milkfish, and piping coffee or hot chocolate. ⊠ *432 San Andres St. at Roxas Blvd., Malate,* ☎ *2/524–7671. AE, DC, MC, V.*

Seafood

$$–$$$
★ ✕ **Via Mare Seafood Specialty Restaurant.** Via Mare always has the freshest seafood in many gracious, inspired guises. Prime seafood—salmon, trout, Alaskan or Japanese cod, blue marlin, *lapu-lapu* (grouper), *maya-maya* (red snapper), deboned milkfish—are transformed into delights such as saffron-scented seafood bisque crowned with puff pastry, Thai chili crab, and *bacalao a la Vizcaina* (salt cod in the Spanish manner, with olive oil, potatoes, and pimientos). The oyster bar offers them fresh, baked, spiced, and seasoned in myriad ways. ⊠ *Greenbelt Commercial Complex, Paseo de Roxas, Makati City,* ☎ *2/893–2306 or 2/893–2746;* ⊠ *Penthouse, Tektite East Tower, Exchange Rd., Ortigas Center, Pasig City,* ☎ *2/631–7980 or 2/631–7981. AE, DC, MC, V. No lunch Sun.*

Spanish

$$
✕ **El Comedor.** As homey as a family dining room, this restaurant specializes in the Spanish-Filipino cooking (generally served in elite homes) for which its founder, Lourdes Perez del Rosario, is famous. Popular dishes are paella—*Valenciana* (with chicken, pork, and sausages) or *arroz negra* (black with squid ink)—*sopa seca* (soup thick with bread, sausage, and ham), *bacalao a la Vizcaina, caldereta de cordero* (lamb stew), *fabada Asturiana* (bean stew with bacon); and most especially, the *cochinillo asado,* roast suckling pig so tender it is sliced with the edge of a saucer. The service, too, is home-style—friendly and intimate—but professional. ⊠ *GF Anson Arcade, Paseo de Roxas and Pasay Rd., Makati City,* ☎ *2/892–5071 or 2/893–2518. AE, DC, MC, V.*

Thai

$$–$$$
✕ **Flavours and Spices.** This is the grandest of the city's many Thai restaurants. Favorites are a salad of finely crisped catfish with green mango; *tom yum* soups (spiced with lime leaves, lemongrass, and cilantro); chicken in pandan leaf balls; red, green and yellow curries; and *pad thai* (rice noodles and bean sprouts, prawns, scrambled egg, scallions). But try as well the Thai congee, or the hot pot in which meat, seafood, and vegetables are cooked then dipped in a hot sesame-seed sauce. The locals delight in the desserts, kindred to many Philippine sweets: *takho* (steamed rice cakes in banana-leaf cups with coconut cream and sweet corn), crushed-ice desserts like *tub tim grob* (mixed fruit and gelatin) or *ruam-mit* (water chestnuts, sweet potatoes, jackfruit strips and coconut milk). ⊠ *Garden Sq., Greenbelt Commercial Center, Makati City,* ☎ *2/894–5624 or 2/894–5625;* ⊠ *El Pueblo Real de Manila, Julia Vargas Ave., Pasig City,* ☎ *2/632–7153 or 2/632–7154;* ⊠ *Adriatico Sq., Pan Pacific Hotel, Gen. Malvar and Adriatico Sts., Malate,* ☎ *2/536–0625, 2/536–0626. AE, DC, MC, V.*

Lodging

As the largest urban area in the country, metropolitan Manila has lodgings that run the gamut from small, intimate establishments to five-star hotels whose lobbies accentuate the grand and the grandiose. Most hotels are in two areas: the Tourist Belt (Malate and Ermita districts) in downtown Manila or in Makati City, Manila's Wall Street and fashionable residential enclave. Unless otherwise noted, rooms have private baths.

Ermita/Malate

The advantages of staying in the Tourist Belt are Manila Bay, with its fabled sunsets, and the area's assortment of restaurants, bars, clubs, coffeehouses, shops, and such museums as the National Museum and the Metropolitan Museum of Art. The Cultural Center of the Philippines (☞ Nightlife and the Arts, *below*) is right on Roxas Boulevard, the scenic main road that flanks the bay.

$$$$ 🏨 **Century Park Hotel.** The sunny, six-story atrium—with a two-level lobby—has been redone and given expansive marble floors and a giant chandelier. A string quartet serenades lobby loungers every evening from 4 to 8. The rooms, done in muted but cheery tones, are spacious. Ask for one with a full bay view; some rooms overlook the adjacent parking lot and shopping complex. ⊠ *Pablo Ocampo Senior St. (formerly Vito Cruz),* ☎ *2/528–8888,* 𝖥𝖠𝖷 *2/528–1811. 505 rooms, 97 suites. 6 restaurants, bar, coffee shop, deli, pool, exercise room, nightclub, business services. AE, DC, MC, V.*

$$$$ 🏨 **Manila Hotel.** This is where General MacArthur had his unofficial
★   headquarters before World War II. Other luminaries who have stayed here include Ernest Hemingway and Douglas Fairbanks. The lobby exudes an Old World feeling, with floors of Philippine marble, *narra* wood and mahogany ceilings, and mother-of-pearl and brass chandeliers. The MacArthur Club, which is reached by a private elevator, serves complimentary breakfast. Room decor re-creates the colonial era with nostalgic artwork and intricate wood paneling that recalls traditional motifs. The best rooms face the bay and the pool. ⊠ *Rizal Park, adjacent to Quirino Grandstand,* ☎ *2/527–0011,* 𝖥𝖠𝖷 *2/527–0022. 440 rooms, 70 suites. 4 restaurants, bar, pool, 2 tennis courts, exercise room, dock, business services. AE, DC, MC, V.* 🐾

$$$ 🏨 **Hyatt Regency.** Right on the main boulevard, this medium-size establishment has a spare but elegant lobby—graced by capiz chandeliers—that never seems crowded. The rooms all have bay views as well as wood-and-straw headboards and cane chairs. ⊠ *2702 Roxas Blvd.,* ☎ *2/833–1234,* 𝖥𝖠𝖷 *2/833–5913. 261 rooms, 28 suites. 3 restaurants, bar, pool, exercise room, nightclub, business services, meeting rooms. AE, DC, MC, V.*

$$$ 🏨 **Manila Diamond Hotel.** The style of the lobby (or, as the staff calls it, the "tea lounge") is a mix of Art Deco and postmodern. The hotel fronts Manila Bay, and all the rooms have a view of the ocean. Room decor combines dark-wood paneling with Art Deco touches; the eclectic motifs, with both ethnic and modernist designs, verge on the pleasantly gaudy. ⊠ *Roxas Blvd. at J. Quintos St.,* ☎ *2/526–2211,* 𝖥𝖠𝖷 *2/526–2255. 472 rooms, 28 suites. 8 restaurants, bar, pool, sauna, health club, business services, meeting rooms. AE, DC, MC, V.* 🐾

$$$ 🏨 **Westin Philippine Plaza Hotel.** Luxurious and grand—a veritable re-
★   sort without the beachfront—the newly renovated Plaza has an enormous lobby with two levels. Not only is the swimming pool huge, but it also has a snack bar smack in the middle of it as well as slides for the kids. All rooms have terraces with views of either Manila Bay or of reclaimed land; the decor features rattan furnishings and a beige-and-white color scheme. ⊠ *Cultural Center complex, Roxas Blvd.,* ☎ *2/551–5555,* 𝖥𝖠𝖷 *2/551–5610. 609 rooms, 48 suites. 3 restaurants, bar, 3 snack bars, pool, spa, driving range, putting green, 4 tennis courts, health club, nightclub, business services, meeting rooms. AE, DC, MC, V.* 🐾

$$ 🏨 **Adriatico Arms.** This small, cozy hotel, with armchairs in the lobby and a combination coffee shop–deli, is in the heart of the Tourist Belt. The rooms are tastefully—if simply—furnished in basic black and white. The small staff treats guests like family. ⊠ *560 J. Nakpil St. at*

Adriatico St., ☎ *2/521–0736,* FAX *2/525–6214. 28 rooms. Coffee shop. AE, DC, MC, V.*

$$ ⊞ **Heritage Hotel.** The spanking-white Heritage fronts the bay and isn't far from the airport. The smart-looking lobby is done in marble, brass, and colored stone inlays. The decor in the guest rooms repeats the motif of stone and brass, with deep-blue upholstery. ⊠ *Roxas Blvd. at EDSA,* ☎ *2/854–8888,* FAX *2/854–8833. 464 rooms, 28 suites. Restaurant, bar, coffee shop, pool, health club, casino. AE, DC, MC, V.* ☙

Makati City

This district, the business capital of the country and neighbor to the airport, is not as congested as the Tourist Belt. The streets and sidewalks are wide, making it easier than elsewhere to walk around, and the hotels are near the gigantic Makati Commercial Center, which has everything from movie houses to money changers.

$$$$ ⊞ **Hotel Inter-Continental Manila.** Conservative in beige and brown motifs, this hotel reeks of sobriety. The rooms are spacious, if a bit stolid, and have access to the Internet via the TV. Businesspeople can avail themselves of rooms with work stations, fax-scanners, swivel chairs, and office supplies. ⊠ *1 Ayala Ave.,* ☎ *2/815–9711,* FAX *2/812–4389. 338 rooms, 65 suites. 6 restaurants, bar, pool, health club, dance club, business services, meeting rooms. AE, DC, MC, V.* ☙

$$$$ ⊞ **Mandarin Oriental.** The ambience here is discreet and elegant, with
★   a small but stately lobby done in black marble and illuminated by a cut-crystal chandelier. The rooms are scrupulously maintained and similarly refined, with muted but rich colors. The staff is unfailingly professional and courteous, another reason (along with management's sensitivity to noise and security) why it's a favorite with many travelers. ⊠ *Makati Ave. and Paseo de Roxas St.,* ☎ *2/750–8888,* FAX *2/817–2472. 430 rooms, 29 suites. 7 restaurants, bar, pool, exercise room, nightclub, business services, meeting rooms. AE, DC, MC, V.* ☙

$$$$ ⊞ **Manila Peninsula.** The Pen, as Manilans call it, exudes an informal
★   elegance, expressed in the wide lobby—under a giant ceiling shaped like the sun's rays—and the understated furnishings and decor of the well-kept rooms, which are spacious enough to seem more like suites. The lobby is known as a "power spot," where politicians and others in Manila society gather for breakfast or a late-night drink. ⊠ *Makati and Ayala Aves.,* ☎ *2/810–3456,* FAX *2/815–4825. 453 rooms, 47 suites. 4 restaurants, bar, deli, pool, nightclub, business services. AE, DC, MC, V.*

$$$$ ⊞ **New World Renaissance.** This 25-story edifice has what's termed "internationalist" style: ultramodern decor and furnishings meant to make businesspeople feel that they're really not too far from home. All rooms have centralized bedside controls for everything—TV, lights, air-conditioning. The staff is quiet, fast, and efficient. ⊠ *Esperanza St. at Makati Ave.,* ☎ *2/811–6888,* FAX *2/811–6777. 583 rooms, 28 suites. 3 restaurants, bar, coffee shop, lobby lounge, pool, barbershop, beauty salon, health club, business services. AE, DC, MC, V.* ☙

$$$$ ⊞ **Shangri-La Makati.** After the luxurious, soaring, light-filled lobby, the rooms here are something of a disappointment: although they're spacious and sparking clean, they have a bland, modern decor. ⊠ *Ayala Ave. at Makati Ave.,* ☎ *2/813–8888,* FAX *2/813–5499. 608 rooms, 95 suites. 9 restaurants, bar, deli, pool, exercise room, dance club, business services. AE, DC, MC, V.*

$$$ ⊞ **Dusit Hotel Nikko.** Formerly the Nikko Manila Garden, this new incarnation opened in 1997. It has an elegant Spanish-Mediterranean style, including a light-filled lobby with black-marble floors and wrought-iron and wood trim. The staff is very gracious, and the location in Makati Commercial Center—with restaurants, cinemas, bou-

tiques, and department stores—is most convenient. ⊠ *Ayala Center at EDSA,* ☎ *2/867–3333,* FAX *2/867–3888. 542 rooms, 59 suites. 7 restaurants, bar, coffee shop, pool, health club, business services, meeting rooms. AE, DC, MC, V.*

Nightlife and the Arts

The Arts

Good guides to the city's cultural life are the *Expat Weekly* and *What's On in Manila,* distributed free by major hotels, restaurants, and tourist information centers. Check the entertainment pages of the dailies, particularly the Sunday editions.

The **Cultural Center of the Philippines** (⊠ Roxas Blvd. facing Pablo Ocampo Senior St., ☎ 2/832–1125) is the country's premier institution for music, theater, dance, and the visual arts. It has a resident dance company and a theater group. The government-run center also hosts internationally known artists and musicians, sometimes in cooperation with the various cultural arms of the foreign embassies. The center's two art galleries display contemporary and traditional art.

ART GALLERIES

Ateneo de Manila Gallery (⊠ Ateneo de Manila University, Katipunan Rd., Loyola Heights, Quezon City, ☎ 2/924–4432) exhibits a stellar collection of Philippine modern art. **Ayala Museum Galleries** (⊠ Makati Ave. at Ayala Ave., ☎ 2/812–1191 up to 2/812–1197) has works by well-established contemporary artists. **Crucible Gallery** (⊠ SM Megamall, EDSA and Julia Vargas St., Building A, Artwalk, 4th floor, ☎ 2/635–6061) shows contemporary Philippine work. **Galleria Duemila** (⊠ SM Megamall, EDSA and Julia Vargas St., Building A, Artwalk, 4th floor, ☎ 2/633–6687) focuses on young artists. An hour and a half's drive southwest of Manila is the **De La Salle University Museum** (⊠ Area B, Dasmariñas, Cavite, ☎ 2/741–9271, ext. 3141), which has an extensive collection of antique furniture that re-creates an 18th-century elite Philippine household.

Hiraya Art Gallery (⊠ 530 United Nations Ave., Ermita, ☎ 2/523–3331) favors up-and-coming artists whose work incorporates social-consciousness themes. **Luz Gallery** (⊠ Makati Ave. at Ayala Ave., ☎ 2/815–6906) is a well-known venue for established modern artists. The government-run **Museo ng Sining** (⊠ Cultural Center complex, GSIS Building, Roxas Blvd., ☎ 2/891–6161 or ext. 4940) offers a surprising range of Filipino art—from traditional to wildly contemporary.

CONCERTS

Free concerts are given at Rizal Park on Sunday beginning at 5 PM, usually featuring a program of popular Western and Philippine music. Well-known singers and musicians are featured. Paco Park and Puerta Real in Intramuros offer similar programs, at 6 PM on Friday and Saturday respectively, during the dry season.

DANCE

The **Cultural Center of the Philippines** (⊠ Roxas Blvd.) has an acclaimed resident dance company, **Ballet Philippines** (☎ 2/832–3675). Two other ballet companies are **Philippine Ballet Theater**(☎ 2/634–2763) and **Ballet Manila** (☎ 2/525–5967 or 2/512–5031), which performs with Russian flair. The country's premier folk-dance company is **Bayanihan Philippines** (☎ 2/536–8602), with an extensive, stylish repertoire.

FILM

Metro Manila has many cinema houses, but many of the English-language films are either the substandard B type or the Hollywood blockbuster type. Good films do turn up, though. During the two-week **Metro Manila Film Festival** in June and December, only Philippine films (of varying quality) are shown in the cinemas.

The **Alliance Française de Manille** (⊠ 220 Gil Puyat Ave., Makati City, ☎ 2/813–2681), **Goethe Institute** (⊠ 687 Aurora Blvd., Quezon City, ☎ 2/722–4671), **Thomas Jefferson Library** (⊠ 1201 Roxas Blvd., Manila, ☎ 2/523–1001), and **University of the Philippines Film Center** (⊠ Diliman campus, Quezon City, ☎ 2/920–5301 or 2/920–5399) offer free film screenings, ranging from silent classics to contemporary movies. The **Mowelfund Film Institute** (⊠ 66 Rosario Dr., Cubao, Quezon City, ☎ 2/727–1915) holds a yearly film festival, **Pelikula at Lipunan** (Film and Society), with a selection of the best of commercial and independent Philippine films.

THEATER

The **CCP Little Theater** (⊠ Cultural Center complex, Roxas Blvd., ☎ 2/832–1125, ext. 277) performs original works or plays translated into Pilipino. The **Equitable PCIB Theater** (⊠ PCI Bank Tower, Paseo de Roxas, ☎ 2/840–7000 or ext. 2360), presents classical chamber music and intimate dramas. **Repertory Philippines** (⊠ Shangri-La Plaza Mall, Ortigas Ave., ☎ 2/633–4821 or 2/633–4825) usually does Broadway and West End musicals.

Nightlife

Metropolitan Manila is a pleasure-seeker's paradise, with an array of nighttime activities, from the soothing to the sinful. You can listen to jazz or rock, have a drink at a bar while ogling scantily clad performers of either sex, dance madly at a disco, or have a snack and cappuccino in a lively coffeehouse.

BARS

There are really two types of bars in Manila: "girlie" bars with skimpily attired dancers and disco music, and music bar-lounges with varied musical fare. Most of the girlie bars are in Pasay City, along Roxas Boulevard. You'll also find some in Quezon City, around the Tomas Morato–Quezon Avenue intersection. They range from basic pub-cum-strip-joints to upscale places offering high-priced drinks and high-priced hostesses who will drink with gentlemen patrons and listen sympathetically as they unburden their troubles.

Music bar-lounges are scattered throughout Makati, the Tourist Belt, and beyond. **Calesa Bar** (⊠ Hyatt Regency hotel, 2702 Roxas Blvd., ☎ 2/887–8084) has a reputation for launching new and noteworthy singers. **Captain's Bar** (⊠ Mandarin Oriental hotel, Makati Ave. and Paseo de Roxas St., Makati, ☎ 2/750–8888), is favored by businesspeople for its soothing tunes. **Fat Willy's** (⊠ The Fort Bonifacio Center, Taguig, ☎ 2/887–5103 or 2/887–5104) gets the wild crowd in for drinks. **Guernica's** (⊠ 1856 Bocobo St., Malate, ☎ 2/521–4415) features Spanish music, ballads, and folk songs. **Giraffe** (⊠ 6750 Ayala Avenue, Makati, ☎ 2/815–3232) attracts yuppies, and the gay crowd brings it alive in the very late hours. The **Prince of Wales** (⊠ New Plaza Building, Greenbelt, Makati, ☎ 02/815–4274) pub packs in the expats. **Sala** (⊠ 610 J. Nakpil St., Malate, ☎ 2/524–6770; *see also* Dining, *above*), a fine dining place, becomes a bar for the smart set after 9 PM.

CAFÉS

The largest concentration of cafés is in the Malate district, in and around Remedios Circle. During the dry season the café owners sometimes sponsor a street fair, with live music. **Cafe Adriatico** (⊠ 1790 Adriatico St., ☎ 2/525–2509) features Philippine food, classical music, and a low-key atmosphere. **Cafe Caribana** (⊠ J. Nakpil St., ☎ 2/524–8421) has jam sessions and Caribbean-inspired food. The folks at the jungle-theme **Endangered Species Cafe** (✉ Adriatico St., ☎ 2/524–0167) serve good international fare. **Penguin Cafe** (✉ 604 Remedios St. at Bocobo St., ☎ 2/521–2088), which doubles as an art gallery, has a great outdoor patio, an artistic crowd, and good homemade pasta. The Ernest Hemingway cigar room and samba music provide the atmosphere at **Café Havana** (✉ 1903 Adriatico and Remedios Sts., Malate, ☎ 2/521–8097 or 2/524–5526; *see also* Dining, *above*).

CASINOS

Manila has three government-sanctioned casinos, each in a major hotel: **Grand Boulevard** (✉ 1990 Roxas Blvd., ☎ 2/526–8588); **Holiday Inn Hotel** (✉ Maria Orosa St. at United Nations Ave., ☎ 2/526–1212); and **Heritage Hotel** (✉ Roxas Blvd. at EDSA, ☎ 2/854–8888). The casino at the Grand Boulevard occupies the hotel's entire mezzanine, with a room reserved for high rollers. All three casinos are open 24 hours a day; games include baccarat, blackjack, roulette, and poker. You must be 18 to enter (bring your passport), and dress is smart casual (though at the Heritage you might want to err on the "smart" side).

DISCOS

Manila discos tend to be cavernous. The beat is generic and follows Western fashions. The trendiest places combine the disco fever with a few karaoke rooms and, on some nights, ballroom dancing. In Quezon City, a popular gay disco is **Club 690** (✉ 690 Amoranto St. at Biak-na-Bato St., ☎ 2/712–3662), with shows featuring dancers and impersonators. **Euphoria** (✉ Hotel Inter-Continental Manila, Makati Commercial Center, Ayala Ave., ☎ 2/815–9711) is a trendy yuppie hangout. **Cats** (✉ New World Renaissance hotel, Esperanza St. at Makati Ave., ☎ 2/811–6888) is one of the liveliest scenes for disco and ballroom dancing. **Virgin Cafe** (✉ Glorietta IV, Ayala Center, Makati, ☎ 2/893–1841) has three floors: one with a café, a lounge with live band, and the third with an often crowded disco.

FOLK AND ROCK HOUSES

Chatterbox (✉ Robinson's Galleria, Ortigas Center, Pasig City, ☎ 2/633–6068) caters to the college-age grunge set. **Hard Rock Cafe** (✉ 3rd floor, Glorieta III, Ayala Center, Makati City, ☎ 2/893–4661) really offers hard rock, plus American-style snacks and Asian food. **Hive Radio Cafe** (✉ 2284 Pasong Tamo Ext., Makati City, ☎ 2/894–2358) swings to rock and roll. **Hobbit House** (✉ 1801 A. Mabini St., ☎ 2/521–7604) is memorable for its waitstaff of little people and regular roster of folk singers. In Quezon City, the **'70's Bistro** (✉ 46 Anonas St., ☎ 2/922–0492) hosts a mix of students and professionals listening to folk-rock bands.

NIGHTCLUBS AND CABARETS

Manila nightclubs offer floor shows that vary from performances of well-known bands and cultural presentations to highly choreographed "model" shows, in which a lot of skin is bared. **Mondo** (✉ The Fort Bonifacio Center, Taguig, ☎ 2/887–5115) is a New York–style supper club that offers live jazz bands and singers belting out standards. Drag shows are put on at **Politix** (✉ 574 J. Nakpil St., Malate, ☎ 2/524–9819). **Top of the Century** (✉ Century Park Hotel, Pablo Ocampo Senior and Harrison Sts., ☎ 2/528–8888) has well-known jazz and pop singers. **Zamboanga** (✉ 1619 Adriatico St., ☎ 2/521–9836) serves Philippine cuisine and presents regional folk dances.

Outdoor Activities and Sports

Basketball

Basketball is the Philippines' premier sport, an enduring legacy of the American colonial era. Tournaments are held by the professional **Philip-**

pine **Basketball Association** (☎ 2/636–5316) as well as by the **Basketball Association of the Philippines** (☎ 2/524–3977) and the **Philippine Amateur Basketball League (PABL)**. The major courts are the **Rizal Coliseum** (☎ 2/525–2171) in Malate, and the **Ultra Stadium** (☎ 2/636–5316) in Pasig City.

Golf

Visitors are welcome at **Club Intramuros** (☎ 2/527–6613), which has 18 holes right beside the historic walls of Intramuros. Greens fees are P1,200 by day, P2,000 at night (last tee off at 8:30 PM); you can rent clubs for P500. You can play at **Puerto Azul Beach and Country Club** (⊠ Ternate, Cavite, ☎ 2/525–9248), a championship 18-hole course in a tropical resort by the sea (a 90-minute drive from Manila), for P1,800; cart rentals cost P885 and clubs rent for P600–P900. The **Westin Philippine Plaza Hotel** (⊠ Cultural Center complex, Roxas Blvd., ☎ 2/551–5555) has a putting green (P175 an hour) and a driving range (P450 for an hour and 160 balls).

Horse Racing

The **Santa Ana Race Track** (⊠ J. Rizal St., Santa Ana, ☎ 2/890–4015) and the **San Lazaro Hippodrome** (⊠ Manila Jockey Club, Felix Huertas St., ☎ 2/711–1251) feature races on Tuesday and Wednesday evenings and Saturday and Sunday afternoons.

Tennis

The **Westin Philippine Plaza Hotel** (⊠ Cultural Center complex, Roxas Blvd., ☎ 2/551–5555) has four (grass or Multiflex) lighted courts. Court fees are P270 during the day, P370 at night; lessons cost P170 an hour. The **Velayo Sports Center** (⊠ Domestic Airport Rd., ☎ 2/833–4425) has five sheltered, lighted courts on which you can play weekdays for P220–P295 an hour and on weekends for P230–P300 an hour. An hour's lesson costs P150. The **Rizal Memorial Stadium** (⊠ Pablo Ocampo Senior St., Malate, ☎ 2/525–6434) also has courts; call for details.

Shopping

As the nerve center of the country, Manila has all the shopping options, from sidewalk vendors and small retail stores to market districts and shopping centers. Nothing beats shopping in the markets for color, bustle, and bargains—in a word, for atmosphere. Here haggling is raised to a fine art. Located in the older areas of the city, each encompasses several blocks and is a neighborhood unto itself. Crowds can be intense, and, as in any urban area, they include pickpockets. Don't be paranoid; just be alert. Shopping malls are in newer areas, such as Makati's commercial center, and in Quezon City. The malls make up in convenience what they lack in charm; prices are fixed, however, so bargaining is pointless.

Districts and Markets

Baclaran. The many stalls on Roxas Boulevard specialize in ready-to-wear clothing. Prices are supposedly lowest on Wednesday, when the weekly devotions to Our Lady of Perpetual Help are held at the nearby Baclaran Church. The disadvantages of Wednesday shopping are the crowds and worse-than-usual traffic jams.

Divisoria. North of Binondo, this is the largest old-fashioned market district, with everything from fresh produce to cooking utensils and hardware to leather goods and handicrafts. Savvy Manilans come to browse among the assorted stalls, emporia, and department stores until they see what they want at the right price. Be especially careful of pickpockets here.

A. Mabini Street. This street and those just off it have several small antiques and handicraft shops. Some reputable stores are: **Likha Antiques** (⌧ 1415 A. Mabini St., ☎ 2/525–6320), **Padua Gallery** (⌧ 1171 A. Mabini St., ☎ 2/526–7772), **Riba Artifacts** (⌧ 1337 M. H. del Pilar, ☎ 2/523–0084), **Terry Baylosis** (⌧ 1185 San Marcelino, ☎ 2/523–7878 for an appointment), **Tesoro's** (⌧ 1325 A. Mabini St., ☎ 2/524–1475), **Via Antica** (⌧ 1411 A. Mabini St., ☎ 2/522–0869), and **VM Antiques** (⌧ 1153 M. H. del Pilar, ☎ 2/524–8243).

San Andres Market. This 24-hour Tourist Belt market is noted for its tropical and imported fruits. The piles of mangoes, watermelons, custard apples, and jackfruit are bright and neatly arranged. It's pricey, but you can bargain.

Malls and Centers

EDSA Malls. On EDSA, between Shaw Boulevard and Ortigas Avenue, loom three gigantic air-conditioned shopping malls—**Robinson's, Shangri-La Plaza,** and **SM Megamall.** All three have shops selling clothing, electronics, record and books, as well as fast-food areas, fine restaurants, art galleries, cinemas, and several department stores. There's even an ice-skating rink. Being relatively near one another, the three malls make one monstrous bazaar, where sophisticated urbanites, foreigners, and visitors from the provinces all mingle in air-conditioned comfort. Shops and fast-food restaurants close at 9 PM; fine-dining establishments close at 10. The malls themselves shut at midnight, or whenever the last film screening lets out.

Harrison Plaza. This huge Tourist Belt center adjacent to the Century Park Hotel, on Adriatico and Pablo Ocampo Senior streets, has department stores, supermarkets, jewelers, drugstores, boutiques, record and electronics shops, video rentals, restaurants and snack bars, and four movie houses. Opening hours vary, but all shops close at 7:30 PM, except the fast-food restaurants, which are open until 8:30.

LaO Center. Some of the better antiques shops—Katutubo, Tawalisi, Osmundo's, and JoLiza's—are in this center. It's on Arnaiz Avenue in Makati and is open Monday through Saturday 10 AM–7 PM.

Makati Commercial Center. Bounded by Makati Avenue on the west, Ayala Avenue on the north, EDSA on the east, and Pasay Road on the south, this is the biggest shopping center in the country, comprising several malls, a couple of gigantic department stores, two hotels, and a multitude of smaller shops. There are plazas where you can rest your feet and watch humanity stream by. Opening hours vary; shops and fast-food restaurants close at 9 PM, fine-dining establishments close at 10, and the malls themselves close at midnight or so.

Metro Manila A to Z

Arriving and Departing

BY AIRPLANE

Ninoy Aquino International Airport (NAIA; ☎ 2/877–1109), the international air hub of the Philippines, is in Paranaque on the southern edge of Metro Manila. Domestic flights land at **Manila Domestic Airport** (☎ 2/833–9358). For specific information on international arrivals and departures and on domestic carriers and flights, *see* Philippines A to Z, *below.*

From the Airports: The major Manila hotels have shuttles; look around for one before using another means of transport. Cabbies generally charge a fixed fee of P300 or higher for trips to the Tourist Belt. Several taxi fleets have coupon services, with rates averaging P450. (You buy a coupon at the booth outside customs for a fixed price of, say, P350 or P400, for travel from the airport to a designated area in the city.) There are no taxi stands in the arrivals area, so you must go to the departure area on the third level. Limousine service is available for P1,600–P1,700; check at the arrivals hall. For rental cars, Hertz, Avis, and National have booths in the arrival area. To the right of the airport building at the end of the driveway are stops for public buses that pass by the Tourist Belt via Makati. They leave every 15 minutes and cost about P20.

In light traffic, it's a 30-minute ride from the domestic airport to Makati's hotels; getting to the Tourist Belt takes close to an hour. Manila Domestic Airport is a two-building affair with a parking area and a designated taxi line. Here airport police make sure cabbies use their meters. A ride to Makati should cost no more than P100, P150 to the Tourist Belt.

BY BUS

There are about 20 major bus companies in the Philippines and almost as many terminals in Manila. Those closest to downtown Manila and Makati are at Plaza Lawton (now called Liwasang Bonifacio, but bus signboards still say LAWTON) and along a portion of EDSA in Pasay City, not far from Taft Avenue. Another important terminal is farther north on EDSA, at the corner of New York Street, in the district of Cubao, Quezon City.

Bus companies include: **BLTB** (✉ EDSA at Aurora St., Pasay City, ☎ 2/833–5501), **Dangwa** (✉ 1600 Dimasalang, Sampaloc, ☎ 2/743–2227), **Pantranco** (✉ 325 Quezon Blvd. Ext., near Roosevelt Ave., Quezon City, ☎ 2/833–5061), **Philtranco** (✉ EDSA and Apelo Cruz St., Pasay City, ☎ 2/832–2456), **Saulog Transit** (✉ 1377 Quirino Ave., Paranaque, ☎ 2/825–2926, 2/825–2927, 2/825–2928, 2/825–2929, or 2/826–1285), and **Victory Liner** (✉ EDSA at Aurora St., Pasay City, ☎ 2/833–0293 or 2/833–5020).

BY CAR

The best routes for leaving or entering the city are the Epifanio de los Santos Avenue (known as EDSA), the South Superhighway, the C-5 Highway, and the EDSA–North Diversion link. EDSA is the main artery connecting Pasay, Makati, Mandaluyong, Quezon, and Caloocan. The North Diversion begins in Caloocan, at a junction of EDSA, and leads to points north. The South Superhighway originates in Manila, passes through Makati with EDSA as a junction, and leads to points south. C-5 is a circumferential road that connects Pasig (a district adjacent to the EDSA malls) to the South Superhighway and destinations farther south, allowing you to bypass the often congested stretch of EDSA through Makati and Mandaluyong.

Parking has become a problem, with Manila becoming more congested. In Makati, there are parking lots and meter maids collecting P20 to P30 per hour. Be on the lookout for designated tow-away zones in Makati.

BY TRAIN

The main rail terminal, Tutuban Station in the Tondo district, has recently been completely transformed into a shopping mall. The two operational train stations are in the Paco and Makati districts. A commuter train, Metro-Tren, operates on a north–south axis during rush hours, from Paco, in Manila, to Alabang, a southern suburb.

Getting Around

Manila isn't a city for walking, though you can do so within certain areas, particularly in the Tourist Belt, on Roxas Boulevard, and in some parts of Makati. Sidewalks are generally narrow, uneven, and sometimes nonexistent. Instead, choose from a vast array of transportation, public and private, from horse-drawn carriages to elevated trains.

BY BUS AND JEEPNEY

Public buses and jeepneys (a cross between a van and a Jeep) crisscross Metropolitan Manila and are the cheapest form of travel for areas not served by the LRT or the Mass Rail Transit. Buses make sense for longer trips, and jeepneys are best for short ones. For example, a bus is recommended to reach Quezon City from Ermita, but within Ermita, or between districts, take a jeepney. The latter can accommodate 12 to 15 passengers and is perhaps the city's most colorful form of public transport, gaudily decorated and with the driver's favorite English slogan emblazoned in front. Fares average P5 to P10.

BY CAR

Between the frustration and the smoke emissions, traffic jams in Manila can reduce drivers to tears. If you don't have to drive within the city, don't. Public transportation is plentiful and cheap. If you do drive, improvisation—such as sudden lane changing—is the rule rather than the exception. Many of the nonarterial roads are narrow and become clogged during morning (7:30–10) and afternoon (3:30–7:30) rush hours. On the other hand, a car gives you flexibility (though parking is a problem), and you don't have to deal with cabs, some of whose meters may run faster than a speeding bullet.

Some car-rental agencies include: **Ace** (☎ 2/889–0180 or 2/889–0181), **Avis** (☎ 2/525–2206 or 2/844–8498), **Budget** (☎ 2/818–7363 or 2/816–6682), **Dollar** (☎ 2/896–9251), **Executive** (☎ 2/831–5852), **Hertz** (☎ 2/897–5151), and **National** (☎ 2/833–0648). Hiring a chauffeur-driven sedan from an agency for 10 hours will cost you, on the average, P3,000.

BY CARETELA OR CALESA

Good for short hops within a neighborhood are the horse-drawn carriages called calesas and caretelas (larger versions of calesas). They're available mostly in the older neighborhoods, such as Binondo (Chinatown), and they're inexpensive (about P30 a ride).

BY LIGHT RAIL

The **Light Rail Transit** (☎ 2/832–0423) is an elevated, modern railway, with 16 stops on a north–south axis; additional stations are under construction. It's the fastest, cleanest, and safest mode of transport in the city. The southern terminal is at Baclaran in Pasay City, the northern at Monumento in Caloocan City. Currently, most stops are in Manila. Hours of operation are from 5 AM to 9 PM. The fare between any two stations is P12. Each station displays a guide to the routes.

Mass Rail Transit (☎ 2/929–5347), a new north–south line hugging the eastern part of Metro Manila and running above EDSA Highway, opened in February 2000. It operates from 5:30 AM to 10 PM. The fare ranges from P12 to P20.

BY PEDICAB OR TRICYCLE

Pedicabs (bicycles) and motorcycles with attached sidecars (tricycles) are found everywhere and provide amazingly inexpensive (P5–P7) short hops.

BY TAXI AND LIMOUSINE

Taxis aren't as inexpensive as other means of public transport, but they're still fairly cheap: a metered 3-km (2-mi) cab ride should cost about P40 (assuming you don't get caught in a traffic jam, a commonplace occurrence), plus tip. However, although rates are theoretically standard, a number of cab companies tolerate their drivers' tampering with the meters. If you feel the fare registered is exorbitant, say so politely. Often the driver will allow you to pay less than what's shown. Try to take a taxi from the better hotels, where cabs are always waiting and hotel doormen note the taxi number, which is useful in case of problems. **Avis Taxi** (☎ 2/532–5758 or 2/844–4884) is a reputable radio-cab company that adds P35 to the meter rate as a pick-up fee.

Major hotels have limo service and use mostly Mercedes-Benzes or luxury Toyota sedans. Costs are P7,000 to P8,500 for 10 hours.

Contacts and Resources

EMERGENCIES

Doctors: Call the **Philippine Medical Association** (☎ 2/928–2132) for referrals. **Dentists:** The **Philippine Dental Association** (☎ 2/899–6332 or 2/890–4609) can suggest a dentist. Finer hotels also usually have a doctor and/or dentist either on premises or on call.

Hospitals: There are emergency rooms at **Makati Medical Center** (⊠ Corner of Amorsolo and de la Rosa Sts., ☎ 2/815–9911 to –9944) and at **Manila Doctors' Hospital** (⊠ 667 United Nations Ave., near UN station on LRT, Ermita, ☎ 2/524–3011). **Pharmacies: Mercury Drug Store,** a citywide chain, has 24-hour branches in Quiapo, at **Plaza Miranda** (☎ 2/733–2112), and in Makati, at **Guadalupe Commercial Center** (☎ 2/843–4327). **Police:** The **Metropolitan Police Command** now has one line for all emergencies (☎ 166). The **Tourist Assistance Police** (☎ 2/524–1660 or 2/524–1724, 24 hours) can assist in cases of theft, missing luggage, or other untoward incidents.

ENGLISH-LANGUAGE BOOKSTORES

National Book Store is the biggest chain. In the Tourist Belt, try the **Harrison Plaza branch** (⊠ Adriatico and Pablo Ocampo Senior Sts., ☎ 2/524–6871 or 2/525–8205). In Makati, try the **Glorietta Center branch** (☎ 2/892–5767) at the Makati Commercial Center, or the newest outlet, **Powerbooks** (☎ 2/844–4455), with a cybercafé on the second floor. **Filipinas Heritage Bookshop** (⊠ Old Nielson Tower across from Manila Peninsula hotel, ☎ 2/892–1801) specializes in Philippine-published books. **Solidaridad** (⊠ 531 Padre Faura St., ☎ 2/525–5038), owned by well-known novelist F. Sionil José, is frequented by Manila's literati. The store offers political, literary, and popular titles.

TOUR OPERATORS

The average city tour takes five hours and can be arranged by the staff of most hotels or by any of the following travel agencies, which also handle out-of-town tours: **American Express** (⊠ Ground floor, Philam Life Building, in front of Holiday Inn, United Nations Ave., ☎ 2/521–9492), **Baron Travel Corp.** (⊠ Pacific Bank Building, H. V. de la Costa St. and Ayala Ave., Makati, ☎ 2/817–4926), and **Rajah Tours** (⊠ 3/f Physicians' Tower, 533 United Nations Ave., ☎ 2/522–0541).

The **Department of Tourism** (☞ Visitor Information, *below*) can provide a list of English-, Spanish-, Japanese-, French-, Italian-, German-, Indonesian-, and even Hebrew-speaking guides. Guided standard day tours around Manila or to nearby Tagaytay or Pagsanjan cost P650 and up, per person, with lunch included.

Bay Cruise (☎ 2/524–5491) offers a nightly dinner cruise of Manila Bay on a tanker-turned-luxury-cruiser, the *Tennessee Walker.* The boat leaves at 7:30 from the Cultural Center complex bay terminal.

TRAVEL AGENCIES

The agencies that offer guided tours (☞ *above*) are travel agencies as well. There's also the venerable **Thomas Cook** (⊠ G/F Skyland Plaza, Gil Puyat Ave., Makati City, ☎ 2/816–3701 or 2/812–2446).

The **Department of Tourism** has an information center on the ground floor of its main offices (⊠ Tourism Building, Agrifina Circle, Rizal Park, T. M. Kalaw Ave., ☎ 2/524–2384, or 2/524–1703), at the mezzanine and arrival mall of the **Ninoy Aquino International Airport** (☎ 2/877–1009), and at **Manila Domestic Airport** (☎ 2/833–9358). For information on the old walled city, contact the **Intramuros Administration** (☎ 2/527–3155).

SIDE TRIPS FROM METRO MANILA

Las Piñas

12 km (8 mi) south of Manila. Drive south from Rizal Park on Roxas Blvd., turn left on Airport Rd., turn right on Quirino Ave. and continue for 10 km (6 mi) to Las Piñas.

The world's only bamboo organ is housed in Las Piñas's 18th-century **San José Church.** The organ, built in 1795, has 121 metal pipes, 832 bamboo pipes, 22 registers, and a 5-octave manual. Every February the church holds its Bamboo Organ Festival, which features well-known local and international organists. Not far from San José Church is the **Sarao Motor Works,** largest manufacturer of the ubiquitous and gaudy jeepney, its original prototype a converted U.S. Army Jeep. The works are open to the public for free tours weekdays 9–5.

Tagaytay Ridge

60 km (37 mi) south of Manila. Take South Expressway to the Carmona or the Santa Rosa exit; join up with the Aguinaldo Highway, which leads to the town of Silang and right into Tagaytay.

Trees and rice fields run alongside the South Expressway, which heads south from downtown Manila to Tagaytay Ridge, 2,500 ft above sea level. Here you can view what may be the world's smallest volcano, **Taal Volcano.** It's actually a volcano within a volcano: the ridge on which you stand is the rim of a giant caldera that exploded centuries ago, forming the lake below, which encloses Taal, an active volcano. With cool temperatures and scenic vistas, Tagaytay provides welcome relief from Manila's heat and congestion.

Laguna Resorts

★ *Hidden Valley is 75 km (46 mi) southeast of Manila; Villa Escudero is 11 km (7 mi) beyond Hidden Valley. Take South Expressway to its end and turn right toward Lucena City; bear left at the Santo Tomas intersection onto the road to San Pablo City and follow it to Alaminos.*

Tucked in the foothills of two Laguna mountains is the popular **Hidden Valley** resort. Daytrippers and overnight visitors alike come here for the six natural, spring-fed pools with their pristine, bubbly (like soda!) waters whose temperatures range from lukewarm to cool. You can also hike through a rain forest dotted with giant *amlang* trees. If you opt for an overnight stay, there are 22 exquisite and peaceful cottages. The resort also offers fine dining with ever-changing menus. ⊠ *Alaminos, Laguna,* ☎ *2/818–4034 or 2/840–4112,* FAX *2/812–1609.*

You can experience a 1,600-acre rice and coconut plantation at **Villa Escudero.** Just 90 minutes from Manila, the resort makes a perfect day trip; you can also stay overnight in one of the bamboo cottages. Upon arrival you may be greeted by children dressed in traditional outfits and playing native instruments. After being serenaded, visit the on-site museum, with its eclectic and colorful collections of war memorabilia, religious artifacts and altars, paintings, and celadon pottery. For lunch, you can dine on dishes made with fresh local produce and afterward go rafting on a sleepy river and dip your feet in the cool waters of a man-made waterfall. ⊠ *San Pablo, Laguna,* ☏ *2/521–0830 or 2/523–0392.* 🚗 *P728 for a day visit (includes food, entertainment, and museum entry).*

Pagsanjan

★ 130 km (80 mi) south of Manila. Take South Expressway to its end, then turn left toward Calamba (there are signs). Turn right at the first major intersection and follow signs to Pagsanjan.

About an hour and a half southeast of Manila, the town of Pagsanjan was used by Hollywood director Francis Ford Coppola for his epic film *Apocalypse Now* (older residents complain the town hasn't been the same since). Pagsanjan is known for its rapids and the numerous waterfalls that empty into the Magdapio River. The last set, the **Magdapio Falls,** cascade from about 100 ft. You can take to the river in small boats guided through the rapids by skillful oarsmen. A raft trip under the Magdapio Falls into a cave caps off the ride. You might also see villagers bathing and laundering in the river as well as an occasional carabao cooling off. Be sure to dress appropriately, and wrap your camera or other nonwaterproof gear in plastic. Life preservers aren't provided, so think twice about taking children along. The round-trip takes 2½–3 hours, and the fee is P600 per head, two per boat (oarsman appreciate a tip of P100 or so).

Corregidor Island

57 km (26 mi) due west of Manila, one-hour boat ride

In 1942, just months after the bombing of Pearl Harbor, Corregidor—a small island in Manila Bay—became a World War II battleground. It was the last bastion of Filipino and American forces fighting the Japanese. Known as "The Rock," Corregidor still has eerie battle-scarred ruins: cement roads linking the old military installations, bombed-out barracks, and giant mortars. The highlight of a tour of the island—now a national shrine—is the sound-and-light show inside the historical Malinta Tunnel. Day trips, available through **Sun Cruises** (☏ 2/831–8140), cost P1,720 per person, including lunch. You can also stay overnight at the Corregidor Inn.

Legaspi City

545 km (338 mi) southeast of Manila (an hour by plane; about 11 hours by car).

Legaspi City—near the tip of southern Luzon, an hour's flight from Manila—has what may be the world's most symmetrical (and still active) volcano, towering 8,189 ft over the Bicol countryside. Aside from

★ the lure of the two- to three-day climb, **Mt. Mayon** has a volcanology/seismography station at about 2,500 ft, with a rest house that offers panoramic views of the volcano and the surrounding terrain. The station has geological displays relating to volcanoes, earthquakes, and tidal waves. You can also see a seismograph in operation.

Just 5 km (3 mi) northwest of Legaspi City are the **Cagsawa Bell Tower and Ruins,** what remains of a church buried in an 1814 eruption; more than 1,000 people who sought refuge inside perished.

NORTHERN LUZON

In northern Luzon you'll find the rugged Cordillera and the Sierra Madre ranges—with breathtaking views at elevations of 3,000 to 9,500 ft—and the narrow, beautiful, coastal plains of the Ilocos region. This area is home to hard-working, highland peoples, the Cordillerans, who are less Westernized than their lowland counterparts and whose origins can be traced to migratory groups older than the Malays. Over the centuries highland and lowland cultures have mingled through commerce, religion, education, and conflict. Nowhere is this more evident than in Baguio: many of its inhabitants are lowlanders (businesspeople, retirees, artists, students), so you're as likely to hear Pilipino as Ilocano, the regional tongue. At 5,000 ft above sea level among pine-covered slopes, Baguio is a lovely respite from the lowland heat and is a good base from which to explore the rice terraces of Banaue or the towns and Spanish-era churches of the Ilocos region. Note that the region can be chilly at night, especially from November through February, and torrential rains mid-June through October can cause rock slides that make roads impassable.

Baguio

① *246 km (153 mi) north of Manila, 196 km (121 mi) south of Vigan.*

At 5,000 ft above sea level, the air in Baguio is crisp, invigorating, and laden with the fragrance of pine trees. Billed as the "summer capital of the Philippines," this resort city was developed as a hill station during the American colonial era and is now the commercial, educational, and recreational hub of the Cordilleras. Avoid the city during the Christmas holidays and Easter week, when both the population of 280,000 and the prices of everything practically triple.

The **Mansion House** was built in 1908 as the summer residence of the American governor-generals and now serves as a site for local and international conferences. You enter through gates that replicate those of Buckingham Palace in London, and you can wander through the pleasant gardens (including one with roses). On your walk, you'll no doubt sense the leisurely pace and elegance of a vanished era. ⊠ *Leonard Wood Rd.,* ☎ *74/442–2703.* ⊡ *Admission.* ☉ *Daily 8–5.*

Across the road from the Mansion House is the 300-ft-long, pine-tree-bordered **Pool of Pines.** From the vine-covered stone trellis at the far end of the pool, a long, grand staircase leads down to **Wright Park,** the most popular horseback-riding park in town (☞ *also* Outdoor Activities and Sports, *below*).

At **Baguio Botanical Garden** (⊠ Leonard Wood Rd.), a pleasant arboretum a short drive or jeepney ride toward downtown Baguio from Mansion House, you'll find floral displays, ornamental plants, and sculptures of *anitos* (native gods). For a small fee, natives dressed in traditional tribal finery will pose for photos.

From Leonard Wood Road head to **Session Road,** downtown Bagio's steep 1-km-long main street, so named because it was the route to the government session hall during the American colonial era. Today, it's crowded with bazaars, restaurants, movie houses, offices, and cafés. This is where Baguio residents promenade.

From Session Road, a long flight of steps leads up to what may be the Philippines' only cathedral painted a light, cheery pink. With its hints of Norman architecture, **Baguio Cathedral** won't inspire raves, but it is a good perch from which to get a panoramic view of the town. The

0 _____ 50 miles
0 _____ 75 km

N

Babuyan Channel · Pt. Escarpada

ILOCOS NORTE
8 Laoag
3 · Aparri
Currimao **7** Paoay
Sinait
Cabugao · Badoc · 2 · Tuao · Tuguegarao · 5
Bangued · 6 Vigan
Tabuk · 5
Candon · 11
ILOCOS SUR · 5 Sagada · 4 Banga-An · Ilagan
4 · 3 Batad
2 Banaue
LA UNION · Cauayan
San Fernando · Jones
Baguio 1 · Bambang
5
Lingayen Gulf

South China Sea

Philippine Sea

CORDILLERAS

SIERRA MADRE

cathedral was one of the few buildings to survive World War II bombs, and it served for a while as a refugee center and trading place. ⊠ *Post Office Loop,* ☎ *74/442–4256.* ⊘ *Mon.–Sat. 6 AM–8 AM and 5 PM–6 PM, Sun. 5 AM–10 AM and 4 PM–6 PM.*

NEED A BREAK? **Cafe by the Ruins** has ambience and good café-style Filipino and Western-style steaks, salads, seafood, coffee, and cakes. ⊠ *25 Chuntug St.,* ☎ *74/442–5041.*

Beside the cathedral is the old **Post Office,** a tiny stone structure that harks back to colonial days. Down a steep, winding road below the cathedral is the **General Aguinaldo Museum,** named after the leader of the revolution against Spain and the subsequent war against America. Displays include historical photos, memorabilia, and a replica of the first flag of the Philippine Republic. ⊠ *Happy Glen Loop Rd.,* ☎ *74/444–8334.* ⊡ *Admission.* ⊘ *Weekdays 1:30–5.*

★ You haven't fully experienced Baguio until you've visited its **public market,** which is between a hill and Magsaysay Avenue at the bottom of Session Road. A series of alleys with stalls on either side, the market has sections devoted to fish and meat; rice, vegetables, and strawberries, for which Baguio is famous; antiques; dry goods that range from traditional loincloths to army surplus items; and regional handicrafts such as rattan backpacks, silver jewelry, and tribal ornaments. The money changers here offer better rates than hotels or banks.

South of Session Road lies the pleasant oasis of **Burnham Park.** Named for American landscape architect Daniel Burnham, who helped plan the city, the park has spacious grounds that are perfect for an idyllic stroll or a picnic. It's popular with families and crowded on weekends. You can boat on the artificial lake or rent bicycles and go for a ride.

Along the park's western edge you'll find the **Baguio Orchidarium,** where—as the name implies—vendors sell orchids, as well as the new **Pine Tree Park,** where international varieties of conifers are being cultivated for research and display.

The **Club John Hay** (a former U.S. military base) is a placid recreation center. Enjoy these green environs while you can; there are plans to transform the grounds into an upscale resort. ⊠ *Loakan Rd. and South Dr.,* ☎ *74/442–7902 or 74/442–2101.* ☜ *Admission.* ☉ *Daily 8–5.*

Dining and Lodging

$$ ✕ **Barrio Fiesta/Pinoy Hotpot.** You can dine on Philippine dishes, including food served in a hot pot, while admiring or critiquing the 10 giant Igorot wooden statues and other carvings that decorate the interior. ⊠ *North Dr. and Session Rd.,* ☎ *74/442–6049. AE, DC, MC, V.*

$$ ✕ **Bonuan.** In a quiet neighborhood below the cathedral, this establishment specializes in seafood and Philippine cuisine. ⊠ *10-B Happy Glen Loop,* ☎ *74/442–5175. AE, V.*

$$ ✕ **O Mai Kan.** Featuring an all-you-can-eat menu, this establishment offers a style of cooking they call "Mongolian": you fill a large bowl with various meats and vegetables and select the spices you like; the staff cooks it for you. ⊠ *12 Otek St.,* ☎ *74/442–5885. AE, DC, V.*

$ ✕ **Biscotti et Cioccolate.** A variety of coffees, pastries, and home-cooked dishes is served at this tiny, charming café. The paintings hung on the wall here reveal the calling of the owners, two artists. ⊠ *Unit 5, Nevada Sq., near Club John Hay,* ☎ *74/442–7420. No credit cards.*

$ ✕ **Ionic Cafe.** Midway along Session Road, this hip place, favored by students and local bohemians, has good coffee, a full bar, salads, pastas, and sandwiches. Its second-floor windows are excellent for people-watching. ⊠ *Session Rd.,* ☎ *74/442–3867. No credit cards.*

$ ✕ **Solana's Manna.** This bakery sells mountain coffee and products made from *camote* (yam) flour as well as serving breakfast and lunch. ⊠ *Club John Hay,* ☎ *74/442–7902. No credit cards. No dinner.*

$ ✕ **Star Cafe.** The menu at this bright, busy Chinese restaurant is extensive. All the dishes are tasty and most of them are reasonably priced. ⊠ *Session Rd.,* ☎ *74/442–3148. AE, DC, MC, V.*

$$ ☷ **Benguet Prime Hotel.** Right in the heart of busy downtown, this architecturally challenged hotel has no lobby to speak of and little in the way of decor. But what it lacks in charm it makes up for in convenience, and its rooms are spacious and clean. ⊠ *Session Rd. at Calderon Rd.,* ☎ *74/442–7066,* ℻ *74/442–8132. 51 rooms. Restaurant, room service. AE, DC, V.*

$$ ☷ **Burnham Hotel.** Rooms at this small hotel near Session Road are clean and wood-paneled. Avoid those on the ground floor, which can be noisy. ⊠ *21 Calderon Rd.,* ☎ *74/442–2331 or 74/442–5117,* ℻ *74/442–8415. 18 rooms. Restaurant, room service. AE, DC, V.*

$$ ☷ **Mountain Lodge.** In a quiet area, this cozy establishment is decorated with local artifacts and has a dining area with a terrace and a lobby with a fireplace. Guest rooms are clean and simply furnished. ⊠ *27 Leonard Wood Rd.,* ☎ *74/442–4544,* ℻ *74/442–6175. 21 rooms. Restaurant, bar. DC, MC, V.*

$$ ☷ **Munsayac Inn.** Small but well maintained, this family-run hotel has a pleasant ambience. Long patronized by missionaries, the inn will appeal to those who like their lodgings on the quiet side. The rooms are neat, with locally woven blankets, TVs, and refrigerators. ⊠ *125 Leonard Wood Rd.,* ☎ *74/442–2451. 20 rooms. Restaurant, lobby lounge, refrigerators. AE, DC, MC, V.*

$–$$ ☷ **Casa Amapola.** Once a family residence, this pension retains a fam-
★   ily-style informality. What was once the living room is now a lounge where guests meet informally, and there's a terrace where you can break-

fast while watching the fog lift from the surrounding hills. If you want more privacy, ask to stay in one of the three-story chalets with verandas and kitchens. ✉ *46 First Rd., Quezon Hill,* ☎ *74/442–3406,* FAX *74/443–7911. 13 rooms, 3 chalets. Dining room. AE, V.*

$ 🖵 **Tepeyac Hotel.** Placed high among the pine trees and removed from city bustle, Tepeyac has clean, comfy, motel-style rooms and nice pine furnishings in the airy hallways. It's quiet and informal. ✉ *177 Leonard Wood Rd.,* ☎ FAX *74/442–3956. 19 rooms. Café, lobby lounge. AE, DC, MC, V.*

Nightlife and the Arts

THE ARTS

Baguio's lively arts scene, inspired by the tribes and indigenous Cordillera cultures, is a cornucopia of poetry readings, art exhibitions, dance, music, and performance art. Every February the city holds the Flower Festival, centered on Session Road. On alternate years, usually around October, the Fiber Web event showcases hand-loom weavers. The **Baguio Arts Guild** (☎ 74/442–8489) and other civic groups organize the biannual Baguio Arts Festival in late November or early December. **Christine's Art Gallery** (✉ 23 Chuntug St., ☎ 74/443–9656), is a showcase for local contemporary artists.

NIGHTLIFE

Perk Cafe and Pub (✉ Top of Session Rd. YWCA, ☎ 74/442–3568) hosts folk and rock bands on weekends. **Rumors** (✉ 55 Session Rd., ☎ no phone) is a low-key bar-lounge with tasty appetizers; you can also hear live music here from time to time. **Spirits** (✉ 22 Otek St. at Burnham Park, ☎ 74/443–8774 or 2/442–6406) is a lively disco in a rambling, wooden, colonial-era house, which, with its gingerbread details, is itself worth a close look.

Outdoor Activities and Sports

HORSEBACK RIDING

There are ponies and larger horses for both children and adults at **Wright Park**; the fee is P100 an hour. You can ride among the casuarina groves in the park or along a trail around the mountain toward Mansion House. The Baguio "pony-boys" act as guides and/or riding instructors; their hourly fee is about P120.

Shopping

Easter Weaving School (✉ Easter School Rd., ☎ 74/442–4972) sells highland blankets and clothing woven on the premises. For silvercraft, visit **Ibay's** (✉ Lion Center, Governor Pack Rd., ☎ 74/442–7082). At **Munsayac's Handicraft** (✉ 21 Leonard Wood Rd., ☎ 74/442–2451) you'll find wood carvings, brass, and silverware. For items made of ikat, try **Narda's** (✉ 151 Upper Session Rd., ☎ 74/442–2992). **PNKY Woodworks** (✉ Nevada Sq., in front of John Hay, ☎ 74/444–5418) has tasteful wood furnishings—antique and brand-new. The **St. Louis Silver Shop** (✉ St. Louis High School, Assumption Rd., ☎ 74/442–2139) sells conventional, well-crafted silver items. **Tucucan** (✉ Upper Level, Maharlika Building, Baguio Public Market, ☎ 74/442–4169) has unusual artifacts, from baskets to beads.

OFF THE BEATEN PATH | **BALATOC MINES –** Experience the life of a gold miner on a tour of these nonoperational mines, a 40-minute ride via Loakan to the town of Itogon, 17 km (10 mi) southeast of Baguio. First you'll view a small museum with displays of rock samples and mining equipment. Afterward, outfitted in miner's gear, you'll take a train ride into the mine with a guide who explains the milling of gold ore and the production of gold bullion. ✉ *Benguet Lab, 141 Abanao St. Ext., Baguio,* ☎ *74/447–2610.* ⌧ *Admission.* ☉ *Daily 7–4.*

TAM-AWAN VILLAGE – At the area's newest cultural attraction, a 15-minute ride from Baguio's city hall, you can see nine reconstructions of traditional grass-roof houses. You can also learn about the tribal life of the Ifugao—one of the Cordilleras's indigenous peoples—take a traditional-art workshop, and have a great cup of coffee. ⊠ *Pinsao Rd., Pinsao,* ☏ *74/446–2949.* ⌧ *Admission.* ⊙ *Daily 8–5.*

Banaue

★ ❷ *196 km (122 mi) northeast of Baguio on mountain roads with dizzying switchbacks and long unpaved stretches.*

Looking like giant steps to the sky, the Banaue rice terraces are spectacular, man-made paddies terraced into the mountainsides of Mayaoyao and Carballo by the Ifugao, a highland tribe, more than 2,000 years ago. If placed end to end, these terraces would extend for 22,500 km (14,000 mi) or halfway around the world. Some of the terraces can be seen from Banaue itself, but the best views are in the countryside. A 1½-hour hike (ask for directions) or a 20-minute drive from Banaue proper will take you to a scenic viewpoint on a promontory. Wizened Ifugao women in native dress will pose for a little money.

Dining and Lodging

$ ✕ **Cool Winds.** Simple, inexpensive fare is the specialty of this spot near the town market. It's a favorite of locals and backpackers. ⊠ *Town Market,* ☏ *74/386–4023. No credit cards.*

$$ ✕▥ **Banaue Hotel.** Each room here has a terrace and a good view of the town and valley. The decor throughout is reminiscent of that in a country lodge. The informal restaurant serves American-style breakfasts, Continental food, and such Philippine regional dishes as pinakbet. The dining room is large and airy—with bright red decor, native wall hangings, and a garden view—and the service is superb. The hotel also puts on a cultural show of Ifugao dances (free for guests) nightly at 8. Afterward the dancers try to get you to join them. ⊠ *Banaue,* ☏ *74/386–4087 or 74/386–4088;* ☏ *2/812–1984 in Manila. 90 rooms. Restaurant, lobby lounge, pool. AE, DC, MC, V.*

$ ▥ **Banaue View Inn.** In this pleasant inn high above the town, the rooms are comfortable and clean. What distinguishes this place is its family museum, which contains a well-known anthropologist's documents and memorabilia—probably the best cultural attraction in Banaue. ⊠ *Off the rd. to Bontoc,* ☏ *74/486–4078. No credit cards.*

$ ▥ **Sanafe Lodge.** Near the city market, Sanafe is a combination dormitory and hotel, with a small lobby overlooking rice terraces. Private rooms are small but clean; eight of them have private baths. There are two less expensive dorm rooms that sleep eight; they're spartan but also clean. The resident manager is a gold mine of information on the area. ⊠ *Banaue,* ☏ *74/386–4085; 2/721–1075 in Manila. 16 rooms. Restaurant. No credit cards.*

Outdoor Activities and Sports

HIKING

The main outdoor activity in the Banaue area is hiking, and you can hire a guide for about P300 and up, per person. Several well-marked trails go to and through the rice terraces, for hikes that range from a couple of hours to a whole day. Check with the local **visitor information center** for more information (☏ 74/386–4087 or 74/386–4088) or contact the **Banaue Hotel** (☞ Dining and Lodging, *above*), which has a list of treks and guides and even has walking sticks available, free of charge.

Shopping

Near the town market, which has handicrafts stalls, is the small **trade center,** where you'll find such souvenirs as baskets, handwoven backpacks, and wood carvings.

Batad and Banga-An

3 **4** *9 km–16 km (6 mi–10 mi) northeast of Banaue on rough roads.*

Even more spectacular than Banaue are the Ifugao villages of Batad and Banga-An, both set among the rice terraces. To reach them from Banaue you can take a 60-minute jeepney ride along the main and only road to the Banga-An Inn, and then hike the easy trail down to Banga-An (another 30 minutes). Alternatively, you could ask the jeepney driver to drop you at "the junction" from which you can then make the 90-minute hike up to Batad. (Note that for about P40, you can spend the night in an Ifugao rest house in Batad.) En route you'll pass pine-covered slopes; green valleys dwarfed by clouded peaks; far-off, pyramid-shape Ifugao huts improbably perched on crags; and mountain streams irrigating the terraces. Village life goes on pretty much as it has for centuries: rice is planted in age-old rituals and plowed with the help of the ubiquitous water buffalo. Dogs, pigs, and ducks wander about native huts, which are elevated on wooden posts. Handicrafts—rattan backpacks, baskets, and ornaments—are sold for low prices.

Sagada

5 *50 km (31 mi) northwest of Banaue, 150 km (93 mi) northeast of Baguio.*

Deep in the central Cordilleras, among the rice terraces, is a small, tightly knit Igorot community. A favorite with adventurous backpackers, Sagada has several burial caves with hanging coffins, an underground river, waterfalls, limestone formations, and hiking trails. At the edge of the village are fruit orchards, smaller rice terraces, and the occasional *dap-ay*—the circular stone meeting place where village elders once gathered to discuss communal matters. It's worth spending at least two days here to savor the unspoiled charm, the laid-back atmosphere, and the striking scenery—no phones, no malls, no pollution. Just be respectful of local customs: Don't take photographs of people without asking permission. Never point at individuals (it's considered intolerably rude), and, of course, don't disturb the hanging coffins.

You can begin a walk through town from **Masferre's Studio,** 15 minutes south of the town center. A Spanish mestizo who settled in Sagada and married a local, the late Eduardo Masferre chronicled the lives of the Cordilleran peoples for decades, starting in the 1930s. A collection of his photos, which have been exhibited in several countries, is on display here, and prints and postcards are for sale. ✉ *Bontoc-Banga-An Rd.,* ☎ *no phone.* ☞ *Free.* ☉ *Irregular hrs.*

Sagada Weaving, closer to town than Masferre's studio, is a well-known purveyor of such quality hand-loomed products as sturdy backpacks, shoulder bags, and blankets. You can watch the Igorot women skillfully plying their trade, incorporating traditional designs into their weaving. ✉ *Main Rd.,* ☎ *no phone.* ☉ *Daily 9–4.*

Across from Sagada Weaving, a trail winds down to a small valley where it's easy to spot the mouth of **Matangkib Cave** and the burial coffins stored in niches within. Respect for these remains is a must. Enter the cave (you'll need flashlights) and you can hear the roar of an **underground river.**

Not far from Sagada Weaving—proceeding south and on the same side of the main road—is a trail that cuts across a narrow river. The trail leads to the small **Bokong Waterfall,** set amid rice terraces, with a deep pool that's perfect for cooling off in after a day of hiking.

Dining and Lodging

In this small village, most of the restaurants are close to the center of town, near the town hall and the market. Prices are truly a bargain, but credit cards are useless. The lodgings are equally a bargain—the average cost per night is $3–$4—but generally basic, with bunk beds and shared baths.

$ ✕ **Country Cafe.** Come to enjoy the big fireplace and strong local coffee. Short-order meals, ice cream, and homemade cakes are available. ☒ *North of town hall, on rd. to Besao,* ☏ *no phone. No credit cards.*

$ ✕ **Log Cabin Cafe.** This quiet, friendly spot serves very good dishes that reflect some European influence. ☒ *North of town hall, on rd. to Besao,* ☏ *no phone. No credit cards.*

$ ✕ **Shamrock Cafe.** Overlooking the market, this café is one of the oldest in town and offers breakfast, lunch, dinner, snacks, and drinks. ☒ *South of town hall, on rd. to Demang,* ☏ *no phone. No credit cards.*

$ ☷ **Mapiya-aw Pension.** This pleasant guest house is surrounded by striking limestone formations and pine groves. The staff is friendly and helpful and will serve meals on request. ☒ *East of town hall, on rd. to Bontoc,* ☏ *no phone. 12 rooms. Laundry service. No credit cards.*

$ ☷ **Masferre Cafe & Inn.** The rooms here are large, and the restaurant has a view of rice terraces. You'll also find a gift shop that sells postcards and T-shirts. ☒ *South of town hall, on rd. to Demang,* ☏ *no phone. 10 rooms. Laundry service. No credit cards.*

$ ☷ **St. Joseph's Rest House.** The largest accommodation in the area is slightly elevated, with a good view of the town and the Episcopalian church. Rooms are spartan but clean. ☒ *East of town hall, opposite church,* ☏ *no phone. 15 rooms. Laundry service. No credit cards.*

Outdoor Activities and Sports

The Sagada area is perforated with caves and underground rivers, making spelunking the most exciting activity in town. For information about which caves are open or to hire a guide, visit the **Sagada Environmental Guides Association** in the town hall. Rates for a guide depend on the size of the party but are eminently affordable. Hiking is the area's other main outdoor activity; you can hire a guide for this as well, or you can head into the fields and pine groves by yourself.

A pleasant trek would be a leisurely 30-minute walk to **Banga-An.** Take in the fresh air, groves of pine trees, and scenic rice terraces. If you have the stamina, ask the guide to take you through rice terraces to Fedilisan Waterfalls.

Vigan

❻ *196 km (122 mi) north of Baguio, 78 km (48 mi) south of Laoag.*

The capital of the Ilocos Sur province, a scenic four-hour drive from Baguio, is Vigan, a small coastal city that dates from the early years of Spanish colonization. It has some of the best-preserved Spanish-influenced architecture in the country; Manila's Intramuros might look like this had it not been so heavily damaged during World War II. The Viva Vigan Festival, the best time to see Ilocano culture, is celebrated during the first week of May. There's a crafts fair, and several colonial-era homes are opened to the public.

Set in a colonial-era residence that used to be occupied by a revolutionary priest, the **Burgos Museum** has a collection of dioramas, artifacts, and paintings (including a series that depicts a local revolt) relating to the area's history, as well as period furniture. ✉ *Burgos St.,* ☎ *no phone.* ⊠ *Admission.* ⊘ *Tues.–Sun. 9–noon and 1–5.*

It's about a 10-minute walk from the Burgos Ayala Museum to the town's main landmark, the 16th-century **Vigan Cathedral** (also known as the Cathedral of St. Paul), a massive, whitewashed, brick-and-wood structure with a tile roof. Chinese lions guard the portals and the gleaming silver altar within. A short stroll northwest of the cathedral takes you to the **Old Quarter,** which you can explore in about half a day. The buildings have whitewashed brick walls, tile roofs, sliding capiz windows, and lofty interiors. General Luna, Crisologo, De los Reyes, and Bonifacio streets have row upon row of these edifices—perfect backdrops for Westerns or Gothic films, for which, in fact, they have been used.

Dining and Lodging

Seafood dishes and vegetables are the specialty on the Ilocos coast. Try fried squid, shrimp marinated in vinegar and peppers, or the grilled catch of the day. In Vigan's plaza, you can taste the local delicacy, an empanada stuffed with vegetables. Also worth trying are *ipon,* delicious small fish caught seasonally, and pinakbet flavored with bagoong.

$ ✕ **Cool Spot.** Choose one of the tasty regional dishes on display behind a glass counter in this wide, airy, thatch-and-bamboo hut. ✉ *Burgos St.,* ☎ *77/722–2588. No credit cards.*

$$ 🏨 **Cordillera Inn.** The rooms at this inn, a colonial-era building with broad stairways and good views of the Old Quarter, are on the bare side but clean. Climb up to the roof for an excellent panorama. ✉ *General Luna and Crisologo Sts.,* ☎ *77/722–2526. 23 rooms. Restaurant, laundry service. No credit cards.*

$ 🏨 **Villa Angela.** This lovely turn-of-the-century home with period furniture and a pleasant garden has been converted into a pension. The living room has family memorabilia on display. In keeping with the spirit of the place, the rooms have high ceilings, four-poster beds, mosquito nets, and capiz windows. ✉ *Quirino Blvd. at Liberation St.,* ☎ *77/722–2914. 6 rooms. Laundry service. No credit cards.*

Shopping

In the bustling **central market** you'll find the usual assortment of produce and handicrafts. You should also check out the *burnay,* or **potters' district,** about a 15-minute walk from the cathedral. Here you can buy terra-cotta jars and urns from the potters themselves.

Check out **Ciudad Fernandina** (✉ 888 Plaza Burgos, ☎ 77/722–2888), a shop that sells antiques in the Old Quarter. **Lucy's Antique Shop** (✉ 14 Crisologo St., ☎ 77/722–2099) is also in the Old Quarter. You'll find woven items at **Rowilda's Handloom Weaving** (☎ 77/722–2732) right across from the Cordillera Inn. In the town of Santiago, just south of Vigan, there's **Cora's Ethnic Handwoven,** where prized local weaving is for sale.

En Route   North of Vigan are a number of good beaches (most without resorts) near the towns of Cabugao, Sinait, Currimao, and Pangil. Fishermen store their boats and nets on Sinait's white-sand beach, Pug-os.

Paoay

★ ❼   *258 km (160 mi) north of Baguio, 50 km (31 mi) north of Vigan, 20 km (12 mi) south of Laoag.*

Between Vigan and Laoag are towns whose churches are fine examples of what a local writer once termed Filipino baroque—unique, even rococo, combinations of Western and Asian styles. Among the most impressive are Santa Maria, with its 85 stately broad steps, and Magsingal, with a small but intriguing museum nearby. The majestic **Paoay Church** is the real must-see. The crenellations and turrets, massive curlicued buttresses, exterior stairways, and niches are reminiscent of a Javanese temple. Beside this splendid fusion of styles is a belfry made of limestone, used as an outpost during the Revolution of 1896 against Spain and by guerrillas during the Japanese occupation in World War II.

Laoag

⑧ *78 km (48 mi) northeast of Vigan, 278 km (172 mi) north of Baguio.*

Laoag, another coastal Spanish colonial town, doesn't have the wealth of architecture and sights of Vigan. Still, the 17th-century **Laoag Cathedral** and its **Sinking Bell Tower** are worth visiting. The church is heavily buttressed (a protection against earthquakes) and has two exterior stone stairways, urn ornamentation, and foliate capitals. The bell tower north of the church has sunk a little more than a yard, so that its portal is barely visible.

Dining and Lodging

$$$ ✕🏨 **Fort Ilokandia.** This sprawling hotel is made up of several two-story
★   buildings, whose style and room decor suggest the Old Quarter residences of Vigan. Tiled walkways connect the buildings, which are nestled among sand dunes (the hotel has a black-sand beach). The spacious, wood-paneled Pamulinawen restaurant serves solid Philippine dishes—including pinakbet and beef *tapa* (cured, dried strips of meat served with a vinegar-and-garlic sauce)—as well as some Continental fare. ⊠ *Baranggay 37, Calayab,* ☏ *77/772–1166,* 📠 *77/772–1411. 264 rooms. Restaurant, bar, pool, beach, dance club. AE, DC, MC, V.*

OFF THE   **THE BATANES** – The country's northernmost islands, the Batanes, are
BEATEN PATH   closer to Taiwan than to Luzon. The rugged cliffs, rolling grassy fields
                akin to the Scottish moors, scenic coastline, and idyllic towns with
                unique stone-walled homes make for great treks. It's best to visit between
                November and May, the relatively dry season before the onslaught of
                monsoon storms (these isles are in the middle of the typhoon belt). Allow
                yourself extra time here; a sudden wind even in the dry season may
                lead to a flight's cancellation. Mindanao Express (☏ 2/854–6431),
                Laoag Air (☏ 2/551–9729), and Corporate Air (☏ 2/714–2218) fly
                regularly from Manila during the dry season. Chemtrade Aviation (☏
                2/833–1183) flies daily from Laoag and Tuguegarao.

Northern Luzon A to Z

Arriving and Departing

BY AIRPLANE

There are no regular flights going to north Luzon farther than those to San Fernando on **Asian Spirit** (☏ 2/840–3811) or Tuguegarao by **Philippine Airlines** (☏ 2/855–8888). From these two town centers, buses and hired cars are available for northern destinations; the Department of Tourism, located in each town's city hall, can help with arrangements.

BY BUS

A number of bus companies run daily trips from Manila to northern Luzon—particularly to Baguio, Vigan, and Laoag—on an hourly basis. For information, contact the Manila offices of Pantranco or Victory Liner (☞ Metro Manila A to Z, *above*). There are no nonstop bus routes to Sagada from Manila; you have to change in Baguio, at the terminal in front of the market, or catch a jeepney from Banaue. It's about six hours from Manila to Baguio and about ten from Baguio to Sagada.

BY CAR

From Manila it's a relatively smooth six-hour drive to Baguio via the North Diversion Highway, which begins at EDSA, links up to the MacArthur Highway, and leads to the zigzagging Kennon Road. If Kennon is closed for repairs, you can take Naguilian Road or the Marcos Highway (which has a Mt. Rushmore–like bust of the late dictator), farther north along the coast. Add an extra hour for these routes to Baguio. Because of rough road conditions, it isn't advisable to drive to Banaue by Kennon Road.

Getting Around

BY BUS

Buses between towns are numerous and cheap, and most terminals are near the public markets. Buses to and from Manila and Vigan arrive at and depart from Baguio's terminal on Governor Pack Road, at the top of Session Road. You can catch buses to Sagada at Baguio's second terminal on Magsaysay Avenue. For tickets contact **Lizardo Bus Company** (☎ 74/442–2741 or 74/443–8719).

BY CAR

On the coastal plains and around the cities of Baguio, Vigan, and Laoag, the roads range from good to excellent. Northeast of Baguio, however, deeper into the Cordilleras, they can be very bad, and public transportation is a better bet.

BY JEEPNEY

Plentiful and good for short routes, jeepneys begin and end their routes at or near the public market. They can also be hired for out-of-town trips. The average cost of a ride, for about a kilometer (½ mi), is a mere P2.

BY TAXI

Baguio has the region's only cabs—small Japanese models. Rides within the central part of town average P80.

Contacts and Resources

BOOKSTORES

In Baguio city, paperbacks are available at **The Bookmark** (✉ Puso ng Baguio Building, Session Rd., ☎ 74/442–4912).

EMERGENCIES

Fire: ☎ 74/160 or 74/442–2222. **Hospitals: General Hospital** (✉ Governor Pack Rd., Baguio, ☎ 74/169 or 74/442–4216). **St. Louis University Hospital** (✉ Assumption Rd., Baguio, ☎ 74/442–5701). **Pharmacy: Mercury Drug Store** (✉ Session Rd. near Magsaysay Rd., Baguio, ☎ 74/442–4310) is open until 9 PM. **Police:** ☎ 74/166.

TOUR OPERATORS

It's best to arrange tours to and throughout northern Luzon with tour operators and travel agencies in Manila.

VISITOR INFORMATION

Department of Tourism North Luzon (Baguio): (✉ Governor Pack Rd., ☎ 74/442–7014).

THE VISAYAS, MINDANAO, AND PALAWAN

While northerners are known for their industry and frugality, southerners are easygoing, gregarious, and musical. The land and seas are especially fertile, yet some of the worst pockets of poverty are also found here, arising out of centuries-old feudalism, an overdependence on cash crops, and the often tragic effects of militarization in areas where the

New People's Army (NPA) is active. (The Communist/Maoist NPA, around since 1969, has a socialist vision that's violently at odds with the Philippine government.) You need not worry about being caught up in the conflict: armed clashes almost always occur in remote rural areas, and left-wing insurgency is on the decline.

Geographically, the Visayas are the center of the Philippines—bound on the north by Luzon and on the south by Mindanao. This group of islands has some of the best beaches and resorts in the country, unusual natural attractions, and non-Hispanicized minority cultures. The populations of Mindanao (the nation's second-largest island) and Palawan (the westernmost isle) are intriguing mixes of Christians, Muslims, and indigenous cultures. Large areas of both islands have been settled by mostly Christian migrants from Luzon and the Visayas. In Mindanao, this has led to an ongoing radical Muslim secessionist movement, though peace talks are being conducted between the government and leaders of the movement. To really enjoy the region, take the time to appreciate the affectionate, fun-loving ways of its people, explore the beaches and beautiful scenery, and experience the charm of small, often historic towns and cities. Note that the places discussed below are all easily accessible by plane from Manila or from Cebu.

Cebu City

❶ *1 hour by plane from Manila.*

This small but strategically important port has the advantages of a big city—restaurants, shops, lodgings, and businesses—but few of the drawbacks. The "Queen City of the South" and capital of Cebu Island, it's not far from Homonhon, where Ferdinand Magellan claimed the country for Spain in 1521. Founded by the conquistador Miguel Lopez de Legaspi in 1571, Cebu was the first Spanish settlement in the Philippines. Though little is left of the original town, you can still spend a fascinating and rewarding day of sightseeing here. Most of the historical sights are within walking distance of one another in the downtown area near the port.

Fort San Pedro, the country's oldest and smallest fort, was built in 1565. The three bastions with turrets for cannons give it a triangular shape. The parapets afford a good view of the sea—a necessity in the days when the settlement was a target for pirate raids. ⊠ *c/o Philippine Tourism Authority,* ☏ *32/253–3532.* ▣ *Admission.* ☉ *Daily 8–noon and 1–5.*

From Fort San Pedro it's a 10-minute walk to Plaza Rizal, where **Magellan's Cross,** the original cross brought over by the famed Portuguese navigator, is housed. You won't actually *see* the original: residents believe the cross has miraculous powers and used to take slivers from it, so it has been encased within the hollow wooden cross that is suspended from the ceiling of a pavilion. ⊠ *Magallanes St.*

Opposite Magellan's Cross is the 18th-century **Basilica Minore** (closed daily noon–2 PM), built in typical Spanish Baroque style. It houses the nation's oldest Catholic image—that of **Santo Niño,** the Holy Infant—brought over by Magellan and presented to Queen Juana of Cebu. Enshrined in glass and ornamented with gold and precious stones, the icon stands atop a side altar, venerated by a constant stream of devotees. The candle-bearing, middle-age women outside the church will, for a small fee, pray to and dance for the Santo Niño on your behalf. ⊠ *Magallanes St.*

A short stroll from Basilica Minore is the oldest street in the country, named after Cristóbal Colón, otherwise known as Christopher Colum-

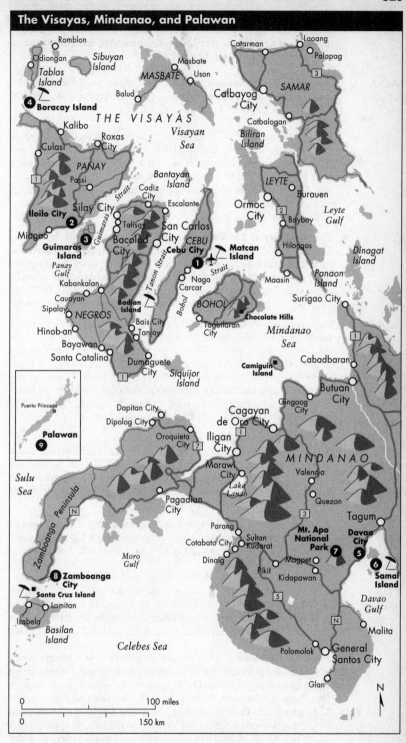

The Visayas, Mindanao, and Palawan

Romblon

Odiongan
Tablas Island

Sibuyan Island

Masbate

MASBATE

Uson

Catarman

Laoang
Palapag

3

4 Boracay Island

Balud

Calbayog City

SAMAR

Kalibo

THE VISAYAS

Catbalogan

Culasi

Roxas City

PANAY

Visayan Sea

Biliran Island

LEYTE

Burauen

Passi

Bantayan Island

Ormoc City

Leyte Gulf

1

Silay City

Cadiz City

2

Baybay

Escalante

Iloilo City

2

Talisay

San Carlos City

CEBU

Hilongos

Miagao

Bacolod City

Cebu City

Matcan Island

Maasin

Dinagat Island

3

Guimaras Island

Panay Gulf

Naga

Carcar

Strait

Panaon Island

Surigao City

Kabankalan

Bohol

BOHOL

1

Cauayan

Sipalay

NEGROS

Badian Island

Chocolate Hills

Cabadbaran

Hinob-an

Bais City

Tanjay

Tagbilaran City

Mindanao Sea

Butuan City

Bayawan

Santa Catalina

Dumaguete City

Siquijor Island

Camiguin Island

Puerto Princesa

Palawan

9

Dapitan City

Dipolog City

Cagayan de Oro City

Gingoog City

1

Oroquieta City

7

Iligan City

MINDANAO

Sulu Sea

Marawi City

Valencia

Zamboanga Peninsula

Lake Lanao

Quezon

Pagadian City

N

3

Tagum

Parang

Sultan Kudarat

Mt. Apo National Park

7

Davao City

5

Cotabato City

Dinaig

Pikit

Magpet

6

Samal Island

8 Zamboanga City

Moro Gulf

Kidapawan

Santa Cruz Island

5

Davao Gulf

Lamitan

N

Malita

Isabela

Basilan Island

Polomolok

General Santos City

Celebes Sea

Glan

N

0 100 miles

0 150 km

bus. Formerly the heart of the Parian District (or Chinatown), **Colón Street** is now downtown Cebu's main drag. Here modernity crowds in on you in the form of movie houses, restaurants, department stores, and other commercial establishments.

NEED A
BREAK?
At the **Lighthouse Restaurant,** a classic Cebu place, you'll find Filipino seafood dishes and a native ambience. ⊠ *Gen. Maxilom Ave.,, ☎ 32/ 233–2383 or 32/233–2386. AE, DC, MC, V.*

From the eastern end of Colón Street, you can walk to **Casa Gorordo,** the former residence of Cebu's first bishop, Juan Gorordo. Now restored, the century-old wood house has a tile roof, capiz windows, a wide veranda, and a fine collection of furnishings from the 18th century. The ground-floor art gallery displays contemporary works by Philippine artists. ⊠ *35 Lopez Jaena St., ☎ 32/255–5630. 🎫 Admission.* ⊙ *Daily 9–noon and 2–5:30.*

★ The **University of San Carlos Museum,** a 20-minute walk from Casa Gorordo, has an extensive collection of seashells, fauna, and relics: local prehistoric stone and iron tools, burial jars, and pottery. Another section focuses on traditional clothing and ornaments of various tribes. ⊠ *Rosario and Junquera Sts., ☎ 32/254–0432. 🎫 Admission.* ⊙ *Weekdays 9–noon and 1:30–5:30; weekends and holidays by appointment.*

Incongruously set in an expensive suburb known as Beverly Hills is a **Taoist Temple,** dedicated to the teachings of the 6th-century BC Chinese philosopher Lao-tzu. You can get here from downtown Cebu by taxi (referred to as a PU, for "public utility") for about P80. A flight of 99 steps leads up to the temple from the road. Come for the panoramic views of the city, the colorful and ornate Chinese architecture, and to have your fortune read. ⊠ *Beverly Hills, ☎ 32/254–6503 or 32/254–6459. 🎫 Free.* ⊙ *Daily 8 AM until dark.*

Dining and Lodging

Sinugba is a Cebuano method of grilling fish and shellfish over coals. Western- and Asian-style dishes are also available. As the second-largest city in the Philippines, Cebu City has a full range of accommodations, and a number of nearby islands, namely Badian and Mactan, have attractive beach resorts.

$$$ ✕ **Lantaw Gardens.** Here you can feast on a splendid, well-priced
★ buffet in an open-air garden setting while enjoying a folk-dance show and scenic views of the city. ⊠ *Cebu Plaza, Nivel Hills, Lahug, ☎ 32/ 231–1231. AE, DC, MC, V.*

$ ✕ **Golden Cowrie.** This informal, screen-enclosed, outdoor establishment serves inexpensive grilled seafood as well as typical Philippine cuisine. ⊠ *Salina at La Guardia St., ☎ 32/233–4243. No credit cards.*

$ ✕ **Grand Majestic.** Dim sum and other Chinese fare are served here at
★ reasonable prices. ⊠ *Archbishop Reyes Ave., ☎ 32/232–1103. AE, DC, MC, V.*

$ ✕ **Vienna Kaffeehaus.** The Austrian proprietor of this establishment
★ has re-created the ambience of a Viennese coffeehouse, complete with Viennese food, newspapers, and magazines. ⊠ *Ground floor., Wayne's Inn, Banilad, Mandaue, ☎ 32/253–1430. No credit cards.*

$$$$ 🏨 **Badian Beach Club.** On Badian Island, just off the southwest coast of Cebu and about a three-hour drive from the city, this resort has a lovely beachfront, scenic bay views, sailboats, and a variety of water sports. A cultural show accompanies the buffet dinners. ⊠ *Badian Island, ☎ 32/254–6309, FAX 32/254–7429. 34 cottages, 16 suites. 3 restaurants, 3-hole golf course, beach, dive shop, snorkeling, boating. AE, DC, MC, V.*

$$$$ 🏨 **Cebu Plaza.** A luxurious hotel, the Cebu Plaza has panoramic views,
★ sprawling grounds, and a clientele consisting mainly of Japanese and
Chinese tourists. The best rooms are those with a view of the city. ⊠
Nivel Hills, Lahug, ☎ *32/231–1231,* FAX *32/231–2071. 417 rooms. 2
restaurants, 3 bars, pool, 2 tennis courts, shops, dance club, meeting
rooms. AE, DC, MC, V.*

$$$$ 🏨 **Maribago Bluewater Beach Resort.** About 30 minutes from the city,
this upscale resort has all the comforts and water sports you could want.
The brightly decorated guest rooms are furnished with locally made
rattan furniture. ⊠ *Buyong St., Maribago, Mactan Island,* ☎ *32/231–
5411,* FAX *32/492–0218. 76 rooms. 3 restaurants, coffee shop, pool, bar-
bershop, driving range, tennis court, exercise room, beach, dive shop,
dock, snorkeling, windsurfing, boating, fishing. AE, DC, MC, V.*

$$$$ 🏨 **Shangri-La's Mactan Island Resort.** On a stunningly landscaped site
near the airport, this palatial luxury resort has its own beach cove, two
lagoon-style swimming pools, and lush tropical gardens. The comfortable, well-maintained rooms are done in tropical motifs and have
such amenities as satellite TV. ⊠ *Punta Engano Rd., Mactan Island,*
☎ *32/231–0288,* FAX *32/231–1688. 490 rooms, 56 suites. 8 restaurants,
bar, coffee shop, 2 pools, massage, 2 tennis courts, exercise room, beach,
dive shop, boating, fishing, nursery. AE, DC, MC, V.*

$$ 🏨 **Marriott Hotel.** A smart business address, this 12-story building is
smack in the heart of the Cebu Business Park, by the doorstep of the
Ayala Shopping Center. Rooms are cheery and modern. ⊠ *Cardinal
Rosales Ave.,* ☎ *32/232–6100,* FAX *32/232–6101. 303 rooms, 22 suites.
2 restaurants, coffee shop, pool, health club, business services, meet-
ing rooms. AE, DC, MC, V.*

$$ 🏨 **Montebello Villa.** This hotel has nice gardens, brightly decorated
rooms, and a cultivated colonial-era ambience. It's in a quiet neigh-
borhood. ⊠ *Banilad,* ☎ *32/231–3681,* FAX *32/231–4455. 142 rooms.
2 restaurants, coffee shop, pool, 2 tennis courts, casino, meeting rooms,
travel services. AE, DC, MC, V.*

$$ 🏨 **Park Place Hotel.** In the heart of downtown, this neat, cozy estab-
lishment is patronized mostly by businesspeople on moderate budgets.
⊠ *Fuente Osmena Ave.,* ☎ *32/253–1131,* FAX *32/253–0119. 114
rooms. Restaurant, bar, café, shops, meeting rooms. AE, DC, MC, V.*

Outdoor Activities and Sports

BEACHES

In and around Cebu are a number of beaches and beach resorts (☞
Dining and Lodging, *above*). Day visitors can use the beaches for
about P50 per person.

TENNIS

Both the Cebu Plaza and Montebello Villa (☞ Dining and Lodging,
above) hotels have tennis courts that nonguests can use for a fee.

Nightlife

BARS

Delta Philippine Dream (⊠ Cebu Yacht Club, Lapu-Lapu City, ☎ 32/
340–3888, FAX 32/340–3083) is a huge cruise ship anchored at a deep-
water dock close to the airport. This floating entertainment complex
has restaurants, bars, and discos. Europeans like the informal **St. Moritz
Bar** (⊠ Gorordo Ave., Lahug, ☎ 32/231–2485), part of a hotel of the
same name. **Thunderdome** (⊠ 175 F. Ramos St., ☎ 32/255–4534) is
a midtown bar favored by yuppies; it has a first-rate sound system.

CASINOS

The decor at the **Waterfront Cebu City Hotel and Casino** (⊠ Salinas
Dr. Ext., Lahug, ☎ 32/233–9424) mimics a picturesque turn-of-the-
century plaza. The action at the gaming tables runs from 5 PM to 5 AM.

You must be 18 years old to enter (bring your passport), and dress is smart casual (no sleeveless T-shirts or shorts allowed). **Montebello Villa** hotel (✉ Banilad, ☎ 32/231–3681) has a small, unremarkable casino with similar age and dress requirements.

DANCE CLUBS

The fashionable set dances at the strobe-lit **Bai Disco** (✉ Cebu Plaza Hotel, Nivel Hills, Lahug, ☎ 32/231–1231, local 5310). **H2O Disco** (✉ Waterfront Cebu City Hotel, 1 Salinas Dr., Lahug, Cebu City, ☎ 32/233–9424) has live bands for the mostly young crowd. **Jukebox** (✉ Grand Convention Center, Archbishop Reyes St., Cebu City, ☎ 32/233–3266) draws in the yuppies.

Shopping

One of the best handicraft stores in the city is the **Cebu Display Center** (✉ 11–13 Magallanes and Lapu-Lapu Sts., ☎ 32/254–1163), which has an excellent collection of regional crafts, particularly items made using shells. Prices aren't inflated for tourists. You may want to visit **Carbon Public Market,** a 20-minute walk from Magellan's Cross and a good place for handicrafts. You can find Cebu's unique crafts at **Regalos de Cebu** (✉ 51 Gorordo Ave., ☎ 32/232–0147).

OFF THE BEATEN PATH | **CHOCOLATE HILLS, BOHOL ISLAND –** These striking limestone hills, which have an average height of 120 ft, look like overturned teacups without handles. About a two-hour bus ride from the market in Tagbilaran City—a half-hour flight from Cebu City, or a 1½-hour ride on Aboitiz's Supercat ferry—the hills turn chocolate-brown during the dry months (February through May). In July they become green again, their grasses nourished by rain.

Iloilo City

❷ *½-hour flight from Cebu City.*

A small and gracious aggregate of six districts, Iloilo (pronounced "*ee-lo-ee*-lo"), the capital of Iloilo Province on Panay Island, has a genteel air and loads of charm. The city and its surrounding area have several noteworthy churches—all accessible by public transportation—where you can get a feel for Iloilo's civic and social pulse.

Near the city center and across from the provincial capitol building is the **Museo Iloilo,** which has an excellent collection of pre-Hispanic artifacts dug up mainly on Panay Island. These include fossils, Stone Age flake tools, and gold death masks. Other exhibits, some supplemented by video presentations, focus on liturgical art and the treasures of a British frigate shipwrecked nearby in the 19th century. ✉ *Bonifacio Dr. at General Luna St.,* ☎ *33/434–7472.* 🎫 *Admission.* ☉ *Daily 8–noon and 1–5.*

Molo Church, in a pleasant park in the downtown Molo district, is a twin-spired Gothic structure erected in the late 19th century. It has an intricate facade, with a kind of domed pergola that's complete with Greek columns. Note the row of female saints that lines the nave.

Jaro Cathedral, 3 km (2 mi) north of downtown, is larger than Molo Church but also shows Gothic influences. In front is a balcony with a statue of the Virgin that locals consider miraculous. Across the street is the church's reconstructed belfry. Nearby is a statue of **Graciano Lopez Jaena,** a journalist who wrote against the Spanish regime and died in Barcelona in 1896, at the outset of the revolution against Spain. Take some time to walk around the district and look at the grand, colonial-style residences, with their intricate grillwork and capiz windows.

The 200-year-old **Miagao Fortress Church,** 40 km (25 mi) south of the city, has two bell towers—of different design, as they were erected by two different friars—that also served as watchtowers against invasions by Muslim pirates. If you promise to be careful, the bell ringer will let you climb one of them. The sandstone facade depicts, amid floral designs, St. Christopher planting a coconut tree.

Dining and Lodging

Iloilo is well known for its *pancit molo* (chicken, pork, and shrimp dumplings in noodle soup), *la paz batchoy* (a tripe stew), *binakol* (chicken-and-coconut soup cooked in a bamboo tube), and pastries.

$ ✕ **Breakthrough sa Baybay.** The tasty dishes at this popular seafood place are served in the open air. ✉ *Santo Nino Norte Rd., Arevalo District,* ☎ *33/337–3027. No credit cards.*

$$ ✕🏨 **Hotel del Rio.** Although modest, this well-run 30-year-old prop-
★ erty is quiet and appealing. The clean, spacious rooms get lovely breezes off the Iloilo River. In the Owari restaurant, the city's best place for Japanese cuisine, local fish is used to good advantage. The more formal Igmaan restaurant serves native cuisine on a breezy terrace with a river view; if you time your meal right, you can also enjoy a beautiful sunset. Afterward, take in the nightlife at the hotel bar. ✉ *M. H. del Pilar St., Molo District,* ☎ *33/335–1171,* 🖷 *33/337–0736. 57 rooms. 3 restaurants, bar, pool, dance club. AE, DC, MC, V.*

$$ 🏨 **Sarabia Manor.** This hotel has a cosmopolitan feel and a friendly, well-informed staff. Ceilings are low, but the rooms are otherwise spacious. The hotel's bar is a good place for a night out. ✉ *General Luna and Ybiernas Sts.,* ☎ *33/335–1021,* 🖷 *33/337–9127. 100 rooms. 3 restaurants, bar, pool, dance club. AE, DC, MC, V.*

$ 🏨 **La Fiesta Hotel.** Florid wrought-iron banisters spiral all the way up this pleasant three-story inn, and cream-color terrazzo tiles are used throughout. Rooms are colorfully decorated. ✉ *M. H. del Pilar St., Molo District,* ☎ *33/338–0044,* 🖷 *33/337–9508. 29 rooms, 2 suites. Restaurant, coffee shop. AE, DC, MC, V.*

Shopping

At **Asilo de Molo Molo** (✉ Avancena St., Molo District, ☎ 33/337–4717 or 33/337-0252), an orphanage for girls, the skills of fine embroidery, especially for church vestments, are taught by nuns. Exquisitely embroidered cloth for dresses and intricate barong tagalogs are sold (at nonnegotiable prices). **Iloilo Producers** (✉ Basa St., ☎ 33/337–0823 or 33/336–2360) gathers native crafts and souvenirs (made of wood, paper, roots, and cloth) in one convenient place. **Sinamay Dealer** (✉ Osmeña St., Arevalo District, ☎ 33/337–4221) is an outlet for fine hand-loomed textiles and runners made from *jusi* (silk), cotton, and pineapple fiber.

Guimaras Island

③ *45-minute boat ride southeast of Iloilo City.*

This lush island, just off the coast of the city, is justly famous for its luscious mangoes. It has a number of fishing villages, rice paddies and cornfields, and a Trappist Monastery that doesn't encourage visitors. It's home to two of the more rustic, if moderately expensive, resorts in the area.

Lodging

$$$ 🏨 **Costa Aguada.** A satellite isle of Guimaras, this 2,200-acre eco-resort has white-sand beaches, a forest, a minizoo, and a turtle nursery. You can participate in water sports, go horseback riding, or play tennis. ✉ *Guimaras Island,* ☎ *2/896–5422 (reservations in Manila),* 🖷 *2/890–5543. 64 rooms. Restaurant, bar, coffee shop, pool, 2 tennis*

courts, health club, horseback riding, beaches, dive shop, snorkeling, boating. AE, DC, MC, V.

$$$ ⛺ **Isla Naburot.** Guest quarters here are in native-style cottages without electricity. The owner's daughter prepares exceptional dishes using mostly homegrown produce or freshly caught fish; she'll urge you to eat till you're near to bursting. Go ahead and indulge; you can work off all that food by participating in one of several water sports. ⊠ *Guimaras Island,* ☎ *33/321–1654,* FAX *33/321–0880. 8 cottages. Dining room, beach, dive shop, snorkeling, fishing. No credit cards.* ✍

Boracay Island

★ ❹ *2 hours by plane and boat from Manila.*

Famous among Europeans, this small, bow-tie-shape island off the coast of Panay has one of the Philippines' most beautiful beaches, with sands as fine and smooth as refined sugar. This is the only attraction, and lazing on the beach or engaging in the water sports available at the various resorts—which range from basic to luxurious—are the main activities.

Lodging

$$$ ⛺ **Friday's Beach Resort.** The island's oldest upscale resort is well maintained. Rooms are in cottages that have a bamboo-and-thatch decor and a terrace. ⊠ *Boracay Island,* ☎ *2/521–2283,* FAX *2/521–1072. 22 rooms. Restaurant, bar, snorkeling, fishing. AE, DC, MC, V.*

$$$ ⛺ **Lorenzo Grand Villa.** This hotel's cliff-top location guarantees two things: a grand view and privacy. The decor throughout is a blend of native and Mediterranean. ⊠ *Boracay Island,* ☎ *2/926–4152. 32 rooms. Restaurant, bar, pool, beach, snorkeling, boating, fishing. AE, MC, V.*

$$ ⛺ **Pink Patio.** Air-conditioned rooms at this motel-like resort, five minutes from the beach, face a pleasant garden. ☎ *2/812–9551,* FAX *2/ 810–8282. 57 rooms. Restaurant, snack bar. AE, DC, MC, V.*

Nightlife

The central section of the beach has several distinctly different establishments: **Bazura Bar** is a disco, sometimes with all-night partying. **Beachcomber** is a mellow spot, often with a folk singer entertaining. **Moondog's Shooter Bar** (☎ 36/288–3409) offers an array of imaginative tropical drinks.

Davao City

❺ *1½ hours by plane from Manila.*

One of the largest cities in the world in terms of area (1,937 square km [748 square mi]), Davao City is busy and booming. It's also probably the most ethnically diverse urban area in the country, with Muslim, Christian, Chinese, and indigenous tribal communities. It's surrounded by banana plantations and fruit and flower farms and bounded on the west by Mt. Apo and on the east by Davao Gulf.

Davao is justly famous for its tropical fruits, especially the durian, said to "smell like hell and taste like heaven." The fruit has an oval shape with a thick yellow-green rind and a creamy white pulp; it smells
★ worse than old gym socks, but it has a caramel taste. The **Madrazo fruit district,** near downtown, is an excellent place to get to know these unusual fruits; most vendors will let you have a sample before you buy.

The large, intricate **Lon Wa Buddhist Temple** has three altars made of Italian marble, gold, and bronze respectively. Photos of deceased faithful are enshrined here. A resident Buddhist monk will tell your fortune if you ask. ⊠ *Rd. to airport,* ☎ *no phone.* 🎫 *Donation requested.*

The **Davao Museum,** not far from the airport and the Insular Century Hotel Davao (☞ Dining and Lodging, *below*), has fascinating displays of tribal artifacts and costumes. ⊠ *Insular Village, Lanag St.,* ☎ *82/235–1876.* ⊡ *Admission.* ◷ *Mon.–Sat. 8–5.*

Philippine Eagle Nature Center, a nonprofit organization in Calinan, about 36 km (22 mi) from the city center, breeds Philippine eagles, an endangered species, in captivity. These majestic birds have 6-ft wingspans, and their diet includes monkeys. The fierce-looking warriors-of-the-air are truly an awesome sight. The center also has captive crocodiles. At the visitors center (at the entrance), you can watch a short documentary on the eagles. ⊠ *Malagos, Calinan,* ☎ *82/221–2030.* ⊡ *Admission.* ◷ *Daily 8–5.*

Dining and Lodging

$$ ✕ **Luz Kinilaw.** Fishermen bring their catches directly to this shore-area restaurant, where the specialties are coal-grilled tuna tail and jaw and sashimi. ⊠ *Salmonan, Quezon Blvd.,* ☎ *82/226–4612. DC, V.*

$ ✕ **Kanaway Restaurant.** The walls of this eatery are adorned with artwork depicting different types of fish—a dead giveaway as to the kinds of delights you'll find on the menu. ⊠ *Magsaysay Park Complex,* ☎ *82/221–8594. DC, MC, V.*

$ ✕ **Molave.** This friendly eatery is well known for its truly greaseless fried chicken. ⊠ *Matina District,* ☎ *82/227–2854. No credit cards.*

$ ✕ **Tai Huat Clay Pot.** The inexpensive and delicious Chinese food here is popular with Davao's Chinese community. ⊠ *141 Magsaysay Ave.,* ☎ *82/226–4576. No credit cards.*

$$$ ⊞ **Insular Century Hotel Davao.** Close to the airport and about 3 km
★ (2 mi) from town, this hotel sits on 20 lush acres with coconut groves, gardens, and a beach. Nearby is a small settlement of the indigenous T'boli. Twice a day tuba gatherers climb the tall trees to collect the sap. The airy rooms, done in native-style decor, have verandas. ⊠ *Lanang,* ☎ *82/234–3050,* ⅺ *82/235–0902. 153 rooms. 3 restaurants, bar, coffee shop, pool, 2 tennis courts, squash, beach, dock, shops, meeting rooms. AE, DC, MC, V.*

$$ ⊞ **Apo View.** This downtown hotel—with its pleasant, busy lobby and its comfortably furnished rooms—is popular with businesspeople. It has many repeat guests. ⊠ *J. Camus and Bonifacio Sts.,* ☎ *82/221–6430; 2/893–1288 (in Manila),* ⅺ *82/221–0748; 2/894–1223 (in Manila). 205 rooms. 2 restaurants, bar, coffee shop, pool, dance club. AE, DC, MC, V.*

$$ ⊞ **Casa Leticia.** This small but friendly establishment has a cozy, casual lobby and clean, well-maintained rooms. The top-floor Toto's Bar and Café—with its photos of rock stars, album covers, and other rock memorabilia—hops almost every night; the owner himself is often the DJ. ⊠ *J. Camus and Palma Gil Sts.,* ☎ *82/224–0501. 41 rooms. Restaurant, bar, coffee shop. AE, DC, MC, V.*

Shopping

The downtown **Aldevinco Shopping Center** is a complex of neat rows of small stores that sell Mindanao tribal crafts, woven mats, brassware, antiques, batik cloth, and wood carvings. A 10-minute walk away is the **Madrazo fruit district** (☞ *above*), where vendors sell tropical fruits.

Samal Island

❻ *15 minutes by motorized launch from the Insular Century Hotel Davao.*

Some of the Davao City area's nicest beaches are on nearby Samal Island. The island has several resorts where you can spend the day or stay overnight. For a schedule of trips to the island, ask at the Insular Century Hotel Davao (☞ Dining and Lodging, *above*).

Lodging

$$$$ 🏨 **Pearl Farm Beach Resort.** Formerly an aquaculture enterprise, this pricey resort has beautifully designed bungalows on a hillside overlooking Davao Gulf. On the grounds is a weaving center of the Mandayas, an indigenous tribe. ☎ 82/231–9976; 82/231–9977; 82/231–9978; 82/231–9979; 2/526–1555 (in Manila), FAX 82/221–9979; 2/526–4484 (in Manila). 73 rooms. Restaurant, bar, pool. AE, DC, MC, V.

$$$–$$$$ 🏨 **Paradise Park and Beach Resort.** This pleasant beach resort, complete with a small zoo, is good for a day trip or an overnight stay. ☎ 82/234–1229, FAX 82/234–2926. 22 rooms. Restaurant, beach. AE, DC, MC, V.

Mt. Apo National Park

❼ *40 km (25 mi) west of Davao City.*

Davao City is a good base from which to explore Mt. Apo, the tallest peak in the country at 9,689 ft. The mountain, considered sacred by the indigenous people that live on and around it, is part of the Mt. Apo National Park. Trails pass through rain forests and sulfur springs. The average time for getting to the summit and back is five days; you can climb at any time of year, but it is best to do so during the dry season between March and May. For essential information and to hire a guide, contact the Davao City tourist office (☞ Visitor Information *in* Visayas, Mindanao, and Palawan A to Z, *below*).

OFF THE   **CAMIGUIN ISLAND–** A three-hour trip from Cagayan de Oro City on the
BEATEN PATH northwest coast of Mindanao, this lovely unspoiled isle is still heavily
             forested and has seven volcanoes. Hibok-Hibok, the largest of them, can
             be climbed with a hired guide. The best place to secure guides is Ardent
             Hot Springs, not far from Mambajao, which is also a good place to
             begin—and end—the climb. Accommodations are basic but cheap and
             clean, and the local people are friendly. There are hot springs, trekking
             opportunities, beaches, and waterfalls.

Zamboanga City

❽ *45-minute flight from Cebu City or Davao City.*

Zamboanga City is famous for its bright flowers (its early name, Jambangan, meant "land of flowers"), which grow profusely in every garden. The roadsides are lined with bougainvillea and bright-red-flowered *gumamela* bushes. It's also a city with a sizable Muslim population, made up mainly of the Yakan, Badjao, Samal, and Tausug tribes; the Christian and Muslim populations live, for the most part, peaceably but in separate enclaves.

Begin exploring the city at **Plaza Pershing,** the town square named after "Blackjack" Pershing, the first American governor of the area. Formerly known as Moroland, the region was said to have spurred the development of the .45 pistol. (Legend has it that fanatic Muslim warriors couldn't be stopped by a .38, hence the need for a more powerful gun.) Two blocks southeast of Plaza Pershing, on Valderrosa Street, is the **city hall;** built by the Americans in 1907, it's a curious combination of Arab and Baroque styles.

East from city hall on Valderrosa Street is **Fort Pilar,** an old Spanish fortress. **Rio Hondo,** beyond Fort Pilar, is a small riverine Muslim village with its own mosque. Many of the houses are on stilts. Men wear white skullcaps, and women wear the distinctive *malong,* a brightly decorated wraparound dress.

North of downtown is **Climaco Freedom Park** (named after a beloved mayor slain many years ago) with its **Ecumenical Holy Hill**. The Stations of the Cross on a roadside cliff lead to a giant white cross at the top, where there's a good view of the city. In **Pasonanca Park,** also north of downtown, you'll find the **Pasonanca Treehouse**. If you contact city hall (☎ 62/991–2295) in advance you can stay here for a night or two (albeit without a bathroom).

About 16 km (10 mi) north of Zamboanga City is the Muslim village of **Taluksangay.** At the back of the town's distinctive red-and-white mosque is a prominent Muslim family's burial plot with headstones shaped like boats and with the ever-present crescent. The community is made up of seaweed gatherers; everywhere piles of seaweed dry in the sun. Stroll along the many catwalks and watch as women weave and sell straw mats. Remember to bargain; prices quoted at first will be high.

Dining and Lodging

Zamboangueños like steamed crabs, barbecued meats, and raw fish marinated in vinegar and hot green peppers.

$$ ★ ✕ **Alavar's.** Run by a husband-and-wife team (he cooks, she manages), this restaurant is justly famous for wonderful seafood. Prawns, clams, and blue marlin are served in this rambling house, but the specialty is *curacha,* crabs in a creamy, sweet-spicy sauce that is the chef's secret. Down your food with refreshing *buko* (young coconut) juice. ⊠ *Don Alfaro St., Tetuan District,* ☎ *62/991–2483. DC, MC, V.*

$ ✕ **Lotus.** Here tasty Filipino and Chinese dishes are served in a pleasant, informal setting. ⊠ *Mayor Jaldon St.,* ☎ *62/991–2510. AE, DC, MC, V.*

$ ✕ **Palmeras.** Feast on barbecued meats—the house specialty—on a pleasant, shady, garden terrace. The waitstaff here is friendly. ⊠ *Santa Maria Rd.,* ☎ *62/991–3284. AE, V.*

$$ ▥ **Grand Astoria Hotel.** Near the airport and 15 minutes from downtown by jeepney, this hotel has sunny, tiled rooms with tropical decor. The staff is friendly and efficient. ⊠ *Mayor Jaldon St.,* ☎ *62/991–2510,* ℻ *62/991–2510. 52 rooms. 2 restaurants, bar, coffee shop, room service. AE, DC, MC, V.*

$$ ▥ **Lantaka.** Right by the waterfront, this establishment has well-appointed rooms and gracious service. The terrace abuts the sea, where Badjaos, a gypsylike tribe, sell mats and seashells from their outrigger boats. Watch the sunset and the sea from the lovely, open-air Talisay Bar. Unfortunately, the hotel cuisine is mediocre. ⊠ *Valderrosa St.,* ☎ *62/991–2033,* ℻ *62/991–1626. 112 rooms. Restaurant, bar, coffee shop, pool, meeting room, travel services. AE, DC, MC, V.*

$ ▥ **Zamboanga Hermosa Inn.** This hotel in a quiet area of the city has a small, informal lobby with a restaurant. Guest rooms are small but comfortably furnished and clean. ⊠ *Mayor Jaldon St.,* ☎ *62/991–2042. 33 rooms. Restaurant, laundry service. DC.*

Shopping

In Zamboanga's colorful **city market** (⊠ Alano St.) you'll find the woven mats (Row C in the handicrafts section has a good selection) for which the city is famous. You'll also find brassware, antiques, items crafted from shells (for which Zamboanga is also noted), and batik from Indonesia. The market is open from dawn to dusk.

San Luis Shell Industries (⊠ San José Rd., ☎ 62/991–1044) has a wide selection of shells. For the tribal weavings prized by Philippine designers, visit the **Yakan Weaving Village,** 7 km (3 mi) from the city on the west coast. The weave is so fine it takes at least a week to finish a yard of cloth. You'll find a good selection of shells at **Zamboanga Home Products** (✉ San José St. at Jaldon, ☎ 62/991–1717).

<table>
<tr><td>OFF THE
BEATEN PATH</td><td>

SANTA CRUZ ISLAND – This small island has a wonderful pink-coral beach, which is open daily 7–4, and a lagoon. At the beach's eastern end is a Muslim burial ground, ornamented with stars, crescents, and tiny boats—to provide passage to the next life. In this life, your passage to the island is best accomplished by renting a *banca*, a native canoe fitted with outriggers, at the Lantaka hotel (☞ Dining and Lodging, *above*). The trip takes 25 minutes; rates are officially set at P400 round-trip. Be sure to pack water and refreshments, as there are no food or beverage stands.
</td></tr>
</table>

Palawan

⑨ *90-minute flight from Cebu City or Manila to Puerto Princesa.*

Shaped like a long dagger, Palawan is the archipelago's westernmost island and one of its most isolated and least developed. Here you'll find beautiful beaches, with excellent snorkeling and diving spots, as well as unique flora and fauna including giant turtles, peacocks, mouse deer, scaly anteaters, purple herons, and seven-color doves. If you really want to get away from it all, you'll find some of the Philippines' most secluded (and often most luxurious) resorts on smaller islands off Palawan's northwestern coast.

The lack of development means that you'll need a little patience on a visit to the island. Outside the island's only city, Puerto Princesa, roads are unpaved and tend to be almost impassable after a heavy rain. (The points of interest listed here are those accessible by public transportation.) And as the island has malaria-bearing mosquitoes, you should take preventive medication before arriving and bring plenty of insect repellent.

The usual port of entry is the capital, **Puerto Princesa.** Although the city is pleasant (it regularly wins honors as the country's cleanest city) and makes a logical hub from which to explore the rest of the island, there isn't a great deal to see in it. The **Palawan Museum** (✉ Old City Hall Building, J. Valencia St., ☎ no phone) does have good ethnographic and crafts displays. Admission is charged.

★ North of the capital is **St. Paul Subterranean National Park,** a national rain forest park with the world's longest known underground river, **St. Paul's River,** most of which runs through St. Paul's Peak, the mountain that comprises almost all of the park. There's a small beach hamlet, **Sabang,** about a three-hour jeepney ride from Puerto Princesa. At Sabang, you can hire a banca to take you to the river and the gigantic caverns—with their stalactite and stalagmite formations—through which it courses. You have to obtain a permit to tour the river and the caves at a ranger station at the mouth of the river. There's no charge for the permit, but be sure to tip the boatmen (P20 or so).

You can also hike from Sabang to the river, about 2 km (1¼ mi) away. A well-marked trail starts from the beach, goes up through rain forest, and emerges at the main ranger station, where you can obtain a visitor's pass. From the station the hike continues by the beach and onto the **Monkey Trail,** a bamboo stairway that winds among limestone rocks and through forest inhabited by monitor lizards, parrots, and—of course—monkeys. *St. Paul Subterranean River National Park office,* ✉ *150 Manalo St., Puerto Princesa,* ☎ *48/433–2409.*

A five-hour bus ride south of Puerto Princesa, near the coastal town of Quezon, are the **Tabon Caves**, discovered in 1962. These caves—numbering about 200 but with only a small number explored—were among the earliest inhabited sites in the country. Although you won't see any artifacts in the caves (most are in the National Museum in Manila), just being here and imagining life millennia ago is a worthwhile experience.

At the Quezon branch of the **National Museum** you can arrange banca trips to the Tabon Caves (prices are reasonable) and view the regional artifacts and marine specimens on display. ⊠ *Admission.* ⊙ *Mon.–Sat. 9–noon and 1–5.*

Dining and Lodging

PUERTO PRINCESA

$$$ ✕ **Cafe Puerto.** This upscale restaurant serves Continental cuisine, including seafood and chops, in one of the city's more formal settings. ⊠ *Rizal Ave.,* ☎ *48/433–2266. AE, DC, MC, V.*

$$ ✕ **Ka Lui's.** Puerto's free spirits hang out here to dine on fresh seafood
★ and delicious fruit shakes served on an airy bamboo veranda. The owner-chef has a small lending library on the premises, with a variety of English-language titles. ⊠ *Rizal Ave.,* ☎ *48/433–2580. No credit cards.*

$$$ 🏨 **Asia World.** Although this concrete structure is incongruous in a city where preserving the environment is an issue, it meets the demands of travelers who prefer urban comforts. Rooms are spacious, air-conditioned, and well maintained. ⊠ *San Miguel National Highway,* ☎ *48/ 433–2212; 2/242–6546 (reservations in Manila),* 🅵🅰🅇 *48/433–2515. 109 rooms, 14 suites. 2 restaurants, bar, coffee shop, pool, tennis court, health club, travel services. AE, DC, MC, V.*

$$ 🏨 **Badjao Inn.** A pleasant low-key atmosphere and a veranda recommend this inn, although many of the rooms are cheerless. ⊠ *350 Rizal Ave.,* ☎ *48/433–2212. 26 rooms. Restaurant, laundry service. AE.*

$$ 🏨 **Casa Linda.** Constructed of bamboo, wood, and thatch, this inn has a veranda, as well as a courtyard garden and parrots. The staff is cheerful and helpful. ⊠ *Trinidad Rd.,* ☎ *48/433–2606. 13 rooms. Restaurant, laundry service. AE.*

$$ 🏨 **Hotel Fleuris.** This new hotel in a three-story, neoclassical-style building downtown has a smoked-glass atrium and lobby. Rooms are well-furnished and comfortable; the food is good; and the service reliable. ⊠ *Lacao St.,* ☎ *48/233–3380. 48 rooms. Restaurant, bar, coffee shop, business services. AE, DC, MC, V.*

ISLANDS OFF THE NORTHERN PALAWAN

$$$$ 🏨 **Amanpulo.** A private island in the Cuyo Archipelago, roughly halfway between northern Palawan and the Visayas' Panay Island, has been turned into a luxurious getaway with gourmet dining and lush surroundings. Here, spacious, secluded casitas—with tropical decor, verandas, cable TV, and VCRs—line white-sand beaches. You have access to golf carts to get around the manicured grounds. ⊠ *Pamalican Island,* ☎ *2/759–4040 (reservations in Manila); 307/734–7333 (reservations in the U.S.);* 🅵🅰🅇 *2/759–4044. 50 casitas. Restaurant, bar, room service, pool, massage, 2 tennis courts, beach, dive shop, snorkeling, boating, fishing, library, meeting rooms. AE, DC, MC, V.* 🐾

$$$$ 🏨 **El Nido.** This resort, spread over two islands off northern Palawan, is in a beautiful marine park and has its own ecological and environmental protection programs, such as a fish nursery. Packages include meals, charter-air transportation, lodging, and the use of water-sports facilities. Guest cottages are patterned after native huts—bamboo, thatch, shell, and wood abound. ⊠ *Miniloc and Lagen Islands, near the town of El Nido,* ☎ *2/894–5644 in Manila. 82 rooms. Restaurant,* *beach, dive shop, dock, snorkeling, windsurfing, boating, fishing. AE, DC, MC, V.*

$$$ 🏨 **Club Paradise.** This resort, on a small isle near the larger Busuanga Island off the coast of northern Palawan, has native-style thatch cottages and rustic surroundings. It's popular with resident expatriates on weekends. ⊠ *Dimakya Island,* ☎ *2/838–4956 (reservations in Manila). 50 rooms. Restaurant, pool, beach, dive shop, dock, snorkeling, boating, fishing. AE, DC, MC, V.*

$$ 🏨 **Marina del Nido.** This homey and isolated resort off the coast of
★ northern Palawan was built in 1994. Sailboats and yachts moor here, and their crews stock up on necessary supplies or just enjoy the resort's cuisine. For landlubbers, there are bungalows (not air-conditioned) built in the native style. The cuisine here is simple but superb. The staff, who are from the local community, can arrange diving and snorkeling tours and camping trips in the rain forest. ⊠ *Malapacao Island,* ☎ *2/831–1487 (reservations in Manila). 4 cottages. Restaurant, snorkeling, boating, fishing. AE, DC, MC, V.*

Nightlife and the Arts

Nightlife in Puerto Princesa is mostly limited to hotels, where people gather in lounges for a drink and conversation. **Bistro Valencia** (⊠ E. Valencia St., ☎ no phone) has local folksingers. Patrons are encouraged to try their vocal cords with the featured singers at **Erick's Sing-Along Bar** (⊠ Rizal Ave. Ext., ☎ no phone). **Kamayan Folkhouse and Restaurant** (⊠ Rizal Ave., ☎ 48/433–2019) serves native dishes as folk bands set the scene. If you're in the mood to dance, check out the discotheque **Prism** (⊠ Asia World hotel, San Miguel National Highway, ☎ 48/433–2111).

Shopping

Along Puerto Princesa's Rizal Avenue, handicrafts, antiques, and baskets can be purchased at Mencoco, Culture Shack, or Karla's. The public market is a good source as well: try Macawili Handicraft for baskets and brassware.

The Visayas, Mindanao, and Palawan A to Z

Arriving and Departing

BY AIRPLANE

Philippine Air Lines (PAL; ☎ 32/340–0190 up to 99 in Cebu City; 82/222–0366 in Davao City) has flights from Manila to major cities in the region. Check with the airline for details about service. **Singapore Airlines/Silk Air** (☎ 32/232–6211 or 32/232–6216 in Cebu City) has direct flights from Singapore to Cebu.

BY BOAT

Cebu City is a busy port and a primary stop for interisland ships. All the major lines have trips between Cebu and ports all over the archipelago. The Cebu–Manila voyage takes 21 hours, Cebu–Davao, 12 hours. Some companies are: **Aboitiz Shipping** (☎ 32/232–0421 up to –0429), **Escaño Lines** (☎ 32/232–8310), **Negros Navigation** (Port Area, ☎ 32/254–8595 in Cebu City; 2/254–0601 or 2/252–0102 in Manila).

High-speed ferry services have transformed interisland traffic, with trips to most central Visayan ports averaging a little less than three hours. **WG&A** (☎ 2/894–3211 in Manila) operates what it calls a SuperFerry service between the cities of Cebu, Iloilo, Davao, and Puerto Princesa; their cruise ships have suites, on-board entertainment, and dining. Other companies include: **Delta Fast Ferries** (☎ 32/232–6295 or 32/232–5237 in Cebu City), **Negros Navigation** (☞ above), **Supercats** (☎

32/233–0972 in Cebu City), and **Waterjet** (☎ 32/245–0568 or 32/245–6660 in Cebu City).

BY BUS
If you can't get enough of bus travel, bridges and ferry service make it possible to travel overland from Manila to Davao City in Mindanao; **Philtranco** (☎ 2/832–2456 in Manila) bus lines make the trip in approximately 44 hours.

Getting Around
BY AIRPLANE
Cebu City's **Mactan International Airport** (☎ 32/340–3486) is the regional hub, providing a crucial link between Manila and Mindanao, other parts of the Visayas, and Palawan. From Cebu, the flight to Iloilo City is 30 minutes; the flight to Zamboanga City is 45 minutes; and flights to Davao City and Puerto Princesa on Palawan Island last an hour. You can arrange flights to the northern Palawan resorts by contacting the resorts directly.

BY BUS
Buses, a main form of public transportation on the islands, usually begin and end their routes in the vicinity of the public market, whether in Cebu or Puerto Princesa. Get to the market early in the morning to secure a good seat. Air-conditioned buses, not as common on islands other than Luzon, are more expensive.

BY CAR
Roads in the urban areas, especially those in and around Iloilo City, are in good shape. The exception is Palawan, where roads are largely unpaved and often impassable during the rainy season. Although having a car gives you freedom and privacy, taxi and jeepney fares are low, and local drivers know the area better than you do. Your best bet—particularly on Palawan—is to travel by "hire-car" in local parlance—by the hour or the day. Ask about going rates at local tourist offices (☞ Visitor Information, *below*).

Car-rental agencies in Cebu City include: **Avis** (☎ 32/231–0941), **Intan Rent a Car** (☎ 32/253–2401 or 32/253–6459), and **Fast Rent a Car** (☎ 32/340–0981).

Agencies in Davao include **Avis** (☎ 82/221–6430).

BY JEEPNEY
Jeepneys generally begin and end their trips at public markets. Fares are very low: a 2-km (1¼-mi) ride within Cebu City costs only P3.

BY TAXI
Taxis in Cebu are metered, while in Iloilo, Zamboanga, and Davao, prices are agreed upon beforehand. The average taxi ride in Cebu costs P80, while trips to Mactan Airport and to out-of-town destinations start at P250. In Davao, a ride to the airport averages P80.

BY TRICYCLE
The tricycle, the ubiquitous motorized pedicab, is good for within-a-neighborhood trips. In Puerto Princesa, however, it's the main form of public transport for trips inside the city or to outside destinations. Prices are negotiable but are generally a bargain.

Contacts and Resources
BOOKSTORES
Bookstores in Cebu City include: **National Bookstore** (✉ Ayala Center, Cebu Business Park, ☎ 32/231–4006) and **Bookmark** (✉ 260 Osmena Blvd., ☎ 32/231–0428). In Puerto Princesa, the **Palawan Museum** (✉ Old City Hall Building, J. Valencia St., ☎ no phone) has a small

library with books on Palawan anthropology and ethnography. **Ka Lui's** (⊠ Rizal Ave., ☎ 48/433–2580) has a collection of paperbacks (left by various travelers) that are lent out on an honor system.

EMERGENCIES

Cebu: ☎ 32/166. **Davao:** ☎ 82/166. **Iloilo:** ☎ 33/166.

TOUR OPERATORS

Trips can be arranged through tour operators and travel agencies in Manila. You can also consult local tourism offices (☞ *below*) for suggestions and a list of guides. In addition, many of the larger hotels have tour operators' desks.

VISITOR INFORMATION

Cebu City (⊠ Ground floor, LDM Building, Lapu-Lapu St., ☎ 32/254–2811 or 32/254–6077). **Davao City** (⊠ 7 Magsaysay Ave. at Magsaysay Park, ☎ 82/221–6798 or 82/221–6955). **Iloilo City** (⊠ Capitol Grounds, Bonifacio Dr., ☎ FAX 33/335–0245). **Puerto Princesa** (⊠ City Hall, ☎ 48/433–2154; Provincial Capitol, ☎ 48/433–2983) . **Zamboanga City** (⊠ Lantaka Hotel, Valderrosa St., ☎ 62/991–0217 or 62/991–0218).

PHILIPPINES A TO Z

Arriving and Departing

By Airplane

AIRPORTS

Manila's **Ninoy Aquino International Airport** (☎ 2/877–1109) is the major international and domestic air hub for the Philippines. Although Cebu City's **Mactan International Airport** (☎ 32/340–3486) is used mainly for domestic flights (which make it the country's second-busiest airport), international flights also use the airport, particularly those from Japan, Singapore, and Australia. The **Laoag International Airport** (☎ 77/771–1162) is now an alternative port of entry into the country for travelers coming from Taipei.

CARRIERS

PAL (☎ 2/855–8888 or 2/832–3011), the national carrier, has drastically reduced its domestic network to only 20 cities and towns. Check with the airline for details about domestic and international service (☞ *also* Air Travel *in* Smart Travel Tips A to Z at the front of this book). **Northwest** (☎ 2/819–7341) has flights to Manila from Chicago and Los Angeles with one stop in either Tokyo or Osaka.

Other carriers with service to Manila include: **China Airlines** (☎ 2/523–8021), **Cathay Pacific** (☎ 2/848–2747), **Japan Airlines** (☎ 2/832–2781), **Korean Air** (☎ 2/815–9261), **Malaysia Airlines** (☎ 2/525–9404), **Singapore Airlines** (☎ 2/810–4951), and **Thai Airways** (☎ 2/812–4744).

FLYING TIMES

Manila is 16 hours from San Francisco; 15 from Los Angeles; 20 hours from Chicago; and 22 hours from New York, Toronto, and Montréal. From London, Manila is a 16-hour trip; flights from Sydney are about 8½ hours.

Getting Around

By Airplane

It's always wise to confirm your domestic flight at least two days in advance. **PAL** (☞ *above*) has traditionally covered most of the archipelago, but owing to the company's recent economic and labor woes, there have been cuts in service. Smaller, privately owned companies have regular flights to some cities and resorts. These include: **Air Philippines** (☎ 2/843–7770 or 2/526–4741), **Asian Spirit** (☎ 2/840–3811), **Cebu Pacific Air** (☎ 2/893–9607), and **Pacific Air** (☎ 2/832–2731, 2/832–2732, or 2/833–2390).

By Boat
Much of the local populace travels by boat, the cheapest way to get from island to island. One-way rates from Manila to Cebu City (a 24-hour trip) range from P2,200 for luxury on **WG&A** SuperFerry (☎ 2/894–3211) to P845 for economy. The same one-way trip by air on PAL costs P2,205 but takes only 70 minutes.

Speed, reliability, and safety vary from line to line. **Aboitiz** (☎ 2/894–3211) and **Negros Navigation** (☎ 2/254–0601) generally have well-kept ships and good records. **Sulpicio** (☎ 2/241–9701) has a lesser reputation.

By Bus
The Philippines has an excellent bus system, with 20 major lines covering the entire archipelago; it's an inexpensive and generally safe way to travel. Service between major destinations is frequent, often on an hourly basis. You can also go island-hopping by bus and ferry. Such routes are usually limited to islands close together, though these days you can get from Manila to Davao City on the Philtranco line in 44 hours.

Manila has several bus terminals. Outside Manila, most terminals are next to public markets. Companies that serve the major routes have coaches with or without air-conditioning. Try **BLTB** (☎ 2/833–5501), **Dagupan Bus Co.** (☎ 2/727–2330 or 2/727–2287), **Pantranco** (☎ 2/743–2227), **Philtranco** (☎ 2/832–2456), and **Victory Liner** (☎ 2/833–0293, 2/833–5019, or 2/833–5020).

By Car
EMERGENCY ASSISTANCE
There are no road-service organizations outside Metro Manila but if your car breaks down, passing motorists and townsfolk will gladly lend a hand. In the capital, call the **Philippine Motor Association** (☎ 2/724–8181 or 2/726–0191) if you have reciprocal Automobile Association membership.

GASOLINE
A gallon costs approximately P50. Gas stations are readily found in and around cities and major towns, with a majority of those in urban areas open 24 hours.

PARKING
Parking can be difficult in Manila. In Makati, there are parking lots (the average cost is P20–P30 for three hours); on some streets meter maids approach you to collect P20 per hour. In other areas of Metro Manila where street parking is available, young men or kids offer to "watch your car" for a few pesos. It's worth it. Major hotels used to provide free parking for guests but now charge major fees. Newer malls have parking levels; fees are nominal.

RENTAL AGENCIES
The larger car-rental agencies represented in the Philippines are: **Avis** (☎ 2/524–5759), **Budget** (☎ 2/818–7363), **Carlines** (☎ 2/810–5421), **Dollar** (☎ 2/896–9251), and **National** (☎ 2/833–0648). On the average, a self-driven car costs about P2,000 per day. Rates vary for chauffeur-driven cars, depending on the agency and the destination.

Road conditions vary from excellent, with smooth cement or asphalt highways (generally around such metropolitan areas as Manila, Cebu City, and Baguio), to bad, where "road" is a euphemism for a dirt track that's dusty and badly rutted in summer and muddy during the rainy season. Although there are official speed limits—95 kph (60 mph) maximum and 55 kph (35 mph) minimum—they are not displayed on highways and are rarely enforced. Use prudence in populated areas and where children or farm animals are nearby.

Driving is on the right, and you must have a valid foreign or international driver's license to rent a car. Be very cautious: locals drive by the motto "Who dares, wins."

By Train
Only Luzon has a railway system, the **Philippine National Railways** (PNR; ☎ 2/361–1125), a single-rail system that has deteriorated. Trains no longer run north of Manila, traveling only south to Guinobatan in Luzon's Bicol region. (Plans have long been drawn to extend rail service north, to La Union, and farther south, to Legaspi City, but they're continuously shelved.) Fares are slightly lower than those for bus travel, but trips take longer.

Contacts and Resources

Customs and Duties
Personal effects (a reasonable amount of clothing and a small quantity of perfume), 400 cigarettes or two tins of smoking tobacco, and 2 liters of liquor may be brought into the Philippines duty-free.

There are restrictions on the export of antiques, religious and historical artifacts, coral, orchids, monkeys, and birds (including endangered species such as the Philippine eagle).

Electricity
Electricity in the Philippines is 220-volt, 60-cycle AC, though major hotels in Manila provide 110 outlets. Wall outlets take a variety of plug styles, including Continental-type plugs, with two round prongs, and plugs with two flat prongs.

Embassies and Consulates
Australia (⊠ Dona Salustiana S. Ty Tower, ground floor, 104 Paseo de Roxas, Makati, ☎ 2/750–2850). **Canada** (⊠ Allied Bank Center, 9th floor, 6754 Ayala Ave., Makati, ☎ 2/810–8861). **New Zealand** (⊠ Far East Bank Center, 23rd floor., Sen. Gil Puyat Ave., Makati, ☎ 2/891–5358). **United Kingdom** (⊠ LV Locsin Building, 15th–17th floor, 6752 Ayala Ave., Makati, ☎ 2/816–7116 or 2/816–4849; ⊠ Maria Luisa Park, Banilad, Cebu City, ☎ 32/346–0525). **United States** (⊠ 1201 Roxas Blvd., Manila, ☎ 2/521–7116; ⊠ Fourth floor, PCI Building, Gorordo Ave., Cebu City, ☎ 32/231–1261).

Health and Safety
Water is usually potable, though in cities such as Manila it's heavily chlorinated. If your stomach is sensitive, you might want to stick to bottled water. On the road be sure to bring water for the trip. The food, whether Western-style or Filipino, shouldn't cause any problems, though it would be better to avoid street offerings, tempting as they may seem. Peeling fresh produce is a good idea.

OTHER PRECAUTIONS

The most common scams occur during currency exchange. In crowded areas, a money belt under your clothing is a good idea, and you should avoid wearing expensive jewelry. Unaccompanied women generally won't be bothered, except, perhaps, by flirts. Still, it's best to dress modestly. Although there are no largely gay areas, gay and lesbian travelers will find that Filipinos aren't really concerned about sexual orientation.

Language, Culture, and Etiquette

The Philippines is an English-speaking country, a legacy of its years as a U.S. colony. Communicating is rarely a problem, either in the cities or in the countryside. A second lingua franca is Pilipino, which is based on the regional language of Tagalog. Spanish is still spoken by many members of the country's elite; in Zamboanga City a form of Creole Spanish known as Chavacano is spoken.

Two simple rules of etiquette will smooth your way: don't point and don't raise your voice. The main principle to bear in mind when in public and in the company of locals is a very Eastern one: never cause anyone to lose face. Filipinos place a premium on what they call Smooth Interpersonal Relations, or SIR. In terms of dress, this being a tropical country, informal attire is fine, but neatness and a well-groomed appearance are musts. Only a few restaurants have a dress code, but shorts, sandals, and tank tops are frowned upon by many establishments. Dress conservatively when visiting churches or mosques.

You'll have no problem taking pictures of most lowland Filipinos—they may even jump in front of your camera. Tribal highlanders, on the other hand, often shy away from being photographed; they may even become angry if you try to photograph them without receiving permission or offering payment for the privilege. In Baguio and Banaue, the costumed tribespeople expect a few pesos for posing.

Mail

POSTAL RATES

For letters to foreign countries, stamps cost P13; the cost is P8 for a postcard or an aerogram.

RECEIVING MAIL

Letters sent care of "poste restante" to the **Manila General Post Office** (✉ Plaza Lawton, Manila, ☎ 2/527–8327 or 2/527–0069) will be held for you. Otherwise, have your mail addressed to you care of **American Express** (✉ Philam Life Building, ground floor, United Nations Ave., Ermita, Manila, ☎ 2/815–4159 or 2/526–8406).

WRITING TO THE PHILIPPINES

In urban areas addresses follow the standard Western format, except that postal codes are infrequently used, and the name of the building is often given in lieu of the street number. For example: XYZ Co., Insular Life Building, Ayala Avenue, Makati, Metro Manila. In rural areas, addresses may seem less than complete to Western eyes (indeed, they may not include a street name, let alone a street number).

Money and Expenses

COSTS

The Philippines remain inexpensive, thanks to low inflation and the weakening of the peso against the dollar due to the economic crisis throughout Asia. Predictably, Metro Manila is the most expensive destination. Other urban areas, such as Baguio and Cebu City, are less expensive, and the surrounding provincial areas are cheapest of all.

Sample Costs: Cup of instant coffee, 25¢; fresh-brewed native coffee, 50¢–$1; bottle of beer, 50¢–$1; Coca-Cola, 60¢; hamburger, $1.50;

2-km (1-mi) cab ride, $1; 2-km (1-mi) bus ride, 50¢; museum admission, 75¢–$3.

CURRENCY

The unit of currency is the peso, made up of 100 centavos. Bills come in denominations of 5, 10, 20, 50, 100, 500, and 1,000 pesos. Coins range from 25 centavos to P5.

The exchange rate at press time was P28 to the Canadian dollar, P41 to the U.S. dollar, P65 to the pound sterling, P24 to the Australian dollar, and P21 to the New Zealand dollar. Licensed money changers in Manila's Tourist Belt, especially those on M. H. del Pilar and A. Mabini streets, often offer better exchange rates than banks. Unless otherwise indicated, prices quoted throughout this chapter are in pesos.

SERVICE CHARGES, TAXES, AND TIPPING

The international airport departure tax is P550, while domestic airports charge, on the average, P50. Hotels add a 10% service charge (as do most restaurants) and a government tax of 13.7%. In addition to a 4% sales tax, a value added tax (VAT) of 10% is charged by all businesses.

Tipping is now an accepted practice, and 10% is considered standard for waiters, bellboys, and other hotel and restaurant personnel. In restaurants and hotels that tack the 10% service charge onto the bill, tipping is optional (though it is customary to leave loose change). At Ninoy Aquino International Airport, you pay P40 per cart, and porters expect P10 for each piece of luggage (in addition to P10 per piece paid to the porter office). Hotel doormen and bellboys should get about the same.

Opening and Closing Times

Most businesses follow the 9 to 5 routine, though a few begin the day at 8. **Banks** are open 9–3. **Museums** have varying hours, though they generally close for an hour or two at midday and are rarely open on Sunday and holidays. Large **post office** branches are open weekdays 8–5 and Saturday 8–noon; hours at smaller branches may differ. **Store** hours vary depending on the type of establishment: shops and supermarkets are usually open 9:30–7:30, with mall stores remaining open till 8; public markets' hours are dawn to dusk. Except on Good Friday, Christmas Day, and New Year's Day, most stores remain open on holidays. Businesses and government offices close for Holy Week.

NATIONAL HOLIDAYS

New Year's Day (Jan. 1), Holy Week—from Maundy Thurs. through Easter Sunday (Apr. 12–15, 2001; Apr. 28–31, 2002); Labor Day (May 1); Independence Day (June 12); All Saints' Day (Nov. 1); Andres Bonifacio Day (Nov. 30); Christmas (Dec. 25); José Rizal Day (Dec. 30).

Passports and Visas

Visas are not required of Australians, New Zealanders, Canadians, or U.K. or U.S. citizens for stays of up to 21 days, provided that travelers have a ticket for a return or onward journey.

Telephones

CALLS TO THE PHILIPPINES

To call the Philippines from overseas, dial the country code, 63, and then the area code. Area codes for some key destinations are: Baguio, 74; Cebu City, 32; Davao City, 82; Iloilo City, 33; Manila, 2; Puerto Princesa, 48; Vigan and Laoag, 77; Zamboanga City, 62.

LOCAL CALLS

Local calls are unmetered, except for those made on a pay phone, which cost P2 for the first three minutes. For directory assistance, dial 114. All operators speak English. Outside of Manila, phone numbers vary in length from five to seven digits—you may even find phone numbers of varying lengths within one town. The Philippines is in the process of updating its phone system, but the conversion is taking place in fits and starts; hence there are still variations.

LONG-DISTANCE AND INTERNATIONAL CALLS

For domestic long-distance calls, you need to go through an operator by dialing 109, unless your phone has direct dialing. The big hotels have direct overseas dialing. Otherwise, dial 108 to reach the operator. Whether or not the party is at the other end, a connection fee of about $1 is charged. International access codes for the Philippines are as follows: **AT&T** (☎ 10512), **MCI** (☎ 10515), and **Sprint** (☎ 10517).

Visitor Information

Before leaving home, Americans and Canadians should contact the **Philippine Center** (✉ 556 5th Ave., New York, NY 10036, ☎ 212/575–7915; ✉ 3660 Wilshire Blvd., Suite 825, Los Angeles, CA 90010, ☎ 213/487–4527; ✉ 447 Sutter St., Suite 507, San Francisco, CA 94108, ☎ 415/956–4060). Visitors from the United Kingdom can contact the **tourism office** in London (✉ 146 Cromwell Rd., SW7 4EF, ☎ 020/7835–1100). In Australia, there's a **tourism office** in Sydney (✉ 301 George St., 2000, ☎ 612/929–6815).

When to Go

The Philippines has two seasons: dry and wet. The dry season generally runs from late October through May, with temperatures ranging from cool and breezy—even chilly—in the northern highlands to scorching hot in the lowland cities. Within this seven-month span, the coolest stretch is from November through February and, since it coincides with winter months in the West, it's also the peak tourist season. Popular spots are crowded, major hotels have high occupancy rates, and airfares are higher. Still, there are plenty of beaches and unspoiled places where crowds are either sparse or nonexistent.

If you enjoy crackling summer heat, then March through May are the best months to visit. The Catholic penitential rites of Lent are observed in late March or early April, climaxing in nationwide rituals during Holy Week, when business and government offices shut down. May is harvest—and fiesta—time. If you find yourself in the Philippines during the rainy season—June through September—note that most of Mindanao lies outside the typhoon belt, which cuts across Luzon and most of the Visayas. Mindanao gets rain, but not much more than during the rest of the year. Manila, on the other hand, is subject to frequent floods, and the highlands of northern Luzon become waterlogged; mud and rock slides frequently make the roads impassable. Be sure to pack a good raincoat and waterproof boots. The following are maximum and minimum temperatures for Manila.

CLIMATE

Jan.	86F	30C	May	93F	34C	Sept.	88F	31C
	70	21		75	24		75	24
Feb.	88F	31C	June	92F	33C	Oct.	88F	31C
	70	21		75	24		74	23
Mar.	91F	33C	July	88F	31C	Nov.	88F	31C
	72	22		75	24		72	22
Apr.	93F	34C	Aug.	88F	31C	Dec.	86F	30C
	74	23		75	24		70	21

FESTIVALS AND SEASONAL EVENTS

The most spectacular festivals are in honor of Jesus Christ, as the Holy Infant (Santo Niño) or Son of God, and the Virgin Mary.

Jan.: Three orgiastic, dancing-in-the-streets carnivals take place this month: the **Ati-Atihan** (third weekend of the month in Kalibo, Aklan), the **Sinulog** (third weekend of the month in Cebu City), and the **Dinagyang** (last weekend of the month in Iloilo City). In all three, the Holy Infant is the object of veneration. Kalibo's Ati-Atihan, the oldest and most popular, is also the noisiest, as competing town bands thump enthusiastically night and day. All three cities get crammed to the gills, and plane, ship, and room reservations must be made two or three months in advance. In contrast, on January 9, the **Black Nazarene** procession of the Quiapo district in Manila is a more somber but equally intense show of devotion, as the faithful compete to pull the carriage holding a statue of Christ that's believed to be miraculous.

Jan.–Mar.: With the **Hari Raya Puasa,** Muslims celebrate the completion of Ramadan, a holy month of fasting and abstention that commemorates the revelation of the Koran to the Prophet Mohammed by the Angel Gabriel. (The Islamic calendar follows the lunar cycle; Ramadan begins and ends on different dates each year.)

Late Mar.–early Apr.: Christ's final sufferings are remembered during the last week of Lent, **Holy Week.** In the central Luzon towns of Bulacan and Pampanga, masked and bleeding flagellants atoning for their sins are a common sight. Groups of old women and children gather at makeshift altars and chant verses describing Christ's passion. The **Turumba** in Pakil, Laguna (held the second Tuesday and Wednesday after Holy Week), honors Our Lady of Sorrows. Devotees dance through the streets trying to make her smile.

May: All over the country, the **Santacruz de Mayo** commemorates St. Helen's discovery of the Holy Cross in 324. The celebrations include colorful processions, complete with floats of each town's patron saint, beautifully gowned young women acting as May queens, and local swains dressed in their Sunday best. One of the more unusual feasts is in Lucban, Quezon Province, where multicolored rice wafers, called *kiping,* are shaped into window ornaments, usually in the form of fruits and vegetables.

Sept.: The **Peñafrancia** (3rd weekend of the month) is the biggest festival in the Bicol region, drawing as many as 10,000 spectators to Naga City in southern Luzon. A procession of floats on the river honors the Virgin of Peñafrancia.

Dec.: 'Tis the season for carolers, midnight masses, and such feasts as the **Maytinis** in the town of Kawit, Cavite—a 90-minute drive from Manila. Christmas Eve is celebrated with 13 colorful gigantic floats. Be there by 6 PM to get a good view.

5 SINGAPORE

Don't let first impressions lead you to write
Singapore off as just another modern
international capital. Although it may no
longer be the exotic, romantic city so vividly
documented by Conrad and Kipling,
Singapore is yet a unique metropolis, where
the flavor, spirituality, and gentle manners of
the East peacefully coexist with the comforts,
conveniences, and efficiency of the West.

By Nigel Fisher

Updated by
Greg Bishop
and Ilsa Sharp

T O ARRIVE IN SINGAPORE is to step into a world where the call to prayer competes with the bustle of capitalism; where old men play mah-jongg in the streets and white-clad bowlers send the ball flying down well-tended cricket pitches; where Chinese fortune-tellers and high-priced management consultants advise the same entrepreneur. This great diversity of lifestyles, cultures, and religions thrives within the framework of a well-ordered society. Singapore is a spotlessly clean—some say sterile—modern metropolis, surrounded by green, groomed parks and populated by 2.9 million orderly and well-regulated people.

Although the Malays, Chinese, and Indians account for 97% of Singapore's population, other ethnic groups—from Eurasians to Filipinos and Thais—contribute significantly to the nation's cultural mix. Understandably, the heritage of the British colonial stay is profoundly felt even though Singapore became a fully independent nation in 1965.

Modern Singapore dates its nascency from the early morning of January 29, 1819, when a representative of the British East India Company, Thomas Stamford Raffles, stepped ashore at Singa Pura (Sanskrit for "Lion City"), as the island was then called, hoping to establish a British trading settlement on the southern part of the Malay Peninsula. There is clear evidence, however, of earlier Malay settlements, and also for an early Chinese presence, such as the 14th-century city of Temasek, which boasted an elegant and prosperous aristocracy. At various times, Singapore fell under the sway of the Javanese and Thai empires. When Raffles arrived, the two sons of the previous sultan, who had died six years earlier, were in dispute over who would inherit the throne. Raffles backed the claim of the elder brother, Tunku Hussein Mohamed Shah, and proclaimed him sultan. Offering to support the new sultanate with British military strength, Raffles persuaded him to grant the British a lease allowing them to establish a trading post on the island in return for an annual rent; within a week the negotiations were concluded. (A later treaty ceded the island outright to the British.) Within three years, the small fishing village, surrounded by swamps and jungle and populated only by tigers, 200 or so Malays, and a scattering of Chinese, had become a boomtown of 10,000 immigrants, administered by 74 British employees of the East India Company.

As Singapore grew, the British erected splendid public buildings, churches, and hotels, often using Indian convicts for labor. The Muslim, Hindu, Taoist, and Buddhist communities—swelling rapidly from the influx of fortune-seeking settlers from Malaya, India, and South China—built mosques, temples, and shrines. Magnificent houses for wealthy merchants sprang up, and the harbor became lined with *godowns* (warehouses) to hold all the goods passing through the port.

By the turn of the century, Singapore had become the entrepôt of the East, a mixture of adventurers and "respectable middle classes." World War I hardly touched the island, although its defenses were strengthened to support the needs of the British navy, for which Singapore was an important base. When World War II broke out, the British were complacent, expecting that any attack would come from the sea and that they would be well prepared to meet it. But the Japanese landed to the north, in Malaya. The two British battleships that had been posted to Singapore were sunk, and the Japanese land forces raced down the peninsula on bicycles.

In February 1942 the Japanese captured Singapore. Huge numbers of Allied civilians and military were sent to Changi Prison; others were marched off to prison camps in Malaysia (then Malaya) or to work on the notorious "Death Railway" in Thailand. The 3½ years of occupation was a time of privation and fear; an estimated 100,000 people died. The Japanese surrendered on August 21, 1945, and the Allied forces returned to Singapore. However, the security of the British Empire was never again to be felt, and independence for British Southeast Asia was only a matter of time.

In 1957 the British agreed to the establishment of an elected 51-member legislative assembly in Singapore. General elections in 1959 gave an overwhelming majority—43 of 51 seats—to the People's Action Party (PAP), and a young Chinese lawyer named Lee Kuan Yew became Singapore's first prime minister. In 1963 Singapore became part of the Federation of Malaysia, along with the newly independent state of Malaysia.

Mainly due to Malays' anxiety over a possible takeover by the ethnic Chinese, the federation broke up two years later and Singapore became an independent sovereign state. The electorate supported Lee Kuan Yew and the PAP time and again. In 1990, Lee resigned after 31 years as prime minister, though as a senior minister he maintains his strong grip. His firm leadership of the party, his social and economic legislation, and his suppression of criticism led to his reputation as a (usually) benevolent dictator; yet Singaporeans recognize that his firm control had much to do with the republic's economic success and high standard of living. Lee is rumored to be grooming his son for the position of prime minister—though the fact that the party is receiving fewer votes than in the past suggests a disaffection with the (virtually) one-party system. In the meantime, Lee's hand-picked successor, Goh Chok Tong, has established a power base of his own during his years as prime minister.

Pleasures and Pastimes

Dining
Eating is an all-consuming passion among Singaporeans, and you'll soon discover why. There's a stunning array of cuisines from around the world, particularly from the three major cultures that make up the island nation: Chinese, Malay, and Indian. It also won't take you long to discover that Singaporeans love spices. But spicy doesn't necessarily mean hot. It can also mean tastes that are mellow, as in thick, rich coconut gravies; pungent, as in Indian curries; tart, as in the sour and hot tamarind-, vinegar-, and lime-based gravies of Thailand, Malaysia, Indonesia, and Singapore; or sweet and fragrant, as in Indian desserts and beverages. Price categories throughout the chapter are based on the following ranges:

CATEGORY	COST*
$$$$	over $36
$$$	$21–$36
$$	$9–$21
$	under $9

All prices are per person for a three-course meal excluding tax, service charge, and drinks.

Gardens and Parks
You can escape from the concrete and glass that is modern downtown Singapore to visit orchid farms or the wonderfully kept Botanic Gardens. If you have a lot of energy, you can hike the trails of Bukit Timah Nature Reserve—the tigers have long gone, but the sounds and smells of the jungle are still here. If you want to see a tiger or two, as well as animals from as far away as the North Pole, Singapore has a world-

class zoo designed in an open format that includes the use of moats, instead of bars, as barriers. The Night Safari is a zoo specifically created for the viewing of nocturnal animals such as tigers and rhinoceros; you can watch them as they wake up at dusk to feed.

Lodging

Although Singapore isn't the same indulgent retreat it once was, it's hard to match the standard of comfort, efficiency of staff, and level of services that Singapore hotels offer. The luxury establishments cater to every whim—and so they should at more than S$300 a night—but you can find good service, freshly decorated rooms, cleanliness, and modern facilities for around S$200. For less money, there are simple, clean hotels (often more personal than the larger ones), with rooms for about S$80. Youth hostels have increased in price of late, to about S$70 a night, but tend to be clean and cosmopolitan. Price categories throughout the chapter are based on the following ranges:

CATEGORY	COST*
$$$$	over $223
$$$	$164–$223
$$	$104–$164
$	under $104

All prices are for a standard double room, excluding 4% tax and 10% service charge.

Shopping

Once upon a time Singapore, a duty-free republic, was a haven for shoppers. And though shopping is still the major pastime, nowadays the shoppers tend to be rich and sassy. Except for a lucky find in an antiques store, bargains are hard to come by. Still, nowhere else will you find so many shops that carry the latest fashions and electronic equipment. Browsing here is as much a pleasure as shopping.

Theme Parks

No other country of Singapore's size has put so much effort into creating attractions for both its citizens and its visitors. A few decades ago, Singapore may have spent millions destroying its heritage buildings, but of late, both the government and private enterprise have spent a fortune re-creating the old face of Singapore, which has already been made over in the name of progress, building up displays like "Images of Singapore" on Sentosa and refurbished conservation areas like Chinatown and Little India.

EXPLORING SINGAPORE

The main island of Singapore is shaped like a flattened diamond, 42 km (26 mi) east to west and 23 km (14 mi) north to south. Near the northern peak is the causeway leading to peninsular Malaysia—Kuala Lumpur is less than four hours away by car. At the southern foot is Singapore city, with its gleaming office towers and working docks. Offshore are Sentosa and some 60 smaller islands—most of them uninhabited—that serve as bases for oil refining or as playgrounds or beach escapes from the city. To the east is Changi International Airport, connected to the city by a parkway lined for miles with amusement centers of one sort or another. Of the island's total land area, more than half is built up, with the balance made up of parkland, farmland, plantations, swamp areas, and forest. Well-paved roads connect all parts of the island, and Singapore city has an excellent public transportation system.

Colonial Singapore

You'll find the heart of Singapore's history and its modern wealth in Colonial Singapore. The area stretches from the skyscrapers in Singapore's financial district to the 19th-century Raffles Hotel, and from the super-modern convention centers of Marina Square to the Singapore History Museum and Fort Canning. Although most of old Singapore has been knocked down to make way for the modern city, in Colonial Singapore most of the major landmarks have been preserved, including early 19th-century buildings designed by the Irish architect George Coleman.

Numbers in the text correspond to numbers in the margin and on the Colonial Singapore map.

A Good Walk

A convenient place to start is at **Collyer Quay** ① ("quay" is pronounced "key") and Clifford Pier, where most European colonizers first set foot on the island. Leaving Clifford Pier, walk up the quay—toward the Singapore River—until you come to the imposing **former General Post Office** ②, also known as the Fullerton Building, built in 1928 of gray stone. Due to construction on and around the building, which is undergoing a transformation into the grand Fullerton Hotel, walking around it is a little difficult. However, with a bit of effort, you should be able to walk to the left of the old post office and so cross the gracious old iron-link **Cavenagh Bridge** ③. If you walk along the river's south bank before crossing the bridge, you'll find what was once a wide towpath and is now a paved pedestrian street of restaurants and bars—**Boat Quay** ④. The second building on your left houses Harry's Bar, which gained international attention in 1995 as a haunt of derivatives trader Nick Leeson, the young whippersnapper who brought down the venerable Barings Bank.

Once over the Cavenagh Bridge, take a left onto North Boat Quay. Slightly back from the river is the huge, white **Empress Place Building** ⑤. A bit farther along the quay is the **statue of Sir Thomas Stamford Raffles** ⑥, who is believed to have landed on this spot in 1819. Turn right onto St. Andrew's Road until you come to **Parliament House** ⑦ on your left, the oldest government building in Singapore, and on your right, **Victoria Memorial Hall** ⑧, built in 1905 as a tribute to Queen Victoria. Across the road is the old **Singapore Cricket Club** ⑨. Just past it, on your right as you continue up St. Andrew's Road, is the **Padang** ⑩, or playing field. To your left are the **Supreme Court** ⑪ and **City Hall** ⑫, two splendidly pretentious, imperial-looking buildings. Continuing northeast on St. Andrew's Road, which runs along the Padang, cross Coleman Street toward the green lawns that surround the Anglican **St. Andrew's Cathedral** ⑬.

Northeast of the cathedral is the huge **Raffles City** ⑭ complex, easily recognized by the towers of the two Westin hotels. Take the MRT underpass north across Stamford Road, and walk through Raffles City to Bras Basah Road. Across the street is the venerable **Raffles Hotel** ⑮. After touring the hotel, continue up Bras Basah Road to Queen Street and make a right to the **Singapore Art Museum** ⑯. After touring the exhibits, cross Bras Basah Road and walk down to Victoria Street, where you'll no doubt find a place to rest and people-watch at the **Chijmes** ⑰ complex. Continue southwest on Victoria Street (it becomes Hill Street after Stamford Road); the **Armenian Church** ⑱ will be on your right just before Coleman Street. From here, stamp collectors should turn left onto Coleman and visit the **Singapore Philatelic Museum** ⑲; culture vultures should go right on Coleman and then right again onto

Singapore City

Orchard Road

Stevens Rd.

NEWTON

Kampong
Java Park

Bukit Timah Rd.

Nassim Rd.

Cairnhill Rd.

Clemenceau Ave.

Claymore Hill

Scotts Rd.

Wilkie Rd.

Tanglin Rd.

ORCHARD

Bideford Rd.

Cavenagh Rd.

Edinburgh Rd.

Orchard Blvd.

Orchard Rd.

Paterson Rd.

One Tree
Hill

SOMERSET

Colonial Singapo

Grange Rd.

Grange Rd.

Exeter Rd.

Oxley

Rise

DHOBY
GHAUT

Rd.

Clemenceau

Fort Canning

Fort
Canning
Park

River Valley Rd.

River Valley Rd.

Zion Rd.

Kim Seng Rd.

River Valley Rd.

Coleman
Bridge

Singapore River

Alexandra Rd.

Havelock Rd.

Havelock Rd.

Havelock Rd.

Havelock Rd.

Pickering St.

TIONG
BAHRU

Tiong Bahru Rd.

New Bridge Rd.

South Bridge Rd.

Henderson Rd.

Outram
Park

Outram Rd.

Jalan Bukit Merah

OUTRAM
PARK

1000 meters

0

0

1000 yards

Neil Rd.

Craig Rd.

Pagar Rd.

Maxwell Rd.

Cecil St.

N

Cantonment

Bahru Rd.

Spottiswoode
Park

TANJONG
PAGAR

Keppel Rd.

Keppel Rd.

Subway & Rail Lines

— North-South MRT line
— East-West MRT line
— Railroad lines
Ⓢ Subway stop

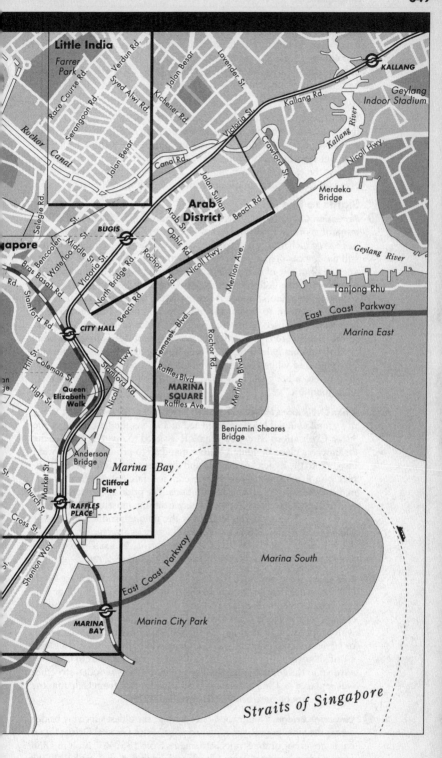

Little India

Farrer Park

Race Course Rd.
Verdun Rd.
Syed Alwi Rd.
Serangoon Rd.
Jalan Besar
Kichener Rd.
Jalan Besar
Lavender St.
Victoria St.

KALLANG

Geylang Indoor Stadium

Rochor Canal

Canal Rd.
Crawford St.
Kallang Rd.
Kallang River
Nicoll Hwy.

Merdeka Bridge

Arab District

Jalan Sultan
Arab St.
Beach Rd.

BUGIS

Geylang River

Selegie Rd.
St.
Middle St.
Victoria St.
North Bridge Rd.
Rochor Rd.
Ophir Rd.
Nicoll Hwy.
Merlion Ave.

apore

Bencoolen St.
Waterloo St.
Bras Basah Rd.
Stamford Rd.

Rd.

CITY HALL

Beach Rd.

Tanjong Rhu

East Coast Parkway

Marina East

Hill
St.
Coleman St.
High St.

Queen Elizabeth Walk

Stamford Rd.
Nicoll Hwy.

Temasek Blvd.
Raffles Blvd.

MARINA SQUARE
Raffles Ave.

Rochor Rd.
Merlion Blvd.

an

Benjamin Sheares Bridge

Anderson Bridge

Market St.
Church St.

St.

Marina Bay

Clifford Pier

RAFFLES PLACE

Cross St.

Shenton Way

East Coast Parkway

Marina South

East Coast Parkway

MARINA BAY

Marina City Park

Marina City Park

Straits of Singapore

Armenian Street to visit the **Asian Civilisations Museum** ⑳. To see the **Singapore History Museum** ㉑ instead, return to Stamford Road and make a left. You may wish to conclude your tour with a stroll through **Fort Canning Park** ㉒, pausing at the European Cemetery and the Tomb of Iskander Shah, and/or a visit to **Clarke Quay** ㉓, south of the park, with its restaurants and shops.

TIMING

This walking tour, with time factored in to wander through the Raffles Hotel and view the exhibits at one or more of the area's four museums, should take a full day. Allow an hour for the Raffles, including time out for a Singapore sling in the Long Bar. Allow at least an hour to view the exhibits at each museum. Remember to buy drinks wherever you can; it's easy to get dehydrated in Singapore's heat.

Sights to See

⑱ **Armenian Church.** More correctly, the **Church of St. Gregory the Illuminator** is one of the most elegant buildings in Singapore. It was built in 1835, which makes it the republic's oldest surviving church, and it's still used occasionally for Armenian Orthodox services. The Armenians were but one of many minority groups that came to Singapore in search of fortune. A dozen wealthy Armenian families (and several non-Christian merchants) donated the funds for the ubiquitous architect George Coleman to design this church. The main internal circular structure is imposed on a square plan with four projecting porticoes. In the churchyard is the weathered tombstone of Agnes Joaquim, who bred the orchid hybrid that has become Singapore's national flower. The pink and white orchid, with a deeper purplish pink center, was discovered in her garden in 1893 and still carries her name: "Vanda Miss Joaquim."

★ ⑳ **Asian Civilisations Museum.** Formerly the Tao Nan School, built in 1910, this grand colonial building reopened in 1997 as the first phase of the Asian Civilisations Museum. (Phase II is slated to open in 2002 at the ☞ **Empress Place Building.**) With a mandate to provide an Asia-wide insight into the legacies of the past and the cultural traditions of the peoples who live in the region, the museum is a fascinating blend of permanent and changing themed exhibitions. The pride of the second floor is a striking Peranakan-culture display from the museum's permanent collection—this fascinating culture is the unique product of blended Chinese and Malay/Southeast Asian influences in art, cuisine, costume, decor, language, and lifestyles. ⊠ *39 Armenian St.,* ☎ *332–3015 or 837–9940.* 🎟 *S$3.* ☺ *Tues., Thurs.–Sun. 9–5:30, Wed. 9–9 PM.* 🐾

❹ **Boat Quay.** Right next to the financial district, along the Singapore River, is this popular new restaurant area with both indoor and outdoor dining. Local entrepreneurs have created a mélange of eateries and nightclubs to satisfy diverse tastes. Between 7 PM and midnight, the area swells with people, who stroll along the pleasant quay, stopping to take a meal or refreshment. At the end of Boat Quay and named after Lord Elgin, a British governor-general of India, **Elgin Bridge** was built to link Chinatown to the colonial quarter. The original rickety wooden structure was replaced in 1863 with an iron bridge imported from Calcutta; the current ferroconcrete bridge was installed in 1926.

❸ **Cavenagh Bridge.** This gracious steel bridge, the oldest surviving bridge across the Singapore River, is named after Major General Orfeur Cavenagh, governor of the Straits Settlements from 1859–67. Built in 1868 from girders imported from Glasgow, Scotland, it was until 1909 the main route across the river; now Anderson Bridge bears the brunt of the traffic.

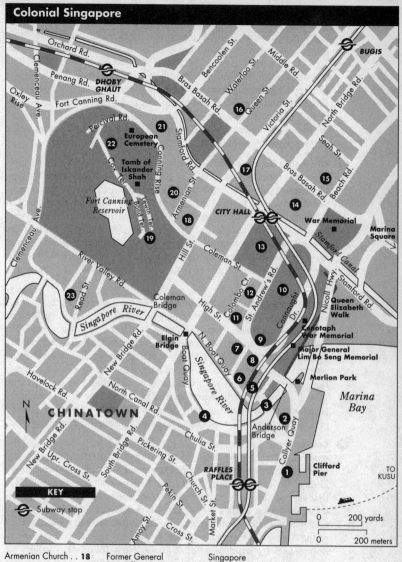

Colonial Singapore

⑰ **Chijmes.** The oldest and core building in this walled complex is the Coleman-designed Caldwell House, a private mansion built in 1840. This, together with other buildings, became in 1852 the Convent of the Holy Infant Jesus, where Catholic nuns housed and schooled abandoned children. The church was added between 1901 and 1903. After World War II, both the convent and the church fell into disrepair. The buildings received a S$100 million renovation and were reopened in 1996 as this shopping and entertainment complex. Today the lovingly restored church is rented out for private functions. The new name "Chijmes" (pronounced "chimes") is an acronym of the convent's name, a nod at the complex's noble past.

⑫ **City Hall.** Completed in 1929, this pompous building, formerly government offices, is now largely desolate, awaiting a new, probably conservation-type purpose. It's popular as a backdrop for young couples' wedding photos. It was here that the British surrender took place in 1942, followed by the surrender of the Japanese in 1945, and here, too, on the Padang field in front, that the great independence rallies of the 1950s were staged. Each year on August 9, the building's steps serve as a viewing stand for the National Day Parade, celebrating Singapore's 1959 independence from Great Britain and the birth of the republic in 1965.

☝ ㉓ **Clarke Quay.** Named in remembrance of Sir Andrew Clarke, the second governor of Singapore, this quay functions as a festival village that offers entertainment, food, and shopping. Here you can observe a tinsmith demonstrating his skill, groove to a blues band in the central square's small gazebo ("The Voodoo Shack"), watch stilt-walkers wobble down pedestrian-only streets, or scout for bargain antiques. The river here is close to being the sleepy waterway it was when Raffles first arrived; cargo vessels are banned from entering. You can board one of the bumboats (small launches) that offer daily 30-minute cruises along the river and into Marina Bay; it's a pleasant ride, and a respite for tired feet.

❶ **Collyer Quay.** Land reclamation through the 19th century pushed the seafront several blocks away from Collyer Quay. At that time, the view from the quay would have been a virtual wall of anchored ships. Today, you look out upon the graceful Benjamin Sheares bridge (1981) that carries the East Coast Parkway from one landfill headland to another, enclosing what's now called Marina Bay. **Clifford Pier,** a covered jetty with high, vaulted ceilings, still reveals some of the excitement of the days when European traders arrived by steamship and Chinese immigrants by wind-dependent junks. Now Indonesian sailors sit around smoking clove-scented cigarettes, and seamen from every seafaring nation come ashore to stock up on liquor and duty-free electronics. The atmosphere here is seedy (this is one of the few places in Singapore where women might feel uncomfortable by themselves). Passengers from the ocean liners no longer come ashore here (they now arrive at the World Trade Centre cruise terminal), but it's still possible to set sail from here on a day cruise around Singapore's harbor and to the outlying islands. Bumboats wallow in the bay, waiting to take sailors back to their ships or carry other visitors wherever they want to go for about S$30 an hour. In **Merlion Park,** at the end of the quay near Anderson Bridge, stands a statue of Singapore's tourism symbol, the Merlion—half lion, half fish. In the evening, the statue—on a point of land looking out over the harbor—is floodlit, its eyes are lighted, and its mouth spews water. You can see an even bigger one on Sentosa Island. This creature is based upon the country's national symbol, the lion (from which the name Singapore was derived). The Merlion symbolizes courage, strength, and excellence.

⑤ Empress Place Building. This huge, white, neoclassical building was meticulously restored as an exhibition hall but is now closed until the year 2002, when it will reopen as Phase II of the ☞ **Asian Civilisations Museum.** Constructed in the 1860s as the courthouse, the building has since had four major additions and has housed nearly every government body, including the Registry of Births and Deaths and the Immigration Department. Virtually every adult Singaporean has been inside this building at one time or another.

② Former General Post Office. The post office recently moved to the suburbs from this imposing edifice—all gray stone and monumental pillars—also called the Fullerton Building, constructed in 1928, the heyday of the British Empire. It's slated to become the grand Fullerton Hotel. To the left as you face the old post office is **Fullerton Square,** a rest stop for cycle-rickshaw drivers and one-time hotbed of political rallies in the 1950s.

☙ ㉒ Fort Canning Park. Fort Canning offers green sanctuary from the bustling city below. It's where modern Singapore's founder Sir Stamford Raffles built his first bungalow and experimented with a trial botanic gardens, echoed by a spice-garden display today. The botany, from massive fig trees and luxuriant ferns to abundant birdlife—piping black-naped orioles and chattering collared kingfishers—are worth lingering over here. You can almost smell the history of the hill in the air. A lively reconstruction of the British army's former underground Far East Command Centre highlights the hill's World War II history. The hill is well signed and trailed, and there are designated picnic areas. A private country club now occupies the former British military Singapore Command and Staff College at the park's edge.

Nostalgic, too, are the remnants of the 19th-century **European cemetery,** weathered tombstones, once divided into areas for Protestants and for Catholics, are now set into a wall around an open field. Deciphering the inscriptions is worth the effort; the young age of some of those at rest there tells a tale of hardship in the conditions faced by the pioneering colonials.

Around the 13th to 14th century, **Fort Canning Rise,** as the hill has been called, was home to the royal palaces of the Malay rulers of the kingdom of Temasek, part of the Srivijayan empire based in Palembang, Sumatra. No doubt they chose this spot not only for its freshwater spring but also for the cool breezes and commanding view of the river. Archaeological excavations have unearthed ancient gold ornaments as well as Chinese trading ceramics on the hill. The last five kings of Singa Pura (Lion City), as the island came to be called, including the legendary Iskandar Shah, are said to be buried there; a sacred shrine, or *kramat* in Malay still marks the spot today. Some dispute this, claiming that Iskandar Shah escaped from Singa Pura before its destruction in 1391. Temasek succumbed to attacks from the Majapahit empire in Java and from the Ayuthia empire of Siam (Thailand).

For several hundred years the site was abandoned to the jungle. It was referred to by the Malays as Bukit Larangan, the Forbidden Hill, a place where the spirits of bygone kings roamed on sacred ground. Then Raffles came: defying Malay superstition, he neatly assumed the mantle of the ancient kings for colonial British rule by establishing his Government House on the rise. Later, in 1859, a fort was constructed; its guns were fired to mark dawn, noon, and night.

OFF THE
BEATEN PATH

MARINA SQUARE – A minicity all its own, built on landfill, Marina Square has three malls and five smart atrium hotels—The Pan Pacific, the Marina Mandarin, The Oriental, The Ritz-Carlton, and the Conrad International Centennial (☞ *also* Lodging, *below*). Suntec City, a mammoth convention center and shopping mall, is rivaled by an even bigger mall, the Millenia (*sic*) Walk, with its three-story duty-free shop. The Marina Square Shopping Mall provides an eclectic mix of boutique bargain shopping. A massive multimillion-dollar performing arts center, The Esplanade, is slated to open in 2002 across the road from this mall and along the Queen Elizabeth Walk, which opened in 1953 to mark the British Queen's coronation. The entire Marina Square/Millenia complex lacks human scale and is pedestrian-unfriendly, cold, and intimidating as a result. A planned creation of the late 1980s and '90s, it doesn't seem to have integrated with the older city yet despite adequate road and pedestrian connections.

❿ Padang. Today the Padang (Malay for "field" or "plain"), which seemingly constitutes the backyard of the ☞ **Singapore Cricket Club,** is used primarily as a playing field. It has traditionally been a social and political hub. Once called the Esplanade, it was only half its current size until an 1890s land reclamation expanded it. During World War II, 2,000 British civilians were gathered here by the Japanese before being marched off to Changi Prison and, in many cases, to their deaths.

Beyond the northeastern edge of the Padang, across Stamford Road and the Stamford Canal, are the four 220-ft (67-meter), tapering, white columns of the **Civilian War Memorial,** known locally as "The Four Chopsticks." The monument honors the thousands of civilians from the four main ethnic groups (Chinese, Malay, Indian, and "others," including Eurasians and Europeans) who lost their lives during the Japanese occupation. Many also suffered terribly when they were sent to help build the Burma–Siam Railway.

Along the Padang's eastern edge, just across Connaught Drive, are several other monuments. The **Major General Lim Bo Seng Memorial** honors a well-loved freedom fighter of World War II who was tortured to death by the Japanese in 1944. The imposing **Cenotaph War Memorial** honors the dead of the two world wars.

❼ Parliament House. George Coleman designed the Parliament House in 1827 as a private mansion for wealthy merchant John Maxwell. He never occupied it, leasing it to the government, which eventually bought it in 1841 for S$15,600. It was the Supreme Court until 1939 and is considered the oldest government building in Singapore. In 1953 it became the home of the then governing Legislative Assembly and the meeting place for Parliament in 1965. The bronze elephant statue on a plinth in front of the building was a gift from King Chulalongkorn of Siam during his state visit in 1871. ⊠ *Corner of High St. and St. Andrew's Rd.,* ☎ *335–8811.* ⬛ *Free.* ☉ *Daily by appointment.* ✎

⓮ Raffles City. Designed by famous Chinese-American architect I. M. Pei, the difficult-to-navigate Raffles City complex of offices and shops contains Asia's tallest hotel, at 700 feet, the Westin Stamford. This is not to be confused with the Westin Plaza, which is in the same building (☞ Lodging, *below*). There's a beautiful view of downtown and the harbor from the Compass Rose restaurant atop the Stamford. Older residents still lament the fact that in 1984 this complex replaced the elegant colonial Raffles Institution school founded by Sir Stamford Raffles himself in 1823.

⓯ Raffles Hotel. Once a "tiffin house," or tearoom, the Raffles Hotel started life as the home of a British sea captain. In 1887 the Armenian Sarkies brothers took over the building and transformed it into one of Asia's grandest hotels. The Raffles has had many ups and downs, especially during World War II, when it was first a center for British refugees, then quarters for Japanese officers, and then a center for released Allied prisoners of war. There's a delicious irony to the Raffles: viewed as a bastion of colonialism, it was not only the creation of Armenians, but in its 130 years of hosting expatriates, it only once had a British manager. Even so, service has been unfailingly loyal to the colonial heritage. Right before the Japanese arrived, the Chinese waiters took the silverware from the dining rooms and buried it in the Palm Court garden, where it remained safely hidden until the occupiers departed.

After the war the hotel deteriorated, surviving by trading on its heritage rather than its facilities. However, in late 1991, after two years of renovation and expansion, the Raffles reopened as the republic's most expensive hotel (S$650 a night and upward). You can no longer just roam around inside. Instead you're channeled through re-created colonial-style buildings to take in a free museum of Raffles memorabilia and then, perhaps, to take refreshment in a reproduction of the **Long Bar,** where the famous Singapore Sling was created in 1915 by the bartender Ngiam Tong Boon. The sling here is still regarded as the best in Singapore; note that your S$17.15 tab includes service and tax, but not the glass—that's another S$8. Also note that some consider the new Long Bar a travesty, with manually operated *punkahs* (fans) replaced by those that are electrically powered. Casual visitors are discouraged from entering the original part of the hotel, via the front reception and lobby area, and nowadays the once lovely Palm Court is not only out of bounds but, to all appearances, devoid of life. If you can brave this atmosphere, the **Tiffin Room** restaurant is worth the effort. For reasonable authenticity outside of the historic hotel core, the **Empire Cafe** and the **Bar and Billiard Room** are much better bets than the Long Bar. You also can simply browse in the arcade's 65 shops, stop by **Doc Cheng's** restaurant for a taste of its "transethnic" cuisine, or head to the tiny **Writers' Bar** for a drink.

⑬ **St. Andrew's Cathedral.** This Anglican church, surrounded by a green lawn, is the third one built on this site. The first was constructed in 1834, and the second was demolished in 1855 after two lightning strikes. (Locals took the bolts from the heavens as a sign. It was suggested that before another place of worship was built, the spirits should be appeased with the blood from 30 heads; fortunately, the suggestion was ignored.) Indian convicts were brought in to construct a new cathedral in the English Gothic style. The structure, completed in 1861, has bells cast by the firm that made Big Ben's, and it resembles Netley Abbey in Hampshire, England. The British overlords were so impressed by the cathedral that the Indian convict who supplied the working drawings was granted his freedom. The church was expanded once in 1952 and again in 1983. Its lofty interior is white and simple, with stained-glass windows coloring the sunlight as it enters. Around the walls are marble and brass memorial plaques, including one remembering the British who died in a 1915 mutiny of native light infantry and another in memory of 41 Australian army nurses killed in the Japanese invasion. Services are held every Sunday. The South Transept has a showcase of historical artifacts and a history video. Guided tours are available.

⑯ **Singapore Art Museum.** When this 1867 building—once the all-boys Catholic St. Joseph's Institution—closed in 1987 it did not reopen as a museum until 1996. (Names of school donors still adorn the porch at the entrance.) When Prime Minister Goh Chok Tung opened it, he described a vision of Singapore "reliving, through its museums, its historic role as an entrepôt for art, culture, civilization, and ideas." The 4,000-piece permanent collection here includes modern art from Singapore and traditional art from other parts of Southeast Asia. The E-mage Gallery has interactive programs that feature 20th-century Southeast Asian art presented on large, high-definition monitors. ⊠ *71 Bras Basah Rd.,* ☎ *332–3222 or 837–9940.* ⌖ *S$3.* ☉ *Tues.–Sun. 9–5:30; Wed. 9–9; free guided tours daily 11 AM and 2 PM, and 3 PM on the weekend.* 🐾

⑨ Singapore Cricket Club. Founded in 1852 and housed in this charming 1884 building with 1907 and 1921 modifications, this club was for a long time the center of social and sporting life for the British community (which had played cricket on the Padang at least from the 1830s). It now has a multiracial active membership of 5,500 and offers facilities for various sports, in addition to bars and restaurants. If you're going to be in Singapore for more than a couple of weeks, you can apply, with the support of a member, for a visiting membership. The club isn't open to the general public, but from the Padang you can sneak a quick look at the deep, shaded verandas, from which members still watch cricket, rugby, and tennis matches.

㉑ Singapore History Museum. Housed in a silver-dome colonial building, this was originally opened as the Raffles Museum in 1887. Included in its collection are 20 dioramas depicting the republic's past, together with the "From Colony to Nation" display on post–World War II developments; the Revere Bell, donated to the original St. Andrew's Church in 1834 by the daughter of American patriot Paul Revere; the 380-piece Haw Par Jade Collection, one of the largest of its kind; the exquisite Farquhar Collection of regional flora and fauna paintings executed in the 19th century; various occult paraphernalia on Chinese secret societies, "Entering the Hung Gate"; ethnographic collections from Southeast Asia; and many historical documents. Enjoy, also, a 35-minute 3-D audiovisual show, "The Singapore Story." ⊠ *Stamford Rd.,* ☎ *332–3659 or 837 9940; 332–3966 for night tours.* ⌖ *S$3 (S$1 extra if "The Singapore Story" or a night tour is included); free guided tour 11 AM Tues.* ☉ *Tues.–Sun. 9–5:30, Wed. till 9 PM.* 🐾

NEED A BREAK?   At the back of the Singapore Art Museum you'll find the **Olio Dome** (☎ 339–0792), a casual breakfast and lunch spot. The Dome, one of several in Singapore, serves a Western menu of soups, salads, and sandwiches—but it really specializes in coffee. A latte goes for S$4.20. You can eat outside on the curving neoclassical porch or inside in a 1920s-style bistro.

⑲ Singapore Philatelic Museum. Housed in a 1907 building, once part of the Anglo Chinese School, is Southeast Asia's first stamp museum. It has a fine collection of local and international stamps as well as an audiovisual theater, a resource center, interactive games, and a souvenir shop. ⊠ *23B Coleman St.,* ☎ *337–3888.* ⌖ *S$2.* ☉ *Tues.–Sun. 9–5:30.* 🐾

⑥ Statue of Sir Thomas Stamford Raffles. This statue near the Empress Place Building on North Boat Quay is on the spot where Raffles purportedly landed in Singapore early on the morning of January 29, 1819. Pause here a moment to observe the contrast between the old and the new. Once this river was the bustling artery feeding Singapore's commercial life, packed with barges and lighters that ferried goods from cargo ship to dock. There were no cranes—the unloading was done by teams of coolies. Swarms of them tottered under their heavy loads, back and forth between lighters and riverside *godowns* (warehouses), amid yells from *compradores* (factotums).

⑪ **Supreme Court.** In the ponderous neoclassical style so beloved of British colonials, the Supreme Court has Corinthian pillars and the look of arrogant certainty. But it was the last such building to be erected in Singapore. Completed in 1939, it replaced the famous Hôtel de l'Europe, a romantic venue of the Conrad era of sailors' derring-do, and then boasting a stunning view of the harbor. The pedimental sculptures of the Greek-templelike facade by Italian artist Cavalieri Rudolfo Nolli portray an allegory of Justice. Inside, the echoing hall and staircase are grand and, high above, the vast paneled ceiling is an exercise in showmanship. All of this was completed just in time for the Japanese to use the building as their headquarters. Thankfully, World War II preempted architect Frank Dorrington Ward's plan to demolish most of the historical buildings around the Padang in favor of a modern complex.

⑧ **Victoria Memorial Hall.** The Memorial Hall was built in 1905 as a tribute to Queen Victoria. Along with the adjacent **Victoria Theatre,** built in 1862 as the town hall, it's currently the city's main cultural center, offering regular exhibitions, concerts, and theatrical performances of all types (☞ Nightlife and the Arts, *below*).

Chinatown

In a country where 77% of the people are Chinese, it may seem strange to name a small urban area Chinatown. But Chinatown was born some 180 years ago, when the Chinese were a minority (if only for half a century) in the newly formed British settlement. In an attempt to minimize racial tension, Raffles allotted sections of the settlement to different immigrant groups. The Chinese were given the area south of the Singapore River. Today, the river is still the northern boundary of old Chinatown; Maxwell Road marks its southern perimeter and New Bridge Road its western one. Before 20th-century land reclamation, the western perimeter was the sea. The reclaimed area between Telok Ayer Street and Collyer Quay–Shenton Way has become the business district, whose expansion has caused Chinese shophouses to be knocked down all the way to Cross Street.

Immigrants from mainland China—many of them penniless and half-starved—were crammed inside a relatively small rectangle. Within three years of the formation of the Straits Settlement, 3,000 Chinese had arrived; this number increased tenfold over the next decade. The Hokkien people, traders from Fukien Province, made up about a quarter of the community. Other leading groups were the Teochews, from the Swatow region of Guangdong Province, and their mainland neighbors, the Cantonese. In smaller groups, the Hainanese, the nomadic Hakkas, and peoples from Guangxi arrived in tightly packed junks, riding on the northeast monsoon winds.

Most immigrants came with the sole intention of exchanging their rags for riches, then returning to China. They had no allegiance to Singapore or to Chinatown, which was no melting pot but, rather, separate pockets of ethnically diverse groups, each with a different dialect; a different cuisine; and different cultural, social, and religious attitudes. In the shophouses—two-story buildings with shops or small factories on the ground floor and living quarters upstairs—as many as 30 lodgers would share a single room, using beds in shifts. Life was a fight for space and survival. Crime was rampant. What order existed was maintained by Chinese guilds, clan associations, and secret societies, all of which fought—sometimes savagely—for control of lucrative aspects of community life.

Not too long ago, all of Chinatown was slated for the bulldozer in the name of "progress." However, selective conservation is now enshrined in government policy both as a way of generating new upmarket commercial space (refurbished old shophouses are now extremely popular with yuppies as offices for everything from law firms to advertising and design companies, and current high purchase prices reflect this fact) and as a necessary part of an enlightened tourism agenda. Besides this, in the later part of the 20th century, both the government and people of Singapore developed more pride in their heritage. They came to recognize that an important way of maintaining Chinese customs and family ties was to conserve the building frameworks in which they once were nurtured. To some extent Chinatown has been recast with the eyes of the 21st century, but much of the old vigor survives at street level.

Numbers in the text correspond to numbers in the margin and on the Chinatown map.

A Good Walk

Begin at the Elgin Bridge, built to link Chinatown with the colonial administration center. At the south end of the bridge, logically enough, South Bridge Road begins. Off to the right is Upper Circular Road, on the left-hand side of which is **Yeo Swee Huat** ① at No. 15, which sells paper replicas of houses, cars, and other worldly goods intended to be burned at Chinese funerals (to be taken with the deceased to the other world for his/her use—you'll encounter other such shops during your walk.) Circular Road, once home to cloth wholesalers, now has bars and restaurants. Walk down **Lorong Telok** ② lane, with its architecturally interesting shops and clan houses, and take a right onto **North Canal Road.** Here are stores that sell Chinese delicacies—dried foods, turtles for soup, sea cucumbers, sharks' fins, and birds' nests. Trace your steps back along North Canal to Chulia Street. Follow it to Phillip Street and turn right to reach the recently restored **Wak Hai Cheng Bio Temple** ③ (1826).

Return to North Canal Road. Continue to New Bridge Road, turn left, and walk past the Furama Singapore Hotel and the People's Park Centre, now home to the Singapore Handicrafts Centre. Cross Upper Cross Street and take a left onto **Mosque Street.** The old shophouses here—now being redeveloped into offices—were originally built as stables. Turn right onto South Bridge Road. The **Jamae Mosque** ④ will be on your right. On the next block is the **Sri Mariamman Temple** ⑤, the oldest Hindu temple in Singapore.

If you take the next right, onto **Temple Street,** you may be fortunate enough to see one of the few remaining streetside scribes in Singapore. At the junction of Trengganu Street, notice the old building on the corner. Reliable sources say this was once a famous **brothel** ⑥. You are now in the core of Chinatown, an area known as **Kreta Ayer.** Trengganu Street leads to the new **Chinatown Complex** ⑦. Leaving the market, walk along **Sago Street** to see more family factories that make paper models to be burned at funerals. Parallel to Sago Street is Sago Lane. There's nothing to see here now, but the street was once known for its death houses, where Chinese waited out their last days.

If you turn right onto South Bridge Road, you'll come to the intersection of **Tanjong Pagar Road** and Neil Road. The **Jinriksha Station** ⑧ was once a rickshaw depot, but it is now a food court. After strolling down Tanjong Pagar Road to see the restored shophouses and trendy restaurants, head back to South Bridge Road. **Smith Street,** on the left, has stores that sell everything from chilies to ground rhinoceros horn. Ann Siang Hill, on the other side of South Bridge Road, is full of old shops and is the site of the **Guild for Amahs** ⑨. From Ann Siang Hill, turn left onto Club Street, and then right at Gemmill Lane. When you get to Telok Ayer Street, turn right, and you'll find the **Nagore Durgha Shrine** ⑩—an odd mix of minarets and Greek columns decorated with fairy lights—built by South Indian Muslims. Continue down the road to the interesting **Thian Hock Keng Temple** ⑪, now integrated with a new housing-shopping complex on Telok Ayer Street. Across from the temple is the China Square Food Centre, home of the unusual House of Mao restaurant (☞ Dining, *below*). A little farther down the street is the **Al Abrar Mosque** ⑫. Walk east along McCallum Street toward the bay and take a left onto Shenton Way. At Boon Tat Street, you'll see the **Lau Pa Sat** ⑬, meaning "Old Market" in local Hokkien-Chinese dialect (derived from the Malay word *pasar*, for "market"), the largest Victorian cast-iron structure in Southeast Asia. Here you can refresh yourself at the food court, then take the subway back to Raffles Place on Collyer Quay.

TIMING

Allow two to three hours for this walk, and factor in a half an hour each for the Wak Hai Cheng Bio, Thian Hock Keng, and Sri Mariamman temples.

Sights to See

⑫ **Al Abrar Mosque.** Also known as Kuchu Palli (the Tamil word for "mosque hut"), this structure dates from 1850. The original mosque, a mere thatched hut built in 1827, was one of the first for Singapore's Indian Muslims.

OFF THE BEATEN PATH

BIRD-SINGING CAFÉS – A special Sunday-morning treat is to take breakfast with the birds. Bird fanciers bring their prize specimens, in intricate bamboo cages, to coffee shops and hang the cages outside for training sessions: by listening to their feathered friends, the birds learn how to warble. Bird-singing enthusiasts take their hobby seriously and, incidentally, pay handsomely for it. For you, it costs only the price of a cup of coffee to sit at a table and listen. One place to try is the Seng Poh Coffee Shop on the corner of Tiong Bahru and Seng Poh roads, west of Tanjong Pagar; arrive at around 9 AM.

⑥ **Brothel.** Reliable sources say this was a famous brothel. Opium dens and brothels played important roles in the lives of Chinese immigrants, who usually arrived alone and worked long days, with little time for relaxation or pleasure. Many immigrants took to soothing their aching minds and bodies at opium dens; as only 12% of the community were women, men often sought female companionship from professionals. Gambling was another popular pastime. (Gambling outside of the various games within the state lottery—which now includes soccer betting—and the official horse-race-betting system, is outlawed by the government today. But the habit dies hard and you can be sure that when you hear the slap of mahjong tiles in a coffeehouse, a wager or two has been made.) Raffles tried to ban gambling, but to no avail—the habit was too firmly entrenched. One legendary figure, Tan Che Seng, who had amassed a fortune subsidizing junks bringing immigrants to work in the warehouses, resolved to give up gambling. As a reminder of his resolution, he cut off half of his little finger. Still, he continued to gamble until his death in 1836!

⑦ **Chinatown Complex.** This market is mobbed inside and out with jostling shoppers. At the open-air vegetable and fruit stands, women—toothless and wrinkled with age—sell their wares. Inside, on the first floor, hawker stalls sell a variety of cooked foods, but it's the basement

Chinatown

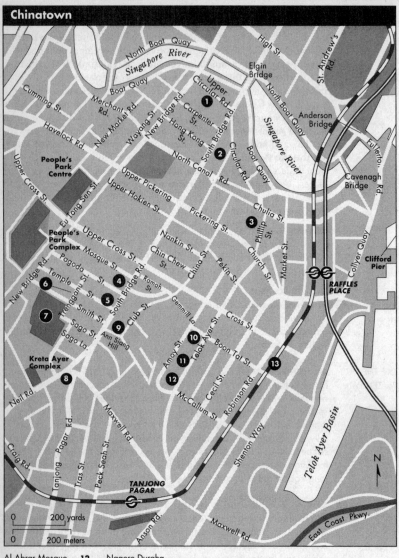

floor that fascinates: here you'll find a wet market—so called because water is continually sloshed over the floors to clean them—where an amazing array of meats, fowl, and fish are bought and sold. Some of the sights may spoil your appetite; at the far left corner, for example, live pigeons, furry white rabbits, and sleepy turtles are crammed into cages, awaiting hungry buyers.

9 Guild for Amahs. Club Street is full of old buildings that continue to house clan associations, including the professional guild for *amahs*. Though their numbers are few today, these female servants were once an integral part of European households in Singapore. Like the *samsui* (women who vowed never to marry)—who until quite recently could still be observed in their traditional red headdresses passing bricks or carrying buckets at construction sites—the amahs choose to earn an independent living, however hard the work, rather than submit to the servitude of marriage. (In traditional Chinese society, a daughter-in-law is the lowest-ranking member of the family.) In the past, when a woman decided to become an amah or samsui, she went through a ritual—a sort of substitute for marriage. Family and friends gathered and even brought gifts. The woman then tied up her hair—to indicate she wasn't available for marriage—and moved to a *gongxi,* or communal house, where she shared expenses and household duties and cared for her sisters.

4 Jamae Mosque. Popularly called Masjid Chulia, the simple, almost austere mosque was built in 1835 by Chulia Muslims from India's Coromandel Coast. So long as it isn't prayer time and the doors are open, you're welcome to step inside for a look (you must be dressed conservatively and take your shoes off before entering; women may need shawls or scarves to cover their heads).

8 Jinriksha Station. This station, built in 1903, was once the bustling central depot for Singapore's rickshaws, which numbered more than 9,000 in 1919. Now there's nary a one, and the station has been converted into a food market on one side and an office block on the other. This is a good place to sit down with a cool drink.

Kreta Ayer. Named after the bullock carts that carried water for cleaning the streets, this is the core of Chinatown.

13 Lau Pa Sat. This market, which looks a lot like a chicken coop, is the largest Victorian cast-iron structure left in Southeast Asia. Already a thriving fish market in 1822, it was redesigned as an octagon by George Coleman in 1834 and redesigned again, as we see it today, in 1894. It has been transformed into a planned food court, with hawker stalls offering all types of Asian fare. By day it's busy with office workers. After 7 PM Boon Tat Street is closed to traffic and the mood turns festive: hawkers wheel out their carts, and street musicians perform.

2 Lorong Telok. Nos. 27, 28, and 29 on this architecturally interesting lane have intricately carved panels above the shop doorways. Across the street are old clan houses whose stonework facades appear to have a Portuguese influence—possibly by way of Malacca (now Melaka), a Portuguese trading post from the 16th century until the Dutch, and then the British, took possession of it.

Mosque Street. The old shophouses here—mercifully spared demolition—were originally built as stables. Now they house Hakka families selling second- or, more likely, third-hand wares, from clothes to old medicine bottles.

10 Nagore Durgha Shrine. This odd mix of minarets and Greek columns was built by South Indian Muslims in 1830. Inside it's now decorated with fairy lights.

Sago Street. At No. 16, Fong Moon Kee, the best *tikar* mats—used by the older Chinese instead of soft mattresses—are sold. They're easy to carry and excellent for picnics, although prices begin at S$60. A cake shop at **No. 34** is extremely popular for fresh baked goods, especially during the Mooncake Festival. Nearby, at **No. 26,** is Ban Yoo Foh Medical Hall, a store that sells dried snakes and lizards, for increasing fertility, and powdered antelope horn, for curing headaches and cooling the body.

Smith Street. Stores here sell chilies, teas, and soybeans. A medicine hall offers ground rhinoceros horn (a controversial product owing to wildlife protection issues) to help overcome impotency (a claim unsupported by science) and pearl dust to help ladies' complexions.

★ ❺ **Sri Mariamman Temple.** The oldest Hindu temple in Singapore, the building has a pagodalike entrance topped by one of the most ornate *gopurams* (pyramidal gateway towers) you are ever likely to see. Hundreds of brightly colored statues of deities and mythical animals line the tiers of this towering porch; glazed cement cows sit, seemingly in great contentment, atop the surrounding walls. The story of this Hindu temple smack in the heart of Chinatown begins with Naraina Pillay, who came to Singapore on the same ship as Raffles in 1819 and started work as a clerk, Singapore's first recorded Indian immigrant. Within a short time, he had set up his own construction business, often using convicts sent over to Singapore from India, and quickly made a fortune. He obtained this site to build a temple on, so that devotees could pray on the way to and from work at the harbor. This first temple, built in 1827 of wood and *attap* (wattle and daub), was replaced in 1843 by the current brick structure. The gopuram was added in 1936. Inside are some spectacular paintings that have been recently restored by Tamil craftsmen brought over from South India. www.gov.sg/heb/temples.html.

Tanjong Pagar Road. The center of an area of redevelopment in Chinatown, the area has 220 shophouses restored to their 19th-century appearance—or rather a sanitized, dollhouselike version of it. They now contain teahouses, calligraphers, mahjong makers, and other shops as well as bars and restaurants. Lively when it first opened, the area has since been somewhat overshadowed by nightlife establishments at Boat Quay and Clarke Quay on the Singapore River.

Temple Street. Here you may be fortunate enough to see one of the few remaining practitioners of a dying profession. Sometimes found sitting on a stool here is a scribe, an old man to whom other elderly Chinese who have not perfected the art of writing come to have their letters written.

⓫ **Thian Hock Keng Temple.** This structure—the Temple of Heavenly Happiness—was completed in 1842 to replace a simple shrine built 20 years earlier. It's one of Singapore's oldest and largest Chinese temples, built on the spot where, prior to land reclamation, immigrants stepped ashore after a hazardous journey across the China Sea. In gratitude for their safe passage, the Hokkien people dedicated the temple to Ma Chu P'oh, the goddess of the sea. Thian Hock Keng is richly decorated with gilded carvings, sculptures, tiled roofs topped with dragons, and fine carved stone pillars. The pillars and sculptures were brought over from China, the exterior cast-iron railings were made in Glasgow, and the blue porcelain tiles on an outer building came from Holland. On either side of the entrance are two stone lions. The one on the left is female and holds a cup, symbolizing fertility; the other, a male, holds a ball, a symbol of wealth. If the temple is open, note that as you enter you must step over a high threshold board. This serves a dual function. First, it forces devotees to look downward, as they should, when entering the temple. Second, it keeps out wandering ghosts—ghosts tend to shuffle their feet, so if they try to enter, the threshold board will trip them.

Inside, a statue of a maternal Ma Chu P'oh, surrounded by masses of burning incense and candles, dominates the room. On either side of her are the deities of health (on the left if your back is to the entrance) and wealth. The two tall figures you'll notice are her sentinels: one can see for 1,000 miles, the other can hear for 1,000 miles. The gluey black substance on their lips—placed there by devotees in days past—is opium, to heighten their senses. While the main temple is Taoist, the temple at the back is Buddhist and dedicated to Kuan Yin, the goddess of mercy. Her many arms represent how she reaches out to all those who suffer on earth. This is a good place to learn your fortune. Choose a number out of the box, then pick up two small, stenciled pieces of wood at the back of the altar and let them fall to the ground. If they land showing opposite faces, then the number you have picked is valid. If they land same-side up, try again. From a valid number, the person in the nearby booth will tell you your fate, and whether you like it or not, you pay for the information. Leave the grounds by the alley that runs alongside the main temple. The two statues to the left are the gambling brothers. They will help you choose a lucky number for your next betting session; if you win, you must return and place lighted cigarettes in their hands.

3 Wak Hai Cheng Bio Temple. Built around 1826 by Teochew Chinese from Guangdong Province and dedicated to the goddess of the sea, this temple was restored in 1998. Its wonderfully ornate roof is covered with decorations—including miniature pagodas and human figures—depicting ancient Chinese villages and scenes from opera. Chinese temples, incidentally, are invariably dusty, thick with incense, and packed with offerings and statuary—evidence of devotees asking for favors and offering thanks for favors granted. To a Chinese, a sparkling clean, spartan temple would suggest unsympathetic deities with few followers. Where burning joss sticks have left a layer of dust and continue to fill the air with scent, the gods are willing to hear requests and grant wishes. If word spreads that many wishes have been realized by people visiting a particular temple, it can, virtually overnight, become the most popular temple in town.

1 Yeo Swee Huat. At No. 15 Upper Circular Road, you'll see a cottage industry designed to help Chinese take care of one obligation to their ancestors: making sure they have everything they need in the afterlife. Here, paper models of the paraphernalia of life—horses, cars, boats, planes, even fake money—are made, to be purchased by relatives of the deceased (you can buy them, too) and ritually burned so that their essence passes through to the spirit world in flames and smoke. Note that although the items may tempt you to chuckle, this custom is a very serious part of Chinese beliefs; try not to offend the proprietors.

Little India

Indians have been part of Singapore's development from the beginning. While Singapore was administered by the East India Company, headquartered in Calcutta, Indian convicts were sent here to serve their time. These convicts left an indelible mark on Singapore, reclaiming land from swampy marshes and constructing a great deal of the city's infrastructure, including public buildings, St. Andrew's Cathedral, and many Hindu temples. The enlightened penal program permitted convicts to study a trade of their choice in the evenings. Many, on gaining their freedom, chose to stay in Singapore.

Other Indians came freely to seek their fortunes as clerks, traders, teachers, and moneylenders. The vast majority came from the south of India—both Hindu Tamils and Muslims from the Coromandel and Malabar coasts—but there were also Gujaratis, Sindhis, Sikhs, Parsis, and Bengalis. Each group brought its own language, cuisine, religion, and customs, and these divisions remain evident today. The Indians also brought their love of colorful festivals, which they now celebrate more frequently and more spectacularly than in India itself. The gory Thaipusam is among the most fascinating (☞ Festivals and Seasonal Events *in* Singapore A to Z *below*).

The area Raffles allotted to the Indian immigrants was north of the British colonial district. The heart of this area—known today as Little India—is Serangoon Road and the streets east and west of it between Bukit Timah and Sungei roads to the south and Perumal Road to the north. Although new buildings have replaced many of the old, the sights, sounds, and smells will make you believe you're in an Indian town.

Numbers in the text correspond to numbers in the margin and on the Little India map.

A Good Walk

Try to plan your walk for a weekday morning, when crowds are at their thinnest and temperatures are at their lowest. Avoid Sunday afternoons, when the neighborhood teems with people. A good starting point is the junction of Serangoon and Sungei roads. As you walk along Serangoon, your senses will be sharpened by the fragrances of curry powders and perfumes, by tapes of high-pitched Indian music, by jewelry shops selling gold and stands selling garlands of flowers. (Indian women delight in wearing flowers and glittering arm bangles, but once their husbands die, they never do so again.) Other shops supply the colorful dyes used to mark the *pottu*—the dot seen on the forehead of Indian women. Traditionally, a Tamil woman wears a red dot to signify that she's married; a North Indian woman conveys the same message with a red streak down the part of her hair. However, the modern trend is for an Indian girl or woman to choose a dye color to match her sari or Western dress. Occasionally you'll see an unmarried woman with a black dot on her forehead: this is intended to counter the effects of the evil eye.

The first block on the left is **Zhujiao Centre** ①, one of the largest wet markets in the city. The streets to the right off Serangoon Road—Campbell Lane and Dunlop Street (home of the highly regarded **Haniffa Textiles** ② at no. 104)—as well as **Clive Street,** which runs parallel to Serangoon, are filled with shops that sell such utilitarian items as pots and pans, rice, spices, brown cakes of palm sugar, red henna powder (a great hair dye), and every other type of Indian grocery imaginable. You'll also see open-air barbershops and tailors working old-fashioned treadle sewing machines, and everywhere you go you'll hear sugar-sweet love songs from Indian movies. Along **Buffalo Road,** to the left off Serangoon, are shops specializing in saris, flower garlands, and electronic equipment. Above the doorways are strings of dried mango leaves, a customary Indian sign of blessing and good fortune. (If you detour down Dunlop Street, to the right off Serangoon Road, you'll come to the **Abdul Gaffoor Mosque** ③, with its detailed facade of green and gold.)

A little farther down Serangoon Road on the left (opposite Veerasamy Road), you'll notice the elaborate gopuram of the **Sri Veeramakaliamman Temple** ④, built in 1881 by indentured Bengali laborers working the lime pits nearby. Take Kinta Road to the **Burmese Buddhist Temple** ⑤ with its 11-ft-tall white marble Buddha. Turn right on Race Course Road to **Farrer Park** ⑥, site of Singapore's original racecourse. Farther along Race Course Road is the charming **Leong San Temple** ⑦, dedicated to the goddess of mercy, Kuan Yin. Across the road is Sakya Muni Buddha Gaya Temple, more commonly referred to as the **Temple of 1,000 Lights** ⑧. Backtrack on Race Course Road to Perumal Road; to the left is the **Sri Srinivasa Perumal Temple** ⑨. Dedicated to Vishnu the Preserver, the temple is easy to recognize by the 59-ft-high monumental gopuram, depicting Vishnu in nine forms. Behind you to your right is the Serangoon Plaza complex on Serangoon Road itself, together with the famed **Mustafa's Centre** ⑩, up Syed Alwi Road, a multistory emporium of goods from both East and West at extremely attractive prices, selling everything from jewelry to electronics and clothing. If you continue along Race Course Road, you'll come to the Banana Leaf Apolo (*sic*), an excellent place for a drink and a curry (☞ Dining, *below*).

TIMING

This whole Race Course Road area is under construction for a new MRT (subway) line and may require a couple of detours while walking. Even so, you should be able to do this tour in three to four hours. Factor in a half an hour extra for the temples.

Sights to See

❸ **Abdul Gaffoor Mosque.** This small, personable temple at No. 41 Dunlop Street has none of the exotic, multicolor statuary of the Hindu temples. But it still woos you with an intricately detailed facade in the Muslim colors of green and gold. When entering, make sure your legs are covered to the ankles, and remember to take off your shoes. Note that only worshipers are allowed into the prayer hall. Out of respect you should not enter during evening prayer sessions or at any time on Friday.

Buffalo Road. Shops here specialize in saris, flower garlands, and electronic equipment. Also along this short street are a number of moneylenders from the Chettiar caste—the only caste that continues to pursue in Singapore the role prescribed to them in India. You'll find them seated on the floor before decrepit desks, but don't let the simplicity of their style fool you: some of them are very, very rich.

❺ **Burmese Buddhist Temple.** Built in 1878, this temple houses an 11-ft Buddha carved from a 10-ton block of white marble from Mandalay. The other, smaller Buddhas were placed here by Rama V, the king of Siam, and high priests from Rangoon, Burma (now called Yangon, Myanmar).

Clive Street. On this byway off Sungei Road, you'll find shops that purvey sugar, prawn crackers, rice, and dried beans. The older Indian women you'll notice with red lips and stained teeth are betel-nut chewers. If you want to try the stuff, you can buy a mouthful from street vendors.

❻ **Farrer Park.** This is the site of Singapore's original racetrack. It's also where the first aircraft to land in Singapore came to rest en route from England to Australia in 1919.

❷ **Haniffa Textiles.** Try this silk shop for a cornucopia of richly colored and ornamented fabrics, scarves, bedspreads, and the like, often at surprisingly affordable prices.

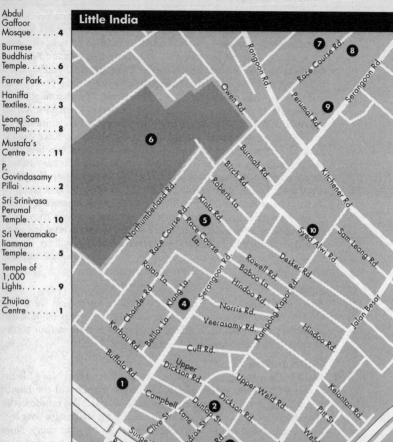

Little India

Its main altar is dedicated to Kuan Yin—also known as Bodhisattva Avalokitesvara—and is framed by beautiful, ornate carvings of flowers, a phoenix, and other birds.

10 Mustafa's Centre. This used to be a humble store favored only by Indian shoppers—until word spread about its low prices and extraordinary variety of goods. It's still unassuming and offers good prices but has expanded to a multilevel store and is patronized by shoppers from all over the world. There's not a lot you can't get here, plus a lot of exotica you might never have thought of, from Indian gold jewelry and saris to Indian foodstuffs and objects for Hindu religious practices.

9 Sri Srinivasa Perumal Temple. Dedicated to Vishnu the Preserver, the temple is easy to recognize by its 60-ft-high monumental gopuram, with tiers of intricate sculptures depicting Vishnu in the nine forms in which he has appeared on earth. Especially vivid are the depictions of Vishnu's manifestations as Rama, on his seventh visit, and as Krishna, on his eighth. Rama is thought to be the personification of the ideal man; Krishna was brought up with peasants and, therefore, was a manifestation popular with laborers in the early days of Singapore. Sri Srinivasa Perumal is very much a people's temple. Inside you'll find devotees making offerings of fruit to one of the manifestations of Vishnu. This is done either by handing the coconuts or bananas, along with a slip of paper with one's name on it, to a temple official, who will chant the appropriate prayers to the deity and place holy ash on your head, or by walking clockwise while praying, coconut in hand, around one of the shrines a certain number of times, then breaking the coconut (a successful break symbolizes that Vishnu has been receptive to the incantation). The Temple is open from 6:30 AM to noon and 6 PM to 9 pm. Dress conservatively, and don't wear shoes inside.

4 **Sri Veeramakaliamman Temple.** Built in 1881 by indentured Bengali laborers working the lime pits nearby, this temple is dedicated to Kali the Courageous, a ferocious incarnation of Shiva's wife, Parvati the Beautiful. Inside is a jet-black statue of Kali, the fiercest of the Hindu deities, who demands sacrifices and is often depicted with a garland of skulls. More cheerful is the shrine to Ganesh, the elephant-headed god of wisdom and prosperity. Perhaps the most popular Hindu deity, Ganesh is the child of Shiva and Parvati. (He was not born with an elephant head but received it in the following way: Shiva came back from a long absence to find his wife in a room with a young man. In a blind rage, he lopped off the man's head, not realizing that it was his now-grown-up son. The only way to bring Ganesh back to life was with the head of the first living thing Shiva saw; he saw an elephant.) Unlike some of Singapore's temples, which are open all day, this one is open only 8 AM–noon and 5:30–8:30 PM. During these times, you will see Hindus going in to receive blessings: the priest streaks devotees' foreheads with *vibhuti,* the white ash from burned cow dung.

8 **Temple of 1,000 Lights.** The Sakya Muni Buddha Gaya is better known by its popular name because, for a small donation, you can pull a switch that lights countless bulbs around a 50-ft Buddha. The entire temple, as well as the Buddha statue, was built by the Thai monk Vutthisasala, who, until he died at the age of 94, was always in the temple, ready to explain Buddhist philosophy to anyone who wanted to listen. The monk also managed to procure relics for the temple: a mother-of-pearl-inlaid cast of the Buddha's footprint and a piece of bark from the bodhi tree under which the Buddha received Enlightenment. Around the pedestal supporting the great Buddha statue is a series of scenes depicting the story of his search for Enlightenment; inside a hollow chamber at the back is a re-creation of the scene of the Buddha's last sermon.

1 **Zhujiao Centre.** One of the largest wet markets in the city, it has a staggering array of fruits, vegetables, fish, herbs, and spices. On the Sungei Road side of the ground floor are food stalls that offer Chinese, Indian, Malay, and Western foods. Upstairs are shops selling brass goods, hardware, shoes, luggage, sports clothing, textiles, and exotic Indian clothing, offering some excellent bargain-priced shopping.

The Arab District

Long before the Europeans arrived, Arab traders plied the coastlines of the Malay Peninsula and Indonesia, bringing with them the teachings of Islam. By the time Raffles came to Singapore in 1819, to be a Malay was also to be a Muslim. Traditionally, Malays' lives have centered on their religion and their villages, known as *kampongs*. These consisted of a number of wood houses, with steep roofs of corrugated iron or thatch, gathered around a communal center, where chickens fed and children played under the watchful eye of mothers and the village elders while the younger men tended the fields or took to the sea in fishing boats. The houses were usually built on stilts above marshes and reached by narrow planks serving as bridges. If the kampong was on dry land, flowers and fruit trees would surround the houses.

All traditional kampongs have fallen to the might of the bulldozer in the name of urban renewal. Though all ethnic groups have had their social fabric undermined by the demolition of their old communities, the Malays have suffered the most, since social life centered on the kampong.

The area known as the Arab District, while not a true kampong, remains a Malay enclave, held firmly together by strict observance of the tenets of Islam. At the heart of the community is the Sultan Mosque, or Masjid Sultan, originally built with a grant from the East India Company to the Sultan of Johor. Around it are streets whose very names—Bussorah, Baghdad, Kandahar—evoke the fragrances of the Muslim world. The pace of life is slower here: there are few cars, people gossip in doorways, and closet-size shops are crammed with such wares as *songkok,* the velvety diamond-shape hats worn by Muslim men; or the lacy white skullcaps presented to *haji,* those who have made the *haj,* as the pilgrimage to Mecca is called; and the tasseled, beaded, and embroidered head-scarflike headgear, *tudong,* favored by devout Muslim women; as well as Indonesian batiks, framed calligraphic verses from holy scriptures, leather bags, and herbs whose packages promise youth, fertility, and beauty.

The Arab District is a small area, bounded by Beach and North Bridge roads to the south and north and spreading a couple of blocks to either side of Arab Street. It's a place to meander, taking time to browse through shops or enjoy Muslim food at a simple café. Much of this neighborhood has undergone extensive renovation since 1996, but this only seems to be adding to the area's quiet charm.

Numbers in the text correspond to numbers in the margin and on the Arab District map.

A Good Walk

This walk begins at the foot of **Arab Street,** a street of specialty shops just off **North Bridge Road.** Wander past the shops and take a right onto Baghdad Street; watch for the dramatic view of the **Sultan Mosque** ① where **Bussorah Street** opens to your left. Leaving the mosque, return to Arab Street and take the first left onto Muscat Street, turn right onto Kandahar Street, and then left onto Baghdad Street. At Sultan Gate, you'll find **Istana Kampong Glam** ②, the sultan's Malay-style palace, built in the 1840s. Baghdad Street becomes Pahang Street at Sultan Gate, where traditional Chinese stonemasons create statues curbside. At the junction of Pahang Street and Jalan Sultan, turn right and, at Beach Road, left, to visit the endearing **Hajjah Fatimah Mosque** ③, built in 1845. It leans at a 6° angle. Return to Jalan Sultan and take a right. Past Minto Road is the **Sultan Plaza** ④, which houses fabric stores. Continue along Jalan Sultan, crossing **North Bridge Road,** to the junction of Victoria Street and the **Malabar Muslim Jama-Ath Mosque** ⑤.

Follow Victoria Street down to **Bugis Street** ⑥. Three blocks beyond where Bugis Street becomes Albert Street—between the Fu Lu Shou shopping complex (whose shops mostly sell clothes) and the food-oriented Albert Complex—is Waterloo Street. Near the corner is the **Kwan Im Thong Hood Cho Temple** ⑦, or just "Kwan Im" for short, one of the most popular Chinese temples in Singapore.

TIMING

This walking tour shouldn't take more than two hours, including stops to look around the temples and mosques. But take your time. This is one of the friendliest areas in Singapore.

Sights to See

★ **Arab Street.** On this street of specialty shops, you'll find baskets of every description—stacked on the floor or suspended from the ceiling. Farther along, shops that sell fabrics—batiks, embroidered table linens, rich silks, and velvets—dominate.

⑥ **Bugis Street.** Until recently, Bugis Street was the epitome of Singapore's seedy but colorful nightlife, famous for the transvestite lovelies who paraded its sidewalks; the government wasn't delighted, though, and the area was razed to make way for a new MRT station. So strong was the outcry that Bugis Street has been re-created (but not really), just steps from its original site, between Victoria and Queen streets, Rochor Road, and Cheng Yan Place. The shophouses have been resurrected; hawker food stands compete with open-fronted restaurants (Kentucky Fried Chicken has a prominent spot on a corner). Closed to traffic, the streets in the center of the block are the places to find bargain watches and CDs; you'll also find the Parco Bugis Junction, an upscale shopping center that's quite a contrast to all the area's dollar stores and souvenir shops.

③ **Hajjah Fatimah Mosque.** In 1845 Hajjah Fatimah, a wealthy Muslim woman married to a Bugis trader, commissioned a British architect to build this mosque. (Hajjah is the title given to a woman who has made the pilgrimage to Mecca.) The minaret is reputedly modeled on the spire of the original St. Andrew's Church in colonial Singapore, but it leans at a 6° angle. No one knows whether this was intentional or accidental, and engineers brought in to see if the minaret could be straightened have walked away shaking their heads. Islam forbids carved images of Allah. The only decorative element usually employed is the beautiful flowing Arabic script in which quotations from the Qur'an (Koran) are written across the walls. This relatively small mosque is an intimate oasis amid all the bustle. It's extremely relaxing to enter the prayer hall (remember to take your shoes off) and sit in the shade of its dome. French contractors and Malay artisans rebuilt the mosque in the 1930s. Hajjah Fatimah, her daughter, and her son-in-law are buried in an enclosure behind the mosque.

② **Istana Kampong Glam.** The sultan's Malay-style palace is more like a big house than a palace. It was built in the 1840s on the site of an even simpler thatched building, to a design by George Coleman. Next door is another grand royal bungalow: the home of the sultan's first minister. Notice its gateposts surmounted by green eagles. Neither building is open to the public—they are awaiting a new life as possible Malay cultural or arts centers—but through the gates you can get a glimpse of the past.

⑦ **Kwan Im Thong Hood Cho Temple.** The dusty, incense-filled interior of this popular temple, commonly known simply as "Kwan Im," its altars heaped with hundreds of small statues of gods from the Chinese pantheon, transports you into the world of Chinese mythology. Of the hundreds of Chinese deities, Kwan Im, more often known as Kuan Yin, is perhaps most dear to the hearts of Singaporeans. Legend has it that just as she was about to enter Nirvana, she heard a plaintive cry from

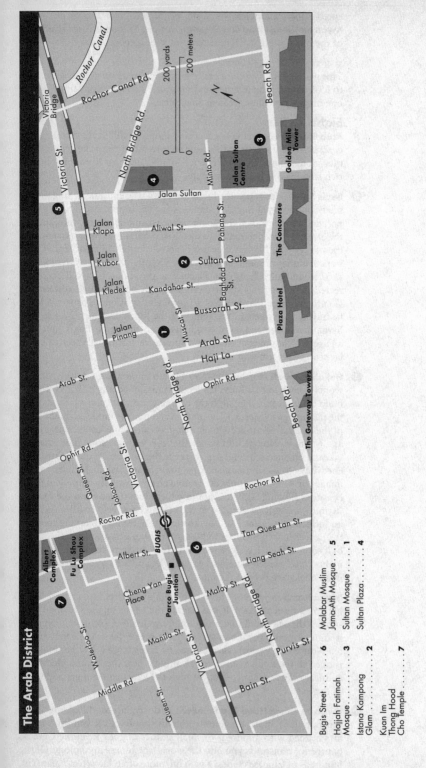

The Arab District

Bugis Street 6
Hajjah Fatimah
Mosque 3
Istana Kampong
Glam 2
Kuan Im
Thong Hood
Cho Temple 7
Malabar Muslim
Jama-Ath Mosque. ...5
Sultan Mosque 1
Sultan Plaza........ 4

Earth. Filled with compassion, she gave up her place in Par[ ] vote herself to alleviating the pain of those on Earth; thereupon, [ ] took the name Kuan Yin, meaning "to see and hear all." People in search of advice on anything from an auspicious date for a marriage to possible solutions for domestic or work crises come to her temple, shake *cham si* (bamboo fortune sticks), and wait for an answer. The gods are most receptive on days of a new or full moon.

For more immediate advice, you can speak to any of the fortune-tellers who sit under umbrellas outside the temple. They'll pore over ancient scrolls of the Chinese almanac and, for a few dollars, tell you your future. If the news isn't good, you may want to buy some of the flowers sold nearby and add them to your bathwater. They're said to help wash away bad luck. A small vegetarian restaurant next to the temple, of the same name, serves good food and delicious Chinese pastries.

❺ Malabar Muslim Jama-Ath Mosque. The land on which this mosque sits was originally granted to the Muslim Indian *Jawi Peranakan* (Malayanised) community in 1848 by Sultan Ally Iskander Shah as a burial ground. The mosque they erected here was abandoned and later taken over by the Malabar Muslims (those with ancestors from India or Ceylon, now Sri Lanka), who rebuilt it in 1962.

North Bridge Road. North Bridge Road is full of fascinating stores that sell costumes and headdresses for Muslim weddings, clothes for traditional Malay dances, prayer beads, scarves, perfumes, and much more. Interspersed among the shops are small, simple restaurants that serve Muslim food. Toward the Sultan Mosque, the shops tend to concentrate on Muslim religious items, including *barang haji,* the clothing and other requisites for a pilgrimage to Mecca.

★ ❶ Sultan Mosque. The first mosque on this site was built early in the 1820s with a S$3,000 grant from the East India Company. The current structure, built in 1928 by Denis Santry of Swan & Maclaren—the architect who designed the Victoria Memorial Hall—is a dramatic building with golden domes and minarets that glisten in the sun. The walls of the vast prayer hall are adorned with green and gold mosaic tiles on which passages from the Qur'an are written in decorative Arab script. The main dome has an odd architectural feature: hundreds of brown bottles, stacked five or more rows deep, are seemingly jammed in neck first between the dome and base. No one seems to know why. Five times a day—at dawn, 12:30 PM, 4 PM, sunset, and 8:15 PM—the sound of the muezzin, or crier, calls the faithful to prayer. At midday on Friday, the Islamic sabbath, seemingly every Malay in Singapore enters through one of the Sultan Mosque's 14 portals to recite the Qur'an. During Ramadan, the month of fasting, the nearby streets, especially Bussorah, and the square before the mosque are lined with hundreds of stalls selling curries, cakes, and candy; at dusk, Muslims break their day's fast in this square. Non-Muslims, too, come to enjoy the rich array of Muslim foods and the party atmosphere.

❹ Sultan Plaza. Inside, dozens of traders offer batiks and other fabrics in traditional Indonesian and Malay designs.

Orchard Road

If "downtown" is defined as where the action is, then Singapore's downtown is Orchard Road. Here are some of the city's most fashionable shops, hotels (which often, like the Hilton, for example, have expensive, upscale malls all their own), restaurants, and nightclubs. The street has been dubbed the Fifth Avenue or Bond Street of Singapore, but, air of luxury aside, it has little in common with either of those older, relatively understated marketplaces for the wealthy. Orchard Road is an ultra-high-rent district that's very modern and very, very flashy—especially at night, when millions of lightbulbs, flashing from seemingly every building, assault your eyes. In addition to all those glittering lights and windows, Orchard Road offers a number of sights with which to break up a shopping trip. Still, if the urge to splurge has overtaken the need to sightsee, you'll find additional information on the malls and stores mentioned in this tour *in* Shopping, *below.*

Numbers in the text correspond to numbers in the margin and on the Orchard Road map.

A Good Walk

Start at the bottom of Orchard Road and head toward the junction with Scotts Road, the hub of downtown. You'll see the enormous **Istana** ①, once the official residence of the colonial governor and now that of the president of the republic. Senior Minister Lee Kuan Yew also keeps his office here. On the other side of Orchard Road, and a few steps down Clemenceau Avenue, is the lovely old **Tan Yeok Nee House** ②. Built in 1885 for a wealthy Chinese merchant, the house has served various purposes, including headquarters for the Salvation Army, but now it's being redeveloped. Turn on Tank Road and continue to the **Chettiar Temple** ③, which houses the image of Lord Subramaniam. Return to Orchard Road and turn left. On the right is Cuppage Road, with a market (open every morning) known for imported and unusual fruit and a row of antiques shops.

Returning once more to Orchard Road, you'll pass the block-long **Centrepoint**; immediately after it is **Peranakan Place** ④, a somewhat diluted celebration of Peranakan culture. A bit farther along and on the other side of Orchard Road is the **Mandarin Singapore** ⑤ hotel, which has an interesting art collection. Immediately after the hotel is the monolithic maroon-colored **Ngee Ann City** ⑥ complex. Cross back to the other side of Orchard Road and follow it to the intersection of Scotts Road, where you'll find **Shaw House** ⑦, which has Isetan as its major anchor. A detour up Scotts Road leads to the landmark **Goodwood Park Hotel,** which offers one of the most civilized high teas in town. Farther up Scotts Road is the **Newton Circus** ⑧ food hawker center.

Retrace your steps to the intersection of Scotts and Orchard roads. Walk up the left side of Orchard Road, past the Wheelock Place building that houses the large **Borders** bookstore, as much a social center as a bookstore. Taxi drivers call this section of Wheelock Place "the rocket," and you'll see why. **Planet Hollywood** opened at Liat Towers on Orchard Road in early 1997 and still gets its share of visiting celebrities. As you continue up Orchard Road, the **Palais Renaissance** will be on your right. Just before Orchard turns into Tanglin, you'll find the **Tanglin Shopping Centre** on your left; the second floor has some of the best antiques shops in town. **Tanglin Mall,** at the junction of Tanglin and Napier roads, has chic boutiques and an excellent food court.

TIMING

Orchard Road has so many shopping diversions that you should allow three to four hours for the walk. Allow half an hour for the Chettiar Temple, and, if you are an antiques fan, at least an hour for the Tanglin Shopping Centre.

Sights to See

Centrepoint. One of the liveliest shopping complexes, spacious and impressive Centrepoint has the **Robinsons** department store as its largest tenant. It also has **Marks & Spencer**; leading watch retailer **The Hour Glass**; leading bookshop **Times the Bookshop**; jewelry, silverware,

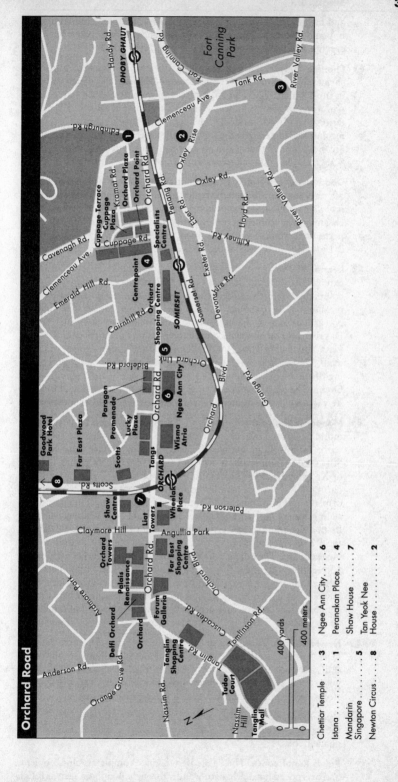

Orchard Road

Chettiar Temple **3**
Istana **1**
Mandarin
Singapore **5**
Newton Circus **8**

Ngee Ann City **6**
Peranakan Place . . . **4**
Shaw House **7**
Tan Yeok Nee
House **2**

and fashion clothing shops; furniture stores that sell Philippine bamboo and Korean chests; and a large basement supermarket. For those craving a Big Mac, a popular **McDonald's** is also here.

❸ Chettiar Temple. This southern Indian temple, home to numerous shrines, is a recent (1984) replacement of the original, which was built in the 19th century. The 75-ft-high gopuram, with its many colorful sculptures of godly manifestations, is astounding. The chandelier-lit interior is lavishly decorated; 48 painted-glass panels are inset in the ceiling and angled to reflect the sunrise and sunset. The temple's daily hours are more limited than those at most Singapore temples; it's open from 8 AM to noon and then again from 5:30 to 8:30.

Goodwood Park Hotel. Though not as well known as the Raffles and 30 years younger (though the building itself dates from 1900), this hotel (☞ *also* Lodging, *below*) is just as much a landmark. Partaking of an elegant afternoon tea here—accompanied by live piano music—is the perfect way to take a break from all that shopping. Tea is served from 2:15 to 5:15 and costs about S$21.

❶ Istana. Built in 1869, this elegant Palladian building set in lush and extensive tropical gardens off Orchard Road once served as the British colonial governor's residence and is now the official residence of the president of the republic. *Istana* means palace in Malay. The building and grounds are open to the public only on fixed holidays: New Year's Day, Hari Raya Puasa (the end of the Muslim fasting month), Chinese New Year, Labor Day, National Day, and the Hindu festival of Deepavali. On the first Sunday of each month, there's a half-hour changing-of-the-guard ceremony at 6 PM on the dot at the main gates on Orchard Road. The office of Singapore's first prime minister, Lee Kuan Yew (he is now the influential Senior Minister, or SM), is at the Istana.

❺ Mandarin Singapore. In the main lobby of this hotel is an exquisite mural delineated by real gold etched into white marble. The 70-ft-long work, by Yuy Tang, is called *87 Taoist Immortals* and is based on an 8th-century Tang scroll. It depicts 87 mythical figures paying homage to Xi Wangmu, Mother of God, on her birthday. While in the Mandarin, you may want to wander around to see the other works of art displayed. In the Mezzanine Lounge is Gerard Henderson's floor-to-ceiling mural *Gift to Singapore*. Henderson, half Chinese and half Irish, also created a powerful series of eight canvases titled *Riders of the World*. Five of these vibrant paintings dominate the wall adjoining the lobby. They depict the untamed and unconquered, including a 13th-century Japanese samurai, a Mandarin of the Ming Dynasty, a 9th-century Moor, and a 20th-century cossack. Don't miss the huge abstract batik mural by Seah Kim Joo, one of Singapore's best-known contemporary artists, that adorns three walls of the Mandarin's upstairs gallery.

❽ Newton Circus. This is one of the best-known hawker centers in town. (The "circus" refers to the rotary, as in Piccadilly Circus.) Some of the stalls are open all day, but the best times to go are either around 9 AM, when a few stalls serve Chinese breakfasts, or after 7 PM, when all the stores are open and the Circus is humming with the hungry.

❻ Ngee Ann City. This mega-mall contains an equally mega-bookshop, the Japanese-owned **Kinokuniya**, which has stacks of English-language books.

Palais Renaissance. The Palais Renaissance complex is chic, opulent, and overpriced but a delight to wander through. Boutiques such as **Ralph**

Lauren, Dunhill, Chanel, and Gucci are for the shopper seeking status labels at high prices.

❹ Peranakan Place. This building on the corner of Orchard and Emerald Hill roads is a somewhat diluted attempt to celebrate Peranakan culture. More interesting is the whole of Emerald Hill Road—a conserved masterpiece of heritage architecture in the Peranakan (also called Straits-born Chinese, Baba, or Nonya) culture style, an innovative blending of Chinese and Malay cultures that emerged in the 19th century as Chinese born in the then Straits Settlements (including Singapore) adopted (and often adapted) Malay fashions, cuisine, and architecture. The area is now a mix of upmarket residences with adaptively renovated shophouses doubling as bars and restaurants, as at Nos. 5 and 7, for instance. Stroll the arcaded street checking out fretted woodwork, pastel wash, ornate wall tiles, and other typical Peranakan touches, such as the unusual carved swing "fence" doors (*pintu pagar*), sometimes with gold-leaf treatments.

☞ Planet Hollywood. The ground floor of the Liat Towers building, formerly home to Galeries Lafayette, the French department store, was transformed into a branch of the now ubiquitous Planet Hollywood. With leopard-print sofas, California cuisine, and film memorabilia adorning the walls, Planet Hollywood remains popular. Teenagers sit across from the entrance waiting for a glimpse of their favorite North American celebrities, who often sign autographs here when in town.

❼ Shaw House. Japan's large Isetan department store is the major anchor in this shopping complex at the corner of Scotts and Orchard roads. There are some interesting specialty boutiques in **Shaw Centre,** the block to the rear of the building bordering Scotts Road and Claymore Hill.

Tanglin Mall. At the corner of Napier and Tanglin roads, this suburban mall was built to cater to the surrounding wealthy neighborhood. It has an excellent food court in its basement.

Tanglin Shopping Centre. There is some excellent shopping here, from fabrics and embroideries collected from the whole region to antiques, carpets, and cameras. The basement level houses restaurants, including the popular Indian vegetarian **Bombay Woodlands.** On one of the upper levels try **Tambuah Mas** for good Indonesian food. The well-known nightspot **Anywhere** is also upstairs, as well as a medical center and **Select Books,** Singapore's only independently owned bookshop, dedicated to books on Asia.

❷ Tan Yeok Nee House. The house was built around 1885 for Tan Yeok Nee (1827–1902), a merchant from China who started out here as a cloth peddler and became a very wealthy man through trade in opium, gambier, and pepper. Whereas most homes built in Singapore at that time followed European styles, this town house was designed in a style popular in South China—notice the keyhole gables, terra-cotta tiles, and massive granite pillars. After the railway was laid along Tank Road in 1901, the house became the stationmaster's. In 1912, St. Mary's Home and School for Girls took it over. Since 1940 the Salvation Army has made the place its local headquarters. The house is now being redeveloped.

Side Trips Around Singapore and Beyond

Although there's a great deal to see and do in Singapore, you may want to escape to areas just outside the city or to small islands just off the coast. A jaunt to the nearby Indonesian island of Bintan—with its pristine shores, mangrove swamps, and hideaway resorts—will no doubt add still more dimension to your Southeast Asia journey.

The East Coast

Two decades ago, Singapore's eastern coastal area contained only co-conut plantations, rural Malay villages, and a few undeveloped beaches. Today, however, it is totally different. At the extreme northeastern tip of the island is Changi International Airport, one of the finest in the world. Between the airport and the city, numerous satellite residential developments have sprung up, and vast land-reclamation projects along the seashore have created a park 8 km (5 mi) long, with plenty of recreational facilities.

Numbers in the text correspond to numbers in the margin and on the East and West Coasts, the Green Interior, and the Sentosa Island maps.

A GOOD TOUR

A trip to the east coast is a relaxing way to spend a morning or after-noon. This two- to three-hour tour is best done by taxi, which will cost you roughly S$8–S$15 each way. Catch a cab at the junction of Nicoll Highway and Bras Basah Road, near the Raffles Hotel and Marina Square.

Nicoll Highway leads onto East Coast Road, and heading east along it, you come to the Kallang area. Cross the Rochor and Kallang rivers by the Merdeka (Independence) Bridge and you'll see, to the left and right, an estuary that was once the haunt of pirates and smugglers. A few shipyards are visible to the left, where the old Bugis trading schooners once anchored. (The Bugis, a seafaring people from the Celebes—now Sulawesi—Indonesia, have a long history as great traders; their schooners, called *prahus*, still ply Indonesian waters.) To the right is the huge National Stadium, where international sporting events are held. Just past the stadium, Mountbatten Road crosses Old Air-port Road, once the runway of Singapore's first airfield. One of the old British colonial residential districts, this area is still home to the wealthy, as attested by the splendid houses in both traditional and mod-ern architectural styles.

Ask the driver to take you up East Coast Parkway, so that you can visit the **Crocodilarium** ① (for still more reptile fun you can head up to the **Singapore Crocodile Farm**) or the **East Coast Park** ②. Stop to eat at the **East Coast Park Food Centre** or the **UDMC Seafood Centre.** Catch another taxi to take you farther east to the infamous **Changi Prison** ③.

SIGHTS TO SEE

❸ **Changi Prison.** This sprawling, squat, sinister-looking place, built in the 1930s by the British, was used by the Japanese in World War II to intern some 70,000 prisoners of war, who endured terrible hardships here. Today it houses some 2,000 convicts, many of whom are here owing to Singapore's strict drug laws. This is where serious offenders are hanged at dawn on Friday.

If you're not part of an organized tour (☞ Tour Operators *in* Singa-pore A to Z, *below*), you can really only visit the **Changi Prison Chapel and Museum,** whose walls hold poignant memorial plaques to those interned here during the war. It's a replica of one of 14 chapels where 85,000 Allied POWs and civilians gained the faith and courage to over-come the degradation and deprivation inflicted upon them by the Jap-anese. The museum contains drawings, sketches, and photographs by POWs depicting their wartime experiences. ☎ 545–1441. ☎ *Dona-tions accepted.* ☉ *Chapel and museum: Mon.–Sat. 10–5; visitors wel-come at 5:30 PM Sun. service.*

Organized guided tours may take you through the old British barracks areas to the former RAF camp. Here, in **Block 151**—a prisoners' hospital during the war—you'll see the simple but striking murals painted by a British POW, bombardier Stanley Warren. (Fax the prison's public affairs department at 764–6119 for approval to view the murals if you're visiting on your own.) The scale of military spending in the 1930s by the British—who put up these well-designed barracks to accommodate tens of thousands of men—is amazing. You can clearly see why the British believed Singapore was impregnable! This is still a military area; most of the barracks are used by Singapore's servicemen during their 2½-year compulsory duty.

❶ **Crocodilarium.** More than 1,000 of the jaw-snapping crocodiles here are bred to be skinned. You can watch crocodile wrestling Tuesday through Sunday at 1:15 and 4:15 PM; a definite feeding time is Tuesday at 11 AM. Naturally, there's a place to buy crocodile-skin bags and belts—at inflated prices. ☎ 447–3722. ⊡ S$2. ⊙ Daily 9–5.

❷ **East Coast Park.** Between the highway and the sea, this park has a wide variety of water sports and other recreational facilities. A cool sea breeze makes it the best place in town for running. (☞ also Outdoor Activities and Sports, below.)

East Coast Park Food Centre. Next to the Europa Sailing Club, this alfresco center offers dining from many stalls and a great view of the harbor.

OFF THE
BEATEN PATH

SINGAPORE CROCODILE FARM – Yet more of these popular creatures—plus alligators, snakes, and lizards—are on view at a 1-acre breeding farm 6½ km (4 mi) northwest of the Crocodilarium. Feeding time is 11 AM Tuesday through Sunday. At the factory, observe the process of turning hides into accessories that—along with imported eel-skin products—are sold at the farm shop. ⊠ 790 Upper Serangoon Rd., ☎ 288–9385. ⊡ Free. ⊙ Daily 8:30–5:30.

UDMC Seafood Centre. This gathering of eight outdoor restaurants is a popular evening destination (☞ also Dining, below).

The West Coast

The satellite city of Jurong is Singapore's main industrial area. It's estimated that more than 70% of the nation's manufacturing workforce is employed here by more than 3,000 companies. Though this may seem an unlikely vacation destination, there are actually several interesting attractions in or around Jurong. A garden environment exists here, demonstrating that an industrial area doesn't have to be ugly.

A GOOD TOUR

West Coast attractions are far from the center of town and far from one another. Allow a half day for each sight (except the Crocodile Paradise, which deserves an hour at most). You can arrange a tour through your hotel or take taxis alone or in combination with the MRT. A cab ride from the center of town to Jurong will cost about S$15. **Haw Par Villa** ④ amusement park is much closer to town than the other sights. The nearest MRT station is Buona Vista Station, from which you must transfer to Bus 200 (though air-conditioned express coach service is available from hotels along Orchard Road). Haw Par Villa is also near one of the main jumping-off points to Sentosa Island, a short ride away, so consider pairing a visit to the villa with one to the island (☞ also Sentosa Island, below).

On another day, you might start with a visit to **Jurong Bird Park** ⑤. An MRT ride to Clementi will cost about S$1.50, depending on where

The East and West Coasts and the Green Interior

Johor Bahru

Causeway

Johor Straits

WOODLANDS

Admiralty Rd. W.

Yishun Ave. 2

Kranji War Memorial

YISHUN

Sarimbun Reservoir

Lim Chu Kang Rd.

Kranji Reservoir

Mandai Rd.

Seletar Reservoir

10

Singapore Zoological Gardens

11

Murai Reservoir

Mandai Orchid Garden

12

Night Safari

Poyan Reservoir

BUKIT PANJANG

Sembawang Rd.

Jalan Bahar

Choa Chu Kang Rd.

Upper Bukit Timah Rd.

Upper Peirce Reservoir

Lower Peirce Reservoir

Upper Thomson Rd.

Kong San Ph Kark S Temple

Bukit Timah

Bukit Timah Expwy.

Pan Island Expwy.

JURONG WEST

Chinese Garden

7

Japanese Garden

8

Singapore Science Centre

9

13

Bukit Timah Nature Reserve

MacRitchie Reservoir

14

Upper Jurong Rd.

Bukit Timah Rd.

Jalan Ahmad Ibrahim

Upper Ayer Rajah Rd.

Holland Rd.

Jurong Reptile Park

5

6

Jalan Buroh

Singapore Mint Coin Gallery

Queensway

Farrer Rd.

Singapore Botanic Gardens

15

Jurong Bird Park

Pandan Reservoir

West Coast Hwy.

Tanglin Rd.

Orchard Rd

Ming Village

Terumbu Retan Laut

Ayah Rajah Rd.

Mt. Faber

Haw Par Villa

4

P. Pesek

P. Merlimau

Telok Blangah Rd.

World Trade Centre Ferry Terminal

P. Ayer Chawan

P. Seraya

P. B

P. Sakra

P. Ayer Merbau

Sentosa Island

P. Bakau

P. Busing

P. Bukom

P. T

P. Ular

P. Hantu

TO
P. SAKENG,
P. SENANG

Sisters' Islands

WEST
MALAYSIA

P. Seletar

Johor Straits

TO DESARU,
MALAYSIA

TO P.
TEKONG

S. Seletar

*P.
Serangoon*

P. Ubin

P. Ketam

*Serangoon
Harbour*

Yio Chu Kang Rd.

PUNGGOL

Punggol Rd.

S. Serangoon

CHANGI

SERANGOON

ng Meng
n Phor
ark See
mple

Central Expwy.

Upper Serangoon Rd.

Tampines Rd.

Loyang Ave.

U. Changi Rd.

**Changi
Airport**

■ **Singapore
Crocodile Farm**

Paya Lebar Rd.

**Changi
Prison**

③

Changi Coast Rd.

Siong Lim
Temple and
Gardens ■

Serangoon Rd.

Pan Island Expressway

BEDOK

New Upper Changi
Rd.

Airport Blvd.

Sims Ave.

East Coast Rd.

Kallang Rd.

Geylang Rd.

KATONG

Mountbatten Rd.

East Coast Parkway

**East Coast
Park Food Centre**

②

N

d Rd.

Nicoll Hwy.

**National
Stadium**

**UDMC
Seafood
Centre**

**East Coast
Park**

① ■

Crocodilarium

**Recreational
Centre**

Straits of Singapore

. Brani

. Tekukor

P. Seringat

Kusu Island

Lazarus Island

St. John's Island

Subway & Rail Lines

- - - - North-South MRT line
——— East-West MRT line
——— Railroad lines
⊖ Subway stop

0   4 miles
0   6 km

you start your journey, and a taxi from here to the park itself will cost another S$5 or so. If you take a taxi the whole way, plan to spend S$30 round-trip. Exploring the park is tiring, so take a break (or two) in one of the on-site restaurants. If you haven't tired of all the fauna, check out the **Jurong Reptile Park** ⑥, directly across the parking lot from the bird park. If, however, you're ready to view some flora, spend your afternoon at the **Chinese Garden** ⑦ and the **Japanese Garden** ⑧ (take the MRT to the Chinese Garden Station to get here).

Alternatively, you could spend your afternoon at the **Singapore Science Centre.** ⑨ If you don't want to spring for a taxi from Orchard Road (about a 20-minute ride), you can take the westbound MRT to the Jurong East Station, and then transfer to Bus 335 or make the 10-minute walk to the Science Centre's Omni-Theatre. Other area sights include the **Singapore Mint Coin Gallery,** where coins are made and displayed, and pottery demonstrations at **Ming Village.**

SIGHTS TO SEE

⑦ Chinese Garden. This 32-acre reconstruction of a Chinese imperial garden (one inspiration for it was the garden of the Beijing Summer Palace) has pagodas, temples, courtyards, and bridges. Lotus-filled lakes and placid streams are overhung by groves of willows. Rental rowboats allow a swan's-eye view of the grounds, and there are refreshment facilities. Within the main garden you'll find the **Ixora Garden,** with several varieties of the showy flowering ixora shrub; the **Herb Garden,** showcasing plants used in herbal medicines; and the **Garden of Fragrance,** where many newlyweds have their photographs taken against stone plaques with auspicious Chinese engravings. If you're coming directly from Singapore, take the MRT to the Chinese Garden stop; it's only a short walk to the garden itself. ☒ *Off Yuan Ching Rd.,* ☎ *264–3455.* ☒ *S$4.50 (includes admission to Japanese Garden).* ☉ *Mon.–Sat., 9–7, Sun. 8:30–7. Last admission at 6 PM daily.*

④ Haw Par Villa. Also known as the Tiger Balm Gardens, the villa presents Chinese folklore in theme-park fashion. Part of an estate owned by two eccentric brothers in the 1930s, after World War II the gardens were opened to the public. They fell into disarray and were sold to a soft-drink-bottling company that spent S$85 million on their transformation. Haw Par Villa was reopened in late 1990, but has since fallen into disarray once again and now awaits a final decision on its fate. For those interested in its bizarre interpretations of Chinese mythology, religion, and social mores, the many odd little tableaux are intriguing. But the villa has very little else to offer, pending its hoped-for revival in the near future. ☒ *262 Pasir Panjang Rd.,* ☎ *774–0300.* ☒ *S$5.* ☉ *Daily 9–5.*

⑧ Japanese Garden. Adjacent to the Chinese Garden, this delightful formal garden is one of the largest of its kind outside Japan. Its classic simplicity, serenity, and harmonious arrangement of plants, stones, bridges, and trees induce tranquillity. (Indeed, the garden's Japanese name, Seiwaen, means "Garden of Tranquillity.") A miniature waterfall spills into a pond full of water lilies and lotus. ☒ *Off Yuan Ching Rd.,* ☎ *264–3455.* ☒ *S$4.50 (includes admission to Chinese Garden).* ☉ *Mon.–Sat. 9–7, Sun. 8:30–7; last admission at 6 PM daily.*

⑤ Jurong Bird Park. Built on 50 landscaped acres, the park hosts the world's largest walk-in aviary, with a 100-ft man-made waterfall (the world's tallest), and another exquisite walk-in Southeast Asian Birds Aviary, where a tropical thunderstorm is simulated daily at noon. More than 8,000 birds from 600 species are here, including impressive displays of hornbills and hummingbirds, a "Parrot Paradise," and penguins. In stark contrast, the view from Jurong Hill is of the factories that crank out Singapore's economic success. For an overview of the park with sweeping vistas, consider taking the 10-minute ride on the Panorail, an air-conditioned monorail train.

If you arrive early, try breakfast at the Lodge on Flamingo Lake or catch the **Lory Feeding** at 9:30, at the huge Waterfall Aviary. From here you can walk over to the **Penguin Feeding** (held at 10:30). At 10 and 11 AM, and again at 3 and 4 PM), you might catch the JBP All Star Bird-Show, at the **Pools Amphitheatre.** The nocturnal-bird house allows a glimpse of owls, night herons, frogmouth, kiwi, and others usually cloaked in darkness. The bee-eaters and starlings are fed at 10:30 AM and 11:30 AM; you can be fed throughout the day at the **Waterfront Cafe** or **Burger King.** ⊠ *2 Jurong Hill, Jalan Ahmad Ibrahim,* ☎ *265– 0022.* 🎫 *S$12, Panorail S$2.* ⊙ *Daily 8–6.* 🐦

👆 ❻ **Jurong Reptile Park.** Singaporeans seem to be fascinated with crocs, and at this 5-acre park you'll find 18-ft specimens. You can feed the crocodiles, watch muscle-bound showmen (and a showlady) wrestle with them, or buy crocodile-skin products at the shop. You can also watch the beasts through glass, in an underwater viewing gallery. But there's more: king cobra snakes, iguana lizards, colorful chameleons, and giant tortoises for starters, more than 50 species in all. A seafood restaurant and fast-food outlets provide refreshments, and there are rides for children. ⊠ *241 Jalan Ahmad Ibrahim,* ☎ *261–8866.* 🎫 *S$7.* ⊙ *Daily 9–6; wrestling at 11:45, 2, and again at 4 on weekends/holidays.* 🐦

Ming Village. At this small complex of buildings not far from the Jurong Bird Park, demonstrations of the art of Chinese pottery-making are given, and copies of Ming Dynasty blue-and-white porcelain are produced and sold. ⊠ *32 Pandan Rd.,* ☎ *265–7711.* 🎫 *Free.* ⊙ *Daily 9–5:30.*

Singapore Mint Coin Gallery. Close to the ☞ Singapore Science Centre and just east of the Boon Lay MRT station, you can watch minting operations. There are also displays of coins, medals, and medallions from Singapore and around the world. ⊠ *20 Teban Garden Crescent,* ☎ *566–2626.* 🎫 *Free.* ⊙ *Weekdays 9:30–4:30.*

👆 ❾ **Singapore Science Centre.** Here, subjects such as aviation, nuclear science, robotics, astronomy, and space technology are entertainingly explored through 650 audiovisual and interactive exhibits. You can walk into a "human body" for a closer look at vital organs or test yourself on computer quiz games. You'll also find a flight simulator of a Boeing 747 and the Omni Theatre, which presents two programs: "Oasis in Space" travels to the beginning of the universe and "To Fly" simulates the feel of space travel. Children of any age are sure to get a thrill from the brave new world of science presented here. ⊠ *Science Centre Rd., off Jurong Town Hall Rd.,* ☎ *560–3316.* 🎫 *S$3; Omni Theatre S$5.* ⊙ *Tues.–Sun. 10–6, Omni Theatre till 9.* 🐦

Into the Garden Isle

Singapore is called the Garden Isle, and with good reason. While giving economic progress more than its fair share of attention, the government has also established nature reserves, gardens, and a zoo. This excursion from downtown takes you into the center of the island to enjoy some of its greenery. If you have only a little time to spare, at least visit the zoo—it's truly exceptional. If you want to learn more about Singapore's natural habitats and plant life, contact the **National Parks Board** (☎ 325– 7473 or 474–1165; www.nparks.gov.sg), the **Nature Society (Singapore)** (☎ 741– 2036; www.post1.com/home/naturesinsingapore), or the **Singapore Environment Council** (☎ 337–6062, 🐦).

Much of Singapore's natural world is miles from the center of the city. Because of the heat, walking through nature here is tiring, so you probably won't be able to see all the sights in one day. Taxis or hotel tours are the favored ways of getting to the orchid garden, the zoo, and the Night Safari—all of which you can tour in the space of an afternoon and an evening. The **Mandai Orchid Garden** ⑩ is a must for flower lovers; a taxi here from the center of town will cost about S$16, or you can take SBS Bus 138 from the Ang Mo Kio MRT station. Spend about an hour here, then visit the **Singapore Zoological Gardens** ⑪. The taxi ride here from the orchid garden will cost about S$6 (though you can also take Bus 138). If you arrive by 3 PM sharp, you'll be in time for tea with an orangutan. You can then get a good look at the zoo before it closes at 6 and head over to **Night Safari** ⑫ for dinner in the restaurant at its entrance (the grounds don't open till 7:30).

To reach the **Bukit Timah Nature Reserve** ⑬ take Bus 171, which departs from the Newton MRT station. From the Orchard MRT station to **MacRitchie Reservoir** ⑭ it's about a S$6.50 taxi ride. Plan to spend about S$4 on a cab to reach the **Singapore Botanic Gardens** ⑮ from the city center, or you can catch Bus 7, 105, 106, 123, or 174 from the Orchard MRT station. Allow two hours for the Botanic Gardens and another two for the reservoir. Allow about three hours for the nature reserve.

On a trip to this area, culture vultures can work in visits to the **Kong Meng San Phor Kark See Temple** and the **Siong Lim Temple and Gardens**; nature lovers can check out the **Seletar Reservoir**; and history buffs can stop by the **Kranji War Memorial.**

⑬ **Bukit Timah Nature Reserve.** If you like your nature a little wilder than what's found in manicured urban parks, then this is the place for you. In these 405 acres around Singapore's highest hill (535 ft), the rain forest runs riot, giving you a feel for how things might have been when tigers roamed the island. Wandering along structured, well-marked paths among towering trees, tangled vines, and prickly rattan palms, you may be startled by a troupe of long-tailed macaques, squirrels, tree-shrews, or, if you're really lucky, a flying lemur. The view from the hilltop is superb. Wear good walking shoes—the trails are rocky, sometimes muddy, paths. You can buy trail maps from the visitor center. ⊠ *177 Hindhede Dr.,* ☎ *800/468–5736.* ☒ *Free.* ⊙ *Daily 8:30–6:30.*

Kong Meng San Phor Kark See Temple. The Bright Hill Temple, as it's commonly known, is a relatively modern complex of Buddhist temples typical of the ornate Chinese style, with much gilded carving. ⊠ *88 Bright Hill Dr., 1½ km (1 mi) west of Bishan MRT station.*

Kranji War Memorial. This cemetery, a tribute to the forces who fought to defend Singapore in World War II, is in the north of the island, near the causeway off Woodlands Road. Rows of Allied dead are grouped with their countrymen in plots on a peaceful, well-manicured hill. A visit here is a touching experience, a reminder of the greatness of the loss in this and all wars.

⊙ ⑭ **MacRitchie Reservoir.** This 30-acre park has a jogging track with exercise areas, a playground, and a tea kiosk. The path around the reservoir is peaceful, with only the warbling of birds and chatter of monkeys to break your reverie. Crocodile-spotting became a favorite pastime after baby crocs were found in the reservoir in early 1996. Don't go in the water. ⊠ *Lornie Rd., near Thomson Rd.,* ☎ *no phone.* ☒ *Free.* ⊙ *Daily dawn–dusk.*

⑩ **Mandai Orchid Garden.** Less than a kilometer down the road from the zoo (TIBS Bus 171 links the two) is a commercial orchid farm. The hillside is covered with the exotic blooms, cultivated for domestic sale and export. There are many varieties to admire, some quite spectacular. However, unless you are an orchid enthusiast, and since it is a good 30-minute taxi ride from downtown, a visit here is worth it only when combined with a visit to the zoo. The ☞ **Singapore Botanic Gardens** are closer to downtown and also have orchids. ✉ *Mandai Lake Rd.,* ☎ *269–1036.* 🎫 *S$2 (refunded if you make a purchase).* ◎ *Weekdays 8:30–5:30.*

★ ☚ ⑫ **Night Safari.** Right next to the ☞ **Singapore Zoological Gardens,** the safari is the world's first wildlife park designed exclusively and especially for night viewing. Here 80 acres of secondary jungle provide a home to 1,200 animals (100 species) that are more active at night than during the day. Some 90% of tropical animals are, in fact, nocturnal, and to see them active—instead of snoozing—gives their behavior a new dimension. Night Safari, like the zoo, uses a moat concept to create open, natural habitats; areas are floodlit with enough light to see the animals' colors, but not enough to limit their normal activity. You're taken on a 45-minute tram ride along 3 km (2 mi) of road, stopping frequently to admire the beasts (some of which, like the deer and the tapirs, can get quite close to the tram) and their antics. On another kilometer or so of walking trails you can observe some of the small cat families, such as the fishing cat; primates, such as the slow loris and tarsier; and the *pangolin* (scaly anteater). Larger animals include the Nepalese rhino (the largest of rhinos, with a single, mammoth horn) and the beautifully marked royal Bengal tigers—which are somewhat intimidating to the nearby mouse deer—*babirusa* (pig deer with curled tusks that protrude through the upper lip), *gorals* (wild mountain goats), and *bharals* (mountain sheep). ✉ *80 Mandai Lake Rd.,* ☎ *269–3411.* 🎫 *S$15.45.* ◎ *Daily 7:30 PM–midnight.*

Seletar Reservoir. Larger and wilder than the MacRitchie Reservoir, the Seletar is the largest and least developed natural area on the island. ✉ *Mandai Rd., near the zoo,* ☎ *no phone.* 🎫 *Free.* ◎ *Daily dawn–dusk.*

★ ⑮ **Singapore Botanic Gardens.** The gardens were begun in 1859 and carry the hallmarks of Victorian garden design—gazebos, pavilions, and ornate bandstands included. This is still one of the world's great centers of botanical scholarship, attracting international scientists to its herbarium and library; the gardens' work on orchid hybridization and commercialization for export has been pathbreaking. Botanist Henry Ridley experimented here with rubber-tree seeds from South America; his work led to the development of the region's huge rubber industry and to the decline of the Amazon basin's importance as a source of the commodity.

Spread over some 128 acres, the grounds contain a large lake (with black swans from Australia), masses of shrubs and flowers, and magnificent examples of many tree species, including fan palms more than 90 ft high. Don't miss the 10-acre natural remnant rain forest. Locals come here to stroll along nature walks, jog, practice tai chi, feed geese, or just enjoy the serenity. There is an excellent visitor center and garden shop, with a restaurant. The newly established **Economic Garden** and eco-lake extension at the Bukit Timah side of Cluny Road is a lovely open site with interesting displays of commercial, culinary, and medicinal crops and herbs. ✉ *Corner of Napier and Cluny Rds.,* ☎ *471–7361 or 471–9943.* 🎫 *Free.* ◎ *Daily 5 AM–midnight.* 🌿

Inside the Botanic Gardens is the 7.4-acre **National Orchid Garden,**
opened in 1995. Here you can see more than 400 orchids and some 2,000
orchid hybrids, a total of 60,000 plants. ⊠ *S$2.* ☉ *Daily 8:30–6.*

★ ☾ ⓫ **Singapore Zoological Gardens.** You get the impression that animals
come here for a vacation and not, as is often the case elsewhere, to serve
a prison sentence. The Singapore zoo, which is set in the middle of natural rain forest with stunning views of nearby reservoir lakes, has an
open-moat concept, wherein a wet or dry moat separates the animals
from the people. (Interestingly, a mere 3-ft-deep moat will keep humans
and giraffes apart, for a giraffe's gait makes even a shallow trench impossible to negotiate. A narrow water-filled moat prevents spider monkeys from leaving their home turf for a closer inspection of visitors.)
Few zoos have been able to afford the huge cost of employing this system, which was developed by Carl Hagenbeck, who created the Ham-
burg, Germany, zoo at the turn of the century. The Singapore zoo has
managed by starting small and expanding gradually. It now sprawls
over 69 acres of a 220-acre forested area.

Try to arrive at the zoo in time for the buffet breakfast. The food itself isn't special, but the company is. At 9:30 AM, Ah Meng, a 24-year-
old orangutan, comes by for her repast. She weighs about 250 pounds,
so she starts by taking a table by herself, but you're welcome to join
her for a snack. (Ah Meng also takes tea promptly at 4.) The zoo has
used massive glass viewing windows to great effect: not only can you
watch polar bears perform "ballet" underwater and pygmy hippos do
less graceful things, but you can also observe big cats like lions and
jaguars in the eye and close up. At the reptile house, be sure to seek
out the Komodo dragon lizards, which can grow to 10 ft in length.
The primate displays are striking, too, and the orangutan enclosure shows
off the world's largest captive orangutan group. New is the educational
"Fragile Forest" exhibit, which displays complete rain forest ecosystems. Some animals are even free-ranging, conditioned to stay in the
zoo by territorial needs, as well as by free food and shelter. In all there
are about 3,000 animals from around 160 species to view.

At the primate-and-reptile show, monkeys, gibbons, and chimpanzees
have humans perform tricks, and snakes embrace volunteers from the
audience. There are performances by fur seals, elephants, free-flying
storks, and other zoo inhabitants at various times throughout the day.
⊠ *80 Mandai Lake Rd.,* ☎ *269–3411 or 269–3412.* ⊠ *S$12; break-
fast or tea with Ah Meng S$15.* ☉ *Daily 8:30–6; breakfast with Ah
Meng Tues.–Sat. 9–10 AM; high tea at 4; animal showtimes 10:30, 11:30
AM, 12:30, 2:30, and 3:30 PM daily; additional times on weekends/hol-
idays.* ⊗

Siong Lim Temple and Gardens. The largest Buddhist temple complex
in Singapore was built by two wealthy Hokkien merchants between
1868 and 1908. Set among groves of bamboo, the temple is guarded
by the giant Four Kings of Heaven, in full armor. There are a number
of shrines and halls, with many ornate features and statues of the
Lord Buddha. The goddess of mercy, Kuan Yin, has her shrine behind
the main hall; another hall houses a number of fine Thai Buddha images. The oldest building in the complex is a small wood shrine containing antique murals of the favorite Chinese legend "Pilgrimage to
the West." ⊠ *184 E. Jalan Toa Payoh, about 1 km (½ mi) east of the
Toa Payoh MRT station.*

Sentosa Island

In 1968 the government decided that Sentosa, the Isle of Tranquillity,
would be transformed from the military area it was into a resort play-

ground, with museums, parks, golf courses, restaurants, and hotels (☞ Lodging, *below*). A lot of money has been spent on development, and some Singaporeans find Sentosa an enjoyable getaway. However, this "pleasure park" is likely to hold little interest for travelers who have come 10,000 miles to visit Asia, a fact lost on the Singapore government. That said, there are two good reasons to visit the island: the visual drama of reaching it—particularly via cable car—and its fascinating wax museum.

In addition to all its historical and scientific exhibitions, Sentosa has a nature walk through secondary jungle; a *pasar malam* (night market) with 40 stalls, open Friday–Sunday 10–6 PM; campsites by the lagoon and tent rentals; and a wide range of recreational activities. You can swim in the lagoon and at a small ocean beach, though owing to all the cargo ships—you'll see hundreds of them anchored off the coast—the waters leave a lot to be desired. If golf is your game, consider a few rounds at the Sentosa Golf Club (☞ Outdoor Activities and Sports, *below*), or putt away on one of WonderGolf's 45 uniquely landscaped greens.

The best way to make the 2-km (1-mi) trip to Sentosa is by cable car (small gondolas that hold four passengers each). Other options include a shuttle bus or taxi via the causeway or a ferry ride (☞ *also* Getting Around *in* Singapore A to Z, *below*). The island's S$6 admission price will get you into many attractions, though some have separate entrance fees. Sentosa has Southeast Asia's first monorail, which operates daily from 9 AM to 10 PM. It has stations close to the major attractions (a recording discusses each sight as you pass it), and unlimited rides are included in the price of the island admission. A free bus can also take you to most of the sights; it runs daily from 7–10:30 at 10-minute intervals. A small train runs along the south coast for about 3 km (2 mi); bicycles are available for rent at kiosks throughout the island; and, of course, you always have your own two feet. For more information about Sentosa and its facilities, call the **Sentosa Development Corporation**'s Sales Department (☎ 275–0388, ✑).

Numbers in the text correspond to numbers in the margin and on the Sentosa Island map.

A GOOD TOUR

This tour will take three to four hours; longer if you linger at the beach or visit VolcanoLand or WonderGolf. Start at the World Trade Centre, where you'll take a ferry or cable car (from the nearby station) to Sentosa. Between the ferry terminal and the cable car station on the Sentosa side are **WonderGolf** and **Asian Village & Adventure Asia** ①, a mini–theme park (the **Fountain Gardens** and **Sentosa Orchid Garden** are also nearby). From Asian Village you can follow the signs to **Images of Singapore** ②, a combined wax, animatronics, and multimedia museum that gives you an idea of Singapore's history and cultures. Close by is the **Butterfly Park and World Insectarium** ③. After seeing all the bugs, board the monorail for a trip to **Underwater World** ④, a popular aquarium. Next to that, you'll find **Fort Siloso** ⑤, an old British fort whose cannons were pointed the wrong way during World War II. From here, take the monorail again to the swimming lagoon.

After a drink at the **Sunset Bar,** where you can sit on the wooden deck, gaze out at the view, and watch the nonstop volleyball, head up the hill behind the bar to the **Merlion** ⑥, Singapore's 10-story mascot. The view from the top is good—the city and the container port on one side, the harbor, the refineries, and the Indonesian islands of Bintan and Batam on the other. Such watery scenery gets you in the mood for the **Mar-**

itime Museum ⑦, which is due east from the Merlion. On the way there, you can stop at **VolcanoLand** or **Fantasy Island.**

SIGHTS TO SEE

❶ Asian Village & Adventure Asia. Adjacent to the ferry terminal, this village contains cultural and architectural displays representing East Asia, South Asia, and Southeast Asia, as well as a mock fisherman's *kelong,* or stilted fishing platform, and a "kids' kampong," where you can fish as well as feed Japanese koi and ducks. In each village, street performances, demonstrations, merchandise, and food stalls do what they can to add life to an eclectic mix that, for example, combines Thai and north Sumatran architecture in one village and a Japanese torii gate and a Chinese teahouse in another. At Adventure Asia you can try more than 8 amusement rides. ⌧ *Asian Village: free. Fisherman's Kelong tour: S$10. Kid's Kampong visit: S$12.50 per hour, more for fishing. Adventure Asia: S$10.* ⊙ *Daily 10–9.*

❸ Butterfly Park and World Insectarium. This park has a collection of 2,500 live butterflies from 50 species, 4,000 mounted butterflies and insects, plus lots of other insects—like tree-horn rhino beetles, scorpions, and tarantulas—that still creep, crawl, or fly. The park has an Asian landscape with a moon gate, streams, and bridges. ⌧ *S$6.* ⊙ *Daily 9–6:30.*

Fantasy Island. This is a great place to escape Singapore's heat. Among other attractions, you'll find a water slide and an action river with whitewater rapids. ⌧ *S$16.* ⊙ *Fri.–Tues. 10:30–7.*

NEED A
BREAK?

You may want to enjoy high tea or an early dinner at the **Rasa Sentosa Food Centre,** open daily 10 AM–10:30 PM, next to the ferry terminal. More than 40 stalls offer a variety of foods for alfresco dining in groomed tropical surroundings.

❺ Fort Siloso. The fort covers 10 acres of gun emplacements and tunnels created by the British to fend off the Japanese. Unfortunately, the Japanese arrived by land (through Malaysia) instead of by sea, so the huge guns were pointed in the wrong direction. The displays have been successfully revamped recently with lots of interactive high-tech audiovisual and animatronic effects. Photographs document the war in the Pacific, and dioramas depict the life of POWs during the Japanese occupation. ⌧ *S$3.* ⊙ *Daily 9–7.*

Fountain Gardens. Several times each evening, visitors to the gardens, conveniently close to the ferry terminal, are invited to dance along with the illuminated sprays from the fountains to classical or pop music. This activity is not for introverts. Performances by traditional-dance groups are sometimes held.

★ **❷ Images of Singapore** This museum stands out from all the rest of Sentosa's attractions. It's best known for its excellent war-history displays, but it offers much more. Galleries trace the development of Singapore and depict the characters who profoundly influenced its history. Though the wax figures aren't the most lifelike, the scenes and the running narrative offer a vivid picture of 19th-century life in Singapore and a rare opportunity, in modern Singapore, to ponder the diversity of cultures that were thrust together in the pursuit of trade and fortune. In the Surrender Chambers, wax tableaux show the surrender of the Allies to the Japanese in 1942 and the surrender of the Japanese to the Allies in 1945. Photographs, documents, and audiovisuals highlight events during the Japanese occupation and the various battles that led to their defeat. Other sections offer faithful depictions of traditional lifestyles and festivals. ⌧ *S$5.* ⊙ *Daily 9–9.* ✎

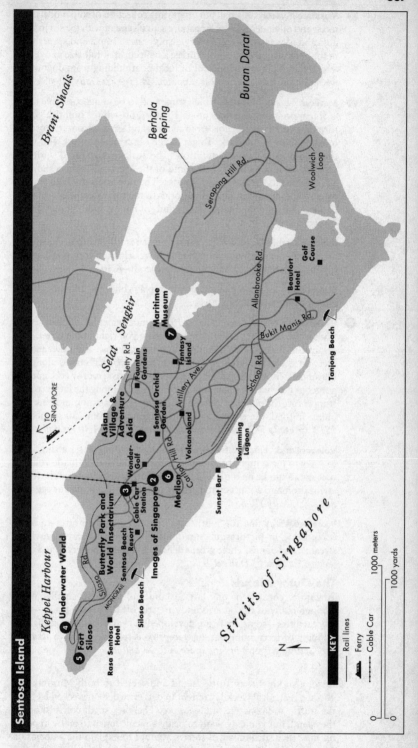

Sentosa Island

Brani Shoals

Buran Darat

Berhala Reping

Woolwich Loop

Seropong Hill Rd

Golf Course

Allanbrooke Rd.

Beaufort Hotel

Maritime Museum **7**

Bukit Manis Rd.

Selat Sengkir

Jetty Rd.

Fountain Gardens

Fantasy Island

Tanjong Beach

TO SINGAPORE

Asian Village & Adventure Asia **1**

Sentosa Orchid Garden

Artillery Ave.

School Rd.

Wonder-Golf **2**

Merlion **6**

Volcanoland

Swimming Lagoon

Keppel Harbour

Underwater World **4**

Butterfly Park and World Insectarium **3**

Cable Car Station

Images of Singapore **2**

Sunset Bar

Fort Siloso **5**

Rasa Sentosa Hotel

Sentosa Beach Resort

Siloso Beach

Siloso Rd.

MONORAIL

Straits of Singapore

KEY
Rail lines
Ferry
Cable Car

1000 meters
1000 yards

N

🐾 ➐ **Maritime Museum.** A small but interesting collection of ship models, pictures, and other items show Singapore's involvement with the sea in business and in war. A fishing gallery displays nets, traps, and spears used in the area throughout the centuries; a collection of full-size native watercraft traces the development of local boatbuilding from dugout canoes to Indonesian *perahus* (sailboats). ✉ *Free.* ☉ *Daily 10–6.*

🐾 ➏ **Merlion.** This monument, which some find to be in questionable taste, is Singapore's tourism mascot—a 10-story, off-white "lion fish" creature that emits laser beams from its eyes and smoke from its nostrils. It even glows in the dark. To get to the observation tower, you walk through a pirate cave exhibition. The walls are covered with TV screens, some showing "The Legend of the Merlion," others showing advertisements for the rest of Sentosa. The ride up to the 10th story is by elevator, then you climb two stories to the top where there's a view of Singapore and the Indonesian islands of Batam and Bintan. ✉ *S$3.* ☉ *Daily 9–10.*

🐾 **Sentosa Orchid Garden.** This exotic garden is filled with orchids from around the world. You'll also find a flower clock, a carp pond, and a Japanese teahouse. ✉ *S$3.50.* ☉ *Daily 9:30–6:30.*

Sunset Bar. Expatriates hang out here to play volleyball and other beach games to the beat of rap music.

🐾 ➍ **Underwater World.** Completed in 1991, Underwater World reverses the traditional aquarium experience by placing you right in the water. Two gigantic tanks house thousands of Asian-Pacific fish and other marine life; you walk through a 100-yard acrylic tunnel that curves along the bottom. There are sharks, giant octopus, stingrays, moray eels, and the gorgeous little weedy sea dragons of Australia. Among the latest crowd-stoppers are the piranhas, electric eels, a *dugong* (sea-cow), and pink dolphins. In total, there are 2,500 marine creatures from 250 species. ✉ *S$13.* ☉ *Daily 9–9; feeding times 11:30 AM, 2, and 4:30 PM daily.* 🐠

🐾 **VolcanoLand.** This multisensory theme attraction creates a simulated journey to the center of the earth, complete with a man-made volcano that spews smoke on the half-hour. There are also exhibits on the Maya civilization and a journey to prehistory to view real dinosaur eggs. ✉ *S$12.* ☉ *Daily 10–8.*

🐾 **WonderGolf.** A first for Southeast Asia, this course features 45 holes for putting in picturesque surroundings, including caves, ravines, streams, and ponds. Three greens deliver different experiences and challenges. ✉ *S$8.* ☉ *Daily 9–9.*

The Outer Islands

Singapore consists of one large island and some 60 smaller ones. Though many of the outer islands are still off the beaten track—with few facilities—some are being developed as beach destinations. Island hopping by ferry, bumboat, or water taxi is relatively easy to arrange. (☞ Getting Around *in* Singapore A to Z, *below*).

KUSU

Kusu, also known as Turtle Island and sacred to both Muslims and Taoists, is an ideal weekday retreat (it gets crowded on weekends) from the traffic and concrete of Singapore. There's a small coffee shop on the island, but you may want to bring a picnic lunch to enjoy in peace on the beach. A number of stories attempt to explain the association with turtles; all the tales in some way relate to a turtle that saved two shipwrecked sailors—one Chinese and one Malay—who washed up on the shore. Turtles now are given sanctuary here, and an artificial pond honors them with stone sculptures.

The hilltop **Kramat Kusu** (shrine) is dedicated to a Malay saint—a pious man named Haji Syed Abdul Rahman, who, with his mother and sister, is said to have disappeared supernaturally from the island in the 19th century. To reach the shrine, you climb the 122 steps that snake up through a forest. Plastic bags containing stones have been hung on the trees by devotees who have come to the shrine to pray for forgiveness of sins and the correction of wayward children. If their wishes are granted, believers must return the following year to remove their bags and give thanks.

Tua Pekong, a small, open-fronted Chinese temple, was built by Hoe Beng Watt in gratitude for the birth of his child. The temple is dedicated to Da Bo Gong, the god of prosperity, and the ever-popular Kuan Yin, goddess of mercy. Here she's also known by her Chinese surname, Sung Tzu Niang ("Giver of Sons"), and is associated with longevity, love of virtue, and fulfillment of destiny. Sung Tzu had a difficult childhood. She was determined to become a nun, but her father forbade it. When she ran away to join an order, he tried to have her killed. In the nick of time she was saved by a tiger and fulfilled her destiny. In gratitude, she cut off her arm as a sacrifice. This so impressed the gods that she was then blessed with many arms. Hence, when you see her statue in many of the Chinese temples in Singapore, she is depicted with six or eight arms. This temple has become the site of an annual pilgrimage. From late October to early November (or in the ninth lunar month), some 100,000 Taoists bring exotic foods, flowers, joss sticks, and candles, and pray for prosperity and healthy children.

PULAU UBIN

Here amid the *kelongs* (fishing huts) and duck and prawn farms the lifestyle for the island's 200 residents hasn't changed much in 30 years. This is a natural haven for plants, birds (145 recorded species), and insects found in its mangrove and forest areas. There are colorful Thai *Ma Chor* temples along the seashore.

ST. JOHN'S ISLAND

St. John's was first a leper colony, then a prison camp. Later it became a place to intern political enemies of the republic, and now it has become an island for picnicking and overnight camping. Without any temples or particular sights, it is quieter than Kusu. Colonial bungalows are available for rent from counters at the World Trade Centre. There are plans to develop camping facilities, which will surely take away some of the peaceful solitude one can experience here now.

SISTERS' ISLANDS

Some of the most beautiful of the southern islands are the best for snorkeling and diving. To get there, you'll have to hire a water taxi (S$50 per hour) at the Jardine Steps or Clifford Pier or take an organized day cruise (check with your hotel). Some of the boatmen know where to find the best coral reefs. If you plan to dive, be advised that the currents can be very strong.

Bintan Island, Indonesia

From the tallest building in Singapore you can see the nearby islands of Indonesia's Riau Archipelago. In 45 minutes, you can cross the straits on a ferry (☞ *also* Getting Around *in* Singapore A to Z, *below*) south to the Batam Islands. Batam is not only a tourist centre but also an important commercial base that includes a duty-free industrial zone. However, Batam and its resorts have been overshadowed by the more interesting island of Bintan.

Today the *orang laut* (sea people; island inhabitants who are descendants of pirates and traders) still live in houses on stilts over the sea—

an interesting contrast to the six modern beach resorts here. Overnight trips to Bintan, more than twice the size of Singapore, can include a stay at a five-star hotel with your own private pool or a more adventurous jaunt in a sampan to the 16th-century palace of a Malaysian sultan. Make hotel reservations as far in advance as possible (☞ Lodging, *below*). You may also want to consider booking a guided tour of the island (☞ Contacts and Resources *in* Singapore A to Z, *below*). Note that citizens of Canada, the United Kingdom, and the United States need only passports for stays in Indonesia of less than one month.

SIGHTS TO SEE

Bintan's main town is **Tanjung Pinang,** where the primary activity is shopping at **Pasar Pelantar Dua.** Tanjung Pinang is a jumping-off point for some interesting nearby sites.

You can take a tour from Tanjung Pinang's Pelentar Pier up the **Snake River** through the mangrove swamps to the oldest **Chinese temple** in Riau. As the boatman poles his way up the small tributary choked with mangroves, the sudden view of the isolated 300-year-old temple with its murals of hell will send chills down your spine. Have the boatman take you back down the river to **Tanjung Berakit,** where tiny huts perch on stilts. Friendly villagers live in spartan homes without electricity or water—this only an hour and a half from Singapore.

Another good stop by motorboat is **Pulau Penyengat** (Wasp Island), once the heart of the Riau sultanate and the cultural hub of the Malay empire. In the 16th century, the Malay sultanate fled here after being defeated by the Portuguese in Malacca. The island is just 15 minutes by motorboat from Tanjung Pinang's Pelentar Pier. Sites include royal graves, the banyan-shrouded ruins of the palace, and the **Mesjid Raya** (Sultan's Mosque)—a bright yellow building that was plastered together with egg yolks.

DINING

Singapore offers the best feast in the East. You'll find restaurants that serve home-grown Nonya (or Peranakan) fare; others that specialize in cuisine from all parts of Asia; and still others that offer European and American dishes. Some cultures consider atmosphere, decor, and service more important than food. In Singapore, however, the food's the thing, and its enjoyment is a national pastime. You're as likely to find gourmet cooking (and high standards of cleanliness) in unpretentious food stalls as you are in elegant eateries.

Many of the poshest restaurants are in hotels. Such establishments offer fine dining, complete with the freshest ingredients, displays of roses and orchids, polished silver and gleaming crystal, waiters dressed in tuxedos, and impeccable service. Several hotels also offer high tea (generally served 3 PM–6 PM at a cost of about S$30 per person without tax or service charge). The Singapore version of this British tradition is usually served buffet style and includes dim sum (called *dian xin* here) and fried noodles as well as finger sandwiches and scones. Standout teas include those at the Four Seasons, Goodwood Park, The Oriental, Raffles, and The Ritz-Carlton.

If you prefer coffee and a casual setting to tea in formal surroundings, you'll be pleased to note that alfresco coffeehouses have taken Singapore by storm. Starbucks, Spinellis, Coffee Club, and Delifrance have locations everywhere and are very popular despite the humidity. Five years ago there was but one outdoor café in the city. People would flock to air-conditioned establishments to seek relief from the heat, just as

Westerners run indoors from the rain or snow. But lately, it has become trendy to meet friends for a coffee or bubble tea—flavored tea with bits of jelly for texture—at outdoor patios, some of which feature a light cool mist sprayed over patrons by large fans. Widespread building restoration has given rise to several chic dining addresses. Boat Quay—a riverside strip of cafés, restaurants, and bars—may well be the busiest place in town at night. Restaurants to look for here include Our Village (North Indian) and House of Sundanese (Sundanese). At Clarke Quay, another massive restoration project, you can dine on a moored *tongkang*, a type of boat that once plied the river; sample the horrible-to-smell but good-to-eat local fruit called durian at Durian House; or try seafood at Key Largo, Thai cuisine at Thanying Restaurant, or Mediterranean fare at Bastiani's. The popular Satay Club, which was located near the Padang, has moved "upstream" to Clarke Quay. Here you can sample a variety of satay sticks with peanut sauce for a small price. Nearby Robertson Quay is slowly beginning to take shape, with new stores and restaurants being built with the charm of the riverside in mind. Other dining areas include Chinatown's Tanjong Pagar—with such trendy restaurants as Da Paolo (Italian) and L'Aigle d'Or (French).

Food is a route to cultural empathy, especially if it's consumed at a stir-fry stall (fondly called "wok-and-roll" stalls) or at a vendor's stall in an open-air hawker center. You'll find many stir-fry stalls—most are half restaurant and half parking lot—on East Coast Road. They open at about 5 PM and serve such simple, freshly cooked dishes as deep-fried baby squid and steamed prawns—accompanied, of course, by fried noodles.

The hawker centers have quite a history. At one time, food vendors moved through the streets, each one serving a single dish (often made using a secret family recipe). A hawker advertised by sounding a horn, knocking bamboo sticks together, or simply shouting. Hearing the sound, people dashed from their houses to place orders. After everyone had eaten, the hawker collected and washed the crockery and utensils and continued up the road. Many hawkers might have passed a house in a day. Several years ago, the government gathered the hawkers into large centers for reasons of hygiene (and rest assured that everything is *very* clean; health authorities are strict). Today, these centers enable you to see the raw materials and watch the cooking methods in stall after stall. Then you simply find a seat at a table, note the table number, relate your order and this number to the vendor, and sit down to wait for your food. (Someone will come to your table to take a drink order.) Though you sometimes pay at the end of the meal, paying when you place your order is more the norm. Most dishes cost S$4 or slightly more; for S$12, you can get a meal that includes a drink and fresh fruit for dessert.

Nearly every major shopping center has a hawker center or food court, although prices there tend to be on the high side. The sheltered hawker center at Marina South has hundreds of stalls. The most touristy open-air center is the raucous, festive Newton Circus. Come here for the experience, but avoid the seafood stalls, which are known to fleece tourists. Feast instead at stalls that offer traditional one-dish meals and that have prices displayed prominently. (When you place an order, specify whether you want a S$2, S$3, or S$4 portion.) Other open-air centers include the historic Lau Pa Sat Festival Market in the downtown financial district, Telok Ayer Transit Food Centre on Shenton Way, and Bugis Square at Eminent Plaza. Indoor, air-conditioned food centers are a great way to beat the midday heat. Those in the Orchard Road area include Picnic in the basement of Scotts Centre and the Food Chain in the basement of Orchard Emerald (opposite and just down from the Mandarin Singapore hotel). The following are dishes and food names that you'll often encounter at hawker centers:

char kway teow—flat rice noodles mixed with soy sauce, chili paste, fish cakes, and bean sprouts and fried in lard.

Hokkien prawn mee—fresh wheat noodles in a prawn-and-pork broth served with freshly boiled prawns.

laksa—a one-dish meal of round rice noodles in coconut gravy spiced with lemongrass, chilies, turmeric, shrimp paste, and shallots. It's served with a garnish of steamed prawns, rice cakes, and bean sprouts.

mee rebus—a Malay version of Chinese wheat noodles with a spicy gravy. The dish is garnished with sliced eggs, pieces of fried bean curd, and bean sprouts.

rojak—a Malay word for "salad." Chinese rojak consists of cucumber, lettuce, pineapple, *bangkwang* (jicama), and deep-fried bean curd—tossed with a dressing made from salty shrimp paste, ground toasted peanuts, sugar, and rice vinegar. Indian rojak consists of deep-fried lentil and prawn patties, boiled potatoes, and deep-fried bean curd, all served with a spicy dip sweetened with mashed sweet potatoes.

roti prata—an Indian pancake made by tossing a piece of wheat-flour dough into the air until it's paper-thin and then folding it to form many layers. The dough is fried until crisp on a cast-iron griddle, then served with curry powder or sugar. An ideal breakfast dish.

satay—small strips of meat marinated in fresh spices and threaded onto short skewers. A Malay dish, satay is barbecued over charcoal and eaten with a spiced peanut sauce, sliced cucumbers, raw onions, and pressed rice cakes.

thosai—an Indian rice-flour pancake that's a popular breakfast dish, eaten with either curry powder or brown sugar.

In sit-down restaurants, plan on small servings of four to five dishes for four people or three dishes for two people. Food is either served family-style—placed all at once at the center of the table so everyone can dig in—or, for more formal meals, served a course at a time, again with diners sharing from a single dish at the center of the table. Each diner is given a plate or bowl of rice. Most Chinese restaurants automatically add a charge of about S$2 per person for tea, peanuts, pickles, and rice.

Most restaurants are open from noon to 2:30 or 3 for lunch and from 6:30 to 10:30 PM (last order) for dinner. Some hotel coffee shops, such as Oscar's at the Conrad International Centennial and the Indian coffee shops along Changi Road, are open 24 hours a day; others close between 2 and 6 AM. At hawker centers, some stalls are open for breakfast and lunch while others are open for lunch and dinner. Late-night food centers such as Eminent Plaza in Jalan Besar are in full swing until 3 AM.

For classic, time-honored cooking minus the usual "service with a smile" and linen tablecloths, head to Geylang in the eastern part of Singapore. Geylang, once part of the city housing brothels and gambling houses, is a bit downscale but is as safe at 3 AM as it is on Orchard Road. Although the privately run brothels are still there, a number of new budget hotels have sprung up and a new housing and shopping development is planned for the area. Hawker stalls abound, serving *kway teow* and noodles and rice of every variety; for the chile eaters, *popiah* or *rojak* are popular choices. On the weekends, Geylang is a 24-hour food fest, in full swing at 2 AM. The locals come here to eat before retiring, and are often seen lining up at their favorite stalls.

The area is full of old Singapore architecture, much of it in various stages of restoration. Nearby is the Malay Village at Paya Lebar MRT stop. Here you will find an excellent variety of Malay/Indonesian special-ties—*nasi goreng, nasi padang, rendang, atchar*—served in copious amounts.

Competition among Singapore's restaurants has kept the overall meal prices low, but liquor has remained expensive. A cocktail or a glass of wine costs S$8–S$12; a bottle of wine is a minimum of S$50. Seafood is inexpensive (though expensive delicacies such as shark's fin, dried abalone, and lobster are served in some Chinese restaurants). Dishes marked "market price" on the menu are premium items. Before ordering, find out exactly how much each dish will cost, and don't be surprised if you're charged for the napkins and cashew nuts that arrive at the start of your meal. Note that smoking is banned in air-conditioned restau-rants and banquet/meeting rooms, though many establishments now offer outdoor patios with a seating area for smokers.

What to Wear

Except at the fancier hotel dining rooms, Singaporeans don't dress up to eat out. The weather calls for lighter wear than a jacket and tie. (Some restaurants tried to enforce a dress code for men but found that their customers went elsewhere to eat. Now an open-neck shirt and a jacket represent the upper limit of formality.) Generally, though, shorts, sleeveless cotton T-shirts, and track suits aren't appropriate for hotel restaurants but are fine for hawker centers and food courts. After the sun goes down, lightweight long pants and evening wear are expected. If you're sensitive to cold, bring a sweater—many restaurants are air-conditioned to subarctic temperatures.

Chinese

$$$$ ✕ **Chang Jiang.** Meals in this Goodwood Park hotel (☞ Lodging, *below*)
★ Shanghainese restaurant are served Western-style (portions are presented on dinner plates, and you don't serve yourself from a central platter). The kitchen staff was trained by the chef of Shanghai's leading restau-rant, Yang Zhou. Recommended dishes are the chicken and goose sur-prise, fresh crabmeat in a yam basket, baby kale with scallops, and sliced beef stir-fried and served with leeks. Presentation is an art here. Even the chopsticks are gold-plated. The service and surroundings are very formal. ⊠ *22 Scotts Rd.,* ☎ *737–7411. AE, DC, MC, V.*

$$$$ ✕ **Hai Tien Lo.** Sit in the right place at this 37th-floor restaurant and you'll get a view of the sea, the Padang, and City Hall. The Cantonese cuisine, the decor, and the service are all extremely elegant: plates are changed with every course, waitresses wear *cheongsams* (Chinese dresses with high collars and side slits) with black with gold trim. For lunch, opt for the dim sum, priced at a premium because of the top-quality ingredients. Other specialties include roast chicken with crispy golden-brown skin and tender, juicy flesh; beef cubes fried with black pepper and oyster sauce; and deep-fried fresh scallops stuffed with minced prawns and tossed in a salty black-bean sauce. The pièce de résistance is Monk Jumps over the Wall—dried abalone, whole chicken, ham, fish stomach lining, dried scallops, and shark's fin steamed together for hours. At S$100 per serving (or S$1,000 for 10 people), it's one of the most expensive dishes in town, but the broth is the best in the world—the really rich simply drink it and leave the rest. ⊠ *The Pan Pacific, Ma-rina Square, 6 Raffles Blvd.,* ☎ *336–8111. AE, DC, MC, V.*

$$$$ ✕ **Jiang Nan-Chun.** On the second floor of the Four Seasons hotel (☞
★ Lodging, *below*), this dining room is home to the innovative creations of one of the youngest master chefs in Singapore, Sam Leong. His de-

Singapore Dining

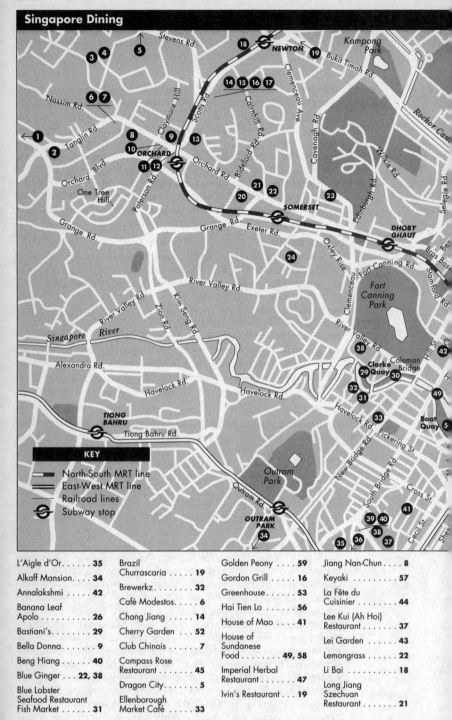

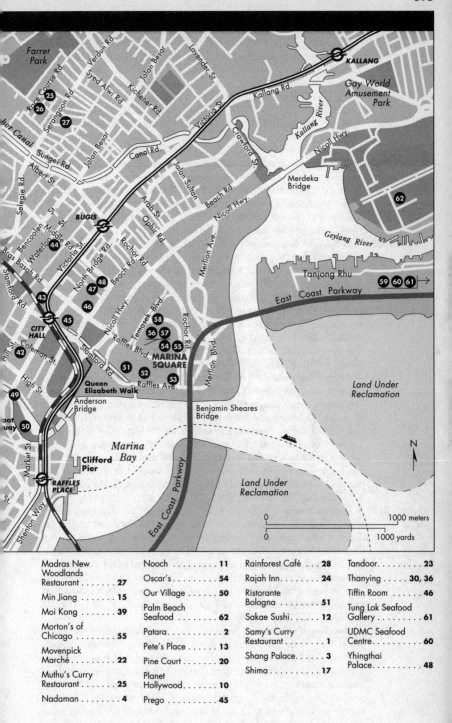

Madras New Woodlands Restaurant 27

Min Jiang 15

Moi Kong 39

Morton's of Chicago 55

Movenpick Marché 22

Muthu's Curry Restaurant 25

Nadaman 4

Nooch 11

Oscar's 54

Our Village 50

Palm Beach Seafood 62

Patara 2

Pete's Place 13

Pine Court 20

Planet Hollywood 10

Prego 45

Rainforest Café . . . 28

Rajah Inn 24

Ristorante Bologna 51

Sakae Sushi 12

Samy's Curry Restaurant 1

Shang Palace 3

Shima 17

Tandoor 23

Thanying 30, 36

Tiffin Room 46

Tung Lok Seafood Gallery 61

UDMC Seafood Centre 60

Yhingthai Palace 48

licious Cantonese food has Thai and Japanese influences. Although a set menu is offered, the restaurant's regular customers often request the chef's favorites, which may include deep-fried scallops with pear sauce, baked oysters with bok choy, or fried prawns with sesame and lime mayonnaise. The presentation is unusual and artistic (the double-boiled seafood soup, for example, is served in a hollowed coconut), the service is attentive, and the ambience is understated and relaxed. ⊠ *190 Orchard Blvd.,* ☎ *734–1110. Reservations essential. AE, DC, MC, V.*

$$$$ ✕ **Shang Palace.** Locals and expats alike frequent this elegant Cantonese dining room in the Shangri-La hotel (☞ Lodging, *below*). Large and decorated in brilliant red and gold, the room can be noisy during a full house, but the delicious food more than compensates. The staff is very knowledgeable about the menu. Try the prawns deep fried with minced shrimp and sesame seeds, or the steamed asparagus served with a poached egg and caviar. For connoisseurs, there are more than 11 Chinese teas from which to choose. ⊠ *22 Orange Grove Rd.,* ☎ *737– 3644. Reservations essential. AE, DC, MC, V.*

$$$–$$$$ ✕ **Li Bai.** The dining room in the Sheraton Towers hotel (☞ Lodging,
★ *below*) evokes richness without overindulgence—deep maroon wall panels edged with black and backlighted, elaborate floral displays, jade table settings, ivory chopsticks. The service is very fine, as is the cooking, which is modern and innovative, yet deeply rooted in the Cantonese tradition. The chef's unusual creations include deep-fried diamonds of egg noodles in a rich stock with crabmeat and mustard greens; fried lobster in black-bean paste; and double-boiled shark's fin with Chinese wine and *jinhua* ham. The restaurant seats approximately 100 people. ⊠ *39 Scotts Rd.,* ☎ *737–6888. AE, DC, MC, V.*

$$$ ✕ **Cherry Garden.** At The Oriental hotel (☞ Lodging, *below*), a
★ wooden-roof pavilion with walls of antique Chinese brick encloses a landscaped courtyard that makes a fine setting for a meal. The artwork is tastefully chosen and displayed, the service is impeccable, and the Hunanese food is a welcome change from the usual Cantonese fare. Try the minced-pigeon broth with dried scallops steamed in a bamboo tube or, in season, served in a fragrant baby melon; the superior Yunnan honey-glazed ham served between thin slices of steamed bread; or the camphor-smoked duck in a savory bean-curd crust. ⊠ *Marina Square, 5 Raffles Ave.,* ☎ *331–0538. AE, DC, MC, V.*

$$$ ✕ **Golden Peony.** "Refined" is the word that best describes everything—from the service and the table settings to the decor and ambience—in the Cantonese dining room at the Conrad International Centennial Singapore hotel (☞ Lodging, *below*). All dishes are exquisitely prepared and ultrafresh. Specialties include deboned crispy chicken with bean curd skin and Yunnan ham (eaten like a sandwich); steamed crab claw in Hua Tiao wine and ginger juice; and steamed Canadian bass and salmon with mushrooms. ⊠ *2 Temasek Blvd.,* ☎ *334–8888 or ext. 7482. AE, DC, MC, V.*

$$$ ✕ **Min Jiang.** Housed in a Chinese pavilion on the grounds of the Goodwood Park hotel (☞ Lodging, *below*), Min Jiang is always packed, thanks to its delicious Szechuan food, fast service, and longtime manageress, the friendly Shirley Neow. The decor is attractive—a restrained and elegant interpretation of Chinese style. The camphor-smoked duck and the long beans fried with minced pork are favorites. Any dish you choose will be pleasing to the palate, and the staff is eager to make recommendations. ⊠ *22 Scotts Rd.,* ☎ *737–7411. AE, DC, MC, V.*

$$$ ✕ **Pine Court.** Baked tench, marinated lamb, and fried dry scallops are just a few of the dishes that distinguish the Pekingese cooking at this restaurant in the Mandarin Singapore hotel (☞ Lodging, *below*). The restaurant's Peking duck is famed for its crisp, melt-in-your-mouth skin and delicate pancake wrapping. Dinner here is the best meal; the more economical lunch (frequently a buffet) is less inspired. The carved-wood wall panels will make you feel as if you're in a Chinese mansion; the acclaimed service is fine and caring. ✉ *333 Orchard Rd.,* ☎ *737–4411. AE, DC, MC, V.*

$$–$$$ ✕ **Dragon City.** Many Singaporeans consider Dragon City to be the best
★ place for Szechuan food. Set in a courtyard and entered through a flamboyant, red, moon-gate door, the large dining room looks Chinese but is not particularly appealing. All artistry is reserved for the food. Choose from such delicious staples as kung po chicken, minced-pork soup in a whole melon, steamed red fish with soybean crumbs, or smoked duck. The service is fast. If you don't quite know how to order your meal, ask for Wang Ban Say, the restaurant's manager and one of the owners. ✉ *Novotel Orchid Inn, Plymouth Wing, 214 Dunearn Rd.,* ☎ *250–3322. AE, DC, MC, V.*

$$–$$$ ✕ **Imperial Herbal Restaurant.** The Chinese believe that "you are what you eat" and that food can be used to maintain or restore health. In the Metropole Hotel's (☞ Lodging, *below*) unique restaurant, an herbalist—rather than a chef—runs the kitchen, and there's a traditional pharmacy near the entrance where herbs are stored (and sold). The menu includes dishes that are decidedly exotic as well as those that are deceptively simple. A must is the delicate quick-fried egg white with scallops and herbs served in a crunchy nest of potato threads. The eel fried with garlic and fresh coriander and the eggplant with pine nuts are equally delicious; the crispy fried ants on prawn toast are not only a conversation piece but totally inoffensive. It's nice to know that the food that's satisfying your taste buds is also doing you good. Beer and wine are available, as are restorative tonics and teas. ✉ *41 Seah St., 3rd floor,* ☎ *337–0491. AE, MC, V.*

$$–$$$ ✕ **Lei Garden.** This aesthetically pleasing restaurant has built up a devoted following with branches in Hong Kong and Kowloon. The food represents the nouvelle Cantonese style with its pristine tastes and delicate textures. One old-fashioned item is the soup of the day, cooked just the way mother did—assuming that mother had the time to stew a soup lovingly for many hours over low heat. The menu also offers a long list of double-boiled tonic soups (highly prized by the Chinese), barbecued meats, and seafood (including a variety of shark's fin dishes). Dim sum is available and extremely popular at lunch; recommendations include Peking duck, grilled rib-eye beef, and fresh scallops with bean curd in black-bean sauce. ✉ *Chijmes, No. 01–24, 30 Victoria St.,* ☎ *339–3822. AE, DC, MC, V.*

$$–$$$ ✕ **Long Jiang Szechuan Restaurant.** Perhaps the greatest draw of this restaurant in the Crown Prince Hotel (☞ Lodging, *below*) is the "all-you-can-eat" offer. For a set price (around S$24), you can sample nearly 40 items on the menu, including hot-and-sour soup, shark's fin soup, smoked duck, and kung po chicken. It's not unlike most other Chinese restaurants in appearance, but the service is above average. ✉ *270 Orchard Rd.,* ☎ *732–1111. AE, DC, MC, V.*

$$ ✕ **Beng Hiang.** At this restaurant in a restored shophouse just outside the financial district, you'll find peasant-style Hokkien cooking: hearty, rough, and delicious. *Kwa huay* (liver rolls) and *ngo hiang* (pork-and-prawn rolls) are very popular and are eaten dipped in sweet plum sauce. *Hay cho* (deep-fried prawn dumplings) are another Hokkien staple. Beng Hiang also serves *khong bak* (braised pig's feet) and what is reputedly the best roast suckling pig in Singapore. ✉ *112–116 Amoy St.,* ☎ *221–6695. Reservations not accepted. No credit cards.*

$$ ✕ **House of Mao.** Opened in the spring of 1998 to great fanfare, this kitschy, pop-art homage to the late dictator is an amalgamation of Warhol meets Julia Child's favorite Chinese (specifically, Hunanese) dishes. The memorabilia and the staff's Red Army uniforms are only two of the reasons to come; the tasty, contemporary Hunanese food is the third. The service can be uneven due to the crowds that have been flocking here since its opening. ⊠ *No. 03-02 China Square Food Centre, 51 Telok Ayer St.,* ☎ *533–0660. Reservations not accepted. AE, DC, MC, V.*

$$ ✕ **Lee Kui (Ah Hoi) Restaurant.** This unassuming storefront restaurant in the heart of Chinatown serves you at large tables (if your party is small, you may have to share a table with others); it's busy, noisy, and often crowded. The distinctive flavors of Teochew cuisine are evident: try the cold crab as a starter, followed by winter melon soup, prawns with young chives and *ngohiang* (minced pork rolls). Your glass of tea will be constantly replenished. It may be helpful to go with a Man-darin-speaking person, as the staff speaks little English. ⊠ *46 Mosque St.,* ☎ *222–3654. Reservations not accepted. No credit cards.*

$$ ✕ **Moi Kong.** At this unpretentious Chinese (Hakka) eatery, try the prawns fried with red-wine lees, the steamed chicken with wine, or the *khong bak mui choy* (braised pork in dark soy sauce with a preserved salted green vegetable), delicious with rice. ⊠ *22 Murray St.,* ☎ *221–7758. Reservations not accepted. AE, DC, V.*

Continental

$$$$ ✕ **Gordon Grill.** The Scottish country/hunting lodge look here is light-
★   ened with apple greens, light-wood chairs, and glass panels etched with delicate drawings of Scottish lairds. The decor is at once formal and casual, lending itself to comfort above all. Tradition is served up here in excellent roast beef and steak, but the menu also surprises with the more adventurous and delicious local pan-fried Ikan Kurau—a white-fish like haddock—served on a bed of spinach, and ratatouille with tape-nade sauce. The lobster thermidor keeps regular patrons coming back for more, sometimes "to go." The sherry trifle is wonderful and the hot-chocolate pudding is a must for chocoholics. ⊠ *22 Scotts Rd.,* ☎ *737–7411. AE, DC, MC, V.*

$$$$ ✕ **Morton's of Chicago** To the dedicated meat eater, Morton's is the ul-timate steakhouse. The Morton's chain consists of 52 restaurants around the globe, one of which has taken up residence on the fourth floor of The Oriental hotel. Morton's old-world charm, played out in dark-wood paneling, linen napkins and tablecloths, and muted lighting, is com-plemented by piped-in jazz music. As the evening progresses, so does the noise level. The Morton's menu is known for its USDA prime aged beef, which is flown in from Chicago (this may account for the high prices, a nonissue for the serious carnivore). An artful presentation of the various cuts of beef is served up by the helpful and friendly staff, who delight in customers' reactions to the size of their orders. A huge loaf of egg-onion bread comes with every meal. Suggestions include shrimp Alexander, which can be ordered as an appetizer or main course, Mor-ton's salad with blue-cheese dressing, and the porterhouse—the signa-ture steak. Portions are huge and pricey, so it is advisable to order extras, like veggies, to share. If you still have room for dessert, try the key lime pie or Godiva hot chocolate cake. ⊠ *Marina Square, 5 Raffles Ave.,* ☎ *339–3740. AE, DC, MC, V. No lunch.*

Eclectic

$$$$ ✕ **Greenhouse.** Saturday nights are smoking with live jazz at the Greenhouse in the lobby of The Ritz-Carlton, Millenia Singapore (☞ Lodging, *below*). While there's nothing special about the decor, the less-than-usual concoctions on offer at the buffet covers all the bases, from Californian to Asian to Mediterranean. Ever had pizza for breakfast? Try one with smoked bacon and egg—a real eye-opener. ⊠ *7 Raffles Ave.,* ☎ *434–5285. AE, DC, MC, V.*

$$$$ ✕ **Oscar's.** Wining and dining take on hedonistic dimensions at Oscar's. This trendy 24-hour restaurant is lively, especially during the popular wine buffet, when for two hours, seven days a week, guests can sample and savor more than 10 types of free-flowing red and white wines during a dinner of international fare (choose from the buffet or à la carte menu). The Sunday brunch boasts more than 70 items to choose from, including breakfast staples such as cereals and Danish, appetizers, soups, salads, and a myriad main courses: sushi, baby lobster and salmon, barbecued and grilled meats, and a delectable array of cakes, tarts, crêpes, and soufflés. Children can entertain themselves at the children's corner while the adults indulge in this epicurean feast. ✉ *Conrad International Centennial Singapore, 2 Temasek Blvd.,* ☎ *334–8888. AE, DC, MC, V.*

$$$ ✕ **Bastiani's.** Mediterranean food with New World accents stars at this
★ restaurant in a restored riverside warehouse. Downstairs there's a comfortable bar and a patio; upstairs the spacious dining room has a terrace (where renegade smokers can indulge in their habit). With its Asian rugs on polished wood floors, eclectic furniture, and open kitchen—hung with garlic, salamis, and the like—Bastiani's has a casual elegance. The menu changes every two months, but it always emphasizes fresh vegetables and herbs; grains such as couscous and polenta; and grilled or baked poultry, red meat, and fish. Pizza is cooked in a wood-fired oven. The more than 4,000 bottles in the wine cellar should satisfy the most fastidious wine buff. ✉ *Clarke Quay,* ☎ *433–0156. AE, DC, MC, V.*

$$$ ✕ **Brazil Churrascaria.** An all-you-can-eat salad bar with hot and cold delights and more meat than you can shake a stick at are the high points of this new find off of Bukit Timah Road. Fifteen different cuts of meat are served every day but Tuesdays, which are dedicated to seafood. A *passador* (roaming waiter) arrives at each table with a huge knife and a skewer filled with sausages for starters. Other passadors serve chicken, garlic-seasoned beef, pork loin, ham, tenderloin, and chicken with bacon, among other meats. If your plate gets empty, you won't have to ask for more—a passador will never pass you by. Beer and wines are available and that Brazilian "rocket fuel," the caipirinha, will surely keep a smile on your face. ✉ *14–16 Sixth Ave., off Bukit Timah Rd.,* ☎ *463–1923, AE, DC, MC, V.*

$$$ ✕ **Brewerkz.** This comfortable, old-style brewery on the river across from Clarke Quay is ideal for indulging in some homemade lager. There are always six varieties on tap in addition to a limited few during any given holiday season. The ample patio outside is well suited for kicking back, or you can play pool indoors while munching on the unique creations by Peruvian chef Eduardo Vargas, who adds his own Latin flavor to regional dishes. ✉ *No. 01–05/06 Riverside Point, 30 Merchant Rd.,* ☎ *438-7438. AE, DC, MC, V..*

$$$ ✕ **Compass Rose Restaurant.** This elegant restaurant is spread out over three floors of the Westin Stamford hotel (☞ Lodging, below); on a clear day, the view from the 70th floor includes Malaysia and some Indonesian islands. Indulge in the luxurious lounge (where high tea and drinks are served) or in the more formal dining room, where artistically presented meals preside. "East meets West" is the theme in such dishes as sautéed veal tenderloin and grilled goose liver, lobster bisque, and broiled king prawns topped with coriander and macadamia pesto. Lunches are considerably less expensive than dinners, and the noontime seafood buffet (S$42) has an amazing variety of dishes. There's always a line at night for seats in the lounge. ✉ *2 Stamford Rd.,* ☎ *338-8585. AE, DC, MC, V.*

$$$ ✕ **Ellenborough Market Café.** A combination of local, Straits Chinese, and international fare awaits you at this roomy eatery. Voted as a runner-up "best dining experience" by the Singapore Tourist Board in 1999, the "market" holds something for everyone. Its varied menu changes regularly. You may find such delicacies as slipper lobster in black-bean sauce, salmon sashimi, beef rendang, or even durian mousse to tantalize you. Both indoor and patio seating is available. A traditional supper buffet stars on Saturday and on the eve of public holidays. It includes teo chew fish porridge and more than 10 choices of *ngoh hiang* (deep-fried morsels). ✉ *Merchant Court hotel, 20 Merchant Rd.,* ☎ *337–2288. AE, D, DC, MC, V.*

$$$ ✕ **Nooch.** The noodle is the theme here, and it comes in several different varieties, including huge bowls of hot curry and Thai- or Japanese-style, all served in a modern, cafeterialike setting. The food is tasty; arrive early, as there is usually a line. ✉ *501 Orchard Rd., No. 02–16 Wheelock Place,* ☎ *235–0880. MC, V.*

$$$ ✕ **Planet Hollywood.** One of the newest in Southeast Asia, Planet Hollywood Singapore offers the usual burgers, wings, and other Western edibles that many vacationers find comforting while far from home. Spend S$15 on your meal and you can enjoy a free movie in a state-of-the-art theater. The Dolby THX sound system is, as the younger set says, "awesome." Kids under six years old eat for free at the Sunday brunch. ✉ *Liat Towers, No. 02–02, 541 Orchard Rd.,* ☎ *732–7827. AE, DC, MC, V.*

$$$ ✕ **Rainforest Café.** Welcome to the latest theme restaurant in Singapore and check out the life-size screeching creatures, more foliage than the local zoo, and a waitstaff sporting safari gear. An international menu awaits while you take in the scenery and wonder where all the strange noises are coming from. Main courses include Sunrise Shrimp pizza loaded with shrimp, peppers, mushrooms, and a sweet mango salsa. Pasta, burgers, and salads are standard fare, but most come with a twist. Dessert lovers—if they dare—can dive into the Seven Wonders of the Rainforest, a sinful concoction of ice cream, hot chocolate cake, hot fudge, caramel, raspberry sauce, whipped cream, banana, and Kit Kat bars. If nothing else, it's a fun place to bring the kids. ✉ *177 River Valley Rd., No. 01–41 Liang Ct.,* ☎ *333–1233. AE, DC, MC, V.*

$$–$$$ ✕ **Club Chinois.** When Tan Zhuan Qing opened the prestigious Club
  ★   Chinois in Shanghai in 1925, he couldn't have imagined that a Singaporean restaurateur, Andrew Tjioe, would model another restaurant on it more than 70 years later. Here, in the Orchard Parade Hotel (☞ Lodging, *below*) you'll find a delectable fusion of Cantonese and French cuisine, aptly directed by famed Canadian chef Susar Lee. The decor is swank and breezy: cream-color tablecloths are accented by turquoise monogrammed napkins and Wedgwood china. Mandarin cha-cha music from the '20s and '30s fills the room as the Armani-clad staff serves delightful dishes. Try the olive-oil-blanched tuna and lobster salad; the soybean bisque with morels; and a chili-marinated rack of lamb with tamarind, orange, and onion marmalade and soft pumpkin cake. ✉ *No. 02–18, 1 Tanglin Rd.,* ☎ *834–0660. AE, DC, MC, V.*

French

$$$ ✕ **L'Aigle d'Or.** Glittering crystal contrasts with gaily decorated floral plates at this small, cheerful restaurant in The Duxton hotel (☞ Lodging, *below*). A five-course *menu dégustation* (sampling menu) for about S$100 may include lobster consommé, sautéed fresh foie gras, baked John Dory fillets, and roast rack of lamb. Desserts come in pairs; you'll rave about the hot lemon soufflé in a chocolate shell. A set lunch menu changes daily and costs about S$36 per person. ✉ *83 Duxton Rd.,* ☎ *227–7678. AE, DC, MC, V.*

$$$ ✕ **La Fête du Cuisinier.** This Creole restaurant, built in the 1870s and reminiscent of New Orleans's French Quarter, is a quiet enclave for a romantic dinner. If the crystal chandeliers, gold-leaf ceiling, Oriental carpets, and Victorian gilded mirrors don't charm you, the duckling Creole, French goose liver terrine with black Perigord truffles, and bananas Foster will. ⊠ *Sculpture Square, 161 Middle Rd.,* ☎ *333–0917. AE, MC, V.*

$$$ ✕ **Mövenpick Marché.** As you enter this well-organized food court you are given a blank check, which you carry around with you as you roam the specialty counters where dishes of pasta, rosti, salads, and desserts are made to order as you wait. Each choice is then added to your check, which is tallied by a cashier when you are ready to leave. If you aren't quite sure what you're in the mood for when you arrive, you'll be totally confused when you get there. Don't despair—there's something for everyone. ⊠ *The Heeren, No. 01–03, 260 Orchard Rd.,* ☎ *737–6996. MC, V.*

Indian

$$$ ✕ **Tandoor.** The food has a distinctly Kashmiri flavor at this luxuri-
★ ous restaurant, where Indian paintings, rust and terra-cotta colors, and Indian musicians (at night) create the ambience of the Moghul court. The tandoor oven, which you can see through glass across a lotus pond, dominates the room. After you order tandoori chicken, lobster, fish, or shrimp—marinated in yogurt and spices, then roasted in the oven—sit back and watch the chef work. Also cooked in the oven is the northern Indian leavened bread called *naan*; the garlic naan is justifiably famous. The tender, spice-marinated roast leg of lamb is a favorite with regulars. Spiced *masala* tea is a perfect ending to the meal. Service is exceptionally attentive. ⊠ *Holiday Inn Park View, 11 Cavenagh Rd.,* ☎ *733–8333. AE, DC, MC, V.*

$$–$$$ ✕ **Annalakshmi.** Run by a Hindu cultural organization, this restaurant in the Excelsior Hotel (☞ Lodging, *below*) is considerably more elegant and more expensive than the average vegetarian eatery. The lunch buffet is very popular with Indian businessmen. At night, the paper-thin *dosai* pancakes are delicious in the special Sampoorna dinner. The selection often includes cabbage curry, *channa dhal* (chickpea stew), *kurma* (a mild vegetable curry cooked with yogurt or cream), *poori* (puffy, deep-fried bread), *samosa* (deep-fried, vegetable-stuffed patties), and *jangri* (a cold dessert). The flavors are delicate; spices are judiciously employed to enhance—rather than mask—the taste. ⊠ *5 Coleman St.,* ☎ *339–9993. AE, DC, MC, V. Closed Sun.*

$$ ✕ **Our Village.** There are considerably more attractive—and expensive—
★ Indian restaurants along Boat Quay, but aficionados swear that the food here is superior. Look for the narrow corridor that leads to the restaurant's elevator, which will take you to the fifth floor and a rooftop terrace that's delightfully cool and has excellent views. The menu contains all the usual North Indian favorites, yet the food, cooked home-style rather than prepared hours in advance, has a particular freshness and intensity of flavor. The *sag paneer* (spinach with homemade cheese) and *bhindi bhartha* (okra) are very good; so are the *naan* and any of the dishes cooked in the tandoor. ⊠ *46 Boat Quay, 4th and 5th floors,* ☎ *538–3058. AE, MC, V.*

$ ✕ **Banana Leaf Apolo.** Along Race Course Road are a host of South
★ Indian restaurants that serve meals on fresh rectangles of banana leaf. This down-home cafeteria-style spot was recently transformed into a stylish restaurant that specializes in fish-head curry (S$18–S$25, depending on the size). The food is fabulous, though it's often so hot that you may wind up with tears streaming down your face. Each person

is given a large piece of banana leaf; steaming-hot rice is spooned into the center; then two *papadam* (deep-fried lentil crackers) and two vegetables, with delicious spiced sauces, are arranged neatly around the rice. Optional extras such as the fish-head curry or spicy mutton may be added. ⊠ *54–58 Race Course Rd.,* ☎ *293–8682. AE, MC, V.*

$ ✕ **Madras New Woodlands Restaurant.** Many locals have quite an al-
★ legiance to this simple restaurant in the heart of Little India. The zesty food is vegetarian, combining northern and southern styles. For a full meal, order a *thali*: a large platter of dosai pancakes served with three spiced vegetables, curd, dhal, *rasam* (hot and sour soup), *sambar* (spicy sauce), sweet *raita* (chopped vegetables with yogurt), and *papadam*. Ask for the *paper dosai,* which is particularly crisp and comes in an enormous roll; it's served with two spiced coconut sauces and a *rasam* and is wonderful enough to make a meal on its own. The milk-based sweetmeats are irresistible. ⊠ *14 Upper Dickson Rd.,* ☎ *297–1594. Reservations not accepted. No credit cards.*

$ ✕ **Muthu's Curry Restaurant.** Curry aficionados argue endlessly over which sibling serves the better food, Muthu or his brother, who owns the Banana Leaf Apolo (☞ *above*) down the street. The decor is similar, and Muthu's also has air-conditioning. ⊠ *78 Race Course Rd.,* ☎ *293–7029. Reservations not accepted. AE, MC, V.*

$ ✕ **Samy's Curry Restaurant.** It's *très* chic to lunch at this restaurant on the grounds that used to be home to the Ministry of Defense, not least because there's no way you can stumble upon it by chance—you have to be in the know. The old, no-fuss, civil-service clubhouse is a legacy of British rule. The decor and service are equally no-fuss. The food—spicy-hot South Indian curries that are served on banana leaves—is excellent. There's no air-conditioning, which means that you sweat it out in true colonial fashion. It's cooler in the evening, but arrive no later than 7 PM for the best dishes. ⊠ *Singapore Civil Service Club House, Block 25, Dempsey Rd.,* ☎ *472–2080 or 296–9391. Reservations not accepted. AE, DC, V. No dinner Thurs.*

Italian

$$$ ✕ **Bella Donna.** Located in the Royal Plaza on Scotts (☞ Lodging, *below*), this popular new Italian eatery has a purposefully laid-back atmosphere. The tile floors, ceiling fans, and open wine racks all add to the airy comfort. Half of the restaurant is outdoor patio seating, which is great for people-watching on Scotts Road. At about 8 PM every night, an acoustic trio emerges and gets the crowd going with Spanish, Italian, and English songs. The next thing you know, the waitstaff is dancing all over the place, and a seemingly spontaneous party has erupted. The lovely presentation of generous salads, prawns, lasagna, and desserts competes for your attention; all are delicious. A daily special lunch menu is available at a 20% discount, and a snack menu, served in the afternoon and late evening, offers a great selection of dishes for only S$9 apiece. ⊠ *25 Scotts Rd.,* ☎ *737–7966. AE, DC, MC, V.*

$$$ ✕ **Pete's Place.** Pete's is well-known in town for its pizza and pasta dishes but more so for its Sunday Italian buffet, where you have an enormous selection of salads, pastas, breads, antipasto, and desserts from which to choose. The restaurant itself, located downstairs and quite dark, is cozy but unremarkable; but never mind, it's the food that entices people here. A wonderful selection is to be found at the salad and antipasto bars. Weekdays and nights you can get a selection of soups and salads for about S$20. Call for specials and selections for the buffet, which are occasionally changed. ⊠ *Grand Hyatt Singapore, 10 Scotts Rd.,* ☎ *730–7113. AE, DC, MC, V.*

$$$ ✕ **Prego.** Save room for the main course at this popular and always crowded large-scale trattoria. Copious amounts of homemade bread arrive after ordering from a varied menu of traditional and nontraditional Italian dishes such as cannelloni and pizza (try lobster) and "create your own" spaghetti. The waitstaff is helpful and friendly. If you arrive without a reservation, be prepared to wait. ✉ *The Westin Plaza, 2 Stamford Rd.,* ☎ *431–5156. AE, DC, MC, V.*

$$$ ✕ **Ristorante Bologna.** The Bologna, in the Marina Mandarin hotel (☞ Lodging, *below*), serves only their homemade pastas and insists on using fresh herbs in such dishes as *agnello al dragoncello* (roast rack of lamb stuffed with snow peas and tarragon). Ingredients are flown in from Italy to ensure authenticity. Waiters in vests provide impeccable service. The decor is light, airy, and luxurious; Renaissance-inspired murals adorn the walls, Carrera marble tiles the floor, and a cascading waterfall tops off the view. ✉ *Marina Square, 6 Raffles Blvd.,* ☎ *338– 3388. Reservations not accepted. AE, DC, MC, V.*

$$–$$$ ✕ **Café Modestos.** Blessed with an unbeatable location on the ground
★ floor of the Orchard Parade Hotel (☞ Lodging, *below*), at the corner of Orchard and Tanglin roads, Café Modestos does more than just wait for folks to wander in. It *draws* them in with its reasonably priced menu of Italian favorites and live entertainment. You can feast on chef Frederico's creative pizza and pasta on the outdoor patio, in the semi-outdoor area (which smokers appreciate), or in the air-conditioned main dining room. There's also a cigar lounge and a wine cellar. Try the carpaccio *di manzo ai funghi misti* (with mushrooms and Parmesan), the linguine *alla modesto* (with assorted seafood), or the *branzino patate e capperi* (sea bass with roasted potatoes in a caper and white-wine sauce). The best pizza has to be the *nera ai frutti di mare* (a squid-ink crust topped with tomatoes and seafood). ✉ *1 Tanglin Rd.,* ☎ *235–7808. AE, DC, MC, V.*

Japanese

$$$ ✕ **Keyaki.** On the rooftop of The Pan Pacific hotel (☞ Lodging, *below*), a Japanese farmhouse has been re-created in a formal Japanese garden with a golden-carp pond. The waitresses in kimonos and the waiters in *happi* coats make you feel as if you're in Japan (despite the European-looking wood chairs). A full spectrum of Japanese cuisine—kaiseki, kobachi, sashimi, shabu shabu, sukiyaki, sushi, tempura, teriyaki, bento, soba, and udon—is artfully presented on a serving dish of just the right color and texture to enhance the meal. The teppanyaki may be the best in Singapore, with a distinctive garlic fried rice and excellent beef, scallops, salmon, and shrimp. ✉ *Marina Square, 7 Raffles Blvd.,* ☎ *336–8111. AE, DC, V.*

$$$ ✕ **Nadaman.** There's nothing quite so exciting as watching a teppa-
★ nyaki chef perform his culinary calisthenics. The Nadaman, in the Shangri-La hotel (☞ Lodging, *below*) offers sushi, sashimi (the fresh lobster sashimi is excellent), teppanyaki, tempura, and *kaiseki* (a formal Japanese banquet). Try one of the *bento* lunches—fixed-price meals (around S$35) beautifully decorated in the Japanese manner and served in lacquer trays and boxes. The decor is distinctly Japanese, and the service is discreetly attentive. ✉ *22 Orange Grove Rd.,* ☎ *737– 3644. AE, DC, MC, V.*

$$$ ✕ **Sakae Sushi.** Not your average conveyer-belt sushi bar. Here it's all order-your-own "on-line" by a touchscreen computer. All the traditional kinds of sushi are here, fresh and tasty. ✉ *Wheelock Place, No. 02– 13 Orchard Rd.,* ☎ *737–6281. AE, MC, V..*

$$–$$$ ✕ **Shima.** Strangely, "German baronial" is perhaps the best way to describe the look of this Japanese restaurant in the Goodwood Park

hotel (☞ Lodging, *below*). Teppanyaki, shabu-shabu, and *yakiniku* (grill-it-yourself slices of beef, chicken, or fish) are the only items on the menu. You sit around a teppanyaki grill, watching the chef at work, or at the shabu-shabu and yakiniku tables cooking for yourself. Copper chimneys remove the smoke and smell. ✉ *22 Scotts Rd.,* ☎ *734–6281/2. AE, DC, MC, V.*

Malay and Indonesian

$$$ ✕ **Alkaff Mansion.** Once the estate of wealthy merchants, this 19th-century house on Mt. Faber Ridge, a short distance southwest of the city center, opened as a restaurant in 1991. You can sit inside under twirling fans or out on a veranda decorated to reflect the diverse tastes of the old Arab traders. Downstairs there's a huge Malay-Indonesian dinner buffet; on the balconies upstairs, 10 sarong-clad waitresses serve a multicourse rijsttafel. Western food—from steaks to seafood bordelaise—is also offered on a three-course luncheon menu and a more elaborate à la carte dinner menu. Overall, the delightful turn-of-the-century ambience and the presentation are more rewarding than the food. ✉ *10 Telok Blangah Green,* ☎ *278–6979. AE, DC, MC, V.*

$$$ ✕ **Tiffin Room.** For a taste of nostalgia and of a typical British "curry tiffin," part of the Malay colonial tradition, a visit to the Tiffin Room in the landmark Raffles Hotel (☞ Lodging, *below*) is a must. Despite its popularity with tour groups, the light, airy restaurant with its marble floors is still gracious; the service is courteous if a fraction slow during busy lunches. The lunch and dinner buffets are tempting spreads of largely Indian dishes. Forget that concession to modern tastes, the salad bar, and head straight for the mulligatawny, a spicy curry soup. There's a large array of spicy (but not necessarily chili-hot) vegetable, meat, poultry, and seafood dishes, and far more pickles, chutneys, and other condiments than a genuine Indian meal would provide. If you've still got room, you can choose from one or two local desserts as well as Indian and international favorites. ✉ *1 Beach Rd.,* ☎ *331–1612. AE, DC, MC, V.*

$$ ✕ **Rajah Inn.** In the lobby of the charming Regalis Court boutique hotel (☞ Lodging, *below*), this surprisingly large Indonesian restaurant is decorated in warm yellow and white tones and has ceiling fans as well as the ubiquitous air-conditioning. Try the *sambal goreng udang* (fried shrimp with chili) for a spicy sensation, *sayur lodeh* (local vegetables cooked in coconut milk), or *kambing gan lembu* (mutton or beef in a mild curry sauce). Prices are very reasonable, but call ahead to make sure the restaurant won't be feeding a tour group at the time you'd like to dine here. ✉ *64 Lloyd Rd.,* ☎ *734–7117. AE, MC, V.*

$–$$ ✕ **House of Sundanese Food.** Sundanese food, born of an isolated
★ province in West Java, is a cuisine apart from the rest of Indonesia. It combines raw, fresh vegetables with meat and fish in a piquant sweet-spicy mix. Order several small dishes and one seafood entrée and share them with your travel companions. You might start with *keredok,* a vegetable salad in a spicy peanut dressing; continue with *taupok goreng isi* (bean-curd-skin rolls stuffed with scallops, prawns, water chestnuts, and mushrooms); and *sedap ikan snapper bakar* (broiled red snapper basted in a sweet sauce). The prices at all three locations are very reasonable, making them hits with the lunchtime business crowd. ✉ *55 Boat Quay,* ☎ *534–3775;* ✉ *Suntec City Mall, No. B1–063, Fountain Terrace, 3 Temasek Blvd.,* ☎ *334–1012;* ✉ *218 East Coast Rd.,* ☎ *345–5020. AE, DC, MC, V.*

Nonya

$$ ✕ **Blue Ginger.** Singapore's most popular Peranakan restaurant has two convenient locations—one in Chinatown, the other on Orchard Road.

Furnishings are stylish and elegant, and colorful paintings by local artist Martin Loh abound. You might try such dishes as *udang goreng tauyu lada* (sautéed prawns with pepper in a sweet soya sauce), *ayam panggang Blue Ginger* (boneless chicken grilled and flavored with spiced coconut milk), and the mouthwatering *ngo heong* (homemade rolls of minced pork and prawns seasoned with five spices). If you're brave, sample the dessert made from the local infamous durian (a large, thorny bit of fruit that smells like old gym socks but has a caramel flavor). At the Tanjong Pagar location, request a second-floor table for an entertaining view of the street below. ✉ *97 Tanjong Pagar Rd.,* ☎ *222–3928; The Heeren, No. 05-02C, 260 Orchard Rd.,* ☎ *835–3928. AE, DC, MC, V.*

$$ ✕ **Ivin's Restaurant.** Housed in the upscale suburb of Bukit Timah, just north of the city center (you'll need a cab to get here), this casual restaurant serves traditional Nonya food à la carte. Specialties include *ayam buah keluak* (chicken in a spicy-sour gravy with a black Indonesian nut that has a creamy texture and the smokiness of French truffles), *babi pongteh* (pork stewed in soy sauce and onions), *udang masak nanas* (prawns cooked with pineapple), and *pong tauhu* (a soup with bamboo shoots and minced chicken, prawn, and bean-curd dumplings). ✉ *19/21 Binjai Park,* ☎ *468–3060. AE, DC, MC, V.*

Seafood

$$$$ ✕ **Tung Lok Seafood Gallery.** Andrew Tijoe's latest venture is for seafood-lovers only. The seafood-packed menu highlights a daily catch that is imported from all over the world. Specialties include crayfish, Maine Atlantic lobster, grouper, green rust, barramundi, sturgeon, and Alaska king crab. A full range of Japanese cuisine is also available. You can take a leisurely walk along East Coast Boardwalk before or after dinner. ✉ *1000 East Coast Pkwy.,* ☎ *246–0555. AE, MC, V.*

$$$ ✕ **Blue Lobster Seafood Restaurant.** The Blue Lobster is for those with large appetites. The Aussie Seafood Luncheon is a "semi-buffet," with a large assortment of lobsters, shrimp, and whitefish available both à la carte and at the buffet. A good variety of Australian wines and beers is also available. A private chef's table and fish market are new additions. ✉ *The Riverwalk, 20 Upper Circular Rd., No. B1–49/50,* ☎ *538–0766. AE, DC, MC, V.*

$$–$$$ ✕ **Palm Beach Seafood.** Forty years ago, this restaurant was on a beach, with tables set under coconut trees—hence the name. It's now in a shopping and leisure complex next to the National Stadium and covers three floors, with its downstairs restaurant seating around 550. What the place lacks in ambience, it more than makes up for in food quality, and the prices may well be the best in town for seafood. The most popular dishes include chili crabs served with French bread to mop up the sauce; prawns fried in black soy sauce or in butter and milk with curry leaves; and deep-fried crisp squid. Don't miss the *yu char kway,* deep-fried crullers stuffed with a mousse of squid and served with a tangy black sauce. ✉ *Leisure Park, 5 Stadium Walk, Kallang Park,* ☎ *344–3088. Reservations not accepted. AE, MC, V.*

$$–$$$ ✕ **UDMC Seafood Centre.** You *must* visit this place at the East Coast Parkway, near the entrance to the lagoon, to get a true picture of the way Singaporeans eat out, as well as real value (prices here are cheaper than in most other seafood restaurants). Walk around the eight open-fronted restaurants before you decide where to eat. Chili crabs, steamed prawns, steamed fish, pepper crabs, fried noodles, and deep-fried squid are the specialties. Restaurants include **Chin Wah Heng** (☎ 444–7967), **Gold Coast Seafood** (☎ 448–2020), **Golden Lagoon Seafood** (☎ 448–1894), **Jumbo Seafood** (☎ 442–3435), **Lucky View Seafood**

Restaurant (☎ 241–1022), and **Red House Seafood Restaurant** (☎ 442–3112). ✉ *East Coast Pkwy. Reservations not accepted. AE, DC, MC, V. No lunch.*

Thai

$$$ ✗ **Lemongrass.** This popular eatery is centrally located and just the thing after a hard day of shopping on Orchard Road. Dishes are made to accommodate all customers, and arrive with varying degrees of heat. Have yours mild or fiery. Either way, specialties like stuffed chicken wings and soft-shelled crabs will not disappoint. On the traditional side, the prawn patties are worth a try. ✉ *No. 05–02A, The Heeren, 260 Orchard Rd.,* ☎ *736–1998. AE, MC, V.*

$$$ ✗ **Patara.** This softly lit, friendly Thai restaurant with marbletop tables is a calming respite where you can sample house specialties like green curry, pineapple rice, and deep-fried pomfret with tamarind sauce. And don't miss the garlic and pepper spareribs, which keep the place on the map. ✉ *No. 03–04 Tanglin Mall, 163 Tanglin Rd.,* ☎ *737–0818. AE, DC, MC, V..*

$$–$$$ ✗ **Thanying.** The owners and chefs at this restaurant in the Amara Hotel
   ★   (☞ Lodging, *below*) are Thai, so it's no wonder that it has such exquisite, aristocratic, Thai decor and that the food (redolent of kaffir-lime leaves, basil, mint, ginger, and coriander) is cooked in the best palace tradition. Indeed, this restaurant has been so successful that the owners have opened a second one on Clarke Quay. Try the *gai kor bai toey* (marinated chicken in pandanus leaves and chargrilled to perfection), an exquisite Thai salad like *yam sam oh* (shredded pomelo tossed with chicken and prawns in a spicy lime sauce), *pla khao sam rod* (grouper, deep-fried until it's so crispy you can practically eat the bones), or one of the Thai curries. And of course, you won't want to miss the sour and hot *tom yam* soup. ✉ *Level 2, 165 Tanjong Pagar Rd.,* ☎ *222–4688;* ✉ *Clarke Quay, Block D,* ☎ *336–1821. AE, DC, MC, V.*

$$ ✗ **Yhingthai Palace.** The no-nonsense decor of this small, simple restaurant—just around the corner from the famous Raffles Hotel—makes it clear that food is the prime concern. Although the service can be slow, the well-prepared and moderately priced food is worth waiting for. The *yam ma muang* (sour mango salad) is an excellent and refreshing dish, while *hor mok talay,* seafood mousse served in charming terra-cotta molds, is light and flavorful. If you enjoy spicy dishes with plenty of herbs, try the *phad kra kai* (stir-fried minced chicken). The *kuay teow phad Thai* (fresh rice noodles fried with seafood) is delicious, and one of the lemony tom yam soups is almost obligatory. ✉ *13 Purvis St.,* ☎ *337–9429. AE, MC, V.*

LODGING

Over the years Singapore has been transformed from a popular tourist destination to a conventioneers' mecca teeming with tour groups and delegates. Singapore's lodging has visibly changed to accommodate this clientele: extensive refurbishment and growth with more varied services has been the trend. With that said, though, luxury still abounds, and there are places where exceptional personal service hasn't completely fallen by the wayside.

Singapore's hotels were once considered inexpensive compared to those in other world-class cities. Today, however, costs rival those in New York or London—a superior double room in a deluxe hotel can run more than S$400 a night; one with a private bath in a modest hotel, about S$150 a night. Further, during conventions and the peak months of August and December, hotel rooms can be scarce and prices can rise.

Still, there are enough discounts and deals that no thrifty visitor should ever have to pay the published price (if you use a travel agent, make sure that he or she asks for a discount). There are also budget hotels with rates less than S$85 a night. The Geylang area east of City Hall has many new low-cost hotels with rooms between S$49 and S$100 a night—some of these are even available for a few hours at a time. And if all you're looking for is a bunk, walk along Bencoolen Street, where there are dormitory-style guest houses that charge no more than S$25 a night, although they seem to be on the way out. (For more information on affordable lodgings, contact the Singapore Tourism Board or STB—*see* Visitor Information *in* Singapore A to Z, *below*— for its annually updated brochure "Budget Hotels.")

Booking ahead—particularly for stays in August and December—will probably save you money and will definitely save you headaches. If, however, you gamble and arrive without reservations, the Singapore Hotel Association has two counters at Changi Airport that are staffed by people who can set you up with a room—often at a discount—with no booking fee.

Establishments in the $$$–$$$$ range offer such amenities as International Direct Dial (IDD) phones with bathroom extensions, TVs with international cable stations, room service, minibars, data ports for modems, no-smoking rooms or floors, in-room safes, and business and fitness centers loaded with the latest equipment. On the flip side, some smaller hotels—particularly those in converted shophouses—have a few rooms that lack windows, so be sure to ask for one that has them. For all of Singapore's high-tech advances—including traffic signals that chirp at you when it's safe to cross the street—there are some establishments that don't offer rooms equipped for people with mobility problems; those that do are indicated below. Unless otherwise noted, all rooms have air-conditioning and private baths.

Singapore

Singapore's hotels have developed in clusters. The best-known grouping is at the intersection of Orchard and Scotts roads. The luxurious Four Seasons is tucked behind the Hilton off Orchard Road, and the recently refurbished Grand Hyatt is on Scotts Road. Close by is the new Traders Hotel, which cuts out the frills and frippery found at luxury hotels, providing all the basic comforts at low rates.

In Raffles City, the megalithic Westins—the Plaza and the Stamford—stare down at the Raffles, the grande dame of Singapore's hotels, and the Inter-Continental's black-and-white marble gleams alongside turn-of-the-century shophouses. At the south end of the Shenton Way commercial district are a number of business-oriented hotels; to the south of the Singapore River, still another cluster has sprung up, one with boutique hotels as well as the Raffles-owned Merchant Court. Marina Square—a minicity created by a reclamation project that pushed back the seafront to make way for the Suntec City convention complex, more than 200 shops, and many restaurants—has a half dozen hotels, including The Pan Pacific and the Conrad International Centennial.

For those of you who can't get enough of Sentosa Island's attractions, there are a couple of hotels to choose from there. If you like shopping and nightlife, then the Orchard and Scotts roads area is for you. If you're attending a convention or simply want an urban landscape with open spaces and river views, Marina Square is the logical choice. If you're doing business in the financial district, a hotel close to Shenton Way is ideal; if your business plans include a trip to the industrial city of

Singapore Lodging

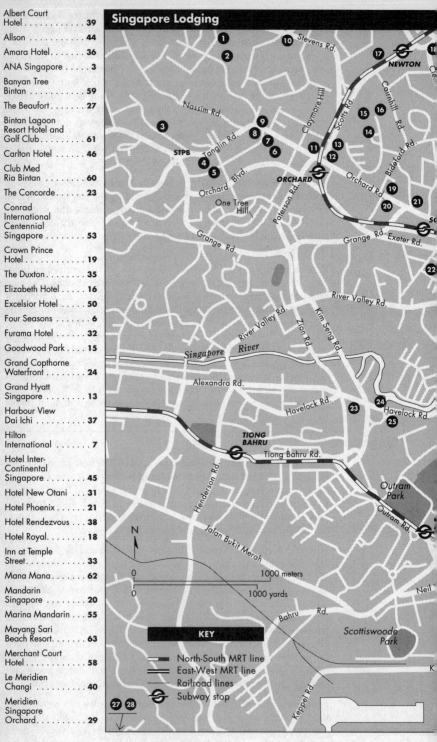

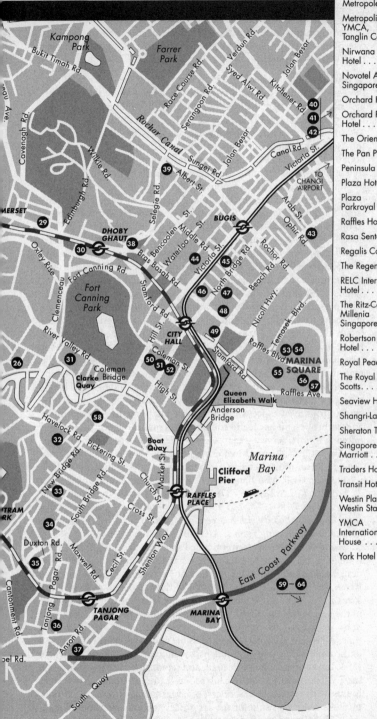

Jurong, then a hotel on the Singapore River is best. Regardless of where you stay, it's easy to get around this compact city. Taxis and public transportation, especially the subway, make it possible to travel between areas swiftly, and no hotel is more than a 30-minute cab ride from Changi Airport.

$$$$ ⊞ **Four Seasons.** Opened in 1995 by the owner of the adjacent Hilton,
★   the Four Seasons is quieter and—dare we say it?—more refined, with luxuries intended to make it outshine the city's older hotels. (Drawn by the modern elegance, Britain's Spice Girls taped a music video here in 1998.) Guest rooms are spacious and gracious, with soft fabrics, peaceful Asian art, large bathrooms, two-line speakerphones with modem hookups, laser video, and CD players. Of the three restaurants, the Cantonese Jiang-Nam Chun (☞ Dining, *above*) is the most memorable for its stunning art deco and art nouveau decor and its exotic fare. Some of the tennis courts are air-conditioned, and there's even a golf simulator. The hotel is linked to Orchard Road via an elevated passageway to the Hilton. ✉ *190 Orchard Blvd., 248646,* ☎ *734–1110,* ℻ *733–0682. 254 rooms, 41 suites. 3 restaurants, bar, 2 pools, 4 tennis courts, health club, shops, business services, meeting rooms. AE, DC, MC, V.*

$$$$ ⊞ **Goodwood Park.** This venerable institution began in 1900 as a club for German expatriates and has since hosted the likes of the Duke of Windsor, Edward Heath, Noël Coward, and the great Anna Pavlova, who performed here. It has recently been renovated to bring its facilities up to world-class standards, with even a foot-reflexology center in the spa. The Parklane Suites, each with a bedroom and a living-dining room, can be rented (for short- or long-term stays) for less than a double room in the main hotel; it is a short walk to the main hotel lobby. The poolside suites, with aged copper wall lamps resembling torches, partial stone walls, and louvered sliding panel blinds of Cape Cod barnwood, are rustic in style. Floor-to-ceiling panel mirrors adorn the entrance walls. The muted lighting, huge terry towels and bathrobes, and peaceful surroundings make for comfortable and relaxing rooms. Service is extremely efficient down to the smallest detail, from the bed turn-down at night to the flashlight in the vanity drawer. Restaurants—which are popular with local diners—include the Gordon Grill, Min Jiang, and Chang Jiang (☞ Dining, *above*). ✉ *22 Scotts Rd., 228221,* ☎ *737–7411; 800/772–3890 (reservations in the U.S.),* ℻ *738–4579. 171 rooms, 64 suites. 8 restaurants, coffee shop, 3 pools, beauty salon, exercise room, spa, baby-sitting, business services, meeting rooms. AE, DC, MC, V.* ✍

$$$$ ⊞ **Grand Copthorne Waterfront.** Billed as a "lifestyle hotel," the Grand is the new kid on the block among a handful of five-star hotels. The design takes full advantage of the hotel's setting on the Singapore River, thus window space is maximized throughout so as to give full focus to the panoramic views; the display from the top floors is one of the best in the city. Light-wood trim, striking modern artwork, and in the deluxe rooms, parquet floors, contribute to the airy light-filled tone. All rooms are wheelchair accessible and have stylishly appointed bathrooms along with the full list of modern amenities: electronic safes, IDD phones, and voice mail, and remote Internet access through the TV. The upper Executive Club rooms feature an exclusive two-story lounge with personalized services, breakfast, and cocktails. A 24-hour business center has state-of-the-art offices and a board room. For edibles, visit Chopsticks for a taste of pan-Asian, or Brio, the main coffee bar, for a more eclectic menu. An Italian restaurant, Pontini Italian Trattoria, has recently opened and promises to be one of the best in the city serving authentic northern Italian cuisine. ✉ *392 Havelock Rd., 169663,* ☎ *733–0880,* ℻ *737–0880. 537 rooms. 3 restaurants, pool,* *hot tub, tennis court, health club, business services, meeting rooms. AE, DC, MC, V.* ✏

$$$$ ▦ **Grand Hyatt Singapore.** Formerly the Hyatt Regency, this centrally located luxury hotel was extensively refurbished in 1998. Room rates here are among the highest in town, but promotional packages are frequently offered. The Grand Wing consists of one-, two-, and three-room apartments with two-line phones, extra bathrooms, work areas, and private mailboxes. Standard rooms are adequate but small. Dine at Pete's Place (☞ Dining, *above*), for excellent pasta dishes; mezza9 for authentic Asian; and Scotts Lounge, for afternoon tea. Travelers with disabilities will find the amenities here to their liking. ⊠ *10–12 Scotts Rd., 228211,* ☎ *738–1234,* ℻ *732–1696. 266 rooms, 427 apartments. 3 restaurants, coffee shop, pool, beauty salon, massage, sauna, 2 tennis courts, badminton, exercise room, squash, business services. AE, DC, MC, V.* ✏

$$$$ ▦ **Hotel Inter-Continental Singapore.** This Bugis Junction hotel, built in 1995, appears to be just another modern, marbleized, posh hotel with all the latest amenities (including facilities for people with disabilities and "cyber-relations" officers, or computer consultants, on call). But in its 83 Shophouse Rooms—each one different from the next—the Peranakan style (the distinctive Malay-Chinese-European mix of design influences) reminds you of Singapore's multicultural heritage. There's a S$10 surcharge a night for a stay in these rooms, but a complimentary American breakfast is included. The remaining guest rooms have classical, clean, European lines. For a surcharge of S$50 a night you'll get more attentive service, a Continental breakfast, and evening cocktails. ⊠ *80 Middle Rd., 188966,* ☎ *338–7600,* ℻ *338–7366. 406 rooms. 3 restaurants, pool, health club, business services, meeting rooms. AE, DC, MC, V.* ✏

$$$$ ▦ **The Oriental.** Inside this pyramid-shape Marina Square hotel, the
★ level of service on everyone's part—from student trainees to seasoned doormen—is second to none. Subdued, modern elegance and personal attention are the hallmarks here. Rooms are understated, with soft hues of peach and green, handwoven carpets, and paintings of old Singapore. Of special note are the Italian-marble-tile bathrooms with phones and radio and TV speakers. One-bedroom suites have lovely sitting rooms and separate washrooms. The Cherry Garden (☞ Dining, *above*) prepares outstanding Hunanese food, and Morton's (☞ Dining, *above*), the Chicago-based steak house, has opened its first Asian branch here. More casual dining is available at Café des Artistes. The Gallery lounge, with its panoramic view of the city and vivid work by local artists adorning the walls, is a restful spot. Note that the hotel has facilities for people with disabilities. ⊠ *5 Raffles Blvd., 039797,* ☎ *338–0066,* ℻ *339–9537. 463 rooms, 60 suites. 3 restaurants, pool, massage, sauna, golf privileges, 2 tennis courts, health club, jogging, business services, meeting rooms, travel services. AE, DC, MC, V.*

$$$$ ▦ **Raffles Hotel.** Opened by the Sarkies brothers in 1887 and visited
★ by such writers as Joseph Conrad, Rudyard Kipling, and Somerset Maugham, Raffles was the belle of the East during its heyday in the '20s and '30s and was declared a national monument in 1987. True to form in this planned republic, millions of dollars have been spent to replace Singapore's noble old charm with a sanitized version of colonial ambience. The new Raffles is a glistening showpiece, especially from the outside; inside, antique furniture blends well with modern amenities (including facilities for people with disabilities). The lobby is divided into two areas: one exclusively for in-house guests and the other for the constant flow of diners and curious tourists. Guest suites have teak floors, 14-ft ceilings, overhead fans, and '20s-style furnishings that tend to be stiff. Some suites are named after famous literary figures who

once stayed here. ⊠ *1 Beach Rd., 189673,* ☎ *337–1886,* FAX *339–7650. 103 suites. 12 restaurants, 3 bars, pool, exercise room, shops, business services. AE, DC, MC, V.* ☜

$$$$ 🏨 **The Ritz-Carlton, Millenia Singapore.** The most dramatic of the lux-
★ ury hotels in Marina Bay is The Ritz-Carlton. It opened in 1996 with 32 floors of unobstructed harbor and city views as well as sculptures by Frank Stella and limited-edition prints by David Hockney and Henry Moore. All rooms are unusually large (travelers with disabilities will appreciate the facilities in some) and have bathrooms that seem better stocked than your local drugstore. For S$60 more a night per single, or S$100 more per double, you can enjoy the complimentary breakfast, noon snacks, afternoon tea, evening cocktails, after-dinner cordials, and personalized concierge services at the Ritz-Carlton Club. For dining, there's Snappers for seafood, the Summer Pavilion for Cantonese cuisine, and the Asian- and European-accented Greenhouse (☞ Dining, *above*). Check out the exclusive health club (local memberships cost S$5,000) and the live jazz in the lobby lounge every evening. ⊠ *7 Raffles Ave., 039799,* ☎ *337–8888,* FAX *338–0001. 609 rooms, 80 suites. 3 restaurants, lounge, pool, spa, tennis court, health club, business services, meeting rooms. AE, DC, MC, V.* ☜

$$$$ 🏨 **Shangri-La.** This hotel has consistently been among Singapore's
★ top three since opening in 1971. To give the other two a run for their money, approximately S$95 million was earmarked in 1998–99 for extensive renovations of this hotel's Tower Wing, pool, lobby areas, and food and beverage outlets. While refurbishments continue, the Valley Wing (built in early 1988) and its 140 rooms is the site of business-as-usual hotel activity. Prime Ministers and presidents have stayed here, but all travelers are treated to the same excellent service. The Coffee Garden, designed after an English conservatory, has light meals and a lunch buffet; you'll find haute Cantonese cuisine in Shang Palace (☞ Dining, *above*) and fine California dining with late-night jazz served at Blu, an eatery on the 24th floor of the Tower Wing; Nadaman (☞ Dining, *above*) serves Japanese fare. (Travelers with disabilities take note: this hotel has amenities for you.) ⊠ *22 Orange Grove Rd., 258350,* ☎ *737–3644; 020/8747–8485 (reservations in the U.K.); 800/942–5050 (reservations in Canada and the U.S.);* FAX *737–3257. 823 rooms. 4 restaurants, bar, putting green, 4 tennis courts, health club, squash, business services, meeting rooms. AE, DC, MC, V www.shangri-la.com.*

$$$$ 🏨 **Sheraton Towers.** The pastel-decorated guest rooms here have all the deluxe amenities, including small sitting areas with a sofa and easy chairs. The Tower Rooms, at about S$60 more, include complimentary butler service and breakfast. The best vantage point for the dramatic cascading waterfall (the rocks are fiberglass) is from the Terrazza restaurant, which has a superb high tea. Other restaurants are Domus for Italian food and Li Bai (☞ Dining, *above*) for refined Cantonese. The hawker stalls at Newton Circus are close by. A large, comfortable lounge has live music in the evening. ⊠ *39 Scotts Rd., 228230,* ☎ *737–6888,* FAX *733–4366. 606 rooms. 3 restaurants, coffee shop, pool, massage, sauna, dance club, business services, meeting rooms. AE, DC, MC, V.* ☜

$$$ 🏨 **ANA Singapore.** Don't be deceived by the antique tapestries and wood-paneled walls in the lobby of this glistening 14-story hotel near the Botanic Gardens and the embassies. It has a full range of modern facilities. Rooms are decorated in light colors and have writing desks, bedside remote controls, and coffee- and tea makers. The Hubertus Grill serves seafood, prime rib, and Continental cuisine; Unkai specializes in Japanese food. ⊠ *16 Nassim Hill, 238467,* ☎ *732–1222,* FAX *732–2222. 445 rooms, 17 suites. 2 restaurants, café, coffee shop, pool, exercise room, dance club, business services. AE, DC, MC, V.* ☜

$$$ 🏨 **The Beaufort.** The remote location of this resort on Sentosa Island is ideal for business seminars and for leisure visitors who wish to escape. Its best feature is the swimming pool, which overlooks the Malacca Straits and is flanked by a romantic, open-air, seafood restaurant. The rooms—down concrete corridors, past pond-filled courtyards, and in two symmetrical low-rise wings—don't share these fine views; instead they look onto tropical parkland. Standard rooms (called deluxe) aren't very large (though bathrooms are of a good size) and have undistinctive pastel furniture. The Garden Rooms have larger bedrooms and work areas with better-quality furniture such as handmade tortoiseshell desks, mosaic tables, and French banquette sofas. There are also four luxurious two-bedroom villas, each with its own pool. (This hotel has facilities for travelers with disabilities.) ⊠ *2 Bukit Manis Rd., Sentosa Island, 099891,* ☎ *275–0331; 800/637–7200 (reservations in the U.S.),* 𝔽𝔸𝕏 *275–0228. 175 rooms, 34 suites, 4 villas. 3 restaurants, pool, 2 tennis courts, exercise room, squash, business services, meeting rooms. AE, DC, MC, V.* 🍴

$$$ 🏨 **Carlton Hotel.** This stark, pristine hotel near Raffles City has achieved a more relaxed ambience than when it first opened in 1988. Your footsteps will still echo through the lobby, but you'll find that the lounges to the side are quiet enclaves for sipping afternoon tea. All the hotel's amenities (including those for travelers with disabilities) are up-to-date. The upper five stories contain concierge floors, with express check-in, complimentary breakfast, and evening cocktails. Published prices have climbed recently; unless you can get a decent discount, they're steep for what the hotel offers. ⊠ *76 Bras Basah Rd., 189558,* ☎ *338–8333,* 𝔽𝔸𝕏 *339–6866. 463 rooms, 14 suites. 2 restaurants, bar, café, coffee shop, lobby lounge, pool, exercise room, business services, meeting rooms. AE, DC, MC, V.* 🍴

$$$ 🏨 **Conrad International Centennial Singapore.** Strategically located in Singapore's new downtown Marina Centre, this luxury five-star business hotel enjoys close proximity to the Singapore International Convention and Exhibition Centre (SICEC), Suntec City, three national museums, famous sightseeing spots, and the central business districts. Numerous original Asian-influenced artworks hang in its public areas, and the rooms are similarly decorated. Each room has a luxurious bathroom and an extensive range of amenities. Travelers with disabilities will appreciate that the hotel has taken their needs into consideration; businesspeople will be grateful for the 24-hour business center and the well-equipped meeting rooms. The Centennial Fitness Club Spa has exercise equipment and a complete range of beauty and body treatments. The 24-hour Oscar's café (☞ Dining, *above*) is known for its popular wine buffet. The Golden Peony (☞ Dining, *above*) features premium Cantonese dim sum. ⊠ *2 Temasek Blvd., 038982,* ☎ *334–8888,* 𝔽𝔸𝕏 *333–9166. 484 rooms, 25 suites. 2 restaurants, pool, exercise room, spa, business services, meeting rooms, travel services. AE, DC, MC, V.* 🍴

$$$ 🏨 **Crown Prince Hotel.** The large, sparse lobby greets you with Italian marble and glass chandeliers. For more drama, glass elevators run along the outside of the building so you can check out the traffic on Orchard Road. Though the pastel rooms are neat and trim, efficiency outweighs warmth here. Long Jiang Szechuan Restaurant (☞ Dining, *above*) offers Szechuan food from a set menu, and Sushi Nogawa is Japanese-owned. ⊠ *270 Orchard Rd., 238857,* ☎ *732–1111,* 𝔽𝔸𝕏 *734–9137. 302 rooms, 9 suites. 3 restaurants, pool, business services, meeting rooms. AE, DC, MC, V.*

$$$ 🏨 **The Duxton.** Singapore's first boutique hotel consists of eight smartly
★ converted shophouses in Chinatown's Tanjong Pagar district. It remains a breath of fresh air: intimate and tasteful, with a whiff of Singapore's

character before it sold out to steel girders and glass. The standard rooms, at the back of the building, are small and have colonial reproduction furniture. You may want to spend the extra S$120 a night for a small duplex suite. Breakfast is included, and afternoon tea is served in the lounge. The excellent French restaurant L'Aigle d'Or (☞ *Dining, above*) is off the lobby. ⊠ *83 Duxton Rd., 089540,* ☎ *227–7678; 800/ 272–8188 (reservations in the U.S.),* FAX *227–1232. 38 rooms, 11 suites. Restaurant, business services. AE, DC, MC, V.* ✇

$$$ 🏨 **Hilton International.** It may be short on glitter and dazzle, but the Hilton's rooms have all the amenities (including those for people with disabilities) of a modern deluxe property and at highly competitive rates. It's near shopping arcades that house some of Singapore's most exclusive boutiques. The rooms on the street side still have views, but those at the back have been blocked by the adjacent Four Seasons. The former Givenchy suites are now Executive Club floors with 72 rooms and suites and a clubroom all decked out in contemporary furniture with warm tones and black steel trim. Executive rooms, many with balconies, have two phone lines and a modem connection. Within the hotel are Checkers Brasserie; rooftop and poolside dining; and the Harbour Grill, which has seafood and French cuisine. ⊠ *581 Orchard Rd., 238883,* ☎ *737– 2233,* FAX *732–2917. 351 rooms, 72 suites. 3 restaurants, 2 bars, pool, health club, business services, meeting rooms. AE, DC, MC, V.* ✇

$$$ 🏨 **Hotel New Otani.** Off by itself on the north bank of the Singapore River, this orange-brick-fronted hotel is striking against the greenery of Fort Canning Park. It attracts many Japanese travelers as part of the Liang Court complex, which houses more than 40 specialty shops, and the large Japanese department store Daimaru. Rooms come with coffee-, tea-, and soup makers. The hotel's location is best suited to business travelers who want to be close to Shenton Way. ⊠ *177A River Valley Rd., 179031,* ☎ *338–3333,* FAX *339–2854. 408 rooms. 2 restaurants, bar, pool, exercise room, business services, meeting rooms. AE, DC, MC, V.* ✇

$$$ 🏨 **Hotel Phoenix.** During recent renovations, the Phoenix installed PCs with Internet access and exercise equipment in all its rooms, as well as a computerized massage chair in each of its executive rooms and suites. In the warmly decorated rooms, beds are dressed in down quilts and have electronic control panels beside them; the Business Executive rooms can be converted into offices during the day. There's no on-site health club, so if the in-room gear isn't enough, take advantage of the free passes to the California Fitness Center two blocks away. The Phoenix Garden Café serves very good local and Western fare, but it can be noisy during dinner, perhaps owing to its basement location. The hotel is in the heart of the Orchard Road district and a five-minute drive to the convention center. ⊠ *277 Orchard Rd., 238858,* ☎ *737–8666,* FAX *732–2024. 290 rooms, 22 suites. Restaurant, bar, patisserie, nightclub, business services. AE, DC, MC, V.*

$$$ 🏨 **Hotel Rendezvous.** Despite some major changes made to address the needs of its business clientele, the Hotel Rendezvous retains something of its '30s past. The rooms are Peranakan in style, with warm and bright colors; the tiles that decorate the walls of many of the bathrooms reflect shades of days gone by. The hotel rises 11 stories in the center of the civic and cultural district. All modern amenitites apply and six meeting rooms of various sizes are available. The lobby and atrium are peaceful places to collect your thoughts or enjoy the sunlight. You can wine and dine at the Straits Café by the Park, which has a delightful Asian buffet. High tea is served on Saturday and a Sunday brunch is very popular with guests and locals alike. The atrium houses a cyber-café; Spago Café and Restaurant, for sandwiches and salads; and Cruisine Steakhouse. ⊠ *9 Bras Basah Rd., 189559,* ☎ *336–0220,* FAX *337–3773.*

300 rooms. 4 restaurants, pool, 2 saunas, hot tub, massage, exercise room, business services. AE, DC, MC, V. 🐾

$$$ 🏨 **Mandarin Singapore.** The grand main lobby has translucent white-and-black Italian marble and a huge mural, *87 Taoist Immortals*, based on an 8th-century Chinese scroll. Guest rooms on the upper floors command fabulous views of the harbor, the city, and Malaysia beyond. The best rooms have VCRs and bedside remote controls; some have amenities for travelers with disabilities. Rooms in the South Tower have black-lacquer furniture with colorful silk cushions. Overall, however, the Mandarin is a little disappointing; tour groups are its mainstay. Dining options include the Pine Court (☞ Dining, *above*); the Top of the M, a revolving restaurant; Chikuyotei, with Japanese fare; the 24-hour Chatterbox coffeehouse; and hawker-stand Chinese food. ⊠ *333 Orchard Rd., 238867,* ☎ *737–4411,* FAX *732–2361. 1,200 rooms. 3 restaurants, coffee shop, pub, pool, beauty salon, massage, sauna, tennis court, exercise room, squash, dance club, business services, meeting rooms. AE, DC, MC, V.* 🐾

$$$ 🏨 **Marina Mandarin.** Here, the John Portman–designed atrium narrows as it ascends 21 floors to a tinted skylight, and the lobby is relatively peaceful. Pastel guest rooms are modern and smart and have coffee- and tea makers; for the best view, ask for a room overlooking the harbor. Rooms on the concierge floor—the Marina Club—cost about 25% more and have such extras as terry robes, butler service, and free breakfast and cocktails. Also available are accommodations for businesspeople who don't need all the extras of the concierge floor but who do need efficient hotel services. The on-site Peach Blossoms restaurant serves Chinese cuisine for lunch and dinner and the Ristorante Bologna (☞ Dining, *above*) has northern Italian fare; the Cricketeer pub is a pleasant place for an evening drink. ⊠ *6 Raffles Blvd., 039594,* ☎ *338–3388,* FAX *339–4977. 575 rooms. 3 restaurants, pub, pool, massage, sauna, 2 tennis courts, exercise room, squash, dance club, business services. AE, DC, MC, V.* 🐾

$$$ 🏨 **Merchant Court.** The trend toward developing "no frills" hotels for business travelers led the Raffles Group to open Merchant Court in 1997. It's across from Clarke Quay and is a free shuttle ride away from the Raffles City Shopping Centre. Standard rooms, albeit small, are comfortable; larger executive rooms have a few more amenities. A stay in a Merchant Club room gets you free use of laptop computers and fax machines as well as complimentary breakfast and cocktails. All rooms have refrigerators for you to stock, and there's a coin-op laundry with video games on the second floor. In addition, the hotel can comfortably accommodate travelers with disabilities. Ellenborough Market Café (☞ Dining, *above*) offers nightly a delightful international, local, and Straits-Chinese buffet of some 35-plus dishes. The fitness facilities are top-notch. ⊠ *20 Merchant Rd., 058281,* ☎ *337–2288,* FAX *334–0606. 470 rooms, 6 suites. Restaurant, 2 bars, refrigerators, pool, exercise room, business services, meeting rooms. AE, DC, MC, V.* 🐾

$$$ 🏨 **Meridien Singapore Orchard.** Slightly away from much of the hustle and bustle on Orchard Road, this hotel captivates guests in the atriumlike lobby with a cascade of flowers descending from the upper floors. A welcome lounge is heavily utilized by air crew and tours. Rooms are done in pastels and have such Asian touches as silk-screen murals; some rooms have balconies loaded with potted plants. Quarters on Le Club Président concierge level have extra amenities such as CD players and fax machines; most bathrooms on these floors have a TV with a perfect view from the tub. In addition to the hotel's dining room, you'll find rotisserie buffets, local specialties, and Western fare in the relaxed Café Georges. The entrance may be difficult to find, but any taxi driver should know it. ⊠ *100 Orchard Rd., 238840,* ☎ *733–8855,*

FAX *732–7886. 407 rooms. 2 restaurants, bar, pool, exercise room, business services. AE, DC, MC, V.*

$$$ 📺 **Orchard Hotel.** Its location close to the activity on Orchard Road, several embassies, and the Botanic Gardens has no doubt contributed to this hotel's popularity. The pastel guest rooms are comfortable and functional, and there are facilities for people with disabilities. Rooms in the 17-story Orchard Wing are larger and more expensive than standard rooms. Rooms on the top four floors are part of the Premier and Harvesters' clubs; amenities here include separate check-in, in-room fax services, and complimentary breakfast and evening cocktails. The formal Hua Ting restaurant offers Cantonese and Shanghainese dishes, and the Orchard and Sidewalk cafés serve light fare till 1 AM. ✉ *442 Orchard Rd., 238879,* ☎ *734–7766,* FAX *733–5482. 680 rooms. Restaurant, 2 cafés, bar, tea shop, pool, exercise room, business services, meeting rooms, travel services. AE, DC, MC, V.* 🐾

$$$ 📺 **Orchard Parade Hotel.** Previously known as the Ming Court Hotel, this 30-year-old property at the corner of Tanglin and Orchard roads underwent a S$40-million transformation that was completed in mid-1998. Mediterranean in style (there's a Spanish feel throughout the place), the rooms are spacious, especially the Junior Suites. Several of these are set aside for families with young children and have one or two extra single beds and a dining area. The hotel's location makes it a favorite with leisure travelers, and all the on-site restaurants are leased to well-known eateries. Club Chinois (☞ Dining, *above*) adds a touch of elegance to this "new" kid on the block. ✉ *1 Tanglin Rd., 247905,* ☎ *737–1133,* FAX *733-0242. 368 rooms, 19 suites. 4 restaurants, bar, coffee shop, dance club, nightclub, meeting rooms, travel services. AE, DC, MC, V.*

$$$ 📺 **The Pan Pacific.** Of the five Marina Square hotels, this one is the largest (which can make it seem impersonal) and the least expensive (which may enable you to overlook its impersonal air). It aims to accommodate the budget traveler and needs of businesspeople alike—from junior executives to senior management. Upper-floor guest rooms have better views and more amenities; those on the Pacific Floor have butler service and complimentary breakfast and cocktails. Guest rooms and meeting rooms have high-speed Internet access with DSL broadband, with speeds up to 50 times faster than a 28.8 Kbps modem. "Cyber butlers" will be happy to assist you with any technical difficulties. Your eatery options include the rooftop Chinese restaurant and the Japanese and Italian dining rooms. ✉ *7 Raffles Blvd., 039595,* ☎ *336–8111,* FAX *339–1861. 784 rooms, 37 suites. 5 restaurants, café, coffee shop, pool, 2 tennis courts, spa, massage, business services, meeting rooms. AE, DC, MC, V.* 🐾

$$$ 📺 **Plaza Parkroyal.** Just ten minutes' walk from notorious Bugis Street, where sailors once strolled with ladies of the night, you'll find the recently refurbished Plaza Parkroyal. The excellent facilities within include a first-class pool and the 7,000 square ft St. Gregory Javana Spa, which offers Balinese-style massages and facials. The Orchid Club floors at the hotel offer special services for the pampered traveler. ✉ *10 Coleman St., 179809,* ☎ *336–3456,* FAX *339–9311. 348 rooms. 2 restaurants, 2 bars, pool, spa, health club, business services, meeting rooms. AE, DC, MC, V.*

$$$ 📺 **The Regent.** A good 10-minute walk from Orchard and Scotts roads, the Regent appeals to those who want a quiet haven. Relaxed, comfortable public rooms are done in soft tones and decked out with Asian carpets and wood paneling. The clubby second-floor cocktail lounge, The Bar, is a peaceful refuge within this refuge. Rooms have pastel color schemes, big beds, writing desks, and marble bathrooms; some have balconies. The Tea Lounge serves, of course, high tea daily.

Capers offers an alfresco setting for its international cuisine, the Summer Palace serves Cantonese cuisine prepared by Hong Kong chefs; and Maxim's de Paris has a Belle Epoque decor and French cuisine. (Travelers with disabilities take note: this hotel has amenities for you.) ⊠ *1 Cuscaden Rd., 249715,* ☎ *733–8888,* FAX *732–8838. 393 rooms, 48 suites. 4 restaurants, bar, lobby lounge, pool, spa, business services. AE, DC, MC, V.* ✍

$$$ 🏨 **Royal Plaza on Scotts.** The lobby here makes a statement with Italian marble floors, two grand staircases, Burmese teak paneling, stained-glass skylights, and handwoven tapestries. Rooms were recently upgraded to the tune of S$20 million, and there are facilities for travelers with disabilities. The Executive Club floor has a private lounge for complimentary breakfast and evening cocktails. Bella Donna (☞ Dining, *above*) is a fun, informal Mediterranean restaurant off the lobby. ⊠ *25 Scotts Rd., 228220,* ☎ *737–7966,* FAX *737–6646. 495 rooms. 2 restaurants, bar, pool, exercise room, business services, travel services. AE, DC, MC, V.* ✍

$$$ 🏨 **Singapore Marriott.** Formerly the Dynasty, this striking 33-story, pagoda-inspired property dominates Singapore's "million-dollar corner"—the Orchard and Scotts roads' intersection. Before Marriott took over, the three-story lobby was done in rich, deep red—the Chinese color for good fortune—with 24 remarkable carved-teak wall panels. Such decoration has been replaced by light-color walls and fake palm trees. Rooms are Western in style, with light-gray carpets, pink vinyl wallpaper, pink-gray upholstery, and ample wood; there are amenities for people with disabilities. The hotel's location—rather than its character—is now its selling point, though it may be the only lodging in the country with an outdoor basketball court. The Crossroads Café is a great spot for people-watching. ⊠ *320 Orchard Rd., 238865,* ☎ *735–5800,* FAX *735–9800. 364 rooms, 19 suites. 2 restaurants, 2 cafés, patisserie, pool, basketball, exercise room, nightclub, business services, meeting rooms. AE, DC, MC, V.* ✍

$$$ 🏨 **Westin Plaza and Westin Stamford.** Catering to business executives, the Plaza is the smaller and higher-priced of these Raffles City twins; the 70-story Stamford, one of the tallest hotels in the world, attracts tours and conventions. These hotels are a hub of their own, with a dozen restaurants—of which the Compass Rose Restaurant (☞ Dining, *above*) is the highlight—more than 100 shops, and convention facilities (including the largest column-free meeting rooms in the world). All rooms have balconies, and the hotel can fulfill the needs of those with disabilities. The 29 Stamford Crest Suites are extremely well appointed with such amenities as a complimentary breakfast and minibar and a separate exercise room. ⊠ *2 Stamford Rd., 178882,* ☎ *339–6633,* FAX *336–5117. Stamford 1,263 rooms; Plaza 764 rooms, 29 suites. 12 restaurants, 2 pools, 6 tennis courts, health club, squash, dance club, business services, convention center, meeting rooms, travel services. AE, DC, MC, V.* ✍

$$ ★ 🏨 **Albert Court Hotel.** Rare in Singapore are small hotels that have gone to the expense and effort of restoring existing structures (and installing facilities for people with disabilities). The Albert Court, which is only a few minutes' walk from Little India, is one. Furnishings are simple, but wood paneling creates a warm, comfortable atmosphere. The staff is enthusiastic, and this attitude infects the mostly European guests. You can relax and grab a bite at the small coffee shop, open from 7 AM to 11 PM. ⊠ *180 Albert St., 189971,* ☎ *339–3939,* FAX *339–3253. 135 rooms, 1 suite. Bar, coffee shop. AE, MC, V.*

$$ 🏨 **Allson.** This hotel's published rates are lower than those at similar hotels, such as the nearby Carlton. All rooms have rosewood furniture and little extras such as coffee- and tea makers and IDD phones. Rooms

on the Excellence Floor are more expensive but more spacious. This hotel has a great location: it's near Raffles City Tower, Marina Square, the historic colonial district, Little India, Bugis Street, and the Arab District, and it's only a 10-minute subway or bus ride to Orchard Road. ⊠ *101 Victoria St., 188018,* ☎ *336–0811,* FAX *339–7019. 450 rooms. 3 restaurants, café, coffee shop, pool, business services. AE, DC, MC, V.*

$$ 🏨 **Amara Hotel.** At the south end of the business district, this 18-story hotel is convenient to the train station and the commercial and port facilities and is one of Singapore's better deals if you get a discount (usually available). Although the hotel itself lacks character, it's part of a vibrant shopping and entertainment complex and close to Chinatown's Tanjong Pagar. Rooms are warm, with pastel colors, large sofas, one king-size or two queen-size beds, and bedside remote-control panels. The Royal Club concierge floor has butler service. Don't miss the nightly S$22 poolside steamboat and barbecue buffet with more than 40 items. (Travelers with disabilities should consider a stay at this hotel.) ⊠ *165 Tanjong Pagar Rd., 088539,* ☎ *224–4488,* FAX *224–3910. 365 rooms. 2 restaurants, coffee shop, pool, tennis court, business services. AE, DC, MC, V.*

$$ 🏨 **The Concorde.** Once appropriately called the Glass Hotel, the Concorde has a glass canopy that curves down from the ninth story over the entrance, which faces southeast for good fortune. Decorated in autumn hues, rooms are modern and have standard amenities. A stay in one on the three executive floors gets you complimentary breakfast and cocktails. For dining and entertainment, head for the fourth floor, where there are French, Japanese, and Chinese restaurants; the Chinese restaurant frequently has floor shows. The hotel lies just south of the Singapore River and west of the business district. ⊠ *317 Outram Rd., 169075,* ☎ *733–0188,* FAX *733–0989. 515 rooms. 3 restaurants, pool, massage, sauna, steam room, exercise room, tennis court, business services, meeting rooms. AE, DC, MC, V.* 🐾

$$ 🏨 **Elizabeth Hotel.** Once the truly budget Queen's Hotel, this establishment in a quiet area off Orchard Road was expanded in 1997 and was given a new name and higher rates. Standard rooms are modest; those in the four-story deluxe wing have refrigerators. Travelers with disabilities will be comfortable here. ⊠ *24 Mt. Elizabeth, 228518,* ☎ *738–1188,* FAX *732–3866. 247 rooms. Restaurant, bar, coffee shop, pool, exercise room, business services, meeting rooms. AE, DC, MC, V.* 🐾

$$ 🏨 **Excelsior Hotel.** This central-city hotel is across the street from nearly 1,000 shops; close to its twin, the Peninsula Hotel (☞ Lodging, *below*); and a block from Raffles City. Guest rooms are reasonably large and well maintained and have safes, minibars, and IDD phones. Its popular Annalakshmi restaurant (☞ Dining, *above*) serves vegetarian Indian fare, and there's a 24-hour café. ⊠ *5 Coleman St., 179805,* ☎ *339–0708,* FAX *339–3847. 271 rooms, 5 suites. 3 restaurants, café, bar, pool, travel services. AE, DC, MC, V.* 🐾

$$ 🏨 **Furama Hotel.** On the doorstep of Chinatown and a 10-minute walk from the commercial district, this modern curvilinear building stands out amid the surrounding shophouses. Tour groups and Japanese businessmen call this place home. The helpful staff will direct you to interesting sights, and there are daily guided walking tours through Chinatown. After hoofing it around, you can rest in the popular poolside café. ⊠ *60 Eu Tong Sen St., 059804,* ☎ *533–3888,* FAX *534–1489. 356 rooms. 2 restaurants, bar, café, pool, beauty salon, sauna, steam room, business services, meeting rooms. AE, DC, MC, V.*

$$ 🏨 **Harbour View Dai Ichi.** If you want to be away from all the hurly-burly but still near the business district, this 29-story hotel will be perfect for you. Rooms are small, neat, and functional; two are in Japanese tatami style (most of the clientele is from Japan), and the hotel's main

restaurant is the Kuramaya. There's also a Continental restaurant. ⊠ *81 Anson Rd., 079908,* ☎ *224–1133,* FAX *222–0749. 416 rooms. 2 restaurants, coffee shop, pool, massage, sauna, exercise room, business services. AE, DC, MC, V.*

$$ ⚏ **Le Meridien Changi.** Aside from its location 10 minutes from the airport, this hotel has no particular merits, except for golfers. Some rooms are designed for the physically challenged. ⊠ *1 Netheravon Rd., 508502,* ☎ *542–7700,* FAX *542–5295. 280 rooms. Restaurant, coffee shop, pool, golf privileges, exercise room, bicycles, baby-sitting, business services. AE, DC, MC, V.*

$$ ⚏ **Novotel Apollo Singapore.** Recently taken over by Novotel, this business-class hotel received an S$80 million face-lift in 1998. Renovations will be completed by the end of 2000. From here it's is a five-minute walk to Chinatown, Clarke Quay, Boat Quay, and the infamous "pub row" of Mohamed Sultan Road. For those doing business at Raffles Place, it is a quick taxi ride and a leisurely stroll back along the Singapore River. Upon entering the hotel you are greeted by the Waterfall Lounge, a relaxing green oasis in the middle of the bustling city. The marble foyer with its huge pillars is art deco–inspired. The rooms are bright and cheerful but simple. Executive Floor rooms are more elaborately decorated, and all rooms have a full range of modern amenities, such as TV satellite, IDD phones, data ports for laptops, and personal safes. A terrace with sundeck, hot tub, wading pool, and a tennis court is set amid a garden landscape. The Luna Coffee House serves Peranakan food with a Western influence. There is an Indonesian buffet for breakfast, lunch, high tea, and dinner. Ask about weekend promotions. ⊠ *405 Havelock Rd., 169633,* ☎ *733–2081,* FAX *732–7025. 480 rooms, 23 suites; 135 deluxe rooms. 3 restaurants, coffee shop, outdoor hot tub, exercise room, dance club, business center. AE, DC, MC, V. www.apollo-hotel.com*

$$ ⚏ **Peninsula Hotel.** The Peninsula Hotel is easily accessible from the financial, shopping, and entertainment districts. The fairly spacious guest rooms are clean, and those on the 17th floor and up have good views. There's no on-site restaurant, but a coffee shop serves the basics, and there are several reasonably priced restaurants nearby. ⊠ *3 Coleman St., 179804,* ☎ *339–0708,* FAX *339–3847. 307 rooms, 8 suites. Coffee shop, in-room safes, minibars, room service, pool, exercise room, nightclub. AE, DC, MC, V.* ✍

$$ ⚏ **Plaza Hotel.** The rooms in this Little Araby hotel include IDD phones, coffee- and tea-makers, and sensor-touch bedside control panels. Service is friendly, though a bit laid-back. The three on-site restaurants offer Cantonese and Thai cuisine, Western and regional fare, and spicy Oriental-style steaks. With a full house, the hotel can be quite lively. There's entertainment in the evenings; if you want to be the evening's entertainment, check out the 18-room Singsation karaoke club. ⊠ *7500A Beach Rd., 199591,* ☎ *298–0011,* FAX *296–3600. 350 rooms. 2 restaurants, 2 bars, refrigerators, pool, steam room, exercise room, business services. AE, DC, MC, V.*

$$ ⚏ **Rasa Sentosa.** A vast, arc-shape building facing the sea, this Sentosa Island resort getaway is popular with both conventions and Singaporean families escaping to the beach for the weekend (room rates are lower during the week). The motel-like rooms are small though all have balconies; ask for a room facing the water, otherwise your view will merely be of a grassy knoll. The main restaurant serves Cantonese fare, and the café dishes up Western and Asian food. Children love this place for its pool with water slides, its playground, its nursery, and its video-games room. Adults appreciate the many recreational activities, including rock-wall climbing, golf, and windsurfing. Travelers with disabilities will find that the hotel caters to their needs as well. You can get to the island on a free shuttle bus from the Shangri-La hotel (☞ Lodging, *above*), which owns this resort. ⊠ *101 Siloso Rd., Sentosa Island 098970,* ☎ *275–0100; 020/8747–8485 (reservations in the U.K.); 800/942–5050 (reservations in Canada and the U.S.),* FAX *275–0355. 459 rooms. 3 restaurants, bar, lobby lounge, pool, massage, health club, Ping-Pong, windsurfing, boating, recreation room, video games, nursery, playground. AE, DC, MC, V.* ☙

$$ 🖼 **Robertson Quay Hotel.** This ten-story circular budget hotel, which opened in 1997, is situated in a serene neighborhood just a short walk away from Chinatown and from the bustling river action of Clarke and Boat quays with their competing music, bumboats, and stores. Rooms in the hotel are basic but comfortable, with the basic amenities, including IDD phone lines, and are wheelchair accessible. The two-room suites are roomier and ideal for families. Ask for a room above the 7th floor to get a great view of the river and the city. There is a small pool overlooking the river and a putting green. An additional S$5 gets you a Continental breakfast served in the lobby. The Home Beach Bar downstairs is equipped with darts, pool, and other table games. ⊠ *15 Merbau Rd., 239032,* ☎ *735–3333,* FAX *738–1515. 150 rooms, 10 suites. Pool, putting green, meeting room. AE, DC, MC, V.* ☙

$$ 🖼 **Seaview Hotel.** Off the East Coast Parkway, midway between Changi Airport and Singapore city, this high-rise hotel is more convenient for travelers in transit than for those here to see the sights. Guest rooms offer the basic amenities, and there are restaurants and shops on the premises and in the area. The nearby East Coast Park offers many outdoor activities, including water-sports facilities. ⊠ *26 Amber Close, 439984,* ☎ *345–2222,* FAX *345–1741. 435 rooms. 2 restaurants, bar, coffee shop, room service, pool, nightclub. AE, DC, MC, V.*

$$ 🖼 **Traders Hotel.** For value (try to take advantage of the frequent pro-
★ motional rates) and service, this hotel is hard to beat. It has all the necessary comforts—including those for travelers with disabilities. Room service is available 24 hours, and scores of restaurants and a supermarket are just steps away. An hourly shuttle to Orchard Road and the MRT station is available for tired sightseers. For seafood and local dishes poolside, check out Ah Hoi's Kitchen for lunch and dinner; Rumpoles serves lunch, snacks, and drinks. Rooms are comfortable, with writing desks and plenty of light from the bay windows. ⊠ *1A Cuscaden Rd., 249716,* ☎ *738–2222; 020/8747–8485 (reservations in the U.K.); 800/942–5050 (reservations in Canada and U.S.),* FAX *831–4314. 543 rooms. Coffee shop, pool, exercise room, business services, meeting rooms. AE, DC, MC, V.*

$$ 🖼 **York Hotel.** Near busy Orchard Road, this classic European hotel is a quiet oasis. The tower has only suites, and the poolside wing has split-level cabanas and rooms surrounding a garden. All guest quarters have two queen-size beds. The White Rose Cafe serves Asian and Western fare. ⊠ *21 Mt. Elizabeth, 228516,* ☎ *737–0511,* FAX *732–1217. 335 rooms, 69 suites. 2 restaurants, bar, pool, beauty salon, sauna, exercise room. AE, DC, MC, V.*

$ 🖼 **Hotel Royal.** This modest hotel has the standard amenities and in-room IDD phones. On the premises is an international forwarding service that can be useful for anyone—especially shoppers—who wish to send excess baggage back home. The hotel is near Newton Circus and is a 20-minute walk from Orchard Road. ⊠ *36 Newton Rd., 307964,* ☎ *253–4411,* FAX *253–8668. 331 rooms. 3 restaurants, coffee shop, minibars, refrigerators, pool, meeting rooms, travel services. AE, DC, MC, V.*

$ 🖼 **Inn at Temple Street.** One of the latest additions to Chinatown's unique
★ boutique hotel scene, the Inn at Temple Street opened in early 1998 and occupies five beautifully restored shophouses. The attractive Per-

anakan decor—a fusion of 19th-century European, Chinese, and Malay furnishings and color schemes—reminds you of the neighborhood's rich cultural traditions. Ask for a room with a view of the street below, which is slated to become a pedestrian mall. ✉ *36 Temple St., 058581,* ☎ *221–5333,* ℻ *225–5391. 42 rooms. Coffee shop, bar, in-room safes, refrigerators. AE, DC, MC, V.*

$ ⌷ **Metropole Hotel.** This very modest, very basic hotel near Raffles City has simply furnished rooms. Rare in budget lodgings, you'll find both a helpful staff and room service. ✉ *41 Seah St., 188396,* ☎ *336–3611,* ℻ *339–3610. 54 rooms. Restaurant, coffee shop, room service. AE, DC, MC, V.*

$ ⌷ **Metropolitan YMCA, Tanglin Centre.** A 10-minute walk from Orchard Road, this YMCA (which admits women) has rooms with air-conditioning and private baths. There are even a few suites. The budget restaurant offers wholesome English breakfasts as well as Chinese, Malay, Nonya, and Western meals. ✉ *Tanglin Centre, 60 Stevens Rd., 257854,* ☎ *737–7755,* ℻ *235–5528. 93 rooms. Restaurant, coffee shop, pool, exercise room, meeting rooms. AE, DC, MC, V.* ✍

$ ⌷ **Regalis Court.** This charming, 43-room boutique hotel—which
★ opened in mid-1997—once housed the Singapore Ballet Academy of British colonial days. The rooms have a Peranakan-inspired decor (earth tones, reds, and browns) with classical European touches and such novel items as reproductions of clunky black telephones and old alarm clocks. You can open your windows (be sure to ask for a room that has them) to the quiet residential neighborhood, and a Continental breakfast is included in the room rate. Only a few minutes' walk from Orchard Road, the hotel is not well known and attracts savvy, independent travelers from around the globe. Check out the Indonesian Rajah Inn (☞ Dining, *above*) restaurant for inexpensive, tasty dishes. ✉ *64 Lloyd Rd., 239113,* ☎ *734–7117,* ℻ *736–1651. 43 rooms. Restaurant, breakfast room, in-room safes, no-smoking rooms. AE, DC, MC, V.* ✍

$ ⌷ **RELC International Hotel.** This is less a hotel than an international
★ conference center often used by Singapore's university for seminars. However, the upper floors contain bargain guest rooms that are large and basically comfortable and have plenty of light. The building is in a residential neighborhood, up a hill beyond the Shangri-La hotel (☞ Lodging, *above*), a 10-minute walk from the Orchard and Scotts roads intersection. Because of its good value, it's often booked, so reservations well in advance are strongly advised. Breakfast is included, and there are coffeemakers in the rooms. ✉ *30 Orange Grove Rd., 258352,* ☎ *737–9044,* ℻ *733–9976. 128 rooms. Coffee shop, coin laundry. AE, DC, MC, V.*

$ ⌷ **Royal Peacock.** Living up to its name, this brightly painted shop-house boutique hotel opened in 1997 on the once notorious Keong Saik Road (it was known for its red lanterns and ladies of the night, who are still here but are in state-controlled brothels). The standard rooms don't have windows, so ask for a deal on a superior or deluxe room (listed at S$125). Breakfast and coffee and tea fixings are included in all prices. The hotel is within the central business district in Chinatown, and it has facilities for travelers with disabilities. ✉ *55 Keong Saik Rd., 089518,* ☎ *223–3522,* ℻ *221–1770. 76 rooms. Bar, café, minibars, business services. AE, DC, MC, V.*

$ ⌷ **Transit Hotel.** At last: a lodging truly geared to bleary-eyed travelers en route to still another destination. This new hotel is *inside* Changi Airport on Level 3 of the departure lounge in Terminal 1. (Note: if you stay here, you don't go through immigration control.) Rooms are clean, fresh, and basic. Rates are for six-hour periods—a double is S$56—and include use of the swimming pool, sauna, and fitness center. Nonguests may also use the pool (S$10), the sauna and showers (S$10),

or just the shower (S$5). ⊠ *Changi Airport, Terminal 1,* ☎ *543–
0911; 0800/96–3562 (reservations in the U.K.); 800/690–6785 (reservations in the U.S.);* FAX *545–8365. Pool, sauna, health club, nursery.
AE, DC, MC, V.*

$ 🖩 **YMCA International House.** This well-run YMCA at the bottom of
Orchard Road offers hotel-like accommodations for men and women—
with double (S$105) and single (S$90) rooms—as well as dormitory-
style quarters (S$25); S$5 will buy you temporary YMCA membership.
All rooms have private baths, color TVs, and IDD phones. In addition
to an impressive gym, you'll find a rooftop pool and squash and bad-
minton courts. There's also a McDonald's at the entrance. ⊠ *1 Orchard Rd., 238824,* ☎ *336–6000,* FAX *337–3140. 111 rooms. Pool,
exercise room, squash. AE, DC, MC, V.*

Bintan Island, Indonesia

Bintan's resorts dot wide sandy beaches on the northern coast. Each
hotel has a wide range of restaurants, bars, and other facilities. Since
there are really only six establishments (the hotels in Tanjung Pinang,
the island's main city, are substandard), book as far in advance as possible. On weekends Singaporeans and expats take full advantage of the
island's clean waters, just 45 minutes from one of the world's busiest
ports.

The resorts accept Singapore dollars for rooms and for meals (price
categories assigned below are based on Singapore dollars), though
credit card purchases for other items may be charged in Indonesian ru-
piahs at, no doubt, a better rate of exchange. The newest resorts, such
as Club Med and Nirwana Resort Hotel, have been offering promotional specials, so always ask about discounts when booking. All resorts have their marketing offices in Singapore, and it's best to make
reservations before arriving on Bintan; for more information, contact
Bintan Resort Management (☎ 543–0039). If, for some reason, you
need to dial an establishment directly, the country code for Indonesia
is 62, and the area code for Bintan is 771.

At press time, plans for shuttle bus service between the resorts were
afoot. If, however, you have to rely on a taxi to get around, you must
book it in advance from a car-rental agency at the ferry terminal. Ask
the front-desk staff of your hotel to help with the arrangements. Although most people come here to relax or frolic in a beach resort environment, consider taking a guided day trip outside of your resort; it
will definitely enhance your Indonesian experience (☞ Tour Operators *in* Singapore A to Z, *below*).

$$$$ 🖩 **Banyan Tree Bintan.** You'll find romance, luxury, and top-notch ser-
★ vice during a stay here. Accommodations are in private, Balinese-style
villas that stand on stilts and overlook a horseshoe-shape bay. Fifty-
five villas have a whirlpool tub on a deck that faces the South China
Sea. The more luxurious Pool Villas also have either a private swimming pool or plunge pool, two bedrooms with king-size beds, a bathroom with a sunken bath, a spacious dressing room, and a kitchen
(though you can make your own meals, most people just ask for a staff
chef to drop by and whip up a special meal or two; there's no grocery
store nearby). Rooms have green and brown color schemes, Indonesian pottery, elevated beds that are draped with mosquito netting, and
sea views—truly idyllic. ⊠ *Site A4, Lagoi, Tanjong Said,* ☎ *462–
4800 (in Singapore); 771/26918 (in Bintan),* FAX *462–2800 (in Singapore); 771/81348 (in Bintan). 72 villas. 2 restaurants, 2 pools, outdoor
hot tub, spa, 18-hole golf course, 2 tennis courts, beach, dive shop,
dock, snorkeling, windsurfing, fishing, meeting rooms. AE, MC, V.* 🐾

$$$ ⛱ **Club Med Ria Bintan.** This resort opened in late 1997 with all the amenities of a luxury Club Med, including many, many water and land activities—there's even a circus school for children, complete with a trapeze that gives parents heart palpitations. The resort is popular with Europeans, Japanese families, and Club Med junkies from around the world, so its staff members are multilingual. You might feel as if you're on the French Riviera: there are numerous chaises longues around the pools and on the private beach; the TV in your room has French satellite television; and wines served at meals are distinctly French. Among the facilities are an excellent children's activity center and a well-equipped exercise room and spa. The general feeling here is that you never need to leave the resort for anything; everything is terribly well organized (great if you want to be involved, not so great if you're seeking solitude). The comfortable rooms have balconies (the sunset views are terrific) and well-equipped baths. ✉ *North coast,* ☎ *738–4222 (in Singapore),* 🖷 *738–0770 (in Singapore). 307 rooms. 4 restaurants, bar, 2 pools, spa, 2 tennis courts, aerobics, archery, health club, beach, water slide, cabaret, dance club, baby-sitting, children's programs, nursery, playground, coin laundry, meeting rooms. AE, MC, V. FAP.* 🐾

$$–$$$ ⛱ **Bintan Lagoon Resort Hotel and Golf Club.** Japanese visitors and locals alike are drawn to the former Hotel Sedona, an enormous villa complex. The property includes two pools—one of them *very* large—water-sports facilities, a spa, a mah-jongg hall, tennis, golf, karaoke, and a children's center. Although right next to the beach, this hotel isn't as aesthetically appealing or relaxed as some of the other resorts. Still, it *is* a golfer's paradise, with two 18-hole courses—one designed by Jack Nicklaus, the other by Ian Baker-Finch—that have driving ranges and putting greens. The stunning view of the Nicklaus course from the golf club's alfresco café is itself inspiring. The rest of the grounds are equally well landscaped; you can rent a bicycle for an hour or two and take a tour of them. Rooms and suites are clean and well kept, if a bit stark in their furnishings; the Sedona Club Suites have huge balconies and sunken tubs. You won't lack for a place to eat: there are seven on-site restaurants that offer a variety of cuisines. ✉ *Pasir Panjang Beach, north coast,* ☎ *226–3122 (in Singapore); 770/691388 (in Bintan),* 🖷 *223–0693 (in Singapore); 62–770/691399 (in Bintan). 401 rooms, 15 suites. 7 restaurants, 2 pools, massage, spa, 2 driving ranges, 2 18-hole golf courses, 2 putting greens, 4 tennis courts, health club, Ping-Pong, volleyball, beach, snorkeling, water slide, windsurfing, jet skiing, fishing, bicycles, billiards, dance club, video games, baby-sitting, children's programs, playground, laundry service, business services, meeting rooms, travel services. AE, DC, MC, V.* 🐾

$$ ⛱ **Nirwana Resort Hotel.** Another new addition to Bintan's north coast is the sprawling former Sol Elite. Rooms are bright, clean, and relatively spacious; those facing the sea have balconies. For about S$100 more a night, you can stay in one of the two- to four-bedroom villas. The public areas are well maintained and cheery; the buildings are painted in dazzling primary colors. To get away from it all, head for the beach; most guests opt for the pool area, so it's often deserted. Organized activities include staff-led lawn games and instruction on how to properly open a coconut. Buffet breakfast in El Patio coffee shop is included in the rates, and the lively Cantores Karaoke Lounge is one of Bintan's few nightspots. ✉ *Nirwana Gardens,* ☎ *374–1308 (in Singapore); 771/770–692505 (in Bintan),* 🖷 *372–1318 (in Singapore). 245 rooms, 14 villas. 2 restaurants, 2 bars, pool, croquet, volleyball, beach, snorkeling, nightclub, video games, playground, business services, meeting rooms, travel services. AE, DC, MC, V. BP.* 🐾

$–$$ ⛱ **Mayang Sari Beach Resort.** Set on a bay with an exquisite palm-lined beach, the relaxed, friendly Mayang Sari is a quiet retreat—the perfect place to read a novel or go beachcombing. The chalet-style cabins have high ceilings, Indonesian teak furnishings, large beds, and private verandas. This, Bintan's first resort property, is reminiscent of what Bali might have been like in the 1960s: tall palm trees lining the beach, friendly service, decent prices, gentle breezes. The on-site Mayang Terrace restaurant serves delicious Indonesian dishes at affordable prices. The gift shop seems to have sporadic opening hours, but again, the price of the goods makes it worth checking out. ⊠ *Northwest coast at Tanjong Tondang,* ☎ *372–1308 (in Singapore),* FAX *372–1318 (in Singapore). 50 cabins. Restaurant, 2 bars, beach, recreation room, baby-sitting, laundry service, meeting room. AE, MC, V.* ❧

$ 🖫 **Mana Mana.** College students and other young Europeans and Australians flock to this resort because of its affordable rates; water-sports enthusiasts of all ages are drawn by the facilities at its beach club. Accommodations are in small, no-smoking huts with TVs and baths (shower only). Most of the cabins are in a garden setting; only the lobby and alfresco restaurant-bar front the beach. The on-site gift shop stocks souvenirs, clothing, knapsacks, and jewelry, but the prices are on the high side. ⊠ *North coast,* ☎ *339–8878 (in Singapore),* FAX *339–7812 (in Singapore). 50 rooms in 25 huts. Restaurant, bar, beach, snorkeling, windsurfing, boating. AE, MC, V.* ❧

NIGHTLIFE AND THE ARTS

The recent Southeast Asian economic crisis certainly looks like history when you survey Singapore's bustling nightlife now. And the scene today is a far cry from when, not so very long ago, Singapore was often branded "boring." There's a genuine hunger for the arts, and the meticulously conserved streets of old Singapore are alive into the wee hours. The Singapore Tourism Board (☞ Singapore A to Z, *below*) has monthly listings of events. You can also find schedules for major performances in the local English-language newspaper, the *Straits Times,* or in the free weeklies *I.S.* and *This Week Singapore,* available at most hotel reception desks. Hit www.happening.com.sg for more information.

Tickets to events are available at box offices or through either of two ticketing agencies: **SISTIC** (☎ 348–5555) or **TicketCharge** (☎ 296–2929)—a credit card is required for bookings by phone. Both of these agencies have Web pages and also counters at major shopping centers.

Nightlife

Singapore's nightlife has evolved into several quite separate nodes: there's the lively Singapore River quayside scene—Boat, Clarke, and Robertson quays, together with Chinatown's Tanjong Pagar district, all crammed with restaurants, music bars, wine bars, and more—and there's the touristy hotel strip of Orchard Road, a mix of sophisticated bars and pounding discos. A former nineteenth-century convent, the Chijmes complex near the Singapore History Museum off Stamford–Bras Basah Roads is a swish venue offering alfresco options, while Holland Village up Holland Road is a trendy little nightlife *coin* all on its own, as is Mohamed Sultan Road, between River Valley Road and the river. Then there's sleazier, more colorful action going on in the east, Katong and Geylang-way, and around Serangoon.

Nightclubs and discos are glitzy and pricey, designed chiefly for the young or those "on the hunt," and are very, very loud, making conversation well nigh impossible. Common, too, is the cover charge or a "first-drink" charge of about S$15 on weeknights and S$25 on weekends. During Happy Hour times, cheaper drinks are customary at most places, so call ahead to find out when they are. *Pace* all feminists, but it's a fact, many places also welcome women (sans male escort) for free or at a reduced rate. Dress codes almost everywhere except the posher hotels are relaxed, even casual, thanks to the humid equatorial climate.

Older Singaporeans favor nightclubs with floor shows and hostesses, jocularly referred to as "public relations officers," who can be "booked" for an hourly fee or a big tip at the end of the evening. Be forewarned that some hostesses may be prostitutes chasing the dollar, and watch out, too, for the custom that requires you to buy a bottle of brandy (a high-status drink with the Chinese), for as much as S$300. Refusal could provoke confrontation.

The truly risqué is underground but alive and well, although the once bawdy Bugis Street is now sanitized. Tourists should take care, but it is possible to observe this underworld in parts of Geylang around the numbered *lorongs* (streets or lanes) and along Desker Road, off Jalan Besar, Serangoon. Red-light districts are literally that, with red lanterns and large, backlit red-on-white house numbers. Some hotels rent rooms in two-hour time slots. Prostitution is illegal but actually tolerated, monitored, and contained, with prostitutes registered and subject to regular medical checks. The gay scene is also extremely active, although again technically illegal (cruisers beware entrapment). Check out Sunday nights at Venom (☞ below), also Why Not? wine bar at 56–58 Tras Street and Taboo Club, 21 Tanjong Pagar Road.

Bars and Pubs

Bang Bang. A new entertainment hub is developing around Prinsep Street, and this two-level pub, with DJ-driven dancing and a pool table upstairs, is part of it. ⊠ *50 Prinsep St., No. 01/01–04,* ☎ *883–0723.* ☜ *No cover charge.* ☉ *Mon.–Thurs. 3 PM–1 AM, Fri.–Sat. 3 PM–3 AM.*

Barcelona. Go Latin at this bar with a Catalan flavor offering salsa music, fine wines, and Havana cigars, not to mention plush, comfy furniture. Live music is featured Wed.–Sat. from 8:30 PM. ⊠ *11 Unity St., No. 01-30/31,* ☎ *235–3456.* ☜ *No cover charge.* ☉ *Mon.–Thurs. 5 PM–1 AM, Fri.–Sat. 5 PM– 2 AM, Sun. 5 PM–midnight.*

Brewerkz. Beer lovers home in on this large pub at Riverside Point, across from Clarke Quay. Brewmaster Scott Robinson offers seven ales and bitters (the most popular is the India Pale Ale) and chef Eduardo Vargas serves eclectic East-West fusion cuisine (the kitchen is open from noon to midnight). The best buy is the set lunch menu (about S$19.95), which includes three glasses of beer and coffee or tea. ⊠ *No. 01-05/06 Riverside Point, 30 Merchant Rd.,* ☎ *438–7438.* ☉ *Sun.–Thurs. noon–1 AM, Fri.–Sat. noon–3 AM.*

Brix. Formerly Brannigan's, this music bar boasting an impressive array of whiskies and wine is as much a magnet as ever for globe-trotters, local lovelies, and sundry smart fun-seekers. The music is familiar Top 40 and soul, R&B and jazz standards, the dance floor packed. ⊠ *Grand Hyatt Singapore, 10–12 Scotts Rd.* ☎ *730–7018.* ☜ *Cover charge: 1st drink S$15 Wed.– Sat. after 9 PM.* ☉ *Weeknights 6 PM–2 AM, weekends 6 PM–3; closed Sun.*

Father Flanagan's. This Irish pub, aptly (or inaptly?) located in the Chijmes old convent complex, serves good pub grub (Irish buffet 11 AM–2:30 PM S$18.50) and a variety of brews. ⊠ *Chijmes complex, lower level, 30 Victoria St.,* ☎ *333–1418.* ☜ *No cover charge.* ☉ *Sun.–Mon. 11 AM to midnight, Tues.–Thurs. 11 AM–1 AM, Fri.–Sat. 11 AM–2 AM.*

Hard Rock Cafe. Hamburgers and light fare are served at this pub-café, and a live band plays in the evenings, with jam sessions on Sunday nights. It's much like other establishments in the chain, with a casual, festive, atmosphere and plenty of rock memorabilia. ✉ *No. 02–01 HPL House, 50 Cuscaden Rd.,* ☎ *235–5232.* ✆ *S$20 cover charge Fri., Sat., and holiday nights after 7 PM includes first drink.* ☉ *Weekdays 11 AM–2 AM, weekends 11 AM–3 AM.*

Ice Cold Beer. Expats tend to gather at this lively pub on a small, historic pedestrian street off Orchard Road. Beers from around the world dominate, ranging S$9–S$12 a pop, and good hot dogs are available for S$6. The music is rock from the '70s and '80s. ✉ *5 Emerald Hill Rd.,* ☎ *735–9929.* ✆ *No cover charge.* ☉ *Nightly 5 PM–2 AM.*

Muddy Murphy's. This one's a longtime favorite, famed for its wine and cheese promotions on the last Wednesday of every month, weekly Sunday Roast lunches, and excellent Irish bands. ✉ *No. B1-01/06 Orchard Hotel Shopping Arcade, 442 Orchard Rd.,* ☎ *735–0400.* ✆ *No cover charge.* ☉ *Mon.–Thurs. 6 PM–2 AM, Sat. 6 PM–3 AM, Sun. 5 PM–1 AM.*

Que Pasa. For wine lovers, this friendly pub with a Spanish ambience is a sure bet. Spanish tapas dishes go for S$6 and up, wines by the glass for S$10. ✉ *7 Emerald Hill Rd.,* ☎ *235–6626.* ✆ *No cover charge.* ☉ *Sun.–Fri. 6 PM–2 AM; Sat. 6 PM–3 AM..*

Discos and Dance Clubs

China Jump. By day, it's a Tex-Mex American-style restaurant; at night, it turns into a busy, yuppy disco featuring retro tunes for the over-25 set, who line up to get in. ✉ *Chijmes complex, interior courtyard, 30 Victoria St.,* ☎ *338–9388.* ✆ *Cover charge: S$25 men, S$20 women Thurs.–Sat. after 10:30 PM.* ☉ *Mon.–Tues. 5 PM–1 AM, Wed.–Fri. 5 PM– 3 AM, Sat. 11 AM–3 AM, Sun. 11 AM–1 AM.*

Europa Music Bar. It's easy to have fun at this busy club where young Singaporeans let down their hair. There are stage shows as well as contests and prizes for the serious drinking crowd. ✉ *No. B1–00 International Building, 360 Orchard Rd.,* ☎ *235–3301.* ✆ *Cover charge: S$14 men, S$12 women Thurs.–Sun.; S$18 men, S$16 women Fri. and Sat. and holidays; no cover charge and one complimentary drink Mon. and Wed.* ☉ *Weeknights 6 PM–1 AM, weekends 6 PM–2 AM.*

Fire. One of Singapore's steady favorites, Fire has live music for a lively, very young and local crowd. You pay for drinks with coupons. Upstairs, would-be artists sing their lungs out in 12 computerized karaoke rooms. ✉ *No. 04-19 Orchard Plaza, 150 Orchard Rd.,* ☎ *235–0155.* ✆ *Cover charge: S$15 men, S$7 women.* ☉ *Nightly 9 PM–3 AM.*

Pleasure Dome. Upscale and expensive with decent live bands, private rooms, and a members' lounge, this club is always busy with the young and well-to-do. The adjoining wine and cigar bar, **Le Château,** is a great place to chill when the crowd gets too noisy. Don't bother going if you're under 25. ✉ *No. B1-02 Specialists Shopping Centre, 277 Orchard Rd.,* ☎ *834–1221.* ✆ *Cover charges vary, but start at S$20.* ☉ *Weeknights 6 PM–3 AM, Sat. 8 PM–3 AM; closed Sun.*

Sparks. An offshoot of the popular Fire disco, this club has karaoke rooms, live music, and laser shows. Foreign dance bands often stop here for one-night shows. ✉ *Ngee Ann City (Takashimaya), Tower B, Level 7,* ☎ *735–6133.* ✆ *Cover charges vary, but start at S$15.* ☉ *Nightly 8 PM–3 AM.*

Venom. This lavish, 10,000-square-ft penthouse disco with Gothic steel-piped architecture is a happening place dishing out techno, hip-hop, garage, and house music, underground London-style. Attitude reigns supreme. Don't bother going unless you're decked out in the latest Italian designer fashions. ✉ *Pacific Plaza Penthouse, 12th floor, 9 Scotts Rd.,* ☎ *734–7677.* ✆ *Cover charges vary, but start at S$20.* ☉ *Tues.–Sun. 9:30 PM–3 AM; closed Mon.*

Zouk, Velvet Underground, and Phuture. It's a bit out of the way, but everyone knows where it is. A huge dance emporium born of renovated warehouses, established for close to a decade now but extensively renovated in 2000, Zouk is an institution of sorts. It's three clubs in one: Zouk for the young; Velvet for the sophisticated disco diva; jampacked Phuture for avant-garde music lovers and frenetic, trippy dancers. Visiting international DJs serve as hosts, and the club consistently gets rave reviews overseas. Taxis wait outside for the 3 AM closing crowd. ⊠ *17 Jiak Kim St.,* ☎ *738–2988.* ☒ *S$20–S$25 cover charge includes two drinks.* ◯ *Wed.–Sat. 7 PM–3 AM; closed Sun.–Tues. Wine Bar open daily.*

Music Clubs

JAZZ

Bar & Billiard Room. Light acoustic jazz complements Singapore's best-known, most historic hotel, in a wood-paneled and brass-fitted Edwardian-English pub ambience, complete with original Victorian billiards tables available for play. The buffet lunch and high tea spreads are scrumptious. ⊠ *Raffles Hotel, 1 Beach Rd.,* ☎ *331–1746.* ☒ *No cover charge.* ◯ *Daily 11:30 AM–12:30 AM; live music starts at 8:30 PM; bar open nightly 6 PM–12:30 AM.*

The Bar at the Regent. Jazz duos and trios often perform at this Four Seasons hotel sister property. ⊠ *The Regent, 1 Cuscaden Rd.,* ☎ *733–8888.* ☒ *No cover charge.* ◯ *Nightly 5 PM–1 AM.*

Harry's Quayside. This is a comfortable place to hang out and listen to a mix of jazz, blues, and old-time rock, with the occasional impromptu jam session thrown in. There are fine waterfront views. ⊠ *28 Boat Quay,* ☎ *538–3029.* ☒ *No cover charge.* ◯ *Sun.–Thurs. 11 AM–1 AM, Fri.–Sat. 11 AM–2 AM; restaurant open 11:30 AM–3 PM; live music starts around 9:30 PM.*

Somerset Bar. The jazz and contemporary music played here has attracted a loyal following, and there's room to sit and relax—a lure for the older crowd. Happy hours are long-lived, 5 PM–8:30 PM. For cocktails, house specials are the Singapore Sling, S$11.80, and Somerset's Sax, S$19.80. ⊠ *Westin Plaza, 3rd floor, 4 Stamford Rd.,* ☎ *338–8585.* ☒ *No cover charge.* ◯ *Nightly 5 PM–2 AM; live music starts around 9 PM.*

ROCK

Anywhere. The resident band, Tania, fronted by Alban and Zul, is a local legend. Powerful renditions of favorite covers are their forte. You'll find wall-to-wall humans, predominantly lone expat males, in this smoke-filled room. ⊠ *No. 04–08 Tanglin Shopping Centre, 19 Tanglin Rd.,* ☎ *734–8233.* ☒ *Cover charge: 1st drink: Mon.–Thurs. S$12, Fri.–Sat. S$18.* ◯ *Mon.–Thurs. 6 PM–2 AM, Fri.–Sat. 6 PM–3 AM; closed Sun.; live music starts around 10:30 PM.*

Bar None. On the site of the former much-loved Fabrice's World Music Bar, now closed, this large bar features a live local band playing Top 40 hits from the '50s till now. It models itself on New York's Blue Note and claims it is a class above techno and karaoke. ⊠ *Marriott Hotel, basement level, 320 Orchard Rd.,* ☎ *831–4656.* ☒ *Cover charge: S$20 weekends and holidays.* ◯ *Tues.–Sun. 7 PM–3 AM, Mon. 7 PM–2 AM; live music starts at 10 PM Tues.–Sun..*

Crazy Elephant. Dedicated to the blues, with occasional forays into R&B and rock, this popular bar also hosts Sunday night jam sessions. Pleasant getaways from the music are possible on the quayside terrace. ⊠ *No. 01–07 Clarke Quay,* ☎ *337–1990.* ☒ *No cover charge.* ◯ *Weeknights 5 PM–1 AM, weekends 5 PM–2 AM; live music starts around 10 PM nightly except Mon.*

Roomful of Blues. Although the music is eclectic, stretching to punk and heavy metal, blues lovers and local musicians flock to this club, especially for Sunday jam sessions. The house special cocktail is the Vertical Smile, for S$25. ⊠ *72 Prinsep St.,* ☎ *837–0882.* ⊠ *No cover charge.* ⊙ *Tues.–Sat. 2 PM–2 AM, Sun.–Mon. 2 PM–12 AM.*

Nightclubs

Apollo Nite Club. This club is patronized by Chinese businessmen with a taste for willowy, sequined Chinese singers and hostesses. Only snacks are served. ⊠ *Novotel Apollo Singapore, 19th floor, 405 Havelock Rd.,* ☎ *235–7977.* ⊠ *Hourly hostess fee S$34; bottle of brandy S$388.* ⊙ *Mon.–Sat. 5 PM–3 AM, Sun. 7:30 PM–3 AM.*

Lido Palace Nite Club. This lavish "palace of many pleasures" offers Chinese cabaret, a band, a DJ-spun disco, hostesses, and karaoke. Only snacks are served. ⊠ *The Concorde hotel, 5th floor, 317 Outram Rd.,* ☎ *732–8855.* ⊠ *Cover charge: 1st drink S$38.* ⊙ *Weeknights 5:30 PM–2:45 AM, weekends 9:30 PM–2:45 AM.*

Neptune Theatre Restaurant. At this sumptuous, two-story club you can dine on Cantonese food or sit in the nondiners' gallery. Local, Taiwanese, and Filipino singers entertain in English and Chinese, joined occasionally by a naughty European dance troupe. It's the only nightclub in Singapore licensed to feature the occasional topless cabaret show. ⊠ *Overseas Union House, 7th floor, Collyer Quay,* ☎ *224–3922 or 737–4411.* ⊠ *Cover charge: drink minimum S$8 with dinner; S$18.50 nondiners.* ⊙ *Nightly 7 PM–11 PM.*

The Arts

Singapore aspires to become the arts hub of Southeast Asia, and it's putting both cash and energy where its mouth is. The maturation and expansion of a professional performing and fine arts school at the **La Salle-SIA College of the Arts** (☎ 344–4300) has helped, as has the government's **National Arts Council** (☎ 270–0722), a prime mover and shaker. The local cultural calendar now hums with action, with strong contributions from an innovative theater scene, the March–April **Singapore International Film Festival** (☎ 222–5953), and the similarly timed, spectacular world ethnic arts showcase, **WOMAD** (World of Music, Arts, and Dance; ✥). Building on domestic Chinese, Malay, and Indian traditions, frequently imported international shows top off a heady cultural mix.

Quality performances of all kinds, from Western and Chinese opera to Indian classical dance and Western plays, take place at the old **Victoria Theatre and Memorial Hall** (⊠ 11 Empress Pl., ☎ 339–6120 for information; 338–8283 for bookings), home to the 85-member Singapore Symphony Orchestra, which is renowned for its large repertoire of well-known classics and works by Asian composers.

Singapore hopes that the downtown, oceanfront **The Esplanade—Theatres on the Bay** (⊠ Singapore Arts Centre Co. Ltd, 2 Raffles Link, No. 01–04, 039392, ☎ 337–3711, 337–0663 for information), due to open in 2002, will become as famous a landmark as Sydney's Opera House. A multimillion-dollar project, it is certainly just as controversial, locally. It will greatly expand arts space in Singapore, with a 2,000-seat theater and a 1,800-seat concert hall, among many other facilities, indoor and outdoor, besides studios and retail and restaurant space.

Indian music, drama, and dance performances are staged during major festivals at the more important temples, including the **Chettiar Temple** (⊠ 14 Tank Rd., ☎ 737–9393), the **Sri Mariamman Temple** (⊠ 244 South Bridge Rd., ☎ 223–4064), and the **Sri Srinivasa Perumal Temple** (⊠ 397 Serangoon Rd., ☎ 298–5771). Dramatic themes come from the ancient epics—tales of gods, demons, and heroes. For more information on Indian cultural events, contact the **Hindu Endowments Board** (☎ 298–5771).

The Substation (✉ 45 Armenian St., ☎ 337–7535 for information; 337–7800 for tickets) offers the nearest thing to "fringe" arts that you'll find in Singapore. It's young and avant-garde. Actors, artists, and musicians often gather here for alfresco drinks (daily from noon to 8:30 PM).

Dance

Periodic performances by companies such as the **Singapore Dance Theatre** (✉ Fort Canning Centre, 2nd floor, Cox Terr., ☎ 338–0611) are given in Fort Canning Park. Take along a picnic—and mosquito repellent—to enjoy the show, which starts at about 7 PM or so.

The **Kala Mandhir Temple of Fine Arts** (☎ 339–0492) and the **Nrityalaya Aesthetics Society** (☎ 336–6537) are Indian dance schools that hold performances regularly throughout the year at different venues. **Sriwana** (✉ No. 02–494 Block 125, 11 Tampines St., ☎ 783–2434) is recognized for its innovative presentations of traditional Malay dances.

Music

ORCHESTRAS

The **Singapore Symphony Orchestra** (☎ 338–1230) gives concerts on Friday and Saturday evenings twice a month at the Victoria Concert Hall. Tickets cost S$8–S$80 and are available at the box office (Monday–Saturday 10–6 and up to 8:30 on the night of a concert) or through SISTIC (☞ *above*). You should also check local listings for performances by the following noteworthy groups: **Singapore Chinese Orchestra** (✉ People's Association, Room 5, Block B, 9 Stadium Link, ☎ 344–8777 or 440–3839); the **Singapore Youth Orchestra** (✉ ECA Branch, No. 02–03, Block 2, 51 Grange Rd., ☎ 831–9606); and the **Singapore Lyric Theatre** (✉ No. 03–06 Stamford Arts Centre, 155 Waterloo St., ☎ 336–1929), which specializes in opera.

CHINESE OPERA

The dramatic *wayangs* (Chinese operas) reenact Chinese legend through powerful movement, lavish costumes, and startling face-paint masks to the accompaniment of clashing gongs and pounding drums, punctuated by wailing flutes and stringed lute- or zitherlike instruments. They depict both myth and history, tell tales of maidens, generals, kings, and demons. Performances are held on temporary stages set up near temples, in market areas, or outside apartment complexes. The backstage area is open to view and you can watch the actors garbing up or applying their heavy makeup. Wayangs are staged all year, but most frequently in August and September, during the Festival of the Hungry Ghosts. Street performances—such as those at Clarke Quay held on Wednesday and Friday at 7:45 PM—are free. You'll need to buy tickets to shows by the **Chinese Theatre Circle** (☎ 323–4862) and other groups that perform at different venues, including the Victoria Theatre and Memorial Hall, throughout the city.

With local Chinese TV programming mostly delivered in Mandarin nowadays, street wayangs—spoken in dialect, though totally different from the conversational dialect—have become popular with the older generation, who rarely have a chance to be entertained in their own language. Do try to seek out a wayang. It's an experience you won't soon forget.

Theater

Theatreworks (☎ 338–4077), noted for the work of director Ong Keng Sen in particular, is the leader of the pack when it comes to profile. Like the highly respected **Practice Performing Arts Centre** (☎ 337–2525), led by veteran Chinese-English bilingual director Kuo Pao Kun, Theatreworks has staged daring cross-cultural and multilingual productions, such as Asian versions of *King Lear* and *Desdemona*, derived from *Othello*. **The Necessary Stage** (☎ 738–6355 or 440–8115), noted for its director, Alvin Tan, and director Haresh Sharma, performs highly experimental works and is an established and respected company.

The **Singapore Repertory Theatre** (✉ Telok Ayer Performing Arts Centre, 182 Cecil St., ☎ 221–5585) is a popular troupe, staging local and international plays and musicals. Its *The Golden Child*, by local playwright David Hwang, went to Broadway.

OUTDOOR ACTIVITIES AND SPORTS

Despite the heat and humidity, Singapore is one of the best cities in Asia for outdoor activities, since it's relatively unpolluted (but watch out for "the haze," which may drift over any time between August and November from forest fires in neighboring Indonesia, making strenuous activity inadvisable). The government has taken care to set aside a significant portion of the island for recreation and 5% for nature conservation, so you can go waterskiing or scuba diving, play beach volleyball or take a jungle hike. Virtually all Singapore hotels have swimming pools, and there are 28 public swimming complexes, some of which are superb. When doing anything outside, be sure to drink lots of water, be prepared for rain always, and try to schedule the most strenuous activities for early morning or late afternoon.

Generous provision of parkland and a total of 7,017 acres of wild nature reserve land, combined with Singapore's naturally lush tropical vegetation, make Singapore much more of an environmental haven than most people realize. Bird-watching is particularly rewarding, with about 350 recorded species to look out for. Two key nature reserve areas: the north-central Bukit Timah Nature Reserve for a safe, well-trailed pocket-size rain forest close to the city, and Sungei Buloh Nature Park, located in the far north, for a wetlands habitat with some impressively large monitor lizards and great bird-watching, especially during the annual north-south migrations, October through April. More information on the great outdoors can be gleaned from the **National Parks Board** (Nature Reserves & Conservation Division; ☎ 474–1165, ✎), based at the Singapore Botanic Gardens, and from the **Nature Society** (☎ 741–2036, ✎). You can pick up a copy of *The Green Map of Singapore*, a guide to Singapore's nature habitats, at the **Singapore Environment Council** (✉ 21 Lewin Terrace, Fort Canning Park, ☎ 337–6062, ✎).

Beaches and Parks

Bintan Island, Indonesia. A quick side trip to Indonesia from Singapore is a snap—the north of Bintan Island is only 45 minutes from Singapore's east coast Tanah Merah Ferry Terminal, its southern half 90 minutes from the World Trade Centre ferry terminal on the southwest coast. The island is a resort haven. You can frolic on its beaches, golf its courses, and experience Indonesian cuisine and culture.

East Coast Park. This park stretches for 20 km (12 mi) on reclaimed land alongside the seafront road on the southeastern coast leading to the airport. It offers a 7.5 km (4.5 mi) sandy beach, restaurants, food stalls, and barbecue pits; daily rental holiday chalets; changing facilities and rest rooms; and almost every recreational facility known to man, including a water-sports lagoon where you can rent sailboards, canoes, kayaks, and sailboats; a 12 km (7 mi) cycle track; a 15 km (9 mi) jogging track; bicycles, skates, and Rollerblades for rent; kite-flying; and fishing points. If you prefer swimming in a pool, the **Aquatic Centre** (☎ 345–6762) has four—including a wave pool—as well as a giant water slide called the Big Splash.

Nearby Islands. The southern islands of **Kusu** and **St. John's** (☞ *also* Exploring, *above*) have reasonable small beaches and swimming facilities. Take the ferry from World Trade Centre. Kusu (☒ $9 for adults) hosts religious shrines, too—beware the ninth lunar month, when hordes of Taoists head for the Tua Pekong temple there, crowding the boats.

Sentosa Island. Billed as Singapore's leisure resort, Sentosa offers a range of recreational facilities in addition to its museums, waxworks, musical fountain, World War II sites, and other attractions (☞ *also* Exploring, *above*). Pleasingly natural in patches but also meticulously landscaped in others, Sentosa is one of the few places in Singapore where you can get up close and personal with three species of carnivorous pitcher plants, besides monkeys and edible-nest swiftlets, among other birds, including immigrant exotica such as Australian cockatoos. There's a beach and a swimming lagoon, with a wide range of water sports available and sports equipment to rent. You can also camp here. The island gets very crowded on weekends.

Participant Sports

Archery

The **Archery Association of Singapore** (☒ 131 Portsdown Rd., ☎ 773–4824), founded in 1967, has 20 affiliated clubs, most of which welcome enthusiasts. The range is open daily and offers floodlit shooting on weeknights. The fee is S$25 for visitors.

Bicycling

Signed **bicycle kiosks** dot designated bike paths. You can rent bikes for about S$3–S$8 an hour, with a deposit of S$20–S$50. There are many such kiosks at East Coast Park, Sentosa Island, Pasir Ris, Bishan, and Pulau Ubin (an island off Singapore's northeast coast that offers mountain or dirt biking). An exciting dirt-biking trail curves around the perimeter of the rain forest at Bukit Timah Nature Reserve (call **National Parks Board** ☎ 391–4488 or 474–1165).

Bowling

There are more than 20 bowling centers in Singapore; the cost per string is about S$2.50 on weekdays before 6 PM, S$3.90 on weekends and after 6 PM weekdays, excluding shoe rental. For general information, contact the **Singapore Tenpin Bowling Congress,** based at the National Stadium (☎ 440–7388). **Jackie's Bowl** (☒ 452B East Coast Rd., ☎ 241–6519) has 20 lanes. Other alleys include **Kallang Bowl** (☒ Leisure-Dome, 5 Stadium Walk, Kallang Park, ☎ 345–0545), **Plaza Bowl** (☒ Textile Centre, 8th floor, Jalan Sultan, ☎ 292–4821), and **Super Bowl Marina South** (☒ 15 Marina Grove, Marina South, ☎ 221–1010), which has 36 lanes.

Fitness Facilities

HOTELS

If you absolutely *have* to work out in a gym, consider a stay at one of these hotels with fabulous fitness facilities. Because most hotel clubs offer annual memberships to Singaporeans, you'll find the facilities busy early in the morning, at midday, and early in the evening.

Four Seasons (☒ 190 Orchard Blvd., ☎ 734–1110). Peter Burwash International pros offer tennis lessons here on indoor, air-conditioned courts. You'll also find two pools (one for adults only), a fully equipped fitness center, massage, a golf simulator, saunas, and steam rooms. Hotel guests pay S$21 plus tax for a Continental breakfast, while club members are served free of charge.

Marina Mandarin (✉ 6 Raffles Blvd., ☎ 338–3388). If you're a guest here, you can play squash or tennis for S$15 per hour before 5 PM (S$18 after that) and then take a free dip in the outdoor pool. Or you can head for the fully equipped gym (free to guests) before relaxing in the steam room or sauna. Massage therapy is an option, too, at S$61.80 per hour.

The Oriental (✉ 5 Raffles Blvd., ☎ 338–0066). Here you'll find tennis courts and a splendid outdoor pool with an underwater sound system and a view of the harbor. The fifth-floor health club includes a hot tub, massage, steam and sauna rooms for men and for women, and all the usual gym equipment. Runners should try the waterfront path on the esplanade across the street from the hotel; maps are provided in your room.

The Ritz-Carlton, Millenia Singapore (✉ 7 Raffles Ave., ☎ 337–8888). The health and fitness club here is so exclusive that it has the highest-priced membership for locals in Singapore: S$4,000 a year (S$5,000 for a married couple). If you're a hotel guest, take advantage of being able to use the state-of-the-art gymnasium, the outdoor pool and Jacuzzi, the sauna, and the steam facilities for free.

Shangri-La (✉ 22 Orange Grove Rd., ☎ 737–3644). Amenities here include a good-size outdoor pool and a smaller indoor one; a fully equipped health club; and a three-hole golf course, where you can jog in the early morning, all free to guests. Tennis and squash cost S$10 per hour. The site also has spacious, separate, "wet" areas—which include saunas, steam rooms, and Jacuzzis—for men and women.

YMCAS/YWCAS

The following YMCA/YWCA complexes have fitness facilities and offer temporary memberships: **Metropolitan YMCA** (✉ 60 Stevens Rd., ☎ 737–7755), which has a swimming pool and free gym use for hotel guests; the **YWCA Fort Canning** (✉ 6 Fort Canning Rd., ☎ 338–4222), which has a pool and tennis court but no gym; and the **YMCA International House** (✉ 1 Orchard Rd., ☎ 336–6000), which offers free pool use to guests, but the gym costs S$10 after 6 PM.

Flying

The **Republic of Singapore Flying Club** (✉ East Camp Building, 140B Seletar Airbase, ☎ 481–0502 or 481–0200) offers visiting membership to qualified pilots, including one-day temporary membership at S$100, and has aircraft available for hire (approximately S$265 per hour, excluding the temporary membership fee, and another $100 for insurance). You can't fly solo unless you have a Singapore license, but planes can be hired with an instructor.

Golf

Golf is largely the sport of a members-only elite in Singapore, so be aware that Singapore's golf clubs can be very smart places, and expensive. Some of the top hotels will make arrangements for their guests to golf at the top-rate local courses. This can include making all the necessary bookings, including equipment reservations, at the club of your choice and arranging for a limousine to take you there. You might check before leaving home to see whether your club has any reciprocal arrangements with a Singapore club. Several courses accept nonmembers, though some limit this to weekdays. Most clubs are open daily 7–7; some offer night golfing until 11. Driving ranges offer practice for as little as S$2 for 50 balls.

Changi Golf Club. This hilly nine-hole course on 50 acres is open to nonmembers on weekdays, with no night golfing available. ✉ *345 Netheravon Rd.,* ☎ *545–5133.* ☎ *Greens fee: S$82.40. Caddy fee: S$20.*

Jurong Country Club. Here you'll find an 18-hole, par-72 course on 120 acres, as well as a driving range. Half the holes are on flat terrain; the other nine are on small hills. It's open to nonmembers. ✉ *9 Science Centre Rd.,* ☎ *560–5655.* ☎ *Greens fee (includes caddy): S$108.15 weekday mornings, S$123.60 afternoons, S$133.90 nights, S$185.40 weekends and holidays.*

Keppel Club. Nonmembers are welcome at this 18-hole course close to the city, which also has a driving range. There is night golfing on Tuesday and Thursday. ✉ *Bukit Chermin,* ☎ *273–5522.* ☎ *Greens fee: S$105 weekdays, S$187 weekends and holidays. Caddy fee: S$40. Driving range: S$5.15 weekdays before 5 PM, S$10.30 after 5 PM and weekends. Closed Mon.*

Seletar Base Golf Club. This is considered the best nine-hole course on the island. If you are not a member of any golf club, you must take a proficiency test held on Monday and Thursday mornings before you can play the course. Otherwise, produce your home club's handicap card. ✉ *244 Oxford St., Seletar Airbase,* ☎ *481–4745.* ☎ *Greens fee (non-Singaporeans): S$45 weekdays, S$60 weekends and holidays. No caddies; trolley fee: S$4.*

Sembawang Country Club. Because of its hilly terrain, this 18-hole, par-72 course is known as the "commando course." The club's squash courts are for members only. The driving range is closed till the end of 2000. There is no night golfing. ✉ *Km 17, 249 Sembawang Rd., Sembawang Airbase,* ☎ *257–0642.* ☎ *Greens fees (includes cart): S$95 weekdays, S$120 weekends and holidays. No caddies; buggy fee: S$15.*

Sentosa Golf Club. Here you can play on the 18-hole **Tanjong course** on the southeastern tip of the island (Tuesdays only for visitors) or the 18-hole **Serapong course** (visitors weekdays only). ✉ *Sentosa Island,* ☎ *275–0022.* ☎ *Greens fees (includes cart): Tanjong S$164.80 mornings, S$185.40 afternoons; Serapong S$123.60 weekday mornings, S$144.20 weekday afternoons, S$226.60 weekends. No caddies.*

Running

Singapore is a great place for runners: there are numerous parks, and a number of leading hotels offer jogging maps. Serious runners can tackle the 15-km (9.3-mi) East Coast Parkway track, then cool off with a swim at the park's sandy beach. One of the most delightful places to run is the Botanic Gardens (off Holland Road and not far from Orchard Road), where you can jog until 11 at night. It's safe for women to run alone. Look right when crossing the road—Singapore drives on the left. There are various big-race events during the year, such as the biennial 42 km (26 mi) Singapore International Marathon in December.

Sailing

Folks at the **Changi Sailing Club** (✉ Netheravon Rd., ☎ 545–2876) can provide general information about sailing. An important sailing facility is **Seasports Centre,** East Coast Park, ☎ 449–1855, offering instruction courses at S$90 for a minimum three persons (windsurfing as well). Sailboats and sunfish can be rented for S$22 for two hours, S$11 per hour thereafter. Sailboat rentals are also available on **Sentosa Island** (☞ Beaches and Parks, *above*).

Scuba Diving

The most interesting (and cleanest) diving is found off nearby islands, though the currents are treacherous. The cost can run anywhere from S$350 to S$600, including scuba equipment, but dives around Pulau Hantu island off Singapore's southern coast may cost less, at S$100-

S$120 per person for two dives, about half a day, including a guide.
For information on local dive opportunities, contact **Marsden Bros.** (☎
475–0050) or **Pro Diving Services** (☎ 291–2261). **Scuba Corner** (✉
No. 02–47 Millenia Walk, 9 Raffles Blvd., ☎ 338–6563) is a dive shop
that runs trips to the outer islands.

Tennis, Squash, and Racquetball

Several hotels have their own tennis and squash courts (☞ Fitness Facilities, *above*), and there are a few public squash and racquetball
courts as well. All the complexes cited below are open 7 AM–10 PM.
At the **Farrer Park Tennis Centre** (✉ 1 Rutland Rd., ☎ 299–4166),
charges are in the S$3.50–S$9.50 per hour range. One public court complex is **Kallang Squash and Tennis Centre** (✉ 52 Stadium Rd., National
Stadium, ☎ 440–6839), where courts cost around S$5–S$10 per hour
for squash, S$3.50–S$9.50 per hour for tennis, depending on the time
of day. At the **Singapore Tennis Centre** (✉ 1020 East Coast Pkwy., ☎
449–9034) court costs range from S$10.50 to S$14.50 per hour. The
Tanglin Tennis Centre (✉ 103E Harding Rd., ☎ 473–7236) charges
S$3.50–S$9.50 per hour.

Waterskiing

The center of activity is Ponggol, a village in northeastern Singapore.
Ponggol Water Ski Centre (✉ 600 17th Ave., Ponggol, ☎ 386–3891)
is open daily 10 AM –6 PM and charges S$80 an hour weekdays, S$90
an hour on weekends for a boat with inboard motor and ski equipment. Another popular place to waterski is along the Kallang River,
where world championships have been held. To take advantage of the
action off Sembawang and the Straits of Johor on the northern coastline, you can also rent equipment, for about S$95 per hour, from
William Water Sports (✉ 60 Jalan Mempurong, Sembawang, ☎ 257–
5859), which is open Wednesday through Monday, 9 AM–6 PM.

Windsurfing

Windsurfing is available at the **SAFRA Resort &Country Club, Changi**
(☎ 546–5880), and on **Sentosa Island** (☞ Beaches and Parks, *above*)
from 9:30 to 6:30. Costs range from around S$10 per hour, plus a S$10
deposit.

Spectator Sports

The **Singapore Sports Council** (☎ 345–7111, ext. 663) is a good source
for information on sporting events, as are the newspapers. Besides the
mainstream sports, there are novelties such as the annual kite-flying
festival.

Cricket

From March through September, matches take place at the center of
the Central Business District every Saturday at 1:30 PM and every Sunday at 11 AM on the Padang grounds in front of the old **Singapore
Cricket Club** (☎ 338–9271), founded in 1852. Entrance to the club
during matches is restricted to members, but you can watch from the
sides of the playing field. Note that the club, not dedicated solely to
cricket, runs lively rugby, soccer, hockey, squash, and other sports
events.

Horse Racing

You'll find on-site racing as well as live telecasts of Malaysian races at
the **Singapore Turf Club,** 30 minutes out of town. There's a strict dress
code: shorts, sleeveless T-shirts, and sandals aren't allowed in the public stands; smart casual (not jeans) is the way to go in the air-conditioned members enclosures (which foreigners need a passport to enter).
✉ *1 Turf Club Ave., Kranji,* ☎ *879–1000.* 🎫 *Public stands S$5 and*

*S$10 (air-conditioned); members enclosures, S$20; no children al-
lowed. ☉ Saturdays 1:30 PM–10 PM, Sundays 1:30 PM–6 PM; night racing Wed. and Sat.*

Polo

The **Singapore Polo Club** (⊠ Thomson Rd., ☎ 256–4530) has both
local and international matches. Spectators are welcome to watch
Tuesday, Thursday, Saturday, and Sunday matches, which are played
after 4 PM. Malaysian royalty may be spotted here playing a chukka—
the designated 7½-minute polo session.

Rugby

Rugby is played on the **Padang** grounds in front of the Singapore Cricket
Club. Kickoff is usually at 3:15 PM and 5:30 PM on Saturday from July
through November. There are 10 teams in the local league.

Soccer

Soccer is the major sport of Singapore, with the added thrill of legal-
ized soccer betting (*Score!*) via the national lottery, Singapore Pools;
important matches take place in the **National Stadium** at Kallang.
Games are played by 12 territorially based home clubs within the local
"S-League." Details are published in the daily papers, and ticket reservations can be made through the Singapore Sports Council (☞ *above*).
The main season is September through March.

Track and Field

Singapore has the **National Stadium** at Kallang for major events as well
as nine athletic centers with tracks. International meets are usually detailed in the daily press. For information and details on how to book
seats for major meets, call the Singapore Sports Council (☞ *above*).

SHOPPING

With an incredible range of goods—brought in from all over the world
and sold in an equally incredible number (and variety) of shops—Singapore is truly a shopping fantasyland. Although you can still find deals
on handcrafted rosewood furniture, Chinese objets d'art, and carpets,
prices for most items are the same as or higher than those in the United
States. You should know the costs of goods you intend to buy—especially photographic and electronic items—at home. Though prices
don't vary much from shop to shop, compare a few shops to feel secure about your price.

Singapore has a knack for reinventing itself overnight. Many of the buildings, shopping centers, and stores seem perpetually new. The name of
the game here is change, and it's expected to continue, so before you
head out for that quaint little antiques shop you discovered last year,
call ahead.

If you have (or wish you had) the money to spend on haute couture,
head over to the Orchard and Scotts roads area to browse in the boutiques of the Hilton International arcade—which leads to the Four Seasons Hotel arcade—where every designer imaginable has a store. A
10-minute walk farther up Orchard Road takes you to the Tanglin Shopping Centre, with its distinctive gift shops. For truly singular gifts
check out the shops around Temple Street and Sago Street in Chinatown, where you'll find such things as Chinese herbal medicines, paper
funerary items, antiques, and religious sculptures.

Stop into at least one of the Watson's drugstores scattered throughout
the city. You'll find bags of prawn chips from Indonesia, tapioca chips
from Malaysia, and lobster balls from Singapore; cookies from Aus-

tralia; mints from England; and candied jellies from Japan. All make great gifts (if they're not eaten before you get them home).

For small, inexpensive souvenirs, take the MRT to the Bugis stop. On one side of Victoria Street is the Parco Bugis Junction—an air-conditioned, semioutdoor, multilevel shopping center. On the other side is an array of market stalls that sells everything from fake designer watches at S$18 each to silk boxer shorts and scarves (three for S$10). "Dollar" stores abound here, and they're full of such inexpensive and indispensable consumer goods as cans of "prickly heat" talcum powder (three for S$1) or packages of one-use, throwaway underwear (S$3 for five pairs).

For real deals, savvy locals flock to the weekly garage sales—usually held by expats leaving the country—advertised in the Saturday classifieds of *The Straits Times*. At these, furniture and goods are sold at bargain-basement prices by people who literally can't take it with them.

Shopping Essentials

Bargaining

Although department stores, chain stores, and some independent stores don't offer discounts—their items are tagged with fixed prices—bargaining is common in Singapore. Shops that are reluctant to offer discounts usually have a FIXED-PRICE STORE sign in their windows (price tags may have the same message). If you don't like to bargain, stick to the department stores, which usually have the lowest initial ("first") price. If you don't mind bargaining, visit a department store first to get an idea of established prices, and then shop around.

Price tags in places that allow bargaining may say "recommended price." Local shops in upscale complexes or malls tend to give a 10%–15% discount on clothes. However, at jewelry stores, the discount can be as high as 40%–50%; carpet dealers also give hefty reductions. At less-upscale complexes, the discounts tend to be greater. Stalls and shops around visitor attractions have the highest initial asking prices, so bargaining here yields deep discounts.

Everyone has his or her own method of bargaining, but in general, when a vendor tells you a price, ask for the discounted price, then offer even less. The person will probably reject your offer but come down a few dollars. With patience, this can continue and earn you a few more dollars off the price. If you don't like haggling, walk away after hearing the discounted price. If the vendor hasn't hit bottom price, you'll be called back.

Complaints

To avoid even having to worry about problems with goods or services, look for shops that have the Singapore Tourism Board's gold circular logo in their windows. This indicates that the retailer has been distinguished for excellent service and fair pricing among other things. Members need to be approved by the **Consumers Association of Singapore** (No. 04–3625, 164 Bukit Merah Central, 150164, ☎ 270–5433) and the tourist board (☞ Visitor Information *in* Singapore A to Z, *below*). If you do end up with complaints about either a serious disagreement with a shopkeeper or defective merchandise, lodge them with the tourist board; rest assured that staff members will follow up on them. **The Retail Promotions Centre** (☎ 458–6377, FAX 458–6393) also handles consumer complaints, mainly from tourists. If you encounter retailer malpractice, you can get full redress through the Small Claims Tribunals—something retailers dread, because the tourist board publishes the names and addresses of miscreants ordered to make redress to visitors.

Electrical Goods

Singapore's current is 220–240 volts at 50 cycles, like that in Australia and Great Britain. Canada and the United States use 110–120 volts at 60 cycles, so before you buy appliances, verify that you can get special adapters, if required, and that these will not affect the equipment's performance. These days, most electrical goods sold are 110–220 volts compatible. Check the sticker on the apparatus you are about to buy.

Guarantees and Receipts

Make sure you get international guarantees and warranty cards with your purchases. Check the serial number of each item against its card, and don't forget to mail the card in. Sometimes guarantees are limited to the country of purchase. If the dealer cannot give you a guarantee, he's probably selling an item intended for the domestic market in its country of manufacture; if so, he has bypassed the authorized agent and should be able to give you a lower price. Though your purchase of such an item isn't illegal, you have no guarantee. If you decide to buy it anyway, be sure to check that the item is in working order before you leave the shop.

Be sure to ask for receipts, both for your own protection and for customs. Though shopkeepers are often amenable to stating false values on receipts, customs officials are wary and knowledgeable.

How to Pay

All department stores and most shops accept these major credit cards— American Express, Diners Club, MasterCard, and Visa—and traveler's checks. Many tourist shops also accept foreign currency; just be sure to check the exchange rates before agreeing to any price—some store owners try to skim extra profit by giving an unfair rate of exchange. Retailers work at a low profit margin and depend on high turnover; they assume you will pay in cash. Except at the department stores, paying with a credit card will mean that your "discounted price" will reflect the commission the retailer will have to pay the credit card company.

Imitations

Copyright laws passed in early 1987 impose stern penalties on the selling of pirated music recordings and computer software. However, Singapore still has a reputation for pirated goods. If you're buying a computer, for example, some stores are quite amenable to loading it with all the software you want. Pirated CDs and video laser discs can be found at certain market stalls, as can incredibly authentic-looking wristwatches from every designer on the globe. The greatest of the fakes is the "solid gold" Rolex, which comes complete with serial number for less than S$100. It looks so good you could have a problem at customs—though you're more likely to have a customs problem (either in Singapore or at home) if it's discovered that you've purchased a counterfeit item.

Shipping

All stores that deal with valuable, fragile, or bulky merchandise know how to pack well. Ask for a quote on shipping charges, which you can then double-check with a local forwarder. Check whether the shop has insurance covering both loss and damage in transit. You might find you need additional coverage. If you're sending your purchases home by mail, check with **Singapore Post** (☎ 800/222–5777), the national postal service, about regulations.

Touts

Touting—soliciting business by approaching people on the street with offers of free shopping tours and special discounts—is illegal (maximum fines are S$5,000, and prison sentences of up to six months are possible). Nevertheless, it continues inside one or two shopping centers, especially Lucky Plaza. Each center has its band of men looking for people to interest in their special stash of fake designer watches. The touts at the top of Tanglin Road can be particularly bothersome. Some taxi drivers tout as well. Avoid all touts and the shops they recommend; a reputable shop doesn't need them. The prices will end up being higher—reflecting the tout's commission—and the quality of the goods possibly inferior.

Shopping Districts

Throughout the city are complexes full of shopping areas and centers. Many stores will have branches that carry much the same merchandise in several of these areas.

Orchard Road

The heart of Singapore's preeminent shopping district, Orchard Road is bordered on both sides by tree-shaded, tiled sidewalks lined with modern shopping complexes and deluxe hotels that house exclusive boutiques. Also considered part of this area are the shops on Scotts Road, which crosses Orchard, and two shopping centers—**Supreme House** on Penang Road and **Singapore Shopping Centre** (which was under renovation at press time).

Orchard Road is known for fashion and interior design shops, but you can find anything from Mickey Mouse watches to Chinese paper kites and antique Korean chests. The interior-design shops have unusual Asian bric-a-brac and such original items as a lamp stand made from old Chinese tea canisters or a pair of bookends in the shape of Balinese frogs. Virtually every Orchard Road complex, with the exception of the Promenade, has a clutch of department stores selling electronic goods, cigarette lighters, pens, jewelry, cameras, and so on. Most also have money changers, a few inexpensive cafés, and snack bars.

Though there's reference to an "Orchard Road price," which takes into account the astronomical rents some shop tenants have to pay, the department stores have the same fixed prices here as at all their branches. Small shops away from the center may have slightly cheaper prices.

Chinatown

Once Singapore's liveliest and most colorful shopping area, Chinatown lost a great deal of its vitality when the street stalls were moved into the **Kreta Ayer Complex** off Neil Road, **Chinatown Complex** off Trengganu Street, and **People's Park Complex** on Eu Tong Sen Street. Still, this neighborhood is fun to explore. The focus is on the Smith, Temple, and Pagoda street blocks, but nearby streets—Eu Tong Sen Street, Wayang Street, and Merchant Road on one side and Ann Siang Hill and Club Street on another—can yield some interesting finds.

Chinese kitchenware can be fascinating, and Temple Street has an abundance of unusual plates, plant pots, teapots, lacquered chopsticks, and so on. Paraphernalia for Chinese funerals is particularly prevalent around Sago Street. Nearby Sago Lane was lined, not so long ago, with "death houses," where elderly people went to await death. This may sound gruesome, but funerary items are among the most creative examples of folk art in the world. They include paper replicas of life's necessities and leisures, to serve the dead in their afterlife. There are some famous craftsmen on Ann Siang Hill. Just around the corner, on

Club Street, are several wood-carvers who specialize in creating idols of Chinese gods. On Merchant Road, a vendor of costumes for Chinese operas welcomes customers. And on Chin Hin Street, you can buy fragrant Chinese tea direct from a merchant.

South Bridge Road in Chinatown is the street of goldsmiths. Dozens of jewelers here specialize in 22K and even 24K ornaments in the characteristic orange color of Chinese gold. Each assistant, often shielded by a metal grill, uses an abacus and a balance to calculate the value of the piece you wish to buy. You must bargain here. South Bridge Road is also home to many art galleries.

Little India

Serangoon Road is affectionately known as Little India. For shopping purposes, it begins at the **Zhujiao Centre,** better known as the KK Market, on the corner of Serangoon and Buffalo roads. Some of the junk dealers and inexpensive-clothing stalls form a bazaar known as Mustafa Centre. This is a fun place to poke about and look for bargains.

All the handicrafts of India can be found on Serangoon Road: intricately carved wood tables, shining brass trays, hand-loomed table linens, fabric inlaid with tiny mirrors, brightly colored pictures of Hindu deities, and garlands of jasmine for the gods. And the sari shops! At dozens of shops here you can get the 6½ yards of voile, cotton, Kashmiri silk, or richly embroidered Benares silk required to make a sari. For the variety, quality, and beauty of the silk, the prices are very low. Other Indian costumes, such as long or short *kurtas* (men's collarless shirts) and Punjabi trouser sets, are unusual and attractive buys. Should you overspend and find yourself with excess baggage, there are several luggage shops on Serangoon Road where you can buy an old-fashioned tin trunk big enough to hide a body in.

Arab Street

The Arab Street shopping area really begins at Beach Road, opposite the Plaza Hotel. This old-fashioned street is full of noteworthy buys. A group of basket and rattan shops first catches your eye. There are quite a few jewelers here, and even more shops selling loose gems and necklaces of garnet and amethyst beads. The main business is batiks (textiles bearing hand-printed designs) and lace.

Brassware, prayer rugs, carpets, and leather slippers are sold in abundance on Arab Street and its side streets, which have appealing names such as Muscat Street and Baghdad Street. Two noteworthy complexes in the vicinity are Beach Road's **Golden Mile Food Centre,** which is devoted to good food on the lower floors and junk and antiques on the top floors, and Jalan Sultan's **Textile Centre,** which offers a wide variety of batiks.

Katong

The quiet east-coast suburb of Katong, just 15 minutes from town via the Pan Island Expressway, has old-fashioned shophouses along its main street, some selling inexpensive children's clothes and one dealing in antiques. Off the main road is the even more old-fashioned Joo Chiat Road, which gets more and more interesting as it approaches Geylang Road. Its shops sell Chinese kitchenware, antiques, baby clothes, and lots of offbeat items. If you walk a short distance down Joo Chiat Road, you will end up at another modern shopping complex, Parkway Parade mall, where modern shops abound and are mixed with outside shopping and hawker stalls. Just beyond that, through an underpass, you can walk to East Coast Park, which provides a nice rest on the beach from a weary day of shopping.

Holland Village

Holland Village, 10 minutes west of town by taxi, is a bit of a yuppie haunt, but it's the most rewarding place to browse for unusual and inexpensive Asian items, large and small. Many shops here specialize in Korean chests. Behind the main street is Lorong Mambong, a street of shophouses jammed with baskets, earthenware, porcelain, and all sorts of things from China and Thailand. One complex to look for in this area is the **Holland Village Shopping Centre** on Holland Avenue. A 10-minute walk along Holland Avenue from Holland Village is **Cold Storage Jelita**, which also has several shops.

Centers and Complexes

Shops in multilevel buildings and shopping complexes are often listed with a numerical designation such as "No. 00–00." The first part of this number indicates what floor the shop is on. The second part indicates its location on the floor. When the phone number of an individual shop is not given in this section, you'll find it listed with the shop under a specific merchandise category, below. Shops in the Orchard area tend to open daily by 10:30 AM. Specialty malls, such as computer-centric Funan Centre and Sim Lim Square, tend to unfold anywhere from 10 AM until noon. Most people shop in the afternoon, after the heat of the day, and when all stores are in full swing; most remain open till 10 PM.

Centrepoint (⊠ 176 Orchard Rd.). This spacious and impressive center has the **Robinsons** department store as its anchor tenant. One of the liveliest complexes, Centrepoint also has jewelry, silverware, and fashion shops; furniture stores that sell Philippine bamboo and Korean chests; and a large basement supermarket.

Delfi Orchard (⊠ 402 Orchard Rd.). Delfi is full of wedding boutiques, art galleries, and jewelry shops. **Royal Selangor Pewter** and **Waterford Wedgwood** are also here, along with a well-stocked golf shop.

Far East Plaza (⊠ 14 Scotts Rd.). This center is where the young and trendy gather to see and be seen. The shops are geared to them, and there's a bargain-basement atmosphere about the place. A forecourt offers fast-food restaurants (including Starbucks, Burger King, and Canadian Pizza—the best in the city), outdoor tables, and entertaining people-watching.

Forum Galleria (⊠ 583 Orchard Rd.). Here you'll find a huge **Toys 'R' Us**, as well as an assortment of boutiques, including **Guess! Kids**.

Funan Centre (⊠ 109 North Bridge Rd.). On North Bridge Road and High Street, near the Peninsula Hotel, this shopping center will thrill computer and information-technology lovers.

The Heeren Shops (⊠ 260 Orchard Rd.). This new complex at Orchard and Grange roads houses a branch of the popular Nonya restaurant, **Blue Ginger**; **Electric City**, an electronics superstore; a huge **HMV** music store; and **True Colours**, a futuristic makeup boutique.

Hilton Shopping Gallery (⊠ 581 Orchard Rd.). Most of Singapore's upscale hotels have a boutique or two in their lobbies, but the Hilton has an extensive shopping arcade full of them. It is home to several top names—**Giorgio Armani, Matsuda, Valentino**—and, through a boutique called **Singora**, many other Italian and French fashion houses. Among its other top-flight tenants are **Davidoff, Dunhill, Gucci, Louis Vuitton,** and **L'Ultimo**. The shopping gallery leads to a similar arcade with still more expensive boutiques that's attached to the Four Seasons.

Liang Court Complex (⊠ 177 River Valley Rd.). Liang Court is off the beaten track but only five minutes by cab from Orchard Road and worth the drive. The department store **Daimaru** is here; half of its floor space has been transformed into selected designer boutiques, such as **Dunhill**, and areas that sell books, silk, pearls, and other specialty items.

Lucky Plaza (⊠ 304 Orchard Rd.). This plaza has gone downhill as many of its shops have moved to trendier, newer buildings. What remains—mostly camera and electronic stores—is geared toward tourists. Plan to bargain furiously, particularly with the jewelers, who are, it seems, involved in a perpetual price-cutting war.

Marina Square. Part of an elegant complex that begins east of the Nicholl Highway downtown (a five-minute walk from the Raffles City MRT station), it includes Millenia Walk (look up to admire the architecture) and houses **Metro**, a large department store that has great sales; **DFS**, a massive duty-free shop; and about 200 small shops, including the English store **Mothercare**.

Ngee Ann City (⊠ 391 Orchard Rd.). Although the Japanese store **Takashimaya** takes up most of this complex, you'll find a number of small boutiques as well.

Orchard Point and Orchard Plaza (⊠ No. 220 and No. 150 Orchard Rd.). These side-by-side centers don't have the popular appeal of some other complexes but will reward dedicated shoppers with good finds. Reptile bags can be found in the basement shops of Orchard Point.

Orchard Towers (⊠ 600 Orchard Rd.). Thai silk, antiques, and leather goods vie for space here with tailors, electronic stores, restaurants, and a food and wine supermarket. Larry Jewelry has some good bargains and fine gems.

Palais Renaissance (⊠ 390 Orchard Rd.). Across the road from the Hilton hotel is this high-fashion center. Targeted at those who seek status labels at high prices, the Palais Renaissance is chic, opulent, and overpriced. It's a delight to wander through regardless of whether you're well heeled or not. Here **DKNY, Gianni Versace, Krizia,** and **Prada** compete as much in the design of their stores as in the design of their merchandise. Perfumes, jewelry, and travel accessories are also expensively represented in this extravagant marbled emporium.

The Paragon (⊠ 290 Orchard Rd.). The glossy Paragon has more than 15 men's fashion boutiques and counts **Gucci** and **Sonia Rykiel** among its more popular tenants. It also has the **Metro** department store.

Parco Bugis Junction (⊠ 230 Victoria St.). Linking the Hotel Inter-Continental and the Bugis MRT station, this shopping center has the Japanese department store **Seiyu** as its major tenant. It also houses a host of boutiques, restaurants, cafés, a Cineplex, and the **Amusement Wonder Park Namco**. Bargain hunters might want to stop by the *pasar malam* (night market) at Bugis Village.

Parkway Parade (⊠ 80 Marine Parade Rd.). This excellent and very attractive center is on Marine Parade Road, 15 to 20 minutes east of town by expressway. On weekdays you can shop here in peace and quiet; on weekends, it's uncomfortably crowded. The focus is on up-to-date and affordable fashions. Things get started around noon.

People's Park Complex and Centre (⊠ Eu Tong Sen St.). Though not new and glossy, this Chinatown center has an international reputation and is always entertaining. Everything is sold here: herbs, Chinese medicines, cameras, stereo equipment, clothes, luggage. Shopkeepers are much more aggressive here than in town, and if you haven't done your homework, you can get taken.

The Promenade (⊠ 300 Orchard Rd.). The elegant architecture (there's a spiral walkway with a gentle slope instead of escalators) here is matched by the elegance of the tenants. Its fashion stores carry some of the hottest names, including **Charles Jourdan, Dolce&Gabbana,** and **Issey Miyake**. Home-decor shops sell superb Asian odds and ends.

Singapore Shopping Complexes and Markets

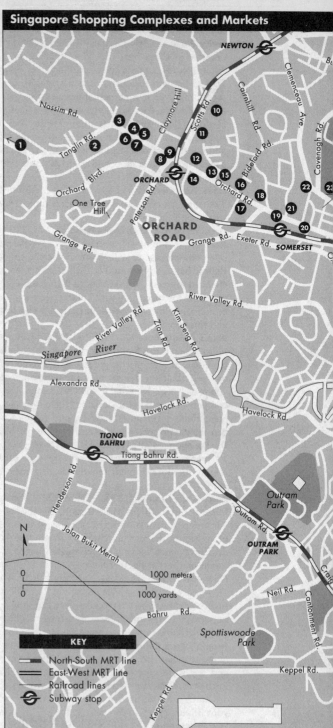

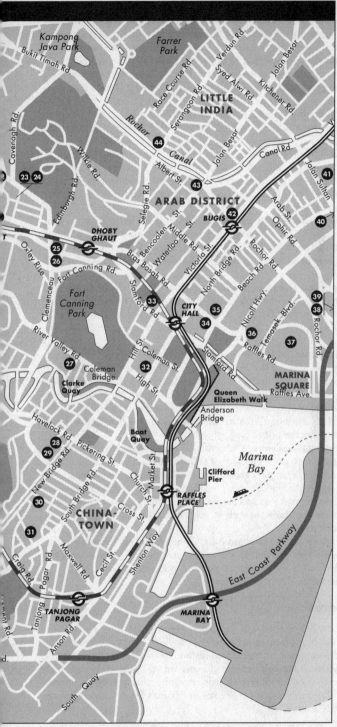

Kampong
Java Park

Farrer
Park

Bukit Timah Rd.

Cavenagh Rd.

Race Course Rd.

Serangoon Rd.

Verdun Rd.

Syed Alwi Rd.

Kitchener Rd.

Jalan Besar

**LITTLE
INDIA**

Rochar

Canal

44

Wilkie Rd.

Edinburgh Rd.

Albert St.

Jalan Besar

Canal Rd.

43

Jalan Sultan

41

23 24

ARAB DISTRICT

Selegie Rd.

St.

St.

BUGIS

42

Arab St.

Ophir Rd.

40

**DHOBY
GHAUT**

Bras Basah Rd.

Waterloo St.

Middle Rd.

Bencoolen St.

Victoria St.

Beach Rd.

Rochor Rd.

Oxley Rise

25

26

Fort Canning Rd.

Stamford Rd.

North Bridge Rd.

Nicoll Hwy.

39

38

**Fort
Canning
Park**

Clemenceau Ave.

33

**CITY
HALL**

35

34

Temasek Blvd.

Rochor Rd.

River Valley Rd.

Hill St.

Coleman St.

36

Raffles Rd.

37

27

Coleman
Bridge

32

High St.

Stamford Rd.

**MARINA
SQUARE**

Raffles Ave.

**Clarke
Quay**

**Queen
Elizabeth Walk**

Havelock Rd.

Pickering St.

**Boat
Quay**

Market St.

Church St.

Anderson
Bridge

28

29

New Bridge Rd.

South Bridge Rd.

Cross St.

**Clifford
Pier**

*Marina
Bay*

30

**CHINA-
TOWN**

Shenton Way

Cecil St.

**RAFFLES
PLACE**

31

Maxwell Rd.

Pagar Rd.

Craig Rd.

Neil Rd.

Anson Rd.

**TANJONG
PAGAR**

East Coast Parkway

**MARINA
BAY**

South Quay

South Quay

Raffles City and Raffles Hotel Arcade. Bordered by Stamford, North Bridge, and Bras Basah roads, this complex has a confusing interior. If you get lost, you're sure to come across many shopping finds, some of them in the Japanese department and grocery store **Sogo.** You'll also find several fashion boutiques, the **Times** bookshop, and a post office branch. Across the road is the Raffles Hotel Arcade, whose 60 boutiques sell high fashion and art. There's also a tourist board office here.

Scotts Shopping Centre (⊠ 6–8 Scotts Rd.). One of the best places in Singapore for affordable fashion that stops just short of haute couture, Scotts also has a basement food court with local and delicatessen food, plus activities and demonstrations to keep shoppers entertained.

Shaw House (⊠ 350 Orchard Rd.). **Isetan,** a large Japanese department store, is the major player in this complex. The **Kinokuniya** bookstore is excellent for volumes on Japan. **Etienne Aigner** is a good place for leather items.

Sim Lim Square (⊠ 1 Rochor Canal Rd.). You can bargain here to your heart's content for anything related to the computer and its add-ons.

Specialists Centre (⊠ 277 Orchard Rd.). This center is the home of the **John Little** department store, better known as JL, and assorted boutiques.

Stamford Court and Stamford House. This corner of North Bridge and Stamford roads has more specialty shopping centers than any other section of downtown Orchard Road. Check out the fine array of furniture and home decor stores here, as well as antiques, sculpture, fine art, and gift shops.

Suntec City Mall. At the corner of the Nicholl Highway and Raffles Boulevard in the Marina Bay area, this large complex is divided into four zones: the Tropics (lifestyle products and services), the Entertainment Centre (housing the French superstore **Carrefour**), the Fountain Terrace (an array of restaurants, pubs, and a food court), and the Galleria (high-end boutiques). You could shop and dine here and not even bother seeing the rest of Singapore.

Tanglin Shopping Centre. This center, where Orchard Road meets Tanglin Road, has a good selection of antiques shops, especially in a small, self-contained section at ground level. **Moongate** is one of Singapore's oldest dealers in fine antique porcelain. **Antiques of the Orient** is the only shop in town that specializes in antique maps. The contemporary interior-design shops, as well as the food court in the basement, are excellent, too.

Wisma Atria (⊠ 435 Orchard Rd.). Come here if only to see the aquarium that wraps around the elevator. If you want to shop as well, this center has such grand names in fashion as **Dior** and **Fendi.** You'll also find the **Isetan** department store.

Department Stores

Singapore has one homegrown chain—**Metro**—that offers a wide range of affordable fashions and household products. When shopping for locally designed and manufactured fashion as well as brands such as Esprit, Metro is the best bet. The designs are up-to-the-minute, and the prices are good by local standards and unbelievably good by international standards. Look for Metros in Far East Plaza, Marina Square, and the Paragon.

Locally owned **Tang's** (⊠ 320 Orchard Rd., ☎ 737–5500), also known as Tang's Superstore or C. K. Tang's, is connected to the Marriott Hotel and subterranean shopping via underground passageways. It looks upscale, but it has some of the best buys in town. Its fashions are, at best, improving, but its accessories are excellent—especially the costume jewelry—and its household products are unsurpassed.

Two Chinese department stores under different ownership, but with the same name, **Overseas Emporium,** are in the **People's Park Complex** (☎ 535–0555) and the **People's Park Centre** (☎ 535–1948). Both offer basically the same goods: Chinese silk fabric, silk blouses, brocade jackets, crafts, children's clothes, and china.

Singaporeans enjoy Japanese department stores. **Isetan**—in **Parkway Parade** (☎ 345–5555), **Shaw House** (☎ 733–1111), and **Wisma Atria** (☎ 733–7777)—always has good specials, and the fashion departments for men and women are well stocked. **Daimaru** (☎ 339–1111), in Liang Court, has some very unusual goods. **Sogo** (☎ 339–1100) opened in Raffles City as did **Seiyu** in the Parco Bugis Junction Complex (✉ 230 Victoria St., Bugis MRT, ☎ 223–2222).

The English **Robinsons** (☎ 733–0888), in Centrepoint, is Singapore's oldest department store. It recently shed its fuddy-duddy image and rethought its pricing and is once again one of the best. **John Little** (☎ 737–2222), at the Specialists Centre, has a full range of offerings but is now targeting the young and trendy. There are still good sales here, however. The **Marks & Spencer** in the basement of Lane Crawford at the corner of Scotts and Orchard is the biggest of several outlets in town.

Markets

Stalls crowding upon stalls in covered, open spaces of the city's **food markets** make for a hectic, colorful scene. The range of foodstuffs is staggering, and some of the items may turn your stomach. The live animals eyed by shoppers will tug at your heartstrings. Usually a food market is divided into two sections: the dry market and the wet market, which has squirming fish, crawling turtles, strutting chickens, and cute rabbits that are sold for the pot (the floors are continually sluiced to maintain hygiene). The wet market at the **Chinatown Complex** is the most fascinating; the dry market at **Cuppage Centre** (on Cuppage Rd., off Orchard Rd.), where the flower stalls are particularly appealing, is a better choice for the squeamish.

The old-style street bazaars are all gone now, but in the **Sungei Road** area, site of the once-notorious Thieves Market, a few street vendors creep back each weekend. The stalls sell mainly inexpensive shirts, T-shirts, children's clothes, and underwear, as well as odds and ends such as inexpensive watches, costume jewelry, and sunglasses. A few sell plastic household items.

The **Kreta Ayer Complex** in Chinatown may be modern, but it has all the atmosphere of a bazaar. All the street vendors from Chinatown were relocated here. The shops sell cassette tapes, clothing from China, toys, and a lot of gaudy merchandise.

Some of Chinatown's elderly junk peddlers refuse to leave the streets. In the afternoon, they line up along **Temple Street** and lay out a strange variety of goods—old bottles, stamps, bits of porcelain or brass, old postcards, and the like—on cloths.

Shops and stalls also cluster at the **Bugis Street** mall and at **Telok Ayer,** but some merchandise tends to be overpriced. Since 1996, several "dollar stores" have opened at Bugis, where items—from Indonesia, Malaysia, Korea, Thailand, and other parts of Asia—that you never thought you'd ever need are for sale. They are great shops for those on a budget who have to pick up several souvenirs for the folks back home.

Specialty Shops

Antiques and Curios

Most antiques stores have a variety of small items—porcelain, brass-ware, idols, and so on—as well as Chinese furniture, which may be of blackwood inlaid with mother of pearl, or red-stained wood with elaborate carvings picked out in gold. Falling halfway between sou-venir shops and antiques stores, curio shops sell a fascinating variety of goods, mainly from China. Reverse-glass paintings, porcelain vases, cloisonné, wood carvings, jewelry (agate, jade, lapis lazuli, malachite), ivory carvings, embroidery, and idols represent just a fraction of their treasures. Note that some curio dealers style themselves as antiques shops, as do some vendors who sell rosewood items or reproduction furni-ture. (Strictly speaking, antiques in Singapore are defined as items that are more than 80 years old.)

If you don't have time to step outside of the Orchard Road shopping mecca, good places to see genuine antiques are the Tanglin Shopping Centre's **Antiques of the Orient** (☎ 734–9351), which specializes in maps, ceramics, and furniture; **Moongate** (☎ 737–6771), which sells porce-lain; and **Tatiana** (☎ 235–3560), which carries primitive art and an-tique Indonesian batik and ikat (a woven fabric of tie-dyed yarns).

For curios, try **Lim's Art & Crafts** (⊠ Ttop floor, ☎ 735–2966) in the Scotts Shopping Centre. For museum-quality Asian antiques, visit the **Paul Art Gallery** in Holland Park (⊠ 68 Greenleaf Rd., ☎ 468–4697). In the east end, about a 20-minute walk on Sims Avenue from the Kallang MRT, is **Poh Antiques and Junks** (⊠ 139 Sims Ave., ☎ no phone), which has Buddhist and Hindu sculptures as well as assorted kitsch from this century. It opens when the owner feels like opening—but even if it's closed when you get there, Sims Avenue around Geylang and Lorong 9 is an interesting neighborhood in which to stroll.

Art

Singapore has more than its share of fine artists. Established names—Chen Wen Hsi for Chinese brush painting, Thomas Yeo for abstract landscapes, and Anthony Poon for contemporary graphics—fetch high prices. Among the artists who are gaining recognition are Wan Soon Kam, Ng Eng Teng (a sculptor who re-creates the human figure in ce-ment, stoneware, and bronze), James Tan (known for his traditional and abstract Chinese brush paintings), and Teng Juay Lee (who spe-cializes in orchids). Nostalgic scenes of the Singapore of yesteryear are captured in watercolors and oils by artists such as Gog Sing Hoi, Ang Ah Tee, and Ong Kim Seng, known for his scenes of the Singapore River and Chinatown. Some delightful paintings can be had for as little as S$300. To contact local artists or find out more about them, call the Singapore National Arts Council at 270–0722.

For a range of art, try **Art Forum** (⊠ 56 Monk's Hill Terr., ☎ 737–3448), but call before visiting. There are also many galleries on South Bridge Road in Chinatown. If you wish to see Chinese calligraphy in the works, Yong Cheong Thye practices his art at the **Yong Gallery** (⊠ 17 Erskin Rd., ☎ 226–1718) in Chinatown.

Other galleries include: **Cicada Gallery of Fine Arts** (⊠ 31 Ann Siang Rd., ☎ 225–6787), **Opera Gallery** (⊠ No. 02–12H, 391 Orchard Rd., ☎ 735–2618), **Plum Blossoms Gallery** (⊠ Raffles Hotel, 1 Beach Rd., ☎ 334–1198), and **Shenn's Gallery** (⊠ 37 Blair Rd., ☎ 223–1233).

Batik

A traditional craft item of Singapore, Malaysia, and Indonesia, batik is now also important in contemporary fashion and interior design. **Blue Ginger Design Centre** (⊠ 1 Beach Rd., ☎ 334–1171) and **Design Batik** (⊠ 1 Beach Rd., ☎ 776–4337), both at the Raffles Hotel, sell clothes and fabrics in modern designs. Blue Ginger is especially innovative, and has opened a branch at the **Merchant Court Hotel** (⊠ 20 Merchant Rd., ☎ 536–4986). **Tang's** department stores (☞ *above*) sell inexpensive batik products, including a wide range of men's shirts. Traditional batik sarong lengths can be bought in the shops on Arab Street and in the **Textile Centre** on Jalan Sultan.

Cameras

Photographic equipment may not be the bargain it once was, but the range of cameras and accessories available can be matched only in Hong Kong. It's especially important that you establish the price at home before buying here. Film and film processing remain excellent buys. All department stores carry cameras, and there are so many in Lucky Plaza that you can do all your comparison shopping in one spot.

For personalized service try **Cathay Photo** (☎ 339–6188) on the second floor of Marina Square. For camera repairs, **Goh Gin Camera Service Centre** (⊠ 150 Orchard Rd., Orchard Plaza, ☎ 732–6155) may be able to help.

Carpets

Carpets are very attractively priced in Singapore. Afghan, Pakistani, Persian, Turkish, and Chinese carpets—both antique and new—are carried by reputable dealers. Carpet auctions, announced in the newspapers, are good places to buy if you know your stuff. In shops, it's acceptable to bargain—in fact, it's integral to the rather lengthy proceedings.

Good shops include: **Amir & Sons** (⊠ No. 03–01, ☎ 734–9112) in Lucky Plaza, **Hassan's** (⊠ No. 03–01, ☎ 737–5626) in the Tanglin Shopping Centre, and **Qureshi's** (⊠ No. 05–12, ☎ 235–1523) in Centrepoint.

Clothing

CASUAL OUTFITS

In department stores and small boutiques all over the island—but especially on Orchard Road—locally made women's fashions and Japanese imports sell for a song. Brands such as Chocolate and Ananas offer colorful, reasonably made, very fashionable garments. Two of the better-known chain stores are the **British India Company** (⊠ 11 Stamford Rd., ☎ 334–6806) and the **East India Company** (⊠ 11 Stamford Rd., ☎ 336–0448), both of which are in the Capitol Building. **Trend** (☎ 235–9446) is a popular Centrepoint boutique.

Shoes are good buys, too, especially in the Metro and Tang's department stores (☞ Department Stores, *above*), but sizes here are smaller than in the West, and some women may have a problem getting the right fit.

HIGH FASHION

Singapore has its own designers, including London-based Benny Ong, who sells through Tang's, and Song & Kelly, a Singaporean/British couple who are winning raves internationally. You should also look for the designs of Jut Ling, Thomas Wee, and Celia Loe in the more upscale department stores and boutiques. For European couture, check the arcades of the Hilton International and the Mandarin, as well as the more fashionable shopping centers, especially the Palais Renaissance.

Boutiques that carry a number of designers include **Club 21** (☎ 738–8778), which has men's and women's fashions and is in the Four Seasons arcade; **Glamourette** (☎ 737–5939) in the Promenade; and **Link** (☎ 736–0645) in the Palais Renaissance.

Men's fashions are represented by **Hermès** (✉ 541 Orchard Rd., ☎ 734–1353) in Liat Towers, **Mario Valentino** (☎ 338–4457) in Marina Square, and **Ralph Lauren** (☎ 738–0298) in Takashimaya.

Jewelry

Singapore is a reliable place to buy jewelry, and there are so many jewelers that prices are competitive. Never accept the first price offered, no matter how posh the store. (All jewelers give enormous discounts, usually 40% or more, but some, especially in hotels, don't mention this until pressed.) The Singapore Assay Office hallmarks jewelry, though the procedure is time-consuming and not many jewelers submit to it unless required for export.

In Chinatown, particularly along South Bridge Road and in People's Park, there are dozens of jewelers who sell 22K gold. Many of these are old family firms, and prices are calculated by abacus based on the weight of the ornament and the prevailing price of gold. The bargaining procedure can take quite some time. On Orchard Road, the jewelry shops are often branches of Hong Kong firms or are local firms modeled along the same lines. They sell 18K set jewelry, often in Italian designs, as well as loose investment stones.

Cartier has shops in Takashimaya (☎ 734–2427) and in **Millenia Walk** in Marina Square (☎ 339–3294). One of the many small jewelers in Takashimaya is the **Hour Glass** (☎ 734–2420), which carries a large selection of designer watches. **Je T'Aime** (☎ 734–2275) in Wisma Atria is a reputable firm. **Larry's** (☎ 732–3222), with branches in Raffles City and other malls, is a popular store. You'll find the antique silver and gold jewelry of the Straits Chinese at **Petnic's** (✉ 41A Cuppage Rd., ☎ 235–6564). **Tiffany & Co.** recently opened a two-story store at Ngee Ann City (☎ 735–8823).

Luggage and Accessories

Luggage is a bargain in Singapore, and every complex contains several stores that carry designer names including Charles Jourdan, Dunhill, Etienne Aigner, and Louis Vuitton. Department stores also carry such brands as Samsonite and Delsey. The **Escada** boutique (☎ 336–8283) at the Promenade and the Millenia Walk has a range of accessories and custom-made luggage.

Pewter and Dinnerware

Malaysia is the world's largest tin producer, and pewter is an important craft item in the region. Modern pewter items are heavily influenced by Scandinavian design. Items range from jewelry and tiny figurines to coffee and tea sets. Sake sets, bowls, vases, ornamental plates, clocks, and traditional beer tankards are also available. Some items are specifically aimed at the tourist trade, such as Raffles plates and Chinese zodiac plaques.

For dinnerware, **Christofle** (☎ 733–7257) is popular and has a boutique in the Hilton. **Royal Selangor Pewter** (✉ Main office: 32 Pandan Rd., ☎ 268–9600), the largest pewter concern in Singapore, has a great product range displayed at the showrooms in the Paragon, Delfi Orchard, Clarke Quay, Raffles Hotel, Marina Square, and Raffles

City. Also try the **Waterford Wedgwood Shop** (⊠ No. 01–01 Delfi Orchard, ☎ 734–8375).

Silk

Chinese silk is easy to find in Singapore. All the emporiums have special departments that sell the fabric or clothes (tailored and ready-to-wear) made from it. **Jim Thompson,** which has outlets in the Raffles Hotel Arcade and in Takashimaya, has a wide range of silks in different weights and types, as well as clothing, including a line specifically designed for the shop.

For Indian silk in sari lengths check out the many shops in the Serangoon Road area. You pay only a fraction of what it would cost elsewhere to buy the 6 meters (6.5 yards) of silk—which could be the thin Kashmiri type or the heavier, embroidered Benares type—required to make a sari.

Thai silk, in different weights for different purposes, comes in stunning colors. Specialty shops sell it by the meter or made up into gowns, blouses, and dresses. The **Siam Silk Company** (⊠ 87 Tanjong Pagar Rd., ☎ 323–4800) is a good place to look.

Tailoring

There are tailors and tailors—what you end up with depends on how well you choose. Tailors who offer 24-hour service rarely deliver, and their quality is often suspect. Another indication of danger is not seeing a tailor on the premises. Anyone can set up shop as a tailor by filling a store with fabrics and then subcontracting the work; the results from such places are seldom felicitous. Allow four to five days for a good job. **Justmen** (☎ 737–4800) in the Tanglin Shopping Centre is one of a number of excellent men's tailors.

SINGAPORE A TO Z

Arriving and Departing

By Airplane

AIRPORTS

The major gateway to Singapore is **Changi International Airport** (☎ 542–1122), which is on the eastern end of the island. The AIRBUS (S$5) runs three different routes to and from all major hotels (☎ 542–1721), 8:20 AM–10:30 PM or 6:30 AM–11:10 PM for the city to airport run, depending on the route, and slightly different hours for the airport to city run. Under normal traffic conditions, the trip to/from the airport by taxi takes 20 to 30 minutes. Fares range from S$13 to S$20, plus a S$3 airport surcharge (S$5 Fri.–Sun. before 5 PM, but not applicable any time for trips *to* the airport). Other surcharges apply when baggage is stored in the trunk or when more than two adults travel in the same cab.

CARRIERS

Singapore Airlines (☎ 223–8888), the national carrier, offers direct, one-stop flights from Los Angeles and New York to Singapore. **United Airlines** (☎ 873–3533) has direct one-stop flights from Los Angeles, San Francisco, and Seattle, and connecting flights (one stop, with a change in Tokyo) from New York and Chicago.

Among the many other airlines that serve Singapore are: **Air New Zealand** (☎ 535–8266), **British Airways** (☎ 839–7788), **Cathay Pa-**

cific (☎ 533–1333), **China Airlines** (☎ 737–2211), **Garuda** (☎ 250–2888), **Japan Airlines** (☎ 221–0522), **Korean Air** (☎ 534–2111), **Malaysia Airlines** (☎ 336–6777), **Northwest Airlines** (☎ 336–3371), **Qantas** (☎ 839–7788), and **Thai Airways International** (☎ 224–9977). For general flight information, call Changi Airport (☎ 542–4422).

FLYING TIMES

Flying west, Singapore is 22 hours from Chicago, 18 hours from Los Angeles, 17 hours from Vancouver, 10½ hours from Auckland and Christchurch, and 8 hours from Sydney. The flying time east from New York is 19 hours; from London it's 13 hours.

By Boat

There are some 14 international cruise lines that visit Singapore, including Crystal Cruises of Los Angeles, Cunardline of New York, and Universal Boss of Hong Kong. The dominant cruise operator out of Singapore to points in Malaysia, Indonesia, and Thailand is **Star Cruises** (✉ 1 Shenton Way, No. 01–02 Robina House, ☎ 223–0002 or 226–1168).

For further information on regional and local cruises or boat services, contact the **Singapore Cruise Centre** at World Trade Centre (☎ 321–2802).

Ferrylink (☎ 545–3622 or 337–1759) plies between Changi Point in Singapore and Tanjong Belungkor in the eastern corner of Johor and other places on the coast of peninsular Malaysia. Most check-ins are an hour before sailing time. From Singapore's Tanah Merah Ferry Terminal, **Berlian Ferries** (☎ 546–8830), **Indo Falcon** (☎ 542–6786), and **Penguin Ferry Services** (☎ 542–7105) offer a four-hour trip to scuba divers' favorite Malaysian island, Tioman. Fares are around S$160 round-trip. From the World Trade Centre Regional Cruise Centre, regular ferries go to the two closest Indonesian islands, Batam and Bintan (☞ *also* Getting Around, *below*).

By Bus

Air-conditioned buses between Singapore and Malaysia are comfortable. The nearest city to Singapore, under an hour, is Johor Bahru ("JB"). The **Singapore-Johor Bahru Express** (☎ 292–8149) runs every seven minutes from 6:30 AM to midnight; the cost is only S$2.10 one way. The **Malacca-Singapore Express** (☎ 293–5915) takes about 4½ hours, costs S$11 one way, and leaves seven times daily. The **Kuala Lumpur-Singapore Express** (☎ 292–8254) leaves mornings, afternoons, and nights from Singapore, is S$25 one way, and takes about six hours.

By Car

If you're driving into Singapore from Malaysia, your Malaysian-registered car must have a valid VEP (Vehicle Entry Permit). Upon entering Singapore, you can obtain a free five-day VEP at the **Land Transport Authority** (LTA; ✉ 10 Sin Ming Drive, ☎ 553–5337 [VEP HQ], 269–0279 [Woodlands], 545–3917 [Changi]) booths at Woodlands Checkpoint or Changi Ferry Terminal. VEPs for weekday nights, weekends, and holidays are also free. Further extensions can be obtained from the LTA booth at ☎ 375–7100, and at designated post offices for S$30 a day. Tolls from S$1–S$2.50 are required on both sides of the Causeway link (Woodlands in Singapore) and the Second Link (Tuas in Singapore). Prepaid toll coupons for the Singapore side are available at post offices and gas stations. Cars driving into Malaysia must not leave Singapore with gas tanks less than three-quarters full. (For more information on driving, ☞ Getting Around, *below*).

By Train

Trains run regularly between Singapore and key cities in western Peninsular Malaysia, including the capital, Kuala Lumpur (called "KL"), and JB. There are four daily departures to JB; the trip takes about an hour and costs roughly S$3 one way. The air-conditioned express train to KL also leaves mornings, afternoons, and nights (sleepers are comfortable). The trip takes about six hours, and the first-class one-way fare is S$68, second-class S$34.For further information, call **Malayan Railway** (☎ 222–5165).

E&OE Services (☎ 392–3500 or 323–4390), the company that operates the *Venice Simplon–Orient Express,* runs the deluxe *Eastern & Oriental Express;* the train travels between Singapore and Bangkok, and on to Chiang Mai, Thailand, once a week, with stops in KL and in Butterworth, Malaysia, permitting an excursion to Penang. The 1,943-km (1,200-mi) journey takes 41 hours. Fares, which vary according to cabin type and include meals, start at S$2,350 per person one way to Bangkok.

Getting Around

By Bicycle-Rickshaw

Bicycle-rickshaws, known as trishaws, number a few dozen. They are considered museum pieces, favored only by tourists, and were last used as serious local transport in the 1960s. They're usually found on Stamford Road in front of the Singapore History Museum and at Bugis Junction. Bargain for the fare; you shouldn't pay more than S$20 for a 45-minute ride. The best time to take a rickshaw ride is 7 PM or later, after the rush hour.

By Boat

Harbor cruises and ferries to Singapore's outer islands, Malaysia, and the Indonesian Riau islands depart from two locations: the **Singapore Cruise Centre** (✉ World Trade Centre, ☎ 270–3918 or 321–2802), a 10-minute drive from the city center, and the **Tanah Merah Ferry Terminal** (✉ Changi Rd., ☎ 345–1210) on Singapore's east coast. (For more information on cruises, ☞ By Boat, *above*).

Singapore River tours, some of them on old Chinese junks, leave from Boat Quay, Clarke Quay, and Clifford Pier; operators include **Eastwind Organisation** (☎ 533–3432), **Singapore River Boat** (☎ 338–9205), **Singapore River Cruises & Leisure** (☎ 336–6111), and **Watertours** (☎ 533–9811).

TO SENTOSA ISLAND

Daily ferries ply the four-minute crossing between the Jardine Steps of the World Trade Centre and Sentosa Island every 20 minutes from 9:30 AM until 9 PM Mon.–Thur., with two extra return ferries weekends and holidays, at 11:15 PM and midnight. The one-way fare is S$1.30. (Admission to the island adds S$6.)

TO THE OUTER ISLANDS

Monday through Saturday, two ferries leave for Kusu from the Singapore Cruise Centre at the World Trade Centre (for schedules phone 862–8322 or 275–0388); on Sundays and holidays there are six ferries. The trip takes about 30 minutes and costs S$9 (including admission to the island). The same ferries that go to Kusu run to St. John's, just over an hour's journey.

You can hire a bumboat (motorized water taxi) for a trip to Pulau Ubin. Take SBS bus 2 from the Tanah Merah MRT station to Changi Point. Then take a bumboat (S$1.50) from the Changi Jetty nearby. To reach

Sisters Island, where there is no regular ferry service, hire a larger water
taxi (S$50 an hour) at Jardine Steps or Clifford Pier.

Ferries directly to any of the resorts on Bintan leave regularly from Singapore's Tanah Merah Ferry Terminal. The round-trip fare for the 45-
minute trip to the resort area is S$45. Do not go without a hotel
reservation and arrangements for land transfer, and remember to take
your passport. The trip to Bintan's main town, Tanjung Pinang, takes
1½ hours and costs about S$58 round-trip. Ferry services include **Bin-
tan Resort Ferries** (☎ 542–4369), **Dino Shipping** (☎ 276–9722), and
Penguin Ferry Services (☎ 542–7105).

By Bus

Reserved bus lanes along the main roads and frequent service—usually every 5 to 10 minutes—make buses quicker than cabs during rush
hours, (and they're always cheaper). The excellent *TransitLink Guide,*
available for S$1.50 at any bookstore or subway (MRT) station, pin-
points major stops. Fares range from S$0.60 to S$1.20 for buses
without air-conditioning and from S$0.70 to S$1.50 for those with
it. Deposit exact change, and remember to collect your ticket. Most
buses run from 6 AM until around midnight. To reach Sentosa Island
by bus, either find a special Sentosa bus (Service E runs down Orchard
Road) or first take a regular bus to the World Trade Centre—number 65 or 143 from Orchard Road—and transfer there onto a shuttle across the causeway. The S$7 round-trip fare includes admission
to the island. Shuttles operate weekdays 7 AM–10:30 PM (till 12:30
AM on weekends).

The S$10 *Tourist Day Ticket* (available at MRT stations and bus in-
terchanges) lets you take up to 12 rides a day on the MRT and bus
system. You must tell the ticketing officer exactly which day you intend to use it as that date will be printed on the ticket.

The red Singapore Trolley bus connects the Orchard Road shopping
belt, the colonial district, the Singapore River, Chinatown, Raffles
Hotel, Clarke Quay, Marina, and Suntec City. It's expensive (S$14.90),
but it does make 22 stops, and your ticket is good for a full day of unlimited travel, as well as a free riverboat tour. You can buy it (you'll
need exact change) when you board or from your hotel concierge.

For all information on bus travel within Singapore, contact the **Singapore Bus Services** (☎ 800/287–2727) or **Singapore Explorer** (☎ 339–
6833).

By Cable Car

You can catch a cable car to Sentosa Island from one of two terminals
on the Singapore side: the **Cable Car Towers** (☎ 270–8855), next to
the World Trade Centre, and the **Mt. Faber Cable Car Station** (☎ 275–
0248). The longer, 13-minute trip from Mt. Faber offers better views,
but there's no bus to the station and it's a long walk up the hill; a taxi
is your best bet. The Cable Car Towers station is accessible by bus:
from Orchard Road, take Bus 65 or 143; from Clifford Pier, Bus 10,
97, 100,125, or 131 to the World Trade Centre; from Chinatown, Bus
61, 84, 143, 145, or 166. Cable cars run regularly daily from 8:30 AM–
9 PM; fares are S$6.90 round-trip, S$5.90 one way.

By Car

With the amount of road rules, regulations, tariffs, tolls, and permit
requirements that seem to change and expand in Singapore every year,
you'd be advised to stick to public transportation. Road congestion
(particularly to and from Malaysia) can be harrowing during rush hours

and on weekends and holidays. Highway names, tariffs, and all licensing schemes are abbreviated, and this can cause great confusion.

To even out traffic flow into the Central Business District (CBD), all cars entering during the restricted hours of 7:30 AM to 7 PM are required to display a valid ALS (Area Licensing Scheme) license. At ALS checkpoints, a yellow light indicates that a part-day license is required; blue and yellow lights indicate that a full-day license is required.

One-day ALS licenses cost S$3 and are available at gas stations, ALS booths, post offices, and 7-Eleven stores.

To relieve congestion between 7:30 AM and 9:30 AM along expressways and busy roads, vehicles passing through Electronic Road Pricing (ERP) gantries on these routes must pay a toll, which is automatically deducted by an in-vehicle unit (IU) from a prepaid cash-card inserted into the IU. Foreign-registered cars can be fitted with a permanent (S$120) or temporary (S$5 daily, deposit S$120) IU on entry to Singapore; cash cards are available at gas stations and 7-Eleven stores. Further information is available from the **ERP Hotline** (☎ 800/553–5226) or **NETS** (☎ 274–1322). A guide to the ALS and ERP is available at the Woodlands Checkpoint on entry to Singapore.

EMERGENCY ASSISTANCE
The **Automobile Association of Singapore** (AAS; ☎ 748–9911) has 24-hour emergency road service.

GASOLINE
Unleaded gas starts at S$1.25 per liter in Singapore. A government ruling requires any car passing the Causeway out of Singapore to drive with at least three-quarters of a tank of gas or be fined; the republic's huge losses in revenue as a result of Singaporeans driving to Malaysia to fill up cheaply led to this unpopular ruling.

PARKING
For visitors, there are two ways of parking: coupon parking and paid parking. Where required, parking coupons should be displayed on the dashboard. Denominations of parking coupons are S$0.45, S$0.90, S$1.80, and S$2 (for overnight parking). Generally, parking rates are S$0.45 per half hour outside the CBD, and S$0.90 per half hour within it. Parking coupons are available from gas stations, post offices, shopping centers, and some shops.

Paid parking is practiced in almost all shopping centers, buildings, and some public parking areas. You basically pay for the amount of time your car is parked. Some shopping centers offer a rebate on your parking charges, as do some hotels.

RENTAL AGENCIES
Rates in Singapore begin at S$65 a day and S$392 a week for an economy car with unlimited mileage. This doesn't include tax on car rentals, which is 3%. You will need an international driving license. The major car-rental companies represented here are Avis, Budget, Hertz, and Sintat. Should you want to look up firms in the Singapore Yellow Pages, check under "Motorcar Renting and Leasing." The following are some local branches of international car-rental agencies: **AB (Budget)** (✉ Pan Pacific Hotel, ground floor, ☎ 334–0019, Changi Airport, Terminal 1 ☎ 543–4431), **National** (✉ Changi Airport, ☎ 543–2331 or 542–8855; ✉ Boulevard Hotel, 200 Orchard Blvd., ☎ 737–1668), **Sime Darby (Hertz)** (✉ Changi Airport, Terminal 2, ☎ 542–5300; ✉ Tudor Court Shopping Gallery, 125 Tanglin Rd., ☎ 1800-734–4646), and **Sintat** (✉ Changi Airport, Terminal 1, ☎ 542–7288; ✉ 60 Bendemeer Rd., ☎ 295–2211 or 295–6288).

ROAD CONDITIONS

For the most part, road conditions are quite good, especially on the expressways. Some streets have fairly deep ditches and may not be well-lit in the evenings.

RULES OF THE ROAD

Driving is on the left-hand side of the road in both Singapore and Malaysia. A valid driving license from your country of residence or a valid International Driver's License is required. Parking coupons (☞ Parking, *above*) should be displayed on the dashboard. The speed limit is 50 kph (31 mph) in residential areas and 80 kph (50 mph) on expressways. Speed cameras are installed throughout the island; fines are comparable to those in, say, New York City or Toronto. Bus lanes or extreme left lanes marked by unbroken yellow lines should not be used by cars during the following hours: weekdays 7:30 AM–9:30 AM and 4:30 PM–7 PM, Saturday 7:30 AM–9:30 AM and 11:30 AM–2 PM.

By Subway

The subway, or MRT, consists of two lines that run north–south and east–west and cross at the City Hall and Raffles Place interchanges. The system includes 48 stations along 83 km (52 mi). All cars and underground stations are air-conditioned, and the trains operate between 6 AM and midnight daily.

You can buy tickets from booths or vending machines in the stations. Large maps showing the station locations and the fares between them hang above each vending machine. There's a S$2 fine for underpaying, so make sure you buy the right ticket for your destination. The magnetic tickets are inserted in turnstiles to let you on and off the platform. Fares start at S$0.70 for about two stations; the maximum fare is S$1.60. The fare between Orchard Road Station and Raffles Place Station (in the business district) is S$0.70. The TransitLink fare card, a prepaid mass-transit ticket, starting at S$12 including a S$2 deposit, can be used on both buses and trains and is available at TransitLink sales offices in MRT stations and at bus interchanges. Any unused fare and the deposit can be refunded at TransitLink offices.

For more information contact: **Singapore Bus Services** (☎ 800/287–2727), **Singapore MRT Ltd.** (☎ 800/336–8900), or **TransitLink** (☎ 800/779–9366).

By Taxi

There are more than 15,000 strictly regulated, metered taxis in Singapore. Taxi fares have been deregulated since 1998, which means that different taxi companies can set their own fares, within reasonable limits monitored by the regulator, the Land Transport Authority. The starting fare for most companies is S$2.40 for the first km (0.9 mi) but thereafter, different companies may charge S$.10 for each subsequent 240 meters (900 ft) or S$.10 for each subsequent 225 meters (820 ft). In the next phase of the fare structure, you might pay S$.10 for every subsequent 225 meters again with one company, or S$.10 for every 200 meters (656 ft) thereafter with another, and so on. Every 30 seconds of waiting time carries a S$.10 charge. You can catch cabs at stands or by hailing them from any curb not marked with a double yellow line. **Radio cabs** are available 24 hours (Tibs ☎ 481–1211, Comfort CabLink ☎ 552–1111, and CityCab ☎ 552–2222). It's often difficult to get through to reserve a cab, so it's better to just hail one or take the bus. A driver showing a red destination label in the window is returning to his garage and can pick up only passengers going in his direction. Drivers don't expect tips.

Be aware of myriad surcharges that may apply. For starters, at peak hours on busy roads, the additional Electronic Road Pricing (ERP) charge will be added to the metered fare, shown on the upper display of the cab's in-vehicle unit. A S$3.20 charge is added for taxis booked by phone (there's an additional S$2 surcharge for every booking half an hour or more in advance). Trips made between midnight and 6 AM have a 50% surcharge, and rides from, *not to,* the airport carry a S$3 surcharge. Unless a taxi displays a yellow permit, a S$1 surcharge is added to fares from the CBD between 5 and 8 PM on weekdays and noon and 3 PM on Saturdays. To the CBD, there's a S$3 surcharge for the purchase of an Area License, which is needed to enter the Restricted Zone between 7:30 AM and 6:30 PM weekdays, between 7:30 AM and 2 PM Saturday, and on the eve of five major holidays. You don't pay the fee if the taxi already has the sticker. Be on the lookout for other charges.

Contacts and Resources

Customs and Duties

ON ARRIVAL

Duty-free allowances include 1 liter each of spirits, wine, and beer (applies to visitors over 18); all personal effects; and less than S$50 in foodstuffs such as chocolates, biscuits, and cakes. The following imports are prohibited: drugs; pornography (including such publications as *Playboy* and *Playgirl*); seditious and treasonable materials; toy coins and currency notes; cigarette lighters of pistol/revolver shapes; reproductions of copyrighted publications, videotapes, records, or cassettes; duty-free cigarettes; and chewing gum in amounts deemed large enough for resale, chewing tobacco and imitation tobacco products, and endangered species of wildlife and their by-products. Special import permits are required for animals, live plants, meats, arms, and controlled drugs. (Penalties for drug abuse are very severe in Singapore—mandatory death for trafficking, defined by possession of fixed amounts—and are rigidly enforced.) Customs is also extremely strict regarding the import of any form of arms, including such items as ceremonial daggers purchased as souvenirs in other countries. These are held in bond and returned to you on your departure. There are no import (or export) restrictions or limitations on the amount of cash, foreign currencies, checks, and drafts.

ON DEPARTURE

Export permits are required for arms, ammunition, explosives, animals, gold, platinum, precious stones and jewelry, poisons, and medicinal drugs. The export of narcotics is punishable by death under Singapore law.

Electricity

The electrical current in Singapore is 220 volts, 50 cycles alternating current (AC), like that in Australia and Great Britain. If you're a resident of North America, bring an adapter and converter; if your appliances are dual voltage, bring just an adapter. Wall outlets take a variety of plug styles, including plugs with two round oversize prongs and plugs with three square-tipped prongs. Many hotels lend guests adapters and converters.

Embassies and Consulates

Most countries maintain a diplomatic mission in Singapore. Call ahead to confirm hours; most are closed Saturday. If you hope to obtain visas for neighboring countries, be aware that the visa-application process at Singapore consular offices may take several days.

Australia (⊠ 25 Napier Rd., ☎ 836–4100). **Canada** (⊠ 80 Anson Rd., ☎ 325–3200). **New Zealand** (⊠ No. 15/06–10, Tower A, 391A Orchard Rd., ☎ 235–9966). **United Kingdom** (⊠ 100 Tanglin Rd., ☎ 473–9333). **United States** (⊠ 27 Napier Rd., ☎ 476–9100).

Emergencies
Ambulance and fire: ☎ 995. **Police:** ☎ 999.

Hospitals and doctors: Most hotels have their own doctor on 24-hour call. Hospitals include: **Gleneagles Hospital** (⊠ 6A Napier Rd., ☎ 473–7222); **Mount Alvernia Hospital** (⊠ 820 Thomson Rd., ☎ 359–7910); **Mount Elizabeth Hospital** (⊠ Mount Elizabeth,, ☎ 737–2666); **Raffles Medical Group** (⊠ 182 Clemenceau Ave., ☎ 334–3337, 24-hour clinic/emergency center; 334–3333, SurgiCentre) has 29 clinics and operates the Raffles SurgiCentre, a private hospital on Clemenceau Avenue near the Dhoby Ghaut MRT station; **Singapore General Hospital** (⊠ Outram Rd., ☎ 222–3322). **Pharmacies:** Some pharmacies are open until 10 PM, although most close at 6 PM. For more information, contact the Singapore Tourism Board (☞ Visitor Information, *below*).

Sentosa Island Ranger Station: ☎ 279–1155.

English-Language Bookstores
Since English is the lingua franca, all regular bookstores carry English-language books. **Borders** (☎ 235–7146) at Wheelock Place on Orchard Road and **Kinokuniya** (☎ 737–5021 or 738–6093) at the Ngee Ann City (Takashimaya) complex at Orchard Road and are both good bets. Other leading local chains are **MPH Bookstores** on Stamford Road (☎ 336–3633) and the **Times the Bookshop** at Centrepoint on Orchard Road (☎ 734–9022). An excellent independent specializing in Asia and frequented by the region's intellectuals is **Select Books** (☎ 732–1515) at Tanglin Shopping Centre, at the western end of Orchard Road.

Singapore has a policy of censorship. Certain books and magazines are banned from being sold or even owned. The multilingual newspaper industry has long been the virtual monopoly of Singapore Press Holdings (SPH), publisher of the only English-language broadsheets, the *Straits Times*, and *Business Times* dailies, as well as *The New Paper* tabloid afternoon paper. This is about to change: the Television Corporation of Singapore, or MediaCorp, partnering with Singapore Telecom and the MRT, is launching a free sheet for MRT commuters, and SPH is responding with another. But all Singapore media are constrained in their reporting and take their cue from the People's Action Party Government, mindful that they work within a framework of considerably less press freedom than in the West.

Health and Safety
FOOD AND DRINK
Tap water is safe, and every eating establishment—from the most elegant hotel dining room to the smallest sidewalk stall—is regularly inspected by the very strict health authorities. But if your stomach is delicate, watch out for the powerful local *chilli sambals* (chili pastes) and take care with shellfish. As anywhere in Asia, it's a good idea to maintain hepatitis immunization.

OTHER PRECAUTIONS
Singapore is a safe place in which to walk around unaccompanied at night. Like everywhere else, however, precautions should be taken after midnight, when subway and bus service stops. Taxis can be flagged, but you'll see more of them in the city center than in the sub-

urbs. Women aren't normally harassed, but conservative attire is recommended in neighborhoods such as Little India and the Arab District in deference to conservative religious customs. Jaywalk at your own risk; Singapore drivers don't slow down or stop to let you cross the street.

Be aware that although you will see garbage on the streets in certain sections of the city, littering is against the law and can nab you a S$1,000 fine. Similarly, consuming food or drink or smoking on the transit systems (this includes subway platforms) is not allowed. Nonsmoking rules are widespread—especially in movie theaters, elevators, lines, offices, and restaurants. Although chewing gum is not sold anywhere, you may bring it in for personal use—just dispose of it properly!

The rights of gays and lesbians aren't protected in Singapore, but gay culture is alive and well, albeit underground, and there is increasing public awareness. Generally though, attitudes are conservative and a discreet "don't ask, don't tell" convention prevails. But if you check out Web sites such as People Like Us (www.plu.singapore.com), Utopia (www.utopia.asia.com/), and Yawning Bread (www.geocities.com/West-Hollywood/5738/), you'll find that there are plenty of places to go. Cruising at swimming pools and big bookshops as well as in bars and on the street is common and relatively upfront, even though there is no gay "neighborhood" per se. When swimming the waters of Singapore's offshore islands, be aware not only of the water quality but also of the strong undercurrents in some places. Although there is virtually no malaria risk in Singapore, there are occasional flare-ups of dengue, or "breakbone fever," so take care to protect yourself at all times from mosquitoes. If you plan to visit Bintan Island, Indonesia, you'll need to take precautions against malaria. Check with your doctor about medication before you leave home and pack plenty of bug spray. Note, however, that resorts on the island will have netting, insect repellent, and mosquito coils.

Language, Culture, and Etiquette

Singapore is a multiracial society with four official languages: Malay, Mandarin, Tamil, and English. The national language is Malay, but the lingua franca is English. It's used in administration, it's a required course for every schoolchild, and it's used in entrance exams for universities. Hence, virtually all Singaporeans speak English with varying degrees of fluency. Mandarin is increasingly replacing the other Chinese dialects, especially among the young. At street level, Singaporeans young and old communicate in "Singlish," a vibrant Singaporean "creole" version of English that has its own cross-cultural vocabulary and structure.

You'd do well to bring along a stash of business cards—it seems like everyone exchanges them, even people who are on vacation. It's proper to offer your business card using both hands with the card facing the recipient. Likewise, when a card is offered to you, accept it with both hands and make it a point to read the card. This shows your respect for the person's title and position.

Don't use your left hand for shaking or giving something to a Malay or an Indonesian, or for eating (that is the hand used to wash the private parts after relieving oneself). It's safer to refrain from kissing or touching the opposite sex, as some communities might be offended. Members of the same sex and community commonly hold hands or interact affectionately, but this is not sexual.

If you're invited for dinner by Chinese friends or business acquaintances, it's proper etiquette to leave some food on the plate or in the bowl, to indicate that your host's generosity is so great, you cannot eat another bite. There's no shame in asking for a knife and fork instead of chopsticks. Chinese tea is generally served throughout the meal. Unlike in the West, dinner-table conversation about money and business is common.

You can get a fuller cultural briefing from the locally published paperback *Culture Shock! Singapore,* part of an excellent series published by Times Books/Times Editions.

Mail

POSTAL RATES

Most hotels sell stamps and mail guests' letters. You can buy postage, stationery, and certain types of driving permits at some post offices. Postage on local letters up to 20 grams (0.8 ounces) is S$0.22. Airmail takes about seven business days to reach North America and Great Britain. An airmail postcard costs S$0.50; larger cards are S$1. A letter up to 20 grams is S$0.35 to Malaysia or Brunei, S$0.40 to other foreign countries. Printed aerogram letters (available at most post offices) are S$0.45. Note that delivery of small packets, printed paper, and parcels (both international and domestic mail) isn't regulated; service for such items is provided by several courier companies as well as Singapore Post.

RECEIVING MAIL

If you know which hotel you'll be staying at, have mail sent there marked "Hold for Arrival." American Express cardholders or travelers' check users can have mail sent care of **American Express International** (✉ The Concourse, No. 18–01/07, 300 Beach Rd., 199555, ☎ 299–8133). Envelopes should be marked "Client Mail." For more postal information, contact the **General Post Office** (GPO; ✉ No. 05–12750 Chai Chee Industrial Park, Chai Chee Rd., 469000, ☎ 448–7733 or 165 to postal inquiries line). The new GPO is in the suburbs; a phone inquiry is your best bet.

WRITING TO SINGAPORE

In 1997, Singapore began using a six-digit postal code; it's important to include this on any correspondence (inquiries to ☎ 800/842–7678; a guide is available from post offices). Addresses can be written either with the number and street following the name of the person or company, with the second or third line used for the name of the building: "XYZ Sales Office, No. 16–00 Cable Car Towers, 3 Maritime Square, Singapore 099254" or "ABC Cable Car (Pte) Ltd., 333 Orchard Rd., No. 03–10 Mandarin Hotel Shopping Arcade, Singapore 238867." Note that in the last address, "No. 03-10" refers to the third floor, office number 10; the abbreviation "Pte" (which is used in many business names) indicates a privately owned company.

Money Matters

COSTS

Singapore ranks up there with other world capitals as far as expenses go. Although good meals cost a little less than you would pay in Paris, hotel room prices are in the New York and London ranges. You can keep costs down by eating at hawker food centers, especially those in the major shopping malls, and by using public transportation. Many hotels offer special promotional rates, corporate rates, or weekend rates; always ask about such deals before booking.

Sample Prices: In moderately priced restaurants, expect to pay: cup of coffee, S$3–S$5; bottle of beer, S$6–S$9; soft drink, S$2.50; bottle of house wine, S$30; sandwich, S$5. Transportation costs are about: 2-km (1-mi) taxi ride, S$4; city bus ride, S$0.70. Museum entrance is generally S$3.

CURRENCY

The local currency is the Singapore dollar (S$), which is divided into 100 cents. Notes in circulation are S$1, S$2, S$5, S$10, S$20, S$50, S$100, S$500, S$1,000, and S$10,000. Coins: S$0.01, S$0.05, S$0.20, S$0.50, and S$1. At press time, the exchange rate was S$0.99 to the Australian dollar, S$1.14 to the Canadian dollar, S$.70 to the New Zealand dollar, S$1.70 to the U.S. dollar, S$2.57 to the pound sterling, and S$1.55 to the Euro.

SERVICE CHARGES, TAXES, AND TIPPING

There's a 3% sales tax, called the Goods and Services Tax (GST). You can get the tax refunded at Global Refund Singapore counters in the airport as you leave the country, for purchases of more than S$300 made at a store or retail chain displaying the Tax Free Shopping sticker (you can pool individual receipts for S$100 or more). (Ask for a Tax Free Shopping Cheque to be completed, and show the goods and the checks at the airport departure terminal for customs inspection.) You can cash the checks at the airport refund counters; opt for a bank check via mail; or ask for a refund to a specific credit card, although a surcharge may be levied for this. This government tax is also added to restaurant and hotel bills, as is a 10% service charge (except by hawker stalls and small restaurants). You're also subject to a S$15 airport departure tax (for travelers to Malaysia, the tax is S$5), which—if it's not already included in the price of your ticket—is payable at the airport (to save time and avoid standing in line, buy a tax voucher at your hotel or any airline office).

Tipping isn't customary in Singapore. It's prohibited at the airport and discouraged in hotels (except for bellboys, who generally receive S$1 per bag) or restaurants that levy the 10% service charge. Unlike in other countries, waitstaffs don't receive a percentage of this service charge, except in the more progressive establishments, which need to retain the best waiters and waitresses. Hence, after experiencing some Singapore service you may begin to wish that tipping was the norm. Taxi drivers don't receive tips from Singaporeans, some of whom become upset when they see tourists tip.

Opening and Closing Times

Businesses are generally open weekdays 9 or 9:30 to 5 or 5:30; a few are also open on Saturday morning. In general, **banks** open weekdays 9:30–3 or 4 and Saturday 9:30–11 AM. However, branches of the Development Bank of Singapore stay open until 3 PM on Saturday, and the bank at Changi Airport is open whenever there are flights. Many **museums** close on Monday; otherwise, they're generally open 9 to 4:30 or 5:30, and often till 9 PM on Wednesdays. Registered pharmacists work 9–6, though some **pharmacies** in the major shopping centers stay open until 10 PM. Of the 87 **post offices** on the island, most are open weekdays 8:30–5 and Saturday 8:30–1. The branch at the airport is open 8–8 and the office at the start of Killiney Road, just off Orchard Road opposite Orchard Point shopping center, is open Sundays and nights. **Shop** opening times vary. Department stores and many shops in big shopping centers are generally open daily from about 10 AM to 9 PM (sometimes later on weekends); smaller shops tend to close on Sunday.

NATIONAL HOLIDAYS

Singapore has 10 public holidays: New Year's Day (Jan. 1), Hari Raya Puasa (Dec. 27, 2000; Dec.16, 2001), Chinese New Year (Jan. 24–26, 2001), Hari Raya Haji (Mar. 6, 2001), Good Friday (Apr. 13, 2001), Labor Day (May 1), Vesak Day (May), National Day (Aug. 9), Deepavali/Diwali (Oct.–Nov.), Christmas Day (Dec. 25).

Passports and Visas

Visas aren't required for stays of up to 14 days for Canadian, U.K., U.S., Australian, and New Zealand citizens. You may automatically be given a 30-day social visit pass upon your arrival if you come from any of these countries; if you arrive in Singapore from Malaysia, Indonesia, or Thailand, your passport may be stamped for only 14 days. Be sure to carry an onward or return air ticket, and sufficient funds. If you require a longer stay, you may apply to **Singapore Immigration** (✉ 10 Kallang Rd., ☎ 800/391–6100) after your arrival. Women who are in an advanced stage of pregnancy (six months or more) should make prior application to the nearest Singapore overseas mission or the Singapore Immigration Department.

To visit Bintan Island, Indonesia, citizens of Great Britain, Canada, the United States, Australia, and New Zealand require only passports for stays of less than one month.

Telephones

CALLS TO SINGAPORE

To call Singapore from overseas, first dial your national IDD access code, then the country code, 65, then the number (Singapore has no area codes). The country code for Indonesia is 62; the area code for Bintan is 771. For Malaysia the country code is 60.

LOCAL CALLS

From a pay phone, the cost is S$0.10; insert a coin and dial the seven-digit number. Hotels charge anywhere from S$0.10 to S$0.50 a call. (There are free public phones at Changi Airport, just past immigration.) Many pay phones only accept phone cards; the coin-operated phones are smaller and frequently found in shopping malls and at information desks. Phone cards (☞ *below*) in a variety of denominations are sold at most kiosks, newsstands, and gift shops. For directory assistance, simply dial 100.

LONG-DISTANCE AND INTERNATIONAL CALLS

To make direct overseas calls dial 001 and then the country code and the number; if you'd like operator assistance, dial 104. To avoid hefty hotel service charges, use the **SingTel** (Singapore Telecom; ☎ 838–3388) phone card if you plan to make lots of long-distance calls during your stay. The cards are available in denominations of S$2, S$5, S$10, S$20, and S$50 and permit you to make both local and overseas calls. The price of each call is deducted from the card total, and your balance is roughly indicated by the punched hole in the card. Phone cards are available from post offices, some newsstands, SingTel customer services outlets, and drugstores.

To save money on calls overseas, use the Home Country Direct service available from your hotel room or any public phone. This puts you in touch with an operator in your home country who places your call, charging either your home phone or your credit card. You can also use pay phones by first depositing S$0.10 and then dialing 8000–111–11 to reach a U.S. operator or 8000–440–440 for a British operator. Note also that some public phones at the airport and many at city post offices accept Diners Club, MasterCard, and Visa.

Tour Operators

A wide range of sightseeing tours covers the highlights of Singapore and are a good introduction to the island. Tours can take two hours or the whole day, and prices range from S$28 to S$80. Most are operated in comfortable, air-conditioned coaches with guides and include pickup and return. Tour agencies can also arrange private-car tours with guides; these are considerably more expensive. There's no need to book tours in advance of your visit; they can be easily arranged through the tour desks in hotels. Also, if you're only in Singapore on a six-hour stopover, the tourist board offers free city tours from Changi Airport. See the STB Desk there.

The following touring companies are recommended: **Gray Line Tours** (☎ 331–8203), **Holiday Tours** (☎ 738–2622), **Malaysia and Singapore Travel Centre** (☎ 737–8877), **RMG Tours** (☎ 220–1661), **SH Tours** (☎ 734–9923), **Singapore Sightseeing Tour East** (☎ 332–3755), **Singapore Trolley** (☎ 339–6833), and **Worldlink Travel**(☎ 299–6698).

Most of these companies market the latest tour ideas (mostly half-day tours, averaging S$30–S$35 per head) being promoted by the Singapore Tourism Board. These include "Flavours of New Asia" (spice gardens, fresh markets, herbalists, and spice shops); "Heartlands of New Asia" (then-and-now contrasts, including villages and Pulau Ubin Island); "Painted Faces" (Chinese street opera, the suppliers of the stage props and mask-makers, an opera performance); "Spirit of New Asia" (multicultural Singapore, the Singapore River, the Asian Civilisations Museum); "The City Experience" (Chinatown, Little India, Orchard Road); and the intriguing "In Harmony with Feng Shui" tour that introduces the arcane world of Chinese geomancy, the auspicious siting or positioning of buildings and interiors, and how it has shaped Singapore city.

Although it's easy to get around Sentosa Island on your own, **Sentosa Discovery Tours** (☎ 277–9654 or 275–0248) offers three-hour guided trips that cover the major attractions. The tours commence every 3½ hours, beginning at 9:30 AM; tickets cost S$39.

If your itinerary includes a trip to Bintan Island, Indonesia, book a day with **Riau Island Adventures** (☎ 270–9937 or 270–3397) for S$100, lunch included. You can make reservations before leaving Singapore or through the concierge at your resort on Bintan. With the company's "Pinang–Penyengat Adventure Cruise," you sail in a traditional Indonesian fishing boat to the bustling old town of Tanjung Pinang, where you can shop in the lively marketplace, followed by a traditional Indonesian lunch on the slow cruise home.

Travel Agencies

BnE Travel Consultants Pte Ltd (✉ No. 05–21, Parklane Shopping Mall, 35 Selegie Rd., 188307, ☎ 339–2123) is well versed in day tours, short side trips from Singapore, and international bookings. (Ask to speak with Mr. Chia and mention the Fodor's Guide.) Many other agencies offer three- and four-day hotel and air excursions to neighboring countries, but you must shop around for the best deal.

Visitor Information

If you are calling from outside the country, you need to add a 0 in front of the prefixes listed here (e.g., "03" for Melbourne), after the IDD access code used in the country you are dialing from. If you are calling from the location of the office, you don't need to dial the prefix at all. Before leaving home, contact the **Singapore Tourism Board (STB)** in **Australia** (✉ 235 Queen St., Level 1, Melbourne, Vic., 3000,

☎ 3/9606–0222, ℻ 3/9606–0322; c/o Sandra Devahasdin PR & Promotions, ✉ Unit 2, 226 James St., Perth, WA 6000, ☎ 8/9228–8166, ℻ 8/9228–8290; ✉ Level 11, AWA Building, 47 York St., Sydney, NSW 2000, ☎ 2/9290–2888, ℻ 2/9290–2555); in **Canada** (✉ 2 Bloor St. West, Suite 404, Toronto, Ontario M4W 3E2, ☎ 416/363–8898, ℻ 416/363–5752, 🖳); in **New Zealand** (✉ Vivaldi World Ltd., 85B Hebron Rd., Waiake, Auckland, 1311, ☎ 9/473–8658, ℻ 9/473–6887); in the **United Kingdom** (✉ Carrington House, 126-130 Regent St., 1st floor, London W1R 5FE, ☎ 207/437–0033, ℻ 207/734–2191); in the **United States** (✉ 590 5th Ave., 12th floor, New York, NY 10036, ☎ 212/302–4861, ℻ 212/302–4801, www.singapore-usa.com; ✉ Two Prudential Plaza, 180 N. Stetson Ave., Suite 2615, Chicago, IL 60601, ☎ 312/938–1888, ℻ 312/938–0086; ✉ 8484 Wilshire Blvd., Suite 510, Beverly Hills, CA 90211, ☎ 323/852–1901, ℻ 323/852–0129).

In Singapore, the **STB** (✉ Tourism Court, 1 Orchard Spring La., Singapore 247729, ☎ 736–6622 or 800/736–2000, 🖳) has staff members ready to answer any questions you may have and to attend to legitimate complaints. The offices are open daily from 8:30 AM to 7 PM. If you're planning a trip to Bintan Island contact the **Indonesian Tourist Promotion Office** (✉ No. 15–07 Ocean Building, 10 Collyer Quay, Singapore 039192, ☎ 534–2837) for tourist, passport and visa, health, and currency information.

When to Go

With the equator only 129 km (86 mi) to the south, Singapore is usually either hot or very hot. The average daily temperature is 80°F (26.6°C); it usually reaches 87°F (30.7°C) in the afternoon and drops to a cool 75°F (23.8°C) just before dawn. The months from November through January, during the northeast monsoon, are generally the coolest. The average daily relative humidity is 84.5%, although it drops to 65%–70% on dry afternoons.

Rain falls year-round, but the wettest months are November through January. February is usually the sunniest month; December, the most inclement.

FESTIVALS AND SEASONAL EVENTS

With so many different cultural and religious groups, Singapore is a city of festivals, from the truly exotic to the strictly-for-tourists. The dates and seasons of many of them vary from year to year according to the lunar calendar; contact the STB (☞ Visitor Information, *above*) for details.

Dec.–Jan.: **Ramadan** is the month of daytime fasting among the city's Muslim population. After sunset, stalls on Bussorah Street and around the Sultan Mosque sell a variety of dishes, including Malay rice cakes wrapped in banana leaves, and fragrant puddings. The **Hari Raya Puasa** festival marks the joyous end to the fast.

Jan.–Feb.: **Thaipusam** celebrates the victory of the Hindu god Subramaniam over the demon Idumban. After night-long ritual purification and chanting, penitents enter a trance and give thanks for favors received or hoped for by piercing their flesh with knives, steel rods, and fishhooks, which they wear during the festival's spectacular 8-km (5-mi) procession. The procession begins at the Perumal temple on Serangoon Road, passes the Sri Mariamman temple on South Bridge Road, and ends at the Chettiar temple, Tank Road, where women pour pots of milk over the image of Lord Subramaniam. The lunar New Year celebration known as the **Chinese New Year** lasts for 15 days, and most shops and businesses close for about a week. The end of the Chinese New Year is marked by the **Chingay Procession.** Chinese, Malays, and Indians all get into the act for this event, complete with clashing gongs, lion dancers, dragons, and stilt-walkers. Check local newspapers for the parade route.

Apr.: **Songkran** (April 18) is a traditional Thai water festival that marks the beginning of the year's solar cycle. In Singapore's Thai Buddhist temples, images of Buddha are bathed with perfumed holy water, caged birds are set free, and blessings of water are splashed on worshipers and visitors. The liveliest (and wettest) celebrations are at Thai Buddhist Temple on Silat Road and Sattha Puchaniyaram Buddhist Temple off Bukit Batok West Avenue 8.

May: **Vesak Day** commemorates the Buddha's birth, Enlightenment, and death. It is the most sacred annual festival in the Buddhist calendar. Throughout the day, starting before dawn, saffron-robed monks chant holy sutras in all the major Buddhist temples and captive birds are set free. Many temples offer vegetarian feasts, to which visitors are permitted. Particularly recommended are the Kong Meng San Phor Kark See temple complex on Bright Hill Drive and the Temple of 1,000 Lights on Race Course Road. Candlelight processions are held at some of the temples in the evening.

June: **Singapore Arts Festival** is an annual international event that features both Asian and Western attractions—concerts, plays, films, Chinese opera—with local and visiting performers. Performances take place throughout the city.

Jul.–Aug.: The "hell gates" open for the Chinese **Festival of the Hungry Ghosts,** a kind of all souls' day when the spirits of the dead wander the earth. The living throng the streets, make elaborate offerings, stage *wayang* (street operas), and loudly auction auspicious objects, anything to placate the ghosts and send them back to hell.

Aug.: **National Day,** the anniversary of the nation's independence, August 9, is a day of processions, fireworks, and dancing. The finest view is from the Padang, where the main participants put on their best show.

Sept.: **The Mooncake Festival,** a traditional Chinese celebration, is named for special cakes richly packed with red-bean or lotus-seed paste, preserved eggs, yam, and nuts. These cakes carried revolutionaries' secret messages in the 14th century. The festival is held on the night of the year when the full moon is thought to be at its brightest. There are lantern-making competitions and special entertainments, including lion and dragon dances.

Sept.–Oct.: During the nine-day **Navarathri Festival,** Hindus pay homage to three goddesses: Parvati, consort of Shiva the Destroyer; Lakshmi, goddess of wealth and consort of Vishnu the Protector; and Saraswathi, goddess of education and consort of Brahma the Creator. At the Chettiar temple on Tank Road, there are performances of classical Indian music, drama, and dance from 7 to 10 PM. On the last evening the image of a silver horse is taken from its home in the temple and paraded around the streets. Thousands take part in the procession, best seen at the Sri Mariamman temple.

Oct.–Nov.: During the **Pilgrimage to Kusu Island,** more than 100,000 Taoist believers travel to the temple of Da Bo Gong, the god of prosperity. If you want to join in, take one of the many ferries that leave from Clifford Pier.

Nov.: **Thimithi** is the spectacular Indian firewalkers' festival honoring classical heroine Draupadi, who walked on fire to prove her fidelity and chastity. Preparations start at 2 AM at Perumal temple on Serangoon Road, but the fire-walking is actually at Sri Mariamman temple,

at South Bridge Road, from about 5 PM. Devotees really do walk on
red-hot burning coals.

Nov.–Dec.: Being a multicultural society, Singapore has taken **Christmas** to heart—and a very commercial heart it is. All the shops are deep
in artificial snow, and a Chinese Santa Claus appears every so often to
encourage everyone to buy and give presents, which they do with zest.
The illuminated decorations on Orchard Road rival even those of
Christian Europe.

6 THAILAND

A dynamic economy and an energetic people whose traditions are rooted in centuries of culture make Thailand the fulcrum of Southeast Asia. No other country in the region has confronted the rush toward industrialization with such genuine reverence for its heritage. Pristine mountain jungles and idyllic virgin beaches contrast with overcrowded beach resorts and red-light districts, and amid the sensory kaleidoscope of the capital, peaceful temple complexes and sophisticated hotels are islands of calm.

By Nigel Fisher

Updated by
Nigel Fisher,
Mick Elmore,
and Lara
Wozniak

THE KINGDOM OF THAILAND is unique among Southeast Asian nations in having developed its culture independently of Western colonialism. As far back as 6800 BC, pottery was being made in Thailand, and excavations at Ban Chiang indicate that bronze was being cast in 2000 BC—about the same time as Mesopotamia is thought to have entered the Bronze Age. The Austroasiatic-speaking Mon inhabited the region; the ancestors of the Thais were still living in southwestern China (they would move during the 6th and 13th centuries into the fertile basin of the Chao Phraya River). The Mon established the area's first recognizable civilization in Dvaravati, a collection of city-states, and their influence stretched over most of present-day Thailand.

The Khmer Empire emerged in the 6th century, expanding its kingdom across modern-day Cambodia and, by the 10th century, into Thailand as well. By the early 13th century, however, the Khmers had outspent themselves on temples and battles with Vietnam. In 1238, two Thai princes overthrew the Khmer outpost at what is now Sukhothai, establishing what is considered the first Thai state and beginning the Sukhothai period. Nineteen-year-old Rama (later known as Ramkhamhaeng, or Rama the Bold) took the throne in 1278 and expanded his kingdom to include parts of Laos, southern Burma (Myanmar), and the southern peninsula around Nakhon Si Thammarat. To protect his northern flank in Chiang Mai, Rama made treaties with the Lanna and Phayao kingdoms.

Not only was Rama an outstanding warrior, but he also made two significant contributions to Thai culture. He revised and adapted the Khmer alphabet to the requirements of the Thai language, and he invited Sri Lankan monks to purify the Khmer-corrupted Theravada (sometimes called Hinayana) Buddhism and establish the religion in a form that is, for the most part, still practiced today.

By 1350, Sukhothai's strength had waned sufficiently for the dynamic young state of Ayutthaya to usurp the reins of power. By 1432 Ayutthaya had sacked Angkor, forcing the Khmers to flee and set up a new capital at Phnom Penh. Sukhothai fell to Ayutthaya in 1438, and for four centuries and 33 kings, Ayutthaya was the heart and brain of Thailand. A brief interlude occurred when the Burmese attacked Ayutthaya in 1568 and defeated the Thais. For 10 years Ayutthaya paid tribute to Burma until King Naresuan amassed a huge army and defeated the Burmese at Nong Sarai in 1593. For the next 150 years, Ayutthaya prospered. In the 1650s, the city's population exceeded that of London and—according to many foreign travelers—with its golden spires, waterways, and roads, it was the most glorious capital not just in Asia, but in all the world.

In 1766 the Burmese attacked the city again. After a 15-month siege, they finally captured Ayutthaya and plundered it. Golden Buddhas were melted down, treasuries ransacked, and buildings burned. Thais who were unable to escape were killed or enslaved; by the time the Burmese left, Ayutthaya's population had dropped from 1 million to 10,000.

Under General Taksin, the Thais regrouped, established a capital on the Chao Phraya River at Thonburi (opposite present-day Bangkok), and set about successfully expelling the Burmese from Thailand. Although he was a commoner, Taksin rose through the ranks as a brave, clever warrior; he was soon crowned king and set out to restore the nation to its past glory. Unfortunately, he went insane and in 1782 Chao P'ya Chakri, a supporter of Taksin and a successful warrior himself, was invited to accept the throne. Taksin was executed (since no one was allowed to touch a king, he was put in a sack and beaten to death), and Chao P'ya Chakri became the first king of the current Chakri dynasty. (The present monarch, King Bhumibol Adulyadej, is the ninth in the line.) One of the first acts of Chao P'ya Chakri, or Rama I (all kings of the dynasty are given the title Rama), was to move the Thai capital to Bangkok.

During the past 200 years, Thailand has had two prime concerns: staving off foreign encroachment on its sovereignty and restructuring its society to meet the demands of industrialization. Despite the economic crisis and devaluation of its currency in 1997, Thailand has managed to succeed quite well at both.

Western powers were first welcomed when they arrived in 1512, but the French (from whom the Thai word *farang,* meaning foreigner, is derived) tried to overthrow the legitimate government and install a puppet regime. As a result, the Thais not only threw out the French but also closed their doors to all outsiders until the middle of the 19th century. When the West again threatened Thailand's sovereignty, King Mongkut (Rama IV, 1851–68) kept the colonial forces at bay through a series of adroit treaties. His efforts were continued by King Chulalongkorn (Rama V, 1868–1910), who secured colonial recognition of Thai sovereignty by ceding to the British a little of what is now Malaysia and to the French a little of Cambodia.

Thailand's other concern was adapting to modern social pressures. Under King Chulalongkorn, slavery was abolished, hospitals and schools were established, and some upper-class Thais received a European education so they could replace Western advisers. Under King Prajadhipok (Rama VII, 1925–35), the world's economic depression brought its share of discontent to Thailand. The pressure for sweeping reform ended in 1932 when a group of mid-ranking military officers demanded the establishment of a constitutional monarchy on lines similar to that of Great Britain.

Since then, quasi-military governments and a strong bureaucracy have administered the country. Changes in government have been by coup as often as by election. Despite such upheavals, the nation's policies have been remarkably consistent in fostering its industrial economy. Since World War II, Thailand has been demonstratively pro-American, receiving in return billions of dollars that increase and decrease proportionately to America's fear of communism. Thailand's own communist rebellion, centered in the poor north, was crushed in the 1980s with harsh military might. Calls for democracy were also met with a heavy hand. Student demonstrators battled with police in 1973 and again in 1976, when hundreds were savagely beaten, many were lynched, and a few were burned alive.

Protests occurring in 1992 against the military-controlled government also met with a bloody crackdown in which as many as 200 demonstrators were killed. This protest, however, had positive results. An elected government (albeit one riddled with corruption) was returned to power, and a new constitution was drawn up—one designed to permit fair elections, reduce corruption, and ensure that the government responds to the people. Only time will tell whether or not it has the desired result.

Throughout all this, the monarchy has been a powerful stabilizing influence. The much-loved king is seen as the father of the nation, and the queen has won the heart of every Thai. The trust and respect at all levels of society for the royal family had a calming effect during the 1992 democracy demonstrations and the economic crisis of 1997–98.

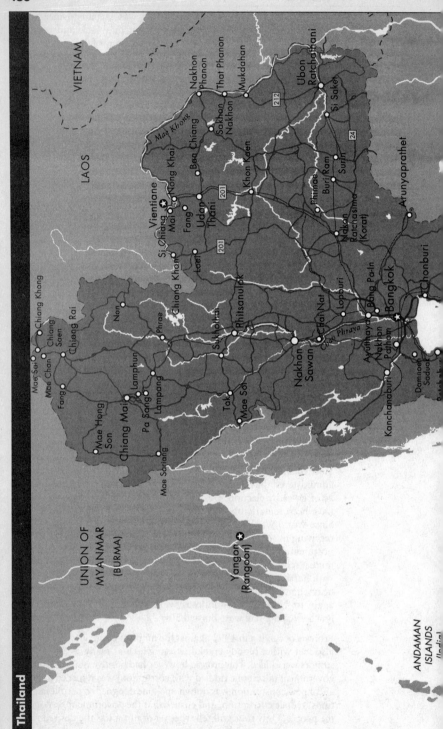

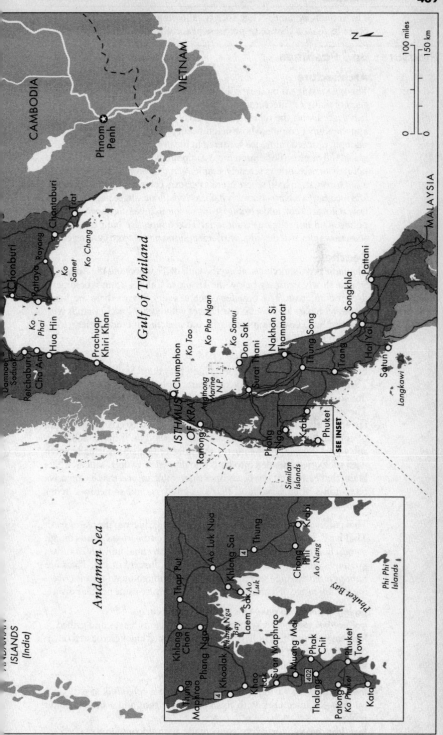

N

100 miles
150 km

CAMBODIA

Phnom Penh

VIETNAM

MALAYSIA

Chonburi
Pattaya Rayong
Chantaburi
Trat
Ko Samet
Ko Chang

Ko Phai

Hua Hin

Prachuap Khiri Khan

Gulf of Thailand

Petchaburi
Cha Am

Damnoen Saduak

Chumphon

Ko Tao

Ko Pha Ngan

Ko Samui

Don Sak

Nakhon Si Thammarat

Songkhla

Pattani

ISTHMUS OF KRA

Ranong

Ang Thong Marine N.P.

Surat Thani

Thung Song

Trang

Hat Yai

Satun

Langkawi

Phang Nga

Krabi

Phuket

SEE INSET

Andaman Sea

ISLANDS (India)

Similan Islands

INSET:

Ao Luk Nua

Khlong Sai

Thung

Krabi

Thap Put

Chong Phli

Ao Nang

Khlong Chon

Khoolak Muang Nga Bay

Ao Luk

Laem Sak

Phuket Bay

Phi Phi Islands

Thung Maphrao Phang Ngo

Khao Lak

Suai Maphrao

Mueng Mai

Phak Chit

Phuket Town

402

Thalang

Ko Phuket

Patong

Kata

The monarchy binds Thai society, allowing the nation, unlike any other in Asia, a chance to progress peacefully into the 21st century.

Pleasures and Pastimes

Architecture

Though staving off modern colonial rule, Thailand has been the beneficiary of many architectural and artistic styles over its 1,000-year history. It is graced with the remains of the early Lanna kingdom in the north and the Khmer empire, whose magnificent *prasats* (temples), now painstakingly restored ruins, are scattered in the lower I-san region. Thailand is also full of *wats* (Buddhist temple compounds), some large and breathtakingly ornate, others serenely simple. Wat compounds usually include a *bot* (ordination hall) where monks perform ceremonies, preach, teach, and meditate; a *viharn* (assembly hall); a *chedi* (dome-shape pagoda), where holy relics are kept; and a *prang* (stupa or spire), towering above the compound. Old nonreligious traditional Thai houses are built of teak and sometimes elevated on stilts, with steep, sloping roofs and curving eaves.

Beaches

Thailand's two shorelines, along the Gulf of Thailand and the Andaman Sea, lie slowly steaming below the Tropic of Cancer, a sun-worshiper's dream come true. The beaches come in every flavor: there are lively scenes with bars and discos; quiet coves with luxury hotels; islands with thatched bungalows; family resorts; and stretches of sands with no footprints at all.

Dining

Food is a consuming passion for Thais; they constantly eat and snack. Throughout the day, roadside food carts replace one another, each vendor stirring up a different tasty morsel, depending on the time of day. The range of Thai cuisine is vast; no restaurant worth its salt has fewer than 100 dishes on its menu. There are seasonal delights, and of course, regional differences and specialties. You'll find a delicious, spicy pork sausage in the north, and northern cuisine is usually eaten with sticky rice kneaded into balls and dipped in various sauces. Thais know that eating out can be cheaper than eating in, and that inexpensive restaurants often serve food that's as good as, and sometimes better than, the fare at fancy places.

Thai cuisine's distinctive flavor comes particularly from the use of fresh Thai basil, lemongrass, tamarind, lime, and citrus leaves. And though some Thai food is as hot as the fires of hell, an equal number of dishes are mild—and the hot ones can be tempered. Instead of salt, Thais use *nam pla,* a fish sauce served with meals. Although by no means covering the full range of Thai cuisine, the following are some popular dishes:

gaeng kieuw wan gai—chicken with green curry
gai hor bai toey—chicken wrapped in pandanus leaves and grilled
kai yang—I-san dish of herb-and-honey-basted chicken roasted on an open fire and cut into small pieces
kung paan tod—flaky, tempura-style prawns
mee krob—crispy fried noodles with shrimp
mieng khum—a variety of herbs wrapped in a *cheaplu* leaf
pu cha—steamed crab with fresh coriander root and a little coconut milk
tom kha gai—a fortifying soup made with coconut milk, chicken, Thai ginger, lemongrass, lime juice, coriander leaves, and chili
tom yam kung—spicy hot-and-sour shrimp soup
yam pla duk foo—deep-fried catfish topped with chili, onion, mango, and tamarind sauce

Price categories throughout the chapter are based on the following ranges:

CATEGORY	COST*
$$$$	over $20
$$$	$10–$20
$$	$4–$10
$	under $4

*per person, including service charge; a 7.5% government tax (VAT) is added to restaurant bills

Lodging

Thailand offers a range of accommodation. On one of the finest beaches in the world, a few dollars can get you a bed cocooned under a mosquito net in a wood hut with a thatched roof. On another beach of equal perfection you can dwell in unbelievable luxury and beauty with smiling, attentive service. In the provincial capitals, expect a clean air-conditioned room with private bath. For $15–$20, you'll get a smaller room with flaking plaster, gurgling plumbing, and instead of air-conditioning a rhythmically wobbling fan.

Price categories throughout the chapter are based on the following ranges:

CATEGORY	COST*
$$$$	over $160
$$$	$100–$160
$$	$60–$100
$	$20–$60
¢	under $20

*per double room, including service and tax

Massage

Every visit to Thailand should include a massage or two—and they come in many different varieties, from gentle kneading of the muscles to joint-breaking pulls. The traditional massage (*nuat boroan*) aims to release blocked channels of energy and uses methods similar to Shiatsu and reflexology. Joint pains and headaches can be eased, but it's also invigorating. The most famous place for a massage is Bangkok's Wat Pho. Those offered at beach resorts tend to be a cross between soothing and traditional.

Shopping

You can get hooked on shopping in Thailand—everything is for sale, and there are so many places to look. Bangkok has fancy shopping centers and department stores, antiques and crafts shops, and markets and street vendors selling watches with recently affixed "Rolex" or "Cartier" trademarks and T-shirts with a crocodile slightly askew. Negotiated prices are irresistibly low. In many large cities and resorts, visiting the Night Market is part of an evening's entertainment. Chiang Mai is a shoppers' paradise with an exceptional Night Bazaar. Except for imported electronics and luxury goods, Thailand's prices, though not duty-free, are considerably lower than Singapore's or Hong Kong's.

Trekking

The forested hills north and west of Chiang Mai would make for good trekking just for their misty, rugged beauty. But here you can take treks of a day or longer to visit isolated villages that are home to the hill tribes, ethnic groups originally from Burma and China who have kept their traditions over the last two centuries.

Exploring Thailand

Most visitors to Thailand experience Bangkok first. The capital city, equidistant from the country's four corners, has become the hub of Southeast Asia. A number of points of interest lie within a day's striking distance of Bangkok. To the west, through forested hills close to the Burmese border, flows the Chao Phraya River (known more famously as the River Kwai). North up the river stand the ruins of the ancient capital Ayutthaya and the Khmer-influenced buildings at Lopburi. To the southwest are Damnoen Saduak's floating market and Nakhon Pathom, where Buddhism first found a home in Thailand. Down both sides of the Gulf of Thailand lie convenient beach resorts.

The vast middle of Thailand stretches from the Burmese border to those of Laos and Cambodia. In the Central Plains stand the restored and partially rebuilt palaces and temples of Thailand's first capital, Sukhothai, and its satellite town, Sri Satchanalai. An hour southeast of Sukhothai is the busy transportation hub of Phitsanulok, east of which lies the vast agricultural Northeast, often referred to as the I-san. Along I-san's southern border are scattered sanctuaries and palaces of the 13th-century Khmer empire.

Chiang Mai is the unofficial capital of northern Thailand, whose culture developed separately from that of the central region. Its temple architecture stems from the Lanna kingdom, which preceded the Thai nation; its food is zestier; and its language is slower. Northern Thailand, particularly the Golden Triangle, where Thailand, Burma, and Laos meet, is hilly, forested, and has stretches of no-man's-land where the opium poppy grows (though production has moved farther into Burma in recent years). Throughout these forests live seven ethnic groups known collectively as the hill tribes. Today they maintain a village life independent of mainstream Thailand.

Beach resorts line the skinny peninsula stretching south from Bangkok to the Malaysia border. For now, three areas—Phuket, on the Andaman Sea; Krabi on the western shore facing it; and Ko Samui, an island in the Gulf of Thailand—have exploited nature's potential, but on these long coastlines the possibilities are endless.

Great Itineraries

IF YOU HAVE 7 DAYS

Spend your first two days in **Bangkok.** Start your first day with the most famous of all Bangkok sights, the Grand Palace, then go on to the ornate Wat Phra Keo and Bangkok's oldest and largest temple, Wat Pho. Explore Chinatown and visit Wat Traimitr. At the Chao Phraya, catch a river bus to the Oriental Hotel and have a cup of tea. In the evening, walk bustling Silom Road to check out the vendor stalls and catch a dinner show of Thai dancing. The next day, go to Wat Benjamabophit, containing Bangkok's much-photographed Marble Temple. Spend the afternoon in the National Museum, and in the evening explore Bangkok's nightlife.

On the third day go to **Ayutthaya,** the glorious former capital. If you intend to head south to a beach resort next, travel to Ayutthaya by bus and return to Bangkok the same day by boat down the Chao Phraya River. For your remaining four days, enjoy sun, sea, and sand at **Phuket** or **Ko Samui,** both of which are short flights from Bangkok.

If you would rather spend your final days seeing more of Thailand's culture and landscape, use your fourth day to continue north by train or bus to **Chiang Mai.** On the fifth day explore the wats of the inner city and in the afternoon check out the craft stores along San Kamphaeng Road. In the evening have a Thai massage, followed by a *khantoke* (northern Thai) dinner and cultural show. On the sixth day rise early and go to Wat Phrathat Doi Suthep, a mountain temple overlooking Chiang Mai. In the afternoon see Wat Chedi Yot and the

National Museum. For the evening's entertainment go to the Night Bazaar. On your final day take an excursion south to the ancient wats at **Lamphun,** and buy cottons at **Pa Sang.**

IF YOU HAVE 10 DAYS

Spend your first two days in **Bangkok** and your third in **Ayutthaya.** Beach lovers can then head south to spend the remainder of their trip at southern beach resorts. If you go overland, break the 12- to 14-hour trip to **Ko Samui** or the Andaman Sea resorts—**Phuket, Krabi,** and **Ko Phi Phi**—with a night or two at the adjoining Gulf Coast resort towns of **Hua Hin** and **Cha' Am;** or fly straight to Phuket and make the six-hour land-and-boat crossing to Ko Samui.

If you head north from Ayutthaya on your fourth day, spend the fifth and sixth days covering the major sights of **Chiang Mai**—not forgetting to shop and have a massage. On the seventh day fly to **Mae Hong Son** and make a three-day, two-night trek among the hill tribes. Or travel by raft to **Chiang Rai** and spend the remaining days relaxing in nearby **Ban Sop Ruak,** exploring the **Golden Triangle.**

IF YOU HAVE 14 DAYS

With a full two weeks you have plenty of options. After spending your first three days in and around **Bangkok,** you could devote your time to some of Thailand's less-developed paradises, like the Gulf Coast's **Ko Chang;** or **Ko Pha Ngan and Ko Tao,** north of Ko Samui; or **Ao Nang,** near Krabi, on the Andaman Sea. You could also combine the best of both worlds: travel north from Bangkok to Ayutthaya and Chiang Mai during the first week, then fly south to **Phuket** or another southern resort for the latter half of your trip.

To see Thailand's traditional heartland, however, visit the Central Plains and I-san. After seeing Ayutthaya and returning to Bangkok, travel by plane or train on your fourth day to **Nakhon Ratchasima** (Korat). Take a day trip the next day to **Prasat Hin Phimae,** the late-11th-century Khmer sanctuary. (If you're short on time, take an early-morning flight to Korat in order to see Phimae the same day.) On your sixth day, travel east by train to Si Saket or Surin, using either as your base for two nights to explore the ancient Khmer sanctuaries of **Prasat Khao Phra Vihan, Prasat Kamphang Yai,** and **Prasat Hin Khao Phanom Rung,** and to visit silk-weaving villages. On the eighth day either take a direct bus or fly via Bangkok to **Phitsanulok** and spend the night there. On the ninth day visit **Old Sukhothai,** then continue north on the tenth to explore **Chiang Mai** and its surroundings for the rest of the trip.

When to Tour Thailand

November through March is the best time to be in Bangkok. The city is at its coolest—85°F—and driest. The Andaman Sea region (Phuket, Krabi, and environs) has two seasons. From May through October (monsoon season), hotel prices are considerably lower, but rough seas can make beaches unsafe for swimming. The peak season is the dry period, from November through April. The rains hit Ko Samui from late October through December—and prices drop by as much as 40%—while its peak season runs from January through early July.

The central and northern parts of Thailand have three seasons. The best time to visit is winter. From November to March the weather is cool in the hills at night. It is hottest and driest from March to May—unbearably so on the plains—and the rainy season, from June to October, makes unpaved roads difficult, especially during September.

Numbers in the text correspond to numbers in the margin and on the maps.

BANGKOK

A foreigner's reaction to the capital is often as confused as the city's geography. Bangkok has no downtown, and streets, like the traffic, seem to veer off in every direction. There's even confusion about the city's name: though to Thais it is Krung Thep, the City of Angels, foreigners call it Bangkok. The oldest quarter clusters along the eastern bank of the Chao Phraya River, which snakes between Bangkok and Thonburi, where the capital was first established after the fall of Ayutthaya in 1767. When King Rama I moved his capital in 1782 across the river, he chose a site that foreign vessels knew from their navigational charts as the village of Bangkok. This settlement—dominated by the Grand Palace and bordered by the Chao Phraya and semicircular *klongs* (canals)—is called Ratanakosin and is today a jumble of streets that lead to palaces, government buildings, temples, and museums.

In the last 25 years, the city has changed enormously. Before Bangkok became *the* R&R destination for American servicemen during the Vietnam War, it had a population of 1.5 million. Then, as U.S. dollars attracted the rural poor and development began, it grew to more than 10 million, nearly 15% of the population and 40 times the size of any other city in Thailand. Nowadays, space in which to live and breathe is inadequate. Bangkok is infamous for its traffic-jammed streets and *sois* (side streets and alleys), and its air pollution is among the worst in the world (policemen directing traffic wear masks). When the economy collapsed in 1997 the traffic situation improved as people sold their cars instead of driving them, and the population shrunk as many returned to the countryside. But as the economy bounces back so does congestion. The skytrain, which opened in December 1999, makes some difference, and a subway system scheduled to open in 2002 should help. However, some streets, particularly Sukhumvit Road and other major arteries, still look like parking lots during much of the day, and as construction reawakens with the reviving economy, the traffic will only get worse.

Even with its growing pains, though, Bangkok gives you a sense of history and timelessness, perhaps because King Rama I set out to build a city as beautiful as old Ayutthaya before the Burmese sacked it. Bangkok's contrasts require an adjustment on your part, but amid the chaos you soon come to appreciate the gentle nature of the Thais and their genuine respect for other people.

Exploring Bangkok

Because confusion is part of Bangkok's fascination, learning your way around is a challenge. It may help to think of Bangkok as an isosceles triangle with the base abutting the S curve of the Chao Phraya River and the apex, pointing east, ending on Sukhumvit Road, somewhere around Soi 40.

Sukhumvit, at the apex of this conceptual triangle, was once a residential neighborhood. In the last two decades, it has developed into a district of hotels, shops, nightclubs, and restaurants while retaining some of its residential atmosphere. The new Bangkok Conference Centre attracts more and more hotels and businesses to this area. Ever since Ramkhamhaeng University opened in the 1970s, Bangkok has sprawled even farther east. Now the area known as Bangkapi is a satellite town, attracting industrial and residential complexes.

Westward, toward the Chao Phraya, are spacious foreign embassy compounds, corporate offices, and modern international hotels. To some this is Bangkok's center, symbolized by the Erawan shrine, where everyday Thais worship and traditional dancers perform for a small fee. South of the shrine is Bangkok's largest green area, Lumphini Park, an oasis in an urban jungle. A bit farther still, stores, offices, and more hotels are closely packed. Now you reach the older sections of Bangkok. On the southern flank runs Silom Road, a shopping and financial district; Suriwongse (pronounced *Suriwong*) Road, with more hotels, parallels it. Between them lies the entertainment district of Patpong. Continue farther and you reach the riverbank and four of Bangkok's leading hotels: the Royal Orchid Sheraton, the Oriental, the Shangri-La, and the Peninsula (across the river).

Going west along Rama I Road in the center of the triangle, you pass the Siam Square shopping area and the National Stadium. Continue south toward the Hualamphong Railway Station, and between it and the river lies Chinatown, a maze of streets with restaurants, goldsmiths, small warehouses, and repair shops.

In the northern part of the triangle, moving westward, you pass through various markets before reaching government buildings, the Victory Monument, Chitlada Palace, the Dusit Zoo, the National Assembly, the National Library, and, finally, the river. Slightly south of this route, you can go west from the Democracy Monument to the National Museums and Theatre near the river, and then south to the Grand Palace and Wat Phra Keo.

Knowing your exact destination, its direction, and approximate distance are important in negotiating tuk-tuk (three-wheeled taxi) fares and planning your itinerary. Note, however, that many sights have no precise written address and the spelling of road names changes from map to map and even street sign to street sign, thus Ratchadamri Road can be spelled *Rajdamri*, Ratchadamnoen is also *Rajdamnern*, Charoen Krung can be *Charoennakorn* or even *New Road*, and so on. Crossing and recrossing the city is time-consuming, and many hours can be spent in traffic jams. Above all, remember that Bangkok is enormous, and distances are great; it can take a half hour or more to walk between two seemingly adjacent sites.

Old Bangkok Along the Chao Phraya

Bangkok's major sightseeing attractions are within a short distance of the Chao Phraya River in the part of Bangkok that was founded in 1782. Chinatown is also here. On the tour described below you'll experience one of Bangkok's greatest pleasures: after getting good and hot visiting a temple or two, you'll be refreshed by crossing the cool Chao Phraya on a ferryboat before tackling another.

A GOOD TOUR

Start at the **Grand Palace** ①, Bangkok's major landmark, and go on to the adjoining **Wat Phra Keo** ②. Then walk south on Sanamchai Road (or take a taxi) to **Wat Pho** ③. From Wat Pho, walk west to the river and then north (toward the Grand Palace) about 250 yards to the Tha Thien jetty and take the ferry across to **Wat Arun** ④. Return by the same ferry to the eastern shore and take a tuk-tuk to **Chinatown.** Get out at Pahuraht Road, and as you take in the sights, walk east, then zigzag left to Yaowarat Road, and continue east until it leads into Charoen Krung. On the opposite corner stands **Wat Traimitr** ⑤.

TIMING

This is a full day's sightseeing. Ideally, you would begin early in the morning, take a break for lunch to escape the heat of midday, and end the excursion in the late afternoon. You might spend as much as 90 minutes each at the Grand Palace and Wat Phra Keo. Wat Pho will only

Exploring Bangkok

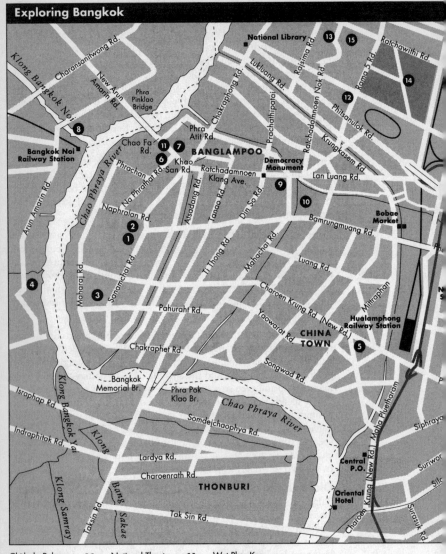

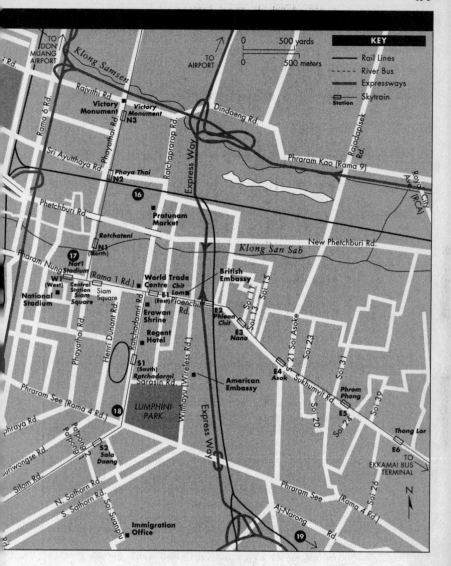

TO DON MUANG AIRPORT

r Rd.

Klong Samsen

Rajvithi Rd.

Rama 6 Rd.

TO AIRPORT

0   500 yards
0   500 meters

KEY
—— Rail Lines
- - - River Bus
▬▬ Expressways
▭ Skytrain
Station

Dindaeng Rd.

Victory Monument
Victory Monument N3

Phayathai Rd.

Ratchaprarop Rd.

Express Way

Phraram Kao (Rama 9)

Royal City Ave. (RCA)

Rajadapisek Rd.

Sri Ayutthaya Rd.

Phaya Thai N2

16

Pratunam Market

New Phetchburi Rd.

Phetchburi Rd.

Ratchateni
N1 (North)

Klong San Sab

Pharam Nung

17 Nat'l Stadium

W1 (West)

Central Station Siam Square

Siam Square

Rama 1 Rd.

World Trade Centre
E1 Chit
Lom
Ploenchit Rd.

British Embassy

Soi 11
Soi 13
Soi 15

National Stadium

Phayathai Rd.

Henri Dunant Rd.

Ratchadamri Rd.

Erawan Shrine

Regent Hotel

Witthayu (Wireless Rd.)

E2 Phleon Chit

E3 Nana

Soi Asoke

Soi 21
Soi 23
Soi 31

S1 (South)
Ratchadarmi

Sarasin Rd.

American Embassy

E4 Asok

Sukhumvit Rd.

Phrom Phong

Soi 39

Pharam See (Rama 4 Rd.)

18

LUMPHINI PARK

E5
Soi 20
Soi 24

Thong Lor
E6

phraya Rd.

Phraya Rd.

Patpong
Patpong 2

S2 Sala Daeng

TO EKKAMAI BUS TERMINAL

N

uriwongse Rd.

Silom Rd.

N. Sathorn Rd.
S. Sathorn Rd.

Soi Suanplu

Immigration Office

Phraram See (Rama 4 Rd.)

Aj-Narong

Soi 26

Rd.

19

take a half hour, unless you have an hour-long massage. Allow time to climb the prang at Wat Arun (unless you suffer from vertigo). Chinatown is a maze of streets and markets, so two hours of wandering can pass by quickly, though nonshoppers may find 30 minutes sufficient. Wat Traimitr can be a 15-minute stop, or you might like to sit there a while and restore your spirit. Some of Bangkok's sights close in the middle of the day, so plan accordingly. Much of Chinatown closes down during Chinese New Year.

SIGHTS TO SEE

Chinatown. When its buildings were the tallest in the land, Chinatown used to be Bangkok's prosperous downtown, but, as the city grew, new, taller office buildings sprang up farther east, and the neighborhood lost some of its bustle. Red lanterns and Chinese signs still abound, and modest restaurants line the streets. Pahuraht Road is full of textile shops, with nearly as many Indian dealers here as Chinese, and Yaowarat Road, the main thoroughfare, is crowded with gold and jewelry shops. The Thieves Market, at the northwest end of Yaowarat Road, used to sell antiques bargains; it has become more utilitarian in its wares, but it's still fun to browse.

❶ Grand Palace. In 1782, when King Rama I moved the capital across the river from Thonburi, he built this palace and walled city, which subsequent Chakri monarchs enlarged. The compound is open to visitors, but all the buildings, which are used only for state occasions and royal ceremonies, are not. The official residence of the king—he actually lives at Chitlada Palace in north Bangkok—is the Chakri Maha Prasart palace, whose state function rooms are sometimes open to visitors on special occasions. The Dusit Maha Prasart, on the right, is a classic example of palace architecture, and Amarin Vinichai Hall, on the left, the original audience hall, is now used for the presentation of ambassadors' credentials. Note the glittering gold throne. ⌧ *Admission.* ⊙ *Daily 8:30–3:30.*

❹ Wat Arun. The Temple of the Dawn is inspiring at sunrise; it is even more marvelous toward dusk, when the setting sun casts amber tones. The temple's architecture is symmetrical, with a square courtyard containing five Khmer-style prangs, the central prang (282 ft) surrounded by its four attendant prangs in the corners. All five are covered in mosaics of broken pieces of Chinese porcelain. Energetic visitors climb the steep steps of the central prang for the view over the Chao Phraya, and the less ambitious linger in the small park by the river, a peaceful spot to take in the sights and smells and watch the sun go down, though the best view is from across the river with the sun setting behind Wat Arun. ⌧ *Admission.* ⊙ *Daily 8:30–5:30.*

★ ❷ Wat Phra Keo. No building within the Grand Palace compound excites such awe as the adjoining Temple of the Emerald Buddha, the most sacred temple in the kingdom. No other wat in Thailand is so ornate and so embellished with murals, statues, and glittering gold. As your wat experience grows, you may decide that you prefer the simplicity of some other wats, but you'll never quite get over Wat Phra Keo's elaborate richness.

As you enter the compound, take note of the 20-ft-tall helmeted and tile-encrusted statues in traditional Thai battle attire standing guard. They set the scene—mystical, majestic, and awesome. Turn right as you enter, and notice along the inner walls the lively murals depicting the whole *Ramayana* epic (*Ramakien* in Thai).

The main chapel, with its gilded three-tier roof, dazzles your eyes. Royal griffins stand guard outside, and the perfect symmetry of the shining gold stupas in the court gives a feeling of serenity. Inside sits the Emerald Buddha. This most venerated image of Lord Buddha is carved from one piece of jade 31 inches high. No one knows its origin, but history places it in Chiang Rai in 1464. From there it traveled first to Chiang Mai, then to Lamphun, and finally back to Chiang Rai, where the Laotians stole it and took it home with them. Eventually, the Thais sent an army to get it back, and it reached its final resting place when King Rama I built the chapel. The statue is high above the altar and visitors can see it only from afar. Behind the altar and above the window frames are murals depicting the life and eventual enlightenment of the Buddha.

At the back of the royal chapel you'll find a detailed scale model of Angkor Wat. 🖼 *Admission.* ⊙ *Daily 8:30–11:30 and 1–3:30.*

Just east of the Grand Palace compound is the **City Pillar Shrine,** containing the foundation stone (Lak Muang) from which all distances in Thailand are measured. The stone is believed to be inhabited by a spirit that guards the well-being of Bangkok.

★ ❸ **Wat Pho, or Wat Phra Jetuphon.** The Temple of the Reclining Buddha, the largest wat in Bangkok, houses the largest—151 ft—Reclining Buddha in the country. Especially noteworthy are his 10-ft feet, with the 108 auspicious signs of the Buddha inlaid in mother-of-pearl.

Walk beyond the chapel containing the Reclining Buddha and enter Bangkok's oldest open university. A hundred years before Bangkok was established as the capital, a monastery was founded to teach classical Thai medicine. The school still gives instruction in natural methods of healing. Around the walls are marble plaques inscribed with formulas for herbal cures, and stone sculptures squat in various postures demonstrating techniques for relieving pain.

The monks still practice ancient cures, and the **massage school of Wat Pho** has become famous. A massage (B200) lasts one hour, growing more and more pleasurable as you adjust to it. Masseurs and masseuses are available daily 8–6. Massage courses of up to 10 days are also available.

Don't be perturbed by the tall statues that good-naturedly poke fun at farangs. Referred to as Chinese rock sculptures, these gangling twice-life-size figures depict the most evil demons, which scare away all other evil spirits. With their top hats, they look farcically Western and, in fact, were modeled after the Europeans who plundered China during the Opium Wars.

These statues guard the entrance to the northeastern quarter of the compound and a very pleasant three-tier temple containing 394 seated Buddhas. Usually a monk sits cross-legged at one side of the altar, making himself available to answer questions (in Thai). On the walls, bas-relief plaques salvaged from Ayutthaya depict stories from the *Ramayana*. Around this temple area are four tall chedis, decorated with brightly colored porcelain, each representing one of the first four kings of the Chakri dynasty. 🖼 *Admission.* ⊙ *Daily 7–5.*

NEED A BREAK?	When you're ready for refreshment, try the pleasant **snack bar** in the northeastern part of the compound, which serves delicious chilled coconut milk.

★ ❺ **Wat Traimitr.** The main Temple of the Golden Buddha has little architectural merit, but off to the side, next to the money-changing wagon, is a small chapel containing the world's largest solid-gold Buddha, cast about nine centuries ago. Weighing 5½ tons and standing 10 ft high, the statue gleams with such richness and purity that even the most jaded are inspired by its strength and power (and value). The statue, sculpted in Sukhothai style, is believed to have been brought first to Ayutthaya. When the Burmese were about to sack the city, it was covered in plaster, and two centuries later, still in plaster, it was thought to be just another statue. When it was being moved to a new temple in Bangkok in the 1950s it slipped from a crane and was left in the mud by workmen. In the morning, a temple monk, who had dreamed that the statue was divinely inspired, went to see the Buddha image. Through a crack in the plaster he saw a glint of yellow, and soon discovered that the statue was pure gold. ⌨ *Admission.* ☉ *Daily 9–5.*

Museums and Wats

Slightly inland from the river and north of the Grand Palace stands a cluster of government buildings. The neighborhood, in itself not particularly attractive, is made even less appealing by the jammed traffic on weekdays, but you must not miss the National Museum, with Thailand's most valued historic treasures and a great collection of Southeast Asian art. There are also two unusual temples a little farther east.

A GOOD TOUR

The **National Museum** ⑥ should be seen early in your visit. The **National Art Gallery** ⑦ is opposite. Next, take a ferry across the Chao Phraya to visit the **Royal Barges** ⑧, coming back the same way. You can walk or take a tuk-tuk east, past the National Museum and the Democracy Monument, to **Wat Rachanada** ⑨. Then walk east, across Maha Chai Road, to **Wat Saket** ⑩, a notable landmark of the old city. Come back to the **National Theatre** ⑪, next to the National Museum, for a classical Thai dance or drama performance.

TIMING

The route is fairly compact. The museums are close together, and though it's not more than a 15-minute walk, you can take a tuk-tuk or taxi to Wat Rachanada. Wat Saket is just a block away. Allow a good two or three hours at the National Museum and just under an hour at the National Art Gallery. Both are closed on Monday, Tuesday, and public holidays. Then, after lunch, visit Wat Rachanada and Wat Saket. It will take at least an hour by taxi from the Sukhumvit area to reach the National Theatre, and 40 minutes from the Silom Road area via the river bus.

SIGHTS TO SEE

⑦ National Art Gallery. Opposite the National Theatre, the National Art Gallery exhibits both modern and traditional Thai art. ⌨ *Chao Fa Rd.,* ☎ *02/281–2224.* ⌨ *Admission.* ☉ *Tues.–Thurs. and weekends 9–4.*

★ **⑥ National Museum.** By far the best place to acquaint yourself with Thai history and art is the National Museum, which has one of the world's best collections of Southeast Asian art in general, and Buddhist and Thai art in particular. Most of the great masterpieces of the Sukhothai and Ayutthaya periods and works from the northern provinces are here, leaving up-country museums rather bare. You'll also have a good opportunity to trace Thailand's long history, beginning with the ceramic utensils and bronzeware of the Ban Chiang civilization (3000–4000 BC). The main building was built in 1783 as a palace for surrogate kings (a position abolished in 1874). You might go first to the artifact gallery, at the left of the ticket counter, for a historical overview. Afterward, explore the galleries that portray the Dvaravati and Khmer periods. These will prepare you for the different styles of Thai art, from the Sukhothai period (1238–mid-14th century) on. ⌨ *Na Phra That Rd.,* ☎ *02/224–1333.* ⌨ *Admission.* ☉ *Wed.–Sun. 9–4. Cafeteria. Free 90-min orientation tours in English start at the bookshop 9:30 AM Wed.–Thurs.*

⓫ **National Theatre.** Classical Thai dance and drama can usually be seen here on the last Friday and Saturday of each month, but it is best to call for the schedule or ask your hotel staff (☞ Nightlife and the Arts, *below*). ⊠ *Na Phra That Rd.,* ☎ *02/224–1342.*

❽ **Royal Barges.** These splendid ceremonial barges are berthed in a shed on the Thonburi side of the Chao Phraya River. The boats, carved in the early part of the 19th century, take the form of mythical creatures in the *Ramayana.* The most impressive is the red-and-gold royal flag barge, *Suphannahongse* (Golden Swan), used by the king on special occasions, including the Royal Barge procession each November. Carved from a single piece of teak, it measures about 150 ft and weighs more than 15 tons. Fifty oarsmen propel it along the Chao Phraya River, accompanied by two coxswains, flag wavers, and a rhythm-keeper. ☎ *02/424–0004* ⌧ *Admission.* ⊙ *Daily 8:30–4:30.*

❾ **Wat Rachanada.** Across from Wat Saket, this Temple of the Metal Castle intentionally resembles the mythical castle of the gods. According to legend, a wealthy and pious man built a fabulous castle, Loha Prasat, from the design laid down in Hindu mythology for the disciples of the Buddha. Wat Rachanada, built in metal, is meant to duplicate that castle and is the only one of its kind remaining. There are stalls selling amulets that protect the wearer from misfortune—usually of the physical kind, though love amulets and charms are also sold. They tend to be rather expensive, but that's the price of good fortune. ⌧ *Admission.* ⊙ *Daily 8–6.*

❿ **Wat Saket.** East of the Democracy Monument you'll find the Temple of the Golden Mount, a notable landmark of the old city and, for a long time, the highest point in the city. King Rama III started construction of this mound and temple, which were completed by Rama V. To reach the gold-covered chedi, you must climb an exhausting 318 steps winding around the mound. Don't even attempt it on a hot day, but on a cool, clear day, the view from the top is magnificent. Every November, at the time of the Loi Kratong festival, there is a popular temple fair (*ngan wat*), with food stalls and stage shows. ⌧ *Admission.* ⊙ *Daily 8–5.*

Scattered Bangkok

Bangkok sprawls, seemingly without rhyme or reason, in delightful chaos. Neighborhoods as we know them in the West do not exist. Once you leave the Chao Phraya River, you are in a mix of the old and the new, amidst the glitz of new wealth and the simplicity of poverty. Temples, factories, palaces, office buildings, and private houses may all be found on one block. Unfortunately, getting from one major sight to another takes time, usually spent in stalled traffic.

A GOOD TOUR (OR TWO OR THREE)

It makes sense to treat the widely spaced sights in scattered Bangkok as a smorgasbord from which to select a sight or two when you're nearby. You might go first to one of Bangkok's most photographed temples, **Wat Benjamabophit** ⑫, northeast of the Democracy Monument. Then it's a short tuk-tuk ride to **Vimarnmek Mansion** ⑬, the largest teak structure in the world. On your way there, you'll probably pass by **Chitlada Palace** ⑭, on the right. On the other side of the road is the **Dusit Zoo** ⑮. West of the zoo is **Banglampoo,** where backpackers gravitate, a fascinating insight into what Western culture can produce. The **Suan Pakkard Palace** ⑯ is on the south side of Sri Ayutthaya Road, between Phayathai and Ratchaprarop roads; its five traditional Thai houses make a nice contrast to Vimarnmek Mansion. **Jim Thompson's House** ⑰ is west of Siam Square. If cold-blooded reptiles strike your fancy, visit the **Pasteur Institute** ⑱, a snake farm a little west of Lumphini Park. **Muang Boran** ⑲ can give you a one-day tour by miniature of the rest of Thailand if you don't have time to see the real thing.

SIGHTS TO SEE

Banglampoo. Backpackers from around the world gather here, near the Chao Phraya just north of Ratchadamnoen Road. It's not really Bangkok; it's a human zoo, and Thais apparently go there to look at strange Westerners. It's also where the movie *The Beach* begins, as well as a source for the latest in travel tips. Many agencies here can book inexpensive travel and tours. The main thoroughfare, Khao Sahn Road, is full of cafés, secondhand bookstalls, and inexpensive shops. In the evening, the streets are full of food stands catering to young Westerners. Off Khao Sahn Road, hundreds of small guest houses rent tiny rooms for B150 to B300 a night.

⑭ **Chitlada Palace.** When in Bangkok, the king resides at Chitlada Palace, which covers the whole block across from the Dusit Zoo. The public is not permitted, and you are only able to see high walls and the honor guards as you drive by.

⑮ **Dusit Zoo.** When you are exhausted by Bangkok's traffic and want to rest in a pleasant expanse of greenery, pay a visit to the Dusit Zoo (Khao Din Wana). Children can ride elephants (not the white ones, which are of "royal blood"), and you can sit at one of the shaded cafés. ☎ *02/ 281–0021* ▣ *Admission.* ☉ *Daily 8:30–6.*

⑰ **Jim Thompson's House.** American Jim Thompson, once an architect in New York, joined the OSS in World War II and went to Asia. After the war, he stayed on and took it upon himself to revitalize Thailand's moribund silk industry. His project met with tremendous success, which in itself would have made him a legend. In 1967 Thompson went to the Malaysian Cameron Highlands for a quiet holiday and was never heard from again.

Thompson imported parts of up-country buildings, some as old as 150 years, to construct his compound of six Thai houses. Three are exactly the same as their originals, including details of the interior layout. With true appreciation and a connoisseur's eye, Thompson then furnished them with what are now priceless pieces of Southeast Asian art. The entrance is easy to miss: at the end of an unprepossessing lane, leading north off Rama I Road, west of Phayathai Road, the house is on your left. It is down the street from the National Stadium skytrain station. ▣ *Soi Kasemsong 2,* ☎ *02/612–3668.* ▣ *Admission.* ☉ *Mon.– Sat. 9–4:30.*

⑲ **Muang Boran** (Ancient City). About an hour's drive (20 km/12 mi) southeast of the city is a park shaped like Thailand. You enter at the country's southern tip and find throughout the park, placed more or less as in geographical reality, 108 smaller but proportionally correct replicas of Thailand's most important architectural sites and monuments. You really need wheels—the area is too vast to cover on foot. Small, discreetly placed restaurants are scattered throughout the grounds, and crafts are sold in a "traditional Thai village." Allow a good four hours to cover most of the sites. By car, take the Samrong–Samut Prakan expressway and turn left at the Samut Prakan intersection onto Old Sukhumvit Road. At km 33, Muang Boran is on your left. Or, take air-conditioned bus No. 11 and get off at Pak Nam to transfer to a small bus, No. 36, which passes in front of the city. You can take a tour arranged by your hotel, or, better yet, four can hire a car and driver for about B1,000. ▣ *Old Sukhumvit Rd., Samut Prakan,* ☎ *02/323– 9252.* ▣ *Admission.* ☉ *Daily 8–5.*

☪ ⑱ **Pasteur Institute.** In 1923, the Thai Red Cross established this snake farm, where venom is milked and stored as an antidote for people kissed by poisonous snakes. At the top end of Suriwongse Road (corner of Rama IV and Henri Dunant), it was the second in the world (the first was in Brazil). There are daily slide shows before the milking sessions at 11 AM, with a second show on weekdays only at 2:30 PM. You can watch the handlers work with deadly cobras, kraits, and pit vipers; you can also get typhoid, cholera, and smallpox vaccinations here. ✉ *1871 Rama IV Rd.,* ☎ *02/252–0161.* ✄ *Admission.* ☼ *Weekdays 8:30–4:30, weekends and holidays 8:30–noon.*

★ ⑯ **Suan Pakkard Palace.** Five antique teak houses, built high on columns, complement the perfectly kept, undulating lawns, shimmering lotus pools, and lush shrubbery. The serene atmosphere makes Suan Pakkard one of the most relaxing places in which to absorb traditional Thai culture. The center of attraction, the Lacquer Pavilion, at the back of the garden, contains gold-covered paneling with scenes from the life of the Buddha, and the other houses display porcelains, Khmer stone heads, old paintings, and Buddha statues. ☎ *02/245–4934.* ✄ *Admission.* ☼ *Daily 9–4.*

⑬ **Vimarnmek Mansion.** This is the largest teak structure in the world, moved to its present location early last century by King Rama V. The three-story suburban mansion is now in the center of administrative Bangkok, next to the National Assembly building, because the capital has grown so much. The place fits its name, "Castle in the Clouds," its extraordinary lightness enhanced by a reflecting pond. King Rama V's fascination with Western architecture shows in its Victorian style, but the building retains an unmistakably Thai delicacy. Most of the furnishings were either bought in the West or given by European monarchs. Some are exquisite—porcelain, handcrafted furniture, and crystal—and some have novelty value, like the first typewriter brought to Thailand. Exhibitions of Thai dancing take place daily at 10:30 and 2. ☎ *02/628–6300.* ✄ *Admission.* ☼ *Daily 9:30–3:15.*

★ ⑫ **Wat Benjamabophit.** Bangkok's most photographed wat, the Marble Temple, was built in 1899 and is where Thailand's present king came to spend his days as a monk before his coronation. Statues of the Buddha line the courtyard, and the magnificent interior has cross beams of lacquer and gold, but Wat Benjamabophit is more than a splendid temple. The monastery is a seat of learning that appeals to Buddhist monks with intellectual yearnings. ✄ *Admission.* ☼ *Daily 7–5.*

Dining

Thais are passionate about food—finding the out-of-the-way shop that prepares some specialty better than anyplace else, then dragging groups of friends to share the discovery, is a national pastime. The tastes and smells of Thai food are all around you, day and night, since Thais always seem to be eating.

Until your digestion adjusts to the food, steer clear of stands in markets and at roadsides. Most are safe, but as a general rule, you should stick to cooked food. The clean, well-maintained food shops on major roads and in shopping centers rarely cause problems and will give you a chance to taste authentic versions of popular Thai dishes at very low prices.

Though Bangkok's water is potable, it's best for visitors to drink bottled. Clear ice cubes with holes through them are made with purified water, and most restaurants use them.

Restaurants usually stop serving dinner at 10:30 PM, but you will find many local places stay open until midnight and later. For price categories, *see* Pleasures and Pastimes, *above*.

Chinese

$$$ ✕ Dynasty. Government ministers and the local business establishment come here to feast on outstanding Cantonese cuisine. In addition to the main dining area, 11 quiet rooms provide unsurpassed locations for business lunches or dinners (nine of them accommodate 10 people each, the other two hold up to 50). The red carpeting, heavy traditional Chinese furniture, carved screens, and porcelain objets d'art contribute to the quietly elegant atmosphere. The Peking duck and shark's-fin dishes, prepared by two first-rate Hong Kong chefs, are among the draws. Seasonal specialties include everything from "hairy crab" (October–November) to "Taiwanese eels" (March), with only fresh ingredients used. The service is efficient and friendly without being obtrusive. ⊠ *Central Plaza Hotel, 1695 Phaholyothin Rd.,* ☎ *02/541–1234. Reservations essential. AE, DC, MC, V.*

$$$ ✕ Mayflower. Captains of industry, royalty, and heads of state are among the regular customers of the five stylishly opulent private rooms and main dining area of the Mayflower. The carved wood screens and porcelain vases set a tone of simple-but-luxurious refinement perfectly in keeping with the outstanding Cantonese food. To provide the best service possible, a computerized record is kept of the guests—of their food preferences, the size of their families, important anniversaries, etc. Two of the best items on the menu are the piquant abalone-and-jellyfish salad, and the Drunken Chinese Chicken—steamed, skinned, and boned chicken doused with Chinese liquor and served with two sauces, one sweet and one spicy. The shark's-fin soup and the dim sum are also worth sampling. An excellent wine list assumes price is no object. Two- to three-day advance notice is required for private rooms. ⊠ *Dusit Thani Hotel, Rama IV Rd.,* ☎ *02/236–0450. Reservations essential. AE, DC, V.*

$$$ ✕ Royal Kitchen. The Royal Kitchen consists of a number of small, el-
★ egant dining rooms where everything, right down to the silver chopsticks, has been carefully considered. The menu is a reference resource for southern Chinese delicacies, including *mieng nok,* with finely minced, seasoned pigeon served on individual fragrant leaves. At lunchtime, dim sum is served, and it, too, is probably Bangkok's best, as beautifully presented as it is subtle in taste. ⊠ *N. Sathorn Rd., opposite YWCA and Thai Oil,* ☎ *02/234–3063. Reservations essential. Jacket and tie. AE, DC, MC, V.*

$$$ ✕ Sui Sian. The Sui Sian serves great, if a tiny bit inconsistent, Cantonese cuisine. Certainly the decor, the service, and the design of both the main dining area and the private rooms make it a good spot for lunch or dinner meetings. The main dining rooms with bamboo-tile eaves give the feel of a courtyard, an impression reinforced by the jade trees on display. The Peking duck is particularly good. If you're in an extravagant mood, try the pricey Ancient Master Jumps the Wall—a soup incorporating black chicken, deer tendons, abalone, shark's fin, dried scallops, fish maw, turtle, sea cucumber, mushrooms, and a selection of secret Chinese herbs. ⊠ *Landmark Hotel, 138 Sukhumvit Rd.,* ☎ *02/254–0404. AE, DC, MC, V.*

$$–$$$ ✕ Hok Thean Lauo. A shuttle boat runs guests across the Chao Phraya from the River City Shopping Centre to one of Bangkok's top Cantonese restaurants. It's nicest to sit at a table by the window, watching the rice barges labor up and down the river. Hok Thean Lauo is known for its dim-sum lunches, especially on Sunday. Waiters continually pass your table offering you small baskets of delicacies. If you're not selective, you'll probably spoil your appetite for the next two days.

⊠ *762 Ladya Rd., Klongsam,* ☎ *02/437–1121. Reservations essential Sun. AE, DC, MC, V.*

$$ ✕ **Jade Garden.** Fine Cantonese cuisine at good value makes this restaurant well worth visiting for dim-sum brunch or dinner. The superb dishes are made without the aid of MSG, a rarity in this part of the world. The decor is similarly assured in its effects, with a remarkable wood-beam ceiling and softly lighted Chinese print screens. Private dining rooms are available with advance notice; otherwise ask for the corner table in the main dining room—it's partly partitioned off and affords extra privacy. Two good dinner specials are fried Hong Kong noodles and pressed duck with tea leaves. Look for the monthly "special promotion" dish featuring seasonal ingredients. ⊠ *Montien Hotel, 54 Suriwongse Rd.,* ☎ *02/233–7060. AE, DC, MC, V.*

$$ ✕ **Shangrila.** The menu has a wide range of dishes, from Peking duck
★ to thinly sliced pork with garlic, but it is hard to pass up the marvelous dim-sum selection. Waiters will help you choose, but it's difficult to make a mistake. Service is pleasantly attentive even when a high-powered politician comes in and is fawned over. The restaurant's split level and small size make it a more comfortable Chinese place than many in this neighborhood, and the bright white tablecloths and gleaming glassware make for an upbeat dining experience. ⊠ *154/4-7 Silom Rd.,* ☎ *02/234–9147 or 02/234–9149. AE, DC, MC, V.*

$$ ✕ **Tien Tien.** For years, Tien Tien has catered to a busy business lunch trade. Dinner is good, too, if you happen to be in the neighborhood, but the decor doesn't get much beyond white tablecloths and red walls. The roast pork is superb: have it any which way you want, but it's so juicy and tender that simple steamed rice is a sufficient complement. The Peking duck is also a must; its skin is crisp and the pancakes light and fluffy. ⊠ *105 Patpong, Silom Rd.,* ☎ *02/234–8717. MC, V.*

$ ✕ **Coca Noodles.** On evenings and weekends, this giant, raucous restaurant is full of Chinese families eating a daunting variety of noodle dishes with noisy gusto. Both wheat- and rice-based pastas are available in abundance, in combination with a cornucopia of meats, fish, shellfish, and crunchy Chinese vegetables. Try some of the green, wheat-based noodles called *mee yoke,* topped with a chicken thigh, red pork, or crabmeat. You can also prepare yourself an intriguing Chinese variant of sukiyaki on a gas ring built into the table. ⊠ *In Siam Square Shopping Centre facing 461 Henri Dunant Rd.,* ☎ *02/251–6337 or 02/251–3538. Another branch is at 6 Soi Tantawan, Suriwongse Rd.,* ☎ *02/ 236–0107. No credit cards.*

$ ✕ **Prachak.** Families from wealthy neighborhoods send their maids
★ here to bring back the superb roast duck (*ped*) and red pork (*moo daeng*) for dinner. By 6 PM there's often no duck or pork left. Nobody comes here for the tile floors and bare walls; it may even strike you as a little grungy—but the food is fine. The problem is in *finding* this hole-in-the-wall restaurant. It is across from Bangrak Market (beside the Shangri-La hotel), diagonally across the road from a 7-Eleven store. Two can dine well for $6. The present owner, grandson of the founder, speaks just a little English. ⊠ *1415 Charoen Krung (New Road), Silom Bansak,* ☎ *02/234–3755. Reservations not accepted. No credit cards.*

Eclectic

$ ✕ **The Siam Diary.** A convenient social spot if you are at the upper end of Silom or Sathorn roads (it's between the two, one block in from Rama IV Road), this cozy Thai-style pub and restaurant has a convivial atmosphere that attracts local expats and Thais. You can sit at the bar or at tables, and the food is a mixture of Thai and Western, from fried noodles to hamburgers. On Friday and Saturday, a trio plays jazz until shortly after midnight. ⊠ *14/10 Soi Saladeang, Rama IV,* ☎ *02/663– 5348. MC, V.*

486

Bangkok Dining and Lodging

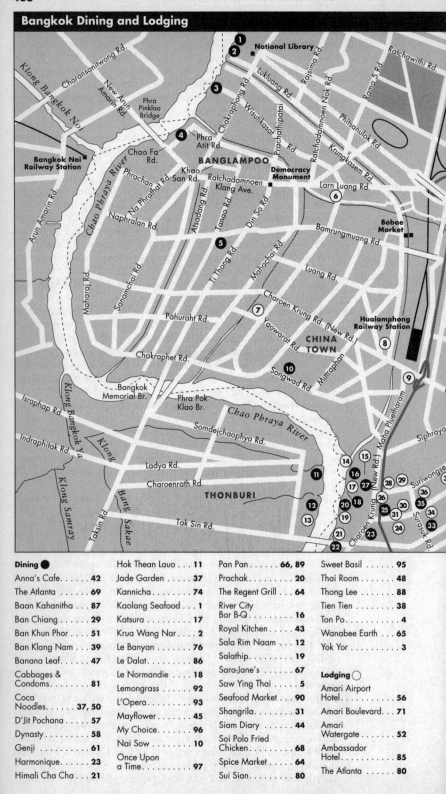

Dining ●

Anna's Cafe **42**
The Atlanta **69**
Baan Kahanitha . . **87**
Ban Chiang **29**
Ban Khun Phor . . **51**
Ban Klang Nam . **39**
Banana Leaf. . . . **47**
Cabbages &
Condoms. **81**
Coca
Noodles. **37, 50**
D'Jit Pochana . . **57**
Dynasty **58**
Genji **61**
Harmonique. **23**
Himali Cha Cha . . **21**

Hok Thean Lauo . . . **11**
Jade Garden **37**
Kannicha **74**
Kaolang Seafood . . . **1**
Katsura **17**
Krua Wang Nar . . . **2**
Le Banyan **76**
Le Dalat. **86**
Le Normandie . . . **18**
Lemongrass **92**
L'Opera **93**
Mayflower **45**
My Choice. **96**
Nai Sow **10**
Once Upon
a Time. **97**

Pan Pan **66, 89**
Prachak. **20**
The Regent Grill . . **64**
River City
Bar B-Q. **16**
Royal Kitchen . . . **43**
Sala Rim Naam . . . **12**
Salathip **19**
Sara-Jane's **67**
Saw Ying Thai . . . **5**
Seafood Market . . . **90**
Shangrila. **31**
Siam Diary **44**
Soi Polo Fried
Chicken. **68**
Spice Market **64**
Sui Sian. **80**

Sweet Basil **95**
Thai Room **48**
Thong Lee **88**
Tien Tien **38**
Ton Po **4**
Wanabee Earth . . **65**
Yok Yor **3**

Lodging ○
Amari Airport
Hotel. **56**
Amari Boulevard. . **71**
Amari
Watergate **52**
Ambassador
Hotel. **85**
The Atlanta **80**

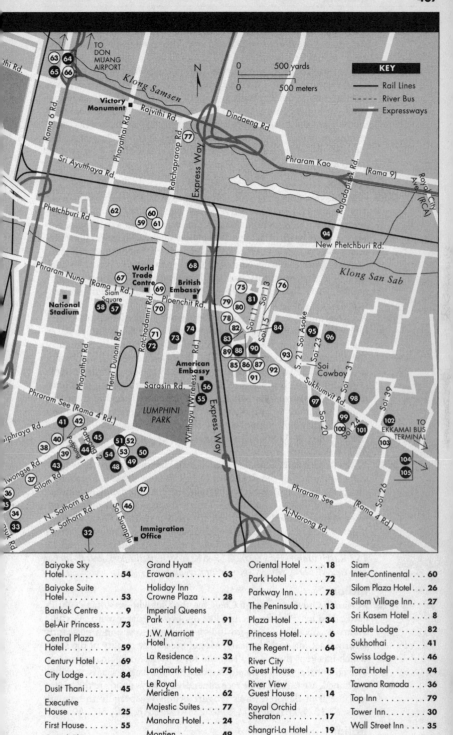

$ ✕ Thai Room. This time capsule opened during the Vietnam War, in 1966, when it was packed in the evening with GIs on R&R. Not a molecule of the decor has changed since then, and it is not unusual to see a veteran of that war quietly reminiscing. Around him, however, will be local residents and tourists in from the tawdry riot of Patpong. The Mexican food is a peculiar hybrid of Mexican and Thai cuisines, and the result is not unpleasing. Some of the Italian items, like the eggplant parmigiana, are very good by any standard, and the Thai food can be excellent. Local clients feel great affection for this one-of-a-kind restaurant, which stays open until midnight. ⊠ *30/37 Patpong 2 Rd. (between Silom and Suriwongse Rds.),* ☎ *02/233–7920. Reservations not accepted. AE, DC, MC, V.*

French

$$$$ ✕ Le Banyan. Come here—a warm, intimate, and vaguely colonial old Thai house—for first-rate French cooking. The chef occasionally experiments with Asian influences, adding an accent of lemongrass, ginger, or Thai basil. A large silver-plated duck press normally takes center stage in the dining room. Pressed duck à la Rouennaise, in a sauce prepared with the juices of the bird and red wine, is one of the duck specialties. Pan-fried foie gras and king lobster make delicious alternatives. ⊠ *59 Sukhumvit Soi 8,* ☎ *02/253–5556. Reservations essential. AE, DC, MC, V. Closed Mon. Dinner only.*

$$$$ ✕ Le Normandie. This legendary restaurant perched atop the Orien-
★ tal Hotel commands a panoramic view across the Chao Phraya River. Michelin three-star chef Georges Blanc is the restaurant's permanent consultant and, periodically, the most highly esteemed chefs in France take over in the kitchen. These artists usually import ingredients from home, and at such times the restaurant's patrons feast on phenomenal French cuisine. Even when no superstar chef is on the scene, the food is remarkable, with the menu often including rare dishes taught to Le Normandie's master chef by the visiting chefs. ⊠ *48 Oriental Ave.,* ☎ *02/234–8690. Reservations essential. Jacket and tie. AE, DC, MC, V. No lunch Sun.*

$$$$ ✕ The Regent Grill. With a terrace overlooking the imaginatively landscaped grounds of the Regent of Bangkok Hotel, this is a strikingly designed, high-fashion French restaurant. Though the menu emphasizes grilled dishes, from time to time it features such memorable entrées as fresh goose liver in raspberry vinegar (which can be specially ordered a day or so in advance). Excellent endive salads and lobster dishes, one with a subtle goose-liver sauce, are regularly featured. ⊠ *155 Ratchadamri Rd.,* ☎ *02/251–6127. Reservations essential. Jacket and tie. AE, DC, MC, V. No dinner weekdays.*

Indian

$$ ✕ Himali Cha Cha. Though Cha Cha, the chef who was once Nehru's cook, died in 1996, his recipes live on, now prepared with matching ability by his wife. Northern Indian cuisine is served in a pleasantly informal setting with the usual Mogul decor. The quality of the food, which has kept the place a favorite for a decade, remains top-notch. The tandoori chicken is locally famous, and the daily specials, precisely explained, are usually to be recommended. Always good are the breads and the fruit-flavored *lassis* (yogurt drinks)—especially the mango ones. ⊠ *1229/11 New Rd.,* ☎ *02/235–1569. AE, DC, MC, V.*

Italian

$$ ✕ L'Opera. Specializing in a variety of homemade pastas, this family bistro draws a loyal clientele of expats. The staff takes pride in working here, and many of them have remained over the years despite cutthroat competition. This is a fine spot to eat when you have a craving for tortelli, large ravioli stuffed with spinach and cheese, or *spadar-rata*, a combination of seafood with garlic-and-white-wine sauce. The bay window table is nice but, given its proximity to the air-conditioner, you might want to wear a sweater. ⊠ *53 Sukhumvit Soi 39,* ☎ *02/ 258–5606. AE, DC, MC, V.*

$$ ✕ **Pan Pan.** The two branches of this Italian food and ice cream chain are enormously popular. They are decorated with Italian kitchen items and spices, and the relaxed atmosphere in both places invites intimate talk. The long list of generous and delicious pasta dishes includes linguine with a sauce of salmon, cream, and vodka that is a taste of high-calorie heaven, and "Chicken Godfather," with a cream-and-mushroom sauce, similarly disappointment-proof. But save room for the ice cream, which is of the thick, dense, Italian type. The branch on Sukhumvit Road offers an antipasto buffet and a large selection of extremely rich desserts. ⊠ *6–6/ 1 Sukhumvit Rd., near Soi 33,* ☎ *02/258–9304 or 02/258–5071;* ⊠ *45 Soi Lang Suan, off Ploenchit Rd.,* ☎ *02/252–7104. AE, DC, MC, V.*

Japanese

$$$ ✕ **Genji.** Bangkok has many good Japanese restaurants, although a number of them give a chilly reception to outsiders. Genji is a happy exception. The fact that it's in a large international hotel shouldn't deter culinary purists—it has an excellent sushi bar and several small private rooms. Try especially the succulent grilled eel. Set menus for lunch and dinner are well conceived, and Japanese breakfasts are also served. ⊠ *Hilton International, 2 Wireless Rd.,* ☎ *02/253–0123. Reservations essential. AE, DC, MC, V.*

$$$ ✕ **Katsura.** This elegant little place overlooking the Chao Phraya River is favored by Japanese and Westerners alike. Though there are three small private rooms, ask for a table by the river, especially at night. There are teppanyaki and sushi counters in the main dining room, where diners will feel entirely comfortable eating alone. The menu offers a number of the chef's inventions, such as sushi with shrimp eggs, a treat for both the eyes and the palate. The *gyuniku-yudofu* (a hot pot of sliced beef, bean curd, and vegetables) and *dobin mushi* (steamed seafood custard served in earthen teapots) are two other favorites. ⊠ *Royal Orchid Sheraton, 2 Captain Bush La.,* ☎ *02/234–5599. AE, DC, MC, V.*

Thai

$$$ ✕ **Lemongrass.** Elegance and a certain adventurousness have made this restaurant a favorite with Thais and resident Westerners. Embellished with Southeast Asian antiques, the dining rooms and the garden have plenty of atmosphere. Over the years the cuisine has become geared to the milder palate of Westerners, which makes for a good introduction to Thai food. Be sure to try a glass of *nam takrai,* the cold, sweet drink brewed from lemongrass. ⊠ *5/1 Sukhumvit Soi 24,* ☎ *02/258– 8637. AE, DC, MC, V.*

$$$ ✕ **Sala Rim Naam.** Definitely an upscale restaurant for visitors, this
★ elegant *sala* (room), across the river from the Oriental Hotel, realizes many of the images conjured by the word *Siam.* The dishes are so beautifully presented that eating them feels like vandalism. Try some of the hot-and-sour salads, particularly the shrimp version called *yam koong.* Make reservations for 7:30 PM and plan to stay on for the beautifully staged Thai dancing. The B1,400 set menu is excellent. Lunch at the Sala Rim's delicious buffet is always less crowded and, during the hot season, special and rarely found light Thai recipes called *Khon Chere* are offered. ⊠ *Use free boat from Oriental Hotel,* ☎ *02/437–6211. Reservations essential weekends and Oct.–late-Feb. AE, DC, MC, V.*

$$$ ✕ **Salathip.** Built as a Thai pavilion, with a veranda facing the Chao Phraya River, this restaurant provides an ambience that guarantees a romantic evening. Be sure to reserve a table outside. Though the food may not have as much hot chili as some like, it hasn't been adulterated to suit Western tastes. On Sunday night, there's possibly the best buffet in Bangkok. ⊠ *Shangri-La Hotel, 89 Soi Wat Suan Phu, New Rd.,* ☏ *02/236–7777. Reservations essential for veranda. AE, DC, MC, V. No lunch.*

$$$ ✕ **Seafood Market.** This vast restaurant still feels like the fish supermarket it used to be. You take a cart and choose from an array of seafood—crabs, prawns, lobster, clams, oysters, flat fish, snapperlike fish, crayfish—and vegetables. The waiter takes it away and cooks it any way you like. Typically your eyes are bigger than your stomach, so select with prudence, not gusto. Though the fluorescent lighting gives it the ambience of a giant canteen, people pack the tables because the prices are reasonable and the fish is fresh. Beware of Johnny-come-latelies who also call themselves Seafood Market and pay taxi and tuk-tuk drivers to divert you to their establishments. ⊠ *388 Sukhumvit Soi 24,* ☏ *02/258–0218. Reservations not accepted. AE, DC, MC, V.*

$$–$$$ ✕ **Ban Klang Nam.** This open-sided restaurant along the river is just
★   upstream from the Hanging Bridge (you'll need a taxi to get here). Choose a table next to the railing overlooking the river; you can also sit out on the patio dock or further inside. The mee krob, so difficult to make well, is delicious. The fired sea bass in garlic and pepper, snapper in an oyster sauce, and kung paan tod are all superb, as is the smooth tom yam kung. ⊠ *3792/106 Pharam (Rama) 3, Soi 14,* ☏ *02/292–0175 or 02/292–2037. Reservations essential. AE, MC, V.*

$$ ✕ **Baan Kahanitha.** Half the pleasure of eating here is in the ambience and attentive service. Wood paneling, old Thai prints, blooming orchids, antique copper, and tableware from Thai kilns create just the right mood for a relaxing evening. The food is strictly Thai, explained well in the English menu and by the English-speaking waiters, although it has been compromised recently to appeal to Westerners, with a resulting absence of Thai diners. Ask for the complimentary appetizer mieng khum. The fried soft-shell crabs in a hot-and-sour sauce and the gaeng kieuw wan gai are two of the better choices. The tom kha gai is wonderfully rich, with just enough lime and lemongrass. ⊠ *3/1 Sukhumvit 23, Soi Prasan,* ☏ *02/258–4181. MC, V.*

$$ ✕ **Ban Chiang.** The decor here is turn-of-the-century Bangkok, and the painted walls are adorned with prints, photographs, and a pendulum clock. The extensive menu can be quite spicy: examples are the roast-duck curry and the shrimp-and-vegetable herb soup. The fried fish cakes and grilled prawns are milder, as is the gai hor bai toey. The service is not a strong point, and you need to know your way around a Thai menu to order a balanced set of dishes. ⊠ *14 Srivieng Rd.,* ☏ *02/236–7045. MC, V.*

$$ ✕ **Ban Khun Phor.** If you're in the Siam Square area, try this popular bistro diagonally across from the Novotel. The wooden tables mix with European Victoriana and Thai artifacts. The menu is varied, with such standard favorites as tom kha gai, roast duck with red curry, and even spicy stir-fried boar's meat. The best dish is the spicy crab soup. ⊠ *458/7–9, Soi 8, Siam Sq.,* ☏ *02/250–1733. Reservations not accepted. MC, V.*

$$ ✕ **Cabbages & Condoms.** Don't be misled by the restaurant's name or disconcerted by the array of contraceptive devices for sale. C&C fundraises for Thailand's birth-control program, the Population & Community Development Association. You'll find the Thai food here excellently prepared, with such dishes as chicken wrapped in pandanus leaf, crisp fried fish with chili sauce, and shrimp in a mild curry sauce. There's a simply decorated dining room and a pleasant garden with bench tables under shady trees—one of the few places in Bangkok to sit outside without noise and air pollution. ⊠ *10 Sukhumvit Soi 12,* ☏ *02/251–0402. AE, DC, MC, V.*

$$ ✕ **D'Jit Pochana.** This branch of the D'Jit Pochana restaurant chain is convenient for those staying near the airport. The restaurant has numerous rooms—including several large private rooms suitable for business dinners—on different levels. Request a room with a view of the garden and its pond and fountain; other rooms overlook the road. Among the many specialties are gai hor bai toey and tom kha gai. ⊠ *26/368–80 Gp 6 Phaholyothin Rd.,* ☎ *02/531–1644. AE, DC, MC, V.*

$$ ✕ **Harmonique.** You can eat on the terrace or on the ground floor of this small house near the river. The decoration, from flowers tumbling out of vases to chests scattered with bric-a-brac, gives the feeling of casual ease that you could expect in Western Europe, but here it is, down a small soi off Charoen Krung, just left of the General Post Office. The menu is small, but what there is is made with care. Foreign tourists come here from the Oriental and Royal Orchid Sheraton and are ably assisted by Madame in selecting the right courses. Try the crisp fish sautéed in garlic, the mild crab curry, or the Chinese cabbage topped with salted fish—all are excellent. ⊠ *22 Charoen Krung Soi 34,* ☎ *02/237–8175. AE.*

$$ ✕ **Kaloang Seafood.** This local favorite is a little off the beaten track, but it's worth the effort if you want the genuine flavor of riverside Bangkok and good seafood as well. Beginning at the National Library, a soi leads down to the open-air restaurant, built on a ramshackle pier. Fans and the breeze off the river keep things comfortably cool most evenings. The more observant customer will notice right away that almost all the waitstaff are transvestites. Service is friendly and competent, if initially somewhat disconcerting. The grilled seafood platter is both generous and cheap, and the grilled giant river prawns are also a bargain. Try the yam pla duk foo. It is rather spicy, but it complements cold beer as few things in this world do. ⊠ *2 Sri Ayutthaya Rd.,* ☎ *02/281–9228. AE, DC, MC, V.*

$$ ✕ **Krua Wang Nar.** This riverside restaurant serves some of the best seafood in town. It is also near the National Museum and Grand Palace. Krua Wang Nar is noisy in the evenings, and the decor is fairly appalling (with pillars and plaster mermaids and several TVs blaring away at once), and the service can sometimes be a little smarmy. However, a prime location on the river, a comfortable, air-conditioned dining section, and high-quality food make this restaurant very popular with Thais and growing numbers of foreigners. Everything listed on the extensive menu is good, particularly the *pla somlee pow* (baked cottonfish with ginger and garlic) and *pae sa pla chon* (steamed serpenthead fish with vegetables). ⊠ *17/1 Chao Fa Rd.,* ☎ *02/224–8552. MC, V.*

$$ ✕ **My Choice.** Middle-class Thais with a taste for their grandmothers' traditional recipes flock to this restaurant all day. The *ped aob,* a thick soup made from beef stock, is particularly popular, but foreigners may prefer the *tom kha tala,* a hot-and-sour dish with shrimp, served with rice. The interior is plain, with Formica tables; it's nicer to sit outside. ⊠ *Sukhumvit Soi 36,* ☎ *02/258–6174. AE, DC, MC, V.*

$$ ✕ **River City Bar B-Q.** As you're seated on the roof of the River City Shopping Centre, a waiter brings a burner and hot plate, and a mound of different meats and vegetables. You use your chopsticks to grill the food. Order some appetizers to nibble on while dinner is cooking—the northern Thai sausage is excellent. Tables at the edge of the roof have romantic views of the Chao Phraya River. ⊠ *5th floor, River City Shopping Centre,* ☎ *02/237–0077 ext. 240. MC, V.*

$$ ✕ **Spice Market.** The decor re-creates a once-familiar sight—the inte-
★ rior of a well-stocked spice shop, with sacks of garlic, dried chilies, and heavy earthenware fish-sauce jars lined up as they were when the only way to get to Bangkok was by steamer. The authentic recipes are tempered to suit the tender mouths of Westerners, but you may ask for your dishes to be prepared full-strength; a chili logo on the menu indicates

peppery dishes. The curries are superb, and there is a comprehensive selection of old-fashioned Thai sweets. From mid-January to the end of March, try the *nam doc mai* (mango with sticky rice and coconut milk); knowledgeable foreigners arrange trips to Bangkok at this time of year just for this dessert. ⊠ *Regent of Bangkok Hotel, 155 Ratchadamri Rd.,* ☎ *02/251–6127. Reservations essential. AE, DC, MC, V.*

$$ ✕ **Ton Po.** This is open-air riverside dining without tourist trappings.
★ Ton Po (Thai for the Bo tree, of which there is a large, garlanded specimen at the entrance) has a wide, covered veranda on the Chao Phraya. To get the breeze that blows even on the hottest days, try to wangle a riverside table. Many of the dishes are well known, and none more so than the *tom khlong plaa salid bai makhaam awn,* a delectable, very hot and sour soup made from a local dried fish, chili, lime juice, lemongrass, young tamarind leaves, mushrooms, and a full frontal assault of other herbal seasonings. Less potent but equally good are the gai hor bai toey and *haw moke plaa* (a type of curried fish custard, thickened with coconut cream and steamed in banana leaves). ⊠ *Phra Atit Rd.,* ☎ *no phone. Reservations not accepted. AE, DC, MC, V.*

$–$$ ✕ **Anna's Cafe.** When owner Tuay David Wibusin's career in finance abruptly ended with the economic collapse in 1998, he decided to open a restaurant that exuded optimism and cheer. By separating the dining areas with walls and plants, he created an ambiance of lighthearted intimacy. Though there is a smattering of European dishes, most of the fare is modern Thai. The gaeng kieuw wan gai is mild and served with a salted boiled egg to counter its sweetness. The *tod mun kung* (fried prawn cakes) served with stir-fried vegetables and fried rice makes for a full and tasty meal. A good appetizer to share is the yam pla duk foo. ⊠ *118 Soi Saladaeng (at the top of Silom Rd.),* ☎ *02/632–0619. AE, DC, MC, V.*

$–$$ ✕ **Kannicha.** The contemporary decor of white tablecloths, lighting that highlights the tropical plants, and waiters wearing scarlet braces over their white shirts set the tone for sophisticated Thai fare. The menu is wide and varied. While reading it, choose an appetizer such as mieng khum or the delicious kung paan tod. Main dishes range from sea bass in "sauce of three tastes" to pork sautéed in garlic and young pepper. ⊠ *17 Sukhumvit Soi 11,* ☎ *02/651–1573. AE, MC, V.*

$–$$ ✕ **Once Upon a Time.** This is an inexpensive place to relax and enjoy Thai food on a plant-filled terrace next to a pool. Inside, the dining room has Thai antiques and floor-to-ceiling wood walls decorated with period photos of the Thai royal family, movie stars, and beauty queens. The music is traditional Thai, both taped and live. The menu is good, and authentically Thai. The timid often order the chopped pork with chili sauce or the beef fillet with pickled garlic. *Miang kham,* a traditional snack of dried shrimp, dried coconut, peanuts, pineapple, chili pepper, and sweet tamarind sauce rolled together in a green leaf, makes an excellent appetizer. ⊠ *Juladis Tower, 7th floor, Soi 19, Phetchburi Rd.,* ☎ *02/255–4948. AE, DC, MC, V.*

$–$$ ✕ **Sara-Jane's.** Sara, formerly of Massachusetts, married a Thai 20 years ago and started a restaurant in 1986. In 1998 her success led to the opening of a new restaurant just down from the American Embassy. In the ground-floor shopping mall of a large office building, Sara-Jane's open dining room has sparse decor. It is designed to accommodate lots of people for lunch, though many also stop for dinner. The menu celebrates I-san food, with many types of salad served with *larb,* a mince made from pork, chicken, tuna, or other meat and fish. One favorite is the yam pla duk foo. For those who want European fare, Sara-Jane also offers Italian food. ⊠ *Ground floor, Sindhorn Tower 1, 130–132 Wireless Rd.,* ☎ *02/650–9992. No credit cards.*

$–$$ ✕ **Wanabee Earth.** White tablecloths and striped wallpaper in gold and white give a bright, fresh feel while the vine-covered trellises separating the tables break up the squareness of the dining room. Thais come here to choose from the range of foods drawn from the four regions of Thailand: for example, spicy salads from the Northeast, southern Thai fried fish, an array of noodle dishes from the Central Plains, and tasty sausages from the North. ⊠ *63/12 Soi Langesuan 2, Ploenchit,* ☎ *02/652–2939. MC, V.*

$–$$ ✕ **Yok Yor.** Dine aboard a grounded vessel on the Chao Phraya, reached by a gangplank. The well-cooked Thai food is served with dispatch, and the cool darkness of the river lends a romantic, exotic aura. There's live music from 6 PM on, and Japanese, Chinese, and some European dishes are also served, though few Westerners eat here. The management also runs a dinner-and-music cruise along the Chao Phraya every night (8:30–10:30; B70 plus cost of food), aboard a 400-seat boat. ⊠ *Wisutikasat Rd. at Yok Yor Pier (next to Bank of Thailand),* ☎ *02/ 281–1829 or 02/282–7385. No credit cards.*

$ ✕ **The Atlanta.** Though simply a coffee shop in a budget hotel, the Atlanta serves Thai cooking that is surprisingly good, thanks to the reclusive innkeeper, Charles Henn, a food fanatic. The menu, which explains the ingredients and their origin, makes interesting, amusing reading. Don't pass up the tom yam kung here—it's especially smooth. Classical jazz is played at dinner, followed by a movie of some repute. New vegetarian dishes are being added every week to the menu, which, if Henn has his way, will soon be recognized as the best in Bangkok. ⊠ *78 Sukhumvit Soi 2,* ☎ *02/252–1650 or 02/252–6069. No credit cards.*

$ ✕ **Banana Leaf.** This is not only the best restaurant in this shopping complex, but it's worth making tracks for if you are in the vicinity of upper Silom Road. The people lining up to get in aren't coming for the decor. It's just bare, painted walls, but the harried waiters and waitresses give quick, friendly service, and there's delicious Thai food at low prices. Try the baked crab with glass noodles, hen's fingers salad, spicy papaya salad, grilled black band fish, or grilled pork with a coconut milk dip. ⊠ *Basement level, Silom Complex, Silom Rd.,* ☎ *02/ 231–3124. No credit cards.*

$ ✕ **Nai Sow.** The best tom yam kung is found here, a Chinese-Thai restaurant next door to Wat Plaplachai in Chinatown. Chefs come and go, but the owner, who never divulges his recipes to his chefs, makes the essential mixture—which includes the fatty juices from the prawns—in secret. Other equally tasty dishes range from curried Thai beef to a mix of sweet-and-sour mushrooms. For an unusual and delicious dessert, finish with the fried taro. Forget decor and ambience: round tables and chairs are about the only furnishings. You come here to eat and talk. ⊠ *3/1 Maitrichit Rd.,* ☎ *02/222–1539. Reservations not accepted. MC, V.*

$ ✕ **Saw Ying Thai.** This place has been open for almost 60 years, and many of its clientele have been regulars for decades. It is rare to find a tourist here, and even long-term expat customers are few. The menus on the wall are in Thai only, and none of the staff speaks English, so try to bring a Thai friend. Be sure to order the *kai toon,* a chicken soup with bamboo sprouts. Also memorable are the *plaa du thawd krawb phad phed* (crisp-fried catfish stir-fried with curry spices and herbs) and the *khai jio neua puu* (an omelette full of crabmeat). This charming restaurant would rate a star if it were more accessible in language or location. ⊠ *Corner of Bamrungmuang and Tanao Rds.,* ☎ *no phone. Reservations not accepted. No credit cards.*

$ ✕ **Soi Polo Fried Chicken.** Although its beat-up plastic tables, traffic
★ noise, and lack of air-conditioning make this small place look like a sure thing for stomach trouble, it is one of the city's most popular lunch spots for nearby office workers. The reason: its world-class fried chicken flavored with black pepper and plenty of golden-brown, crisp-

fried garlic. The chicken should be sampled with sticky rice and perhaps a plate of the restaurant's excellent *som tam*, a hydrogen bomb of hot-and-sour raw papaya salad from the Northeast. Try to get here a bit before noon, or landing a table will be a problem. ⊠ *Walk into Soi Polo from Wireless Rd. (the restaurant is the last of the shops on your left as you enter the soi),* ☎ *no phone. Reservations not accepted. No credit cards. No dinner.*

$ ✕ **Thong Lee.** This small but attractive shophouse restaurant has an air-conditioned upstairs dining area. Although prices are very low, Thong Lee has a devoted upper-middle-class clientele. The menu is not adventurous, but every dish has a distinct personality—evidence of the cook's artistry and imagination. Almost everyone orders the *muu phad kapi* (pork fried with shrimp paste); the *yam hed sod* (hot-and-sour mushroom salad) is memorable but very spicy. ⊠ *Sukhumvit Soi 20,* ☎ *no phone. Reservations not accepted. No credit cards.*

Vietnamese

$$-$$$ ✕ **Sweet Basil.** It is worth making the long trek down Sukhumvit to
★ Soi 62 for the splendidly presented Vietnamese fare, in a fresh setting of crisp white tablecloths, glistening silver and glassware, and ferns and flowers. Try the *bo la lat* (brochettes of beef wrapped in a pungent leaf) and the *ban cuon tom* (dumplings stuffed with shrimp and mushrooms), or the more usual but still delicious salads and crunchy *cha gio* (spring rolls with a sweet, tangy sauce). This is a smart restaurant where Thais dress up for a special meal. ⊠ *23 Sukhumvit Soi 62,* ☎ *02/176–5490. Reservations essential. AE, DC, MC, V.*

$$ ✕ **Le Dalat.** This very classy Vietnamese restaurant, once a private house,
★ consists of several intimate and cozily decorated dining rooms. Much Vietnamese cuisine is based on flavor juxtapositions striking to the Western palate, and here it's all served up with style. Try *naem neuang*, which requires you to take a garlicky grilled meatball and place it on a round of *mieng* (edible thin rice paper wrapper), then pile on bits of garlic, ginger, hot chili, star apple, and mango, spoon on a viscous sweet-salty sauce, and wrap the whole thing up in a lettuce leaf before eating. The restaurant has become a favorite with Bangkok residents. ⊠ *51 Sukhumvit Soi 23, opposite Indian Embassy,* ☎ *02/260–1849. Reservations essential. AE, DC, MC, V.*

Lodging

The economic and currency crisis of 1997–98 lowered prices in dollars or sterling at hotels whose clientele is mostly Thais and other Asians. Hotels with mostly an American or European clientele (especially the luxury hotels) raised their prices to offset the devaluation of the baht. Now, though, even hotels that quote prices in baht have started to raise their rack rates. Nevertheless, prices fluctuate enormously, and if business is down, huge discounts are offered. The best bargains are probably found in the $$–$$$ categories.

That said, Bangkok hotel prices are still lower than those in Singapore and Hong Kong and are not expensive by European standards. Rates at fabulous deluxe hotels are about the equivalent of $250 for a double. Those in the $80–$100 range also have fine service, excellent restaurants, health clubs, and business facilities. For $40 to $50, you can find respectable lodgings in a hotel with an efficient staff. Rooms in small hotels with limited facilities are available for around $10, and, for those willing to share a bathroom, guest houses are numerous.

The four main hotel districts are next to the Chao Phraya River and along Silom and Suriwongse roads; around Siam Square; in the foreign-embassy neighborhood; and along Sukhumvit Road. Other areas, such as Khao San Road for inexpensive guest houses favored by back-packers, and across the river, where modern high-rise hotels are sprouting up, are not included in the following list. For price categories, see the price chart at the start of this chapter.

$$$$ 🏨 **Dusit Thani.** This low-key 23-story hotel with distinctive, pyramid-style architecture is the flagship property of a Thai group that manages Dusit and Princess hotels. An extensive shopping arcade, a Chinese restaurant, and an elegant Thai restaurant occupy the street level. One floor up, the lobby, reception area, and a sunken lounge overlook a small garden. The pool is in a central courtyard filled with trees, a peaceful oasis amid Bangkok's frenzy. (But be aware that the construction of a subway and the attendant traffic diversion has made the Dusit area a mess.) The Dusit Thani is particularly noted for its spacious, though very high priced, Landmark suites, furnished in classical Thai tradition with handcrafted furniture, but the standard rooms are due for refurbishing. The service is not up to past standards. ⊠ *Rama IV Rd., 10500,* ☎ *02/236–0450; 800/223–6800 U.S. reservations; 212/838–3110 in N.Y.,* ℻ *02/237–5837. 510 rooms and 30 suites. 7 restaurants, bar, coffee shop, in-room VCRs, pool, health club, shops, nightclub, business services, meeting rooms. AE, DC, MC, V.* ♨

$$$$ 🏨 **Grand Hyatt Erawan.** The Grand Hyatt is built on the site of the old Erawan Hotel, next to the Erawan shrine. The typically Hyatt lobby is a stylish four-story atrium with a domed, stained-glass roof and decorated with an extensive art collection. Service is efficient. Guest rooms are large, with window bays for a desk and a couple of chairs. The wood floors are strewn with area rugs, and each room has original art. Messages are displayed on a TV monitor, and the bathrooms have separate showers, oversize tubs, and dressing areas. The three Regency floors offer concierges and other services. The rooms with the best view look over Lumphini Park and the racetrack, though you can hear the traffic on Ratchadamri Road. With the new skytrain not too far away, the lower-floor rooms can be noisy. Restaurants abound. The Italian fare at Spasso, developed by a Milanese chef, is especially creative and a lunch here is recommended whether you stay in the hotel or not. The pool terrace is covered with ferns and plants, and a physical therapist manages the elaborate health club. ⊠ *494 Ratchadamri Rd., 10330,* ☎ *02/254–1234; 800/233–1234 U.S. reservations,* ℻ *02/253–5856. 389 rooms and suites. 3 restaurants, bar, pool, 2 tennis courts, health club, squash, business services, meeting rooms. AE, DC, MC, V.* ♨

$$$$ 🏨 **Landmark Hotel.** Though it calls itself high-tech, the Landmark's generous use of teak in its reception areas creates an ambience suggestive of a grand European hotel. Guest rooms, unobtrusively elegant, are geared to the international business traveler, with good desks and TV/video screens that can tune in to information banks linked to the business center. With a staff of 950, service is attentive. The hotel's elegant Hibiscus restaurant has a view of the city and serves European fare, and a jazz trio accompanies drinks and light meals in the Huntsman Pub. ⊠ *138 Sukhumvit Rd., 10110,* ☎ *02/254–0404,* ℻ *02/253–4259. 395 rooms and 55 suites. 4 restaurants, coffee shop, snack bar, pool, sauna, health club, squash, shops, business services, meeting rooms. AE, DC, MC, V.* ♨

$$$$ 🏨 **Oriental Hotel.** The Oriental has set the standard for which all other ★ Bangkok hotels strive. Part of its fame stems from its past guests, and today's roster features heads of state and film stars. Its location on the Chao Phraya is unrivaled; the original building, now the Garden Wing, has been refurbished, and the rooms here—and the main building's luxury suites—are the hotel's best. Among its well-known restaurants are China House; Sala Rim Naam across the river, renowned for its Thai food; and Le Normandie, the best French restaurant in Bangkok. In addition, the hotel has a riverside barbecue every night. The Oriental radiates elegance and provides superb service, though in recent years some of the crispness and panache have disappeared, perhaps because the staff is continually wooed away by other hotels. You can attend a Thai cooking school here, as well as afternoon seminars on Thai culture. The smart spa across the river (next to the Sala Rim) lets you indulge in all sorts of luxurious treatments. The hotel has a helicopter service ($150) to and from the airport. ⊠ *48 Oriental Ave., 10500,* ☎ *02/236–0400; 71/537–2988 U.K. reservations; 800/223–6800 U.S. reservations,* FAX *02/236–1937. 398 rooms. 8 restaurants, 2 pools, 2 tennis courts, health club, jogging, squash, nightclub, business services, helipad. AE, DC, MC, V.* ✆

$$$$ 🖫 **The Peninsula.** The Peninsula opened its doors in 1999 with all the latest in hotel technology, from fax machines in every room to bedside fingertip controls that operate the lights, TV, and opening and closing of curtains. Bathrooms not only have a separate shower stall but also a TV with a mist-free screen at one end of the bathtub, as well as a hands-free telephone. The spacious rooms look out onto the river and the skyscraper-infested jungle that Bangkok has become. Because the Peninsula is on the Thonburi side of the Chao Phraya, opposite the Oriental, the Shangri-La, and the heart of Bangkok, you'll need to take the free hotel shuttle boat across the river every time you come and go (a possible nuisance, or a retreat from Bangkok's chaos). Dining options at the hotel are adequate, though not exceptional, with the Cantonese (a formal restaurant) and Pacific Rim (contemporary American cuisine) restaurants, and a dining room–coffee shop. Barbecue buffets are often held in the evening. The hotel has a long, attractive swimming pool stretching inland from the river with *salas* where guests can sit in sun or shade. ⊠ *333 Charoennakorn Rd., Klonsan, 10600,* ☎ *02/861–2888,* FAX *02/861–2355. 370 rooms. 3 restaurants, bar, health club, business center, meeting rooms, helipad. AE, DC, MC, V.* ✆

$$$$ 🖫 **The Regent.** Long one of Bangkok's leading hotels, the Regent is in
★   the embassy district, which is now the geographical center of the city. You enter by mounting palatial steps into a formal lobby where local society meets for morning coffee and afternoon tea, and where Thai classical art adds serenity to sophisticated luxury. Service is exemplary. Off a delightful courtyard there are shops and restaurants, including the popular Spice Market. The large rooms are decorated with Thai silk upholstery, and bathrooms have a separate shower. Some of the best rooms overlook the racetrack, but choose one on a high floor, since the new skytrain blocks the view for rooms on the first three floors. There are also four "cabana rooms," whose private patios look onto a small garden with a lotus pond. In the concierge club lounge (extra charge), there's an extensive library, concierge services, excellent breakfasts, and complimentary hors d'oeuvres. Be sure to have the Regent's fragrant-oil massage. ⊠ *155 Ratchadamri Rd., 10330,* ☎ *02/251–6127,* FAX *02/253–9195. 363 rooms. 3 restaurants, pool, massage, health club, shops, business services. AE, DC, MC, V.* ✆

$$$$ 🖫 **Le Royal Meridien.** The new Royal Meridien charges about 20% more than the adjacent 30-year-old Meridien, which has had its day. Because the new hotel is having trouble filling its rooms, special promotional rates often reduce the cost of a hotel room by 50%. The large guest rooms have bathrooms with a separate shower stall. The executive floor, which costs 20%–25% more than standard floors, has added amenities including a fax machine with a dedicated line. Executive-floor guests can also use the pleasant lounge with great city views and have complimentary breakfasts and evening cocktails. The hotel, which seems less than oriented to the individual traveler, has a 2,000-person capacity

ballroom and meeting rooms with the latest technology. Its leading restaurant, run by a Hong Kong chef, prides itself on tables than can seat 10 to 24 people. The rooftop pool, however, is intimate. ⊠ *973 Ploenchit Rd., Lumphini, Pathumwan, 10330,* ☎ *02/656–0444,* FAX *02/656–0555. 381 rooms. 2 restaurants, pool, spa, health club, business services, meeting rooms. AE, DC, MC, V.*☻

$$$$ ▣ **Royal Orchid Sheraton.** Of the hotels offering riverfront luxury this 28-story palace is more oriented toward tour groups than its neighbors, the Oriental and the Shangri-La. All rooms face the river and are well appointed—the namesake flowers are everywhere. The decor, low-key peaches and creams, is a little boring. Standard rooms tend to be long and narrow, with a slightly cramped feeling, but if you go for a deluxe room, you'll be paying the same price as if you were staying at the Oriental or Shangri-La. The restaurants are almost too numerous to mention, but the Thai Thara Thong is memorable, with subtle classical music accompanying your meal. You could equally well choose Japanese, Indian, or Italian cuisine. A glassed-in bridge leads to the River City Shopping Centre next door. ⊠ *2 Captain Bush La., 10500,* ☎ *02/266–0123 or 02/237–0022,* FAX *02/236–8320. 771 rooms. 3 Restaurants, 2 bars, coffee shop, 2 pools, 2 tennis courts, health club, shops, business services, meeting rooms, helipad. AE, DC, MC, V.*☻

$$$$ ▣ **Shangri-La Hotel.** For decades the Oriental could safely claim to be Bangkok's finest hotel; then came the challenge by a spate of new hotels, of which the Shangri-La was one of the first and best. The initial enthusiasm has passed—it's looking a little tired these days, the smiles seem permanently fixed, and the fairly large guest rooms, decorated in pastels, are showing signs of age. The staff is nevertheless professional and efficient, and the spacious marble lobby with crystal chandeliers is a relief from the congestion of Bangkok. The lobby lounge, with its floor-to-ceiling windows, offers a marvelous panorama of the Chao Phraya River. The gardens are an oasis whose peace is interrupted only by the riverboat traffic. In the opulent Krungthep Wing, a separate tower across the gardens, all guest rooms have fax outlets and balconies overlooking the river. ⊠ *89 Soi Wat Suan Phu, New Rd., 10500,* ☎ *02/236–7777,* FAX *02/236–8579. 801 rooms and 65 suites. 13 restaurants, 4 bars, 2 pools, 2 tennis courts, health club, squash, shops, business services, helipad. AE, DC, MC, V.*☻

$$$$ ▣ **Sheraton Grande Sukhumvit.** The Grande Sukhumvit soars 33 floors above the business-shopping-embassy area. The light-flooded guest rooms, on the upper floors, are a far cry from typical boxlike hotel rooms; each has a spacious bathroom angled off the bedroom, and the entrance hall and walk-in wardrobe have interesting diagonals. In these "Deluxe" rooms, a 24-hour butler service will bring you coffee or iron your clothes at the push of a button. You'll never go hungry here: the street-level entrance has Riva's, a restaurant and bar offering live music and contemporary cooking; off the marble lobby on the first floor, the Orchid Café has an international buffet; on the second floor you can choose Italian or Chinese, or have tea in the lounge or cocktails in the rotunda. On the third floor, the health club and the deep-blue, serpentine swimming pool are laid out in an Oriental garden, which is also the setting for the Thai restaurant and, in the winter (dry) months, a barbecue. ⊠ *250 Sukhumvit Rd., 10110,* ☎ *02/653–0333,* FAX *02/653–0400. 445 rooms. 4 restaurants, pool, health club, business services. AE, DC, MC, V.*☻

$$$$ ▣ **Sukhothai.** On six landscaped acres off Sathorn Road (a high-traffic area with no tourist attractions), this hotel attempts to recapture the glory of Thailand's first kingdom in its architecture and ambience, but it does not quite succeed. It does, however, offer quiet; the clutter and chaos of Bangkok seem a world away from its numerous court-

yards. The hotel's Thai restaurant is set in a pavilion in an artificial lake, but for all its elegance, it feels a bit stiff and pretentious. Public areas have stern pillars, sharp right angles, and prim little tables laid for tea. The dining room for Continental and grilled fare is comfortable, but prices are high. Standard rooms are spacious but not exceptionally well furnished. The one-bedroom suites ($400) have splendid, oversize, teak-floor bathrooms with "his and her" washbasins and mirrors. Most of the guest rooms face one of the pond-filled courtyards. ⊠ *13/3 South Sathorn Rd., 10120,* ☎ *02/287–0222,* FAX *02/287–4980. 136 rooms and 76 suites. 2 restaurants, pool, massage, sauna, tennis court, health club, squash. AE, DC, MC, V.* 🐾

$$$–$$$$ 🏨 **Amari Watergate.** This flagship hotel of the Amari group is at the top range of its price category, with quality to match—ask for the promotional rate. Guest rooms are spacious and comfortable, furnished in rich fabrics. Bathrooms are also quite large, though the separate shower stall is too small for two. The executive floor has a lounge where complimentary breakfast and cocktails are served. The two main restaurants are Italian and Thai; in the latter, the menu specializes in fare from the four major regions in Thailand. The coffee shop serves a buffet. The swimming pool is one of the largest in Bangkok hotels. ⊠ *847 Phetchburi Rd., 10400,* ☎ *02/653–9000,* FAX *02/653–9045. 575 rooms. 3 restaurants, pool, health club, business services, meeting rooms. AE, DC, MC, V.* 🐾

$$$–$$$$ 🏨 **Baiyoke Sky Hotel.** Although the hotel brags that it is the tallest in the world (at 88 stories), completed hotel rooms begin on the 22nd floor and end at the 36th. The empty 40 or so floors don't yet have guest rooms. However, a Japanese restaurant is on the 78th floor and a buffet is on the 79th. Hotel guests must pay B50 to get up there (nonguests pay B100) and that includes a visit to the revolving observation deck on the 84th floor. The rooms are very plainly furnished and not particularly restful to the spirit. However, they are spacious and the bathrooms have a separate shower stall. The one-bedroom suites are disappointing—while they have lots of storage space, the bedrooms may remind you of boarding school. The lobby, on the 18th floor, has a coffee shop open 24 hours. The Baiyoke Sky Hotel is in many ways a symbol of Thailand's billionaires who built for self-glorification until their bubble economy burst. ⊠ *222 Ratchaprarop Rd., Rajthawee, 10400,* ☎ *02/656–3000,* FAX *02/656–3555. 170 rooms and 30 suites. 3 restaurants, pool, business services. AE, DC, MC, V.* 🐾

$$$–$$$$ 🏨 **J. W. Marriott Hotel.** The last thing Bangkok needed in late 1997 was a new luxury hotel, but it got this one, and though normally it would be in the $$$$ price category, it has priced itself lower to win some business. Although sparkling with modern technological conveniences, such as two telephone lines per room and a separate shower stall in the bathrooms, the Marriott does not stand out. Rooms are standard, though a firm king-size bed makes for good sleeping. It's worth an extra B800 to stay on the Executive Floors (16–24). Though the rooms are the same as others, guests check in and out in the executive lounge and are offered complimentary breakfast, afternoon tea, and evening cocktails. The fitness center is superb, with saunas and the latest equipment for retooling the body. Restaurants include the Cantonese Man Ho, the White Elephant Thai restaurant, and the informal JW's California, with an open kitchen and contemporary cuisine. ⊠ *4 Sukhumvit Soi 2, 10110,* ☎ *02/656–7700,* FAX *02/656–7711. 446 rooms. 3 restaurants, bar, pool, sauna, health club, business services, meeting rooms. AE, DC, MC, V.* 🐾

$$$–$$$$ 🏨 **Westin Banyan.** Although the lobby is on the ground floor and the dining room is one floor below, the rest of the hotel starts on the 33rd floor of a skinny building reaching up 60 floors. With no other buildings around and way above the smog level, the light-filled guest

rooms—all of which are suites—have sweeping views of the city. The generous use of wood, from large desks to walk-in closets, give a warm feel to the rooms. With TVs in both the bedroom and the sitting-work area, a two-line telephone system with data port, and an in-room printer-fax-scanner, there is little need for the business center. Large bathrooms have a separate shower stall. For the indulgent, there is a fully equipped fitness center and spa, as well as a sun deck on the 53rd floor with a current pool and whirlpool. You can watch the lights on the Chao Phraya River and the city skyline from the excellent Chinese restaurant (on the 60th floor) or the bar lounge (on the 59th). ✉ *21/100 South Sathorn Rd., 10120,* ☎ *02/679–1200,* FAX *02/679–1199. 198 rooms. 2 restaurants, bar, pool, spa, health club, business services, meeting rooms. AE, DC, MC, V.* ✍

$$$ 🏨 **Amari Airport Hotel.** If you need to stay within walking distance of the airport, this is your only option. A covered passageway leads from the International Terminal to the hotel, which is modern and utilitarian, with a helpful staff. Rooms are functional and efficient. The daytime (8 AM–6 PM) rate for travelers waiting for connections is B600 for stays up to three hours, and video screens in public areas display schedules of flight arrivals and departures. ✉ *333 Chert Wudhakas Rd., Don Muang 10210,* ☎ *02/566–1020,* FAX *02/566–1941. 440 rooms. 2 restaurants, coffee shop, pool, nightclub, meeting rooms. AE, DC, MC, V.* ✍

$$$ 🏨 **Amari Boulevard.** This hotel is just in from Sukhumvit Road, down a one-way soi and close to the tourist action. The original building opened in 1990 and the glass pyramid-shape tower, known as the Krungthep Wing, opened in 1992. The use of dark wood in rooms in the older part give a traditional ambiance. Particularly attractive are those overlooking the pool. The new tower is more modern and airy, with pastel furnishings. The bathrooms here are also slightly larger and have a separate shower stall. The new wing costs an extra B1,000. The ground floor lobby is vast, with plenty of sitting areas, and the casual Peppermill restaurant serves a range of Thai, Japanese, and international dishes. ✉ *2 Sukhumvit Soi 5, 10400,* ☎ *02/255–2930,* FAX *02/255–2950. 315 rooms. Restaurant, bar, pool, health club, business services, meeting rooms. AE, DC, MC, V.* ✍

$$$ 🏨 **Ambassador Hotel.** This hotel—one of Bangkok's biggest, with three wings of guest rooms, a complex of restaurants, and a shopping center—is virtually a mini-city, which may explain the impersonal service and limited helpfulness of the staff. Milling convention delegates in the colossal lobbies contribute to the businesslike atmosphere. Guest rooms are compact, decorated in standard pastel. The Tower Wing offers the most comfort and should be chosen over the lower-price Sukhumvit Wing, which is exposed to the noise from busy Sukhumvit Road. Be aware that the least expensive rooms are very small. You may also want to select a room above the sixth floor to avoid noise from the hotel's popular clubs: the Dickens Pub garden bar, the Flamingo Disco, and The Club for rock music. ✉ *171 Sukhumvit Soi 11–13, 10110,* ☎ *02/254–0444,* FAX *02/253–4123. 1,026 rooms and 24 suites. 12 restaurants, coffee shop, snack bar, pool, massage, 2 tennis courts, health club, business services, meeting rooms. AE, DC, MC, V.*

$$$ 🏨 **Central Plaza Hotel.** Given its location in the middle of one of the city's fastest-growing business districts, most of the hotel's clientele are business travelers. The west side of the hotel has a view of the former Railway Golf Course; the remaining sides look out on the city's hell-bent horizontal and vertical growth. The refreshingly cool, green lobby is a welcome hideaway, the atmosphere enhanced by the soothing white noise of a cascading waterfall. Rooms are graceful, with understated floral designs; Thai prints, bronze mythological figures, and temple-dog lampstands remind guests that they are in Thailand. The two floors of the Dynasty Club offer even better accommodations, with large, handsomely furnished sitting areas, stereo units, minibars, kitchen facilities, and dining areas plus valet service and lounge access. Among the hotel's numerous restaurants and bars is Dynasty, a popular spot for Chinese cuisine. ⊠ *1695 Phaholyothin Rd., 10210,* ☎ *02/541–1234,* FAX *02/541–1087. 421 rooms. 3 restaurants, pool, health club, business services, meeting rooms. AE, DC, MC, V.*

$$$ 🏨 **Holiday Inn Crowne Plaza.** Located next to the Gem Tower, the Holiday Inn has two towers: the smaller of the two, the Plaza Tower, is over 20 years old with cheaper and smaller rooms than the newer Crowne Tower, which opened in 1991. You can usually get a 50% discount on published rates, making a stay here good value. Not so otherwise. Even the newer tower shows signs of wear. The high ceilings and vast spaces of public areas make it seem rather like New York's Grand Central Station and the hotel survives by catering to airline staff and tour groups. However, the two executive floors are geared to the business traveler, with check-in and -out at the concierge desk in the executive lounge. Rooms have light color schemes, plenty of lamps, lots of draperies, and a bathroom with separate shower stall. The executive suites are ill-conceived—the bathroom and bedroom are smaller to make up for the extra sitting area. ⊠ *981 Silom Rd., 10500,* ☎ *02/238–4300,* FAX *02/238–5289. 385 rooms in the Plaza Tower, 341 rooms in the Crowne Tower. 3 restaurants, pool, 2 tennis courts, health club, business services, meeting rooms. AE, DC, MC, V.* 🐾

$$$ 🏨 **Imperial Queens Park.** The largest hotel in Bangkok stands with its two towers just off Sukhumvit and next to a small park (ideal for jogging). With seven restaurants, numerous shops, two swimming pools, a vast lobby, and more space for meetings and conventions than other Bangkok hotels, the Imperial Queens Park is a city in itself. Standard rooms are reasonably spacious and well laid out, with a good-sized desk, but the nicer (more expensive) rooms are the junior corner suites, with a separate work area and plenty of natural light. Many of the rooms have whirlpool tubs (of the dated variety) and a separate shower stall. Rooms have only one telephone line, which doubles as a data port. To fill its 1,400 rooms, management makes special arrangements for long-term (a month or more) guests. ⊠ *199 Sukhumvit Soi 22, 10110,* ☎ *02/261–9000,* FAX *02/261–9530. 1,090 double rooms and 310 suites. 7 restaurants, pool, 2 tennis courts, health club, business services, convention center, meeting rooms. AE, DC, MC, V.* 🐾

$$$ 🏨 **Montien.** This hotel across the street from Patpong, convenient to the corporations along Silom Road, has been remarkably well maintained over its two decades. The concierge is particularly helpful. The guest rooms are spacious, though not decoratively inspired. They do, however, have private safes. Prices are slightly higher than you would expect, but the hotel will give discounts. It's also the only hotel with in-house fortune-tellers who will read your palm or your stars for B250. ⊠ *54 Suriwongse Rd., 10500,* ☎ FAX *02/234–8060. 500 rooms. 2 restaurants, coffee shop, pool, nightclub, business services, meeting rooms. AE, DC, MC, V.* 🐾

$$$ 🏨 **Narai Hotel.** Conveniently near the business, shopping, and entertainment areas on Silom Road, this friendly, modern hotel offers utilitarian but comfortable rooms. At the low end of this price category, the hotel is a good value, given its cheerful rooms and high level of service. The most distinguishing feature is Bangkok's only revolving restaurant, La Rotonde Grill, on the 15th floor. ⊠ *222 Silom Rd., 10500,* ☎ *02/257–0100,* FAX *02/236–7161. 490 rooms and 10 suites. 3 restaurants, coffee shop, pool, health club, nightclub, business services. AE, DC, MC, V.* 🐾

$$$ 🏨 **Siam Inter-Continental.** On 26 landscaped acres in the center of Bangkok, the Siam Inter-Continental has a soaring pagoda roof and beautiful gardens. Its modern Thai architecture, lofty lobby, and sense of space make this hotel stand out. Each of the air-conditioned rooms is stylishly decorated with teak furniture, a trim, upholstered wing chair and love seat, and a cool blue color scheme. Especially attractive are the teak-panel bathrooms with radios, telephones, and hair dryers. ⊠ *967 Rama I Rd., 10330,* ☎ *02/253–0355,* FAX *02/253–2275. 411 rooms and suites. 4 restaurants, 2 bars, pool, driving range, putting green, health club, jogging, meeting rooms. AE, DC, MC, V.* ✍

$$ 🏨 **Bel-Air Princess.** Two hundred yards down Soi 5 from clamorous Sukhumvit is this quiet, well-managed hotel. It gets its fair share of tour groups, but for the most part the lobby and lounge are cool and peaceful, and the downstairs restaurant is a good place to relax over a light meal. Northern Indian cooking, lightly spiced for Western taste, is served in the formal Tiffin Room. Spacious, carpeted guest rooms, with two queen-size beds or one king, are large enough for a round table and chairs as well as the standard TV-cabinet-desk. Personal safes, in-house movies, hair dryers, and tea- and coffeemakers are pluses, and the bowl of fruit on each landing is a nice touch. Rooms at the back of the hotel overlook Soi 7 and beyond; front rooms overlook the pool. ⊠ *16 Sukhumvit Soi 5, 10110,* ☎ *02/253–4300,* FAX *02/255–8850. 160 rooms. 2 restaurants, bar, pool, health club. AE, DC, MC, V.* ✍

$$ 🏨 **Century Hotel.** Its location in the northern part of downtown is convenient to the airport. The rooms, though neat and clean, are small and dark. The coffee shop–bar is open 24 hours, a plus for travelers with early morning flights. ⊠ *9 Ratchaprarop Rd., 10400,* ☎ *02/246–7800. 240 rooms. Bar, coffee shop, pool. AE, DC, MC, V.*

$$ 🏨 **City Lodge.** There are two City Lodges off Sukhumvit, one on Soi 9 and this one, a tad better, on Soi 19. Both are part of the Amari hotel group, but aimed at the frugal traveler. The charmless, compact rooms are functional, designed for efficiency of space. Business services are minimal, but you can use those at the nearby sister hotel, the Amari Boulevard (as well as its swimming pool). The coffee shop–restaurant specializes in Italian food at dinner. ⊠ *Sukhumvit Soi 19, 10110,* ☎ *02/254–4783,* FAX *02/255–7340. 35 rooms. Restaurant. AE, DC, MC, V.* ✍

$$ 🏨 **Grand China Princess.** One good reason for staying in Chinatown is that it's the center of old Bangkok, with lots of exotic turn-of-the-century Asian ambience. Another reason is this hotel. It occupies the top two-thirds of a 25-story tower from which the guest rooms have panoramic views of the city. Room 2202, for example, gives you a morning view of the Temple of the Dawn, the Golden Mount, and Wat Tuk. Since the rooms form a segment of a circle, they are interestingly shaped. The furnishings are unexciting but functional, and all the rooms have safes and satellite TV. The bathrooms are on the small side. Service is friendly, and the reception floor (10th) has a welcoming bar, lounge, and coffee shop. Carpeted in a huge lotus design, the restaurant, Siang Ping Loh (Cantonese and Szechuan fare), is well worth a visit in its own right. ⊠ *215 Corner of Yaowarat and Ratchawongse Rd., Samphantawongse, 10100,* ☎ *02/224–9977,* FAX *02/224–7999. 155 rooms. Restaurant, coffee shop, health club, business services. AE, DC, MC, V.* ✍

$$ 🏨 **La Residence.** You would expect to find this small town-house hotel on the Left Bank of Paris, not in Bangkok. Though it's a little overpriced, La Residence suits the frequent visitor who wants a low-key hotel. The staff, however, can be abrupt at times. The guest rooms are small, but the furnishings—pale-wood cabinets, pastel draperies—give them a fresh, airy feel. The restaurant, with Thai and European food, also serves as a sitting area for guests. ⊠ *173/8–9 Suriwongse Rd., 10150,* ☎ *02/233–3301. 23 rooms. Restaurant, laundry service. AE, DC.*

$$ 🏨 **Swiss Lodge.** This small hotel off Silom Road near the Dusit Thani is the closest equivalent to a boutique hotel in Bangkok. Rooms are furnished in light colors that give a crisp, fresh look. Single rooms are really

the size of small doubles; doubles are a bit larger, so as to fit in king-size beds. All rooms have built-in safes, bathrobes, and ample work space, and the telephone line can be transferred to your computer. Bathrooms are compact but fully equipped. Half of the guest-room floors are no-smoking. A very small outdoor pool and sundeck are on the fifth floor, and a helpful business center has computer facilities and a small meeting room for up to six people. The second floor has a bar lounge. On the ground floor, a coffee shop–style dining room serves Thai and Continental food. ⊠ *3 Convent Rd., 10500,* ☎ *02/233–5345,* ☒ *02/236–9425. 57 rooms. Restaurant, bar, pool, business services. AE, DC, MC, V.* ⊛

\$\$ 🏨 **Tara Hotel.** This hotel is in the developing restaurant-and-nightlife section of Sukhumvit Road. The lobby is spacious, lined with teak carvings. The check-in lounge serves tea or coffee while formalities are completed. Guest rooms, which are on the small side, are decorated in pastels; many overlook the eighth-floor terrace garden with swimming pool. ⊠ *Sukhumvit Soi 26, 10110,* ☎ *02/259–0053,* ☒ *02/259–2900. 200 rooms and 20 suites. Restaurant, coffee shop, pool, meeting rooms. AE, DC, MC, V.* ⊛

\$\$ 🏨 **Tawana Ramada.** Although this hotel has hosted tourists for many years, continual refurbishing keeps the rooms looking smart. You can choose double or king-size beds. Bathrooms are satisfactory rather than grand. Each room has a safe and cable TV, but, unlike many Bangkok hotels, no in-room tea/coffeemaker. A few rooms have a balcony (not worth the extra cost) overlooking the very modest pool. Published rates are a hefty B4,000, though the majority of guests—package tour clients—don't pay anywhere near that amount. Ask for a corporate rate. The hotel's location, in the heart of the Silom-Suriwongse business and entertainment district, gives easy access to Bangkok's sights. The coffee shop stays open until 2 AM and the Grill offers an international buffet of some repute for B312. ⊠ *80 Suriwongse Rd., 10500,* ☎ *02/236–0361,* ☒ *02/236–3738. 265 room. 2 restaurants, pool, health club, business services, meeting rooms. AE, DC, MC, V.*

\$\$ 🏨 **Wall Street Inn.** Its moderate rates (at the low-end of this price range) and location in the business district make the Wall Street Inn an option. Japanese travelers make up the greatest percentage of guests, due perhaps to the many Japanese offices and nightclubs in the immediate area. Standard rooms are small and windowless, but functional. Furnishings in natural-grain wood are reasonably attractive, though the walls are bare. Bathtubs in the plain bathrooms are cramped. Deluxe rooms have full-size tubs and windows, though the quality of the view may make you wonder if windows are a good thing. There is no pool or health club, but the hotel has a traditional Thai massage parlor, and Lumphini Park is nearby for jogging. ⊠ *37/20–24 Soi Suriwong Plaza, Suriwongse Rd., 10500,* ☎ *02/235–6068,* ☒ *02/236–3619. 75 rooms. Coffee shop, massage, business services. AE, DC, MC, V.*

\$–\$\$ 🏨 **Baiyoke Suite Hotel.** Many a traveler has passed through this skyscraper hotel and it shows, and its location off Pratunam market and shopping complex may be a tad inconvenient. However, with a promotional price of B1,600, it's good value, especially if you plan to be in Bangkok for some time. The rooms are large and sparsely furnished, with a separate sitting area, pantry-style sink, and cooking area. The hotel's lobby is on the fifth floor, the pool on the 11th. Rooms on the higher floors have panoramic views of the city. At the very top is a revolving restaurant (under separate management). ⊠ *130 Ratchaprarop Rd., Rajthawee,, 10400,* ☎ *02/255–0330,* ☒ *02/254–5553. 202 suites. Restaurant, pool, business center. AE, MC, V.*

\$–\$\$ 🏨 **Bangkok Centre.** There are few hotels around the Hualamphong Railway Station, in part because it is not a desirable area in which to stay. However, if you do need a place to rest close by, the Bangkok Centre has clean rooms, though the furnishings and decor are in need of a complete overhaul. The main restaurant offers Brazilian fare and is known for its buffet lunch. The day rate (to rest between trains) is B500, less than half the normal rate. ⊠ *328 Pharam 4 (Rama 4), 10500,* ☎ *02/ 238–4848,* FAX *02/236-1862. 80 rooms. Restaurant, coffee shop, pool, meeting rooms. AE, DC, MC, V.*

$–$$ 🏨 **Manohra Hotel.** An expansive and spotless marble lobby is one of the nicest things about this hotel between the river and Patpong. Rooms have pastel walls, patterned bedcovers, and dark-green carpets. There is a roof garden for sunbathing and the Buccaneer Night Club for evening action. A word of caution: if the Manohra is fully booked, the staff may suggest its new sister hotel, the Ramada (no relation to the American-managed Ramada) on New Road. Decline unless you are desperate; it is overpriced and has small, poorly designed rooms. ⊠ *412 Suriwongse Rd., 10500,* ☎ *02/234–5070,* FAX *02/237–7662. 230 rooms. 2 restaurants, coffee shop, indoor pool, nightclub, meeting rooms. AE, DC, MC, V.*

$–$$ 🏨 **Park Hotel.** Although the lobby area, lounge, and bar are far from being designer decorated, this hotel has a fresh crispness to it not often found in its price category. Ample light makes the guest rooms cheerful, and bathrooms are small and clean. The deluxe doubles have space for a desk. There is also a small pool in the garden. ⊠ *Sukhumvit Soi 7, 10110,* ☎ *02/255–4300,* FAX *02/255–4309. 139 rooms. Restaurant, bar, coffee shop, pool, travel services. MC, V.*

$–$$ 🏨 **Princess Hotel.** This small, smart hotel in the Grand Palace part of town is close to major tourist attractions. The immediate vicinity, which is dominated by numerous small merchants, is deserted in the evening. You can dine in one of the four hotel restaurants (Chinese, Italian, Japanese, and Thai-Western) or take a short taxi ride to a number of fine riverside restaurants. The small lobby has gardens on two sides, and recessed crystal chandeliers and potted plants complete the tranquil ambience. The rooms have subdued color combinations that set off the dark-wood furnishings. Spacious, well-lighted desks provide adequate work space. The bathrooms and tubs, however, are very small, with rust stains beginning to appear. All the deluxe rooms, costing 8% more, have balconies facing the pool. Executive rooms are on the Princess Floor, which has its own private lobby and breakfast room. Special discounted rates, about half the published rates, are usually available. ⊠ *269 Larn Luang Rd., 10100,* ☎ *02/281–3088,* FAX *02/280–1314. 160 rooms. 4 restaurants, pool, business services. AE, DC, MC, V.* ✧

$–$$ 🏨 **Silom Plaza Hotel.** This hotel in the shopping area on Silom Road has an open lobby area with a lounge. The compact rooms have modern decor in soft colors; the more expensive ones have river views. The hotel caters to business travelers who want to be close to Silom Road. Service is quick. The facilities are limited, but all the entertainment you could wish for is nearby. ⊠ *320 Silom Rd., 10500,* ☎ *02/236–0333,* FAX *02/236–7562. 209 rooms. Restaurant, coffee shop, indoor pool, sauna, health club, meeting rooms. AE, DC, MC, V.*

$–$$ 🏨 **Silom Village Inn.** Clean, neat, and friendly, with extremely reasonable
★ prices (about B1,000, with the invariable discount) describes this small hotel. The king-size beds leave just enough space for a desk and a couple of chairs. Bathrooms are new and functional. Choose a room at the back of the hotel to avoid the Silom Road street noise. The reception desk staff is helpful and reliable at taking messages. A small restaurant is good for breakfast and snacks and also serves Italian food, but the Seafood Village Plaza next door is tempting. ⊠ *Silom Village Trade Centre, 286 Silom Rd., 10500,* ☎ *635–6810/7,* FAX *02/635– 6817. 34 rooms. Restaurant. AE, DC, MC, V.*

$–$$ ⊡ **Tower Inn.** The hotel's name is appropriate; it is a tall skinny build-
ing on Silom Road near the Thai International Airways office. The top
floor has a health club and swimming pool from which you can glimpse
the Chao Phraya River. The reception desk, bar, and small lounge are
on the ground floor, and the coffee shop (Thai and Continental food)
is on the second floor. The rooms are as spacious as those at the
Shangri-La, with plenty of light flooding in from picture windows. The
furnishings, however, are utilitarian—two queen-size beds and a cab-
inet that holds the TV and serves as a desk. The bathroom is smallish—not one to linger in. You can usually negotiate a 30% discount
with no trouble at all, which brings the room rate down to about B1,400.
⊠ *533 Silom Rd., 10500,* ☎ *02/237–8300,* FAX *02/237–8286. 150 rooms.
Restaurant, pool, health club, travel services. AE, DC, MC, V.*

$ ⊡ **The Executive House.** Though it offers only limited services, this hotel's
reception staff will sometimes help with travel questions, and the coffee shop will deliver food to your room until midnight. The rooms are
spacious for the price, the air-conditioning works, and, even if the decor
is drab and a bit run-down, the rooms on the upper floors have plenty
of light. The penthouse rooms—on the 15th–18th floors—are flooded
with it. Rooms with a river view are B200 more than those with a city
view. Over the last few years, room prices have steadily increased, with
no improvement in facilities, and the lack of tourist services makes this
hotel more suited for visitors already familiar with Bangkok. The hotel
is next to the Manohra Hotel, down a short driveway. ⊠ *410/3–4 Suriwongse Rd., 10500,* ☎ *02/235–1206,* FAX *02/236–1482. 120 rooms.
Coffee shop. MC, V.*

$ ⊡ **First House.** Tucked behind the Pratunam market on a soi off Phetch-
buri, the First House offers excellent value for a full-service hotel in this
price range. The small lobby serves as a meeting place where guests can
read the complimentary newspapers. Off to the left, the Saranyuth coffee shop-restaurant, open 24 hours, serves Thai and Western dishes. The
compact rooms are carpeted and amply furnished but so dark as to be
depressing during the day. Bathrooms are clean, though patches of
rough plaster and drab fixtures don't encourage leisurely grooming. But
the reasonable rates, the security, and the helpfulness of the staff all contribute to making this hotel worth noting. ⊠ *14/20–29 Phetchburi Soi
19, Pratunam, 10400,* ☎ *02/254–0303,* FAX *02/254–3101. 84 rooms.
Coffee shop, travel services. AE, DC, MC, V.*

$ ⊡ **Majestic Suites.** On Sukhumvit between Soi 4 and Soi 6, Majestic
Suites has no actual suites, only studio, superior, and deluxe rooms.
Those barely large enough to fit a queen-size bed run just over B1,000;
the much larger deluxe rooms cost B1,800 and have the added touches
of coffeemaking facilities and bathrobes. All rooms have safes, minibars, and hair dryers. Furnishings are bright and fresh—the hotel
opened in 1999. Rooms at the back are quieter but have no view, whereas
the street side, though noisier, has lots of action to watch. ⊠ *110
Sukhumvit Rd., 10110,* ☎ *02/656–8220,* FAX *02/656–8201. 55 rooms.
Bar, coffee shop, business services. AE, DC, MC, V.* ✍

$ ⊡ **New Trocadero.** This hotel, between Patpong and the Chao Phraya
River, has been a Westerner's standby for decades—and the furnishings have borne the brunt. The smallish rooms have queen-size-plus
beds and clean bathrooms. Service is friendly, and there's a helpful travel-
tour desk in the lobby. The New Trocadero is associated with two adjacent, very similar hotels, the Peninsula and the Fuji. ⊠ *343 Suriwongse
Rd., 10500,* ☎ *02/234–8920,* FAX *02/236–5526. 130 rooms. Coffee shop,
pool, travel services. AE, DC, MC, V.*

$ ⊡ **Parkway Inn.** Amid the commotion on Sukhumvit stands this small,
boutique-style hotel above a tailor's shop and next to the Landmark
Hotel. The reception desk, a small bar lounge, and two bedrooms are

on the first floor. The other 22 rooms (priced just under B1,000) are on the floors above. Though not very large, the rooms don't seem cramped. Furnishings are comfortable and include cable TV and a refrigerator. The tiled bathrooms are compact but more than adequate. If you can do without looking on busy Sukhumvit, rooms at the back are the quietest. ⊠ *132 Sukhumvit Rd., 10400,* ☎ *02/255–3711,* 𝔽𝔸𝕏 *02/254–2180. 24 rooms. Bar. AE, MC, V.*

$ 🏨 **Plaza Hotel.** This building used to be an apartment complex until fifteen years ago, when it was turned into a hotel—rooms on the seventh floor and above still have a kitchen counter and sink. Though the furnishings are hardly inspiring, the size of the rooms easily accommodates the king-size beds. The staff are low-key and friendly. Though the lobby area and corridors are a little shabby, its convenient location in the heart of the Silom/Suriwongse business and entertainment district makes the Plaza very good value at B1,000 a night. ⊠ *118 Suriwongse Rd., 10500,* ☎ *02/235–1760,* 𝔽𝔸𝕏 *02/237–0746. 158 rooms. Coffee shop, pool. AE, DC, MC, V.*

$ 🏨 **Stable Lodge.** Down a small, partly residential street off Sukhumvit Road, this small, quiet hotel seems more like a guest house. Videos are shown in the lounge in the evening. Since the new owners acquired the property (formerly Mermaid's), prices have climbed to around B1,000. Rooms are clean and neat with queen-size beds. The more expensive rooms have private balconies, and those at the back are the quietest. A pool in the garden is an added attraction. The coffee shop serves Thai and Western food all day, and there is a garden barbecue at night. ⊠ *39 Sukhumvit Soi 8, 10110,* ☎ *02/653–0017,* 𝔽𝔸𝕏 *02/253–5125. 40 rooms, most with private baths. Restaurant, pool. AE, MC, V.*

$ 🏨 **Top Inn.** In a busy section of Sukhumvit, this new hotel has small, air-conditioned rooms for B850. Rooms have either twin beds or one queen. A TV, refrigerator, and a couple of chairs make up the furnishings. Bathrooms are compact, but tiled and clean. Notwithstanding the smallness of the rooms, the newness of the hotel and its cleanliness makes it a possible choice if you really want to be close to the nightlife of Sukhumvit and Soi 4. Rooms at the back are the quietest. ⊠ *128 Sukhumvit Rd., 10110,* ☎ *02/656–8290,* 𝔽𝔸𝕏 *02/253–6077. 12 rooms. Coffee shop. AE, MC, V.*

¢ 🏨 **The Atlanta.** Charles Henn, a part-time professor, caters to visiting
★ scholars and frugal travelers who often return again and again. The dining room and lobby are straight out of the 1950s, with leatherette banquettes and a circular sofa. Beyond the lobby is the garden, with tables and chairs and even desks for budding authors, as well as an excellent swimming pool. The accommodations are simple and without TV, but they're clean (rooms were repainted in 1998 and 1999) and very spacious for the rock-bottom rates. Some rooms have air-conditioning, some have fans and ventilators, and some have balconies; most have personal safes. In the dining room, classical music is played before 5 PM, jazz thereafter, and a movie from Henn's videotape collection is shown after dinner. The menu, which explains the ingredients of each dish, makes interesting reading (Henn is a food critic), and the Thai food is superb, with a wide vegetarian selection. In the crass glitter of modern Bangkok, the Atlanta is an oasis—and one of the best values in town. ⊠ *78 Sukhumvit Soi 2, 10110,* ☎ *02/252–1650 or 02/252–6069,* 𝔽𝔸𝕏 *02/656–8123 or 02/255–2151. 59 rooms. Restaurant, pool, travel services. No credit cards.*

¢ 🏨 **River City Guest House.** It's a shame this small hotel, a block from the water's edge, has no view of the river. But then if it did, the price of a room would probably quadruple. As it is, B500 gives you a modest air-conditioned room with a double bed, and a table and chair. The small bathrooms have hot and cold water showers and exposed plumbing for decoration! Ask for a room with a window. The trick is to find the hotel: walk upriver from the Sheraton, past the River City Shopping Centre, and as the soi bends to the right, the hotel is on the right. This location gives you easy access to the marvelous sois of Chinatown and the river ferries, and puts you within walking distance of Suriwongse and Silom roads. ⊠ *11/4 Soi Rong Nam Khang 1 (Soi 24), Charoen Krung Rd., 10100,* ☎ *02/235–1429,* FAX *02/237–3127. 17 rooms with bath or shower. Coffee shop. MC, V.*

¢ 🏨 **River View Guest House.** Down a tiny soi on the edge of Chinatown and just one house in from the Chao Phraya River, this family-run hotel is unique for being a budget hotel with river views. The rooms are shabby but clean. The river-view rooms (B450) are fan-cooled and without a full bathroom, and the rooms with only a limited view of the river have air-conditioning and a bath (B700). Tiny rooms with shared bathrooms cost only B150. The coffee shop, on the eighth floor, has a spectacular view since this is where the Chao Phraya makes a turn. This hotel is not for everyone, and there aren't many Westerners around. It could also use refurbishing. The easiest way to find it is to walk upriver from the Royal Orchid Sheraton, keeping as close to the river as you can. After about 1,000 yards, you'll see the guest house's sign pointing down a soi on the left. ⊠ *768 Soi Panurangsri, Songvad Rd., 10100,* ☎ *02/ 234–5429,* FAX *02/236–6199. 37 rooms, half with bath. Restaurant. V.*

¢ 🏨 **Sri Kasem Hotel.** Across the klong from Hualamphong Train Station, this small hotel is ideally located if you come in on a late train or are departing early in the morning. The building is old and so is the hotel—don't expect modern amenities. However, the sparsely furnished rooms are air-conditioned, the bathrooms are clean, the staff is helpful, and the price is right. ⊠ *1860 Krung Kasem Rd., 10500,* ☎ *02/225–0132,* FAX *02/225–4705. 26 rooms. Coffee shop. No cards.*

Nightlife and the Arts

The English-language newspapers, the *Bangkok Post* and *The Nation,* have good information on current festivals, exhibitions, and nightlife. TAT's weekly *Where* also lists events. Monthly *Metro* magazine has an extensive listings section and offers reviews of new hot spots.

Nightlife

The law requires that bars and nightclubs close at 2 AM, but Bangkok never sleeps, and many restaurants and street stalls stay open for late-night carousing. The city is awash with bars catering to all tastes, from the Oriental Hotel's classy Bamboo Bar right down to the sleaze of watching sex acts while you drink. Soi 55 (also called Soi Thonglor), off Sukhumvit Road, has several good bars and nightclubs. Soi Sarasin, across from Lumphini Park, is packed with friendly pubs and cafés that are popular with yuppie Thais and expats. And it's only in Bangkok that would you ever find a phenomenon like Royal City Avenue (called "RCA"). By about 11 PM this strip, nearly deserted by day, used to be thronged with thousands of young Thais walking up and down among the 160 bars lining the avenue and blaring loud music. With the economic crisis of 1997, RCA lost its wild gaiety and many bars closed, but as the economy regains its strength and newer nightspots go stale, people are returning to RCA and its ever-ready drinking and music joints.

Unfortunately, tourism has been accompanied by the most lurid forms of nightlife geared to the male tourist. Live sex shows, though officially banned, are still found in three areas of Bangkok. Patpong is the biggest, and it includes three streets that link Suriwongse and Silom roads. Patpong 1 and 2 are packed with go-go bars that have hostesses by the dozen. Sex shows are generally found one flight up. Patpong 3 caters mostly to gays but also to lesbians. Note that Patpong is quite safe and well patrolled by police, and it even has a Night Market where Thais take visiting friends to shop. Soi Cowboy, off Sukhumvit Road at Soi 21, is a less raunchy, more easygoing version of Patpong. The bars are considerably tamer; some have go-go dancers, whereas others are good for a quiet beer, with or without a temporary companion. Nana Plaza, at Soi 4 off Sukhumvit Road, is the most popular with expats and expanded in the late '90s. The plaza is now packed with three floors of bars; most of them have hostesses, but there are some quieter places, too. The newest bars have spilled out along Soi 4 itself. All three nightspots are near skytrain stations, but keep in mind that the trains stop just after midnight. Watch out for scams if you indulge, including aggressive hostesses, touts that promise a lot for a little money, and the copying of credit cards (it's best to pay with cash).

BARS AND PUBS

You can get a decent pint of (chilled) beer and pub grub at the **Bobbies Arms** (⊠ Car Park Blvd., second level, Patpong 2 Rd., ☎ 02/233–6828). On weekends, a live band plays, and various excuses are made for a party—anything from St. Patrick's Day to St. George's Day. A good place to start carousing is **Brown Sugar** (⊠ 231/20 Soi Sarasin, ☎ 02/250–0103). The popular **Bull's Head Pub** (⊠ Sukhumvit Soi 33, near the Phrom Phong skytrain station, ☎ 02/259–4444) offers a Quiz Night on the second Tuesday of each month. Amid the swinging nightlife of Nana (Soi 4), **Bus Stop** (⊠ 14 Sukhumvit Soi 4, ☎ 02/251–9222) is a pleasantly relaxed pub with outdoor seating and grilled fare. Two large TVs play sports channels, and hostesses are not pushy.

For years now, **Delaney's Irish Pub** (⊠ 1/5–6 Convent Rd., near the Sala Daeng skytrain station, ☎ 02/266–7160) has been standing room only during evening music hours. Beers include Guinness on tap, and good Western food is served. The **Hard Rock Cafe** (⊠ Siam Sq., ☎ 02/254–0830) remains popular for Western food and music. **The Hemingway Bar & Grill** (⊠ Sukhumvit Soi 55, ☎ 02/392–3599), modeled on a log cabin, is popular with Thais and expats. **The Londoner Brew Pub** (⊠ 591 UBCH Building, in the basement, Sukhumvit Rd. at the corner of Soi 33, ☎ no phone) makes its own "real ale." British fare is served at tables, booths, and the bar.

The Old Dragon (⊠ 29/78–81 Royal City Ave., ☎ 02/203–0972), or Old Leng, is filled with oddities, from wooden cinema seats to etchings of Chinese characters on old mirrors. The owner claims that only the music machines, cash register, and most of the guests are younger than 50 years. The food served is a mix of Chinese and Thai (snacks are also available). **Route 66** (⊠ 29/37 Royal City Ave., ☎ 02/203–0407 or 02/203–0407) celebrates the famous American highway and is often packed. **Saxophone Pub & Restaurant** (⊠ 3/8 Victory Monument, Phayathai Rd., near the Victory Monument skytrain station, ☎ 02/246–5472) offers great music and good food and proves popular with locals and expats. The **Old West Saloon** (⊠ 231/17 Soi Sarasin, ☎ 02/252–9510) re-creates the atmosphere of America's Old West aided by a four-piece band and a happy hour.

CABARET

The largest troupe of performing transvestites is reputed to be the **Calypso Cabaret** (⊠ In the Asia Hotel, 296 Phayathai Road, ☎ 02/653–3960 or 02/653–3962 before 6 PM; 02/216–8937 or 02/216–8938 after 6), with nightly shows at 8:15 and 9:45. For live bands and internationally known nightclub artists, try the **Tiara** (⊠ Rama IV Rd., ☎ 02/236–0450, ext 2449), the Dusit Thani's penthouse restaurant.

CULTURAL SHOWS

Silom Village (⊠ 286 Silom Rd., ☎ 02/234–4448), open 10 AM–10 PM, may be rather touristy, but it appeals also to Thais. The block-size complex has shops, restaurants, and performances of classical Thai dance. At a couple of the restaurants, chefs cook tasty morsels in the open—you select what suits your fancy or order from a menu. Silom Village also has a cultural show at **Ruan Thep** (☎ 02/635–6313). Dinner starts at 7 and showtime is at 8:30. Dinner and a show costs B450; the show only is B350.

DANCE CLUBS

Although most hotels have discos that were popular in the mid '90s, there are better places to dance, including several good dance bars on RCA (☞ *above*). **Concept CM2** (⊠ Siam Square 392/44 Rama 1, Soi 6, ☎ 02/255–6888) is a posh nightclub in the Novotel Siam. If you want to really cut loose try **Deeper** (⊠ 82 Silom Rd. Soi 4, ☎ 02/233–2830). The in-crowd goes to **Taurus** (⊠ Sukhumvit Soi 26, ☎ 02/261–3991).

DINNER CRUISES

Boats built to look like traditional Thai houses or refurbished rice barges serve a Western or Thai dinner while cruising the Chao Phraya River. Hotel staff make reservations, as these two-hour evening cruises are usually strictly for tourists. **The Horizon** (⊠ Shangri-La Hotel, 89 Soi Wat Suan Phu, New Rd., ☎ 02/236–7777) has cruise departures at 8 PM. **The Manohra Moon** (⊠ Marriott Royal Garden Riverside Hotel, 257/1–3 Charoen Krung Rd., Thonburi ☎ 02/476–0021 or 02/476–00222, ext. 1416) has lunch (B800) and dinner (B1,200) cruises. **Yok Yor** (☞ Dining, *above*) is one of the few cruises likely to be all Thai.

JAZZ BARS

For a quiet drink accompanied by easy-listening live jazz try the Oriental Hotel's **Bamboo Bar** (⊠ Oriental Lane, ☎ 02/236–4000). **Fabb Fashion Cafe** (⊠ In the Mercury Tower, 540 Ploenchit Rd., near the Chidlom skytrain station, ☎ 02/658–2003) plays jazz in the early evening and offers good Thai and Western food. **Witch's Tavern** (⊠ Sukhumvit Soi 55, down from the Thong Lor skytrain station, ☎ 02/391–9791) has classical jazz in a cozy Victorian atmosphere. It also serves hearty English fare.

The Arts

CLASSICAL THAI DANCE

Thai classical dance is the epitome of grace. Themes for the dance drama are taken from the *Ramayana*. A series of controlled gestures uses eye contact, ankle and neck movements, and hands and fingers to convey the stories' drama. It is accompanied by a woodwind called the *piphat*, which sounds like an oboe, and percussion instruments.

Various restaurants offer a classical dance show with dinner. **Baan Thai** (⊠ Sukhumvit Soi 22, ☎ 02/258–5403) is popular for those staying at hotels in the eastern part of Bangkok. At the **National Theatre** (⊠ Na Phra That Rd., ☎ 02/221–5861 or 02/224–1342), performances are given most days at 10 AM and 3 PM, and special performances are also held on the last Friday of each month at 5:30 PM. The **Sala Rim Naam** (☞ Dining, *above*) in the Oriental Hotel puts on a beautiful show with an excellent dinner.

Outdoor Activities and Sports

Participant Sports

GOLF

There are good golf courses in and around Bangkok, and although weekend play requires advance booking, tee times are usually available during the week. Greens fees are approximately B700 weekdays and B1,500 weekends, with caddy fees about B100. **Krungthep Sports Golf**

Course (✉ B.P. 522, 10 Huamark, ☎ 02/374–6063) is attractively laid out with fairways flanked by bougainvillea and pine trees, and elevated greens surrounded by sand traps. The **Navatanee Golf Course** (✉ 22 Mul Sukhaphiban 2 Rd., Bangkapi, ☎ 02/374–7077), designed by Robert Trent Jones, is thought to be the most challenging. The **Rose Garden Golf Course** (✉ 4/8 Sukhumvit Soi 3, ☎ 02/253–0295) is a pleasant, undemanding course.

HEALTH CLUBS

The **Clark Hatch Athletic Club** has branches at Thaniya Plaza (✉ Silom Rd., ☎ 02/231–2250); Charn Issara Tower II (☎ 02/308–2779); Amari Watergate Hotel (☎ 02/653–9000); Amari Atrium Hotel (☎ 02/718–2000); Century Park Hotel (☎ 02/246–7800); and Chaengwatana Sports Club (☎ 02/962–6100). The **Grand Hyatt Erawan** (✉ 494 Ratchadamri Rd., ☎ 02/254–1234 ext 4437) has the best health-and-fitness facility of any Bangkok hotel. The **Peninsula** (✉ 333 Charoennakorn Rd., Klonsan, ☎ 02/861–1111, ext. 6011) also has a good fitness center.

JOGGING

For a quick jog, the small running track at many hotels may be the best bet. Stay off the grass in all city parks; you can run alone safely in the parks during the day but not at night. **Chatuchak Park's** loop is 4 km (2½ mi), but it is north of the city. **Lumphini Park,** whose pathways are paved, is about 2 km (1¼ mi) around and is popular with serious joggers. **Sanam Luang,** in front of the Grand Palace, is a popular park for runners. The **Siam Inter-Continental Hotel's** jogging track in its parkland gardens is one of the most attractive.

MASSAGE

Traditional Thai massage is very common in Bangkok and will generally be Wat Pho style. Go for two hours for the full effect. Hotel staff can usually recommend where to go.

The massage (B200) given at the famous **Wat Pho school** is the best bargain and an experience not to be missed. A very gentle massage in very genteel surroundings may be had at the new **Oriental Spa** (✉ In the Oriental Hotel, 48 Oriental Ave., ☎ 02/236–0400). Here in wood-paneled sophistication you can get facials, hydrotherapy, mud and seaweed wraps, and herbal treatments, from the "Jet Lag Solution" at B2,000 to a full day's pampering for $200. A most relaxing massage, with oils, is available at the **Regent Hotel** (✉ 155 Ratchadamri Rd., ☎ 02/251–6127).

Spectator Sports

HORSE RACING

Horse racing is a popular pastime in Bangkok, where each meeting has up to 12 races, and public betting is permitted. The **Royal Bangkok Sports Club** (✉ Henri Dunant Rd. between Rama I and Rama IV roads, ☎ 02/251–0181) and the **Royal Turf Club** (✉ On the north side of Phitsanulok Rd. just east of Rama V Rd., ☎ 02/280–0020) hold races on alternating Sundays.

THAI BOXING

The national sport of Thailand draws an enthusiastic crowd in Bangkok, where bouts are the real thing, unlike some Thai boxing shows you may see in tourist resort areas. Understanding the rules is close to impossible; it's fast and furious, and the playing of traditional music heightens the drama. Daily matches alternate between the two main stadiums. **Lumphini stadium** (✉ Rama IV Rd., ☎ 02/251–4303) has matches on Tuesday, Friday, and Saturday at 6 PM and Sunday at 1 PM. **Ratchadamnoen stadium** (✉ Ratchadamnoen Nok Rd., ☎ 02/281–4205) has bouts on Monday, Wednesday, and Thursday at 6 PM. Tickets (B100–500) may be bought at the gates.

Shopping

Even if you don't feel like buying, browsing through the markets is fascinating. Everything is for sale—from fake Rolex watches for the equivalent of a few bucks to Paris originals costing thousands. And aside from the wonderfully cheap mass-produced knockoffs of international brands, you'll find good-quality merchandise made in Thailand: jewelry, silks, silverware, leather, and Oriental antiques are just some examples.

Tourists can now reclaim the 7.5% VAT (Value Added Tax) at the airport on store-bought items if they have a receipt for the merchandise. Ask about the VAT refund when you buy goods. If you still want the convenience of a big duty-free shop try **King Power International Group** (⊠ 4 Ratchadamri Rd., 7th floor, Patumwan, ☎ 02/252–3633 up to 8), which has a large array of goods on the top floor of the World Trade Centre and is open daily 9:30 AM to 10:30 PM. The merchandise is rather expensive, and you miss the fun of bartering at street stalls. Most clerks speak a bit of English. You pay for the items at the shop, then pick them up at the airport when you leave. To buy, you need your passport and airline ticket, and you need to pay for goods at least eight hours before leaving the country.

Districts

The main shopping areas are along Silom Road and at the Rama IV end of Suriwongse for jewelry, crafts, and silk; along Sukhumvit Road for leather goods; along Yaowarat Road in Chinatown for gold; and along Silom Road, Oriental Lane, and Charoen Krung Road for antiques. The Oriental Plaza and the River City Shopping Centre have shops with collector-quality goods; the shops around Siam Square and at the World Trade Centre attract middle-income Thais and foreigners. Peninsula Plaza, across from the Regent Hotel, has very upscale shops, and the newest and glitziest complex is Thaniya Plaza, between Silom and Suriwongse roads, near Patpong. If you're knowledgeable about fabric and cut, you can find bargains at the textile merchants and tailors who compete along Pahuraht Road in Chinatown and Pratunam off Phetchburi Road. Although prices are inflated for tourists, Patpong 1 is a lively market for cheap goods. You'll see locals buying here, too, from 6 PM until well into the night. Stalls are also set up in the afternoon and evening along Silom Road, selling tourists knockoff designer ware.

Markets

You can buy virtually anything at the **Chatuchak Weekend Market** (⊠ Chatuchak Park, Phaholyothin Rd.), across the street from the northern terminus of the skytrain and near the Northern Bus Terminal. Sometimes you'll find great fashion buys, including items made from *mudmee* silk (ikat weave, where thread is tie-dyed before weaving) that would sell in America for five times the price. Even if you don't buy, a visit will open your eyes to exotic foods, flowers, and Thai life. Though open on Friday from 5 to 9 PM and weekends from 9 AM to 9 PM, Bangkok's largest market is best visited on Saturday and Sunday in the late morning.

Pahuraht Cloth Market (⊠ Off Yaowarat Rd.), operated mostly by Indians, is known for its bargain textiles, batiks, and buttons. An auctioneer with a microphone announces when everything at a particular stall will be sold at half price, and the shoppers surge over to bid. Hundreds of stalls and shops jam the sidewalk daily at **Pratunam Market** (⊠ Corner of Phetchburi and Ratchaprarop Rds., near the Indra Regent and Amari Watergate hotels). The stacks of merchandise consist mainly of inexpensive clothing—jeans for $5 and shirts for $4. It's a good place to meet Thais, who come in the evening to shop and eat tasty, inexpensive Thai and Chinese street food.

Soi Sampeng (⊠ Parallel to Yaowarat Rd.) has toys, household goods, clothes, and lots of fabrics—it is Bangkok's best-known and oldest textile center. Antiques (both old and new) are found on **Ta Chang Road,** where there's also jewelry made by Thailand's northern hill tribes. **Ta Phra Chan** (⊠ Near Wat Phra Keo), where the Weekend Market used to be, still has booths selling antiques and assorted goods. Between Yaowarat and Charoen Krung in Chinatown lies the so-called **Thieves Market** (Nakorn Kasem), an area of small streets with old wood houses, where you can buy anything from hardware to porcelains. Bargains are hard to find nowadays, but these small, cluttered streets are fascinating. Bargain hard!

Specialty Stores

ART, CRAFTS, AND ANTIQUES

Note that Thai antiques and old images of the Buddha need a special export license. Suriwongse Road, Charoen Krung Road, and the Oriental Plaza (across from the Oriental Hotel) have many art and antiques shops, as does the River City Shopping Centre. Original and often illegal artifacts from Angkor Wat are sometimes sold there too.

Don't miss **123 Baan Dee** (⊠ 123 Fuengnakorn Rd., ☎ 02/221–2520) in the old town, in a restored small teak house. Antique silks, ceramics, beads, pictures, and other fascinating artifacts abound on two floors, and there's a small ice-cream parlor at the back. **Peng Seng** (⊠ 942 Rama IV, at the Suriwongse Rd. intersection, ☎ 02/234–1285) is one of the most respected dealers of antiquities in Bangkok. Prices may be high, but articles are likely to be genuine. **Rasi Sayam** (⊠ 32 Sukhumvit Soi 23, ☎ 02/258–4195), in an old teak house in a garden, has a wonderful collection of fine Thai crafts.

CLOTHING AND FABRICS

Thai silk gained its world reputation only after World War II, when technical innovations were introduced. Two other fabrics are worth noting: mudmee silk, produced in the Northeast, and Thai cotton, which is soft, durable, and easier on the wallet than silk.

Design Thai (⊠ 304 Silom Rd., ☎ 02/235–1553) has a large selection of silk items in all price ranges—a good place for that gift you ought to take home (you can usually manage a 20% discount here). For factory-made clothing, visit the **Indra Garment Export Centre** (⊠ Ratchaprarop Rd., behind the Indra Regent Hotel), where hundreds of shops sell discounted items.

The **Jim Thompson Thai Silk Company** (⊠ 9 Suriwongse Rd., ☎ 02/234–4900) is a prime place for silk by the yard and ready-made clothes. There is no bargaining and the prices are high, but the staff is knowledgeable and helpful. A branch store has opened in the Oriental Hotel's shopping arcade.

Napajaree Suanduenchai studied fashion design in Germany; 20 years ago she started the **Prayer Textile Gallery** (⊠ Phayathai Rd., near Siam Square, ☎ 02/251–7549) where her mother's dress shop had been for 14 years before that. She makes stunning traditional clothes in naturally dyed silks and cottons and in old fabrics from the north, Laos, and Cambodia.

The custom-made suit in 24–48 hours is a Bangkok specialty, but the suit often hangs on the shoulders just as one would expect from a rush job. If you want an excellent cut, give the tailor more time. The best in Bangkok is **Marco Tailor** (⊠ 430/33 Siam Square, Soi 7, ☎ 02/252–0689), where, for approximately B17,000, your suit will equal those made on Savile Row.

For women's apparel, **Stephanie Thai Silk** (⊠ 55 Soi Shangri-La Hotel, New Rd., Bangrak, ☎ 02/234–0590 or 02/233–0325) is a respected shop which can deliver in 24 hours, though allowing more time is recommended. It has its own wide selection of silks but you can bring your own material. A skirt with blouse and jacket made of Thai silk starts at B5,000.

JEWELRY

Thailand is a world center for gems, exporting more colored stones than anywhere in the world, and the jewelry trade has taken off in the past decade. Be aware of deals that are too good to be true; they probably are. Scams are common and it's best to stick with established businesses. If you have any complaints, see the tourist police. There are countless gem and jewelry stores on Silom and Suriwongse roads, with a large concentration of gem dealers in the Jewelry Trade Centre on Silom Road.

A long-established jewelry firm is **Johny's Gems** (⊠ 199 Fuengnakorn Rd., ☎ 02/224–4065). If you telephone, he'll send a car to pick you up (a frequent practice among the better Bangkok stores), or you can walk to the shop if you are in the vicinity of Wat Phra Keo. **Oriental Lapidary** (⊠ 116/1 Silom Rd., just across and a little down the street from the Jewelry Trade Centre, ☎ 02/238–2718) has a long record of good service. **Pranda Jewelry** (⊠ 333 Soi Rungsang, Bangna-Trad Rd., ☎ 02/361–3311) is a well-established store with separate branches for gems and jewelry. **Than Shine** (⊠ 84/87 Sukhumvit Soi 55, ☎ 02/381–7337), run by sisters Cho Cho and Mon Mon, offers classy and new wave designs.

LEATHER

Leather is a good buy in Bangkok, with some of the lowest prices in the world, especially for custom work. Crocodile leather is popular, but be sure to obtain a certificate that the skins came from a domestically raised reptile; otherwise U.S. Customs may confiscate the goods. The River City Shopping Centre has a number of leather shops. For shoes and jackets, try the 20-year-old **Siam Leather Goods** (⊠ In the River City Shopping Centre, ☎ 02/233–4521).

PRECIOUS METALS

Chinatown is the place to go for gold. Most shops are authentic (they wouldn't survive there as anything but); still, insist on a receipt. There is no bargaining for gold. For bronze try **Siam Bronze Factory** (⊠ 1250 Charoen Krung Rd., ☎ 02/234–9436).

Bangkok A to Z

Arriving and Departing

BY AIRPLANE

At **Don Muang Airport international terminal,** next to the domestic terminal, you'll find an array of desks where you can arrange for taxis into Bangkok and transport to other destinations; a reservation desk for Bangkok hotels (no fee); and a **Tourist Authority of Thailand (TAT)** desk with free brochures and maps. Both terminals have luggage-checking facilities (☎ 02/535–1250, but only Thai is spoken).

There's a tax of B500 for international departures and B30 for domestic departures.

Thai Airways International (⊠ 485 Silom Rd., ☎ 02/280–0060) is the national airline, and most of its flights go through Don Muang. It has direct flights from the West Coast of the United States and from London, and it also flies daily to Hong Kong, Singapore, Taiwan, and Japan.

The U.S. carrier with the most frequent flights is **Northwest Airlines** (✉ 153 Ratchadamri Rd., Peninsula Shopping Plaza, 4th floor, ☎ 02/ 254–0789). It has service through Tokyo (with a minimal stopover) from New York, Detroit, Seattle, Dallas, San Francisco, and Los Angeles. Northwest also has a round-Asia fare, in conjunction with local airlines, which lets you hop from one capital to another. **Singapore Airlines** (✉ Silom Centre Building, 2 Silom Rd., ☎ 02/236–0440), flies to Bangkok through Singapore. **British Airways** (✉ 990 Rama IV Rd., ☎ 02/636–1747), flies nonstop to Bangkok from London. The three airlines are among the 70 or so now serving Bangkok, with more seeking landing rights. A new international airport, southeast of the city, is scheduled to open in 2004.

The airport has more than its share of hustlers out to make a quick baht, who often wear uniforms and tags that make them seem official. They will try to get you to change your hotel to one that pays them a large commission, perhaps claiming your intended hotel is overbooked. They will hustle you into overpriced taxis or limousines. Do not get taken in.

BETWEEN THE AIRPORT AND TOWN

By Bus: An airport bus service (B70) runs approximately every 30 minutes between Don Muang and four sectors of downtown Bangkok. A1 travels to Ratchadamri and Silom roads. A2 covers the central area that includes the Victory Monument and Chinatown. A3 goes down Sukhumvit. A4 weaves its way to Hualamphong, the main train station. A detailed listing of each route is available from the airport TAT office and at the bus stop outside the arrivals hall. You can also catch local air-conditioned buses (B15) on the main road that passes the airport.

By Helicopter: For about $150, with a three person minimum, you can fly between the airport and the Peninsula, Oriental, Royal Orchid Sheraton, and Shangri-La hotels, but new expressways have greatly diminished the need for this service.

By Taxi: Don Muang is 25 km (15 mi) from the city center. The highways are often congested, and the trip can take from 30 minutes to more than an hour. State your destination at the counter on the curb (at either terminal) and obtain a voucher; a driver will lead you to the taxi. The fare on the meter (be sure that the meter is turned on) for downtown Bangkok depends on the exact destination and, to some extent, the time of day. Count on B200–B250 plus a B50 expressway toll charge and a B50 airport surcharge. Taxis to the airport from downtown Bangkok do not have the airport surcharge, and will cost approximately B200.

By Train: Bangkok Airport Express trains make the 35-minute run every 90 minutes from 8 AM to 7 PM. Check the schedule at the tourist booth in the arrival hall. The fare is B100. You can also take the regular trains from 5:30 AM to 9 PM. The fare is B5 for a local train and B13 for an express. The train is rarely convenient as there are few hotels near the train station.

BY BUS

Bangkok has three main bus terminals. **Northern Bus Terminal** (✉ Phaholyothin Rd., behind Chatuchak Park, ☎ 02/279–4484), called Morchit, serves I-san, Chiang Mai, and the north. **Southern Bus Terminal** (✉ Pinklao-Nakomchaisri Rd., Talingchan, ☎ 02/391–9829), in Thonburi, is for Hua Hin, Ko Samui, Phuket, and points south. **Eastern Bus Terminal** (✉ Sukhumvit Soi 40, ☎ 02/391–2504), called Ekkamai, is for Pattaya, Rayong, and Trat province.

Hualamphong Railway Station (✉ Rama IV Rd., ☎ 02/223–0341), the city's main station, serves mostly long-distance trains. **Bangkok Noi** (✉ Arun Amarin Rd., ☎ 02/411–3102), on the Thonburi side of the Chao Phraya River, is used by local trains to Hua Hin and Kanchanaburi.

Getting Around

Both the skytrain, which opened along two central city routes in December 1999, and the river, when available, are good options to beat the traffic. New expressways have eased the congestion somewhat, particularly from the airport to hotels on the river. If you do join the traffic, timing is a consideration, with roads at their worst during rush hours, 7–10 AM and 4–7 PM. A subway system is scheduled to open in 2002.

BY BOAT

Water taxis and ferries ("river buses") ply the Chao Phraya River. The taxis are long-tail boats (so called for the extra-long propeller shaft that extends behind the stern) that you can hire for about B400 an hour. The river-bus fare is based on zones, but B5 will cover most trips that you are likely to take. At certain ferry piers (*tha*) you will also pay a B1 jetty fee. The jetty adjacent to the Oriental Hotel is a useful stop. You can get to the Grand Palace in about 10 minutes and half a dozen stops, or to the other side of Krungthon Bridge in about 15 minutes. It is often the quickest way to travel north–south. It is also a few degrees cooler on the water.

BY BUS

Though buses can be very crowded, they are convenient and inexpensive. For a fare of only B3.50 (any distance) on the ordinary non-air-conditioned buses and B6 to B16 on the air-conditioned ones, you can go virtually anywhere in the city. Micro Buses are smaller, air-conditioned, do not permit standing passengers, and charge B20 for any distance. Buses operate from 5 AM to around 11 PM. The routes are confusing, but usually someone at the bus stop will know the number of the bus you need to catch. You can pick up a route map at most bookstalls for B35. Be alert for purse snatchers and pickpockets on buses.

BY MOTOTAXI

At the head of many sois you will often find a gang of motorbikers. These "soi boys" began by taking passengers down the sois, but their operations have expanded to take you anywhere in Bangkok, although they can still pick up passengers only at their soi. The physical risk and discomfort limit their desirability, but, if you are late for a date, they are the fastest means of transport in congested traffic. Ask for a helmet. Fares, to be negotiated, are about the same as, or perhaps a little less than, taxi fare.

BY SAMLOR

These unmetered three-wheeled polluters, called tuk-tuks, are slightly cheaper than taxis and are best used for short trips in congested traffic. But the drivers are tough negotiators, and unless you are good at bargaining you may well end up paying more than for a metered taxi. Tuk-tuk drivers often offer "tours" at a bargain rate and take the unsuspecting to gem shops and tailors who, of course, give the drivers a commission.

BY SKYTRAIN

The skytrain opened on December 5, 1999, the King's birthday. With two intersecting lines, it covers 23 km and has 25 stations. It has shrunk the city for those who can pay the fare (B10 to B40), determined by the distance you travel. The routes above Sukhumvit, Silom, and Phaholyothin roads make traveling in those areas a breeze. The skytrain does not go through the old part of town, however, because it is considered too unsightly (you certainly can't miss the huge concrete pillars). The skytrain runs from 5 AM to midnight.

BY TAXI

Nowadays most taxis are metered, and you should take only these. The tariff for the first 2 km (1.2 mi) is set at B35 and then increases a baht for about every 50 meters. If the speed drops to under 6 kph, there is a surcharge of one baht per minute. A typical journey of about 5 km (3 mi) runs B60.

Contacts and Resources

EMERGENCIES

Ambulance: ☎ 02/252–2171 up to 5. **Fire:** ☎ 199. **General emergencies:** ☎ 1155. **Police:** ☎ 191.

In an emergency, you are advised to contact the **Tourist Police** (✉ Tourist Service Centre, 4 Ratchadamnoen Rd., ☎ 02/1155) rather than the local police. There are Tourist Police mobile units in major tourist areas.

Dentists: Bangkok has a number of dental clinics, among them **Ambassador Dental Clinic** (✉ 171 Sukhumvit Soi 11, Ambassador Plaza, ☎ 02/255–2279) and **Thaniya Dental Centre** (✉ 4th floor, Thaniya Plaza, 52 Silom Rd., ☎ 02/231–2100). If you want a private dentist, see **Khun Phira Sithiamnuai** (✉ President Park Dental Clinic, Mahogany Tower, President Park, Sukhumvit 24, ☎ 02/661–1156), who did his training and internship in Massachusetts.

Hospitals: Bangkok Adventist Hospital (✉ 430 Phitsanulok Rd., ☎ 02/ 281–1422). **Bangkok Christian Hospital** (✉ 124 Silom Rd., ☎ 02/233– 6981 or 02/233–6989). **The Bangkok Nursing Home** (✉ 9 Convent Rd., ☎ 02/233–2610 or 02/233–2609). **Chulalongkorn Hospital** (✉ Rama IV Rd., ☎ 02/252–8181). **Nonthavej Hospital,** (✉ 30/8 Ngam-wong-wan Rd., Bangkhen Nonthaburi, ☎ 02/951–8575), out toward Don Muang Airport, has qualified doctors and an excellent staff accustomed to overseas patients.

Pharmacies: There is no shortage of pharmacies in Bangkok. Compared with the United States, fewer drugs require prescriptions, but if you need one, the prescription must be written in Thai. Be aware that over-the-counter drugs are not necessarily of the same chemical composition as those in the United States. **Foodland Supermarket Pharmacy** (✉ No. 9 Patpong 2 Rd., ☎ 02/233–2101; ✉ 1413 Sukhumvit Soi 5, ☎ 02/254–2247) stays open all night. The ubiquitous **7-Eleven, AM/PM,** and other 24-hour stores carry nonprescription medications.

ENGLISH-LANGUAGE BOOKSTORES

The English-language dailies the *Bangkok Post* and *The Nation* and the monthly *Metro* are available at newsstands.

Asia Books has a wide selection of books and magazines at branches throughout the city. Two convenient locations are 221 Sukhumvit Soi 15) ☎ 02/651–0428) and the Peninsula Plaza, adjacent to the Regent Hotel (☎ 02/253–9786). **Bookazine** is a chain with a good selection and several locations, including one in the CP Tower (✉ 313 Silom Rd., ☎ 02/231–0016). **Kinokuniya Books** (✉ Emporium Shopping Complex, Sukhumvit Rd., at the corner of Soi 24 and connected to the Phrom Phong skytrain station, ☎ 02/664–8554) has one of the largest selections of books.

GUIDED TOURS

Virtually every major hotel has a travel desk that books tours in and around Bangkok, though you can easily visit many of the sights independently. With slight variation, the following tours of the city are usually offered: the half-day City and Temples tour (Wat Pho, Wat Benjamabophit, Wat Traimitr, but not the Grand Palace); the Grand Palace and Emerald Buddha tour; and a Thai Dinner and Classical Dance tour.

TELEPHONES

The level of English remains limited even in Bangkok, so patience will serve you well. Telephone information from an English-speaking operator is available by dialing 13, but getting through is often difficult.

TRAVEL AGENCIES

For significant purchases, you may want to use a large, established agency. Major hotels can arrange itineraries or recommend a good travel agent. **Diethelm** (⊠ Kian Gwan Building 11, 140/1 Wireless Rd., across from the US Embassy, ☎ 02/255–9150). **East West Siam** (⊠ Building One, 11th Floor, 99 Wireless Rd., ☎ 02/256–6153 or 02/256–6155). **World Travel Service** (⊠ 1053 Charoen Krung Rd., ☎ 02/233–5900).

VISITOR INFORMATION

The **Tourist Authority of Thailand (TAT)** (⊠ Le Concord Building, 202 Ratchadaphisek Rd., Huay Kwang, 10320, ☎ 02/694–1222, FAX 02/694–1220), open 8:30 to 4:30, tends to have more in the way of colorful brochures than hard information, but it can supply useful material on national parks and various routes to out-of-the-way destinations. A tourist hot line (dial 1155—open 24 hours a day) provides information on destinations, accommodations, festivals, arts, and culture. You may also use the hot line to register complaints or request assistance from the tourist police. There is also a TAT branch at the international terminal at **Don Muang Airport** (☎ 02/523–8973), open 8 AM to half-past midnight.

SIDE TRIPS OUT OF BANGKOK

Though the fascination of Bangkok never really dulls, there comes a time when you want to escape the clouds of pollution and find fresher fields. Sophisticated seaside resorts at Cha' Am and Hua Hin are a few hours away, pristine beaches on Ko Samet and Ko Chang, a day's journey. But exotic markets in Damnoen Saduak, religious centers at Nakhon Pathom, Kanchanaburi's forested jungles laced with waterfalls, and ancient temples and palaces in Ayutthaya and Lopburi can all be seen on day trips from the City of Angels.

West of Bangkok

Don't bother visiting the floating market in Bangkok; head out through rice paddies and water buffalo to Damnoen Saduak in the province of Ratchaburi, where the colorful scene is a photographer's fantasy. The area around Nakhon Pathom has been settled for millennia—the city was founded before the time of Christ. Kanchanaburi Province, farther west, is so beautiful that you may want to go hiking and thoroughly explore its gorges and waterfalls, or even take an overnight rafting trip.

Damnoen Saduak

① *109 km (65 mi) southwest of Bangkok.*

At Damnoen Saduak, hire a *ruilla pai* (sampan) for about B300. Then, for an hour or more, lazily travel the canal and witness true gridlock: a mess of boats trying to shove their way along the klong as sampan

Lopburi
Nakhon Ratchasima
Erawan Waterfall
Saraburi
Ayutthaya
Bang Pa-In
Prachin Buri
Kanchanaburi
Sai Yok
Nakhon Pathom
Bangkok
Chachoengsao
Ratchaburi
Damnoen Saduak
Chonburi
BURMA (MYANMAR)
Phetchaburi
Ko Phai
Ko Lan
Pattaya
Cha'Am
Sattahip
Rayong
Ban Phe
Hua Hin
Ko Samet
Chantaburi
Sam Roi Yod N.P.
Laem Ngop
Trat
Gulf of Thailand
Ko Chang
Prachuap
0   50 miles
0   75 km
N
Ko Mak
Ko Kut
CAMBODIA

vendors sell fresh vegetables, meats, and clothes. Farmers' wives dressed in baggy pants, long-tail shirts, and straw hats sell produce from their boats, paddling back and forth, or rather pushing and barging their way through the congestion. Other women, cooking tasty treats on little stoves, sit ready to ferry sustenance to the hungry. The scene couldn't be more authentic and colorful.

If you want to rest, a wharf alongside the klong has tables and chairs. Buy your drinks from the stall and your food from any one of the *ruilla pai.* Go early because by 11 AM, you will have seen the best of Damnoen Saduak; any longer and the novelty of exotica wears thin and irritation at the vendors' aggressive commercialism sets in.

Nakhon Pathom

56 km (34 mi) west of Bangkok.

Nakhon Pathom is reputed to be Thailand's oldest city, dating from 150 BC. Its main attraction is **Phra Pathom Chedi,** the tallest Buddhist monument in the world—at 417 ft, it stands a few feet higher than the Shwe Dagon Chedi in Burma. The first chedi on this site was erected in the 6th century, but the large chedi you see today, built in 1860, encases the ruins of the original. It also marks the first center of Buddhist learning on the Thai peninsula, established here about 1,000 years ago.

The man responsible for reconstructing the chedi was King Monghut (Rama IV), who, when he was a monk, understood the historical role Phra Pathom Chedi had played in the the establishment of Buddhism in Thailand. Believing that the chedi, then in a state of disrepair, contained the Buddha's holy ashes, he ordered that it be incorporated into the new one. In the outer courtyard are four viharn facing in different directions and containing images of Lord Buddha in various postures.

The terraces around the temple complex are full of fascinating statuary, including a Dvaravati-style Buddha seated in a chair, and the museum contains some interesting Dvaravati (6th–11th century) sculpture. Occasionally, classical Thai dances are performed in front of the temple, and during the Loi Krathong festival, bazaars and a fair are set up in the adjacent park. ⊙ *Museum Wed.–Sun. 9–noon and 1–4.*

Sanan Chan Palace, just west of Phra Pathom Chedi, was built during King Rama IV's reign. The palace is closed to the public, but the surrounding park is a lovely place to relax in the shade before heading back to Bangkok.

Rose Garden

🕓 *25 km (15 mi) east of Nakhon Pathom, 32 km (19 mi) west of Bangkok.*

On the Bangkok Road out of Nakhon Pathom is the Rose Garden, a complex that replicates a Thai village. Amid flowering gardens of 20,000 rosebushes, there are traditional Thai houses and a stage where a "cultural show" of dance, Thai boxing, sword fighting, and a wedding ceremony is performed at 2:45. The park also has a hotel, restaurants, swimming pools, and playground activities. The B250 admission is fairly steep, but you can while away a few pleasant hours, especially with children, in this somewhat sterile re-creation of Thailand. There is a daily afternoon tour from Bangkok. ✉ *195/15 Soi Chokchai Chongchamron, Rama III Rd. (Bangkok booking office),* ☎ *02/295–3261.* ▨ *Admission.* ⊙ *Daily 8–6.*

Next door to the Rose Garden and equally as commercial are the ele-
🕓 phant roundups and crocodile shows at the **Samphran Elephant Ground & Zoo.** Though there is lots else to see, the elephants steal the day. A score of these great pachyderms haul logs, play football, and dance on their hind legs. The finale reenacts the Yutha Harti, the 16th-century elephant-back battle between King Naresuan and a Burmese prince-invader. During the 40-minute show a soundtrack explains the role of elephants in Thai history, including their centuries-long role as domestic beasts of burden. ✉ *Km 30, Petchkasem Rd.,* ☎ *02/295–2938 or 02/295–2939 for reservations.* ▨ *Admission.* ⊙ *Daily 10–4.*

Kanchanaburi

❸ *140 km (87 mi) west of Bangkok.*

Kanchanaburi Province's jungles, rivers, and waterfalls make it one of Thailand's most beautiful regions. But it is also known for the Death Railway built during World War II and immortalized in the movie *The Bridge Over the River Kwai,* adapted from Pierre Boulle's novel. About 16,000 Allied prisoners-of-war and between 50,000 and 100,000 slave laborers were forced by the Japanese to construct a rail link through the jungles of Thailand and Burma. One person died for every railway tie on the track. There are two Allied cemeteries where the remains of 8,732 POWs are buried.

Don't expect to see the bridge from the 1954 movie, which was filmed in a river gorge in Sri Lanka. A reconstructed bridge, still in use, is in Kanchanaburi town where the Kwai Noi and Kwai Yai rivers meet to form the Mae Khlong River. It has arched steel spans which the Japanese brought from Java late in the war. They rebuilt the two square center sections after the war to replace those destroyed by Allied bombs. The original bamboo bridge that inspired the book and movie was a few hundred meters downstream. You can walk across the new bridge, which is next to a plaza, with restaurants, souvenir shops, and jewelry stores.

The **Kanchanaburi War Cemetery,** next to noisy Saengchuto Road just south of the train station, has row upon row of neatly laid-out graves of 6,982 Australian, British, and Dutch prisoners of war. The remains of the American POWs were returned to the United States during the Eisenhower administration. They are all remembered at a commemorative service here every April 25, Australia's Anzac Day.

The **Japanese War Memorial Shrine** is near the bridge, 1 km (½ mi) northwest of the Kanchanaburi War Cemetery. Be sure to read the plaque on the Japanese War Memorial—it has an English translation.

About 2 km (1 mi) downriver from the bridge and in town is the **JEATH War Museum** (JEATH is an acronym for Japan, England, America, Australia, Thailand, and Holland). Founded by a monk from the adjoining temple, the museum consists of a reconstructed bamboo hut—the type used to house the POWs—and a collection of utensils, railway spikes, clothing, aerial photographs, newspaper clippings, and illustrations designed to show the conditions under which the POWs lived during the construction of the Death Railway. ⊠ *Admission.* ☉ *Daily 8–5.*

The **Chong-Kai War Cemetery,** on the grounds of a former POW hospital and graveyard, is a sadly serene site with simple, neatly organized grave markers of Commonwealth soldiers. Though rarely visited because it's a little out of the way, it is worth the trek. Hire a tuk-tuk, or take the ferry across the river from the pier below the park off Patana Road and walk just over 500 meters down the road. The cemetery will be on your left.

Walk inland from Chong-Kai about 1 km (½ mi) to find **Wat Thum Khao Pun,** one of the best cave temples in the area. A small temple stands outside and a guide entices you into the cave, where calm images of the Buddha sit between the stalagmites and stalactites.

Dining and Lodging

Most of the restaurants for tourists are near the River Kwai Bridge or farther downstream where the Kwai Noi and Kwai Yai join to form the Mae Khlong. Because most foreigners visit Kanchanaburi on day trips, hotels, which line the riverbanks, are designed primarily for Thai families. A few of the resorts offer thatched bungalows on the river that have river views by day but tend to be hot and muggy at night.

$ ✕ **Pae Karn Floating Restaurant.** For authentic Thai food, try this little restaurant on a floating dock at the river's edge just at the confluence of the Kwai Noi and Kwai Yai rivers. The food is better than in tourist restaurants around the bridge, but the decor amounts to no more than plain walls and a few tables. ⊠ *Song Kwai Rd.,* ☎ *no phone. No credit cards.*

$ ✕ **River Kwai Floating Restaurant.** The most attractive—and crowded—open-air restaurant is to the right of the bridge. Fish dishes, either cooked with Thai spices or lightly grilled, dominate the menu. The specialty is *yeesok,* a fish found in the Kwai Yai and Kwai Noi rivers. Try to arrive before the tour groups, and request a table alongside the river. ⊠ *River Kwai Bridge,* ☎ *034/512595. No credit cards.*

$$ ✕🏨 **River Kwai Village.** Nestled in the heart of the jungle in the River Kwai Valley, this resort village consists of five one-story log cabins and a few guest rooms on rafts. All non-raft rooms have air-conditioning and are simply furnished in teak, with colored stones embedded in the walls. The cafeteria-style restaurant offers a combination of Thai and Western dishes, but it's more fun to eat at the casual restaurant on one of the anchored floating rafts. The resort will supply transportation from Bangkok and arrange tours of the area. ⊠ *72 Moo 4, Tambon Thasao, Amphoe Sai Yok, Kanchanaburi 71150,* ☎ *034/634454 up*

to 6; 02/251-7552 Bangkok reservations, FAX *034/591054. 60 rooms and 7 raft houses. 2 restaurants, pool, meeting rooms, travel services. AE, DC, V.* ❧

$$$ 🏨 **Felix River Kwai Resort.** This luxury hotel was first managed by Sofitel and then by a Thai group. It is still going through growing pains, but it does have a tranquil setting along the bank of the river in sight of the bridge. Polished wood floors and wicker headboards give a cool airiness to the rooms. Each has two queen beds or one king, as well as a private safe and cable TV. A large free-form pool amid tropical plants sets the relaxing scene. The hotel is within walking distance of most of Kanchanaburi's attractions. ✉ *9/1 Moo 3, Tambon Thamakham, Kanchanaburi 71000,* ☎ *034/515061 or 034/515002; 02/675–6990 Bangkok reservations,* FAX *034/515095. 150 rooms. Restaurant, pool, massage, health club. AE, DC, MC, V.* ❧

$$–$$$ 🏨 **The Pavilion Rim Kwai Thani Resort.** Between downtown Kanchanaburi and the Erawan Waterfall, this new resort caters to upscale Bangkok residents wanting to retreat into the country and still have their creature comforts. Tropical flora surrounds the hotel, and the infamous River Kwai flows serenely past. Guest rooms are sparsely furnished, which, along with the shining wood floors, gives a fresh, sparkling ambiance. The large dining room serves Thai and Western dishes. ✉ *79/2 Moo 4, Km 9 Ladya-Erawan Rd., Tambon Wangdong, Kanchanaburi 71190,* ☎ *034/515772,* FAX *034/515774. 200 rooms. Restaurant, pool, 2 tennis courts, exercise room. AE, MC, V.*

$$ 🏨 **Kasem Island Resort.** Within view of the town is this resort, perched on an island in the middle of the river. You can choose to stay in a room, bungalow, or raft-house. ✉ *44 Thaichumpon St., Kanchanaburi 71000,* ☎ *034/513359; 02/255–3604 Bangkok reservations. 29 rooms, 10 bungalows, and 19 rafts. Restaurant. MC, V.*

$$ 🏨 **River Kwai Hotel.** On the main road through town is Kanchanaburi's first big hotel. It is a comfortable place, but far from the river and popular with tour groups. ✉ *284/4–6 Saengchuto Rd., Kanchanaburi 71000,* ☎ *034/513348,* FAX *034/511269. 150 rooms. Restaurant, travel services. AE, MC, V.*

Outdoor Activities and Sports

RAFTING

Rafting trips on either the Kwai Yai or Mae Khlong rivers, which take at least a full day, let you experience the tropical jungle in a leisurely way. The rafts, which resemble houseboats, are often divided into sections for eating, sunbathing, and diving. Be careful when swimming—the currents can have a whirlpool effect and suck a swimmer down. The cost of a one-day trip starts at about B300. Longer trips are also available. Make advance reservations through the TAT office or a travel agent. Booking through a responsible travel agent may cost more, but you'll be more likely to get a raft in good condition and a skipper familiar with the currents.

Shopping

Blue sapphires from the Bo Phloi mines, 45 km (28 mi) north of Kanchanaburi, are generally a good buy, but prices are marked up at the shops in the plaza before the bridge. You're better off buying the sapphires at the small shops in the center of town or in Bangkok.

Erawan Waterfall

❹ *65 km (40 mi) northwest of Kanchanaburi (Rte 3199).*

If you want to visit some of the spectacular countryside of Kanchanaburi Province, make the trip out to the Erawan Waterfall, perhaps the most photographed in Thailand. It is in the beautifully forested

Khao Salop National Park and is at its best in early autumn. You can take a tour bus from Kanchanaburi or the public bus (No. 8170), which leaves every hour for the 90-minute journey. It's a 1½-km (1-mi) walk or taxi ride to the foot of the falls. Allow two hours to climb up all seven levels of the falls, and wear tennis shoes or similarly appropriate footwear. The rock at the top is shaped like an elephant; hence the name Erawan, which refers to the god Indra's three-headed elephant.

Five kilometers (3 miles) up the road from the Erawan Waterfall is the 300-ft **Sri Nakharin Dam,** with its power station and vast reservoir. A tour boat makes a two-hour excursion on the reservoir to the **Huay Khamin Falls.**

OFF THE
BEATEN PATH
SAI YOK NOI – The trip out of Kanchanaburi to this waterfall (also called Kao Phang) is a memorable one, since you travel the 77 km (46 mi) on the Death Railway. The train leaves each day at 10:33 AM, passing through jungle landscape and by rushing waterfalls as it clings to the mountainside on a two-hour run that is not for the faint-hearted. From Nam-Tok, the last stop, it's a 1½-km (1-mi) walk to Sai Yok Noi. Although a lot smaller than the Erawan falls, it offers pools for swimming during the rainy season (May–Aug.), the best time to visit. On weekends the area is packed with Thai families. The bus back to Kanchanaburi takes half the time of the train.

North from Bangkok

Thailand's most glorious period began when Ayutthaya became the kingdom's seat of power in 1350. Toward the end of the 16th century, Europeans described the city, with its 1,700 temples and 4,000 golden images of the Buddha, as more striking than any capital in Europe. In 1767, the Burmese conquered Ayutthaya and destroyed its temples with such vengeance that little remained standing. The city never recovered, and today it is a small provincial town with partially restored ruins. The site is particularly striking at sunset, when the silhouetted ruins glow orange-brown and are imbued with a melancholy charm.

People usually visit these sites on excursions from Bangkok or on the way to Thailand's northern provinces. Try to get an early start for Ayutthaya to see as much as possible before 1 PM, when the heat becomes unbearable. Then take a long lunch and, if you have time, continue into the late afternoon and catch the sunset before you leave. Most people, though, find that a morning is sufficient. For a three-hour tour of the sights, tuk-tuks can be hired for about B500; a four-wheel samlor (small bicycle cab) costs a bit more than B700. English-speaking guides can be hired around the station. A popular excursion to Ayutthaya from Bangkok, run by the Oriental, Marriott Royal Garden Riverside, and Shangri-La hotels, takes you by cruise one way and bus the other; going by bus and coming back by boat is the better choice. A tour of a couple of Ayutthaya's sights and of the Bang Pa-In Palace is included, along with lunch on the cruise boat. It makes for a hassle-free day, and the boat trip is wonderful, but it gives you very little time actually visiting what you spend most of the day traveling to see.

Ayutthaya

⑤ *72 km (45 mi) north of Bangkok.*

Ayutthaya lies within a large loop of the Chao Phraya River as it meets the Pa Sak and Lopburi rivers. To completely encircle their capital by water, the Thais dug a canal along the northern perimeter, linking the Chao Phraya to the Lopburi. Although the new provincial town of Ayutthaya, which has a railway station, is on the east bank of the Pa Sak, most of Ayutthaya's ancient temples and ruins are on the island. An exception is Wat Yai Chai Mongkol, a B20 tuk-tuk ride southeast of the railway station.

Wat Yai Chai Mongkol was built in 1357 by King U-Thong for meditation. After King Naresuan defeated the Burmese by beheading their crown prince in single-handed combat on elephants in 1593, he enlarged the temple. The complex was totally restored in 1982, and with the neatly groomed grounds, smart new monks' quarters, and the contemporary images of the Buddha lining the courtyard, it looks a little touristy, an impression not helped by several souvenir shops, a beverage stand, and a host of tour buses from Bangkok. Notice how the chedi is leaning; it was restored without replacing the foundations and is, under the increased weight, sinking. Linger a while to pay your respects to the Reclining Buddha, and be sure to enter the new sala to look at a painting (1988) of the battle with the Burmese (Thai soldiers are dressed in red uniforms). ▨ *Admission.* ☉ *Daily 8–5.*

★ The road continues to **Wat Phanan Choeng,** a small temple on the banks of the Lopburi, which predates Ayutthaya's flowering. In 1324, one of the U-Thong kings, who had arranged to marry a daughter of the Chinese emperor, came to this spot on the river; instead of entering the city with his fiancée, he arranged an escort for her. But she, thinking that she had been deserted, threw herself into the river in despair and drowned. The king tried to atone for his thoughtlessness by building the temple. The story has great appeal to Thai Chinese, many of whom make romantic pilgrimages here. ▨ *Admission.* ☉ *Daily 8–6.*

From the main road, go left and cross over the bridge to the island. Continue on Rojana Road for about 1½ km (1 mi) to the **Chao Phraya National Museum.** Though Ayutthaya's best pieces are in Bangkok's National Museum, a guided visit here can highlight the evolution of Ayutthaya art over four centuries. ▨ *Admission.* ☉ *Wed.–Sun. 9–noon and 1–4.*

Just beyond the Chao Phraya National Museum, turn right onto Si Samphet Road. Pass the city hall on the left and continue for 1 km (½ mi) to **Wat Phra Si Samphet,** easily recognizable by the huge parking lot. The shining white-marble building south of Wat Phra Si Samphet not only looks modern, it is. Built in 1956, **Viharn Phra Mongkol Bopitr** houses a large bronze image of the Buddha, one of the few that escaped the destruction wrought by the Burmese.

Wat Phra Si Samphet was the largest wat in Ayutthaya and the temple of the royal family. Built in the 14th century, in 1767 it lost its 50-ft Buddha, Phra Sri Samphet, to the Burmese, who melted it down for its gold—374 pounds' worth. The chedis, restored in 1956, survived and are the best examples of Ayutthaya architecture. Enshrining the ashes of Ayutthaya kings, they stand as eternal memories of a golden age. The architectural design of Wat Phra Si Samphet was used in the construction of Wat Phra Keo at Bangkok's Grand Palace. Beyond the monuments is a grassy field where the royal palace once stood. The field is a cool, shady place in which to walk and picnic. The foundation is all that remains of the palace that was home to 33 kings. ☉ *Daily 8–5.*

Before you leave, visit some of the stalls in the **market** behind the souvenir stands; you'll find a marvelous array of vegetables, fruits, and other foods. After wandering around, stop at the café at the viharn end of the market for refreshments—try the chilled coconut in its shell.

From the large coach park, Naresuan Road crosses Si Samphet Road and continues past a small lake to nearby **Wat Phra Mahathat,** on the corner of Chee Kun Road. Built in 1384 by King Ramesuan, the monastery was destroyed by the Burmese, but in 1956 during a restoration project, a buried chest was found containing a relic of Lord Buddha, golden Buddha images, and other objects in gold, ruby, and crystal that are now housed in Bangkok's National Museum. If you climb up what is left of the monastery's 140-ft prang, you'll be able to envision just how grand the structure must have been. You can also admire neighboring **Wat Raj Burana,** built by the seventh Ayutthaya king in memory of his brother.

Continue east on Naresuan Road, now called Chao Phnom Road, to the Pa Sak River. Either go left up U-Thong Road to **Chandra Kasem Palace,** or go right to the bridge. The reconstructed 17th-century palace is Ayutthaya's second national museum.

For an educational overview of the Ayutthaya period, stop in at the new **Ayutthaya Historical Study Centre,** near the Teacher's College and the U-Thong Inn. Financed by the Japanese government, the center functions as a museum and a place of national research. Models of the city as a royal capital, as a port city, as an administrative and international diplomatic center, and as a rural village are displayed. ✉ *Rotchana Rd.,* ☎ *035/245123.* ▨ *Admission.* ⊙ *Tues.–Sun. 9–4:30.*

About 5 km (3 mi) north of Ayutthaya is the **Elephant Kraal,** Thailand's only intact royal kraal, last used during King Chulalongkorn's reign in 1903 to hold wild elephants to be trained for martial service.

Dining and Lodging

Romantics may want to stay in Ayutthaya to see the ruins at night. Since most tourists arrive from Bangkok around 10 AM and depart at 4 PM, those who stay are treated to genuine Thai hospitality. Don't expect luxury, however; Ayutthaya has only modest hotels and simple Thai restaurants.

$$ ✕ **Pae Krung Kao.** If you want to dine outdoors on Thai food and watch the waters of the Pa Sak, this is the better of the two floating restaurants near the bridge. You can also come here for a leisurely beer. ✉ *4 U-Thong Rd.,* ☎ *035/241555. AE, MC, V.*

$ ✕ **Tevaraj.** For good, spicy Thai food, head for this unpretentious restaurant behind Ayutthaya's railway station. The fish dishes and the tom kha gai are excellent. ✉ *74 Wat Pa Kho Rd.,* ☎ *no phone. No credit cards.*

$$$$ ✕▨ **The Manohra Song.** The 60-ft wreck of an old teak rice barge has, with the help of lots of taste and even more money, been brought back to life as a luxury cruiser on the Chao Phraya. For a day and a half, eight passengers are pampered by a chef and their own guide, amid mahogany, silks, and antique furnishings, as they watch the world drift by between Bangkok and Ayutthaya. ✉ *Manohra Cruises, Marriott Royal Garden Riverside Hotel, 257/1–3 Charoen Nakorn Rd., Thonburi, Bangkok 10600,* ☎ *02/476–0021 or 02/276–0022 Bangkok reservations,* FAX *02/4761120 or 02/460–1805. 4 suites. AE, MC, V. AP.*

$$ ▨ **Krungsri River Hotel.** For a long time the U-Thong Inn was the only reasonably smart hotel in Ayutthaya, but it had its drawbacks. The Krungsri is a welcome addition, and it is conveniently close to the train station. The spacious marble-floor lobby is refreshingly cool, and the rooms, albeit not special in any way, are clean, fresh, and furnished with modern amenities. For atmosphere, choose a room overlooking the river. Because Ayutthaya has few overnight visitors, try to negotiate a discounted rate. ✉ *27/2 Rojana Rd., Ayutthaya 13000,* ☎ *035/ 242996,* FAX *035/243777. 200 rooms. Restaurant. MC, V.*

Bang Pa-In

❻ *20 km (12 mi) south of Ayutthaya.*

A popular attraction outside Ayutthaya is the Bang Pa-In Summer Palace, within well-tended gardens in an architectural complex of striking variety. The original palace, built by King Prusat (1630–55) on the banks of the Pa Sak, was used by the Ayutthaya kings until the Burmese invasion. After being neglected for 80 years, it was rebuilt during the reign of Rama IV (1851–68) and became the favored summer palace of King Chulalongkorn (Rama V, 1868–1910) until tragedy struck. Once, when the king was delayed in Bangkok, he sent his wife ahead on a boat, which capsized, and she drowned. She could easily have been saved, but because a royal person was sacrosanct she could not be touched by a commoner on pain of death. The king could never forgive himself. He built a pavilion in her memory; be sure to read the touching inscription engraved on the memorial.

King Chulalongkorn was interested in Europe and its architecture, and many Western influences are evident here. The most beautiful building, however, is the **Aisawan Thippaya,** a Thai pavilion that seems to float on a small lake, its series of staggered roofs leading to a central spire. It is sometimes dismantled and taken to represent the country at worldwide expositions.

Phra Thinang Warophat Phiman, nicknamed the Peking Palace, stands to the north of the Royal Ladies Landing Place in front of a stately pond. The replica of a palace of the Chinese imperial court, it was built from materials custom-made in China—a gift from Chinese Thais eager to win the king's favor. It contains a collection of exquisite jade and Ming-period porcelain.

Take the cable car across the river to the **Wat Nivet Thamaprawat,** built by King Chulalongkorn in Gothic style. Complete with a belfry and stained-glass windows, it looks as much like a Christian church masquerading as a Buddhist temple. ☒ *Admission to Bang Pa-In Palace Complex.* ☉ *Tues.–Thurs. and weekends 8–3.*

The **Bang Sai Folk Arts and Craft Centre** was set up by the queen in 1976 to train and employ families in handicraft skills. Workers at the center demonstrate their technique and make and sell products available throughout Thailand at the Chitrlada handicraft shops. The crafts on sale include fern-vine basketry, wood carvings, dyed silks, and handmade dolls. It also has a small restaurant and a park, a pleasant place for a picnic, although it is crowded on weekends with Thai families. ☒ *24 km (14½ mi) south of Bang Pa-In on the Chao Phraya River,* ☏ *035/366092.* ☒ *Admission.* ☉ *8:30–4, closed Mon.*

Lopburi

❼ *75 km (47 mi) north of Ayutthaya, 150 km (94 mi) north of Bangkok.*

Lopburi is one of Thailand's oldest cities: the first evidence of its habitation dates from the 4th century. After the 6th century, its influence grew under the Dvaravati rulers, who dominated northern Thailand until the Khmers swept in from the east. From the beginning of the 10th century until the middle of the 13th, when the new Thai kingdom drove them out, the Khmers used Lopburi as their provincial capital. During the Sukhothai and early Ayutthaya periods, the city's importance declined until, in 1664, King Narai made it his second capital to escape the heat and humidity of Ayutthaya. He employed French architects to build his palace; consequently, Lopburi is a strange mixture of Khmer, Thai, and Western architecture.

Lopburi is relatively off the beaten track for tourists. Few foreigners stay overnight, but there is one reasonable hotel, the Lopburi Inn. The rarity of foreigners may explain why locals are so friendly and eager to show you their town—and to practice their English! Bicycle samlors are available, but most of Lopburi's attractions are within easy walking distance.

Wat Phra Si Mahathat, built by the Khmers, is behind the railway station. It underwent so many restorations during the Sukhothai and Ayutthaya periods that it's difficult to discern the three original Khmer prangs—only the central one is intact. Several Sukhothai- and Ayutthaya-style chedis are also within the compound. ⌨ *Admission.* ☉ *Daily 8:30–4:30.*

Walk diagonally through Wat Phra Si Mahathat to **Narai Ratchaniwet Palace.** The preserved buildings, which took from 1665 to 1677 to complete, have been converted into museums. Surrounding the buildings are castellated walls and triumphal archways grand enough to admit an entourage mounted on elephants. The most elaborate structure is the **Dusit Mahaprasat Hall,** built by King Narai to receive foreign ambassadors. The roof is gone, but you'll be able to spot the mixture of architectural styles: the square doors are Thai and the domed arches are Western.

The next group of buildings in the palace compound—the **Chan Phaisan Pavilion** (1666), the **Phiman Monghut Pavilion** (mid-19th century), and the row of houses once used by ladies of the court—are now all museums. The ladies' residences now house the **Farmer's Museum,** which exhibits regional tools and artifacts seldom displayed in Thailand. ⌨ *Admission.* ☉ *Wed.–Sun. 9–noon and 1–4.*

North across the road from the palace (away from the station), you'll pass through the restored **Wat Sao Thong Thong.** Notice the windows of the viharn, which King Narai changed to imitate Western architecture. Beyond the wat and across another small street is **Vichayen House,** built for Louis XIV's personal representative, De Chaumont. The house was later occupied by King Narai's infamous Greek minister, Constantine Phaulkon, whose political schemes eventually caused the ouster of all Westerners from Thailand. When King Narai was dying in 1668, his army commander, Phra Phetracha, seized power and beheaded Phaulkon. In the attack, the Vichayen House and its ancillary buildings, including a Roman Catholic church, were nearly destroyed. ⌨ *Admission.* ☉ *Wed.–Sun. 9–noon and 1–4.*

Walk east on the road between Wat Sao Thong Thong and Vichayen House to **Phra Prang Sam Yot,** a Khmer Hindu shrine and Lopburi's primary landmark. The three prangs symbolize the sacred triad of Brahma, Vishnu, and Shiva. King Narai converted the shrine into a Buddhist temple, and a stucco image of the Buddha sits serenely before the central prang once dedicated to Brahma.

About 250 meters down the street facing Phra Prang Sam Yot and across the railway tracks is the **San Phra Kan shrine.** The respected residents of the temple, Samae monkeys, often perform spontaneously for visitors. These interesting animals engage in the human custom of burying their dead.

Dining and Lodging

Accommodations in Lopburi are used mostly by Thai traveling salesmen. Except for the hotel dining rooms, Lopburi restaurants are sidewalk cafés serving Thai and Chinese food. Menus are written in Thai, but you can point to what you want in glass cases at the front of the restaurant.

$$ ⊞ **Lopburi Inn.** This is the only hotel in Lopburi with air-conditioning and modern facilities. Even so, don't expect your room to have much more than a clean bed and a private bath. The dining room serves Thai and Chinese food, and the hotel has achieved a certain fame by having an annual dinner party for the town's resident monkeys. ⊠ *28/9 Narai Maharat Rd.,* ☎ *036/412300,* ☒ *036/411917. 142 rooms. Restaurant, coffee shop. AE, DC, V.*

The Western Gulf Coast

In the 1920s the royal family built a palace at Hua Hin on the western shore of the Gulf of Thailand. The royal entourage would travel from Bangkok on special trains, and high society followed. Those were Hua Hin's glory days. After World War II, Pattaya's star ascended, and Hua Hin became a quiet town once more, but Pattaya's seedy reputation has made Thais and foreign visitors reconsider Hua Hin and its neighbor Cha' Am as desirable beach resorts close to the capital. After a building boom in the 1990s, the coastline is now dotted with high-rise hotels and weekend condominiums.

During the day, Hua Hin is a busy market town, but most tourists are at the beach. They come into town in the early evening to wander through the bazaars before dinner. There is no beachfront road to attract boisterous crowds, so stretches of beach remain deserted. The drop-off slopes down gently, and the waters are usually calm. The only drawback is the occasional invasion of jellyfish—check for them before you plunge in. The nightlife here is restricted mostly to hotels, though a few bars have opened in recent years. Most foreign visitors stay at hotels in Hua Hin rather than at self-contained resorts, where you need a car or taxi to take you into town.

Hua Hin

❽ *189 km (118 mi) south of Bangkok.*

The king and queen spend the month of April and celebrate their wedding anniversary at the royal summer palace, on the northern boundary of Hua Hin. The palace was completed in 1928 by King Rama VII, who named it Klai Kangwol ("far from worries"). Four years later, while he was staying at Klai Kangwol, the army seized control in Bangkok and demanded that he relinquish absolute power in favor of a constitutional monarchy. He agreed, and the generals later apologized for their lack of courtesy.

The highway to the southern provinces passes through the center of Hua Hin. In fact, it's the town's main street, with shops and cafés lining the sidewalk; a congested street of market stalls and buses runs parallel to it. The **Chatchai street market** is fun to walk through. In the morning vendors sell meats and vegetables; then, from early evening, all sorts of wares, from food to trinkets, are offered. Toward the southern end of town, across the tracks from the quaint wooden railway station, lies the respected **Royal Hua Hin Golf Course** (⊠ Damnernkasem Rd., Prachchuabkirikhan, ☎ 032/512475). Nonmembers can play the par-72 course for B800–B1,200; you can rent clubs, and there's a coffee lounge for refreshments.

Tourist shops and moderately priced hotels line both sides of Damnernkasem Road, leading to the **public beach.** On your way to the beach, keep your eyes open for Naresdamri Road, just before the Sofitel, where Damnernkasem Road becomes closed to traffic. Turn left down Naresdamri Road, which is parallel to and a block from the beach, and walk past several inexpensive hotels and the 17-story Melia Hua

Hin, and a few hundreds meters farther you'll find **Fisherman's Wharf.** It's abuzz in the morning, when the catch comes in. Naresdamri Road is active at night with restaurants and a few bars.

Near the intersection of Damnernkasem and Naresdamri roads is the **Sofitel Central Hua Hin Resort,** formerly the Royal Hua Hin Railway Hotel, which put up royalty and Thailand's elite during the town's heyday. The magnificent Victorian-style colonial building was portrayed as the hotel in Phnom Penh in the film *The Killing Fields.* Be sure to wander through its well-tended gardens and along its verandas.

If you look south along the coast, you'll see a small headland, **Khao Takiab,** and a small island, **Ko Singto.** You can reach the headland by *songthaew* (a pickup truck with two benches), but the best way to get there is to hire a pony and trot along the beach. The 7-km (4-mi) stretch passes hotels and villas and then becomes virtually deserted until you eventually reach Khao Takiab's beach, where three tall condominiums have been built. At the end of the beach, where restaurant stalls abound, dismount for the steep climb past a large statue of the Buddha to the small Buddhist monastery—the views are worth the climb. Then, try to rent a fishing boat at the base of Khao Takiab to cross over to Ko Singto, where you are guaranteed a catch within an hour.

OFF THE BEATEN PATH

KHAO SAM ROI YOD NATIONAL PARK – The rice fields, sugar palms, pineapple plantations, and crab farms that make up this park are about 40 km (25 mi) south of Hua Hin. The plains of the park were depicted in the movie *The Killing Fields* as the site of Pol Pot's murderous reeducation schemes. The charming fishing village of **Wang Daeng** is typical of coastal Thailand 20 years ago, and south of Wang Daeng, the countryside is even more magnificent, with jungle-clad hills and a curving shoreline. Try to get as far south as the picturesque fishing village of **Ao Noi.** Beyond that is the pleasant, sleepy town of **Prachuap** (about 90 km/56 mi south of Hua Hin), which has little appeal for the tourist except for staggering panoramic views from the hills behind its bay.

Dining and Lodging

The restaurants along Naresdamri Road in Hua Hin offer a warm ambience and good value, especially for fresh seafood. For Western food, it's best to eat at one of the major hotels. On Thai holiday weekends, reservations are a must. During peak season—October through mid-March—the prices at hotels are nearly double those in the off-season.

$$$ ✕ **Fisherman's Seafood Restaurant.** The nautical decor sets the tone of the Royal Garden Resort's restaurant, which serves excellently prepared clams, lobsters, mussels, sea tiger prawns, and crabs. Depending on your taste, these can be cooked with Thai spices (such as lobster with garlic and peppers) or simply grilled. ⊠ *107/1 Phetkasem Rd.,* ☎ *032/511881. AE, DC, MC, V.*

$$ ✕ **Sang Thai.** For interesting seafood dishes—from grilled prawns with bean noodles to fried grouper with chili and tamarind juice—this open-air restaurant down by Fisherman's Wharf is popular with Thais. The extensive menu is appealing, but you need to ignore the ramshackle surroundings and floating debris in the water. Don't miss the *kang* (mantis prawns). ⊠ *Naresdamri Rd.,* ☎ *032/512144. DC, MC, V.*

$-$$ ✕ **Chao Lay.** Of the many outdoor pier restaurants, this one is consistently good. The fish is fresh, the cooking exact, and the service friendly (many of the staff speak English). The pier stretches out into the sea a little farther than at the other restaurants, which seems to allow for more cooling breezes. There is an ample selection of dishes, from spicy to tame, from prawns to snapper, and from hot pork curry to mild chicken in coconut milk. ⊠ *15 Naresdamri Rd.,* ☎ *032/513436. No credit cards.*

$$$$ 🏨 **Chiva-Som.** *Condé Nast Traveler* named it the top health resort in
★ the world in 1999, so in less than five years Chiva-Som has become a
world-class spa. The resort centers on health treatments and a whole-
some diet, but the setting on the beach in tasteful and comfortable lodging will do you a world of good, too. ⊠ *73/4 Petchkasem Rd., Hua
Hin 77110,* ☎ *032/536536; 02/381–4459 or 02/381–4460 Bangkok
reservations,* FAX *032/381154. 57 rooms and suites. Restaurant, pool,
massage, spa. AE, DC, MC, V.* 🐟

$$$$ 🏨 **Royal Garden Resort.** Adjacent to the Sofitel, this hotel has accommodations and service equal to those of its neighbor, but because
it doesn't have the colonial ambience, the rates are a few hundred baht
less. The hotel tends to draw a younger set, attracted by the nightclub
and the proximity to the beach. Guest rooms are decorated with modern, unimaginative furniture. The Market Seafood Restaurant is less
elegant than Sofitel's Salathai, but it serves better food. ⊠ *107/1
Phetkasem Rd., Hua Hin 77110,* ☎ *032/511881; 02/476–0021
Bangkok reservations,* FAX *032/512422. 215 rooms. 2 restaurants, bar,
coffee shop, pool, 4 tennis courts, snorkeling, boating, nightclub, playground. AE, DC, MC, V.* 🐟

$$$$ 🏨 **Sofitel Hua Hin Resort.** Even if you don't stay here, the Old World
★ charm of this tasteful hotel is worth a visit. Wide verandas fan out in an
arc, following the lines of the wooden building, and open onto gardens
leading down to the beach. The gardens are splendidly maintained by
30 gardeners, with scores of different plants and topiary figures that look
like shadows at night. The lounges around the reception area are open
to sea breezes. The best guest rooms are those on the second floor with
sea views though the newest are in the 60-room modern wing, which
was completed in 1998. The units in an annex across the street, run by
the Central Village Hotel, offer 41 less attractive but also less expensive
one- and two-bedroom bungalows. ⊠ *1 Damnernkasem Rd., Hua Hin
77110,* ☎ *032/512021; 02/233–0974 Bangkok reservations,* FAX *032/
511014. 214 rooms. 2 restaurants, bar, coffee shop, pool, 4 tennis courts,
snorkeling, boating, nightclub, meeting rooms. AE, DC, MC, V.* 🐟

$$$–$$$$ 🏨 **Dusit Resort & Polo Club.** Although this resort opened in early 1991,
★ the polo grounds and riding stables have yet to be added. Perhaps not
so many guests will actually play polo, but the game establishes the
tone—smart, exclusive, and luxurious. The spacious lobby serves as a
lounge for afternoon tea and evening cocktails, drunk to the soft tunes
of house musicians. Beyond an ornamental lily pond is the swimming
pool with bubbling fountains, and beyond that is the beach. The main
dining room serves Thai, Chinese, and European fare. Off to the left
is the San Marco, an alfresco Italian restaurant; to the right is the Ben-
jarong, in a traditional Thai-style pavilion. All the guest rooms have
private balconies and a pool or sea view. There's shuttle service to Hua
Hin and car service to Bangkok. ⊠ *1349 Petchkasem Rd., Cha' Am,
Petchburi 76120,* ☎ *032/520009; 02/636–3333 Bangkok reserva-
tions,* FAX *032/520296. 298 rooms and 10 suites. 5 restaurants, 2 bars,
in-room safes, pool, wading pool, 5 tennis courts, steam room, exer-
cise room, squash, boating, parasailing, waterskiing, meeting rooms.
AE, DC, MC, V.* 🐟

$$$–$$$$ 🏨 **Melia Hua Hin.** Towering over Hua Hin, this 17-story hotel has great
rates during the off-season, as low as B1,000. In-season rates are a lit-
tle lower than the Sofitel's. The Melia is a mass-market hotel, popu-
lar with many European tour groups. Its rooms are spacious (a minimum
of 42 square meters [450 square ft]), modern, and functional. The la-
goon-like pool dominates the garden, and the small sandy beach shares
its limited space with vendors and tourists from other hotels. ⊠ *33 Nares-*

damri Rd., Hua Hin 77110, ☎ 032/511612, ℻ 032/511135. 297 rooms. 3 restaurants, pool, 2 tennis courts, health club, squash, nightclub, meeting rooms. AE, DC, MC, V. 🐌

$$$–$$$$ 🏨 **Regent Cha' Am.** This beach resort has everything from water sports to gourmet dining to shopping arcades. Some guest rooms are in bungalows, a number of which face the beach, while others are in one of two 12-story buildings set back from the beach. Gardens separate the bungalows, the main building, two large outdoor pools, and two smaller outdoor pools. The Lom Fang restaurant, overlooking the lake at the back, serves excellent fish with a spiced curry-and-lime sauce. The more formal restaurant, the Tapien Thong Grill Room, offers seafood and steak. In the evening, a small group sings Western songs in Thai. The hotel has its own car service from Bangkok. ⊠ *849/21 Cha' Am Beach, Petchburi, ☎ 032/451240; 02/251–0305 Bangkok reservations, ℻ 032/471492; 02/253–5143 Bangkok reservations. 630 rooms and 30 suites. 3 restaurants, coffee shop, 4 pools, snorkeling, boating, nightclub. AE, DC, MC, V.* 🐌

$$$ 🏨 **Pran Buri Seaview Beach Resort.** A collection of small bungalow units facing the beach south of Hua Hin comprises this isolated holiday complex. The first row, facing the beach, is the best. Though simply furnished, guest rooms have their own terraces, minibars, telephones, and TV with VCR. The main lodge contains the bar-lounge and dining room, where Thai, Chinese, and Western dishes are served. The atmosphere is laid-back and fun. ⊠ *9 Parknampran Beach, Prachuapkhirikhan 77220, ☎ 032/631765; 02/233–3871 Bangkok reservations, ℻ 02/235–0049. 60 rooms. Restaurant, bar, pool, 2 tennis courts, health club, snorkeling, boating, meeting rooms. AE, DC, MC, V.*

$ 🏨 **Jed Pee Nong.** This hotel, on the main tourist street, has bungalow cottages in its courtyard. Rooms have huge beds and not much else, but the price is right. The terrace restaurant facing the street stays open late and is a popular spot from which to watch the parade of vacationers walking past. ⊠ *17 Damnernkasem Rd., Hua Hin 77110, ☎ 032/ 512381, ℻ 032/53063. 44 rooms. Restaurant, coffee shop. MC, V.*

$ 🏨 **Sirin.** At B1,500 during high season, B890 in low season, this ordinary hotel with a helpful staff is a bargain. It's on the main tourist avenue, a block from the beach. The air-conditioned rooms are plain but clean and light, and the bathrooms are reasonably large. Although there is a dining room (which doubles as a lounge), you'll probably want to go out for dinner. ⊠ *18 Damnernkasem Rd., Hua Hin 77110, ☎ 032/511150 or 032/512045, ℻ 032/513571. 35 rooms. Restaurant. AE, DC, MC, V.*

¢ 🏨 **All Nations.** Of the backpacker hangouts in Hua Hin, this is about the best. You'll find local expats coming by for a drink or breakfast. Rooms are clean, and while none have private bathrooms, there is a large bathroom on each floor, and only two or three rooms per floor. The expat owner has set up a computer corner where guests and nonguests can, for a fee, access e-mail. ⊠ *10–10/1 Dechanuchit Rd., Hua Hin 77110, ☎ 032/512747, ℻ 032/53474. 11 rooms. Restaurant, bar. No credit cards.*

The Eastern Seaboard

As the Bangkok metropolitan area becomes more and more congested, the Eastern Seaboard is growing rapidly, with most of the economic development around Chonburi and Rayong. The coast—chiefly the resort of Pattaya—has long been the attraction, with water sports, fairgrounds, and nightlife, but Pattaya has so exemplified the seedier aspects of tourism and so rapidly outpaced its infrastructure that many travelers continue into Chantaburi and Trat provinces. Not all the coastline is particularly attractive, and cultural sites are few and far between, but there are fishing villages along the way, a few decent beaches, delightful islands offshore, and inland provincial capitals for supplies. Except for buying gemstones in Chantaburi and Trat, tourists come for beach pleasures. The following destinations are arranged in order of their proximity to Bangkok.

Pattaya

9 *147 km (88 mi) southeast of Bangkok.*

Five decades ago, Pattaya was a fishing village on an unspoiled natural harbor. Discovered by affluent Bangkok residents, it became a weekend playground, replacing the southwest coast as a vacation destination. Then came the Vietnam War, when thousands of American soldiers sought release and recreation. With air and naval bases nearby, U.S. servicemen hit the beaches at Pattaya in droves, and the resort became a boomtown of uncontrolled development.

Pattaya's unbridled sex trade, its crowds, and its water pollution began to erode its appeal, and business dropped off. Now, after a few years in the doldrums, Pattaya is getting busier, with conventioneers and many tourists from Eastern Europe. Pattaya has something tacky for everyone, the most obvious being its many bars and nightclubs catering to foreign males (conveniently located on the side streets are dozens of clinics to treat venereal diseases). The highway from Bangkok was recently expanded but still remains congested; on weekends the two-hour trip often takes four. Raw sewage still seeps into the once-crystal-clear bay, though the government and private enterprises have started a cleanup process with water- and sewage-treatment plants. Most of the hotels are now connected to a sewage system and the water quality is slowly improving. But another problem now faces Pattaya: foreign underworld gangs, generally referred to by Thais as the "Mafia," are a law unto themselves, with the Russian mafia coming out on top.

If Pattaya were anywhere else but Thailand, it would be positively distasteful. But it *is* in Thailand, and somehow what is gross is made acceptable by the smiling Thais. Pattaya can be divided into three sections: the northernmost, Naklua Beach, still attracts locals but has recently expanded, with bars and restaurants that cater to foreigners—particularly Germans and some backpackers. On a small promontory south of the Dusit Resort Hotel is the curving bay of Pattaya, along which runs Beach Road, lined with palm trees on the beach side and modern resort hotels on the other. At the southern end of the bay is the fun part of town—bars, nightclubs, restaurants, and open-front cafés dominate both Sunset Avenue (the extension of Beach Road) and side streets.

Parallel to Beach Road runs Pattaya 2 Road, the main commercial street, which becomes more crowded with traffic and shops the farther south you go. Continuing through town, Pattaya 2 Road climbs a hill leading past Buddha Park on the left and then descends to quieter Jontien Beach, which has attracted condominium developers and hotels along its stretch of white sand.

Tourist attractions abound in Pattaya. The number of open-air bars will astound you. Massage parlors line Pattaya 2 Road. And there are a dozen or so attractions designed for families. One such diversion is the **Elephant Kraal,** where 14 pachyderms display their skill at moving logs in a two-hour show. There are also demonstrations by war elephants, an enactment of ceremonial rites, and the capture of a wild elephant. Everything is staged, but it's always fun to see elephants at work and at play, and though it's unsettling to see them in the city, they and their mahouts have little other choice in making a living. ⊠ *On main hwy., 5 km (3 mi) from Pattaya,* ☎ *038/249818. Tickets and transport: Tropicana Hotel Elephant Desk, Pattaya 2 Rd.,* ☎ *038/ 428158.* ☑ *Admission.* ⊙ *Show daily at 2:30.*

Ů **Nong Nuch Village** has a cultural folk show, an exhibition of monkeys picking coconuts, elephants bathing, and a small zoo and aviary. Two restaurants, one Thai and one Western, serve refreshments on rolling grounds covered with coconut trees. Despite its touristy nature, the village provides a pleasant break from sunbathing on the beach, particularly if you're traveling with children. Hotels will arrange transportation for morning and afternoon visits, since it is 15 km (9 mi) south of Pattaya, at the 163-km marker on Highway 1. Or you can contact the office in Pattaya (☎ 038/429321) opposite the Amari Nipa Resort on Pattaya Klang Road. ⊠ *163 Sukhumvit Hwy., Bang Saray,* ☎ *038/709358.* ☑ *Admission.* ⊙ *Daily 9–5:30; folk show daily 10 AM and 3 PM.*

Ů **Ripley's Believe It or Not Museum** (⊠ Royal Garden Plaza, 218 Beach
Ů Rd., South Pattaya, ☎ 038/710294) offers an adventure through 10 theme galleries that lasts about an hour. The **Million Years Stone Park and Crocodile Farm** (⊠ 22/1 Mu, Nongplalai, Banglamung, ☎ 038/ 422957) has gigantic, grotesque-shape rocks decorating a large garden, and a man-catching-crocodile show performed every hour from
Ů 11 AM to 5 PM. The **Pattaya Monkey Training Centre** (⊠ 151 Km., Soi Chaiyapruk, Sukhumvit Rd., ☎ 038/756367) has shows at 9, 11, noon, 1, 2, and 5. The pig-tailed monkeys, who live about 40 years, are trained for harvesting coconuts, a 12-month course, but are also taught a few other entertaining tricks and are popular with tour groups.

Ů The **Bottle Museum** is actually quite special. Pieter Beg de Leif, a Dutchman, has devoted 14 hours a day for the last 15 years to creating more than 300 miniatures—tiny replicas of famous buildings and ships—in bottles. ⊠ *79/15 Moo 9, Sukhumvit Rd.,* ☎ *038/422957.* ☑ *Admission.* ⊙ *Daily 10–9.*

Dining and Lodging

$$$ ✕ **Bruno's.** This restaurant and wine bar, which replaced Dolf Riks, a Pattaya institution, is well on its way to being an institution itself. Bruno promises to keep the same warm, friendly atmosphere; you can still chat at the bar and dine on top-quality food. The difference is in the cooking. Riks was Indonesian-influenced; Bruno's uses Swiss recipes. ⊠ *463/28 Sri Nakorn Centre, N. Pattaya (turn down cul-de-sac beside Pattaya Bowl),* ☎ *038/361073. AE, DC, MC, V.*

$$$ ✕ **Peppermill Restaurant.** Tucked away next to P. K. Villa, this distinctly French restaurant takes a classical approach to dining, with an emphasis on flambéed dishes. More creative dishes such as fresh crab in a white-wine sauce and poached fillet of sole with a lobster tail are also served. Dinner is a special occasion here, particularly if complemented by a good bottle of wine from the respectable cellar. ⊠ *16 Beach Rd.,* ☎ *038/428248. AE, DC, MC, V. No lunch.*

$$ ✕ **Angelo's.** For Italian food, this is a good choice. The Milanese owner presides over the dining room, and his Thai wife is the chef. Her fortes are lasagna and a wonderful fish casserole. ⊠ *N. Pattaya Rd.,* ☎ *038/429093. MC, V.*

$$ ✕ **Nang Nual.** Next to the transvestite nightspot Simon Cabaret is one of Pattaya's better places for seafood, cooked Thai-style or simply grilled. A huge array of fish is laid out as you enter the restaurant. Point out what you want and say how you want it cooked. There's a dining room upstairs, but you may want to eat on the patio overlooking the sea. For carnivores, the huge steaks are an expensive treat. Menu photographs of the finished products will overcome any language barrier. Similar

dishes are found at Nang Nual's Jontien Beach branch, near the Sigma Resort. ⊠ *214–10 S. Pattaya Beach Rd.,* ☎ *038/428478. AE, MC, V.*

$$ ✕ **PIC.** Dine in classic teak pavilions on a wide range of Thai dishes like delicious deep-fried crab claws and spicy eggplant salad. The food can be hot or mild, and if you are averse to chilies, try the succulent white snapper on vegetables, scented with ginger and salted prunes. ⊠ *Soi 5, Beach Rd.,* ☎ *038/428387. AE, DC, MC, V.*

$$ ✕ **Tak Nak Nam.** This floating restaurant in a Thai pavilion at the edge of a small lake has an extensive menu of Chinese and Thai dishes. Live classical Thai and folk music plays while you dine on such specialties as steamed crab in coconut milk or blackened chicken with Chinese herbs. ⊠ *252 Pattaya Central Rd., next to Pattaya Resort Hotel,* ☎ *038/429059. MC, V.*

$ ✕ **Sportsman Inn.** If you want some down-home English cooking, this is the best spot in Pattaya. The steak-and-kidney pie, bangers-and-chips, and fish-and-chips are well prepared, as testified to by the many ex-pats who get their daily sustenance here. ⊠ *Soi Yod Sak (Soi 8),* ☎ *038/361548. No credit cards.*

$$$$ 🏨 **Royal Cliff Beach Hotel.** Pattaya's most lavish hotel, 1½ km (1 mi) south of town on a bluff jutting into the Gulf, is a self-contained resort with three wings. The 84 one-bedroom suites in the Royal Wing (double the price of standard rooms in the main building) have butler service, in-room breakfast at no charge, and reserved deck chairs. The Royal Cliff Terrace wing has two-bedroom and honeymoon suites with four-poster beds. The swimming pool sits on top of a cliff overlooking the sea. ⊠ *Jontien Beach, Pattaya, Chonburi,* ☎ *038/250421; 02/282–0999 Bangkok reservations,* 🖷 *038/250141. 700 rooms and 100 suites. 4 restaurants, 3 pools, sauna, miniature golf, 2 tennis courts, jogging, squash, 2 beaches, windsurfing, boating, shops. AE, DC, MC, V.*♨

$$$ 🏨 **Dusit Resort.** On a promontory at the northern end of Pattaya
★ Beach, this large hotel has superb sea views. The beautifully laid-out grounds with two pools that run around the promontory add to the pleasure. Though the rooms are in need of some cheerful refurbishing, they have large bathrooms, balconies, oversize beds, and sitting areas. The Landmark Rooms are larger and have extensive wood trim. The Empress restaurant serves sophisticated Cantonese fare against the panoramic backdrop of Pattaya Bay. This retreat is only a B5 songthaew ride from all of Pattaya's tourist action. ⊠ *240/2 Pattaya Beach Rd., Pattaya, Chonburi 20260,* ☎ *038/425611; 02/236–0450 Bangkok reservations,* 🖷 *038/428239. 500 rooms and 28 suites. 4 restaurants, 2 pools, massage, sauna, 3 tennis courts, health club, Ping-Pong, squash, windsurfing, boating, shops, billiards. AE, DC, MC, V.*♨

$$$ 🏨 **Montien.** Though not plush, this hotel is centrally located and designed to take advantage of the sea breezes. With the hotel's generous off-season discounts, a room with a sea view can be one of the best values in town. The air-conditioned section of the Garden Restaurant has a dance floor and stage for entertainment. ⊠ *Pattaya Beach Rd., Pattaya, Chonburi 20260,* ☎ *038/361340 up to 54; 02/233–7060 Bangkok reservations,* 🖷 *038/423155. 320 rooms. 2 restaurants, bar, coffee shop, snack bar, pool, 2 tennis courts, meeting rooms. AE, DC, MC, V.*

$$$ 🏨 **Royal Garden Resort.** This modern resort in downtown Pattaya, a block from the beach, gives the feeling of great space by having both a large, open lobby and lounge, and a garden full of trees with a pool in its center. The carpeted bedrooms are standard, furnished in light colors with enough room for a coffee table and two chairs; a balcony looks over the pool and garden to the sea. Next door is the Royal Garden Plaza, a shopping and entertainment complex. ⊠ *218 Beach Rd., Pattaya, Chonburi 20260,* ☎ *038/412120; 02/476-0021 Bangkok reservations,* 🖷 *038/429926. 300 rooms. 2 restaurants, bar, pool,* *beauty salon, 4 tennis courts, health club, business services, meeting rooms, travel services. AE, DC, MC, V.* ✍

$–$$ ⛱ **Palm Lodge.** This started as a no-frills hotel, but its central yet quiet location has prompted the owners to expand and improve the facilities. Now the hotel offers modern rooms with TVs and minibars. Bathrooms are tiled and clean. The outdoor pool is smallish but pleasantly laid out in a shady garden; besides, the sea is just across the road. ⊠ *Mu 9, Beach Rd., Pattaya, Chonburi 20260,* ☎ *038/428780,* 𝔽𝔸𝕏 *038/421779. 80 rooms. Coffee shop, pool, laundry service. MC, V.*

$ ⛱ **Chris Guest House.** Owned by an Englishman, this small hotel offers clean, inexpensive (B500), air-conditioned rooms with private baths—ask for one of the new rooms. The friendly atmosphere makes this the top choice in the budget category. On the ground floor there's an open-front lounge-restaurant-bar where old roués gather at a round table chaired by Chris to review the world of sex and sin. Though it's only half a block from the sea, it is nevertheless quietly secluded, with its own garden down a small soi. ⊠ *185 Soi 13, Pattaya Beach Rd., Pattaya, Chonburi 20260,* ☎ *038/429586,* 𝔽𝔸𝕏 *038/423653. 15 rooms. Restaurant, bar. No credit cards.*

$ ⛱ **Diamond Beach Hotel.** In the heart of Pattaya's nightlife, amid discos and cafés, this hotel is a bastion of sanity. Rooms are clean, and security guards make female guests feel safe. The staff, however, is not particularly friendly or helpful—perhaps that's why you can often find a room here when other hotels are full. ⊠ *373/8 Pattaya Beach Rd., Pattaya, Chonburi 20260,* ☎ *038/428071,* 𝔽𝔸𝕏 *038/424888. 126 rooms. Restaurant, massage, travel services. No credit cards.*

Nightlife and the Arts

Entertainment in Pattaya revolves around its hundreds of bars, cafés, discos, and nightclubs, most of which are at the southern end of the beach and a couple of blocks inland. Bars and clubs stay open past midnight, and some are open much later. Drinks for any hostess who joins you are B100. Pattaya has confronted its AIDS problem, but the disease is still a serious concern. The city is also the center of criminal gangs. Caution is therefore advised for night revelers! For something other than the common girlie bars try **Tony's Entertainment Complex** (⊠ Walking Street Rd., South Pattaya, ☎ 038/425795), next to the Royal Garden Plaza, which has live bands, a beer garden, and a disco. **Dalaney's Pattaya** (⊠ In the Royal Garden Resort, 218 Beach Rd., ☎ 038/710641) has food, beer, and a large-screen TV for sports fans.

Outdoor Activities and Sports

BUNGEE JUMPING

If you like the thrill, try **Kiwi Thai Bungee Jump** (⊠ Off the main road to Jontien Beach, ☎ 038/250319). You are hoisted in a metal cage to a height of 150 ft; then you jump. Just remember to attach your rubber harness first.

GOLF

Laem Chabang International Country Club (⊠ 106/8 Moo 4 Beung, Srirach, Chonburi, ☎ 038/372273) has a professionally maintained course near Pattaya. Thailand's longest course (6,800 yards), the **Royal Thai Navy Course** (⊠ Phiu Ta Luang Golf Course, Sattahip, Chonburi, ☎ 02/466–1180 or 02/466–2217, ext. Sattahip), is 30 km (18 mi) from Pattaya. With rolling hills and dense vegetation, it's considered one of the country's most difficult. The **Siam Country Club** (⊠ 50 Moo 9 T. Poeng A., Banglamong, Chonburi, ☎ 038/418002), close to Pattaya, offers a challenging course with wide fairways but awkward water traps and wooded hills.

WATER SPORTS

All kinds of water sports are available, including windsurfing (B200 per hr), waterskiing (B1,000 per hr), and sailing on a 16-ft Hobie catamaran (B500 per hr). Private entrepreneurs offer these activities all along the beach, but the best area is around the Sailing Club on Beach Road. Jet skiing and parasailing are dangerous and shouldn't be tried for the first time here. Operators of parasailing boats tend to be inexperienced, making sharp turns or sudden stops that bring the parachutist down too fast. Be on the lookout for unscrupulous operators who rent a defective machine and hold the customer responsible for its repair or loss. The water near the shore is too polluted for diving and snorkeling.

En Route　Take highway H3 south for about 20 km (12 mi) and turn right at the 165-km marker for **Bang Saray.** The village consists of jetties, a fishing fleet, a small temple, and two narrow streets running parallel to the bay. Fully equipped game-fishing crafts are tied to the jetty, and photos to prove fishermen's stories are posted in the area's two hotel bars, Fisherman's Lodge and Fisherman's Inn. It costs about B2,500 to charter one of the faster fishing boats for the day. If you just want to soak up the scene, stop next to the main jetty at the Ruam Talay Restaurant. Windsurfers can be rented at the beach, just north of the bay at the Sea Sand Club. H3 goes through Sattahip, a Thai naval base. Avoid it by taking bypass H332, which passes through countryside full of coconut groves and tapioca plantations, to **Rayong** (50 km/31 mi east of Sattahip), a booming market town famous for seafood and nam plaa, the fermented fish sauce Thais use to salt their food. Since the early 1990s, this area has become a center of economic growth, with industrial estates offering tax and customs breaks to investors. About 20 km (12 mi) east of Rayong is the small village of **Ban Phe,** whose beaches and self-contained resorts attract Thai families. Ban Phe is the jumping-off point for Ko Samet.

Ko Samet

⑩ *30 mins by ferry from Ban Phe, which is 223 km (139 mi) southeast of Bangkok.*

Two ferries (B30) from Ban Phe make the crossing to Ko Samet. One goes to Na Duan on the north shore, the other to An Vong Duan halfway down the eastern shore. All the island's beaches are an easy walk from these villages. Indeed, from the southern tip to the north is a comfortable three-hour walk. Ko Samet is known for its beaches; its other name is Ko Kaeo Phitsadan ("island with sand like crushed crystal"), and its fine sand is in great demand by glassmakers. The island has many bungalows and cottages, with and without electricity. Make sure that yours has mosquito netting: come dusk, Ko Samet's mosquitoes take a fancy to tourists. Restaurants set up along the beach in the late afternoon offer an opportunity to laze a little more. Seafood is the best choice but menus cater to all tastes. While you dine, the tide will inch its way up to your table in the sand, and your feet could be wet before you leave.

Lodging

¢　☷ **Vong Duan Resort.** Vong Duan (also spelled Wong Deuan) beach is a cove with lots of bungalow accommodation. The Vong Duan Resort is the biggest and has the largest staff. Its bungalows, which are on stilts and have air-conditioning and fans, are a degree better than its neighbors'. The beach has a smaller, more relaxed crowd than some other parts of the island. Although the hotel has a restaurant, all the seafood restaurants lining the beach are pretty good. ⊠ *Vong Duan Beach,* ☎ *038/651777. 30 bungalows. Restaurant. No credit cards.*

Chantaburi

⑪ *100 km (62 mi) east of Rayong; 180 km (108 mi) east of Pattaya.*

Buses from Rayong and Ban Phe make the 90-minute journey to the pleasant provincial town of Chantaburi. Its gem mines are mostly closed now, but it has become renowned as a trading center for gems. Rubies and sapphires still rule, but stones from all corners of the world are now traded here. Gem Street, in the center of town, is fascinating: in small storefronts, you'll see traders sorting through gems and making deals worth hundreds of thousands of baht. The street becomes a gem market on Fridays and Saturdays with buyers and sellers from all over the world. The province of Chantaburi has few beach resorts of note, and those cater mostly to Thais. Laem Sadet, 18 km (11 mi) from Chantaburi, is the most popular, and its accommodations range from small bungalows to low-rise hotels. Chantaburi is once again becoming a gateway to the western part of Cambodia as Thailand's neighbor opens up.

Lodging

$$ 🏨 **KP Grand Hotel.** Though this 18-story business hotel has no charm, it does have modern facilities, large guest rooms with two single beds or a king, and attentive service. It's on the eastern side of town, but within walking distance of Gem Street. ✉ *35/200-201 Theerat Rd., 22000,* ☎ *039/323201,* 📠 *039/323214. 200 rooms. 2 restaurants, bar, pool, health club, meeting rooms. AE, DC, MC, V.*

En Route Beyond Chantaburi lies Trat, Thailand's easternmost province. Hemmed in by the Khao Banthat mountain range, the region is waiting to be discovered by tourists. The provincial capital, **Trat,** two hours plus from Chantaburi, is a small town whose interest is as a market and transport center. For travelers, it is where buses arrive from and depart for Bangkok, and where songthaews leave for the 20-minute trip to Laem Ngop, the port for ferries to Ko Chang.

Ko Chang

★ **⑫** *1 hr by ferry from Laem Ngop, which is 15 km (9 mi) southwest of Trat; Trat is 400 km (250 mi) southeast of Bangkok.*

Ko Chang (Elephant Island) is Thailand's second largest island (Phuket is the biggest). It is also the largest and most developed of the 52 islands that make up Mu Ko Chang National Park, many of which are not much more than hummocks protruding from the sea. These islands are still being discovered by Westerners and local tourists and have not yet been spoiled by the honky-tonk commercialism found in Pattaya, Phuket, and Ko Samui. The infrastructure is basic and accommodations rustic. You can book lodgings on these islands in Laem Ngop, where you buy your ferry ticket. Most of the tourists who make the trip here (a good eight hours from Bangkok) are backpackers and young Thais looking for inexpensive vacations.

Ko Chang's best beaches are on the western shore. Haad Sai Khao (White Sand Beach) attracts mostly backpackers who pay B100 a night for a cot in huts crammed together along the narrow beach. Haad Khlong Phrao is next, with a long, curving beach of pale golden sand. Accommodations here are spaced farther apart and tend to be larger and more expensive. Farther down and at the end of the only road on the island is Haad Kai Bae. Here, the beach, with both sand and pebbles, has a very gentle drop-off—safe for nonswimmers. A couple of small, uninhabited islands offshore make the views attractive, and accommodations range from a few air-conditioned bungalows to small huts.

One of the most beautiful islands is tiny **Ko Wai** (three hours by ferry from Laem Ngob), resplendent with idyllic beaches, tropical flora, and fantastic coral reefs. **Ko Ngam,** also small, is shaped like a butterfly and has waters of different hues. **Ko Kradat** has little development except for one bungalow resort. **Ko Mak,** a little larger than the other islands, has a small village and a couple of basic resorts with bungalows. **Ko Kut,** the second largest of the Ko Chang group, is mountainous.

Lodging

Booking agents at travel agencies in Laem Ngob port can make reservations for you on the Ko Chang islands.

$$$ ⊞ **Ko Chang Resort.** One of the first comfortable resorts to be built on Ko Chang is a self-contained complex on the edge of the bay, with clean, rustic bungalows around a reception lounge and dining room. The rate for the air-conditioned units is fairly steep, and the small ones are very cramped. The advantage of the resort is that you can make the booking in Bangkok; it also has its own boat service to the island. ⊠ *Ko Chang, Trat 23120,* ☎ *01/211–3834; 02/276–1233 Bangkok reservations,* ⅏ *02/276–6929 in Bangkok. 45 rooms. Restaurant. MC, V.*

$–$$$ ⊞ **Sea View Resort.** Choose either a small, fan-cooled thatched bungalow just back from the sands of Kai Bae Beach or a larger air-conditioned unit with a private bath 100 yards inland on a slight rise. The resort is at the far end of the beach and is therefore quieter than the others. It has an attractive terrace restaurant and a very gentle, sloping, sandy beach—too gentle for many. ⊠ *Ko Chang, Trat 23120,* ☎ *038/538055; 02/256–7168 Bangkok reservations,* ⅏ *02/276–6929 in Bangkok. 32 rooms. Restaurant. MC, V.*

¢–$$ ⊞ **Kae Bae Hut Bungalows.** Accommodations run the gamut from tiny ★ B50 bungalows back from the beach to much larger ones with air-conditioning and private baths facing the beach. Because the bungalows are near the center of Kae Bae Beach, guests can wander over to nearby restaurants for meals and entertainment, although the restaurant's food is the best on the beach and the staff the friendliest. ⊠ *Ko Chang, Trat 23120,* ☎ *No phone. 25 rooms. Restaurant, dive shop. No credit cards.*

Side Trips out of Bangkok A to Z

Arriving and Departing

By Airplane

HUA HIN AND CHA' AM

The Hua Hin airport will open again in 2001 after an expansion and renovation. Charter flights and private aircraft will be welcome, and Bangkok Airways or another of Thailand's airlines may return with regular flights. The airport is near town.

PATTAYA

Bangkok Airways (⊠ 60 Queen Sirikit National Convention Centre, New Ratchadaphisek Rd., Bangkok, ☎ 02/229–3434) has a daily flight from Ko Samui, which lands at U-Tapao Airport, 50 km (30 mi) east of Pattaya. **Silk Air** (☎ 02/236–0440 in Bangkok; 053/276–459 in Chiang Mai; 076/213891 in Phuket) has flights between Singapore and Pattaya every Tuesday, Wednesday, Friday, and Saturday. There are also chartered flights from Europe.

By Boat

AYUTTHAYA

Though you can go by rail or road, the nicest way to get there (at least one-way) is by tourist boat along the Chao Phraya River (☞ Tour Operators, *below*).

By Bus and Minibus

AYUTTHAYA

Buses leave Bangkok's Northern Terminal every 30 minutes between 6 AM and 7 PM for Ayutthaya and Lopburi. Minibuses frequently leave Ayutthaya's Chao Prom Market for Bang Pa-In starting at 6:30 AM. The 50-minute trip costs B10.

DAMNOEN SADUAK, NAKHON PATHOM, AND KANCHANABURI

Public buses, some air-conditioned, leave from Bangkok's Southern Bus Terminal every 20 minutes starting at 6 AM for Damnoen Saduak's bus station. The fare is B30, B90 air-conditioned. From there, walk along the canal for 1½ km (1 mi) to the floating market or take a taxi boat at the pier for B10. Buses leave Bangkok from the same terminal every 20 minutes for the 2½-hour trip to Kanchanaburi. Buses also run to Nakhon Pathom from Damnoen Saduak.

HUA HIN AND CHA' AM

Buses, air-conditioned and non-air-conditioned, leave Bangkok's Southern Bus Terminal every half hour during the day for the three-hour trip to **Hua Hin's terminal** (✉ Srasong Rd., ☎ 032/511654).

KO CHANG

For the various islands of the Ko Chang group, take a bus from Bangkok's Eastern Bus Terminal for the five- to six-hour trip to Trat, where you pick up a songthaew for the 20-minute run to the ferries at Laem Ngob. Schedules vary, but if you can get to Laem Ngob by 1 PM (take the first bus from Bangkok, at 6 AM), you should find a ferry that afternoon going to Ko Chang and the other islands. The last bus out of Bangkok is at 11 PM, which gets you to Trat at 4 or 5 AM, in time for coffee at the market before a songthaew, usually loaded with housewives and vegetables, leaves for Laem Ngob to connect with the 7 AM ferry.

PATTAYA AND KO SAMET

Buses depart every half hour from Bangkok's Eastern Bus Terminal, arriving at **Pattaya's bus station** (✉ North Pattaya Rd., ☎ 038/429877). The fare is B77. From the bus station, songthaews will take you into downtown Pattaya for B30—tell the driver where you want to go. A bus runs between Don Muang Airport and Pattaya (B120) every two hours from 7 AM to 5 PM, and direct buses run between Nakhon Ratchasima (Korat) and Pattaya's northern bus station on Central Pattaya Road.

Most hotels in Bangkok and Pattaya have a travel desk that works directly with a minibus company. Minibuses leave approximately five times a day and cost B200 per person. An Avis minibus that departs from Bangkok's **Dusit Thani Hotel** (✉ Rama IV Rd., ☎ 02/236–0450) for its Pattaya property is open to nonguests.

Direct buses make the three-hour trip between Pattaya's hotels and Bangkok's Don Muang Airport every two or three hours from 6 AM to 9 PM. **Thai Limousine Service** (✉ ticket desk at airport, or in Pattaya, ☎ 038/421421) has the cleanest, most reliable air-conditioned buses. The cost is B200.

For Ko Samet, buses leave frequently from Bangkok's Eastern Bus Terminal for Ban Phe to connect with the ferry. From Pattaya, try the **Malibu Travel Centre** (✉ Post Office La., ☎ 038/423180), which has daily 8 AM departures for B150. You can also take the local bus or a car to Ban Phe.

By Car and Taxi

DAMNOEN SADUAK, NAKHON PATHOM, AND KANCHANABURI

You can arrange to be picked up by a private car or taxi in Bangkok and reach the Damnoen Saduak market by 9 AM, before the tours arrive. Speak to your concierge, who will usually have a good resource. The cost for two people will be no more than a tour-bus fare and can be as low as B1,500 round-trip. If you keep the car to visit both Nakhon Pathom and Kanchanaburi, the cost will be about B2,000.

HUA HIN AND CHA' AM
A few hotels, such as the Regent and Dusit Thani, run minibuses (which nonguests may use) between their Bangkok and Cha' Am or Hua Hin properties for a flat fee of B450. Otherwise, you can hire a car and driver for approximately B2,500 to or from the Bangkok airport.

PATTAYA
Taxis to Pattaya from either Don Muang Airport or downtown Bangkok will ask B2,500, which can be quickly renegotiated to B1,800 or less. Coming back costs about B1,000.

By Train
AYUTTHAYA
Between 4:30 AM and late evening, trains depart frequently from Bangkok's Hualamphong station, arriving in Ayutthaya 80 minutes later. Since Don Muang Airport lies between the two cities, many travelers coming back from Chiang Mai visit Ayutthaya and then get off at the airport to fly to their next destination. Trains from Bangkok regularly make the 70-km (42-mi) run to Bang Pa-In railway station, from which a minibus runs to the palace. Three morning and two afternoon trains depart from Hualamphong station for the three-hour journey to Lopburi. The journey from Ayutthaya takes just over an hour. Trains back to Bangkok run in the early and late afternoon.

DAMNOEN SADUAK, NAKHON PATHOM, AND KANCHANABURI
Trains from Bangkok's Hualamphong and Noi stations stop in Nakhon Pathom. Trains for Kanchanaburi leave Noi Station at 8 AM and 1:55 PM. The State Railway of Thailand also runs a special excursion train (B75) on weekends and holidays; it leaves Hualamphong Station at 6:15 AM and returns at 7:30 PM, stopping at Nakhon Pathom, the River Kwai Bridge, and Nam-Tok, from which point minibuses take you to Khao Phang Waterfall. There is no train to Damnoen Saduak.

HUA HIN AND CHA' AM
The train from Bangkok's Noi Station takes four long hours to reach Hua Hin's delightful wooden **train station** (✉ Damnernkasem Rd., ☎ 032/511073). Trains leave Bangkok at 12:45 PM and 2:45 PM and depart Hua Hin for the return trip at 2:20 PM and 4 PM.

Getting Around

Ayutthaya
For a three-hour tour of the sites, tuk-tuks can be hired within the city for about B400.

Hua Hin and Cha' Am
Local buses make it easy to travel between Cha' Am and Hua Hin, as well as to points south of Hua Hin. Taxis are available, but samlors are more convenient for short distances. You can walk to most of the sights in town, but if you are staying at a resort hotel in Cha' Am, use the hotel shuttle bus or take a taxi. Tours to nearby attractions can be arranged through your hotel.

Kanchanaburi
Attractions around Kanchanaburi are accessible both on foot and by samlor. Buses leave from the town's **terminal** (✉ Saeng Chuto Rd., ☎ 034/511387) every half hour for most of the popular destinations.

Pattaya

Songthaews cruise the two main streets, parallel to the beach. The fare is B5 in town, and B10 between Naklua and Pattaya; for the Royal Cliff Resort, the fare is about B50, and to Jontien Beach, it's at least B100. Sedans and jeeps can be rented for B700–B900 a day, with unlimited mileage. **Avis** (⊠ Dusit Resort Hotel, Pattaya, ☎ 038/429901) and **Budget** (⊠ Sai Two Rd., Pattaya, ☎ 038/720613) offer insurance, though not all rental companies do. Motorbike rentals cost about B250 a day but getting around by bike is risky.

Contacts and Resources

Emergencies

AYUTTHAYA

Tourist Police (☎ 035/242352). **Ratcha Thani Hospital** (⊠ 111 Moo 3, Rotchana Rd., ☎ 035/335555 or 035/335560).

HUA HIN AND CHA' AM

Tourist Police (☎ 032/515995). **Hua Hin Hospital** (⊠ Phetkasem Rd., ☎ 032/511743).

PATTAYA

Tourist Police (⊠ Pattaya 2 Rd., ☎ 038/429371; 1699 for emergencies). **Hospital and ambulance** (☎ 191).

Tour Operators

Tours of Ayutthaya and Bang Pa-In take a full day. You can travel the 75 km (46 mi) both ways by coach or in one direction by cruise boat and the other by coach. The best combination is to take the morning coach to Ayutthaya for sightseeing before the day warms up, and return down the river. The most popular trip is aboard the overnight *Manohra Song* (⊠ Managed by the Marriott Royal Garden Resort, 257/1–3 Charoen Nakorn Rd., Thonburi, Bangkok, ☎ 02/476–0021/2). Day trips with the *Oriental Queen* (⊠ Managed by the Oriental Hotel, 48 Oriental Ave., Bangkok, ☎ 02/236–0400) cost B1,900. You can book either of these cruises with any travel agent.

The **Chao Phraya Express Boat Co.** (⊠ 2/58 Aroon-Amarin Rd., Maharat Pier, Bangkok, ☎ 02/222–5330) runs a Sunday excursion to Bang Pa-In Summer Palace, which leaves the pier at 8:30 AM and arrives in time for lunch. On the downriver trip, it stops at the Bang Sai Folk Arts and Craft Centre and arrives in Bangkok by 5:30 PM.

All the major hotels have arrangements with tour operators who organize morning trips to Damnoen Saduak, sometimes combined with the Rose Garden, or Kanchanaburi and the bridge over the River Kwai. These tours pick you up at about 8 AM and cost B700. A full day is usually necessary to visit the Allied war cemeteries and the infamous bridge, and to tour the gorgeous countryside.

Visitor Information

Ayutthaya Tourist Authority of Thailand (TAT) (⊠ Si Sanphet Road, ☎ 035/246076 or 035/246077), open daily 9–5. **Cha' Am TAT** (⊠ 500 Petchakasem Rd., ☎ 032/471005 or 032/471006), open daily 8:30–4:30. **Kanchanaburi TAT** (⊠ Saeng Chuto Rd., ☎ 034/511200). **Pattaya TAT** (⊠ 382/1 Mu 10 Chaihat Rd., ☎ 038/427667 or 038/428750), open daily 9–5.

NORTHERN THAILAND

Northern Thailand is the scene of an ancient sophisticated culture and intellectual center existing side by side with agrarian peoples stepping slowly into the industrial age. Chiang Mai is the gateway to the region: many travelers stay a month or longer, making excursions and

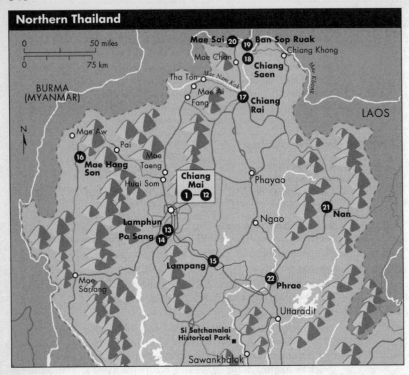

Northern Thailand

returning there to rest. Guest houses and smart hotels accommodate them, and well-worn tracks lead into the surrounding tribal villages. The opium trade still flourishes, flowing illegally into southern Thailand en route to the rest of the world. For the tourist, however, the attractions are trekking in forested hills laced with rivers, the cultures of the hill tribes, and the cool weather. (Those who also seek the poppy often find themselves languishing in a Chiang Mai prison.)

The hill tribes around Chiang Mai have been visited so frequently that they have lost some of their unique character. You need to go farther afield, to areas around Tak, near the Burmese border, and Nan to the east, to find villages untainted by tourism. Two paved highways from Chiang Mai and daily flights have opened up the region, and even Mae Hong Son, west of Chiang Mai, known for its sleepy pace and the regular gathering of hill tribes, is developing its tourist trade.

The Golden Triangle (*Sop Ruak* in Thai), the area where Thailand, Laos, and Burma meet, has long captivated the Western imagination. The opium poppy still grows here, albeit on a much diminished scale, and the hill tribes that cultivate it are semiautonomous, ruled more by warlords than by any national government. Today, the tribes of Laos and Burma retain their autonomy, but Thailand's corner of the Golden Triangle has become a tourist attraction, with the tribes caught up in the tide of commercialism. Chiang Rai is the closest city. In 1990 it had only one luxury hotel; now there are at least three resort complexes, and two more have been built where the rivers converge, overlooking Laos and Burma.

Chiang Mai and West to the Border

Most visitors fly from Bangkok to the walled, moated city of Chiang Mai (though many are discovering the pleasant overnight train) and make short excursions to the smaller towns south and southeast; we cover those spots in that order. People also come to see Chiang Mai's ancient buildings and stay to shop. Then, if there's time, they drive or fly west to Mae Hong Son to visit the nearby hill-tribe villages.

Chiang Mai

❶ *696 km (430 mi) north of Bangkok.*

Chiang Mai's rich culture stretches back 700 years to the time when several small tribes, under King Mengrai, banded together to form a new "nation" called Anachak Lanna Thai. They first made Chiang Rai (north of Chiang Mai) their capital but moved it in 1296 to the fertile plains between Doi Suthep mountain and the Mae Ping River and called it Napphaburi Sri Nakornphing Chiang Mai.

Lanna Thai eventually lost its independence to Ayutthaya and, later, Burma. Not until 1774—when the Burmese were driven out—did the region revert to the Thai kingdom. After that, it developed independently of southern Thailand. Even the language is different, marked by a relaxed tempo. In the last 50 years communications have grown between Bangkok and Chiang Mai; the small, provincial town has exploded beyond its moat and gates, and some of its innocence has gone.

Chiang Mai can be explored easily on foot or by bicycle, with the occasional use of buses, tuk-tuks, or taxis for getting to attractions outside the center. Most wats are free and are usually open sunup to sundown.

❷ **Wat Phrathat Doi Suthep** is perched high up—3,542 ft—on Doi Suthep, a mountain 16 km (10 mi) northwest of Chiang Mai that overlooks the city. It is a 30-minute drive—you can take a songthaew from Chuang Puak Gate at the corner of Manee Napparat and Chotana roads on the north side of the city—and then a cable-car ride (if the cable car is completed) or steep climb up 304 steps to the chedi. The stone balustrade, added in 1577, is in the form of *nagas* (mythical snakes that control the irrigation waters in rice fields), inlaid with scales of brown and green tiles.

A special relic here makes Wat Phrathat one of the four royal wats: in the 14th century, when a relic of Lord Buddha was being installed at Wat Suan Dok, it split into two, and a white elephant was sent to find a new location for the second piece. The animal stomped his way up Doi Suthep, circled three times in a counterclockwise direction and knelt down, marking the chosen spot. A chedi was built, then later enlarged and followed by other shrines to make a large and glorious complex that dazzles the eyes with gold, red, and green mosaics and a glittering gold-plated chedi. Murals depict scenes from the life of the Buddha.

❸ **Phuping Palace,** the summer residence of the Thai royal family, is across a valley from Wat Phrathat. Though the palace cannot be visited, the gardens are open on Friday, Sunday, and public holidays, unless any of the royal family is in residence. The blooms are at their best in January.

❹ **Wat Umong,** south off Suthep Road, is the most fun temple in Chiang Mai. According to local lore, a monk named Jam liked to go wandering in the forests. This irritated King Ku Na, who often wanted to consult with Jam. In order to be able to seek advice at any time, the king built this forest wat for the monk in 1380. Along with the temple structures, tunnels were constructed and decorated with paintings, fragments of which may still be seen. Beyond the chedi is a pond filled with hungry carp. Throughout the grounds are snippets of "wisdom" on posted signs.

Chiang Mai

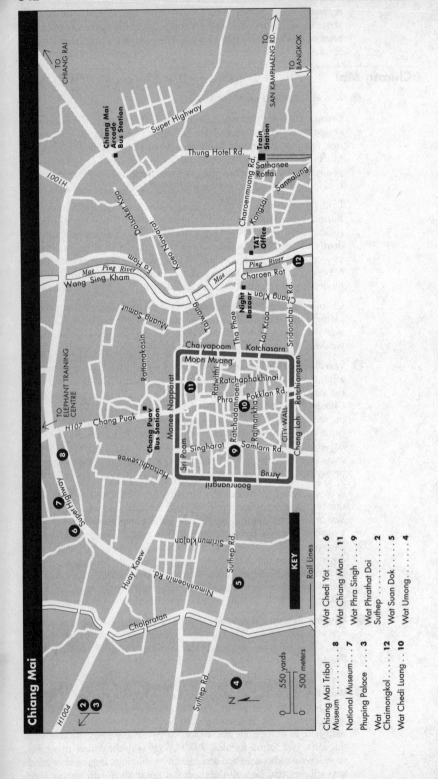

KEY

—— Rail Lines

⑤ **Wat Suan Dok,** on Suthep Road, is one of the largest of Chiang Mai's temples, said to have been built on the site where bones of Lord Buddha were found. Some of these relics are reportedly housed in the chedi; the others went to Wat Phrathat. At the back of the viharn is the bot housing Phra Chao Kao, a superb bronze Buddha cast in 1504. Chiang Mai aristocrats are buried in stupas in the graveyard.

⑥ On the superhighway between its intersection with Huay Kaew Road and Highway 107 stands Wat Photharam Maha Viharn, more commonly known as **Wat Chedi Yot.** Meaning Seven-Spired Pagoda and built in 1455, it is a copy of the Mahabodhi temple in Bodh Gaya, India, where the Buddha achieved enlightenment; the seven spires represent the seven weeks that he subsequently spent there. The sides of the chedi have marvelous bas-relief sculptures of celestial figures.

⑦ From Wat Chedi Yot you can walk to the recently renovated **National Museum,** a northern Thai-style building containing many statues of Lord Buddha and a huge Buddha footprint of wood with mother-of-pearl inlay. The upper floor's archaeological collection includes a bed with mosquito netting used by an early prince of Chiang Mai. ✉ *Admission.* ⊙ *Weekdays 8:30–noon and 1–4:30.*

⑧ Up Chang Puak Road (take a tuk-tuk) is Rachanangkla Park and the **Chiang Mai Tribal Museum.** Until 1998, more than 1,000 pieces of traditional crafts from the hill tribes, collected over the past 30 years, had been hidden away in a small museum at Chiang Mai University. This fine collection—farming implements, colorful embroidery, weapons, hunting traps, and a variety of drums and musical instruments—is now displayed in its own building by the lake in the park. ✉ *Rachanangkla Park, Chang Puak Rd.,* ☎ *053/221933.* ✉ *Admission.* ⊙ *Mon.–Sat. 8:30–4.*

★ ⑨ Chiang Mai's city walls contain several important temples—all within walking distance of one another. At the junction of Ratchadamnoen and Singharat roads, in the middle of town, stands Chiang Mai's principal monastery, **Wat Phra Singh,** containing the Phra Singh Buddha image. Its serene and benevolent expression has a radiance enhanced by the light filtering into the chapel. Be sure to note the temple's facades of splendidly carved wood, the elegant teak beams and posts, and the masonry. In a large teaching compound, student monks often have the time and desire to talk.

⑩ On Phra Pokklao Road, between Rajmankha and Ratchadamnoen roads, stands **Wat Chedi Luang.** In 1411, a vision commanded King Saen Muang Ma to build a chedi "as high as a dove could fly." He died before it was finished, as did the next king, and, during the following king's reign, an earthquake knocked down 100 ft of the 282-ft chedi. It is now a superb ruin. Don't miss the naga balustrades at the steps to the viharn, considered the finest of their kind.

⑪ **Wat Chiang Man,** Chiang Mai's oldest (1296) monastery and typical of northern Thai architecture, has massive teak pillars inside the bot. Two important images of the Buddha sit in the small building to the right of the main viharn. Officially, they are on view only on Sunday, but sometimes the door is unlocked.

★ ⑫ The rarely visited **Wat Chaimongkol,** along the Mae Ping River and near the Chiang Mai Plaza Hotel, is small, with only 18 monks in residence. Its little chedi contains holy relics, but its real beauty lies in the serenity of the grounds.

Ⓒ If you have not seen an "elephant camp" elsewhere, visit the **Elephant Training Centre** about 20 km (12 mi) northwest of Chiang Mai at Mae Sa. As commercial and touristy as it is, elephants are so magnificent that the show (B80) cannot fail to please. Action begins at 9:40 AM, when mahouts bring their animals to the river for a frolic in the water and a thorough wash down. The elephants then stage a dull demonstration of dragging in 20-ft teak logs and nudging them into a pile. At the end of the show, the audience feeds them bananas. You can also ride an elephant around the camp or take a one-hour trek through the forest. Lunch at the **Mae Sa Valley Resort** (⊠ In the valley, ☎ 053/291051, FAX 053/290017), which has thatched cottages in beautiful gardens where vegetables are grown. The owner's honey-cooked chicken with chili is particularly good.

Dining

All the top hotel dining rooms serve good Continental and Thai food, but for the best Thai cuisine, go to the restaurants in town. Several good bistro-style restaurants serving northern Thai cuisine are across from the Rincome Hotel on Nimanhaemin Road, about 1½ km (1 mi) northwest of downtown. Also try the food at the Anusan Market.

$$–$$$ ✕ **Baen Suan.** Off the San Kamphaeng Road (the shopping-factory street), and a B40 tuk-tuk ride from downtown, sits a northern-style teak house in a peaceful garden. The excellently prepared food is from the region. Try the hot Chiang Mai sausage, broccoli in oyster sauce, green curry with chicken, and shrimp-and-vegetable soup. ⊠ *51/3 San Kamphaeng Rd.,* ☎ *053/242116. Reservations essential. No credit cards.*

$$–$$$ ✕ **The Gallery.** North along the Mae Ping from the Riverside and the Good View is the third in a line of pleasant, shaded, waterside restaurants. This one is also an art and antiques gallery. The terraces down toward the river have a secluded feeling, and the food is Thai, with some northern Thai dishes to spice up the menu. ⊠ *25–29 Charoen Rat Rd.,* ☎ *053/248601. AE, DC, MC, V.*

$$ ✕ **Arun Rai.** This is the best-known restaurant in Chiang Mai for northern Thai cuisine. Its success has inspired the owner to roof half of his space, but you still should not expect great ambience; the focus is on the food. Try the papaya salad, *tabong* (boiled bamboo shoots fried in batter), *sai oua* (pork sausage with herbs), or the famous frogs' legs fried with ginger. The menu is available in English. The Arun Rai often has the delicacy *rod fai* (fried banana worms), which you may want to try. ⊠ *45 Kotchasarn Rd.,* ☎ *053/276947. Reservations not accepted. No credit cards.*

$$ ✕ **The Good View.** Of the three terraced restaurants in a row along the Mae Ping River, this one in the middle is the prettiest and the quietest and has the best view. You can sit on the shaded deck just outside the restaurant or down toward the water on varying levels. A broad menu with both Thai and Western dishes should satisfy all comers. ⊠ *13 Charoen Rat Rd.,* ☎ *053/302764. MC, V.*

$$ ✕ **Hong Tauw Inn.** Linger in the relaxing, intimate atmosphere as you try dishes from northern Thailand and the Central Plains. There is an English menu, and the owner speaks English fluently. Excellent Thai soups, crispy *pla mee krob* (fried fish with chili), and *nam phrik ong* (minced pork with chili paste and tomatoes) are among the popular dishes. ⊠ *Across from Rincome Hotel, 95/17–18 Nantawan Arcade, Nimanhaemin Rd.,* ☎ *053/218333. MC, V.*

$$ ✕ **Huen Phen.** The small rooms in this restaurant, once a private
★ home, are full of old handicrafts which, if not antiques, are wonderful decorative artifacts. Be sure to browse through each dining room before settling in, either inside or in the garden, to study the extensive menu. The *kaeng hang lae* (northern pork curry) with *kao neeu* (sticky rice) is a specialty; *larb nua* (spicy ground beef fried with herbs) and deep-fried pork ribs are two more good dishes to try. ⊠ *112 Rachamongka Rd., Phrasing,* ☎ *053/277103. MC, V.*

$$ ✕ Kaiwan. Not many Westerners come here, but the food is held in
★ high esteem by Thais. The best place to sit is upstairs at one of the pic-
nic tables under the stars. Try the not-so-spicy beef curry (*kaeng mat
sa man*) or the zesty fried fish (*pla tot na phrik*). ⊠ *181 Nimanhaemin
Rd. Soi 9, near the Rincome Hotel,* ☎ *053/221147. MC, V.*

$$ ✕ Len Pae. If you've made the shopping trip along San Kamphaeng Road
and want a relaxing lunch, this floating restaurant on an artificial lake
hits the spot. Gentle breezes off the water keep the temperature down.
The best tables are those on the piers extending into the lake. The fare
is northern Thai with a variety of spicy sausages and fried freshwater
fish, as well as less spicy Chinese food. ⊠ *114 Moo 2 Sanklang, Chiang Mai–San Kamphaeng Rd.,* ☎ *053/338641. No credit cards.*

$$ ✕ Nang Nuan. Though this large restaurant has tables indoors, it's pleas-
ant to sit on the terrace facing the Mae Nam Ping. Because it's 3 km
(2 mi) south of Chiang Mai, you'll need to take a tuk-tuk or taxi, but
the tom kha gai and the *yam nua* (beef salad) are worth the trip.
Grilled charcoal steaks and fresh seafood (displayed in tanks) are also
on the menu. ⊠ *27/2 Ko Klang Rd., Nonghoy,* ☎ *053/281955. AE,
DC, MC, V.*

$$ ✕ Riverside. In a 100-year-old teak house on the bank of the Mae Nam
Ping, this restaurant serves primarily Western food given zest by the
Thai chef. The casual, conversation-laden atmosphere attracts young
Thais and Westerners, and with lots of beer flowing, the food gets only
partial attention. Choice tables are on the deck, with views of Wat
Phrathat on Doi Suthep in the distance. There's live light jazz and pop
music after 7 PM. ⊠ *9–11 Charoen Rat Rd.,* ☎ *053/243239. Reser-
vations not accepted. No credit cards.*

$$ ✕ Whole Earth. On the second floor of an attractive old Thai house
in a garden, this long-established restaurant serves delicious vegetar-
ian and health foods and a few nonveg dishes for the carnivorous, such
as *kai tahkhrai* (fried chicken with lemon and garlic). Many are In-
dian dishes—try the eggplant masala. The inside dining room is air-
conditioned, and the balconies take full advantage of any breezes (but
you should ask for a mosquito coil under your table). The service is
sometimes slow. ⊠ *88 Sridonchai Rd.,* ☎ *053/282463. Reservations
not accepted. No credit cards.*

$ ✕ Supotana Kaun. For superb northern Thai food you must travel 7
★ km (4½ mi) north on the Chiang Dao road (Hwy. 107) and also put
up with traffic noise, zero decor, and crates of empty bottles lying around,
but the food is worth it. The *phad thai* (stir-fried noodles) is so crisp
and delicate it melts in your mouth, and the fish with a hot-and-sour
sauce is delicious. Try the "1,000-year-old eggs" (actually eggs buried
in mud for three months and called *kai yean ma*, which means "eggs
washed in horse's urine"). ⊠ *Chiang Dao Rd., at traffic light where
road from Chiang Mai Sports Complex joins from left,* ☎ *053/210980.
No credit cards.*

Lodging

With Chiang Mai on every tourist's itinerary, a variety of hotels flour-
ishes, and construction is ongoing. Some hotels add a surcharge in Jan-
uary and February, which brings prices here close to those in Bangkok.
Lodgings cluster in four districts. The commercial area, between the
railway station and the Old City walls, holds little interest for most
tourists. The area between the river and the Old City has the largest
concentration of hotels and is close to most of the evening street ac-
tivity. Within the city walls small hotels and guest houses offer simple,
inexpensive accommodations. The west side of town, near Doi Suthep,
has attracted the posh hotels; it's quieter but also far from many points
of interest. Taxi and tuk-tuk drivers will try to get you to change your

hotel for one they recommend (which gives them a commission), and hotels that don't pay them off (the River View Lodge and Gap's House are two) often have their clients misrouted.

$$$$ 🔳 **Regent Chiang Mai.** In the lush Mae Rim Valley, 20 minutes north
★ of Chiang Mai, the most attractive hotel in northern Thailand nestles in 20 acres of landscaped gardens amid lakes, lily ponds, and terraced rice paddies. An arc of 16 two-story buildings in traditional Lanna style contains the suites, each with an outdoor *sala* (Thai gazebo) just perfect for breakfast and cocktails. Rooms are furnished with rich Thai cottons and Thai art; floors are polished teak. Huge bathrooms overlook a garden. The main restaurant, Sala Mae Rim, serves beautifully presented Thai dishes and offers sweeping views of the valley. Another restaurant beside the pool is popular for light meals. Once you're here, even catching the shuttle bus to Chiang Mai center seems too much effort, and therein lies its disadvantage: isolation from the rest of the world. ⊠ *Mae Rim-Samoeng Old Rd., 50180,* ☎ *053/298181,* FAX *053/ 298189. 67 suites. 2 restaurants, bar, pool, 2 tennis courts, health club. AE, DC, MC, V.* 🍃

$$$ 🔳 **Chiang Mai Orchid Hotel.** This is a grand hotel in the old style, with teak pillars in the lobby. Rooms are tastefully furnished and trimmed with wood. The Honeymoon Suite is often used by the Crown Prince. You can choose to eat at either the formal Continental restaurant, Le Pavillon; the Japanese restaurant; or the informal Thai coffee shop. You'll find entertainment in the lobby bar or the cozy Opium Den. The hotel is a 10-minute taxi ride from Chiang Mai center. ⊠ *100–102 Huay Kaeo Rd., 50000,* ☎ *053/222099; 02/245–3973 Bangkok reservations,* FAX *053/221625. 260 rooms and 7 suites. 2 restaurants, coffee shop, 2 bars, pool, beauty salon, sauna, health club, business services, meeting room. AE, DC, MC, V.*

$$$ 🔳 **Imperial Mae Ping Hotel.** Festoons of lights sweep down from the building's towering heights to the vast courtyard and gardens below. Here, in the outdoors, buffet dinner is served and, in the beer garden, Philippine bands drown out any street noise. Classical and hill-tribe dancing are performed at the far end of the garden. Inside the hotel are three more restaurants—European, Chinese, and Japanese. With 371 rooms to fill in the center of town, the Imperial caters to package tours, particularly Japanese, but the modern, functional bedrooms are well kept and the staff is surprisingly even-tempered. ⊠ *153 Sridonchai Rd., 50100,* ☎ *053/270160; 02/261–9460 Bangkok reservations,* FAX *053/270181. 371 rooms. 4 restaurants, bar, beer garden, coffee shop, pool, meeting rooms. AE, DC, MC, V.* 🍃

$$$ 🔳 **Royal Princess.** Formerly the Dusit Inn and still part of the chain, this hotel is ideal if you'd like to step out of the front door and into the tumult of Chiang Mai's tourist center. The famous Night Bazaar is a block away, and street vendors are even closer. The rooms lack natural light, making them a little dreary, but the staff is well trained and helpful, the lobby is pleasant, the cocktail lounge has a pianist in the evenings, and the Jasmine restaurant serves the best Cantonese fare in Chiang Mai. ⊠ *112 Chang Rd., 50000,* ☎ *053/281033; 02/233– 1130 Bangkok reservations,* FAX *053/281044. 200 rooms. 2 restaurants, pool, meeting rooms, airport shuttle. AE, DC, MC, V.* 🍃

$$ 🔳 **Chiang Inn.** Behind the Night Bazaar and set back from the street, the Chiang Inn has quiet rooms (the higher up the better). They are reasonably spacious and decorated in local handwoven cottons. La Grillade serves Thai-influenced French cuisine in a formal atmosphere, and the more casual Ron Thong Coffee House serves Thai and Western dishes. The hotel is usually swamped with tour groups, to which its facilities are geared. ⊠ *100 Chang Khlan Rd., 50000,* ☎ *053/270070;*

02/251–6883 Bangkok reservations, FAX *053/274299. 170 rooms and 4 suites. 2 restaurants, pool, nightclub, meeting rooms, travel services. AE, DC, MC, V.*

$$ ⊞ **River View Lodge.** Facing the Mae Nam Ping across a grassy lawn,
★ this lodge is an easy 10-minute walk from the Night Bazaar. Some seasoned travelers say it's the best place to stay in the city. The rooms are tastefully done with wood furniture crafted in the region and terra-cotta floor tiles; the more expensive ones have private balconies overlooking the river. Though neither elegant nor luxurious, there's a restful simplicity here that's a far cry from the standard uniformity in most of the city's high-rise hotels. The small restaurant is better for breakfast than for dinner, and the veranda patio overlooking the pool and river is good for relaxing with a beer or afternoon tea. The owner speaks nearly fluent English and will assist in planning excursions. ⊠ *25 Charoen Prathet Rd. Soi 2, 50000,* ☎ *053/271109,* FAX *053/279019. 36 rooms. Restaurant, pool. AE, DC, MC, V.*

$$ ⊞ **Zenith/Suriwongse.** Around the corner from the Royal Princess, near the Night Bazaar, this hotel recently underwent a refurbishment that brought it up to first-class standards. Its association with the French hotel chain attracts European tour groups, and the staff makes a game attempt to speak French. The rooms, done in pastels, are bright and cheery, and the hotel compares favorably with the Royal Princess. ⊠ *110 Chang Khlan Rd., 50000,* ☎ *053/270051; 02/251–9883 Bangkok reservations; 800/221–4542 U.S. reservations,* FAX *053/270063. 166 rooms and 4 suites. Restaurant, coffee shop, travel services, airport shuttle. AE, DC, MC, V.*

$–$$ ⊞ **Galare Guest House.** This guest house on the Mae Ping riverfront
★ has many advantages: its good location (within five minutes' walk of the Night Bazaar); small but clean rooms with air-conditioning and fans; a shady garden in which to relax; and a restaurant facing the river. It offers more charm and personal service than many of the other city hotels, and it's the best value in town. ⊠ *7 Charoenprathet Rd. Soi 2, 50100,* ☎ *053/818887,* FAX *053/279088. 35 rooms. Restaurant. MC, V.*

$–$$ ⊞ **Grand Apartments.** With reasonable rates by day or by month (B4,000 per month), this new building in the old city is good for an extended stay. Its air-conditioned rooms are efficient and clean, and guests have access to telex and fax machines, and a laundry room. ⊠ *24/1 Prapklao Rd., Chang Puak Gate, 50000,* ☎ *053/217291,* FAX *053/ 213945. 36 rooms. Café, coin laundry. MC, V.*

$–$$ ⊞ **Montri Hotel.** Near the Tha Pae Gate, the Montri has clean, utilitarian rooms with adequate bathrooms. Rooms at the back are quietest. The coffee shop–restaurant opens at 6 AM for those wanting breakfast before an early departure. ⊠ *2-6 Ratchadamnoen Rd., 50200,* ☎ *053/ 211069,* FAX *053/217416. 46 rooms. Restaurant. MC, V.*

$–$$ ⊞ **River Ping Palace.** The complex of Thai buildings at this welcoming little guest house shows you what Chiang Mai was like 50 years ago. It's owned by a Frenchman and his Thai wife. Food is served at any time in the pleasant open-air restaurant. The wooden structures have smallish rooms decorated with old Thai furnishings and artifacts—very personal, if a bit fussy. The best room, No. 3, costs B1,600; in the smaller ones (B1,200), there's very little space around the double bed. The guest house is a B30 tuk-tuk ride south of the Night Bazaar. ⊠ *385/2 Charoen Phrathat Rd., Chang Klan 50100,* ☎ *053/274932,* FAX *053/204281. 5 rooms, most with bath. Restaurant. MC, V.*

$ ⊞ **Gap's House.** This collection of traditional wood houses is like a tiny shady village within the walls of old Chiang Mai. Room No. 5 overlooks a junglelike plant nursery and tiny vegetable garden; one room has a fishpond, another an old Thai bed on its veranda. A lively rooster and a bilingual mynah bird add to the rural atmosphere, and antique bric-a-brac is scattered around the open breakfast-sitting area. Mr. Gap, the owner, either likes you or not—immediately. The rooms are furnished with an odd assortment of antiques, giving a homey, well-worn feel. Bathrooms are basic, with cement floors and rudimentary showers, and breakfast comes with the room. Treks or excursions can be arranged, and the garden bar is often full of happy travelers swapping stories. English is spoken here, but don't speak it too loudly or get too rowdy—Gap might throw you out! ⊠ *4 Ratchadamnoen Rd. Soi 3, 50200, ☎ 053/278140. 18 rooms. Bar. MC, V.*

$ ⊞ **Mountain View Guest House.** Within the Old City and just inside the Chang Puak Gate is this oasis of a guest house with simple but clean rooms. It has its own garden and a little restaurant where the friendly staff will prepare basic food for you. ⊠ *105 Sriphum Rd., 50200, ☎ 053/212–8666, FAX 053/222635. 15 rooms. No credit cards.*

$ ⊞ **Roong Ruang Hotel.** You step into the courtyard of this little garden hotel right off Tha Pae Road, the scene of a lot of Chiang Mai's action. Two-story wings with overhanging eaves and galleries for sitting flank the courtyard, where motorbikes and a few cars can be parked. All rooms have hot water and satellite TV; some have fans (B350) and some are air-conditioned (B450). The owner, who speaks English, owns the neighboring cybercafé and will order breakfast if you want it. ⊠ *398 Tha Pae Rd., 50000, ☎ 053/234746 or 053/232017, FAX 053/252409. 25 rooms. No credit cards.*

¢ ⊞ **Lai Thai.** On the edge of the Old City walls, a 10-minute walk from the Night Bazaar, this friendly guest house has air-conditioned or fan-cooled rooms around a garden courtyard. Bare, polished floors and simple furniture give them a fresh, clean look, and those at the back are quietest. The casual open-air restaurant serves Thai, Western, and Chinese food. ⊠ *111/4–5 Kotchasarn Rd., 50000, ☎ 053/271725, FAX 053/272724. 120 rooms. Restaurant, motorbikes, coin laundry, travel services. MC.*

Nightlife and the Arts
BARS AND PUBS

Aside from the "love places," of which Chiang Mai has its share, there are several pubs and bars, some with live music and food. To listen to live jazz, drop in at the casual European-style **Bantone** (⊠ 99/4 Moo 2, Huay Kaew Rd., ☎ 053/224444). **Bubbles** (⊠ Charoen Prathet Rd., ☎ 052/270099), in the Pornping Tower Hotel, is a lively disco for the young at heart. The Chiang Mai Orchid Hotel's dance club, **Club 66** (⊠ 100–102 Huay Kaeo Rd., ☎ 053/222099), aspires to attract a stylish, sophisticated crowd. At the **Cozy Corner** (⊠ 27 Moon Muang Rd., ☎ 053/277964), the pub atmosphere, chatty hostesses, and beer garden with a waterfall are all popular with the patrons, who come for hamburgers and beer.

You may leave messages for fellow travelers at **The Domino Bar** (⊠ 47 Moon Muang Rd., ☎ 053/278503), an English-style pub serving snacks. For those who want to visit each branch of the famous chain, there is a **Hard Rock Cafe** (⊠ 66/3 Loi Kroh Rd., near Thape Gate, ☎ 053/206103) in Chiang Mai. Described by *Newsweek* as "one of the world's best bars," **The Pub** (⊠ 189 Huay Kaew Rd., ☎ 053/211550) can get a little crowded. Still, for draft beer, good grilled steak, and a congenial atmosphere, this place is hard to beat. With its location next to the Mae Ping River and small bands that perform throughout the evening, the **Riverside** (☞ Dining, *above*) is popular.

At **The Hill** (⊠ 92–93 Bumrungburi Rd., ☎ 053/277968), in a large, mostly covered courtyard, Thais while away the evening listening to a live band (usually with Thai vocalists). The cement floors are scattered with bench tables, a wooden bridge crosses a stream that divides the cavernous area, and a balcony attracts the more demonstrative couples. Entertainers perform on an artificial hill with rocks and ferns. You buy tickets at a kiosk, then collect your food, beer, and soft drinks from stands (bring your own bottle and pay a corkage fee if you want the hard stuff).

KHANTOKE DINNER AND DANCING

No first visit to Chiang Mai should omit a khantoke dinner. The menu is usually sticky rice, which you mold into balls with your fingers; delicious *kap moo* (spiced pork skin); a super-spicy dip called *nam phrik naw,* with onions, cucumber, and chili; and *kang ka,* a chicken-and-vegetable curry—all accompanied by Singha beer. The dinner usually includes performances of Thai or hill-tribe dancing (or both). An evening's diversion usually starts at 7, costs B650 for two, and requires reservations.

Tour buses deposit middle-aged Westerners at the **Blue Moon** (✉ 5/3 Moon Muang Rd., ☎ 053/278818) for a very routine performance of a dance show that includes a troupe of transvestites. One much-publicized "dinner theater" puts on a repertory of dancing and a khantoke dinner at the back of the **Diamond Hotel** (✉ 33/10 Charoen Prathet Rd., ☎ 053/272080). Tour groups come here because there are good explanations of the symbolism in the dancing. The best place in the center of Chiang Mai to eat a khantoke dinner and see hill-tribe and classical Thai dances is the **Khum Kaew Palace** (✉ 252 Pra Pok Klao Rd., ☎ 053/214315). The symbolism of each dance is explained in Thai and English. The building is a distinctive traditional northern Thai house, where you sit cross-legged on the floor or at long tables. The **Old Chiang Mai Cultural Centre** (✉ 185/3 Wualai Rd., ☎ 053/ 275097), designed like a hill-tribe village, has nightly classical Thai and authentic hill-tribe dancing, after a khantoke dinner.

MASSAGE

Chiang Mai is a good place to try a **traditional Thai massage,** practiced since the time of the Buddha and believed to ameliorate problems ranging from epilepsy to backaches and tension. A simple hour massage costs B200, a two-hour rubdown is B400. **Petngarm Hat Wast** (✉ 33/10 Charoen Prathet Rd., ☎ 053/270080), in the Diamond Hotel, offers a range of traditional and herbal massages. Good massages with or without herbs are given at **Suan Samoon Prai** (✉ 105 Wansingkham Rd., ☎ 053/252716).

Shopping

Chiang Mai, Thailand's foremost shopping center, is known for many crafts. Lacquerware was traditionally used to make betel-nut sets; the bamboo frame would be covered with layer upon layer of red lacquer and decorated with black. Nowadays trays and jewelry boxes are popular items. Jade comes from Burma: the softer jade is carved into chopsticks, figurines, and Buddha images, the harder and more translucent jade is used for jewelry. Silver is hammered into plates and cups as well as chunky jewelry, priced according to weight (silver runs about B10 per gram). Paper made from silk, cotton, or mulberry leaves is used to make writing paper and umbrellas. Celadon, often known as greenware, is a variety of stoneware developed in China over 2,000 years ago. Much of Chiang Mai's woodcarving is pretty junky, but fine workmanship can be found in **Baan Tawai,** a village of small workshops devoted to woodcarving (go 13 km/8 mi south down Highway 108 to Hang Dong and then east for a couple of km). Silk prices are higher here than in I-san, and for mudmee, wait until you get to the Northeast. Two-ply silk for shirts and skirts runs about B375 a meter and four-ply silk for suits runs about B500 a meter. Rough cotton, usually from Pa Sang, is B60 a meter. Even if merchandise is priced, there is always room for negotiation. Most shops honor major credit cards, and a discount for cash is often possible.

The **Golden Mile** is a 16-km (10-mi) stretch of the road that runs east to San Kamphaeng. Large emporiums on both sides sell silver, ceramics, cottons and silks, woodcarvings, hill-tribe crafts and artifacts, lacquerware, bronzeware, and hand-painted umbrellas. You can watch the goods being made at factory workshops, which is alone worth the trip. Taxi drivers know the stores and any of them will happily spend a couple of hours taking you around for B50 to B100. The driver receives a commission each time he brings tourists to a store, whether they buy or not.

The **Night Bazaar** is a congestion of stalls and one of Thailand's most exciting markets. There are crafts made in rural villages throughout Burma, Laos, and northern Thailand—but inspect the goods thoroughly for minor flaws. The clothing can be very inexpensive, and, at times, good quality. Some objets d'art are instant antiques, but there are real ones, too. **Lanna Antiques** (⊠ Booth No. 2 on the second floor) has a good selection. Behind the stalls is a sort of courtyard, with restaurants and some good hill-tribe products.

Some of your best buys can come from patient browsing among the downtown shops north of Tha Pae Road, but there are also larger shopping venues. The **Chiang Inn Plaza** (⊠ Chiang Khlan Rd.), across from the Chiang Inn in the center of town, is a modern shopping center where you can buy well-crafted goods. At the **Rimping Superstore Chotana** (⊠ 171 Chang Puak Rd., ☏ 053/210377), established retailers sell quality goods at fixed prices.

En Route A few miles south of Chiang Mai, before you reach Lamphun, a small road marked by a Shell station on the corner leads west to **Wat Chedi Liem,** a five-tier wat built by King Mengrai in the 13th century, and probably copied from Wat Chama Devi in Lamphun. Approximately 3 km (2 mi) past Wat Chedi Liem, on a small island in the Mae Nam Ping, is the **McKean Leprosarium,** which has treated leprosy sufferers since 1908 and is internationally recognized as a model self-contained community clinic. Don't worry about catching the disease—visitors are perfectly safe. The community itself is inspiring: some 200 patients have their own cottages on 160 secluded acres, with medical facilities, occupational therapy workshops, stores, and a church. The Leprosarium is open weekdays 8 to noon and 1 to 4, and Saturday 8 to noon; donations are requested.

Lamphun

🔞 *26 km (16 mi) south of Chiang Mai.*

Minibus songthaews (B10) go from Chiang Mai to Lamphun. It's also a pleasant day's trip to drive south on Highway 106, a shady road lined by 100-ft rubber trees, past Lamphun to Wat Phra Baat Takpa.

Lamphun claims to be the oldest existing city in Thailand (but so does Nakhon Pathom). Originally called Nakhon Hariphunchai, it was founded in AD 680 by the Chamdhevi dynasty, which ruled until 1932. Unlike Chiang Mai, Lamphun has remained a sleepy town, consisting of a main street with stores, several food stalls, and not much else. The town is known for its *lamyai* (longan), a sweet cherry-size fruit with a thin shell. The fruit is celebrated in early August with the Ngam Lamyai festival, with floats, a beauty pageant, and a drum-beating competition. In the nearby village of **Tongkam,** the "B10,000 lamyai tree" nets its owner that sum in fruit every year. Buy yourself a jar of lamyai honey; you'll be in for a treat.

Lamphun's architectural prizes are two temple monasteries. Two kilometers (1¼ miles) west of the town's center is **Wat Cham Devi**—often called Wat Kukut (topless chedi) because the gold at its top has been removed. You'll probably want to take a samlor down the narrow residential street to the wat. Since it is not an area where samlors generally cruise, ask the driver to wait for you.

Despite a modern viharn at the side of the complex, the monastery has a lovely weathered look. Suwan Chang Kot, to the right of the entrance, is the most famous of the two chedis, built by King Mahantayot to hold the remains of his mother, the legendary Queen Cham Devi, first ruler of Lamphun. The five-tier sandstone chedi is square; on each of its four sides, and on each tier, are three Buddha images. The higher the level, the smaller the images. All are in the 9th century Dvaravati style, though many have obviously been restored. The other chedi was probably built in the 10th century, though most of what you see today is the work of 12th-century King Phaya Sapphasit.

Wat Phra That Hariphunchai is dazzling. Enter the monastery from the river, through a parking lot lined with stalls selling food, clothing, and mementos. Through the gates, guarded by ornamental lions, is a three-tier, sloping-roof viharn, a replica (built in 1925) of the original, which burned in 1915. Inside, note the large Chiang Saen–style bronze image of the Buddha and the carved *thammas* (Buddhism's universal principals) to the left of the altar.

Leave the viharn by walking to the right, past what is reputedly the largest bronze gong in the world, cast in 1860. The 165-ft Suwana chedi, covered in copper plates and topped by a golden spire, dates from 847. A century later, King Athitayarat, the 32nd ruler of Hariphunchai, raised it and added more copper plating to honor the relics of Lord Buddha inside. On top of the chedi, he added a nine-tier umbrella, gilded with 14 pounds of pure gold. The monk who brought the relics from India is honored with a gold statue in a nearby chamber. He's also remembered for his potbelly—legend has it that he made himself obese so that his youthful passion for women wouldn't interfere with his concentration on the Buddha's teachings.

At the back of the compound—which leads to a shortcut to the center of town—there's another viharn with a standing Buddha, a sala housing four Buddha footprints, and the old museum. The new museum, just outside the compound, has a fine selection of Dvaravati stucco work and Lanna antiques. ✉ *Admission.* ☉ *Museum: Wed.–Sun. 8:30–4.*

NEED A BREAK? For lunch or a cold drink, go back through Wat Hariphunchai to the main road along the Kwang River and choose any one of the string of cafés.

Pa Sang

 12 km (7½ mi) south of Lamphun, 38 km (19 mi) south of Chiang Mai.

Many visitors go to Pa Sang, down Highway 106 from Lamphun, to shop for locally produced cottons with traditional designs and to watch the weaving. Songthaews (B10) ply the route all day. Although in recent years the better stores have moved to Chiang Mai and the selection has diminished, you can find both cloth by the yard and ready-made clothing. A shirt with a batik pattern goes for B100, while dresses run about B175.

More contemporary clothing and household items can be found at **Nandakwang Laicum,** a market on the right-hand side as you enter town.

Five kilometers (3 miles) south of Pa Sang on Highway 106 is **Wat Phra Bhat Takpa,** commonly known as the Temple of Buddha's Footprint. The energetic can climb the 600 steps to the hill-top chedi, but the main attraction is the two huge imprints of Lord Buddha's foot, indented in the floor, inside the temple at the right of the car park. As you enter, buy a piece of gold leaf (B20), which you can paste in the imprint and make a wish.

Lampang

⑮ *65 km (40 mi) southeast of Lamphun, 91 km (59 mi) southeast of Chiang Mai.*

During Rama VI's reign, carriage horses were imported from England. The quaint image of horse-drawn carriages in the town's streets is still promoted by tourism officials, but the 21st century has come to Lampang, and a superhighway connects this busy metropolis to Chiang Mai and Bangkok. Concrete houses and stores have replaced the wooden buildings, cars and buses have taken over the streets, and only a few horses remain. Still, its wats, shops, and the few old-style wooden houses are sufficiently pleasant that you may wish to spend the night. Hotels in Lampang are the best you'll find between Chiang Mai and Phitsanulok.

Despite its modernization, Lampang has some notable Burmese architecture remaining. Opposite the Thai International Airways office is **Wat Phra Fang,** easily recognizable by its green corrugated-iron roof on the viharn and its tall white chedi, decorated with gold leaf. Surrounding the chedi are seven small chapels, one for each day of the week. Inside each chapel is a niche with images of the Buddha.

A well-preserved example of Lampang's Burmese architecture is **Wat Sri Chum.** Pay particular attention to the viharn: the eaves have beautiful carvings, and its doors and windows have elaborate decorations. Inside, gold-and-black lacquered pillars support a carved-wood ceiling, and to the right is a bronze Buddha cast in the Burmese style. Red-and-gold panels on the walls depict country temple scenes.

North of town, on the right bank of the River Wang, is **Wat Phra Kaeo Don Tao,** dominated by its tall chedi, built on a rectangular base and topped with a rounded spire. Of more interest, however, are the Burmese-style shrine and adjacent Thai-style sala. The 18th-century shrine has a multi-tier roof rising to a point. Inside, the walls are carved and inlaid with colored stones; the ornately engraved ceiling is inlaid with enamel. The Thai sala, with the traditional three-tier roof and carved-wood pediments, houses a Sukhothai-style reclining Buddha.

Legend suggests that the sala was also home to the famous Emerald Buddha (Phra Keo). In 1436, when King Sam Fang Kaem was transporting the statue from Chiang Rai to Chiang Mai, his elephant reached Lampang and refused to go any farther. The statue remained here for the next 32 years, until the succeeding king managed to get it to Chiang Mai.

If you are driving to Chiang Mai and want a tranquil rural rest stop, stop on the north side of town at **Wat Chedi Sao,** a charming, peaceful monastery named after its 20 small white chedis.

☾ Farther up the road toward Chiang Mai, at the 32 km post, is the **Elephant Conservation Centre** at Baan Tung Kiewn. Not only was this the first center to train elephants and to have a hospital specializing in pachyderm care, but it is one of the best places to see an elephant show. The elephants are first bathed; then, under instructions from mahouts, they drag and stack logs. (By the time elephants are 15 years old, they understand some 40 different commands.) There are daily shows at 9:30 and 11 and an extra show on weekends at 2. Money from admission (B75) and elephant rides goes toward supporting the hospital. ☎ *054/227051.* ⌧ *Admission.* ⊙ *Daily 8–4. Closed Mar.–May.*

Wat Phra That Lampang Luang, south of Lampang, is one of the most venerated temples in the north. You'll spot the chedi towering above the trees, but the viharn to the left is more memorable. The carved wood facade and two-tier roof complement its harmonious proportions; note the painstaking workmanship of the intricate decorations around the porticoes. The temple compound was once part of a fortified city founded in the 8th century by the legendary Princess Chama Devi of Lopburi and destroyed about 200 years ago by the Burmese. The temple museum has excellent wood carvings, but its treasure is a small emerald Buddha, which some claim was carved from the same stone as its counterpart in Bangkok. ⌧ *Admission.* ⊙ *Tues.–Sun. 9–4. Closed Mon.*

Dining and Lodging

$$$ ✕ **Krua Thai.** Take a samlor to this stylish and popular restaurant in a northern Thai–style house. Locals gather in the many small, heavily timbered dining rooms to eat spicy northern Thai food. There are some Chinese dishes to offset the heat of chilies. ⌧ *Phahonyothin Rd.,* ☎ *054/226766. MC, V.*

$$ ✕ **Baan Rim Nam.** The name means "home by the river," and that is exactly what this traditional wood house was before it became an atmospheric restaurant. The menu offers good, not-too-spicy Thai food and international dishes. ⌧ *328 Thip Rd.,* ☎ *054/322501. MC, V.*

$ ✕ **Riverside.** A clutter of wooden rooms with verandahs over the riverbank gives a charm to this pub-style restaurant, which serves tasty Thai and European fare at moderate prices. Or just come in for a relaxing beer. ⌧ *328 Tipchang Road,* ☎ *no phone. No credit cards.*

$ ✕ **U-Ping.** The fun local place to eat is this open-sided restaurant on the main street, across from the access road to the Thip Chang hotel. Sports fans gather here to dine on the varied and well-prepared Thai food and drink the evening away while watching local and international matches on the half dozen TVs suspended from the ceiling. ⌧ *Thakraw Noi Rd.,* ☎ *054/226824. No credit cards.*

$$–$$$ ⌂ **Lampang River Lodge.** Set on the banks of the Wang River and a small lake, this resort is 6 km (3½ mi) south of town. A tremendous effort has been made to develop the gardens and build the hotel to blend in with nature. Wood furnishings give the ambiance of a rustic retreat, and there are serene bungalows overlooking the lake. The other rooms are set in rows among the gardens and are usually assigned to tour groups, which flock into the hotel just before dinner. The restaurant is a vast, open-sided room; the set dinner is pricey and not very good. It's better to eat in town, but first, have a cocktail at the bar overlooking the river. ⌧ *330 Mu 11, Tambol Champoo, 52000,* ☎ *054/226922,* ℻ *054/226922. 47 rooms. Restaurant, bar. AE, MC, V.*

$$ ⌂ **Thip Chang.** Stay here only if the Wienthong Hotel is full, since the Thip Chang has aged badly and is in need of a complete overhaul. Most rooms have two double beds, a coffee table, and a couple of chairs. A few of the staff members speak some English, but often not with a smile. The coffee shop stays open until 1 AM, and the restaurant serves respectable Western, Thai, and Chinese food. It is sometimes fully booked by tour groups. ⌧ *54/22 Thakraw Noi Rd., 52000,* ☎ *054/226501,* ℻ *054/ 225362. 120 rooms. Restaurant, bar, coffee shop, pool. AE, MC.*

$$ ⌂ **Wienthong Hotel.** Currently the best city hotel, the Wienthong has comfortable rooms and public areas. Rooms are kept clean and fresh, despite the continual flow of tour groups. The restaurant is the best in town for Western food. ⊠ *138/109 Phahonyothin Rd.,* ☎ *054/225801,* FAX *054/225803. 178 rooms. Restaurant. AE, MC, V.*

¢ 🖭 **No. 4 Guest House.** The friendly owner of this old, Thai-style teak house with a garden teaches English at the local school. ⊠ *54 Pamai Rd., Vieng Nuea,* ☎ *no phone. 25 rooms with shared bath. Breakfast room. No credit cards.*

Shopping

Lampang is known for its blue-and-white pottery, which is sold in Bangkok and Chiang Mai at a hefty markup. Buy it here at shops in the city center, or visit any of the 60 factories in town. Generally, a samlor driver will take you to these factories for a few baht, since he receives a commission if you buy something. **Ku Ceramic** (⊠ 167 Mu 6, Phahonyothin Rd., ☎ 054/218313) has a good selection.

Doi Inthanon National Park

57 km (36 mi) southwest of Chiang Mai.

Doi Inthanon is Thailand's highest mountain (8,464 ft) and the habitat of many species of plants, animals, and birds. From the park entrance on the main road, you can either drive the steep, 48-km (30-mi) toll road to the top or take a minibus from Chom Thong, beyond the park's turnoff. It's a good idea to rent a minibus if you wish to see the Mae Ya waterfall, because the road there—12 km (7½ mi) of unpaved tracks—can be impassable. An easier waterfall to reach is Mae Klang, which has three tiers of falls. The turnoff is 6 km (3½ mi) from the entrance.

Mae Hong Son

⑯ *270 km (169 mi) northwest of Chiang Mai via Pai, 368 km (230 mi) via Mae Sariang, 924 km (574 mi) north of Bangkok.*

This sleepy market town close to the Burmese border where villagers trade vegetables and wares is like the Chiang Mai of 30 years ago, but it is developing quickly. Already it has two comfortable hotels, several small resorts, and at least a dozen guest houses. Tourists usually spend only a night or two here, though a few foreign travelers have embraced the gentle pace and stayed a month or more. Mae Hong Son means "province of the three mists," and it is a good base from which to trek through the jungles to less commercialized hill-tribe villages. A word of warning: around late March and April, farmers set brush fires in the surrounding hills to clear the land. The smoke can make breathing unpleasant and often prevents the scheduled Thai International Airways planes from landing at Mae Hong Son airport.

If you take a 15-minute walk up the winding stepped path to the top of Doi Kong Mu, Mae Hong Son's highest hill, you will be rewarded first by restful views as you sit in the small shaded pavilion, then by the marvelously varied structures of **Wat Phra That Doi Kong Mu,** a gleaming white temple inhabited by white plaster demons with gaping scarlet mouths. A kiosk sells bottled water and film. In town, after you stroll around the lake and look at the two temples, there is little to do but have coffee or eat at one of the restaurants on the main street and observe daily life. A few stores sell hill-tribe jewelry, textiles, and a few garments, but the merchandise is more of the souvenir variety than art. (Art objects are bought by dealers directly from the villages and shipped to Chiang Mai or Bangkok.) In the morning the local market has a colorful array of fruits, vegetables, and people.

Aside from the lush countryside, waterfalls, and caves around Mae Hong Son, the tourist lure is **visiting hill-tribe villages,** especially those of the

Karen Long Necks (also called Padong), whose women wear brass bands around their necks, making them exceptionally long. Most of the Karen Long Necks are in Burma—an estimated 3,000 families. In Thailand there are three villages, all near Mae Hong Son, with a total of 36 Long Neck families, all of whom are accustomed to posing for photographs. Some visitors find there's an ethical dilemma in going to these villages, since tourism may perpetuate what some find to be a rather barbaric custom. At the same time, tourist dollars also help to feed these Karen refugees from Burma. There is a B300 fee for entering a village; half of it goes to the village, the other half to the local warlord, who uses the money to fund his army. With as many as 150 tourists a day in peak season, a village can make good money by exhibiting their long-neck women.

Long Neck Karens have a legend that their ancestors were descended from the god of wind and a female dragon, and it is thought that the women extend their necks to imitate the dragon. The brass bands may also be a sign of wealth. Girls start to wear bands at six, adding another every three years until they are 21. They are never removed, even after death, except for cleaning, or in the case of adultery, when the woman's relatives, out of shame, will forcibly remove them.

The easiest village to reach is one with six families, upriver from Mae Hong Son beyond the village of Nam Pieng Din. By arrangements made through your hotel or a local guide, you travel by boat, with a guide, for the 90-minute trip. The cost is approximately B1,300.

The second village is near the Shan village of Nai Soi. Getting there is a two-hour, four-wheel-drive journey, followed by a 30-minute hike (an experienced rider traveling with a guide can go by motorbike, over a rough trail and a swinging bridge). The cost is B1,500.

Families living in the third village, at Huey Sautea, arrived in 1995, fleeing factional fighting in Burma. The village is relatively easy to reach by a 50-minute drive in the dry season, but if it rains, the track becomes extremely muddy and waters must be forded. The cost is B1,000.

Within a three-hour drive of Mae Hong Son, the Shans, Lanna Thais, Karens, and Hmongs (Meo) also have villages, which are usually visited on guided treks of three or more days. You can leave the choice of village up to the guide—each has his favorites—but you should ask him whether he speaks the village language and discuss fully with him what is planned and how strenuous the trek will be. Since guides come and go, and villages tend to change in their attitude toward foreigners, what is written today is out of date tomorrow (☞ Outdoor Activities and Sports, *below*).

Dining and Lodging

$–$$ ✕ **Bai Fern.** For food and live music together this is the most popular restaurant in town, both with Thais and foreigners. The dining room is large, with paneled walls and teak columns. Subdued lights and whirling fans add to the festive mood. The staff is surprisingly helpful, anxious for you to enjoy the food. Most of the menu is Thai, and spicy dishes can be adapted to Western tastes on request. ⊠ *87 Khun Lum Praphas Rd.,* ☎ *053/611374. MC, V.*

$ ✕ **Kai-Mook.** Just off the main street, this is the best restaurant for al-
★ fresco dining and excellent northern Thai cooking. Of the 10 or so restaurants along this street, Kai-Mook has the freshest and tastiest food. ⊠ *71 Khun Lum Praphas Rd.,* ☎ *053/612092. No credit cards.*

$$–$$$ ☷ **Rooks Holiday Hotel and Resort.** This former Holiday Inn, about 1½ km (1 mi) out of town off the main road to Khun Yuam, teems with tour groups; activity focuses around the pool in the daytime and in the disco at night. Rooms are standard, boring, slightly depressingly furnished in blue, and well worn but clean. The best of them have private balconies that overlook the gardens and the pool. Service is a little sloppy, but many of the staff speak English. ✉ *114/5–7 Khun Lum Praphas Rd., 58000,* ☎ *053/611390,* FAX *053/611524. 144 rooms. Restaurant, pool, nightclub, travel services. AE, DC, MC, V.*

$$ 🏨 **Tara Mae Hong Son.** Though slightly less expensive than the Rooks
★ Holiday Hotel, this hotel is considerably more attractive. Its classic northern Thai architecture, with a huge lobby and broad open porches, makes it very airy. The restaurant, which serves good Thai food—both northern and Bangkok—has a glassed-in section for chilly mornings and evenings. It faces the terraced valley, as does the beautifully landscaped pool. The decor emphasizes wood, with polished floors and bamboo chairs and tables. The service is enthusiastic and helpful. The hotel is 3 km (2 mi) out of town, slightly beyond Rooks. ✉ *149 Moo 8 Tambon Peng Moo, 58000,* ☎ *053/611473; 02/254–0023 Bangkok reservations,* FAX *053/611252. 104 rooms. Restaurant, pool, travel services. AE, DC, MC, V.*

$–$$ 🏨 **Rim Nam Klang Doi.** On the Pai River, 5 km (3 mi) out of town, is one of the better rural resorts that offers good value. Many of the rooms overlook the river; others have views of the tropical landscaped grounds. There are fan-cooled rooms with a private hot-water shower—you really don't need the more expensive air-conditioned rooms. A minivan shuttles you to town or back for B100. ✉ *Ban Huay Dua, 58000,* ☎ *053/ 612142,* FAX *053/612086. 34 rooms. Restaurant. MC, V.*

$ 🏨 **Piya Guest House.** The most comfortable guest house in the area, with the best location, faces serene Jong Kham lake in the center of Mae Hong Son. The owner, Piya Grongpherpoon, has let the fan-cooled rooms around the courtyard deteriorate slightly (they cost only B250) and paid more attention to the air-conditioned rooms, each with a clean private bath, that face the garden and cost B550. Outside tables at the restaurant face the lake; those inside share space with a pool table. ✉ *1 Soi 6, Khun Lum Praphat Rd., 58000,* ☎ *053/611260,* FAX *053/612308. 11 rooms, most with bath. Restaurant. No credit cards.*

¢ 🏨 **Jean's Guest House.** This is truly a basic bungalow guest house for backpackers on the cheap, where a tiny room with a fan goes for B100. The advantage of staying here is that Jean speaks fluent English and can often serve as a good resource for finding local guides. ✉ *6 Prachautith Rd., 58000,* ☎ *053/611662. 9 rooms. No credit cards.*

Outdoor Activities and Sports

TREKKING

In the 1960s a few intrepid travelers in northern Thailand started wandering the hills and staying at the villages; by 1980, tour companies were organizing guided groups and sending them off for three- to seven-day treks. Days are spent walking forest trails between villages, where nights are spent as paying guests. Accommodation is in huts, and at best a wooden platform with no mattress is provided. Food is likely to be a bowl of sticky rice and stewed vegetables. Travel light, but be sure to take sturdy hiking shoes, warm clothes (it can become very cold at night), mosquito repellent, and perhaps some disinfectant soap, in case the huts are grubby.

The level of difficulty varies: you might traverse tough, hilly terrain for several hours, or travel by jeep, and then take an easy 30-minute walk to a village. An elephant ride or a half day on a raft may be thrown in to give a sense of adventure.

Typically, the easier the trek the more commercial the village, though villages unsaturated by Westerners is ever-dwindling. Because areas quickly become overtrekked and guides come and go, the only way to select a tour is to talk to other travelers and try to get the latest information. What was good six months ago may not be good today.

Unless you speak some Thai, know the local geography, and understand something of the native customs, don't go alone: you risk being robbed, or worse, by bandits. Use a certified guide, and since he determines the quality of the tour, it's important to pick one who's familiar with local dialects and who knows which villages are the least tourist-ridden. He should also speak English well. It is also imperative that you discuss the villages and route; that way you'll at least seem to know the ropes. You can usually tell whether the guide is knowledgeable and respects the villagers, but question him thoroughly about his experience before you sign up.

Chiang Rai and the Golden Triangle

Chiang Rai's raison d'être is as a base for visiting tribal villages and exploring the Golden Triangle. This area, remarkable for its natural beauty and friendly villagers, is relatively easy to explore on your own. The following itinerary goes from Chiang Rai to Chiang Saen and up to the apex of the triangle, Sop Ruak. It then continues west along the Burmese border to Mae Sai and back to Chiang Rai. You can hire a taxi or take a public bus, though many people rent jeeps or motorbikes.

Chiang Rai

17 *180 km (112 mi) northeast of Chiang Mai, 780 km (485 mi) north of Bangkok.*

King Mengrai, who founded the Lanna kingdom, built Chiang Rai in 1256. According to legend, a runaway royal elephant stopped to rest on the banks of the Mae Nam Kok River. Considering this an auspicious sign, King Mengrai placed his capital where the elephant stopped. In the 15th century the area was overrun by the Burmese, who stayed until 1786. Architecturally, little can be said for this city of two-story concrete buildings. Most of the famous old structures are gone. Wat Phra Keo once housed the Emerald Buddha that is now in Bangkok's Grand Palace, and a precious Buddha image in the 15th-century Wat Phra Singh has long since disappeared. Today, Chiang Rai is a market town that works during the day and is fast asleep by 10 PM, though a recently established night bazaar, just off Phaholyothin Road, has crafts stalls and open-air dining.

The Akha, Yao, Meo, Lisu, Lahu, and Karen tribes all live within Chiang Rai province. Each has a different dialect, different customs, handicrafts, costumes, and a different way of venerating animist spirits. Only in the past two decades have the tribes been confronted with global capitalism. Now, the villagers are learning to produce their handicrafts commercially for eager buyers in exchange for blue jeans and other commodities. You can visit some villages on day trips or make two- to five-day guided treks to the more remote ones (☞ Outdoor Activities and Sports, *above*).

Dining and Lodging

$ ✕ **Honarira.** If you decide not to eat at the night bazaar, then this restaurant is by far Chiang Rai's best for a casual outdoor meal under an umbrella of small trees. The extensive menu (also in English) is a mix of northern and mainstream Thai, so you might start with some spicy sausages and follow with *pla tod chon* (deep-fried serpent-head fish) and red curry beef. ✉ *402/1-2 Banphaprakan Rd.,* ☎ *053/715722. No credit cards.*

$$$–$$$$ 🏨 **Dusit Island Resort.** Sitting on 10 acres on an island in the Kok river,
★ the Dusit Island has all the amenities of a resort, including the largest
outdoor pool in the north, plus quick access to town. The building's
three wings give all the guest rooms a stunning view of the river. Fur-
nished in a modern rendition of traditional Thai, the spacious rooms
have private safes and large marble baths. The formal dining room of-
fers Western cuisine and a panoramic view; a Chinese restaurant serves
Cantonese food; and the Island Cafe, where a buffet breakfast is served,
has rather disappointing Thai and Continental food all day. If you ar-
rive in Chiang Rai by river, the boatman can drop you off at the hotel's
pier, except in periods of low water. ✉ *1129 Kraisorasit Rd., Chiang
Rai 57000,* ☎ *053/715777; 02/238–4790 Bangkok reservations,* 🗎
*053/715801 or 02/238–4797. 271 rooms. 3 restaurants, 4 bars, pool,
beauty salon, massage, 2 tennis courts, health club, shops, nightclub,
meeting rooms, airport shuttle, car rental. AE, DC, MC, V.*

$$$ 🏨 **Little Duck Hotel.** The first luxury resort in Chiang Rai screams its
modernity. Guests are often conventioneers who mill around the huge
lobby, far removed from the world outside. The rooms are bright and
cheery, with light-wood fixtures and large beds. Service is brisk and
smart, and the travel desk organizes excursions into the neighboring
hills. ✉ *450 Super Highway Rd., Amphoe, Muang, Chiang Rai 57000,*
☎ *053/715620; 02/255–5960 Bangkok reservations,* 🗎 *053/712639.
350 rooms. 2 restaurants, coffee shop, pool, tennis court, meeting
rooms, travel services. AE, DC, MC, V.*

$$–$$$ 🏨 **Rimkok Resort.** Because it's across the Mae Nam Kok river and a
10-minute drive from town, the hotel, on extensive grounds, has more
appeal for tour groups than for independent travelers. The main building is designed in modern Thai style with palatial dimensions—a long,
wide lobby lined with boutiques leads to a spacious lounge and dining area. Guest rooms are in wings on both sides, and most have views
of the river from their picture windows. ✉ *6 Moo 4 Chiang Rai
Tathorn Rd., Rimkok Muang, Chiang Rai 57000,* ☎ *053/716445; 02/
279–0102 Bangkok reservations,* 🗎 *053/715859. 248 rooms. 4 restaurants, bar, pool, shops, meeting rooms, car rental. AE, DC, MC, V.*

$$–$$$ 🏨 **Wiang Inn.** In the heart of town, this comfortable, well-established
hotel has a small outdoor pool, a pleasant sitting area, and a restaurant serving Chinese, Thai, and Western food. Spacious bedrooms, now
slightly worn, made this the top hotel in Chiang Rai until the two resort hotels opened; it is still the best hotel within the town itself. ✉
893 Phaholyothin Rd., Chiang Rai 57000, ☎ *053/711543,* 🗎 *053/
711877. 260 rooms. Restaurant, pool, health club, nightclub, travel
services. AE, DC, V.*

$ 🏨 **Golden Triangle Inn.** Don't confuse this guest house with the backpackers
hangout at Ban Sop Ruak. This is a comfortable little place that is all too
popular—advance reservations are necessary—since it is ideally situated
in the center of town. Rooms have private bathrooms and are either air-
conditioned or fan-cooled, and since the guest house is set back from the
road, there is no traffic noise. The restaurant-lounge offers Thai and Western fare. Next door is a travel agency of the same name that arranges treks
and visas into Laos. ✉ *590 Phaholyothin Rd., Chiang Rai 57000,* ☎ *053/
711339,* 🗎 *053/713933. 20 rooms. No credit cards.*

Chiang Saen

🔞 *59 km (37 mi) north of Chiang Rai, 239 km (148 mi) northeast of Chiang Mai, 935 km (581 mi) north of Bangkok.*

An hour outside Chiang Rai, on the banks of the Mae Khong River,
is Chiang Saen, a one-street town that in the 12th century was home
to the future King Mengrai. Only fragments of the ancient ramparts

survived destruction by the Burmese in 1588, and the remainder was ravaged by fire in 1786, when the last of the Burmese were ousted.

Only two ancient chedis remain standing. Just outside the city walls is the oldest chedi, **Wat Pa Sak,** whose name (*sak* means "teak") reflects the 300 teak trees that were planted around it. The stepped pyramid, which narrows to a spire, is said to enshrine holy relics brought here when the city was founded. Inside the walls stands the imposing octagonal 290-ft high 14th-century **Wat Phra That Luang.**

Next door to Wat Luang is the **National Museum,** which houses artifacts from the Lanna period (Chiang Saen style), as well as some Neolithic finds. The museum also has a good collection of carvings and traditional handicrafts from the hill tribes. ⌧ *Admission.* ◷ *Wed.–Sun. 9–4.*

Lodging

¢ ▥ **Chiang Saen Guest House.** One of several guest houses in this area, the Chiang Saen was among the first on the scene and is still a gathering point for travelers, especially at its riverside restaurant. However, the rooms have become very shabby. The helpful owner is well informed on trips in the area. ⌧ *45 Tambon Wiang, Amphoe Chiang Saen, Chiang Rai 57150,* ☎ *053/650146. 10 rooms and 3 bungalows. No credit cards.*

¢ ▥ **Gin's Guest House.** The best guest house in Chiang Saen is a couple of kilometers north of town and is run by a local schoolteacher. The main house has attractively furnished, spacious rooms. Less-expensive smaller rooms are available in A-frame buildings in the garden. A simple breakfast is offered and, if you give advance notice, dinner is available. ⌧ *Sop Ruak Rd., Chiang Saen, Chiang Rai 57150,* ☎ *053/ 650847. 12 rooms. No credit cards.*

OFF THE BEATEN PATH

CHIANG KHONG AND BAN HOUIE SAN – The recently paved road east out of Chiang Saen parallels the Mae Khong en route to **Chiang Khong,** with magnificent views of the river and Laos on the other side. Bus songthaews plough the 53-km route; make the trip in the morning to avoid crowded midday songthaews. You can also hire a speedboat to go down the river, a thrilling three hours of slipping between the rocks and rapids. Not too many tourists make the journey, especially to villages inhabited by the local Hmong and Yao tribes. Across the river from Chiang Khong is the Laotian town of **Ban Houie Sai,** from which beautiful antique Lao textiles and silver jewelry are smuggled to Thailand. Locals are permitted to cross the river; foreigners require Laotian visas. Fifteen-day visas can be acquired in Chiang Khong from **Ann Tour** (⌧ 6/1 Moo 8, Saiklang Road, ☎ 053/655198) within one business day. Numerous guest houses in Chiang Khong accommodate overnight visitors. **The Bamboo** (⌧ 71/1 M.1 Huaviang, ☎ 053/ 791621), on the riverside, has thatched bungalows with hot and cold water (B250) and a pleasant restaurant-lounge. If you don't go to Laos, you could drive directly back to Chiang Rai, but retracing your steps north from Chiang Khong will give you a different view of the wild, rugged, and beautiful scenery along the Mae Khong that is actually more dramatic than that around the Golden Triangle.

Ban Sop Ruak (The Golden Triangle)

⑲ *8 km (5 mi) north of Chiang Saen.*

Turning left (north) at the T junction in Chiang Saen will take you to Ban Sop Ruak, a village in the heart of the Golden Triangle where the opium warlord Khun Sa once ruled. A decade ago, Thai troops forced him back to Burmese territory, but visitors still flock here to see this notorious region, and the village street is lined with souvenir stalls to lure them from their buses. The only evidence of opium that you are likely to see will be at the new **Opium Museum** in the center of town that's open daily from 7 to 6. A commentary in English details the growing, harvesting, and smoking of opium, and many of the exhibits, such as carved teak opium boxes and jade and silver pipes, are fascinating. Even if you don't stay overnight, pay a visit to the new **Golden Triangle Resort Hotel,** which has some of the best views over the confluence of the Mae Sai, Mae Ruak, and Mae Khong rivers, and into the hills of Burma and Laos. Another good viewing point is the pavilion along the path leading from behind the police station.

Lodging

$$$ **Le Meridien Baan Boran Hotel.** This distinctive resort hotel, on a ★ hill off the Mae Sai road 12 km (7 mi) out of Chiang Saen, looks out over the confluence of the Ruak and Mae Khong rivers to the mysteries of Burma and Laos. All the hilltop guest rooms share the hotel's panoramic views. They have corner table-desks, couches, coffee tables, and picture windows opening onto balconies. Bedside panels hold controls for the TV and lights. The central building houses the Yuan Lue Lao restaurant, serving Thai and Western fare, and in high season the more formal Suan Fin offers elaborate Thai and European dishes. People meet in the evening in the cocktail bar and the Opium Den bar. ⊠ *Chiang Saen, Chiang Rai 57150,* ☎ *053/784084; 02/653–2201 Bangkok reservations,* FAX *053/784090 or 02/653–2208. 106 rooms and 4 suites. 2 restaurants, 2 bars, in-room safes, pool, 2 tennis courts, health club, squash, meeting rooms, travel services, airport shuttle, car rental. AE, DC, MC, V.*

$$–$$$ **Imperial Golden Triangle Resort Hotel.** The views of the forested hills across the rivers are splendid from this resort. The architecture is northern Thai, with plenty of wood throughout. The superior ("executive") rooms have private balconies overlooking the Golden Triangle; third-floor rooms have the best view. The hotel has an elegant dining room called the Border View, but it's more fun sitting out on the deck, sipping Mae Khong whiskey and imagining the intrigues in villages across the border. Classical Thai dance is performed in the evening. ⊠ *222 Ban Sop Ruak, Chiang Saen, Chiang Rai,* ☎ *053/784001; 02/261–9000 Bangkok reservations,* FAX *053/784006 or 02/261–9518. 74 rooms. 2 restaurants, pool, travel services. AE, DC, MC, V.*

Mae Sai

㉑ *25 km (15 mi) west of Ban Sop Ruak, 60 km (36 mi) north of Chiang Rai.*

By minibus—or your car or motorbike—from Ban Sop Ruak you can travel west on a semipaved, dusty, but easy road to Mae Sai, along the Mae Sai River. Mae Sai is a border market town where merchants trade goods with Burmese from Tha Kee Lek village. For the best view across the river into Burma, climb up to **Wat Phra That Doi**—the 207-step staircase starts from behind the Top North Hotel.

Non-Thais may cross the river to visit **Tha Kee Lek** on a one-day visa, obtainable at the bridge for $10. It's a smaller version of Mae Sai, selling the same goods. For $30 plus a mandatory purchase of $100 worth of Burma's Foreigner Exchange Certificates, you can get a three-night visa that lets you travel north to **Kengtung,** a quaint town with British colonial structures alongside old Buddhist temples. The trip on the unpaved road (163 km/101 mi) takes four to five hours in the dry season and up to eight from June through November.

Dining and Lodging

$$ ✕ **Rabiang Kaew.** Set back from the main road by a wooden bridge, this restaurant built in the northern style has a certain Old World charm. Artifacts adorning the dining room add to its rustic style, and the Thai fare is well prepared. ✉ *356/1 Phaholyothin Rd. (across from the Krung Thai Bank)*, ☎ *053/731172. MC, V.*

$ ✕ **Rim Nam (RiverSide) Restaurant.** Its open terrace above the Mae Sai, overlooking Burma, makes this restaurant a good choice for relaxing with a beer. The Thai food, however, is only passable. ✉ *Phaholyothin Rd.*, ☎ *053/731207. No credit cards.*

$$ 🏨 **Wang Thong.** This hotel on the riverbank opened in 1993, hoping to cash in on the relaxing of trade restrictions with Burma. Choose a guest room high up on the river side, and you can spend the day idly watching the flowing waters and the flowing pedestrian traffic across the bridge. The hotel is designed for upscale business travelers. Its rectangular rooms are modern and functional, and though the restaurant offers only average fare, it has Western dishes as well as Thai and Chinese. ✉ *299 Phaholyothin Rd., Mae Sai, Chiang Rai 57130*, ☎ *053/733388,* FAX *053/733399. 148 rooms. Restaurant, coffee shop, pool. MC, V.*

$ 🏨 **Mae Sai Guest House.** Backpackers rank this riverside guest house, 1 km (½ mi) west of the bridge, as the best in Mae Sai. It has clean bungalows and some river views. A small garden area surrounds the bungalows, and the main building housing the office also has a casual dining room. ✉ *688 Wiengpangkam, Mae Sai, Chiang Rai 57130*, ☎ *053/732021. 20 cottages with communal showers. No credit cards.*

$ 🏨 **Northern Guest House.** When the Mae Sai Guest House is full, this is a good second choice, with a helpful owner. It's on the way back to town from the Mae Sai, and it has small (there's just enough room for a bed) but clean bungalows. A few have their own shower and toilet. The veranda-style dining room is pleasant in the evenings, and the river flows at the edge of the garden. ✉ *402 Tumphajom Rd., Mae Sai, Chiang Rai 57130*, ☎ *053/731537. 26 cottages, a few with bath. Dining room. No credit cards.*

$ 🏨 **Tip Sukon House.** Just down the road to the left (west) of the bridge is this concrete structure, on the left and perched on the hill. Most rooms face Burma, but the ones on the top floor have the best view from their balconies. The rooms are bare but clean, and there is hot and cold water in the bathroom. There is no restaurant, but breakfast coffee is served in the reception area. ✉ *774 Moo 1, Shailamjay Rd., Mae Sai, Chiang Rai 57130*, ☎ *053/642816. 23 rooms. No credit cards.*

Shopping

Thais take household goods and consumer products across the river, and the Burmese bring sandalwood, crafts, raw jade, and rubies. Though you may want to set a foot in Burma, the prices and quality of the goods will not be better than in Mae Sai, which has better prices than Chiang Mai. **Mengrai Antique** (✉ Phaholyothin Rd., close to the bridge, ☎ 053/731423) is a good store. On the east side of Phaholyothin Road, opposite the Tourist Police, is the **Thong Tavee Jade factory.** Mae Sai is also justifiably proud of its sweet strawberries, which ripen in December or January.

Cheng Dao Cave

5 km (3 mi) from Mae Sai.

From Mae Sai, it's a 1½-hour local bus ride back to Chiang Rai, or you can take an air-conditioned express bus to Chiang Mai (via Chiang Rai) that takes about five hours. If you are traveling back to Chiang Rai by car or motorbike, drive to the **Cheng Dao Cave Temple,** known for its Buddha carvings and monstrous stalactites. Farther up the dirt road you come to the **Monkey Temple,** where playful monkeys will snatch anything that sparkles.

DOI TUN – Just south of Mae Chan, between Mae Sai and Chiang Rai, look for the right-hand turnoff to Highway 149, a steep, rough road that runs 17 km (11 mi) up to **Phra That** on Doi Tun, one of the highest peaks in northern Thailand. En route, stop at the Akha Guest House to inquire about road conditions to the top. The drive is awe-inspiring; at the summit, mist cloaks monks chanting at the temple, which was built in 911. This has become one of the area's most revered shrines. If you don't feel like driving, you can arrange in Mae Chan for a car to take you.

Nan

㉑ *270 km (167 mi) southeast of Chiang Rai, 318 km (197 mi) east of Chiang Mai.*

Near the Laos border lies the city of Nan, a provincial capital founded in 1272 by the court of Laos—though according to local legend, the Lord Buddha, passing through Nan valley, spotted an auspicious site for a temple to be built. By the late 13th century Nan was brought into Sukhothai's fold, but it maintained a fairly independent status into the 20th century. Only in the last two decades has a modern road been cut from Phrae to bring this region into closer communication with authorities in Bangkok. Nan province is rich in teak plantations and fertile valleys that produce rice and superb oranges. The town of Nan itself is small; everything is within walking distance, and daily life centers on the morning and evening markets. The Nan River, which flows past the eastern edge of town, is ignored by the tourist industry, except for a couple of riverbank restaurants with overpriced food. The most popular time to visit the Nan is in October during the traditional boat races.

To get a sense of the region's art visit the **National Museum,** housed in the former palace of the Nan royal family. The collection has a good array of wood and bronze Buddha statues, textiles, musical instruments, ceramics, and other works of Lanna art, all of which are explained in English. ✉ *Phalong Rd.* ✇ *Admission.* ☉ *Wed.–Sun. 9–12 and 1–5.*

★ The most astounding temple in Nan is the beautiful **Wat Pumin** on Phalong Road. The cruciform bot, built in 1596, is small and quite intimate. You climb a flight of steps flanked by two superb nagas, their heads guarding the north entrance and their tails the south. The temple was extensively renovated in 1865 and 1873, and at the end of the 19th century murals picturing everyday life and the commoner's view of the world were painted on the inner walls. The images range from the traumas of Buddhist hell and men with oversize testicles to a starving farang clasping a tool for premasticating food; from hunting scenes to views of courtly life. These are simple murals totally unlike the sophisticated art found in Bangkok's Grand Palace. The unknown artist is presumed to be from southern Yunan. The bot's central images are also quite unusual—four Sukhothai Buddhas in the vanquishing Mara position, facing the cardinal compass points.

Nan is dotted with other wats. **Wat Hua Wiang Tai** on Sumonthewarat Road is the gaudiest, with a naga running along the top of the security wall and lively murals painted on the viharn's exterior. **Wat Suan Tan** in Tambon Nai Wiang district has a 15th-century bronze Buddha image and is the scene for fireworks during Songkran. **Wat Ming Muang** on Suriyaphong Road contains the city pillar (lak muang). **Wat Chang Kham** on Suriyaphong has a large chedi supported by elephant buttresses.

Lodging

$–$$ ⊡ **Dhevaraj.** The first international hotel in Nan has been modernized to become the hotel of choice. While the City Park Hotel is newer and has a pool, it is a good mile out of town and has a deserted, empty feel unless a tour group has descended on it. Dhevaraj, on the other hand, is in the center of town across from the market and is a meeting point for locals as much as tourists. A coffee shop is open from 6 AM to midnight and the courtyard dining room serves dinner in a romantic setting. The rooms are quite respectable, with small but modern bathrooms. ⊠ *T44 Sumonthevaraj Rd., 50000,* ☎ *054/710094,* FAX *054/710212. 154 rooms with bath. 2 restaurants. MC, V.*

$ ⊡ **Nanfah Hotel.** This old wooden Chinese hotel, a relic of the past, is worth a visit, even if you are disinclined to stay in its rather dark, bare rooms with their dated bathrooms. A live band plays in the lounge-restaurant at night. That, of course, does not help those trying to sleep in the rooms above, but rooms at the back of the hotel are quiet. The wide-plank floors are of a bygone age and a balcony overlooks the street. Marvelous antiques are scattered around the hotel, and the owner, who also has a souvenir and artifact shop in the lobby, is a delightful host. ⊠ *438 Sumonthevaraj Rd., 55000,* ☎ *054/772640. 14 rooms with shower. No credit cards.*

Phrae

㉒ *235 km (145 mi) south of Chiang Rai, 201 km (125 mi) southeast of Chiang Mai, 118 km (73 mi) southwest of Nan.*

Phrae (pronounced "prayer") is off the main tourist beat, a market town in a narrow rice valley on the road to Nan. The town's recorded history starts in the 12th century, when it was called Wiang Kosai, the Silk Cloth City. It remained an independent kingdom until the Ayutthaya period. Remains of these former times are seen in the crumbling city walls and moat, which separate the old city from the new commercial sprawl. On the northeastern edge of town stands **Wat Chom Sawan,** a beautiful monastery built during the reign of King Rama V (1868–1910) and designed by a Burmese architect. The bot and viharn are combined to make one giant sweeping structure. Phrae's oldest building is **Wat Luang,** near the city wall and moat. Though it was founded in the 12th century, renovations and expansions completely obscure the original design, and the only original section is a Lanna chedi with primitive elephant statues. A small museum on the grounds contains sacred Buddha images, swords, and texts; a monk will take you around, but he is likely to speak only Thai.

On a hilltop in Tambon Pa Daeng, 10 km (6 mi) southeast of town, stands another ancient wat, **Wat Phra That Cho Hae.** It was built in the late 12th century, and its 108-ft chedi is coated in gold sheet. The chedi is linked to the viharn, a later construction, which has a series of murals depicting scenes from the Buddha's life. The revered Buddha image is said to increase a woman's fertility. Cho Hae is the name given to the cloth woven by the local people, and in the fourth lunar month (June) the chedi is wrapped in this cloth and an annual fair is held. Two kilometers (1 mile) from Wat Cho Hae is another smaller wat, **Wat Phra That Chom Chang,** whose chedi is said to contain a strand of Lord Buddha's hair.

About 9 km (6 mi) west of Phrae's center, in the hamlet of Tambon Pa Maet on highway 1023, is **Ban Prathap Chai,** billed as one of the largest teak structures in the world. Although that may be an exaggeration, this composite of nine old houses was constructed from 130 huge teak posts, and the rooms inside are a beautiful example of traditional Thai housing. Much of the compound is given over to shops, some of which have weaving and crafts of good quality.

There is a **Night Market** at Pratuchai Gate with numerous stalls offering cheap, tasty food.

Lodging

$–$$ ⊞ **Nakorn Phrae Tower Hotel.** Although Phrae is not a tourist town, you'll find all the creature comforts one might expect in the leading hotel of a provincial capital. Bedrooms have either two queen-size beds or a king and are furnished with chairs, desks, minibars, and TVs. Bathrooms are small, tiled, and functional. The restaurant serves Thai, Chinese, and Western fare, and you can have drinks in the lounge or at a small bar. ⊠ *3 Muanghit Rd., 54000,* ☏ *054/521321,* 𝖥𝖠𝖷 *054/523503. 139 rooms. Restaurant, bar, meeting rooms. AE, DC, MC, V.*

Northern Thailand A to Z

Arriving and Departing

The State Railway links Chiang Mai to Bangkok and points south but goes no farther north. As the trip from Bangkok takes about 13 hours and there's little to see but paddy fields, overnight sleepers are the best trains to take, and they are very comfortable. On most routes buses are faster and cheaper than trains, but if time is short, take a plane. Don't leave your valuables unattended on either bus or train. Petty thievery is common.

By Airplane

CHIANG MAI AND NEARBY; MAE HONG SON

In peak season, flights to Chiang Mai are heavily booked. The airport is about 10 minutes from downtown, a B80 taxi ride. **Thai Airways International** (⊠ 240 Prapokklao Rd., ☏ 053/211044; 02/234–3100 in Bangkok) has 10 or more flights daily from Bangkok (about one hour; B1,700), and direct daily flights from Phuket. It also has a twice weekly service to Kumming, China. **Bangkok Airways** (☏ 053/281519; 02/229–3434 in Bangkok) flies daily from Bangkok, with a stopover in Sukhothai. **Lao Aviation** (☏ 053/418258) offers two flights a week to Vientiane.

Silk Air (☏ 053/276459) has direct flights from Singapore. **Air Mandalay** (☏ 053/818049) flies three times a week from Mandalay, Burma (book through a travel agent).

Thai Airways International has a daily flight between Bangkok and Lampang. It also has several flights between Bangkok and Mae Hong Son, and two flights daily between Chiang Mai and Mae Hong Son. In March and April, smoke from slash-and-burn fires often prevents planes from landing at the airport.

CHIANG RAI

Thai Airways International (☏ 054/711179) has two nonstop flights daily from Bangkok (B1,820) and two from Chiang Mai (B230). Taxis meet incoming flights, but most tourist hotels have their own shuttle vans waiting for guests.

By Boat

CHIANG RAI

The most exciting way to reach Chiang Rai is on a combination bus and boat trip. You leave Chiang Mai at 6:30 AM for a four-hour trip on a local bus to Tha Thon, north of Fang (or you can hire a car and driver for about B1,200 and leave your Chiang Mai hotel at 8 AM). In Tha Thon, after lunch at the restaurant opposite the landing stage, you leave on a long-tail boat at 12:30 PM (buy your ticket at the kiosk). These public boats hold about 12 passengers, sitting in the bottom, and the fare is B160 per person. You may hire your own boat for B1,600, which you will have to do if you arrive after 12:30 PM. The trip down the Mae Nam Kok River to Chiang Rai takes five hours, going through rapids and passing a few hill-tribe villages. Bring bottled water, an inflatable cushion, and a sun hat. The more adventurous can travel by unmotorized raft (best during October and November, when the water flows quickly), staying overnight in villages on the three-day journey.

By Bus

CHIANG MAI AND NEARBY; MAE HONG SON

The trip between Bangkok and Chiang Mai takes about 11 hours and costs approximately B300. More comfortable, privately run air-conditioned buses cost B470. State-run buses leave from Bangkok's **Northern Bus Terminal** (⊠ Phaholyothin Rd., ☎ 02/279–4484). Some of the private buses use Bangkok's Banglampoo section of town as the drop-off and pick-up point. An express bus to Mae Hong Son leaves in the morning for the five- to six-hour trip (B175) from Chiang Mai's **Arcade bus terminal** (☎ 053/274638 or 053/242664), which also serves Bangkok, Chiang Rai, and Chiang Rai province. **Chiang Phuak terminal** (☎ 053/211586) serves Lamphun, Fang, Tha Ton, and destinations within Chiang Mai province.

The easiest way to reach Lamphun from Chiang Mai is to take the minibus songthaew (B10), which leaves every 20 minutes from across the TAT office on Lamphun Road. Both air-conditioned and non-air-conditioned buses connect Lampang to Thailand's north and northwest and to Bangkok. The bus station is 3 km (2 mi) away—take a samlor into town—but the ticket offices are in Lampang.

CHIANG RAI

Buses run throughout the day from Chiang Mai. The express takes 2½ hours and costs about B80; the local takes 3½ hours and is even cheaper.

By Car

MAE HONG SON

The road to Mae Hong Son from Chiang Mai has 1,273 arm-wrenching bends but is also very scenic; the northern route through Pai (4 hours) is shortest and most attractive; the southern route—Highway 108 through Mae Sariang—is easier driving but takes about two hours longer.

By Train

CHIANG MAI AND NEARBY

Trains for the north depart from Bangkok's Hualamphong Railway Station and arrive in **Chiang Mai station** (⊠ Charoenmuang Rd., ☎ 053/245563). Overnight sleepers leave Hualamphong at 3 PM, 6 PM, 8 PM, and 10 PM, arriving at 5:35 AM, 7:20 AM, 9:05 AM, and 1:05 PM. Return trains leave at 2:50 PM, 4:25 PM, 5:25 PM, and 11:30 PM and arrive in Bangkok at 5:55 AM, 6:25 AM, 6:50 AM, and 2:55 PM. (Departure times are subject to minor changes.) The overnight trains are invariably well maintained, with clean sheets on the rows of two-tier bunks. The second-class carriages, either fan-cooled or air-conditioned, are comfortable (the fare is B625). First class (two bunks per compartment) is twice the price. The Nakhonphing Special Express (no first class) leaves Bangkok at 7:40 PM and arrives in Chiang Mai at 8:25 AM (return trip departs at 9:05 PM and arrives in Bangkok at 9:40 AM). The tuk-tuk fare to the center of town is about B25.

Most Bangkok–Chiang Mai trains stop at Phitsanulok and at Lamphun, where a bicycle samlor can take you the 3 km (2 mi) into town for B30.

The train to Lampang from Chiang Mai takes approximately 2½ hours; from Bangkok, it takes 11 hours, and from Phitsanulok, 5 hours.

Getting Around

Chiang Mai and Nearby

Compact Chiang Mai can be explored easily on foot or by bicycle, with the occasional use of public or other transport for temples, shops, and attractions out of the city center. A car, with a driver and guide, is the most convenient way to visit the five key temples outside Chiang Mai, the elephant camp, the hill-tribe villages, and the Golden Mile craft factory–shopping area. If you hire a taxi for a day (B1,000–B1,400, depending on mileage), negotiate the price in advance or, better yet, arrange it the evening before and have the driver collect you from your hotel in the morning. Do not pay until you have completed the trip. More and more tourists are renting four-wheel-drive vehicles. Driving is easier than it may first appear, though pedestrians and unlighted vehicles make it hazardous at night. Two major car-rental agencies in Chiang Mai are **Avis** (⊠ Chiang Mai Airport, ☎ 053/201574) and **Hertz** (⊠ 90 Sridornchai Rd., ☎ 053/279474).

Motorcycles are also popular. Rental agencies are numerous, and most small hotels have their own agency. Shop around to get the best price and a bike in good condition. Remember that any damage to the bike that can be attributed to you will be, including its theft. Most trips in a tuk-tuk within Chiang Mai should cost less than B30. Songthaews follow a kind of fixed route, but will go elsewhere at a passenger's request. Name your destination before you get in. The cost is B5.

In the small town of Lamphun all the sights are within a B20 bicycle samlor ride.

Chiang Rai

Taxis and bicycle samlors are always available in Chiang Rai and in the surrounding small towns. Buses depart frequently for nearby towns (every 15 minutes to Chiang Saen or to Mae Sai, for example), or you can commission a taxi for the day.

Lampang

Horse-drawn carriages are available for tourists at a rank outside the government house, although some are usually waiting at the train station. The price for a 15-minute tour of central Lampang is B30. The hourly rate is approximately B100. The easiest and least expensive way to get around, however, is by samlor.

Mae Hong Son

Mae Hong Son is very small; everything is within walking distance, although you may need a tuk-tuk or taxi to take you into town from your hotel. Tourists usually take trips to the outlying villages and sights with a guide and chauffeured car. Should you hire a jeep, be sure that its four-wheel drive is in working order. Less expensive, if you want to explore on your own, are motorbikes, which can be rented from one of the shops along the town's main street. Be careful: the main roads have gravel patches, the side roads are rutted and, in the rainy season, you must also contend with mud.

Contacts and Resources

Emergencies

CHIANG MAI AND NEARBY
Police and ambulance (☎ 191). **Tourist Police** (⊠ 105/1 Chiang Mai–Lamphun Rd., ☎ 053/248974 or 1699). There are also tourist police

boxes in front of the Night Bazaar and in the airport. **Lanna Hospital** (✉ 103 Superhighway, ☎ 053/211037).

CHIANG RAI
Police (☎ 053/711444). **Chiang Rai Hospital** (☎ 053/711300). **Over Brook Hospital** (☎ 053/711366).

MAE HONG SON
Thai Tourist Police (✉ Rajadrama Phithak Rd., ☎ 053/611812).

Tour Operators

Every other store in Chiang Mai seems to be a tour agency, so you'd be wise to pick up a list of TAT-recognized agencies before choosing one. Each hotel also has its own travel desk and association with a tour operator. Since it is the guide who makes the tour great, arrange to meet yours before you actually sign up. This is particularly important if you are planning a trek to the hill-tribe villages. Prices vary quite a bit, so shop around, and carefully examine the offerings. Unreliable tour operators often set up shop on a Chiang Mai sidewalk and disappear after they have your money, so *use* your TAT-approved list. **Summit Tour and Trekking** (✉ Thai Charoen Hotel, Tapas Rd., ☎ 053/233351) and **Top North** (✉ 15 Soi 2, Moon Muang Rd., ☎ 053/278532) offer good tours at about B350 a day (more for elephant rides and river rafting). **World Travel Service** (✉ Rincome Hotel, Huay Kaeo Rd., ☎ 053/221–1044) is reliable.

The four major hotels in Chiang Rai and the Golden Triangle Resort in Chiang Saen organize minibus tours of the area. Their travel desks will also arrange treks to the hill-tribe villages with a guide. Should you prefer to deal directly with a tour agency, try **Golden Triangle Tours** (✉ 590 Phaholyothin Rd., Chiang Rai 57000, ☎ 053/711339).

Travel Agencies

In Chiang Mai, **ST&T Travel Centre** (✉ 193/12 Sridonchai Rd., ☎ 053/251922), on the same street as the Chiang Plaza Hotel, is good for plane, train, or bus tickets.

Visitor Information

In Chiang Mai you'll find an office of the **Tourist Authority of Thailand** (TAT) (✉ 105/1 Chiang Mai-Lamphun Rd., ☎ 053/248604) on the far side of the river. For information in Chiang Rai try the **Tourist Information Centre** (✉ Singhakhlai Rd., ☎ 053/711433).

THE CENTRAL PLAINS AND I-SAN

Inasmuch as Bangkok is the economic heart of Thailand, and the south its playground, the soul of the country lives in the vast central area, symbolized by rice fields worked by farmers and their water buffalo, that stretches from the Burmese border to Cambodia. In the western part of this region, at Sukhothai, Thailand's first kingdom was established when the Khmer empire was defeated. The eastern part, known as the I-san, close to Cambodia and the Khmer capital of Angkor Wat, was slower in being absorbed into the new Thai nation. Its many Khmer ruins present a different aspect of Thailand. Other parts of the I-san have been influenced by the culture of what is now Laos.

The shift of power, first to Ayutthaya and then to Bangkok, left both the western and eastern regions of this central area to become rural backwaters. Modern international hotels are few and far between, yet some of Thailand's most fascinating historic sites are here. Sukhothai takes first place, since it was the nation's first capital, but there are other architectural treasures that span half a millennium of Thai history.

Central Plains

The early history of Thailand lies in the plains due north of Bangkok, where the Thai nation was founded at Sukhothai in 1238. After 112 years the seat of government was transferred briefly to Phitsanulok, then south to Ayutthaya. In recent times, Phitsanulok has grown into a major provincial capital, whereas Sukhothai has become a small farming community. Fortunately, the wats and sanctuaries of Old Sukhothai still remain, and their careful restoration displays the classical art of early Thailand.

Phitsanulok

❶ *377 km (234 mi) north of Bangkok.*

For a brief span, Phitsanulok was the kingdom's capital, after the decline of Sukhothai and before the consolidation of the royal court at Ayutthaya in the 14th century. Farther back in history, Phitsanulok was a Khmer outpost called Song Kwae—only an ancient monastery remains. The new Phitsanulok, which had to relocate 5 km (3 mi) from the old site, is a modern provincial administrative seat with few architectural blessings. Two outstanding attractions, however, merit a visit: Phra Buddha Chinnarat and the Pim Buranaket Folklore Museum. Phitsanulok is also the closest city to Sukhothai with modern amenities and communications, which makes it a good base for exploring the region.

A major street runs from the railway station to the Kwae Noi River. The newer commercial area is along this street and a little farther south, around the TAT office. North of this main street are the market and **Wat Phra Si Ratana** (commonly known as Wat Yai). Take a samlor to Wat Yai from the railway station or your hotel, but pay no more than B20. The temple is close to the river, on the city side of Naresuan Bridge.

Built in 1357, Wat Yai has developed into a large monastery with typical Buddhist statuary and ornamentation. Particularly noteworthy are the viharn's wooden doors, inlaid with mother-of-pearl at the behest of King Boromkot in 1756. Behind the viharn is a 100-ft prang that you can climb, but you cannot see the Buddha relics, which are in a vault.

All this is secondary, however, to what many claim is the world's most beautiful image of the Buddha, **Phra Buddha Chinnarat,** cast during the late Sukhothai period. The statue, in the Mara position, was covered in gold plate by King Eka Thossarot in 1631. According to folklore, the king applied the gold with his own hands. The statue's grace and humility are overpoweringly serene. The black backdrop, decorated with gilded angels and flowers, only increases this impression. It's no wonder that so many copies of the image have been made, the best known of which resides in Bangkok's Marble Temple. The many religious souvenir stands surrounding the bot make it hard to gain a good view of the building itself, but the bot has a fine example of the traditional three-tier roof with low sweeping eaves, designed to diminish the size of the walls, accentuate the nave, and emphasize the image of the Buddha. ▨ *Free.* ☉ *Daily 8–6.*

From Wat Yai, walk south along the river, where numerous tempting food stalls line the bank, particularly in the evening. On the far side of the bank you'll see many houseboats, which are popular among Thais. Disregarding the Naresuan Bridge, some Thais still paddle across in sampan ferries. Two blocks after the post office and communications building—from which you can make overseas calls—is a small park. Turn left and the railway station is straight ahead.

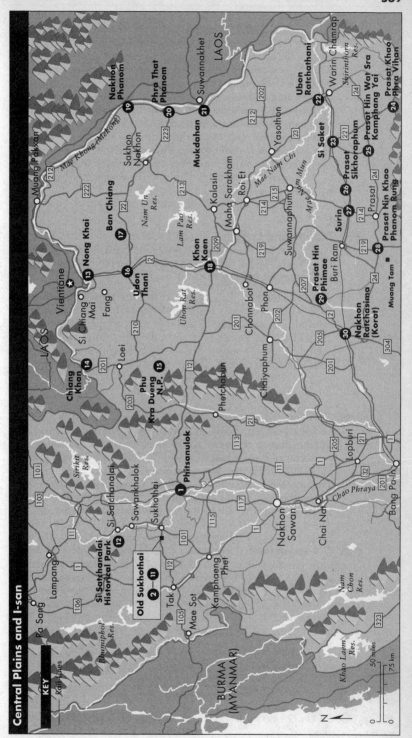

Central Plains and I-san

KEY

Rail lines

LAOS

BURMA (MYANMAR)

Nakhon Phanom **19**

Phra That Phanom **20**

Suwannakhet **21**

Muang Pakxan

Mae Khong (Mekong)

212

202

Ubon Ratchathani **22**

Warin Chamrap

Sirindhorn Res.

Prasat Khao Phra Vihan **24**

Prasat Hin Wat Sra Kamphang Yai

24

212

Sakhon Nakhon

223

Mukdahan **20**

Yasothon

23

Si Saket **23**

221

Prasat Sikhoraphum **25**

Ban Chiang **17**

22

Nam Un Res.

213

Kalasin

Maha Sarakham

Roi Et

Mae Nam Chi

214

215

Suwannaphum

Nam Mun

Prasat **26**

Surin **27**

214

Prasat Hin Khao Phanom Rung **28**

Nong Khai **13**

16

Udon Thani

2

Lam Pao Res.

Khon Kaen **18**

209

219

Buri Ram

219

Muang Tam

Vientiane

Si Chiang Mai

Fang

210

Ubon Rat Res.

Chonnabot

Phon

202

207

Prasat Hin Phimae **29**

2

Nakhon Ratchasima (Korat) **30**

24

LAOS

Chiang Khan **14**

201

Loei

Phu Kra Dueng N.P. **15**

12

Chaiyaphum

Phetchabun

205

201

304

Siriikit Res.

101

103

111

Sawankhalok

Si Satchanalai

21

113

Phitsanulok **1**

111

Lopburi

21

32

205

201

Bang Pa-in

1

Sukhothai

Si Satchanalai Historical Park **12**

Old Sukhothai **2 11**

101

115

117

Nakhon Sawan

Chai Nat

Chao Phraya

201

Lampang

1

12

Tak

Kamphaeng Phet

1

Nam Chon Res.

Pa Sang

106

105

Mae Sot

Bhumiphol Res.

Khao Laem Res.

323

N

0   50 miles

0   75 km

Phitsanulok also has an unheralded museum that alone justifies a visit to the city. The **Pim Buranaket Folkcraft Museum** (Sergeant-Major Thawee Folk Museum) is a 15-minute walk south of the railway station, on the east side of the tracks. In the early 1980s, Sergeant-Major Khun Thawee traveled to small Thai villages, collecting traditional tools, cooking utensils, animal traps, and crafts that are rapidly disappearing, and crammed them into a traditional Thai house and barn. For a decade nothing was properly documented; visitors stumbled through tiger traps and cooking pots. Then Khun Thawee's daughter graduated from college and came to the rescue: The marvelous artifacts are now systematically laid out, and displays show how the items were used—from the simple wood pipes hunters played to lure their prey to elaborately complex rat guillotines. The daughter or her assistant will explain the ingenuity of the contraptions and the cultural norms embedded in the household implements. ⊠ *Donations requested.* ⊙ *Daily 9–5.*

Dining and Lodging

Phitsanulok lacks fine dining establishments, and most travelers eat at their hotels, though the Night Market, along the river by Naresuan Bridge, has food stalls and carts.

$$ 🏨 **Amarin Nakhon.** Only two blocks from the train station, this hotel fulfills all the basic needs. It had a little face-lift in 1998, making it more cheerful. The staff is helpful and the rooms are clean. Each has two queen-size beds, leaving little space for other furniture. The coffee shop stays busy 24 hours a day, serving late-night customers from the hotel's basement disco. U.S. Army personnel use this hotel during visits to the Thai military base on the outskirts of town. ⊠ *3/1 Chao Phraya Rd.,* ☎ *055/258588,* ⅏ *055/258945. 130 rooms. Restaurant, coffee shop, nightclub. AE, DC, MC, V.*

$$ 🏨 **Pailyn Hotel.** Phitsanulok sprouted several new hotels in the late 1990s and this is the best, if only because it's downtown and within walking distance of most of the city's attractions. Rooms are quite large, with picture windows—choose a higher floor for a view of the Nan River. Furnishings are in pastels and the larger rooms have two queen beds. The large lobby and coffee shop can be a scene of great activity in the morning as tour groups depart, and in the evening the disco attracts locals and tourists. ⊠ *36 Baromatrailokart Rd., 65000,* ☎ *055/ 253411; 02/215–7110 Bangkok reservations,* ⅏ *055/258185. 125 rooms. 2 restaurants, nightclub, meeting rooms. AE, DC, MC, V.*

$–$$ 🏨 **Rajapruk Hotel.** Of the modest hotels in town, this one is quieter and more refined, with newer furnishings. The owner's wife is American, and many staff members speak a little English. Guest rooms are decorated with wood and warm colors that accentuate the hotel's intimacy. The small restaurant off the lobby is good for light meals; a formal restaurant serves Thai and Chinese food. The hotel's main drawback is its location, away from the town center on the east side of the railroad tracks. ⊠ *99/9 Pha-Ong Dum Rd.,* ☎ *055/258477; 02/251–4612 Bangkok reservations,* ⅏ *055/251395. 110 rooms. Restaurant, coffee shop, pool, beauty salon, nightclub, car rental. AE, DC, MC, V.*

Old Sukhothai

❷ *56 km (35 mi) northwest of Phitsanulok, 427 km (265 mi) north of Bangkok.*

An hour from Phitsanulok by road, Sukhothai has a unique place in Thailand's history. Until the 13th century, most of Thailand consisted

of many small vassal states under the suzerainty of the Khmer Empire based in Angkor Wat. But the Khmers had overextended their resources, allowing the princes of two Thai states to combine forces. In 1238 one of the two princes, Phor Khun Bang Klang Thao, marched on Sukhothai, defeated the Khmer garrison commander in an elephant duel, and captured the city. Installed as the new king of the region, he took the name Sri Indraditya and founded a dynasty that ruled Sukhothai for nearly 150 years. His youngest son became the third king of Sukhothai, Ramkhamhaeng, who ruled from 1279 to 1299 (or possibly until 1316), and through military and diplomatic victories expanded the kingdom to include most of present-day Thailand and the Malay peninsula.

The Sukhothai (Sukhothai means "the dawn of happiness") period was relatively brief—a series of eight kings—but it witnessed lasting accomplishments. The Thais gained their independence, which was maintained despite the empire building of Western powers. King Ramkhamhaeng formulated the Thai alphabet by adapting the Khmer script to suit the Thai tonal language; Theravada Buddhism was established and became the dominant national religion; and, toward the end of the Sukhothai dynasty, such a distinctive Thai art flourished that the period is known as Thailand's Golden Age of Art.

By the mid-14th century, Sukhothai's power and influence had waned, and Ayutthaya, once its vassal state, became the capital of the Thai kingdom. Sukhothai was gradually abandoned to the jungle, and a new town of Sukhothai developed 10 km (6 mi) away. In 1978, a 10-year restoration project costing more than $10 million created the Sukhothai Historical Park. New Sukhothai, where all intercity buses arrive, is a small, quiet market town where most inhabitants are in bed by 11 PM. The vast historical park (70 square km/27 square mi) has 193 historic monuments, of which about 20 can be classified as noteworthy and six have particular importance.

Frequent songthaew buses from New Sukhothai will drop you on the main street just outside the park entrance, about 500 yards from the museum. The best way to tour the park is by bicycle; you can rent one from a store along the main street.

The restaurant across the street from the museum is your last chance for refreshment until you reach the food stalls at the center of the Historical Park. It's a good idea to take a bottle of water with you into the park—cycling in the sun is hot work. The park's main entrance is at the east end of the main street, and the terminus for the tourist tram is at this entrance. The admission ticket does not permit reentry. Begin your tour with the museum.

③ Most of the significant pieces of Sukhothai art are in Bangkok's National Museum, but the **Ramkhamhaeng National Museum** has enough to demonstrate the gentle beauty of this period. The display of historic artifacts helps visitors form an image of Thailand's first capital city, and a relief map gives an idea of its geographical layout. ▨ *Admission.* ⊙ *Wed.–Sun. 9–noon and 1–4.*

④ For the modern Thai, Sukhothai represents a utopian state in which man is free, land is plentiful, and life is just. The spiritual center of this utopia is magical **Wat Mahathat.** Sitting amid a tranquil lotus pond, it is the largest and most beautiful monastery in Sukhothai. Enclosed in the compound are some 200 tightly packed chedis, each containing the funeral ashes of a nobleman, and towering above them, a large central chedi, notable for its bulbous, lotus-bud prang. Around the chedi are friezes of 111 Buddhist disciples, hands raised in adoration. Probably built by Sukhothai's first king, Wat Mahathat owes its present form to a 1345 remodeling by King Lö Thai, who erected the lotus-bud chedi to house two important relics—the Hair Relic and the Neck Bone Relic—brought back from Sri Lanka by the monk Sisatta. This Sri Lankan-style chedi became the symbol of Sukhothai and classical Sukhothai style. Copies of it were made in the principal cities of its vassal states, signifying a magic circle emanating from Sukhothai, the spiritual and temporal center of the empire.

Thais imagine Sukhothai's government as a monarchy that served the people, stressing social needs and justice. Slavery was abolished, and people were free to believe in their local religions, Hinduism and Buddhism (often simultaneously), and to pursue their trade without hindrance. In the 19th century, a famous stone inscription of King
⑤ Ramkhamhaeng was found among the ruins of the **Royal Palace** across from Wat Mahathat. Sometimes referred to as Thailand's Declaration of Independence, the inscription's best-known quote reads: "This Muang Sukhothai is good. In the water there are fish, in the field there is rice. The ruler does not levy tax on the people who travel along the road together, leading their oxen on the way to trade and riding their horses on the way to sell. Whoever wants to trade in elephants, so trades. Whoever wants to trade in horses, so trades."

⑥ Sukhothai's oldest structure may be **Wat Sri Sawai.** The architectural style is Khmer, with three prangs—similar to those found in Lopburi—surrounded by a laterite wall. (Laterite, made from red porous soil that hardens when exposed to air, is the building material used most in Sukhothai.) The many stucco Hindu and Buddhist images and scenes suggest that Sri Sawai was probably first a Hindu temple, later converted to a Buddhist monastery, and that Brahmanism probably played an important role throughout the Sukhothai period.

❼ Another one of Sukhothai's noteworthy attractions is the striking and peaceful **Wat Sra Sri,** which sits on two connected islands encircled by a lotus-filled lake; the rolling, verdant mountains beyond add to the monastery's serenity. The lake, called Traphong Trakuan Pond, supplied the monks with water and served as a boundary for the sacred area. A Sri Lankan-style chedi dominates six smaller chedis, and a large, stucco, seated Buddha looks down a row of columns, past the chedis, and over the lake to the horizon.

Even more wondrous is the **walking Buddha** by the Sri Lankan-style chedi. The walking Buddha is a Sukhothai innovation and the most ephemeral of Thailand's artistic styles. The depiction of the Buddha is often a reflection of political authority and is modeled after the ruler. Under the Khmers, authority was hierarchical, but the kings of Sukhothai represented the ideals of serenity, happiness, and justice. The walking Buddha is the epitome of Sukhothai's art: Lord Buddha appears to be floating on air, neither rooted on this earth nor placed on a pedestal above the reach of the common people. Later, after Ayutthaya had become the capital, statues of Buddha took on a sternness that characterized the new dynasty.

❽ Just beyond the northern city walls is **Wat Phra Phai Luang,** second in importance to Wat Mahathat. This former Khmer Hindu shrine was converted into a Buddhist temple. Surrounded by a moat, the sanctuary is encircled by three laterite prangs, similar to those at Wat Sri Sawai—the only one that's intact is decorated with stucco figures. In front of the prangs are the remains of the viharn and a crumbling chedi with a seated Buddha on its pedestal. Facing these structures is the *mondop* (square structure with a stepped pyramid roof, built to house religious relics), once decorated with Buddha images in four different poses. Most of these are now too damaged to be recognizable; only the reclining Buddha still has a definite form.

❾ The **Wat Si Chum,** southwest of Wat Phra Phai Luang, is worth visiting for its sheer size. Like other sanctuaries, it was originally surrounded by a moat. The main sanctuary is dominated by the Buddha in his Mara position. The huge stucco image is one of the largest in Thailand, measuring 37 ft from knee to knee. Enter the mondop through the passage inside the left inner wall. Keep your eyes on the ceiling: more than 50 engraved slabs illustrate scenes from the *Jataka* (stories about the previous lives of Lord Buddha).

❿ On the east side of the park, the most notable temple is **Wat Traphang Thong Lang.** The square mondop is the main sanctuary, the outer walls of which boast beautiful stucco figures in niches—some of Sukhothai's finest art. The north side depicts the Buddha returning to preach to his wife; on the west side, he preaches to his father and relatives. Note the figures on the south wall, where the story of the Buddha is accompanied by an angel descending from Tavatisma Heaven.

⓫ Also on the east side of the park beyond the moat is **Wat Chang Lom.** The bell-shape chedi is raised on a square base atop now-damaged elephant buttresses (a few of the elephants have been reconstructed). In front of the chedi is a viharn and solitary pillars; the remains of nine other chedis have been found within this complex.

Dining and Lodging

Old Sukhothai has no smart restaurants, but there are many inexpensive cafés and food stalls. Old Sukhothai also has one hotel, but most visitors stay in New Sukhothai, where there's some evening entertainment and where, across from the long-distance bus stop, there are a number of good Thai food eateries in and around the covered marketplace. For the best coffee in the province, visit the rustic **Dream Coffee Shop** (⊠ Singhawat Road), across from the Sawat Phong Hotel.

$$ ✕⌂ **Northern Palace.** The best of New Sukhothai's indifferent lodgings is this small, modern hotel on the Phitsanulok road, close to the town center. Rooms have twin beds and are furnished in light colors and kept clean. The staff speaks a little English, and the bar and dining room serves as an evening gathering spot—often with live music—for locals and foreigners. The dining room offers mostly Chinese and Thai food. ⊠ *43 Singhawat Rd., 64000,* ☎ *055/612081,* FAX *055/ 612038. 81 rooms. Restaurant, pool, nightclub. MC, V.*

$$ ⌂ **Pailyn Sukhothai Hotel.** This modern building tries to incorporate Thai architecture, but the result is characterless. Nevertheless, it has the most creature comforts of any hotel in the area and most of the better tour groups stay here. It has a shuttle to the historic area. The big negative is that it's off by itself between Old and New Sukhothai, with no place of interest in the vicinity. ⊠ *Jarodvithithong, Sukhothai 64210,* ☎ *055/613310; 02/215–5640 Bangkok reservations,* FAX *055/ 613317. 238 rooms. 3 restaurants, pool, massage, sauna, health club. MC, V.*

$–$$ ⌂ **Thai Village House.** This compound of thatched bungalows is usually stuffed with tour groups. Consequently, the staff is impersonal and unhelpful. The hotel's advantage is its location—a five-minute bicycle ride from the Historical Park. Guest rooms (most are air-conditioned) have two queen-size beds and little else except for private bathrooms. The open-air dining room is pleasantly relaxing when tour groups aren't around. ⊠ *214 Jarodvithithong Rd., Muang Kao 64000,* ☎ *055/ 611049 or 055/612075,* FAX *055/612583. 123 rooms. Restaurant, shops. MC, V.*

$ ⌂ **Anasukho.** Down a narrow soi on the south side of the river in New Sukhothai, this small guest house is run by a friendly Thai couple. The wood floors and beams and the small garden add to the feeling that this could be your home away from home. No food is served, but tea and coffee are always available. ⊠ *234/6 Jarodvithithong Rd. and Soi Panison, Sukhothai 64000,* ☎ *055/611315. 3 rooms with shared bath. No credit cards.*

$ ⌂ **River View Hotel.** Steps away from the private bus terminal in the center of the new town, this very basic and rather institutional hotel is currently the best and most convenient budget choice. (Neighboring Chinawat has deteriorated in the last couple of years.) The air-conditioned rooms are clean, and each has a private shower. There is a restaurant, but it's better to eat in the market across the street. ⊠ *92 Nikorn Kasem Rd., 64000,* ☎ *055/61156,* FAX *055/613373. 32 rooms. Dining room. No credit cards.*

Si Satchanalai Historical Park

⑫ *57 km (35 mi) north of Sukhothai.*

With its expanse of mown lawns, Sukhothai Historical Park is sometimes criticized for being too well groomed—even the ruins are neatly arranged. Si Satchanalai is less so; spread out on 228 acres on the right bank of the Mae Yom River, it remains a quiet place with a more ancient, undisturbed atmosphere. Si Satchanalai may be reached either as part of a tour from Sukhothai—Chinawat Hotel offers a day minibus tour—or by local bus. If you go by bus, get off in Sawankhalok and take a taxi to the historical park, using it to visit the various sites inside. For the more energetic, bicycles may be rented from the shop close to the signpost for Muang Kao Si Satchanalai. Accommodations near the park are only expensive bungalow-type guest houses.

Si Satchanalai, a sister city to Sukhothai, was usually governed by a son of Sukhothai's reigning monarch. Among its many monuments are a few to search out. At the right of the entrance, **Wat Chang Lom,** with its 39 elephant buttresses, shows strong Sri Lankan influences. The main chedi was completed by 1291; as you climb the stairs, you'll find seated images of the Buddha. The second important monument, **Wat Chedi Jet Thaew,** across the road and to the south of Wat Chang Lom, has seven rows of lotus-bud chedis, in a ruinous state, that contain the ashes of members of Si Satchanalai's ruling family. **Wat Nang Phya,** to the southeast of Wat Chedi Jet Thaew, has well-preserved floral reliefs on its balustrade and stucco reliefs on the viharn wall. On your way back out, stop at **Wat Suam Utayan** to see a Si Satchanalai image of Lord Buddha, one of the few still remaining.

I-san

The sprawling northeast plateau, known as I-san, is rarely visited by tourists. Comprising one third of Thailand's land area, 17 provinces, and four of the kingdom's most populous cities, the Northeast is also Thailand's poorest region. Life, for the most part, depends on the fickleness of the monsoon rains; work is hard and scarce. For many, migration to Bangkok has been the only option. Most tuk-tuk drivers in Bangkok are from I-san, and the bars of Patpong are filled with its daughters, sending their earnings back home.

The people of the Northeast, burned by the scorching sun and weathered by the hard life, are straightforward and direct, passionate and obstinate. Their food is hot and spicy, their festivals are robust, and their regional language reflects their closeness to Laos. I-san's attractions are: the Khmer ruins, which have been only partially restored; national parks; the Mae Khong river; and the traditional way of life. While there are hotels in every major town, they are mostly characterless, designed for the business traveler. In Si Saket, however, in the heart of the I-san's Khmer ruins, a boutique guest house called Manee's Retreat recently opened, paving the way for a new way to see rural, traditional Thailand.

Travelers in Bangkok who are short on time may want to limit their visit to Nakhon Ratchasima (Korat), only four hours away by train, which can serve as a base for trips to the nearby Khmer ruins at Phimae. Surin and Si Saket, a little farther away, are also good bases from which to visit more Khmer ruins. Our itinerary begins in the far north at Nong Khai on the Mae Khong, then loops west via Loei and the national park, to Udon Thani and Khon Kaen, then back to the Mae Khong at Nakhon Phanom. Next it roughly follows the Mae Khong south along the Laotian border to Ubon Ratchathani before turning west to Si Saket and Surin along the Mun River and the Cambodian border, through an area full of Khmer ruins, and back to Korat.

The new bridge into Laos at Nong Khai has stimulated local trade, and shoppers will find interesting goods there and also at Mukdahan. The handmade lace and tie-dyed mudmee cottons may tempt you, as may such oddities as large washbowls made of aluminum recycled from downed U.S. aircraft. Nong Khai is also a good source for silver. For silk, try Udon Thani and its nearby silk-weaving villages, Khon Kaen, and Si Saket.

Foreigners can cross into Laos at Nong Khai, Nakhon Phanom, and Mukdahan. They require Laotian visas, which can be obtained from the Laotian Embassy in Bangkok, the consulate in Khon Kaen, and (currently) in Nong Khai and at the Friendship Bridge.

Nong Khai

⓭ *615 km (381 mi) northeast of Bangkok, 356 km (221 mi) north of Korat.*

Nong Khai has a delightful frontier-town atmosphere: because Laos has been closed to the world for so long, you feel as if you're at the end of the line. However, times are changing. Laos is opening up, seeking co-operation with Thailand and encouraging tourist travel. Previously the only connection was a scurry of ferries from Tha Sadet, the boat pier, which has a small immigration and customs shed. Now the traffic crosses the Mae Khong on the Friendship Bridge, which opened in 1994, joining Nong Khai and Vientiane, Laos's capital, in a sweeping arc. (If you go across, note that driving in Laos is on the right-hand side.) Non-Thais need Laotian visas. You can get 15-day visas at the Laotian border or, for a slightly higher charge, in Nong Khai (ask at your hotel), but you need to show that you have a return ticket and ample funds to support yourself in Laos. The bridge is about 5 km west of town; a shuttle bus runs to the bridge and Thai passport control from the local bus station. The opening of this bridge has not changed Nong Khai very much, however, as the expected surge in tourism has not occurred.

Fanning out from Tha Sadet, the boat pier, on Rim Khong Road, are market stalls with goods brought in from Laos. On Nong Khai's main street, Meechai Road, old wooden houses—for example, the governor's residence—show French colonial influences from Indochina. **Wat Pho Chai,** the best-known temple, houses a gold image of the Buddha, Luang Pho Phra Sai, that was lost for many centuries in the muddy bottom of the Mae Khong. Its rediscovery, part of the local lore, is told in pictures on the temple's walls. **Village Weaver Handicrafts,** next to the temple, employs 350 families in the production of indigo-dyed mudmee cotton. You may want to take a B50 tuk-tuk ride 5 km (3 mi) along the Nong Khai–Phon Pisai Road west of town to visit **Wat Khaek** (also called Sala Kaew Koo), something of an oddity created by Luang Pu, a monk who believes that all religions should work together. The temple's gardens are a collection of bizarre statues representing gods, goddesses, demons, and devils from many of the world's faiths, though the emphasis is on Hindu gods.

Lodging

$$ 🏨 **Mekong Royal.** The gleaming white building standing back from the river 2 km (1 mi) out of town was built on the unfulfilled promise that the Friendship Bridge would bring tourists by the busload to Nong Khai. While the furnishings and architecture may not enthrall you, the rooms are spacious, amenities are new, and most of the rooms have great views over the Mae Khong into Laos. Best of all is the large pool, so refreshing in the blistering heat of the I-san. The hotel is part of the Holiday Inn chain. ✉ *222 Jomanee Beach, 43000,* ☎ *042/420024; 02/272–0087 or 02/272–0089 Bangkok reservations,* FAX *042/421280; 02/272–0090 in Bangkok. 198 rooms. Restaurant, pool, meeting rooms. AE, DC, MC, V.*

$ 🏨 **Phanthawi.** This is Nong Khai's downtown business hotel. Don't expect more than clean rooms with either air-conditioning or fans. The beds suffice rather than being really comfortable, and the furnishings are sparse. The restaurant, on the open-front ground floor, also serves as a sitting area. The staff speaks limited English, but enough to direct guests to the appropriate bus stations. ✉ *Haisoke Rd., 43000,* ☎ *042/411568,* FAX *042/411568. 67 rooms. Restaurant. MC, V.*

En Route You can take a marvelous scenic trip west along the Mae Khong, on the old dirt road with your own wheels, or on Highway 211 by bus, to **Si Chiang Mai,** 50 km (31 mi) from Nong Khai. This sleepy backwater is famous for producing spring-roll wrappers—you'll see the white translucent rice flour everywhere, spread out on mats to dry. Just out of Si Chiang Mai at road marker 83 you come to **Wat Hin Maak Peng,** a meditation temple run by *mae chee,* Buddhist nuns, and farther on you'll come to **Than Thon waterfall,** a series of rapids in a stream, where Thais picnic and bathe.

Chiang Khan

⑭ *235 km (146 mi) east of Nong Khai, 50 km (31 mi) north of Loei.*

Continuing west from Si Chiang Mai, you'll cross into Loei province and soon come to Chiang Khan, on the banks of the Mae Khong. The village has retained much of its rural charm with old wooden houses along the river. On the eastern edge of town are scores of restaurants with seating areas facing the river and Laos. Downriver, a series of rapids tests the skill of boatmen. From Chiang Khan the road turns south to Loei, the provincial capital, a major stop on bus routes in all directions.

Dining and Lodging

$–$$ ✕🏨 **Chiang Khan Hill Resort.** On two acres atop the banks of the Mae
★ Khong, commanding marvelous views of a series of rapids and the Laotian countryside, this resort is worth a trip in its own right. Rooms are in octagonal bungalows, the choicest being the ones with a clear view of the river. The bungalows have a king-size bed, a coffee table and comfortable chairs by the window, and a small but modern bathroom. There's an excellent open-air restaurant where the deep-fried shrimp cakes are crispy and delicious, the *somtan* (a relish) tingles with lime, and the chicken dishes are made from free-range birds. ⊠ *Kaeng Khut Khu, 28/2 Mu 4, Chiang Khan,* ☎ *042/821285,* 🖷 *042/821414. 40 rooms. Restaurant. MC, V.*

Phu Kra Dueng National Park

⑮ *70 km (42 mi) south of Loei, off the Loei–Khon Kaen highway.*

Loei province's main attraction is Phu Kra Dueng National Park, a lone, steep-sided mountain topped by a 60-square-km (23-square-mi) plateau nearly a mile above sea level. It's wonderfully cool up here, and the profusion of flowers during March and April is brilliant. You reach the plateau by a 9-km (5½-mi) hike through lightly forested fields of daisies, violets, orchids, and rhododendrons, and on top there are well-marked trails to scenic overlooks at the edge of the escarpment. The park is closed during the rainy season (July through October).

Udon Thani

⑯ *564 km (350 mi) northeast of Bangkok, 51 km (32 mi) south of Nong Khai.*

As a major U.S. Air Force base during the Vietnam War, Udon Thani grew in size and importance and, though diminished, the American military presence remains in a few glitzy bars and in the half Thai–half American young people. A popular hangout for them is the Charoen Hotel on Pho Si Road, where pop singers perform nightly. Tourists come to Udon Thani chiefly as a place to stay while visiting Ban Chiang. The town is known for its *kai yang* (roast chicken), the best of which can be found at the stalls on the corner of Phrajak and Mukkhamontri roads. There is a Western-style shopping center at Jaroensri at the junction of Pho Si and Tahaan roads. At the **Udon Cultural Centre** (⊠ Tahaan Road, away from the clock tower) of Udon Teacher's College, an exhibit of photographs and artifacts illustrates daily life and regional folk crafts. To buy silk, go to **Ban Na Kha,** a village of silk weavers, about 14 km (8 mi) north on the Nong Khai road.

Ban Chiang

⑰ *60 km (36 mi) east of Udon Thani.*

The chief attraction near Udon Thani is Ban Chiang, where archaeological finds of "fingerwhorl" pottery, skeletons, jewelry, and flint and
iron weapons suggest a civilization here more than 7,000 years ago.
UNESCO declared it a Heritage Site in 1992. The pottery in particular—red-on-cream with swirling geometric spirals—indicates that this
civilization was ahead of its time in cultural development, and even
more intriguing is that copper bells and glass beads found here are similar to some found in North and Central America. This poses the question: Did Asians trade with Americans 7,000 years ago, or even migrate
halfway around the world? You can reach Ban Chiang from Udon Thani
on the local bus, or take a car and driver for about B600. The excavation site is a short walk away at **Wat Pho Si Mai.** The larger of the
two **museums** in the center of the village has English explanations. 🖼
Admission. 🕙 *Wed.–Sun. 9:30–4:30.*

OFF THE
BEATEN PATH   One hour by bus northwest of Udon Thani is a 1,200-acre mountain
park at **Ban Phue,** where you can rent a motorbike (B40) to get to the
top of the mountain, 8 km (5 mi) away. The park is covered with rocks
of all sizes, some shaped into Buddhist and Hindu images. **Wat Phra
Buddha Baht Bua Bok,** at the top of the hill, is named after the replica of
the Buddha's footprint at its base; its 131-ft pagoda is in the style of the
revered Wat That Phanom, farther to the east. Take the path to the right
of the temple, and within a km (½ mi), you'll reach a **cave** with a series
of stick-figure and silhouette paintings thought to be 4,000 years old.

Khon Kaen

⑱ *449 km (278 mi) northeast of Bangkok, 110 km (68 mi) south of Udon
Thani.*

South of Udon Thani on the road to Nakhon Ratchasima lies Khon Kaen,
whose rapid growth has been assisted by the Thai government in its effort to develop the Northeast. It is now Thailand's third largest city. Though
essentially a businessperson's town, Khon Kaen is also known for its mudmee silk, celebrated each December with a silk fair. At **Chonnabot,** 50
km (30 mi) to the south, you can see the silk being processed, from its
cocoon stage through its spinning and dying to its weaving on hand looms.
If you don't have time to make the trip, visit **Rin Thai Silk** (⊠ 412 Na-
muang Rd., southeast of the Sofitel, ☎ 043/220705 or 043/221042), an
emporium that carries mudmee silks and cottons, both new and old; ready-
to-wear items; and local goods, all at reasonable prices.

Lodging

$$–$$$ 🏨 **Sofitel Raja Orchid.** This splendid 25-story hotel dominates the sky-
line. The soaring lobby is centered by a stylized lotus, the symbol of
the I-san, sculpted of glass and copper, silver and gold, and rising like
a huge Christmas tree from a marble pool. Carved woods and handwoven silks add to the luxury, as does the five-bedroom Royal Suite,
with its own helipad. You can try Thai, Chinese, Vietnamese, or international cuisine in the sleek restaurants, and in the underground entertainment complex you can drink beer at the Kronen Brauhaus
microbrewery, air your lungs at Studio 1 Karaoke, or dance in the dazzling lights at the Wow! Fun House. ⊠ *9/9 Prachasumran Rd., 44000,*
☎ *043/322155; 800/221–4542 in U.S., FAX 043/322150. 300 rooms.
5 restaurants, 3 bars, pool, health club, dance club, business services,
meeting rooms. AE, DC, MC, V.* 🍴

¢–$ 🏨 **Roma Hotel.** An inexpensive place near the bus station, this hotel has a helpful staff, large, sparsely furnished rooms, and bathrooms with hot and cold water. Air-conditioned rooms are better kept up than the fan-cooled ones. ⊠ *50/2 Klangmuang Rd., 40000,* ☎ *043/237177,* FAX *043/243458. 46 rooms. Coffee shop. MC, V.*

Nakhon Phanom

⑲ *740 km (459 mi) northeast of Bangkok, 252 km (156 mi) east of Udon Thani.*

Approximately three hours east of Udon Thani by bus is Nakhon Phanom, a sleepy market town on the banks of the Mae Khong with the best hotel in the area. Foreigners are now allowed to cross the Mae Khong into Laos on one of the regularly scheduled ferries, as long as they have a visa.

Lodging

$$–$$$ 🏨 **Mae Nam Khong Grand View.** The most expensive of Nakhon Phanom's hotels is a modern construction along the river. The concrete structure is not pleasing to the eye, but the carpeted guest rooms are spacious and the tiled bathrooms are modern and clean. The restaurant serves Thai and Western menus, and a live band plays in the nightclub on weekends. ⊠ *527 Sunthon–Wichit Rd.,* ☎ *042/513564,* FAX *042/511037. 116 rooms. Restaurant, nightclub. AE, MC, V.*

$–$$ 🏨 **Si Thep Hotel.** This hotel is a good alternative if you don't want to pay luxury prices. The property is about 400 yards from the Mae Khong river, back from a side street off the main road, so all the rooms are quiet. Rooms are standard and the well-used furnishings are slightly depressing, but everything is clean, including the bathrooms. The restaurant has a terrace if you want the evening air instead of air-conditioning. ⊠ *708/11 Si Thep Rd.,* ☎ *042/512395,* FAX *042/511346. 87 rooms. Restaurant. MC, V.*

Phra That Phanom

⑳ *50 km (31 mi) south of Nakhon Phanom.*

Take the bus from Nakhon Phanom to Mukdahan to get to Phra That Phanom, northeast Thailand's most revered shrine. No one knows just when Phra That Phanom was built, though archaeologists trace its foundations to the 5th century. The temple has been rebuilt several times—it now stands 171 ft high, with a decorative tip of gold weighing 22 pounds. A small museum to the left of the grounds houses its ancient bells and artifacts. Once a year, droves of devotees arrive to attend the Phra That Phanom Fair during the full moon of the third lunar month, and the village becomes a mini-metropolis, with the stalls of market traders and makeshift shelters for the pilgrims.

Ten kilometers (6 miles) back toward Nakhon Phanom is the small village of **Renu Nakhon,** which has along its main street a row of showrooms and cottage industries similar to those at San Kamphaeng in Chiang Mai. They sell an extensive range of products, including cotton and silk dresses, quilted blankets, and ceramics.

Mukdahan

㉑ *40 km (24 mi) south of Phra That Phanom.*

Mukdahan, Thailand's newest provincial capital, is across the Mae Khong from the Laotian town of Suwannakhet. It buzzes with stalls and shops all along the riverfront, selling goods brought in from Laos—a fascinating array of detailed embroidery; lace; lacquered paintings, trays, and bowls; cheap cotton goods; and a host of souvenir items.

When you're not shopping, sample some Thai and Laotian delicacies from one of the numerous riverfront food stalls. Non-Thais with a visa for Laos can cross the Mae Khong.

Lodging

$$ 🏨 **Mukdahan Grand Hotel.** The only Western-style hotel in town is this modern concrete building. Though the staff speaks little English, they are welcoming and helpful. Rooms are plain but adequately furnished with twin- or king-size beds, and a table and chairs. The restaurant serves a buffet breakfast, and Thai and Western dishes for lunch and dinner. ✉ *70 Songnang Sanid Rd., 49000,* ☎ *042/612020,* 🖷 *042/612021. 200 rooms. Restaurant. AE, MC, V.*

Ubon Ratchathani

㉒ *181 km (112 mi) south of Mukdahan, 227 km (141 mi) east of Surin.*

A three-hour bus ride south from Mukdahan takes you to Ubon Ratchathani, southern I-san's largest city. Its best-known tourist attraction is the Candle Procession in late July, when huge beeswax sculptures of Buddhist-inspired mythical figures are paraded through town. At other times, especially after the rainy season, locals make for the food stalls of **Haad Wat Tai Island,** in the middle of the Mun River, connected to the shore by a rope bridge (B1) that sends shivers of apprehension through those who cross. Try the local favorites: *pla chon,* a fish whose name is often translated as "snakehead mullet," or, if your stomach is feeling conservative, the ubiquitous kai yang. Temple enthusiasts should visit both the Indian-style pagoda **Wat Nong Bua,** a copy of one in Bodh Gaya, India, and **Wat Maha Wanaram** (Wat Pa-Yai), which houses a revered Buddha image named Phra Chao Yai Impang, believed to have magical powers. Check out the wax float at the rear of the chedi, used in the Candle Procession.

Lodging

$$ 🏨 **Patumrat Hotel.** Though the nearby Regent Palace is the newest luxury hotel in town, the Patumrat's service and ambience guarantee its position as Ubon's leading hotel. The drawback, as is the Regent's, is its location, a 20-minute walk from the center of town. ✉ *173 Chayangkun Rd., 34000,* ☎ *045/241501,* 🖷 *045/243792. 137 rooms. Restaurant, coffee shop. AE, DC, MC, V.*

$ 🏨 **Rajthani Hotel.** This modest hotel used by business travelers and tourists is downtown on the main street. The uncarpeted rooms are simply furnished but clean, and bathrooms have hot and cold water. The clerks at the reception desk are friendly but unable to provide much tourist information. ✉ *297 Khuan Thani Rd., 34000,* ☎ *045/244388,* 🖷 *045/243561. 100 rooms. Restaurant. No credit cards.*

$ 🏨 **Sri Kamol Hotel.** A five-minute walk from the TAT, this clean, modern hotel in the center of town has carpeted rooms with twin- or king-size beds. The furnishings are standard—there's a table with two chairs and a minibar with a small TV on top. The staff is welcoming, and a few of them speak English well. You can often negotiate a discount of 25% on the price of a room. ✉ *26 Ubonsak Rd., 34000,* ☎ *045/255804,* 🖷 *045/243793. 82 rooms. Restaurant. No credit cards.*

Si Saket

㉓ *40 km (24 mi) west of Ubon Ratchathani, 571 km (357 mi) northeast of Bangkok.*

With the exception of a brand new Buddhist temple, said to be one of the grandest in the Northeast, the town of Si Saket is known more for its pickled garlic, pickled onion, somtam, and, of course, kai yang than its architecture. But in early March, when the colorful lamduan flower blooms, the town comes alive in a riot of yellows and reds, and locals celebrate with the three-day Lamduan Festival. Si Saket can also be used as a base from which to visit Khmer ruins.

$$ ✕⌂ **Manee's Retreat.** In the center of a small village surrounded by
★ paddy fields, Manee has built a stylish wooden house on 9-ft stilts for Westerners who want to see the Thailand that most tourists never get a chance to see. There are only two bedrooms—ideal for two couples traveling together. You can eat Thai or Western food on the balcony, but most visitors eat under the house, often joined by locals who come to check out the foreign guests. Daily activities are arranged by Manee— who speaks fluent English—to fit your interests. Activities include: a trip to the Khmer ruins; a visit to the elephant camp at Surin; and participating in village ceremonies. You can even try your hand at planting rice. Discuss what you want to do before making reservations. Prices vary according to the program but count on about $250 a day for two (that includes everything from food to local transportation). Travel from Bangkok can also be arranged. ⌂ *Ban Nong Wa, Moo 13/29, Kluey Kwang, Huey Tap Tan, Si Saket 33120,* ☎ *01/834–5353. 2 rooms. No credit cards. All-inclusive.*

Prasat Khao Phra Vihan

★ ㉔ *125 km (86 mi) southeast of Si Saket.*

Both Thailand and Cambodia claim that Prasat Khao Phra Vihan is on their soil. The World Court awarded it to Cambodia—but because access from that side requires scaling a cliff, you get to the site from Thailand! The temple is on the outskirts of Guntharalak. Although the 12th-century sandstone laterite ruins are in a state of neglect, enough remains in this commanding location to let your imagination fly back nine centuries to when the Khmer ruled much of southeast Asia. Because brigands and disbanded soldiers caused security problems, the site was closed until 1999. Now you can go by car or by bus from Si Saket down Highway 221 to Guntharalak. You'll need to show your passport to get to the temple. The stiff hike up very steep steps will be rewarded by the summit's sweeping views over Cambodia's jungles. ⌂ *Admission.*

Prasat Hin Wat Sra Kamphang Yai

㉕ *40 km (25 mi) south of Si Saket.*

Prasat Hin Wat Sra Kamphang Yai (Stone Castle), just outside Ban Sa Kamphang, is in better condition than many of the other Khmer sanctuaries in I-san. Thailand's Department of Fine Arts has restored it, re-creating what has been lost or stolen over the last 900 years. Particularly spectacular are the lintels of the middle stupa, which depict the Hindu god Indra riding his elephant Erawan. The main gate, inscribed with Khom letters, is estimated as 10th-century, built during the reign of King Suriyaworamann. The temple behind the prasat is a Thai addition, its walls covered with pictures illustrating Thai proverbs.

Prasat Sikhoraphum

㉖ *85 km (52 mi) west of Si Saket, 40 km (24 mi) east of Surin.*

On the main road west, between Si Saket and Surin, is Prasat Sikhoraphum, a five-prang Khmer pagoda built in the 12th century. The central structure has engraved lintels of Shiva, as well as depictions of Brahma, Vishnu, and Ganesha. Shoppers may want to detour south to **Ban Butom,** 12 km (7½ mi) before Surin, where villagers make straw baskets to be sold in Bangkok. They'll be happy to demonstrate their skill and sell you their wares.

Surin

⊘ *227 km (141 mi) west of Ubon Ratchathani, 190 km (120 mi) east of Korat.*

Surin is famous for its annual elephant roundup in the third week of November. The roundup is essentially an elephant circus, albeit an impressive one, where elephants perform tricks in a large arena and their mahouts reenact scenes of capturing wild elephants. The main show starts at 7:30 AM.

If you want to see elephants at other times, you must travel to **Ban Ta Klang,** a village 60 km (37 mi) north of Surin, off Highway 214. After 36 km (22 mi), at Ban Krapo, take a left and go another 24 km (15 mi) to Ban Ta Klang, home of the Suay people, who migrated from southern Cambodia several centuries ago and whose expertise with elephants is renowned. Until recently, teams of Suay would go into Cambodia to capture wild elephants and bring them back to train them for the logging industry. But civil turmoil in Cambodia and the elephants' vast appetites have led to their replacement by heavy machinery—the animals and their mahouts have become little more than a tourist attraction here and throughout Thailand. Many an elephant and his mahout now travel to Bangkok and even as far as Phuket, where tourists pay B20 to feed the animal a banana or B400 to take an hour's ride.

Recently, TAT and Thai Airways International contributed funds to establish an **Elephant Study Centre** in Ban Ta Klang. A mobile medical unit there provides basic treatment so the animals won't have to go to the elephant hospital in Lampang. There are elephant shows on weekends at the newly built arena. Performances are tentatively scheduled during the winter months for 9:30 AM on Saturday, though times do change, so inquire first (☎ 044/512925 or 044/516053).

On your return south from Ban Ta Klang, 15 km (10 mi) before Surin a small road leads off to the left to **Ban Choke,** a village once famous for its excellent silk. Silver jewelry is now also made there. You can find bargains in bracelets and necklaces with a minimal amount of negotiation.

Lodging
$$ ⌹ **Tharin Hotel.** Surin's newest (and only high-rise) hotel is a 10-minute walk from the center of town. Light flooding in through tall windows reflects off the polished marble in the lobby and reception areas. Rooms are done in light pastels or burnt browns and have wall-to-wall carpeting, TV, telephones, and a table and two chairs. Bathrooms are large. Ask for a corner room and you'll have good city views and lots of light. In the evening, the Darling Cocktail Lounge attracts local swells, and the disco swings on weekends. ⊠ *60 Sirirat Rd., 32000,* ☎ *045/514281,* 🖷 *045/511580. 160 rooms and 35 suites. Restaurant, bar, coffee shop, sauna, nightclub, meeting rooms. AE, MC, V.*
$ ⌹ **Petchkasem Hotel.** Though the Tharin Hotel has smarter creature comforts, the Petchkasem is in the center of town between the bus and railway station. The carpeted guest rooms have air-conditioning, refrigerators, color TV, and not much else. The lobby is a pleasant sitting area, and the staff is helpful. In the evening, hostesses serve drinks in the Bell Cocktail Lounge. ⊠ *104 Jitbamroong Rd., 32000,* ☎ *045/*

511274, FAX 044/511041. 162 rooms. Restaurant, lobby lounge, pool, nightclub, meeting rooms. AE, MC, V.

¢ 🔲 **Pirom Guest House.** The owners, who speak English well, make this a choice place to stay if you don't mind very basic accommodation. The Piroms will enthusiastically explain the I-san and its traditions to their guests. Mr. Pirom often arranges tours to off-the-beaten-track villages. There are five small, fan-cooled rooms (no private baths) in the old-fashioned teak house, but you'll spend most of your time in the garden or in the small, homey dining room. The guest house is two blocks west of the market. (The Piroms may move into a newer, larger house, but they will keep the same telephone number.) ✉ *242 Krungsrinai Rd., 32000, ☎ 044/515140. 6 rooms. Breakfast room. No credit cards.*

Buri Ram

98 km (60 mi) west of Surin, 349 km (220 mi) northeast of Bangkok.

The provincial capital of Buri Ram, less than an hour west of Surin by train or bus, is a rather uninteresting town with little reason for an overnight stay. However, being connected to Bangkok by rail and the Northeast by bus, it is a gateway for those visiting the nearby Khmer prasats.

Prasat Hin Khao Phanom Rung

28 *60 km (34 mi) south of Buri Ram, 65 km (39 mi) southwest of Surin, 90 km (54 mi) east of Korat.*

The restored hilltop sanctuary of Prasat Hin Khao Phanom Rung is 7 km (4½ mi) by bus or taxi from the village of Nang Rung. It is a supreme example of Khmer art, built in the 12th century under King Suriyaworamann II, one of the great Khmer rulers, and restored in the 1980s at a cost of $2 million. It's one of the few Khmer sanctuaries without later Thai Buddhist additions. The approach to the prasat sets your heart thumping—you cross an imposing naga bridge and climb majestic staircases to the top, where you are greeted by the magnificent Reclining Vishnu lintel. This lintel, spirited away in the 1960s, reappeared at the Chicago Art Institute, and after 16 years of protests and negotiations was finally returned to its rightful place in Thailand. Step under the lintel and through the portal into the double-walled sanctuary. Intricate carvings in a style similar to those found in Lopburi cover the interior walls, and in the center of the prasat stands the great throne room dedicated to Lord Shiva.

Prasat Phanom Rung has become very popular with Thais, and in their footsteps have come scores of souvenir and food vendors adjacent to the car park.

Scattered in the area are other Khmer prasats in various stages of ruin, overgrown by vegetation. One of these has been rescued from nature's consumption and prettified by Thailand's Department of Fine Arts. **Prasat Muang Tam** (15 minutes by car south of Phanom Rung; no public bus makes this trip), estimated to be 100 years older than its neighbor, started off as a 10th-century Hindu sanctuary. Its main building symbolically represents the universe, with lesser towers emanating from the center. Today four towers remain, containing Hindu carvings of Shiva and his consort Uma, Varuna on a swan, Krishna with cows, and Indra on the elephant Erawan. The complex is flanked by ceremonial ponds, with five-headed nagas lying alongside.

Prasat Hin Phimae

㉙ *54 km (34 mi) north of Korat; buses leave for Phimae every 15 mins between 6 AM and 6 PM for the 1¼-hr trip.*

Prasat Hin Phimae, the other great Khmer structure of the Northeast (along with Phanom Rung), was probably built sometime in the late 11th or early 12th century, and though the ruins have been restored, they have not been groomed and manicured. To enter the prasat through the two layers—the external sandstone wall and the gallery—is to step back eight centuries, and by the time you reach the inner sanctuary, you're swept up in the creation and destruction of the Brahman gods engraved on the lintels. Gate towers (*gopuras*) at the four cardinal points guard the entrances, with the main one facing south, toward Angkor. The central white sandstone prang, 60 ft tall, flanked by two smaller buildings, one in laterite, the other in red sandstone, makes an exquisite combination of pink and white against the darker laterite, especially in the light of early morning and late afternoon. The principal prasat is surrounded by four porches, whose external lintels depict Hindu gods and scenes from the *Ramayana*. Inside, the lintels portray the religious art of Mahayana Buddhism.

Though I-san covers a third of Thailand, only recently has it been given any attention for its heritage as part of the Khmer empire. In the 1990s, with the support of Princess Maha Chakri Sirindhorn, the excellent **Phimae National Museum** was founded. Its two floors contain priceless treasures from the early settlers of I-san and from the Dvaravati and Khmer civilizations—notably great works of Khmer sculpture. The museum's masterpiece is a stone statue of King Jayavarman VII of Anghor Thom, found at Phimae. More boundary stones, lintels, and friezes are stacked outside in the garden, and though less interesting to the casual visitor, they are definitely worth a walk past. ✉ *Tha Songkran Rd.,* ☎ *044/471167.* ▦ *Admission.* ☉ *Tues.–Sun. 9–4.*

You may want to drive about 2 km (1⅓ mi) from the ruins to see **Sai Ngam,** the world's largest banyan tree, whose mass of intertwined trunks supports branches that cast a shadow of nearly 15,000 square ft. Some say that it is 3,000 years old. On weekends, the small park nearby has stalls selling *patnee* (noodles) and fried chicken for picnics.

Dining and Lodging

$ ✕ **Tieu Pai.** Phimae ducks are well known for their succulence, and the grilled duck here is worth the trip to Phimae. Other items, such as tom yam kung, supplement the duck dishes. You can sit in the hot shade outside or in the air-conditioning inside. In neither case should you expect ambiance. The restaurant is 100 meters beyond the Phimae Museum and across the bridge over the Mun River. ✉ *Ta Pisu, Ban Lek,* ☎ *044/471983. No credit cards.*

$ ▣ **Phimae Hotel.** Phimae has limited tourist facilities and only very basic hotels, of which the Phimae is about the best, but that isn't saying much. The rooms are clean, but that musty odor of neglected up-country hotels pervades. Only a bottom sheet is provided, along with a blanket, which, with the air-conditioning, you'll need. You may want to request two extra sheets and place the well-used blanket between them. (In these older up-country hotels, management usually supplies extra sheets without cost or question.) ✉ *305/1–2 Haruthairom Rd., 30100,* ☎ *044/471306,* ℻ *044/471918. 40 rooms. No credit cards.*

Nakhon Ratchasima

30 *54 km (34 mi) southwest of Phimae, 259 km (160 mi) northeast of Bangkok.*

Most tourists use Nakhon Ratchasima (also called Korat) as a base for visiting Phimae and Phanom Rung. With a population of over 300,000, it is I-san's major city and Thailand's second largest, considered the gateway to the Northeast. You will probably not want to spend many daytime hours here, but between 6 and 9 PM, head to the **Night Bazaar** in the center of town. A block-long street is taken over by food stands and shopping stalls and is crowded with locals. The huge **local bazaar** for clothes and general merchandise is also fun to walk through. It's on the left-hand side of Chomsuranyart Road; take a right at the end of the Night Bazaar and walk for 200 meters.

A side trip to **Pak Thongchai Silk and Cultural Centre,** 32 km (20 mi) south of Korat, offers a chance to see the complete silk-making process, from the raising of silkworms to the spinning of thread and weaving of fabric. You can also buy silks at some 70 factories in the area. Try the **Srithai Silk** showroom (⌧ 333 Subsiri Rd., ☎ 044/441588) in Pak Thongchai. For ceramics, drive out to the village of **Ban Dan Kwian,** 15 km (10 mi) southwest on Route 224. The rust-color clay here has a tough, ductile texture and is used for reproductions of classic Thai designs. **Suwanee Natewong** (⌧ 34 Moo 4, Dan Kwian Chok Chai, ☎ 044/375203), on the left as you enter town from Korat, has a wide selection of interesting designs and will ship your purchases if you cannot take them with you.

Korat also serves as a base for trips to **Khao Yai National Park,** southwest of town, which covers 2,168 square km (833 square mi) in four provinces, providing fresh air, hiking, and four golf courses for Thais needing a break from Bangkok.

Lodging

$$–$$$ 🏨 **The Royal Princess.** The newest (1994) hotel in town started off well, but cutbacks by the Dusit-Princess hotel group have brought in inferior management; the Sima Thani now has the edge. The expansive lobby gives way to a comfortable lounge. The coffee shop overlooks a small garden and rectangular pool, and the surrounding concrete buildings create a strong glare in the noonday sun. The large rooms are furnished in pastels, and most have two queen-size beds or one king. Bathrooms are functional. The formal restaurant serves the best Cantonese food in town. The hotel's drawback, like that of the Sima Thani, is that it's 3 km (2 mi) from downtown. ⌧ *1/37 Surenarai Rd., 30000,* ☎ *044/256629,* ℻ *044/256601. 186 rooms. Restaurant, coffee shop, pool, 2 tennis courts, health club, business services, meeting rooms. AE, DC, MC, V.* 🐾

$$–$$$ 🏨 **Sima Thani Hotel.** On the outskirts of Korat (a B40 tuk-tuk ride from the Night Bazaar), this sparkling hotel is well-accustomed to tourists and businesspeople. It is designed around a hexagonal atrium lobby. Furnishings in the guest rooms are comfortably unobtrusive. Each room has two queen-size beds, a table and chairs, and a good working desk (but an inadequate reading lamp). Bathrooms come with hair dryers and telephones. The coffee shop–dining room is open 24 hours, the Chinese restaurant is Cantonese, and best of all is the extensive evening buffet outdoors, with musicians and classical I-san dancers every night except Monday. Most of the staff knows some English, and service is extremely professional. ⌧ *Mittraphap Rd., Tambon Nai Muang, 30000,* ☎ *044/243812,* ℻ *044/251109. 135 rooms. Restaurant, coffee shop, piano bar, pool, massage, health club, meeting rooms. AE, DC, MC, V.*

$$ 🏨 **Rooks Korat.** Even if you're not a golfer, you may well prefer staying at this resort and country club 28 km (17 mi) southwest of Korat. (A songthaew will run you out there for B200.) The cozy, comfortable rooms look out over the par-72 golf course, and the patio with table and chairs is ideal for breakfast or a sundowner. The resort has a good swimming pool, and the terrace alongside it is a pleasant spot for dinner. The restaurant serves adequate food, including excellent crispy fried free-range chicken. Rooks' cost is about half that of the Royal Princess in Korat, and on weekdays, golf greens fees may be included in the room rate. All the prasats around Korat are easily accessible. ✉ *Km 22, Korat–Pakthonchai Rd., Ban Laemluak, 30000,* ☎ *01/212–0254, 01/212–2468, or 01/222–1371,* 📠 *01/222–1371. 62 rooms. Restaurant, pool, golf course. MC, V.*

$ 🏨 **Chansurang.** In the heart of town, minutes away from the Night Bazaar, this was once Korat's main hotel. It then deteriorated, but recent renovations have smartened up the rooms and added modern amenities. The lobby area has been redesigned, and the reception staff gives clients a warm welcome. The restaurant serves Thai dishes, including I-san specialties, and Western food. ✉ *2701/2 Mahadthai Rd., 30000,* ☎ *044/257060,* 📠 *044/252897. 157 rooms. Restaurant, pool. MC, V.*

The Central Plains and I-san A to Z

Arriving and Departing

By Airplane

I-SAN

All air traffic to the Northeast radiates from Bangkok, with daily flights on **Thai Airways International** (☎ 02/232–8000 in Bangkok) between the capital and Khon Kaen, Udon Thani, Buri Ram, Nakhon Phanom, Ubon Ratchathani, and Korat.

PHITSANULOK

With three direct flights each day, Thai Airways International connects Phitsanulok with Bangkok (B920) and Chiang Mai (B650). Taxis meet incoming flights.

SUKHOTHAI

The airport, between Sukhothai and Si Satchanalai, is a 35-minute ride from Sukhothai. **Bangkok Airways** (☎ 02/229–3456 in Bangkok) operates a daily direct flight to Sukhothai from Bangkok and Chiang Mai. Alternatively, you can use **Thai Airways International** (☎ 02/232–8000 in Bangkok) into Phitsanulok and take an hour-long bus or taxi ride to Sukhothai.

By Bus

I-SAN

Many of the towns in the Northeast are served by direct air-conditioned and non-air-conditioned buses from Bangkok's **Northern Bus Terminal** (✉ Phaholyothin Rd., ☎ 02/279–4484). Bus fares are slightly lower than train fares. From Phitsanulok, there is daily service to Loei and then on to Khon Kaen and Nong Khai. There are also daily direct buses that connect Chiang Mai and the Northeast's major provincial capitals like Mukdahan and Buri Ram.

From Korat, Thailand is your oyster. There are direct buses to Bangkok (256 km/159 mi), Pattaya (284 km/176 mi), Rayong (345 km/214 mi), Chiang Rai (870 km/539 mi), Chiang Mai (763 km/473 mi), and Phitsanulok (457 km/283 mi).

PHITSANULOK

Buses run frequently to Phitsanulok from Chiang Mai, Bangkok (Northern Terminal), and Sukhothai. Bus service also connects Phitsanulok to eastern Thailand. Long-distance buses arrive and depart from the intercity bus terminal, 2 km (1¼ mi) northeast of town.

SUKHOTHAI

The bus to New Sukhothai from Phitsanulok departs from the intercity bus terminal, makes a stop just before the Naresuan Bridge, and arrives an hour later; you can take a minibus songthaew at the terminal to Old Sukhothai. Buses go directly to New Sukhothai from Chiang Mai's **Arcade Bus Station** (☎ 053/242664); the trip takes five hours and costs B100. The bus trip from Bangkok's **Northern Bus Terminal** (☎ 02/279–4484) takes seven hours and costs B140.

By Train

I-SAN

The Northeastern Line has frequent service from Bangkok to I-san. All trains go via Don Muang airport and Ayutthaya to Kaeng Khoi Junction (the stop after Saraburi), where the line splits. One track goes to Nakhon Ratchasima, continuing east to Buri Ram, Surin, and Si Saket before terminating at Ubon Ratchathani; the other line goes north, stopping at Bua Yai Junction, Khon Kaen, and Udon Thani before arriving at Nong Khai. Both routes have daytime express and local trains and an overnight express train with sleeping cars. The Ubon Ratchathani sleeper leaves Bangkok at 9 PM to arrive at 7:05 AM and departs from Ubon Ratchathani at 7 PM to arrive in Bangkok at 5:20 AM. The Nong Khai sleeper departs from Bangkok at 7 PM to arrive at 7:10 AM and on the return trip leaves Nong Khai at 6:35 PM to be back in Bangkok at 6:10 AM.

PHITSANULOK

Phitsanulok is about halfway between Bangkok and Chiang Mai. On the rapid express, it takes approximately six hours from either city. Some trains between Bangkok and Phitsanulok stop at Lopburi and Ayutthaya, enabling you to visit these two historic cities en route. A special express train between Bangkok and Phitsanulok takes just over five hours. Tickets for this service, which cost 50% more than those for regular second-class travel, can be purchased at a separate booth inside the Bangkok or Phitsanulok station; reservations are essential.

Getting Around

I-san

Between cities, there are buses throughout the day, from about 6 AM to 7 PM. Bicycle samlors and songthaews are plentiful in towns. A car with driver can be rented in the major provincial capitals. Reputable self-drive car firms are few and far between—in Nakhon Ratchasima, try **L.A. Trans Services** (☎ 044/267680), which will bring the car to your hotel.

Unless you have your own transportation, the Khmer ruins are best visited by taxi or pick-up, which can be hired for the day (so you can visit more than one site) at railway and bus stations in Buri Ram, Si Saket, and Surin. Always negotiate the price in advance, and bargain hard.

Phitsanulok

Most sights in Phitsanulok are within walking distance, but bicycle samlors are easily available. Bargain hard—most rides are about B20. Taxis are available for longer trips; you'll find a few loitering around the train station.

Sukhothai

Bicycle samlors are ideal for getting around New Sukhothai, but take a taxi (B120) or minibus songthaew (B5) to Old Sukhothai (Muang Kao) and the Historical Park. Minibus songthaews depart from New Sukhothai's bus terminal, 1 km (½ mi) on the other side of Prarong Bridge.

The best means of transportation around the Historical Park is a rented bicycle (B30 for the day). If you don't have much time, you can hire a taxi from New Sukhothai for B300 for a half day. Drivers know all the key sights. Within the park, a tourist tram takes visitors to the major attractions for B20.

Contacts and Resources

Emergencies

NAKHON RATCHASIMA

General Emergencies (☎ 191). **Police** (☎ 044/242010). **Maharat Hospital** (⊠ Chang Phuak Rd., ☎ 044/254990).

NONG KHAI

Police (☎ 042/411020). **Nong Khai Provincial Hospital** (⊠ Meechai Rd., ☎ 042/411504).

PHITSANULOK

Police (☎ 055/240199). **Phitsanuwej Hospital** (⊠ Khun Piren Rd., ☎ 055/252762).

SUKHOTHAI

Police (☎ 055/611199). **Sukhothai Hospital** (☎ 055/611782).

UBON RATCHATHANI

Police (☎ 045/254216). **Rom Gao Hospital** (⊠ Auparat Rd., ☎ 045/254053).

Visitor Information

Contact Tourist Authority of Thailand (TAT) offices for the Tourist Police. **Nakhon Ratchasima TAT** (⊠ 2102–2104 Mittraphap Rd., 30000, ☎ 044/213606). **Phitsanulok TAT** (⊠ 209/7–8 Boromtrailokanat Rd., 65000, ☎ 055/252742), open weekdays 9–4:30. **Ubon Ratchathani TAT** ⊠ 264/1 Khuan Thani Rd., 34000, ☎ 038/377008).

THE SOUTHERN BEACH RESORTS

The resorts of southern Thailand's long peninsula between the Andaman Sea and the Gulf of Thailand are pure hedonism. Everything is here for the wanting, from luxury hotels to dirt-cheap bungalows, from water sports to golf, from sleazy bars to elegant dining rooms, from beaches washed by azure waters to verdant hills, from exotic fruit to bountiful seafood and, regrettably, pizza and hamburgers.

Phuket and Phuket Bay Resorts

Backpackers discovered Phuket in the early 1970s. The word got out about its long, white, sandy beaches and cliff-sheltered coves, its waterfalls, mountains, clear waters, scuba diving, fishing, seafood, and fiery sunsets. Entrepreneurs built massive developments, at first clustering around Patong, then spreading out. Most formerly idyllic deserted bays and secluded havens now have at least one hotel, and hotels are still being built despite a shortage of trained staff and an overburdened infrastructure. Prices have escalated to a point where staying here costs about half as much as in Bangkok. Even the local Director of Tourism admits that Phuket has become overpriced. Charter flights continue to bring tourists from Europe, especially Germany, and during peak season Phuket's 20,000 hotel rooms are jammed to capacity and hotel's add a "peak surcharge" to room rates. Phuket's popularity endures, however, perhaps because it is large enough (so far) to absorb the influx, though more and more visitors are cutting their visits short and moving to less commercial pastures nearby, such as the Phi Phi Islands or Ao Nang and its 83 offshore islands. Peaceful Phang Nga Bay, north of Phuket, is famous for its karst formations—outcroppings of limestone rising 900 ft straight up from the sea—and offshore caves accessible only by boat.

Phuket is linked to the mainland by a causeway. Its indented coastline and hilly interior make the island seem larger than its 48-km (30-mi) length and 21-km (13-mi) breadth. Before tourism, Phuket was already making fortunes out of tin mining (it is still Thailand's largest tin producer) and rubber plantations. Although the west coast, with its glittering sand beaches, is committed to tourism, other parts of the island still function as normal communities, largely untainted by the influx of foreign vacationers. Typically, tourists go directly to their hotels on arrival, spend most of their vacation on the beach, and make only one or two sorties to other parts of Phuket. Renting a car for a couple of days can be a good idea if you want to see the island. Sights and beaches are listed in a counterclockwise itinerary, beginning with Phuket Town, the provincial capital and only real town on the island.

Phuket Town

❶ *862 km (539 mi) south of Bangkok.*

About one-third of the island's population lives in Phuket Town, the provincial capital, but very few tourists stay here. The town is busy, and drab modern concrete buildings have replaced the old Malay colonial-type architecture. Most of the shops and cafés are along Phang-Nga and Rasda roads. By bus, you arrive in Phuket on the eastern end of Phang-Nga Road.

Phuket Town's main street (where many hotel shuttles drop you off) is Rasda Road, and the sidewalk tables in front of the Thavorn Hotel provide a good place to do a little people-watching while sipping a cold beer. Going east from there along Rasda Road, an immediate right puts you on Phuket Road, with the TAT office and Tourist Police on the left. West on Rasda Road after the traffic circle (Bangkok Circle) you come to Ranong Road, with the **local market** on the left, an aromatic riot of vegetables, spices, meats, and sellers and buyers. On the next block of Ranong Road is the **Songthaew Terminal,** where you get the minibus to Patong, Kata, Kamala, Karon, and Surin beaches. Songthaews for Rawai and Nai Harn beaches stop at Bangkok Circle. The **Provincial Town Hall,** diagonally across town from the market, was used as the French Embassy in the movie *The Killing Fields.*

The most relaxing way to see Phuket Town and the island's interior **❷** may be from the top of **Khao Rang** (Rang Hill) northwest of town.

Dining and Lodging

$ ✕ **Natural Restaurant.** It's worth coming into Phuket Town just to dine at this characterful eatery, which has been described as a Swiss Family Robinson tree house, Thai style. Thick vegetation conceals any concrete, signs disappear behind branches, and a waterfall drowns out customer noise. The fare is Thai and good. Though there is an English menu, farangs are rarely seen. A map just southwest of the Central Market will help you find the restaurant. ✉ *62/5 Soi Phutom, Bangkok Rd.,* ☎ *076/224287. No credit cards. Closed Mon.*

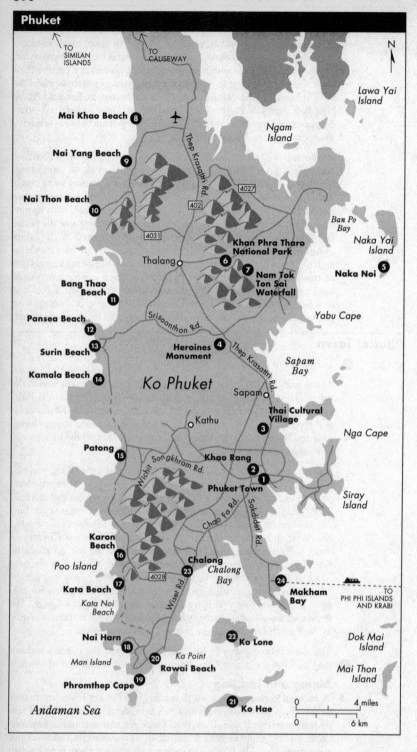

TO
SIMILAN
ISLANDS

TO
CAUSEWAY

N

Lawa Yai
Island

Mai Khao Beach ⑧

Ngam
Island

Nai Yang Beach ⑨

Thep Krasatti Rd.

4027

402

Nai Thon Beach ⑩

Ban Po
Bay

Naka Yai
Island

4031

Thalang

Khan Phra Tharo
National Park

⑥

⑦ Nam Tok
Ton Sai
Waterfall

Naka Noi ⑤

Bang Thao
Beach ⑪

Srisoonthon Rd.

Yabu Cape

Pansea Beach ⑫

Heroines
Monument ④

Thep Krasatti Rd.

Surin Beach ⑬

Sapam
Bay

Kamala Beach ⑭

Ko Phuket

Sapam

Thai Cultural
Village

Kathu

③

Nga Cape

Patong ⑮

Wichit Songkhram Rd.

Khao Rang
②
①
Phuket Town

Chao Fa Rd.

Sakdidej Rd.

Siray
Island

Karon
Beach ⑯

Poo Island

Chalong
⑳

4028

Chalong
Bay

⑳

Makham
Bay

TO
PHI PHI ISLANDS
AND KRABI

Kata Beach ⑰

Kata Noi
Beach

Nai Harn ⑱

Man Island

⑳

Ka Point

Rawai Beach

⑳ Ko Lone

Dok Mai
Island

Mai Thon
Island

Phromthep Cape ⑲

Andaman Sea

㉑ Ko Hae

0   4 miles

0   6 km

$$$ 🏨 **Metropole.** If you come to Phuket Town on business, you should stay at the best and newest hotel. A sparkling, crisp, marble lobby greets you; there's a spacious lounge bar for cool comfort during the day, and a karaoke bar for fun at night. The very handsome Chinese restaurant, the Fortuna Pavilion, offers a dim-sum lunch. For Western food in a steak-house atmosphere, try the Metropole Café. Guest rooms are bright, with picture windows and pastel furnishings. ⊠ *1 Soi Surin, Montri Rd., Phuket Town 83000,* ☎ *076/214022,* FAX *076/215990. 248 rooms. 2 restaurants, lobby lounge, pool, health club, business services, meeting rooms. AE, DC, MC, V.*

Thai Cultural Village

❸ *5 km (3 mi) north of Phuket Town.*

The Thai Cultural Village has a 500-seat amphitheater, where it presents various aspects of southern Thai culture: classical Thai dance, shadow puppet shows, Thai boxing exhibitions, sword fighting, an "elephants-at-work" show, and more. ⊠ *Thepkasati Rd.,* ☎ *076/214860.* 🎟 *Admission.* ⊘ *Show times: 10:15, 11, 4:45, 5:30.*

Heroines Monument

❹ *12 km (7 mi) north of Phuket Town.*

On the airport highway at a crossroads, you'll notice a statue of two women. In 1785 these sisters rallied the Thais to ward off a siege by the Burmese, who had sacked Ayutthaya four years earlier.

The **National Museum** nearby has exhibits displaying the way of life and history of Phuket, including dioramas of the heroines. ☎ *076/ 311426.* 🎟 *Admission.* ⊘ *Wed.–Sun. 10–4.*

Naka Noi

❺ *26 km (16 mi) northeast of Phuket Town.*

By taking the road east at the crossroads you'll arrive at Ban Po Bay, where you can take a 20-minute boat ride to Naka Noi, the Pearl Island. After you tour the island and perhaps look in at the Pearl Extracting Show at 11 AM, visit the small **restaurant** (☎ *076/213723)* for refreshments. Lodging is also available.

Khan Phra Tharo National Park

❻ *19 km (12 mi) north of Phuket Town.*

Turning inland from Ban Po on the small, partially unpaved road heading for Thalang, you'll traverse Khan Phra Tharo National Park, the last remaining virgin forest on Phuket.

❼ You may want to stop at **Nam Tok Ton Sai Waterfall,** a few minutes off the road. It's a popular picnic spot all year, but the falls are best during the rainy season.

Mai Khao Beach

❽ *37 km (23 mi) northwest of Phuket Town.*

From Thalang, a few miles northwest of the Heroines Monument intersection, the main road continues north to the airport and the causeway. If you take the airport road west for 5 km (3 mi) to the shore, you'll get to Mai Khao Beach. This is Phuket's northernmost beach and the island's largest, often ignored by Western tourists because at low tide it turns slightly muddy, and its steep drop-off makes it unpopular with swimmers. The absence of farangs attracts Thais, who appreciate its peacefulness. Giant sea turtles like it, too: they come between November and February to lay their eggs.

Nai Yang Beach

❾ *34 km (20 mi) northwest of Phuket Town.*

Nai Yang Beach is really a continuation south of Mai Khao—making a 10-km (6-mi) stretch of sand. It curves like a half-moon, with casuarina trees lining the shore. It is popular with Thais, and it now has a resort, Pearl Village. Another, larger resort is under construction, perhaps spelling an end to the beach's quiet.

Nai Thon Beach

❿ *30 km (18 mi) northwest of Phuket Town.*

Tucked in the center of a headland that separates Nai Yang and Bang Tao Bay is Nai Thon Beach. Its rough waters keep swimmers away, and the village remains a peaceful fishing port.

Bang Thao Beach

⑪ *22 km (14 mi) northwest of Phuket Town.*

South of the headland sheltering Nai Thon, the shore curves in to form Bang Thao Beach, formerly the site of a tin mine. Chemical seepage had left the place an ecological disaster, and it remained an eyesore until about 10 years ago, when a Thai developer bought the land and started a cleanup. He built one hotel, then another, and another, until the whole bay became a resort area with five major hotels and their 2,000 rooms and 27 restaurants. All the hotels—the Banyan Tree, Dusit Laguna, Laguna Beach Club, Sheraton Grande Laguna, and Allamanda—cater to the affluent tourist. A free shuttle service travels between them, guests can use the pool facilities of any hotel in the group, and a cross-dining plan permits guests of one hotel to dine at any other. The Dusit and the Sheraton have the best beaches.

Dining and Lodging

$$$$ ✕🏨 **Banyan Tree Phuket.** Of the five resort hotels on Laguna Beach, this is the most exclusive—and expensive. It's built along classical European lines, but with teak floors and Thai fabrics. Many guests come for rejuvenation treatments that include herbal massages, special diets, and exercise. When not being pampered at the spa, you can stay in your private villa—a secluded enclave whose bathroom, with an extra outdoor shower, is as big as the huge bedroom. The king-size bed is enthroned on a raised platform and, lying on it wrapped in your toga, you look out onto your private garden. At the end of the garden there's a open-sided gazebo where, if the mood takes you, a masseuse will come and perform miracles on your body. Thirty-four of these villas have their own 9-by-3-meter pools (B5,000 extra). Should you tire of the hotel's two restaurants, you can join the hoi polloi at any of the restaurants at the other Laguna Beach hotels and bill your meals to your room. Your only worry will be the mosquitoes, who'll visit your ankles when the sun goes down. ✉ *33 Moo 4 Srisoonthorn Rd., Cherngtalay, Thalang, Phuket 83110,* ☎ *076/324374,* 📠 *076/324356. 98 villas. 2 restaurants, pool, massage, spa, 5 tennis courts, health club, squash. AE, MC, V.* 🏊

$$$ ✕🏨 **Dusit Laguna.** Facing a mile-long beach and flanked by two lagoons, this hotel is popular with upscale Thais seeking refuge from the more commercial Patong and with foreigners who want to stay in a sedate, quiet resort yet like to be near a more lively hotel (the Sheraton) when the mood strikes. The hotel rooms, with picture windows opening onto private balconies, have pastel decor and spacious bathrooms. There's barbecue dining on the terrace and, after dinner, dancing to the latest beats. European fare is served at the Junkceylon; Thai cuisine, to the tune of traditional Thai music, is served in the Ruen Thai restaurant. Evening entertainment changes nightly and may consist of a song-and-dance troupe of transvestites or classical Thai dance. The cross-dining plan with the other four resorts in the Laguna complex extends your choices of where to eat and be entertained. ⊠ *390 Srisoonthorn Rd., Cherngtalay, Thalang, Phuket 83110, ☎ 076/324320; 02/236–0450 Bangkok reservations, ⅜X 076/324174. 233 rooms and 7 suites. 4 restaurants, pool, putting green, 2 tennis courts, windsurfing, boating, meeting rooms, travel services. AE, DC, MC, V.* ✎

$$$ ╳⊡ **Sheraton Grande Laguna.** Another Laguna Beach hotel, this one is built around a lagoon. The beach is just across a grassy lawn, and a 323-meter narrow pool meanders through the hotel complex before opening up into two larger, swimmable pools. The large rooms are furnished minimally and decorated with indigenous art. All have small private balconies. Bathrooms have a sunken tub that looks appealing but takes forever to fill, so you tend only to use it for a shower. The service is swift and polite. For more privacy and personal attention, rent one of the 85 one- or two-bedroom "villa suites" in a separate enclave with its own pool, and receive a complimentary breakfast as well as evening cocktails. Guests can dine at a range of restaurants, the best of which is the Marketplace, a group of food stands that present a sampling of Asian foods, from grilled Thai lobster to Mongolian hot pot. There are several other casual restaurants; the more formal Tea House for Chinese seafood; and, for Thai food, the Chao Lay, built on stilts over the lagoon. ⊠ *Bang Thao Bay, 10 Moo 4 Srisoonthorn Rd., Cherngtalay, Thalang, Phuket 83110, ☎ 076/324101, ⅜X 076/324108. 258 rooms and 85 suites. 5 restaurants, 2 pools, 18-hole golf course, 4 tennis courts, windsurfing, boating, nightclub. AE, DC, MC, V.* ✎

Pansea Beach

★ ⑫ *21 km (12 mi) northwest of Phuket Town.*

South of Bang Thao, in a small bay sheltered by a headland, stretches Pansea Beach, virtually a private enclave for two splendid hotels.

Dining and Lodging

$$$$ ╳⊡ **Amanpuri.** For taste and elegance, there is no finer place in Thailand—nor any quite as expensive. The most basic accommodation costs $370, but a room with a better view costs $850. The completely open main building, with polished floors, modern bamboo furniture, and thatch roof, looks over a serene, black-lined swimming pool surrounded by tall palms. A sweeping staircase leads down to the secluded beach. Guests stay in individual pavilions, staggered up the hillside and reached by an elevated boardwalk whose style is distinctly Thai, with broad eaves and swooping roofs. Each suite has a private sundeck with a gazebo; the furnishings are handcrafted of local woods. A split-level bar perched on the hill has a romantic view of the sunset across the Andaman Sea, and in the beautiful dining room the culinary delights prepared by an enthusiastic French chef (with an Italian touch) will tempt you to return. Try the fresh fish on a bed of vegetables, topped with a sauce sparked by fresh ginger and lemongrass. Thirteen privately owned villas, each with several bedrooms and a pool, are also rented out. ⊠ *Pansea Beach, Cherngtalay, Phuket 83110, ☎ 076/324333; 02/ 287–0226 Bangkok reservations; 800/447–7462 U.S reservations, ⅜X*

076/324100. 40 pavilions and 30 villas. 2 restaurants, bar, pool, 2 tennis courts, windsurfing, boating, shops, travel services. AE, V. ✇

$$$$ ⊞ **Chedi.** There's a special ambience and superior service here, a re-
★   sort that is exclusive without being overly formal and stiff. As you enter
the lobby, you are greeted by a sweeping view of the Andaman Sea and
a hexagonal pool, with gardens below that abut the sands of the virtually private beach. Although all the chalets along the hillside face the
sea, it is hidden from most of them by swaying palms. One that does
have a sea view is No. 106. Each chalet has its own sundeck; the interior is but pleasantly uncluttered and accentuated by shining wood
floors and woven palm walls. The bathrooms, a bit skimpy, have only
showers and no baths. The Chedi used to be a bargain but the rates
have steadily climbed to around $220—still, that is $150 cheaper than
the Amanpuri next door. ⊠ *118 Moo 3, Pansea Beach, Cherngtalay,
Phuket 83110,* ☎ *076/324017,* ⅎⅩ *076/324252. 110 rooms. Restaurant, outdoor café, pool, 2 tennis courts, windsurfing, boating, business services, meeting rooms. AE, DC, MC, V.* ✇

Surin Beach

⑬ *20 km (12 mi) northwest of Phuket Town.*

Surin Beach, adjoining Pansea Beach to the south, has a long stretch
of golden sand, but it's not good for swimming because of strong currents. On the headland south of Surin you'll find several small, romantic
coves. Each requires a climb down a cliff, where, with luck, the tiny
beach surrounded by palms and rocks is your personal haven. One particularly peaceful cove is **Laem Sing.**

Kamala Beach

⑭ *18 km (11 mi) west of Phuket Town.*

South of a headland below Surin Beach is Kamala Beach, a small curving strip of sand with coconut palms and a few bungalows, a resort
hotel, and a delightful, tiny, open-air restaurant called the White Orchid. Beyond this restaurant a small dirt road leads over a rugged cliff
to Patong—passable, but very tricky and not advised even if you are
an experienced dirt-track motorcyclist. It's best to drive back to the
main road that sweeps its way down the west coast.

Dining

$ ✕ **White Orchid.** At the far end of the Kamala Bay Terrace Resort, be-
★   yond the Kamala Hotel, where the road peters out to a rutted track, is
Eed's little restaurant, with six or seven tables under a thatched cover
and two more sitting under palm trees at the water's edge. The menu is
limited to what Eed buys that day in the market. If she has the tiger prawns,
be sure to have those, and start with her spring rolls. Although most of
what she and her sister cook is Thai, she does a couple of Western dishes
as well. All is clean, and Eed will prepare the food according to your
taste. Not only is Eed warm and welcoming, but she speaks English and
French, too. ⊠ *Kamala Bay,* ☎ *01/892–9757. No credit cards.*

$ ⊞ **Seaside Inn.** A line of bungalows facing a courtyard constitutes this
motel-like inn, in the center of Kamala village, just across the road from
the beach. The owner is helpful, and the air-conditioned rooms are modern and clean, with tiled floors. The queen-size beds have firm mattresses, the minibar supports the cable TV, and there is a small kitchenette
for preparing simple meals. The large bathrooms have hot and cold
water, and the accommodation here is a bargain at B1,000—far below
the prices generally charged on Phuket. ⊠ *88/6 Moo 3, Rimhad Rd.,
Kamala Beach, Phuket 83000,* ☎ ⅎⅩ *076/270894. 14 rooms. MC, V.*

Nightlife

The newest extravaganza on the island is **Phuket Fantasea** (✉ 99 Moo 3, Kamala Bay, ☎ 078/271222), a Las Vegas-type show with Thai chorus girls doing modern and classical dance, 30 elephants doing animal tricks, and humans doing magic tricks, all for B1,000. ✑ *Admission.* ◷ *Open daily 5:30–10:30* PM. *Showtime 9* PM.

Patong

⑮ *13 km (8 mi) west of Phuket Town.*

Patong is Phuket's mini Pattaya, complete with German restaurants, massage parlors, hustlers selling trinkets, and places like Tatum's, a combined coffeehouse, disco, and go-go dance floor. A half-mile radius around Soi Bangla has 150 bars and a number of gay clubs. The 90 lodgings, ranging from deluxe hotels to small cottages—more than 6,000 double rooms in all—attest to Patong's popularity among charter groups. From about 7 PM on, the main street is lined for about 3 km (2 mi) with stalls selling, among other things, junk jewelery, wood carvings, and watches. Restaurants down side streets offer seafood and Western food, and beyond these, one bar crowds out another. Special buses bring hotel guests to Patong for the evening, allowing time for dinner, shopping, and a turn around the café-bars, which are full of hostesses of both sexes.

Dining and Lodging

$$ ✕ **Baan Rim Pa.** For classical Thai cooking, come to this restaurant on a cliff at the north end of Patong Beach. The large, open terrace is one of the most attractive settings on Phuket, and the food is prettily presented in traditional style. In fact, the head chef started the Thai Cooking School and has constructed set menus to make ordering simpler for non-Thais. Therein lies the warning: if you like hot and spicy fare, you may be disappointed. ✉ *100/7 Kalim Beach Rd., Patong,* ☎ *076/340789. AE, MC, V.*

$$ ✕ **Chao Lay at Coral Beach Hotel.** Perched on a bluff overlooking the Andaman Sea and the beach, the Chao Lay open-front restaurant is an ideal spot to enjoy fantastic views and Thai cooking. Dishes include tom kha gai, mee krob, spring rolls, and grilled seafood. ✉ *104 Moo 4, Patong Beach,* ☎ *076/321106. Reservations essential. AE, DC, MC, V.*

$$ ✕ **Mallee's Seafood Village.** This restaurant in the center of Patong offers a wide-ranging international menu. Two Thai dishes worth trying are the charcoal-grilled fish in banana leaves and the steamed fish in a tamarind sauce. If you want Chinese food, try the shark steak in a green-pepper sauce; for European fare, consider the veal sausage with potato salad. On the other hand, you may simply want to sit at one of the sidewalk tables and indulge in pancakes with honey. ✉ *94/4 Taweewong Rd., Patong,* ☎ *076/321205. AE, DC, MC, V.*

$$ ✕ **Suang Sawan.** Since they cater to vacationing foreigners, restaurants in Phuket are usually not as good (or as cheap) as those in Bangkok or other parts of Thailand. What distinguishes restaurants here is location—as is the case with Suang Sawan. Sitting above the sea, north of Patong, the panorama of coastline below makes this a splendid place to dine on seafood. Try the *pla gaprong nam manao* (sea bass steamed in a spicy lime broth). ✉ *255 Phrabarama Rd., Patong,* ☎ *076/344175. MC, V.*

$$$ ✕🏨 **Diamond Cliff Hotel.** North of town and away from the crowds, this is one of the smartest and most architecturally pleasing resorts in Patong. The beach across the road has mammoth rocks that create the feeling of several private beaches. The swimming pool is built on a ledge above the main part of the hotel, providing an unobstructed view of the coast. Rooms are spacious, full of light, and decorated in pale colors that accentuate the open feel of the hotel. Dining is taken seriously,

with fresh seafood cooked in European or Thai style. Guests can eat indoors or on the restaurant's terrace looking out to sea. ⊠ *61/9 Kalim Beach, Patong, Kathu District, Phuket 83121,* ☎ *076/340501; 02/ 246–4515 Bangkok reservations,* ☎ *076/340507. 140 rooms. Restaurant, bar, lobby lounge, pool, boating, travel services. AE, MC, V.* ⊛

$$ 🏨 **Paradise Resort.** There are many similar moderately priced hotels in Patong. This one on the strip facing the beach has more appeal than those in the thick of restaurants, shops, and bars. The Paradise has reasonably large rooms and clean bathrooms, a pool, and a coffee shop–dining room for light Thai and Western fare. ⊠ *93 Taweewong Rd. (next to the Holiday Inn), Patong, Phuket 83121,* ☎ *076/340172,* ☎ *076/295467. 16 rooms. Restaurant, pool, travel services. MC, V.*

$$ 🏨 **Phuket Cabana.** This hotel's attraction is its location: in the middle of Patong, facing the beach. Both guests and staff are laid-back, but the basic resort amenities are here, with a good tour desk and a reputable dive shop to arrange outings. Modest rooms are in chalet-type bungalows furnished with rattan tables and chairs. The Charthouse restaurant serves grilled Western food and a decent selection of Thai dishes. ⊠ *80 Taweewong Rd., Patong Beach, Phuket 83121,* ☎ *076/340138,* ☎ *076/340178. 80 rooms. Restaurant, pool, dive shop, travel services, airport shuttle. AE, MC, V.*

$ 🏨 **Bangla Bang.** If you want to be encircled by the bars and restaurants of Patong and want your lodgings cheap, try this hotel, down a small soi and therefore relatively quiet. The air-conditioned rooms are clean, with enough space for a queen-size bed or two twins. Bathrooms have hot water. The owner is chatty and knows the local scene. ⊠ *29/ 2 Bangla Rd., Patong, Phuket 83150,* ☎ *076/344528,* ☎ *076/344529. 17 rooms. MC, V.*

Karon Beach

🔟 *20 km (12 mi) southwest of Phuket Town.*

Over the headland south of Patong is beautiful Relax Bay, surrounded by verdant hills and virtually taken over by the huge Le Meridien Hotel. Occasionally, cruise ships anchor offshore, doubling the already large crowd of vacationers. A little way farther south is Karon Beach, divided into two sections: Karon Noi, a small area under development with a rather scruffy beach, and Karon Yai. Because of its good swimming and surfing, the latter part is becoming increasingly popular, and several hotels and a minitown have sprung up, making it just another strip of beach with hotels and some shops one block in from the seafront.

Dining and Lodging

$$ ✕ **On the Rock.** This 100-seat restaurant on three levels, perched on the rocks overlooking Karon Beach, is wonderfully romantic. Three baby reef sharks glide lazily in an aquarium tank, glancing at the diners. Seafood is the specialty: try the *her thalee kanom khrok* (mackerel with fresh tomato and onion) and the *pla goh tod na phrik* (snapper in a pepper and chili sauce) with rice. Those not partial to Thai fare can choose Italian pasta dishes. ⊠ *Marina Cottages, south end of Karon Beach,* ☎ *076/381625. AE, MC, V.*

$$$$ 🏨 **Le Meridien.** This self-contained resort occupying a small bay is designed to keep you so fully occupied that you never need to bother with the rest of Phuket. The U-shape bay is very pretty, though undercurrents can curtail swimming and the water is often rather murky. Most of the hotel guest rooms, which are furnished in rattan and teak, have lovely sea views. Guests (mostly on packaged holidays from Europe) seem to focus, however, on the two large swimming pools, complete with an is-

land planted with palm trees. The complex, on 48 acres with long passageways and multiple shops, restaurants (buffet meals are the norm), and bars, has the feel of an international vacation camp, but if you're looking for one place to meet all your holiday needs, Le Meridien could be your answer. ✉ *Karon Beach, Box 277, Phuket 83000,* ☎ *076/ 340480,* FAX *076/340479. 470 rooms. 7 restaurants, 3 bars, 2 pools, 4 tennis courts, health club, squash, meeting rooms. AE, DC, MC, V.* 🐾

$–$$ 🖭 **Marina Cottages.** The 50 small cottages here, straddling the divide
★ between Karon and Kata beaches, all have verandas with views of either the ocean or palm trees. Those closer to the beach are more spacious than those up the hill, but all have air-conditioning, tiled floors, balconies, and private bathrooms. The pool, nestled among rock outcroppings, is surrounded by tropical foliage. Though prices have increased, this hotel remains one of the better values on the island. ✉ *Box 143, Phuket 83000,* ☎ *076/330625,* FAX *076/330516. 104 rooms. 2 restaurants, pool. AE, MC, V.* 🐾

$ 🖭 **Ruan Thep Inn.** Just a stone's throw from the beach is a small collection of air-conditioned bungalows with decent-sized rooms and clean bathrooms. A small restaurant satisfies the appetite, though there are plenty more eateries a short walk north, in the heart of Karon Beach. ✉ *120/4 Moo 4, Patak Rd., Karon Beach, Phuket 83000,* ☎ *076/330281. 14 rooms. MC, V.*

Kata Beach

⑰ *22 km (13 mi) southwest of Phuket Town.*

Kata Beach is the next beach south of Karon Beach. The sunsets are as marvelous as ever, but the peace and quiet are fading fast. Club Mediterranée has been followed by other large hotels, but there are still stretches of sand with privacy, and the center of town has only a modest number of bars. Nearby, on lovely Kata Noi Beach (*noi* means "little") in the shelter of a forest-clad hill, is the Kata Thani Hotel, popular with tour groups.

Dining and Lodging

$$$ ✕🖭 **Boathouse Inn & Restaurant.** With all 33 rooms looking onto Kata
★ Beach, an excellent Thai restaurant facing the Andaman Sea, and a relaxing beach bar, this small hotel is a very comfortable retreat. The Thai-style architecture adds a traditional touch to the otherwise modern amenities, such as bedside control panels and a Jacuzzi pool. Guest rooms are furnished in reds and browns and have air-conditioning, private safes, and bathrooms with baths and massage showers. Though the restaurant is air-conditioned, it's best to sit on the veranda listening to gentle music from a small band. Try the *kung thot keeow:* fried shrimp paste with green curry, full of herbs and spices, garnished with basil leaves and strips of red chili, and served on thin, crisp pastry shells. The hotel also offers Thai cooking courses. ✉ *2/2 Patak Rd., Kata Beach, Phuket 83100,* ☎ *076/330015; 02/253–8735 Bangkok reservations.,* FAX *076/330561. 36 rooms. Restaurant, bar, beauty salon, travel services. AE, DC, MC, V.* 🐾

$ ✕🖭 **Friendship Bungalows.** A four-minute walk from the beach, two rows of single-story buildings contain modest, sparsely furnished, but spotlessly clean rooms, each with its own bathroom (there is usually hot water). The owners are extremely hospitable and encourage guests to feel at home. The small restaurant-bar on a terrace offers good Thai food; Western food is also available. Your leftovers will probably be enjoyed by the two monkeys on the restaurant's wall, who play there all day. ✉ *6/5 Patak Rd., Kata Beach, Phuket 83130,* ☎ *076/330499. 23 rooms. Restaurant. No credit cards.*

$$–$$$ 🏨 **Kata Beach Resort.** The fact that this hotel is owned by a Thai fam-
ily (rather than a conglomerate) is reflected in staff loyalty and their
enthusiasm for the hotel, which in turn makes the guest feel truly welcome. All rooms have balconies, but try to get a room that looks out
to sea and faces Crab Island. Even if your wedding was a long time
ago, the honeymoon rooms are a good choice for view and space. Your
one complaint here will be the tantalizing smell of the breakfast buffet wafting through the lobby in the morning. The Nero restaurant is
worth a dinner when you need a break from buffet dining. The beach
is long and wide, and most water sports are provided free of charge
by the hotel. ✉ *5/2 Moo, Patak Rd., Kata Beach, Phuket 83100,* ☎
076/330530, 🖷 *076/330128. 267 rooms. 3 restaurants, pool, health
club, water sports. AE, MC, V.* ✨

$$–$$$ 🏨 **Kata Thani.** Practically all of Kata Noi is taken up by this resort.
All the large guest rooms have balconies facing the beach, though this
means walking down long corridors to reach your room from the
lobby. Between the hotel rooms and the sandy, golden beach are grass
lawns and two large pools, one with a pool bar. There are street restaurants when you tire of the three hotel dining rooms. (The hotel has another self-contained building, the Bhuri, which is back from the beach
and not particularly recommended.) ✉ *3/24 Patak Rd., Kata Noi, Phuket
83100,* ☎ *076/330124,* 🖷 *076/330426. 433 rooms. 3 restaurants, 2
pools, 4 tennis courts, health club, water sports. AE, MC, V.* ✨

Nai Harn

★ ⑱   *18 km (11 mi) southwest of Phuket Town.*

The road south of Kata cuts inland across the hilly headland to drop
into yet another gloriously beautiful bay, Nai Harn. Protected by Man
Island, this deep bay has been a popular anchorage for international
yachtsmen. On the north side, a huge, white-stucco, stepped building,
the Phuket Yacht Club, rises from the beach in stark contrast to the
verdant hillside. From the Yacht Club's terrace, the view of the sun dropping into the Andaman Sea is superb. The public beach, with a few
stalls for snacks, is good for sunning and swimming.

Dining and Lodging

$$$$ ✕🏨 **Royal Meridien Phuket Yacht Club.** Set in a picturesque, westward-
facing bay, this stepped, modern, luxury hotel (now managed by Meridien) looks like an ambitious condominium complex. Architecture
aside, its comfort, service, amenities, and secluded location make it extremely pleasant. A 1998 refurbishment has brought this hotel back
up to speed even though it has lost its role as headquarters for the King's
Regatta in December. The guest rooms are large and have separate sitting areas and private balconies overlooking the beach and the islands
(balconies on upper floors are completely secluded). Make a point of
dining in the Chart Room, an open-sided restaurant that overlooks the
bay. Try the baked fresh fish stuffed with prawns in a tasty mixture of
Thai spices. ✉ *Nai Harn Beach, Phuket 83130,* ☎ *076/381156; 02/
251–4707 Bangkok reservations; 071/537–2988 in U.K.; 800/526–6566
in U.S.,* 🖷 *076/381164. 100 rooms and 8 suites. 2 restaurants, bar,
pool, 2 tennis courts, spa, health club, windsurfing, boating, travel services. AE, DC, MC, V.* ✨

Phromthep Cape

⑲   *18 km (11 mi) southwest of Phuket Town.*

From the cliff top at Phromthep Cape, the southern point of Phuket Island, the panorama includes Nai Harn Bay and the island's coastline.

At sunset, the view is supreme. This evening pilgrimage has become so popular that policemen organize parking, and a row of souvenir stands lines the parking lot. But once you get away from the congestion, you can enjoy the colors of the setting sun in contemplative solitude.

Rawai Beach

20 *16 km (10 mi) southwest of Phuket Town.*

Around the corner from Phromthep, facing south, is Rawai Beach, whose shallow, muddy beach is not very attractive, but whose shoreline, with a fishing village set in a coconut grove, has the charm you may have wanted to find in Phuket.

At the southern end of Rawai Beach lies the small village of **Chao Le**, whose inhabitants are descendants of the original tribes of Phuket. Called Chao Nam (Water People) by the Thais, they tend to shy away from the modern world, preferring to stay among their own. They are superb swimmers, able to fish at 90 ft in free dives. One of the three tribes of the Chao Nam is believed to be descended from the sea gypsies who pirated 17th-century trading ships entering the Burmese-Singapore waters. Of the three Chao Nam villages on Phuket, the one at Rawai Beach is the easiest to visit.

East of Rawai is **Ka Point.** Most of the promontory is owned by the huge Mercure Hotel Phuket Island Resort, a virtual town with several restaurants, two swimming pools, and a minibus to take guests from one facility to another.

Ko Hae

21 *8 km (5 mi) offshore from Chao Le.*

Cruise boats leave Rawai and Chalong, farther up the coast, for popular Ko Hae (Coral Island), 30 minutes from shore, which has clear water for snorkeling and superb beaches for sunbathing. There is a café on the island and a resort with 40 bungalows.

Ko Lone

22 *6 km (4 mi) north of Ko Hae.*

North of Ko Hae is Ko Lone, another island reached by boat from Rawai or Chalong, with a 30-room resort on its northern shore. Hiring a boat for half a day costs B800.

Chalong

23 *11 km (7 mi) south of Phuket Town.*

Chalong Bay is a huge, horseshoe-shape bay, whose entrance is guarded by Ko Lone and whose waters are the temporary resting place for yachts making passage from Europe to Asia. Commercial fishing boats also anchor here, and you can catch a boat to Ko Hae and Ko Lone from the jetty. The town of Chalong has several good, inexpensive, outdoor seafood restaurants—try Kan Eang for delicious crabs and prawns. Boats also make the short run over to Ko Raya, a small, tranquil island where Jet Skis are banned. The island has a couple of spotless beaches, Ao Tok (best for sunsets) and Ao Siam. Should you wish to spend the night, five small resorts can accommodate you at prices ranging from B500 to B1,000. Book through **Pal Travel Services** (☎ 076/340551 ext. 1150).

A bit inland from Chalong Bay you'll find **Wat Chalong,** the largest and most famous of Phuket's 20 Buddhist temples—all built since the

19th century. It enshrines the gilt statues, wrapped in saffron robes, of two revered monks who helped quell an 1876 rebellion.

Dining

$$ ✕ **Jimmy's Lighthouse Bar and Grill.** This pub-restaurant, formerly called Latitude 8, is still a hangout for sailors, though many of the sailing crowd now go next door to the marina, and the crowd that gathers here is partly tourists. The food, both Thai and Western, has improved, and it's good both for lunch and dinner. ⊠ *45/33 Chao Fa Rd., Chalong,* ☎ *076/381709. No credit cards.*

$$ ✕ **Kan Eang.** There are now two Kan Eang restaurants in Chalong.
★ Thais make a point of going to Kan Eang 1; the food is more authentic and spicier than at nearby Number 2, which is next door and in from the bay. At Number 1, get a table next to the seawall under the coconut palms and order some delicious seafood. Choose spicy dishes carefully, and be sure that your waiter understands whether you want Thai *pet* (spicy hot) or to farang taste. Include the succulent and sweet crabs in your order. ⊠ *Chalong,* ☎ *076/381323. AE, MC, V.*

Makham Bay

㉔ *11 km (6 mi) east of Chalong Bay, 9 km (5 mi) south of Phuket Town.*

East of Chalong Bay lies a peninsula with the town of Makham Bay, where you can catch the ferryboat to the Phi Phi Islands and then on to Krabi.

OFF THE
BEATEN PATH

THE SIMILAN ISLANDS – With some of the world's most interesting marine life, these islands off the west coast of Phuket in the Andaman Sea are renowned for snorkeling and diving. No hotels are permitted, though there are camping facilities. The underwater sights rival those of the Seychelles and the Maldives, and visibility ranges from 60 to 120 ft. You'll dive in water 10 ft deep down to about 120 ft. The most comfortable way to visit the islands is to take a cruise boat with a sleeping cabin from Phuket. You can also travel 80 miles north of Phuket airport to the mainland and up the coast to Tha Talamu in Phang Nga province, from where boats make the 70-minute run out to the islands on day trips. Over the last few years, the mainland coast has blossomed with hotels and dive operators, and it has its own lovely beaches for swimming and sunning. The **Khaolack Laguna Resort** (⊠ 27/3 Moo 1, Bang Naisie, Takua Pah, Phang Nga 82100, ☎ 076/420200, ℻ 076/420206) has 58 cottages and 32 hotel rooms amid tropical foliage and set back from the sandy cove, as well as a pool and restaurant.

Ko Phi Phi

In Phuket Bay, 90 mins southeast of Phuket Town; 2 hrs southwest of Krabi.

The Phi Phi Islands used to be idyllic retreats, with secret silver-sand coves, unspoiled beaches, and limestone cliffs dropping precipitously into the sea. But their proximity to busy Phuket and the easy 90-minute journey by ferry from Makham Bay have meant that tourists coming to escape Phuket's commercialism simply bring it with them. Ko Phi Phi became in some ways the poor man's Phuket, with very modest bungalow accommodations for the budget traveler, but in the late 1990s the cheap bungalows on the better beaches gave way to more expensive accommodations and backpacker lodgings were pushed to the outskirts of the main shopping street and the bays beyond. The main street, crowded with gift shops, travel agencies, and inferior restaurants, is extremely tacky, but even so it draws tourists in droves, and in high season, Ko Phi Phi is a zoo.

Of the two main islands, only **Phi Phi Don** is inhabited. It's shaped like a butterfly, with two hilly land portions linked by a wide sandbar, 2 km (1¼ mi) long. Most accommodations and the main mall with its shops and restaurants are on this sandbar, where boats come into a village called **Ton Sai**. No vehicles are allowed on the island; you can disembark at hotels on the north cape if you wish. In the evening, visitors stroll up and down the walkway along the sandbar, where small restaurants display the catch of the day on ice outside. Later in the evening, bars and discos keep the young from their beds. Away from Ton Sai, where travel is either by serious hiking or by boat, Ko Phi Phi quiets down with some very high-priced resorts, such as the P. P. Palm, in an oasis of greenery fronting a beach.

The most popular way to explore is by either a cruise boat or a long-tail boat that seats up to six people. One of the most exciting trips is to the other main island, **Phi Phi Lae.** The first stop is **Viking Cave,** a vast cavern of limestone pillars covered with what look like prehistoric drawings but are actually only a few centuries old, depicting Portuguese or Dutch cutters. The boat continues on, gliding by cliffs rising vertically out of the sea, for an afternoon in **Maya Bay.** Here the calm, clear waters, sparkling with color from the live coral, are ideal for swimming and snorkeling. You can take a 45-minute trip by long-tail boat to circular **Bamboo Island,** with a superb beach around it. The underwater colors of the fish and the coral are brilliant. The island is uninhabited, but you can spend a night under the stars.

Dining and Lodging

Restaurants on Phi Phi consist of a row of closely packed one-room cafés down the narrow mall. The menus offer mostly fish dishes—you choose your fish from the ice bin outside, and the chef cooks it according to your instructions. Prices are well under B200 for two people, including a couple of Singha beers. The open-air restaurants to the left of the pier cost more, but the food is essentially the same. The two luxury accommodations are off by themselves, 15 minutes by boat or a stiff 45-minute hike from the isthmus.

$$$–$$$$ ✕🏠 **P. P. Palm Beach Travelodge Resort.** This isolated retreat built on a terrace at the north end of the island has standard double rooms, as well as larger deluxe rooms in bungalows with sea views at twice the price. All rooms are air-conditioned and have small refrigerators and color TV. A new management is refurbishing all rooms with the intention of making this the most exclusive resort on Ko Phi Phi. The terraced restaurant, serving Thai and European cuisines, has splendid views of the sea, and the fish is absolutely fresh. ✉ *Cape Laemthong, Phi Phi, 81000,* ☎ *01/229–1052; 076/214654 Phuket reservations,* ᴀ̄ *01/229–1922. 100 rooms. Restaurant, snorkeling, windsurfing, boating, travel services. AE, V.*

$$–$$$ 🏠 **PP Princess.** In the center of the isthmus, this complex of bungalows in a coconut grove looks a little like a modern housing development, but its air-conditioned units with shiny wood floors are spacious and comfortable. The main building houses a restaurant and a huge lobby where guests, sometimes arriving in large groups, are processed before being shunted off to their bungalows. The complex faces Lohdalum Bay, though only a few bungalows have views. ✉ *Lohdalum Bay, Phi Phi, 81000,* ☎ *075/622079,* ᴀ̄ *075/612188. 79 rooms. Restaurant, bar, dive shop. AE, DC, MC, V.*

$$ 🏠 **Cabana Hotel.** Facing the sea amid coconut palms, this property offers smart accommodations in the center of Phi Phi at Ton Sai village, just five minutes from the ferry docks. Rooms are either in the hotel around the swimming pool or in small wood bungalows with a more rustic flavor—the ambience is set by the cane furniture. All rooms have air-conditioning. The outdoor restaurant, like most other restaurants on the island, specializes in fish. ⊠ *Ton Sai Beach, Phi Phi, 81000,* ☎ *075/620634,* FAX *075/612132. 100 rooms. Restaurant, pool. AE, DC, MC, V.*

$$ ☐ **Pee Pee Island Village.** This hotel on the north cape offers modest accommodations in small thatched bungalows. It provides the same water sports and tours as its neighbor, P. P. Palm Beach, but the atmosphere here is more laid-back—and the hotel less expensive. The views are less impressive, however, although guests do have panoramas of the sea and palm-clad hills. ⊠ *Cape Laemthong, Phi Phi, 81000,* ☎ *01/476–7517; 076/215014 in Phuket,* FAX *01/229–2250. 65 rooms. Restaurant, snorkeling, boating, travel services. AE, V.*

$ ☐ **Andaman Beach Resort.** About a 15-minute walk east from the pier is Laem Hin and a small beach that escapes most of the human traffic of Ton Sai. The Andaman has a range of comfortable bungalows, each with their own bathroom, on a lawn that reaches down to the sand. ⊠ *Laem Hin Beach, Phi Phi, 81000,* ☎ *01/228-4368,* FAX *01/ 228–4368. 33 bungalows. No credit cards.*

Krabi

867 km (538 mi) south of Bangkok, 180 km (117 mi) southeast of Phuket, 43 km (27 mi) by boat east of Ko Phi Phi.

Krabi, the provincial capital of the region, lies across Phuket Bay on the mainland. Once a favorite harbor for smugglers bringing alcohol and tobacco from Malaysia, it has become a fishing port and gateway to the province's islands, particularly Ko Lanta and Ko Phi Phi, and the famous beaches at and around Ao Nang. Krabi is a pleasant, low-key town, but most visitors stop here only to do some shopping, cash traveler's checks, arrange onward travel, and catch up on the news at one of the restaurants on Uttarakit Road. With the opening in 1999 of an airport 12 km (7½ mi) from town, however, one can expect Krabi to mushroom in size and increase its tourist infrastructure.

Between Krabi and Ao Nang Beach lies **Susan Hoi** (Shell Cemetery Beach), aptly named for the 75-million-year-old shells that have petrified into bizarrely shaped rock slabs.

Dining and Lodging

$$ ✕ **Isouw.** This floating restaurant just across from the Night Market can be a cool place in which to sit, enjoy lunch, and watch the river traffic. It specializes in grilled fish with sweet-and-sour sauce, and the mee krob here has an abundance of fresh, sweet shrimp. ⊠ *Krabi,* ☎ *075/611956. Reservations not accepted. No credit cards.*

$–$$ ☐ **Thai Hotel.** Though it is primarily for business travelers, this new hotel ranks as Krabi's best. If you've missed your onward connections, the location is convenient—just a block from the pier. Rooms are uniform and have a two-tone blue color scheme. Many have a queen-size as well as a single bed, just in case you bring your mother-in-law. Bathrooms are modern and functional. ⊠ *7 Isara Rd., 81000,* ☎ *075/611474,* FAX *075/620564. 151 rooms. Restaurant. MC, V.*

$ ☐ **Grand Tower Hotel.** Extremely popular with backpackers of all ages, this modern, five-story guest house has large, fan-cooled rooms and clean, modern bathrooms. The café serves basic Western fare, and the tour desk operators are knowledgeable. Many of the long-distance private bus companies stop here. ⊠ *73/1 Uttarakit Rd.,* ☎ *075/ 621456,* FAX *075/611741. 40 rooms with bath. Restaurant, travel services. MC, V.*

Ao Nang

★ *20 km (12 mi) from Krabi Town.*

Ao Nang, less than 20 minutes (a B20 songthaew ride) by road from Krabi, was discovered by backpackers in the early 1990s. Now it's being discovered by land speculators. Already, smart modern hotels have replaced most of the thatched bungalows, and the rutted roads are paved. Further growth can be expected with the opening of the Krabi airport. But even with the development, the beaches here are some of Thailand's most attractive, and the fascinating 83 offshore islands and limestone karsts will always remain. Days are spent on the beach or exploring the islands by boat. The snorkeling and scuba diving is good, particularly around Turtle Island and Chicken Island. Long-tail boats for hire line the beaches for trips to other islands or to other beaches along the coast.

Around a headland farther on from Ao Nang Bay is **Haad Noppharat Thara,** a beach (and part of a National Park) less populated than Ao Nang that's famous for its rows of casuarina trees. You can walk out to the little rocky island at low tide, but don't linger there too long. When the tide comes in, so does a current. For total seclusion, hire a long-tail boat to take you (15 minutes) to the offshore islands. You can also take a boat back toward Krabi to the beaches of **Nam Mao and Railay** (the shuttle boat between Ao Nang and Railay costs B30). You can stay at Railay, in the luxury Rayavadee Resort or in a backpacker-type bungalow, and have a meal at one of the restaurants.

Dining and Lodging

$$$$ ✕🍴 **Rayavadee Premier Resort.** A true retreat laid out on 26 land-
★ scaped acres, this resort is on the mainland but is accessible only by boat (20 minutes from Krabi town or 10 minutes from Ao Nang Bay). Its gardens and coconut groves lead down to white-sand beaches on three sides. Such privacy comes dearly: prices start at $330. Circular Thai-style pavilions have spacious living rooms downstairs and curving staircases to the magnificent bedrooms and sumptuous bathrooms with huge, round tubs. The use of highly polished wood and tile floors adds to the cool luxury. Because nearly all the pavilions are between the two beaches that flank the headland, you are never more than a five-minute walk from a beach. Krua Pranang, the Thai restaurant in a breezy pavilion, serves food as exciting as it is delicious. For an appetizer, try the *mieng kana* (Chinese broccoli leaves filled with lime, chili, shallots, and ginger) or the fried sweetened beef and papaya salad served with steamed rice. For entrées, the steamed fish with pickled plum and the tom kha gai are two tasty choices. If you plan to arrive at the hotel directly from Bangkok, you will need to fly into Phuket by 3:30 PM, have a hotel car take you the two hours to a ferry landing, and then take a 10-minute boat ride to the resort. ✉ *67 Mu 5, Susan Hoy Rd., Tambol Sai Thai, Krabi 81000,* ☎ *075/620740,* ℻ *075/620630. 98 pavilions. 2 restaurants, bar, snack bar, in-room safes, in-room VCRs, pool. AE, DC, MC, V.* ✇

$$–$$$ ✕🍴 **Krabi Resort.** What was once a small collection of thatched cottages on Ao Nang has mushroomed into a large resort. Rows of attractive wood bungalows are staggered back from the beach. (The first two rows closest to the beach cost 15% more, at B3,000.) Furnishings are wood and wicker. A concrete two-story building at the back of the property offers 40 standard hotel rooms for the same price as the bungalows in the last two rows. There is also a pool in the garden. The restaurant, popular with guests from other hotels, is alongside the beach adjoining several other dining establishments, all of which specialize in local seafood. ✉ *55–57 Pattana Rd., Amphoe Muang, Krabi 81000,* ☎ *075/*

637030; 02/208–9165 Bangkok reservations, FAX 075/637051. 103 rooms. Restaurant, pool, boating, nightclub. DC, MC, V.

$ ✕🔟 **Emerald Bungalows.** On the quiet, sandy beach of Haad Noppharat, just north of Ao Nang, this hotel offers an array of bungalows with private baths. Those facing the beach are the best and most expensive (B1,200). The restaurant serves seafood and Thai dishes and is the place for socializing and reading. ✉ Haad Noppharat Beach, Moo 4, Tambol Ao Nang (2/1 Kongca Rd., Krabi 81000), ☎ 075/611106. 36 rooms. Restaurant. No credit cards.

$$–$$$ 🔟 **Ao Nang Villa.** At the other end of the beach from the Krabi Resort, where bungalows used to be stands a three-story hotel facing the beach, which curves around a good-size swimming pool and gardens. All rooms have balconies facing the pool. The restaurant pavilion, in gardens of its own next door, serves dinner both under its roof and on the surrounding lawn. A few good twin-bed bungalows still remain, kept only for those in the know. These are fan-cooled and smallish, but with private bathrooms (cold water only) and full access to all the hotel's amenities; they can, with some negotiation, be a great bargain. ✉ 113 Ao Nang Beach, Krabi 81000, ☎ 075/637270, FAX 075/637274. 62 rooms. Restaurant, pool, tennis court. MC, V.

$$ 🔟 **Ban Ao Nang Resort.** The rooms at this three-story hotel are quite large and have decent bathrooms. All but a few are air-conditioned; the others come with a fan and are about B500 cheaper. The nicest rooms overlook the swimming pool. Those at the back have views of tropical undergrowth and are only to be taken as a last resort. The staff is friendly and helpful. The beach and the main street of Ao Nang are 100 meters down a slight hill. Meals are served buffet-style. ✉ 31/3 Moo 2, Ao Nang, Krabi 81000, ☎ 075/637072, FAX 075/637070. 108 rooms. Restaurant, pool. MC, V.

$$ 🔟 **Phra Nang Inn.** Krabi's prices have doubled in the last two years, and this hotel is no exception, but it does have rustic charm and a good location across the road from the beach. Rooms are furnished in soft colors, some with four-poster and some with two queen-size beds. The staff is extremely accommodating; hopefully their attitude won't change with the new management. The dining room serves Thai and international fare. ✉ 119 Mu 2, Ao Nang, Krabi 91000, ☎ 075/637130, FAX 075/637134. 83 rooms. Restaurant. AE, DC, MC, V. 🍃

¢–$ 🔟 **Railay Bay Bungalows.** This is one of a couple of modest resorts facing the same pretty beach as the Dusit Rayavadee. (Cocos, the cheapest, with tiny units and shared baths, gets an active, friendly, back-packing clientele.) The Railay Bay's bungalows start at B400 for a small fan-cooled unit that's back from the beach and go up to B700 for a larger unit closer to the water. There is even one air-conditioned bungalow at B1,600. The two tightly packed rows of bungalows are perpendicular to the beach, extending inland from the beachfront restaurant, which serves inexpensive seafood, Thai dishes, and European breakfasts. ✉ Railay Beach, Ao Nang, Krabi 81000, ☎ 01/228–4112, FAX 01/228–4516. 30 rooms. Restaurant. No credit cards.

¢ 🔟 **Inter House.** On the small street that runs parallel to the beach road are a number of guest houses. Inter House is noteworthy for its friendly owner, Mrs. Chotika Boonrungsri, and the clean, fan-cooled rooms that are large enough for two queen-size beds (B500). It has no restaurant, but there is a local Thai eatery next door. ✉ 245/11 Moo 2, Ao Nang Arcade, Ao Nang, Krabi 81000, ☎ 075/637508 or 01/968–9846. 5 rooms. No credit cards.

¢ 🔟 **Jinda Guest House.** Cheap bungalows are hard to find in Ao Nang, but there are four guest houses in a row up the main street, 200 yards from the beach. There isn't much difference between them; they all charge B200 for a fan-cooled room and shared bathroom. You may want to try the Jinda first, since breakfasts here are quite reasonable and the owner speaks a little English. ⊠ *Moo 2, Ao Nang, Krabi 81000,* ☎ *01/607–8556. 9 rooms with shared bath. No credit cards.*

Phang Nga Bay

★ *100 km (62 mi) north of Phuket, 93 km (56 mi) northwest of Krabi.*

Phang Nga Bay, made famous by the James Bond movie *The Man with the Golden Gun,* lies at the top of Phuket Bay. There are little islands to explore, as well as offshore caves and startling karst formations rising out of the sea. You really need a full day to see everything and to appreciate the sunsets, which are particularly beautiful on **Ko Mak.**

The best—really the only—way to visit this bay is by boat. A number of agencies on Phuket run half-day trips, or you can hire a boat locally. There are two inlets, just before you reach Phang Nga town, from which long-tail and larger boats depart. Most tour buses go to the western inlet, where costs run B1,300 for two hours (you're unlikely to see the Kao Kien cliff paintings), negotiable to B900. The second inlet, signposted "Ferry," has fewer foreign tourists and better prices—about B800 for three hours. **Mr. Kean** (☎ 076/43061) is a reliable organizer who rides around in his songthaew. Most tourists don't arrive from Phuket until 11 AM, so if you get into the bay before then, it will be more or less yours to explore, with a boatman as your guide. To get an early start, you may want to stay overnight in the area.

There are several key sights. **Ko Panyi** has a Muslim fishing village built on stilts, restaurants charging 300% above a reasonable price, and lots of souvenir shops selling high-priced junk. The beautiful **Ko Phing Kan,** now known as James Bond Island, is well worth a visit. **Ko Tapu** looks like a nail driven into the sea. **Tham Kaeo grotto** is an Asian version of Capri's Blue Grotto. **Kao Kien** has overhanging cliffs with primitive paintings, thought to be 3,500 years old, of elephants, fish, and crabs. **Tham Lot** is a large cave with stalactites that have been carved into an archway large enough for cruise boats to pass through.

Dining and Lodging

$$ ✕▥ **Phang Nga Bay Resort.** This modern hotel's raison d'être is as a base for exploring the bay, and you can hire a boat here to do so. It's on an estuary 1½ km (1 mi) from the coast, and it doesn't have panoramic views, but the rooms are comfortable and modern, the bathrooms are clean and large, and the dining room serves reasonable Chinese, Thai, and European food. ⊠ *20 Thaddan Panyee, Phang Nga 82000,* ☎ *076/440723 or 01/917–4147,* ℻ *076/440726. 88 rooms. Restaurant, coffee shop, pool, 2 tennis courts. AE, MC, V.*

¢ ▥ **Phang-Nga Bay National Park.** Before the dock area and the Phang Nga Bay Resort is the Phang Nga National Park, with chalet-style accommodation. There are two units to each chalet, and each unit has two bedrooms. The rooms are spartan and the mattresses very hard. Bathrooms have squat toilets (don't use toilet paper—it clogs the drains), and showers are bowls of cold water poured over your body—all typical aspects of traditional Thai living that are not for everyone. The restaurant alongside a tidal creek has superb, spicy Thai food. ⊠ *80 Mu 1, Phang Nga Bay 82000,* ☎ *076/411136. 6 rooms. Restaurant. No credit cards.*

Ko Samui and Nearby Islands

In the southern Gulf of Thailand lies Ko Samui, the world's coconut capital, discovered by backpackers several years ago and now regarded as an alternative to Phuket. Already too commercial for some people, it still has far fewer hotels, restaurants, and bars than Phuket, and it is a haven of tranquillity compared with seedy Pattaya. The island's best food, both Thai and Western, is found at the major hotels; the greatest number of local restaurants are in Chaweng, but little distinguishes one from another. Just look to make sure that the seafood is fresh. Lamai Beach has a noisy and more developed nightlife. The quieter beaches, such as Bophut, are on the island's north shore. The TAT has a list of guest houses on the islands, and most travel agencies can make reservations at some of them and at the hotels.

Ko Samui is half the size of Phuket, and could be easily toured in a day. But tourists come for the sun and beach, not for sightseeing, and they usually stay put. We cover the island clockwise. The best beaches, with glistening white sand and clear waters, are on the east coast; the others have either muddy sand or rocky coves. The waters around Ko Samui are already less clear than they were years ago, but the sea surrounding the smaller islands nearby is still crystal clear. Ko Pha Ngan, north of Ko Samui, though in the process of being discovered by tourists and land developers, is still one of the world's most idyllic places. Ko Tao, north of Ko Pha Ngan, is now a haven for backpackers and has fantastic snorkeling. The tiny islets of the Angthong Marine National Park, east of Ko Samui, are also superb for snorkeling and scuba diving.

New Port

❶ *500 km (310 mi) south of Bangkok, 20 km (12 mi) by boat east of Don Sak, which is 27 km (18 mi) from Surat Thani.*

The car ferry from Don Sak on the mainland arrives at New Port, south of the main town, Na Thon. Unless a hotel van is waiting for you, take a songthaew first to Na Thon, and then another to reach your final destination.

Na Thon

❷ *30 km (18½ mi) by boat east of Surat Thani, 6½ km (4 mi) north of New Port.*

Compared with the other sleepy island villages, Na Thon is a bustling town. The passenger ferry from Surat Thani docks here; shops, travel agencies, and restaurants line the waterfront, and local businesses and banks are on the parallel street one block back. Though Na Thon has a hotel, tourists seldom stay in town.

Maenam

❸ *10 km (6 mi) northeast of Na Thon.*

On the north coast east of Na Thon, the first major tourist area is Maenam. Its long, curving, sandy beach is shaded by trees and lapped by gentle waters that are great for swimming. Inexpensive guest houses and the luxury Santiburi resort share the 5-km (3-mi) stretch of sand.

Lodging

$$$$ 🏨 **Santiburi.** Set on 23 acres of gardens paralleling the beach is an ex-
  ★   clusive hideaway. The standard suites are private bungalows with highly polished wood floors, even in the huge bathrooms, which have two black washbasins, black oval bathtubs, and separate black-tile shower stalls— a typical case of modern Thai opulence. The contemporary Thai furnishings give an open feel that's enhanced by a glass panel between the living room and bedroom. Sliding doors to the patio add to the openness at the expense of privacy. Each bungalow has its own TV, VCR, and CD player, with free CDs and videotapes. The main building, a mod-

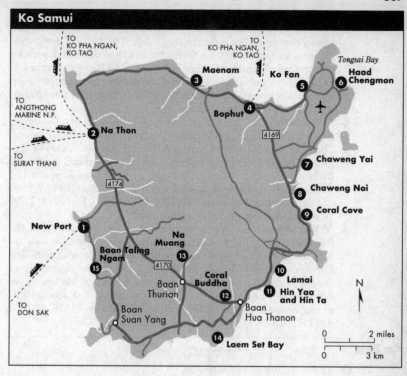

Ko Samui

ern Thai pavilion overlooking the oval swimming pool, has European and Thai restaurants—the Sala Thai has superb dishes. Guests also amble up to the beach bar for informal meals. From this secluded resort oasis you can walk to the main road and take a songthaew to any part of the island. ⊠ 12/12 Moo 1, Tambol Maenam, Ko Samui 84330, ☎ 077/425031; 02/238–4790 Bangkok reservations; 800/223–5652 in U.S., FAX 077/425040. 75 suites. 2 restaurants, snack bar, pool, 2 tennis courts, health club, squash, boating. AE, DC, MC, V. ☜

Bophut

4 *11 km (7 mi) east of Na Thon.*

A small headland separates Maenam from the next bay, Bophut. The beach is quite narrow but wide enough for sunbathing and jogging. During rainy season the runoff waters make the sea slightly muddy, but otherwise this village community is a low-key resort in contrast to the burlesque of Chaweng beach. Prices here are also less than in Chaweng or Lamai. Hotels and guest houses range from backpacker hangouts to fancier places, and a line of pleasant restaurants faces the seafront. Bophut also serves as the point from which high-speed boats go to Ko Tao every morning at about 8:30.

Dining and Lodging

$–$$ ✕ **La Sirene.** For a touch of French cooking—the owner is from Nice—try this small bistro on the waterfront. A four-course menu beginning with some homemade pâté followed by medallions of beef or pork in a mustard sauce, salad, and then dessert runs about B220. À la carte dishes, including Thai ones, are also offered. A few tables are inside, but the delight is to sit on the deck overlooking the boats moored a few yards offshore. ⊠ 65/1 Bophut Beach, ☎ 077/425301. No credit cards.

$ ✕ **Happy Elephant.** Owner Khun Sasothon displays the day's seafood specialty on ice in front of his Thai restaurant. Choose the fish and specify how you'd like it done, have a drink at the bar, and then, when dinner is ready, sit outside on the deck above the beach and dine under the stars, watching the twinkling lights of Ko Pha Ngan across the sea. Other dishes are also served—the *tom yam pla nam sai* (clear spicy soup with fish) is strongly recommended. ✉ *79/1 Moo 1, Bophut Beach,* ☎ *077/245347. No credit cards.*

$ ⊞ **The Lodge.** Looking a bit like an English roadside inn, this small, two-story, vine-clad hotel has clean, modern rooms, all facing the sea. The spacious air-conditioned rooms (B1,000) have minimal but adequate furnishings and wood floors, with ceiling fans and lockboxes. Bathrooms have both showers and tubs, with hot and cold water. The TV has CNN, and best of all, each room has a balcony. ✉ *91/1 Moo 1, Bophut Beach, Ko Samui 84140,* ☎ *077/425337,* ℻ *077/425336. 10 rooms. Restaurant, bar. No credit cards.*

$ ⊞ **Peace Bungalows.** Just to the west of the main street of Bophut, the Pupaiboon family has a collection of bungalows. The smaller ones are fan-cooled; the larger ones are air-conditioned and popular with Thai families. All are well-maintained and clean. The large grass lawn shaded by coconut palms leads down to the beach. It has one of the better hotel restaurants on the island, serving zesty Thai food as well as international dishes. ✉ *Bophut Beach, Ko Samui 84320,* ☎ *077/ 425357,* ℻ *077/425343. 36 rooms. Restaurant. MC, V.*

Ko Fan

❺ *18 km (11 mi) east of Na Thon.*

On the north shore of Ko Samui near the northeast tip is Ko Fan, a little island with a huge sitting **Buddha image** covered in moss. Try to visit at sunset, when the light off the water shows the statue at its best. Back across the causeway, on the beach facing the seated Buddha, there are a number of guest houses and bungalows frequented by backpackers who find Bophut too noisy and expensive.

Haad Chengmon

❻ *20 km (12½ mi) east of Na Thon.*

Continue east along the north coast to Haad Chengmon (*haad* means "beach"), which is dominated by the headland Laem Rumrong. This is the end of the road for the few songthaews that take this route, and few tourists come here. The several guest houses and one upscale resort scattered along the shoreline don't disturb the peace and tranquillity.

Dining and Lodging

$$$$ ✕⊞ **Tongsai Bay Hotel.** The Tongsai Bay is an elegant resort retreat whose service is not as good as it should be for the price. Set on 25 acres stepped up from the bay, it has whitewashed, red-tile hillside cottages with balconies looking out to sea (when the view is not blocked by foliage), and 24 rooms in the three-story main building. The cottage rooms are stylishly furnished, and some of the split-level rooms incorporate the natural rock wall, although they are too closely clustered together. The dining room has beautiful views; reserve a table on the terrace. Ko Samui is known for huge succulent oysters and king prawns, and Tongsai gets the best. The duck in tamarind sauce is also excellent. A shuttle will take you to Na Thon and Chaweng. ✉ *Tongsai Bay, Ko Samui 84140,* ☎ *077/421451; 02/254–0023 Bangkok reservations,* ℻ *077/421462; 02/253–3190 Bangkok reservations. 80*

rooms. Restaurant, bar, pool, 2 tennis courts, windsurfing, boating. AE, DC, MC, V.

$$$ ⊡ **Boat House Hotel.** This imaginative property across the bay from Tongsai comprises 34 rice barges converted into duplex suites. The whale-like boats in tightly packed rows 100 yards in from the shore look like a Jonah's nightmare, but onboard, they're superb. Each has an enclosed upper deck with a lounge and wet bar and, below, a sitting area, bedroom, and large bathroom with a grand oval tub. The hulls are original; the uncluttered interiors and upper decks are new, with highly polished teak and mahogany beams and paneling. The double beds are just a foot off the floor, while high above are suspended fishing nets. Another 176 rooms were built in two wings between the barges and the road. They're less expensive (B3,200 versus B5,400 for a barge suite) but have no sea view. Coral reefs are exposed at low tide, but the swimming is safe and in sheltered waters. The hotel is a little off the beaten track. ⊠ *Chengmon Beach, Ko Samui, Surat Thani 84140,* ☎ *077/ 421451; 02/254–0023 Bangkok reservations,* ☒ *077/421462. 34 boat suites, 176 rooms. 2 restaurants, pool, 4 tennis courts, windsurfing, boating, travel services. AE, DC, MC, V.*

Chaweng

20 km (12½ mi) east of Na Thon.

If you have your own transportation—and don't mind bumping over rutted, unpaved surfaces—the road continues around the peninsula for 6 km (3¾ mi) to Chaweng Beach (also served by songthaew from Bophut). Of the 11 beach areas of Ko Samui, Chaweng has the finest glistening white sand. It is also the most congested, crammed with guest houses, hotels, shops, restaurants, and tourists. All this commercial activity enlivens both sides of the one unpaved road, a block in from the beach. It could be seen as a miniature version of Patong Beach on Phuket, but in contrast to the tacky, neon-lit commercialism there, the chaotic mishmash of buildings and shacks on Chaweng's strip is more fun and more Thai.

❼ **Chaweng Yai** (*yai* means "large"), the northernmost section, is separated from Chaweng Noi (*noi* means "little") by a small point, Laem Koh Faan. Chaweng Yai is divided by a reef into two sections, of which the northern one is a quiet area popular with backpackers. The southern part is crowded with hotels and scantily clad tourists, young and old (Thais find it offensive that Western women sunbathe topless, and although they usually say nothing, they smile scornfully). Here you will find anything you want, from scooter rentals to money changers and nightclubs, like the currently popular **Reggae Pub** (☎ 077/422331), with its many bars and dance floors.

❽ South of this busy beach is **Chaweng Noi,** which is not as fully developed and whose beach has more lively waves. The salt air has yet to be tainted by the odor of suntan oil, but there are already many hotels and more on the way.

Dining and Lodging

$ ✕ **Nakorntorung.** There are prettier places to dine than this open-sided restaurant with concrete floor, Formica-topped tables, and toilet rolls for napkins, but it is hard to find better seafood, Thai curries, and soups. That's why locals come here, as does a smattering of Westerners who recognize good food and are not put off by the service—the staff is friendly and helpful, just slow. The restaurant is on the main street in the southern part of town, diagonally across from the Beachcomber Resort. ⊠ *2 Chaweng Beach Rd., Chaweng,* ☎ *077/422500. No credit cards.*

$$$ 🏨 **The Imperial Samui.** This resort is attractively laid out at the top of a landscaped garden terrace with steps leading down to the beach. Guest rooms, which fan out from the main building, are standard, with modern furnishings and little appeal except for the view of the beach. One disadvantage is that wherever you go on the property, you must go up or down steps. Attention is focused on the swimming pool, which contains a small island, complete with three coconut trees. The hotel is at the south end of Chaweng Noi, where the beach isn't crowded and the sea is clean. The restaurant tends to serve too many boring, although bountiful, buffets. ⊠ *Chaweng, Ko Samui 84140,* ☎ *077/421390,* FAX *02/253–3190 Bangkok reservations. 77 rooms. Restaurant, bar, pool, windsurfing, boating. AE, DC, MC, V.* 🍴

$$$ 🏨 **Poppies.** At the far southern end of Chaweng is without doubt the most attractive of all its hotels. Though away from the noisy hoi polloi, it's within walking distance of shops and nightlife. Each cottage has either a queen or two twin beds and a living room with a sofa bed. Cottages have air-conditioning and a ceiling fan. Roof panels, doors, and floors are all teak, and Thai cotton and silk are used. Bathrooms have a sunken tub and shower set in marble. With a ratio of 3.5 staff members to every cottage, you can be assured that service is swift and attentive. Poppies restaurant, between the pool and the beach, offers seafood, Thai, and international fare served either under the sky or in the sala-style dining room. ⊠ *South Chaweng Beach, Box 1, Chaweng, Ko Samui 84320,* ☎ *077/422419,* FAX *077/422420. 26 cottages. Restaurant, pool. AE, MC, V.* 🍴

$$ 🏨 **Amari Palm Reef Hotel.** The part of Chaweng beach on which this hotel is set is too shallow for swimming; you must walk 500 yards south for that. Half the rooms, in two wings that overlook the pool and garden, are simply functional, with small bathrooms and showers only. The more attractive accommodations are across the road from the beach in small compounds of teak, Thai-style bungalows. Mattresses are on low platforms above the polished mahogany floor. The large cottages have sleeping lofts, air-conditioning, and small terraces. The hotel has a swimming pool with a swim-up bar. The dining room (mostly Western fare) is one floor up, with a view; the Thai restaurant is in a wood-paneled room to the rear. The staff is enthusiastic and friendly. ⊠ *14/ 3 Moo 2, Tambon Bophut, Chaweng, Ko Samui 84140,* ☎ *077/ 422015; 02/255–4588 Bangkok reservations,* FAX *077/422394. 104 rooms. 2 restaurants, bar, 2 pools, 2 tennis courts, squash. MC, V.* 🍴

$$ 🏨 **Central Samui Hotel.** Set back from the beach, this hotel may not be quite as smart as its neighbor, the Imperial Samui, but it costs less. Guest rooms come with fans or, for a few more dollars, air-conditioning. Equipment for water sports is available, and the restaurant offers views over the gulf. ⊠ *Chaweng Noi Beach, Ko Samui 84140,* ☎ *077/ 421384,* FAX *077/421385. 50 rooms. Restaurant, bar, coffee shop, windsurfing. AE, MC, V.*

$–$$ 🏨 **Fair House.** This hotel on the beach at Chaweng Noi used to have small, simple bungalows with air-conditioning. Only a couple of these are left, and a modern resort has been constructed, separated from the beach by a swimming pool. Furnishings are simple but adequate—queen-size or twin beds, two cane chairs, a small coffee table, and a TV on the minibar. Showers have hot and cold water. The open-front dining room has broad sea views, and the Thai cuisine—with a few Western dishes—is remarkably good. ⊠ *Chaweng, Ko Samui 84140,* ☎ *077/ 422327,* FAX *077/422255. 36 rooms. Restaurant, bar, pool. MC, V.*

$ 🏨 **Montien.** Decent-sized bungalows, each with a patio given privacy by tropical foliage, line up perpendicular to the beach. Well-placed bedside lights make for easy reading indoors. A separate washbasin just outside the bathroom is convenient, and there's a hot-water shower.

The ambience is spare, but at B1,200 the Montien is good value, especially if you want to be in the heart of Chaweng's action. ⊠ *5 Moo 2, Chaweng, Ko Samui 84140,* ☎ *077/422169,* ℻ *077/422145. 25 rooms. Restaurant, bar. MC, V (adds 5% to bill).*

$ ⌂ **O. P. Bungalow.** Among the inexpensive bungalow hotels that line the middle part of Chaweng Beach protected by a reef, this quiet property is efficiently run, and it has clean, simple rooms with hot-water showers. The narrow property has four rows of cottages stretching back from the beach to the road (rates are higher closer to the beach). The rooms have tile floors and most have twin beds. Room 502, with a double bed and close to the beach, is a good one to request. An open-sided coffee shop down at the beach has reasonably priced Thai and Chinese food. ⊠ *111 Chaweng Beach Rd., Chaweng, Ko Samui, Surat Thani 84320,* ☎ *077/422424,* ℻ *077/422425. 38 rooms. Restaurant. No credit cards.*

Coral Cove

⑨ *21 km (13 mi) southeast of Na Thon.*

Beyond the Imperial Samui Hotel is Coral Cove, popular with scuba divers. But you don't have to be a diver to enjoy the underwater scenery: just walk waist-high into the water and look through a mask to see the amazing colors of the coral. For a Thai seafood lunch, walk up the rocks to Coral Cove Bungalows, where you also can rent snorkeling equipment.

Lamai

⑩ *18 km (11 mi) southeast of Na Thon.*

A rocky headland separates Chaweng from Ko Samui's second most popular beach, Lamai. It lacks the glistening white sand of Chaweng, but its clear water and rocky pools made it the first area to be developed on Ko Samui (investors later shifted their get-rich plans to Chaweng). Lamai has more of a steeply shelving shoreline than Chaweng, so few families come here, but it does make the swimming better. It's not as honky-tonk or congested as Chaweng, though there are plenty of restaurants and bars and enough shops to stir your acquisitive instincts.

Every visitor to Ko Samui makes a pilgrimage to Lamai for yet another reason: at the point marking the end of Lamai beach stand two rocks,
⑪ named **Hin Yaa** (Grandmother Rock) and **Hin Ta** (Grandfather Rock). Erosion has shaped the rocks to resemble weathered and wrinkled intimate private parts. It's nature at its most whimsical.

Lodging

$–$$ ⌂ **Golden Sand Beach Resort.** The open lobby and reception area of this hotel are off Lamai's main street. Guest rooms, in two-story buildings, angle out from the reception room and overlook a palm-fringed garden. Although the rooms are small, most have air-conditioning (a few less expensive ones are fan-cooled) and each has its own balcony and private bathroom with a shower. The most expensive rooms have a sea view. The coffee shop offers Thai, Chinese, and Western fare, and a beach bar stays open late. ⊠ *124/2 Lamai Beach, Ko Samui, Surat Thani 84310,* ☎ *077/424031,* ℻ *077/424430. 82 rooms. Coffee shop, bar. MC, V.*

$–$$ ⌂ **Pavilion.** Not too far from the action but far enough to offer a little respite from the tawdriness of downtown, the Pavilion has standard rooms in its hotel and some more expensive but much nicer octagonal thatched bungalows on its grounds. The hotel restaurant has good seafood and the beachside pool is a nice alternative to the sands. ✉ 120 Lamai Beach, Ko Samui 84310, ☎ 077/424427, ℻ 077/424211. 45 rooms. Restaurant, pool. MC, V.

En Route   About 4 km (2½ mi) from Lamai beach, at the small Chinese fishing village of Baan Hua Thanon, the road that forks inland (the direct route ⑫ to Na Thon) leads to the **Coral Buddha,** a natural formation carved by years of erosion. Beyond the Coral Buddha, toward Na Thon, lies the village of Baan Thurian, famous for its durian trees, where a track to the right climbs up into jungle-clad hills to the island's best waterfall, ⑬ **Na Muang.** The 105-ft falls are spectacular—especially just after the rainy season—as they tumble from a limestone cliff to a small pool. You can bathe in the pool, getting cooled by the spray and warmed by the sun. For a thrill, swim through the curtain of falling water; you can sit on a ledge at the back to catch your breath.

Laem Set Bay

⑭ *17½ km (11 mi) south of Na Thon.*

This small rocky cape on the southeastern tip of the island is away from the crowds. It's a good 3 km (2 mi) off the main circle road, and without your own transport, it's hard to reach, but it's worth the effort to get there to have a meal at the Laem Set Inn. You may also want to visit the nearby **Samui Butterfly Garden,** two acres of meandering walks enclosed by nets that take you through kaleidoscopic clouds of butterflies. ▥ *Admission.* ☉ *Daily 10–4.*

Dining and Lodging

$–$$$$ ✕▥ **Laem Set Inn.** The Perrys (he's British, she's Thai) have created a unique retreat here, with widely varying rates. The buildings are reconstructions of traditional Thai houses or genuine old houses they saved from destruction. The top-priced Kho-Tan suite (two bedrooms, B9,250), an old rosewood house found on nearby Kho-Tan and reassembled here overlooking the sea, has its own pool. Another suite was made from the old Ko Samui post office. The small, thatched cottages (B1,250) with woven bamboo walls are more modest, with small bathrooms and showers only, but they have lofts for a child or for storage. Dining is given serious attention, and the kitchen has won accolades from the international press. The beach is a mix of sand and coral, with a picturesque sprinkling of rocks. The inn provides kayaks, snorkeling equipment, and mountain bikes at no charge. ✉ *110 Moo 2, Hua Thanon, Ko Samui, Surat Thani 84310,* ☎ *077/424393 or 077/ 233300,* ℻ *077/424394. 4 rooms, 3 suites, 9 cottages. Restaurant, pool, snorkeling, boating, bicycles. MC, V.*

Baan Taling Ngam

⑮ *3 km (2 mi) south of New Port.*

The south and west coasts are less developed; their beaches are not so golden, the water not so clear, and the breezes not so fresh. But there is one very good reason for coming to the west coast, and that is a luxury hotel directly west of the village of Baan Taling Ngam, on a pretty stretch of shore with magnificent views.

Dining and Lodging

$$$$ ✕▥ **Le Royal Meridien Baan Taling Ngam.** The name of this expensive luxury hotel, now under Meridien management, means "home on a beautiful cliff," which eminently suits the small and appealing hotel set dramatically on a 200-ft cliff facing west across the sea. Sunsets are phenomenal—be sure you come at least once for a sundowner. The equally stunning swimming pool is set so that its water, flowing over one side,

seems to disappear over the cliff. Most of the 42 guest rooms are built into the cliffside, and each has a private terrace. The contemporary furnishings are given warmth by a generous use of wood paneling. Seven suites and a pool down by the beach are reached by golf carts, and above the main building there are 33 private, two-bedroom villas that the hotel leases. You'll dine elegantly on Thai and European fare at the Lom Talay; seafood is served at the more casual Promenade. Baan Taling Ngam is secluded, and some may find it inconveniently far from most of the island's attractions—you'll need transportation whenever you leave the property. ⊠ *295 Moo 3, Baan Taling Ngam, Ko Samui 84140,* ☎ *077/ 423019; 0800/40–40–40 in U.K.; 800/225–5843 in U.S.,* FAX *077/ 423220. 42 rooms, 7 suites, 33 villas. 2 restaurants, pool, 2 tennis courts, health club, travel services. AE, DC, MC, V.* ✍

OFF THE
BEATEN PATH

ANGTHONG MARINE NATIONAL PARK – You should take one full day for a trip out to the 40 islets that make up the Angthong Marine National Park, which covers some 250 square km (90 sq mi). The water, the multicolor coral, and the underwater life are amazing, and the rocky islets form weird and wonderful shapes. Boats leave Na Thon daily at 8:30 AM for snorkeling and scuba diving; the cost is B250 and the trip takes about one hour.

Ko Pha Ngan

12 km (7½ mi) by boat north of Ko Samui.

Since Ko Samui is no longer off the beaten track, travelers looking for the simple beach life now head for Ko Pha Ngan, which is at the turning point of its development. A decade ago, the few international wanderers stayed in fishermen's houses or slung hammocks on the beach. Now cheap, simple guest bungalows have sprung up on most of the best beaches, and investors are buying up beach property. Land worth a million baht three years ago can bring as much as 45 million baht today. For now, though, the lack of transportation to and on the island limits Ko Pha Ngan's transformation, and one of the world's most idyllic places has yet to be spoiled.

Since the island's unpaved roads twist and turn, it's easier to beach-hop by boat. In fact, if you want to find the beach that most appeals to you, take a ferry trip around the island—it takes about nine hours with stops along the way. The southeast tip of the island is divided by a long promontory into **Haad Rin West** and **Haad Rin East,** the island's most popular and crowded areas, sometimes referred to as the backpackers' ghetto. Boats from **Thong Sala,** the major town, take 40 minutes to reach Haad Rin East; their departure is timed to meet arriving passengers from the interisland boat.

If Haad Rin is too crowded, catch the onward boat up the east coast to **Haad Tong Nai Pan,** a perfect horseshoe bay divided by a small promontory. On the beach of the southern and larger half are several guest houses
★ and a couple of small restaurants. The northern bay, **Tong Nai Pan Noi,** is the smaller and quieter of the two. Telephone cables have yet to link it with the world, and though there is a road, no self-respecting kidney will take the incessant bouncing of the four-wheel-drive vehicle negotiating its curves and ruts. Glistening white sand curves around the turquoise waters of this half-moon bay, and coconut trees behind the beach hide the houses of the villagers. At the ends of the bay are two small resorts.

Dining and Lodging

$ ✕ **Pannoi's.** The owner of this local restaurant goes fishing in the evening for the next day's menu. The guests, barefoot and shirtless, sit at rough-hewn wood tables set in the sand. A meal may consist of tender and succulent *ma pla* (horsefish, much like snapper) and a plateful of barbecued prawns with garlic and pepper. ⊠ *Haad Tong Nai Pan Noi,* ☎ *no phone. No credit cards.*

$–$$ ✕🏠 **Panviman Resort.** This resort has thatched cottages and stone-and-
★   stucco bungalows (B3,500), some cooled by fan and others by air-conditioning. Each bungalow has a balcony, a large bedroom, and a spacious bathroom with a cold-water shower. During the day, electricity is turned off and the rooms become stifling, but who wants to be inside? There are also twin-bed, fan-cooled hotel rooms (half with ocean views) that cost B1,200. The circular wood restaurant, cooled by the breezes blowing over the promontory, serves Western food, but the Thai dishes are better and more extensive. Ask for a light hand in the chili department. Guests gather here to watch a nightly video. ⊠ *Haad Tong Nai Pan, Ko Pha Ngan,* ☎ 🖷 *077/377048,* ☎ *02/587–8491 Bangkok reservations,* 🖷 *02/587–8493 in Bangkok. 15 rooms, 10 bungalows, 15 cottages. Restaurant. MC, V.*

$ 🏠 **Tong Tapan Resort.** These small thatched cottages on stilts perched on the side of the hill are home to international backpackers. ⊠ *North end of Haad Tong Nai Pan Noi,* ☎ *no phone. 22 rooms. No credit cards.*

Ko Tao

47 km (29 mi) by boat north of Ko Pha Ngan.

Small Ko Tao is an island 4 km (2½ mi) wide and 8 km (5 mi) long, with unpaved roads. Only five years ago the island was likened to a second home for Robinson Crusoe. Today it is inundated with backpackers, hanging out and dreading the day when they might actually have to go to work. It's on the scheduled route of ferries out of Ko Pha Ngan and Ko Samui, and two boats a day make the three-hour (express boat) or six-hour (regular ferry) run between Ko Tao and Chumphon on the mainland. The island used to make its living from coconuts, but tourism is taking over despite the rugged interior and few beaches, and more than two dozen small bungalow developments offer basic accommodation. Since the peace and quiet has gone, the main reason to come here is the snorkeling. In fact, speedboats now leave from Ko Samui's Bophut pier at 8:30 AM, taking snorkelers on day trips to Ko Tao and neighboring Ko Nang Yuan (about B1,300).

Most of the bungalows on Ko Tao are on **Haad Sai Ri,** a sweeping crescent beach north of **Ban Mae Hut,** the village where the ferries dock. One of the better places is **Sea Shell Bungalows** (☎ 01/229–4621). Rooms here (B800) are fan-cooled and have private bathrooms. On the south shore of the island at **Haad Chalok Kao,** the **Ko Tao Cottage International Dive Resort** (☎ 01/229–3662, 🖷 01/229–3751) has fan-cooled bungalows for less than B1,000 a night. If both of these are full, go to the Ko Tao Tourism Centre, a commercial travel office, and ask the owner, Khun Aka, to find you a bungalow. This office is to the right as you exit the ferry terminal building and about 165 yards up the dirt road.

Ko Nang Yuan is a teeny island, or rather three islands linked by a sandbar, where the snorkeling is excellent. It's 15 minutes off the north coast of Ko Tao and tends to be flooded with visitors arriving on the 10 AM ferry who depart at 4 PM. The only residents on the island are guests at the **Ko Nang Yuan Dive Resort** (☎ 01/229–5085, 🖷 01/229–5212), which has simple rooms at B800 and more spacious ones with air-conditioning at B2,500. It's the only lodging on the island, so make sure you can stay there *before* the last ferry leaves.

Chumphon

400 km (240 mi) south of Bangkok, 50 km (21 mi) by boat east of Ko Tao.

Chumphon is often seen as the gateway to the south since trains and buses connect it to Hua Hin and Bangkok in the north, to Surat Thani and Phuket farther south, and to Ranong to the southwest. Ferries to Ko Tao dock at Pak Nam at the mouth of the Chumphon River, 11 km (7 mi) southeast of town. Most boat services run a free shuttle between the docks and the city. **Songserm Travel Centre** (⌧ 66/1 Thatapao Hotel, Chumphon, ☎ 077/502764) coordinates its ferry with its bus service to and from Bangkok.

You'll find little of specific interest in Chumphon, but people here are very friendly. If you are overnighting here or have a couple of hours before catching onward transportation, visit the Night Market. If you have more time, just north of Chumphon there's an excellent beach, **Ao Thong Wua Laen,** with a superb hotel. You can catch a songthaew (B25) on the street across from the bus station or take the hotel's minivan (B120). The curving beach is 3 km (2 mi) of white-yellow sand with a horizon dotted by small islands famous as the nesting place of swifts. Swifts make nests that the Chinese like to serve as bird's nest soup. Never venture onto these islands—they are patrolled by armed guards who will shoot you on sight to protect the fortune of the concessionaire. Just offshore is, however, safe. Dive boats go out to nearby reefs where there is some spectacular coral.

There are several restaurants and guest houses along Thong Wua Laen beach as well as picnic and camping spots. But even on national holidays the beach is far from crowded.

Lodging

$–$$ ▣ **Chumphon Cabana Resort.** This excellent resort at the south end of Thong Wua Laen beach consists of 40 bungalows hidden in lush foliage and another 100 hotel rooms in three low-rise buildings. Each of the hotel rooms has a private balcony. Furnishings are simple but pleasant, and the bamboo-walled bungalows are especially romantic. The public areas are open-sided and spacious, but most guests, when not out diving or getting some sun, sit around the airy, open restaurant beside the beach. The staff is super friendly and, even if you are not staying at the hotel, will help you make travel arrangements. The hotel also should be commended for spending a few extra million and building an ecologically friendly resort with an infrastructure designed to protect the environment. A PADI-registered dive shop is attached to the hotel. ⌧ *69 Moo 8, Saplee, Pathui, Chumphon 86230,* ☎ *077/ 560245 up to 9,* ℻ *077/560247,* ☎ ℻ *02/427–0122 Bangkok reservations. 140 rooms. Restaurant, dive shop, meeting rooms. MC, V.*

¢ ▣ **Marokot.** This is not the most luxurious or the most prestigious hotel in Chumphon, but the rooms are clean, the air-conditioning is efficient, the queen-size beds are firm and comfortable, and the bathrooms have hot and cold water. The staff is very helpful and the hotel's location is a short walk from Songserm's bus and ferry pickup point, the city bus terminal, and the Night Market. Best of all, the price for a room is only B300. ⌧ *102–112 Thannon Songkla, 86000,* ☎ *077/503628,* ℻ *077/ 570196. 46 rooms, most with air-conditioning. No credit cards.*

Southern Beach Resorts A to Z

Arriving and Departing

By Airplane

KO SAMUI

The island's small airport, on the northeast tip, is served by **Bangkok Airways** (☎ 077/425012 at Ko Samui airport; 02/229–3456 in Bangkok), which runs five very expensive flights daily between Bangkok and Ko Samui (B3,950 one way), between Phuket and Ko Samui (B2,550 one way), and between Singapore and Ko Samui (about B14,000). Reservations are crucial during peak periods. **Thai Airways International** (☎ 077/273355) flies to Surat Thani on the mainland, from which you must transfer to Ko Samui.

Taxis meet arrivals; the price is fixed (usually B200) for trips to various parts of the island. Some hotels have a limo or van service at the airport, but these cost the same as a taxi. Songthaews sporadically go between the airport and Na Thon for B30.

KRABI

Krabi has a new airport into which **Thai Airways International** (☎ 076/620070) runs two flights a day to and from Bangkok.

PHUKET

Bangkok Airways (✉ Yaowarat Rd., Phuket Town, ☎ 076/212311 or 076/212341) now offers two flights daily between Chiang Mai and Phuket, Ko Samui and Phuket, and U-Tapao (Pattaya) and Phuket. **Thai Airways International** (✉ 78 Ranong Rd., Phuket Town, ☎ 076/211195 domestic, 076/212499 international) has daily 70-minute flights from Bangkok and 30-minute flights from Hat Yai. The airline also has direct flights from Chiang Mai, Penang (Malaysia), and Singapore.

Phuket's airport is at the northern end of the island. Most of the hotels are on the west coast, and many send minivans to meet arriving planes. These are not free—just convenient. For Phuket Town (32 km/20 mi southeast of the airport) or Patong Beach, take a Thai Airways minibus—buy the ticket (B80 and B120, respectively) at the transportation counter in the terminal. Songthaews run sporadically between the airport and Phuket Town for B30.

By Boat

Songserm Travel Centre (☞ Travel Agencies, *below*) operates many of the boats to and from Ko Pha Ngan, Ko Tao, Ko Phi Phi, and Ko Samui.

KO PHA NGAN AND KO TAO

From Surat Thani, Songserm express boats depart for Thong Sala on Ko Pha Ngan at 7 AM, 9 AM, and 2 PM (sometimes more often), stopping en route at Na Thon on Ko Samui. From Chumphon on the mainland, two ferries (one Songserm express taking just over two hours and one slow boat taking just over six hours) travel daily to Ko Tao and on to Ko Pha Ngan and Ko Samui. (These ferries are frequently cancelled during the monsoon season.) From Ko Samui, you can also take a small ferryboat from Bophut to Haad Rin at about 10 AM, and in good weather (but not when the seas are high), a long-tail boat leaves Maenam for Haad Tong Nai Pan at about 9 AM. A speedboat seating a score of passengers departs for Ko Tao every morning from Bophut at 8:30.

The State Railway offers a combined ticket that takes you by train to Chumphon and by ferry to Ko Tao and Ko Pha Ngan.

KO PHI PHI

Boats leave Makham Bay on Phuket twice a day (9:30 and 1) for the two-hour journey; those run by Songserm Travel Centre are the best. Two to four ferries a day make the two-hour trip between Krabi and Phi Phi Don.

KO SAMUI

From Surat Thani, two ferries cross to Ko Samui. The Songserm passenger boat leaves several times a day for Na Thon from its terminal 8 km (5 mi) out of town (a Songserm bus collects passengers from the row of travel agencies on the Surat Thani waterfront). The ride takes about two hours, after which the ferry goes on to Ko Pha Ngan. The other ferry, which takes cars and cargo, leaves from Donsak, 45 minutes by bus from Surat Thani, and lands at New Port. This ferry takes about 90 minutes. Combined bus-ferry tickets are available from one of the many tour or bus companies in Surat Thani. The last ferry to Ko Samui leaves around 4 PM, and the last ferry from Ko Samui departs at 3 PM. Times vary, so be sure to check the schedule.

KRABI AND AO NANG

Two to four ferries a day make the two-hour run between Krabi and Ko Phi Phi. Bookings can be made on the dock at Phi Phi Don or any travel agency; the fare is B160. Ferries also go once a day between Ko Phi Phi and Ao Nang.

By Bus

KRABI AND AO NANG

Air-conditioned buses depart from Bangkok's Southern Bus Terminal at 7 PM and 8 PM for the 819-km (509-mi) journey (B850) to Krabi, which takes about 12 hours. From Phuket, buses usually leave in the morning for the 180-km (112-mi) trip (B150). Songthaews go from Krabi to Ao Nang for about B20.

PHANG NGA BAY

First get yourself to the one-horse town of Phang Nga, served by frequent buses from Krabi and Phuket, then take a songthaew 10 km (6¼ mi) to the bay. At the bay, hire a long-tail boat to tour the islands.

PHUKET

Non-air-conditioned buses leave throughout the day from Bangkok's Southern Bus Terminal. One air-conditioned bus leaves in the evening. Tour companies also run coaches that are slightly more comfortable, and often the price of a one-way fare includes a meal. The bus trip from Bangkok to Phuket takes 12–13 hours. A bus plies between Phuket and Surat Thani with timed connections for the Ko Samui ferry. There's also service between Phuket and Trang, Hat Yai, and Satun.

SURAT THANI

This town, at the crossroads of railway and bus lines, is the jumping-off point for many southern beach resorts. Buses from Bangkok's Southern Bus Terminal cost less than the train (about B255 for air-conditioned buses), but they are also less comfortable. Private tour companies use more comfortable, faster buses. Express buses also go to Surat Thani from Phuket (5 hrs), Krabi (4 hrs), and Hat Yai (7 hrs).

By Train

KO SAMUI

The State Railway of Thailand sells a combined ticket that includes rail fare (a berth in air-conditioned second class), bus connection, and ferry ride, for B610. Passengers leave Bangkok at 7:15 PM and arrive in Ko Samui at about 10 AM the following day.

The closest train station is at Surat Thani, where trains connect to Bangkok and Singapore. A bus service links Phuket with Surat Thani (5 hr) and the overnight train, which takes 11 hours to Bangkok. The State Railway of Thailand, in conjunction with Songserm Travel Centre, issues a combined train (second-class air-conditioned sleeper) and bus ticket (B670).

SURAT THANI

Many express trains from Bangkok's Hualamphong railway station stop at Surat Thani on their way south. The journey takes just under 12 hours, and the best trains are the overnighters that leave Bangkok at 6:30 PM and 7:20 PM, arriving in Surat Thani soon after 6 AM. First-class sleeping cabins are available only on the 7:20 train. Two express trains make the daily run up from Trang and Hat Yai in southern Thailand.

Getting Around

Ko Pha Ngan
The twisting, rutted, unpaved roads can be painful for the bony. You may want to consider using the long-tail boats out of Thong Sala that travel to all the bays on the island.

Ko Phi Phi
On these islands the way to get around is on foot or by cruise boat or long-tail boat.

Ko Samui
Na Thon is the terminus for songthaews, which take either the north route around the island via Chengmon to Chaweng on the east coast, or the southern route along the coast to reach Lamai. Between Chaweng and Lamai you change songthaews at a transfer point for either the northern or southern route. The fare from Na Thon to Chaweng, the most distant point, is B30. Songthaews for the northern trip start from the waterfront north of the pier; those on the southern route start from south of the pier.

After about 6 PM songthaews become private taxis, and fares need to be established before setting out. During the day, songthaews may be rented as private taxis. The trip from Na Thon to Chaweng, for example, costs B250.

If you really want to explore Ko Samui, it's best to rent your own transportation. Jeeps are expensive (around B1,200 plus B175 for the Collision Damage Waiver [CDW]), but they're the safest, although most people choose motor scooters (about B175 per day), which can be rented at most of the resorts. Gravel, potholes, and erratic driving make riding dangerous, and each year some travelers return home with broken limbs, and though crash helmets are now mandatory, some never return at all.

Avis has counters at the Santiburi Hotel (☎ 077/425031), the Imperial Tongsai Bay Hotel (☎ 077/421451), and at the airport. **Hertz** is represented at the airport and at most of the luxury resorts.

Phuket
Ten-seat songthaews have no regular schedule, but all use Phuket Town as their terminal. Songthaews leave from Ranong Road near the day market and Fountain Circle, plying back and forth between most beaches; a few also make the trip to the airport. If you want to get from one beach to another, you will probably have to go back into Phuket Town and change songthaews. Fares range from B20 to B40.

Taxi fares are usually fixed between different destinations. If you plan to use taxis frequently, get a list of fares from the TAT office, because drivers are not above charging more. A trip from Phuket Town to Patong Beach is B140 and to Bang Tao is B200.

Your own transport is, of course, the most convenient for exploring. If on motor scooter, watch out for potholes and loose gravel that can cause a spill; crash helmets are required by law. Some minor roads are not paved. Many hotels have rental desks, but their prices are 25%–40% higher than those outside hotels or in Phuket Town, where a scooter costs B150 a day and a jeep is B750.

At **Pure Car Rent** (⊠ 75 Rasda Rd., Phuket Town, ☎ 076/211002), prices for a jeep start at B770 per day, plus a CDW of B120 per day. Motor scooters begin at B150 a day. The larger, 150-cc scooters are safer. **Avis** (☎ 076/327358), **Budget** (☎ 076/205396), and **Hertz** (☎ 076/321190) have offices at the airport, as well as at some hotels.

Contacts and Resources

Emergencies
General Emergencies: ☎ 1699.

KO SAMUI
Tourist Police (☎ 077/421281 in Na Thon). **Hospital** (☎ 077/421230); also **Surat Thani Hospital** (☞ *below*).

PHUKET
Police (☎ 076/212046). **Tourist Police** (☎ 1699). **Ambulance** ☎ (076/212297). **Bangkok Phuket Hospital**(☎ 076/254421).

SURAT THANI
Tourist Police (☎ 077/281300 or 1699). **Surat Thani Hospital** (⊠ Surat-Phun Phin Rd., ☎ 077/272231).

Guided Tours
A half-day Phuket sightseeing tour includes Wat Chalong, Rawai Beach, Phromthep Cape, and Khao Rang. Other half-day tours take in the Thai Cultural Village and the cultured-pearl farms on Naka Noi Island. Make arrangements at your hotel.

A full-day boat tour goes from Phuket to Phang Nga Bay and other islands. **World Travel Service** (☞ Travel Agencies, *below*) runs a comprehensive tour to Phang Nga Bay. Another full-day tour visits the Phi Phi Islands for swimming and caving. The daylong Ko Hav (Coral Island) tour takes you snorkeling and swimming.

Full-day cruises to the Similan Islands, costing B1,500, are run by **Songserm Travel Centre** (☞ *below*). The boat trip takes about 10 hours from Phuket, and about four hours from Thap Lamu Port, two hours north on the west coast. **Marina Divers** (⊠ Karon Villa Hotel, Karon Beach, Phuket, ☎ 076/381625) runs diving trips to the Similan Islands. The **Siam Cruise Co.** (⊠ 33/10–11 Chaiyod Arcade, Sukhumvit Soi 11, Bangkok 10110, ☎ 02/255–8950) operates two- and three-night cruises to the Similans on the luxury cruise ship *Andaman Princess*. **PIDC Divers** (⊠ 1/10 Viset Rd., Chalong Bay, Phuket, ☎ 076/381219), operates the 66-ft MV *Andaman Seafarer* for four- and six-day live-aboard dive excursions that cost approximately $520 and $720, respectively.

Travel Agencies
Chan Phen Tour (⊠ 145 Uttarakit Rd., Krabi, ☎ 075/612404, FAX 075/612629) is one of a number of travel agencies on Uttarakit Rd. **Chok Anan** (⊠ Ratchadamnoen Klang Ave., Bangkok, ☎ 02/281–2277)

runs buses from Bangkok to Surat Thani. **Dive Deep** (✉ Chaweng Beach Resort, Ko Samui, ☎ 077/230155) runs trips from Ko Samui to Angthong National Marine Park, Ko Tao, and Sail Rock. **Lao Ruam Kij** (✉ 11 Khongka Rd., ☎ 075/611930) is a travel agency in Krabi.

Songserm Travel Centre (✉ 121/7 Soi Chapermla, Phyathai Rd., Bangkok 10400, ☎ 02/252–9654 and 02/251–8994) has branches in Ko Pha Ngan (✉ Ferry terminal, Thong Sala, ☎ 077/281639); Ko Samui (64/1–2 Na Thon, ☎ 077/421316); Phuket (✉ 51 Satoon Rd., Phuket Town, ☎ 076/222570, FAX 076/214391); and Surat Thani (✉ In the ferry terminal, ☎ 077/272928).

Travel Accommodation Centre (✉ Seafood Village, Ao Nang, ☎ 075/637311, FAX 075/637311) is extremely knowledgeable and helpful in finding lodging on east coast resorts, including Phuket. **World Travel Service** (✉ Hotel Phuket Merlin, Phuket Town, ☎ 076/212866, ext. WTS; Phuket Yacht Club, ☎ 076/214020, ext. WTS) is reliable.

Visitor Information
Ko Samui TAT (✉ Na Thon, ☎ 077/421281). **Krabi TAT** (✉ Uttarakit Rd., ☎ 075/612740). **Phuket TAT** (✉ 73–75 Phuket Rd., near bus terminal, Phuket Town, ☎ 076/212213). The TAT desk at Phuket airport offers limited help. The **Surat Thani TAT** office (✉ 5 Talat Mai Rd., ☎ 077/281828) also handles Ko Phi Phi, Ko Pha Ngan, and Ko Tao.

THAILAND A TO Z

Arriving and Departing

By Airplane
AIRPORTS

The major gateway to Thailand is Bangkok's **Don Muang International Airport** (☎ 02/535–2081).

CARRIERS

About 70 airlines serve Bangkok, and more are seeking landing rights. The U.S. carrier with the most frequent flights is **Northwest Airlines** (☎ 800/447–4747). It has direct service through Tokyo (with a minimal stopover) from New York, Detroit, Seattle, Dallas, San Francisco, and Los Angeles. Northwest has a round-Asia fare, in conjunction with local airlines, which lets you hop from one capital to another.

To fly from the West Coast, contact **Cathay Pacific** (☎ 800/233–2742), **Northwest Airlines** (☎ 800/447–4747), **Thai Airways International** (☎ 800/426–5204), or **United Airlines** (☎ 800/241–6522).

For departures from the East Coast, contact **Asiana Airlines** (☎ 800/227–4262), **China Airlines** (☎ 800/227–5118), **EVA Air** (☎ 800/695–1188), **Gulf Air** (☎ 800/553–2824), **Japan Airlines** (☎ 800/525–3663), **Korean Air** (☎ 800/438–5000), **Northwest Airlines** (☞ *above*), and **Singapore Airlines** (☎ 800/742–3333).

Daily departures to Thailand from London are scheduled aboard **British Airways** (☎ 020/8897–4000; 0345/222111 outside London), **Qantas** (☎ 0345/747767 or 0800/747767), and **Thai Airways** (☎ 020/7499–9113).

From Australia, you can fly **British Airways, Qantas,** and **Thai Airways International.**

FLYING TIMES

Bangkok is 17 hours from San Francisco, 18 hours from Seattle and Vancouver, 20 hours from Chicago, and 22 hours from New York and

Toronto; 11 hours from London; and 10 hours from Sydney. Add more time for stopovers and connections, especially if you are using more than one carrier.

Getting Around

By Airplane

The major domestic carrier is **Thai Airways International** (✉ 485 Silom Rd., Bangkok, ☎ 02/232–8000). Its planes connect Bangkok with all major cities and tourist areas in Thailand, except Ko Samui. **Bangkok Airways** (✉ 60 Queen Sirikit National Convention Centre, New Ratchadaphisek Rd., Klongotey, Bangkok, ☎ 02/229–3456 or 02/229–3434) has numerous daily flights between Bangkok and Ko Samui, using 40-seat planes. It also flies daily between Ko Samui and Phuket, daily from Bangkok to Angkor Wat in Cambodia, twice a week to Krabi, and three times a week to Chiang Mai via Sukhothai. Its fares are competitive with those of Thai Airways. The new and fast-growing **Angel Airlines** (☎ 02/535–6287 at Don Muang airport office) flies between Bangkok and Chiang Mai, Phuket, Udon Thani, and Singapore; between Chiang Mai and Phuket, Udon Thani, and Singapore; and between Phuket and Singapore.

On popular routes during peak times, flights are often fully booked. Make reservations well in advance, reconfirm flights when you arrive in Thailand, and get to the airport well before departure time—the airlines have started giving away the seats of late passengers to standby-ticket holders. Thai Airways has a good on-time record, but during the rainy season there may be delays.

AIR PASSES

The Thai Airways **Discover Thailand Pass** ($179 for four internal flights) must be purchased outside Thailand. Virtually all planes go through Bangkok, except for the daily nonstop service between Chiang Mai and Phuket. Be aware that if you fly from Chiang Mai to Surat Thani, you must change planes in Bangkok and thus use two of your flights.

By Bicycle Rickshaw

For short trips, bicycle rickshaws are a popular, inexpensive form of transport, but they become expensive for long trips. (Note that they aren't allowed in central Bangkok.) Fares are negotiated, and it is imperative to be very clear about what price is agreed upon. Drivers have a tendency to create a misunderstanding leading to a nasty scene at the end of the trip.

By Bus

Long-distance buses are cheaper and faster than trains and reach every corner of the country. For example, the nine-hour trip between Chiang Mai and Bangkok is between B300 and B570, depending on which travel agent you use. The level of comfort depends on the bus company. Air-conditioned buses are superior but are always so cold that you'll want an extra sweater.

By Car

Cars are available for rent in Bangkok and in major tourist destinations, but the additional cost of hiring a driver is small and the peace of mind great. If a foreigner is involved in an automobile accident, he or she—not the Thai—is likely to be judged at fault.

In Chiang Mai, Ko Samui, Pattaya, and Phuket, hiring a jeep or motorcycle is convenient, but be aware that motorcycles skid easily on gravel roads. A sign in Ko Samui posts the year's count of foreigners

who never made it home from their vacation! Crash helmets are now
required, and this law is periodically enforced, particularly in Phuket.

GASOLINE

A liter of gasoline costs B14–B16. Many gas stations stay open 24 hours
and have clean toilet facilities. Many also have minimarkets that sell
snacks, beer, and whiskey.

PARKING

In cities, the larger hotels, restaurants, and department stores have garages
or parking lots. Rates vary, but count on B10 an hour. If you purchase
anything parking is free, but you must have your ticket validated.

RENTAL AGENCIES

Rates from international franchises begin at $39 a day and $336 a week
for an economy car with unlimited mileage, not including tax (7%) or
the Collision Damage Waiver (about $10 a day). One-way rentals
with drop-offs in most major cities are offered by the major rental companies. It is better to rent your car in Thailand, as you can usually get
a discount and can rent from small local agencies for about $20 a day,
including insurance.

The major companies represented in Thailand are **Avis** (☎ 800/230–
4899; 800/272–5871 in Canada; 01344/707070 in the U.K.), **Budget**
(☎ 800/527–0700), and **Hertz** (☎ 800/654–3001; 800/263–0600 in
Canada; 0345/555888 in the U.K.).

ROAD CONDITIONS

The major roads in Thailand tend to be very congested, and street signs
are often in Thai only. But the limited number of roads and, with the
exception of Bangkok, the straightforward layout of cities combine to
make navigation relatively easy. Driving at night in rural areas, especially north and west of Chiang Mai and in the south beyond Surat
Thani is not advised.

RULES OF THE ROAD

If your current driving license is not written in English, an international
driving license is required. Driving is on the left; speed limits are 60
kph (37 mph) in cities, 90 kph (56 mph) outside, and 110 kph (70 mph)
on expressways.

By Samlor

Usually called tuk-tuks for their spluttering sound, samlors are three-
wheel cabs that are slightly less expensive than taxis and, because of
their maneuverability, the most rapid form of travel through congested
traffic. All tuk-tuk operators drive as if your ride will be their last, but,
in fact, they are remarkably safe. Tuk-tuks are not very comfortable,
though, and they subject you to the polluted air, so they're best used
for short journeys.

By Taxi

Most Bangkok and Chiang Mai taxis now have meters installed, and
these are the ones tourists should take. (Note that taxis waiting outside hotels in these areas may play a con game, claiming that they've
been waiting at the hotel and missing other fares so must charge extra.)
In other cities, fares are still negotiated. Never enter the taxi until the
price has been established. Most taxi drivers do not speak English, but
all understand the finger count. One finger means B10, two is for B20,
and so on. Ask at your hotel what the appropriate fare should be. Never
pay more than what the hotel quotes, as they will have given you the
high price. If in doubt, accept 65%–75% of the cabbie's quote.

With any form of private travel, never change your initial agreement on destination and price unless you clearly establish a new "contract." Moreover, if you agree to the driver's offer to wait for you at your destination and be available for your onward or return journey, you will be charged for waiting time, and, unless you have fixed the price, the return fare can be double the outbound fare.

By Train

The State Railway of Thailand has three lines, all of which terminate in Bangkok. The Northern Line connects Bangkok with Chiang Mai, passing through Ayutthaya and Phitsanulok; the Northeastern Line travels up to Nong Khai, at the Laotian border, with a branch that goes east to Ubon Ratchathani; and the Southern Line goes all the way south through Surat Thani—the stop for Ko Samui—to the Malaysian border and on to Kuala Lumpur and Singapore, a journey that takes 44 hours. (There's no train to Phuket, though you can go as far as Surat Thani and change to a scheduled bus service.) For information on schedules and passes, call the **Bangkok Railway Station,** (☎ 02/223–3762 or 02/223–0341 for booking office; 02/220–4334 or 02/220–1690 for information).

Most trains offer second- and third-class seats, and some of the overnight trains to Chiang Mai, to the northeast, and to the south have first-class sleepers with two berths per compartment. Second-class sleepers have multiple couchettes, with sheets and curtains for privacy, and are surprisingly comfortable. They cost about half the price of first-class, and most Western travelers choose them. Do not leave valuables unguarded on these overnight trains.

Fares are reasonable. An air-conditioned, second-class couchette, for example, for the 14-hour Bangkok–Chiang Mai journey costs B625; first class is B1,190. Reservations are strongly advised for all long-distance trains.

RAIL PASSES

The State Railway of Thailand offers two types of rail passes. Both are valid for 20 days of unlimited travel on all trains in either second or third class. The **Blue Pass** costs B1,100 for second class and does not include supplementary charges such as air-conditioning and berths; for B3,000, the **Red Pass** does.

You need to book seats even if you are using a rail pass; reservations are required on some trains, and they're a good idea in peak season on popular routes.

Contacts and Resources

Customs and Duties

If you are bringing any foreign-made equipment from home, such as cameras, it is wise to carry the original receipt with you or register it with U.S. Customs before you leave (Form 4457). Otherwise, you may end up paying duty on your return.

One liter of wine or liquor, 200 cigarettes or 250 grams of smoking tobacco, and all personal effects may be brought into Thailand duty-free. Visitors may bring in any amount of foreign currency; amounts taken out may not exceed those declared upon entry. Narcotic drugs, pornographic materials, and firearms are strictly prohibited.

The export of more than B50,000 in Thai currency is prohibited, as is the export of antiquities or Buddha images without a permit. Antiques stores can arrange the formalities, but expect the process to take 3–5 days.

Electricity

Some new U.S.-purchased electrical equipment has a built-in transformer; older items will need a converter and adapter. All computer users should carry a surge protector. The electrical current in Thailand is 220 volts, 50 cycles alternating current (AC); wall outlets take either plugs with two flat prongs, like those in the United States, or Continental-type plugs, with two round prongs.

Embassies and Consulates

Most nations maintain diplomatic relations with Thailand and have embassies in Bangkok; a few have consulates also in Chiang Mai. Should you need to apply for a visa to another country, the consulate hours are usually 8–noon.

In Bangkok: Australian Embassy (⊠ 37 Sathorn Tai Rd., ☎ 02/287–2680); **British Embassy** (⊠ 1031 Wireless Rd., ☎ 02/253–0191); **Canadian Embassy** (⊠ Abdulrahim Bldg., 15th floor, 990 Rama IV, ☎ 02/636–0540); **New Zealand Embassy** (⊠ 93 Wireless Rd., ☎ 02/254–2530); **United States Embassy** (⊠ 120–122 Wireless Rd., ☎ 02/205–4000).

In **Chiang Mai: Australian Consulate** (⊠ 165 Sirman Khalajan, ☎ 053/221083); **British Consulate** (⊠ 201 Airport Business Park, 90 Mahidon, ☎ 053/203–405); **U.S. Consulate** (⊠ 387 Wichayanom Rd., ☎ 053/252629).

Health and Safety

FOOD AND DRINK

In Thailand, the contamination of drinking water, fresh fruit, and vegetables frequently causes traveler's diarrhea. Stay away from ice (unless it was made from bottled water), uncooked food, and unpasteurized milk and milk products; drink only water that has been bottled or boiled for at least 20 minutes.

OTHER PRECAUTIONS

If you plan to visit rural areas, where there's questionable sanitation, you'll need a vaccination as protection against hepatitis A. Take extra precautions against malarial mosquitoes in both Ko Samet and northern Thailand. The U.S. Centers for Disease Control recommend chloroquine (analen) as an antimalarial agent. In areas with malaria and dengue, also carried by mosquitoes, take mosquito nets, wear clothing that covers the body, apply repellent containing DEET, and use a spray against flying insects in living and sleeping areas.

Be aware that a high percentage of sex workers in Thailand are HIV positive, and unprotected sex is extremely risky.

Thais are seldom violent against farangs, and you can feel secure walking at night. You may be charged too much or cheated in various ways (we mention a few imaginative scams), but your life and limb won't be in danger, except perhaps from speeding vehicles.

Language, Culture, and Etiquette

Thai is the national language, a tonal language with its own alphabet. What may sound to a foreigner as "krai kai kai kai" will mean to a Thai, said with the appropriate pitch, "who sells chicken eggs?" In polite conversation, males use the word "krap" to end a sentence or to acknowledge what someone has said. Females use "ka." It is easy to learn a few phrases, such as "sawahdee krap" or "sawahdee ka" (good day) and "khop khun krap" or "khop khun ka" (thank you). With the exception of taxi drivers, Thais who work with travelers generally speak enough English for basic communication.

Thais believe in accommodation rather than confrontation. Demands, displays of anger, and any behavior that upsets harmony are frowned upon. Though you might see two grown women or, more rarely, men holding hands (an ordinary custom), publicly shown affection, hetero- or homosexual, is out of place, as is nudity. There are few respectable venues for gays and lesbians to meet and socialize, and the prevalence of AIDS makes the raunchy ones dangerous. Discretion is the order or the day—and night.

Mail

POSTAL RATES

The airmail postcard rate to the United States and Canada is B12; to the United Kingdom, Australia, and New Zealand, B9. Airmail letters cost B19 to the United States and Canada; B17 to the United Kingdom, Australia, and New Zealand. Allow about two weeks.

RECEIVING MAIL

You may have mail sent to you at: Poste Restante, General Post Office, Bangkok, Thailand. There's a B1 charge for each letter collected, B2 for a parcel.

WRITING TO THAILAND

Thais put their last name first, so be sure to write the recipient's surname in capital letters and underline it. The elements of an address may include a building, then a street and a soi (a street, or alley, running off a main road), both with numbers, and a suburb or city district.

Money and Expenses

COSTS

The cost of visiting Thailand is very much up to you. It is possible to live and travel quite inexpensively if you do as Thais do—eat in local restaurants, use buses, and stay at non-air-conditioned hotels. Once you start enjoying a little luxury, prices jump drastically. For example, crossing Bangkok by bus is a 10¢ ride, but by taxi the fare may run to $10.

Sample Prices. Continental breakfast at a hotel, $8; large bottle of beer at a hotel, $6 (in a local restaurant, under $2); bottles of water start at 25¢; a bowl of noodles with slices of pork at a street stall, 50¢; a meal in a local restaurant, $4 for two (two or three dishes plus a bowl of rice); a similar meal in a smartish restaurant, $13; 2-km (1-mi) taxi ride, $1.50; local bus ride, 10¢–20¢; museum entrance, 50¢–$2.

CURRENCY

The basic unit of currency is the baht. There are 100 satang to one baht. There are six different bills, each a different color: B10, brown; B20, green; B50, blue; B100, red; B500, purple; and B1,000, beige. Coins in use are 25 satang, 50 satang, B1, B5, and B10. The B10 coin has a gold-colored center surrounded by silver.

All hotels will convert traveler's checks and major currencies into baht, though exchange rates are better at banks and authorized money changers. The rate tends to be better in Bangkok than up-country and is better in Thailand than in the United States.

At press time, the exchange rate was B23 to the Australian dollar, B28 to the Canadian dollar, B18 to the New Zealand dollar, B44 to the U.S. dollar, and B63 to the pound sterling.

Changing old (even in good condition) $100 U.S. bills is increasingly difficult as they have apparently been successfully counterfeited. Bring the new, "big head" bills.

To report lost or stolen credit cards, contact the following: **American Express** (☎ 02/273–0022). **Diners Club** (☎ 02/238–3660). **Master**

Card (☎ 02/246–0300; 001–800–118–870663 toll free). **Visa** (☎ 02/256–7326 or 02/246–0300).

SERVICE CHARGES, TAXES, AND TIPPING

A 10% Value Added Tax (VAT) is built into the price of all goods and services, including hotel stays and restaurant meals. Officially, you should be able to get the VAT on store-bought purchases refunded at the airport as long as you have receipts, but in practice, the tax is essentially nonrefundable. The top hotels are beginning to include a service charge in their bills, including their restaurant bills, but otherwise, tips are left up to you. In Thailand, tips are generally given for good service, except when a price has been negotiated in advance. A taxi driver is not tipped unless hired as a private driver for an excursion. With metered taxis in Bangkok, however, the custom is to round the fare up to the nearest 5 baht. Hotel porters expect at least a B20 tip, and hotel staff who have given good personal service are usually tipped. A 10% tip is appreciated at a restaurant when no service charge has been added to the bill.

Opening and Closing Times

Thai and foreign **banks** are open weekdays 8:30–3:30, except for public holidays. Most **commercial concerns** in Bangkok operate on a five-day week and are open 8–5. **Government offices and post offices** are generally open 8:30–4:30 with a noon–1 lunch break. Many **stores** are open daily 8–8. **Museums** tend to close on Monday, otherwise they are open 9–4. **Wats** are generally open to visitors from 7 or 8 in the morning to 5 or 6 PM.

NATIONAL HOLIDAYS

New Year's Day (Jan. 1); Chinese New Year (Feb. 8, 2001; Feb. 26, 2002); Magha Puja (on the full moon of the third lunar month); Chakri Day (Apr. 6); Songkran (Apr. 13–15); Coronation Day (May 5); Visakha Puja (May, on the full moon of the sixth lunar month); Queen's Birthday (Aug. 12); King's Birthday (Dec. 5). Government offices, banks, commercial concerns, and department stores are usually closed on these days, but smaller shops stay open. Many shops close on election days.

Passports and Visas

Australian, Canadian, U.K., and U.S. citizens need only a valid passport and an onward ticket to enter Thailand for stays of up to 30 days; New Zealanders can stay for 90 days with a valid passport and an onward ticket. The **Immigration Division** (✉ Soi Suan Phlu, Sathorn Rd., Bangkok, ☎ 02/287–3101) issues Thai visa extensions, but if you overstay by a few days, don't worry; you'll simply pay a B200 per diem fine as you go through emigration on departure.

Telephones

CALLS TO THAILAND

To call Thailand from overseas, dial the country code, 66, and then the area code, omitting the first 0.

LOCAL AND LONG-DISTANCE CALLS

Public telephones are available in most towns and villages and take B1 coins or both B1 and B5 coins. Some accept only phone cards, which are sold at newsstands and convenience stores. Long-distance calls can be made only on phones that accept both B1 and B5 coins.

For a long-distance call in Thailand, dial the area code and then the number. For international calls from a pay phone, you must use the Lenso yellow phones (common in Bangkok and major resort areas). Otherwise, to make overseas calls, you should use either your hotel switchboard—Chiang Mai and Bangkok have direct dialing—or the overseas telephone facilities at the central post office and telecommunications building. You'll find one in all towns. For assistance, dial 100/ 233–2771. For local telephone inquiries, dial 100/183, but you will need to speak Thai.

When calling the States, you can dial the following **access numbers** to reach a U.S. long-distance operator: **AT&T** (☎ 0019–991–1111); **MCI** (☎ 001–999–1–2001); **Sprint** (☎ 001–999–13–877). Many hotels block these access numbers and charge as much as 400% more than a calling card for calls placed from your room. If the hotel operator claims that you cannot use any phone card, ask to be connected to an international operator, who will help you to access your phone card, or try calling your phone company collect. If collect calls are also blocked, call from a pay phone in the hotel lobby. Some locations in Bangkok have AT&T USADirect phones, which connect you directly with an AT&T operator.

Visitor Information

Contact the offices of the **Tourism Authority of Thailand (TAT)** (✉ 5 World Trade Centre, Suite 3443, New York, NY 10048, ☎ 212/432–0433, FAX 212/912–0920; ✉ 611 North Larchmont Blvd., 1st floor, Los Angeles, CA 90004, ☎ 213/461–9814, FAX 213/461–9834). Inquiries from Canada should be directed to the Los Angeles office. In the U.K., contact the **Thailand Tourist Board** (✉ 49 Albemarle St., London W1X 3FE, ☎ 020/7499–7679).

Australians and New Zealanders should contact the Sydney **TAT office** (✉ 75 Pitt St, Sydney 20000, NSW, ☎ 2/9247–7549).

When to Go

Thailand has two climatic regions: tropical savannah in the northern regions and tropical rain forest in the south. The three seasons run from hot (March through May) to rainy (June through September) to cool (October through February). Humidity is high all year, especially during the hot season. The cool season is pleasantly warm in the south, but in the north, especially in the hills, it can be quite chilly. The cool season is the peak season. Prices can be twice as high then as in the low seasons, and hotels are often fully booked.

CLIMATE

Following are average temperatures for Bangkok. The north will generally be a degree or two cooler.

Jan.	89F	32C	May	93F	34C	Sept.	89F	32C
	68	20		77	25		75	24
Feb.	91F	33C	June	91F	33C	Oct.	88F	31C
	72	22		75	24		75	24
Mar.	93F	34C	July	89F	32C	Nov.	88F	31C
	75	24		75	24		72	22
Apr.	95F	35C	Aug.	89F	32C	Dec.	88F	31C
	77	25		75	24		68	20

FESTIVALS AND SEASONAL EVENTS

The festivals listed below are national and occur throughout the country unless otherwise noted. Many events follow the lunar calendar, so dates vary from year to year.

Jan.: New Year celebrations are usually at their best around temples. In Bangkok, special ceremonies at Pramanae Ground include Thai dancing.

Feb.: Magha Puja commemorates the day when 1,250 disciples spontaneously heard Lord Buddha preach the cardinal doctrine on the full moon of the third lunar month.

Apr.: Songkran marks the Thai New Year and is an occasion for setting caged birds and fish free, visiting family, dancing, and water-throwing, in which everyone splashes everyone else in good-natured merriment. The festival is at its best in Chiang Mai, with parades, dancing in the streets, and a beauty contest.

May: On the full moon of the sixth lunar month, the nation celebrates the holiest of Buddhist days, Visakha Puja, commemorating Lord Buddha's birth, enlightenment, and death. Monks lead the laity in candlelight processions around their temples.

Aug.: On the 12th, Queen Sirikit's birthday is celebrated with religious ceremonies at Chitlada Palace, and the city is adorned with lights.

Nov.: Held on the full moon of the 12th lunar month, Loi Krathong is the loveliest of Thai festivals. After sunset, people make their way to a body of water and launch small lotus-shape banana-leaf floats bearing lighted candles, to honor the water spirits and wash away the sins of the past year. Of all Bangkok's fairs and festivals, the Golden Mount Festival is the most spectacular, with sideshows, food stalls, bazaars, and large crowds of celebrants.

Dec.: On the 5th, the King's birthday, a trooping of the colors is performed in Bangkok by Thailand's elite Royal Guards.

7 VIETNAM

The midday downpour is a given. The lush green of the landscape is only one sign that you're in monsoon country. Another is the relentless flooding. But these are conditions the Vietnamese have learned to abide, even to revere. For thousands of years, they have followed the dictates of the predictable climate, plowing, planting, and harvesting when the weather tells them to. Foreign oppressors have come and gone, but the rhythmic cycle of the seasons endures.

V IETNAM IS A COUNTRY ON THE MOVE. The introduction of economic reforms—known as *doi moi*, meaning "new change"—more than a dozen years ago acted as a catalyst, releasing the energies of the nation left behind after decades of war and isolation. Now wherever you travel in Vietnam—in the towns, the cities, and the countryside—you will see people on the go.

From the rows of *pho* (noodle soup) stalls lining the sidewalks to the numerous vendors selling postcards to the huge neon signs advertising Western chic, it is apparent that the drive to make it in this new era cuts across social boundaries. Billboards hawking everything from Lifebuoy soap and Heineken beer to the newest luxury apartments tower above streets jammed with motorbikes, bicycles, and more and more cars. It seems as if, once the sun rises, the entire population is up within an hour rushing headlong into another day.

It is especially in the main cities—Hanoi, Haiphong, Danang, and most of all Ho Chi Minh City (formerly Saigon)—that you see this headlong rush. But travel just 16 km (10 mi) into the countryside and you still see farmers sowing rice with water buffalo, and duck herders wooing their flocks across roads where the only hazards are passing bicycles. These scenes are no less exhilarating than those in the booming cities.

For Vietnam is a country of stunning beauty, with a pristine coastline of golden beaches stretching 3,225 km (2,000 mi) from tip to tail along the South China Sea. To the north, Vietnam borders China along the rugged Hoang Lien mountain chain (the Tonkinese Alps), a breathtaking landscape of deep valleys and tall, mysterious peaks shrouded in mist. Down the country's enormous arched spine are forest-covered highlands, which can be as deliciously cool as a European spring. These mountains, as well as those in the north, are home to Vietnam's 53 ethnic minority groups—the Black Thai, Flower H'mong, Ede, and Muong, among others—whose traditional way of life is today under siege by the forces of development: some have been removed from their land to make way for power stations and the ever-encroaching Kinh majority. Change has been thrust on others by severe deforestation of much of the highlands and mountains. The majority of Vietnamese, however, live along the coast and in the country's two major deltas—the Red River Delta in the north and the Mekong Delta in the south. Here the land fans out into patchworks of vivid-green, wet rice paddies; fruit orchards; and fishing hamlets inhabited by a thousand generations of farmers and fisherfolk.

In the midst of this beautiful country, stark reminders of the high price paid by the Vietnamese people for their independence are never far away. Although few visible signs of the damage sustained by Vietnam remain, every town has its monument to war, be it a captured American jet fighter or a victorious North Vietnamese tank. And dotting the cities and countryside are huge Soviet-style memorials recognizing the millions that died in the country's most recent struggle against outside forces.

For 2,000 years the country has been fending off foreign invaders, most notably the Chinese, French, Japanese, and Americans. The Chinese were the first to invade, and by the time they were driven out by Ngo Quyen in AD 938 they had ruled the country for a millennium. During the following centuries the Vietnamese migrated south in ever increasing numbers, battling with the kingdoms of Champa and Angkor as they went. These expansionist ambitions led to conflicts between competing Vietnamese lords—the Nguyen and the Trinh.

The French entered the scene in the late 18th century by invitation of the Nguyen lords, who sought assistance in crushing a rebellion. By the mid-19th century, the French had taken over by force, annexing large parts of Vietnam to create the colony of Cochin China and the protectorates of Annam and Tonkin. The Japanese occupation during World War II interrupted the French domination, briefly. With Japan's surrender, the French returned to rule Vietnam, but not without conflict: Ho Chi Minh had declared Vietnamese independence in 1945, and by 1946 anti-French sentiment developed into the French-Indochina War.

The French were soundly defeated by General Vo Nguyen Giap and the Vietminh at Dien Bien Phu in 1954, and the country was split in two under the Geneva Accords that same year. Cold War concerns drew the American military into Vietnam, which led to full-scale U.S. involvement in the Vietnam War. But American firepower only reinforced the conviction among many North Vietnamese that they would not be defeated. And the 1968 Tet Offensive was the turning point. Though the collective push by northern forces and the Communist Vietcong in the south was eventually rebuffed, American sentiment turned against intervention and favored withdrawal. By 1973 most U.S. troops had left the country, and the Saigon regime fell in 1975.

But strife did not end there for the Vietnamese. Following Khmer Rouge border incursions in 1978, Vietnam "volunteers" invaded Cambodia late in that year and within a few weeks reached Phnom Penh, effectively ending the "killing fields" of Pol Pot. (Hanoi set up a de facto Vietnamese occupational government that ruled Cambodia until 1989.) In response to Vietnam's involvement in Cambodia, the Chinese invaded northern Vietnam in 1979, devastating much of the countryside and leveling many towns and villages near the border. But the Vietnamese quickly repulsed the Chinese and for the first time in decades lived in relative peace. They were not, however, without a new set of visitors: the Soviets.

Now that the Soviets have departed, what becomes evident is the amazing resilience of the Vietnamese people. When you visit Vietnam, you can't help marveling at their endurance. Slender, silk-clad women bear yokes hung with baskets of rice weighing twice their own weight; they build roads, protected only by a conical hat and a perfectly white handkerchief tied over nose and mouth.

And in the cities, you have to admire their panache—well-primped teenage girls ride the backs of their friends' Hondas, wearing spaghetti-string halter tops, eye-popping bell-bottoms, and five-inch chockablock heels. Don't be surprised to encounter a pair of bareheaded men careening on a motorbike through city traffic at the height of a midday downpour, the driver tooting his horn with a soggy cigarette in his mouth, his companion, arms outstretched, balancing a large pane of glass on his knees. That mixture of practicality and bravado, in some ways the essence of Vietnam, is what's taking the country into the future.

Pleasures and Pastimes

Beaches

Unlike Thailand and other Southeast Asian countries, Vietnam lacks a highly developed beach culture. Although there are incredible coral reefs, sea life, and surf (Danang was the site of an international surfing competition in 1994), there are few places that rent gear or give surfing or scuba-diving lessons. However, some towns along the coast—especially Nha Trang, which does have a few dive shops, and China Beach near Danang—are beginning to grow.

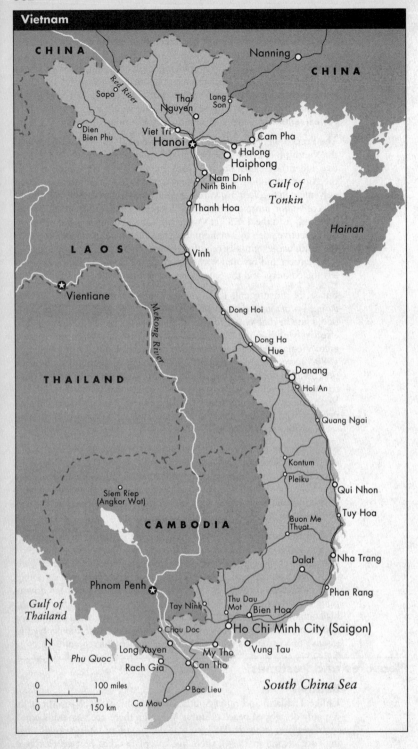

Vietnam

Dining

Seafood is delicious, abundant, and cheap all over Vietnam, particularly in coastal towns like Nha Trang, Danang, and Halong Bay. But the dish that reigns supreme is *pho,* the ubiquitous noodle soup that can safely be called Vietnam's national dish. In addition to pho, noodles, and spring rolls (called *nem* in the north, and *cha goi* in the south), rice (*com*) is another staple, served with anything and everything. Beef, pork, and chicken are generally of high quality in the cities, but out in the provinces they can be tough. Dog meat isn't as inexpensive or plentiful as you might think; just watch out for dishes that contain *thit cho.* Instead of soy sauce, the seasoning of choice is *nuoc mam,* inadequately translated as fish sauce, a clear amber liquid pressed out of large barrels of anchovies and salt.

To taste pho and other favorites, you need only step out of your hotel and into the streets. The best meals in Vietnam aren't usually found in elegant restaurants or hotel dining rooms but at stalls on every street corner and in the marketplace. Family-run restaurants and cafés everywhere serve seafood, delicious and curious meats, and tasty *an chay* (vegetarian dishes). A number of upscale Vietnamese and international restaurants have opened in Ho Chi Minh City and Hanoi, but finding top-notch Western food elsewhere is difficult. Cities like Haiphong, Danang, and Nha Trang are entering the realm of international cuisine with varying degrees of success.

CATEGORY	COST*
$$$$	over $25
$$$	$15–$25
$$	$7–$15
$	$2–$7
¢	under $2

Per person for a three-course dinner, including 10% tax and 5% service but not drinks

Lodging

Graham Greene did much to romanticize hotel life in Vietnam in *The Quiet American.* But aside from the Continental Hotel in Ho Chi Minh City, immortalized in Greene's book, and a handful of other older institutions, including the Sofitel Metropole in Hanoi, hotels in Vietnam have little Old World charm or mystery. The focus today is on newness; the vast majority of joint-venture, international-standard hotels are less than five years old. And unfortunately many of the older hotels that have survived the wrecking ball have fared poorly from years of neglect, bad management, and lack of funds.

Until a few years ago, hotels in Vietnam were not known for good service. The recent influx of foreign tourists and the increasing number of international hotel chains have improved matters, though service in many of the state-run hotels still leaves much to be desired. Resorts have been developed along the coast—the best so far near Phan Thiet, Nha Trang, and on China Beach near Danang—and in the mountain town of Dalat.

Besides surprisingly pricey international properties, Vietnam has a selection of midsize, midlevel hotels and guest houses, especially in cities and popular tourist areas, that are generally state-run and are acceptable for a night's sleep. "Minihotels" are usually a better option. These privately owned, often family-run operations range from utilitarian to plush; they usually provide friendly service, spotless if basic rooms, IDD phones, private bathrooms, air-conditioning, and a homey environment. In small towns or rural areas off the beaten track, expect much more basic digs.

The rates quoted below are for accommodations in summer. Reservations are recommended during July and August and particularly during Tet, the lunar new year (January or February); prices often go up at that time. Rates sometimes include breakfast. Many of the larger, international hotels, particularly in Hanoi, aren't always fully booked and should be ready to give you a better room rate than listed.

CATEGORY	COST*
$$$$	over $200
$$$	$100–$200
$$	$50–$100
$	$25–$50
¢	under $25

All prices are for a standard double room, including 10% tax and 5% service.

Shopping

There is plenty to buy in Vietnam, though perhaps not of as high quality as elsewhere in Southeast Asia. Custom-made clothing, unique handicrafts such as delicate blue-and-white ceramics, elegant black-and-red lacquerware, colorful textiles made by ethnic minority groups, and intricate wood carvings can be found at rock-bottom prices. In addition, Vietnam—particularly Hanoi—has a booming contemporary arts scene, though paintings can get pricey. Bargaining is virtually mandatory in all but the most exclusive shops.

Exploring Vietnam

The best way to see Vietnam is to use the major cities as your base for trips into the outlying regions. Begin in Hanoi, the capital, and travel north to south, against the tourist tide, for less crowding and more choice. Hanoi is the most sober and ideologically driven of Vietnam's cities, but the French influence still reverberates in this beautiful tree-shaded town. Possible trips out of Hanoi include two-day boat excursions through the limestone archipelagoes of Halong Bay and trekking tours through breathtaking scenery in the Hoang Lien Mountains, where, in towns like Sapa, ethnic minorities live.

South along the coast, Hue is perhaps the country's most culturally attractive city. Its wide boulevards lead to the vestiges of the Imperial City, where elite mandarins ruled, and the romantic Perfume River takes you out of town to their remarkable, mysterious tombs. South of working-class Danang, site of the lovely Cham Museum of Art, lie spectacular stretches of coastline, such as China Beach, and Hoi An, a delightful centuries-old port town. This living, working museum is blessed with a beautiful beach and estuary, a remarkably intact historic center, and nearby Cham ruins. The south-central coast (the area around Nha Trang) is also known for its beaches and ruins. From Hoi An or Nha Trang you can visit the resort town of Dalat and take a trip through the central highlands up the spine of the country to the mountain towns of Pleiku and Kontum. Like the northern Alps, these towns are surrounded by spectacular mountains and rivers. They're populated by ancient Malayo-Polynesian hill tribes who still use working elephants.

Ho Chi Minh City, still called Saigon by people who live in it, is the engine of Vietnam, with a population of over 6 million. An exuberant mix of the old and the new, the crass and the sophisticated, it betrays its thoroughly Western heritage as the former capital of French Cochin China and of South Vietnam. From the city you can head to the Mekong Delta on day trips or longer, cruising by palm-lined hamlets and punting through magnificent, ancient mangrove forests.

Great Itineraries

Even under the most stringent time constraints, touring just the two major cities would not only be unsatisfying, but would misrepresent the country as a whole.

IF YOU HAVE 3 DAYS

Spend one or two days in Ho Chi Minh City, using it as a base for a day trip either to the Cu Chi Tunnels and the Caodai Holy See in Tay Ninh, or through the Mekong Delta on a boat. Another option is to spend a day and a half in Hue and a day and a half in Hoi An, which is a three-hour car trip from Hue. You could also easily spend your time in Hanoi, with an overnight trip to Halong Bay, Vietnam's premier natural wonder.

IF YOU HAVE 7–10 DAYS

Spend one day in Ho Chi Minh City, taking a day trip to the Cu Chi Tunnels and the Caodai Holy See in Tay Ninh, or into the Mekong Delta. Fly to Hue for two days; tour the ancient citadel and the Nguyen dynasty tombs and pagodas. A trip to the perfectly preserved 18th-century city of Hoi An is well worth your time. Fly or take an overnight train to Hanoi. From Hanoi you could take a day trip to the Perfume Pagoda or make an overnight excursion to Halong Bay.

WHEN TO TOUR VIETNAM

Vietnam's microclimates can make it hot and dry in one area while it's monsoon season in another. March–April and September–November have the best weather in the largest number of regions. Weather in the north is finest around August to December; it rains for much of the rest of the year, although not as heavily as in the south. It can get quite chilly in the north January–March. Dry season in the south (about November–June) is best; during the monsoons much of the Mekong Delta and central highlands are impassable. (☞ When to Go *in* Vietnam A to Z, *below.*)

Numbers in the text correspond to numbers in the margin and on the maps.

HANOI

By Michael Mathes and Elka Ray

658 km (408 mi) north of Hue, 763 km (473 mi) north of Danang, 1,710 km (1,060 mi) north of Ho Chi Minh City.

Hanoi, the self-appointed stronghold of "true" Vietnamese, anti-imperialist culture, has learned to covet satellite TV and blue jeans. The country's leaders let in a flood of overseas investment from Hong Kong, Malaysia, Singapore, Taiwan, and even the United States and Australia, and now the capital of the Socialist Republic of Vietnam relishes its newfound economic liberalization despite itself. Although Western fashions, music, and food have managed to elbow their way into the once-impenetrable north, Hanoi is appealing because it retains its ancient culture, French colonial architecture, broad tree-lined boulevards, and beautiful lakes.

The city dates to the 7th century, when Chinese Sui dynasty settlers occupied the area and set up a capital called Tong Binh. In 1010 King Ly Thai To is said to have seen a golden dragon ascend from Hoan Kiem Lake. The dragon is a traditional Chinese symbol of royal power, and the king took the omen literally: he relocated his capital to the shores of the lake, the site of present-day Hanoi, and named his new city Thang Long, or "City of the Ascending Dragon." During the 11th century the old citadel was built, and 36 villages, each with its own specialized vocation, sprang up to service the royal court. This is the origin of the 36 streets that define the city's Old Quarter.

In 1428 King Le Loi is said to have driven Vietnam's Chinese over-lords from the country with the help of a magic sword from heaven. Celebrating his success after the war with a boating excursion on Hoan Kiem Lake, Le Loi was confronted by a gigantic golden tortoise that retrieved the sword for its heavenly owner. Thus the lake became known as the Lake of the Restored Sword, or Ho Hoan Kiem. In 1789 the Chinese reconquered Hanoi, but not for long. Nguyen Hue, leader of a rebellion in Tay Son (in the south), drove the Manchu invaders out of the country and crowned himself King Quang Trung. Officially, however, by then the country was led by the Nguyen dynasty, which moved the capital to Hue under the rule of Gia Long in 1802. This chapter in northern Vietnam's history was in part orchestrated by the French, who began to play a stronger role in the political and com-mercial fabric of the country.

The French usurped more and more control, setting up the protectorate of Annam in 1883–84, which meant the Hue royalty held the reins but only under the auspices of French rule. In the following years the French set up their administration and used Hanoi as the Eastern Cap-ital, or Dong Kinh (the origin of Tonkin), of French Indochina. The Chinese character of the city was basically eliminated as the French filled in canals between Hanoi's many lakes and created a plain on which to remake the capital in their own mold. They constructed the large villas and administrative buildings that cluster in the streets around the present-day Presidential Palace and the Ho Chi Minh Mausoleum, as well as the grid of wide boulevards south of Hoan Kiem Lake. These streets and structures remain, and they continue to give the city a somewhat dilapidated but still striking colonial-era feel.

Once the French were defeated at Dien Bien Phu, Hanoi was again de-clared the capital of Vietnam. From 1954 until 1975 it was the seat of the Democratic Republic of Vietnam, or North Vietnam, from which Ho Chi Minh initiated his struggle to reunify the country. Despite Amer-ican attempts to smash the Communist administration by bombing it from the air, the city survived the war with most of its grandeur re-markably intact. The post-1975 socialist order sought to seal off the city and, after the war with China in 1979, expel the ethnic Chinese, although many of these predominantly mercantile families had lived in Vietnam for generations.

In the decades after 1975 relations with the Soviet Union were strength-ened. Tens of thousands of Russian advisers came to live in Hanoi and other parts of the country, leaving their mark in such buildings as the Viet Xo Cultural Palace and massive infrastructure projects such as the Hoa Binh hydroelectric power station. But the '80s were tough times for Hanoians and everyone else. Natural disasters and international isola-tion led to near mass starvation. Come nightfall, city streets were deserted. Entrepreneurs were jailed for capitalist tactics they used to make ends meet.

Then in 1986, following the lead of Gorbachev's perestroika in the So-viet Union, the government suddenly took a bold "reform or perish" approach and proclaimed *doi moi*, the move to a market economy. The Soviet Union dissolved soon thereafter, taking with it billions of dol-lars of desperately needed foreign aid. But foreign investors had already started preliminary explorations of one of the world's largest untapped markets, and more and more foreign investment started coming, es-pecially after the American embargo was lifted in early 1994.

More than a decade of economic reforms has changed the attitudes of the ruling party members considerably, and reformist city leaders are learning the ways of capitalism quickly—perhaps too quickly, according to some of the aging Communist Party cadres and conservative critics who pride themselves on their city's being the seat of Vietnam's socialist revolution. But few can argue that the last decade of change in Hanoi has been anything short of a godsend. In the past six years, as the economy has continued to open and the people have gained increasing amounts of disposable income, the city has modernized rapidly.

Nonetheless, Hanoi remains a city of academics, artists, diplomats—and contradictions. You'll see people carrying new TVs on the backs of their Honda motorbikes, but you'll also see people carrying hundreds of pounds of rice on bicycles with no brakes. People may zoom around all day doing business, but they also take time out for long discussions over a cup of coffee in a café. Pete Peterson, once a prisoner in the Hanoi Hilton, has been the U.S. ambassador to Vietnam since 1997. On a Sunday you may see him cruising to a noodle shop on his motorbike with his Vietnamese-Australian wife. Octogenarian General Giap, who defeated the French at Dien Bien Phu, is involved in Vietnam's developing telecommunications industry. Like everyone else in Hanoi and all over Vietnam, General Giap is aware of his history but is moving on with the times.

Exploring Hanoi

Hanoi is divided into four main districts, or *quan*. The Hoan Kiem District, named after the lake at its center, is the hub of most local and tourist activity. Just north of the lake is the Old Quarter, a charming cluster of ancient streets. South of the lake is the modern city center, once the French Quarter, which houses grand colonial-style villas that have been turned into hotels and offices. The Ba Dinh District, west of the Old Quarter, contains the zoo, the Ho Chi Minh Mausoleum, the Presidential Palace, and areas around West Lake, a picturesque body of water north of the Ba Dinh and Hoan Kiem districts. The Hai Ba Trung District, in the southeast part of Hanoi, is a calm, elegant residential area, whose primary attraction is Lenin Park. The Dong Da District, to the southwest, is where the Temple of Literature can be found.

Getting around Hanoi on foot is not out of the question, but it can be tiring. So if you intend to stick within the Old Quarter or elsewhere in Hoan Kiem District, break up your walks with a cyclo (pedicab) ride or two. Otherwise consider taking taxis, or if the weather is good and you're feeling a little more gung ho, rent a bicycle or hop on the back of a *xe om* (motorcycle taxi).

The Old Quarter

When Vietnam gained its independence from China in the 11th century, King Ly Thai To built his palace here, and the area developed as a crafts center. Artisans were attracted from all over the northern part of the country and formed guilds based on specialized trades and village affiliation. This area is referred to as the 36 Streets—actually now there are nearly 70. To this day the streets are still named after the crafts practiced by the original guilds. Note the slim buildings called tunnel or tube houses—with narrow frontage but deceiving depth—which combine workshops, storefronts, and living quarters. They were built this way because each business was taxed according to the width of its storefront. In addition to the specialty shops, each street has religious structures reflecting the beliefs of the village from which its guilds came.

A GOOD WALK
Begin your walk in the northern section of the Hoan Kiem District, at the **Dong Xuan Market** ① on Hang Chieu Street. From here you can dive right into the bustle of the ancient streets—but be careful in the

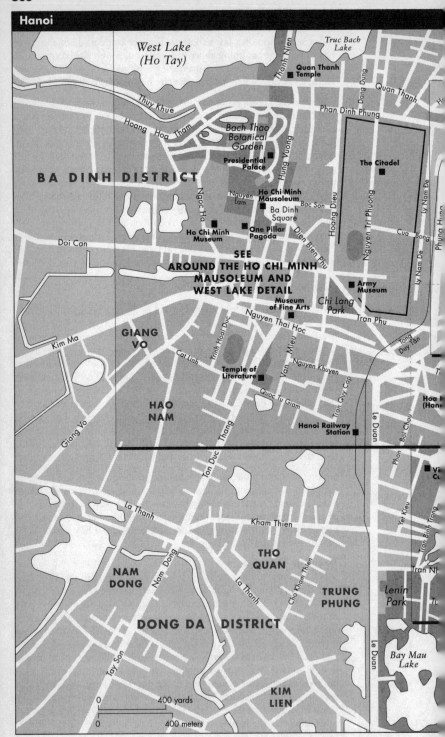

West Lake
(Ho Tay)

Truc Bach
Lake

Quan Thanh
Temple

Quan Thanh

Thanh Nien

Thuy Khue

Phan Dinh Phung

Dung Duong

Hoang Hoa Tham

Bach Thao
Botanical
Garden

Hung Vuong

The Citadel

BA DINH DISTRICT

Presidential
Palace

Ngoc Ha

Nguyen
Lam

Ho Chi Minh
Mausoleum

Ba Dinh
Square

Bac Son

Hoang Dieu

Nguyen Tri Phuong

Ly Nam De

Doi Can

Ho Chi Minh
Museum

One Pillar
Pagoda

Dien Bien Phu

Cua Bong

Ly Nam De

Phung Hung

**SEE
AROUND THE HO CHI MINH
MAUSOLEUM AND
WEST LAKE DETAIL**

Army
Museum

Kim Ma

**GIANG
VO**

Museum
of Fine Arts

Chi Lang
Park

Tran Phu

Nguyen Thai Hoc

Cat Linh

Trinh Hoai Duc

Van Mieu

Nguyen Khuyen

Tong
Duy Tan

Hoa
(Han)

Giang Vo

**HAO
NAM**

Temple of
Literature

Quoc Tu Giam

Tran Quy Cap

Le Duan

Boi Chau

Hanoi Railway
Station

Phan

Vi
Cu

Ton Duc Thang

La Thanh

Kham Thien

Yen Kieu

Tran Binh Trong

**NAM
DONG**

Nam Dong

**THO
QUAN**

Cho Kham Thien

La Thanh

**TRUNG
PHUNG**

Tran Nl

Lenin
Park

DONG DA DISTRICT

Tay Son

0   400 yards

0   400 meters

**KIM
LIEN**

Le Duan

Bay Mau
Lake

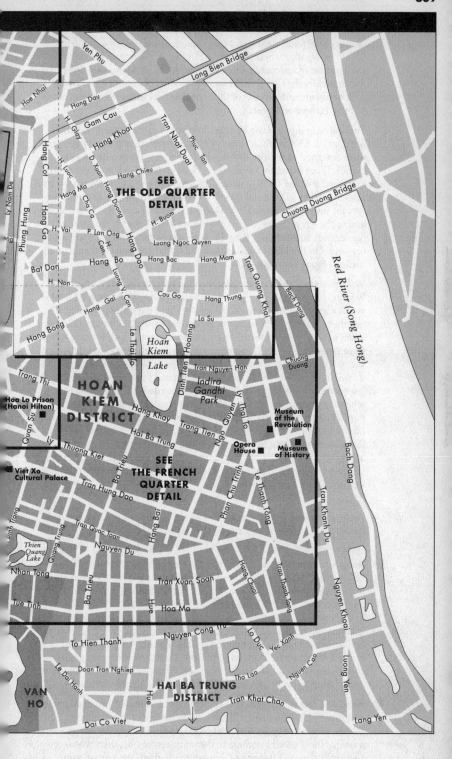

Yen Phu

Long Bien Bridge

Hoe Nhat

Hang Dau

H. Gioy Gam Cau

Hang Khoai

H. Luoc D. Xuan Hang Duong Tran Nhat Duat Phuc Tan

Hang Cot

Hang Chieu

Hang Ma Cha Ca

SEE
THE OLD QUARTER
DETAIL

Phung Hung

H. Vai P. Lan Ong H. Buom

Hang Ga H. Can. Luong Ngoc Quyen

Bat Dan Hang Bo Hang Dao Hang Bac Hang Mam Tran Quang Khai

H. Non Luong V. Can

Hang Bong Cau Go Hang Thung Bach Dang

Hang Gai Lo Su

Le Thai To Hoanng

Hoan
Kiem
Lake

Red River (Song Hong)

Trang Thi

HOAN
KIEM
DISTRICT

Dinh Tien Tran Nguyen Han Chuong
Duong

Hoa Lo Prison
(Hanoi Hilton)

Quan Su

Ly

Hang Khay Indira
Gandhi
Park

Ngo Quyen Ly Thai To

Museum
of the
Revolution

Thuong Kiet

Trang Tien

Hai Ba Trung

Opera
House

Museum
of History

Viet Xo
Cultural Palace

Ba Trieu

SEE
THE FRENCH
QUARTER
DETAIL

Phan Chu Trinh

Le Thanh Tong

Bach Dang

Tran Hung Dao

Hang Bai

Dinh Tong

Bui Thi

Tran Quoc Toan

Nguyen Du

Hang Chua

Tran Thanh Tang

Tran Khanh Du

Nguyen Khoai

Thien
Quang
Lake

Ba Trieu

Tran Xuan Soan

Nhan Tong

Tue Tinh

Hue

Hoa Ma

Luong Yen

Nguyen Cong Tru

Lo Duc Yec Xanh

To Hien Thanh

Tho Lao

Nguyen Cao

Le Dai Hanh Doan Tran Nghiep

VAN
HO

Hue

HAI BA TRUNG
DISTRICT

Tran Khat Chan

Dai Co Viet

Lang Yen

Chuong Duong Bridge

traffic! From the intersection of Hang Chieu and Dong Xuan streets, head south on Dong Xuan, which immediately turns into Hang Duong (Sugar) Street and then into Hang Ngang Street. Spare a moment for 48 Hang Ngang, where President Ho Chi Minh wrote his country's Declaration of Independence. Continue south, to **Hang Dao Street** ②, which divides the Old Quarter and serves as a convenient corridor from which to venture down any of the appealing side streets. Once you come to busy **Hang Bac Street** ③, turn left.

Turning right down Hang Be Street brings you to the historic boat-building district. The bamboo rafts, called *cai mang,* that you may see here were designed especially for the shallow rivers, lakes, and swamps of Hanoi. From Hang Be Street take a right on Cau Go Street, the southeast border of the Old Quarter. This neighborhood was known for its flower market in colonial times, a vestige of which can be found before the intersection with Hang Dao Street. Just beyond this flower mart and to the left is the northern tip of **Hoan Kiem Lake** ④, the focal point for legends surrounding King Le Loi's encounter with the Ho Guom tortoise. On the left, or east, side is the distinctive red footbridge that leads to **Ngoc Son Temple** ⑤.

Walk back to Cau Go Street and through the chaotic intersection here. Beyond this roundabout, Cau Go becomes **Hang Gai Street** ⑥, where you'll want to spend some time if you're shopping for embroidery, silk, or other souvenirs or if you want to wander through some art galleries. From here turn right (north) on Hang Hom Street, which leads to **Hang Quat Street** ⑦. This area is home to a few of the oldest musical instrument shops still standing in the Old Quarter. (Some shops here have turned to the more profitable business of selling paints and solvents.) A quick jog to the left on Hang Non Street brings you to Hang Thiec Street, where utilitarian tin chests and utensils dangle from every doorway. Farther north, this street becomes Thuoc Bac Street. The street has maintained quite a bit of its French-era Art Deco frontage. Eventually this street meets **Hang Ma Street** ⑧, which gets its name from the paper goods and fake money made for burning to appease ancestral spirits. Heading east on Hang Ma takes you back to Hang Chieu Street and, to the left, the Dong Xuan Market.

TIMING
Because the Old Quarter is filled with shops, this 3-km (2-mi) route is the kind of walk that could take two hours or 10.

SIGHTS TO SEE
❶ **Dong Xuan Market.** Once conveniently accessible by riverboat, this market, the oldest (1947) and largest still standing in the city, has seen trading with the whole of Southeast Asia. "Still standing" may not be the appropriate term; the huge structure was destroyed by a massive fire in 1994 on July 14, Bastille Day. The fire displaced 3,000 workers, caused millions of dollars in damage and losses, and took five human lives and an untold number of exotic animals. The market reopened in December 1996; today it looks more like a concrete shopping mall but continues to offer all manner of local and Western goods. ✉ *Dong Xuan and Hang Chieu Sts., Hoan Kiem District.* ☉ *Daily 6–6.*

❸ **Hang Bac Street.** This street was originally dominated by silversmiths and money changers and still has a wide variety of jewelry shops. The Dong Cac jewelers' guild was established here in 1428, and it later erected a temple (now gone) in tribute to three 6th-century brothers whose jewelry skills, learned from the Chinese, made them the patron saints of Vietnamese jewelry. The Hanoi Cai Luong Theatre, at the corner of Ta Hien Street, is still in operation. Check inside for showtimes.

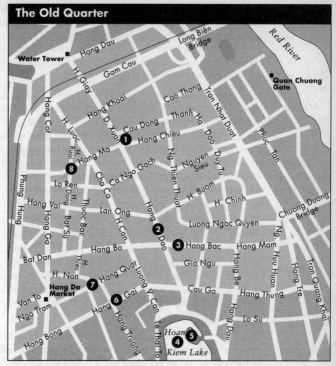

The Old Quarter

② Hang Dao Street. Since the 15th century, when it was one of the original silk-trading centers, Hang Dao Street has been known for its textiles. When the French colonized Vietnam, Hang Dao Street became the center for all traffic in silk, with massive biweekly trade fairs. Indians who settled here at the turn of the 21st century introduced textiles from the West, and today the street features ready-to-wear clothing in addition to bolts of silk.

★ **⑥ Hang Gai Street.** The Street of Hemp now offers a variety of goods, including ready-made silk, lovely embroidery, and silver products. With plenty of art galleries, crafts stores, and souvenirs, this is ground zero for tourists on foot.

⑧ Hang Ma Street. Here you can find *ma*, delicate paper replicas of material possessions made to be burned in tribute to one's ancestors. These faux luxury villas and Honda motorbikes can be found alongside more practical merchandise such as imported party decorations and kites.

★ **⑦ Hang Quat Street.** The Street of Fans now features a stunning array of religious paraphernalia, including beautiful funeral and festival flags. This is one of the most atmospheric streets in Hanoi during holiday seasons.

★ **④ Hoan Kiem Lake** (Ho Hoan Kiem or Ho Guom). The spiritual, legendary, and social heart of Hanoi, Hoan Kiem Lake, the Lake of the Restored Sword, is one of the most enchanting spots in the city. Vietnamese of all ages delight in recounting the legend of how the Lake of the Restored Sword got its name: 15th-century war hero Le Loi used a magic golden sword from heaven to vanquish Chinese invaders. While Le Loi was boating on the lake in celebration of his successful martial exploits, a gigantic tortoise rose from the depths and retrieved the blade for its heavenly owner. Taking a dip is not advised—not to mention illegal. Hanoi's sewer and plumbing systems are stressed to the limit, and the water is polluted. Unless drastic measures are taken, it may be only a matter of time before the lake's turtles—revered by locals as a link to Hanoi's legend-heavy past and proclaimed by scientists to be a species unto themselves—disappear forever.

❺ Ngoc Son Temple (Den Ngoc Son). Enjoy a lazy game of Chinese checkers with the old gentlemen who frequent the courtyard of this quiet and well-manicured 18th-century shrine, whose name means "jade mountain." On an island in Hoan Kiem Lake, it is one of Hanoi's most picturesque temples. In the pagoda's anteroom is a 6-ft-long stuffed turtle that locals pulled from Hoan Kiem Lake in 1968. ⊠ *Dinh Tien Hoang St., Hoan Kiem District.* 🖾 *12,000d.* ☉ *Daily 8–8, later for festivals and 1st and 5th days of every lunar month.*

The French Quarter

Although much of the French Quarter's appeal lies in its grand but aging colonial architecture, the area is fast becoming a leading diplomatic and commercial section of the city. As you walk through this airy, surprisingly green district, note the considerable international presence here: more than a dozen embassies occupy renovated villas or compounds in the grid of avenues south of Hoan Kiem Lake, and 20-story office buildings have begun to shadow the streets of this lovely part of town.

A GOOD WALK

This 4-km (2½-mi) walk, beginning southeast of Hoan Kiem Lake, ends not where it begins but on the west side of the lake, still in the heart of the city. If you've arranged for a driver to pick you up afterward, tell him to meet you in front of the Nha Tho Lon, the Grand Cathedral—also known as St. Joseph's.

Start on the steps of the downtown area's grandest building, the restored **Opera House** ⑨. From the Opera House steps turn sharply to the right and follow Trang Tien Street east to its end. Here, at No. 1, is the **Museum of History** ⑩, which houses some of Vietnam's dearest artifacts. Just up Trang Tien Street, at 25 Tong Dan Street, is the **Museum of the Revolution** ⑪.

Return to the huge intersection in front of the Opera House. From here head south on Phan Chu Trinh Street—that's the second road on the left if you're looking west from the Opera House steps. Turn right onto **Tran Hung Dao Street** ⑫. If you're pressed for time or want to rest your legs, hop into a cyclo here for a 1-km (½-mi) ride down Tran Hung Dao to Quan Su Street (it should cost a maximum of 10,000d, but you could try to bargain it down to 5,000d). If you choose to walk, you'll discover that this stretch of Tran Hung Dao Street is an embassy row of sorts.

At the intersection of Tran Hung Dao and Quan Su is the **Viet Xo Cultural Palace** ⑬, the Soviet Union's most striking architectural contribution to this district. At the end of Tran Hung Dao Street is the dreary Ga Hanoi, the main railway station whose name comes from the French: *gare.* Now travel north on Quan Su Street to the nearby **Ambassador's Pagoda** ⑭. At Ly Thuong Kiet Street turn right, then left about 300 ft later at Hoa Lo Street. This is the site of what's left of the infamous **Hoa Lo Prison** ⑮, the turn-of-the-21st-century "fiery furnace" that the French euphemistically called La Maison Centrale and that American prisoners of war sardonically nicknamed the Hanoi Hilton.

From Hoa Lo continue east on Ly Thuong Kiet for another block and a half. On the left is the entrance to a bustling market with CHO 19–

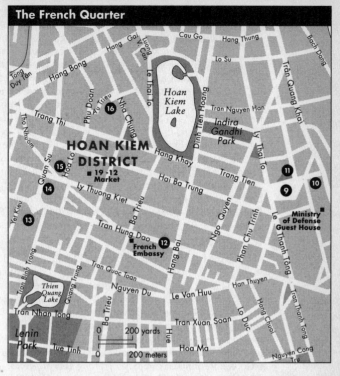

The French Quarter

12 (December 19th Market) written in red lettering on a flaking gray sign. (If you want to skip the market, continue down Ly Thuong Kiet Street and take a left on Quang Trung Street.) The north end of the market spills out onto Hai Ba Trung Street, named after the rebellious and heroic Trung sisters, who led a short-lived revolt against the Chinese in AD 40. Turn right on this street and then left on Quang Trung Street; at No. 1 is the main Vietnam Airlines ticketing office. Beyond Trang Thi Street, the road merges with Nha Chung Street. Continuing north on Nha Chung brings you to the Hoan Kiem District Culture Center (Nha Van Quan Hoan Kiem), a Soviet-style dance hall. Another 650 ft or so and you've reached **St. Joseph's Cathedral** ⑯, a proud but tired-looking stone-and-cement edifice that fronts a small square. From here it's just a two-block walk east to Hoan Kiem Lake or two blocks north to busy Hang Gai Street in the Old Quarter.

TIMING

This is a full-morning walk that could extend into the afternoon if you're keen on Vietnamese history. The museums, including the one at Hoa Lo Prison, are closed on Monday and at lunchtime. If you must see all three museums on this walk and you have other afternoon plans, start early. You can also save time by hopping in a cyclo or taxi.

SIGHTS TO SEE

⑭ **Ambassador's Pagoda** (Chua Quan Su). This stately prayer house once served the many ambassadors who called on the Le kings. As the pagoda is in part dedicated to a monk who is said to have saved King Ly Than Tong from his deathbed, many older women come here to pray for good health, especially on the first and 15th evenings of every month of the lunar calendar. ☒ *73 Quan Su St., Hoan Kiem District,* ☎ *04/825–2427.* ☒ *Free.* ☉ *Daily 7:30–11:30 and 1:30–5:30.*

⓯ **Hoa Lo Prison** (Hanoi Hilton). There's not much left of the infamous "Hanoi Hilton," the prison that once housed captured American servicemen during the Vietnam War, including U.S. Air Force pilot Douglas "Pete" Peterson, who at press time was rounding out his tenure as the first U.S. ambassador to Hanoi. These days it's the focal point of what the government plans as the central business district of the emerging metropolis of Hanoi. What does remain, however, is a small section of the old jail, which is now the **Hoa Lo Prison Museum,** and the tree under which Do Muoi, the aging former General Secretary of the Communist Party, used to sit while writing epithets on the backs of leaves during his imprisonment by the French during the years of Vietminh resistance. If you're looking for historical detail about the prison, bring your own well-informed guide; those available at the museum are far more inclined to talk about the size of the cells than reveal any nuggets about what once took place behind the musty yellow walls. ⊠ *1 Hoa Lo St., Hoan Kiem District,* ☎ *04/824–6358.* ⊠ *Free.* ⊘ *Tues.–Sun. 8:30–11 and 1:30–4:30.*

⓾ **Museum of History** (Bao Tang Lich Su). Opened in 1932 as the museum of the École Française d'Extrême Orient, this building has served in its present capacity since 1958, when the French finally handed it back to Hanoi authorities. It houses treasures from early history, particularly Vietnam's Bronze Age, and modern Vietnamese culture. Visiting the museum can be a frustrating experience: there is far too little explanatory text, and English-language translation is lacking. You would be best served accompanied by a translator and, if possible, a historian. The museum was undergoing a major redesign at press time, so look out for new exhibits. ⊠ *1 Trang Tien St., Hoan Kiem District,* ☎ *04/825–3518.* ⊠ *10,000d.* ⊘ *Tues.–Sun. 8:45–11:45 and 1:15–4:30.*

⓫ **Museum of the Revolution** (Bao Tang Cach Mang). Built in 1926 to house the French tax office, this cavernous museum opened its doors in 1959. Exhibits focus on specific events or periods in Vietnam's arduous road to independence. Fortunately, just about all the exhibits have English and French commentary, so a few hours in here can be a great learning experience. On the other hand it may be difficult to swallow some of the museum section titles. English-language guided tours must be arranged in advance. ⊠ *25 Tong Dan St., Hoan Kiem District,* ☎ *04/825–4151.* ⊠ *10,000d.* ⊘ *Sat. 8–11:30, Tues.–Fri. and Sun. 8–11:30 and 1–4.*

⑨ **Opera House** (Nha Hat Lon). The centerpiece of French architecture in Hanoi and one of the grandest buildings in the city, the Hanoi Opera House is a small-scale version of the Paris Opéra designed by Charles Garnier and completed in 1875. The Hanoi structure, finished in 1911, incorporates the same grand elements of Napoleonic architectural style. Despite (or because of) the theater's French history, its steps were the site of frequent denunciations against colonial rule. Today the Opera House is positively glowing after a three-year restoration. Seeing a show may be the only way to get into the Opera House, however, as its doors are usually closed. ⊠ *Trang Tien St., Hoan Kiem District,* ☎ *04/824–8029.*

⓰ **St. Joseph's Cathedral** (Nha Tho Lon). French missionaries built the cathedral in the late 19th century and celebrated the first mass here on Christmas Day in 1886. The small but beautiful panes of stained glass were created in Paris in 1906. Also of note is the ornate altar, with its high gilded side walls. The creaky wooden front doors open for Sunday Mass, but if you're visiting at midday, you'll have to walk through the iron gates to the left of the main entrance and enter through the side door. ⊠ *Nha Tho St., Hoan Kiem District,* ☎ *04/828–*

5967. ⊙ *Mass Sun. at 4:30 AM, 5:30 AM, 7 AM, 10 AM, and 6 PM, Mon.–Tues. and Thurs. at 5:30 AM, Wed. and Fri.–Sat. at 5:30 AM and 6 PM.*

NEED A
BREAK?

Café Moca (✉ 14–16 Nha Tho St., Hoan Kiem District, ☎ 04/825–6334), opposite St. Joseph's Cathedral, serves excellent coffee plus Vietnamese, Western, and Indian cuisine in an airy ambience. Mr. Binh, Moca's charming young maître d', is a small-talk pro, but he's also a veteran of the Hanoi restaurant scene and will do what it takes to please. All he needs now is to change the unwieldy chairs.

⑫ Tran Hung Dao Street. Once called Rue Gambetta, Tran Hung Dao Street is now named after the revered 13th-century Vietnamese warrior who repulsed Kublai Khan's Mongol hordes at a legendary battle on the Bach Dang River, near present-day Haiphong. The boulevard is lined with a number of diplomatic missions; among them, fittingly, is the French embassy. Others are of the Philippines, Indonesia, India, Iraq, and Cambodia.

⑬ Viet Xo Cultural Palace (Cung Van Hoa Viet-Xo). Never one to downplay its influence, the Soviet Union assisted with the design and construction of this "workers' cultural palace," which was inaugurated September 1, 1985. The rigid 120-room white colossus stretches from Yet Kieu Street to Tran Binh Trong Road. The palace is actually three structures: the performance building houses a 1,200-seat concert hall, while the study and technology buildings contain a library, a conference hall, and an observatory. ✉ *91 Tran Hung Dao St., Hoan Kiem District,* ☎ *04/825–3787.* ⌾ *Free.* ⊙ *Daily 8–noon and 1–4:30.*

Around The Ho Chi Minh Mausoleum

Ask a cyclo or taxi driver to take you from Hoan Kiem Lake to the Ho Chi Minh Mausoleum, in Ba Dinh District. As you travel northwest on Dien Bien Phu Street, you'll leave the tightly woven fabric of the Old Quarter behind and find yourself surrounding by sweeping French-era villas and massive ocher-color government buildings. At the end of Dien Bien Phu Street is the minimally landscaped Ba Dinh Square, in the center of which flutters Hanoi's largest Vietnam flag. One can almost hear the echoes of Ho Chi Minh's voice ringing out over loudspeakers to the half million northern Vietnamese who gathered to hear Uncle Ho's Declaration of Independence on September 2, 1945. On the west side of the square is the mausoleum itself.

A GOOD WALK

Start at the **Ho Chi Minh Mausoleum** ⑰. Once you have passed by the unflinching guards and through the mausoleum itself, you'll be directed through large iron gates and toward **Ho Chi Minh's Residence** ⑱, which is in the tranquil wooded compound of the **Presidential Palace** ⑲. Although you are welcome to Uncle Ho's house, the palace itself is off-limits, as is much of the surrounding parkland. Behind the Presidential Palace, however, is the large **Botanical Garden** ⑳, which is open to the public, although the entrance is a bit far away, on Hoang Hoa Tham Street. A short pathway leads from Ho Chi Minh's house to **One-Pillar Pagoda** ㉑, the reconstructed Buddhist tower in the center of a small square lake. To the left is Dien Huu Pagoda; this charming but seldom-visited temple sits in the shadow of the architecturally baffling **Ho Chi Minh Museum** ㉒.

Walk out the front doors of the museum and down the steps toward Ba Dinh Square. Turn right on Hung Vuong Street, the road in front of the mausoleum. Ahead and to the left is the six-story International Press Center. But turn left just before that building, on Le Hong Phong Street. At No. 11 on this wide, tree-lined boulevard is the International

Around the Ho Chi Minh Mausoleum and West Lake

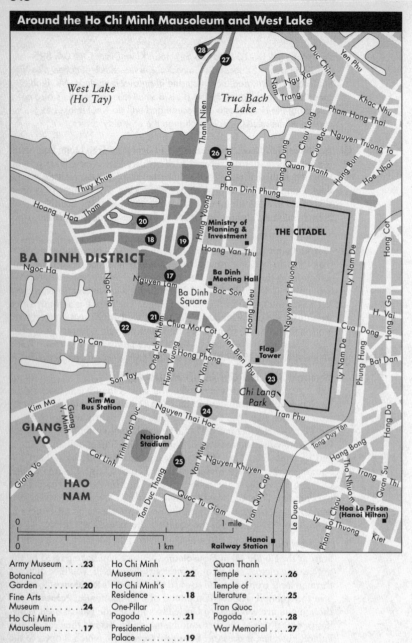

Conference Center, where the gathering of French-speaking nations, known as the *Francophonie,* was held in November 1997. Le Hong Phong leads back to Dien Bien Phu Street, where you should bear right. In about 200 yards you'll reach shady Chi Lang Park, where there's a statue of Vladimir Ilyich Lenin, one of the last still standing. Lenin appears to be leaning resolutely toward the **Army Museum** ㉓, just across the street. To the left is the 100-ft tower known as the Flag Pillar, the surviving remnant of the Nguyen dynasty citadel, which has become a historic symbol of the city.

From the Army Museum, retrace your steps to the intersection of Le Hong Phong, Dien Bien Phu, and Hoang Dieu streets. Turn left on Hoang Dieu and continue, past the Chinese embassy on your right, until you reach very busy Nguyen Thai Hoc Street. One block to the right is the **Fine Arts Museum** ㉔, set back in a courtyard. From here the **Temple of Literature** ㉕ is just across the street, secluded behind a low stone wall. To get to the entrance, proceed south down Van Mieu Street, opposite the art museum, and turn right on Quoc Tu Giam Street.

TIMING

Three hours should be enough to get from the Ho Chi Minh Mausoleum to the Fine Arts Museum, provided you don't venture over to the Botanical Garden. Leave at least another 30–40 minutes for the Temple of Literature. Or conversely, you could start at the Temple of Literature—it opens in the summer at 7:30, in winter at 8—and make your way up to the Botanical Garden or to West Lake, taking in the sights along the way. The only real delay is lining up to view Uncle Ho (keep in mind, too, that his mausoleum is closed in the afternoons).

SIGHTS TO SEE

㉓ **Army Museum** (Bao Tang Quan Doi). The Army Museum is an intriguing example of Vietnam's continuing obsession with publicizing its past military exploits. The museum buildings were once used as French military barracks. Adjacent to the museum is the **Hanoi Flag Pillar.** Built in 1812, the pillar escaped destruction by the French when they leveled much of the citadel. ⊠ *28 Dien Bien Phu St., Ba Dinh District,* ☎ *04/823–4264.* ≦ *10,000d.* ☉ *Weekends and Tues.–Thurs. 8–12 and 1:30–4:30.*

㉚ **Botanical Garden** (Vuon Bach Thao). This 50-acre park behind the Presidential Palace was designed by French landscape engineers in 1890. Athletes in search of exercise congregate here. Between dusk and closing time—10 PM—the island retreat in the center of the park is definitely rated R. ⊠ *Entrance on Hoang Hoa Tham Rd., Ba Dinh District.* ≦ *2,000d.* ☉ *Daily 7 AM–10 PM.*

★ ㉔ **Fine Arts Museum** (Bao Tang My Thuat). The evolution of Vietnamese art is sparingly, if not lovingly, chronicled in this musty three-story museum, which opened in 1966 after serving as a boardinghouse for French girls living in Indochina. ⊠ *66 Nguyen Thai Hoc St., Ba Dinh District,* ☎ *04/823–3084.* ≦ *10,000d.* ☉ *Daily 9:15–6.*

★ ⑰ **Ho Chi Minh Mausoleum** (Lang Chu Tich Ho Chi Minh). It's hard to overstate Ho Chi Minh's heroic stature among the Vietnamese and the significance of his mausoleum. Although the number of citizens queuing up to see their late president has dropped significantly in the last few years, thousands of Vietnamese still visit the revered site each year to pay homage to "Uncle Ho." Had officials followed his wishes, this structure may never have been built, as Ho Chi Minh had expressed in his will his desire to be cremated. But the preservation of the Vietnamese leader and his memory has gone the way of such other Communist figureheads as Lenin, Stalin, and Mao. Ho's embalmed body, touched up now and again in Russia, is virtually the only thing inside the mausoleum. The structure itself is a squat, cold, gray cubicle ringed by columns and topped by a flat square frieze adorned with the words "*Chu Tich* (President) Ho Chi Minh" in red plum marble.

When you enter the mausoleum, be aware of the strict propriety expected of visitors. Although Vietnamese pilgrims move in a solemn single-file procession, foreigners must sign in at an office at No. 8 Hung Vuong Street, south of the mausoleum, then leave their possessions at another checkpoint closer to the actual tomb, where uninformative brochures are for sale. Your purchase of them amounts to your entrance donation. No cameras, hats, or bags of any kind may be brought into the building, and you are expected to behave respectfully. This means not wearing shorts or tank tops or putting your hands in your pockets while inside. Talking is also forbidden, and once inside the chilly room containing Ho's corpse you are discouraged from lingering for more than a few moments in front of the glass. ⊠ *Enter at corner of Hung Vuong and Le Hong Phong Sts., Ba Dinh District,* ☎ *04/845-5128.* ☑ *4,000d donation expected.* ⊙ *Weekends and Tue.–Thurs. 8 AM–11 AM. Usually closed Oct. and/or Nov., when Ho's body is in Russia for maintenance.*

㉒ Ho Chi Minh Museum (Bao Tang Ho Chi Minh). Opened on May 19, 1990, on what would have been Ho's 100th birthday, this complex was established, in the language of the brochure that you can take on entering, "to satisfy the Vietnamese people's desire to express their deep gratitude to the President." This museum is a must-see—if only for 15 minutes—on the Uncle Ho circuit. You must leave your cameras and bags at the reception area. There is an interesting gift shop. ⊠ *3 Ngoc Ha St. (also accessible from Chua Mot Cot St.), Ba Dinh District,* ☎ *04/846-3752.* ☑ *5,000d.* ⊙ *Weekends and Tues.–Thurs. 8–11 and 1:30–4.*

⑱ Ho Chi Minh's Residence (Nha Bac Ho). After 1954 Ho Chi Minh had the run of the Presidential Palace, but the ostentation was too much for the ascetic president. Instead, he preferred the humble former home of the palace's electrician, where he lived for four years. Then, the story goes, in 1958 Ho Chi Minh moved to this simple but tastefully designed wooden house on stilts, which served as his living quarters and work space until his death in 1969. Regardless of Ho Chi Minh's faith in the accuracy of the city's antiaircraft gunners, some doubt must be thrown on the claim that Ho Chi Minh spent so much time in this open-air sanctum while American bombers targeted Hanoi during the Vietnam War. Indeed, Ho's Politburo ordered the construction of a nearby bomb shelter, later dubbed House No. 67. Legend holds that Uncle Ho refused to use the shelter as a home, preferring to confer with the Politburo in this fortified bunker but to sleep in his stilt house. You may want to purchase a 20,000d booklet entitled *The Living Quarters and Working Place of President Ho Chi Minh,* available at the entrance gate to the house. Though overwrought, it's actually quite informative. ⊠ *Hung Vuong Rd., Ba Dinh District.* ☑ *3,000d.* ⊙ *Daily 7:30–11 and 1:30–4.*

㉑ One-Pillar Pagoda (Chua Mot Cot). The French destroyed this temple, once known as Lien Hoa Tower but now exclusively referred to as One-Pillar Pagoda, on their way out in 1954. It was reconstructed by the new government and still commemorates the legend of Emperor Ly Thai Tong. It is said that the childless emperor dreamed that Quan Am, the Buddhist goddess of mercy and compassion, seated on a lotus flower, handed him a baby boy. Sure enough, he soon met and married a peasant woman who bore him a male heir, and in 1049 he constructed this monument in appreciation. The distinctive single pillar is meant to represent the stalk of the lotus flower, a sacred Vietnamese symbol of purity. ✉ *Ong Ich Kiem St., Ba Dinh District.* 🎟 *Free.* ⊙ *Daily 7–5:30.*

⑲ **Presidential Palace** (Cung Chu Tich). Constructed from 1900 to 1906, the bright, mustard-yellow building served as the living and working quarters of Indochina's governors-general. When Ho Chi Minh returned to Hanoi after the defeat of the French in 1954, he refused to live in the palace itself and chose the more modest quarters of the palace electrician. Today the building is used for formal international receptions and other important government meetings; it's not open to the public. ✉ *Hung Vuong Rd. and Hoang Van Thu St., Ba Dinh District.*

★ ㉕ **Temple of Literature** (Van Mieu). An unusually well-preserved example of Vietnamese architecture, this monument to Confucius was built in 1070 by Emperor Ly Thanh Tong. Soon after its construction, it became the site of Vietnam's first university, Quoc Tu Giam, which specialized in training students—many of them sons and daughters of emperors and other high-ranking dignitaries—to pass the rigorous examinations for government and civil-service posts. The achievements of several centuries of the university's doctoral recipients are recorded on 82 stelae (stone slabs), which rest on stone tortoises. The French later used the building as, appropriately, their school of civil administration. On the far side of this temple is the site of what was the Van Mieu Library, largely destroyed by bombing raids in 1954. At press time the library, a small museum, and lecture halls were being renovated. ✉ *Quoc Tu Giam St., Dong Da District,* ☎ *04/845–2917 or 04/823–5601.* 🎟 *12,000d; 20,000d for an English-speaking guide.* ⊙ *Summer, daily 7:30–6; winter, daily 8–5.*

West Lake

About 3 km (2 mi)—10 minutes by taxi or motorbike—northwest of Hoan Kiem Lake lies West Lake (Ho Tay), another body of water that's steeped in legend. It is said a giant golden calf from China followed the peals of a monk's bronze bell to this spot. When the ringing stopped, the calf lost its direction and kept walking in circles, creating the basin of West Lake. Like Hoan Kiem's tortoise, the calf is said to still dwell in the lake.

Development is changing the face of the shore, however, as luxury hotels and high-rent villas eat away at the traditional communities such as the flower village of Nghi Tam, near the Kim Lien Pagoda. The lake itself is a weekend boating spot for Vietnamese families. Afterward they stop in one of the floating restaurants for snails boiled in lemon leaves.

A GOOD WALK

Start your walk at the beginning of the wide causeway of Thanh Nien Street, which divides West Lake from the smaller Truc Bach Lake. Along the way note the floating seafood restaurants and the neon signs of the times—billboards for beer and computers. At the very beginning of Thanh Nien duck into ornate **Quan Thanh Temple** ㉖.

Staying on the same side of the street, walk for about five minutes to reach an unnamed **War Memorial** ㉗ to antiaircraft gunners stationed on the roof of a nearby factory who shot down 10 American planes in 1967. Walk about 650 ft, then cross the street to Hanoi's oldest pagoda, the delightful **Tran Quoc Pagoda** ㉘, on an islet jutting into West Lake. From there it's a 10- to 15-minute walk back to the beginning of Thanh Nien Street.

If you're up for walking at least part of the way back into the center of town from here, then go along Phan Dinh Phung Street. This beautiful shaded avenue leads past sprawling French villas and Chinese mandarin mansions, many occupied by long-serving party members, as well as the gracious but seldom-used Gothic North Door Cathedral (Cua Bac).

TIMING

The causeway can be traversed in about 20 minutes, but allow for an hour if you want to peek around the temples. Allow 90 minutes if you want to rent a dilapidated paddleboat from the quay on the Truc Bach side. The walk from the southeast corner of West Lake to the water tower at the edge of the Old Quarter is another 15–25 minutes.

SIGHTS TO SEE

㉖ **Quan Thanh Temple** (Chua Quan Thanh or Chan Vu Quan). Built by King Ly Thai To in the 11th century, this much-made-over temple was once known as the Temple of the Grand Buddha. Above the ornamented main gate is a 1677 replica of the bronze bell that supposedly lured the West Lake's legendary golden calf from China. ⊠ *Quan Thanh and Thanh Nien Sts., Ba Dinh District,* ☎ *04/823–4378.* ☒ *5,000d donation.* ☉ *Daily 8–4:30.*

㉘ **Tran Quoc Pagoda** (Chua Tran Quoc). Hanoi's oldest temple and an active monastery dates from the 6th century, when King Ly Nam De had a pagoda, named Khai Quoc, built on the bank of the Red River. More than a thousand years later, excessive erosion of the riverbank caused King Le Kinh Tong to move the pagoda to Goldfish (Ca Vang) Islet on West Lake, and a subsequent Le king renamed it Tran Quoc. ⊠ *Thanh Nien St., Tay Ho District.* ☒ *5,000d donation.* ☉ *Daily 8–4:30.*

㉗ **War Memorial.** If you're interested in Vietnam War history, head for this small memorial between West Lake and Truc Bach Lake; it marks the capture of one of the war's most famous POWs. On October 26, 1967, Navy lieutenant commander John McCain's jet fighter was shot down, sending him parachuting into Truc Bach Lake. Suffering from badly broken bones and severe beatings, he was imprisoned in the Hanoi Hilton for more than five years. He went on to become an Arizona senator and made an unsuccessful bid for the Republican nomination in the 2000 presidential race. He's also been a vocal advocate of reconciliation between the United States and his former captors. ⊠ *Thanh Nien St., Ba Dinh District.*

Dining

The concept of an international cuisine industry is new to the capital despite the decades-long imposing presence of a culinary superpower: France. Fresh baguettes—and they're wonderful and cheap—are just about the only food link to that era. Virtually everything else at the international level has sprung up in the last half dozen years, leaving a Hanoi establishment's standing far more dependent on expatriate word of mouth and successful international management skills. Even the Vietnamese restaurants in Hanoi—and there are dozens of treats that await you—are confined to similar strictures; the hardscrabble north has understandably been preoccupied with more pressing concerns than cuisine throughout most of this century. Keep such issues in perspective and you should be pleasantly surprised.

Though the establishments listed below have staying power, you should call before heading out to a particular restaurant, as Hanoi places shut down as suddenly as they open. In addition, it's not uncommon for owners and managers to change, transforming the whole restaurant— for better or worse. Hanoi's top hotels—particularly the Sofitel

Metropole, the Hilton Hanoi Opera, the Melia, the Guoman, the Daewoo, Horison, and Meritus Westlake—have high-quality dining rooms.

Cafés

$$ ✕ **Au Lac Café.** It's the perfect location for breakfast, an afternoon break, or an after-dinner espresso—at a table on the outdoor terrace of this café across from the new wing of the Sofitel Metropole. Don't confuse it with the copycat next door, the Diva Café, and pray it doesn't rain. ⊠ *57 Ly Thai To St., Hoan Kiem District,* ☎ *04/825–7807. No credit cards.*

$$ ✕ **Moca Café.** Thanks to this two-story café, the street facing St. Joseph's Cathedral is infused with the smell of roasting coffee beans. An airy interior, good coffee, and a huge menu of Western, Vietnamese, and Indian dishes keep this café packed. Your best bet is the Indian food. ⊠ *14–16 Nha Tho St., Hoan Kiem District,* ☎ *04/825–6334. MC, V.*

¢ ✕ **Café 252.** This is the famous breakfast spot where Catherine Deneuve hung out while filming *Indochine.* Some say it has lost a dose of charm since remodeling in early 1998, but Mr. Chi and company still serve good pastries and the best fresh yogurt in town. ⊠ *252 Hang Bong St., Hoan Kiem District,* ☎ *04/825–0216. No credit cards.*

Eclectic

$$ ✕ **Al Fresco.** This colorful south-of-the-border-cum-pizza restaurant a block south of Hoan Kiem Lake gets high marks for its eclectic East-meets-West dining, coupled with a casual open-air ambience. Al Fresco's may be the most popular foreign restaurant in Hanoi because of its jumbo portions of ribs, pasta, T-bone steak, Mexican salad, and pizza. ⊠ *23L Hai Ba Trung St., Hoan Kiem District,* ☎ *04/826–7782. No credit cards.*

$$ ✕ **Red Onion Bistro.** Hanoi's most gregarious chef, American Bobby Chin, dishes up California-style cuisine on the fourth floor of a newly built office and residential tower. Favorites include pan-fried tuna with wasabi mashed potatoes, nachos, and a tray of Mediterranean appetizers. The attached bar, Fat Jax, stays open past midnight—late by Hanoi standards. ⊠ *Somerset Grand Hanoi, 4th floor, 49 Hai Ba Trung St., Hoan Kiem District,* ☎ *04/934–2342. AE, MC, V.*

French

$$ ✕ **Café des Arts de Hanoi.** Run by an amiable Frenchman, this cozy ★ restaurant is popular with Hanoi's French expatriates. Terra-cotta floors, wooden tables, and regularly changing exhibits of paintings by local artists give the place a homey feel. The menu features such typical French fare as *croque monsieur* (ham and cheese sandwich dipped in egg and sautéed in butter), beefsteak with fries, and a delicious pastis-flavored shrimp dish. ⊠ *11B Bao Khanh La., Hoan Kiem District,* ☎ *04/828–720. AE, MC, V.*

$$ ✕ **Hoa Sua.** Walk through a front courtyard off the street to find this ★ restaurant serving both French and Vietnamese food. It's a favorite of Francophiles and French expatriates. More than a restaurant, it's a humanitarian project: young people—particularly orphans—in need of assistance are trained as waiters and cooks. Outdoor seating is available on a terra-cotta patio surrounded by palms; the inside is equally charming, with wrought-iron furniture. Though the customer-server ratio often seems to be one-to-one, service is erratic. Reservations are recommended for Sunday brunch. ⊠ *81 Tho Nhuom St., Hoan Kiem District,* ☎ *04/824–0448. No credit cards.*

Ice Cream

¢ ✕ **Fanny's Ice Cream.** For the best ice cream in town, head for this charming, French-managed café across the street from Hoan Kiem Lake. The offerings, all made with natural ingredients and no preservatives, include unique local flavors like young rice, and tamarind, along with old favorites such as coffee, rum raisin, and wickedly rich dark chocolate. ⊠ *48 Le Thai To St., Hoan Kiem District,* ☎ *04/828–5656. No credit cards.*

Indian

$$ ✕ **Khazana.** This restaurant in the center of town is an opulent tribute to North Indian cuisine. Indian art and music add color to the elegant dining room, but it's the food that keeps people coming back. The tandoori chicken is outstanding, while the mutton dishes—actually made with goat meat (the traditional Indian recipes use mutton)—melt in your mouth. The slightly higher-than-average prices are justified both by the quality and quantity of food; the set lunches are an excellent value. ⊠ *41B Ly Thai To St., Hoan Kiem District,* ☎ *04/824–1166. MC, V. No lunch Sun.*

$ ✕ **Tandoor.** This small Indian restaurant in the Thuy Loi minihotel makes up for its lack of ambience with a wonderful yet inexpensive menu. Food is prepared fresh, with hand-ground spices. You can't go wrong with anything here, but fluffy garlic naan bread, tender chicken *masala,* and eggplant curry are particularly good. The fish *tikka* in red sauce and the chicken kebab marinated in yogurt are also sensational. ⊠ *24 Hang Be St., Hoan Kiem District,* ☎ *04/824–5359. MC, V.*

Italian

$$$ ✕ **Il Grillo.** This popular Italian-run eatery serves authentic prosciutto and grappa. The rib-eye steak is highly recommended, as are the homemade pasta dishes. The restaurant has cheerful, cozy decor—like a cabin in the Dolomites. Reservations are recommended, especially for Sunday night. ⊠ *116 Ba Trieu St., Hai Ba Trung District,* ☎ *04/822–7720. AE, MC, V.*

$$$ ✕ **Luna D'Autunno.** Hanoi's newest Italian eatery offers covered outdoor seating on a terra-cotta terrace, as well as indoor tables. The layout feels a bit like a cafeteria, but the food is excellent. Try one of their fat sandwiches or the exquisite platter of marinated vegetables with feta cheese, or go all out with a four-cheese pizza. On Friday nights there's a jazz band, followed by live piano on Saturday evenings. ⊠ *11B Dien Bien Phu St., Ba Dinh District,* ☎ *04/823–7338. AE, MC, V.*

$$ ✕ **Mediterraneo.** Delicious, reasonably priced Italian food is served in the bright, California-like atmosphere of this central eatery. Along with the best *bruschetta* (toasted bread with olive oil and various toppings) in town, the Italian hosts serve excellent cappuccinos, thin-crust pizzas cooked in a wood-burning oven, and an interesting array of homemade grappas—try licorice or peach. ⊠ *23 Nha Tho St., Hoan Kiem District,* ☎ *04/826–6288. MC, V.*

Japanese

$$$ ✕ **Saigon Sakura.** The stamp of approval here is the number of expatriate Japanese regulars who frequent this take-off-your-shoes restaurant. A clean Zen decor, good-value lunch sets, and an attentive staff make this a Hanoi favorite. Private dining is available upstairs. ⊠ *17 Trang Thi St., Hoan Kiem District,* ☎ *04/825–7565. MC, V.*

$$ ✕ **Ky Y.** Low prices encourage overindulgence in sushi or sashimi at this Japanese equivalent of a friendly neighborhood diner. The lunch specials are a steal at less than $6. Seating is at low tables on tatami mats or at a long polished bar. ⊠ *29 Phu Dong Thien Vuong St., Hai Ba Trung District,* ☎ *04/978–1386. AE, DC, V.*

Mediterranean

$$$$ ✕ **Press Club, The Dining Room.** Modern Mediterranean cuisine and ★ fine wines are served in this elegant restaurant evoking the 1930s. Eat inside in the tasteful, wood-paneled dining room or outside on the ter-

race surrounded by palms. International managers and chefs, including visiting chefs from many of the region's finest hotels, ensure topnotch food and service. The pepper squid is a refreshing appetizer, as is the marinated seafood. For dessert try homemade ice cream or a juicy apple tart. ✉ *59A Ly Thai To St., Hoan Kiem District,* ☎ *04/934–0888. AE, D, MC, V.*

Spanish

$$ ✕ **La Salsa Tapas Bar and Restaurant.** This is Hanoi's latest Fridaynight hot spot, where you can nibble on small servings of seviche, zesty meatballs, and marinated mushrooms, or choose an entrée of warm duck salad, pan-fried salmon, or lamb tenderloin. If you're not in the mood to see and be seen, avoid the cozy downstairs bar and hide out in the quieter upstairs dining room. ✉ *25 Nha Tho St., Hoan Kiem District,* ☎ *04/828–9052. AE, MC, V.*

Thai

$ ✕ **Bangkok-Hanoi.** The Bangkok-Hanoi feels authentic: the chef is from Thailand, Thai decorations and music fill the little eatery, and you'll even find ice-cold Singha beer. The spicy salads are excellent. For dessert try a dish of sweet taro or pumpkin in coconut milk. ✉ *52A Ly Thuong Kiet St., Hoan Kiem District,* ☎ *04/934–5598. No credit cards.*

¢ ✕ **Van Anh Thai Food.** Although there's no decor to speak of, this small restaurant has gained a cult following among Hanoi's expats. Feast on incredibly cheap Thai delights such as spicy seafood soup, leaf-wrapped chicken, fried fish cakes, and spicy papaya salad. It's very clean and, thanks to all the fluorescent lights, very bright. ✉ *5A Tong Duy Tan St., Hoan Kiem District,* ☎ *04/928–5163. No credit cards.*

Vegetarian

$–$$ ✕ **Vegetarian Restaurant Com Chay Nang Tam.** An unusual array of vegetarian dishes, many prepared to resemble meat (careful: some actually have meat), is served in the back of a dimly lit villa. The warm corn squares are a pleasing starter, and the "ginger fish," made of tofu, is a good main course. Be aware that they go heavy on the oil. ✉ *79A Tran Hung Dao St., Hoan Kiem District,* ☎ *04/826–6140. No credit cards.*

Vietnamese

$$$ ✕ **Emperor Restaurant.** Located off the street in a renovated French villa, the Emperor provides arguably the most beautiful and romantic setting in all of Hanoi. Climb the curved wooden staircase and enter the elegant, high-ceilinged Vietnamese-style dining room; downstairs the resident jazz band plays in the Emperor Pub. The food is as impressive as the decor, with plenty of seafood dishes and Hue specialties, including the delectable Hue spring rolls. ✉ *18B Le Thanh Tong St., Hoan Kiem District,* ☎ *04/826–8801. AE, MC, V.*

$$ ✕ **Brother's Cafe.** This gorgeous eatery is located in an old, tile-roof pagoda that abuts a quiet courtyard. At night the courtyard is lit by candles. Diners help themselves to a large buffet of hot and cold dishes, including lots of seafood, pork, and chicken, plus five kinds of Vietnamese salads. The $5 lunch buffet includes a glass of juice, whereas the $10 dinner buffet includes a glass of wine. ✉ *26 Nguyen Thai Hoc St., Ba Dinh District,* ☎ *04/733–3866. MC, V. No lunch Sun.*

$$ ✕ **Cha Ca La Vong.** Right in the thick of the Old Quarter is Hanoi's most famous purveyor of *cha ca* (boneless Red River fish cubes marinated in dill, grilled—with an alarming disregard for safety—at your table, and served with rice noodles and peanuts). The grease-covered walls add to the authentic, pungent experience. Don't wear your best threads; you'll likely be wearing some of that grease by evening's end. ✉ *14 Cha Ca St., Hoan Kiem District,* ☎ *no phone. No credit cards.*

$$ ✕ **Nam Phuong.** Definitely aimed more at tourists than at a local clientele, this restaurant offers a good introduction to Vietnamese cuisine. While portions of the tasty and beautifully presented dishes (such as the beef in coconut milk served in a coconut) are disappointingly scanty, the villa setting is lovely and musicians play traditional instruments while you dine. ⊠ *19 Phan Chu Trinh St., Hoan Kiem District,* ☎ *04/824–0926. AE, MC, V.*

$$ ✕ **Seasons of Hanoi.** English manager Justin Wheatcroft has done wonders with this antiques-filled restaurant, where French elegance meets Vietnamese charm in a beautifully restored 1902 villa. The coconut and lemongrass chicken curry is a rich choice, and the fish baked in a clay pot is excellent. Some nights the place is packed with tour groups, so phone ahead. ⊠ *95B Quan Thanh St., Ba Dinh District,* ☎ *04/835–5444. AE, MC, V.*

$ ✕ **Dac Kim Bun Cha.** After souvenir shopping on Hang Bac Street, con-
★ sider having lunch at this four-story Old Quarter institution. Ordering shouldn't be hard: the restaurant serves only two dishes, and locals say both are tops. Bun cha (grilled pork patties with rice noodles) is served with heaping plates of herbs and lettuce; as a side dish, try the huge pork- and crab-filled spring rolls. ⊠ *1 Hang Manh St., Hoan Kiem District,* ☎ *no phone. No credit cards. No dinner.*

$ ✕ **Cafe Que Huong.** Popular with both locals and foreigners, this relaxed restaurant serves typical Vietnamese fare in a villa with an attached courtyard. On warm summer nights sit at an outdoor table beneath a roof of thatched palm and order the excellent, tender fried squid; wash it down with a cold beer. ⊠ *42 Tang Bat Ho St., Hai Ba Trung District,* ☎ *04/971–1444. No credit cards.*

Lodging

Hoan Kiem District

$$$$ 🏨 **Hotel Sofitel Metropole Hanoi.** The exquisitely renovated Metropole,
★ built by the French in the early 1900s, combines Old World European grandeur with modern convenience. And you can't beat the location, in the heart of Hanoi. The impeccably decorated rooms with French-style shuttered windows are luxurious if not overly spacious. ⊠ *15 Pho Ngo Quyen St., Hoan Kiem District,* ☎ *04/826–6919,* ℻ *04/826–6920. 244 rooms. 2 restaurants, 2 bars, air-conditioning, in-room safes, minibars, refrigerators, room service, pool, dry cleaning, laundry service, concierge, business services, meeting rooms, travel services, airport shuttle, car rental. AE, DC, MC, V.*

$$$ 🏨 **Hilton Hanoi Opera.** So convincingly does the design of this hotel complement that of the nearby Opera House that many newcomers take it for an original French building. The rooms are both tasteful and comfortable. Within the hotel are a bakery, a fancy Chinese restaurant, and a French bistro. What really makes this hotel stand out, however, is its location. Where else can you float in the swimming pool and look out at the Opera House? ⊠ *1 Le Thanh Tong St., Hoan Kiem District,* ☎ *04/933–0500,* ℻ *04/933–0530. 269 rooms. 3 restaurants, 2 bars, air-conditioning, in-room safes, minibars, room service, pool, health club, dry cleaning, laundry service, concierge, business services, meeting rooms. AE, D, MC, V.* 🐾

$$–$$$ 🏨 **Guoman Hotel.** Since opening in 1997, this well-run and centrally located hotel has become very popular with business travelers. The rooms are pleasant, and the service is efficient. The main restaurant, Café Paradise, turns out good and reasonably priced international fare. An outdoor café features nightly barbecues. ⊠ *83A Ly Thuong Kiet St., Hoan Kiem District,* ☎ *04/822–2800,* ℻ *04/822–2822. 149 rooms. 3 restaurants, bar, air-conditioning, in-room safes, minibars, room service, health club, laundry services. AE, DC, MC, V.*

$$–$$$ ⊞ **Hoa Binh Hotel.** In a grand old building, the Hoa Binh is poised to accommodate an upscale crowd but seems to be lacking an experienced staff. The spacious rooms are clean and have high ceilings, but they betray sloppy renovations. However, the hotel is efficient, well maintained, and wins points for nostalgic charm. Ask about discount room rates for longer stays. ⊠ *27 Ly Thuong Kiet St., Hoan Kiem District,* ☎ *04/825–3315,* FAX *04/826–9818. 88 rooms. Restaurant, bar, air-conditioning, minibars, massage, sauna, dry cleaning, laundry service, business services, car rental. AE, MC, V.*

$$–$$$ ⊞ **Melia Hanoi.** Although many of Hanoi's newly opened luxury hotels have low occupancy rates, this new, glitzy, 23-story hotel tower is consistently busy. The secret? What it lacks in charm it makes up for in price. After discounts, guests receive top-notch facilities and service at minihotel prices. One restaurant serves international cuisine; the other specializes in Chinese and Thai food and hosts a popular nightly Thai dinner buffet. ⊠ *44B Ly Thuong Kiet St., Hoan Kiem District,* ☎ *04/934–3343,* FAX *04/934–3344. 308 rooms. 2 restaurants, air-conditioning, in-room safes, minibars, room service, pool, health club, dry cleaning, laundry service, concierge, business services, meeting rooms. AE, D, MC, V.*

$$ ⊞ **Chains First Eden Hotel.** Located in the Old Quarter, this hotel is an excellent point of departure for walking tours. The rooms themselves have all the amenities, but unfortunately also have darkly oppressive furniture and curtains that may induce flashbacks to the 1970s. Deluxe rooms contain individual fax machines. All in all, although it was built in 1996, this hotel feels a bit faded. ⊠ *3A Phan Dinh Phung St., Hoan Kiem District,* ☎ *04/828–3896,* FAX *04/828–4066. 42 rooms. Restaurant, air-conditioning, minibars, laundry service, travel services. AE, DC, MC, V.*

$$ ⊞ **Saigon Hotel.** A joint venture of Saigon Tourist and the Hanoi Rail-
★ way, this property offers friendly service and, despite the concrete '60s architecture, a pleasant ambience. Rooms are standard hotel-style, bordering on the dull. The rooftop garden is a terrific place for an evening drink, but you may feel like the only one in on the secret up there. ⊠ *80 Ly Thuong Kiet St., Hoan Kiem District,* ☎ *04/826–849,* FAX *04/ 826–6631. 44 rooms. Restaurant, 2 bars, air-conditioning, in-room safes, minibars, refrigerators, room service, massage, sauna, dry cleaning, laundry service, business services, meeting rooms, travel services, car rental. AE, DC, MC, V.*

$$ ⊞ **Sunway Hotel.** Unassuming but modern, the Malaysian-invested Sun-
★ way, which opened in February 1998, is aiming its quiet charms and conveniences at the business traveler. It has triple-glazed windows, drinkable tap water, and fax-modem desk outlets in all rooms. Decor is unremarkable but ultimately acceptable, and the hotel dining room offers good international fare and theme buffets. ⊠ *19 Pham Dinh Ho St., Hoan Kiem District,* ☎ *04/971–3888,* FAX *04/971–3555. 143 rooms. Restaurant, bar, in-room safes, minibars, refrigerators, room service, exercise room, dry cleaning, laundry service, business services, meeting rooms, travel services, car rental. AE, DC, MC, V.*

$–$$ ⊞ **Galaxy Hotel.** Built in 1918, this granite-face hotel has been fully
★ renovated to accommodate business travelers and seems wholly modern. The comfortable rooms have typical hotel decor and are quieter than you'd suspect given the hotel's proximity to the bustling Old Quarter; some have garden views. ⊠ *1 Phan Dinh Phung St., Hoan Kiem District,* ☎ *04/828–2888,* FAX *04/828–2466. 60 rooms. 2 restaurants, bar, air-conditioning, in-room safes, minibars, room service, dry cleaning, laundry service, concierge, business services, meeting rooms, travel services, car rental. AE, DC, MC, V.*

$–$$ 📺 **Prince Hotel.** This smallish, comfortable minihotel has simple but elegant rooms, nice bathrooms, and an enthusiastic, English-speaking staff. The balconies block the noise from the street. It's near the train station and not too far from the city center. ⊠ *96A Hai Ba Trung St., Hoan Kiem District,* ☎ *04/824–8314,* ℻ *04/824–8323. 25 rooms. Restaurant, bar, air-conditioning, minibars, refrigerator, dry cleaning, laundry service, business services, car rental. AE, DC, MC, V.*

$–$$ 📺 **Thuy Nga Hotel.** Just a stone's throw from the central Hoan Kiem Lake, this upscale minihotel is a gem. Service is efficient and friendly, and the rooms are tastefully decorated with wooden furniture and plush carpeting. Some of the standard rooms lack windows, so be sure to ask ahead. It's worth splurging on the top-floor $70 VIP suite, which has a large terrace with a stunning view over the lake. ⊠ *4 Ba Trieu St., Hoan Kiem District,* ☎ *04/934–1256,* ℻ *04/934–1262. 20 rooms. Restaurant, air-conditioning, in-room safes, minibars, laundry service. AE, DC, MC, V.*

¢–$ 📺 **Phan Thai Hotel.** Modern minihotel conveniences, inoffensive decor, balconies, and a friendly staff make this a very decent accommodation. The top floors provide a fabulous view of Old Quarter roofs and the Long Binh train and bicycle bridge. ⊠ *44 Hang Giay St., Hoan Kiem District,* ☎ *04/824–3667,* ℻ *04/826–6677. 16 rooms. Restaurant, air-conditioning, minibars, laundry service, travel services, car rental. AE, DC, MC, V.*

¢–$ 📺 **Win Hotel.** At the top end of the budget accommodations, the Win,
★   just a short skip from Hoan Kiem Lake, is immaculate and homey all at once. Carved hardwood furniture, high ceilings, clean baths, and a fluffy dog in the lobby will make you feel at home. An added bonus is its location next to Café Nhan, which is famous for its avocado shakes and rocket-fuel coffee. ⊠ *34 Hang Hanh St., Hoan Kiem District,* ☎ *04/ 828–7371 or 04/828–7150,* ℻ *04/824–7448. 8 rooms. Air-conditioning, fans, minibars, laundry service, travel services, car rental. MC, V.*

¢   📺 **Camellia II Hotel.** This well-run, well-maintained minihotel, located near Hang Da Market in the thick of the Old Quarter, has clean, bright rooms and a friendly staff. There's a glossy feel to everything here—shiny new bathrooms, lots of glazed wood, and an abundance of satin. Although the hotel is not exactly tasteful, given the price, it's hard to quibble. ⊠ *31 Hang Dieu St., Hoan Kiem District,* ☎ *04/828– 5704,* ℻ *04/828–5777. 12 rooms. Air-conditioning, fans, minibars, laundry service. MC, V.*

¢   📺 **Lavender Hotel.** It's hard to find fault with this cheery minihotel, located around the corner from Xoi Alley—a street lined with noodle and rice shops that stay open late. The friendly manager, Mr. Thang, speaks great English and runs a tight ship: the rooms are clean and bright with big windows and sparkling bathtubs. Rooms in the front have balconies. ⊠ *3D Tong Duy Tan St., Hoan Kiem District,* ☎ *04/828– 6723,* ℻ *04/828–6046. 12 rooms. Air-conditioning, fans, minibars. AE, MC, V.*

¢   📺 **Vinh Quang Hotel.** Aside from the cheap East-West fusion decor, the Vinh Quang offers neat, efficient rooms and a great central location. Front rooms have balconies overlooking the color and activity of Hang Quat Street, one of the most charming and lively streets in the Old Quarter. Some of the smaller back rooms are windowless. ⊠ *24 Hang Quat St., Hoan Kiem District,* ☎ *04/824–3423,* ℻ *04/825– 1519. Restaurant, bar, air-conditioning, fans, minibars, laundry service, travel services. AE, MC, V.*

Around Lenin Park

$$–$$$ 📺 **Hotel Nikko Hanoi.** With its sleek and airy lobby offering a peek into a tiny Japanese garden, this 15-story hotel is a shining example of understated Japanese elegance. The rooms are both simple and luxurious, with plenty of light, tasteful wooden furniture, and large closets. The corner suites have spacious bathrooms that overlook Lenin Park across the street. ⊠ *84 Tran Nhan Tong St., Hai Ba Trung District,* ☎ *04/822–3535,* FAX *04/822–3555. 260 rooms. 3 restaurants, bar, air-conditioning, in-room safes, minibars, room service, pool, sauna, health club, dry cleaning, laundry service, concierge, business services, meeting rooms. AE, DC, MC, V.*

$$ 🖬 **Green Park Hotel.** This hotel's exterior, painted a terrifying shade of green, hides a truly charming interior, where the marble-floor lobby is always full of fresh flowers and staff members will go out of their way to make you feel at home. The rooms—some of which look toward nearby Lenin Park—are spacious, quiet, and, given the hotel's exterior, surprisingly tasteful. Front rooms have larger windows and are slightly larger than back ones, but all rooms are pleasant. The corner suites are especially wonderful, with light streaming in from all directions and large, luxurious bathrooms. The top-floor restaurant serves Asian and Western food and has a lovely view over Lenin Park and Thuyen Quang Lake. ⊠ *48 Tran Nhan Tong St., Hai Ba Trung District,* ☎ *04/822–7725,* FAX *04/822–5977. 40 rooms. Restaurant, air-conditioning, in-room safes, minibars, room service, massage, dry cleaning, laundry service, concierge, business services, meeting room, travel services. AE, DC, MC, V.*

Around the Ho Chi Minh Mausoleum/Ba Dinh District

$$$$ 🖬 **Hanoi Daewoo Hotel.** The pool here—the longest in Southeast
★ Asia—is just one example of how over-the-top this hotel is. The Daewoo offers plenty of space—from the open marble lobby to the four restaurants. Rooms are big and lavishly decorated. The main drawback is its distance from downtown; although there is a shuttle service, it doesn't run frequently enough. ⊠ *360 Kim Ma St., Ba Dinh District,* ☎ *04/831–5000,* FAX *04/831–5010. 411 rooms. 4 restaurants, 2 bars, air-conditioning, in-room safes, minibars, refrigerators, room service, pool, hot tub, sauna, aerobics, health club, dance club, dry cleaning, laundry service, concierge, business services, meeting rooms, travel services, car rental. AE, DC, MC, V.*

$$ 🖬 **Hanoi Horison Hotel.** Known as the "Emerald City" because of its impressive green glass-fronted facade, the Horison is a joint Vietnamese-Indonesian project. Rooms are luxurious, if not overly large, and are done in soothing pastels. In the spacious lobby, which has a marble floor and Indonesian artwork, there is a bakery that serves good pastries. The hotel also has an international restaurant and the Chimney Pub, which occasionally has live music. ⊠ *40 Cat Linh St., Ba Dinh District,* ☎ *04/733–0808,* FAX *04/733–0688. 350 rooms. Restaurant, bar, lobby lounge, air-conditioning, in-room safes, minibars, room service, pool, tennis court, exercise room, laundry service, business services, meeting rooms, travel services. AE, DC, MC, V.*

Around West Lake

$–$$$ 🖬 **Ho Tay Villas.** These villas, 5 km (3 mi) outside Hanoi on West Lake, offer peaceful accommodations that feel like a cross between an elegant estate and a socialist summer camp. The grounds are gorgeous, with lots of flowering trees and wild birds. Rooms are clean, with all the amenities, although perhaps a little musty from age and proximity to the lake. ⊠ *Dang Thai Mai St., Quan Tay Ho,* ☎ *04/845–2393,* FAX *04/823–2126. 75 rooms. Restaurant, bar, air-conditioning, fans, minibars, tennis court, laundry service, meeting rooms, travel services. MC, V.*

$$ 🖬 **Hanoi Club.** Well-appointed rooms at this swank private sports club offer spectacular sunset views over West Lake and include the use of the club's plush facilities. The only drawback? With two tennis courts,

squash courts, a huge gym, a golf driving range, an outdoor pool, and sailboats to keep you busy, you'll have trouble finding time to sightsee. ⊠ *76 Yen Phu St., Tay Ho District,* ☎ *04/823–8115,* FAX *04/823–8390. 12 rooms. 3 restaurants, bar, air-conditioning, in-room safes, minibars, room service, pool, massage, driving range, 2 tennis courts, health club, squash, boating, dry cleaning, laundry service, meeting rooms. AE, MC, V.*

$$ 🏨 **Meritus Westlake Hotel.** Stunning views of Truc Bach and West lakes and a central location are two of the highlights of this luxury hotel. The guest rooms are comfortable and tasteful, but what makes this hotel stand out is its swimming pool. Set on the fourth floor with a view over the neighboring lakes, the pool has a retractable roof, making it the only hotel pool in Hanoi that can be used year-round. There are two restaurants serving Chinese and Western food, as well as a top-floor bar with a great view of the city. ⊠ *1 Thanh Nien St., Ba Dinh District,* ☎ *04/823–8888,* FAX *04/829–3888. 322 rooms. 2 restaurants, bar, air-conditioning, in-room safes, minibars, room service, pool, massage, health club, dry cleaning, laundry service, concierge, business services, meeting rooms, travel services. AE, DC, MC, V.*

$ 🏨 **Dragon Hotel.** It's hard to imagine Mother Theresa, who stayed here in 1996, surrounded by so much extravagance—a many-armed statue of the Goddess of Mercy, carp-filled pools, gold dragon statues—and that's before you get into the room. With ornately carved wooden furniture, institutional carpeting, and mirrors beside the beds, the rooms are a tribute to tackiness. It's not all in bad taste, however: the staff is friendly, the rooms overlook a leafy canal, and there's a lovely terracotta patio strung with birdcages. ⊠ *9 Tay Ho Rd., Ba Dinh District,* ☎ *04/829–2954,* FAX *04/829–4745. 23 rooms. Air-conditioning, in-room safes, laundry service, travel services. AE, MC, V.*

Nightlife and the Arts

The Arts

OPERA, THEATER, AND CIRCUS

Chuong Vang Theater of Hanoi (⊠ 72 Hang Bac St., Hoan Kiem District, ☎ 04/825–7823) has performances of *cai luong–* and *tuong–* style shows on Saturday evenings. Tuong, a classical art form developed in central Vietnam, usually focuses on Vietnamese legends; music is minimal. Cai luong, the "renovated opera" that emerged in the early 20th century, is more similar to Western dramas and operas.

Hanoi National Opera (⊠ 15 Nguyen Dinh Chieu St., Ba Dinh District, ☎ 04/826–7361), a tiny, simple drama house, seats 50 guests. *Cheo* operas (folk operas with tragic and comic elements) and traditional music concerts are usually staged on Monday, Wednesday, and Friday at 8 PM, but call or stop by to confirm. This theater will arrange special performances for groups of 10 or more. Tickets cost 50,000d.

Hanoi Opera House (Nha Hat Lon; ⊠ 1 Trang Tien St., Hoan Kiem District, ☎ 04/993–0113) is worth a visit, no matter what happens to be showing. This beautifully restored French building hosts regular classical music concerts, ballets, and Western and Vietnamese operas, plus a variety of singers. Tickets usually cost between 80,000d and 150,000d.

☾ **Municipal Water Puppet Theater** (⊠ 57 Dinh Tien Hoang St., on northeast shore of Hoan Kiem Lake, Hoan Kiem District, ☎ 04/825–5450) is the best place to see the thousand-year-old art of *roi nuoc,* or water puppetry. If you're in Hanoi on a package tour, it's likely you're already scheduled for a show. If not, get your tickets early (40,000d, including a tape of the music), as they sell out. The curtain goes up at 8 every night but Monday, and there's a 9:45 AM matinee on Sunday;

occasionally there are 6 PM shows as well. There's a fee for taking pictures or videotaping.

Traditional Music Club (✉ 15B Nguyen Dinh Chieu St., Hai Ba Trung District, ☎ 04/826–7361) features cheo operas, folk songs, and traditional dancing. Shows start at 8 PM on Monday, Wednesday, and Friday and cost $4 for foreigners.

☞ **Vietnam Circus** (Rap Xiec; ✉ Tran Nhan Tong and Tran Binh Tong Sts., at north end of Lenin Park, Hoan Kiem District, ☎ 04/822–0268) offers an evening of guaranteed entertainment. In winter, bring a jacket. Shows last two hours and are held Wednesday–Sunday at 8 PM; ticket prices range from 15,000d to 30,000d.

Youth Theater (Nha Hat Tuoi Tre; ✉ 11 Ngo Thi Nham St., Hoan Kiem District, ☎ 04/825–4673) focuses mainly on contemporary drama, although music and dance are sometimes performed. About a dozen foreign theater groups perform here annually. Thursday–Sunday the theater hosts comedy acts aimed at children, for which tickets cost 30,000d.

Nightlife

BARS AND PUBS

Emotion Cybernet Cafe (✉ 52 Ly Thuong Kiet St., Hoan Kiem District, ☎ 04/934–1066) offers Internet access, cheap food and drinks, and a large-screen TV that's regularly tuned in to soccer matches.

Fat Jax Bar (✉ Somerset Grand Hanoi, 4th floor, 49 Hai Ba Trung St., Hoan Kiem District, ☎ 04/934–2342), located in the Red Onion Bistro (☞ Dining, *above*), attracts a mellow crowd of expats and businesspeople. It stays open late and has a pool table.

Jazz Club (✉ 31 Luong Van Can St., Hoan Kiem District, ☎ 04/828–7890) is owned by one of Hanoi's best-known jazz musicians, Quyen Van Minh. Nightly live jazz, performed by both local and foreign musicians, is the big draw here.

The Library Bar, Press Club (✉ 59A Ly Thai To St., Hoan Kiem District, ☎ 04/934–0888) has plush couches, an unobtrusive staff, and a menu of fancy (and expensive) cocktails and Cuban cigars. On Friday evenings the attached terrace hosts an after-work happy hour popular with Hanoi's expats; a live jazz band plays Friday nights.

Le Maquis (✉ 2A Ta Hien St., Hoan Kiem District, ☎ 04/828–2598), a tiny, casual, bar in the heart of Hanoi's backpacker district, is easy to find thanks to the many Russian Minsk motorcycles parked out front (this is the official headquarters of Hanoi's Minsk motorcycle club). This a fine place to go for a drink, a snack, and some travel advice.

Met Pub (✉ 15 Ngo Quyen St., Hoan Kiem District, ☎ 04/826–6919), on the Ly Thai To Street side of the Metropole Hotel, is where high-rolling businesspeople watch satellite TV at the wood-panel bar and middle-aged expats drink martinis and listen to live jazz.

Polite Pub (✉ 5 Ngo Bao Khanh St., Hoan Kiem District, ☎ 04/825–0959) is the hangout of choice for Hanoi's young, groovy expats, who lounge at the bar listening to rock or alternative tunes or challenge each other to games of Foosball and pool. On weekends, the Polite Pub is often packed from 9 PM to midnight, before Apocalypse Now (☞ Dance Clubs, *below*) goes into full swing.

R&R Tavern (✉ 38A Cua Dong St., Hoan Kiem District) is a Hanoi institution. The pub offers an all-American menu of nachos and burgers, draft beer, darts, and Grateful Dead classics.

Spotted Cow (✉ 23C Hai Ba Trung St., Hoan Kiem District, ☎ 04/824–1028) is the bar of choice for committed frat-brother types. Cheap draft beer, darts, and plenty of rowdy fun can be found at this small, Australian-run joint.

DANCE CLUBS

Apocalypse Now (⊠ 338 Ba Trieu St., Hai Ba Trung District, ☎ 04/821–6416) trades on the mystique of the Francis Ford Coppola movie with Vietnam War props—a helicopter coming out of one wall, murals of choppers, and more. Black paint and no windows add to the bomb-shelter atmosphere, where expatriates hunker down for drinking and dancing until almost dawn. Until 11 PM you'll be blasted with rock oldies, which give way to dance hits and techno as the night wears on. Despite—or because of—its sweaty, meat market feel, this club is very popular on weekends after 11 PM.

Dong Da Magic (⊠ 3 Thai Thinh St., Dong Da District, ☎ 04/563–0257) is not just a nightclub; it also features a 100-seat cinema, a video arcade, a high-tech disco, a party room, cheap beer and drinks, and lots of hyped-up teenagers. Multiple levels of glitzy dance rooms will keep your adrenaline pumping until the bread vendors start shouting "Banh me nao!"

Metal Night Club (⊠ 57 Cua Nam St., Dong Da District, ☎ 04/824–1975) has the stainless-steel panels and rivets to back up its name. The music, however, is not metal but Asian techno and dance hits. Local young people pack the place on weekends.

New Century (⊠ 10 Trang Thi St., Hoan Kiem District, ☎ 04/928–5285) is Hanoi's hippest new night spot, thanks to slick industrial decor, dry ice, lasers, and the best light show in town. The latest dance hits plus techno keep the mainly local crowd bopping on the dance floor.

Outdoor Activities and Sports

Biking

Vietnamese bikes and the ubiquitous Chinese Phoenix bicycles are for sale all over town for about $40 to $60. In Hanoi, cheap-o Chinese-made mountain bikes are for sale on Ba Trieu Street.

Memory Café (⊠ 33 bis Tran Hung Dao St., Hoan Kiem District) rents bicycles—as do many other backpacker-oriented cafés and minihotels.

Golf

King's Island Golf & Country Club (⊠ Dong Mo, Son Tay town, Ha Tay Province, about 45 km (28 mi) west of Hanoi, ☎ 034/834–666) is a gorgeous 18-hole lakeside course surrounded by the beautiful Tan Vien Mountains. Greens fees are $50 for guests on weekdays and $80 on weekends. Caddy fees add an extra $8, and renting clubs will set you back another $20. Guests reach the club via a scenic boat trip across a reservoir.

Lang Ha Golf Driving Range (⊠ 16A Lang Ha St., Ba Dinh District, ☎ 04/835–0909) charges diehards $10 for the chance to practice their shots.

Health Clubs and Swimming Pools

A few major hotels in Hanoi allow you to purchase one-day memberships (about $10–$17) to their exercise facilities, even if you aren't staying at the hotel: **Clark Hatch Fitness Center** (⊠ Hotel Sofitel Metropole Hanoi, 15 Ngo Quyen St., Hoan Kiem District, ☎ 04/826–6919, ext. 8881); **Daewoo Hotel Fitness Center** (⊠ Hanoi Daewoo Hotel, 360 Kim Ma St., Ba Dinh District, ☎ 04/831–5000, ext. 3309); **Meritus Lifestyle Club** (⊠ Meritus Westlake Hanoi, 1 Thanh Nien St., Ba Dinh District, ☎ 04/823–8888, ext. 5380).

Running

The best places to run in the city are around Lenin Park, off of Tran Nhan Tong Street; the Botanic Garden (☞ Around the Ho Chi Minh

Mausoleum, *above*); and Hoan Kiem Lake (☞ The Old Quarter, *above*). Early risers can join the runners on the streets between 5 and 6:30 AM, but be aware that joggers are expected to be off the streets by 7 AM.

Soccer

No sport captures the attention and hearts of the Vietnamese quite like soccer. The religiously followed semi-professional national league packs them in at the 20,000-capacity **National Stadium** (⊠ Nguyen Thai Hoc and Trinh Hoai Duc Sts., Ba Dinh District). The season runs roughly from October to May, but watch for news of international friendlies, which are occasionally played in Hanoi.

Shopping

Markets

Dong Xuan Market (Cho Dong Xuan; ⊠ Dong Xuan St., Hoan Kiem District) is a textile center, but sells food and all sorts of items for the home. **Hang Da Market** (⊠ Hang Da St., Hoan Kiem District) sells imported liquor, food, flowers, and pottery; there's also a colorful bird market. **Hom Market** (Cho Hom; ⊠ Pho Hue and Tran Xuan Soan Sts., Hai Ba Trung District), the biggest and most crowded market in town, sells everything from candles to plastic tubs. **19–12 Market** (Cho 19–12; ⊠ Ly Thuong Kiet St. between Hoa Lo and Quang Trung Sts., Hoan Kiem District), the December 19th Market, has food and items for everyday use.

Shopping Districts

The area north of Hoan Kiem Lake is bustling with tiny shops carrying everything from shoes to clothes to antique timepieces. Hanoi is Vietnam's fine-arts capital, and running along the southern part of Hoan Kiem Lake, where Hang Khay Street turns into Trang Tien Street, are several arts-and-crafts galleries and antiques shops (note, however, that it is illegal to take antiques out of the country without permission from the government). You can find paintings and watercolors, as well as crafts such as lacquerware and puppets, on Trang Tien and Hang Khai streets. Any number of shops along Hang Gai and Duc Loi streets, not far from Hoan Kiem Lake, can inexpensively produce custom-made clothes. Hang Gai is also good for souvenirs and antiques. Hand-embroidered linens are found on Hang Gai Street, which turns into Hang Bong Street. Hang Bong is the place to find trendy fashions from Hong Kong and Korea. Most souvenir and silk shops in the tourist area of the Old Quarter are open until about 10 PM on weekends.

Specialty Shops

ART

When buying art in Vietnam, be careful of fakes. Paintings by Vietnam's most famous painters—Bui Xuan Phai, Nguyen Tu Nghiem, and Le Thiet Cuong—are widely copied. **Apricot Gallery** (⊠ 40B Hang Bong St., Hoan Kiem District, ☎ 04/828–8965). **Co Xanh** (Green Palm Gallery; ⊠ 51 Hang Gai St., Hoan Kiem District, ☎ 04/826–7116). **Hanoi Studio** (⊠ 13 Trang Tien St., Hoan Kiem District, ☎ 04/934–4433). **Mai Gallery** (⊠ 3B Phan Huy Chu St., Hoan Kiem District, ☎ 04/825–1225). **Red River Gallery** (⊠ 71A Nguyen Du St., Hai Ba Trung District, ☎ 04/822–9064). **Salon Natasha** (⊠ 30 Hang Bong St., Hoan Kiem District, ☎ 04/826–1387). **Trang An Gallery** (⊠ 15 Hang Buom St., Hoan Kiem District, ☎ 04/826–9480). **Van Gallery** (⊠ 25–27 Trang Tien St., Hoan Kiem District, ☎ 04/825–1532).

CLOTHING AND ACCESSORIES

Some international fashion boutiques like Louis Vuitton have sprung up in Hanoi's top hotels. It's possible to have clothes made to order with enough time (one day to three weeks, depending on what you want made and how busy the tailor is). Keep in mind that you will need to return to have the clothes fitted. Good tailors include the following: **Cao Minh** (✉ 47 Tran Hung Dao St., Hoan Kiem District, ☎ 04/824–2727); **Co** (✉ 18 Nha Tho St., Hoan Kiem District, ☎ 04/828–9925); **Jade** (✉ 219 Hang Bong St., Hoan Kiem District, ☎ 04/828–8335); **Le Minh Silk** (✉ 79–111 Hang Gai St., Hoan Kiem District, ☎ 04/828–8723); **Phuong Anh** (✉ 56 Hang Hom St., Hoan Kiem District, ☎ 04/826–1556).

La Boutique and The Silk (✉ 10F Dinh Liet St., Hoan Kiem District, ☎ 04/934–323; ✉ 6 Nha Tho St., Hoan Kiem District, ☎ 04/928–5368) has a colorful selection of Laotian silk scarves and clothing made from ethnic minority fabrics. **Ipa Nima** (✉ 30B Nguyen Huu Huan St., Hoan Kiem District, ☎ 04/934–0876) carries funky and fashionable handbags, as well as other accessories. **Kenly Silk** (✉ 108 Hang Gai St., Hoan Kiem District, ☎ 04/826–7236) sells silk and linen clothes. **Khai Silk** (✉ 121 Nguyen Thai Hoc St., Ba Dinh District, ☎ 04/823–3508; ✉ 96 Hang Gai St., Hoan Kiem District, ☎ 04/823–3508) is where the Princess of Thailand shops for fine silk clothing and linens. **Song** (✉ 7 Nha Tho St., Hoan Kiem District, ☎ 04/828–9650) is a beautiful French-owned boutique stocked with women's clothing in silk, cotton, and linen.

EMBROIDERY

Tan My (✉ 66 Hang Gai St., Hoan Kiem District, ☎ 04/825–1579) is one of the most famous embroidery shops in Hanoi. **Tuyet Lan** (✉ 65 Hang Gai St., Hoan Kiem District, ☎ 04/825–7967) does beautiful embroidery, especially children's bed sheets and baby clothes.

HANDICRAFTS

Craft Link (✉ 43 Van Mieu St., Ba Dinh District, ☎ 04/843–7710) has a terrific selection of crafts, proceeds from which go to the ethnic minority women who make them. **Craft Window** (✉ 99 Nguyen Thai Hoc St., Ba Dinh District, ☎ 04/733–5286; ✉ 6 Nha Chung St., Hoan Kiem District, ☎ 04/828–9477) stocks ethnic minority crafts, beaded handbags, and beautiful embroidered greeting cards. **KAF** (✉ 318 Ba Trieu St., Hoan Kiem District, ☎ 04/822–0022) sells quality reproductions of antique Buddha statues and lacquerware. **Lan Vietnamese Handicrafts** (✉ 26 Au Trieu St., Ba Dinh District, ☎ 04/828–9278) carries patchwork quilts made by youngsters with disabilities.

Hanoi A to Z

Arriving and Departing

BY AIRPLANE

Many international airlines fly into Hanoi's **Noi Bai International Airport** (☎ 04/886–5318), about 35 km (22 mi) north of the city. **Vietnam Airlines** (✉ 1 Quang Trung St., Hoan Kiem District, ☎ 04/825–0888 or 04/832–0320) serves Danang, Dien Bien Phu, Ho Chi Minh City, Hue, Nha Trang, and Vinh. **Pacific Airlines** (✉ 100 Le Duan St., Dong Da District, ☎ 04/518–1503) is Vietnam's smaller domestic carrier.

Vietnam Airlines runs bus service from the airport into Hanoi; the trip takes about 40 minutes, and tickets are 30,000d. Airport Taxi has a booth in the airport terminal; the trip into central Hanoi cost $10 or less. Minibuses to the airport depart from the Vietnam Airlines office (☞ *above*); book a seat in advance. Or call **Airport Taxi** (☎ 04/873–3333), which will get you to Noi Bai for $8.

BY BUS

Buses may be dirt cheap in Vietnam, but they are also uncomfortable and unreliable. For information, contact **Hanoi Bus Company** (✉ 32 Nguyen Cong Tru St., Hai Ba Trung District, ☎ 04/971–4590). **Rainbow Services** (✉ 42 Nha Chung St., Hoan Kiem District, ☎ 04/826–8752), a popular tour company, will take you all the way from Hanoi to Ho Chi Minh City on an air-conditioned bus for $30. **Sinh Café** (✉ 56 Hang Be St., Hoan Kiem District, ☎ 04/824–2457) operates tour buses between Hanoi and Ho Chi Minh City. A $33–$38 open ticket allows you to break up your journey at several points—including Nha Trang, Dalat, Hoi An, and Hue—between the two cities.

Gia Bat Bus Station (Ben Xe Gia Bat; ✉ Giai Phong St., Hai Ba Trung District, ☎ 04/864–1467) serves most southern routes. **Gia Lam Bus Station** (Ben Xe Gia Lam; ✉ Ben Xe St., Gia Lam District, ☎ 04/827–1529) serves northern routes. **Kim Ma Bus Station** (Ben Xe Kim Ma; ✉ Nguyen Thai Hoc and Giang Vo Sts., Ba Dinh District, ☎ 04/845–2846) provides service to the northwest.

BY CAR OR MINIBUS

It's unlikely that you'll arrive in or leave Hanoi by car, but if you want to hire a car or minibus and driver, contact any hotel, large travel agency such as **Vietnam Tourism,** or one of the tourist cafés (☞ Tour Operators and Travel Agencies, *below*).

BY TRAIN

The ticket office at the main Hanoi train station, **Ga Hanoi** (✉ Le Duan St., at the west end of Tran Hung Dao St., Hoan Kiem District, ☎ 04/825–3949), is open 7:30–11:30 AM and 1:30–3:30 PM. There's a special counter where foreigners buy tickets, and some of the schedules are even in English. Another, smaller train station, up the tracks from the main one, serves northern routes.

Trains leave four times daily for Ho Chi Minh City (soft berth $139, 40 hrs), but only one is an express (32 hrs). It stops at major cities such as Vinh, Hue, Danang, and Nha Trang. Purchase a day in advance to ensure a seat. Other destinations include Lang Son ($4, twice daily, 5 hrs); Lao Cai (hard berth $18, weekend-only soft sleeper $25; daily, 11 hrs); and Haiphong ($4, seven times daily, 2 hrs).

Getting Around

BY BICYCLE

Bikes can be rented at hotels and cafés in the center of town for around 10,000d per day. Make sure the bike you get has a lock.

BY CYCLO

Cyclos are a good way to get around Hanoi; the fare for a short ride should run under 10,000d. Bear in mind that taxis charge 14,000d for two kilometers and bargain accordingly. And make sure you're both on the same wavelength when talking money: unsuspecting travelers have been known to agree to a fare of 10,000d, only to have the cyclo driver later claim the agreed-upon figure was $10.

BY MOTORBIKE

Motorbike taxis, known as xe om, are one way to get around—if you're brave. They'll find you. Many hotels and tourist cafés also rent motorcycles (☞ Vietnam A to Z, *below*). Try the **Mai Linh Café** (✉ 22 Cau Go St., Hoan Kiem District, ☎ 04/824–4554) or the **Memory Café** (✉ 33 bis Tran Hung Dao St., Hoan Kiem District, ☎ 04/826–5854).

BY TAXI

The moment you step into a cab, the meter (all cabs in Hanoi should be metered) reads 14,000d or 15,000d; after that rates run about

5,600d per km (½ mi). A trip across town will cost you about 25,000d. Hail a cab (a good place is outside major hotels) or order a taxi by phone from the following: **Airport Taxi** (☎ 04/873–3333); **City Taxi** (☎ 04/822–2222); **Red Taxi** (☎ 04/856–8686); **Taxi CP** (☎ 04/824–1999); and **Taxi PT** (☎ 04/856–5656).

Contacts and Resources

CURRENCY EXCHANGE

Most major international and large national banks in Hanoi have a currency exchange. Hotels, too, can change money, as can some jewelry shops. But don't change money with the black-market money changers who gather around the General Post Office (GPO) and will try to shortchange you. Many of Hanoi's shops and upscale restaurants accept both dollars and dong.

Major banks in Hanoi include the following: **ABN-AMRO Bank** (✉ 360 Kim Ma St., Daeha Business Center, Ba Dinh District, ☎ 04/831–5250, FAX 04/831–6874), **ANZ Bank** (Australia New Zealand Bank; ✉ 14 Le Thai To St., Hoan Kiem District, ☎ 04/825–8190, FAX 04/825–8189), **Bank of America** (✉ 27 Ly Thuong Kiet St., Hoan Kiem District, ☎ 04/824–9316, FAX 04/824–9322), **Citibank** (✉ 17 Ngo Quyen St., Hoan Kiem District, ☎ 04/825–1950, FAX 04/824–3960), **Deutsche Bank** (✉ 53 Quang Trung St., Hoan Kiem District, ☎ 04/826–8554, FAX 04/826–8652), **Standard Chartered Bank** (✉ 49 Hai Ba Trung St., 8th floor, Hoan Kiem District, ☎ 04/825–8970, FAX 04/825–8880), **VID Public Bank** (✉ 2 Ngo Quyen St., Hoan Kiem District, ☎ 04/826–6953, FAX 04/826–8228), and **Vietcom Bank** (Bank for Foreign Trade of Vietnam; ✉ 23 Phan Chu Trinh St., Hoan Kiem District, ☎ 04/934–3137, FAX 04/824–1395).

EMBASSIES

Australia (✉ 8 Dao Tan St., Van Phuc Compound, Ba Dinh District, ☎ 04/831–7755, FAX 04/831–7709). **Canada** (✉ 31 Hung Vuong St., Ba Dinh District, ☎ 04/823–5500, FAX 04/823–5333). **New Zealand** (✉ 32 Hang Bai St., Hoan Kiem District, ☎ 04/824–1481, FAX 04/824–1480). **United Kingdom** (✉ 31 Hai Ba Trung St., Hoan Kiem District, ☎ 04/825–2510, FAX 04/826–5762). **United States** (✉ 7 Lang Ha St., Ba Dinh District, ☎ 04/843–1500, FAX 04/843–1510).

EMERGENCIES

Ambulance (☎ 15). **Fire** (☎ 14). **Police** (☎ 13).

Medical facilities in Hanoi are not up to international standards. A few foreign-run medical clinics offer basic treatment—at Western prices—and can arrange for emergency medical evacuation to Singapore or elsewhere in the region. **Emergency Viet Duc Hospital** (Benh Vien Viet Duc; ✉ 40 Trang Thi St., Hoan Kiem District, ☎ 04/825–5956). **Hanoi Family Medical Practice** (✉ A-1 Bldg., Van Phuc Diplomatic Compound, Suite 109–112, Kim Ma Rd., Ba Dinh District, ☎ 04/843–0748; 09/040–1919 for emergency mobile phone). **International SOS** (✉ 31 Hai Ba Trung St., Hoan Kiem District, ☎ 04/934–0555). **Vietnam International Hospital** (Benh Vien Quoc Te Viet Nam; ✉ Phuong Mai Rd., next to Bach Mai Hospital, Hai Ba Trung District, ☎ 04/574–0740; 04/574–1111 for emergencies).

ENGLISH-LANGUAGE BOOKSTORES

Look for books in English at the following: **The Gioi Publishers Bookshop** (✉ 46 Tran Hung Dao St., Hoan Kiem District, ☎ 04/825–1289), **Hieu Sach Hanoi** (✉ 34 Trang Tien St., near the Sofitel Metropole, Hoan Kiem District, ☎ 04/824–1615), **State Bookshop** (✉ 44 Trang Tien St., Hoan Kiem District, ☎ 04/825–4282), and **Tien Phong** (✉ 175 Nguyen Thai Hoc St., Ba Dinh District, ☎ 04/943–2337).

MAIL

The **General Post Office** (Buu Dien Trung Vong; ⊠ 75 Dinh Tien Hoang St., Hoan Kiem District, ☎ 04/825–7036) has phone, fax, and express-mail services (open daily 6:30 AM–8 PM). Dozens of branch post offices dot the city.

TOUR OPERATORS AND TRAVEL AGENCIES

The following travel agencies offer visitor information, transportation and hotel bookings, car and bus rentals, guided tours, private tour guides, and visa extensions. Tourist cafés, which are mainly walk-in businesses, have many of the same services but usually at lower prices.

Buffalo Tours (⊠ 11 Hang Muoi St., Hoan Kiem District, ☎ 04/828–0702) conducts kayaking and trekking tours. The French-run **Exotissimo Travel** (⊠ 26 Tran Nhat Duat St., Hoan Kiem District, ☎ 04/828–2150, FAX 04/828–2146) handles upscale tours. **Green Bamboo Café** (⊠ 2B Trang Thi St., Hoan Kiem District, ☎ 04/824–9179, FAX 04/826–4949) offers some of the best tour services in the city. **Hanoi Tourism** (⊠ 18 Ly Thuong Kiet St., Hoan Kiem District, ☎ 04/826–1627, FAX 04/824–1101; marketing office ⊠ 1 Ba Trieu St., Hoan Kiem District, ☎ 04/824–2330 or 04/826–5244, FAX 04/825–6418) is a big state-run agency. **Queen Cafe** (⊠ 65 Hang Bac St., Hoan Kiem District, ☎ 04/826–0860, FAX 04/826–0300) currently wears the Hanoi tourist-café crown. **Rainbow Services** (⊠ 42 Nha Chung St., Hoan Kiem District, ☎ 04/826–8752, FAX 04/826–4949) is one of the best budget tourist cafés in town. **Saigon Tourist** (⊠ 55B Phan Chu Trinh St., Hoan Kiem District, ☎ 04/825–0923, FAX 04/825–1174 for tours) is the largest agency in Vietnam. **TF Handspan–TF Travel** (⊠ 116 Hang Bac St., Hoan Kiem District, ☎ 04/828–1996) is a well-run tour company that offers kayaking, rafting, and adventure tours. **Vietnam Tourism** (⊠ 30A Ly Thuong Kiet St., Hoan Kiem District, ☎ 04/825–6916, FAX 04/825–7583) is a large state-run agency.

SIDE TRIPS FROM HANOI

Once you have seen the sights in Hanoi, it's time to jump off into the countryside—the "real" Vietnam—on day trips, using the city as your base. Less than an hour out of the capital in any direction brings you to stretches of rice paddies interrupted only by villages and jagged rocky outcrops. Trips organized by Hanoi's tourist cafés and travel agencies are usually the most time-efficient way to see this region.

Perfume Pagoda

60 km (37 mi) southwest of Hanoi.

Considered Vietnam's most important Buddhist site, the Perfume Pagoda (Chua Huong) is the largest of a cluster of shrines carved into the limestone of the Huong Tich Mountains. In the late spring the trails leading up to the shrines are clogged with thousands making their pilgrimage to pray to Quan Am, the goddess of mercy and compassion.

From the shores of the Yen River, you are ferried to the site, 4 km (2½ mi) away, on sampans that seem to be made of flimsy aluminum. After a spectacular ride past boats laden with fruit and farmers at work in their fields, you are let off at Chua Tien Chu. From there, follow a stone path uphill to the various pagodas and shrines. Three kilometers (2 miles) later you reach the Perfume Pagoda.

Hoa Lu

113 km (70 mi) south of Hanoi.

Hoa Lu, which in the 10th century became the first capital of independent Vietnam, is known as "Halong Bay without the water." The stunning natural beauty—limestone karsts rising from green rice paddies—and the historic interest of Hoa Lu's status as a 10th-century seat of power make for a worthwhile excursion. Much of the ancient capital of Hoa Lu has been destroyed or has succumbed to the forces of nature, but the two sanctuaries that do survive hint at the tastes of the emperor and his court.

Many travel agencies in Hanoi arrange tours to Hoa Lu that include entry tickets, lunch, and a boat ride on a lovely river that winds between terraced rice paddies and passes through historic limestone grottoes. It takes less than two hours to get there. You can also rent a car or take the train. If you're en route to Hue, you can stop off at nearby Ninh Binh, visit Hoa Lu, and reboard the next night for the rest of the trip.

Halong Bay and Cat Ba Island

★ *160 km (99 mi) east of Hanoi, 55 km (34 mi) northeast of Haiphong.*

Halong Bay's 3,000 islands of dolomite and limestone cover a 1,500-square-km (579-square-mi) area extending across the Gulf of Tonkin nearly to the Chinese border. According to Chinese legend this breathtaking land- and seascape (similar to the Guilin area of China) was formed by a giant dragon that came barreling out of the mountains toward the ocean. Geologists are more likely to attribute the formations to sedimentary limestone that formed here between 300 and 500 million years ago, in the Paleozoic Era. Boat trips through Halong Bay are the main attraction; they are often part of organized tours from the capital, and can be arranged by hotels or travel agencies in Hanoi or in the town of Halong City.

One of Halong Bay's most remarkable formations is **Cat Ba Island,** 420 square km (162 square mi) of wildly steep spines of mountains, narrow valleys and waterfalls, lush wetlands, golden beaches, and one of Vietnam's most beautiful national parks. In 1938 a French archaeologist found traces of an ancient fishing culture on the island dating from the end of the Neolithic Era. Today the population of more than 12,000 continues to subsist on fishing and rice and fruit cultivation, but tourism is quickly becoming Cat Ba's new cash crop. The park was established in 1986 to protect about half of the island. Included in these ecosystems are tropical evergreen forests, 15 kinds of mammals (including wild boars and hedgehogs), 200 species of fish, 21 species of birds, and 640 species of plants.

Hiring a car and driver in Hanoi or going with an organized tour (the fees are prepaid and a hike is mapped out) are the easiest ways to visit the area. Many of the roads have been upgraded in the last few years, and travel to Halong Bay now takes just three and a half hours, making it a possible (albeit tiring) day trip from Hanoi. However, you'll probably want to stay overnight in Halong City if your destination is Halong Bay; those going only to Cat Ba Island should go to Haiphong, the port city 100 km (62 mi) east of Hanoi, where daily ferries make the two- to four-hour trip.

Lodging

$$$ ⚑ **Halong I Hotel.** The grande dame of Halong properties, this French
★   colonial restoration is evocative of a more sublime era. Don't expect
     fawning service here. Thankfully the whole place is quiet—except for

the strains of karaoke wafting up from the roadside below. Try to book the Catherine Deneuve Room, where the French actress stayed while filming *Indochine.* ⊠ *Halong Rd.,* ☎ *033/846–320,* FAX *033/846–318. 23 rooms. Restaurant. AE, MC, V.*

$$$ 🏨 **Halong Plaza Hotel.** This modern luxury hotel has a spacious front lobby with a glass-front entryway looking out onto the bay. Most of the rooms, too, have views of the bay, though some face the more industrial back side. ⊠ *8 Halong Rd.,* ☎ *033/845–810,* FAX *033/846–867. 200 rooms. 2 restaurants, bar, in-room safes, minibars, no-smoking room, pool, massage, exercise room, dance club, laundry service, business services, meeting rooms. AE, MC, V.*

$$$ 🏨 **Heritage Halong.** This eight-floor, glitzy, international hotel soaks up much of the package-tour business in Halong Bay. Rooms are clean; those on the top floors in front have lovely views of the distant islands. ⊠ *88 Halong Rd.,* ☎ *033/846–888,* FAX *033/846–999. 101 rooms. Restaurant, café, pool. AE, MC, V.*

$ 🏨 **Vuon Dao Hotel.** Ask for one of the top-floor rooms with a view of the sea at this three-story hotel run by Halong Tourist Company, the state-run travel agency. Breakfast is included in the room rate. ⊠ *Halong Rd.,* ☎ *033/846–427,* FAX *033/846–287. 77 rooms. Restaurant, air-conditioning. MC, V.*

Sapa

35 km (22 mi) south of Lao Cai town, 170 km (105 mi) northeast of Dien Bien Phu, 350 km (217 mi) northwest of Hanoi.

Ringed by Vietnam's tallest peaks, Sapa is an enchanting hill-tribe village that has become the de facto tourist capital of the far northwest. It is part of the northwestern province of Lao Cai, which means "town of sand," and a 90-minute drive from the provincial capital—a dreary border town of 30,000 people also known as Lao Cai. A pilgrimage to Sapa offers a glimpse of the country's most breathtaking mountain scenery as well as some of its ethnic minority cultures—the H'mong, the Dao, the Tay, the Giay, the Muong, the Thai, the Hoa (ethnic Chinese), and the Xa Pho. The hill tribes cultivate rice and ginger and hunt wild game by traditional methods; they continue as they always have to worship the soul of rice, their ancestors, and the spirits of earth, wind, fire, rivers, and mountains. To see them in their traditional style of dress—layers of indigo-dyed, brilliantly embroidered cotton; elaborate headdresses; and silver adornments—is to feel yourself caught in a time warp. Every Saturday there's a colorful market in Sapa; be sure to plan your trip so that it coincides.

The French dubbed the area around Sapa the "Tonkinese Alps." In 1922 colonial authorities displaced the minority residents and began building villas for themselves in the town, turning it into a kind of health resort and retreat from Hanoi's heat and the depot for a nearby mine. Between the end of French colonial rule in 1954 and national reunification 22 years later, the North Vietnamese government made weak attempts to grant the ethnic minorities political representation and the same constitutional rights as the majority Kinh population—provided they took up the struggle against the U.S.-backed Saigon regime. Since 1975 the government has pursued "integration" programs, providing free limited education and health care.

The protection of Sapa's cultural diversity and the environment seems to have little place on the state agenda, however. It appears that tourism may corrupt the integrity of the local populace and upset the area's fragile ecology. Some of the minority groups practice slash-and-burn agriculture, and along with the depredations of two centuries of outside interests, this has already reduced the virgin forest to a mere 12-square-km (4½-square-mi) area. Further destruction would be tragic, considering the area's remarkable natural gifts.

Sapa is part of the Nui Hoang Lien Nature Reserve, a mountainous 7,400-acre landscape covered by temperate and subtemperate forests. The reserve provides a habitat for 56 species of mammals—including tigers, leopards, monkeys, and bears—and an impressive 150 species of birds (don't expect a bird-watching bonanza, however). Among the area's geological resources are marble; calcium carbonate; and kaolinite, or China clay, used in the making of porcelain. Guided walking tours of the nature reserve are recommended and are easily arranged through hotels in town.

Sapa is also the departure point for Mt. Fansipan, Vietnam's tallest peak at 10,372 ft. Hiking the mountain requires little technical expertise, but it does take three or four days, as you must depart from Sapa and hike down into the valley, then hike back up the other side. Bring your own tent and sleeping bag and warm clothes. You'll also want an experienced guide to help you navigate the wet, chilly mountainside and suggest the best route and places to camp. Hiking Fansipan is serious business and should not be taken lightly. Ask for details at the Auberge Hotel or the Green Bamboo Hotel (☞ Dining and Lodging, *below*).

One of the best ways to get to Sapa is with a tour organized by a travel agency or tourist café in Hanoi. By car, the trip takes 10 hours on Highway 1 to Lao Cai, then 90 minutes from Lao Cai on Highway 4. If you don't want to lose a whole day driving to Sapa, take the overnight train to Lao Cai. Most comfortable is the "luxury" train on Friday night (11 hrs; departs at 8:15 PM), on which you get a soft sleeper in a four-person compartment for about $25. Tickets cannot be purchased more than two days in advance, so go to Ga Hanoi (☞ Hanoi A to Z, *above*) Thursday morning. Minibuses can take you from the Lao Cai train station to Sapa (35 km/22 mi; 25,000d). You can buy your return ticket in Sapa (and check train and bus schedules) at the small post office next to Phan Xi Pan Hotel. Unfortunately, the night train from Lao Cai to Hanoi has only hard sleepers. Buses from Sapa to the Lao Cai train station depart at 6:30 AM and 2 PM, but you can also share a bus or jeep with other travelers and leave at the time you want.

Dining and Lodging

$$ ✕☱ Hotel Victoria Sapa. The premier hotel in Sapa, the Victoria caters to the fancy of its guests. The hotel, a French-designed pleasure palace on a hilltop overlooking town, has spacious, clean, and tastefully decorated rooms with inviting bathtubs, satellite TVs, and heaps of amenities. A posh restaurant serving European and Vietnamese cuisine adorns the main hall, as does a gift shop for those who don't want the hassle of bargaining for souvenirs. The hotel also has its own tour package in which guests stay in private luxury sleeper and dining cars on the train to and from Hanoi. ⊠ Overlooking town, ☎ 020/871–522, ℻ 020/871–539. 77 rooms. Restaurant, bar, air-conditioning, room service, pool, sauna, tennis court, laundry service. AE, DC, MC, V. ✍

¢ ✕☱ Auberge Hotel. The best thing going in Sapa, this popular hotel
★ has exquisite views of the mountains. Rooms, particularly on the third floor, are cozy and clean and have functioning fireplaces. Breakfast is by far the top culinary event in the restaurant: you can feast on standard Vietnamese fare, including excellent spring rolls, while soaking up rays out on the terrace. The owner, Mr. Trung, and his son can help with all sorts of travel information. Reservations are a must. One major fault: Mr. Trung can't say "no," so overbooking is a serious problem. He rarely leaves anyone in the lurch, though you may find your-

self with a room in the annex or in another minihotel altogether. ⊠ *Main road,* ☎ *020/871–243,* ℻ *020/871–282. 12 rooms. Restaurant, laundry service, travel services, car rental. No credit cards.*

¢ ⊞ **The Green Bamboo.** Run by the Green Bamboo Café in Hanoi, this mountainside accommodation has small, sunny rooms decked out with satellite televisions, new but simple furniture, and private bathrooms. If you're looking for a quiet getaway, however, stay elsewhere on weekends. Reservations, which are recommended, can be made at the Green Bamboo Café in Hanoi (⊠ 2B Trang Thi St., Hoan Kiem District, ☎ 04/824–9179, ℻ 04/826–4949, ✎). ⊠ *Main road,* ☎ *020/ 871–411. 28 rooms. Bar, café, laundry service, travel services. No credit cards.*

HUE

Updated by
Craig Thomas

108 km (67 mi) north of Danang, 140 km (87 mi) north of Hoi An, 1,097 km (680 mi) north of Ho Chi Minh City, 689 km (427 mi) south of Hanoi.

Bisected by the Perfume River and 13 km (8 mi) inland from the South China Sea in the foothills of the Annamite Mountains (Truong Son Mountains), Hue (pronounced *hway*) stands as a reminder of Vietnam's imperial past. The seat of 13 Nguyen dynasty emperors between 1802 and 1945, Hue was once Vietnam's splendid Imperial City. Although it was devastated by the French in the 19th century and in the 1940s, and by fighting between the North Vietnamese and the Americans in 1968, the monument-speckled former capital has a war-ravaged beauty. Imperial splendor may be long gone, but a walk by the old citadel and into the emperor's palace can still conjure up images of eras past.

As early as the 2nd century BC, Hue was home to rulers: it was the seat of command for the Chinese Han army and was called Tay Quyen. By the 2nd century AD, Hue was captured by local chieftains, who renamed it K'ui Sou. Between the 10th and 14th centuries, the Cham and the Vietnamese fought for its control, and by the 15th century, the Vietnamese had succeeded and renamed it Phu Xuan. In 1558 Hue became the capital of a region ruled by Lord Nguyen Hoang, which established control of South Vietnam by the Nguyen lords. (During this time, the Nguyen lords, who controlled South Vietnam, and the Trinh lords, who controlled North Vietnam—fought for control of the whole country.)

Late in the 18th century, the Nguyen lords were temporarily defeated in the Tay Son Rebellion, which arose from a general sentiment of discontent with both Nguyen and Trinh rule. The Tay Son emperor, Quang Trung, ruled in Hue from 1786 to 1802, when the ousted Lord Nguyen Anh returned, with French backing. At the same time, Nguyen Anh captured Hanoi from the Tay Son rebels, who had defeated the Trinh and the Chinese-backed Ly dynasty. In 1802, Nguyen Anh anointed himself Emperor Gia Long and made Hue the capital of a newly united Vietnam. Twelve Nguyen dynasty emperors followed him to the throne until the monarchy was abolished in the mid-20th century. Their impressive tombs and pagodas and the Imperial City are reminders of the important role Hue once played in the nation's affairs.

It was under Emperor Gia Long's rule that the city's architectural identity was established—and the prospect of French colonial rule in Vietnam initiated. With guidance, ironically from the French architect Olivier de Puymanel, Gia Long designed and built the city's surrounding fortress (the citadel), in the style of the Forbidden City in Beijing. The result was a fairly modern structure that looked centuries old.

In the 1830s, voices of dissent arose against the French presence in Vietnam. The French responded by attacking Hue in 1833 (they had been looking for an excuse to assert their claims to the country in exchange for assisting Gia Long to the throne) and making the country—particularly Tonkin and Annam—into a protectorate. During this time, a Western-style city was established across the river from the citadel to accommodate the French forces; some of these old French colonial buildings are still standing. In 1885, after repeated disagreements between the French and the emperors of Hue, the French pillaged the Royal Court, burned the Royal Library, and replaced Emperor Ham Nghi with the more docile Emperor Dong Khanh.

It was the Tet Offensive of 1968, however, that really destroyed large parts of the Imperial City. During one of the fiercest battles of the Vietnam War, the Vietcong forces occupied the city for 25 days, flying their flag in defiance and massacring thousands of suspected Saigon Government sympathizers. The South Vietnamese and the Americans moved in to recapture the city with a massive land and air attack and in doing so further destroyed many of Hue's architectural landmarks. Overall, more than 10,000 people died in the fighting, many of them civilians.

Though much of the Imperial City was reduced to rubble, many sections still exist, and Hue's main draw continues to be the remnants of its glorious past. Today tourists keep the city thriving. There are many hotels and numerous cyclo drivers who can give you a tour of the Imperial City for only 50,000d. On top of it all, Hue is known for its outstanding cuisine.

Exploring Hue

Hue itself is quite small, and you can easily get around the Imperial City on foot. To visit the sprawling, majestic, imperial tombs down the Perfume River—the Tomb of Tu Duc and the Tomb of Minh Mang—and the Thien Mu Pagoda on the outskirts of Hue, you need to go by boat or car—or by motorbike or bicycle, if you are more adventurous.

A Good Walk

You'll probably be staying on the right (east) bank of the Perfume River, so you should begin your walk at the Phu Xuan Bridge and Le Loi Street. Cross the bridge to the west bank, turn left on Tran Hung Dao Street, and walk toward the entrance to **The Citadel,** which is circled by a moat and ramparts. Along the way you'll see on your left the 122-ft **Flag Tower.** The citadel contains the Imperial City (where mandarins and the royal family conducted affairs of state), within which is the **Forbidden Purple City,** where the royal family lived. Cross the moat and pass through the Ngan Gate (Cua Ngan). After entering, you'll see four of the Nine Holy Cannons on your right. These bronze cannons commemorate the four seasons; the other five depict the Chinese elements—earth, water, wood, metal, and fire. Make your way along to the entrance of the **Imperial City.**

Enter this mostly ruined complex through the Noontime, or Royal, Gate (Cua Ngo Mon) and take an immediate left toward the **Nine Dynastic Urns,** symbols of the formidable Nguyen dynasty. Head back toward the entrance and turn left across the Golden Water Bridge (Trung Dao Bridge), once used only by the emperor. Straight ahead is one of the few intact structures in the Imperial City: the intricately decorated **Palace of Supreme Harmony.**

Exit the palace through the back of the gift shop. On either side of the path leading to the entrance of the Forbidden Purple City are the Halls of the Mandarins, where those court officials dressed in special attire before paying homage to the emperor. Through the courtyard in front of the halls, you can see the vast empty expanse that once was the Forbidden Purple City. To your right is the Royal Theater, or Festival Hall, which is largely intact; behind it stands the partially restored **Royal Library.**

Heading east from the Royal Theater, exit the Imperial Enclosure through the beautiful and ornate Eastern Gate (Hien Nhan Mon). Make a right on Doan Thi Diem Street and then take the first left on Le Truc Street to get to the **Imperial Museum.**

Make a left out of the Imperial Museum and then another left onto Dinh Tien Hoang Street. Follow the street through what feels like a quiet suburban residential neighborhood for about 1 km (¾ mi). At the intersection with Tinh Tam Street is Tinh Tam Lake, overgrown with lotus flowers in spring and summer. Across Dinh Tien Hoang Street is another lake, Tang Tau, with a small island containing the Ngoc Huong Pagoda.

TIMING

This walk should take about four hours at a leisurely pace. Go in early morning or late afternoon to avoid the midday heat.

Sights to See

The Citadel (Kinh Thanh). Seeking to secure his empire, Emperor Gia Long built this 1½-square-mi citadel with a 65-ft-wide moat in the heart of Hue in 1805. Gia Long was assisted in the design by the French architect Olivier de Puymanel, and the result is a combination of French military architect Vauban's work and classical Chinese architecture. Enclosed in the citadel is the **Imperial City, or Imperial Enclosure** (Hoang Thanh), where official government activity took place. Within it is the **Forbidden Purple City** (☞ *below*), which was the private sanctuary of the emperors and their families. ⊠ *Free.*

Flag Tower (Cot Co). This 122-ft structure, Vietnam's tallest flagpole, is one of the symbols of Hue. It was originally built in 1809 to serve as the Imperial Palace's central observation post. Like much of Hue, it has a history of being destroyed: it was toppled by a typhoon in 1904, rebuilt in 1915, destroyed again in 1947, and built anew in 1949. When the city was occupied by the Vietcong during the Tet Offensive of 1968, the National Liberation Front flag flew from the Flag Tower. The interior is closed to the public. ⊠ *In front of 23 Thang 8 St., facing Ngo Mon Gate.*

Forbidden Purple City (Tu Cam Thanh). This royal enclave was almost entirely destroyed during the Vietnam War and is now largely a wide-open field. In its day it housed members of the imperial family and the concubines and eunuchs who served them. Anyone else who entered was executed. After the 1968 Tet Offensive, only the Royal Theater (Duyet Thi Duong) and the intimate and partially restored ☞ **Royal Library** behind it remained intact. ⊠ *In Imperial City.* ⊠ *Included in admission to Imperial City.* ☉ *Daily 7–5.*

Imperial City (Hoang Thanh). The Imperial City, or Imperial Enclosure, was once a complex of palaces and pavilions where civil and religious ceremonies took place and the region was governed. Now it betrays disappointingly few remnants of past glory beneath the sporadic vegetation that is taking over the ruins. There are four gateways into the Enclosure: the **Gate of Peace** (Cua Hoa Binh), **the Gate of Humanity** (Cua Hien Nhian), the **Gate of Virtue** (Cua Chuong Due), and the **South Gate** (Ngo Mon). ⊠ *Inside citadel.* ⊠ *55,000d.* ☉ *Daily 7–5.*

Imperial Museum. This beautiful wooden structure was built in 1845 and houses miscellaneous royal knickknacks such as wooden incense boxes, many inlaid with mother-of-pearl. ✉ *Dinh Cong Trang St., close to intersection of Doan Thi Diem St.* ☎ 22,000d. ⊙ *Daily 7–noon and 1:30–5.*

Nine Dynastic Urns (Cuu Dinh O The-Mieu). Cast in 1835 and weighing approximately 5,000 pounds each, these urns are dedicated to rulers of the Nguyen dynasty. Emperor Gia Long, the founder of this dynasty, is featured on the elaborately decorated central urn. ✉ *To left of the south gate into Imperial City.* ☎ *Included in admission to Imperial City.* ⊙ *Daily 7–5.*

Palace of Supreme Harmony (Thai Hoa Dien). In the 19th century, this wooden palace, the site of special events, ceremonies, and festivals for the new moon, was where the emperor received dignitaries. Now it houses a gift shop. ✉ *In the Imperial City.* ☎ *Included in admission to Imperial City.* ⊙ *Daily 7–5.*

Royal Library (Thai Binh Lau). The Royal Library, past the Palace of Supreme Harmony, on your right, is one of the few largely intact buildings in the Imperial City, although there are no books or other furnishings left. ✉ *In Imperial City.* ☎ *Included in admission to Imperial City.* ⊙ *Daily 7–5.*

Thien Mu Pagoda. This Mahayana Buddhist temple contains one of Hue's most famous monuments, the seven-story, octagonal Phuoc Nguyen Tower, built in 1844 by Emperor Thieu Tri at a peaceful spot overlooking the Perfume River. Each of the tiers is dedicated to a different human incarnation of the Buddha, and the main sanctuary houses a splendid, large Laughing Buddha. *About 2½ km (1½ mi) southwest of Citadel on left bank of Perfume River.* ☎ *Free.* ⊙ *Daily 7–5.*

Tomb of Minh Mang. Another Hue classic, this tomb is one of the most palatial, with numerous pavilions and courtyards in a beautiful pine forest. The route to the burial site is bordered with sculptures of mandarins, elephants, and lions. *About 11 km (7 mi) south of Hue and 1½ km (1 mi) inland on left bank of Perfume River.* ☎ 50,000d. ⊙ *Daily 8–5.*

★ **Tomb of Tu Duc.** This tomb, one of Hue's most visited, has a lake and pine forest. Built in 1867 by thousands of laborers, it was once Tu Duc's second residence, to which he escaped to commune with nature and write poetry. You, too, may end up spending an hour here just wandering around the grounds. *About 5 km (3 mi) south of Hue, on right bank of Perfume River.* ☎ 50,000d. ⊙ *Daily 8–5.*

OFF THE
BEATEN PATH

DMZ – About 100 km (62 mi) north of Hue is the DMZ (Demilitarized Zone), site of some of the heaviest fighting of the Vietnam War. The DMZ was established following the terms of the 1954 Geneva Accords, in which Vietnam was split in two along the 17th parallel at the Ben Hai River. Though it was supposed to have been temporary, enforced only until the elections in 1956, it existed until the country was reunified in 1975.

South and west of the DMZ are areas that may be familiar for the bitter fighting that took place here: Con Thien, Camp Carroll, the Rockpile, Hamburger Hill, Quang Tri, and, above all, Khe Sanh. One of the biggest battles of the war—and one of the most significant American losses—took place at Khe Sanh in 1968.

The DMZ Tour Office (☞ *Hue A to Z, below*) organizes trips to the area.

Dining and Lodging

Hue's cuisine, distinguished by the elegant radial symmetry of its presentation, is said to be the most sophisticated in Vietnam. Two specialties are *banh khoai*, a rice pancake filled with shrimp and pork, and *bun bo Hue*, a dish of rice noodles and broth topped with pork, beef, and pork rinds. Most of Hue's hotels are on the right (east) bank of the Perfume River. You have an excellent selection from which to choose in all price ranges, and you can often swim in a hotel's pool for a small fee, even if you're not staying there.

Dining

$$$ ✕ **Century Riverside Hotel Restaurant.** Perhaps the most upscale dining establishment in Hue, the Century serves two particularly tasty dishes: grilled fish in banana leaves and superb spring rolls. ⊠ *49 Le Loi St.,* ☎ *054/823–390. AE, MC, V.*

$$ ✕ **Club Garden.** A dimly lit street leads you to the entrance of this small restaurant, where you can get a fabulous fixed-price five-course dinner for less than $10. The seafood and fish dishes are particularly good, as are the pork buns. ⊠ *12 Vo Thi Sau St.,* ☎ *054/826–327. No credit cards.*

$$ ✕ **Huong Giang Hotel Restaurant.** From the windows of this spacious third-floor restaurant you get great views of the Perfume River. Large portions of very solid Vietnamese food and Western dishes, such as chicken and french fries, are served. Reserve ahead if you want a seat by the window. ⊠ *51 Le Loi St.,* ☎ *054/822–122. AE, MC, V.*

$ ✕ **Am Phu.** Excellent traditional Vietnamese cuisine is served at this restaurant. The nonglamorous atmosphere keeps this place relatively free of Western tourists. Although there are no prices listed on the menu, most dishes cost about 30,000d. ⊠ *35 Nguyen Thai Hoc St.,* ☎ *054/ 825–259. No credit cards.*

$ ✕ **Lac Thanh Restaurant.** Packed with tourists and teeming with postcard and cigarette vendors, this dive (and its next-door copycat) serves the tastiest and cheapest meals in Hue. Some notable dishes include Asian basics like shrimp and vegetables over crispy noodles. ⊠ *6A Dien Tien Hoang St.,* ☎ *no phone. No credit cards.*

$ ✕ **Ngoc Anh.** This open-air restaurant—the Vietnamese version of a sidewalk café—serves high-quality Vietnamese and Chinese food in a relaxed atmosphere. The sizzling-hot clay-pot seafood special is exceptional. ⊠ *29 Nguyen Thai Hoc St.,* ☎ *054/822–617. No credit cards.*

$ ✕ **Tong Phuoc Nen.** Although soup—particularly different versions of eel soup—is the specialty of the house, you can also order a variety of fish dishes. Diners include somewhat adventurous tourists and lots of Vietnamese teenagers. ⊠ *20 Ba Trieu St.,* ☎ *054/825–264. No credit cards.*

¢ ✕ **Banh Beo Ba Cu.** Don't be put off by the grungy interior of this restaurant. The quality of the decor is in inverse proportion to the quality of the food. This favorite among locals serves only eight dishes, all specialties of the region. Particularly memorable is the *banh uot thit nuong* (grilled meat rolled in pastry). ⊠ *47 Nguyen Hue St.,* ☎ *no phone. No credit cards.*

¢ ✕ **Banh Khoai.** This two-table, family-run food stall serves some of the best banh khoai in town. The meat-filled rice pancake topped with bean sprouts comes to the table piping hot. Break it up with chopsticks into your small rice bowl, add the greens and sauce, and eat. ⊠ *2 Nguyen Tri Phuong St., off Hanoi St.,* ☎ *no phone. No credit cards.*

¢ ✕ **Bun Bo Hue.** Close to the center of Hue, this very downscale sidewalk food stall serves wonderful bun bo Hue. There's no menu, as this is the only dish served. ⊠ *11B Ly Kiet St.,* ☎ *no phone. No credit cards.*

¢ ✕ **Mai Huong.** Although it may not live up to your fantasy of a Parisian patisserie, this small "coffee shop" is a good place for a slice of coconut cake and a cup of tea. ✉ *14 Nguyen Tri Phuong St.,* ☎ *no phone. No credit cards.*

Lodging

$$–$$$ 🏨 **Century Riverside Inn.** Although this large Western-style hotel on the river is the most luxurious in town, it's not opulent by Western standards. But it is very clean and comfortable. Ask for a room with a view of the river. ✉ *49 Le Loi St.,* ☎ *054/823–390,* FAX *054/823–399. 158 rooms. 2 restaurants, bar, minibars, refrigerators, room service, pool, massage, tennis court, dry cleaning, laundry service. AE, MC, V.*

$$ 🏨 **Dong Da Hotel.** This spacious hotel on a quiet street corner falls somewhere between a minihotel—one of the new, privately owned small places popping up all over Vietnam—and a Western-style accommodation. Rooms are clean and modern and have simple Japanese-style furnishings. All have TVs. ✉ *15 Ly Thuong Kiet St.,* ☎ *054/823–071,* FAX *054/ 823–204. 37 rooms. 2 restaurants, bar, air-conditioning, laundry service, travel services, car rental. AE, MC, V.*

$$ 🏨 **Hoa Hong Hotel II.** Almost as comfortable as its more expensive neighbors, the Century Riverside and the Huong Giang, this new hotel has similarly styled, semiluxurious, nondescript rooms. Though the hotel is not on the water, it's tall enough so that many rooms have excellent views of the river. In the restaurant are nightly shows of traditional music and dance. ✉ *1 Pham Ngu Lao St.,* ☎ *054/824–377,* FAX *054/ 826–949. 60 rooms. Restaurant, dry cleaning, laundry service, travel services. MC, V.*

$$ 🏨 **Huong Giang Hotel.** Large rooms with traditional Vietnamese-style
★   decor and the most helpful staff in Hue make this hotel, on the north end of the east bank, the most pleasant in town. Request one of the renovated older rooms—they're better than the newer ones around the pool. The hotel also has a very good restaurant and rooftop bar-garden with panoramic views of the river. The travel office in the hotel is exceptional. ✉ *51 Le Loi St.,* ☎ *054/832–220,* FAX *054/821–426. 102 rooms. 2 restaurants, 2 bars, outdoor café, pool, tennis court, dry cleaning, laundry service, travel services. AE, MC, V.*

$ 🏨 **A Dong Hotel 1.** This pleasant, clean, and airy minihotel is a great budget alternative. Though there's nothing particularly charming about the place, it does have large, basic, immaculate rooms. It scores big, however, with fresh fruit and flowers delivered daily to your room. The staff speaks very little English but is eager to please. ✉ *1 Chu Van An St.,* ☎ *054/824–148,* FAX *054/828–074. 7 rooms. Restaurant, bar, air-conditioning, minibars, refrigerator, laundry service, travel services, car rental. No credit cards.*

$ 🏨 **Dong Duong (Indochina) Hotel.** It's just as clean and pleasant as its
★   hotel counterpart, the Huong Giang Hotel (☞ *above*), but the Dong Duong has larger rooms and a more intimate environment. The cozy, sunny rooms are arranged around a small garden. Staying here, you sacrifice having access to recreational facilities, but you get the feel of a small inn and easy access to the center of town. ✉ *3 Hung Vuong St.,* ☎ *054/826–070,* FAX *054/826–074. 12 rooms. Restaurant, air-conditioning, fans, minibars, refrigerators, laundry service, travel services, car rental. AE, MC, V.*

$ 🏨 **Saigon Hotel.** Don't be put off by the strangely decorated restaurant (with a neon backlit cow's head) in this minihotel. Rooms are sunny and squeaky clean, and the bathrooms are in excellent condition and have tubs. ✉ *32 Hung Vuong St.,* ☎ *054/821–007,* FAX *054/821–009. 20 rooms. Restaurant, air-conditioning, fans, laundry service, travel services, car rental. No credit cards.*

¢–$ ▣ **Hoa Hong I.** The smaller and less luxurious of the Hoa Hong family of hotels, this place has comfortable rooms and bathrooms with tubs as well as IDD phones. Just ignore the fake-flower finishing touches and the overly cutesy pastel decor. ✉ *46C Le Loi St.,* ☎ *054/824–377,* ℻ *054/826–949. 56 rooms. Restaurant, air-conditioning, minibars, refrigerators, laundry service, travel services. No credit cards.*

¢–$ ▣ **Hung Vuong Hotel.** Both backpackers and nonbackpackers stay here, especially those taking the Sinh Café bus (☞ Hue A to Z, *below*), which drops off and picks up passengers at the hotel. There's a variety of clean rooms in a wide price range. The hotel adjoins the Thua Thien–Hue Tourism office and is near downtown Hue. ✉ *2 Hung Vuong St.,* ☎ *054/823–866,* ℻ *054/825–910. 70 rooms. Restaurant, air-conditioning, minibars, refrigerators, laundry service, travel services, car rental. No credit cards.*

Hue A to Z

Arriving and Departing
BY AIRPLANE
Vietnam Airlines (✉ 7 Nguyen Tri Phuong St., ☎ 054/846–320) flies to Hue's Phu Bai Airport, 15 km (9 mi) south of the city center, from Ho Chi Minh City (1 hr; $70; twice a day, seven days a week); Hanoi (50 mins; $70; once or twice a day, seven days a week); and Dalat (1 hr 20 mins; $105 one way; 2 times a week). The schedule changes frequently, so confirm departure times a day or two before your flight. Taxis will take you into town for about 80,000d.

BY BUS
The **Sinh Café bus** (✉ Hung Vuong Hotel, 2 Hung Vuong St., Hue, ☎ 054/823–866) stops in Hue on both its northbound and southbound routes (Hanoi to Hue takes about 12 hrs and costs $12; the trip from Ho Chi Minh City takes about 3 days, costs $40, and includes stops in Dalat and Nha Trang).

BY TRAIN
Trains from all over Vietnam come into the **Hue Railway Station** (Ga Hue; ✉ On right bank at southwest end of Le Loi St.). The ticket office is open daily 7:30 to 5. Four trains depart daily for Ho Chi Minh City (24 hrs, $40–$60 for a sleeping berth), and four depart daily for Hanoi (15 hrs, $40–$50 for a sleeping berth).

Getting Around
BY BICYCLE
An easy way to get around Hue is by bicycle, which you can rent from the Century Riverside Inn (☞ Lodging, *above*) and from a stand across the street from the Hung Vuong Hotel.

BY CAR OR MINIBUS
You can rent a minibus with a driver to take you to Hoi An, Danang, the imperial tombs, or other points near Hue; the cost is approximately $25–$50 for the trip, depending on the kind of vehicle, its age, and whether it has air-conditioning. The additional cost of the services of a guide is $25–$50.

BY CYCLO
You can always find a cyclo outside hotels or cruising along the right bank. For 20,000d you should be able to get pretty much anywhere, although you will always have to negotiate. The Century Riverside Inn (☞ Lodging, *above*) posts suggested cyclo prices for those who hate to bargain.

Taxis are metered. Expect to pay a few dollars for trips around town. Call **Hue Taxi ATC** (☎ 054/824–500 or 054/833–333) to arrange a ride, or just hail one on the street, though they are not always easy to find.

Contacts and Resources

CURRENCY EXCHANGE

The **Thua Thien–Hue branch of Vietcom Bank** (ICBV; ⊠ 46 Hung Vuong St., ☎ 054/822–281) changes money and gives cash advances on Visa and MasterCard. It's open weekdays 7 to 11 and 1:30 to 3:30. You can also exchange money at most hotels.

EMERGENCIES

In case of emergency, contact **Benh Vien Trung Uong Hue** (Hue General Hospital; ⊠ 16 Le Loi St., ☎ 054/822–325). Some of the doctors speak English.

If you need to fill a prescription, the woman working at **Thuoc Tay** (⊠ 5 Hung Vuong St.) speaks better French than English, but she is very helpful, especially if you write down what you need.

TOUR OPERATORS

A number of agencies organize boat trips on the Perfume River, which include stops at the tombs and the Thien Mu Pagoda. Most depart at 8 AM daily and cost about 40,000d, excluding tomb and pagoda entry fees, which can cost as much as 50,000d each.

VISITOR INFORMATION AND TRAVEL AGENCIES

The following travel agencies arrange cars with drivers, tours of Hue, boat tours along the Perfume River, and excursions to the DMZ. **DMZ Tour Office** (⊠ 26 Le Loi St., ☎ 054/825–242). **Huong Giang Company** (⊠ 17 Le Loi St., ☎ 054/820–188, FAX 054/823–102). **Thua Thien–Hue Tourism** (Cong Ty Du Lich Thua Thien–Hue; ⊠ 30 Le Loi St. [and a branch at 2 Hung Vuong St.], ☎ 054/822–369, 054/822–288, or 054/822–355).

THE CENTRAL COAST

The region south of Hue includes the port city of Danang, with an outstanding museum of Cham culture; the Cham ruins at My Son; the famous China Beach; and the delightful town of Hoi An, a well-preserved 18th-century trading village on the sea, where families have lived in the same homes for more than 200 years.

The portion of the south-central coast lying between Hoi An and Nha Trang is an area with few tourist attractions but often breathtaking scenery and seemingly endless white-sand beaches. If you're traveling by car between the two cities, don't miss the opportunity to visit the Son My Memorial, built in remembrance of the brutal My Lai massacre. Farther inland, the central-highland towns of Pleiku and Kontum are good bases from which to explore the villages of the hill tribes.

Danang

108 km (67 mi) south of Hue, 30 km (19 mi) north of Hoi An, and 972 km (603 mi) north of Ho Chi Minh City.

Danang, an important port town at the end of the 19th century, may be familiar to you as a U.S. Air Force base during the Vietnam War. Today, it is a slightly run-down city that offers little in the way of sights except for the wonderful Cham museum. The city also has the region's largest airport and is a good jumping-off place for Hoi An and other points of interest in the region.

★ On display at the **Cham Museum** are artifacts from the ancient Kingdom of Champa, which existed from the 2nd to the 18th centuries around present-day Danang, Nha Trang, and Phan Rang. The Cham adopted many elements of Indian art and Sanksrit as their sacred language, and their religion combines native beliefs with elements of Indian culture and early Hindu thought (the god Shiva is often represented). Their kingdom stretched from the north of Hue to the Mekong Delta in the 10th and 11th centuries, between the Khmer to the south and the Viet to the north. In the 12th century, the Cham were under frequent attack by the Khmer. In the 13th century, backed by the Chinese, the Viet attacked in the north but were defeated in 1377 when the Cham reached an agreement with the Chinese. The Cham presence was substantial until the 1400s, when they were conquered by the Viet. After that, their influence receded until they were finally overthrown by the Viet in the 1700s. Remnants of the sandstone-and-brick towers built for Hindu worship by the Cham can still be found along the central coast, and descendants of the Cham continue to live in the highlands and along the coastal lowlands.

The Cham Museum was founded by the French in 1915 to exhibit Cham sculptures and fragments of temples and towers unearthed by archaeologists. Exhibits are arranged chronologically, reflecting the changing seats of power in the kingdom, from Emperor Indrapura to Tra Kieu to My Son to Khuong My. The highly sensual, innovative, and expressive works from Tra Kieu's reign (7th century) and that of My Son (8th–9th centuries) and the abundant sandstone carvings of the god Shiva show the prosperity of the Kingdom of Champa.

As you walk through the museum, note that the Cham Buddha is displayed on a throne in an imperial pose, with his feet flat on the ground, not in the traditional lotus position. This subtle difference in Buddha styles reflects the Cham belief in the spiritual continuum between crown and divinity—the nobility were thought to be "higher up" because they were more directly connected to God. The symbol of fertility, Uroja (meaning female breast), which you will also see throughout the museum, reveals the esteem afforded women in Cham culture. ⊠ *Intersection of Tran Phu and Le Dinh Duong Sts.* 🚃 *20,000d.* ⊙ *Daily 8–6.*

OFF THE BEATEN PATH
My Son – About 70 km (42 mi) southwest of Danang, or 45 km (28 mi) due west of Hoi An, are the My Son Cham ruins: former temples and towers dedicated to kings and divinities, particularly Shiva, who was considered the founder of the Kingdom of Champa. With more than 70 brick structures, of which some 20 remain in recognizable form today, My Son was the most important religious and architectural center of the Kingdom of Champa. Although extensively damaged by American bombing during the war, the My Son complex still retains vestiges of its former glory. Seeing both the Cham Museum and the temples of My Son will enable you to fully appreciate the wonders of Cham culture.

Lodging

$$ 🏨 **Bamboo Green.** A welcome addition to Danang's desultory lodging scene, this brand-new hotel is only a five-minute walk from the Cham Museum. Rooms are large and tastefully decorated, and the satellite TVs and efficient room service give you the feeling that you've briefly stepped out of Vietnam. ⊠ *158 Phan Chu Trinh St.,* 🕾 *0511/822–997,* 𝖥𝖠𝖷 *0511/822–998. 46 rooms. Restaurant, bar, air-conditioning, minibars, refrigerators, room service, massage, dry cleaning, laundry service, business services, travel services, car rental. AE, MC, V.*

Marble Mountains

11 km (7 mi) southwest of Danang, 19 km (12 mi) north of Hoi An.

Five beautiful limestone peaks, known as the Marble Mountains, rise
above the beach south of Danang. A visit here can easily be combined
with a trip to China Beach (☞ *below*). The Marble Mountains, named
for the five basic elements of Chinese philosophy—earth, water, fire,
wood, and metal—are riddled with caves. Over the centuries the **caves**
(dong) in the Thuy Son Peak have been turned into temples and shrines.
The first to use them were the Cham, who turned them into Hindu
shrines, but more recently, Buddhists have taken over, adorned, sanc-
tified, and inhabited them.

The path leading to the various cave-pagodas is not particularly strenuous. It leads you into a cave filled with Buddhas, bathed in ethereal
light from an opening high above, and then through the mountain into
other shrines and out to spectacular views below. Polite children in traditional school uniforms may take you by the hand and lead you
through the various caves, at the end offering you the "best price. . . for
you only" for such marble souvenirs as miniature Marble Mountains
and small mortar-and-pestle sets. ⊠ *About 11 km (7 mi) south of
Danang; 19 km (12 mi) north of Hoi An off Hwy. 1.* ✉ *10,000d.*

China Beach

12 km (7 mi) southeast of Danang, 25 km (15 mi) north of Hoi An.

Yes, the TV show *China Beach* was based on this place, but the China
Beach that was an R&R resort for U.S. soldiers during the Vietnam
War is actually 5 km (3 mi) north of what is now called China Beach
(Bac My An). Activity here is limited to lazing on the sand and surfing. Surfboards can be rented from the Furama Resort, as can bicycles. It's best for nonsurfers between May and July, when the water is
placid.

Lodging

$$$ ⊞ **Furama Resort.** This is one of Vietnam's premier resorts, a favorite
★   with the country's expatriates. Right on the beach, it comprises a
group of French Vietnamese–style villas surrounding an artificial la-
goon. The interior evokes the French colonial era, with a Vietnamese
influence: shuttered windows, cane furniture, ceiling fans, and Viet-
namese artifacts. The resort has a shuttle service from Danang's air-
port and can organize tours for you to Danang, Hoi An, and even Hue.
⊠ *68 Ho Xuan Huong St.,* ☎ *0511/847–333; 08/821–1888 in Ho Chi
Minh City,* FAX *0511/847–666. 200 rooms. 2 restaurants, 2 bars, in-
room safes, minibars, room service, pool, sauna, driving range, 4 ten-
nis courts, health club, surfing, bicycles, dry cleaning, laundry service,
meeting rooms, travel services. AE, MC, V.*

Hoi An

*138 km (86 mi) south of Hue, 30 km (19 mi) south of Danang, and
965 km (598 mi) north of Ho Chi Minh City.*

Perhaps the most delightful of all Vietnamese towns, riverside Hoi An
defies the insidious pace of modernization. The 18th-century houses,
pagodas, and assembly halls built by the early Chinese communities
remain in pristine condition; the bustling market makes you feel you've
gone back in time. The many galleries selling the works of local artists
and the numerous cafés give the town a strong bohemian feel. Hoi An
offers great cuisine and is probably the most tourist-friendly town in
the whole country. The whole town can easily be navigated on foot in

an hour, but plan to spend more time in Hoi An than you think you'll need, since it's easy to fall in love with the place.

Hoi An, or Faifo as it was called, is a composite of many foreign influences. From the 2nd to 10th centuries, it was an important port town under the control of the Kingdom of Champa. During the 14th and 15th centuries, when the Cham and the Vietnamese fought for control, Hoi An ceased to be a trading center, but peace in the 16th century again saw the arrival of ships from all over Asia and Europe, bringing merchants in search of silk, porcelain, lacquer, and medicinal herbs.

During the Tay Son Rebellion in the 1770s, Hoi An was severely damaged, but it was speedily rebuilt and once again became a major international port, where for two centuries Chinese, Japanese, Dutch, and Portuguese merchants came to trade. During the off-season, the merchants set up shop, and foreigners' colonies began to develop along the riverfront. To this day, ethnic Chinese make up a significant portion of the population. In the late 1800s, the French arrived and made Hoi An an administrative post. Then, when the Thu Bon River began to silt up, Danang gradually eclipsed Hoi An as the area's major port.

The Old Town, a combination of Vietnamese, Japanese, and Chinese architectural styles, is reserved for pedestrians, bicycles, and motorbikes—the perfect place for a walk. Get a map from your hotel or from the tourist office at the corner of Nguyen Hue Street and Phan Chu Trinh Street. Here you can also find an English- or French-speaking guide and buy the combined entrance ticket (50,000d) to the wonderful mix of Chinese assembly halls and temples, museums, and old teak houses. The ticket admits you to four of the sites and the Japanese Bridge, which is actually a public thoroughfare. Once you buy the combined entrance ticket, you may purchase an additional entry ticket to any sight for 10,000d.

A GOOD WALK

After purchasing your tickets, head to the small colonial-era **Museum of History and Culture,** approximately one block from the tourist office, at the corner of Tran Phu and Nguyen Hue streets. Walk across the courtyard filled with birdcages to get to **Quan Cong Temple,** dedicated to a deified Chinese general. Leave through the front entrance to find yourself directly opposite the **Central Market,** one of Vietnam's most pleasant.

Leave the market, and walk east on Tran Phu Street until you get to No. 178, the **Assembly Hall of the Hainan Chinese Congregation.** Continue east on Tran Phu Street, which turns into Nguyen Duy Hieu Street after it intersects with Hoang Dieu Street. Just past the intersection on the left, at No. 157, is the **Chaozhou Assembly Hall,** with its fine wood carvings. Turn around and go back west on Tran Phu Street; cross Nguyen Hue and walk past charming small houses with teak columns and tile roofs. On your right is the colorful **Assembly Hall of the Fujian Chinese Congregation,** now a temple devoted to Thien Hau, the goddess of the sea. Continue along Tran Phu street until you come to No. 64, the **Chinese All-Community Assembly Hall** on your right; as its name implies, it was used as a meeting place for all the Chinese communities in Hoi An. Farther along on your left will be the ancient **Quang Thang House,** at No. 77.

At No. 80 is the Diep Dong Nguyen House, now the **Museum of Trade Ceramics,** and then, past Le Loi and Nhi Trung streets, on the north side, is the **Assembly Hall of the Cantonese Chinese Congregation.** Farther along Tran Phu Street, past a row of souvenir shops and the intersection with Nhi Trung Street, is the fascinating **Japanese Bridge.**

Keep going on Tran Phu Street, which becomes Nguyen Thi Minh Khai Street. At No. 4 is the **Old House of Phung Hung,** where eight generations of one family have lived for more than 200 years. Turn around and head back east on Tran Phu Street. Take the small road that forks in front of the Japanese Bridge (Chau Van Thuong Street) to get to Nguyen Thai Hoc Street. At No. 101 is the **Old House of Tan Ky.** Continue east on Nguyen Thai Hoc Street and then make a left onto Le Loi Street. Cross Phan Chu Trinh Street; on the corner is the **Tran Family Chapel.**

SIGHTS TO SEE

Assembly Hall of the Cantonese Chinese Congregation. The main altar of this hall, founded in 1786, is dedicated to Quan Cong, a revered General of the Chinese Han dynasty. ⊠ *176 Tran Phu St., at Nguyen Thai Hoc St.* 🎫 *In combination ticket.* ⊘ *Daily 8–5.*

Assembly Hall of the Fujian Chinese Congregation. Built as a meeting place, this hall later became a temple dedicated to Thien Hau, the Fujian goddess of the sea and protector of fishermen. Thien Hau is represented in the mural near the entrance. Another mural depicts six Fujian families who fled from China to Hoi An in the 17th century. The gate is newer: it was built in 1975. ⊠ *Opposite 35 Tran Phu St.* 🎫 *In combination ticket.* ⊘ *Daily 8–5.*

Assembly Hall of the Hainan Chinese Congregation. This hall, founded by Chinese from Hainan, was constructed in 1883 in memory of more than 100 merchants who were mistakenly killed because they were thought to be pirates. ⊠ *At east end of Tran Phu St., before intersection with Nguyen Duy Hieu St.* 🎫 *In combination ticket.* ⊘ *Daily 8–5.*

Central Market. Hoi An's wonderful market is one of the most enjoyable in Vietnam. The aisles are lined with silk shops that can fill custom clothing orders for little money in less than 24 hours (but beware of "cotton" that's part synthetic and "silk" that's really polyester). In the center are fresh and dried fruit and flowers; the daily catch is down by the river; and miscellaneous batteries, pajamas, and bicycle pumps pop up all over. ⊠ *Intersection of Tran Quy Cap and Tran Phu Sts.* ⊘ *Daily 6–dusk.*

Chaozhou Assembly Hall (Trieu Chau). Built by the Chaozhou Chinese community in 1776, this hall exemplifies Chinese wood carving of this period at its finest. ⊠ *157 Nguyen Duy Hieu St.* 🎫 *In combination ticket.* ⊘ *Daily 8–5.*

Chinese All-Community Assembly Hall (Chua Ba). This hall was built in 1773 as a meeting place for the Cantonese, Chaozhou, Fujian, Hainan, and Hakka families living in Hoi An. ⊠ *64 Tran Phu St.* 🎫 *In combination ticket.* ⊘ *Daily 8–5.*

Japanese Bridge (Cau Nhat, or Lai Vien Kieu). One of the city's landmarks, this red-painted, covered wooden bridge was originally built in 1593 by the Japanese to link their section of town to the Chinese quarter. Two small altars at one end are topped by charming statues of dogs and those at the other by statues of monkeys. A small temple on the north side is dedicated to Tran Vo Bac De (god of the north), revered by sailors because he controls wind and rain. ⊠ *Tran Phu St., west of Nhi Trung St.* 🎫 *In combination ticket.* ⊘ *Daily 8–5.*

Museum of History and Culture. This small museum—housed in just one large room—provides a great introduction to Hoi An and its culture. On display are ancient bowls, cups, and other ceramics, many of them archaeological artifacts. ⊠ *7 Nguyen Hue St.* 🎫 *In combination ticket.* ⊘ *Daily 8–5.*

★ **Museum of Trade Ceramics.** The ancient Diep Dong Nguyen House has been converted into a terrific small museum dedicated to the history of ceramics in Hoi An. The collection includes ancient wares, some of them recovered from shipwrecks in the surrounding waters, and a large assortment of household objects, such as bowls and vases. ⊠ *80 Tran Phu St.* 🎫 *In combination ticket.* ☉ *Daily 8–5.*

Old House of Phung Hung. Eight generations of the Phung Hung family have lived here since the house was built in 1780. Note the Japanese influences in the roof, the Chinese influences in the balcony, and the Vietnamese architectural style of the walls. ⊠ *4 Nguyen Thi Minh Khai St.* 🎫 *In combination ticket.* ☉ *Daily 8–5.*

Old House of Tan Ky. One of the oldest in Hoi An, this private house has remained largely unchanged in the 200 years since it was built. Seven generations of the Tan Ky family have lived here. ⊠ *101 Nguyen Thai Hoc St.* 🎫 *In combination ticket.* ☉ *Daily 8–5.*

Quan Cong Temple. Founded in 1653 by the Chinese community, this temple is dedicated to Quan Cong, a revered general of the Chinese Han dynasty. The carp, symbolic of patience in Chinese mythology, is displayed throughout. ⊠ *24 Tran Phu St.* 🎫 *In combination ticket.* ☉ *Daily 8–5.*

Quang Thang House. Another of Hoi An's ancient family homes, built about 300 years ago, has beautiful wood carvings on the walls of the rooms surrounding the courtyard. ⊠ *77 Tran Phu St.* 🎫 *In combination ticket.* ☉ *Daily 8–5.*

Tran Family Chapel. This structure, built in 1802, is dedicated to the worship of the Tran family's deceased ancestors. Tours are given in English by members of the Tran family. ⊠ *21 Le Loi St.* 🎫 *In combination ticket.* ☉ *Daily 8–5.*

Dining and Lodging

$$ ✕ **Han Huyen Floating Restaurant.** It's a pleasure to sit on the breezy deck of this docked boat, whose menu serves Chinese and Vietnamese dishes, and specializes in game. ⊠ *Bach Dang St.,* ☎ *0510/861–462. No credit cards.*

$$ ✕ **Tam Tam Café.** This restaurant-cum-bar is the perfect place to unwind after a day of sightseeing. The French proprietor oversees the preparation of steaks, homemade pastas, and traditional French and Italian dishes. Set in a tastefully restored former tea warehouse, the Tam Tam is also a good spot to while away the warmer hours of the day playing pool or reading with a cold drink. ⊠ *110 Nguyen Thai Hoc St.,* ☎ *0510/862–212. No credit cards.*

$$ ✕ **Vinh Hung Restaurant.** A peaceful oasis across the street from the Cantonese Assembly Hall, this restaurant serves superb seafood and such local specialties as White Roses, a delicious shrimp dumpling said to resemble a rose. Have a drink on the shady terrace, hung with bougainvillea and cages of singing birds, and watch the world go by. ⊠ *147B Tran Phu St.,* ☎ *0510/862–203. No credit cards.*

$ ✕ **Café Can.** Café Can, located along the riverfront, serves fantastic meals at absurdly low prices. The seafood here is excellent, particularly the fish served in banana leaves and the steamed crab. ⊠ *74 Bach Dang St.,* ☎ *0510/861–525. No credit cards..*

$ ✕ **Café des Amis.** There is no menu at the Café des Amis. Instead, your
★ waiter will ask if you want seafood or a vegetarian meal, then start bringing you food. Be warned: visitors who eat here on their first night in Hoi An have a tendency to not try anywhere else. The waterfront location makes for a great atmosphere. ⊠ *52 Bach Dang St.,* ☎ *0510/861–616. No credit cards.*

$ ✕ **Faifoo.** Come here for refreshing fruit shakes, as well as a great multicourse sampler menu of chicken and pork dishes, all for next to nothing. ⊠ *104 Tran Phu St.,* ☎ *0510/861–548. No credit cards.*

$ ✕ **Restaurant Thanh.** This open-air riverfront restaurant makes a splendid flounder (or whatever white fish happens to be fresh that day) cooked in banana leaves. The decor consists of shiny black and gold pillars, pink walls, paper lanterns, and a voluptuous, tumbling thunbergia vine. But the candlelight ambience is frequently disrupted by postcard vendors. ⊠ *76 Bach Dang St.,* ☎ *0510/861–366. No credit cards.*

$$$ ⌷ **Victoria Hoi An Resort.** Although not yet complete at press time, this resort, part of the Victorian Hotel & Resorts chain, is scheduled to open on Cua Dai Beach early in 2001. Most of the 100 bungalow units will have views of the sea. ☎ *Ho Chi Minh City office 08/990–1350. 100 bungalows. Restaurant, bar, pool, tennis court, business services, meeting rooms, travel services. AE, MC, V.* ⊛

$$–$$$ ⌷ **Hoi An Hotel.** This hotel offers the best accommodation in town. Rooms are comfortable, spotless, and spacious, with IDD phones and satellite TV. The outstanding Hoi An tourist office is in the lobby. At press time the hotel was scheduled to open villas on Cua Dai Beach by the middle of 2001. ⊠ *6 Tran Hung Dao St.,* ☎ *0510/861–445,* ℻ *0510/861–636. 130 rooms. Restaurant, fans, pool, bicycles, laundry service, travel services, car rental. AE, MC, V.*

$–$$ ⌷ **Hai Yen Hotel.** One of a number of new hotels on the road to the beach, the Hai Yen has spacious and inexpensive suites and an almost rural setting, with rice fields just a few steps away. ⊠ *22A Cua Dai St.,* ☎ *0510/862–445,* ℻ *0510/862–443. 33 rooms. Restaurant, bar, minibars, travel services, car and motorbike rental. AE, MC, V.*

$ ⌷ **Cua Dai Hoi An Hotel.** One of the nicest accommodations in town, this plush minihotel has spotless, sunny rooms, many with balconies. Both the beach and the town center are just a bike ride away (you can rent bicycles at the hotel). ⊠ *18A Cua Dai St.,* ☎ *0510/862–231,* ℻ *0510/862–232. 17 rooms. Restaurant, air-conditioning, fans, bicycles, laundry service, travel services. No credit cards.*

$ ⌷ **Thanh Binh.** This centrally located hotel has clean rooms that get plenty of light. Get here early: the hotel often fills up by noon with budget travelers. ⊠ *1 Le Loi St.,* ☎ *0510/861–740. 14 rooms. Air-conditioning, fans, laundry service, travel services, car rental. No credit cards.*

$ ⌷ **Thien Trung.** This hotel is very close to the bus station and only a short bike ride from the old town. Rooms are neat and bright. ⊠ *63 Phan Ding Phung St.,* ☎ *0510/861–720 or 0510/861–769. 16 rooms. Restaurant, air-conditioning, fans, laundry service, travel services, car rental. No credit cards.*

$ ⌷ **Vinh Hung Hotel.** This Chinese-inspired hotel near the Japanese Bridge has dark wood paneling and carvings and a smiling Buddha in the lobby. Rooms are sunny and cheerfully decorated. The owners also run the popular Vinh Hung Restaurant on the corner. ⊠ *143 Tran Phu St.,* ☎ *0510/861–621,* ℻ *0510/861–893. 12 rooms. Restaurant, bar, air-conditioning, fans, laundry service, travel services. MC, V.*

Son My Memorial

110 km (68 mi) south of Hoi An.

My Lai, a sleepy hamlet about 13 km (8 mi) east of the city of Quang Ngai in the Son My district, is a site infamous for the worst atrocity carried out by American forces during the war in Vietnam. On the morning of March 16, 1968, U.S. troops entered the Son My area (including My Lai, Thuan-Yen, and other hamlets), which was thought to be a stronghold of the Vietcong, and massacred hundreds of Vietnamese civilians—mostly women and children—in an act that has come to symbolize the often senseless brutality that accompanied the conflict in Vietnam. (The term "Vietcong," used by the Americans and the Republic of South Vietnam, is used in this chapter because it is probably most familiar. It means, loosely, Vietnamese "Commies." The National Liberation Front [NLF] was the official name of the group fighting the southern government.)

The Son My Memorial is dedicated to the victims of the massacre at My Lai and lies about 10 km (6 mi) east of National Highway 1A. The road leading to the memorial begins next to the My Tra Hotel (☞ Lodging, *below*). The memorial itself is set on the grounds of the former hamlet of Thuan-Yen, where many of the worst crimes took place. In striking contrast to the terrible events that occurred here, the memorial is set against a quiet and pastoral backdrop.

Lodging

$–$$ ☷ **My Tra Hotel.** This surprisingly modern and efficient hotel is conveniently located for visits to the Son My Memorial and nearby lovely Bien Khe Beach. The rooms are clean but simple, with watercolors of traditional scenes of rural Vietnamese life. ⊠ *Hwy. 1, north of Quang Ngai across the Tra Khuc Bridge,* ☎ *055/842–985,* 𝔽𝔸𝕏 *055/842–980. 70 rooms. Restaurant, bar, air-conditioning, minibars, massage, tennis court. MC, V.*

Pleiku and Kontum

Kontum is 155 km (96 mi) south of Danang; Pleiku lies 30 km (18 mi) south of Kontum.

Both Kontum and Pleiku are good bases from which to stage trips to the region's remaining forests and the villages of the many hill tribes that live in the area. Day hikes in the surrounding forests and multiday treks with overnight stays in the homes of hill-tribe villagers can be arranged through local tour agencies. You can also arrange for guided tours of the numerous former battlefields from the Vietnam War that dot the area.

Pleiku, the larger of the two towns with about 50,000 residents, has more in the way of accommodations and dining options; sleepy Kontum has much less bustle.

Lodging

¢–$ ☷ **Dakbla Hotel.** This lime-green hotel lies just over the bridge that leads you into Kontum from Pleiku. The rooms are clean, and the staff speaks English. Inside the Dakbla there's a branch of the Kontum Tourist Company, which can arrange treks and visits to the hill-tribe villages in the area. ⊠ *2 Phan Dinh Phung St., Kontum,* ☎ *060/863– 333,* 𝔽𝔸𝕏 *060/863–336. 30 rooms. Restaurant, air-conditioning, minibars, laundry service, travel services. No credit cards.*

¢–$ ☷ **Hung Vuong Hotel.** The convenient and relatively modern Hung Vuong is on the main road as you enter Pleiku on Highway 19. The hotel houses the Gia Lai Tourist Company, which can arrange treks and other guided tours of the surrounding area. ⊠ *215 Hung Vuong St., Pleiku,* ☎ *059/824–270,* 𝔽𝔸𝕏 *059/827–170. 20 rooms. Restaurant, air-conditioning, minibars, travel services. No credit cards.*

Central Coast A to Z

Arriving and Departing

Vietnam Airlines (⊠ 35 Tran Phu St., Danang, ☎ 0511/821–130, 𝔽𝔸𝕏 0511/832–759) flies to Danang's airport, 3 km (2 mi) southwest of the city, from Ho Chi Minh City (daily), Hanoi (daily), and Nha Trang (four times a week). A regular taxi to the airport should cost no more than 50,000d; to reserve one, call **Airport Taxis** (☎ 0511/825–555), Danang's most reliable taxi company.

You can fly from Ho Chi Minh City (daily) or Hanoi (daily) to Hue's **Phu Bai Airport**, 15 km (9 mi) south of the city center, via **Vietnam Airlines** (✉ 7 Nguyen Tri Phuong St., Hue, ☎ 054/846–320). **Taxis** are available at the airport to take you into town; the cost is generally about 80,000d.

Vietnam Airlines (✉ 55 Quang Trung St., Pleiku, ☎ 059/845–9823) flies three times a week from both Hanoi and Ho Chi Minh City to Pleiku; there are also direct flights from Danang.

BY BUS

The convenient and cheap Sinh Café buses (☞ Hue A to Z, *above*) run between Hoi An and Hue, with stops at key sites in between.

BY CAR

Hue is about two hours north of Danang, and Hoi An is less than one hour south. China Beach and the Marble Mountains are easily accessible by car from Danang, as are Hoi An and the Son My Memorial. You can also drive to Kontum and Pleiku from Danang, but be prepared for a rough ride if you take Highway 14, the direct route. You can make arrangements at most hotels and through the **Danang Tourism Services Co.** (✉ 76 Hung Vuong St., ☎ 0511/823–993 or 0511/825–653, ℻ 0511/821–312).

Getting Around

See Arriving and Departing, *above,* for information about renting cars with drivers; motorbikes can also be rented from many hotels and travel agencies. In Hoi An, **Mr. Loc** (✉ 141 Tran Phu St., ☎ 0510/861–447), can see to all your motorbike or taxi needs and even arrange a trip to My Son by boat. In Danang, taxi drivers hang out at the Cham Museum (count on about $15 for the day), or you can take a taxi from the airport to Hoi An, stopping at Marble Mountains and China Beach.

NHA TRANG

Though it's a bustling city with a long stretch of developed beachfront, Nha Trang has its charms: swarms of high-school students bike to and from classes, and hordes of teenagers play soccer in the few waterfront lots that have not been turned into tourist sights. Recreational attractions include swimming, scuba diving, snorkeling, and boat trips to neighboring islands—lush enclaves with isolated beaches and groves of palm trees. Recent dynamiting of coral reefs by fishermen has made scuba diving a bit disappointing, though still interesting. For a good day trip you can travel by boat up the Cai River, which is wonderfully tropical, with lush palm forests lining the banks; it was reputedly the model for the journey upstream in *Apocalypse Now.*

Exploring Nha Trang

The beautiful **Long Son Pagoda,** built in the late 19th century and reconstructed a number of times since, is the town's most famous sight. A giant Buddha beckons you up a flight of stairs, at the top of which is a panoramic view of Nha Trang. The entrance to the pagoda itself is down below. The resident monks give tours of the main sanctuary. ✉ *About 550 yards west of railroad station, opposite No. 15 on 23 Thang 10 St.* ▣ *Free.* ☉ *Daily 8–noon and 2–4.*

One of the better preserved Cham ruins in Vietnam, the **Po Nagar Cham Towers** (Nha Trang Huu Duc), also called the Mother Goddess or Lady of the City Towers, was originally a 2nd-century site of Hindu worship. The present buildings were constructed between the 7th and 12th centuries. Of the original eight towers, four remain, in various states of preservation. The towers still serve as an active shrine for Vietnam's remaining Cham community and for Chinese and Vietnamese Buddhists. ⊠ *On north side of Cai River over Hai Ra and Xom Bong bridges.* 🕾 *6,000d.* ⊘ *Daily 8–5.*

The **Hon Chong Promontory** affords good views of the coastline and the surrounding islands; it's on the same side of the river as the Po Nagar Cham Towers. ⊠ *About ½ km (⅓ mi) from the intersection of Nguyen Dinh Chieu and 2 Thang 4 Sts.* 🕾 *10,000d.* ⊘ *Daily 8–4.*

A boat trip to the surrounding **islands**—Mieu Island (Tri Nguyen Island), Mun Island, Tam Island, and Monkey Island (Dao Khi) can be arranged through any number of hotels and travel agencies (☞ Contacts and Resources *in* Nha Trang A to Z, *below*). **Mama Hahn's Boat Trips** are reputed to be the most fun, though a bit bawdy; book through the Nha Trang Sailing Club (☞ Dining and Lodging, *below*) or your hotel.

North of town are two somewhat isolated and less developed **beaches, Doc Let** (30 km/19 mi), and the spectacular **Dai Lanh** (83 km/51 mi). To reach them it's best to hire a car and driver or simply catch a cab.

Dining and Lodging

$$ ✕ **Ngoc Suong.** This establishment a block from the beach serves the
★ best and the freshest seafood in town. Fish salad, made from marinated local seafood, is the specialty. ⊠ *16 Tran Quang Khai St., not far from Tran Phu St.,* 🕾 *058/954–516. No credit cards.*

$$ ✕ **Nha Trang Sailing Club.** The liveliest of all the seaside cafés/restau-
★ rants in town, the Sailing Club is popular with expats, locals, and tourists. It's the place to go for food like burgers, pizzas, and even sushi. Diving trips can be arranged through the office just behind the restaurant. ⊠ *72–74 Tran Phu St.,* 🕾 *058/826–528. No credit cards.*

$ ✕ **Lac Canh.** Each table in this smoke-filled restaurant has a charcoal grill on which you make your own cheap and delicious marinated seafood and meat dishes. Just be prepared for one odd habit: diners pile empty beer bottles and other leftovers on the floor after they're done with them. ⊠ *11 Hang Ca St.,* 🕾 *058/821–391. No credit cards.*

¢ ✕ **Banana Split.** This small sidewalk café—open for breakfast, lunch, and dinner—serves ice-cream sundaes, omelettes, chicken, and burgers. It's a destination for Western travelers looking to meet other people. Boat trips and other travel arrangements can be made here. ⊠ *58 Quang Trung St.,* 🕾 *058/829–115. No credit cards.*

$$$ 🏨 **Ana Mandara Nha Trang Resort.** This beachfront resort is the classi-
★ est and most comfortable place to stay in Nha Trang. Reminiscent of Balinese- and Thai-style resorts, it has private thatched cottages. ⊠ *60 Tran Phu St.,* 🕾 *058/829–829,* 🕿 *058/823–629. 68 rooms. Restaurant, in-room safes, minibars, room service, pool, bicycles, motorbikes, library, dry cleaning, laundry service, meeting rooms, travel services. AE, MC, V.* 🐾

$$ 🏨 **Nha Trang Lodge Hotel.** Rooms at this hotel across the street from the ocean are perfectly clean and comfortable, with satellite TVs and IDD phones; some even have views of the sea. The lobby, however, is incredibly tacky, and the decor is reminiscent of roadside motels across the United States. But it's still a nice place to stay. ⊠ *42 Tran Phu St.,* 🕾 *058/810–500,* 🕿 *058/828–800. 124 rooms. Restaurant, air-con-*

ditioning, room service, in-room safes, minibars, dry cleaning, laundry service, travel services. AE, MC, V.

$$ 🏨 **Yasaka Saigon–Nha Trang Hotel.** Unwieldy name aside, this brand-new hotel across the street from the beach is one of the nicest accommodations in town. Rooms are spacious and tastefully decorated and have wide-screen TVs. Don't be afraid to bargain a bit on the price as this hotel is still trying to establish its reputation. ⊠ *18 Tran Phu St., ☎ 058/820–090, FAX 058/820–000. 174 rooms. 2 restaurants, tennis court, exercise room, dance club. AE, MC, V.*

$–$$ 🏨 **Haiyen Hotel.** Although it caters to large cruise ships full of Asian tourists, this big waterfront hotel looks like it has not been touched since the '70s. Nonetheless, rooms are passable—meaning they are reasonably clean and have basic amenities such as TVs. ⊠ *40 Tran Phu St., ☎ 058/822–828, FAX 058/821–902. 107 rooms. 2 bars, dining room, lobby lounge, outdoor café, air-conditioning, fans, minibars, refrigerators, room service, pool, beauty salon, massage, sauna, dance club, dry cleaning, laundry service, meeting room, travel services, car rental. MC, V.*

$ 🏨 **Seaside Hotel.** A plush minihotel just south of town on the coast, this place has some of the most tastefully decorated rooms in Nha Trang; a number even have ocean views. No services are offered, however, and the staff sleeps in the lobby at night. Nonetheless, it's one of Nha Trang's best in its price range. ⊠ *96 Tran Phu St., ☎ 058/821–178, FAX 058/ 828–038. 15 rooms. Restaurant, air-conditioning, fans, laundry service. No credit cards.*

¢ 🏨 **Sao Mai.** If you're looking for a cheap but clean establishment, Sao Mai may be for you. The rooms are basic, a fact that is reflected in the price, but the family that runs this lodging is genuinely nice and eager to please. ⊠ *99 Nguyen Thien Thuat St., ☎ 058/827–412. 12 rooms. Air-conditioning, fans, bicycles, motorbikes, travel services. No credit cards.*

Outdoor Activities and Sports

The Blue Diving Club (⊠ 40 Tran Phu St., Coconut Grove, ☎ 058/825–390, FAX 058/824–214), a well-run Professionally Approved Diving Institute (P.A.D.I.) center, offers beginning scuba instruction in English and French and arranges guided excursions for all diving levels.

Nha Trang A to Z

Arriving and Departing

BY AIRPLANE

The easiest way to get to Nha Trang is by plane. **Vietnam Airlines** (⊠ 12B Hoang Hoa Tham St., Nha Trang, ☎ 058/823–797) flies twice daily between Nha Trang and Ho Chi Minh City, and three times a week to Danang.

BY BUS

The **Sinh Café bus** (☞ Getting Around by Bus *in* Vietnam A to Z, *below*) links Ho Chi Minh City with Dalat and then Nha Trang.

BY CAR

Nha Trang is 448 km (278 mi) north of Ho Chi Minh City along Highway 1 (9 hrs by car) and 1,250 km (775 mi) south of Hanoi. Danang is 541 km (335 mi) north of Nha Trang (10 hrs by car). A car and driver can be hired from hotels and from private and state-run travel agencies (☞ Contacts and Resources, *below*).

BY TRAIN
Nha Trang is served three times daily by both express and local trains from Hanoi and Ho Chi Minh City. A soft sleeper to Ho Chi Minh City costs $25–$35; to Hanoi it costs $80–$100, depending on whether you take the express or the local train. The express train between Ho Chi Minh City and Nha Trang takes 12 hours, the local 22 hours; between Hanoi and Nha Trang, the express takes 24 hours and the local 32. Purchase tickets at **Nha Trang Railway Station** (⊠ 26 Thai Nguyen St., ☎ 058/822–113).

Getting Around

The easiest way to get around Nha Trang is by cyclo, which you can find all over town. Be sure to bargain to get the best rate. Or you can rent a bicycle at any travel agency and at most hotels for about 10,000d a day. Hiring a car with a driver is necessary only to go to one of the beaches outside town. You can rent a motorbike, with or without driver, for about 70,000d a day from travel agencies and hotels.

Contacts and Resources

TRAVEL AGENCIES
Ha Phuong Tourist Café (⊠ 5A Tran Hung Dao St., ☎ 058/827–814) arranges bus trips to points north and south of Nha Trang as well as boat trips to the nearby islands. **Sinh Café** (⊠ 10 Biet Thu St., ☎ 058/811–981) can arrange tours to the islands and other points of interest in and around Nha Trang; they also do cash advances.

THE CENTRAL HIGHLANDS AND DALAT

Extending north and south from Dalat is the region known as the central highlands, an unspoiled landscape dotted with ethnic minority villages and religious complexes. Part of the southern end of the Truong Son range, this area of mountains, streams, lakes, and waterfalls covers the provinces of Lam Dong, Dac Lac (Dak Lak), Gia Lai, and Kon Tum; the region includes the towns of Pleiku and Kongtum (☞ The Central Coast, *above*). It is one of the few parts of the country where it is cool enough to wear a sweater, even in summer. The mountain resort of Dalat, the principal town, is somewhat shabby, but its lovely scenery continues to appeal.

Dalat

308 km (191 mi) north of Ho Chi Minh City, 205 km (127 mi) southwest of Nha Trang.

Named for a river of the native Lat people, Dalat was "discovered" in the early part of this century by Alexandre Yersin, a protégé of the French scientist Louis Pasteur, and quickly became a vacation spot for Europeans escaping the infernal heat. During the Vietnam War the city was the favorite nonpartisan resting spot for high-ranking Vietcong and South Vietnamese officers.

Dalat today is a favorite of Vietnamese honeymooners, and attempts are being made to transform it into an international tourist destination. An 18-hole golf course is already in place, new hotels have been built, and old colonial villas are being converted into guest houses. The city vaguely resembles a small French town and is blessed with lovely weather, but it provides kitsch in unspoiled, unself-conscious abundance. The endless flora and fauna are mocked by plastic replicas decorating the white cars of the wedding processions that pass two or three times a day. Panoramic views of majestic mountains and placid lakes are often interrupted by incongruous Vietnamese dressed as American cowboys offering a ride and a photo opportunity.

Exploring Dalat

Dalat's prime sight is its market, which ranks among Vietnam's best. Several places outside downtown are also worth a visit, but since these are spread out across hilly Dalat, it's a good idea to hire a car with a driver and a guide. Decide what you want to see and leave the exact itinerary to your guide.

Dalat surrounds the dam-generated **Xuan Huong Lake** (Ho Xuan Huong), named for a 17th-century Vietnamese poet known for her daring attacks on the hypocrisy of social conventions. Circumscribed by a path and adjoining a beautiful 18-hole golf course, the lake is a hub of leisurely activity (including paddleboating).

The official center of Dalat is the picturesque **Central Market,** with its small collection of restaurants. Locals come here to buy and sell chickens, fruit, vegetables, and specialties such as dried strawberries. ⊠ *Nguyen Thi Minh Khai St.*

Bao Dai's Summer Palace (Biet Dien Quoc Truong) is a wonderfully preserved example of modernist architecture. The yellow palace, built in 1933, still contains the original French furnishings of Emperor Bao Dai, the last emperor of the Nguyen dynasty, who ruled, with the support of the French, from 1926 to 1955. ⊠ *Le Hong Phong St.,* ☎ *063/ 822–125.* ▨ *5,000d.* ☉ *Daily 8–5.*

The **Lam Ty Ni Pagoda** is the home of the multitalented, multilingual monk Vien Thuc, known as the Mad Monk of Dalat. An artist, poet, landscape architect, craftsman, and religious scholar, Vien Thuc is a living legend who will show you around and, if you're not careful, sell you one of his watercolors. ⊠ *2 Thien My St.* ▨ *Free.* ☉ *Daily 9–5.*

One of Dalat's smaller waterfalls, lovely **Cam Ly Falls** is unfortunately somewhat kitschy and crowded with Vietnamese and Western tourists and kids selling gum and dried meat, a Dalat treat.

If you love gardens, go to the European-style **Dalat Flower Garden** (Vuon Hoa Dalat), near the northeast end of Xuan Huong Lake. ⊠ *2 Phu Dong Thien Vuong St.,* ☎ *063/822–151.* ▨ *4,000d.* ☉ *Daily 7–5.*

If you're a train buff or just want to see what Dalat was like in the 1920s, visit the **Crémaillère Railway** (Ga Da Lat). These days the train goes (8 AM departure) only to **Trai Mat,** an ethnic minority village 8 km (5 mi) east of Dalat (you must hire a whole train car for $15 to take a ride). ⊠ *½ km (⅓ mi) east of Xuan Huong Lake.* ▨ *10,000d to view station.* ☉ *Daily 8–5.*

The **Thien Vuong Pagoda** (Chua Tau Thien Vuong), southeast of town, is surrounded by gardens atop a steep mountain with great views. It was built in 1958 by the Chaozhou Chinese congregation. ⊠ *About 3 km (2 mi) southeast of center of town, following Khe Sanh St.* ▨ *Free.* ☉ *Daily 9–4.*

A favorite of Vietnamese honeymooners is **Prenn Falls** (Thac Prenn). In the crowded park surrounding the falls you can frolic over rope bridges and under the falls themselves, or hike up the short path to a makeshift zoo. ⊠ *South of Dalat on Hwy. 20; look for Prenn Restaurant.* ▨ *6,000d.* ☉ *Daily 8–4:30.*

The Valley of Love (Thung Lung Tinh Yeu) is a popular pilgrimage site for Vietnamese honeymooners. On a walk around the lovely green valley you can see Vietnamese couples being photographed with locals on horseback dressed as cowboys. ⊠ *Approximately 3 km (2 mi) north of Xuan Huong Lake, following Phu Dong Thien Vuong St.* ▨ *6,000d.* ☉ *Daily 7:30–4.*

Dining and Lodging

$$ ✕ **Thanh Thanh.** This pleasant though unspectacular Vietnamese restaurant is one of the few formal establishments in Dalat. Because it's recommended by most of the local guides and hotel concierges, it's often filled with Western tourists. One of the better dishes on the menu is the tasty sugarcane shrimp. ✉ *4 Tang Bat Ho St.,* ☎ *063/821–836. No credit cards.*

$–$$ ✕ **Maison Hoa.** Billing itself as a "restaurant de famille," this friendly place with its English-speaking owner is a welcome oasis. It's well located, close to the Central Market, and the Vietnamese-French food is very good. ✉ *6 Duong 3 Thang 2,* ☎ *063/822–934. No credit cards.*

$ ✕ **Lyla Restaurant.** With both European and Vietnamese fare, Lyla is one of the better dining choices in Dalat. Try the *xa lat tron thit bo* (mixed salad with beef). Set on a hill, this restaurant overlooks the Central Market. ✉ *18A Nguyen Chi Thanh St.,* ☎ *063/834–540. No credit cards.*

$$$$ ✕▨ **Sofitel Dalat Palace.** Reminiscent of a French château, the Sofitel
★ is one of the best hotels in Vietnam. Overlooking Xuan Huong Lake, it has been renovated to recapture the grandeur and elegance of its original 1922 French design. Spacious rooms with tasteful antique reproductions, original moldings, and unobtrusive modern conveniences, combined with impeccable service, make it a great place to stay. The French-influenced food in the beautiful Le Rabelais ($$) does not quite live up to its flawless service or impressive wine list. ✉ *12 Tran Phu St.,* ☎ *063/825–444,* ℻ *063/825–666. 43 rooms. Restaurant, café, lounge, piano bar, pub, in-room safes, minibars, no-smoking room, room service, 18-hole golf course, 2 tennis courts, mountain bikes, baby-sitting, dry cleaning, laundry service, concierge, business services, meeting rooms, travel services, airport shuttle. AE, MC, V.*

$$$ ▨ **Novotel.** A sister hotel of the tonier Sofitel Dalat Palace, the Novo-
★ tel Dalat offers first-class, if somewhat small, rooms within walking distance of town and the golf course. The rooms are sleekly functional, though luxurious, with high ceilings, gleaming hardwoods, and brass touches. ✉ *7 Tran Phu St.,* ☎ *063/825–777,* ℻ *063/825–888. 144 rooms. Restaurant, café, bar, lobby lounge, in-room safes, minibars, 18-hole golf course, 2 tennis courts, laundry service, meeting rooms, business services, travel services. AE, MC, V.*

$$ ▨ **Golf 3 Hotel.** Located right in the center of town, the Golf 3 offers excellent, spacious, and fairly inexpensive rooms; having said that, the rooms are a bit on the kitschy side. The enormous sunken tubs in the deluxe rooms are reason enough to stay here. ✉ *4 Nguyen Thi Minh Khai St.,* ☎ *063/826–042,* ℻ *063/830–396. 72 rooms. Restaurant, bar, café, beauty shop, massage, dance club, business services, travel services, airport shuttle. AE, MC, V.*

$$ ▨ **Hang Nga Guesthouse.** Each of the unique rooms is an animal all its own—light your fire in an eagle's egg fireplace while momma eagle spreads her wings over the chimney. At this small guest house and art gallery close to the center of town, the wacky architecture makes for a cheerful lodging alternative in an amusing ambience. ✉ *3 Huynh Thuc Khang St.,* ☎ *063/822–070. 10 rooms. Restaurant, travel services. No credit cards.*

The Central Highlands

The western part of the central highlands is home to a large population of ethnic minorities, dubbed Montagnards (mountain people) by the French. They are largely nomadic farmers who live an isolated existence in tribal villages. Some have been in Vietnam for thousands of years; others came from neighboring Cambodia and Laos several centuries ago.

Steep, slippery steps lead to excellent views of the 300-ft **Dambri Falls.** The falls are about 75 km (47 mi) southwest of Dalat and 233 km (144 mi) northwest of Ho Chi Minh City. ⊠ *10,000d.* ☉ *Daily 7–5.*

Southeast of Dalat on Highway 20, just before you get to the semiarid twin cities of Phan Rang–Thap Cham, are the **Po Klong Garai Cham Towers,** four well-preserved Hindu temples that are remnants of a 13th-century Cham temple built during the reign of Cham King Jaya Simhavarman III, when the Kingdom of Champa ruled this part of Vietnam. ⊠ *Off Hwy. 20.* ⊠ *20,000d.* ☉ *Daily 8–5.*

The Central Highlands and Dalat A to Z

Arriving and Departing

BY AIRPLANE

Vietnam Airlines (San Bay Lien Khuong; ⊠ 5 Truong Cong Dinh St., Dalat, ☎ 063/822–895) flies daily between Dalat's Lien Khuong Airport (30 km/18 mi south of town) and Ho Chi Minh City.

BY BUS

The **Dalat Tourist/Lamdong Tourist Company** (☞ Getting Around, *below*) runs daily minibus service between Dalat and Ho Chi Minh City. **Sinh Café** (☞ Getting Around by Bus *in* Vietnam A to Z, *below*) connects Dalat to Ho Chi Minh City.

Getting Around

The best way to get around Dalat's narrow, hilly roads is by hired car and driver with a guide or on a rented motorbike. Try the **Dalat Tourist/Lamdong Tourist Company** (⊠ 4 Tran Quoc Toan St., ☎ 063/ 822–125, ☎ 063/822–661), which can also arrange a tour of the city.

HO CHI MINH CITY

by Andrew Chilvers

Arriving in Ho Chi Minh City can be a bewildering experience. At the airport the bustle of the crowds and the throngs of taxi drivers competing for business can be jarringly disorienting, especially if you're jet-lagged. But don't be put off—confusion and chaos are at the very heart of the city.

Once romantically referred to by the French as the Pearl of the Orient, Ho Chi Minh City is still called Saigon by almost everyone who lives here. The city has a more cosmopolitan feel than Hanoi, although much of its French colonial quality is vanishing beneath the rapidly rising skyline. History, however, has bequeathed the city a kaleidoscopic melting pot of styles. For dinner you have your choice of not only Vietnamese food but also hamburgers, fine French cuisine, or black caviar at one of the Russian restaurants. Then you can head to one of the sleek, Western-style bars opening monthly.

At the teeming markets, tropical fruits, king cobras, barbecued dogs, and a hundred other such items are for sale; the sidewalks are crammed with noodle stands, cafés, and vendors selling fresh glasses of beer (*bia hoi*) for as little as 25¢. The roads are often gridlocked with motorbikes, scooters, bicycles, cyclos, buses, and an increasing number of cars. All kinds of people travel around by bicycle or motorbike: women dressed in traditional *ao dais* (straight-cut silk gowns worn over flowing pants), long gloves, and conical hats; and whole families—mother, father, and two children—all squeezed on one seat. Everyone seems to be going somewhere, no matter what time of day.

Ho Chi Minh City stretches northwest as far as Cu Chi, in Tay Ninh Province, and south to the upper reaches of the Mekong Delta. The part of the city known as Saigon comprises only Districts 1 and 3 (there are 14). Bordered by the Thi Nghe Channel to the north, the Ben Nghe Channel to the south, and the Saigon River to the east, the city has served as a natural fortress and has been fought over by countless people during the past 2,000 years. The ancient empire of Funan made it a trading post, and the Khmer kingdom of Angkor transformed Prey Nokor, as it was called, into a flourishing trade center protected by a standing army. By the 14th century, while under Khmer rule, the city attracted Arab, Cham, Chinese, Malay, and Indian merchants. It was then known as the gateway to the Kingdom of Champa, the sister empire to Angkor.

In 1674 the Nguyen lords of Hue established a customs post at Prey Nokor to cash in on the region's growing commercial traffic, and Saigon (the Vietnamese name) became an increasingly important administrative post. The building in 1772 of a 6-km (4-mi) trench on the city's western edge (now District 5) marked the shift in the south from Angkor to Nguyen rule, and Vietnamese consolidation increased in 1778 with the development of Cholon, Saigon's Chinese city, as a second commercial hub. The Nguyen lords moved their power base from Hue to Saigon in 1789, after attacks by Tay Son rebels, who were unhappy with Nguyen rule. The rebels massacred most of the Nguyen clan and took control of the government—briefly. In 1802, Prince Nguyen Anh, the last of the Nguyen dynasty, defeated the Tay Son ruler—with French backing—regaining power and uniting Vietnam. He moved the capital back to Hue and declared himself Emperor Gia Long.

Gia Long's request for French help in quelling the Tay Son rebels came at a price. In exchange, he promised the French territorial concessions. Though the French Revolution and the Napoleonic Wars temporarily delayed any French claims, the concessions eventually cost Vietnam dearly. In 1859, tired of waiting for what they felt they deserved, the French seized Saigon and made it the capital of their new colony, Cochin China. This marked the beginning of an epoch of colonial-style feudalism and indentured servitude for many Vietnamese and ethnic minorities.

The catastrophe that was to overtake Saigon and the whole of Vietnam during the latter half of the 20th century was a direct result of French colonial interference. But despite France's role, the Vietnamese to this day, both north and south, maintain deep sentimental ties with French culture and art, as is apparent across the country. And perhaps even more surprising, they graciously welcome Americans with friendly interest, seemingly without rancor or blame.

Nowadays, without colonial or military occupation, the Saigonese are living life to the fullest—and trying to make money. This most Western of all Vietnamese cities has a broad range of international cuisine and Western-style high-rise buildings, although reminders of the past still poke through the headlong rush into capitalism. The Hotel Continental, immortalized in Graham Greene's *The Quiet American*, continues to stand on the corner of Rue Catinat (now Dong Khoi), the most famous thoroughfare of old Indochina. The city still has its central opera house and the old Hôtel de Ville, and it is still dotted with the bunkers and watchtowers of its more recent violent past.

Exploring Ho Chi Minh City

Ho Chi Minh City is not noted for tourist attractions. Although several of its sights should not be missed, its particular appeal is in its street

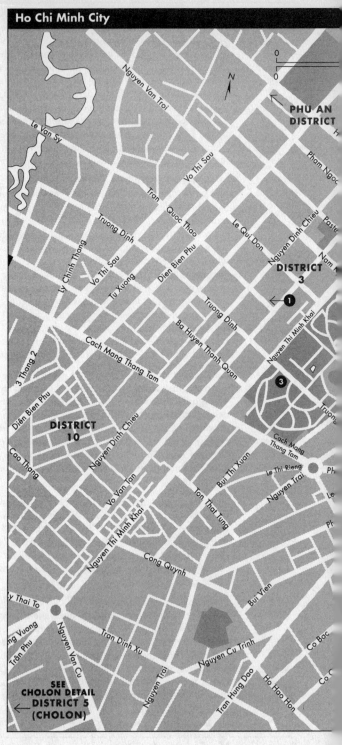

Ho Chi Minh City

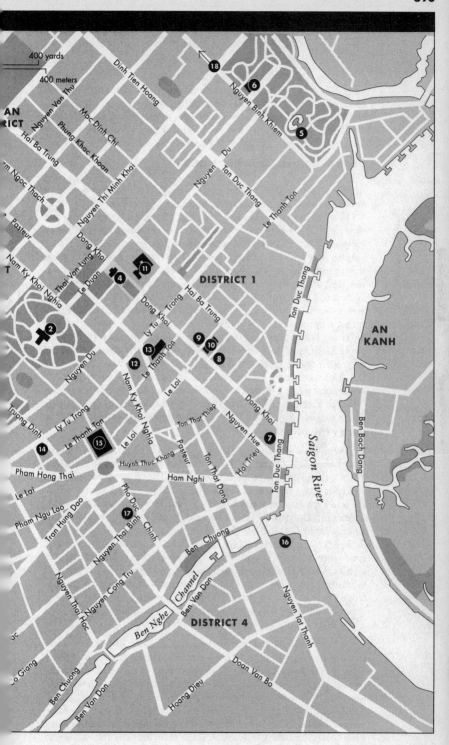

life. From early morning to late at night, the sidewalks are home to hawkers and barbers, noodle sellers and street artists, in a kaleidoscopic maze, with Western-style commerce right alongside traditional trades and practices.

Of the city's 14 districts, the three of most interest to visitors are Districts 1 and 3 (downtown Saigon) and District 5 (Cholon). The city's rather daunting layout and chaotic traffic tend to discourage leisurely walking, and the intermittent taxi, cyclo, or motorbike ride (6,000d– 10,000d) is an enjoyable alternative. Any of the walks below could be done as a cyclo ride, an option particularly recommended on hot days.

Central Saigon (Districts 1 and 3)
A GOOD WALK

Although slightly away from the center, the provocative **War Remnants Museum** ① makes a good starting point. From here head northeast on Vo Van Tan Street toward tree-lined Nam Ky Khoi Nghia Street, and turn right. You will soon see the grounds of the modern **Reunification Palace** ②. Directly behind it is the old French sports club, the Cercle Sportif, now known as **Cong Vien Van Hoa Park** ③; to enter the park, turn right off Nguyen Du Street, which is a one-way road running alongside the palace. Walk through the park into the grounds of the palace and on to Le Duan Boulevard. Walk northeast; after passing Pasteur Street, you'll see the back of **Notre Dame Cathedral** ④, with its pink spires. Continue on Le Duan Boulevard. A couple of blocks past Hai Ba Trung Boulevard is the new U.S. consulate, which was built where the U.S. embassy once stood. The embassy was the site of one of the most memorable images of the war, after the capture of Saigon: the U.S. ambassador, an American flag clutched to his chest, rushing into a helicopter waiting on the roof, while marine guards pushed back mobs of South Vietnamese who had been assured evacuation. Continue on to the sprawling grounds of the **Zoo and Botanical Garden** ⑤ and the **History Museum** ⑥.

From the main entrance of the complex, walk southeast on Nguyen Binh Khiem Street to the intersection with Le Thanh Ton Street. Make a right, then take the first left at Ton Duc Thang Street, which turns and runs along the Saigon River. Walk south along the waterfront to the late 19th-century **Hotel Majestic** ⑦, at the intersection of Ton Duc Thang and Dong Khoi streets. Turn right at Nguyen Hue Boulevard and make the first left onto Hai Trieu Street, also known as Whiskey Row. Take a right on Ham Nghi Street, where a bunch of international food stores (No. 64 is a good one) are jam-packed with Western specialties. Make a right onto Ton That Dang Street, where you can find everything from live eels to laundry detergent at the market that extends along intersecting Huynh Thuc Khang Street, a kind of electronics arcade. Continue a block past Huynh Thuc Khang Street, to Ton That Thiep Street, in the Indian quarter, and turn right.

Cross Nguyen Hue Boulevard, and turn left on Dong Khoi Street, which extends from the river to Notre Dame Cathedral. Along Dong Khoi Street is the **Delta Caravelle** ⑧, once a favorite haunt of war correspondents at cocktail hour. Opposite the Caravelle is the **Hotel Continental** ⑨. Although a shadow of its former self, it's still worth a visit. Sandwiched between the two at the end of Le Loi Boulevard is the **Municipal Theater** ⑩, recognizable by its inverted dome. Farther up Dong Khoi Street, past the Continental, is the main branch office of Saigon Tourist, on the corner of Le Thanh Ton Street. Next comes Notre Dame Cathedral—the front of the church this time. The beautiful French colonial **Central Post Office** ⑪ is on the right side of the square in front of the cathedral.

With your back to the cathedral, turn right on Nguyen Du Street, then take the first left onto Pasteur Street, and the first right onto Ly Tu Trong Street to get to the neoclassic **Museum of the Revolution** ⑫, or Army Museum. Return to Pasteur Street, and turn right to get to Le Thanh Ton Street and the **Old Hôtel de Ville** ⑬, now the People's Committee building. Follow Le Thanh Ton Street southwest and make a right on Truong Dinh Street. In the middle of the block on your left is the **Mariamman Hindu Temple** ⑭, the last functioning one in the city. Backtrack on Le Thanh Ton Street to where the busy **Ben Thanh Market** ⑮ spills out into the surrounding street.

TIMING

The walk could take a day or more, depending on how much time you spend at the sights.

SIGHTS TO SEE

★ ⑮ **Ben Thanh Market** (Cho Ben Thanh). Every imaginable item is sold here—look for a cheap meal, a hat, even live snakes. The market building was built in 1914 by the French. The best time to visit is first thing in the morning. ⊠ *At circular intersection of Le Loi Blvd., Pham Ngu Lao St., and Ham Nghi Blvd., District 1.* ☉ *Daily 7–7.*

★ ⑪ **Central Post Office** (Buu Dien Truing Tam). This classic French colonial building was completed in 1891; inside is a huge map of old Indochina. To mail letters, enter the less romantic, Soviet-era expansion at 117 Hai Ba Trung Street. ⊠ *At the top of Dong Khoi St. opposite Notre Dame Cathedral, District 1.* ☉ *Daily 7:30–7:30.*

☞ ③ **Cong Vien Van Hoa Park.** Huge tamarind trees line the road leading up to this park, which resembles a botanical garden. As the Cercle Sportif, the elite sporting club of the French bourgeoisie in colonial times, this park was barred to Vietnamese people. Today the sports club has tennis courts, a swimming pool, a gym and weight room, and a colonial clubhouse. To use the facilities will cost you no more than a dollar. ⊠ *Entrance on 115 Nguyen Du St., District 1.*

⑧ **Delta Caravelle.** This recently renovated hotel is now the most popular in the city, with its ideal location and its modern cafés and bars. It was renowned in the 1960s as home to most of the foreign correspondents during the Vietnam War. During the 1968 Tet Offensive, several U.S. marines were killed here; journalists filmed the battle from the rooftop. The same rooftop is now the city's most popular bar, **Saigon, Saigon.** ⊠ *19 Lam Son Sq., District 1,* ☎ *08/823–4999.*

Dong Khoi Street. Once named Rue Catinat, this was French colonial Saigon's Fifth Avenue or Rodeo Drive. During the Vietnam War it was Tu Do Street, the center of the infamous red-light district. These days the street remains the center of the Old City, but most of the old-time bars have been replaced by restaurants and tourist-oriented shops.

NEED A
BREAK?
    The **Paris Deli** (⊠ 31 Dong Khoi St., District 1, ☎ 08/829–7533) is a
    European-style café serving excellent cappuccinos and pastries.

⑥ **History Museum** (Vien Bao Tang Lich Su). Although the front door leads you right to a statue of ubiquitous "Uncle Ho," this museum is dedicated to Vietnamese history from the earliest inhabitants to 1930, when the Communist Party was established. Half the museum covers the history of the nation as a whole, while the other half focuses on the art and artifacts of southern Vietnam; the ethnography section is particularly interesting. The neo-Vietnamese structure was built by the French in 1929, and much of the current collection was compiled by the French Far Eastern Institute. ⊠ *2 Nguyen Binh Khiem, District 1,*

☎ *08/829–8146 or 08/829–0268.* ✉ *10,000d.* ⊙ *Tues.–Sat. 8–11:30 and 1:30–4:30, Sun. 8:30–11:30.*

★ ❾ **Hotel Continental.** In French colonial days, the Hotel Continental's open terrace (now simply a sidewalk), shaded by broad tamarind trees, was the town's most sought-after lunch spot. During the Vietnam War, journalists and diplomats met on the terrace to discuss the latest events. Graham Greene's *The Quiet American* was set here. ✉ *132–134 Dong Khoi St., District 1,* ☎ *08/829–9201.*

★ ❼ **Hotel Majestic.** Built in the late 19th century, the Majestic was one of the first French colonial hotels, and it still has the elegant decor of its origins. The hotel's rooftop bar provides magnificent views of the Saigon River and the Thu Thiem swamp district opposite. ✉ *1 Dong Khoi St., District 1,* ☎ *08/829–5512.*

⑭ **Mariamman Hindu Temple** (Chua Ba Mariamman). Vivid statues and colorful floral offerings at this temple create a microcosm of India in the streets of Saigon. Before its return in the early '90s to the Hindu community, the government used the temple as a factory for making incense and processing dried fish. ✉ *45 Truong Dinh St., District 1.* ⊙ *Daily 7–7.*

❿ **Municipal Theater** (Nha Hat Thanh Pho). This colonial-style theater was built as the opera house in 1899. Later it housed the National Assembly of South Vietnam until it became a theater again after 1975. ✉ *Intersection of Le Loi Blvd. and Dong Khoi St., District 1,* ☎ *08/ 825–1563.*

⑫ **Museum of the Revolution** (Bao Tang Cach Mang). Constructed in 1886 as the residence for the French governor of Cochin China, the building is now a museum dedicated to the Vietnamese struggle against the French and Americans. The displays are in Vietnamese, but you'll easily get the message. The neoclassical building itself is as interesting as many of the exhibits inside: it has huge columns outside and high-ceilinged ballrooms from the 19th century inside. Beneath the building, in the concrete bunkers and tunnels connecting to the Reunification Palace, President Ngo Dinh Diem and Ngo Dinh Thuc hid before their capture and execution in 1963. ✉ *65 Ly Tu Trong St., District 1,* ☎ *08/829–9741.* ✉ *Free.* ⊙ *Tues.–Sun. 8–4:30.*

❹ **Notre Dame Cathedral** (Nha Tho Duc Ba). This neo-Romanesque cathedral, prominent on the Saigon skyline, was built by the French in 1880 on the site of an old fort. Spanish, Portuguese, and French missionaries introduced Catholicism to Vietnam as early as the 16th century, and today Vietnam's 9 million Catholics are Asia's largest Christian population after the Philippines. The Mass celebrated at 9:30 AM on Sunday is quite a spectacle. ✉ *Top of Dong Khoi St., District 1.*

⑬ **Old Hôtel de Ville.** Built by the French between 1901 and 1908 to be Saigon's City Hall, this yellow-and-white colonial-style building now houses the city's main governing body and is known as the Ho Chi Minh City's People's Committee office. It's not open to the public. ✉ *Intersection of Le Thanh Ton and Nguyen Hue Sts., District 1.*

❷ **Reunification Palace** (Hoi Truong Thong Nhat). This modern palace—the symbolic center of the South Vietnamese government—was the scene of the dramatic seizure of Saigon by the National Liberation Front in 1975, when tanks smashed down the gates and an NLF flag was draped over the building's balcony. The president's mansion, designed by the European-influenced modernist architect Ngo Viet Thu in 1962, is classic '60s architecture. It was built after President Diem's own air force bombed him in the old French palace in an assassination attempt, and he decided he had an "image problem." It wasn't completed until after his death. Although tours are free to Vietnamese, foreigners must pay. ✉ *Visitors' entrance on 106 Nguyen Du St., District 1,* ☎ *08/ 829–4117.* 🎫 *10,000d.* ☉ *Daily 7:30–10:30 and 1–4.*

❶ War Remnants Museum (Nha Trung Bay Toi Ac Chien Tranh Xam). You may instinctively shy away from this museum, which is dedicated to publicizing the horrors perpetrated by U.S. armed forces during the Vietnam War. You'll probably come away with mixed feelings about the one-sided propaganda—ashamed of the U.S. actions, angry about the Vietnamese inaccuracies in depicting them, or both. But it's a must-see if you're curious about the war. ✉ *28 Vo Van Tan St., District 3,* ☎ *08/829–5587.* 🎫 *10,000d.* ☉ *Tues.–Sun. 7:30–11:45 and 1:30–4:45.*

🅒 ❺ Zoo and Botanical Garden (Thao Cam Vien). The fauna here does relatively well, and the flora thrives in its natural subtropical niche. After seeing the lackluster array of live animals, visit the eerie "taxidermy-go-round," where you can ride stuffed animals. ✉ *Nguyen Binh Khiem St. at Le Duan Blvd., District 1.* 🎫 *2,000d.* ☉ *Daily 8–5:30.*

Circling Old Saigon

This tour covers the sights around the periphery of Old Saigon. South of District 1, on the broad waterfront along the Saigon River, is a less palatial section of the old city where the old docks and customs houses used to be. This was also the old banking district, and you can still see the colonial-era Hong Kong and Shanghai Banking Corporation, and Banque d'Indochine buildings. You might want to hire a cyclo to take you to some of the sights in this area.

SIGHTS TO SEE

❶⑥ Ho Chi Minh Museum (Khu Luu Niem Bac Ho). The museum building itself, nicknamed the "Dragon House" (Nha Rong) for its architectural design, is far more interesting than most of the displays of Uncle Ho's personal belongings. It was constructed in 1863 as the original French customs house; Ho Chi Minh (1890–1969) passed through here in 1911 on the way to his 30-year sojourn around Europe and America. ✉ *On Saigon Port at 1 Nguyen Tat Thanh St., by quayside on Ben Nghe Channel at far end of Ham Nghi Blvd., District 4,* ☎ *08/829–5740.* 🎫 *10,000d.* ☉ *Tues.–Sun. 8:30–11:30 and 1:30–4.*

❶⑦ Art Museum (Bao Tang My Thuat). Considering its grand colonial setting, this museum is a disappointment. The building is in classic French-Vietnamese architectural style (European-type stucco and Asian design). The first and second floors cover propaganda art of the Soviet socialist-realist variety. But the reason to visit the museum is on the third floor, where you'll find antique statues and other relics of the pre-Vietnamese south, objects from the ancient Funan and Chmer civilizations, and some good Cham art. ✉ *97A Pho Duc Chinh St., District 1,* ☎ *08/822–2577.* 🎫 *10,000d.* ☉ *Tues.–Sun. 7:30–11:30 and 1:30–4.*

★ ❶⑧ Emperor Jade Pagoda (Chua Ngoc Hoang or Phuoc Hai Tu). Also known as the Tortoise Pagoda, this structure—the finest Chinese pagoda in Saigon—was built by the Cantonese community in 1909. Taoist, Buddhist, and ethnic myths provide the subjects for the pagoda's multitude of statues and carvings. Take a moment to note the main altar, the side panel's depiction of hell and, in the side room, the miniature female figures who represent the range of human qualities. ✉ *73 Mai Thi Luu St., District 3.* 🎫 *Free.* ☉ *Daily dawn–dusk.*

Cholon (District 5)

Southwest of central Saigon lies Cholon (District 5), a commercial mecca that's still the center of Chinese culture in Vietnam. Negotiate a price of about 55,000d with a cyclo driver to take you on a tour of the pagodas and mosques concentrated around Nguyen Trai Street and Tran Hung Dao Boulevard. Pagodas are seldom shut to the public, and most monks begin their prayers early in the morning, so you are generally welcome to enter a pagoda at any time of day. There are no admission fees, but it is traditional to give a donation. When you've seen enough pagodas, tell your guide or cyclo driver, so you won't be taken to every single one. Spend the rest of the day exploring Cholon's streets, markets, shophouses (stores that double as the owners' homes), and restaurants, with their distinctive Chinese appeal.

A GOOD WALK

Begin at the bustling **Binh Tay Market** ⑲, and when you leave, turn left and walk east along Phan Van Khoe Street until you get to Phung Hung Street; take a left and follow it until you reach the **Ong Bon Pagoda** ⑳, where you can pay your respects to the guardian of happiness and virtue. Leaving the pagoda, walk east on Hai Thuong Lan Ong Boulevard to the old colonial **Post Office** ㉑. Walk north up Chau Van Liem Boulevard to Tran Hung Dao Boulevard, the center of Cholon, with its street markets and old, small shophouses (and some newer, taller ones).

Continue north past Nguyen Trai Street (the heart of Cholon's pagoda district); turn right on small Lao Tu Street to reach the **Quan Am Pagoda** ㉒, known for its elaborately decorated scenes. Head south on Luong Nhu Hoc Street to the **Ha Chuong Hoi Quan Pagoda** ㉓, at No. 802, one of the many temples devoted to the goddess of the sea. Take a left on Nguyen Trai Street and walk along until you come to the **Thien Hau Pagoda** ㉔, at No. 710, where sailors used to come before they went out to sea. Continue past the intersection of Trieu Quang Phuc Street, to No. 678, on the left, the **Nghia An Hoi Quan Pagoda** ㉕, famous for its detailed woodwork. On the other side of the street, at No. 118, is the **Tam Son Hoi Quan Pagoda** ㉖, dedicated to the goddess of fertility. Keep on Nguyen Trai Street, past the intersection of Ly Thuong Kiet Boulevard, until you reach the **Cholon Mosque** ㉗.

TIMING

Depending on how interested you are in pagodas, this walk could take up to three or four hours.

SIGHTS TO SEE

⑲ **Binh Tay Market** (Cho Binh Tay). Cholon's main market is in a colonial-era, Chinese-style building. The street outside is a frenzy of activity; inside you have to wend your way through very narrow aisles. ⊠ *On Hau Giang Blvd., District 6.* ⊙ *Daily, usually 5 AM–8 PM.*

㉗ **Cholon Mosque.** Built in 1932 by Tamil Muslims, the Cholon Mosque now serves Saigon's Indonesian and Malaysian Muslim community. ⊠ *641 Nguyen Trai St., at Ly Thuong Kiet Blvd., District 5.*

㉓ **Ha Chuong Hoi Quan Pagoda.** Like many pagodas built by Fujian congregations, this one is dedicated to Thien Hau, goddess of the sea and protector of fishermen and sailors. Its four stone pillars encircled by painted dragons were brought from China when the pagoda was constructed in the 19th century. ⊠ *802 Nguyen Trai St., District 5.*

㉕ **Nghia An Hoi Quan Pagoda.** Built by the Chaozhou Chinese congregation in 1872, this pagoda is worth seeing for its elaborate woodwork. There is a large figure of the deified Chinese general Quan Cong's sacred red horse, as well as representations of Quan Cong himself with two guardians. ⊠ *678 Nguyen Trai St., District 5.*

★ ⑳ **Ong Bon Pagoda** (Chua Ong Bon or Nhi Phu Hoi Quan). Many deities are represented at this pagoda, but the main attraction is Ong Bon him-

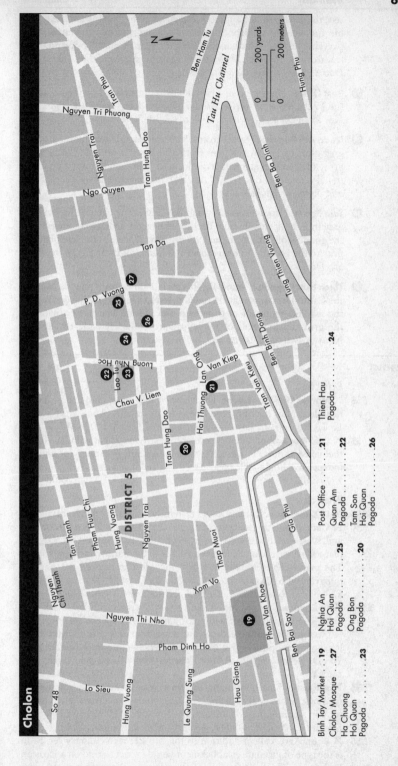

Cholon

N

200 yards
200 meters
0
0

Ben Ham Tu
Tau Hu Channel
Ben Ba Dinh
Hung Phu

Nguyen Tri Phuong
Tran Phu
Tran Hung Dao
Nguyen Trai
Ngo Quyen
Tan Da
Tung Thien Vuong
P. D. Vuong
Ben Binh Dong
Luong Nhu Hoc
Lao Tu
Van Kiep
Chau V. Liem
Tran Van Kieu
Hai Thuong Lan Ong
Gia Phu
Tran Hung Dao
DISTRICT 5
Tan Thanh
Pham Huu Chi
Hung Vuong
Nguyen Trai
Nguyen Chi Thanh
Xom Vo
Thap Muoi
Phan Van Khoe
Nguyen Thi Nho
Ben Bai Say
Pham Dinh Ho
So 48
Lo Sieu
Hung Vuong
Le Quang Sung
Hau Giang

27
25
26
24
22 23
21
20
19

Binh Tay Market . . . 19
Cholon Mosque . . . 27
Ha Chuong
Hoi Quan
Pagoda 23

Nghia An
Hoi Quan
Pagoda 25
Ong Bon
Pagoda 20

Post Office 21
Quan Am
Pagoda 22
Tam Son
Hoi Quan
Pagoda 26

Thien Hau
Pagoda 24

self, the guardian of happiness and virtue. Ong Bong is also responsible for wealth, so people bring fake paper money to burn in the pagoda's furnace in his honor, hoping the year ahead will bring financial rewards. ⊠ *264 Hai Thuong Lan Ong Blvd. (parallel to Tran Hung Dao St.), at Phung Hung St., District 5.*

㉑ **Post Office.** This modernist building was constructed by the French in the 1920s. ⊠ *Intersection of Hai Thuong Lan Ong Blvd. and Chau Van Liem Blvd., District 5.* ☉ *Daily 7:30–7:30.*

㉒ **Quan Am Pagoda.** Dating from 1816, this pagoda was built by a congregation of Fujian refugees from China. It is notable for its busy array of scenes in lacquer, ceramic, gold, and wood illustrating traditional Chinese stories. ⊠ *12 Lao Tu St. (parallel to Huong Vuong Blvd. and Nguyen Trai St.), District 5.*

㉖ **Tam Son Hoi Quan Pagoda** (Chua Ba Chua). The Chinese Fujian congregation built this lavishly decorated pagoda dedicated to Me Sanh, the goddess of fertility, in the 19th century. Women—and some men— pray to the goddess to bring them children. ⊠ *118 Trieu Quang Phuc St., District 5.*

㉔ **Thien Hau Pagoda** (Chua Ba). This early 19th-century pagoda built by the Cantonese congregation is dedicated to Thien Hau, the goddess of the sea and protector of fishermen and sailors. The turtles living on the grounds, symbols of longevity, are considered sacred. ⊠ *710 Nguyen Trai St., District 5.*

Dining

Eclectic

$$$ ✕ **Marine Club Restaurant.** The Marine Club, decked out in garish nautical decor, has the only wood-burning pizza oven in Saigon. ⊠ *17A4 Le Thanh Ton St., District 1,* ☎ *08/829–2249. AE, DC, MC, V.*

$$ ✕ **Café Mogambo.** A quirky restaurant-cum-burger-bar with an African theme, Mogambo is a favorite with Americans homesick for a good, inexpensive home-style meal. ⊠ *20 Thi Sac St., District 1,* ☎ *08/825– 1311. MC, V.*

French

$$$$ ✕ **Le Camargue.** Romantic and tastefully done, the French-influenced
★ Le Camargue is an exciting culinary forum. The cuisine is a mix of East and West—with a good wine list to match. Dine out on the elegant, plant-filled terrace of the restored villa or in the warmly lit dining rooms. The menu changes daily but may include pan-roasted sea bass or tamarind-glazed crab cake. ⊠ *16 Cao Ba Quat St., District 1,* ☎ *08/ 823–3148. Reservations essential. AE, DC, MC, V. No lunch.*

$$$$ ✕ **Le Caprice.** Stodgy but run like a Swiss timepiece, this landmark provides Saigon's expat elite with unoriginal but fine French cuisine, passé but well-maintained hotel decor, and a beautiful view of the Saigon River. It's worth stopping by just to have a drink. ⊠ *Landmark Building, 5B Ton Duc Thang St., 15th floor, District 1,* ☎ *08/822–8337. AE, DC, MC, V.*

$$$ ✕ **Augustin.** Small, intimate, and filled with comfortably solo expats reading the newspaper at the bar, Augustin serves tasty French bistro food to a predominantly international crowd. ⊠ *10 Nguyen Thiep St., District 1,* ☎ *08/829–2941. AE, DC, MC, V. No lunch Sun.*

$$$ ✕ **Bi Bi.** An excellent addition to the city's French culinary set, Bi Bi is the type of intimate establishment you'd expect to find on a Parisian backstreet. This is more than just a restaurant or café: people come here to eat, gossip, play cards, drink pastis, and snack on oysters flown in each day from Brittany. The steak, served with french fries, may not be very French but is still a popular dish. ✉ *8A/8D2 Thai Van Lung St., District 1,* ☎ *08/829–2747. AE, DC, MC, V.*

$$ ✕ **La Fourchette.** A small and extremely intimate affair, La Fourchette, with only six tables, is more a café than a restaurant. The cuisine is good, not great, but its friendly atmosphere more than compensates. ✉ *9 Ngo Duc Khe St., District 1,* ☎ *08/829–8143. AE, DC, MC, V.*

Italian

$$$ ✕ **Ristorante Pendalesco.** Most dishes here are Italian, but the restaurant also caters to other cuisines for the international crowd. This is slightly off the beaten path in District 3, but its fine cuisine and intimate atmosphere are always popular, so it's a good idea to book ahead. ✉ *142B Vo Thi Sau St., District 3,* ☎ *08/820–3552. AE, DC, MC, V.*

Japanese

$$$$ ✕ **Sakura.** This has fast become the most popular sushi bar in town. With all the ingredients flown in fresh every day, Sakura is expensive by local standards, but worth it nonetheless. ✉ *40 Mac Thi Boui St., District 1,* ☎ *08/822–2182. AE, DC, MC, V.*

Russian

$$ ✕ **'A' The Russian Restaurant.** Saigon's premier Russian establishment has surprisingly good food—Siberian *pelmeni* (dumplings), beef Stroganoff, and caviar with black bread—at very reasonable prices. Endless amounts of vodka also flow. ✉ *361/8 Nguyen Dinh Chieu St., District 3,* ☎ *08/835–9190. MC, V.*

Thai

$$–$$$$ ✕ **Chao Thai.** This sensational restaurant serves the finest Thai food in the city. The cuisine is equal to the setting: a mock Thai longhouse decorated with *apsara* dancers and wood carvings. ✉ *16 Tai Van Lung St., District 1,* ☎ *08/824–1457. AE, MC, V.*

Vegetarian

¢   ✕ **Bodhi Tree II.** Bodhi serves vegetarian delights in a quaint alley just off Pham Ngu Lao Street. The eggplant sautéed with garlic, the vegetable curry, and the braised tofu in a clay pot are superb. The fresh-fruit shakes are meals in themselves. ✉ *175/6 Pham Ngu Lao St., District 1,* ☎ *08/839–1545. No credit cards.*

Vietnamese

$$$ ✕ **Blue Ginger.** Dine on excellent Vietnamese cuisine in an elegant set-
★   ting with an international clientele. Traditional music shows are performed at 7:30. ✉ *37 Nam Ky Khoi Nghia St., District 1,* ☎ *08/829–8676. AE, DC, MC, V.*

$$$ ✕ **Lemongrass.** An expat and tourist favorite, Lemongrass serves ex-
★   cellent Vietnamese food in a French-bistro atmosphere. Almost everything on the short menu is delicious, but the spicy mixed-seafood soup deserves special praise. ✉ *4 Nguyen Thiep St., District 1,* ☎ *08/822–0496. AE, DC, MC, V. No lunch.*

$$$ ✕ **Vietnam House.** Very popular with travelers and expats, Vietnam House serves a wide selection of hearty noodle dishes and other Vietnamese standards in a glossy Eurasian-style dining room. Live traditional music is performed every night upstairs. ✉ *93 Dong Khoi St., District 1,* ☎ *08/829–1623. MC, V.*

$ ✕ **Restaurant 13.** This local and expat hangout, on a quiet road just off Dong Khoi Street, serves delicious traditional food in a no-nonsense setting. ✉ *11–17 Ngo Duc Ke St., District 1,* ☎ *08/829–1417. No credit cards.*

$ ✕ **Thi Sach Street Cafés.** Thi Sach Street is a must if you love seafood. From 5 PM onward the top part of Thi Sach Street, where it borders Le Thanh Ton Street, is literally impassable with street restaurants. Best bets are the steamboat (boiling broth in which seafood is cooked at your table), freshwater crabs, and colossal tiger prawns. ⊠ *Thi Sach St., District 1,* ☎ *no phone. No credit cards.*

¢ ✕ **Pho Hoa.** If you're not quite game for the sidewalk-food-stall eating experience, this open-air noodle kitchen is the next best thing. Just say "chicken," "beef," or "pork," or point to whatever looks good at the next table. ⊠ *260C Pasteur St., District 3,* ☎ *08/829–7943. No credit cards.*

Lodging

Central Saigon (Districts 1 and 3)

$$$$ ⊞ **Delta Caravelle.** This recently renovated hotel has quickly become the most popular accommodation in the city. Ideally located opposite the historic opera house, the new hotel is part of an international chain catering to tourists and businesspeople. The rooftop bar, Saigon Saigon, is an excellent place to unwind and gives great views across the downtown area. ⊠ *19 Lam Son Sq., District 1,* ☎ *08/823–4999,* FAX *09/824–3999. 335 rooms. 2 restaurants, bar, café, lobby lounge, air-conditioning, in-room data ports, in-room safes, in-room VCRs, minibars, room service, pool, massage, sauna, exercise room, business services, meeting rooms. AE, DC, MC, V.* ⊗

$$$$ ⊞ **Hotel Continental.** If it's history you're after, stay at the French
★ colonial-style Continental: Graham Greene's classic *The Quiet American* was set here, and it was a meeting place of journalists and diplomats during the Vietnam War. But because the hotel was renovated by the state-run Saigon Tourist agency, it remains a shadow of its former self—the decor and finishing lack the finesse and expert renovations of the hotel's international counterparts. Rooms facing the street are very noisy; ask for one overlooking the inner courtyard. ⊠ *132–134 Dong Khoi St., District 1,* ☎ *08/829–9201,* FAX *08/829–9252. 87 rooms. 2 restaurants, lobby lounge, air-conditioning, in-room safes, minibars, no-smoking rooms, refrigerator, room service, dry cleaning, laundry service, concierge, business services, meeting rooms, travel services. AE, DC, MC, V.*

$$$$ ⊞ **Hotel Majestic.** The Majestic, on the waterfront overlooking the Saigon
★ River, is one of Vietnam's great colonial hotels. As with the Continental, the hotel was renovated by Saigon Tourist, so it still lacks the service expertise of the international chains. Nevertheless, the hotel's charm persists. Rooms, with their high ceilings and the original woodwork, strike a delicate balance between airy and intimate. Be sure to have a drink at the rooftop bar overlooking the river. ⊠ *1 Dong Khoi St., District 1,* ☎ *08/829–5512,* FAX *08/829–5510. 122 rooms. 2 restaurants, 2 bars, lobby lounge, outdoor café, air-conditioning, in-room safes, minibars, no-smoking rooms, refrigerators, room service, pool, massage, sauna, exercise room, piano, dry cleaning, laundry service, concierge, business services, meeting rooms, travel services. AE, DC, MC, V.*

$$$$ ⊞ **New World Hotel Saigon.** The New World's central location—
★ across the street from the Ben Thanh Market—makes it very popular, particularly with tour groups and businesspeople. ⊠ *76 Le Lai St., District 1,* ☎ *08/822–8888,* FAX *08/823–0710. 541 rooms. 3 restaurants, bar, lobby lounge, air-conditioning, in-room safes, minibars, no-smoking floor, refrigerators, room service, pool, massage, sauna, driving range, tennis court, exercise room, motorbikes, nightclub, piano, baby-sitting, dry cleaning, laundry service, concierge, business services, meeting rooms, travel services, airport shuttle, car rental. AE, DC, MC, V.*

$$$$ ⊞ **Riverside Renaissance.** This brand-new chain hotel has a lovely lo-
★ cation overlooking the river. The Riverside Renaissance offers all the comforts you'd expect of a newly built international hotel, but it lacks

the colonial flair of some of the older hotels in the city. ✉ *8–10 Ton Duc Thang St., District 1,* ☎ *08/822–0033,* ᴍ *08/823–5666. 349 rooms. Restaurant, bar, lobby lounge, air-conditioning, in-room safes, minibars, no-smoking rooms, refrigerators, room service, massage, sauna, exercise room, dry cleaning, concierge, business services, meeting rooms, travel services. AE, DC, MC, V.*

$$$$ ⊞ **Saigon Prince Hotel.** Rooms at the Saigon Prince are more spacious ★ and have higher ceilings and finer finishing touches than many of the other luxury hotels in the city. But the hotel has fewer facilities. The lobby bar is a nice spot for a calm midafternoon break, whether you're staying at the hotel or not. ✉ *63 Nguyen Hue Blvd., District 1,* ☎ *08/ 822–2999,* ᴍ *08/824–1888. 203 rooms. Dining room, sushi bar, lobby lounge, air-conditioning, in-room safes, minibars, no-smoking rooms, refrigerators, room service, hot tub, massage, sauna, steam room, exercise room, nightclub, dry cleaning, laundry service, concierge, business services, meeting rooms, travel services. AE, DC, MC, V.*

$$$$ ⊞ **Sofitel Plaza.** A high-ceilinged, spacious lobby leads to the first ★ floor and the Aromasia, a restaurant serving Western and Asian cuisine. The Sunday brunches are the best value in the city. There's also a pool bar here. Rooms have satellite TVs and IDD phones. Conveniently situated, the Sofitel is opposite the U.S. consulate. ✉ *17 Le Duan Blvd., District 1,* ☎ *08/824–1555; 08/824–1666 in the U.S.,* ᴍ *08/ 823–2333. 280 rooms, 12 suites. 3 restaurants, 2 bars, air-conditioning, pool, massage, sauna, health club, laundry service, business services, meeting rooms. AE, MC, V.*

$$$ ⊞ **Mercury Hotel.** The Mercury combines warmth and elegance with modern conveniences. Rooms are reasonably sized and decorated in a luxurious yet utilitarian and unoriginal style. The hotel is closer to the budget traveler's haven—Pham Ngu Lao Street—than to the congregation of upscale hotels and restaurants around Le Loi and Nguyen Hue boulevards. ✉ *79 Tran Hung Dao St., District 1,* ☎ *08/824–2525,* ᴍ *08/822–3312. 104 rooms. 2 restaurants, bar, lobby lounge, air-conditioning, in-room safes, minibars, no-smoking rooms, refrigerators, room service, massage, health club, dry cleaning, laundry service, baby-sitting, business services, meeting rooms, travel services. AE, DC, MC, V.*

$$–$$$ ⊞ **Rex Hotel.** The Rex stands as a monument to Saigon's recent history. Originally a French garage, it later became a hotel and then the base for American operations during the Vietnam War. Its conference room was the scene of the daily press briefings, or "five o'clock follies," and in 1976 the unification of the country was announced in the same room. Today the hotel is filled with glorious kitsch: stuffed animals, statues, and crown-shape lamp shades. Even if you don't stay here, it's worth a peek, and you should go up to the rooftop bar. ✉ *141 Nguyen Hue Blvd., District 1,* ☎ *08/829–2185,* ᴍ *08/829–1469. 207 rooms. 2 restaurants, lobby lounge, air-conditioning, in-room safes, minibars, no-smoking rooms, refrigerators, room service, pool, beauty salon, massage, sauna, steam room, nightclub, dry cleaning, laundry service, concierge, business services, travel services. AE, DC, MC, V.*

$$ ⊞ **Grand Hotel.** Although more modest than the Majestic or the Continental hotels, this pleasant old colonial establishment evokes a bygone era of Francophone Saigon in the heart of the old Rue Catinat. Unfortunately, like the other colonial-era hotels here, the Grand is state-owned and suffers accordingly. The rooms are light and airy, with real character. But the service is indifferent, and the dining room should be avoided. Still, as locations go, this is as central as you can get. ✉ *8 Dong Khoi St., District 1,* ☎ *08/823–0163,* ᴍ *08/823–5781. 135 rooms. Dining room, air-conditioning, in-room safes, massage, sauna, health club, laundry service, business services. AE, DC, MC, V.*

$$ 🏨 **Mondial Hotel.** The renovated Mondial has small, tidy standard rooms. In the lobby are various large bas-relief wooden sculptures of dragons and mythical Vietnamese warriors. The hotel's Skyview restaurant has traditional Vietnamese dancing and music nightly. ⊠ *109 Dong Khoi St., District 1,* ☎ *08/829–6291,* FAX *08/829–6273. 40 rooms. Restaurant, lobby lounge, air-conditioning, in-room safes, room service, nightclub, dry cleaning, laundry service, travel services. AE, DC, MC, V.*

$$ 🏨 **Norfolk Hotel.** This superslick establishment is between the Ben Thanh Market and the Hôtel de Ville in central Saigon. White and chrome dominate. Rooms are impeccable and comfortable, if small and simple. Facilities are oriented primarily to businesspeople; there is even a resident interpreter. ⊠ *117 Le Thanh Ton St., District 1,* ☎ *08/829–5368,* FAX *08/829–3415. 109 rooms. Restaurant, bar, lobby lounge, sports bar, air-conditioning, in-room safes, minibars, massage, sauna, health club, baby-sitting, dry cleaning, laundry service, business services, meeting rooms, travel services. AE, DC, MC, V.*

$ 🏨 **Mogambo Guest House.** This minihotel above the restaurant of the same name (☞ Dining, *above*) is run by an American and is very popular with—guess who?—Americans. Like most of these small establishments, the Mogambo is unexceptional looking but has clean rooms that are suitable for a good night's sleep. ⊠ *20 Thi Sach St., District 1,* ☎ *08/825–1311. 10 rooms. Restaurant, air-conditioning. MC, V.*

$ 🏨 **Phuong Duong Hotel.** Another one of the city's minihotels, this one, too, is bare bones but comfortable and clean. Rooms have IDD phones and satellite TV. ⊠ *55B Nguyen Van Thu St., District 1,* ☎ *08/822–2437,* FAX *08/822–1346. 10 rooms. Restaurant, air-conditioning. MC, V.*

$ 🏨 **Spring Hotel.** In the hub of a major dining and nightlife area in District 1, this cozy, family-run minihotel has squeaky-clean rooms with new moldings and fixtures made to look old. Some rooms have nice views of the street below, but the standard ones with no windows are much less expensive. ⊠ *44–46 Le Thanh Ton St., District 1,* ☎ *08/829–7362,* FAX *08/821–1383. 38 rooms. Bar, dining room, lobby lounge, air-conditioning, in-room safes, room service, travel services. AE, DC, MC, V.*

Cholon (District 5)

$$$$ 🏨 **Hotel Equatorial.** This luxury hotel is in an odd location—on the edge of Cholon, about 15 minutes from the downtown area. To date, bookings have been somewhat scarce because of this. Nonetheless, the hotel is one of the best in town. It also has Vietnam's nicest health club and a half-Olympic-size swimming pool. ⊠ *242 Tran Binh Trong St., District 5,* ☎ *08/839–7777,* FAX *08/839–0011. 333 rooms. Bar, café, lobby lounge, air-conditioning, minibars, refrigerator, room service, pool, health club, nightclub, piano, dry cleaning, laundry service, business services, meeting rooms, travel services, car rental, free parking. AE, DC, MC, V.*

$$ 🏨 **Arc En Ciel Hotel.** This neon-clad hotel is done up in a mishmash of modern, '60s, and Chinese interior decor, with accommodations on the higher end of utilitarian. But overall it's a good deal—if you want to stay in Cholon. ⊠ *52–56 Tan Da St., District 5,* ☎ *08/855–0332,* FAX *08/855–2424. 91 rooms. Restaurant, bar, lobby lounge, outdoor café, air-conditioning, in-room safes, room service, beauty salon, massage, sauna, exercise room, nightclub, dry cleaning, laundry service, concierge, business services, meeting rooms, travel services. AE, DC, MC, V.*

$ 🏨 **Prince Hotel.** Not to be confused with the Saigon Prince in District 1, this small-time "royal" lodging in the middle of Chinatown provides charm and efficiency cheaply. Unlike many hotel restaurants, the Prince's dining room actually serves good food. ⊠ *29 Chau Van Liem St., District 5,* ☎ *08/855–6765,* FAX *08/856–1578. 25 rooms. Restaurant, bar, lobby lounge, outdoor café, air-conditioning, in-room safes, minibars, refrigerator, room service, travel services. AE, DC, MC, V.*

Phu Nuan District

$$$$ ⊡ **Garden Plaza Hotel.** Only about 10 minutes from the airport, this international establishment is one of the best. It's a good 15 to 20 minutes from downtown. ⊠ *309 Nguyen Van Troi St., Phu Nhuan District,* ☎ *08/842–1111,* FAX *08/842–4370. 157 rooms. Restaurant, lobby lounge, pub, air-conditioning, in-room safes, minibars, no-smoking rooms, refrigerators, room service, pool, massage, sauna, exercise room, motorbikes, dry cleaning, laundry service, concierge, business services, meeting rooms, travel services, airport shuttle, car rental. AE, DC, MC, V.*

$$$$ ⊡ **Omni Saigon Hotel.** Built in the former CIA headquarters, with walls
★   so thick mobile phones won't work, the Omni is one of the city's finest hotels. It has the essence of French elegance, with a hint of glitz and a touch of '60s bunker architecture. More important, it's one of the few international hotels to have sent its staff abroad for training, which shows in its excellent service. ⊠ *251 Nguyen Van Troi St., Phu Nhuan District,* ☎ *08/844–9222,* FAX *08/844–9198. 248 rooms. 3 restaurants, lobby lounge, pub, air-conditioning, in-room safes, minibars, no-smoking rooms, refrigerators, room service, pool, beauty salon, massage, sauna, exercise room, motorbikes, nightclub, piano, baby-sitting, dry cleaning, laundry service, concierge, business services, meeting rooms, travel services, airport shuttle, car rental. AE, DC, MC, V.*

Nightlife and the Arts

Saigon's nightlife is thriving. But nightclubs here are subject to the erratic rules laid down by the authorities. One week they are open, and the next they are classified as social evils and are all shut down. Nightclub owners take this in stride. Check in "Time Out," the weekly English-language supplement in the *Vietnam Investment Review,* for up-to-date information.

The Arts

MUSIC AND THEATER

The only regular venue in town for classical music performances is the **Conservatory of Music** (Nhac Vien Thanh Pho Ho Chi Minh; ⊠ 112 Nguyen Du St., District 1, ☎ 08/839–6646); the seasons runs September–June. Built in 1899 by the French as an opera house and later used as the home of the National Assembly of South Vietnam, the **Municipal Theater** (Nha Hat Thanh Pho; ⊠ intersection of Le Loi and Dong Khoi Sts., District 1, ☎ 08/829–1249) became a theater again in 1975.

Nightlife

BARS AND CLUBS

Apocalypse Now (⊠ 2C Thi Sach St., District 1), one of the oldest clubs in Saigon, is loud, fun, and always packed with a cross section of expatriates, tourists, amiable pimps, and local prostitutes. Note: take a taxi, not a cyclo, back to your hotel (cabs line up outside); cyclo drivers have been known to steal from drunken foreigners. Leave any jewelry, including watches, at your hotel.
Bar No. 5 (⊠ Ly Tu Trong St., District 1), on the edge of the downtown area, is one of the latest favorites with expats and tourists. Located in an old French bungalow, it's partly open to the outside and is a good place to start the night on balmy tropical evenings.
Bar Rolling Stones (⊠ 177 Pham Ngu Lao St., District 1), in the backpacker area of town, serves cheap beer and spills out onto the street with loud music. If you sit outside, hold your bag in your lap or wind the straps around your ankles.
Café Latin (⊠ 25 Dong Du St., District 1) is a multilevel tapas bar with constructivist decor and fine Australian and French wines.

Café Mogambo (✉ 20 Thi Sach St., District 1, ☎ 08/825–1311), run by an American expat and his Vietnamese wife, is a kind of self-parodying Reno-style roadside stop where you can get good draft beer in a kitschy environment all dressed up with African decor.

Le Camargue (✉ 16 Cao Ba Quat St., District 1, ☎ 08/823–3148), although really more a restaurant (☞ Dining, *above*), has an excellent terrace bar and a pool table. A recent addition is a tapas bar, called Vasco's, on the ground floor.

Catwalk (✉ New World Hotel, 76 Le Lai St., District 1) has private karaoke dens where you can sing to your heart's content and a dance floor where dry ice creates a moody atmosphere.

Globo (✉ 6 Nguyen Thipe St., District 1, ☎ 08/822–8855) looks like it could be in Paris and is very popular with the city's fashionable French set.

Hard Rock Cafe (✉ 24 Mac Thi Buoi St., District 1), though not official, does a booming business with expats and tourists.

Long Phi (✉ 163 Pham Ngu Lao St., District 1) is one of the few bars in town to attract expats, Vietnamese, and backpackers.

O'Brien's (✉ 72A2 Hai Ba Trung St., District 1), is a popular bar decked out with a trendy Parisian-style interior. It also has a garden terrace where you are served excellent pizzas straight out of the oven.

Q Bar (✉ In the side of the Municipal Theater, off Dong Khoi St.)—a hip spot that looks like it could be in New York, London, or Paris—has become one of Saigon's not-to-be-missed. Bar food is served.

Sheridan's Irish House (✉ 19 Le Thanh Ton St., District 1), in the downtown area, is a traditional Irish pub serving Guinness and, oddly, dim sum.

HOTEL BARS

A more civilized alternative to Saigon's bar scene is one of the many rooftop establishments at the city's hotels. Particularly noteworthy hotel bars include those in the **Caprice Hotel** (✉ Landmark Building, 5B Le Ton Duc Thang St., District 1); the Saxophone Bar at the **New World Hotel** (✉ 76 Le Lai St., District 1); the fifth-floor veranda at the **Rex Hotel** (✉ Khach San Ben Thanh St., District 1); the piano bar at the **Saigon Prince** (✉ 63 Nguyen Hue Blvd., District 1); and the Saigon, Saigon on the rooftop of the **Delta Caravelle** (✉ 19 Lam Son Sq., District 1).

Outdoor Activities and Sports

Golf

There are two 18-hole golf courses outside Saigon. **Vietnam Golf and Country Club** (✉ Ap Gian Dan, Long Thanh Mi Ward, District 9, ☎ 08/825–2951), in the outlying district of Thu Duc, 10 km (6 mi) north of Saigon, costs about $50 a day for a game. **Song Be Golf Resort** (✉ 254B Nguyen Dinh Chieu St., ☎ 06/585–5802), 20 km (12 mi) outside the city, has swimming pools, tennis courts, and restaurants. The cost for a day is $50.

Health Clubs and Swimming Pools

Cercle Sportif (✉ In Cong Vien Hoa Park, District 1) has tennis courts, a swimming pool, and a gym with a weight room; you can use the facilities for less than $1. **Hotel Equatorial** (✉ 242 Tran Binh Trong St., District 5, ☎ 08/839–7777) has the best gym in town and a half-Olympic-size pool. The cost is $15 for the day. **Hotel Majestic** (✉ 1 Dong Khoi St., District 1, ☎ 08/829–5514) has a small pool and gym that you can use as long as you order something from the bar. **New World Hotel Saigon** (✉ 76 Le Lai St., District 1, ☎ 08/822–8888) charges $12 for use of its small pool and standard gym.

Jogging

Hot, crowded, polluted Saigon isn't really a good city for jogging, though some Vietnamese do go out around 5 AM, before the traffic begins. If you are set on running, contact the Hash House Harriers club, which meets every Sunday outside the **Century Hotel** (⊠ 68A Nguyen Hue Blvd., ☎ 08/845–3886).

Shopping

Ho Chi Minh City is a good place to have casual clothes made or to have designer apparel copied. The city is famous also for its lacquerware and wood carvings. Dong Khoi Street between Le Loi Boulevard and the river is lined with art galleries and shops selling jewelry, lacquerware, wood carvings, and other souvenirs to mostly tourists (which doesn't mean there aren't good finds). No matter where you shop, if you are buying a large number of items, be sure to bargain. But be polite; the debate over prices is expected to be a very civil and friendly process. Also, most shops will take dollars or dong, though they often list prices in dollars only.

Department Stores

On the ground floor of the huge **Tax Department Store** (Cua Hang Back Hoa; ⊠ intersection of Nguyen Hue St. and Le Loi Blvd) you can change travelers' checks and find all kinds of souvenirs. But the best bargains in Vietnam are on the two upper floors: designer clothes and sneakers made in China but redirected to Vietnam; nice, inexpensive bags; and 24-hour tailors.

Markets

Clothing, shoes, bags, wood carvings, lacquerware, food, and more are available at the large **Ben Thanh Market** (Cho Ben Thanh; ⊠ intersection of Le Loi Blvd., Pham Ngu Lao St., and Ham Nghi Blvd., District 1). Keep careful watch of your belongings; pickpockets have been known to strike. **Cholon's Binh Tay Market** (Cho Binh Tay; ⊠ Hau Giang Blvd., District 6) has all kinds of items—kitchenware, baskets, toys, hats, shoes, and food. The charming **open-air market** on Ton That Dam Street, between Huynh Thuc Khang Street and Ham Nghi Boulevard in District 1, has everything from fish and produce to plastic toys and cleaning products. On the north side of Ham Nghi Boulevard, between Ho Tung Mau and Ton That Dam streets, you can find all kinds of international foods at the tiny, jam-packed European-style **specialty food shops.** For an assortment of **electronic equipment,** try Huynh Thuc Khang Street, Nguyen Hue Boulevard, and Pasteur Street.

Specialty Shops

ANTIQUES

It's against the law for foreigners to take antiques (anything older than 21 years plus a day) out of Vietnam without special permission from the Ministry of Culture. It's also very difficult to distinguish between genuine and fake items, especially on Dong Khoi Street, where both sell at comparable prices. In particular, beware of restored antique timepieces, which often have a 1950s Rolex face, for example, covering the much cheaper works of a '70s Seiko.

Nguyen Frères (⊠ 2A Le Duan Blvd., District 1, ☎ 08/821–3716) sells antiques and replicas. Most popular items include beautiful French-Vietnamese antique and reproduction furniture and a range of prints of old colonial Saigon. Without doubt, it's the finest shopping of its kind in town.

ART

Taking fine art out of the country isn't as problematic as taking out antiques, but have a receipt for your purchase to show customs just in case. Many art galleries can be found on Dong Khoi Street and the surrounding area. Canvases fetch as little as $30 and as much as $15,000. **Anh** (⊠ 135 Nguyen Hue Blvd., District 1, ☎ 08/821–3716) sells ethnic folk art and fabrics. **ATC** (Art Tourist Services; ⊠ 172 Nam Ky Khoi Nghia St., District 3, ☎ 08/829–6833; ⊠ 29B Dong Khoi St., District 1, ☎ 08/829–2695; ⊠ 2 Cong Truong Quoc St., District 3, ☎ 08/829–6833) is a national art organization. **Dong Phuong Gallery** (⊠ 135 Nam Ky Khoi Nghia St., District 1, ☎ 08/822–1716). **Fine Arts Museum** (⊠ 97A Pho Duc Chinh St., District 1, ☎ 08/821–0001). **Galerie Lotus** (⊠ 43 Dong Khoi St., District 1, ☎ 08/829–2695). **Hong Hac Art Gallery** (⊠ 9A Vo Van Tan St., District 3, ☎ 08/824–3160). **Saigon Art Gallery** (⊠ 77 Mac Thi Buoi St., District 1, ☎ 08/822–6048).

CLOTHING

Linh Phuong Maison de Couture (⊠ 38 Ly Tu Trong St., District 1, ☎ 08/824–2985) is very reliable for custom-made clothing for adults and children. **Tropic** (⊠ 73A Le Thanh Ton St., District 1, ☎ 08/829–7452) carries contemporary and traditional clothing as well as some home furnishing items. **Zakka** (⊠ 23 Dong Khoi St., District 1, ☎ 08/829–8086), next to the Hotel Majestic, sells fabric and beautifully designed clothing, shoes, and bags (with a Western influence).

HOUSEWARES

Home Zone (⊠ 41 Dinh Tien Hoang St., District 1, ☎ 08/822–8022) sells stylish silverware, furnishings, and other housewares. **Mai Huong** (⊠ 73 Le Thanh Ton St., District 1, ☎ 08/829–6233) is the place to go for beautifully embroidered tablecloths and bedspreads. **Q Home** (⊠ 65 Le Loi St., 2nd floor, District 1, ☎ 08/821–4883) has colorful, contemporary-style ceramics.

LACQUERWARE

Several galleries sell lacquerware on Dong Khoi Street (from No. 137 to No. 145) and in the Phu Nhuan District on Nguyen Van Troi Street (and on its continuation, Cong Hoa Street). **Heritage** (⊠ 53 Dong Khoi St., District 1) has beautiful contemporary-looking lacquerware and outstanding replicas of antique Buddhas and statuary. **Tay Son** (⊠ 198 Bo Thi Sau St., District 3, ☎ 08/820–2524) is a large lacquerware distributor with a wide selection and good prices.

SHOES

Tran Van My (⊠ 95 Le Thanh Ton St., District 1, ☎ 08/822–3041) is the place to go for ready-made, custom-made, embroidered, and leather shoes and sandals.

Ho Chi Minh City A to Z

Arriving and Departing

BY AIRPLANE

Many international airlines fly into Ho Chi Minh City's **Tan Son Nhat Airport** (⊠ Hoang Van Thu Blvd., Tan Binh District, ☎ 08/844–3179), 7 km (4 mi) outside of central Saigon. **Vietnam Airlines** (⊠ 116 Nguyen Hue St., District 1, ☎ 08/829–2118, FAX 08/823–0273), the Vietnamese national carrier, has international flights from Ho Chi Minh City as well as domestic flights to the following destinations: Buon Ma Thuot, Cantho, Dalat, Danang, Haiphong, Hanoi, Hue, Nha Trang, Phu Quoc, Pleiku, and Qui Nhon. Prices range from $60 to $150. It's best to book several days in advance and to reconfirm your flight; you can always change your reservation at branch offices all over the city.

To get to the airport from downtown, use the free hotel shuttle service if you're staying at one of the mid-range or high-end hotels. Or, choose an official-looking taxi from the throngs waiting outside. Though many now have meters, you should still try to negotiate a price before getting in: about $5–$8 (you can pay in dong or dollars), depending on the number of passengers and pieces of luggage. The ride takes about 20 minutes, depending on traffic.

BY BUS

Traveling by public bus around Vietnam is not recommended. You're better off taking one of the minibuses that leave from the bus stations (make reservations a day in advance through your concierge, a travel agent, or a travel café), or even better, a tour bus organized by one of the travel agencies or tourist cafés (☞ Travel Agencies, *below*).

BY TRAIN

From Ho Chi Minh City there is local train service to Nha Trang, Qui Nhon, and Hue. The slightly faster **Reunification Express** goes to many of the larger coastal towns, from Phan Rang–Thap all the way north to Hanoi. Trains arrive and depart from the **Saigon Railway Station** (Ga Saigon; ✉ 1 Nguyen Thong St., District 3, ☎ 08/823–0105), about 1 km (½ mi) from central Saigon. The **ticket office** (✉ 275C Pham Ngu Lao St., District 1, ☎ 08/832–3537) is open daily 7:15–11 and 1–3, though it's best to ask a travel agent to call for ticketing and information. Note that Saigon Tourist does not provide any train service information.

Getting Around
BY BICYCLE

Hotels often rent out bicycles or can at least suggest where to rent decent ones. Those available from shops on the street are generally unreliable.

BY BOAT

Boats touring the Saigon River start at 50,000d an hour and are available at the riverside on Ton Duc Thang Street, between Ham Nghi Boulevard and Me Linh Square. Negotiate an exact price with the owners before boarding. Ask at travel agencies for advice about choosing the best trips.

BY BUS

Public buses are the cheapest way to get around town, though not the fastest, most convenient, or most pleasant. Service is often erratic and painfully slow, and the buses generally have no air-conditioning and are often crammed full of people. You're better off taking a cyclo or a taxi. Nevertheless, it's important to know about the **Saigon–Cholon line,** which you are most likely to use; it starts in Me Linh Square at the Tran Hung Dao intersection and ends up at Cholon's Binh Tay Market. Tickets, available on board, cost 2,000d; look for signs reading XE BUYT (bus stop).

BY CAR

Taxis and cyclos provide the best means of getting around the city. You may want to be driven to sights around Saigon, though most people use a car only for excursions outside the city. You can hire a car and driver from one of the hotels or travel agencies (☞ Travel Agencies, *below*).

BY CYCLO

Although cyclos, or pedicabs, are only supposed to charge 2,000d per km (½ mi), 5,000d–10,000d is a decent rate (this includes the tip) for just about any destination within the same district. Cyclo drivers frequently speak English very well and can provide informative city tours for a small price (a generous half-day rate is about 30,000d–55,000d)—bargaining is advised. Drivers will wait for you when you visit sights; just don't leave any valuables in the cyclo. If you are happy with your driver, you can make arrangements to have him pick you up the next day.

BY MOTORBIKE

One of the quickest ways around the city is riding on the back of a motorbike taxi, known as a Honda *om* or *xe om*. This service usually costs about 10,000d. Motorbike drivers are everywhere; they'll just drive up alongside you and ask where you're going. You can also rent your own motorbike from any number of cafés, restaurants, and travel agencies, especially Sinh Café and Ann's Tourist.

BY TAXI

Taxis are available in front of all major hotels. Nowadays most taxis have meters, and most drivers speak a little English. An average journey across town starts at 20,000–40,000d. The best taxi companies are: **Saigon Taxi** (☎ 08/844–8888) and **Vina Taxi** (☎ 08/811–0888 or 08/842–2888). Other recommended companies include: **Airport Taxi** (☎ 08/825–4250); **Giadinh Taxi** (☎ 08/822–6699); and **Saigon Tourist** (☎ 08/822–2206).

Contacts and Resources

CONSULATES

Australia (⌧ 5B Ton Duc Thang St., District 1, ☎ 08/829–6035). **Canada** (⌧ 203 Dong Khoi St., District 1, ☎ 08/824–2000). **New Zealand** (⌧ 41 Nguyen Thi Minh Khai St., District 1, ☎ 08/822–6905). **United Kingdom** (⌧ 21 Le Duan Blvd., District 1, ☎ 08/829–8433). **United States** (⌧ 5 Le Duan St., District 1, ☎ 08/822–9433).

CURRENCY EXCHANGE

Although they don't always offer the best exchange rate, hotels are usually the easiest places to change money; they can also change traveler's checks. Banks and the small exchange shops offer the most competitive rates. Don't change your money on the black market. Many tourists lose out to sharks because the high dong denominations can be confusing for the first-time visitor.

Major banks in Ho Chi Minh City include: **ANZ Bank** (Australia New Zealand Bank; ⌧ 11 Me Linh Sq., District 1, ☎ 08/829–9316); **Citibank** (⌧ 8 Nguyen Hue St., District 1, ☎ 08/824–2118); **Hong Kong Bank** (⌧ 75 Pham Hong Thai St., District 1, ☎ 08/829–2288); **Standard Chartered Bank** (⌧ 203 Dong Khoi St., District 1, ☎ 08/829–8383); and **Vietcom Bank** (⌧ 29 Chuong Duong St., District 1, ☎ 08/823–0310). International ATMs can be found at ANZ Bank and Hong Kong Bank.

EMERGENCIES

Ambulance (☎ 15). **Police** (☎ 13).

Round-the-clock medical treatment is available at **Asia Emergency Assistance** (AEA; ⌧ Han Ham Building, 65 Nguyen Du St., District 1, ☎ 08/829–8520), a clinic run by Western doctors. **Cho Ray Hospital** (⌧ 201B Nguyen Chi Thanh St., District 5, ☎ 08/554–4137 or 08/554–4138) has regular and 24-hour emergency treatment. **International SOS Assistance** (⌧ Han Ham Building, 65 Nguyen Du St., District 3, ☎ 08/829–8520 for emergencies; 08/829–4386 for the clinic) can help with emergency care and evacuations.

My Chau Pharmacy (⌧ 389 Hai Ba Trung St., District 1, ☎ 08/822–2266), recommended by the Travel Medical Consultancy, is open daily 7:30 AM–10 PM.

For lost credit cards, contact **Vietcom Bank** (☎ 08/829–3068 or 08/822–5413), which is affiliated with Western banks.

A few bookstores in Ho Chi Minh City sell English-language books. Many traveling street vendors have English–Vietnamese phrase books and dictionaries, travel guides, Graham Greene's *The Quiet American,* and other books on Vietnamese culture and history. **Xuan Thu** (⊠ 185 Dong Khoi St., District 1, ☎ 08/822–4670) sells international newspapers and periodicals and Vietnamese–English phrase books. **Xunhasaba** (⊠ 76E Le Thanh Ton St., District 1), the largest foreign magazine and newspaper distributor in town (it also doubles as a tailor shop), sells nice, inexpensive art books and some novels (mostly classics) in English. Look carefully in Cholon (among other places) for shops buying and selling used paperbacks in English.

The **Central Post Office** (⊠ 2 Cong Xa Paris St., District 1), next to Notre Dame Cathedral, is open daily 7:30–5:30.

Travel agencies can arrange wonderful guided tours outside the city. For excellent tours to the Mekong Delta and the Cu Chi Tunnels and for various customized trips—some for as little as $5 per day including lunch—check itineraries and schedules at the Saigon Tourist budget office or at any number of cafés and small travel agencies on Pham Ngu Lao Street.

Ann's Tourist (⊠ 58 Ton That Tung St., District 1, ☎ 08/833–2564, FAX 08/832–3866) could very well be your only tourist-information stop. The company arranges tours around Ho Chi Minh City and throughout the entire country; rents cars; books flights; arranges visa extensions; and provides all the historical, cultural, and orientation material you could possibly need. It's open Monday–Saturday 8–6, and Sunday 9–11.

Exotissimo (⊠ 28 Dinh Tien Hoang St., District 1, ☎ 08/825–1723, FAX 08/825–1684) is a more upscale tour operator headquartered in Hanoi but with an office in Saigon. **Peregrine Tours** (⊠ 24/9 Pham Ngoc Thach St., District 3, ☎ 08/829–6086 or 08/822–8464, FAX 08/829–6158), run by Australian John Powell, specializes in adventure tours as well as the more common package trip. **Vidotours** (⊠ 41 Dinh Tien Hoang St., District 1, ☎ 08/829–1438, FAX 08/829–1435) specializes in upscale package tours and individual trips all over the country with excellent tour guides.

Saigon Tourist (⊠ main office: 49 Le Thanh Ton St., District 1, ☎ 08/823–0100, FAX 08/822–4987; budget office [in Café Apricot]: ⊠ 187 Pham Ngu Lao St., ☎ 08/835–4535) is the big government-run travel service. It can arrange just about everything you might need. Note that besides the price, the only difference between the luxury and budget excursions seems to be the size of the bus. It's open daily 7:30–6:30.

Other offices and agencies include: **Getra Tour Company** (⊠ 86 Bui Vien St., District 1, ☎ 08/835–3021); **Thanh Thanh Travel Agency** (⊠ 205 Pham Ngu Lao St., District 1, ☎ 08/836–0205); and **Vietnam Tourism** (⊠ 234 Nam Ky Khoi Nghia St., District 3, ☎ 08/829–0776, FAX 08/829–0775).

Kim's Cafe (⊠ 272 De Tham St., District 1) organizes inexpensive trips to regions such as the Mekong Delta. **Sinh Café Travel** (⊠ 179 Pham Ngu Lao St., District 1, ☎ 08/835–5601) has Vietnam's greatest travel deal: a $33–$38 open-ended ticket good for bus travel the length of the country. The café is open daily 7 AM–11 PM.

SIDE TRIPS FROM HO CHI MINH CITY

Cu Chi Tunnels

65 km (40 mi) northwest of Ho Chi Minh City via Hwy. 22.

The Cu Chi Tunnels—a 250-km (155-mi) underground network of field hospitals, command posts, living quarters, eating quarters, and trapdoors—stand as a symbol of the Vietcong's ingenuity in the face of overwhelming odds.

These tunnels, first used in the late '40s against the French, made it possible for the Vietcong in the '60s to not only withstand massive bombings and to communicate with other distant Vietcong enclaves but to command a sizable rural area that was in dangerous proximity (a mere 35 km, or 22 mi) to Saigon. After the Diem regime's ill-fated "strategic hamlet program" of 1963, disenchanted peasants who refused to move fled to Cu Chi to avoid the aerial bombardments. In fact, the stunning Tet Offensive of 1968 was masterminded and launched from the Cu Chi Tunnels nerve center, with weapons crafted by an enthusiastic assembly line of Vietcong-controlled Cu Chi villagers.

Despite extensive ground operations and sophisticated chemical warfare—and even after declaring the area a free-fire zone—American troops were unable to control it. In the late '60s, though B-52 bombing reduced the area to a wasteland, the Vietnamese Communists and the NLF managed to hang on.

The guided tour includes a film that documents the handiwork of "American monsters" and an array of booby traps demonstrated by former Vietcong soldiers. The claustrophobic might consider skipping the crawl through the hot, stuffy, and tight tunnels (though sections have been expanded to allow for tourists' bigger bodies). Amazingly, in these same tunnels many Vietnamese survived for months and even years.

The easiest and best way to visit is on a tour arranged through one of the travel agencies or tourist cafés (☞ Travel Agencies in Ho Chi Minh City A to Z, *above*), since the trip is identical at every agency. A day trip, which will run you about $40 per person, will generally combine the tunnels with a visit to the Caodai Holy See, in neighboring Tay Ninh (☞ *below*).

Tay Ninh

95 km (59 mi) northwest of Ho Chi Minh City via Hwy. 22.

The town of Tay Ninh is home to Caodaism—an indigenous hybrid religion based on the major Eastern and Western religions—and to its
★ impressive, brightly colored temple, the **Caodai Holy See.** Founded in 1926 by a mystic named Ngo Minh Chieu, Caodaism is a fusion of a Mahayana Buddhist code of ethics with Taoist and Confucian components. Sprinkled into the mix are elements of Islam, Roman Catholicism, the cult of ancestors, Vietnamese superstition, and over-the-top interior decoration, encompassing a fantastic blend of architectural styles.

Caodai has grown from its original 26,000 members to a present-day membership of 3 million. Meditation and communication with spiritual worlds via earthly mediums or seances are among its primary practices. Despite its no-holds-barred decorative tendencies, Caodaism emphasizes abstinence from luxury and sensuality as well as vegetarianism as means of escaping the reincarnation cycle. Although the priesthood is strictly nonprofessional, members of the clergy are celibate.

Perhaps most important, the Caodaists believe the divine revelation has undergone three iterations: God's word presented itself first through Lao Tse and other Buddhist, Confucianist, and Taoist players; then through a second set of channelers such as Jesus, Muhammad, Moses, Confucius, and the Buddha. Whether because of the fallibility of these human agents or because of the changing set of human needs, the Caodaists believe the divine transmission was botched. They see themselves as the third and final expression, the "third alliance between God and man." Since anyone can take part in this alliance, even Westerners like Joan of Arc, Victor Hugo, and William Shakespeare have been added to the Caodai roster.

The noon ceremony (others are held at 6 AM, 6 PM, and midnight) is one of the most fascinating and colorful religious vignettes to which you'll ever be privy as a tourist. A finely tuned hierarchical procession of men and women of all ages parades through the temple's great hall, where great painted columns twined with carved dragons support sky-blue arched vaults; panels of stained glass with a cosmic-eye motif punctuate the walls. You are permitted to watch and take snapshots from the mezzanine.

Generally a visit to Tay Ninh is part of a day trip to the Cu Chi Tunnels (☞ *above*) arranged through one of the travel agencies in Saigon. A guide will accompany you, explain the history of the Caodai sect, and take you through the temple.

Mekong Delta

The northern delta, centered around My Tho and Can Tho, the region's capital, is accessible and can be managed in a day trip. Fruit grows here in abundance: orchards full of mangoes, jackfruit, lemons, custard fruit, dragon fruit, pineapples, durians, and papayas. Lush green rice paddies stretch for miles. In the Mekong's remote southern section, steamy mangrove swamps and thick palm forests thrive on the flat, flooded delta, making the area difficult to navigate.

The heart of the delta is the Mekong River, also known as Song Cuu Long, or River of the Nine Dragons. The river carries with it and deposits every second 2,500 to 50,000 cubic yards of fertile soil, which created the delta and continues to make it grow. Descending from the Tibetan plateau, the Mekong River runs through China, separates Burma from Laos, skirts Thailand, passes through Cambodia, and flows through Vietnam into the South China Sea. As it enters Vietnam, the river divides into the Tien Giang (Upper River), which splinters at My Tho and Vinh Long into several seaward tributaries; and the Hau Giang (Lower River), which passes through Chau Doc, Long Xuyen, and Can Tho to the sea.

The Khmer once ruled this region but were slowly pushed out by the Vietnamese over the centuries. Uncertainty about who would have sovereignty over the Mekong Delta lasted until 1954, when the French handed over the area to the new country of South Vietnam. The Khmer have been disgruntled ever since. Under Pol Pot's rule in Cambodia, the Khmer again laid claim to the delta as their ancestral land, and there were frequent skirmishes between Khmer Rouge and Vietnamese soldiers along the border.

Most organized tours of the northern delta region include boat trips through the river tributaries to islands, such as Tan Long Island, crisscrossed with paths leading through orchards. Often you will stop to have a snack of exotic fruit and tea at someone's farm stand or home. You might visit a beekeeper or see rice noodles being made. Another popular stop on many tours is the Island of the Coconut Monk (Ong Dau Dua), about 2 km (1 mi) from My Tho, where you can have a full meal or a snack with rice wine and honey. Only ruins remain of a garish, eclectic religious complex built in the 1940s by a monk named Nguyen Thanh Nam, who was said to have once lived for years on nothing but coconuts.

There are only two ways to get to the Mekong Delta, both of which must be arranged from Ho Chi Minh City: you can hire a private car with driver and guide through a travel agency or participate in an organized tour. The most scenic parts of the Mekong Delta are accessible only by boat. Boat trips are generally part of any prearranged tour or can be set up by your guide. Be sure to keep an eye on your bags and valuables during your boat trip.

VIETNAM A TO Z

Arriving and Departing

By Airplane

AIRPORTS

At present there are no direct flights between Vietnam and North America. International flights from North America into Vietnam typically connect through hubs like Bangkok, Singapore, Manila, Hong Kong, Kuala Lumpur, and Taipei and fly into Ho Chi Minh City's Tan Son Nhat Airport or Hanoi's Noi Bai Airport.

Major hubs for domestic air travel are Ho Chi Minh City, Hanoi, and Danang, but there is also service to Ban Me Thuot, Dalat, Dien Bien Phu, Haiphong, Hue, Nha Trang, Phu Quoc Island, Pleiku, Qui Nhon, and Vinh.

AIRPORT TAXES

Every time you fly into or out of an airport in Vietnam, on a domestic or an international flight, you must pay an airport tax. The airport tax is 20,000d for domestic flights and $10 or 140,000d for international flights.

CARRIERS

Current international carriers with flights to Vietnam include: **Asiana Airlines** (☎ 800/227–4262), **Cathay Pacific Airways** (☎ 800/233–2742 in the U.S.; 800/268–6868 in Canada), **China Airlines** (☎ 800/227–5118), **Korean Air** (☎ 800/438–5000), **Malaysia Airlines** (☎ 800/552–9264), and **Singapore Airlines** (☎ 800/742–3333). **Continental** (☎ 800/231–0856), **Northwest Airlines** (☎ 800/225–2525), and **United Airlines** (☎ 800/241–6522) have flights into Tokyo, Singapore, and Bangkok, which then connect with regional carriers.

There are no direct flights to Vietnam from the United Kingdom. Bangkok and Hong Kong are the easiest connection points. Contact **British Airways** (☎ 0345/222–111), **Cathay Pacific** (☎ 0345/581–581), or **Thai Airways International** (☎ 020/7491–7953).

Domestic routes in Vietnam are flown by **Vietnam Airlines** (✉ 1 Quang Trung St., Hoan Kiem District, Hanoi, ☎ 04/825–0888; ✉ 116 Nguyen Hue St., District 1, Ho Chi Minh City, ☎ 08/829–2118) and the smaller **Pacific Airlines** (✉ 100 Le Duan St., Dong Da District, Hanoi, ☎ 04/518–1503; ✉ 177 Vo Thi Sau St., District 1, Ho Chi Minh City, ☎ 08/820–0978).

It's a good idea to confirm both domestic and international flights 48 hours in advance. Also, be sure to arrive at the airport early; Vietnam

Airlines' check-in counters close 30 minutes before the scheduled boarding time. During rainy season avoid flying in late afternoon and early evening, when storms generally occur.

Flying time from Los Angeles to the Southeast Asian hub of Bangkok is approximately 18 hours, Chicago to Bangkok is 20 hours, and New York to Bangkok is 22 hours. Bangkok to Ho Chi Minh City takes 1 hour.

By Train

Trains leave Hanoi for Beijing twice weekly (55 hrs, $58–$88). The northeastern border crossing is at Dong Dang, just north of Lang Son. You'll need a standard tourist visa to enter China from Vietnam.

Getting Around

By Bus

Though an extensive and dirt-cheap public bus system serves every nook and cranny of the country, the buses are often overcrowded, cramped, unbearably hot, and notoriously loud. They also break down like clockwork and operate under arbitrary schedules. Air-conditioned minibuses, only slightly more expensive, are often available at or near most bus stations. An even better option is to take the more convenient, reliable, and infinitely more comfortable privately run tour buses organized by travel agencies, tourist offices, and travel cafés to most destinations. Even the most budget-conscious backpackers opt for the minivans or tourist buses.

Sinh Café Travel (☞ Hanoi A to Z and Ho Chi Minh City A to Z, *above*), runs the Sinh Café bus. For $33–$38 you get an open-ended ticket enabling you to break your journey for as long as you want at several points—Nha Trang, Dalat, Hoi An, Hue, and Ninh Binh—between Ho Chi Minh City and Hanoi.

By Car

At present, you, as a tourist, are not permitted to drive a car yourself. A rented car automatically comes with a driver who will, hopefully, speak some English. Cars and minivans with drivers are readily available from private and state-run travel agencies, tourist offices, and through most hotels in bigger cities. You're charged either by the kilometer or by the day, or both. A daily rate runs anywhere from $30 to $60, depending on the make of the car, the city in which you rent it, whether it has air-conditioning, and your bargaining skills. The agreed-on price should include gas and tolls (clarify all this before you set off).

The backbone of Vietnam's road system is Highway 1, extending from near the Chinese border, north of Hanoi, through Ho Chi Minh City and to the heart of the Mekong Delta. The major roads are for the most part paved, but they are still slow going (96 km/60 mi takes 1½–2 hrs). Those in the north are far worse than those in the south, where the U.S. war effort built or paved many of them, but even the southern ones are suffering from neglect. In early 2000, construction began on a second North–South route, the Truong Son Highway, which will follow the famous Ho Chi Minh Trail from the northern province of Ha Tay to Ho Chi Minh City.

By Cyclo

Cyclos, the bicycle-powered buggies that are unfortunately on the verge of becoming outlawed, provide the most entertaining and cheapest means of transportation in Vietnam. Although cyclo drivers are supposed to charge 2,000d per km (½ mi), they definitely deserve more since many double as informed English-speaking tour guides. Plan to pay 15,000d–25,000d per hour. Bargaining is advised, but it's worth giving the guys a break (and a tip).

On Foot
The best way to get through traffic on foot is to walk at a steady pace across the street and, of course, to watch out; the oncoming vehicles will have a better chance of avoiding you if the drivers can get a sense of where you will be going next. If you stop suddenly, it's harder for drivers to judge where you are in relation to them.

By Motorbike
One of the quickest ways to get around Vietnam's major cities is to ride on the back of a motorbike taxi. This service usually costs about 10,000d. They'll drive up alongside you and ask where you're going and whether you're interested in a ride.

You can also rent motorbikes and scooters in major cities at most travel agencies and some hotels for about 55,000d to 100,000d a day. A deposit is usually required along with a passport or a photocopy of one. But don't part with your deposit until you are convinced the place is legitimate (which usually means it has a line of motorbikes for rent and a standard ticket they give to all customers). Temporary insurance for tourists is almost nonexistent, and your own auto insurance generally does not apply. Make sure your medical insurance covers motorbike accidents, even if you are only a passenger. And ask for a helmet. When riding a motorbike, use your skills of prediction, timing, weaving, and of course honking. And always give trucks, army jeeps, and buses the right-of-way.

By Taxi
Metered taxis are common in Hanoi and Ho Chi Minh City and are becoming more common in smaller cities. Fares are quoted in dong. Although tipping is not required, some cabbies have developed a habit of "not having change" in the hope you'll tell them to keep it. Though many cabbies act like reckless kings of the road, taxis are the safest way to get around the cities.

By Train
The 2,600-km (1,612-mi) rail system, built by the French, goes north–south, serving coastal towns between Hanoi and Ho Chi Minh City; another line goes both northwest and northeast (and on to China) from Hanoi. The main drawback is that the trains are slow. The quickest one, the Reunification Express, takes 36–44 hours between Hanoi and Ho Chi Minh City, depending on how many stops it makes. Trains are good for overnight trips such as the hops between Hanoi and Hue, Hanoi and Lao Cai, and Ho Chi Minh City and Nha Trang.

You'll need separate tickets for each destination, and it's a good idea to book ahead, especially for overnight travel. When traveling long distances, reserving a soft-berth sleeper or soft seat is worth the small extra fare. You may want to take food and water with you, although they are available on some trains or from vendors in stations, and the fares on some routes include boxed meals.

Contacts and Resources

Customs & Duties
Upon entering Vietnam you'll be given a yellow customs declaration slip and a blue departure slip. You need these to get out of the country, so don't lose them. Don't bring weapons, pornographic materials, or anything that could be considered subversive into Vietnam, as you

may receive a hefty fine, be detained, or in extreme cases, jailed. It's a good idea to declare cameras, camcorders, laptop computers, and any other expensive electronics that you want to take out of the country again, though it's not required. Keep receipts for all your purchases. Upon leaving Vietnam and reentering your country, be ready to show customs officials what you've bought. It is illegal to export antiques (anything older than 21 years and a day) and wooden furniture unless you get special permission from the Ministry of Culture to do so. If you buy an item that looks like an antique, be sure to get a note from the store owner stating that it is not.

Health and Safety

CRIME

Although it is widely accepted that Vietnam is safe for tourists, pick-pocketing and bag snatching are becoming serious problems in Ho Chi Minh City and even in Hanoi. Don't wear conspicuous jewelry. Walk with your bag on the shoulder away from the curb, and keep your hand or ankles through the straps when in a cyclo, as snatch-and-ride theft (on a motorbike) is common. Put your wallet in your front pocket or in a zipped-up bag, and be alert in busy markets or crowds. Children or elderly people may act as decoys or pickpocket you themselves. When in a street café, keep your hands through the straps of your bag or put the strap around your neck, so no one can grab it. If someone does steal your bag, don't pursue the thief; bag snatchers often carry knives.

As for cyclos, don't go with a driver you don't feel comfortable with, and don't travel by cyclo after dark, especially in cities. Leave passports, cameras, laptop computers, and other valuables in your hotel room's safe, in the hotel's safe, or with the front desk. It is wise to leave your passport in your hotel and carry only a photocopy with you. It's safe to walk around cities at night—even for women—but you should avoid dark, deserted streets. Minihotels in popular tourist areas such as Halong Bay seem to be thief magnets, so always keep your doors and windows locked.

FOOD AND DRINK

Be careful of what you eat and drink in Vietnam. Fresh, leafy vegetables are known to carry parasites, so avoid those of dubious origin or those likely to have been washed in tap water. Also, try to eat only fruit that has a peel. Drink only bottled water. Ice from Western-style restaurants is usually fine, but many visitors avoid it altogether. Note that monosodium glutamate (MSG) is used in many dishes in Vietnam, particularly in pho (noodle soup). That said, dining at street food stands can be as safe or safer than eating in restaurants, especially in cities. Be more careful away from urban areas. Most of all, use common sense and pick a food stand, restaurant, or café that looks clean, is crowded, and has fresh food.

MEDICAL CARE

Check with the Centers for Disease Control and your physician about current health risks in Vietnam and recommended vaccinations before you go.

Vietnam's medical infrastructure is not up to international standards. Hospitals and pharmacies are often undersupplied and out of date. Only a handful of Vietnamese doctors have top-quality Western training. Foreign insurance is very rarely accepted, so you should expect to pay immediately in cash or by credit card. Foreign-run medical clinics offering basic treatment and 24-hour on-call services can guide you to local hospitals for more serious problems and can arrange for emergency evacuation. Embassies have duty officers on call who can assist with

logistics. If you get sick outside Hanoi or Ho Chi Minh City, get yourself to those cities as soon as possible.

Language

Vietnamese, or *kinh,* is written in a Roman-based script called *quoc ngu,*
devised by a French Jesuit scholar in the 17th century. Before that, the
Vietnamese used a system called *nom,* which drew on the Chinese system of characters. Although the letters may look familiar and the words
sometimes be recognizable, the tonal spoken language is quite foreign to
Western ears. Barring a few exceptions in tones and words, written Vietnamese is homogenous throughout the country, though accents differ dramatically, particularly between north and south. It's best to use a phrase
book as a point-and-show device, though a little Vietnamese goes a long
way. English is by far the most widely used language in the tourist trade.

Mail

Packages mailed to and from Vietnam will probably be scrutinized at
the post office. Videotapes, books, and compact discs are especially sensitive. Count on about two weeks, sometimes longer, for mail to arrive in the West from Vietnam. The main post offices in Hanoi and Ho
Chi Minh City have *poste restante,* where you can have mail sent to
you from abroad.

Express mail services to Vietnam can take from four to seven days. **DHL**
(✉ 778 Lang Rd., Dong Da District, Hanoi, ☎ 04/775–3999; ✉ 4
Huynh Huu Bac St., Tan Binh District, Ho Chi Minh City, ☎ 08/844–
6303). **FedEx** (✉ 6B Dinh Le St., Hoan Kiem District, Hanoi, ☎ 04/
826–4952; ✉ 26 Truong Son St., Tan Binh District, Ho Chi Minh City,
☎ 08/848–5888). **UPS** (✉ 4C Dinh Le St., Hoan Kiem District, Hanoi,
☎ 04/824–6483; ✉ 80F Nguyen Du St., District 1, Ho Chi Minh City,
☎ 08/829–4321).

On average, a postcard or letter to the United States costs about
16,000d; one to Europe costs about 13,000d. Stamps are sold at post
office (*buu dien*) branches, which are generally open daily 6 AM–8 PM,
and at many hotels and shops. Usually the postal clerk will cancel the
stamps on your letter and give it back to you to put into the slot. This
prevents the stamps being peeled off your letter for resale and your letter thrown away.

Money and Expenses

The Vietnamese unit of currency is the dong (abbreviated as d throughout this guide), which comes in 100d, 200d, 500d, 1,000d, 2,000d,
5,000d, 10,000d, 20,000d and 50,000d notes. Since a 50,000d note
is worth just over $3, you have to lug around quite a few notes. It's a
good idea to keep plenty of 5,000d, 10,000d, and 20,000d notes
handy for cyclos, cabs, and snacks.

The official rate at press time was about 14,400d to the U.S. dollar,
9,400d to the Canadian dollar, and 20,700d to the British pound. Although traveler's checks are accepted at many places, cash—in the form
of U.S. dollars or dong—is much more widely used. It's best to bring
at least a few hundred dollars in cash or as much as you feel comfortable
carrying. A money belt is good idea. The Bank for Foreign Trade of
Vietnam, or Vietcom Bank, has branches all over the country and
gives the official government rate. Although they don't often have the
best exchange rates, hotels are convenient places to change money. You
can usually get the highest exchange rates in gold or jewelry shops. At

many places you'll get a better exchange rate with higher-denomination bills.

FORMS OF PAYMENT

Credit cards have yet to catch on as a normal form of payment with ordinary merchants (ask first), but they are accepted at large hotels, upscale restaurants, better shops, large tour operators, and airline agencies. Hotels and shops sometimes insist on a service charge of up to 4% if you pay by credit card, however. MasterCard and Visa are the most widely accepted cards. Cash is definitely needed in rural areas and small towns.

Technically it is illegal for many establishments to accept payment in anything but dong, but such rules are widely ignored. U.S. dollars are accepted almost everywhere, except at state enterprises—including train stations—which take only dong. You should carry both dong and dollars with you at all times.

WHAT IT WILL COST

Vietnam is still a relatively inexpensive destination. Though some upscale international hotels in Ho Chi Minh City and Hanoi cost more than $200 per night, many minihotels and guest houses there charge less than $20, and elsewhere they're even cheaper. Food can be a steal. If you eat at small local restaurants, street-side cafés, food stalls, or markets, you'll pay between $1 and $4. A meal at an upscale restaurant, including wine, costs an average of $10–$15. Be aware that Vietnam has an official dual-pricing system, so foreigners often are expected to pay more than double what locals do for trains, buses, flights, other goods and services, and admission fees.

Sample Costs: a cup of coffee in a street café will cost you 2,500d (20¢); a cyclo ride will generally cost from 5,000d to 10,000d (from 35¢ to 70¢) per km (½ mi); a liter of beer is 2,500d (20¢); bottled beer goes for between 12,000d and 25,000d (about $1–$2); and a bowl of noodles from a food stall is 5,000d (35¢).

National Holidays

The traditional lunar new year, known as Tet in Vietnam and celebrated throughout much of Asia, falls in January or February, depending on the lunar calendar. Other national holidays include: New Year's Day (January 1), the anniversary of the founding of the Vietnamese Communist Party (February 3); Liberation Day (April 30), commemorating the day the North Vietnamese army took Saigon; International Workers Day, or May Day (May 1, the date following Liberation Day, which means a two-day holiday); Ho Chi Minh's birthday (May 19); National Day (September 2); and Christmas Day (December 25).

Opening and Closing Hours

Most banks, offices, and government-run agencies are open weekdays 8–4:30. Museums are often closed on Sunday and Monday. Post offices are open seven days a week. Cafés and restaurants are open all day, almost every day, and small family-run shops seem to stay open indefinitely, primarily because living and working quarters are often one and the same. Most sidewalk stalls serving breakfast and lunch finish by 2 and reopen for dinner at 4. You can always find late-night noodle stands. Bars and nightclubs usually close at about 1 AM or whenever the last customer leaves.

Passports & Visas

To get into Vietnam, you need a passport and a visa. You are no longer required to carry your passport with you at all times, though most hotels will ask you for your passport when you check in.

Obtain a visa from the **Vietnam Embassy** (✉ 1233 20th St. NW, Suite 400, Washington, DC 20036, USA, ☎ 202/861–0694, FAX 202/861–1297; ✉ 12–14 Victoria Rd., London W8-5RD, England, ☎ 020/7937–1912, FAX 020/7937–6108; ✉ 226 Maclaren St., Ottawa, ON, Canada, K2P 0L9, ☎ 613/236–0772, FAX 613/236–2704). The standard processing fee is $65 for a two-week turnaround and $80 for a four- or five-day rush turnaround. Officially the embassy is only supposed to grant 30-day visas (that you may be able to extend once you're in Vietnam), but persistent callers have been known to receive two-month visas.

Telephones

The country code for Vietnam is 84. Some city codes are: Dalat, 063; Danang, 0511; Haiphong, 031; Halong Bay, 033; Hanoi, 04; Ho Chi Minh City, 08; Hoi An, 0510; Hue, 054; Nha Trang, 058; Phan Thiet, 062; Vung Tau, 064.

CALLING HOME

To call overseas from Vietnam, dial 00 + the country code (1 for the United States) + the area code + the number. Vietnam time is 12 hours ahead of Eastern Standard Time and 16 hours ahead of Pacific Standard Time.

International phone calls from Vietnam cost a small fortune. Many hotels have international direct dial (IDD) phones, but a better option is to buy phone cards at the telephone companies that are usually in or near post offices, and use them on special phones inside the phone company offices or in hotel lobbies. Card calls to the United States, Europe, and Canada cost $3.10 for the first minute and $2.20 for each additional minute. As of press time, access numbers for reaching U.S. long-distance operators do not work in Vietnam, though the phone companies claim otherwise. Collect calls are not allowed.

CALLING VIETNAM

To call Vietnam from overseas, dial the international access code (011 from the United States) + the country code 84 + the area code without the first 0 + the number.

Tipping

Tipping at restaurants is not common in Vietnam, although many upscale places are starting to add a service charge and/or gratuity to bills. If this hasn't been done and the service is good, you might consider leaving 5%–10%. Chambermaids and porters usually appreciate a small tip, though as you go farther north you may find that hotel employees will refuse tips, waving them off with a perplexed grin. Although it is not necessarily expected, tour guides are more than happy to receive a tip. Many cyclo drivers will request in English a "souvenir" after you've paid the agreed amount.

Travel Agencies and Visitor Information

As of yet, there is no official source of tourist information abroad, but you might try calling the Vietnam Embassy (☞ Passports & Visas, *above*). The *Vietnam Economic Times,* available internationally, provides some business information of interest to tourists. In Vietnam, travel agencies, tourist cafés, and hotels are your best sources of information.

Almost every city and province has a state-run tourist agency that does everything from booking trains, planes, and automobiles to arranging guided tours and extending visas. The larger firms (**Vietnam Tourism, Saigon Tourist, Hanoi Tourism**) are huge agencies with fingers in many pies, but they are often pricey, slow, and not very helpful. In some smaller provinces, they're the only game in town. Hotels, big and small, are frequently affiliated with a travel agency or have their own travel services. In larger cities, there are also excellent, privately run travel agencies. Tourist cafés, though primarily oriented toward budget travelers, have many of the same services as large travel agencies and generally the best information, the widest selection of tours and day trips, and the lowest prices.

In Hanoi and Ho Chi Minh City travel agencies can provide English-speaking guides for about $15 a day. You may also be approached on the street by former U.S. Army interpreters or by cyclo drivers who will ask 50,000d for a day's work as a guide. This is a viable option, but make sure you understand their English by conducting an informal interview before you agree on a fee. Tourist agencies in cities like Hue, Danang, Halong Bay, and Haiphong all claim they can provide English-speaking guides. But outside the main cities, it's definitely hit or miss.

Vietnam Veterans

The **Vietnam Veterans of America Foundation** (VVAF) (⊠ 8605 Cameron St., Suite 400, Silver Spring, MD 20910 USA, ☎ 301/585–4000, FAX 301/585–0519; ⊠ 51 Ly Thai To St., Hanoi, ☎ 04/934–1607, FAX 04/934–1606) is involved in building long-lasting ties and increasing understanding between Vietnamese and Americans. Veterans returning to Vietnam are encouraged to contact the Hanoi or Maryland office. At least once a year VVAF organizes tours to Vietnam; contact the Maryland office for information.

When to Go

During the festival of Tet, the lunar new year, accommodations are scarce; and museums, offices, and shops tend to close for days at a time.

Vietnam's climate varies widely from region to region; the best time of year in northern Vietnam is from September to December, when it's not so humid. Chilly, wet weather begins in January and continues through March. Sticky heat is common from May to early September, and flooding can be expected in the summer. The central highlands are cool year-round and dry from December to March. Along the central coast, the rainy season runs from December to February; dry heat is the norm from June to October. In the south the best weather is from December to April. May to November generally brings the wet season and sporadic showers, usually during lunchtime. The rain shouldn't discourage you from visiting the south during this time (especially in late fall), though flooding in the Mekong Delta can make traveling there difficult. Overall, the best time of year to visit all of Vietnam is September–December and March–April.

The following are average daily maximum and minimum temperatures for Hanoi and Ho Chi Minh City.

Climate in Vietnam

HANOI

Jan.	66F	19C	May	84F	29C	Sept.	82F	28C
	54	12		72	22		68	20
Feb.	66F	19C	June	88F	31C	Oct.	81F	27C
	55	13		73	23		68	20
Mar.	70F	21C	July	86F	30C	Nov.	75F	24C
	59	15		73	23		63	17
Apr.	77F	25C	Aug.	84F	29C	Dec.	70F	21C
	66	19		73	23		59	15

HO CHI MINH CITY

Jan.	84F	29C	May	88F	31C	Sept.	82F	28C
	68	20		75	24		73	23
Feb.	86F	30C	June	84F	29C	Oct.	82F	28C
	70	21		73	23		72	22
Mar.	88F	31C	July	82F	28C	Nov.	82F	28C
	72	22		73	23		70	21
Apr.	90F	32C	Aug.	82F	28C	Dec.	82F	28C
	75	24		73	23		68	20

8   OTHER DESTINATIONS

Pagodas in Burma, Khmer sanctuaries in Cambodia, and ancient Buddhist temples in Laos are begging to be rediscovered. Closed to visitors for decades, these countries are now opening their frontiers. Untainted, as yet, by mass tourism, their peoples greet outsiders with warmth and hospitality.

By Nigel Fisher

ALTHOUGH CAMBODIA, LAOS, AND BURMA (Myanmar) are opening themselves up to international trade and tourism, they're still secondary destinations on most Southeast Asian itineraries. Many tour companies offer trips to these countries, but you can also travel independently; it's much easier than you would think. So long as you travel within secure areas, it's also reasonably safe (although banditry and guerrilla warfare make some provinces and towns—including Phnom Penh—dangerous). Locals—not yet inured to countless visiting foreigners—volunteer assistance and a friendly welcome. Moreover, because these countries are not yet commercialized and caught up in the West's techno-consumerism, you can still experience the best of Southeast Asia's traditions and cultures. The easiest way into any of these countries is through Bangkok.

Dining

Price categories throughout the chapter are based on the following ranges (as a number of the countries covered have unstable currencies, prices are quoted in dollars):

CATEGORY	COST*
$$$$	over $20
$$$	$10–$20
$$	$4–$10
$	under $4

*Per person for a three-course dinner, excluding tax, service, and drinks.

Lodging

Price categories throughout the chapter are based on the following ranges:

CATEGORY	COST*
$$$$	over $160
$$$	$100–$160
$$	$60–$100
$	$20–$60
¢	under $20

*For a standard double room in high season, excluding service charge and tax.

BURMA (MYANMAR)

The tale of modern Burma is a sad one. When it achieved independence from Great Britain in 1948, it was the rice bowl of Asia and potentially the richest country in the region. But the only person who had the strength of leadership and nobility of purpose to unite the independent-minded ethnic groups and establish a democracy was Aung San, and he was assassinated a few months before Burma was granted full sovereignty. Political squabbling, ethnic fighting, and communist terrorism became the rule, and in 1962 a military coup was engineered by General Ne Win, who for years presided over flagrant abuses of human rights and the disintegration of the country's economy. Although he resigned as president in 1982, his influence is still felt.

Popular resolve against the one-party rule of the Burmese Socialist Programme Party (BSPP), chaired by Ne Win, boiled over in 1988, and democratic demonstrations swept through the country. The government attacked the demonstrators—approximately 12,000 people disappeared or were killed—and the military seized absolute power on September 18, 1988. Since then the State Law and Order Restoration Council (SLORC), a military junta, has ruled by terror. Surprisingly,

SLORC permitted elections in 1990, expecting that their party would win. They miscalculated. Although the two leaders of the National League for Democracy (NLD), Aung San Suu Kyi and U Tin U, had been under detention since July 1989, the NLD won 82% of the 13 million votes cast. As expected, SLORC refused to hand over power and has tightened its grip, imprisoning any who speak out, many of whom "just disappear." Over the last several years, various organizations have given Burma the lowest human-rights rating of any country in the world.

Aung San Suu Kyi (daughter of Aung San) won the Nobel Peace Prize in 1991 for her fight to win her people's freedom. During—and for five years following—her party's 1990 victory, she lived under house arrest in Rangoon, and today her movement and communication are fiercely restricted. In August 2000, military personnel stopped her car and let the air out of her tires as she was on her way out of Rangoon to meet with supporters; she camped in her car for nine days in protest (as she has done three times before). She was then escorted back to her home, and she and eight other members of the NLD were placed under house arrest—again.

Herein lies your dilemma: by visiting Burma, you are likely contributing to the coffers of SLORC and its oppression of the people. Aung San Suu Kyi argues that foreign money (and that includes tourist dollars) should not be spent in Burma while SLORC denies freedom and human rights to the people. Others argue that so long as tourists purchase goods and services from the people and not from government-owned facilities, tourism may assist the Burmese in eventually overthrowing the SLORC dictatorship. Bear in mind, though, that even owners of hotels and other tourist facilities have to pay a foreigner head tax to SLORC when you use their services.

Pleasures and Pastimes
ARCHITECTURE
Burma is a land of pagodas—although "pagoda" is actually an English term and slightly misleading. The generic Burmese term for a Buddhist holy structure is *paya*, of which there are two types, the *zedi* and the *pahto*. Pahto is usually translated as "temple" or "shrine." Monks are not necessarily in attendance, nor do Buddhists *worship* in the Western sense. Rather, they go to a shrine (which can be a building of almost any shape) for contemplation and meditation. The other pagoda form, the zedi (also known as a *chedi* or stupa), is a solid, bell-shape structure raised on a series of terraces and crowned by a golden finial called a *hti*. Zedis house important Buddhist relics—either objects taken from the Buddha or such holy materials as Buddha images and prayer tablets.

A paya can have both pahtos and zedis; Rangoon's Shwedagon Pagoda, for example, is a famous Mon zedi (the central one) that's surrounded by numerous pahtos where the devout go to pray. Most pagodas are open from dawn to dusk and are free, though at some, such as the Shwedagon, foreigners are required to make a donation.

DINING
Burmese food is disappointing. It has none of the intrigue and subtleties of Thai cuisine. Rice and rice noodles are the staples. Curries—of chicken, meat, or fish fried in peanut oil—are the usual substantive dishes. Unfortunately, these do not use all the herbs and spices found in Indian curries, at best limiting themselves to garlic, onions, tomatoes, turmeric, ginger, and chili peppers. Every meal comes with a bowl of clear soup to offset the oiliness of the curries. If you don't like curries, seafood or

simple fried chicken is your best, if not only, bet. In Rangoon and Mandalay, Western food is served in hotel dining rooms; in the smarter restaurants, Chinese recipes and perhaps a few Western dishes will be on the menu. In the larger provincial capitals and resorts, you'll find Chinese cooking, but in smaller towns, you won't have that choice.

LODGING
Burma has only recently opened its doors to tourists, so hotels outside the major tourist areas are few and far between, and pretty grungy. In the main tourist areas (Pagan, Inle Lake, Mandalay, and Yangon) you can find international-standard hotels, though these are often ugly. The only super first-class hotel in the country is the Strand in Rangoon—and it costs a bundle.

In the late 1990s, there was a rush to build hotels in Rangoon, as well as in Mandalay and Bagan; now there are too many. In other areas, you'll find places with little more than a bed, ceiling fan, and basic plumbing in the private bathrooms. Perhaps because they're limited in number, these basic hotels are surprisingly expensive—about $35 a night. Even the cheapest accommodation in Rangoon, where the bathroom is shared, runs $20 a night; in the country, a room with a cot, mosquito net, and washbasin costs $10 to $15.

THE PEOPLE
The greatest pleasure in Burma is meeting the people—excluding the military, of course. The Burmese are exceedingly congenial, polite, and generous in a way reminiscent of the Thai attitude toward visitors in the 1950s. They are eager to talk, to help, and to welcome you to their country. They give unstintingly of their warm sincerity—often all they have to give, considering the average per capita income of around $100 a year. Most are devout Buddhists who take their religion seriously by practicing good thoughts and deeds every day.

SHOPPING
Burma's range of goods is limited. While crafts are least expensive at the place where they are made, in Rangoon you can find lacquerware, tables, trays, and chests from Pagan; Shan shoulder bags, many from the Inle Lake region; and wooden chests made throughout Burma. Precious gems, for which Burma is known, are really no cheaper than in Thailand, and unless you are a gemologist, the risk of being taken is great.

Great Itinerary
Moving swiftly, you can cover the major sights in Rangoon, Mandalay, Pagan, and Inle Lake in little over a week. This certainly does not do justice to all the sights or allow you to take in the depth of Burma's fascination, but it will be a sound introduction. Our coverage of Burma includes only these most popular destinations, all of which have a substantial tourist infrastructure. For those willing to rough it a bit, Burma has a lot more to offer, from beaches at Ngapali and Chaung Tha to the architectural wonders of Mrauk U.

IF YOU HAVE 10 DAYS
On day one, fly into **Rangoon** from Bangkok in the morning; in the afternoon, stroll around downtown, visit the National Museum, and shop at Bogyoke Aung San Market. Take dinner at a restaurant on Kandawgyi Lake and catch a "cultural show." Start the next day at the Shwedagon Pagoda, and in the afternoon, take a tour of the outer townships to get a sense of the expanding city and to visit small pagodas.

On the morning of the third day, fly to **Pagan.** Spend that afternoon, all of the next day, and the following morning visiting a few of the 2,000 monuments in the Pagan Architectural Zone. On the afternoon of the fifth day, fly or go by road to **Mandalay.** For the sixth day, visit the pagodas at the foot of Mandalay Hill and then tour the hills in **Sagaing,** visiting the monasteries and taking in the breathtaking views. On the way back, stop at U Bien Bridge in **Amarapura.** For the seventh day take the ferry up the Ayeyarwady (Irrawaddy) to **Mingun** for its monuments and the world's largest uncracked bell. Return to Mandalay for the afternoon; pay homage to the Buddha at the Mahamuni Pagoda, and visit Shwe Kyaung palace. On day eight, fly out of Mandalay to serene **Inle Lake.** Leave on the morning of the 10th day for Bangkok, changing planes in Rangoon.

Rangoon (Yangon)

Only some 5 million people live in Rangoon, the capital, so named by the British (the name Yangon, meaning "end of strife," was given to the city in 1755 by King Alaungpaya after defeating enemy forces in the south; both names are used here). The city spreads over a wide expanse, comprising teak forests, gardens, wide boulevards, lakes, parks, and pagodas. Without the SLORC soldiers, the economic despair, and the crumbling buildings, Rangoon could be an attractive place to live.

Rangoon is relatively new as a capital. The British chose it in 1885 for its proximity to the sea, just 32 km (20 mi) away, and its natural defensive position: the Rangoon River encases the city on its west and south side, and the Pazundaung Canal, which flows south into the Rangoon River, flanks the east side. The city's heart is clustered close to the riverbanks. Here colonial architecture is dwarfed by the buildings put up in the boom created by foreign capital. Since 1992, when capitalist-minded General Than Shwe became the head of SLORC, foreign investment and imports have been flooding into the city. People still move slowly, but the traffic is building. One wonders if Rangoon will go the way of Asian cities, bounding into the 21st century with neon lights, traffic jams, and concrete high rises.

Downtown is built on a grid system: minor north–south streets are numbered, whereas the other streets often have both a pre- and post-independence name. Expect to be confused. The city is divided into townships; aside from the downtown area, the most important townships are Dagon (with the Shwedagon Pagoda, several embassies, and a couple of hotels) and, slightly farther out, Bahan (with more hotels).

Your downtown landmark should be the **Golden Sule Pagoda** (Sule Paya). Its octagonal shape rises 150 ft above the surrounding shops, and the central stupa is said to contain a hair of the Buddha. The complex has been rebuilt so often that no one truly knows when it was begun, but some suggest it may have been as long as 2,000 years ago. 🖼 *Free.* ⊙ *Dawn–dusk.*

★ The country's best-known and most venerated pagoda is the **Shwedagon Pagoda,** erected northwest of the city center about 2,500 years ago to house eight sacred hairs of the Buddha. Its golden stupa, on Singuttara Hill, rises to 320 ft, dominating the skyline, and its spiritual power reaches out to all of Burma. Thousands come to pay homage each year.

At first, the pagoda was only 30 ft high, but successive monarchs have added to it, committing their empire's coffers to its restoration and elaboration. The dome is now covered with about 70 tons of gold, and the gilded hti on top is studded with rubies, sapphires, and topaz. The gold-and-silver weather vane is decorated with 1,100 diamonds; its orb is encrusted with 4,350 small diamonds and crowned with one of 76 carats.

Entrance to Shwedagon Pagoda is by four stairways, but foreigners may use only the southern one, from Pagoda Road (elevators are available). You enter the pagoda at the **Temple of the Konagama Buddha,** named for one of the four Buddhas that the Burmese believe preceded Siddhartha Gautama (the Buddha whose teachings are referred to today). From there, as you circle to the left around the golden stupa, you pass through a religious fairyland of pavilions and shrines, sculpted images, and small stupas. Plan on at least two hours here, which will allow you only to duck in and out of the two dozen or more small shrines. A guide is strongly recommended; otherwise you'll miss many of the fascinating details and intricacies of the Buddhist iconography. ▨ *Admission.* ⊙ *Daily 6 AM–10 PM.*

At the **Chauk Htat Gyi Pagoda,** a short distance beyond the Shwedagon Pagoda, lies a reclining Buddha image, one of the largest in Burma. The original figure, built in 1907, suffered such damage from climate over the years that it was demolished in 1957 and rebuilt in 1966. ▨ *Shwegondine Road.*

The **National Museum,** a five-minute walk from the historic Strand Hotel, contains the Mandalay regalia from Burma's last royal court and other artifacts. The showpiece is King Thibaw's 26-ft-high Lion Throne, which was originally in the Royal Palace at Mandalay. Once displayed in London's Victoria and Albert Museum, it was returned to Rangoon in 1964. ▨ *26 Pansodan St.* ▨ *Admission.* ⊙ *Weekdays 10–3.*

Bogyoke Aung San Market, Rangoon's largest and liveliest (still called by its old name, Scott's Market), throbs with activity, and it is here, more than anywhere else in Rangoon, that the depressed economy and oppressive rule of SLORC seem to be forgotten. In its maze of covered alleys, you'll find a huge collection of crafts from all over Burma, including the Shan states and Upper Burma. There are numerous jewelry stalls: search for **Su Yadana** (▨ 58 West D Hall), whose owners are honest, fair, extremely helpful, and speak some English. Locals come to Bogyoke Market for dry goods, black-market items, gold, and clothes. Some stalls will change dollars at the black-market rate.

Botahtaung Pagoda (*Bo* means "leader" and *tahtaung* means "a thousand") commemorates the thousand military leaders who escorted relics of the Buddha brought from India more than 2,000 years ago. The present Botahtaung is hollow, and inside you can walk through a sort of mirrored maze with glass showcases containing many of the ancient relics and artifacts that were sealed inside the earlier pagoda. Above this interesting interior, the golden spire rises 132 ft.

The **Kaba Aye Pagoda,** dedicated to world peace (*Kaba Aye*), was built in 1952 for the Sixth Buddhist Synod, held in 1954–56 to coincide with the 2,500th anniversary of the Buddha's enlightenment. The 111-ft pagoda also measures 111 ft around its base. It stands about 11 km (7 mi) north of the city, a little beyond the Inya Lake Hotel. **Mahana Guha,** an enormous artificial cave, 455 by 370 ft, was built close to the Kaba Aye Pagoda in the same compound. The Sixth Buddhist Synod was held here; participants recited the entire Theravada Buddhist scripture, known as the Tipitaka. In **North Okkalapa,** a satellite town about 20 minutes' drive west from the city center, there is a whole cluster of spired pagodas and sculptured figures, of which the **Mai-Lamu Pagoda,** which has giant images depicting the Buddha's earlier lives, is the most famous.

Dining and Lodging

$$ ✕ **Green Elephant.** This restaurant's popularity is based on its garden setting and its reasonably good menu, which has Chinese, Burmese,

and Western dishes. Try the lime salad and the river prawn curry. Arrive about 8 PM, when the air is cooler, and spend a couple of hours relaxing over a dinner served by friendly, attentive waiters. ⊠ *12 Inya Rd.,* ☎ *01/530263. No credit cards.*

$$ ✕ **Lone Ma Lay Restaurant.** One of several restaurants known more for its "cultural show" than its cuisine, Lone Ma Lay usually has a good repertoire of traditional regional dances and contemporary acts (shows start around 8 PM). Food here is better than at most dinner-show establishments; it has a number of Chinese dishes to supplement the Burmese. The restaurant also serves breakfast. It's just up the bank from Kandawgyi Lake, so the lights dance prettily on the water and a cool breeze wafts through the open-sided dining room. ⊠ *Natmauk Rd., Kandawgyi Lake,* ☎ *01/250357. Reservations essential. No credit cards.*

$ ✕ **Nan Yu.** Local businessmen come for lunch at this spot in the center of Rangoon. The hybrid Burmese-Chinese cooking is good; hot-and-sour fried prawns and fried chicken with green chili are good bets. A meal for two runs about $10, including a Mandalay beer. The decor is plain, but the tables have white cloths and a few photographs decorate the walls. ⊠ *81 Pansodan St.,* ☎ *01/577796. No credit cards.*

$ ✕ **Pole Star.** This restaurant is not fancy by any stretch, but it does make the attempt to present itself smartly, with blue tablecloths on neatly lined-up tables and clean walls hung with pictures. The fare is Burmese and quite good, without excessive oil. Fish dishes, when available, are good choices, and the chicken curry is made with an exciting mixture of spices. The extensive menu will certainly have something to tempt you. ⊠ *No 81, Lanthit St.,* ☎ *01/222095. No credit cards.*

$$$$ ✕⊞ **Strand Hotel.** The cost of a room here for one night is exorbitant—
★ three times the nation's annual per-capita income—but if you do treat yourself, you'll find the experience worth the tab. Founded in 1901, the Strand reached its zenith in the 1920s, but after Burmese independence it deteriorated into little more than a boardinghouse. In the early '90s, when the property was completely renovated, the Strand returned to (and surpassed) its former glory. You'll find all the conveniences of the 21st century, done with impeccable Edwardian sensibilities. A tie and jacket at dinner are de rigueur, and sipping a pink gin in the wood-paneled bar is appropriate. Throughout, 20-ft-high ceilings, potted palms, lazy overhead fans, and wicker furnishings suggest colonial elegance. In the huge guest rooms—on two floors, each with a valet on duty at all times—king-size beds rest on polished teak floors, and spacious tile baths have separate shower and tub. The dining room is pleasantly formal, and the food is the best you'll eat in Burma. Much of the produce is imported, and there is a reasonable wine selection. The attentive staff will assist you in negotiating Burma, whether you're a business traveler or a tourist. ⊠ *92 Strand Rd.,* ☎ *01/220065; 800/ 447–7462; 212/223–2848 in the U.S.; 0800/282684 in the U.K.;* FAX *01/22424. 32 suites. 2 restaurants, bar, room service, laundry service, business services, travel services. AE, DC, MC, V.*

$$$ ⊞ **Kandawgyi.** This newly reconstructed hotel on Kandawgye Lake, about 2 km (1 mi) from downtown, has become a popular choice for those who wish to avoid the noise that downtown Yangon's hotels suffer. The modern guest rooms have little charm, but the view of the lake makes up for that. The restaurant has mostly Western food, with a couple of Burmese curries thrown in for good measure. For idling time away, there are three bars, including one poolside. ⊠ *Kan Yeik Tha Road,* ☎ *01/249255, 01/249256, or 01/249257,* FAX *01/242776. 310 rooms. Restaurant, 3 bars, pool, health club, business services. AE, MC, V.*

$$$ ⊞ **Traders Hotel.** The Traders hotels, a division of the Shangri-La
★ group, provide top-quality accommodation without the frills (and

concomitant price tag) of a five-star hotel. This 22-story property has all the modern facilities, including 24-hour medical service, and in-house movies. Four restaurants provide Burmese, Japanese, international, Cantonese, and Italian fare. Guest rooms are of ample size, comfortable, and functional. ⊠ *223 Sule Pagoda Rd.,* ☎ *01/242828,* FAX *01/242800. 500 rooms. 4 restaurants, pool, health club, business services, meeting rooms. AE, MC, V.*

$$–$$$ ⊞ **Ramada.** Rooms at this new, modern hotel near the airport have either one king-size or two twin beds. Lighting, air-conditioning, and television are controlled from the bedside panel. The brasserie serves international fare all day long; you can cool off at the poolside bar. The hotel offers a useful luggage service: leave behind that extra case while you go up-country. ⊠ *Airport Estate, Mingaladon Township,* ☎ *01/666699,* FAX *01/663675. 120 rooms. Restaurant, bar, pool, exercise room, business services. AE, MC, V.*

$$ ⊞ **Thamada.** The management of this hotel, part of the New World Group, is efficient and geared to meet business travelers' needs. Rooms are compact, especially singles, but the feeling is one of cleanliness. The location is convenient, across the boulevard from the central railway station and a five-minute walk from the Traders Hotel. Prices are negotiable, so don't pay the printed rate. ⊠ *5 Signal Pagoda Rd.,* ☎ *01/ 243639,* FAX *01/245001. 58 rooms. Restaurant. AE, DC, MC, V.*

Inle Lake

Nyaung Shwe, the main lake town, is 23 km (14 mi) southwest of Taunggyi, the capital of the Shan state. Taunggyi is 350 km (217 mi) northeast of Rangoon, a 16-hour bus trip, and 150 km (95 mi) southeast of Mandalay, an eight-hour trip.

Surrounded by mountains in the Shan state, which borders Thailand, Laos, and China, Inle Lake is one of the most beautiful in Asia. It is magical and serene and is often spoken of in the same breath as the lakes of Kashmir. If beauty isn't attraction enough, the inhabitants are interesting and friendly. The narrow body of water—30 km (18 mi) north to south and only 8 km (5 mi) wide—supports nearly 200 villages with a total population of 150,000.

Although the lake is in the Shan state, those that live on its shores are not Shan, but a Mon people known as the **Intha** (Sons of the Lake). The Intha developed an ingenious way of farming the lake: they weave the rubbery tubes of hyacinths and rushes into gigantic mats, then dredge fertile mud from the lake's bottom and lay on a layer of humus. This floating garden is then staked in the water near a family's home. They also fish, with a unique style that involves rowing and using a large conical net simultaneously. With one leg wrapped around the oar, an Intha fisherman is able to move through the hyacinths cluttering the lake while leaving one hand free to control the net. When the fisherman spots a shoal of fish, down goes the net, allowing him to spear dinner at his leisure.

A major religious festival is held here for two weeks in October. An ornamental barge carrying the image of the mythical "karaweik" bird and four sacred figures covered in gold from Phaungdaw U pagoda tours the lake. The figures are thought to have been brought from Malaya by the 12th-century king Alaungsithu. After the big boat finishes the tour, the leg-rowers, both men and women, gather for a regatta. The festival is held with great pomp and pageantry. Fairs and dances are also held.

Visitors, unlike sacred figures, can tour the lake all year round. Boats depart at about 8 AM for a five-hour tour past floating gardens, one-leg rowers, and small lakeshore communities. Most tour boats head for the village of Ywama, where there is a colorful floating market every five days. This is the ideal day to take the tour, but you'll have to be persistent to find out which day the market is being held—the guides often claim that there is a market every day. There will be places to stop for refreshment and lunch and you'll need to be firm with your boatman on just how many shops and artist studios you want to see. Take a hat to wear under the merciless midday sun. You can hire a boat through your hotel for about US$10 or choose one at random for slightly less. An admission ticket to the lake is US$4 per person, payable at the tourist office at the pier in Nyaung Shwe, which puts the money into the junta's pockets.

Dining and Lodging

$ ✕ **Bigdrum.** Shan food is served in this thatched restaurant with plain wood floors, a bar, and a jukebox. Posters and maps on the wall add some color, but otherwise the decor is basic. The food is good, however, and usually you can try the best of the fish caught in Inle Lake. If you are less adventurous, you can choose from the Chinese dishes on the menu. The restaurant is next to the Golden Duck and the Queen Lodging House. ⊠ *Nyaung Shwe, Inle Lake,* ☏ *no phone. No credit cards.*

$ ⊞ **Golden Express Hotel.** This small two-story hotel on a shady street has a front courtyard where you can park your bike. The proprietor speaks some English, and the rooms are bright, with shiny satin bedspreads, print curtains, and colorful layers of linoleum. If you stay in room 105 you can watch the procession of monks at dawn with their begging bowls. Breakfast is included in the rate. ⊠ *Road to Pier,* ☏ *no phone. 11 rooms. Breakfast room. No credit cards.*

¢ ⊞ **Gypsy Inn.** This small, family-owned hotel is across from the lake's canal and only 20 yards from the pier where the tour boats come and go. The owner, who built the house himself in 1995, is extremely friendly—giving guests rides on the back of his motorbike and running them to the airport (for a fee) when his car is free. Rooms are basic but clean, and they have a private shower. They tend to be dark and gloomy, but the hotel's balcony looking out to the canal more than makes up for that. Free breakfast is served in the morning; coffee, tea, and beer are available all day. ⊠ *82 Canal Rd., Win Quarter, Nyaung Shwe,* ☏ *no phone. 11 rooms. No credit cards.*

Pagan

450 km (279 mi) north of Rangoon. 193 km (120 mi) southwest of Mandalay, a four-hour drive by car or six-hour trip by local bus. An express boat, departing in the early morning, makes the 10-hour river run between Mandalay and Bagan.

On the banks of the Ayeyarwady River stands astonishing, extensive Pagan (also called Bagan), once the seat of the mighty Myanmar kingdom, established by King Anawrahta (1044–77), the 42nd ruler of the Pagan dynasty. Pagan was probably founded around 849, but its Golden Age began when Anawrahta defeated his rivals, primarily the Mons from the south, and expanded his borders to include most of present-day Burma. Wealth poured in, and the building of pagodas began. At the same time, Anawrahta introduced Theravada Buddhism, and he was wise enough to incorporate into the cosmic whole of Buddhism the worship of *nats*, guardians of the spirit world that were part of the traditional animist Burmese religion.

After about two centuries of dominance, corruption began to eat away at the Pagan dynasty. The final blow came when Kublai Khan, the great Mongol lord, demanded that Pagan pay tribute to him. Pagan's ruler, the pompous King Narathihapati (1256–87), refused, and executed the Khan's messenger. Kublai Khan's army attacked, and the Pagan royal family fled.

Today more than 2,000 stupas, shrines, and monasteries remain from the 6,000 built during the Pagan dynasty, covering an immense area
★ of 10,000 acres (or about 16 square mi) now known as the **Pagan Archeological Zone.** So as not to tire of seeing yet another stupa or shrine, limit yourself to a few of the most interesting and best preserved. Admission to the Pagan Archeological Zone is US$10. Transport is either by hired car, rented bicycle, or bullock cart. The latter is romantic, but even well-padded bones begin to crunch after four hours.

Erected in 1091, the **Ananda Temple** was reconstructed after the devastating earthquake of 1979. The central square has 175-ft sides and rises in terraces to 168 ft. In the center of the cube are four vestibules, each with a standing Buddha that is 31 ft high, representing the four Buddhas who attained Nirvana prior to Gautama Buddha. Only the images facing north and south are original; the east- and west-facing images are replacements for figures destroyed by fires. The base and the terraces are decorated with glazed tiles depicting Jataka tales, stories of Gautama Buddha's prior lives. In the western sanctum, there are life-size statues of the shrine's founder, Kyannzittha.

Tradition has it that a holy tooth, collarbone, and frontlet relics of the Buddha are enshrined in the **Shwezigon Pagoda.** The chronicles relate that the tooth was presented by the King of Ceylon, and that King Anawrahta placed the bone relic on a jeweled white elephant and, making a solemn vow, said, "Let the white elephant kneel in the place where the holy relic is fated to rest!" It was at Shwezigon that the elephant knelt, and that is where Anawrahta built the pagoda. Anawrahta used this shrine to assimilate the old worship of nats into the new faith: inside are murals of nats riding mythical animals. On the terraces are plaques with scenes from Jataka tales.

The highest shrine in Pagan is the 200-ft-tall **Thatbyinnyut Temple,** built in the mid-12th century and repaired in 1979. The small shrine to the northeast known as the "tally pagoda" was built with one brick for every 10,000 used in the main shrine and is, in theory, one ten-thousandth its big brother's size.

Dining and Lodging

Dining options in Pagan are limited; most are associated with a hotel. For now, the River View and the Kumadara are the top spots.

$$ ✕ **River View.** The tables here are outside, along the Ayeyarwady, and candles provide the light (it's hard to see what you are eating—go with the mood and have faith). The Burmese curries and fish dishes are nicely prepared—not as oily as you often find—but service can be slow. ☎ *062/70099. Reservations essential. No credit cards.*

$$ ✕🏨 **Kumadara.** Scattered around the small garden behind the main building of this property are three long chalet-type bungalows that house the guest rooms. These accommodations are quite basic, but each has cheerful draperies and bedcovers, and a small balcony. The bathroom has a good shower, which usually streams hot water. The restaurant—in the main house with the bar and reception—has quite good Western and Asian food and after-dinner cultural dance and puppet shows. ⊠ *Dawna St., Pyu Saw Hte Quarter, Pagan,* ☎ *062/70080,* 🆕 *01/97486 in Rangoon. 42 rooms. Restaurant, bar. No credit cards.*

$ 🏨 **Queen Saw Guest House.** This small guest house in the village of New Pagan (where, in 1990, villagers were forcibly relocated from the Archaeological Zone) is owned by a very friendly, if rather shy, Burmese couple. The fan-cooled rooms are clean—choose one with a terrace—and the bathrooms have lukewarm showers. ✉ *Shwe Laung Kyan Sittya, New Pagan, Nyaung U,* ☎ *062/70032. 8 rooms. Breakfast room. No credit cards.*

Mandalay

193 km (120 mi) northeast of Pagan, 580 km (362 mi) north of Rangoon. The long-distance bus from Mandalay to Rangoon takes about 13 hours. The train takes about 14.

In 1857 King Mindon decided to fulfill a sacred prophecy that a great city would be built at the foot of Mandalay Hill on the eastern bank of the Ayeyarwady River. All signs were auspicious for a great capital, and the time seemed right: it was the 2,400th anniversary of the Buddha's attaining enlightenment. King Mindon designed his new capital as a fortified city in a form of a square. It is said that, following tradition, the king had 52 people buried alive beneath the four corners of the site to become guardians of the city. More prosaic protection was afforded by a moat, 225 ft wide and 11 ft deep. The battlements were made of brick and mud and rose to a height of 25 ft. Entrance was through 12 gates, three on each side and equidistant from one another. In the center was the king's palace. Four years after the foundations were laid, King Mindon moved his capital and his court, plus 15,000 of his subjects, to Mandalay.

The city's guardians, however, did not do their job: the British attacked the city 25 years later and annexed all of Upper Burma. Mindon's palace, renamed Fort Dufferin, became the British colonial barracks. Later, the Japanese made the palace their command headquarters, which prompted the British to drop bombs on it, and the ensuing fire destroyed a third of the city. For the next 40 years, the grounds and moat became not much more than a garbage dump. It wasn't until 1996 that the moat was cleaned out, largely in an effort to promote tourism and the "Visit Myanmar Year" campaign; the labor was provided by conscripted locals and chained convicts.

Part of the **Royal Palace,** in the center of the city, is being partially reconstructed in cement at great expense and should offer an idea of what the original looked like. A sense of the beauty of the old palace can be gleaned from the scale model, made in 1952 and kept in an iron cage to the west of the old palace. The Lion Throne and several tons of regalia are in the National Museum in Rangoon.

The **Shwe Nandaw Kyaung** (Golden Palace Monastery) was the only palace of King Mindon that escaped bombing in World War II. It had been moved from the fortified city's grounds after King Mindon had inauspiciously died in it. The spectacular building has carved teak, mosaics, and pillars, which are each a single trunk of teak. The original lacquering and gilding can still be seen on the pillars and walls. ✉ *62nd St., south of Mandalay Hill and due west of Fort Mandalay.* ☞ *Admission.* ☉ *Daily 8–4.*

Near the foot of Mandalay Hill is the **Kyauktawgyi Pagoda,** famous for its huge Buddha statue carved from a single block of marble. Near the Kyauktawgyi Pagoda is the **Kuthadaw Pagoda,** built in 1857. King Mindon wanted to make Mandalay the world center of Buddhism, and he built the complex to house the entire Tipitaka, the Buddhist teachings. These are inscribed on marble slabs and enshrined in 729 miniature pagodas. For this reason, the Kuthadaw is often referred to as the world's largest book.

The religious heart of Mandalay is the **Mahamuni Pagoda,** on the south side of town, which houses Mandalay's most venerated image of the Buddha. According to the Burmese, the image is one of only five that were molded to the actual likeness of Guatama Buddha. However, so much gold leaf has been affixed to the statue by the thousands of devotees who pay their respects each day that the shape of the body is now distorted. Only the gleaming, polished bronze face remains untouched. The approach to the shrine is lined with stalls and astrologers' booths. Follow the lines of pilgrims to the small room where the venerated Mahamuni image sits. Only men are permitted in this room; women must go off to the side and look upon the Buddha from a balcony. Before entering, men can pick up some gold leaf to apply to the surface while walking around the image. ⊠ *84th St., 5 km (3 mi) south of Fort Mandalay.* 🎫 *Admission.* ⏰ *Daily 8–5.*

Zegyo Market, in the downtown area, is the most popular shopping center in Mandalay. Here you can buy fine handicrafts and jewelry of Burmese origin, not to mention all kinds of consumer goods made in China, India, and Thailand. For those keen on collecting souvenirs, Phayagyi bazaar is much to the purpose, stocking articles for worship and prayer to the Buddha. The bazaar is near the Great Maha Muni Pagoda, next to Zegyo Market.

Lodging

$$$ ✕🏨 **Novotel.** After renovations, this arc-shape building is now one of Burma's better modern hotels. Large, functional guest rooms have modern bathrooms and picture windows that face the hotel's gardens or Mandalay Hill (those at the back have the best view, with a pagoda or two in the distance). The "superior" rooms are even larger and worth the extra price. The hotel's best feature is a restaurant, where the influence of the French management prevails. It's the only place in Mandalay for good European food; you may also want to try the Burmese buffet at lunch, where an array of dishes offers a crash course in the nation's cuisine. ⊠ *10th Street, Oo Boke Taw Quarter, Aung Myea Township,* ☎ *02/35638,* 📠 *02/35671. 206 rooms. 2 restaurants, pool, health club, business services. AE, MC, V.*

Amarapura

19 km (12 mi) south of Mandalay.

Until King Mindon moved his court to Mandalay, Amarapura (the City of Immortals) was the capital of Upper Burma. Not much is left of the Old Town—a new township has taken its place. Most of the important buildings were dismantled and reassembled in Mandalay.

It's worth spending a couple of hours at the **U Bien Bridge.** The two-century-old footbridge, made from teak planks salvaged from yet another former capital, Ava, crosses the Taung Thaman Lake. If you make the 1¼-km (¾-mi) hike, your reward will be the charming **Kyauktawgyi Pagoda,** with its immense jade Buddha inside. After you see the pagoda you can hang around the base of the bridge, where Burmese families come for afternoon picnics or eat at one of the several outdoor restaurants.

Ava

10 km (6 mi) southwest of Mandalay.

A few miles downriver from Mandalay stands what remains of Ava, one of the three cities around Mandalay, each of which formerly served as capital. In 1364, sometime after the fall of Pagan, Ava became the capital and remained the most important town in Upper Burma for the next four centuries. The city was largely demolished by an 1838 earthquake, and what did remain was dismantled and taken to Amarapura. Still discernible are the Namyin Watch Tower and some city walls. Only the **Maha Aungmye Bonzan monastery,** built of brick and stucco, remains intact, glaring white in the sun, but of little interest inside.

Sagaing

16 km (10 mi) west of Mandalay, across the Ayeyarwady River.

With a dozen monasteries and nunneries and 600 pagodas, Sagaing is regarded as the spiritual center of Burma. To reach the city, you'll travel across the 2,400-ft Ava Bridge, built by the British in 1934 and still the only bridge to cross the Ayeyarwady. (A new bridge is being built at Pyay, halfway between Rangoon and Mandalay.) Sagaing is a township, once the capital of an independent Shan state, and the area around it is known as the Sagaing Hills. On the tops and crests of these hills are the religious centers, some of which have tremendous views overlooking the Ayeyarwady. One of the best views is from **Soon U Ponya Pagoda** on Shin Bin Man Kai hill.

The largest of the pagodas is **Kaungmudaw** (10 km/6 mi outside the town of Sagaing), built in 1636 by King Thalun and said to contain a tooth and strands of hair from the Buddha. Its perfectly hemispherical dome rises 150 ft; some government guides claim that it was modeled after the Mahaceti Stupa in Sri Lanka, although others say it represents the perfect and ample breast of King Thalun's favorite queen. Around the base of the stupa are 812 stone pillars, each of which has a small hollow for an oil lamp. At one time these lights illuminated the huge dome. Also around the base are 120 niches containing the images of nats. Over the last nine centuries, Buddhist kings and governments have tried to downplay the role of nats, but their worship is so embedded in Burmese culture that appeasing the nats is still part of everyday life.

The **Hsinmyashin Pagoda,** known as the Elephant Pagoda, is between the town of Sagaing and Kaungmudaw. Twenty-foot-high elephants stand guard at the gates of the temple, built in 1429 to house religious relics brought from Sri Lanka. The elephants fell down, however, in 1985, when they failed to prevent the wrath of an earthquake. Much of the pagoda has since been restored, and it's one of the few where you can enter the relic chamber to see the display of votive tablets and images.

Mingun

13 km (8 mi) north of Mandalay by boat.

A popular day trip out of Mandalay is the hour-long boat ride up the Ayeyarwady to Mingun. Boats leave from Mandalay's Ma Yan Chan jetty from 8 AM on. You can either hire your own boat for about 1,000 kyats or take a public boat for 100 kyats. The hour on the river goes quickly as you pass by fishing communities on the riverbanks and bamboo rafts floating downriver to destinations as far off as Rangoon.

King Bodawpaya, the predecessor to King Mindon, expanded his kingdom by conquering Arakan; to celebrate, he had 20,000 Arakanese slaves build the **Mingun Pagoda.** He ran out of cash by 1819 and abandoned the project long before it reached its projected 500-ft height. Nevertheless, with each of its four sides measuring 450 ft, it was and still is the largest brick-base structure in the world. You can climb the 150 ft to the unfinished top for the views, but it's really just the sheer mass of this vanity that's impressive.

King Bodawpaya also commissioned an enormous **bell** to go with his pagoda. Finished in 1790 and hung on teak uprights, the bell weighed approximately 100 tons. It proved too much for the teak supports, though, and the 1838 earthquake brought it to the ground. Now, hung on chains and housed in a pavilion, it remains the largest uncracked bell in the world. Give the bell a tap and hear its superb resonance.

The **Hsinbyame Pagoda** was built in 1816 by Bagyidaw, King Bodawpaya's grandson, in memory of his wife. It's a long way up the covered staircase to the shrine, an ascent you should think of as climbing Mount Meru, the center of the earth in Buddhist cosmology. Your earthly reward will be breathtaking views of the village below and of the timeless flow of the Ayeyarwady.

Burma A to Z

Arriving and Departing

BY AIRPLANE

The only way into Burma, other than by stepping off the occasional cruise ship or visiting a border town over the Thai frontier, is by plane. **Rangoon Airport** is on the northern edge of town, a 500 kyats ($4) taxi ride from downtown.

Carriers. **Thai Airways International** (☎ 01/255499 or 01/66266 in Rangoon, 02/234–3100 in Bangkok) has two daily flights from Bangkok to Rangoon; round-trip fare is around US$230. **Myanma Airways** (☎ 01/525488 in Rangoon, 02/630–0338 in Bangkok) also flies between Bangkok and Rangoon for the same price. **Malaysia Airways,** (☎ 01/525488 in Rangoon) in partnership with Myanma Airways, offers three flights a week from Kuala Lumpur to Rangoon; a round-trip ticket costs about US$180. **Air Mandalay** (☎ 01/525488 in Rangoon, 02/271–4375 in Bangkok) operates a daily flight between Chiang Mai and Mandalay for about US$220, round-trip.

At press time, there were no nonstop flights to Burma from North America or Britain, although several major airlines (among them British Airways, Lufthansa, and JAL) were in negotiations.

Getting Around

BY AIRPLANE

Government-owned **Myanma Airways** (✉ 77–91 Sule Pagoda Rd., Yangon, ☎ 01/283997), the privately owned **Air Mandalay** (✉ 146 Damazedi Rd., Bahan Township, Yangon, ☎ 01/525488), and **Yangon Airways** (✉ 22–24 Pamsodan St., Yangon, ☎ 01/700359) connect Burma's tourist destinations. There are direct flights from both Mandalay and Rangoon to Pagan and to Heho, the airport nearest Inle Lake, 40 km (24 mi) from Taunggyi and 18 km (11 mi) from Nyaung Shwe. Air Mandalay has the best reputation of the three.

BY BUS OR CAR

Regularly scheduled buses run between Burma's towns and cities. Self-drive rental cars are not available, but you can hire cars with a driver. Travel agencies and tour operators can make the arrangements. The cost is about $40 to $50 a day; the driver will appreciate a gratuity of $5 a day. Roads are generally paved between the major destinations covered in this chapter. Off the main roads and in the Pagan Archaeological Area, expect gravel and potholes.

BY TRAIN

Tickets need to be purchased in advance. There is no first class on the train.

Contacts and Resources

CUSTOMS AND DUTIES

Tourists may bring into Burma 200 cigarettes, 50 cigars or ½ lb of tobacco, one quart of spirits, and one pint of perfume or eau de cologne. You are allowed to bring pets that are accompanied by health certificates. You may import unlimited amounts of foreign currency, but no local currency (kyats). The export of religious artifacts requires a permit, and you must show the bill of sale for any precious stones you are taking out of the country.

ELECTRICITY

The electrical current in Burma is 220 volts AC, 50Hz. You can expect occasional blackouts.

EMBASSIES AND CONSULATES

British Embassy (✉ Box 638, 80 Strand Rd., Yangon, ☎ 01/295300, FAX 01/289566). **Australian Embassy** (✉ 88 Strand Rd., Yangon, ☎ 01/273521). **Embassy of the United States of America** (✉ Box 521, 581 Merchant St., Yangon, ☎ 01/282055–9 or 01/282182, FAX 01/280409). Canada and New Zealand are represented by the British Embassy.

EMERGENCIES

Ask your hotel or tour operator first for help in the case of medical and police emergencies. Provincial towns have clinics, but major medical emergencies are best attended to in Mandalay or Rangoon. Try the **Rangoon General Hospital,** a historic landmark (✉ Bogyoke Aung San St., ☎ 01/281722), or the **Diplomatic Hospital** (✉ Kyaikkasan Rd., ☎ 01/250149). Better yet, get back to Thailand for hospital treatment. If your passport is stolen or lost, notify your embassy immediately. The emergency telephone numbers in Rangoon are: ambulance, 192; fire, 101; police, 199.

HEALTH AND SAFETY

Don't drink tap water; bottled water is readily available. Stick to foods that are cooked. Crime is very rarely directed against foreigners, though the military police may shake you down for a bribe. Beware of people who want to talk politics. It is said that one out of eight Burmese is an informer for the military junta.

LANGUAGE, CULTURE, AND ETIQUETTE

The national language, Burmese, uses a non-Roman phonetic alphabet that is difficult for Westerners to read or write. Speaking Burmese is equally difficult, since it is tonal; in that regard it's similar to Thai. An amazing number of Burmese, particularly those in the travel industry, speak English. Burmese are very conservative in their dress: always smart and neat, never flaunting nakedness. Tourists should follow suit, especially in religious places—no short shorts or sleeveless shirts, for example. Shoes and socks should be removed before entering a temple. Feet are always seen as being a repository for bad things, so as in Thailand, it's insulting to point your feet at anyone and ill-mannered to put your feet on top of furniture. Never touch a person's head or the head of a Buddha image. So far in Burma, there's no discernible accommodation for or recognition of homosexuals. Discretion is evidently the rule, and public affection, hetero- or homo-, is frowned on.

MAIL

The easiest way to send mail in Burma is to hand it to your hotel reception clerk, who will often have postage stamps, too. In Yangon you can drop it in the pillar-boxes at the corners of all main roads and streets. The Central Post Office is at 39 Bo Aung Kyaw Street, at the corner of Strand Road. Mail is collected at 11 AM and 2 PM. Airmail letters (preprinted, prestamped forms, 3.50 kyats each) can be mailed anywhere. Basic overseas postage: Yangon to Australia/Canada/New Zealand/U.K./U.S. is 5 kyats. Yangon to Thailand/Hong Kong/Japan/Taiwan/Korea/Malaysia/Singapore is 4 kyats. All post offices are open weekdays 9:30–4:30. Addresses usually contain the block number of the office or housing unit, followed by the street, and then the township, which is often a subdistrict of the major city.

MONEY MATTERS

Costs. Burma can be surprisingly expensive. International-style hotels charge $150 and up for a double room, and even budget hotels with not much more than a cot and a shared bath charge as much as $30 in Rangoon. Air travel within Burma is expensive; fares between Rangoon and Mandalay are approximately $100. However, bus and rail travel is very inexpensive—and uncomfortable. Taxis run about 100 kyats per kilometer. Local beer (Mandalay is the best) costs 180 kyats in a local café. At a hotel, an imported beer will cost about $4.

Currency. Burmese currency comes in kyats (pronounced chi-ats). Notes include the following denominations: 5, 10, 15, 20, 45, 50, 90, 100, and 500. (The 45 and 90 banknotes were the inspiration of Ne Win, who considered those numbers to be lucky.)

The official rate of exchange is 6 kyats to the U.S. dollar—the only Western currency in common circulation—but no traveler uses the official rate (it's designed to allow the Junta personnel to buy cheap imports). Instead, you're required to buy, with cash or traveler's checks, $300 worth of Foreign Trading Certificates (FTCs), which each cost a dollar. You can then change these for Burmese currency at international hotels, where you'll get the unofficial rate of about 175 kyats per dollar. FTCs cannot be converted easily back to dollars.

If you do not have to buy FTCs, don't. You're better off with cash, which, on the black market (really more of a gray market), can be exchanged at a rate of about 185 kyats to the U.S. dollar. (Other currencies and traveler's checks are rarely accepted.) Most independent travelers change the minimum required amount into FTCs and use the black market to convert dollars into kyats for any remaining needs. Those traveling on prepaid package tours may be exempt from the FTC minimum-purchase requirement. (Your Burmese visa indicates to immigration whether or not you're on a tour.)

Keep in mind that you can always pay in dollars—most hotels and travel operators prefer it. International hotels and airlines require payment in dollars or FTCs. Credit cards are rarely accepted, except at international hotels. ATMs are *not* linked to such networks as Cirrus and Plus; it is possible to obtain cash from a bank with a MasterCard or Visa, but the rate of exchange is poor, the commission fees are high, and the paperwork is time-consuming.

Service Charges, Taxes, and Tipping. Government tax is 10% on hotels and restaurants. A service charge of 10% is added to the bill in tourist hotels. Tipping is not a widespread custom in Burma, but there are times when a gratuity is expected: a bellboy would like 100 kyats to take your luggage to your room, and the driver of your car may expect 500 kyats per day.

OPENING AND CLOSING TIMES

Offices tend to be open weekdays 9:30–4:30. Similar hours are kept by museums. Banks are open weekdays 10–2. Official holidays are Independence Day (Jan. 4); Union Day (Feb. 12); Peasants' Day (Mar. 2); Armed Forces Day (Mar. 27); Thingyan, Water Festival and Myanmar New Year (Apr. 13); May Day (May 1); Martyrs' Day (July 19); National Day (Nov. 2); Christmas Day (Dec. 25).

PASSPORTS AND VISAS

All foreign nationals need a visa. Visitors from North America, Great Britain, Australia, and New Zealand can obtain a 30-day tourist visa within 48 hours from most embassies and consulates. The cost is approximately $10. Contact the **Union of Myanmar embassies** in Australia (✉ No. 22, Arkana St. , Canberra, A.C.T 2600, ☎ 06/2733751); Canada (✉ 85, Rang Rd., The Sandringham , Ottawa, Ontario KIN 816, ☎ 326436); Thailand (✉ 132, N. Sathorn Rd., Bangkok 10500, ☎ 02/337250); the United Kingdom (✉ 19A, Charles St., Mayfair, London WLX 8ER, ☎ 0891/600306); or the United States (✉ 2300 S. St. NW, Washington, DC 20008, ☎ 202/332–9044 and ✉ 10 E. 77th St., New York, NY 10021, ☎ 212/535–1310).

TELEPHONES

To call Burma from overseas, dial the country code, 95, and then the area code, omitting the first 0. Calling Burma is expensive—about $7 a minute from Pacific Rim countries, North America, and Europe. Phoning out of Burma is also costly and time-consuming as there are not sufficient international lines available. Many of the international hotels have better access to lines, but you'll pay through the nose. Public telephones, available at the airports, railway stations, and department stores, are good only for domestic calls. Coins are used. When calling long distance from inside Burma, dial the "0" of the area code.

TOUR OPERATORS AND TRAVEL AGENCIES

Abercrombie & Kent (✉ 4th fl., Silom Plaza, 491/29–30 Silom Rd., Bangkok 10500, ☎ 02/266–7660, FAX 02/266–7854; ✉ 1520 Kensington Rd., Suite 212, Oak Brook, IL 60521, ☎ 630/954–2944 or 800/323–7308, FAX 630/954–3324) arranges custom trips through Burma, including cruises up and down the Ayeyarwady.

Journeys International (✉ 4011 Jackson Rd., Ann Arbor, MI 48103, ☎ 313/255–8735 or 800/255–8735) has 8- and 15-day tours as well as group packages for 5 to 28 people. Unlike many U.S. tour operators, they don't use government guides, vehicles, and hotels—a plus in our book.

A very special, albeit expensive, way to visit the sights of Pagan and Mandalay is by taking the river cruise ship *The Road to Mandalay*, operated and owned by the **Orient-Express Hotels, Trains, & Cruises** (☎ 800/524–2420 U.S.; 020/7620–0003 U.K., FAX 020/7620–1210), the same company that operates the luxury train between Singapore and Bangkok. The ship, originally used on the Rhine, accommodates 138 passengers in 72 air-conditioned cabins, with en suite bathrooms and personal safes. On board there is a dining room (dress for dinner, please), swimming pool, and bar. The ship makes the day-and-a-half run on the Ayeyarwady between Mandalay and Pagan; you sleep on board for the two nights that it's berthed in Mandalay and the two in Pagan. All sightseeing tours with guides are in the package. The company is not affiliated with the Burmese government.

VISITOR INFORMATION

If asked, the Union of Myanmar embassies (☞ Passports and Visas, *above*) will forward basic tourist information along with your visa application. The Burmese ministry of tourism is an arm of the SLORC and is not set up to assist travelers.

WHEN TO GO

The cool season is from late November through February, with temperatures in the 70°–85°F (22°–30°C) range. The hot season is March and April, when the mercury can peak at 110°F (46°C). May to October is the rainy season, which often makes the up-country roads impassable for a day or two.

The best festival is Thingyan, the Water Festival, which celebrates the Burmese New Year, in April. The Burmese get carried away in dousing each other and being doused with water, and for three days the country comes practically to a standstill.

CAMBODIA

As the seat of the Khmer empire from the 9th to the 13th century, Cambodia developed a complex society based first on Hinduism and then on Buddhism. After the decline of the Khmers and the ascendancy of the Siamese, Cambodia was colonized by the French in the 19th century and become part of Indochina. Shortly after the end of World War II, during which the Japanese had occupied Cambodia, independence became the rallying cry for all of Indochina. Cambodia became a sovereign power with a monarchy and an elected government.

In the early 1970s, the destabilizing consequences of the Vietnam War led Cambodia's political factions to take up arms. A very bloody civil war ensued, with the barbaric Khmer Rouge, under the French-educated Pol Pot, emerging as victors. A regime of terror followed. Under a program of Mao Tse Tsung–inspired reeducation centered around forced agricultural collectives, hundreds of thousands of Cambodians died through torture and execution or from malnutrition and exhaustion in the camps. More than a third of Cambodians were killed during the Pol Pot regime.

Vietnam, unified under the Hanoi government, eventually intervened in 1978, partially defeated the Khmer Rouge, and brought back Prince Sihanouk as head of state. The United Nations was brought in as a peace-keeping force, and in 1996 a government was formed through democratic elections. In 1997, Hun Sen toppled the elected government, but political pressure forced new elections—monitored by the international community—in late summer 1998. Hun Sen won a plurality amid charges of election rigging and, through coercive tactics, formed a government. After the death of Pol Pot in mid-1998, the Khmer Rouge presence and its threat to the country's stability diminished. Some of its leaders are still at large; two are in prison awaiting trial, but Hun Sen is slow to bring them to justice for fear of exposing existing leaders who also committed crimes against humanity. It remains to be seen whether foreign investment and the development of tourism will follow, whether domestic problems will be solved, and how the international community will continue to accept Hun Sen's hard-line rule.

The civil wars and Pol Pot's madness have caused Cambodia to be the sick man of Southeast Asia. Roads that were once paved have deteriorated to dirt tracks. Investment has been slow in coming. Tourism has been Cambodia's big hope, but building the infrastructure has only just begun. To boot, many visitors find that Cambodians are less than sincere when it comes to money; expect to be ripped off, hustled, and maybe robbed during your stay.

Great Itinerary

Four days in **Siem Reap** allows for a leisurely appreciation of the Khmer complexes at **Angkor.** You can get a brief view of **Phnom Penh** in one day and night, but flight connections may require you to spend one night in Phnom Penh on the way to Siem Reap and one night on your return.

Phnom Penh

As the capital of the Kingdom of Cambodia, Phnom Penh is strategically positioned in the center of the country at the confluence of four branches of the Mekong River. Though it was founded in 1434, Phnom Penh is a small city with only a million inhabitants. During the Pol Pot regime's forced emigration of people from the cities, Phnom Penh had less than a thousand residents; buildings and roads deteriorated and are still in a mess. Traffic is like a complex ballet in which only the dancers understand the moves that make even crossing the street a thrilling achievement. There are only a few notable sights here, which you can easily cover in a morning; you can cover the ghoulish reminders of the recent genocide in the afternoon.

According to legend, a wealthy woman named Penh found four statues of the Buddha washed up on the banks of the Mekong, and in 1372 she commissioned a sanctuary to house them. **Wat Phnom,** Penh's temple, stands on a 90-ft knoll, visible from all parts of the city to which it gave its name: Phnom Penh means "Hill of Penh."

The **Royal Palace,** now the home of Prince Sihanouk, is a 1913 reconstruction of the one built in 1886. Though the royal palace itself is closed to the public, **Wat Phra Keo** (Temple of the Emerald Buddha), in the southern courtyard of the palace grounds, is open. The temple is often referred to as the Silver Pagoda because of the 5,000 silver blocks (6 tons of pure silver) that make up the floor. At the back of the temple is the venerated **Emerald Buddha**—some say it's carved from jade, while others hold that it's Baccarat crystal. Nearby is a 200-pound, solid-gold Buddha studded with 10,000 diamonds. Along the wall of the courtyard enclosing the temple complex are murals depicting scenes from the Hindu epic the *Ramayana.* ⊙ *Tues.–Sun. 7–11 and 2–5.*

If the Silver Pagoda is a tribute to Cambodia and its civilization, the **Toul Sleng Holocaust Museum** (⊠ Street 113, Boeng Keng Kang 3, Chemkar Mora, ☎ 023/300698) is a horrific reminder of the cruelty that humans are capable of. Once a neighborhood school, the building was seized in 1975 by Pol Pot's Khmer Rouge and turned into a prison; during its four years of operation as an interrogation center, some 20,000 Cambodians were tortured here. It's a scary thought that some of the guards who did the torturing were only 10 years old: if they survived, they're in their mid-30s today and probably walking the streets of Phnom Penh. Only seven prisoners of Toul Sing survived; none are still living. The bodies of those that died under torture were tossed into the school's garden and playing fields; those that survived the torture went to the extermination camp outside of town called **Choeung Ek,** now known as the Killing Fields. A memorial stupa stands at Choeung Ek, 14 km (9 mi) southwest of Phnom Penh, filled with the skulls of Cambodians exhumed from the mass graves. Be warned that this is an extremely disturbing sight to behold: the cracked skulls, the tree where young children were killed, and the pits where hundreds of bodies were piled on top of each other defy explanation. ⊙ *Daily 8–11 and 2–5.*

The **National Museum,** a red building constructed in 1917 in the Khmer style, contains the nation's treasure of archaeological finds, from the pre-Angkor periods of Funan and Chenia (5th–9th centuries), the Indravarman period (9th–10th centuries), the classical Angkor period (10th–13th centuries), and the post-Angkor period up to the present. ⊙ *Tues.–Sun. 8–11 and 2–5.*

Lodging

$$$$ 🏨 **Cambodiana.** This Sofitel-managed hotel is the best property in town. Its location along the Mekong River adds to its desirability. Reserve a room with a view. Rooms are comfortably modern, and most

have a separate shower. Restaurants offer Cantonese and French-inspired Western options. ✉ *313 Sisowath Quay,* ☎ *023/426288; 800/221–4542 in the U.S.,* FAX *023/426290. 300 rooms. 3 restaurants, pool, 2 tennis courts, business services, meeting rooms, travel services. AE, MC, V.*

$$$ 🏨 **Royal Phnom Penh.** Close to the Mekong River, the hotel has the good fortune to be set among beautifully tended gardens. The rooms have been completely refurbished. ✉ *26 August Site, Samdech Sothearoh Blvd. Sankat Tonle Bassac,* ☎ *023/360026,* FAX *023/360036. 40 rooms. Restaurant, pool, travel services. AE, MC, V.*

$ 🏨 **Soriya Thmey Hotel.** The 34-room Soriya Thmey is the city's best value. Large and clean rooms have air-conditioning that usually works and private bathrooms with hot water. The staff is honest and friendly, and, like most hotels here, the reception staff will arrange sightseeing trips and make bookings for you up to Siem Reap by boat. There's a pleasant bar on the ground floor. ✉ *79 Trasak Phaem Rd. 63, Sangkat Boeung Raing, Khan Daun Penh,* ☎ *023/210268,* FAX *023/212481. 34 rooms. Bar. No credit cards.*

Shopping

While in Phnom Penh, find some time to visit a market or two. The largest is the **Central Market,** an art deco–style structure in the center of the city that sells foodstuffs, household goods, fake antiques, and some silver and gold jewelry; it's most active in the morning. **O Russel Market** has lots of food stalls and small shops selling jewelry. For serious shopping, go to **Tuol Tom Pong Market,** which has real and fake antiques, carved-wood furniture, and small Buddha statues.

Angkor Temple Complex

★ *322 km (201 mi) north of Phnom Penh.*

If Angkor had been discovered before the late 19th century, it certainly would have been classified as one of the Seven Wonders of the World. The Khmer Empire reached the zenith of its power, influence, and creativity from the 9th to 13th centuries, and Angkor, the seat of the Khmer kings, was one of the largest capitals in Southeast Asia. In all there are some 300 monuments scattered in all directions through the surrounding jungle. Only the largest and best preserved are mentioned here. Admission to the complex costs $20 per day. After 4 PM, admission is free as long as you purchase a ticket for the following day. This permits you to catch the sunset at Angkor Wat.

If you are very energetic, have only one day, and want to cover as much as possible, then visit Angkor Thom and its two vast temple complexes, Bayon and Baphuon, in the early morning hours. Visit Banteay Srei by midday; Ta Prohm, a wonderful 12th-century temple that has been reclaimed by the jungle, by midafternoon; and Angkor Wat, which faces west and is best seen and photographed as the sun sinks, in the evening.

To get around, you need to hire transport and a guide. It's best to link up with a group traveling in a minivan, but you can hire a car and driver in Siem Reap for about $23 a day, plus another few dollars for going the extra distance to Banteay Srei. A motorcycle with a driver costs $6 a day (though they will ask for more). Bicycles may be rented, but make sure that you know where you're going. *Never stray off the beaten paths*—live land mines still dot the area.

Siem Reap, meaning "Siam Defeated," is a small market town that is usually the base for visits to the Khmer monuments at Angkor, just 8 km (5 mi) away. During the Khmer Rouge era of the late 1970s, Siem Reap was largely destroyed and abandoned. With the Khmer Rouge's retreat into the jungles, hotels have reopened and the accommodation and feeding of visitors has become big business. The current building boom will put another three mammoth hotels as well as a mass of small hotels and guest houses on the market by 2002, so prices may drop. About 90% of the town is dependent upon tourism: expect ingratiating smiles to lure you to buy, rent, or stay, and a sour face if you do not. Like the rest of Cambodia, prices for foreigners are inflated; negotiation is necessary, and even then the relative value for your money is questionable. Except as a base to visit Angkor, Siem Reap has little going for itself.

Angkor Thom

Angkor Thom was the last great Khmer City before the empire began to fall apart in the 13th century. The **Bayon** is the mystical and focal heart of the former capital, built by King Jayavarman VII (reigned 1181–1200). The central tower has 53 secondary towers, on each of which are four huge, strangely smiling faces of Bhodisattava Avalokitesvara in the likeness of Jayavarman. On the outer walls of the central sanctuary and on the inner walls of the laterite enclosure are marvelous bas-reliefs—1½ km (¾ mi) of them in all. On the outer walls, the depictions are of the common person pursuing his mundane life; on the inner walls, the gods do legendary deeds.

The **Baphuon** was built in the 12th century, shortly before Bayon, by King Udayadityavarman II (reigned 1050–66). This is a fine example of poor planning: architects erected the monument on a hill without the proper supports. When the earth shifted, collapse was inevitable. Much of what is there today is collapsed stone forming a chaotic ruin in the form of a pyramid with remarkable stone reliefs. Walk out past the moats and through the southeastern gate and you'll enter the Royal Enclosure. This vast rectangular yard was the epicenter of the Angkor empire. At the northeastern corner is what was perhaps a cremation tower but is now known as the Terrace of Leper King. The 23-ft-high platform is carved with *apsaras* (dancing maidens) and mythological animals known to have inhabited the upper slopes of Mt. Meru, the Hindu and Buddhist center of the cosmos. To the north is the Terrace of the Elephants, which was used as a reviewing stand, where dignitaries sat and watched the proceedings. The walls, measuring 1,150 ft long and 10 ft high, are sculpted with scenes of hunting elephants, water buffalo, and lions.

Ta Prohm

Ta Prohm has been kept more or less as it was when French explorers rediscovered Angkor at the end of the 19th century. Vines twist through pillars, and trees block out the sun. Here you can easily be transported back 800 years to the time when King Jayavarman VII had this structure built to honor his mother. Though you wouldn't know it today, this complex had 566 stone dwellings, 39 major sanctuaries, 18 chief abbots, 2,740 priests, 2,202 assistants, and 615 dancing girls to assist the priests. With all the sounds of the jungle around you and knotted trees contending for space, you can easily become lost and bewildered. Don't stray too far!

Angkor Wat

As in typical Khmer architecture, the plan of Angkor Wat is simple and audacious. The five towers are the central element of the complex, forming a lotus bud (the emblem of the Cambodian flag). The reliefs of the lower gallery show scenes of daily life and war. The celebrated apsaras surround the monument.

Angkor Wat was founded at the beginning of the 12th century and is the best preserved of the Khmer temples. It was erected by King

Suryavarman II (reigned 1112–52) and dedicated to the Hindu god Vishnu. Like all the major monuments at Angkor, the buildings form a complex representing the Hindu (and Buddhist) universe. The central shrines symbolize Mt. Meru, while the gates and cloisters depict the successive outer reaches of cosmic reality. Moats represent the seven oceans that surround Mt. Meru.

Angkor Wat is reached by an impressive causeway, an avenue lined with balustrades in the form of serpents. The complex itself rises in three concentric enclosures; wander around the terraces and marvel at the images of Hindu deities and of the Buddha, many of which have lost their heads to looters. Other amazing sculptures cover the 1-km-long (½-mi-long) open colonnaded gallery. This collection depicts the Hindu epics and Suryavarman's earthly deeds, both of which are celebrated by dancing apsaras.

Architecture and the fine reliefs symbolize the richness, power, and prosperity of the Khmer empire during this period, but such was the tremendous outlay required to build Angkor Wat that it nearly bankrupted the empire. It took 30 years to recover, and it was King Jayavarman VII who had the energy to revitalize the kingdom.

OFF THE
BEATEN PATH

BANTEAY SREI – If you have the time, visit Banteay Srei (Citadel of Women), northeast of Angkor Wat, a magnificent 10th-century temple dedicated to Shiva. The fine sculptures of rosy sandstone are surprisingly realistic and very well preserved. You can also make this a lunch stop—there are several cafés from which to choose. A hired car will cost about $5, a motorbike $2. The route is mostly, if not completely, free of land mines.

Dining and Lodging

Hotel builders always rush to fill a vacuum, even before there is a need, and so there's a variety of new accommodations on the airport road and in Siem Reap proper, ranging from budget guest houses and stylish renovations to the luxurious palace Grand Hotel d'Angkor.

$$$$ ✕🏨 **Grand Hotel d'Angkor.** This grande dame, built in 1930 and long fallen on hard times, was occupied by Khmer Rouge guerillas and then by the Vietnamese army. It has since been rejuvenated and is open for business, complete with gorgeous Taj Mahal–inspired gardens, silken fabrics, and Oriental carpets throughout. It is the most expensive hotel in Angkor—to the point of ridicule by the locals (basic rooms start at $360 and climb up to $2,000 for a suite). Most rooms have balconies that overlook either the swimming pool or the (developing) countryside. Dinners often are disappointingly buffet-style. ⊠ *1 Vithel Charles de Gaulle,* ☎ *063/963888,* ℻ *063/963168. 150 rooms. Restaurant, pool, travel services. AE, MC, V.*

$$$$ 🏨 **Angkor Village Resort.** If you want a hotel with charm in this dusty, rather ugly, town, then this is your only option. The hotel's French architect interpreted Khmer art as a complex of wood bungalows surrounding a sala used for dining and relaxing. The use of the teak makes this a warm and welcoming hotel. However, the standard rooms are rather small; better to pay for a superior room that is considerably larger. All rooms have air-conditioning, attractive bathrooms (no tub, just shower) and are furnished with Khmer artifacts. The restaurant offers local, Thai, and some international cuisine. Cultural shows are performed in the hotel's theater. ⊠ *Sangkat Svay Dong Kum,* ☎ *063/963563,* ℻ *063/360104. 18 rooms. Restaurant, pool, theater. MC, V.*

¢ 🏨 **Phnom Kaosan Guest House.** This is one of the better guest houses in Siem Reap. The rooms in the new building are large and fresh. All rooms have overhead fans, and each has a fair-sized bathroom. Corner room No. 21 is the best, with lots of windows and ventilation. Travelers here consist of expats living in Asia and some backpackers; conversations in the sitting-dining pavilion are usually lively. The food, Western, Thai, and Khmer, is adequate. ✉ *078, Group 8, Vihea Chen Village, Suay Dang Kum,* ☎ *012/898694,* FAX *no fax. 15 rooms. Restaurant. No credit cards.*

Cambodia A to Z

Arriving and Departing

BY AIRPLANE

Thai Airways International (☎ 023/214359 in Phnom Penh; 02/232–8000 in Bangkok) flies twice daily between Bangkok and Pochentong (PNH), Phnom Penh's International airport, 10 km (6 mi) from the city. Flights are quite heavily booked, so try to reserve in advance. **Bangkok Airways** (☎ 023/427429 in Phnom Penh; 02/229–3456 in Bangkok) and **Royal Air Cambodge** (☎ 023/428055, 023/428229 in Phnom Penh; 02/653–2261 in Bangkok), also fly this route. Royal Air Cambodge also operates internationally to Kuala Lumpur, Singapore, Ho Chi Minh City, and Hong Kong. **Malaysia Airlines** (☎ 023/426688 in Phnom Penh; 03/746–3000 in Kuala Lumpur; 02/263–0565 in Bangkok) flies from Kuala Lumpur; **Vietnam Airlines** (☎ 04/825–0888 in Hanoi; 08/829–2118 in Ho Chi Minh City) from Hanoi and Ho Chi Minh City. **Lao Aviation** (☎ 021/212050 in Vientiane) flies from Vientiane. **Bangkok Airways** (☎ 063/380191 in Siem Reap) flies daily direct from Bangkok to Siem Reap. A tax of US$20 is levied on all international departures, US$10 for domestic departures. A taxi to reach downtown is US$7, a motorbike is US$2.

BY BUS OR CAR

Road travel between Phnom Penh and Ho Chi Minh City, Vietnam, either by hired car or by bus, poses no problem; it's only a matter of time and rough, bumpy travel. The bus trip is certainly cheap—approximately $10—and in four hours you're at the Vietnamese border. You walk across and get another bus on the other side for a five-hour ride to Ho Chi Minh City. You can hire a car and driver at most travel agencies or from the **General Directorate of Tourism** in Phnom Penh (☎ 023/426107) for about $50 for the trip to the border, but it's not always easy to find a car in Vietnam to take you to Ho Chi Minh City.

Getting Around

The road to Siem Reap from Phnom Penh is open, but a very rough nine hours by pick-up truck or bus. Most travelers find it more comfortable to fly or go by boat; the latter is the most interesting way and costs $25. High-speed ferries to Siem Reap and other destinations depart from the Psar Cha Ministry of Transport Ferry Landing between 102 and 104 streets, and go to Kompong Cham, Kratie, Stung Treng, Kompong Chanang, and Phnom Krom. Because of the present rise in crime, intercity boat travel should be restricted to the fast boats to Kompong Cham and Kratie.

From Siem Reap, you can go by road to the Thai border at Poipet, 150 km (95 mi) away, cross into Thailand and take a tuk-tuk (40 baht) to Aranyaprathet, where buses go to Bangkok and other destinations. The journey by pick-up to the border costs $7 inside the cab or $5 outside in the back and takes six hours (because the dirt road is so abysmal, often requiring the driver to slip off the road and go along a river bed). Note that in the rainy season, the road can be impassable. You can take buses (or a hired car) to Cambodia's southern towns on the Gulf of Thailand, and it's also possible, by bus and ferry, to enter Thailand's

Trat province. Those planning such a trip should inquire in Phnom Penh about conditions, which are continually changing.

Buses to Phnom Penh suburbs leave from the bus station at 182 Street (open 5:30 AM–7:30 PM). Cruising taxis are nonexistent, but service taxis can be hired at the Psar Chabam Pao Shared-Taxi Station between 367 and 369 streets. Few drivers speak English; fewer yet speak some French. Visitors can arrange to hire cars with a driver, with or without air-conditioning, from the General Directorate of Tourism for about US$40–US$50 per day.

Contacts and Resources

CUSTOMS AND DUTIES

Tourists are allowed to bring into Cambodia 200 cigarettes, 50 cigars, or ½ pound of tobacco, and one quart of alcoholic liquor. You are not allowed to bring in or take out local currency. The export of antiques or religious objects requires a permit.

ELECTRICITY

Electrical current is 220 volts AC, 50Hz. Power cuts are frequent. Outside Phnom Penh and Siem Reap, electricity is often only up from around 6:30 PM to 9:30 PM.

EMBASSIES AND CONSULATES

Australian Embassy (⊠ Villa II, Street 254, Chartaumuk, Daun Penh District, Phnom Penh, ☎ 023/213470). **British Embassy** (⊠ 29 Street 275, Phnom Penh, ☎ 023/427124). **Canada** (⊠ 48 Street 172, Phnom Penh, ☎ 012/810731). **Embassy of the United States of America** (⊠ 27 EO Street 240, Phnom Penh, ☎ 023/216436). New Zealanders should contact the British Embassy.

EMERGENCIES

For medical and police emergencies, use the services of your hotel. The best advice if you do get sick is to get back to Thailand as fast as possible, but if you wish to consult an English-speaking doctor, visit Dr. Gavin Scott at the **Tropical & Travellers Medical Clinic** (⊠ 88 Street 108, Wat Phnom Quarter, Phnom Penh 3, ☎ 023/366802; mobile 015/912100). In the case of a lost passport, immediately notify your embassy.

HEALTH AND SAFETY

Just under half a million people enter Cambodia every year, either as tourists or on business. Although travel in parts of Cambodia is not advised—the killings and kidnappings of a number of Western tourists in recent years attest that remnants of the Khmer Rouge still roam the forests—neither Phnom Penh nor the Khmer ruins at Angkor are considered particularly dangerous. Robbery, though, is becoming more common in Phnom Penh. Cambodia's security is not especially efficient, and you're asking for trouble if you walk the streets alone at night or put your trust in the smiling hustler who knows all the right phrases to convey such interest in your well-being. Watch your health, too; drink bottled water and avoid uncooked food and vegetables.

LANGUAGE, CULTURE, AND ETIQUETTE

The Cambodian language is based on the Khmer phonetic alphabet and is tonal. Within the tourist industry, English is spoken and, to a lesser degree, French. Many in Phnom Penh speak some English, from their dealings with the U.N. forces. Many of the older Cambodians know some French. As elsewhere in Southeast Asia, confrontational behavior and displays of anger are considered bad manners, as is nakedness and bare limbs at religious sites. Homosexuality is tolerated but not encouraged, and public displays of affection should be avoided.

Airmail to Europe takes 4–5 days; to the United States 7–10 days. The Post & Telephone Office (PTT) in Phnom Penh is across from the Hotel Monorom at the corner of Achar Mean Boulevard and 126 Street; it's open 7–noon and 1–11. The main post office in Phnom Penh is on the west side of 13 Street between 98 Street and 102 Street and is open 6:30 AM–9 PM weekdays.

MONEY MATTERS

Costs. Hotel prices in Phnom Penh and Siem Reap are quite high, around $180 a night, for very average accommodation (rated first-class by the government). A spartanly furnished room with a private bathroom in a cheaper hotel runs about $30 or less with negotiation. A room in a guest house costs about $8. Western-style restaurants are also fairly expensive for very ordinary fare; expect to pay $20 a head. Local food is inexpensive. Air travel is expensive; buses are very inexpensive, but they're also uncomfortable. Taxis run about $2 per kilometer, or you can hire a car with driver for about $20 if you cover less than 25 km (15 mi). Local beer costs $1.50 in a local café. At a hotel, an imported beer will cost about $4.

Currency. The monetary unit in Cambodia is the rial, but U.S. dollars are in demand and it is best to take lots of low-denomination bills. Payment in dollars is required by hotels and airlines. At press time, the exchange rate was approximately 3,900 rials to the U.S. dollar, but you do better to pay all your bills in dollars since vendors and hotels use a higher rate.

Tipping. A bellboy would like a dollar for carrying your luggage. Guides may expect a fee of $5 for a day's sightseeing. At tourist hotels, gratuities are included in the cost of meals and accommodation.

OPENING AND CLOSING TIMES

Business hours are 7–11:30 and 2–5:30 weekdays. Generally, post office hours are weekdays 7:30–noon and 2:30–5. Public holidays for 2001 are: New Year's Day (Jan. 1); International Women's Day (Mar. 8); Cambodian New Year (Apr. 13); Labor Day (May 1); Visak Bochea (Buddha's Birthday; May 17); Sep Bonn Phchum Ben (International Children's Day; Sept. 23); Constitution Promulgation Day (Sept. 24); Taing Tok Ceremony (Oct. 20–22); Paris Peace Agreement (Oct. 23); King's Birthday (Oct. 31); Independence Day (Nov. 9); Human Rights Day (Dec. 10).

PASSPORTS AND VISAS

All visitors are required to have a passport and a one-month visa, obtainable from the **Embassy of Cambodia** (⊠ 4500 16th St. NW, Washington, DC 20001, ☎ 202/726–7742).

Visas are also available for around $20 at travel agencies in Bangkok, who apply at the **Royal Cambodian Embassy** (⊠ 185 Rajdamri Rd., Lumpini, Patumwan, Bangkok, 10330 Thailand, ☎ 02/254–6630, FAX 02/253–9859). Allow five days. You can also collect a visa when you arrive at the airport in Phnom Penh. You'll need one passport-size photograph of yourself.

TELEPHONES

To call Cambodia from overseas, dial the country code, 855, and then the area code, omitting the first 0. The Phnom Penh code is 023. Calling overseas is very expensive, and you cannot do it from public telephones. If you have to make a call, either go to the main post office or, more conveniently, use your hotel's switchboard. Public phones take coins. For long-distance calls within the country, dial the zero as part of the area code.

Though you'll spend less money making your own plans, you can make tour arrangements (round-trip flight from Bangkok, Phnom Penh hotel, day trip to Angkor Wat, and visas) through a travel agency in Bangkok for approximately US$530. Recommended (but expensive) is **Abercrombie & Kent** (✉ 4th fl., Silom Plaza, 491/29–30 Silom Rd., Bangkok 10500, ☎ 02/266–7660, FAX 02/266–7854; ✉ 1520 Kensington Rd., Suite 212, Oak Brook, IL 60521, ☎ 630/954–2944 or 800/323–7308, FAX 630/954–3324).

A good travel agent is your best bet for assistance with travel in Cambodia. You may want to visit the knowledgeable, though expensive, **Diethelm Travel Ltd.** (✉ House 65, Street 240, Box 99, Phnom Penh, ☎ 023/219151.).

The dry, cool season runs from November through February, with temperatures between 65°F (18°C) and 80°F (27°C). It heats up to around 92°F (33°C) from March through May. June is the beginning on the monsoon season, with downpours for an hour or two on most days, and continues through October; temperatures range from 80°F (27°C) to 95°F (35°C).

LAOS

Of all the peoples in Southeast Asia, Laotians seem the most gentle and peace-loving. But this tiny landlocked nation, not much larger than Great Britain, has for centuries been a strategic battleground. Most recently, during the Vietnam War, the U.S. Air Force, in a vain attempt to disrupt the Ho Chi Minh Trail, dropped more tons of bombs on Laos than were dropped on Germany during World War II. Since the end of the Vietnam War, the People's Democratic Party has ruled the country, first on Marxist-Leninist lines and now on the basis of limited pro-market reforms. Overtures are being made to the outside, particularly to Thailand and China, to assist in developing the country—not an easy task.

Some changes are taking place. A new airport is underway, and the road from Vientiane north to Luang Prabang, Laos's ancient capital, has been paved—though it still takes six to seven hours to make the 150-mi journey. New hotels are opening, and the Friendship Bridge over the Mekong from Thailand's northern town of Nong Khai has made Vientiane, the capital, accessible to trade from the south. Other border crossings have also opened up. The average annual per-capita income of $170 and a rugged landscape that makes transportation and communications extremely difficult have long made the countryside of Laos a sleepy backwater; but Luang Prabang has already become a tourist hub and is likely to become more so in the years to come.

Great Itinerary
If you limit your visit to the sights of Vientiane and Luang Prabang, a minimum of three days is required: one in Vientiane and two in Luang Prabang. However, we recommend that you consider taking another day or two to make the Mekong river trip from Luang Pranbang to Ban Huai Sai (across from Chiang Khong in Thailand).

Vientiane

Vientiane is the quietest Southeast Asian capital. It's modern and small, with none of the imposing sights that you find in Bangkok. Notwithstanding the imports slipped in from Thailand and the occasional burst of pop music coming from newly acquired stereos, Vientiane's pace is as slow as the Mekong, which flows through town. On the avenue that runs along the north bank of the river, or close to it, is where you will want to stay and wander in the evenings.

To immerse yourself in Vientiane, visit the morning **market** (Talat Sao) in the center of town, less than 1,000 yards northeast of the Presidential Palace and the bank of the Mekong.

The one temple worth finding is **Wat Phra Keo,** a name that has good reason for being similar to one in Bangkok's Royal Palace: the original Wat Phra Keo temple here was built in 1565 to house the Emerald Buddha taken from the Thais by the Lao; the Buddha was recaptured by the Thai army in 1778 and taken to Bangkok. The present temple dates from 1936 and has become a national museum. On display are Lao wood sculptures and a vast array of Buddhas in different styles, including a Laotian interpretation of the walking Buddha first developed in Thailand's Sukhothai. There are also wonderful images of Khmer deities and a 16th-century door carved with Hindu images. ⊙ *Tues.–Sun. 8–11:30 and 2–4:30.*

Dining and Lodging

$$ 🏨 **Novotel Vientiane.** This French-managed hotel between the airport and downtown is convenient and efficient, if not exactly charming. Everything is modern and spotless. It's not a place to linger, but for a stopover waiting for an outbound flight, you can't do better. ✉ *Unit 9, Samsenthai Rd.,* ☎ *021/213570,* ℻ *021/213572. 209 rooms. 2 restaurants, pool, dance club, business services, meeting rooms. AE, MC, V.*

$$ 🏨 **Tai-Pan.** In an ideal spot in the heart of Vientiane and facing the Mekong River, this 44-room hotel, which opened in 1994, offers personal and attentive service, largish rooms neatly decorated in pale blue-greys and yellow, and a convenient dining room. The concierge and front desk are extremely helpful in fulfilling the needs of the businessperson and/or tourist. ✉ *22/3 Francois Ngin Rd., Ban Mixay,* ☎ *021/216907,* ℻ *21/216223. 44 rooms. Business services, meeting rooms. MC, V.* ⊛

$–$$ 🏨 **Heuan Lao.** This new guest house, built specially to accommodate the influx of travelers yet to come, has large rooms that are both air-conditioned and fan-cooled. Bathrooms are modern and clean. ✉ *Friendship Hwy.,* ☎ *no phone. 15 rooms. Breakfast room. No credit cards.*

$ 🏨 **Lane-Xang.** The hotel promotes itself as a five-star hotel at the cost of a three-star, but these days, the hotel is looking very tired. It remains a good choice for the price, especially if you can have a large room overlooking the Mekong. And while the furnishings are worn and the high ceilings of the rooms in need of paint, the rooms are of decent size, the bathrooms are clean, and the staff is polite and attentive. ✉ *Fangum Rd.,* ☎ *021/214102,* ℻ *021/214108. 109 rooms. Restaurant, travel services. MC, V.*

Luang Prabang

230 km (144 mi) north of Vientiane.

Most visitors to Laos don't go to see Vientiane, the present-day capital, but to see the ancient capital of Luang Prabang, a sleepy town of about 21,000 inhabitants that sits high on the banks of a peninsula where Nam Khan meets the Mekong. It is still, at least unofficially, the historic, religious, and artistic capital. Some 30 temples remain intact, making it a pleasant place to tour on a rented bicycle for a couple of days. Be prepared to be cheek to jowl with other tourists. With each passing year, the increase in visitors seems to overwhelm the town. Despite hundreds of guests houses, finding accommodation can be a challenge in peak season.

Start with a visit to the **Royal Palace Museum,** the former palace of the Savang family. (King Savang Vattana and his family were exiled to northern Laos in 1975 and have not been heard from since.) The most prized exhibit is the **Pha Bang,** a gold Buddha just inches under 3 ft tall and weighing more than 100 pounds. Its history goes back to the first century, when it was cast in Sri Lanka; it was brought to Luang Prabang in 1353 as a gift to King Fa Bang. This event is celebrated as the introduction of Buddhism to Laos, and Fa Bang is venerated as the protector of the faith. Also on display are excellent friezes removed from local temples, Khmer bong drums, elephant tusks with carved images of the Buddha, and a Sukhothai–style standing Buddha. The eclectic assortment of items also includes, in the Queen's reception room, teacups presented by Mao Tse Tung and medals from Lyndon Johnson. In the king's reception room, the walls are covered with murals painted in the 1930s, depicting scenes of traditional Lao life.

Luang Prabang's most awesome temple is **Wat Xieng Thong.** Constructed in 1559, it's one of the few structures to have survived centuries of marauding Chinese and Thais. Low, sweeping roofs overlap to make complex patterns and create a feeling of harmony and peace. There are marvelous interior mosaics, and decorated wooden columns support the ceiling, which is covered with wheels of *dhamma,* which represent the Buddha's teaching.

Several small **chapels** at the sides of the main hall contain images of the Buddha; the bronze 16th-century reclining Buddha was displayed in the 1931 Paris Exhibition. On the back wall of this chapel is a mosaic, an unusual creation that commemorates the 2,500th anniversary of the Buddha's birth with a depiction of Lao village life. Another chapel, near the compound's east gate, contains the royal family's funeral statuary, including funeral urns and a 40-ft wooden chariot used as a hearse. The walls of the chapel are noteworthy for their gilt panels etched with erotic scenes from the *Ramayana.*

Dining and Lodging

In addition to the hotels listed below, Luang Prabang has masses of small guest houses, mostly run by families, of similar quality and atmosphere.

$ ✕ **Duang Champa.** Across the street from the Nam Khan River, this town house has been converted into a restaurant. With high ceilings, wood floors, and white tablecloths, it has the ambience of a French brasserie. The menu, except for the few Lao dishes, reinforces that feeling. Steak à poivre with an order of sautéed potatoes or the chicken in a red wine sauce are good bets. Be sure to have the house salad with its fragrant dressing. Orders can be à la carte or, at a more reasonable price, from the set menu. ✉ *Thanon Kingkitsarath,* ☎ *071/212420. MC, V.*

$$ 🏨 **L'Auberge Calao.** This charming guest house was resurrected from a ruined mansion originally built by a Portuguese merchant in 1906. Four guest rooms upstairs open onto a colonnaded veranda, and all have air-conditioning. There is one small, fan-cooled room on the ground floor. Wholesome breakfasts are served; only snacks thereafter, but there are several restaurants down by the river, just 150 yards away. ✉ *River Rd.,* ☎ *071/212100. 5 rooms. Bicycles. No credit cards.*

$$ 🏨 **Villa Santi.** Formerly a royal palace and often called by its previous
★   name, Villa de la Princesse, the Villa Santi has been converted into a very commodious hotel and civilized place to have dinner. Although it may not offer modern five-star luxury, the rooms are simply fur-

nished—with old-fashioned twin beds and table and chairs—in pleasing good taste. Hallways have bric-a-brac that, if not antique, certainly create that atmosphere, and it's a treat to have drinks in the garden. The staff is wonderfully helpful, and the manager, Sant Inthavong, is anxious to please. The new annex around the corner is equally attractive; it looks as comfortably Old World as the main building. ⊠ *Rue Sakkarine, BP 681,* ☎ *071/212267,* ℻ *071/252158. 25 rooms. Restaurant. No credit cards.*

Pak Ou Caves

25 km (15 mi) up the Mekong from Luang Prabang.

In high limestone cliffs above the river are two sacred caves stuffed with Buddha statues. The lower cave, **Tham Thing,** is accessible from the river by a stairway and has enough daylight to allow you to find your way around. The stairway continues to the upper cave, **Tham Phum,** for which you will need a flashlight.

It takes about two hours by slow boat, one hour by speedboat, to reach the caves. Along the way you pass small villages, and you'll probably stop at **Xang Hai** for refreshment. Be forewarned: the village makes *Lao Lao,* a potent, fermented rice drink. Try it, but don't try to dilute it with unfiltered water—better a temporarily swimming head than stomach troubles.

Side Trip to Northern Thailand

Growing in popularity is the Mekong River trip between Luang Prabang and Ban Huai Sai, across the river from Chiang Khong in Thailand. The scenery is splendid: high hills clad in foliage and rocky islands in mid-river are a continual feast for the eyes. Only a few villages line the river; these isolated pockets of habitation are havens of wonder. Only one village has established itself as a stopover for foreigners. That is Pakbeng, halfway between Luang Prabang and Ban Huai Sai.

There are two ways to make the journey: either by regular boat, which holds about 50 passengers, or by speedboat, which seats about four. The regular boat takes 12 hours over two days. The night is spent at Pakbeng in very basic lodgings—guest houses with only cold water and limited electricity. The speedboats make the journey between Luang Prabang and Ban Huai Sai in six hours. Speedboats, while thrilling for the first hour, become extremely uncomfortable after the novelty wears off. Passengers must sit uncomfortably on hard seats; the engine noise is deafening (ear plugs are advised); and the wind and spray can be chilling. Take a warm, waterproof windbreaker, and get a life jacket and crash helmet with a visor from the boatsman. With a speedboat, you can still overnight at Pakbeng and the following day either continue with a speed- or regular boat. For the regular boat, the fare is about 750 baht; the speed boat is 1,300 baht.

There is also a twice-weekly flight between Luang Prabang and Ban Huai Sai, and for those travelers with cushions as bottoms, there are the uncomfortable Laotian buses that travel the rutted road between the two towns.

Laos A to Z

Arriving and Departing
You can fly from Bangkok to Vientiane's Wattai Airport, 4 km (2½ mi) from the city, on **Thai Airways International** (☎ 021/225271 in Vien-

tiane; 02/234–3100 in Bangkok). The national airline, **Lao Aviation** (☎ 021/212050 in Vientiane; 02/236–9821 in Bangkok), also connects Vientiane to Bangkok and to Hanoi, Phnom Penh, and Ho Chi Minh City. Departure tax is US$10.

You can enter Laos from Northern Thailand by crossing the Friendship Bridge at Nong Khai. Buses and taxis wait on the Laotian side to make the run into Vientiane, 19 km (12 mi) away—about 150 baht by taxi.

Getting Around

Though you can go by road from Vientiane to Luang Prabang, it takes six to seven hours to make the 242-km (150-mi) trip along the meandering, but paved, road up into the mountains. Missing out on some great scenery, many people prefer to fly on Lao Aviation, which has daily flights out of Vientiane in the morning for approximately $50. Irregularly, river ferries also ply the waters between Vientiane and Luang Prabang; it takes three nights upstream and two nights coming down the Mekong. You can also charter a speedboat, but the discomfort keeps most from choosing this option. The fare is about $10 on the slow boat and you must bring your own food. You are also supposed to have a pass, but it's rarely requested.

Contacts and Resources

CUSTOMS AND DUTIES

Tourists are allowed to bring into Laos 200 cigarettes, 50 cigars, or ½ lb of tobacco, and one quart of spirits. Bringing in or taking out local currency is prohibited, as is the export of antiques and religious artifacts without a permit.

ELECTRICITY

The electrical current is 220 volts AC, 50Hz. Outside of Vientiane and Luang Prabang, electricity is uncertain, and even in Luang Prabang there are frequent late-afternoon outages in hot weather.

EMBASSIES AND CONSULATES

Embassy of the United States of America (✉ BP 114, rue Bartholomé, Vientiane, ☎ 021/212 581). Australian, British, Canadian, and New Zealand residents should contact their respective embassies in Bangkok for assistance in Laos.

EMERGENCIES

For medical and police emergencies, use the services of your hotel. In serious medical emergencies, get to Thailand as soon as possible. In the case of a lost passport, immediately notify your embassy.

HEALTH AND SAFETY

As in all of Southeast Asia, it's advisable to drink bottled water and keep away from uncooked foods. Laos is fairly free of crime in the tourist areas, though traveling by road puts you at risk of highway thieves. Trekking is increasingly popular in Laos, but beware: there are still many unexploded mines and bombs left over from the Vietnam War. Don't photograph anything that may have military significance.

LANGUAGE, CULTURE, AND ETIQUETTE

In tourist hotels, the staff speak some English. You will also find a smattering of English speakers in the shops and restaurants. A few old-timers know some French. The national language, Lao, is tonal; although a few words are similar to Thai, most are not, and the alphabet differs. Dress respectfully, and remove your shoes before entering a temple. Take your lead from these gentle, hospitable people and avoid displays of anger or confrontational behavior. Everyone should also avoid public displays of affection, which are considered offensive.

MONEY MATTERS

Costs. Anticipate spending $75 for a double room in a Western-style hotel that has private bathrooms. Dinner with Western food costs $18; in a local restaurant, a meal will cost less than $4. A local beer runs $1.50.

Currency. The local currency is the kip. It suffers inflationary pressure and continually drops against the dollar. Hence, dollars are preferred and are always used to pay hotel and airline bills. The Thai baht is accepted in Vientiane, Luang Prabang, Pakbeng, and Ban Huai Sai. Kip cannot be changed back into a hard currency. At press time the official exchange rate was 196 kip to the Thai baht and 7,600 kip for US$1. Credit cards are accepted at only the more expensive establishments in the larger cities.

Tipping. Give bellboys a dollar. Guides expect $5 for a day's sightseeing. At tourist hotels, gratuities are included in the cost of meals and accommodation.

OPENING AND CLOSING TIMES

Business hours are 7–11:30 and 2–5:30 weekdays, and post offices keep the same schedule. Laotian public holidays are: New Year's Day (Jan. 1); Army Day (Jan. 24); Lao New Year (Water Festival, Apr. 13–15); Labor Day (May 1); National Day (Dec. 2).

PASSPORTS AND VISAS

All visitors to Laos need a passport and visa. Most travelers obtain their visas in Bangkok, but for $50 you can get one at Vientiane airport, at the Friendship Bridge in Nong Khai, and also in Chiang Khong (near Chiang Rai) and Khon Kaen in northeastern Thailand. The process can be time-consuming—usually three days in Bangkok, 24 hours at Chiang Khong, and three hours in Khon Kaen. Sometimes the immigration officials want to see evidence that you have sufficient funds for your travels in Laos and an air ticket out of the country. Tourist visas are good for 15 days and can be extended for another 15. Because the rules are continually changing, it's advisable to contact the **Embassy of the Lao People's Democratic Republic** (✉ Consular Section, 2222 S. St. NW, Washington, DC 20008, ☎ 202/667–0076) for the most recent entry requirements.

You can also apply for visas through a travel agency in Bangkok; allow three business days for processing. In Rangoon, you can deal directly with the Laotian embassy and get a visa in about two days for $20. Many travelers heading for Thailand from Hanoi prefer the cheaper five-day transit visa (which is, in any case, the only type issued from Hanoi), because with it they can fly cheaply from Hanoi to Vientiane and then take the Friendship Bridge across the Mekong to Nong Khai, Thailand—as opposed to paying US$180 for a flight from Hanoi to Bangkok.

TELEPHONES

To call Laos from overseas, dial the country code, 856, and then the area code, omitting the first 0. The outgoing international code is 00, but IDD phones are rare. If you have to make an international call from Laos, use your hotel's switchboard. This is a good idea even for local calls, since there are few pay phones.

TOUR OPERATORS

You can make tour arrangements (round-trip flight from Bangkok to Vientiane and Luang Prabang, hotels, guides, and visas) through a travel agency in Bangkok for approximately US$800. Recommended is **Abercrombie & Kent** (✉ 4th fl., Silom Plaza, 491/29–30 Silom Rd., Bangkok

10500, ☎ 02/266–7660, FAX 02/266–7854; ✉ 1520 Kensington Rd., Suite 212, Oak Brook, IL 60521, ☎ 630/954–2944 or 800/323–7308, FAX 630/954–3324). **Journeys International** (✉ 4011 Jackson Rd., Ann Arbor, MI 48103, ☎ 313/255–8735 or 800/255–8735) also organizes tours to Laos.

VISITOR INFORMATION

A good travel agency in Bangkok is your best source of information on Laos (☞ Tour Operators, *above*).

In Laos, you can get limited information from the **National Tourism Authority of the Lao People's Democratic Republic** (✉ BP 3556, Avenue Lang Xang, Vientiane, ☎ 021/212248). In Luang Prabang, try the **Luang Prabang Tourism Office** (✉ 72 Sisavangvong Rd., ☎ 071/212198). The office runs one- to six-day river tours that are worth checking out.

WHEN TO GO

The dry season is from December through May and is much cooler—even chilly at night—than the rainy season. Sudden downpours occur from June through November.

9   PORTRAITS OF SOUTHEAST ASIA

Southeast Asia at a Glance: A Chronology

Religion in Southeast Asia

Books and Videos

SOUTHEAST ASIA AT A GLANCE: A CHRONOLOGY

20,000 BC   First evidence of human settlement in the Philippines.

6000   Rice cultivation begins in Southeast Asia.

3000   Use of bronze begins in Thailand.

c. AD 150   Coastal Indonesians establish direct trade with South India. Early Malayan rulers adopt Indian Sanskrit.

c. 400   Chinese inscriptions from Province Wellesley (along the coast of the Malay Peninsula) indicate the presence of Mahayana Buddhism.

c. 638–700   Empire of Srivijaya emerges on Sumatra and power extends to the Malay Peninsula and small archipelagoes to the south; West Java and southwest Borneo are influenced. Eighth-century inscriptions attest to "Old Malay," the earliest-known use of national language in Southeast Asia.

c. 775–856   Under the Sailendra dynasty, Central Java prospers; great monuments are built by followers of Mahayana Buddhism.

1000–1100   Suryavarman I of Angkor conquers the area that is now Thailand and Laos. Old Javanese literature flourishes.

1100–1200   Singapore Island becomes a prosperous trading center, while Kediri is chief political center in East Java. Khmer temples are built at Lopburi (the region now occupied by Thailand and Laos).

1230   A Theravada Buddhist becomes ruler of Ligor (now Malaysia).

1291   Marco Polo arrives in Pasai, in northern Sumatra.

1292–93   Mongols attack Java. Northern Sumatran states adopt Islam.

1293   Majapahit, near the present-day town of Modjokerto, is founded as the capital of the eastern Javanese kingdom.

1350–78   The Siamese kingdom of Ayutthaya is founded and shortly thereafter conquers the state of Sukhothai.

1364   The Nagarajertagama (Old Javanese survey of Indonesian culture) is completed.

1402–1500   Melaka (Malacca), along the southwestern coast of the Malay Peninsula, becomes the greatest international trading center in eastern world and is the greatest diffusion center of Islam; Islam spreads throughout Sumatra and eastward to the Sulu Archipelago in the southern Philippines. Buddhist reforms begin in the Burma region.

1431   Brahman political advisors are brought to Ayutthaya (capital of Siam), and the king becomes a divine monarch; the Siamese sack Angkor.

1511   The Portuguese conquer Melaka.

1521 Ferdinand Magellan, on the first voyage to circumnavigate the globe, reaches what is now the Philippines; he is slain in battle by a local chieftain, Lapu-Lapu.

1525–36 Spanish expeditions under Charles V claim the Philippines.

1596 The Dutch arrive in Indonesia.

1600–1700 Ayutthaya becomes the principal port of Far East. The French, under Louis XIV, exchange embassies with Siam; the European influence on Southeast Asia increases.

1633 The Dutch blockade Melaka, but don't gain control until 1641, when the Portuguese surrender the city.

1688 Siam enters a period of comparative isolation, not to be broken until the 19th century.

1767 The Burmese destroy Ayutthaya, and the Sino-Siamese Phy Tak Sin becomes monarch; Siam's capital moves to Thonburi.

1781 The Philippines enter a time of prosperity as the state holds a monopoly on the cultivation, manufacture, and sale of tobacco.

1782 The Chakri dynasty is established in Siam.

1795 Great Britain takes over Melaka.

1807 Organized by Herman Willem Daendels (governor general), the Indonesian highway is constructed along northern coast of Java.

1811 British troops occupy Java.

1819 Under the East India Company, Singapore becomes a new British port south of Melaka.

1824 Britain returns Indonesia to the Dutch.

1826–32 Singapore joins with Penang and Melaka (both in present-day Malaysia) to form the Straits Settlements; the territory then becomes the seat of government.

1834 After years of clandestinely trading sugar and other tropical produce with Europe, Manila enters the world trade market.

1851 Siam's King Rama IV begins to reestablish previously severed diplomatic relations with Western powers.

1896–1901 The Philippines experience a countrywide revolt led by the Katipunan Society; José Rizal, the Philippines' national hero, is executed by the Spanish; General Emilio Aguinaldo declares the Philippines independent of Spain; instead of independence, sovereignty changes hands and the United States takes control. Though Aguinaldo's troops refuse to recognize the transfer, the United States forces collapse of Filipino resistance.

1907–09 Siam cedes Laos and Cambodia to France, and recognizes British control over Kedan, Kelantan, Perlis, and Terengganu.

1916　The Philippines adopt a bicameral legislature.

1922　Singapore is chosen as the principal base for defense of British interests in the Far East.

1932　A Western-educated minority stages a revolution in Siam, replacing absolute monarchy with a constitutional monarchy, though there's little change in policy.

1935　Primary education is made compulsory throughout Thailand.

1941–42　Japan occupies most of Southeast Asia (Malaya, the Philippines, Hong Kong, Singapore, Taiwan, Burma, Indochina).

1945–49　Indonesia stages resistance against Dutch and declares independence. Singapore is liberated from the Japanese by Great Britain.

1946　The Straits Settlements are disbanded and Singapore becomes a separate colony; Melaka and Penang are incorporated into Malaya. The Republic of the Philippines becomes independent. U.S. economic assistance to Thailand begins (more than $2 billion of aid is sent between 1950 and 1975.)

1947–57　Thailand enters a time of political unrest and flux of government policy until finally, in 1957, a state of national emergency is declared; Field Marshal Phibun is ousted and new elections are held.

1947–66　Indonesia's Communist Party becomes increasingly powerful, with several coup attempts; in 1965, political tension climaxes with a coup that leads to more than 100,000 deaths. Sukarno is replaced by Suharto, and Indonesia's Communist Party is banned.

1948–60　The Federation of Malaya is proclaimed; Malaya enters a 12-year state of emergency as the Malayan Communist Party begins a widespread terrorist campaign and attacks police stations, plantations, and communication facilities; thousands are murdered, including High Commissioner Sir Henry Gurney in 1951.

1953–57　Ramon Magsaysay is elected President of Philippines; defeats Communist insurgents, the Huks.

1954　In the hope of presenting a united front to forestall Communist aggression, the Southeast Asia Treaty Organization (SEATO) is formed. Singapore's People's Action Party (PAP) is established under the leadership of Lee Kuan Yew.

1958–63　Despite dissension among leading politicians, Thailand's economy grows under generals Sarit Thanarat and Thanom Kittikachorn.

1959　Lee Kuan Yew wins general elections (agreed upon by Great Britain in 1957) and becomes Singapore's first prime minister.

1963–65　Malaysia is established, joining together the Federation of Malaya, Singapore, Sabah, and Sarawak; after two years Singapore secedes and becomes an independent sovereign state.

1965   Ferdinand Marcos takes office as president of the Philippines. Singapore leaves the Federation of Malaysia.

1968   The Association of Southeast Asian Nations (ASEAN) is formed.

1972   Martial law, imposed by Philippine president Marcos, stifles dissent but increases armed insurgency. The country prospers for a while but by the 1980s falls into deep recession.

1973–76   Continual student demonstrations, strikes, and political assassinations occur in Thailand.

1974   Unrest erupts in Indonesia when students stage street demonstrations against the visit of Japan's premier.

1975   North Vietnam defeats the South; Vietnam is unified.

1977   SEATO is disbanded.

1978   Vietnam invades Cambodia, ousting Pol Pot and the Khmer Rouge.

1979   Elections for the lower house of legislature are held in Thailand.

1983   Benigno Aquino Jr., the Philippines' opposition leader, is assassinated when he returns from exile; Marcos's downfall begins.

1984   Great Britain agrees that Hong Kong will revert to China in 1997.

1986   In a bloodless, four-day February Manila uprising known as "People Power," the Marcoses are forced into exile. The popular Corazon Aquino, widow of Benigno Aquino Jr., wins victory as president, and democratic rule is restored.

1989   Burma changes its name to Myanmar; places Aung San Suu Kyi under house arrest.

1990   A powerful earthquake causes major destruction in Philippines.

1991   Military coup d'état in Thailand. Aung San Suu Kyi of Burma is awarded the Nobel Peace Prize. Mt. Pinatubo, dormant for 600 years, erupts in the Philippines, and this affects the global climate.

1992   Thais take to the streets in bloody demonstrations, forcing the military junta out of power and holding democratic elections. In the first freely held presidential elections since 1969, Fidel V. Ramos succeeds Corazon Aquino as president of the Philippines.

1993   U.N.-sponsored elections take place in Cambodia.

1994   The United States lifts its embargo on Vietnam. The last U.S. military base in the Philippines is shut down, ending almost a century of U.S. military presence in the country.

1995   Burma's Aung San Suu Kyi is released from house arrest. Thailand holds general elections. The United States establishes full diplomatic relations with Vietnam.

1996 Two activists—Bishop Carlos Ximenes Belo and José Ramos-Horta—from the Indonesian island of Timor are awarded the Nobel Peace Prize.

1997 A regional financial crisis starts in July in Thailand and spreads through ASEAN.

1998 Pol Pot, the notorious head of the Khmer Rouge, dies in his sleep in one of the jungles of Cambodia. Indonesia's President Suharto steps down after 32 years in power. His resignation is followed rioting that left more than 1,000 dead in Jakarta, Medan, and Solo.

RELIGION IN SOUTHEAST ASIA

L IKE THE SHIFTING PATTERNS in a kaleidoscope, the rituals, ceremonies, prayers, and customs of all the world's major religions meet the eye of a visitor to Southeast Asia. Intrepid travelers will spend many hours "doing temples," and their weary feet will carry them up hundreds of steps and through miles of courtyards. Their cameras will click unceasingly, recording images of the Buddha, of Jesus, of Rama, and of the pantheon of Hindu and Chinese gods. They will take pictures of mosques with golden domes and of minarets festooned with loudspeakers. At night, if they are in Malaysia or Indonesia, they may turn on the TV and listen to a Koran-reading competition.

A quick glance at the calendar in Singapore demonstrates the impact of multiple faiths on a modern society. The government of multiracial Singapore is basically Chinese. The only holiday when these hardworking people close up shop altogether is the Chinese new year. Nevertheless, the government recognizes holidays sacred to four religions, and important Buddhist, Islamic, and Hindu occasions are public holidays.

After all, the fact that it has been 2,000 years since the birth of Christ is not particularly meaningful for most Asians. Muslims date the era from the year of Muhammad's hegira in AD 622. The Buddha's birth was in 563 BC. Many Asian calendars are bilingual, with Arabic numerals and Christian dates on one side and Chinese, Buddhist, or Islamic dates on the other. In Thailand, the cornerstones of important buildings usually carry two dates. Christian dating, like the English language, is used for business, banking, and all international transactions.

The calendar plays an important part in the lives of the people, because elements of astrology (both Hindu and Chinese) are considered when making important decisions. Statesmen, kings, and peasants refer to astrologers or *bomohs* or *dukuns* for help. The Chinese and Thais, for example, attach great importance to the year of a person's birth within a 12-year cycle, each year represented by an animal.

In most of Asia, time is regarded as cyclical, whereas for most Occidentals it is linear. For people in the Judeo-Christian and Islamic traditions, each life is an entity—a unit—created at a specific moment in time. Death is the termination of the physical life of that individual, while the soul may continue to exist through eternity. The conditions of the afterlife, according to Christian and Muslim belief, depend in large part on the individual's behavior during his or her earthly sojourn. Christians, according to most dogmas, believe in resurrection—but not reincarnation. And here is where the great schism between Eastern and Western thought begins. Hindus and Buddhists assume that life, as well as time, follows a cycle. The soul may endure over the course of many lives. Often the conditions of the new life depend on the behavior of the soul in its previous body. A Christian seeks eternal life through the teaching of Christ. A Buddhist seeks *nirvana,* or release from all suffering, and follows the teachings of the Buddha.

Buddhism

Buddhism, a nontheistic philosophy, is tolerant of other faiths and beliefs. Thus elements of older religions turn up in the practices and customs of Buddhists. The cyclical notion of time and the idea of reincarnation are in keeping with older Hindu and Vedic beliefs. Indeed, the Buddha was born a Hindu prince, and much of his teaching was aimed at a reform of the structure and complexities of Hinduism.

The "historical Buddha" ("buddha" actually means an awakened or enlightened being) was born **Siddhartha Gautama** about 563 BC, near the border of Nepal. A wealthy prince, he lived in luxury, married, and had a son. Like many people of his class, he had been protected from viewing the harsher aspects of life. Legend has it that one day he went out from the palace and for the first time saw poverty, sickness, and death. Overwhelmed by these realities, he renounced his worldly position and became a wandering mendicant. After years of fasting, begging, and traveling, he sat down under a *bodhi* tree and sank into a deep meditation lasting 49 days. At last he achieved enlightenment, and Siddhartha became a buddha.

The answer he found after his contemplation was that to escape from suffering and misery, human beings must eliminate craving and attachment. In this world, he maintained, misery is caused by craving for desirable situations and aversion to unwanted ones. This craving and aversion results in wrong thought and misdirected action. Thus, in order to achieve nirvana, an individual must purify him- or herself at a deep level, through meditation. At the same time, the follower should renounce evil action and strive to follow a moral code, which also serves as a foundation for the practice. The **Five Precepts** in Buddhist teaching prescribe guidelines for right living. They are not to kill, steal, do sexual wrong, lie, or use any intoxicants. Each life an individual passes through is another chance to move closer to nirvana.

Forms of Buddhism

As it spread from northern India throughout Asia, Buddhism branched into many schools and sects. The basic divisions are Theravada Buddhism (sometimes called Hinayana, or "Lesser Vehicle"), Mahayana ("Greater Vehicle"), and Tantric Buddhism.

Theraveda Buddhism, the "way of the elders," emphasizes that each person must seek salvation through enlightenment, attained by meditation and a morally upright life. Theravada is a monastic religion, and people enter religious communities (the *sangha*) for mutual guidance and support.

Myanmar (Burma) and Thailand are both Buddhist countries where religion forms an integral part of life. In Thailand, for example, it's customary for every young man who can to spend at least three months of his youth as a monk, when he will eat only the food he has received as "merit" offerings by the people early in the morning. The remainder of the day is spent in study, prayer, and meditation. Buddhist monks appear at every official function, whether it be the opening of a village school or the inauguration of a military airfield.

Mahayana Buddhism originated in India but developed in China, Korea, and Japan. The tradition acknowledges that most people do not have the fortitude to achieve enlightenment on their own, and so followers of Mahayana sects such as the Pure Land School call upon the aid of saints to help them to salvation. These saints, called bodhisattvas, are fully enlightened beings who have voluntarily postponed their own entry into nirvana to help others along the way. In Southeast Asia, most Mahayana temples, such as the famous Ayer Hitam Temple in Penang (Malaysia), were founded by Chinese immigrants. These temples are filled with images of Kuan Yin, the goddess of mercy, and other bodhisattvas, which have become objects of devotion among the faithful.

Tantric Buddhism is a subsect of Mahayana Buddhism; it in turn has divided into various sects that are found most prominently in Tibet, but also in northern Burma as well as in China and Japan. Tantric Buddhism is also centered on monasteries, and emphasizes secret rituals designed to combat demons and overcome evil.

Hinduism

Hindu belief in reincarnation forms the basis of religious practice and faith. Unlike the Buddhist concept of nirvana, the Hindu notion is one of attained deliverance. Hindu dogma teaches that the soul can be released from the wheel of life only by the observance of dharma—doing one's duty according to one's position in life. The aim of each existence is to perform the dharma of that life so correctly that the soul will be rewarded with a higher station in the next life.

Hindu Deities

The Hindu godhead consists of a holy trinity: Brahma the Creator, Vishnu the Preserver, and Shiva the Destroyer. Each god appears in a number of different forms, or incarnations, and has a consort and many minor deities attached to his worship. Brahma is usually depicted with four heads to indicate his creativity and intellect. Vishnu is usually pictured with four arms, stressing his versatility and strength. His consort is the popular goddess of wealth and fortune, Lakshmi. Shiva is probably the most popular of the three, and the most widely worshiped. As he is the god of both destruction and regeneration, he is thought to be sympathetic to the human condition. In his incarnation as Shiva Nataraja, Lord of the Dance, he dances continuously to keep the world in existence.

His consort is worshiped in several forms and is a source of comfort and inspiration. Her more familiar names are Kali, Parvati, or Dewi. Shiva has two sons: Ganesha, the elephant-headed god of knowledge and "remover of obstacles," and Subramaniam, god of war. Worship of the deities takes place daily in the home and in the temple on festival days. Thaipusam, which pays homage to Subramaniam, is celebrated widely in Singapore and Kuala Lumpur. The other major Hindu holiday is Deepavali, the autumn festival of lights.

Hinduism in Southeast Asia

Hindu-Brahmanic influence, which can be seen throughout Southeast Asia, is a relic of historical kingdoms that came under Indian influence in the 6th to 10th centuries. In Thailand some of these Hindu traditions came from the great Khmer kingdom that flourished in the 9th to 12th centuries. Thai royalty retains several court Brahman priests as a holdover from the times when they advised the king on heavenly omens. In modern times, these priest-astrologers advise only on special matters affecting the royal family and in connection with public ceremonies such as the annual opening of the plowing season, celebrated in Bangkok on the Pramane Ground.

The Hindu influence in Indonesia dates back to the powerful Srivijaya kingdom, which controlled much of Sumatra and the Malay Peninsula in the 10th century. In Java, a succession of empires combined several aspects of Hindu and Buddhist traditions so that in some instances Shiva, the Hindu god of destruction and regeneration, became merged with the Buddha—as can be seen in the temple at Prambanan near Yogyakarta.

The grounds of the Prambanan temple provide the setting for performances of a modern dance-drama based on the *Ramayana* and held during the summer months. One of two great Sanskrit epics (the other being the *Mahabharata*), the *Ramayana* narrates the life and adventures of Rama, an incarnation of Vishnu descended to earth in human form to subdue the demon Ravanna. The *Ramayana* story is narrated in dance, painting, and sculpture throughout Southeast Asia.

Hinduism on Bali

The advent of Islam in the 16th century, and its rapid spread thereafter, extinguished Hinduism in Indonesia except on the island of Bali. Balinese religion is a rich mixture of Hindu mythology, animist beliefs, and an underlying awe of nature and God as manifest in the great volcano Gunung Agung. The Balinese, who accept the Hindu concept of Kali Yug—the last of the four great epochs before the end of the world—believe that in such times as these it is imperative to maintain a proper reverence for all the gods and spirits who dwell on the island, for their anger can be very destructive. Many Balinese believe that both the eruption of the volcano in 1963 and the wave of killings during the civil unrest in 1965 occurred because of religious improprieties.

Balinese Hinduism has absorbed so many local island deities that it has very little in common with Hinduism as observed by other communities in Southeast Asia. The two most famous local deities of Balinese Hinduism are the witch Rangda and her adversary, the lionlike beast called Barong. The Barong Kris dance performed daily at Batubulan is a modern, secular version of the very sacred *calonerang* exorcistic dance-drama that is used by the Balinese to protect their villages from evil; calonerang is rarely seen by outsiders, because it's performed at midnight at village crossroads and in graveyards. Both versions depict a struggle between Rangda, the personification of darkness and evil, and the protective Barong; the struggle always ends in a draw, because in the mortal world neither good nor evil can completely triumph.

Islam

Despite its long cultural and historical role, Hinduism is a minority religion in Southeast Asia today. The reason for this was the great Islamic expansion during the 15th and 16th centuries, when part of the Malay Peninsula (including the four southernmost provinces of Thailand), all of the Indonesian archipelago (with the exception of Bali), and the southern islands of what is today the Philippines became Muslim.

Islam, which is monotheistic, exclusive, and highly moralistic, came as quite a contrast to the pantheism of the Hindu and Buddhist religions it replaced. With the advent of Islam, the way of life in these areas changed. Some of the more obvious changes were in the calendar, the status of women, and the role of the state in regulating citizens' behavior.

The Islamic Calendar

The Islamic calendar is divided into 12 lunar months, as is the Chinese, so that all festivals move forward every year. Unlike the Chinese calendar, however, the Muslim lunar calendar does not make any accommodation to the solar year by adding "leap months" (7 months during the course of every 19 years). Muslim holidays, therefore, move forward 11 days each year, which explains why Muslims do not celebrate a fixed New Year's Day. Coincidentally, this system ensures that the month of fasting, Ramadan, rotates through the seasons and therefore is never confused with local planting or harvest festivities, which hark back to pagan customs and would be considered taboo for orthodox Muslims.

Islam and Women

Islam is often seen in the West as a religion that oppresses women. Muslims, however, contend that men and women are treated differently but equally. In Islam's Arabian homeland, the laws of the Koran regarding women were originally designed to protect their personal dignity and legal rights. Women were expected to cover their hair (but *not* necessarily to wear a veil; that is a later development that varies widely in the Islamic world according to local custom) and to be modest in their dealings with outsiders. They were given the legal right to own property and protection from arbitrary divorce. Muslim men may have up to four wives, if they can afford to support them and treat them all equally.

Islamic law, however, clearly makes women not only separate, but also inferior. The Koran states: "Men have authority over women because God has made the one superior to the other . . . so good women are obedient." Among some orthodox groups in Southeast Asia, unmarried women are strictly segregated from men in schools and social organizations, and married women are expected to avoid any dealings with men outside their own families. But other groups have adapted Islamic law to local custom; among the Minangkabau of Sumatra and Malaysia, for example, women own most of the property and have a strong voice in community affairs. In other cases, women have received some protection from the strictness of Islamic law through parliamentary women's-rights legislation.

Islam and the State

In Southeast Asia, Malaysia and Brunei are avowedly Islamic nations; Indonesia has no official religion, but the population is overwhelmingly Muslim. Government departments include a bureau of religious affairs. Indonesia's constitution requires that every citizen must profess belief in a single deity. This law is inconvenient for the Chinese and Balinese, who have been forced rather artificially to add a "supreme deity" to their elaborate pantheons. In recent years many Chinese have become Christian to avoid harassment.

The Koran

Islam, like Christianity, is based on a specific holy scripture: the Koran, or Qu'ran, which is a collection of the words of God as revealed to his prophet, Muhammad. To a devout Muslim the book is the holy of holies, and much time is spent reading and studying it. The book must be treated with reverence, never handled carelessly, and should never be placed beneath any other books. One should never drink or smoke while the Koran is being read aloud, and it should be heard in respectful silence. In many villages children are taught to memorize great numbers of verses, and Koran competitions are annual events.

The Five Pillars of Islam

The Koran and Muslim tradition set forth the Five Pillars of Islam: the Profession of Faith, the Five Daily Prayers, the obligation to fast, the obligation to make the pilgrimage, and the obligation to give alms. The **Profession of Faith** is the familiar doctrine of the Unity of God, which is heard in every mosque and from every minaret: There is no God but Allah; Muhammad is his prophet.

The **Five Daily Prayers** are made at specific times of day: at dawn, at noon, in the afternoon, at sunset, and at night. One must pray kneeling and bowing in the direction of Mecca (of course, in this part of the world, that means turning west, not east). Because the Koran demands cleanliness before prayer (preferably a total bath, but if this is not possible then a ritual cleansing of face, hands, and feet), you'll see tanks and basins of water outside all mosques.

The third Pillar of Islam is **fasting.** The ninth month of the year, Ramadan, is set aside for ritual fasting. For 30 days all adult Muslims are enjoined against taking any food, drink, or cigarettes from dawn to dusk. During this month, work efficiency tends to drop, because in addition to being hungry and thirsty, many Muslims are also sleepy because they have stayed up much of the night eating. Adherence to the tradition is quite strict, and in some villages special police prowl the streets looking for secret munchers. The Koran does, however, give dispensation to the sick and to those who must take a meal in the course of their work. The end of Ramadan is the great feast, Hari Raya Puasa. After a morning visit to the mosque, the family returns home for a memorable feast that more than makes up for the month of deprivation.

The fourth Pillar is the duty to make a **pilgrimage to Mecca.** Obviously for many Muslims in Southeast Asia this is an expensive and long journey, and therefore the pilgrimage is obligatory only for those who can afford it. Nevertheless, because of the honor and prestige accorded to those who have made the journey and because the pious regard it as a religious duty, every year thousands of men and women, many of them old, board pilgrim ships and planes for the long journey. Those who return are addressed as Haji (or Hajjah for women), indicating that they have fulfilled their obligation. The last Pillar is **almsgiving,** similar to the Christian custom of tithing. In Malaysia this money is collected by the Department of Religious Affairs and is used for welfare projects for the poor.

Christianity

Because of its claims to universal validity and the simplicity of its faith, Islam swept through the islands of Southeast Asia up to the Philippines, where it ran head-on into the Spanish Catholic Church. With the establishment of Spanish authority in Manila on June 3, 1571, Islam encountered a nearly impenetrable barrier to further expansion.

The Filipinos often pride themselves on having the only Catholic country in Asia, as well as the most westernized. The Filipinos accepted the Catholic teaching for a variety of reasons. In the first place, Catholicism did not have to contend with an organized, established religion because most of the indigenous beliefs involved ancestral spirits and nature gods; they offered neither a systematic theology nor a firm promise of salvation. So for the Filipino, acceptance of the new religion did not involve any deeply traumatic rejection of old ways. In fact, many of the older customs were absorbed into Catholic ritual. The second factor was the language problem. The islands were a hodge-podge of languages and dialects. Catholic schools, which taught Spanish as well as the catechism, gave the Spanish colonial authorities a means of unifying the country both religiously and linguistically. Furthermore, the church offered protection from marauding pirates and outlaw gangs—one of the terms for new Christians was "those who live under the bells." On the other hand, the Spanish friars were notorious for their abuses—one of the factors that contributed to the 1896 revolution.

As you travel through the Philippine countryside, you'll see some huge, stark, very un-Roman-looking cathedrals. These are the churches of an indigenous Christian faith, the Iglesia ni Kristo, which incorporates nationalistic feelings into a Protestant liturgy. It is estimated to have almost a million members.

Elsewhere in Southeast Asia, Christian missionaries, both Catholic and Protestant, followed the colonizing European powers. The lovely churches in Macau, Melaka (Malacca), parts of Indonesia, and along the coastal regions of Sri Lanka—where nearly all the fisherfolk are Catholic—are remnants of the Portuguese presence.

Missionary work in Southeast Asia did not disappear with the departure of the colonial powers. Indeed, in certain areas proselytizing church groups are now more active than ever. Much current missionary effort is directed toward the peoples living in remote mountains and jungles, where pagan practices still prevail. Though Islam is Malaysia's national religion, the East Malaysian states are predominantly Christian.

Changing Times

Religion no longer plays the role in Southeast Asia that it once did, when personal identity was established by an individual's spiritual tenets. Educational, national, and professional ties have superseded the bonds that rituals in the home and ceremonies in the community once forged. Overcrowding in the cities has pushed people closer together, sometimes with unfortunate results, when vastly different customs clash with one another. The call to prayer, when amplified over a loudspeaker, becomes noise pollution to some ears; the clanging cymbals accompanying a Chinese funeral are equally unwelcome to the ears of others.

During these transitional times a visitor to Southeast Asia has a unique opportunity to observe and participate in the customs, rituals, and ceremonies of many different religions. Sensitivity and good manners are still essential. Don't try to enter a religious building if the people within ask you not to. Don't intrude on or photograph people at prayer. Remove your shoes when entering a mosque, wear a waist sash when entering a Balinese temple, and always dress modestly.

Throughout Southeast Asia, religion has nevertheless remained a more important feature of day-to-day social activity than it has in most of the West. Although the forms and nature of this religious feeling vary widely within the region, most of the population is actively involved in it. There is still a strong sense of traditional values, reflected in fundamental social attitudes.

BOOKS AND VIDEOS

Books

Southeast Asia

The Travelers' Guide to Asian Customs and Manners, by Kevin Chambers, advises on how to dine, tip, dress, make friends, do business, and bargain in Asia, Australia, and New Zealand. *Shopping in Exotic Places,* by Ronald L. Krannich, Jo Reimer, and Carl Rae Krannich, discusses all major shopping districts and tells how to bargain and how to pack.

Video Night in Kathmandu, by Pico Iyer, is a delightful collection of essays on the *Time* correspondent's travels through Southeast Asia. Highly recommended works on history include *Southeast Asia,* 3rd edition, by M. Osborne; *Southeast Asia: A History* by Lea E. Williams; *A Modern History of Southeast Asia* by Clive J. Christie; and *Nations and States in Southeast Asia* by Nicholas Tarling.

In *Beyond Belief,* a follow-up book to *Among the Believers,* V. S. Naipaul conveys the effects of Islam in Indonesia, Malaysia, Iran, and Pakistan. His account is full of the people he encounters on his travels and their stories.

A Fortune-Teller Told Me, by Tiziano Terzani, is a part travel, part philosophical narrative in which a journalist makes a voyage to Asia where he moves about on foot and by train and boat and rediscovers the land, the people, and his own needs and desires.

Southeast Asia inspired Joseph Conrad's works, including the novels *An Outcast of the Islands, Lord Jim, The Shadow-Line, Victory, Almayer's Folly,* and *The Rescue,* and the short stories "Karain," "The Lagoon," "Youth," "The End of the Tether," "Typhoon," "Flak," "The Secret Sharer," and "Freya of the Seven Isles."

SouthEast Asia Wildlife is a collaborative effort by a number of the regions' top naturalists and explorers detailing the wildlife, national parks, and tourist facilities of Indonesia, Malaysia, Singapore, Thailand, and the Philippines. *Soul of the Tiger,* by Jeffrey McNeely and Paul Spencer-Wachtel, describes stories behind the region's customs and beliefs.

Cambodia

Cambodia: Report from a Stricken Land, by Henry Kamm, is a perceptive, angry account of the last 30 years—how the world betrayed Cambodia, and its leaders picked it clean.

Indonesia

Anthology of Modern Indonesian Poetry, edited by B. Raffle, provides insight into Indonesian society. Christopher Koch's *The Year of Living Dangerously* is a historical novel of the chaotic state of Indonesia in 1965. *The Religion of Java,* by Clifford Geertz, is a modern classic that describes the religious and social life of the Javanese.

Underwater Indonesia, by Kal Muller, is the best guide to diving in the archipelago—a must-read for anyone planning to scuba dive or snorkel here. Anne Richter's *The Arts & Crafts of Indonesia* is a beautifully photographed guide to handicrafts, costumes, and arts throughout the islands. *Adventuring in Indonesia,* by Holly S. Smith, is a guide to the nature and culture of the islands, including many national parks. Eliot Elosofan's *Java Diary,* Frances Yeager's *Jungle Woman,* and John MacKinnon's *In Search of the Red Ape* are classic accounts of explorers discovering wildlife and culture on Java, Sumatra, and Borneo, respectively.

Malaysia

Denis Walls and Stella Martin's *In Malaysia* is a dramatic novel set in Malaysia. Somerset Maugham's *Ah King and Other Stories* and *The Casuarina Tree* are two volumes of short stories that capture the essence of colonial life in Malaya. *Kalimantan,* by C. S. Godshalk, is a fictional account of an Englishman who establishes a private raj on the north coast of Borneo in the 19th century.

Philippines

In Our Image, by S. Karnow, and *The Philippines,* by Onofre D. Corpuz, are good standard texts on the history of the nation. An excellent book dealing with the 1986 People Power revolution is *Endgame,* by Ninotchka Rosca, while José Sison's *The Philippine Revolution* places the People Power phenomenon in the context of earlier history. *Waltzing with a Dictator,* by

R. Bonner, is an in-depth study of the relationship between the United States and the Philippines. Also try Bryan Johnson's *The Four Days of Courage: The Untold Story of the People Who Brought Marcos Down.* D. Schirmer's *Philippine Reader* is a good collection of left-wing essays. *Playing with Water: Love and Passion on a Philippine Island,* by James Hamilton Patterson, is a fascinating account of a year's stay on a small island.

Singapore

Maurice Collis's *Raffles* is a rich biographical account of the founder of Singapore. *Singapore Malay Society,* by T. Li, is a solid historical reference. *Saint Jack* is a novel by Paul Theroux set in Singapore. JoAnn Meriwether Craig's *Culture Shock! Singapore* is a must for anyone spending more than a few days in the island nation.

Thailand

Monsoon Country is a contemporary novel by Pira Sudham, who portrays life in the northeast of Thailand. For insights into Thai culture and everyday life, read Denis Segaller's *Thai Ways* and *More Thai Ways.* For a humorous account of an expatriate's life in Thailand in the 1950s, read *Mai Pen Rai,* by Carol Hollinger. An excellent account of life in northern Thailand is provided by Gordon Young in *The Hill Tribes of Northern Thailand.*

Vietnam

Anthony Gray's *Saigon* takes the reader through all the major events from the 1920s to 1975. Neil Sheehan, a former *New York Times* reporter in Vietnam offers a very comprehensive look at America's involvement in Vietnam in *The Bright Shining Lie.*

Videos

Cambodia's troubles and America's involvement in Southeast Asia are examined in *The Killing Fields* (1984), journalist Sydney Schanberg's tale of the search for his Cambodian aide, Dith Prahn, who was left behind when Pnomh Penh fell to the Khmer Rouge in 1975. As a follow up to this movie, a must-see is Spaulding Gray's *Swimming to Cambodia* (1987). Gray weaves poetry, humor, political discussion, and personal confessions into an entertaining, insightful monologue linked to his small role in *The Killing Fields,* and to U.S. military aggression and the situation in Cambodia.

In *Indochine* (1991), Catherine Deneuve portrays a French colonial plantation owner who loses her way of life and her adopted Vietnamese daughter to the 1930s conflicts that begin to change the face of Southeast Asia. Linda Hunt won an Oscar for her performance as a male photographer covering strife-ridden Indonesia just before Sukarno's rule fell to Suharto in 1965 in *The Year of Living Dangerously* (1982). She plays alongside Mel Gibson and Sigourney Weaver. In *Beyond Rangoon* (1995), an American doctor (Patricia Arquette) finds herself caught up in the conflict between Burma's ruling fascist regime and the dissident democratic movement.

There have been many films made about the military horrors of the Vietnam War, including the classic *Apocalypse Now* (1979), *Platoon* (1986), and *Full Metal Jacket* (1987). *Born on the Fourth of July* (1989) conveys the aftereffects of this war on the men who fought it.

VOCABULARY

To properly experience the culture of a foreign country, one must feast on its cuisine, learn the history of its monuments, and speak its native tongue. Southeast Asian languages, like its history, are as diverse as its people and customs.

To simplify communications, Fodor's has compiled a vocabulary chart of six languages you may encounter throughout your travels in the region. This easy-reference listing includes important words and significant phrases in English, Cantonese, Malay (which is usually similar to Indonesian), Mandarin, Tagalog, and Thai. Use the phonetical chart to assist you in getting around, asking directions, and dining out.

Note: In Bahasa Indonesia, the letter "c" is pronounced as "ch"; hence, *capcai*, a spicy vegetable dish, is pronounced "chap chai." Also the letter "y" is pronounced as "j"; thus, "Yogyakarta" is pronounced "Jogjakarta."

	English	Cantonese	Malay/Indonesian

Basics

	English	Cantonese	Malay/Indonesian
Yes/No	hai/mm'hai	ya/**tee'** -dak
Please	m'goy	**see**-la/**min**-ta
Thank you (very much).	doy-jeh/fehseng doh jeh	**tree**-ma **ka**-say (**ban**-yak)
You're welcome.	foon ying	**sa**-ma **sa**-ma
Excuse me.	dai'm jee	ma-fkan sa-ya
Hello	wa´	apa khabar or "hello"
Goodbye	joy geen	se-**la**-mat **ja**lan/ se-**la**-mat **ting**-gal

Numbers

One	yaht	sa-too
Two	eee	doo-a
Three	som	tee-ga
Four	say	em-pat
Five	m'	lee-ma
Six	look	e-nam
Seven	chut	tu-juh
Eight	baht	la-pan/**de**-lah-pan
Nine	gou	sem-bee-lan
Ten	sup	se-pu-luh

Days and Time

Today	gäm-yät	**ha**-ree ee-nee
Tomorrow	ting-yat	**ay**-sok (also **bay**-sok)
Yesterday	chum-yät	kel-**mar**-in/ke-**mar**-in
Morning	joo-joh	**pa**-gee
Afternoon	ahn-joh	**pe**-tang
Night	man-hak	**ma**-lam
Monday	lye bye **yaht**	**ha**-ree **iss**-nin/ **ha**-ree se-nin
Tuesday	lye bye **ee**	**ha**-ree se-**la**-sa
Wednesday	lye bye **som**	**ha**-ree **ra**-boo
Thursday	lye bye **say**	**ha**-ree **ka**-mees
Friday	lye bye m	**ha**-ree **ju**-ma-at
Saturday	lye bye **look**	**ha**-ree **sab**-too
Sunday	lye bye **yaht'**	**ha**-ree **a**-had (also **ha**-ree **ming**-gu)

Mandarin	Tagalog	Thai	English
shee/pu shee	oh-oh/hin-deé	khrap/mai khrap (M)/kha/mai kha(F)	Yes/No
ching	pah-keé	karoona	Please
sy-eh sy-eh nee	(mah-rah-ming) sah-lah-maht	khob (M)/kha (F) khun khrap	Thank you (very much).
boo sy-eh	wah-lahng ah-noo-mahn	mai pen rai	You're welcome.
too-eh pu-shee	pah-oó-manh-hiń po	kaw-tōd	Excuse me.
way	kuh-moos-tah/ heh-ló	sa-wat dee khrap (M)/sa-wat dee kha (F)	Hello
tsay jen	pah-ah-lam nah pó	sa-wat dee khrap (M)/sa-wat dee kha (F)	Goodbye
ee	ee-sah	nung	One
err	dah-lah-wah	song	Two
san	taht-loh	sam	Three
soo	ah-paht	see	Four
woo	lee-mah	hah	Five
lee-oo	ah-neem	hōk	Six
chee	pee-toh	jet	Seven
bah	wah-ló	paat	Eight
joo	see-yahm´	kao	Nine
shur	sahm-poó	sip	Ten
chin tien	nga-yohn	wannee	Today
ming tien	boó-kahss	proong nee	Tomorrow
tso tien	kah-há-pon	moo-ah-wannee	Yesterday
shang wu	oo-mah-gah	torn-chao	Morning
sha wu	hah-pon	torn bai	Afternoon
wan shang	gah-beh	torn moot	Night
lee-pa-ee	loó-ness	wan-chan	Monday
lee-pa-ayr	mahr-tess	wan-ung-khan	Tuesday
lee-pa-san	moo-yehr-koh-less	wan-poot	Wednesday
lee-pa-soo	hoo-whé-bess	wan-pru-roo-hud	Thursday
lee-pa-wu	bee-yehr-ness	wan-sook	Friday
lee-pa-ee-oo	sah-bah-doh	wan-sao	Saturday
lee-pa-tien	leeng-goh	wan-ar-teet	Sunday

English	Cantonese	Malay/Indonesian

Useful Phrases

English	Cantonese	Malay/Indonesian
Do you speak English?	nay gäng m' gäng ying män	**ta**-hoo-kah ber-ba-**ha**-sa **Ing**-gris?
I don't speak . . .	ah m' woiy gäng gäng doong wah.	**sa**-ya **tee**-dak ber-**cha**-kap ba-**ha**-sa
I don't understand.	äh m' sic	**sa**-ya **tee**-dak fa-ham/men-**ger**-ti
I don't know.	äh m' jee	**sa**-ya **tee**-dak **ta**-hoo
I am American/British.	ä hay may gäc yan/ying gäk yan	**sa**-ya **o**-rang Amerika/**Ing**-gris
I am sick.	ä beng **jah**	**sa**-ya **sa**-kit
Please call a doctor.	m goy nay gew yee sung	**see**-la ta-**lee**-pon **dok**-ter
Have you any rooms?	nay yaw mohfäng	**bi**-lik **a**-da
How much does it cost?	gay´ däh chien	**har**-ga-nya ber-**a**-pa
Too expensive	gai´ gway	ter-**la**-loo **ma**-hal
It's beautiful.	hoh leng	**chan**-tik
Help!	bong jô	**to**-long
Stop!	ting jee	ber-**hen**-ti

Getting Around

English	Cantonese	Malay/Indonesian
How do I get to . . .	deem yerng huy . . .	ba-gai-ma-na boh-lay per-gee-ke . . .
. . . the train station?	fäw ché jäm	**stay**-shen **kray**-ta a-pee dee **ma**-na
. . . the post office?	yaw jing gook	pe-**ja**-bat pos dee **ma**-na
. . . the tourist office?	le hang se´	ja-bat-ban pe-**lan**-chong/**kan**-tor **tor**-is dee **ma**-na
. . . the hospital?	yee´ yuen	**roo**-mah **sa**-kit dee **ma**-na
Does this bus go to . . . ?	ga ba se´ huy m huy . . .	a-da-kah bis ee-nee per-gee ke . . .
Where is the W.C.?	say soh gahn herng been doh	**tan**-das/way say **a**-da dee **ma**-na
Left	jäh	**kee**-ree
Right	yäw	**ka**-nan
Straight ahead	chiem mein	troos

Mandarin	Tagalog	Thai	English
nee fweh sho yung yoo má	mah-roo-nohng hoh kay-yohng mahg-Ing-glehs?	khun pood pas-sa ung-grid dai-mai	Do you speak English?
wo pu fweh sho (thai kway yoo)	hin-deé a-koh mah-roo-nohng mahg-tah-gah-lohg	phom (M)/chan (F) mai pood pasa Thai mai dai	I don't speak . . .
wo pu lee-oo chee-ay	hin-deé koh nah-ee-een-tin-deé-hahn	phom (M)/chan (F) mai kao chai	I don't understand.
wo pu tung	hin-deé koh ah-lahm	phom/chan mai roo	I don't know.
wo sher may kwo jen/ing kwo jen	ah-ko ay Ah-meh-ree-kah-noh/Ing-glehs	phom/chan pen (American/ ung-grid)	I am American/British.
wo sheng ping ler	ah-ko ay may sah-kit	phom/chan mai sa-bai	I am sick.
ching chow ee sung lin	pah-kee-tah-wahg ang dook-tohr	dai-prod re-ak moa mai	Please call a doctor.
nee hay yoo fwang chien ma	may-roh-ohn kah-yong mang-ah kuh-wahr-toh	khun-mee hong-mai	Have you any rooms?
to shaw chien	mahg-kah-noh?	tao rai	How much does it cost?
tao kwa la	mah-hal mah-shah-doh	pa-eng goo-pai	Too expensive
chen pee-ow lee-ang	mah-gahn-dah	soo-ay	It's beautiful.
choo-ming	sahk-loh-loh	choo-ay doo-ay	Help!
ting	hin-toh	yoot	Stop!
wo tsen yang tao . . .	pah-pah-no pah-poon-tah sah . . .	phom/chan ja pai . . . dai yangngai	How do I get to . . .
. . . fwa chu chan	ee-stah-syon nahng tren	sa-tai-nee rod-fai	. . . the train station?
. . . yu choo	post oh-pis/tahn-gah-pahn nahng koh-reo	pai-sa-nee	. . . the post office?
. . . kuan kuang choo	oh-pee-see-nah nahng too-ris-moh	sam-nak-ngan tóng-tee-oh	the tourist office?
. . . ee-yuen	oh-spee-tal	rohng-phayar baan	. . . the hospital?
chu pu pa shur tao . . . ma	poo-moo-poon-tah bah ee-tohngboos sah . . .	rod-mai-nee pai-nai . . . chai mai	Does this bus go to . . . ?
chaw soo tsai na lee	sah-ahn ahng bahn-nyoh	hong-nam tee-nai	Where is the W.C.?
tso	kah-lee-wah	sai	Left
yoo	kah-nahn	kwah	Right
ching sung chien tson	dee-reh-tsoh	trong-pai	Straight ahead

INDEX

Icons and Symbols

★ Our special recommen-
dations
✕ Restaurant
🏠 Lodging establishment
✕🏠 Lodging establishment
whose restaurant war-
rants a special trip
👶 Good for kids (rubber
duck)
☞ Sends you to another
section of the guide for
more information
✉ Address
☎ Telephone number
🕐 Opening and closing
times
💲 Admission prices
💻 Sends you to
www.fodors.com/urls
for up-to-date links to
the property's Web site

Numbers in white and black
circles ③ ❸ that appear on
the maps, in the margins, and
within the tours correspond
to one another.

A

Abdul Gaffoor Mosque, *364,
365*
Adiyawarman Museum, *159*
Adventure tourism, *8*
Affandi Museum, *58*
Agastya Art Institute, *64*
Agung Rai Museum of Art
(ARMA), *95–96*
Air Keroh, *227*
Air travel, *xii–xiv, xvii, 9.*
☞ *Also* specific
countries; transportation
in cities and areas
Aisawan Thippaya pavilion,
524
Al Abrar Mosque, *359*
Alor Setar, Malaysia, *219–
220*
Amarapura, Burma, *734*
Ambar Budaya Crafts Center,
64
Ambarita, Indonesia, *154*
Ambassador's Pagoda
(Hanoi, Vietnam), *642,
643*
Ampenan, Indonesia, *117–
119*
Amusement parks
Brunei, 262
Singapore, 377, 380
Ananda Temple, *732*

Angkor Temple Complex, *16,
742–743*
Angkor Thom, *743*
Angkor Wat, *743–744*
Angthong Marine National
Park, *613, 618*
Ao Nang, Thailand, *603–
605, 617*
Ao Thong Wua Laen,
Thailand, *615*
Apartments, *xxv*
Archery, *431*
Armenian Church
(Singapore), *347, 350*
Army Museum (Hanoi,
Vietnam), *647*
Art galleries and museums
Alor Setar, 219–220
Bang Pa-In, 524
Bangkok, 480
*Brunei Arts and Handicrafts
Centre, 261*
Hanoi, Vietnam, 647
Ho Chi Minh City, 697, 708
Jakarta, 30, 32, 33, 34–35
Kuala Lumpur, 183, 186, 188
Langkawi, 221
Lombok, 121
Manila, Philippines, 302
Pinang, 212
Singapore, 9, 380, 381, 388
Ubud, 95
Yogyakarta, 58, 61
Art Museum (Bao Tang My
Tuat) (Ho Chi Minh
City), *672*
Arts. ☞ Specific cities and
countries
Asian Civilisations Museum,
9, 14, 350
Asian Village & Adventure
Asia, *385, 386*
Assembly Hall of the
Cantonese Chinese
Congregation, *679, 680*
Assembly Hall of the Fujian
Chinese Congregation,
679, 680
Assembly Hall of the Hainan
Chinese Congregation,
679, 680
Astana, *245*
Automatic teller machines
(ATMs), *xxvi*
Ava, Burma, *734–735*
Ayutthaya, Thailand, *521–
524*
dining, 523
emergencies, 539
lodging, 524
transportation, 538
visitor information, 539
Ayutthaya Historical Study
Centre, *523*

B

Baan Hua Thanon, Thailand,
612
Baan Taling Ngam, Thailand,
612–613
Baba and Nyonya Heritage
Museum, *229*
Baguio, Philippines, *312–316*
Baguio Botanical Garden,
312
Baguio Cathedral, *312–313*
Baguio Orchidarium, *314*
Bajaj travel, *163*
Bako National Park, *246*
Balai Besar, *219*
Balai Nobat, *219*
Balatoc Mines, *315*
Bale Kambang (Floating
Pavilion), *105*
Bale Kunung, *124*
Bali, Indonesia, *74–115*
arts, 81, 87, 101
beaches, 105–106
Bedulu, 94–95
Candidasa, 106–107
crafts villages, 92–94
dance, 81, 86–87
Denpasar, 91–92
*dining, 78, 82–84, 88–89, 92,
96–99, 104, 105–106, 107,
108–109*
*English-language bookstores,
113*
emergencies, 113
Gunung Batur, 103–104
internet, mail, telephones, 113
Jimbaran, 75, 78–80
Klungkung, 105
*Kuta, Legian, and Seminyak,
81–88*
*lodging, 78–79, 83–86, 89–90,
92, 98–100, 104, 105–106,
107, 108, 110*
money matters, 112
*nightlife, 79, 81, 86–87, 90,
100–101*
Nusa Dua, 80–81
*outdoor activities and sports,
81, 87, 90, 101*
pharmacies, 113
Sanur, 88–91
*shopping, 79–80, 81, 87–88,
90–91, 92, 101–102*
Tampaksiring, 103
transportation, 110–112
Ubud, 95–102
visitor information, 115
Bali Barat National Park,
110
Bali Museum, *92*
Bali Seni Negeri, *219–220*
Balina Beach, *105–106*
Ballalompoa Museum, *137*
Bamboo Island, *601*
Ban Butom, *582*

Na Thon, Thailand, *606*
Nagore Durghe Shrine
  (Singapore), *359, 361*
Nai Harn, Thailand, *598*
Nai Thon Beach, *592*
Nai Yang Beach, *592*
Naka Noi, Thailand, *591*
Nakhon Pathom, Thailand,
  517–518, 537–538
Nakhon Phanom, Thailand,
  579
Nakhon Ratchasima,
  Thailand, *585–586, 588*
Nan, Thailand, *562–563*
Nanggala, Indonesia, *143*
Narai Ratchaniwet Palace,
  525
Narmada Taman Temple
  complex, *118*
National Art Gallery
  (Bangkok), *480*
National Monument
  (MONAS) (Jakarta), *33,
  34*
National Museum
  (Bangkok), *14, 480*
National Museum (Chiang
  Mai, Thailand), *543*
National Museum (Chiang
  Saen, Thailand), *559*
National Museum (Jakarta),
  33, 34
National Museum (Manila),
  292
National Museum (Nan,
  Thailand), *562*
National Museum (Palawan),
  333
National Museum (Phnom
  Penh), *741*
National Museum (Phuket),
  591
National Museum (Rangoon,
  Burma), *728*
National Parks
Angthong Marine National
  Park, *613, 618*
Bako National Park, *246*
Bali Barat National Park, *110*
Brunei, *8*
Cat Ba Island, *666*
Doi Inthanon National Park,
  554
Gunung Mulu National Park,
  250–251
Java, *52*
Khan Phra Tharo National
  Park, *591*
Khao Salop National Park,
  521
Khao Sam Roi Yod National
  Park, *527*
Khao Yai National Park, *585*
Kinabalu Park, *256–257*
Mt. Apo National Park, *330*
Phu Kra Dueng National
  Park, *577*
St. Paul Subterranean
  National Park, *332*

Taman Negara, *236–237*
Ulu Temburong National
  Park, *262*
National Theatre (Bangkok),
  480, 481
Nature reserves
Bandung, *53*
Bukit Timah Nature Reserve
  (Singapore), *382*
Danum Valley Conservation
  Area, *258*
Hutan Rekreasi (Recreational
  Forest), *227*
Jurong Bird Park, *377, 380–
  381*
Jurong Reptile Park, *380, 381*
Nui Hoang Lien Nature
  Reserve, *668*
Orangutan Rehabilitation
  Station, *149, 151*
Philippine Eagle Nature
  Center, *329*
Pulau Moyo, *125*
Sepilok Orang-Utan
  Rehabilitation Center, *257*
Nature tourism, *8*
Negri Sembilan, Malaysia,
  226–227
Neka Gallery, *95*
New Port, Thailand, *606*
Newton Circus, Singapore,
  372, 374
Ngee Ann City complex, *372,
  374–375*
Nggela, Indonesia, *129*
Nghia An Hoi Quan Pagoda,
  698
Ngoc Son Temple (Hanoi,
  Vietnam), *640, 642*
Nha Trang, Vietnam, *684–
  686*
Niah Caves, *250*
Night Safari (Singapore),
  15, 382, 383
Nightlife. ☞ Specific cities
  and countries
Nine Dynastic Urns (Cuu
  Dinh O The-Mieu), *670,
  672*
Nong Khai, Thailand, *576–
  577, 588*
Nong Nuch Village, Thailand,
  531
Northern Borneo, *242–268.*
  ☞ Also Sabah; Sarawak
emergencies, *266–267*
English-language bookstores,
  267
transportation, *264–266*
visitor information, *268*
Northern Luzon, Philippines,
  312–321
arts, *315*
dining, *314, 316, 318, 319, 320*
emergencies, *321*
English-language bookstores,
  321
lodgings, *314–315, 316, 318,
  319, 320*

nightlife, *315*
outdoor activities and sports,
  315, 316, 318
shopping, *315, 317, 319*
transportation, *320–321*
visitor information, *321*
North Okkalapa, Burma, *728*
Notre Dame Cathedral (Ho
  Chi Minh City), *694, 696*
Nui Hoang Lien Nature
  Reserve, *668*
Nusa Dua, *80–81*
Nusa Tenggara, Indonesia,
  115–133
arts, *121*
dining, *119, 121–122, 124,
  125, 126, 127, 128*
emergencies, *132*
English-language bookstores,
  132
lodging, *119–120, 121–122,
  123–124, 125, 126, 127,
  128–129*
nightlife, *120–121*
outdoor activities and sports,
  121, 122, 127
sightseeing in, *115–117*
shopping, *118–119*
transportation, *129–131*
visitor information, *133*

O

Old House of Phung Hung,
  680, 681
Old House of Tan Ky, *680,
  681*
One-Pillar Pagoda, *645,
  648–649*
Ong Bon Pagoda, *698, 700*
Opera House (Hanoi,
  Vietnam), *642, 644*
Opium Museum, *560*
Orangutan Rehabilitation
  Station, *149, 151*
Outdoor activities and sports.
  ☞ Outdoor activities and
  sports under specific
  countries and cities;
  specific sports

P

Pa Sang, Thailand, *551–552*
Pabalsenam, Indonesia, *142*
Packing, tips for, *xxvi–xxvii*
Paco Park, *292*
Padang, Indonesia, *159–160*
Padangbai, Indonesia, *105*
Pagan, Burma, *731–733*
Pagan Archeological Zone,
  16, 732
Pagodas. ☞ Temples
Pagsanjan, Philippines, *311*
Pahang, Malaysia, *233–237*
Pak Ou Caves, *751*
Pak Thongchai Silk and
  Cultural Centre, *585*
Palace of Supreme Harmony
  (Thai Hoa Dien), *670,
  672*

NOTES